Fodor's

ESSENTIAL CARIBBEAN

Welcome to the Caribbean

Yes, the Caribbean is famous for gorgeous beaches, but that's not all that lures travelers back year after year. The string of islands that arcs from Turks and Caicos to Aruba includes dozens of individual nations, each with a unique history, cuisine, and way of life. If you want to do more than soak up the sun on a white-sand beach, the Caribbean offers an abundance of sea and shore experiences, from snorkeling off remote cays to sipping cocktails under a palm tree. Whatever you choose, the tropical warmth and relaxed pace guarantee an enchanting vacation.

TOP REASONS TO GO

★ **Beaches:** Nearly every island has a beach that ranks among the world's best.

★ **Resorts:** There's everything from luxurious beachfront hideaways to simple inns.

★ **Water Sports:** Diving, sailing, snorkeling, and kayaking can be enjoyed year-round.

★ **Island Culture:** History and folklore give each island a unique identity.

★ **Nature:** Lush rain forests and mountains make for great hiking and bird-watching.

★ **Parties:** Beach bars, carnivals, and celebrations galore enliven the scene.

Contents

1 EXPERIENCE THE CARIBBEAN...... 9
20 Ultimate Experiences............ 18
What's Where 12
Best Resorts in the Caribbean 26
The Caribbean's
Best Outdoor Activities............. 28
Best Beaches in the Caribbean 30
Top Golf Courses in the Caribbean .. 32
11 Places to Experience
Carnival in the Caribbean........... 34
Best Dive and Snorkel
Destinations in the Caribbean....... 36
Kids and Families 38

2 TRAVEL SMART 49
Know Before You Go 50
Getting Here and Around 52
Essentials 55
Renting a Villa 62
Weddings 64
On the Calendar.................... 65
Contacts........................... 68

3 ANGUILLA......................... 69
Welcome to Anguilla 70
Island Snapshot.................... 72
Planning........................... 74
Anguilla 76
Activities 92

4 ANTIGUA AND BARBUDA 95
Welcome to Antigua and Barbuda .. 96
Island Snapshot.................... 98
Planning........................... 99
Antigua.......................... 103
Barbuda 123

5 ARUBA 125
Welcome to Aruba 126
Island Snapshot................... 128
Planning.......................... 130
Oranjestad........................ 134
Manchebo, Druif,
and Eagle Beaches 143
Palm Beach, Noord, and
Western Tip (California Dunes)..... 148
Savaneta and San Nicolas.......... 157
Arikok National
Park and Environs................. 159
Activities 160

6 BARBADOS..................... 167
Welcome to Barbados............. 168
Island Snapshot................... 170
Planning.......................... 173
Bridgetown and the Garrison 179
Hastings, Rockley, and Worthing... 185
St. Lawrence Gap 189
Oistins and the
Surrounding South Point Area 192
Crane and the Southeast 194
Holetown and Vicinity 196
Speightstown..................... 201
East Coast........................ 204
Central Interior 207
Activities 210

7 BONAIRE....................... 215
Welcome to Bonaire 216
Island Snapshot................... 218
Planning.......................... 220
Bonaire........................... 224
Activities 235

8 BRITISH VIRGIN ISLANDS....... 241
Welcome to British Virgin Islands.. 242
Island Snapshot................... 244
Planning.......................... 246
Tortola........................... 248
Side Trips from Tortola 264
Virgin Gorda 264
Jost Van Dyke 273
Anegada 278
Cooper Island..................... 281
Guana Island 282
Norman Island.................... 282

9 CAYMAN ISLANDS 283
Welcome to Cayman Islands....... 284
Island Snapshot................... 286
Planning.......................... 287
Grand Cayman—West Section..... 291
Grand Cayman—The
Eastern Districts 314
Cayman Brac 331
Little Cayman 338

10 CURAÇAO 343
Welcome to Curaçao 344
Island Snapshot 346
Planning 348
Willemstad 354
East End 364
West End 368

11 DOMINICAN REPUBLIC 375
Welcome to Dominican Republic ... 376
Island Snapshot 378
Planning 380
Santo Domingo 384
The Southwest 393
The Southeast Coast 393
Punta Cana 399
North Coast 409
Samaná Peninsula 420
Activities 428

12 GRENADA 437
Welcome to Grenada 438
Island Snapshot 440
Planning 442
St. George's 447
Elsewhere on Grenada 451
Carriacou 465
Petite Martinique 471

13 GUADELOUPE 473
Welcome to Guadeloupe 474
Island Snapshot 476
Planning 478
Grande-Terre 483
Basse-Terre 494
Marie-Galante 500
Îles des Saintes 504

14 JAMAICA 511
Welcome to Jamaica 512
Island Snapshot 514
Planning 516
Montego Bay 521
Falmouth 528
Runaway Bay 530
Ocho Rios 532
Port Antonio 541

Fodor's Features

Flavors of the Caribbean 40

Kingston 545
Port Royal 553
Blue Mountains 554
South Coast 555
Negril 559
Activities 568

15 MARTINIQUE 577
Welcome to Martinique 578
Island Snapshot 580
Planning 582
Fort-de-France 587
Le François 594
Les Trois-Îlets 595
Le Diamant 602
Le Marin 603
Ste-Anne 603
Ste-Luce 604
Balata 605
St-Pierre 606
Le Morne Rouge 608
Macouba 608
Ste-Marie 609
Tartane 610
Le Carbet 611
Le Prêcheur 613
Activities 613

16 PUERTO RICO.................... 617
Welcome to Puerto Rico........... 618
Island Snapshot................... 620
Planning.......................... 622
San Juan.......................... 625
Río Grande........................ 644
El Yunque......................... 645
Luqillo........................... 648
Fajardo........................... 649
Vieques........................... 652
Culebra........................... 656
Dorado............................ 658
Arecibo........................... 659
Rincón............................ 660
Boquerón.......................... 663
Aguadilla......................... 663
Isabela........................... 664
Ponce............................. 665
Guánica........................... 669
San Germán........................ 670

17 ST. BARTHÉLEMY................. 671
Welcome to St. Barthélemy........ 672
Island Snapshot................... 674
Planning.......................... 676
Gustavia.......................... 682
Anse de Toiny..................... 689
Colombier......................... 690
Corossol.......................... 690
Flamands.......................... 691
Gouverneur........................ 692
Grand Cul de Sac.................. 692
Grande Saline..................... 693
Lorient........................... 694
Pointe Milou...................... 695
St-Jean........................... 695
Activities........................ 699

18 ST. KITTS AND NEVIS............ 701
Welcome to St. Kitts and Nevis.... 702
Island Snapshot................... 704
Planning.......................... 706
St. Kitts......................... 709
Nevis............................. 724

19 SAINT LUCIA.................... 737
Welcome to Saint Lucia........... 738
Island Snapshot................... 740
Planning.......................... 743
Rodney Bay and the North......... 748
Castries.......................... 752
Marigot Bay....................... 760
Soufrière and the
Southwest Coast................... 761
Vieux Fort and the East Coast...... 770
Activities........................ 772

20 ST. MAARTEN
AND ST. MARTIN................. 779
Welcome to
St. Maarten and St. Martin........ 780
Island Snapshot................... 782
Planning.......................... 784
St. Maarten (Dutch Side).......... 789
St. Martin (French Side).......... 802
Activities........................ 815

21 TURKS AND CAICOS ISLANDS... 819
Welcome to
Turks and Caicos Islands.......... 820
Island Snapshot................... 822
Planning.......................... 824
Providenciales.................... 827
Parrot Cay........................ 850
Pine Cay.......................... 851
North Caicos...................... 852
Middle Caicos..................... 854
South Caicos...................... 855
Grand Turk........................ 856
Salt Cay.......................... 863

22 UNITED STATES
VIRGIN ISLANDS................. 865
Welcome to
United States Virgin Islands....... 866
Island Snapshot................... 868
Planning.......................... 870
St. Thomas........................ 873
St. John.......................... 899
St. Croix......................... 918

INDEX 943

ABOUT OUR WRITERS. 959

MAPS

The Caribbean 10–11
The Greater Antilles. 12–13
The Lesser Antilles. 14–15
Windward Islands. 16–17
Anguilla 78–79
Antigua. 104–105
Palm Beach, Noord, and Western Tip (California Dunes) 136–137
Oranjestad, Manchebo Beach, Druif Beach, and Eagle Beach 150
Bridgetown and The Garrison. 180–181
Hastings, Rockley, Worthing, St. Lawrence Gap, Oistins, South Point, Crane, and the Southeast. 186–187
Holetown, Speightstown, and Vicinity 202
East Coast and Central Interior. 208
Bonaire. 222–223
Tortola, Scrub Island, and Guana Island 250–251
Virgin Gorda 266–267
Cayman Islands - George Town and West Bay. 300
Grand Cayman - Seven Mile Beach 304
Grand Cayman Eastern Districts . . . 317
Cayman Brac and Little Cayman . . . 332
Curaçao 350–351
Willemstad 356
Santo Domingo 392
The Southwest and The Southeast Coast 394
Punta Cana 400
North Coast. 410
Samaná Peninsula 421
Grenada 448–449
Carriacou and Petite Martinique . . . 466
Grande-Terre and Basse-Terre 484–485
Marie-Galante and Îles des Saintes. 505
Montego Bay 524
Falmouth, Runaway Bay, and Ocho Rios 534–535
Port Antonio, Kingston, Port Royal, and Blue Mountains. 548–549
South Coast 558
Negril 566
Fort-de-France. 590
Martinique. 596–597
Old San Juan 626–627
Greater San Juan 636–637
Puerto Rico 646–647
Greater Ponce 666
St. Barthelemy 678–679
St. Kitts. 710
Nevis. 730
Rodney Bay and the North, Castries, and Marigot Bay 754–755
Soufrière and the Southwest Coast and Vieux Fort and the East Coast 766
St. Maarten (Dutch Side) 790–791
St. Martin (French Side) 804
Providenciales. 830–831
Grand Turk. 858
St. Thomas 876–877
Charlotte Amalie 880
St. John 904–905
St. Croix 920–921

Chapter 1

EXPERIENCE THE CARIBBEAN

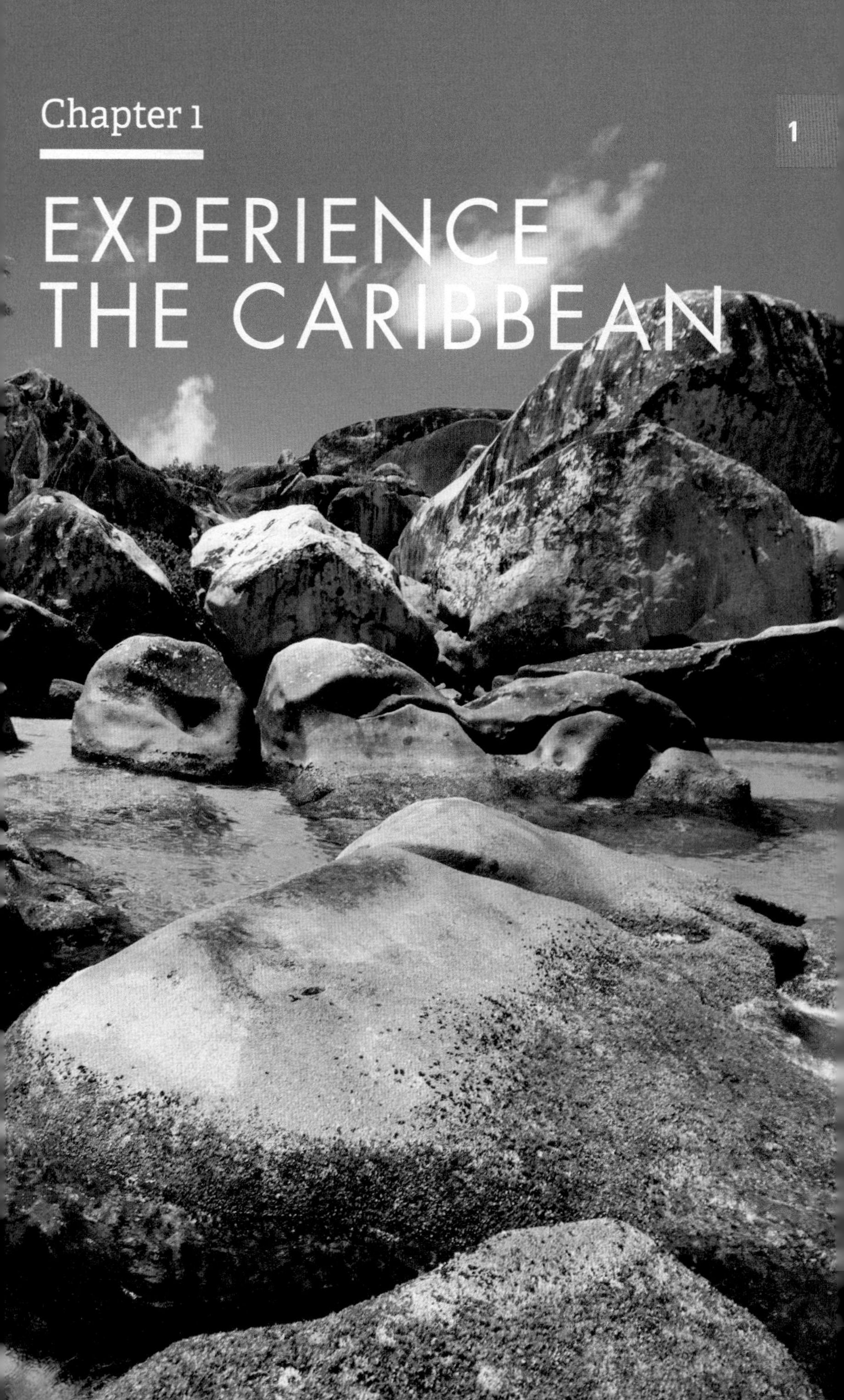

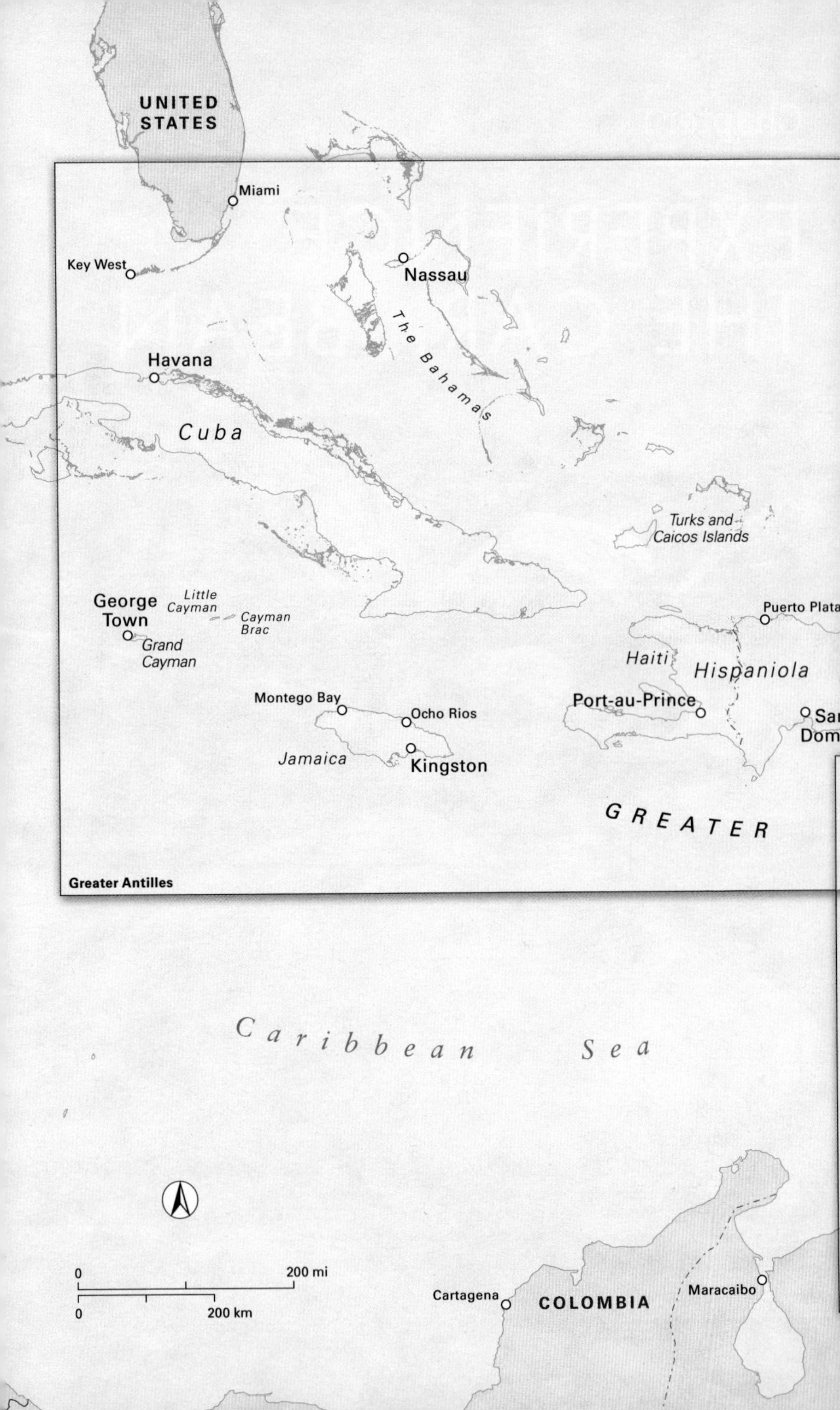

UNITED STATES
Miami
Key West
Nassau
The Bahamas
Havana
Cuba
Turks and Caicos Islands
George Town
Little Cayman
Cayman Brac
Grand Cayman
Puerto Plata
Haiti
Hispaniola
Montego Bay
Ocho Rios
Port-au-Prince
Jamaica
Kingston
GREATER
Greater Antilles
Caribbean Sea
0
200 mi
0
200 km
Cartagena
COLOMBIA
Maracaibo

The Caribbean

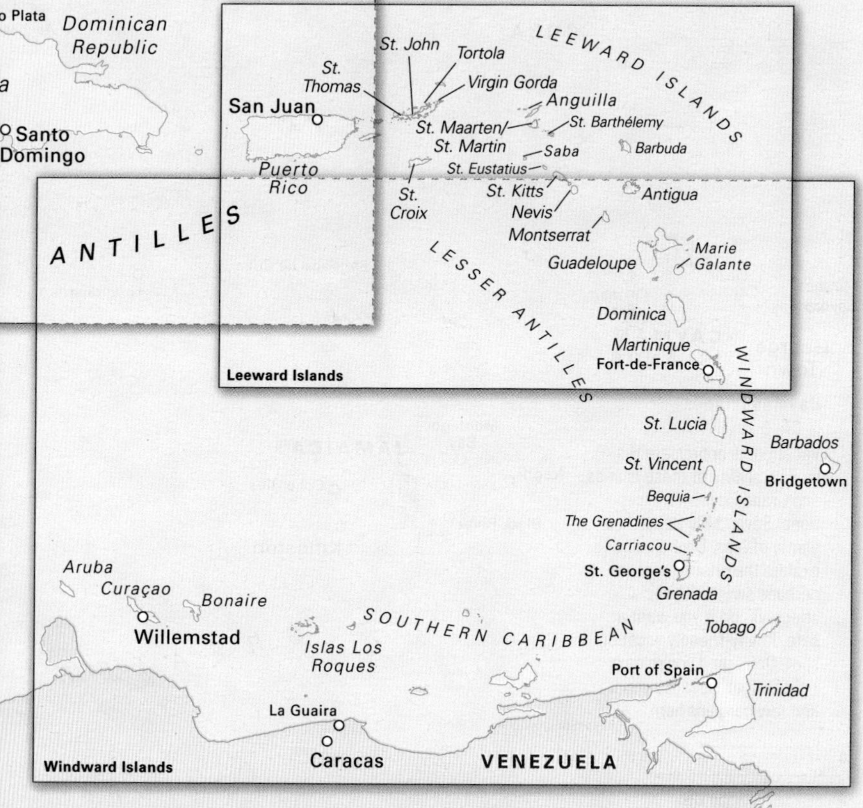

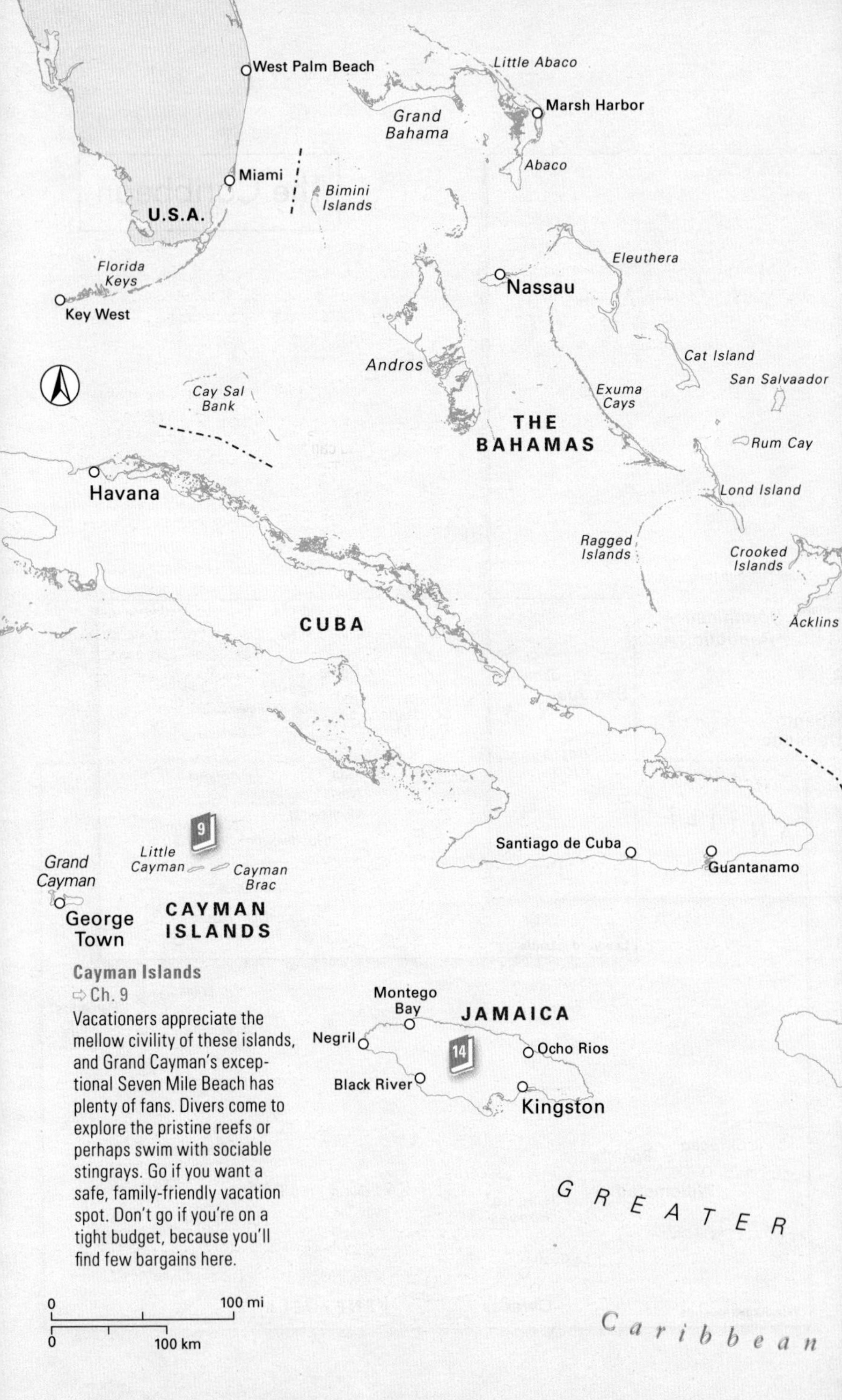

Cayman Islands

⇨ Ch. 9

Vacationers appreciate the mellow civility of these islands, and Grand Cayman's exceptional Seven Mile Beach has plenty of fans. Divers come to explore the pristine reefs or perhaps swim with sociable stingrays. Go if you want a safe, family-friendly vacation spot. Don't go if you're on a tight budget, because you'll find few bargains here.

THE GREATER ANTILLES

The four islands closest to the United States mainland—Cuba, Jamaica, Hispaniola (Haiti and the Dominican Republic), and Puerto Rico—are also the largest in the chain of islands that stretches in an arc from the Florida Keys to Venezuela. The Cayman Islands, just south of Cuba, are included in the Greater Antilles group. We also include Turks and Caicos Islands, which are part of the Lucayan Archipelago. Visit Fodors.com for coverage of Haiti and Cuba.

Dominican Republic ⇨ Ch. 11
This island is blessed with pearl-white beaches and a vibrant Latin culture. Go for the best-priced resorts in the Caribbean and a wide range of activities that will keep you moving day and night. Don't go if you can't go with the flow: Things don't always work here, and not everyone speaks English.

Jamaica ⇨ Ch. 14
Easy to reach and with resorts in every price range, Jamaica is an easy choice for many travelers. Go to enjoy the music, food, beaches, and sense of hospitality that's made Jamaica one of the Caribbean's most popular destinations. Don't go if you can't deal with the idea that a Caribbean paradise still has problems of its own to solve.

Puerto Rico ⇨ Ch. 16
San Juan is hopping day and night; beyond the city, you'll find a sunny escape and slower pace. Party in San Juan, relax on the beach, hike the rain forest, or play some of the Caribbean's best golf courses. You have the best of both worlds here, with natural and urban thrills alike. So go for both—just don't expect to do it in utter seclusion.

Turks and Caicos Islands ⇨ Ch. 21
Miles of white-sand beaches surround this tiny island chain, only nine of which are inhabited. The smaller inhabited islands are reminiscent of some long-forgotten era of Caribbean life. Go for deserted beaches and excellent diving on one of the world's largest coral reefs. Don't go for nightlife and a fast pace. And don't forget your wallet—this isn't a budget destination.

WHAT'S WHERE

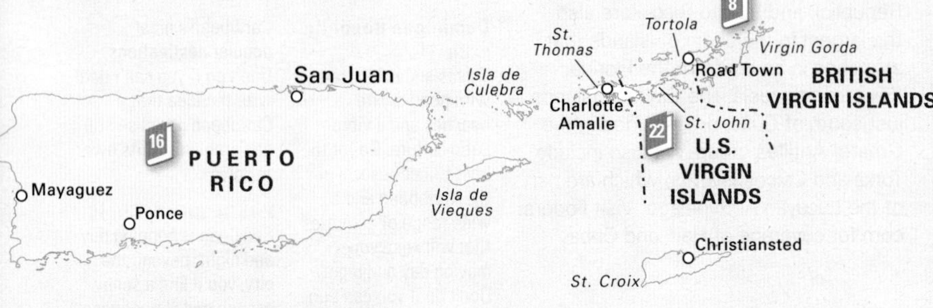

THE LESSER ANTILLES AND THE LEEWARD ISLANDS

Smaller in size but larger in number than the Greater Antilles, the Lesser Antilles make up the bulk of the Caribbean arc. From the Virgin Islands in the north to Trinidad and Tobago in the south, these islands form a barrier between the Atlantic Ocean and the Caribbean Sea. The Lesser Antilles are further divided into the Leeward Islands (Anguilla, Antigua and Barbuda, B.V.I., Guadeloupe, Montserrat, Saba, St. Barth, St. Eustatius, St. Kitts and Nevis, St. Maarten/St. Martin, and U.S.V.I.), the northern islands in the chain; the Windward Islands, farther south in the chain; and the ABCs (Aruba/Bonaire/Curacao), southwest of the Windwards. The Leewards and Windwards are also referred to as the Eastern Caribbean. On any of these islands, the best beaches are usually located on the Caribbean (leeward) side. Visit Fodors.com for coverage of Montserrat, Saba, and St. Eustatius.

Anguilla ⇨ Ch. 3
With miles of brilliant beaches and a range of luxurious resorts (even a few that mere mortals can afford), Anguilla is where the rich, powerful, and famous go to chill. Go for the fine cuisine in elegant surroundings, great snorkeling, and a funky late-night music scene. Don't go for shopping and sightseeing. This island is all about relaxing and reviving.

Antigua and Barbuda ⇨ Ch. 4
Beaches are bone-white and beckoning—there's one for every day of the year—and can be either secluded or hopping with activity. History buffs and nautical nuts will appreciate English Harbour, which sheltered Britain's Caribbean fleet in the 18th and 19th centuries. Go for those beaches but also for sailing. Don't go for local culture, because all-inclusives predominate. Lovely as they are, these islands are more for tourists than travelers.

British Virgin Islands ⇨ Ch. 8
The lure of the British Virgins is exclusivity and personal attention, not lavish luxury. Even the most expensive resorts offer a state of mind rather than state-of-the-art. So go with an open mind, and your stress may very likely disappear. Also go if you love sailing...and island hopping. Don't go if you expect glitz or stateside efficiency. These islands are about getting away, not getting it all.

Guadeloupe ⇨ Ch. 13
An exotic, tropical paradise, butterfly-shaped Guadeloupe is covered by lush rain forest and blessed with a rich Creole culture that influences everything from dancing to food. Go if you want to experience another culture—and still have your creature comforts and access to fine beaches. Don't go if you want five-star luxury, because it's rare here.

St. Barthélemy ⇨ Ch. 17
If you come to St. Barth for a taste of European village life, not for a conventional full-service resort experience, you will find yourself richly rewarded. Go for excellent dining and wine, great boutiques with the latest fashions, and an active vacation. Don't go for big resorts—and make sure your credit card is platinum.

0 50 mi

0 50 km

ATLANTIC OCEAN

Anguilla 3

West End Village

St. Maarten

St. Martin

Marigot

20

Philipsburg

Gustavia

17 St. Barthélemy

Saba

St. Eustatius

Oranjestad

LEEWARD ISLANDS

St. Kitts 18

Basseterre

Nevis

Charlestown

Barbuda 4

Antigua

St Johns

English Harbour

Montserrat

Grande-Terre

Le Désirade

Guadeloupe

Abymes

Pointe-à-Pitre

13

Petite Terre

Basse-Terre

Basse-Terre

Marie Galante

Grande-Bourg

Les Saintes

Portsmouth

Dominica

Roseau

Martinique

15

St Pierre

Fort-de-France

St. Kitts and Nevis ⇨ Ch. 18

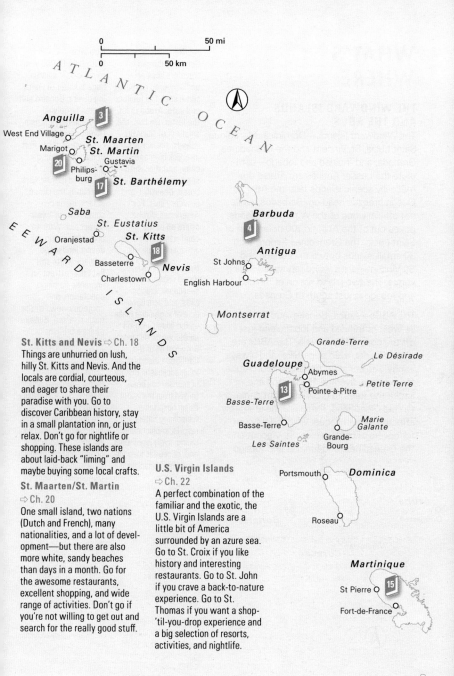

Things are unhurried on lush, hilly St. Kitts and Nevis. And the locals are cordial, courteous, and eager to share their paradise with you. Go to discover Caribbean history, stay in a small plantation inn, or just relax. Don't go for nightlife or shopping. These islands are about laid-back "liming" and maybe buying some local crafts.

St. Maarten/St. Martin ⇨ Ch. 20

One small island, two nations (Dutch and French), many nationalities, and a lot of development—but there are also more white, sandy beaches than days in a month. Go for the awesome restaurants, excellent shopping, and wide range of activities. Don't go if you're not willing to get out and search for the really good stuff.

U.S. Virgin Islands ⇨ Ch. 22

A perfect combination of the familiar and the exotic, the U.S. Virgin Islands are a little bit of America surrounded by an azure sea. Go to St. Croix if you like history and interesting restaurants. Go to St. John if you crave a back-to-nature experience. Go to St. Thomas if you want a shop-'til-you-drop experience and a big selection of resorts, activities, and nightlife.

WHAT'S WHERE

THE WINDWARD ISLANDS AND THE ABCS

The Windward Islands—Dominica, Martinique, Saint Lucia, St. Vincent and the Grenadines, Grenada, and Trinidad and Tobago—complete the Lesser Antilles arc. These dramatically scenic islands face the Atlantic Ocean breezes head-on. Barbados, while not officially one of the Windward Islands, pokes out of the Atlantic 100 miles east of Saint Lucia. The Grenadines—more than 30 small islands between Grenada and St. Vincent—are a world-renowned sailing venue. The two-island nation of Trinidad and Tobago is just south of Grenada.

The ABCs—Aruba, Bonaire, and Curaçao—lie west of Trinidad and Tobago and just off the coast of Venezuela. The ABCs are unusually dry, even desertlike, and always windy. The constant trade winds on Aruba, for example, average 15–35 mph and cause the trees to grow at a right angle. On the other hand, these islands are rarely affected by hurricanes. Visit Fodors.com for coverage of Dominica, St. Vincent and the Grenadines, and Trinidad and Tobago.

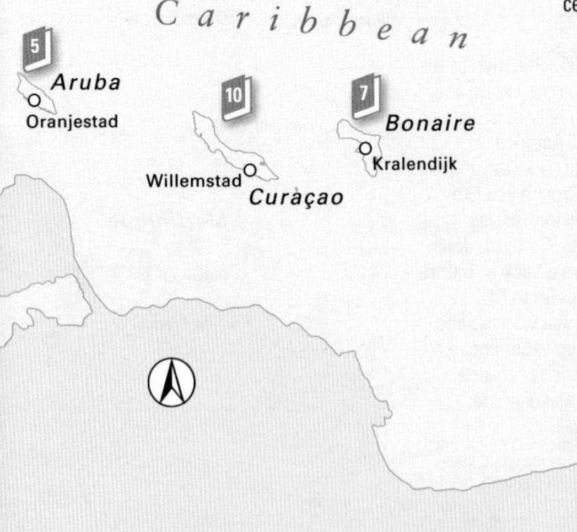

Aruba ⇨ Ch. 5
Some Caribbean travelers seek an undiscovered paradise; some seek the familiar and safe. Aruba is for the latter. On this, the smallest of the ABC islands, the waters are peacock blue and calm, and the white sandy beaches are broad, beautiful, and powdery soft. For Americans, Aruba offers all of the comforts of home—and lots of casinos.

Barbados ⇨ Ch. 6
Broad vistas, sweeping seascapes, craggy cliffs, and acre upon acre of sugarcane make up the island's varied landscape. In this most British of all of the Caribbean islands, a long, successful history of tourism has been forged from the warm Bajan hospitality, welcoming hotels and resorts, sophisticated dining, lively nightspots, and, of course, magnificent sunny beaches.

Bonaire ⇨ Ch. 7
With only 15,000 year-round citizens and a huge number of visiting divers, Bonaire still seems largely untouched by tourism. Divers come for the clear water, profusion of marine life, and great dive shops. A protected marine park surrounds the island; in fact, many dive spots feature "walk-in" access. With an arid, almost surreal desert landscape, brilliant white salt flats that attract an immense flamingo population, and gorgeous views of the turquoise sea, Bonaire offers a brilliant holiday setting for landlubbers, too.

Curaçao ⇨ Ch. 10
Rich in heritage and history, Curaçao easily blends quaint island life and savvy city life, along with wonderful weather, spectacular diving, and charming beaches. Dutch and Caribbean influences

are everywhere, but there's also an infusion of touches from around the world—particularly noteworthy in the great food. Willemstad is the picturesque capital and a treat for pedestrians, with shopping clustered in areas around the waterfront.

Grenada ⇨ Ch. 12
The spice business is going strong, but tourism is just as important. On this truly laid-back island, you'll spend your days splashing in the surf on spectacular Grand Anse Beach, exploring the lush rain forest, and enjoying nutmeg-flavored everything (drinks, ice cream, syrups, sauces...). Resorts are mostly small and charming. St. George's, the island's capital, boasts what is often considered the most beautiful harbor in the Caribbean.

Martinique ⇨ Ch. 15
Excellent cuisine, fine service, highly touted rum, and lilting Franco-Caribbean music are the main draws in Martinique. Go if you're a Francophile drawn to fine food, wine, and sophisticated style. Don't go if you are looking for a bargain and have little patience. Getting here is a chore, but there are definitely rewards for the persistent.

Saint Lucia ⇨ Ch. 19
One of the greenest and most beautiful islands in the Caribbean is, arguably, also the most romantic. The scenic southwestern and central regions are mountainous and lush, with dense rainforest, endless banana plantations, and fascinating natural sites. In the north, some of the region's most appealing resorts are interspersed with dozens of delightful inns that welcome families as well as lovers and adventurers.

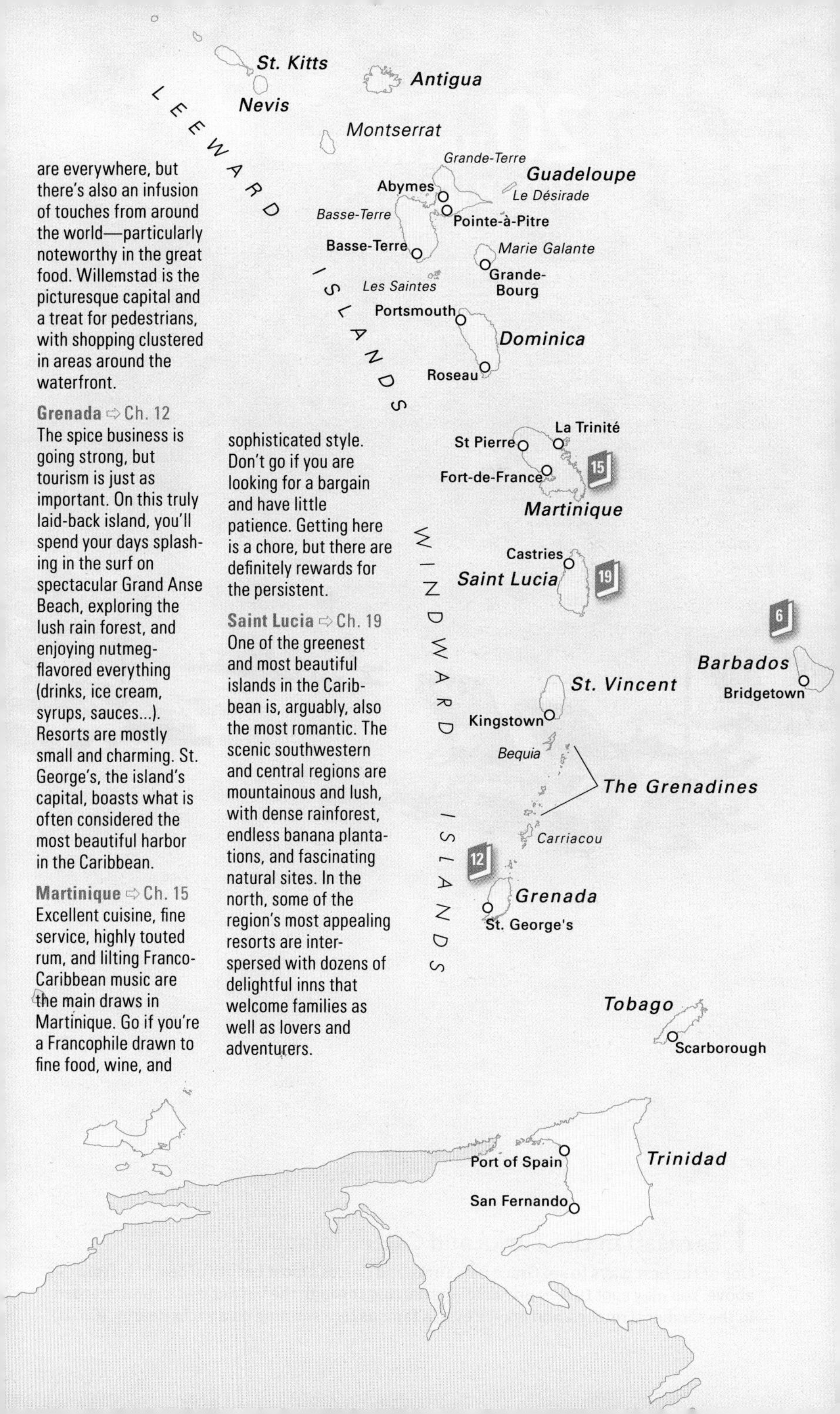

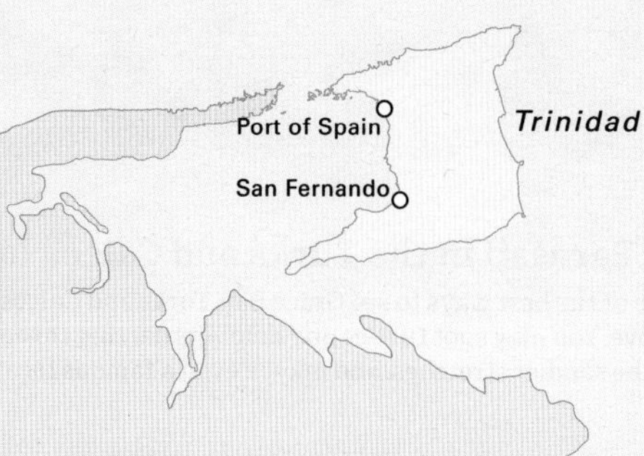

20 ULTIMATE EXPERIENCES

The Caribbean offers terrific experiences that should be on every traveler's list. Here are Fodor's top picks for a memorable trip.

1 Parasail in the Turks and Caicos Islands

One of the best ways to see Grace Bay, Turks and Caicos's most beautiful beach, is from above. You may spot turtles and dolphins darting through the barrier reef's coral, starfish in the sandier stretches, and maybe even a famous face sunning on a yacht nearby. (Ch. 21)

2 Snorkel in the Cayman Islands

There are plenty of snorkel sites in the Cayman Islands to spot colorful reefs and tropical fish, including Grand Cayman's popular Stingray City. (Ch. 9)

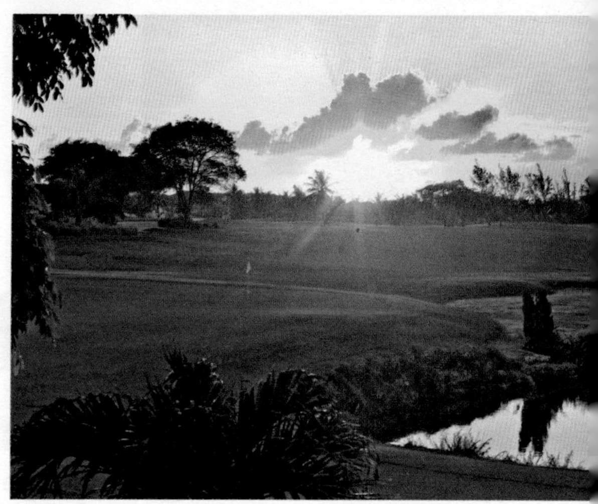

3 Golf in Barbados

Barbados boasts five PGA Standard golf courses, some of which are designed by legends like Tom Fazio and Robert Trent Jones Jr. (Ch. 6)

4 Whale-Watch in the Dominican Republic

The DR boasts the Caribbean's largest whale-watching industry; from January through March, more than 200 humpback whales migrate from Iceland and North America to reproduce in Samaná Bay. (Ch. 11)

5 Hike in Guadeloupe

Nearly 200 miles of trails twist through Guadeloupe National Park's practically untouched terrain past waterfalls, forests, and the tallest peak in the Lesser Antilles—La Grande Soufrière. (Ch. 13)

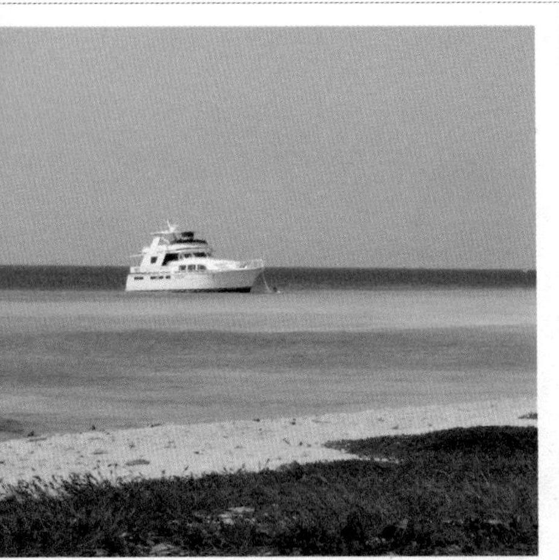

6 Cruise to Little Curaçao

Take a catamaran tour to the deserted coral atoll known as Klein (Little) Curaçao, which lies about 15 miles off Curaçao's southeastern tip. The main reason to visit? The beach, of course! (Ch. 10)

7 Dine in St. Maarten/St. Martin

For an island measuring a mere 37 square miles, it's impressive that St. Maarten/St. Martin has more than 400 restaurants. You'll find the best in St. Martin's village of Grand Case. (Ch. 20)

8 Explore History in St. Kitts and Nevis

Known as the "Gibraltar of the West Indies," St. Kitts's Brimstone Hill Fortress is worth a stop. And Nevis's biggest claim to historical fame? It's the birthplace of Alexander Hamilton. (Ch. 18)

9 View Underwater Art in Grenada

The Underwater Sculpture Park off Moliniere Point is home to 75 different statues that are a favorite spot for divers but still shallow enough to be viewed while snorkeling. (Ch. 12)

10 Sunbathe in Anguilla

The eel-shaped island (named for the French word, anguille) is lined by 33 white-sand beaches, many of which rank among the world's 10 best. (Ch. 3)

11 Windsurf in Bonaire

Stunning Lac Bay, a windsurfer's dream, has an endless sweep of turquoise water, much of it waist-deep, and a constant stiff breeze. (Ch. 7)

12 Sail in Saint Lucia

Take a catamaran from Rodney Bay to Soufrière to visit all the natural sights, including the botanical garden, sulphur baths, and drive-in volcano—and get a waterside view of the famed Pitons. (Ch. 19)

13 Feel Irie in Jamaica

Reggae was born in Jamaica in the 1960s and has become the "heartbeat" of its people. The familiar, pulsing rhythm can be heard everywhere, from jerk shacks to the island's famed summer reggae festival. (Ch. 14)

14 Go Off-Roading in Aruba

Hop on an ATV and zip through abandoned gold mines and past twisted divi-divi trees and cacti in Aruba's desert-like Arikok National Park, which covers 20 percent of the island. (Ch. 5)

15 Sail in the BVI

The BVI has earned its reputation as the "Sailing Capital of the Caribbean," with the Sir Francis Drake Channel ensuring plenty of safe anchorages and several untouched islands and secluded cays to explore. (Ch. 8)

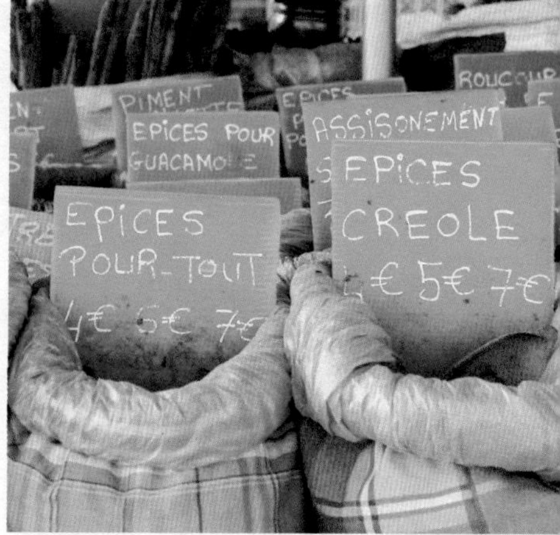

16 Window-Shop in St. Barth

Even if you can't splurge on a new bag at Dolce & Gabbana or a timepiece at Rolex, you can still indulge in fantastic window shopping at the island's 200-plus (duty-free) luxurious boutiques. (Ch. 17)

17 Enjoy French Fare in Martinique

Cuisine in Martinique mixes the island's French heritage with Caribbean creole. In the capital of Fort-de-France, savor the local flavors at Grand Marché, the island's largest market. (Ch. 15)

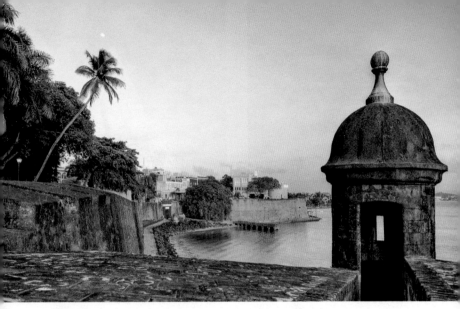

18 Soak Up History in Puerto Rico

In the second-oldest city in the "New World," Old San Juan's historic district is a maze of cobblestone streets crowned by two 500-year-old forts, El Morro and San Cristóbal. (Ch.16)

19 Catch the Sunset Party in Antigua

The 490-foot-high Shirley Heights Lookout point hosts a weekly Sunday evening party, which shows off one of the most scenic views of the water below. (Ch. 4)

20 Sail and Shop in the USVI

Sailing is a popular pastime around St. John; but if shopping is more your thing, head to Charlotte Amalie (St. Thomas) and Christiansted (St. Croix) for art and duty-free finds. (Ch. 22)

Best Resorts in the Caribbean

JADE MOUNTAIN, SAINT LUCIA

If vistas of the Pitons and the shimmering sea aren't enough to woo you, perhaps an infinity pool in your room will. All of Jade Mountain's 24 guest sanctuaries (optional all-inclusive) have open fourth walls and individually designed swimming pools. *(Ch. 19)*

ZOËTRY AGUA PUNTA CANA, DOMINICAN REPUBLIC

It's hard NOT to find an all-inclusive resort in the Dominican Republic, but Zoëtry Agua Punta Cana blows its neighbors out of the water. The picturesque setting is just the beginning. Prepare to be spoiled! Your personal butler is on hand to satisfy all your needs—whether that's arranging horseback riding or pampering massages. *(Ch. 11)*

GALLEY BAY RESORT & SPA, ANTIGUA

Galley Bay Resort & Spa is exactly what you envision in an adults-only Caribbean vacation. Food is plentiful and delicious, and cocktails are dangerously good. Paddleboards and kayaks are a great way to burn off all those piña coladas, and the staff is eager to cater to your every whim. If you're seeking after-dark excitement, the Sea Grape hosts live music. *(Ch. 4)*

COBBLERS COVE, BARBADOS

Cobblers Cove, on Barbados's magical Platinum Coast, is an exercise in understated elegance with sherbet-hued facades, breezy decor, and lush tropical gardens. If you want a massive resort, look elsewhere, because this is a B&B/half-board jewel with an optional all-inclusive package—and thoughtful touches like afternoon tea. *(Ch. 6)*

ROUND HILL, JAMAICA
Round Hill isn't the typical all-inclusive, with shiny yellow wristbands and fluorescent daiquiris. Instead, this family-friendly resort proffers an all-inclusive option that's an excellent value and allows travelers to fully settle into vacation mode knowing everything is covered. *(Ch. 14)*

CASA DE CAMPO, DR
Casa de Campo is one of those treasures that doesn't just have returning guests; it has die-hard loyalists. Why? Because this sprawling 7,000-acre sanctum boasts first-class facilities that include an 18-hole golf course, tennis courts, a fitness center, and a spa. *(Ch. 11)*

THE CAVES, JAMAICA
A far cry from all-you-can-eat buffets and jam-packed schedules, this grown-up getaway offers an intimate all-inclusive experience geared toward couples. Expect cliff-side cottages, cerulean seas, and warm hospitality. *(Ch. 14)*

JUMBY BAY, ANTIGUA
Heralded as the crème de la crème of all-inclusives, this 300-acre private island off the north coast of Antigua is where celebs go for paparazzi-free downtime and discrete decadence—well, that along with exceptional service and a backdrop of unblemished beauty. *(Ch. 4)*

CURTAIN BLUFF, ANTIGUA
Breathtaking beaches and turquoise waves are complemented by sophisticated rooms and award-winning cuisine at Curtain Bluff. In fact, gourmet dining is a major selling point. Health-focused travelers will appreciate dedicated wellness concierges, nutritious menus, and calorie-burning activities. *(Ch. 4)*

TAMARIJN ARUBA ALL-INCLUSIVE, ARUBA
At one of Aruba's original and most popular family-friendly all-inclusives—and a sister resort to the Divi Aruba—children under 12 stay free when accompanied by two adults. Druif Beach is gorgeous, all nonmotorized water sports are included, and there's a 30-foot tall climbing tower on the beach. *(Ch. 5)*

The Caribbean's Best Outdoor Activities

WATER SPORTS
The Caribbean is *the* place for water sports—kayaking, paddleboarding, windsurfing, kitesurfing, snorkeling—and rates at beachfront lodgings usually include free use of nonmotorized equipment.

HORSEBACK RIDING
Horseback riding on the beach as the sun sets is a quintessential Caribbean dream that can become reality in Anguilla, Aruba, the Dominican Republic, Guadeloupe, Jamaica, Martinique, Puerto Rico, St. Kitts and Nevis, Saint Lucia, St. Maarten/St. Martin, Turks and Caicos Islands, and the U.S. Virgin Islands.

ZIPLINING
Fly with the birds above the rain forest canopy, passing occasional waterfalls and wildlife as you zip from platform to platform tethered to a zipline in Antigua, the Dominican Republic, Jamaica, Puerto Rico, St. Kitts, Saint Lucia, and St. Maarten/St. Martin—with more islands coming on board all the time.

BOATING AND SAILING
Whether you charter a boat or captain a vessel yourself, the Caribbean's many secluded bays and inlets are ideal for boating and sailing. From either the USVI or the BVI, for example, you can explore more than 100 islands and cays within a 50-nautical-mile radius. Cruising to a different beach or yacht harbor every day is a truly unique way to experience the Caribbean. Antigua and St. Lucia host major sailing regattas each year, attracting international sailors.

DIVING AND SNORKELING
The best conditions for diving and snorkeling—clear water, lots of marine life, and numerous wreck sites—can be found throughout the Caribbean's crystalline waters. Some of the best spots are in the Cayman Islands, as well as in Bonaire, Curaçao, Saint Lucia, and the Virgin Islands (both U.S. and British).

WHALE-WATCHING
Samaná, in the northeastern Dominican Republic, is revered for its shimmering water, Champagne-hued sand, and superior sportfishing. But its signature aquatic activity is world-class whale-watching in season (January through March), as pods of humpbacks mate and calve. Other opportunities for a whale-watching trip include Guadeloupe, Jamaica, Martinique, Puerto Rico, Saint Lucia, and the Turks and Caicos Islands.

There are trails for every level of hiker in Antigua.

FISHING

Fish—barracuda, bonefish, billfish, dolphin, kingfish, marlin, sailfish, swordfish, tarpon, wahoo, yellowfin tuna, or the ravenous lionfish (a threat to local species, but delicious)—are biting year-round in the Caribbean, and half- and full-day deep-sea, reef, and coastal fishing charters are available on almost every island. Many billfish are catch-and-release; sometimes, you can take your catch back to your resort where the chef will prepare it for your dinner.

HIKING

Hiking in the Caribbean is often associated with lush rain forests. That wouldn't be wrong, but on mountainous islands—like Grenada, Guadeloupe, Jamaica, Martinique, Nevis, St. Kitts, and Saint Lucia—an often-challenging hike to a mountain summit or caldera can provide spellbinding views.

BIKES, SCOOTERS, AND ATVS

Many hotels have cruising bikes available for guests to take out for a leisurely spin, but serious mountain bikers will find worthwhile tracks in Barbados, the Dominican Republic, Nevis, Saint Lucia, and the Turks and Caicos Islands. Scooters are available to rent on almost every island in the Caribbean, and they are a great way to see the sights. Daredevils might want to join an ATV excursion in the Dominican Republic, Jamaica, or Saint Lucia.

BIRD-WATCHING

The watching part isn't so active, but hiking through rain forests, up mountain trails, and across savannas will give you the opportunity to see more bird species than you can count—including the nine different parrot species that make their nests in the Caribbean.

Best Beaches in the Caribbean

BOTTOM BAY BEACH, BARBADOS
Barbados has many top-notch beaches, but secluded Bottom Bay Beach is the star. Tucked into a quiet spot at the island's southeastern tip and surrounded by coral cliffs, the beach's pure white sand is soft and studded with swaying palm trees. *(Ch. 6)*

SOROBON BEACH, BONAIRE
This stunning white-sand beach along the southern edge of Lac Bay—on Bonaire's sunny, windy, southeastern coast—is mecca for windsurfers. The water is no more than waist-deep and you'll find covered areas for shade or a picnic. *(Ch. 7)*

PLAYA PORTOMARI, CURAÇAO
This long stretch of white sand on Porto Marie Bay is part of Plantages Porto-Mari, a private estate on the west coast of the island near the village of Sint Willibrordus. A double reef is accessible from shore, making it an excellent place to snorkel or dive. *(Ch. 10)*

SHOAL BAY, ANGUILLA
This tiny island is packed with 33 beautiful beaches, but Shoal Bay on the northwestern coast steals the show with its two-mile-long white-sand beach, crystal-clear water, and family-friendly surf. *(Ch. 3)*

EAGLE BEACH, ARUBA
Aruba's widest beach wins the prize, with striking white sand, aquamarine water, gentle surf, and the iconic divi-divi tree that you see in almost every Aruba photograph. *(Ch. 5)*

PINK BEACH, BARBUDA
Barbuda, sister island to Antigua, is off the beaten track, so its 17 miles of Pink Beach are a hidden treasure unless you're in the know. The unusually soft sand gets its sponginess and hue from eons of crushed pink shells being churned up from the seabed. *(Ch. 4)*

THE BATHS, VIRGIN GORDA, BVI
A small beach adjacent to the giant boulders known as The Baths is perfect for a refreshing swim; snorkelers will see lots of fish. Come early in the day or later in the afternoon to escape most of the day-trippers. *(Ch. 8)*

SEVEN MILE BEACH, GRAND CAYMAN
Along Grand Cayman's picturesque western shore, Seven Mile Beach has long been named one of the best Caribbean beaches—if not *the* best Caribbean beach—period. *(Ch. 9)*

The 17-mile Pink Beach on Barbuda is a hidden treasure.

PLAYA FLAMENCO, CULEBRA, PUERTO RICO
A 50-minute ferry ride from Ceiba, this horseshoe-shaped playa's sparkling white sand and clear turquoise water are surrounded by swaying palms, lush green hills, and the Culebra National Wildlife Refuge. *(Ch. 16)*

ANSE DE GRANDE SALINE, ST. BARTH
Named for the large inland salt pond nearby, the stretch of unspoiled beachfront along the southern shore of St. Barth is public but feels private. *(Ch. 17)*

PINNEY'S BEACH, NEVIS
This long stretch of soft golden sand, shaded by palm trees on one side and lapped by the clear blue sea on the other, is the two-island nation's most popular beach. *(Ch. 18)*

REDUIT BEACH, SAINT LUCIA
This long strand of golden sand is the focal point of Rodney Bay Village. Three resorts line most of the beachfront, but that doesn't preclude public access. Kids (and adults) love Splash Island Water Park, just offshore. *(Ch. 19)*

MULLET BAY BEACH, ST. MAARTEN
Calm and quiet (except for the occasional roar of a passing plane), this beach is perfect for swimming, especially at the northern end, and never too crowded. *(Ch. 20)*

NEGRIL BEACH, JAMAICA
Also called Seven Mile Beach, Negril Beach stretches along the western tip of Jamaica and is the island's finest beach—especially for nude sunbathing. The white sand is soft and smooth, the gentle sea is robin's egg blue, and the sunsets are amazing. *(Ch. 14)*

Top Golf Courses in the Caribbean

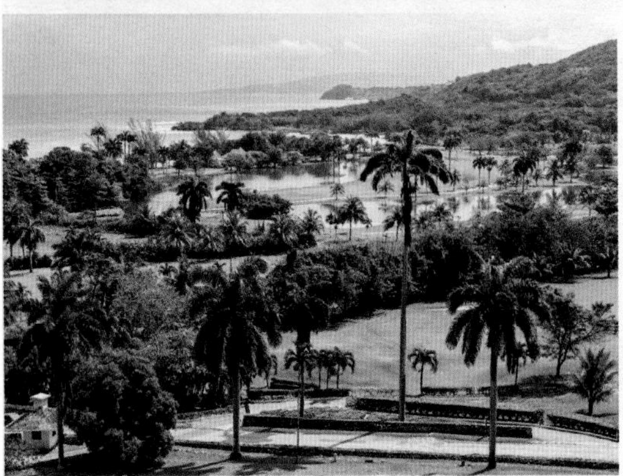

THE TRYALL CLUB GOLF COURSE, JAMAICA
Combine first-class golf with the island's storied history at this Ralph Plummer–designed course, beautifully laid out on the site of a 19th-century sugar plantation 15 miles west of Montego Bay. *(Ch. 14)*

CASA DE CAMPO RESORT, DOMINICAN REPUBLIC
The scenic Teeth of the Dog course, one of the resort's three extraordinary courses designed by the legendary P. B. (Pete) Dye, is considered one of the top courses in the world. *(Ch. 11)*

SANDY LANE COUNTRY CLUB, BARBADOS
Perhaps the Caribbean's most prestigious club, golfers can play the Old Nine, with its small greens and narrow fairways, or one of two Tom Fazio–designed courses—the modern-style Country Club Course or the spectacular Green Monkey (reserved for guests and club members). *(Ch. 6)*

FOUR SEASONS GOLF COURSE, NEVIS
The majestic scenery and unbelievably lush landscaping, along with Robert Trent Jones Jr.'s wicked layout incorporating ravines and sugar mills, make this golfing experience well above par. *(Ch. 18)*

BUCCANEER GOLF COURSE, ST. CROIX, USVI
You'll have a spectacular Caribbean view from 13 of the 18 holes at this challenging, yet very playable, course on the eastern end of the island and not far from Christiansted. *(Ch. 22)*

THE GOLF LINKS AT ROYAL ISABELA, PUERTO RICO
One of the most dramatic courses built in recent years, this challenging course—two distinct 9-hole circuits—features an incomparable setting along the dramatic bluffs on the northwest edge of the island, 70 miles west of San Juan. *(Ch. 16)*

AURORA INTERNATIONAL GOLF CLUB, ANGUILLA
The Caribbean's answer to Pebble Beach—13 of the 18 holes on this challenging Greg Norman course, and Anguilla's only golf course, directly overlook the sea. The course was remastered and a 9-hole course added in 2021; an ecosystem of ponds and lagoons snakes through the course. *(Ch. 3)*

PROVO GOLF CLUB, TURKS AND CAICOS
You'll find stunning scenery—rugged limestone outcroppings and freshwater lakes—along with immaculate greens, lush fairways, and four sets of tees to suit all golfing levels at this top-ranked championship course in Providenciales. *(Ch. 21)*

BARBADOS GOLF CLUB, BARBADOS
A round of golf on a championship course in the Caribbean doesn't have to break the bank. This Ron Kirby-designed, 18-hole public course (returning 9s) built on gently rolling hills on the south coast of the island offers players exciting, affordable golf. *(Ch. 6)*

LA CANA GOLF CLUB, DOMINICAN REPUBLIC
Three 9s—Tortuga, Arrecife, and Hacienda—make up 27 holes of championship golf on this P. B. (Pete) Dye–designed course at Puntacana Resort & Club—the first course in the Caribbean to use grass seed that can be watered with sea water; 14 holes have ocean views. *(Ch. 11)*

11 Places to Experience Carnival in the Caribbean

Nothing brings West Indians together like a party that celebrates their culture. Here are 11 islands that showcase the best of Carnival in the Caribbean—complete with costumes, music, dancing, and great food.

MARTINIQUE

Carnaval de Martinique is a unique celebration of French and African culture that lasts for five days, beginning just before Lent. The fête features parades of costumed revelers, rhythmic music, singing, dancing, mock weddings, along with a King or Vaval, a mannequin made from paper, reeds, or wood that's carried through the festival's parades and burned in a massive bonfire on Fat Tuesday (Mardi Gras). *(Ch. 15)*

SAINT LUCIA

Saint Lucia Carnival is a month-long summer celebration that starts in June with a host of parties and events such as steel band competitions, pageants, and a Junior Carnival. Most revelers and spectators look forward to the last two days of Carnival, in mid-July, when the two-day costumes parade and Road March competition take place. There's a flurry of jewels, beads, and feathers, as performers parade to the sounds of soca, reggae, and calypso music. *(Ch. 19)*

BARBADOS

Crop Over, Barbados's annual festival that is fairly equivalent to Carnival, began more than 300 years ago as a harvest festival on sugar cane plantations during slavery. The festival, which runs over a 12-week period from May through August, includes hundreds of craft and food vendors, musical events, parades, and competitions to determine the festival's King and Queen. The main celebrations take place on the last four days of Crop Over and end on Grand Kadooment Day. *(Ch. 6)*

ARUBA

Aruba's Carnival is a month-long celebration that culminates on the day before Ash Wednesday. The weeks before feature street parades, locally called "jump-ups," that lead up to the Grand Carnival Parade in Oranjestad. The midnight burning of King Momo, a life-size effigy of the spirit of Carnival, signals the end of the season. *(Ch. 5)*

DOMINICAN REPUBLIC

This is not the typical Carnival celebration. Instead of calypso and soca, you'll hear merengue and bachata. Instead of barely-there costumes with jewels and feathers, you'll see traditional Taino costumes and African garments. Parades take place every Sunday in February in all of the major cities; the most popular is El Carnaval de la Vega, in La Vega, the country's third-largest city. *(Ch. 11)*

JAMAICA

Bacchanal, as it is called in Jamaica, has gained a reputation for being one of the Caribbean's most popular and most exciting events—combining all the traditional aspects of a Caribbean Carnival with Jamaican music, food, and vibrant people. The celebrations start as early as January in Ocho Rios and Kingston and end after Easter with the final event, Bacchanal Road March. Locals and tourists alike cover themselves with oil, glitter, and paint and then head out in their costumes to dance in the street to the latest soca and dancehall tunes. *(Ch. 14)*

ST. MAARTEN

The tiny island of St. Maarten (the Dutch side of the two-nation island St. Maarten/St. Martin) comes alive during Carnival season—18 days in April. All festivities—parades, music competitions, reggae and soca bands, vibrant costumes, dancing, drinks, and food—take place at the purpose-built St. Maarten Carnival Village, the island's largest arena. *(Ch. 20)*

CURAÇAO

Carnival Curaçao, a nearly month-long event ending on the eve of Ash Wednesday, features teen and adult King and Queen competitions, a teen Carnival parade, a children's parade, and a number of "jump-ups" (street parties), which all lead up to the two major events: Gran Marcha (Grand Parade) and Marcha di Despedida (Farewell March), which mark the official end of the carnival season. *(Ch. 10)*

PUERTO RICO

Officially called Carnaval Ponceño, this annual weeklong celebration held in the city of Ponce, typically begins the week before Lent and ends on Ash Wednesday. Parties and parades are a daily happening, starting with the Vejigantes (Devil's) Party procession and ending with the Burial of the Sardine (Entierro de la Sardina) ceremony on the day before Ash Wednesday. Many of the traditions, ceremonies, and costumes of Carnaval Ponceño reflect Puerto Rico's Spanish and Catholic roots. *(Ch. 16)*

GUADELOUPE

From the beginning of January to Ash Wednesday, the colorful Carnival festivities liven up the islands of Guadeloupe. The major events—the Opening Parade and the Grand Parade, which feature music, bands, and skimpy costumes with matching headwear—are held in the capital city of Basse-Terre. There are also singing and dancing contests, costumed processions, and a competition to determine the Carnival King and Queen. After the festivities have ended, King Vaval (a symbolic figure for Carnival) is burnt on Ash Wednesday to mark the end of carnival season. *(Ch. 13)*

GRENADA

In early August, the Caribbean island of spice celebrates its very own 10-day Carnival celebration, called Spice Mas. While the pageants and parades are always fun and entertaining, the celebration itself has deep-rooted spiritual links to the island's African, French, British, and Caribbean heritage. If you happen to be in St. George's for Spice Mas, you'll see streets full of calpysonians, steel pan orchestras, costumed frolickers, and other masqueraders covered in black oil, horns, and chains—a Grenadian tradition called "Jab Jab." *(Ch. 12)*

Best Dive and Snorkel Destinations in the Caribbean

BRITISH VIRGIN ISLANDS
In BVI, divers can explore the spectacular corals and sea life within the system of marine parks, the colorful reefs teeming with fish just below the surface, and some amazing wrecks. For snorkelers, The Caves at Norman Island and The Indians, nearby, are terrific sites. *(Ch. 8)*

ANGUILLA
Diving and snorkeling are relatively easy in Anguilla—there's a long barrier reef, sunken wrecks, mini-walls, and seven designated marine parks. Boat trips (dive boat or public shuttle) to nearby cays are another option. *(Ch. 3)*

ARUBA
Intriguing coral formations and rather spectacular shipwrecks—including the 400-foot, World War II-era, German cargo ship *Antilla*—make Aruba a great option for divers and snorkelers. Snorkelers will also find walk-in opportunities at beaches with shallow water (perfect for youngsters), fascinating corals and sponges, and plenty of colorful fish—especially at Baby Beach and around Boca Catalina and Malmok. *(Ch. 5)*

BARBADOS
More than two dozen dive sites attract scuba divers to the reefs and wrecks off Holetown on the island's west coast and Carlisle Bay in the south. Barbados's calm waters are also ideal for snorkeling. On the west coast, Dottin's Reef is easily accessible from shore—especially from the beach at Folkestone Underwater Park & Marine Reserve. *(Ch. 6)*

BONAIRE
Bonaire's fantastic reef diving has been compared to that of Australia's Great Barrier Reef. With more than 63 dive sites, many walk-in accessible, Bonaire Marine Park is a prime spot to glimpse an abundant array of underwater life, including turtles, purple stovepipes, brain coral, and tropical fish. *(Ch. 7)*

CAYMAN ISLANDS
Soaring pinnacles, precipitous walls, beautiful coral-encrusted caverns and grottos, swim-through arches, and more than 200 dive sites (many close to shore), make the Cayman Islands one of the Caribbean's (if not the world's) leading dive destinations. Divers and snorkelers of all abilities particularly enjoy exploring the reefs around Cayman Brac—where divers can inspect the MV *Capt. Keith Tibbetts*, a 330-foot Russian frigate purposely sunk in 1996. *(Ch. 9)*

CURAÇAO
About one-third of the southern coast of Curaçao is a protected marine park, with wall diving, a couple of wrecks, and more. High on the list of boat dives, though, is Mushroom Forest, just off the island's northwest shore, where the coral heads resemble giant mushrooms. For snorkelers, one of the most popular spots is a small sunken tugboat in shallow water at Spanish Water; it's often included in a boat tour but also accessible by land. *(Ch. 10)*

A coral reef off Bonaire's coast is the perfect spot for diving.

GRENADA
Grenada and its sister island, Carriacou, offer some of the region's best diving in the form of wrecks, reefs, and drift dives. On Grenada's west coast, scuba divers swim around—and snorkelers swim above—75 life-size figures in the Underwater Sculpture Park at Molinere Point, the world's first underwater environment of its kind. Nearby Carriacou has 20 dive sites, 15 within a marine protected area, and a pair of intentionally sunk wrecks. *(Ch. 12)*

GUADELOUPE
While dive sites are scattered all around the island, Cousteau Underwater Park is the island's main diving and snorkeling area. Les Saintes, one of Guadeloupe's offshore islands, is also a great place to dive and snorkel; it's known for underwater hills, caves, and trees that actually sway. *(Ch. 13)*

SAINT LUCIA
Superb dive sites are found near The Pitons, on the island's southwestern coast. Snorkelers enjoy exploring the reefs at Anse Cochon, a usual stop on day sails between Rodney Bay and Soufrière; nearby, the *Lesleen M*, a 165-foot freighter, was sunk to become an artificial reef that sits in 60 feet of water. *(Ch. 19)*

TURKS AND CAICOS
The pristine waters surrounding the Turks and Caicos islands—and more than 70 miles of barrier reefs and walls off Providenciales alone—provide some of the region's best diving opportunities. Many of the sites are in protected areas, so the coral remains vibrant and the marine life is plentiful—sea turtles, lobsters, eels, eagle rays, and schools of colorful tropical fish. *(Ch. 21)*

U.S. VIRGIN ISLANDS
Diving off St. Thomas reveals coral-encrusted reefs, archways, caves, rocks, pinnacles, and a couple of intriguing wrecks. On St. John's east end, Eagle Shoals is a beautiful dive. And on St. Croix, a shore dive from Cane Bay reveals coral heads, 19th-century anchors, a colorful reef, and an almost bottomless wall. Every USVI beach offers great snorkeling, but St. John's Trunk Bay Beach has a marked underwater trail that's great for beginners. *(Ch. 22)*

VIEQUES, PUERTO RICO
Many divers and snorkelers head to Vieques or nearby Culebra, two small islands east of Puerto Rico, to explore a colorful underwater world in the company of turtles, dolphins, manatees, spotted eagle rays, puffer fish, and nurse sharks. *(Ch. 16)*

Kids and Families

CHOOSING A PLACE TO STAY

Many resorts, except those that are exclusively for adults, offer kids-free promotions, special restaurant menus, and programs for tots on up to teens.

Let them entertain you. If you prefer to relax while the kids are entertained, choose an all-inclusive, family-friendly resort with a kids' program. For example, **Beaches Resorts** in Providenciales, Turks and Caicos, and in Ocho Rios and Negril, Jamaica, offer kids' programs to match all ages from toddler to teen, outdoor playgrounds, gaming centers, field trips for ages 12 and up such as snorkeling and scuba diving, and *Sesame Street* character appearances. In the Dominican Republic, **Royalton Splash Punta Cana** boasts a world of adventures for kids and parents alike, including the largest water park in the Caribbean. Kids stay free at **Turtle Beach by Elegant Hotels** in Barbados, which has family-size accommodations, a dedicated splash pool for kids, and the complimentary Flying Fish Kids Club featuring interactive games, authentic Bajan experiences, and local crafts. And at **Coconut Bay Beach Resort & Spa** in Saint Lucia, half the 85-acre resort is reserved for families; Cocoland Kidz Club (infant–12 years) features a pirate ship, mini zipline, mini rock wall, a water park with a lazy river and exciting waterslides—but the whole family is involved in "fun nights," with music, dancing, movies, and more. In addition, **Hyatt Regency Aruba Resort Spa & Casino** features Camp Hyatt, where kids ages 3 to 12 can participate in a variety of activities and adventures. **Club Med Punta Cana,** in the Dominican Republic, offers a baby gym, arts-and-crafts programs, dance instruction, a circus school, a teen spa, and more. **Four Seasons Resort Nevis** offers supervised programs such as cake baking, croquet, sea turtle–watching, beach walks, and a supervised lizard hunt—along with story time, a playground with a pirate ship and tree house, a children's menu, even kid-size bathrobes in the bedroom.

DIY. If you'd prefer more of a home base from which to explore the island on your own, choose a family-friendly hotel, condo, or villa near the attractions you'd most like to visit. Condos and villas provide an at-home atmosphere with full kitchens and separate bedrooms, and many include home entertainment systems.

TOP ATTRACTIONS

Museums. In Kingston, Jamaica, teenagers may enjoy the **Bob Marley Museum.** The former home of the late, great, king of reggae music—painted Rastafarian red, yellow, and green—is filled with Marley's personal memorabilia. A 15-minute video presents the singer's life story, along with familiar music clips. The **Barbados Museum** has a Children's Gallery with interactive exhibits on the island's Amerindian past, British colonialism, and sugar industry. The most fun: a "dress-up corner," where kids can don the garb of a Zouave soldier or an African prince.

Fortresses. A long grassy walk leads up to the 500-year-old **Castillo del Morro** (El Morro) Castle, an imposing structure in Puerto Rico's Old San Juan that looks like the Wicked Witch's scary fortress. Venture inside the thick walls and make your way through the ramparts, tunnels, and dungeons. Wax mannequins model historic battle uniforms, and a video shows the history of building and defending this stronghold. Equally imposing is St. Kitts's **Brimstone Hill,** known as the Gibraltar of the West Indies. Ft. George, which sits atop the hill, is built of 7-foot-thick walls of black volcanic stone. Woeful kids can imagine being imprisoned here during a "time-out." From high atop the fort's cannon ways, kids can also search the horizon for the islands of Nevis, Montserrat, Saba, St. Maarten/St. Martin, and St. Barth. And it's always fun to spot the scampering green monkeys that play along the nature trails that wind around this 38-acre site.

Caves. An electric tram takes you into and through Barbados's **Harrison's Cave,** where specially lighted caverns illuminate the stalactites, stalagmites, and underground waterfalls so the caves don't seem too spooky (or confining!). The **Hato Caves** in Curaçao date back to the Ice Age; but today, instead of cavemen, the inhabitants are long-nose fruit bats. Puerto Rico's **Río Camuy Cave Park** tour begins with a short video and then a trolley ride right to the mouth of the cave. Though 200 feet high, the cave is only half a mile long. The walking tour is level and flat, allowing kids' eyes to roam all over without fear of stumbling.

Zoos. Roam freely with the animals at the **Barbados Wildlife Reserve.** This outdoor zoo keeps kids engaged as they walk along shady pathways and spot exotic animals, reptiles, and birds in their natural habitat. There are land turtles, fine-feathered peacocks, green monkeys, parrots, and even a caiman (who does not roam free!). After exploring outside, kids can check out the walk-in aviary and the many natural-history exhibits. On Grand Cayman, **Cayman Turtle Centre** is a marine theme park with tanks and ponds full of turtles; kids can touch and pick up the creatures, swim and snorkel among them, and learn about conservation, too.

Zoo de Martinique, located in a centuries-old estate on the northwest coast of the island, has wild animals from Australia, Africa, and Central and South America—monkeys, jaguars, pumas, lorikeets, raccoons, a great anteater, and hundreds more. Not exactly a zoo, but **The Butterfly Farm**—a beautiful garden filled with fluttering butterflies from around the world—has sites in Aruba and St. Martin. View, firsthand, the life cycle of these amazing insects from egg to caterpillar to butterfly—it's a fascinating experience for the whole family.

Aquariums. Coral World Ocean Park, on St. Thomas, is an interactive aquarium and water-sports center that has a 2-acre dolphin habitat, as well as several outdoor pools where you can pet baby sharks, feed stingrays, touch starfish, and view endangered sea turtles. You can also Snuba, swim with a sea lion, and view an 80,000-gallon coral reef exhibit. **Ocean World Adventure Park,** in Puerto Plata, Dominican Republic, has interactive marine and wildlife programs, including dolphin and sea lion shows, a tropical reef aquarium, stingrays, shark tanks, and more.

Fun parks. Kids will love **Kool Runnings Adventure Park** in Negril, Jamaica, which has 10 waterslides and a ¼-mile lazy-river float ride, as well as a go-kart track and kayaking. There are also outdoor laser combat games, bungee jumping, a "kool kanoe" adventure, a wave pool, and paintball. At Reduit Beach in Saint Lucia, **Splash Island Water Park** is an open-water sports park with colorful, inflatable, modular features that include a trampoline, climbing wall, swing, slide, hurdles, and more. It's thrilling for kids and adults—but mostly kids—and a lifeguard is on duty.

FLAVORS OF THE CARIBBEAN

As a key entry point to the New World, the Caribbean region has a rich culinary tradition that reflects the diversity of its immigrants. This melting pot of Spanish, African, French, English, and Dutch influences has resulted in dishes packed with fresh ingredients and bold, spicy flavors and seasonings.

Local produce is varied and includes lima beans, black-eyed peas, corn, yams, sweet potatoes, cassava, taro, and endless varieties of fruit. Rice and beans are ever-present staples, commonly seasoned with ingredients like curry, cilantro, soy sauce, and ginger. The spice-forward "jerk" style of marinated and rubbed meat, fish, and fowl is prevalent. Jamaica, Haiti, Guadeloupe, and other French Caribbean islands savor goat meat in dishes like goat water, a tomato-based stew, which is the official national dish of Montserrat and a speciality on St. Kitts and Nevis. Fresh-caught seafood from local waters also figures prominently in the cuisine.

Modern menus don't stray too far from tradition, opting instead for clever twists rather than reinvention, like flavoring black beans with tequila and olive oil, or serving rice spiked with coconut and ginger. No matter where your culinary curiosities take you in these islands, plan on a well-seasoned eating adventure.

(opposite) Dasheene Restaurant at Ladera Resort, St. Lucia, (top) Jerk pork, a signature Jamaican dish, (bottom) scotch bonnet peppers.

THE ISLANDS' GLOBAL FLAVORS

Island cuisine developed through waves of wars, immigration, and native innovations from the 15th century through the mid-19th century. Early Amerindian native peoples, the Arawaks and the Caribs, are said to have introduced the concept of spicing food with chili peppers, a preparation that remains a hallmark of Caribbean cuisine. Pepper pot stew was a staple for the Caribs, who would make the dish with *cassareep*, a savory sauce made from cassava. The stew featured wild meats (possum, wild pig, or armadillo), squash, beans, and peanuts, which were added to the cassareep and simmered in a clay pot. The dish was traditionally served to guests as a gesture of hospitality. Today's recipes substitute meats like pig trotters, cow heel, or oxtail.

Caribbean-style curried goat

As European colonization took place, traders and settlers brought new fruits, vegetables, and meats. Their arrival coincided with that of enslaved Africans, en route to the Americas. Every explorer, settler, trader, and slave culturally expanded the palette of flavors. Although Caribbean cooking varies from island to island, trademark techniques and spices unite the cuisine.

SPANISH INFLUENCES

Christopher Columbus sailed to the Caribbean in 1492, at the behest of the Spanish crown. When he returned to colonize the islands a year later, he brought ships laden with coconut, chickpeas, cilantro, eggplant, onions, and garlic. The Bahamas, Hispaniola, and Cuba were among Columbus' first findings, and as a result, Cuba and nearby Puerto Rico have distinctly Spanish-accented cuisine, including *paella* (a seafood- or meat-studded rice dish), *arroz con pollo* or *pilau* (chicken cooked with yellow rice), and white-bean Spanish stews.

Arroz con Pollo

FRENCH TECHNIQUE

As tobacco and sugar crops flourished and the Caribbean became a center of European trade and colonization, the French settled Martinique and Guadeloupe in 1635 and later expanded to St. Barthélemy, St. Martin, Dominica, Grenada, St. Lucia, and western Hispaniola. French culinary technique meets the natural resources of the islands to create dishes like whelk (sea snail) grilled in garlic butter, fish cooked *en papillote* (baked in parchment paper), and *crabs farcis* (land crab meat that is steamed, mixed with butter, breadcrumbs, ham, chilis, and garlic, then stuffed back into the crab shells and grilled).

DUTCH INGENUITY

Beginning in the 1620s, traders from the Dutch East India Company brought Southeast Asian ingredients like soy sauce to the islands of Curaçao and St. Maarten. Dutch influence is also evident throughout Aruba and Bonaire (all have been under Dutch rule since the early 19th century), where dishes like *keshi yeni*, or "stuffed cheese," evolved from stuffing discarded rinds of Edam cheese with minced meat, olives, and capers. Another Dutch-influenced dish is *boka dushi* (Indonesian-style chicken satay), which translates to "sweet mouth" in the islands' Papiamento dialect.

Paella

Boka dushi

Jerk meat

Roti

Whelk

ENGLISH IMPORTS

British settlers brought pickles, preserves, and chutneys to the Caribbean, and current-day chefs take advantage of the islands' indigenous fruits to prepare these items. British influence also is evidenced by the Indian and Chinese contributions to Caribbean cuisine. British (and Dutch) colonists brought over indentured laborers from India and China to work on sugar plantations, resulting in the introduction of popular dishes like curry goat and *roti,* an Indian flatbread stuffed with vegetables or chicken curry.

AFRICAN INGREDIENTS

The African slave trade that began in the early 1600s contributed foods from West Africa, including yams, okra, plantains, breadfruit, pigeon peas, and oxtail. Slave cooks often had to make do with plantation leftovers and scraps, yielding dishes like cow heel soup and pig-foot souse (a cool soup with pickled cucumber and meat), both of which are still popular today. One of the most significant African contributions to the Caribbean table is "jerking," the process of dry-rubbing meat with allspice, Scotch bonnet peppers, and other spices. Although the cooking technique originated with native Amerindians, it was the Jamaican Maroons, a population of runaway African slaves living in the island's mountains during the years of slavery, who developed and perfected it, resulting in the style of jerk meat familiar in restaurants today.

CARIBBEAN'S NATURAL BOUNTY

Soursop

Despite its spicy reputation, Caribbean food isn't always fiery; rather the focus is on enhancing and intensifying flavors with herbs and spices. Food plays a major role in island culture, family life, and traditions, and no holiday would be complete without traditional dishes prepared from the island's natural products.

TANTALIZING TROPICAL FRUIT

Breadfruit, a versatile starch with potato-like flavor, can be served solo—baked or grilled—or added to soups and stews.

Rich **coconut** milk frequently appears in soups, stews, sauces, and drinks to help temper hot, spicy flavors.

The bright pink flesh of the tropical fruit **guava** tastes somewhat like a pear and strawberry combination that is pleasantly sweet when mature. It is used in compotes, pastes, jellies, and (especially) as juice.

The pungent smell of **jackfruit** may be off-putting for some, but its sweet fleshy meat is popular in milkshakes.

Papaya is sweet and floral tasting when ripe; unripe, it can be shredded and mixed with spices and citrus for a refreshing salad. It's often used in fruit salsas that are served with seafood.

Tamarind

The brightly flavored **passion fruit** is commonly puréed and used in sauces, drinks, and desserts.

The dark-green skinned, creamy fleshed **soursop** is known for its sweet-tart juice used in drinks, sorbets, and ice creams.

The fibrous stalks of **sugarcane**, a giant grass native to India, can be consumed in several forms, including freshly extracted juice and processed sugar.

Tamarind is the fruit of a large tree. The sticky pulp of its pod is used in chutneys, curries, and candy to impart a slightly sweet, refreshingly sour flavor.

FARM-FRESH VEGETABLES

Cassava (also called yucca) is used much like a potato in purées, dumplings, soups, and stews. Cassava root flour is made into tapioca.

Chayote is a versatile member of the squash and melon family, often used raw in salads or stuffed with cheese and tomatoes and baked.

Dasheen (taro) is much like a potato, but creamier. It can be added to stews or sliced thinly and fried like a potato chip.

Jackfruit

Fitweed (or French thistle) is a tropical herb related to coriander (cilantro), and is popular in Caribbean seasonings.

Pod-like **okra** is commonly used in *callaloo*, the national dish of Trinidad and Tobago. The creamy, spicy stew is made of leafy dasheen leaves, okra, and crabmeat.

Plantain is a cooking staple across the Caribbean, often sliced, pounded, dipped in a seasoned batter, and deep-fried.

The bright red **sorrel** is boiled, sweetened, and chilled for a traditional Christmas beverage.

Chayote

Curry powder

SWEET AND SAVORY SPICES

Native **allspice**, also called Jamaican pepper, is the dried unripe berry of the evergreen pimento tree. Native Jamaicans once used it to preserve meats, but today it's an essential ingredient in jerk preparations and Caribbean curries.

Curries are intensely seasoned gravy-based dishes originating from India—they are most prevalent on the islands of Jamaica, Trinidad, and Tobago.

Native Carib people pioneered the use of **chili peppers** in the islands for hot, spicy flavoring, using primarily habaneros and Scotch bonnet peppers.

Ginger is used raw or dried and ground into a powder that adds flavor and heat to ginger beer, sweet potatoes, or coconut milk–based sauces.

Allspice

The mix of spices in **jerk** seasoning vary, but typically include scallions, thyme, allspice, onions, and garlic.

The tiny island of Grenada is the second largest exporter of **nutmeg** in the world. Nutmeg often accents sauces, vegetables, drinks, and ice cream.

ISLAND FISH AND SEAFOOD

Bonito is a medium-sized fish in the mackerel family. Atlantic bonito is moderately fatty, with a firm texture and darker color. It's served blackened, grilled (sometimes with fruit-based salsas), or Jamaican jerk style.

On many islands, especially the Bahamas, **conch**—large shellfish—are made into conch fritters, a mix of conch meat, corn meal, and spices that are deep fried and make an excellent snack.

Cascadura fish is a small fish found in the freshwater swamps of Trinidad and Tobago. The fish is typically served in curry with a side of rice or dumplings.

Flying fish are named for the wing-like fins that enable them to glide or "fly" over water. Firm in texture, this fish is typically served steamed or fried. Flying fish is a staple in Bajan cuisine and is found in abdundance off the coast of Barbados.

Salt fish

Conch salad

Kingfish is another word for wahoo, a delicate white fish commonly fished off the coasts of St. Croix and Barbados. Wahoo is served *escabeche* style, marinated in a vinegar mixture, then fried or poached.

Land crab is found throughout the islands. Delicate in flavor, common preparations include curried crab stewed in coconut milk, stuffed crab, and crab soup.

Mahi mahi is fished off the coast of St. Croix. With a subtle, sweet flavor, the firm, dark flesh lends itself to soy sauce glazes and Asian preparations.

Salt fish is a dish made from dried cod, often seasoned with tomatoes, onions, and thyme. Stir-fried ackee (a tropical fruit with nutty-flavored flesh) and saltfish is Jamaica's national dish.

THE RISE OF RUM

The Caribbean is the world center for rum production, with many islands having their own brands and styles of rum. Dozens of rum companies operate throughout the islands. Although larger, mainstream brands like Bacardi, Captain Morgan, and Mount Gay are available on every island, you may have to look locally for the smaller brands. The best-quality rums are dark, aged rums meant for sipping, priced from $30 to $700 a bottle. For excellent sipping rum at the lower end of the spectrum, try Appleton or Rhum Barbancourt. For mixed drinks, use clear or golden-color rums that are less expensive and pair well with fruit juices or cola. Spiced and flavored rums are also popular in cocktails. Here are some of the best rums you'll encounter at an island bar:

Appleton Estate (Jamaica) The Estate VX is an amber-color rum with subtle brown sugar aromas and a smooth, toasted honey finish. Excellent mixer for classic cocktails.

Bacardi (Bermuda, PR) Superior is a clear, mild rum with subtle hints of vanilla and fresh fruits. It is smooth and light on the palate. Best in mixed drinks.

Captain Morgan (PR) Its Black Label Jamaica Rum is dark, rich, and smooth, with strong notes of vanilla. Sip it iced or with a splash of water.

Clarke's Court (Grenada) The Original White is clear with a touch of sweetness and a hint of heat, best used as a mixer.

Ron Barceló

Mount Gay Rum

Cruzan (VI) Less strong and sweet than most rums, the White Rum is smooth, and best suited for mixing.

Havana Club (Cuba) The Añejo 3 Años is deceiving—light in color and body and delicate in flavor. It is a nice rum to sip neat.

Mount Gay Rum (Barbados) Eclipse, the brand's flagship rum, has a golden color with a butterscotch caramel nose and sweet taste on the palate with mouth-warming flavor.

Pusser's (BVI) Self-described as "the single malt of rum," the aged 15-year variety boasts notes of cinnamon, woody spice, and citrus. A good sipping rum.

Rhum Barbancourt (Haiti) Aged 15 years, this premium dark rum is distilled twice in copper pot stills and often called the "Cognac of Rum." Sip it neat.

Ron Barceló (DR) The Añejo is dark copper in color, with a rich flavor, while the aged Imperial boasts notes of toffee on the nose, and a buttery smooth finish.

Shillingford Estates (Dominica) Its most popular product, Macoucherie Spiced, is a blend of rum, the bark of the Bois Bande tree, and spices.

(left) Pusser's Rum, (right) Havana Club

THE ISLANDS' BEST BREWS

Beer in the Caribbean was largely homemade for centuries, a tradition inherited from British colonial rulers. The first commercial brewery in the islands was founded in Trinidad and Tobago in 1947.

In the islands, do what the locals do: drink local beer. Whatever brand is brewed on-island is the one you'll find at every restaurant and bar. And no matter where you go in the Caribbean, there's a local island brew worth trying. Another plus: local brands are almost always cheaper than imports like Corona or Michelob. Most island beers are pale lagers, though you'll find a smattering of Dutch-style pilsners and English-style pale ales. The beers listed below are our top picks for beachside sipping:

Kalik

Banks Beer (Banks Breweries, Barbados) A straw-colored lager that is light tasting with a touch of maltiness on the nose and tongue.

Blackbeard Ale (Virgin Islands Brewing Co., Virgin Islands) This English pale ale–style beer is bright amber in color with a creamy white head. Well-crafted beer with a nice hoppy bite at the finish.

Balashi Beer (Brouwerij Nacional Balashi N.V., Aruba) Refreshingly light, this Dutch pilsner boasts mild flavor, slight sweetness, and subtle hop bitterness.

Legends Premium Lager (Banks Breweries, Barbados) One of the Caribbean's best brews, this golden yellow lager offers crisp hops and a clean finish. Distinctive toasty, malt character.

Carib Lager Beer (Carib Brewery, Trinidad and Tobago) This great beach refresher is a pale yellow color with a foamy head. Fruity and sweet malty corn aromas, it is sometimes referred to as the "Corona of the Caribbean."

Kalik Gold (Commonwealth Brewery LTD., New Providence, Bahamas) Clear straw color with gentle hoppy, herbal notes, this is an easy drinking, warm weather lager.

Medalla Light (Puerto Rico) This bright gold lager is substantial for a light beer. It's a local favorite.

Red Stripe (Jamaica) The Jamaican lager pours golden yellow in color with lots of carbonation. Light bodied, crisp, and smooth.

Banks Beer

Carib Lager Beer

Piton (St. Lucia) Light and sparkly with subtle sweetness, this pale yellow lager is pleasant enough, but barely flavored.

Presidente (Dominican Republic) Slight citrus aroma, light body, and fizziness, plus a clean finish make for easy drinking. Perfect pairing for barbecued meats.

Wadadli (Antigua Brewery Ltd., Antigua and Barbuda) A crisp, light-bodied American-style lager. Toasty malt on the nose.

(left) Red Stripe, (right) Presidente

Did You Know?

During Puerto Rico's Carnaval de Ponce, which takes place every February, revelers wear brightly colored vejigante masks. Vejigantes are Puerto Rican folk characters that appear at festivals; traditional costumes and masks come in green, yellow, and red or red and black.

Chapter 2

TRAVEL SMART

Updated by
Jane Zarem

Know Before You Go

When should I go? When is hurricane season? Should I bring U.S. dollars? You may have a few questions before you head out to vacation in the Caribbean. We've got tips and a few tricks to make sure your trip runs smoothly.

BRING YOUR PASSPORT... AND U.S. DOLLARS
A valid passport is needed to enter any of the Caribbean islands—and to re-enter the U.S.—except for Puerto Rico and USVI. Most non-U.S. islands also require a return or ongoing airline ticket. But don't worry about the local currency. U.S. dollars—but not coins—are widely accepted. Bring small bills, though, as you'll almost always get change in local money—including from an ATM.

ENGLISH IS WIDELY SPOKEN
English is understood, spoken, and written throughout the Caribbean, although French is the preferred language on Guadeloupe, Martinique, St. Barth, and St. Martin. You'll also hear a French Creole patois spoken in Jamaica, Saint Lucia, and Grenada. On the Dutch islands, you'll hear both Dutch and English spoken, while Papiamento (which adds Spanish, Portuguese, French, African, and Arawakan elements to the Dutch/English mix) is the local patois in Aruba, Bonaire, and Curaçao. Spanish, of course, is the most prevalent language in the Dominican Republic and Puerto Rico.

DON'T JUST VACATION IN "HIGH SEASON"
A Caribbean vacation is a great way to escape winter in much of the U.S., but winter is also "high season"—December 15 through April 15, especially the year-end holiday weeks. But wait! Caribbean weather doesn't change much from month to month, although late summer and early fall are generally more humid. So whenever you're in the mood to escape, don't hesitate. "Low season," which is really most of the year, can be quiet; but with lower prices for accommodations and flights. The only caveat: Hurricanes are at their peak in September and October.

NOT ALL ISLANDS EXPERIENCE HURRICANE SEASON
Speaking of hurricanes, when those storms come roaring across the Atlantic in the fall, they usually aim directly at the Leeward Islands, sometimes the Windwards, often the Virgin Islands, and eventually the Greater Antilles. Islands that don't get a direct hit may experience storm surge and serious flooding. Barbados normally escapes hurricanes, although it can experience periods of torrential rain and flooding in the fall; and the southernmost islands—Aruba, Bonaire, and Curaçao—are out of the "hurricane zone," so weather there is always sunny and warm with little rain.

TECHNOLOGY 101
Wi-Fi is available—and usually free—at most resorts and hotels (even small inns) throughout the Caribbean. You can also plug in your charger(s) and any other dual-voltage devices and accessories right in your hotel room. Some islands use U.S. standard current (110v), and many individual hotels have installed 110v plugs in guest rooms. If not, the hotels will usually let you borrow an adapter if you haven't brought your own.

BEACHES—IT'S WHAT YOU CAME FOR
You'll find the pristine white-sand Caribbean beaches of your dreams on the flattest islands—Anguilla, Antigua, Aruba, and Anegada in the BVI. On mountainous islands—Puerto Rico, Jamaica, Saint Lucia—the sand is more golden in color. Islands with a volcanic geology (St. Kitts, Nevis, and Guadeloupe) have stunning

black-sand beaches. As for pink-sand beaches, you'll find them in Barbados, Bonaire, and Barbuda. Nude bathing is accepted on French islands—such as St. Martin, St. Barth, and Guadeloupe—but frowned upon (or illegal) elsewhere, although Negril in Jamaica and Antigua do have beaches with clothing-optional areas.

ISLAND HOP—BY SEA OR BY AIR

A multi-island Caribbean vacation or a day trip to a nearby island is possible, as many islands are in close proximity and have frequent, reasonably priced ferry and/or air service (small planes and sometimes seaplanes). Some Caribbean nations are already multi-island (USVI, BVI, Cayman Islands, Turks and Caicos); some are dual-island nations (Antigua and Barbuda, St. Kitts and Nevis); some have separate off-shore islands (Puerto Rico's Vieques and Culebra, Guadeloupe's Les Saintes and Marie Galante, Grenada's Carriacou and Petite Martinique); and others are just in close proximity (St. Martin and Anguilla, St. Maarten and St. Barth, Saint Lucia and Martinique). Expand your adventure—you'll thank us later.

RENT A VEHICLE

If you're staying in a remote location, but plan to explore, eat out, or visit distant sights or beaches, then definitely consider renting a vehicle—car, jeep, minimoke (beach buggy), or scooter. Be aware, though, that driving can be a challenge on narrow, winding roads on mountainous islands—especially at night and often on the left side of the road, British-style. Taxis and inexpensive public buses (or private vans that operate like buses) are always an option. Taxi drivers are generally well-informed and will take you where you want to go, when you want to go, for as long as you wish, at an hourly rate. Just keep in mind the cost.

THERE'S MORE TO DO THAN LIE ON THE BEACH

Beaches in the Caribbean are the draw, but there's also hiking, ziplining, horseback riding, mountain biking, and bird-watching. There are rain forests, underground caves, botanical gardens, volcanoes (yes, volcanoes), and a plethora of golf courses. And if you dare, try an ATV safari for an exhilarating hour or two.

THESE ISLANDS HAVE HISTORY

Spain, England, France, The Netherlands, even Denmark colonized one or more of the Caribbean islands, and each country left its mark. Understanding an island's history can add depth to your vacation. Forts, garrisons, and military lookouts usually provide the best views of the island and the surrounding sea, but you'll also learn why, when, and by whom the island needed defending. Visiting a plantation, particularly in Barbados and Jamaica, provides perspective on history. Wander around Nelson's Dockyard in Antigua, Old San Juan in Puerto Rico, Scharloo in Curaçao, Brimstone Hill in St. Kitts, even Alexander Hamilton's birthplace in Nevis. Each one provides a fascinating history lesson.

RUM, RUM, RUM, RUM

Whether you take it neat or with a little water; with Coke and a twist of lime; or in a fruity mixture with an umbrella—rum is the alcohol of choice throughout the Caribbean. Many islands produce rum—dozens of brands—and nearly every island has its own brand and distilleries that you can visit—most notably Mount Gay in Barbados, Appleton Estate in Jamaica, and Casa Bacardi in Puerto Rico but also smaller operations like Cruzan in St. Croix and Bounty in Saint Lucia. Bottoms up!

CORAL REEF-SAFE SUNSCREEN IS A MUST

Coral reefs are dying at an alarming rate, and one of the major contributors is sunscreen—more specifically the chemicals oxybenzone and octinoxate. Luckily, numerous companies like Sun Bum, Blue Lizard, and Thinksport offer reef-safe alternatives. So check those labels before you buy your next bottle.

Getting Here and Around

Air

Many carriers fly nonstop or direct routes to the Caribbean from major international airports in the United States, including Atlanta, Boston, Charlotte, Chicago, Dallas, Fort Lauderdale, Houston, Miami, New York (JFK), Newark, Philadelphia, Phoenix, and Washington (Dulles). If you live elsewhere in the United States, you'll have to make a connection to get to your Caribbean destination. It's also not uncommon to make a connection in the Caribbean, most often in Puerto Rico (San Juan), Jamaica (Montego Bay), Barbados, Antigua, or St. Maarten.

Some interisland flights will be on small planes operated by local or regional carriers, some of which may have code-share arrangements with major airlines from the United States. Or you can confidently book directly with the local carrier, using a major credit card, either online or by phone.

Some regional airlines may make multiple stops, accepting and discharging passengers and/or cargo at each small airport or airstrip along the way. This is not unusual—nor is the sometimes unreliable schedule that these smaller airlines may follow. Flights can be late—or even depart early—without apology or explanation. Be sure to confirm your flights on interisland carriers, as you may be subject to their whims; for example, if no other passengers are booked on your flight, particularly if the carrier operates "scheduled charters," you'll be rescheduled on another flight or at a different departure time that is more convenient for the airline—which may be earlier or later than your original reservation. If you're connecting from an interisland flight to a major airline, be sure to include a substantial buffer of time for possible delays.

Typical Nonstop Travel Times by Air	New York	Miami
Puerto Rico	3¾ hours	2½ hours
Jamaica	4 hours	1¾ hours
Saint Lucia	4½ hours	3¾ hours
Aruba	4¾ hours	2¾ hours
Punta Cana, D.R.	4 hours	2½ hours
Grand Cayman	4 hours	1½ hours
Turks and Caicos	3¾ hours	1¾ hours

Boat

Interisland ferries are an interesting and often less expensive way to travel around certain areas of the Caribbean, but they are not offered everywhere. A few destinations are reached only by ferry (St. John in the U.S. Virgin Islands and Anguilla, for example). In most cases, service is frequent (either daily or several times daily).

MAJOR FERRY ROUTES

Ferries connect: Puerto Rico with the outlying islands of Vieques and Culebra; St. Thomas with Water Island, St. John, and St. Croix and with Tortola, Virgin Gorda, Jost Van Dyke, and Anegada in the British Virgin Islands; the various islands of the British Virgin Islands with each other and with St. Thomas and St. John in the U.S. Virgin Islands; St. Martin/St. Maarten with Anguilla and St. Barth; St. Kitts with Nevis; Antigua with Barbuda; Guadeloupe with La Désirade, Marie-Galante, and Îles des Saintes (Les Saintes), as well as with Martinique and Saint Lucia; Saint Lucia with Guadeloupe and Martinique; Grenada with Carriacou and Petite Martinique; and limited ferry service in the Turks and Caicos Islands (Provo and North Caicos, Grand Turk and Salt Cay). In most cases, service is frequent—either daily or several times daily.

 Bus

Some islands—Aruba and Barbados, for example—have excellent public bus service, with large, modern buses traveling main routes on regular schedules. Many other islands offer "bus" service in privately owned 16-passenger vans that are regulated by the government and travel along regular routes. Bus travel is inexpensive—the equivalent of $1 or $2 or even less, depending on the destination—and can be an interesting experience, as well. While mainly used by local people, bus travel is perfectly safe for island visitors.

 Car

Your own valid driver's license works in some countries, but temporary local driving permits are required in several Caribbean destinations (Anguilla, Antigua, Barbados, the British Virgin Islands, Cayman Islands, Grenada, Nevis, St. Kitts, and Saint Lucia). You can secure the temporary permit at rental agencies or local police offices upon presentation of a valid license and small fee. Saint Lucia requires a temporary permit only if you don't have an International Driving Permit (available from AAA), but you will need to have the permit stamped at the airport.

On islands with British heritage—Antigua and Barbuda, Barbados, British Virgin Islands, Cayman Islands, Jamaica, Saint Lucia, Turks and Caicos—and (oddly enough) U.S. Virgin Islands, driving is on the left, British style. On other islands, drive on the right—U.S. style. Seat belts are universally required, as are car seats for children.

CAR RENTAL

Major U.S. car rental agencies operate on many islands throughout the Caribbean, but local agencies are also reliable and offer a variety of cars, jeeps, and beach buggies at competitive prices. Most, if not all, agencies offer children's car seats and provide free pickup service from your hotel.

■ TIP→ For a green alternative, consider renting an electric car. On islands like St. Barth, they're becoming fashionable—and charging stations are popping up around the island. Electric cars rent for about $85 per day.

GASOLINE

Gasoline is sold by the liter throughout the Caribbean, with roughly four liters equaling one U.S. gallon. Per-gallon equivalent prices range from about $3.50 in Puerto Rico to as high as $9 or more elsewhere. As at home, gas prices in the Caribbean fluctuate according to the world market.

ROAD CONDITIONS

Island roads vary throughout the Caribbean. Most often, you'll find narrow, two-lane roads; but modern highways are found on some islands like Puerto Rico and Barbados. On mountainous islands (Jamaica and Saint Lucia, for example), the roads are often winding and steep, with hairpin turns and narrow or no shoulders. On many islands, signage is nonexistent. In and around cities, even on small islands, traffic can be heavy during "rush hours."

Getting Here and Around

ROADSIDE EMERGENCIES

If you're in an accident, especially if there are injuries, call the police or ambulance service for that island. For general roadside assistance, whether you've lost your car keys or have a flat tire, run out of gas or need a jump start, call your rental car company—most of which have an after-hours telephone number.

RULES OF THE ROAD

Other than driving on the right (or left) side of the road, general rules of the road are to wear your seat belt, follow the speed limits, and always be courteous. On back roads in the countryside, drive slowly and watch for pedestrians, small animals (goats, dogs, and chickens), blind curves, oncoming traffic, and buses/vans picking up or dropping off passengers. You'll always hear a lot of horn-beeping, but that's mainly taxi drivers saying "hello" as they pass each other.

Ride-Sharing

Uber is branching out into the Caribbean, initially in the Dominican Republic, Puerto Rico, and Jamaica. In Barbados, you can use the BeepCab app to hail and pay for the nearest taxi. RIDE Caribbean, based in Saint Lucia, is a mobile ride-sharing and payment service with plans to operate elsewhere in the Caribbean.

Scooter

Scooters can be a fun way to get around the islands (Bonaire, BVI, St. Barth), and many places offer day rates. Just remember to pay attention to road rules: Drive on the left on an island with British heritage—Antigua, Barbados, BVI, Cayman Islands, Grenada, Jamaica, Saint Lucia, Turks and Caicos—and (oddly enough) USVI. And wear sunblock and a helmet. A valid driver's license and cash deposit or credit card may be required.

Taxi

Taxi rates are fixed by the government on most islands, but you should always ask whether the price quoted is in U.S. or local currency. Taxi drivers often go through tourism training, whether required or by choice, and can provide a comfortable and personalized island tour at a reasonable hourly rate.

Essentials

Addresses

Finding an address on some small islands may be difficult, as street signs are often nonexistent. Local residents are usually very helpful, though, when you're trying to find your way. Postcards, letters, and packages often take weeks to reach their destination, whether sending them to or from the Caribbean. Many islands have added postal codes to mailing addresses, but it's taking quite awhile for local people to actually use them. In the meantime, postal codes are not always required for the mail to go through.

Dining

As the entry point to the "New World," the Caribbean presents a rich and diverse culinary history. The blending of Spanish, African, East Indian, French, English, and Dutch influences has resulted in a cuisine that focuses on fresh, local ingredients and bold, spicy flavors and seasonings.

Despite its spicy reputation, Caribbean food isn't always fiery; rather, the focus is on enhancing and intensifying flavors with local herbs and spices. Food plays a major role in island culture, family life, and traditions; no holiday would be complete without traditional dishes prepared from the island's local products.

Local produce is varied and includes both familiar and unfamiliar vegetables (pigeon peas, corn, yams, sweet potatoes, breadfruit, plantains, cassava, callaloo, christophene/chayote, and dasheen/taro) and familiar and unfamiliar fruits (citrus, mangoes, bananas, melons, pineapple, guava, coconut, papaya, passion fruit, soursop, mammy apples, and tamarinds). Rice and beans are often seasoned with curry, cilantro, soy sauce, or ginger. The hot and spicy "jerk" style of preparing meat, fish, and fowl is prevalent. You'll find barbecued chicken (legs, especially) nearly everywhere, and fresh-caught seafood is ubiquitous. Modern menus don't stray far from tradition, opting instead for clever twists rather than reinvention—perhaps spiking black beans with tequila and olive oil or flavoring rice with coconut and ginger. No matter your culinary curiosities, plan on a well-seasoned eating adventure.

MEALS AND MEALTIME

Hotel and resort breakfasts are usually served buffet-style between 7 and 10 am, although an à la carte menu is often available. Lunch is usually served between 12 noon and 2 or 2:30 pm, often at a beachfront grill. And dinner usually starts at 6 pm in hotels, resorts, and independent restaurants. In the fanciest restaurants, people tend to dine late—from 8 pm onward.

PAYING

Your bill at most dining establishments in the Caribbean will include a 10-15% service charge, although you may want to add a bit more for exceptional service. If the bill doesn't include the service charge, a 10–15% tip is recommended on most islands. In Puerto Rico and the U.S. Virgin Islands, a 15–20% tip is more common. At all-inclusive resorts, you've paid in advance—although butlers and spa personnel may accept tips.

RESERVATIONS AND DRESS

If dining at a particular restaurant at a particular time is important to you (especially if the restaurant is particularly small), make a reservation. Some resorts have a "fine-dining" or extremely popular on-site restaurant that requires reservations. A few extraordinary restaurants may require reservations months in advance. Beachwear is not welcome in restaurants, except at beachfront grills;

Essentials

always wear a shirt or cover-up. At dinner, gentlemen should wear long pants and a collared shirt; ladies, a sundress or dress slacks. A jacket for men is rarely, if ever, required—perhaps around the holidays at the fanciest resorts.

Health and Safety

Dengue, chikungunya, and zika have all been reported throughout the Caribbean. We recommend that you protect yourself from these mosquito-borne illnesses by keeping your skin covered and/or wearing mosquito repellent, particularly if you plan to trek through the rainforest. The mosquitoes that transmit these viruses are as active by day as they are by night.

COVID-19 has disrupted travel since March 2020, and travelers should expect sporadic ongoing issues. Always travel with a mask in case it's required, and keep up to date on the most recent testing and vaccination guidelines for whatever island you're traveling to in the Caribbean.

Immunizations

Children should be up-to-date on their routine immunizations (DTaP, MMR, influenza, chicken pox, and polio), and all visitors to the Caribbean must have a valid proof of COVID 19 vaccination; it's important to verify the most recent requirements with your physician before you travel.

Lodging

WHEN TO RESERVE

The most popular properties book as much as a year in advance, particularly during the holiday weeks and school vacation periods, due to the high number of repeat guests—many of whom request the same room every year. Many high-end or popular chain resorts, such as Four Seasons, Ritz-Carlton, and Sandals properties, also book well in advance for peak periods. The most difficult time to find a well-priced room is typically around the Christmas and New Year's holidays, when minimum-stay requirements of one to two weeks may be common and room rates are the most expensive.

For the typical Caribbean resort, though, two months is usually sufficient notice. In popular mass-market destinations such as Punta Cana or Negril, a couple of weeks may be enough advance notice. Of course, it's easiest to find an acceptable room in the busiest destinations by virtue of the sheer number of rooms available at any given time. Although waiting until the last minute doesn't always net bargains, flexibility and timing can sometimes pay off with either a deep discount (usually at a larger resort) or a room category upgrade.

FEES AND ADD-ONS

Every island charges an accommodations tax or VAT ranging from 7% to 15%, whether you stay in a bed-and-breakfast inn, hotel, guesthouse, resort, or private villa. In addition, most Caribbean hotels and resorts tack on a service charge, usually 10%. The service charge isn't quite the same as a tip for service, so it is customary at most resorts (all-inclusives being an exception) to tip the staff. Expect taxes and service charges to add at least 20% above the base rate for a room. So-called "energy" surcharges are also not uncommon.

A growing trend is the "resort fee." You may encounter it anywhere but particularly at large resorts with lots of activities. Resort fees are almost universal in San Juan, Puerto Rico, but are less popular elsewhere. The fee, which can range from $5 to $50 per night, presumably covers the costs of services and resort facilities. These add-ons aren't always mentioned when you book, so be sure to inquire.

PICKING THE BEST ROOM

On virtually every island, especially at beachfront lodgings, the price increases as the beach access or ocean view improves. You could save $100 or more per night by choosing a garden-, mountain-, or town-view room. But regardless of the view, be sure to ask about the property's layout. For example, if you want to be close to the "action" at many larger resorts, whether you have mobility concerns or just need to satisfy your gambling or gamboling itch, the trade-off might be noise—whether from screaming kids jumping in the pool or DJs pumping reggae at the bar. Likewise, saving that $100 may not be worth it if your room faces a busy thoroughfare. If you have any specific desires or dislikes, discuss them thoroughly and ahead of time with the reservations staff.

TYPES OF LODGINGS

Condos and Time-Shares Condo resorts offer both extra space (kitchens, sofa beds, and more) and superior savings for families or small groups traveling together. In fact, condos dominate the sensuous sweeps of Grand Cayman's Seven-Mile Beach, Provo's amazing Grace Bay in the Turks and Caicos, Palm Beach in Aruba, and elsewhere. Some condos are time-share properties, but not all time-shares require you to sit through a sales pitch.

Inns and B&Bs Historic inns come in all shapes and sizes. The old Spanish colonial capitals of Santo Domingo in the Dominican Republic and San Juan, Puerto Rico, have converted monasteries. Puerto Rico also offers affordable lodgings in its paradors; patterned after the Spanish system, most of them are historically and/or culturally significant buildings—such as old-time thermal baths or working coffee plantations. Longtime sailing and whaling destinations, such as Antigua, offer their own bits of history adapted to modern comfort; and Guadeloupe, Martinique, and St. Croix feature converted sugar plantations. St. Kitts and Nevis, in particular, are prized by Caribbean connoisseurs for their restored greathouse plantation inns, often with a resident expat owner who enhances your experience with amusing anecdotes and insider insights.

Most islands run the gamut, offering a full range of glitzy resorts, chic boutique hotels and inns, historic hostelries, family-run B&Bs, condo resorts, self-catering apartments, and private villas.

Private Villas Another popular option for families or those seeking a good bargain are private villas. Self-catering on more expensive islands such as St. Barth (where villas usually cost much less than hotels) means saving on dining costs, though a car is often necessary. Many villas have private pools with stunning sea views and/or beachfront access.

Hotels and Resorts Most prevalent in the Caribbean are large hotels and resorts, including all-inclusives, that are usually positioned strategically on the beach or on a golf course. Some have a theme: couples, families, spa retreat, etc. You'll find familiar chain hotels in all price categories—from Ritz-Carlton to Comfort Suites.

ALL-INCLUSIVE OR NOT?

The AI ("all-inclusive") concept is especially prominent in Jamaica, the Dominican Republic, Antigua, and Saint Lucia; but throughout the Caribbean, hotels and resorts that are not entirely AI often offer an AI rate option. For those who have only a week for vacation, the allure is obvious: a hassle-free, prepaid vacation that includes accommodations, meals, unlimited drinks, entertainment, and most activities. And you tend to get what you pay for. AIs range from hedonistic, high-tech luxury to bare-bones, beachfront bang-for-the-buck, with prices to match. Some AI resorts are intimate, romantic hideaways for couples; some emphasize sporting options; others cater to families; and still others cater to singles ready to mingle in a nonstop party atmosphere.

But there are caveats. Few AIs offer *everything* for free. That spa treatment, the scuba trip, the sunset cruise, or the tour of the nearby plantation may not be included. Moreover, there can be surcharges for dining in some restaurants.

AI resorts appeal mostly to travelers who just want to get away and bask in the sun, rum punch within easy reach. AIs are generally not for more adventuresome types who seek interaction with the locals and immersion in their culture—nor are they good for people who want to eat local food, since most AI travelers rarely leave the resort's boundaries.

$ Money

The U.S. dollar is the official currency in Puerto Rico, the U.S. Virgin Islands, the Turks and Caicos Islands, and the British Virgin Islands. The Eastern Caribbean Dollar is the official currency in Anguilla, Antigua and Barbuda, Grenada, St. Kitts &and Nevis, and Saint Lucia. The euro is the official currency of Guadeloupe, Martinique, St. Barth, and St. Martin (French side only). Other countries—Aruba, Barbados, Bonaire, Cayman Islands, Curaçao, St. Maarten (Dutch side only), Dominican Republic, and Jamaica—have their own unique currencies.

On Grand Cayman you'll usually have a choice of Cayman or U.S. dollars when you take money out of an ATM and may even be able to get change in U.S. dollars. On most other islands (other than those that use the euro), U.S. paper currency (not coins) is generally accepted. When you pay in dollars, however, you'll almost always get change in local currency; so it's best to carry bills in small denominations. The exceptions are at airports, which will generally make every attempt to give you change in U.S. dollars, if you wish. Canadian dollars and British pounds are occasionally accepted, but don't count on this as the norm. If you do need local currency (say, for a day trip to one of the French islands), take money out of a local ATM for the best rate. With regard to the EC dollar, Cayman dollar, Aruba florin, Netherlands Antillean guilder, and Barbadian dollar, the exchange rate is fixed; so it makes little difference if you exchange your money in your hotel or at a bank (or, indeed, at all). The exchange rates for the Dominican peso and Jamaican dollar fluctuate.

ATMs can be found on all islands; due to persistent problems with fraud, however, American debit and ATM cards may be blocked in Jamaica. On some islands, ATMs offer the option of taking out either local currency or U.S. dollars. Major credit cards are widely accepted at hotels, restaurants, shops, car-rental agencies, and other service providers throughout the Caribbean. The only places that might not accept U.S. dollars are open-air markets or tiny shops in out-of-the-way villages—but even they will often accept U.S. dollars, albeit at a slightly less favorable rate of exchange.

Packing

It's hot, hot, hot in the Caribbean, so pack sleeveless or short-sleeved shirts, shorts, lightweight slacks, beach sandals, bathing suits, and a beach cover-up. For evenings, gents should pack collared shirts and long pants; for ladies, sundresses or dress slacks and tops. Pack a pair of shoes for evening, too, as you may find yourself dancing! It's always a good idea to bring a light wrap, although it's unlikely you'll need it. Bring tennis shoes, hiking shoes, and reefwalkers if you have those activities in mind. Bring your medicine, sunscreen, sunglasses, and personal items. Most hotels have shops where you can purchase sundries if you forget something, and many have lending libraries where you can borrow (or swap) a book; pharmacies and markets are also easily accessible. Pack light, though. Bring only what you need—or know you'll wear.

Passport

All Caribbean islands require travelers to have a valid passport, except for U.S. citizens traveling to Puerto Rico and/or the U.S. Virgin Islands, which are U.S. territories. Most islands also require travelers to have a valid return or ongoing ticket.

Telephones

Most U.S. cell phones will work in the Caribbean, though roaming charges can be expensive—about $3 per minute or part thereof. U.S. carriers offer short-term international packages, which reduce the cost of overseas calls. And buying a local SIM card for your own unlocked phone is a less expensive alternative if you're planning an extended stay or expect to make a lot of local calls. Top-off services for pay-as-you-go phones are readily available throughout the islands.

The most common carriers are Digicel and Flow, but others include CHIPPIE, Claro, MIO, Orange, and SETAR. AT&T, T-Mobile US, and Verizon also have a presence.

More Content

Looking for more Caribbean content? Check out Fodors.com for guides to Dominica, Montserrat, Saba, St. Eustatius, St. Vincent and the Grenadines, and Trinidad and Tobago, as well as the Bahamas.

Visa

Visas are NOT required by Caribbean nations for travelers with a passport issued by the United States, nearly all European countries, much of South America, or parts of Asia. Passport holders from the Middle East, African nations, most of Asia, or parts of Central and South America must apply for a tourist visa.

Visitor Information

ELECTRICITY

The electric current varies throughout the Caribbean. Anguilla, Barbados, British Virgin Islands, Jamaica, St. Maarten, and U.S. Virgin Islands use 110 volts, 50 cycles; Cayman Islands, Dominican Republic, Puerto Rico, and Turks and Caicos use 120 volts, 60 cycles; and Aruba and Curaçao use 127 volts, 60 cycles. (All are U.S. standard). The electric current on Martinique, Saint Lucia, and St. Martin is 220 volts, 50 cycles; on Antigua and Barbuda, Guadeloupe, St. Barth, and St. Kitts and Nevis, 230 volts, 50 cycles. (All are U.K. standard, requiring a square, three-pin plug). Dual-voltage computer and phone chargers or other appliances require a plug adapter, which you can often borrow from the hotel. For North American appliances that are not dual-voltage, you'll also need a transformer to convert the voltage. More and more hotels and resorts have added 110-volt outlets for general use but sometimes only for electric razors. Many hotels and resorts also provide USB ports, iPod docking stations... even Alexa.

EMERGENCIES

In an emergency, call 911 on most islands. Exceptions are: in Antigua, the British Virgin Islands, Saint Lucia, and Turks and Caicos, the emergency number is 999; in Barbados, call 211; in Jamaica, call 119; in Guadeloupe or Martinique, call 17; and in St. Barth, call 18.

TIME ZONES

The Cayman Islands, Jamaica, and the Turks and Caicos Islands are all in the Eastern Standard Time zone. All other Caribbean islands are in the Atlantic Standard Time zone, which is one hour later than Eastern Standard. Caribbean islands don't observe daylight saving time; during that period (March through October), when Eastern Standard Time is turned back one hour, Atlantic Standard Time and Eastern Daylight Time are the same.

When to Go

The Caribbean high season is traditionally winter—from December 15 to April 15—when you're guaranteed the most entertainment at resorts and the most people with whom to enjoy it. High season is also the most fashionable, most expensive, and most popular time to visit—and most hotels are heavily booked. You should make reservations at least two or three months in advance for the very best places (sometimes a year in advance for the most exclusive spots). Hotel prices can drop 20% to 50% after April 15; airfares and cruise prices also fall. Saving money isn't the only reason to visit the Caribbean during the off-season. Many islands now schedule their carnival, music festivals, and other events during the off-season. Late August, September, October, and early November are the least crowded months—but the weather then is also the most unpredictable. Some hotels and resorts actually close during September and October.

CLIMATE

The Caribbean climate is fairly constant. The average year-round temperature for the region ranges from 78°F to 88°F. The extremes are 65°F low, 95°F high; but, as everyone knows, it's the humidity, not the heat, that makes you suffer—especially when the two go hand in hand. The high-season months of December through April generally provide warm, sunny days with little humidity. The off-season months, particularly August through November, are the most humid. As part of the late-fall rainy season, hurricanes occasionally sweep through the Caribbean. Check the news daily and keep abreast of brewing tropical storms. The southernmost Caribbean islands are generally spared the threat of hurricanes, although they may experience storm-surge flooding. The rainy season consists mostly of brief showers interspersed with sunshine. You can watch the clouds thicken, feel the raindrops, then have brilliant sunshine dry you off, all while remaining on your lounge chair. A spell of overcast days or heavy rainfall is unusual.

HURRICANE SEASON

The Atlantic hurricane season lasts from June 1 through November 30, but it's rare to see a large storm in either June or November. Most major hurricanes occur between August and October, with the peak season in September.

Avoiding Storms. Keep in mind that hurricanes are rarer the farther south you go. The ABC Islands (Aruba, Bonaire, and Curaçao) and Grenada are least likely to get a direct hit from a hurricane, although it's never a certainty that you'll avoid storms by going south. Grenada, for example, was severely affected by Hurricane Ivan in 2004—the island's first direct hit in nearly 50 years. Surprisingly, Barbados is unlikely to be affected by hurricanes, although it lies out in the Atlantic, all by itself, 100 miles east of its nearest neighbor. Barbados can, however, experience heavy rain and flooding in September and October; accordingly, many hotels close during that period.

Airlines. Airports are usually closed during hurricanes and flights are canceled, which results in a disruption of the steady flow of tourists in and out of affected islands. If you are scheduled to fly into an area where a hurricane is expected, check with your airline regularly and often. If flights are disrupted, airlines will usually allow you to rebook for a later date. You will not get a refund if you have booked a nonrefundable ticket nor, in most cases, will you be allowed to change your ticket to a different destination; rather, you will be expected to reschedule your trip for a later date.

Hotels and Resorts. If a hurricane warning is issued and flights to your destination are disrupted, virtually all Caribbean resorts will waive cancellation and change penalties and allow you to rebook your trip for a later date. Some will allow you to cancel if a hurricane threatens to strike, even if flights aren't canceled. Some will give you a refund if you have prepaid for your stay, while others will expect you to rebook your trip for a later date. Some large resort companies—including Sandals and SuperClubs—have "hurricane guarantees," but they apply only when flights have been canceled or when a hurricane is sure to strike.

Travel Insurance. If you plan to travel to the Caribbean during the hurricane season, it is wise to buy travel insurance that allows you to cancel for any reason. This kind of coverage can be expensive (up to 10% of the value of the trip); but if you have to prepay far in advance for an expensive vacation package, the peace of mind may be worth it. Just be sure to read the fine print; some policies don't kick in unless flights are canceled and the hurricane strikes, something you may not be assured of until the day you plan to travel. To get a complete cancellation policy, you must usually buy your insurance within a week of booking your trip. If you wait to purchase insurance until after the hurricane warning is issued, it will be too late.

Track Those Hurricanes. To keep a close eye on the Caribbean during hurricane season, several websites track hurricanes as they progress: 🌐 www.accuweather.com, 🌐 hurricanetrack.com, 🌐 nwww.nhc.noaa.gov, and 🌐 www.weather.com.

Renting a Villa

In the Caribbean, the term *villa* may describe anything from a traditional cottage to a luxurious architectural wonder but almost always means a stand-alone accommodation, often privately owned. Villa rentals provide some of the region's most desirable accommodations from both a comfort and an economic point of view. We recommend considering this option, especially if you're traveling with your family or a group of friends. A villa accommodation provides a lot more space, much more privacy, and a better sense of the island than you would get at a hotel—and usually at a fraction of the per-person cost. Factor in the ability to fix simple meals, snacks, and drinks, and the savings really add up.

WHAT DOES IT COST?

Rental rates vary widely by island and by season. In-season rates range from a few hundred dollars for a simple one-bedroom cottage to more than $40,000 a week for a multiroom luxury home. Many full-service resorts offer villas of varying sizes on their property; although pricey, that can be an excellent choice if you want the best of both worlds—full service and facilities but also space and privacy. In many cases, renting a villa at a resort will cost less than renting three or four individual rooms—and you can still have a waiter deliver your rum punch to a beach chair or enjoy access to a high-tech fitness room.

WHAT'S INCLUDED?

Villas are generally furnished nicely, have updated bathrooms and full kitchens, and are equipped with linens, kitchen utensils, TV, other entertainment devices, and Wi-Fi access. The sophistication of all of the above is factored into the price; the more luxurious the digs, the higher the price.

Upscale rental villas often have small, private plunge pools (few are beachfront); daily housekeeping service (except Sunday) is included in the quoted price. On some islands, including the Dominican Republic, Jamaica, and Barbados, two or even three staff members are common. Inquire about the villa's staff and, right from the start, specify particular needs or expectations such as start times and specific or additional duties such as laundry, cooking, or child care.

HOW DO YOU RENT?

Some owners rent their properties directly (e.g., www.airbnb.com, www.vrbo.com, www.ownerdirect.com) but, in general, we recommend renting a villa through a reputable local agency that both manages and maintains the properties and has an office with local staff to facilitate and troubleshoot on your behalf should something go wrong. Lavish catalogs or websites with detailed descriptions and photographs of each villa can help assuage any concerns about what to expect. The agent will meet you at the airport, bring you to the villa, explain and demonstrate the household systems, and (for a fee) stock the kitchen with starter groceries. Some agencies provide comprehensive concierge services, will arrange or recommend car rentals, and help you find additional staff such as chefs or babysitters or yoga instructors. Some of the larger companies even host a weekly cocktail party where renters can meet each other and form a community to share local information or socialize. Local villa-rental companies are listed and recommended throughout this guide.

CHOOSING A VILLA

Your hunt will no doubt start on the Internet. A simple search for "villa rental [island name]" will get you started. The tourist board of each island can also provide a list of reputable local rental agents. It pays to seek out reputable companies, especially if you are a first-time renter.

Villa-rental websites allow you to see pictures of available villas and often have a chat feature where a knowledgeable representative will help you sort the listings according to your requirements. But use caution: Sometimes the rental agent isn't personally familiar with the villas that the agency represents; rather, they consolidate listings from other sources.

THINGS TO CONSIDER WHEN SEARCHING FOR A VILLA

How many people are in your family/group? How many bedrooms do you need? Must they be of equal size? Must all bedrooms be attached to the house? If you are two couples, you might want to specify that you'll need two master suites. If you are traveling with young children, you won't want them in a separate bedroom pavilion. Definitely confirm the types of beds in each room; couples may prefer queens or kings, whereas kids would be happy in single beds. Those looking for a bit more privacy might prefer bedrooms in a guesthouse or small cottage that's separate from the main house.

What location do you prefer? Do you want to be right on a beach? Do you want to walk to town? Will proximity to a particular activity, such as golf or scuba diving, enhance your vacation? Are you willing to rent a car to get around?

What are your requirements for electronics and appliances? Do you require a TV? Wi-Fi? Or would you be okay with something less connected? Do you want a dishwasher? A microwave? How about an outdoor gas grill, or is charcoal sufficient?

Is the villa child-friendly? Ask whether the rooms have direct access to the pool area, as that might not be a safe choice for younger kids who could open a sliding door and enter the pool area unsupervised. Are you comfortable having a pool at all? Most Caribbean villas don't have childproof security gates around pools or pool alarms. If the villa has two floors, are the rooms best suited for kids on the same floor as the master suite?

What specific issues about your destination will affect your villa choice? Personal security may be an issue in some areas of the Caribbean. Evaluate the location of potential rentals in relation to known problem areas—and ask if the villa has an alarm system. A surprisingly low rental rate on an otherwise expensive island could be a red flag.

Will you really be comfortable on your own? The final thing to consider is your relative travel hardiness and that of your traveling companions. Is this your first time in the destination? Do you relish or dread the idea of navigating local markets? Will you miss having a concierge to help arrange things for you? Do you really want to be faced with a sink full of dishes a few times a day? Will your kids be happy without a hotel full of peers? What about you?

Weddings

The Caribbean is one of the most popular venues for destination weddings. Many resorts offer attractive packages for couples to create their ultimate island-paradise wedding. As an added bonus, many islands and resorts either provide or will recommend an experienced wedding planner. Some resorts will even lend you a dress! So whether you picture an intimate beachfront ceremony for two or a full-blown affair, you can confidently leave the details to a professional and simply concentrate on exchanging your vows.

FINDING A WEDDING PLANNER

Hiring a wedding planner to handle all the logistics—from the preliminary paperwork right down to the final toast—allows you to relax and truly enjoy your big day. The best planners will advise you about legalities (residency requirements, fees, etc.), help organize the marriage license, and hire the officiant—plus arrange for venues, flowers, music, refreshments, or anything else your heart desires. Planners typically have established relationships with local vendors and can bundle packages with them, which can save you money. Many resorts have on-site wedding coordinators. But there are also many independents available, including those who specialize in certain types of ceremonies—by locale, size, religious affiliation, and so on. Island tourism boards often maintain an online list of names, and a simple "Caribbean weddings" Google search will yield scores more. What's important is that you feel *comfortable* with your coordinator. Ask for references—and call them. Share your budget. Ask coordinators how long they've been in business, how much they charge, how often you'll meet with them, and how they select vendors. Above all, request a detailed list—in writing—of what they'll provide. If your vision of the dream wedding doesn't match that coordinator's services, try someone else.

MAKING IT LEGAL

Your goal is to tie the knot, not to get tied up in red tape. So it is important to be mindful of the legalities involved. Specifics vary widely, depending on the type of ceremony you want (civil ones are invariably less complicated than religious services) and the island where you choose to wed. In the Dominican Republic, for example, key documents must be submitted in Spanish: unless you enlist a translator, your wedding will be conducted in Spanish, too. On the French-speaking islands (Guadeloupe, Martinique, St. Barth, and St. Martin), language issues are further compounded by stringent residency requirements, which can make marrying there untenable.

There are, however, **standard rules** that apply throughout the islands:

Most places will expect you to produce valid passports and a certified copy of your birth certificates as proof of identification when applying for a marriage license (the exceptions being Puerto Rico and the U.S. Virgin Islands, where a government-issued picture ID will suffice for American citizens).

If either partner is under 18 years old, parental consent is generally required; in some cases (e.g., Puerto Rico), the parents of minors must be present.

If either partner is divorced, the original (or certified) divorce or annulment decree is required.

If either is a widow or widower, an original death certificate is required. (In certain locales, an *apostille* stamp confirming the authenticity of such documents must be attached.)

On the Calendar

January

Carnival. January through April, many islands—Aruba, Curaçao, Dominican Republic, Guadeloupe, Jamaica, Martinique, St. Croix, St. Maarten—celebrate Carnival with parties, cultural events, and street parades.

Cayman Cookout. The Cayman Islands calendar literally gets cooking with the celebrity-heavy event co-organized by Eric Ripert. 🌐 caymancookout.com

Fiestas de la Calle San Sebastián, Puerto Rico. The fiestas feature four nights of live music, as well as food festivals and *cabezudos* parades. 🌐 www.discoverpuertorico.com

St. Barth Music Festival. Showcasing a wide variety of musical and dance performances, the festival is usually held the second and third weeks of the month. 🌐 www.stbartsmusicfestival.org

February

The Holetown Festival, Barbados. The weeklong event commemorates when the first European settlers arrived in Barbados in 1627. 🌐 www.holetownfestivalbarbados.org

Moonsplash, Anguilla. Visiting musicians join regional reggae superstar Bankie Banx for this annual music festival. 🌐 www.whatwedoinanguilla.com

March

BVI Spring Regatta and Sailing Festival. More than 60 boats from the Caribbean, the U.S., and Europe participate in three days of racing. 🌐 www.bvispringregatta.org

St. Maarten Heineken Regatta. As many as 300 sailboats from around the world compete. 🌐 heinekenregatta.com

April

Antigua Sailing Week. One of the world's top regattas. 🌐 www.sailingweek.com

Batabano, Cayman Islands. Cayman explodes with color with its take on Carnival. 🌐 www.caymancarnival.com

Carnival, St. Maarten. The 19-day celebration starts right after Easter with a parade and music competition.

Carnival, St. Thomas. Expect to see plenty of Mocko Jumbies, St. Thomas's colorful stilt walkers, during Carnival, which takes place right after Easter. 🌐 www.vicarnivalschedule.com/stthomas

Festival del Mar, Anguilla. Celebrate Anguilla culture during this Easter weekend festival at Island Harbour. 🌐 www.ivisitanguilla.com

Saborea Puerto Rico. Puerto Rico's largest culinary event is a three-day extravaganza held in San Juan. 🌐 www.saboreapuertorico.com

St. Barth Film Festival. Celebrate Caribbean-made documentaries and feature films. 🌐 www.stbarthff.org

May

Anguilla Regatta. The national love for boat racing peaks at this 3-day event. 🌐 www.ivisitanguilla.com/festivals-and-events

Puerto Rico Restaurant Week. Dozens of restaurants celebrate the island's cuisine with a three-course prix-fixe menu. 🌐 www.puertoricorestaurantweek.com

On the Calendar

Saint Lucia Jazz. One of the Caribbean's largest musical events. 🌐 www.stlucia.org/experiences/festivals-events

Soul Beach Music Festival, Aruba. Annual Memorial Day weekend festival featuring international artists. 🌐 www.soulbeach.net

June

La Fête de la Musique, Martinique. Celebrate the island's musical traditions with free concerts and parties. 🌐 www.frenchcaribbean.com/martinique

St. Kitts Music Festival. The island's biggest event draws international performers and music lovers alike. 🌐 www.stkittsmusicfestival.com

July

Anguilla Summer Festival. A 10-day carnival starting in late July and the island's most anticipated event of the year. 🌐 whatwedoinanguilla.com/calendar/anguilla-summer-festival

Bastille Day, St. Martin. Parades, ceremonies, and celebrations commemorate July 14, with more revelry on Grand Case Day, July 21. 🌐 www.welove-saintmartin.com

Carnival, St. John. The island celebrates with plenty of street celebrations and a huge parade on the 4th of July. 🌐 www.usvifestivals.vi/st-john

Crop Over, Barbados. A monthlong festival of music and parades, similar to Carnival, begins in July and ends on Kadooment Day (a national holiday). 🌐 ncf.bb/crop-over

Nevis Culturama Festival. This is the island's weeklong summer carnival. 🌐 www.culturamanevis.com

Saint Lucia Carnival. Celebrated mainly in Castries and Gros Islet, expect costumes, music, and the usual hedonism. 🌐 www.stlucia.org/experiences/festivals-events

August

Antigua Carnival. An elaborate, 10-day summer event with eye-catching costumes and fierce musical competitions. 🌐 www.antiguacarnival.com

Curaçao North Sea Jazz Festival. The event features big-name stars of jazz and pop music. 🌐 www.curacaonorthseajazz.com

Emancipation Festival, BVI. Also known as August Festival, this event commemorates the abolition of slavery throughout the British Empire in 1834, including some 5,000 slaves in the BVI.

SpiceMas, Grenada. Grenada's annual carnival is the island's premier cultural event, celebrated for a week in early August. 🌐 spicemasgrenada.com

St. Barth Summer Sessions. This event features 30 top musicians from around the world over 10 days. 🌐 www.frenchcaribbean.com/st-barthelemy/Things-to-Do/Local-Events

Tour Cycliste International de la Guadeloupe. The Caribbean's 10-day answer to the Tour de France runs over 800 miles on both Grande-Terre and Basse-Terre. 🌐 www.guadeloupecyclisme.com

September

European Heritage Days, Martinique. The culmination of two months of heritage weekends, public and private historical monuments and sites are celebrated with three days of cultural activities, guided tours, and experiences. 🌐 www.jep-martinique.org

October

Barbados Food & Rum Festival. The annual festival in the "Culinary Capital of the Caribbean" attracts international chefs, gastronomes, and local rum ambassadors. 🌐 www.visitbarbados.org/barbados-food-and-rum-festival

Dominican Winter Baseball Season, Dominican Republic. Well-known for its star baseball players, the DR's professional baseball series starts in October and extends through January. 🌐 www.godominicanrepublic.com/events

The Moorings Interline Regatta, BVI. Kick off the boat-racing season with this annual regatta in the Caribbean's sailing capital. 🌐 www.moorings.com/regattas-and-events/interline-regatta

Pro-AM Regatta, BVI. Enjoy the boat races at this annual event off the Bitter End Yacht Club on Virgin Gorda, which matches amateurs with America's Cup skippers. 🌐 www.beyc.com/play-at-sea/regattas

November

Caribbean Food and Wine Festival, Turks and Caicos. Chefs and vintners attend this revelry-filled long weekend. 🌐 turksandcaicostourism.com/caribbean-food-and-wine-festival

KLM Curaçao Marathon. The marathon and half-marathon courses go along the waterfront, across the famous Queen Emma pontoon bridge, and then across the Juliana Bridge—one of the world's highest. 🌐 curacaomarathon.com

Pirates Week Festival, Cayman Islands. The massive 11-day party on three islands (over three weekends) features parades, costume competitions, street dances, fireworks, and more. 🌐 www.pirateweekfestival.com

St. Barth Gourmet Festival. This international gourmet food festival lures 10 renowned chefs (and visitors) to the island. 🌐 saintbarthgourmetfestival.com

Turks and Caicos Conch Festival. Held in Blue Hills on Provo, the event celebrates the islands' national symbol and #1 export. 🌐 turksandcaicostourism.com/turks-and-caicos-conch-festival

December

Atlantic Rally for Cruisers, Saint Lucia. The finish of the world's largest ocean-crossing race is marked by a week of festivities at Rodney Bay. 🌐 www.worldcruising.com/arc/event.aspx

Crucian Christmas Festival, St. Croix. A nearly monthlong celebration coincides with the island's Christmas Carnival, ending January 6 with a huge parade. 🌐 www.vicarnivalschedule.com

Martinique Jazz Festival. The Caribbean's longest-running jazz festival is held in even-numbered years. 🌐 www.frenchcaribbean.com/martinique

Maskanoo, Turks and Caicos. On Boxing Day, the day after Christmas, live bands, parades, and fireworks erupt in Grace Bay. 🌐 turksandcaicostourism.com/maskanoo

Sugar Mas, St. Kitts and Nevis. The two-island nation celebrates its national carnival for six weeks, winding up just after New Year's Day. 🌐 www.stkittstourism.kn/about/events/st-kitts-nevis-national-carnival

Contacts

Air

MAJOR AIRLINES

Air Canada ☎ 888/247–2262 🌐 www.aircanada.com. **American Airlines** ☎ 800/433–7300 🌐 www.aa.com. **Caribbean Airlines** ☎ 800/920–4225 🌐 www.caribbean-airlines.com. **Delta Airlines** ☎ 800/241–4141 🌐 www.delta.com. **JetBlue** ☎ 800/538–2583 🌐 www.jetblue.com. **Spirit Airlines** ☎ 855/728-3555 🌐 www.spirit.com. **United Airlines** ☎ 800/864–8331 🌐 www.united.com.

SMALLER/REGIONAL AIRLINES

Air Antilles ☎ 590/590–38–4322 in Guadeloupe airantilles.com. **Air Caraïbes** ☎ 0820/835–835 in French West Indies 🌐 www.air-caraibes.com. **Air Sunshine** ☎ 800/327–8900 🌐 www.airsunshine.com. **Aruba Airlines** ☎ 297/290–8300 in Aruba. **Caicos Express Airways** ☎ 649/941–5730 in the Turks and Caicos, ☎ 305/677–3116 in U.S. 🌐 www.caicosexpress.com. **Cape Air** ☎ 800/227–3247, ☎ 284/495–2100 in BVI, ☎ 508/771–6944 outside U.S and USVI 🌐 www.capeair.com. **Cayman Airways** ☎ 345/949–2311 in the Cayman Islands, ☎ 876/613–9105 in Jamaica, ☎ 800/422–9626 in U.S. 🌐 www.caymanairways.com. **Grenadine Alliance** ☎ 246/228–5544 in Barbados 🌐 www.grenadine-air.com. **InterCaribbean Airways** ☎ 888/957–3223 in U.S. and USVI, ☎ 649/946–4999 in Turks and Caicos 🌐 www.intercaribbean.com. **LIAT** ☎ 268/480–5582 in Antigua, ☎ 246/428–1644 in Barbados, ☎ 888/844–5428 elsewhere in the Caribbean, ☎ 268/480–5601 in U.S. 🌐 www.liat.com. **Seaborne Airlines** ☎ 866/359–8784 or 787/946–7800 🌐 www.seaborneairlines.com. **St. Barth Commuter** ☎ 590/590–275–454 or ☎ 590/590–878–072 in St. Barth 🌐 www.stbarth-commuter.com. **SVG Air** ☎ 268/562–8033 in Antigua, ☎ 246/247–3712 in Barbados, ☎ 473/444–3549 in Grenada, ☎ 784/457–5124 in St. Vincent 🌐 www.flysvgair.com. **Winair** ☎ 721/545–4237 in St. Maarten 🌐 www.fly-winair.sx.

Visitor Information

Anguilla Tourist Office 🌐 www.ivisitanguilla.com. **Antigua & Barbuda Department of Tourism** 🌐 www.antigua-barbuda.org. **Aruba Tourism Authority** 🌐 www.aruba.com. **Barbados Tourism Marketing**. 🌐 visitbarbados.org. **Tourism Corp. of Bonaire** 🌐 www.tourismbonaire.com. **BVI Tourism Board** 🌐 www.bvitourism.com. **Cayman Islands Department of Tourism** 🌐 www.caymanislands.ky. **Curaçao Tourist Board** 🌐 www.curacao.com. **Dominican Republic Ministry of Tourism** 🌐 www.godominican-republic.com. **Grenada Tourism Authority** 🌐 www.puregrenada.com. **Comité du Tourisme des Iles de Guadeloupe** 🌐 www.lesilesdeguadeloupe.com. **Jamaica Tourist Board** 🌐 www.visitjamaica.com. **Comité Martiniquais du Tourisme** 🌐 www.martinique.org. **Puerto Rico Tourism Company** 🌐 www.discoverpuertorico.com. **St. Barths Online** 🌐 www.st-barths.com. **St. Kitts and Nevis Hotel and Tourism Association** 🌐 www.stkittsnevishta.org. **Saint Lucia Tourism Authority** 🌐 www.saintlucia.org. **St. Martin Tourist Office** 🌐 www.st-martin.org. **St. Maarten Tourism Department** 🌐 www.vacation-stmaarten.com. **Turks and Caicos Islands Tourist Board** 🌐 www.turksand-caicostourism.com. **USVI Division of Tourism** 🌐 www.visitusvi.com.

Chapter 3

ANGUILLA

Updated by
Riselle Celestina

Sights	Restaurants	Hotels	Shopping	Nightlife
★★★★☆	★★★★☆	★★★★☆	★★★☆☆	★★☆☆☆

WELCOME TO ANGUILLA

TOP REASONS TO GO

★ **Beautiful Beaches:** Miles of brilliant beach ensure you have a high-quality spot on which to lounge.

★ **Great Restaurants:** The dining scene offers both fine dining and delicious casual food on and off the beach.

★ **Fun, Low-Key Nightlife:** A funky late-night local music scene features reggae and string bands.

★ **Upscale Accommodations:** Excellent luxury resorts coddle you in comfort.

★ **Hidden Bargains:** You'll find a few relative bargains for both food and lodging if you look hard enough.

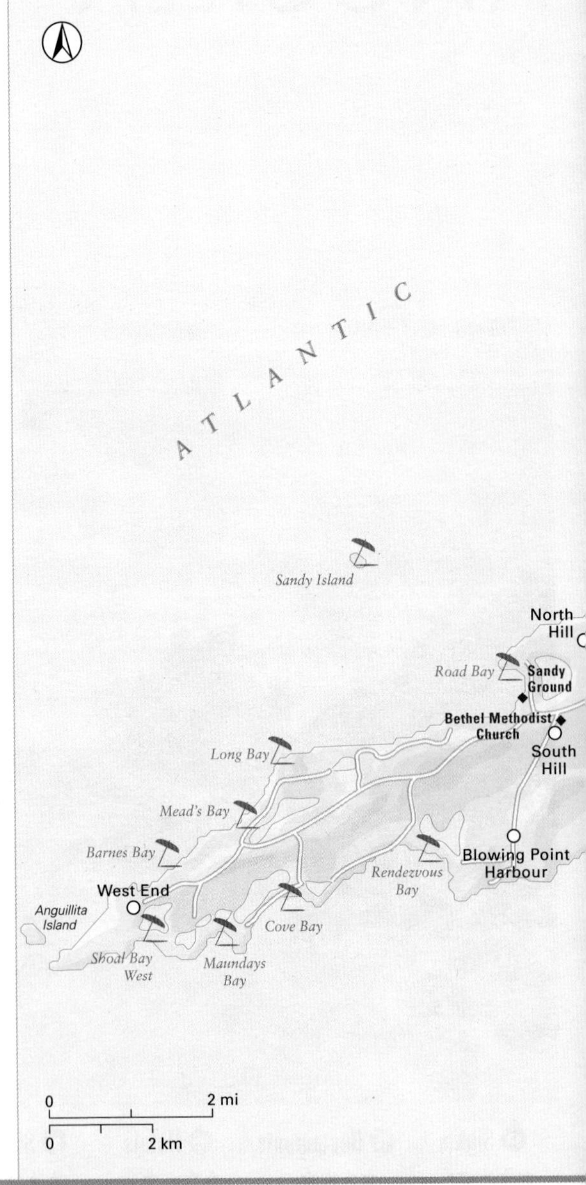

OCEAN

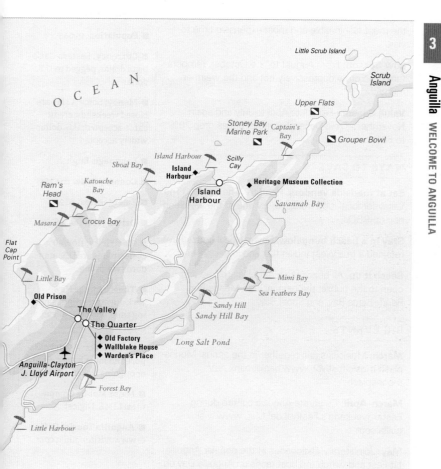

Little Scrub Island

Scrub Island

Upper Flats

Stoney Bay Marine Park

Captain's Bay

Grouper Bowl

Island Harbour

Scilly Cay

Shoal Bay

Island Harbour

Heritage Museum Collection

Ram's Head

Katouche Bay

Island Harbour

Savannah Bay

Masara

Crocus Bay

Flat Cap Point

Little Bay

Mimi Bay

Sea Feathers Bay

Old Prison

Sandy Hill

Sandy Hill Bay

The Valley

The Quarter

Old Factory

Wallblake House

Warden's Place

Long Salt Pond

Anguilla-Clayton J. Lloyd Airport

Forest Bay

Little Harbour

Caribbean Sea

ISLAND SNAPSHOT

WHEN TO GO

High Season: Mid-December through mid-April is the most fashionable and most expensive time to visit.

Low Season: From August to late October, temperatures can grow oppressively hot and the weather muggy.

Value Season: From late April to July and again November to mid-December, hotel prices drop 20% to 50%.

WAYS TO SAVE

Eat at roadside vendors. Head to "The Strip" in The Valley for local food trucks, or try one of the weekend pop-up BBQs.

Stay in a beach bungalow. Several local hotels have retained a true West Indian flair and lower prices.

Beach it up. All beaches on Anguilla are free and open to the public; the best include Meads Bay, Rendezvous Bay, and Shoal Bay.

BIG EVENTS

March: Musicians join together in the annual Moonsplash music festival. www.bankiebanx.net/moonsplash

March–April: Celebrate Anguilla culture during Easter weekend's Festival del Mar. www.ivisitanguilla.com

May: Join literary aficionados at the popular Anguilla Lit Fest and watch the boat races on Anguilla Day on May 30th. www.ivisitanguilla.com

May: The national love for boat racing peaks at the annual Anguilla Regatta. www.anguilla-regatta.com

July–August: Anguilla Summer Fest features two weeks of pageants, parades, and fireworks.

AT A GLANCE

- **Capital:** The Valley
- **Population:** 15,045
- **Currency:** Eastern Caribbean dollar; pegged to U.S. dollar
- **Money:** Some ATMs are closed weekends; credit cards accepted; U.S. dollar widely accepted
- **Language:** English
- **Country Code:** ☎ *1 264*
- **Emergencies:** ☎ *911*
- **Driving:** On the left
- **Electricity:** 110v/60 cycles; plugs are U.S. standard two-prong
- **Time:** Same as New York during daylight saving time; one hour ahead otherwise
- **Documents:** A valid passport and must have a return or ongoing ticket
- **Major Mobile Companies:** LIME, Digicel
- **Anguilla Tourist Office:** *www.ivisitanguilla.com*

Peace, pampering, great food, and a wonderful local music scene are among the star attractions on Anguilla (pronounced an- *gwill*-a). Beach lovers may become giddy when they first spot the island from the air; its blindingly white sand and lustrous blue-and-aquamarine waters are mesmerizing. And if you like sophisticated cuisine served in casually elegant open-air settings, this may well become your culinary Shangri-la.

The island's name, a reflection of its shape, is most likely a derivative of *anguille,* which is French for "eel." (French explorer Pierre Laudonniere is credited with having given the island this name when he sailed past it in 1556.) In 1631 the Dutch built a fort here, but so far no one has been able to locate its site. English settlers from St. Kitts colonized the island in 1650, with plans to cultivate tobacco and, later, cotton and then sugar. But the thin soil and scarce water doomed these enterprises. Except for a brief period of independence, when it broke from its association with St. Kitts and Nevis in the late 1960s, Anguilla has remained a British colony ever since.

From the early 1800s various island federations were formed and disbanded, with Anguilla all the while simmering over its subordinate status and forced union with St. Kitts. Anguillians twice petitioned for direct rule from Britain and twice were ignored. In 1967, when St. Kitts, Nevis, and Anguilla became an associated state, the mouse roared; citizens kicked out St. Kitts's policemen, held a self-rule referendum, and for two years conducted their own affairs. To what *Time* magazine called "a cascade of laughter around the world," a British "peacekeeping force" of 100 paratroopers from the Elite Red Devil unit parachuted onto the island, squelching Anguilla's designs for autonomy but helping a team of royal engineers stationed there to improve the port and build roads and schools. Today Anguilla elects a House of Assembly and its own leader to handle internal affairs, and a British governor is responsible for public service, the police, the judiciary, and external affairs. Some tourists may still be wondering whose responsibility it is to repair roads, some of which are absolute patchworks.

The territory of Anguilla includes a few islets (or cays, pronounced "keys"), such as Scrub Island, Dog Island, Prickly Pear

Cay, Sandy Island, and Sombrero Island. The 15,000 or so island residents are predominantly of African descent, but there are also many of Irish background, whose ancestors came from St. Kitts in the 1600s. Historically, because the limestone land was unfit for agriculture, attempts at enslavement never lasted long; consequently, Anguilla doesn't bear the scars of slavery found on so many other Caribbean islands. Instead, Anguillians became experts at making a living from the sea and are known for their boatbuilding and fishing skills. Tourism is the stable economy's growth industry, but the government carefully regulates expansion to protect the island's natural resources and beauty. New hotels are relatively small, select, casino-free, and generally expensive; Anguilla emphasizes its high-quality service, serene surroundings, and friendly people.

Planning

Getting Here and Around

AIR

American Airlines' inaugural flight from Miami to Anguilla in 2021 marked the beginning of nonstop flights to Anguilla from the United States. American has two to three flights per week from Miami, depending on the time of year. You can also get here fast by flying to St. Maarten's Princess Juliana International SXM Airport and taking a nearby ferry to Anguilla, about a half-hour ride away. Air Sunshine also flies several times a day from St. Thomas and San Juan, Cape Air from St.Thomas once a week, and Anguilla Air Services flies from St. Maarten and St. Barth. Silver Airway flies in from San Juan. TransAnguilla provides scheduled flights throughout the Caribbean.

LOCAL AIRLINE CONTACTS Air Sunshine. ☎ *800/327–8900* ⊕ *www.airsunshine.com.* **Anguilla Air Services.** ☎ *264/498–5922* ⊕ *www.anguillaairservices.com.* **Tradewind Aviation.** ☎ *800/376–7922, 203/267–3305* ⊕ *www.flytradewind.com.* **TransAnguilla Airways.** ☎ *264/497–8690* ⊕ *www.transanguilla.com.*

AIRPORT Clayton J. Lloyd International Airport. ☎ *264/497–3510* ⊕ *www.gov.ai/airport.php.*

BOAT AND FERRY

Public ferries run frequently between Anguilla and Marigot on French St. Martin. Boats leave from Blowing Point on Anguilla three times daily (same from Marigot, St. Martin) between 7 am and 6 pm. You pay a $23 departure tax before boarding ($5 for day-trippers coming through the Blowing Point terminal—but be sure to make this clear at the window where you pay), in addition to the $20 one-way fare. Fares require cash payment. Children under 12 years of age are $10. On very windy days the 20-minute trip can be fairly bouncy. The drive between the Marigot ferry terminal and the St. Maarten airport is vastly faster thanks to the causeway (bridge) across Simpson Bay lagoon. Transfers by speedboat to Anguilla are available from a terminal right at the airport at a cost of about $85 per person (arranged directly with a company or through your Anguilla hotel). Private ferry companies listed below run four or more round-trips a day, coinciding with major flights, between Blowing Point and Princess Juliana airport in Dutch St. Maarten. On the St. Maarten side they will bring you right to the terminal in a van, or you can just walk across the parking lot. These trips are $75 one-way or $130 round-trip (cash only) and usually include departure taxes. There are also private charters available.

CONTACTS Funtime Ferry. ☎ *264/497–6511* ⊕ *www.funtimecharters.com.* **GB Ferries.** ☎ *264/235–6205, 321/406–0414 in U.S.* ⊕ *www.gbferries.com.* **Link Ferries.** ☎ *264/772–4901* ⊕ *www.linkferry.com.*

CAR

Although many of the rental cars on-island have the driver's side on the left as in North America, Anguillian roads are like those in the United Kingdom—driving is on the left side of the road. It's easy to get the hang of, but the roads can be rough, so be cautious, and observe the 30 mph (48 kph) speed limit. Roundabouts are probably the biggest driving obstacle for most. As you approach, give way to the vehicle on your right; once you're in the roundabout, you have the right of way.

Car Rentals: A temporary Anguilla driver's license is required to rent a car—you can get into real trouble if you're caught driving without one. You get it for $20 (good for three months) through any of the car-rental agencies at the time you pick up your car; you'll also need your valid driver's license from home. Rental rates start at about $45 to $55 per day, plus insurance.

CONTACTS Avis. ✉ *Airport Rd.* ☎ *264/497–2642* 🌐 *www.avisanguilla.com.* **Moke Anguilla.** ✉ *Meads Bay, West End Village* ☎ *264/581-5000* 🌐 *www.mokeanguilla.com.*

TAXI

Taxis are fairly expensive, so if you plan to explore many beaches and restaurants, it may be more cost-effective to rent a car. Taxi rates are regulated by the government, and there are fixed fares from point to point, listed in brochures the drivers should have handy and published in local guides. It's about $22 from the airport or $28 from Blowing Point Ferry to West End hotels. Posted rates are for one or two people; each additional passenger adds $5, and there is a $1 charge for each piece of luggage beyond the allotted two. You can also hire a taxi for a flat rate of $28 an hour. A surcharge of $4 applies to trips between 6 pm and midnight. After midnight it's $10. You'll always find taxis at the Blowing Point Ferry landing and the airport at the taxi dispatch, but you'll need to call for hotel and restaurant pickups and arrange ahead with the driver who took you if you need a late-night return from a nightclub or bar.

CONTACTS Maurice & Sons Exquisite Taxi Services. ☎ *264/235–2676, 264/476-0505* 🌐 *www.msexquisiteshuttle.com.*

Health and Safety

Dengue, chikungunya, and zika have all been reported throughout the Caribbean at some time. Although there have been no cases in recent years, we recommend that you protect yourself from these mosquito-borne illnesses by keeping your skin covered and/or wearing mosquito repellent. The mosquitoes that transmit these viruses are as active by day as they are by night. Many locals swear by a product called "Mosquito Milk," a roll-on insect repellent available at many Caribbean pharmacies; it has a lemongrass fragrance mosquitoes seem to hate.

Hotels and Resorts

Anguilla is known for its luxurious resorts and villas, but there are also some places that mere mortals can afford (and a few that are downright bargains).

Resorts. Anguilla is known for luxurious, expensive resorts.

Villas and rentals. Private villa rentals are becoming more common and are improving in quality of design and upkeep every season as development on the island accelerates. Condos, with full kitchens and multiple bedrooms, are great for families or for longer stays.

Hotel reviews have been shortened. For full information, visit Fodors.com.

What It Costs in U.S. Dollars			
$	$$	$$$	$$$$
RESTAURANTS			
under $12	$12–$20	$21–$30	over $30
HOTELS			
under $275	$275–$375	$376–$475	over $475

Visitor Information

CONTACTS Anguilla Tourist Board. ✉ *Coronation Ave., The Valley* ☎ *264/497–2759* 🌐 *www.ivisitanguilla.com.*

Anguilla

Sights

Exploring Anguilla is mostly about checking out the spectacular beaches and resorts. The island has only a few roads. Locals are happy to provide directions, but using the readily available tourist map is the best idea. Visit the Anguilla Tourist Board, centrally located on Coronation Avenue in The Valley.

You can take a free, self-guided tour of the Anguilla Heritage Trail, consisting of 10 important historical sights that can be explored independently in any order. Wallblake House, in The Valley, is the main information center for the trail, or you can just look for the large boulders with descriptive plaques.

Heritage Museum Collection
HISTORY MUSEUM | **FAMILY** | A remarkable opportunity to learn about Anguilla, this tiny museum (complete with gift shop) is painstakingly curated by Colville Petty. Old photographs and local records and artifacts trace the island's history over four millennia, from the days of the Arawaks. High points include historical documents of the Anguilla Revolution and photo albums chronicling island life, from devastating hurricanes to a visit from Queen Elizabeth in 1964. You can see examples of ancient pottery shards and stone tools along with fascinating photographs of the island in the early 20th century—many depicting the heaping and exporting of salt and the christening of schooners—and a complete set of beautiful postage stamps issued by Anguilla since 1967. ✉ *East End at Pond Ground* ☎ *264/235-7440* 🎫 *$10* ⏲ *Closed Wed., Thu., Sat. and Sun.*

Island Harbour
MARINA/PIER | Anguillians have been fishing for centuries in the brightly painted, simple, handcrafted fishing boats that line the shore of the harbor. It's hard to believe, but skillful pilots take these little boats out to sea as far as 50 or 60 miles (80 or 100 km). Late afternoon is the best time to see the day's catch, and there are a couple of good, laid-back beach restaurants here.

■ TIP→ Scilly Cay, the classic little offshore restaurant offering sublime lobster and Eudoxie Wallace's knockout rum punches, is still hoping to reopen following Hurricane Irma. They have already completed some rebuilding: stay tuned. ✉ *Island Harbor Rd.*

Sandy Ground
BEACH | Almost everyone who comes to Anguilla stops by this central beach, home to several popular open-air bars and restaurants, as well as boat-rental operations. This is where you catch the ferry for tiny Sandy Island, 2 miles (3 km) offshore for about $40 round-trip. ☎ *264/476–6534* 🌐 *www.mysandyisland.com.*

Beaches

Anguilla's beaches are among the best and most beautiful in the Caribbean. You can find long, deserted stretches suitable for sunset walks and beaches lined with lively bars and restaurants—all surrounded by crystal-clear warm waters in several shades of turquoise. The sea is calmest at 2½-mile-long (4-km-long)

Did You Know?

Anguilla, about 150 miles east of Puerto Rico, has 33 beaches, each more beautiful than the last.

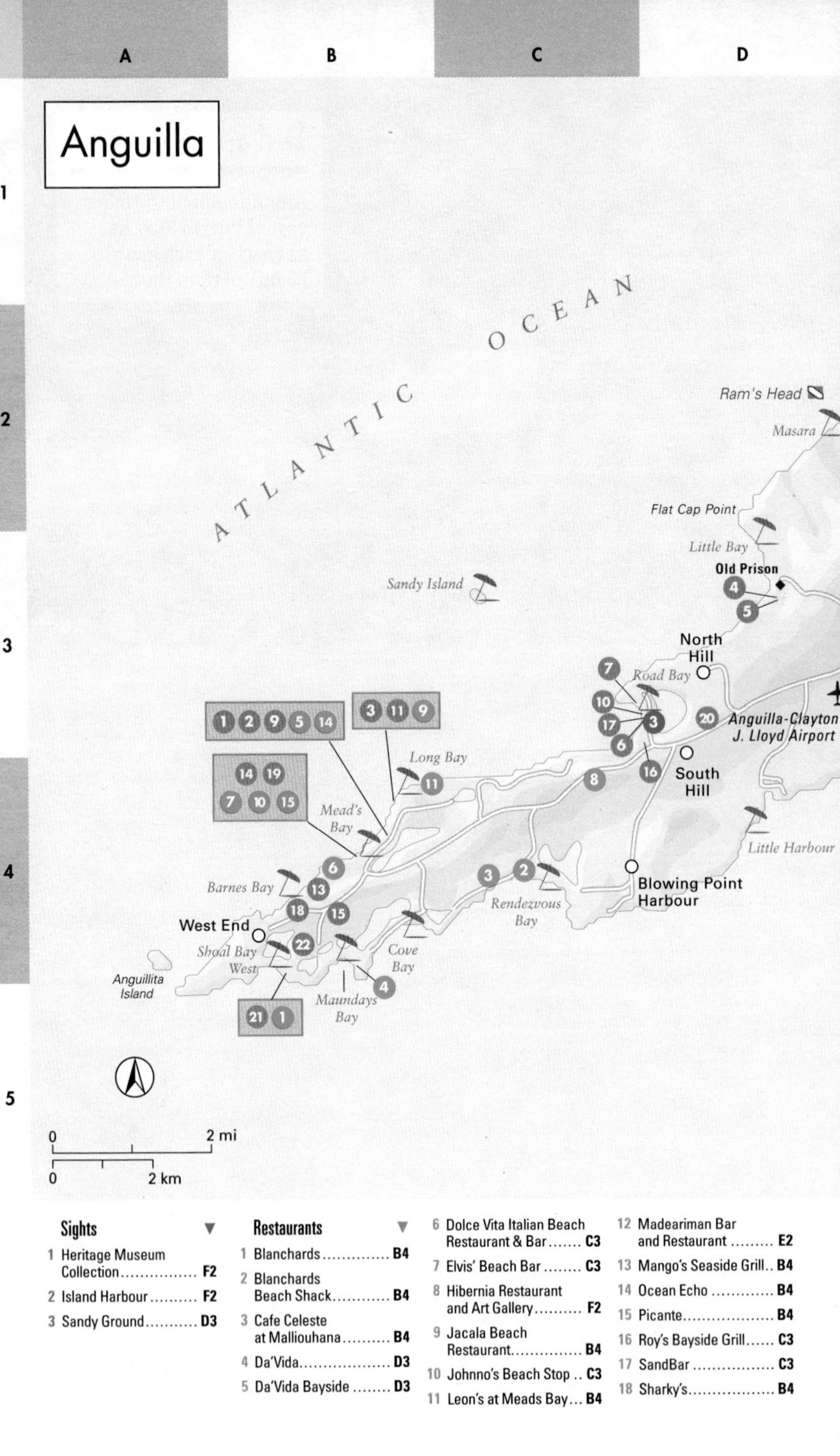
A
B
C
D
1
2
3
4
5
Anguilla
ATLANTIC OCEAN
Ram's Head
Masara
Flat Cap Point
Little Bay
Old Prison
Sandy Island
North Hill
Road Bay
Anguilla-Clayton J. Lloyd Airport
South Hill
Long Bay
Mead's Bay
Little Harbour
Barnes Bay
Blowing Point Harbour
Rendezvous Bay
West End
Shoal Bay West
Cove Bay
Anguillita Island
Maundays Bay
0
2 mi
0
2 km
Sights
1 Heritage Museum Collection F2
2 Island Harbour F2
3 Sandy Ground D3
Restaurants
1 Blanchards B4
2 Blanchards Beach Shack B4
3 Cafe Celeste at Malliouhana B4
4 Da'Vida D3
5 Da'Vida Bayside D3
6 Dolce Vita Italian Beach Restaurant & Bar C3
7 Elvis' Beach Bar C3
8 Hibernia Restaurant and Art Gallery F2
9 Jacala Beach Restaurant B4
10 Johnno's Beach Stop .. C3
11 Leon's at Meads Bay ... B4
12 Madeariman Bar and Restaurant E2
13 Mango's Seaside Grill .. B4
14 Ocean Echo B4
15 Picante B4
16 Roy's Bayside Grill C3
17 SandBar C3
18 Sharky's B4

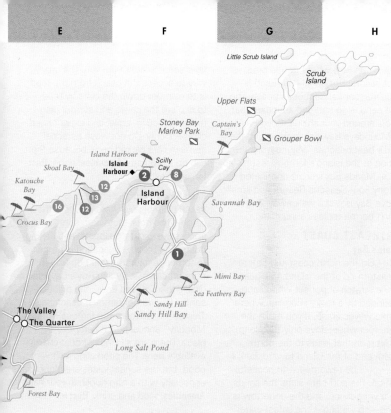

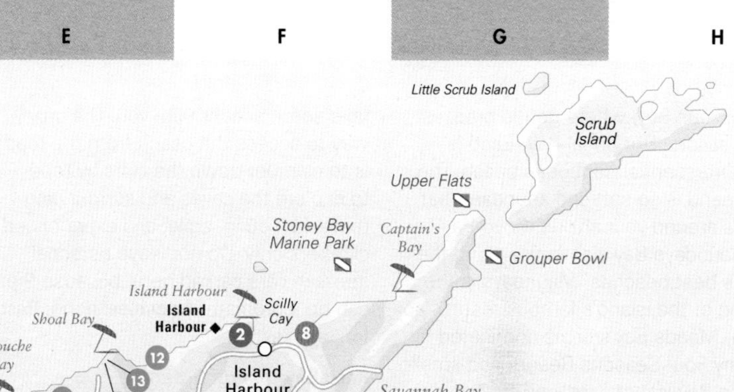

19 Straw Hat B4
20 Tasty's D3
21 Trattoria Tramonto Restaurant B4
22 Veya and Meze at Veya B4

Hotels ▼

1 Altamer B4
2 Anguilla Great House Beach Resort C4
3 Aurora Anguilla Resort & Golf Club C4
4 Belmond Cap Juluca ... B4
5 Carimar Beach Club B4
6 Four Seasons Resort and Residences Anguilla ... B4
7 Frangipani Beach Resort B4
8 La Vue Inn C4
9 Malliouhana, An Auberge Resort B4
10 Meads Bay Beach Villas B4
11 Quintessence B4
12 Serenity Cottages E2
13 Shoal Bay Villas E2
14 Tranquility Beach B4
15 Turtle's Nest Beach Resort B4
16 Zemi Beach House Hotel & Spa/Residences E2

Rendezvous Bay, where gentle breezes tempt sailors. But Shoal Bay (East) is the quintessential Caribbean beach. The white sand is so soft and abundant that it pools around your ankles. Cove Bay and Maundays Bay also rank among the island's best beaches. Maundays is the location of the island's famous resort Cap Juluca. Meads Bay's arc is dominated by the tony Four Seasons Resort, and smaller Cove Bay is just a walk away. Anguilla doesn't permit topless sunbathing.

NORTHEAST COAST

Captain's Bay

BEACH | On the north coast just before the eastern tip of the island, this quarter-mile stretch of perfect white sand is bounded by a rocky shoreline where Atlantic waves crash. If you make the tough, four-wheel-drive-only trip along the dirt road that leads to the northeastern end of the island toward Junk's Hole, you'll be rewarded with peaceful isolation. The surf here slaps the sands with a vengeance, and the undertow is strong—so wading is the safest water sport. **Amenities:** none. **Best for:** solitude.

Island Harbour

BEACH | For centuries Anguillians have ventured from these sands in colorful handmade fishing boats. Mostly calm waters are surrounded by a slender beach—good sightseeing, but not much for swimming or lounging. But there are a couple of good restaurants (Hibernia, offering dinner, and Falcon Nest, a casual spot for lunch and dinner). **Amenities:** food and drink; toilets. **Best for:** partiers.

NORTHWEST COAST

Little Bay

BEACH | On the north coast, not far from The Valley, this small gray-sand beach is a favored spot for snorkeling and night dives. It's essentially accessible only by water, as it's backed by sheer cliffs lined with agave and creeping vines. The easiest way to get here is a five-minute boat ride from Crocus Bay (about $10 round-trip). There are no amenities, so take some snacks with you. The only way to access the beach from the road is to clamber down the cliffs by rope to explore the caves and surrounding reef—for young, agile, and experienced climbers only. Do not leave personal items in cars parked here, because theft can be a problem. **Amenities:** none. **Best for:** snorkeling.

Road Bay (*Sandy Ground*)

BEACH | The big pier here is where the cargo ships dock, but so do some impressive yachts, sailboats, and fishing boats. The brown-sugar sand is home to terrific restaurants that hop from day through dawn, including Roy's Bayside Grill, Johnno's, and Elvis', the quintessential (and rather famous) beach bar. This beach is where the famous "August Monday" annual beach party takes place. There are all kinds of boat charters available here. The snorkeling isn't very good, but the sunset vistas are glorious, especially with a rum punch in your hand. **Amenities:** food and drink. **Best for:** sunset.

Sandy Island

BEACH | A popular day trip, tiny Sandy Island shelters a pretty lagoon nestled in coral reefs about 2 miles (3 km) from Road Bay/Sandy Ground, with a restaurant that serves lunch and great islandy cocktails. From November through August you can take the shuttle from Sandy Ground ($40 round-trip). There is mooring for yachts and larger sailboats. Small boats can come right in the channel. **TIP→ The reef is great for snorkeling.** **Amenities:** food and drink. **Best for:** partiers; snorkeling; swimming. 🌐 *www.mysandyisland.com.*

★ Shoal Bay

BEACH | **FAMILY** | Anchored by seagrape and coconut trees, the 2-mile (3-km) powdered-sugar strand at Shoal Bay (not to be confused with Shoal Bay West, at the other end of the island) is one of the world's prettiest beaches. You can park free at any of the restaurants, including Tropical Sunset or Gwen's Reggae Bar &

Grill, most of which either rent or provide chairs and umbrellas for patrons for about $20 a day per person (some offer chairs and umbrellas free of charge with lunch). There is plenty of room to stretch out in relative privacy, or you can bar-hop. The relatively broad beach has shallow water that is usually gentle, making this a great family beach; a coral reef not far from the shore is a wonderful snorkeling spot. Sunsets over the water are spectacular. **Amenities:** food and drink. **Best for:** sunset; swimming; walking.

SOUTHEAST COAST

Sandy Hill

BEACH | You can park anywhere along the dirt road to Sea Feathers Bay to visit this popular fishing center. What's good for the fishermen is also good for snorkelers, with a coral reef right near the shore. The beach here is not much of a lounging spot, but it's a favorite spot for local families to picnic. For those with creative culinary skills, it's a great place to buy lobsters and fish fresh from local waters in the afternoon. **Amenities:** food and drink. **Best for:** snorkeling; walking.

SOUTHWEST COAST

★ Maundays Bay

BEACH | The dazzling, platinum-white mile-long beach is especially great for swimming and long beach walks. It's no wonder that the Belmond Cap Juluca, one of Anguilla's premier resorts, chose this as its location. Public parking is straight ahead at the end of the road near Cap Juluca's Pimms restaurant. You can have lunch or dinner here (be prepared for the cost) or, depending on the season, book a massage in one of the beachside tents. **Amenities:** food and drink; parking (no fee); toilets. **Best for:** sunbathing; swimming; walking.

★ Meads Bay

BEACH | **FAMILY** | Arguably Anguilla's premier beach, Meads Bay is home to many of the island's top resorts (Malliouhana, Four Seasons) and a dozen fine restaurants. The powder-soft Champagne sand is great for a long walk and is as beautiful now as it has ever been. Park at any of the restaurants, and plan for lunch. Several of the restaurants offer chaises for patrons. **Amenities:** food and drink; parking (no fee); toilets. **Best for:** sunbathing; swimming; walking.

Rendezvous Bay

BEACH | **FAMILY** | Follow the signs to Anguilla Great House for public parking at this broad swath of pearl-white sand that is some 1½ miles (2½ km) long. The beach is lapped by calm, bluer-than-blue water and a postcard-worthy view of St. Martin. The expansive crescent is home to three resorts; stop in for a drink or a meal at one, or rent a chair and umbrella at one of the kiosks. Don't miss the daylong party at the Dune Preserve, where Bankie Banx, Anguilla's most famous musician, presides. (Jimmy Buffett recorded a concert there several years back, too.) **Amenities:** food and drink; parking (no fee); toilets. **Best for:** sunbathing; swimming; walking.

Shoal Bay West

BEACH | This glittering bay bordered by mangroves and seagrapes is a lovely place to spend the day. The 1-mile-long (1½-km-long) beach offers sublime tranquility with coral reefs for snorkeling not too far from shore. Punctuate your day with lunch or dinner at beachside Trattoria Tramonto and you can use their chairs and umbrellas. Reach the beach by taking the main road to the West End and bearing left at the fork, then continuing to the end. Note that similarly named Shoal Bay is a separate beach on a different part of the island. **Amenities:** food and drink; parking (no fee); toilets. **Best for:** solitude; swimming; walking.

Restaurants

Despite its small size, Anguilla has more than 70 restaurants: stylish temples of haute cuisine; classic, barefoot beachfront grills; roadside barbecue stands;

food vans; and casual cafés. Many have breeze-swept terraces for dining under the stars. Call ahead—in winter to make a reservation and in late summer and fall to confirm whether the place is open. Anguillian restaurant meals are leisurely events, and service often has a relaxed pace, so settle in and enjoy. Most restaurant owners are actively and conspicuously present, especially at dinner.

★ Blanchards

$$$$ | **ECLECTIC** | Creative cuisine, an upscale atmosphere, attentive service, and an excellent wine cellar please the star-studded crowd at Blanchards, one of the best restaurants in the Caribbean. Ever changing but always good, the contemporary menu, with items such as the warm Brussels sprout Caesar and the sesame-crusted sea bass, wins over even the most sophisticated palates. **Known for:** fine dining; the owners' book, "A Trip To The Beach," which has motivated many to visit; exquisite presentation. *Average main: $38 ✉ Meads Bay Beach, Long Bay Village ☎ 264/497–6100 🌐 www.blanchardsrestaurant.com ⏲ Closed Sun. No lunch. Closed end of Aug. to mid. Oct.*

Blanchards Beach Shack

$$ | **AMERICAN** | **FAMILY** | This spin-off on the sands of Meads Bay Beach is the perfect antidote to high restaurant prices. Right next to Blanchards, this chartreuse-and-turquoise cottage serves delicious lunches and dinners of mahi BLT, all-natural burgers, tacos, and terrific salads and sandwiches, and there are lots of choices for children and vegetarians. **Known for:** "the wait" from 12:30 on; beach food with a twist; generous portions. *Average main: $13 ✉ Meads Bay Beach, Long Bay Village ☎ 264/498–6100 🌐 www.blanchardsrestaurant.com ⏲ Closed Sun. and end of Aug. to mid Oct.*

★ Cafe Celeste at Malliouhana

$$$$ | **ECLECTIC** | The romantic open-air setting of Cafe Celeste on a promontory overlooking Meads Bay sets the stage for a memorable meal. The café's dishes are inspired by Mediterranean seafaring cultures, including seafood spaghettini or conch tiradito made with soursop, peppers, scallions, and lime. **Known for:** the stunning view; Malli sunset cocktails; grilled crayfish with lemon butter. *Average main: $36 ✉ Meads Bay Beach, Long Bay Village ☎ 264/497–6111 🌐 aubergeresorts.com/malliouhana/dine/celeste 💳 No credit cards ⏲ Closed late Aug. to Oct.*

Da'Vida

$$$$ | **ASIAN FUSION** | **FAMILY** | Dining at this locally owned, fine dining restaurant on the pristine beach at Crocus Bay is a delight. A semi-open design allows the sounds and smells of the ocean to tantalize your senses while you dine on exquisite Asian-Mediterranean fusion dishes like mushroom and kale risotto and pan seared miso grouper with lemongrass beurre blanc. **Known for:** friendly service; beachside sophistication; tapas and cocktails at the Tamarind Lounge. *Average main: $36 ✉ Crocus Bay ☎ 264/498–5433 🌐 www.davidaanguilla.com ⏲ Closed Mon. and Tues. and from Aug. to Nov.*

Da'Vida Bayside

$$$ | **INTERNATIONAL** | **FAMILY** | Da'Vida Bayside is a nice, more relaxed lunchtime alternative to neighboring Da'Vida. Sitting on the stunning, calm beach at Crocus Bay, this spot is perfect for a stress-free day complete with delicious lunch options and a comprehensive cocktail and mocktail menu. **Known for:** kayak, snorkeling equipment, and kayak rental; unique pizzas, seafood pasta, and frozen drinks; lunch with your feet in the sand. *Average main: $22 ✉ Crocus Bay ☎ 264/498–5433, 264/584-5433 🌐 www.davidaanguilla.com ⏲ Closed Mon. and Tues., no dinner.*

Dolce Vita Italian Beach Restaurant & Bar
$$$$ | **ITALIAN** | **FAMILY** | Serious Italian cuisine and warm and attentive service are provided in a romantic beachside pavilion in Sandy Ground. It all starts with meticulously sourced seafood and freshly made pasta, which stars in classic lasagna, linguine with clams, seafood risotto, and a meatless eggplant parmigiana. **Known for:** beachside dining; fresh catch of the day; Italian wine selection. *Average main: $43* *Sandy Ground, Sandy Ground Village* *264/497–8668* *Closed Sun. and Sept.–mid-Oct. No lunch.*

★ **Elvis' Beach Bar**
$$ | **MODERN AMERICAN** | One of the most famous beach restaurants in the Caribbean, Elvis' is a hub of nightlife on the island, catering to all kinds of visitors and Hollywood A-listers. The bar is actually a boat; you can sit around it or with your feet in the sand under umbrella-covered tables on the beach. **Known for:** Mexican food and potent drinks; the famous Goatchos and goat taco; big screen TVs with sports on. *Average main: $20* *Northern End, Sandy Ground beach* *264/476–0101* *www.elvisbeachbar.com.*

★ **Hibernia Restaurant and Art Gallery**
$$$$ | **ECLECTIC** | Creative dishes are served in this wood-beam cottage restaurant overlooking the water at Anguilla's eastern end. The tables in the intimate dining room face a Balinese-style pool with a fountain, sure to inspire relaxation during dinner. **Known for:** white chocolate and lavender ice cream meringue cake; eclectic dining; can't-miss smoked Caribbean fish appetizer. *Average main: $36* *Harbor Ridge Dr., Island Harbour* *264/497–4290* *www.hiberniarestaurant.com* *Closed Sun. and Mon. and from Aug. to Oct.; no lunch except Tues. and Fri.*

★ **Jacala Beach Restaurant**
$$$ | **FRENCH** | On beautiful Meads Bay, this restaurant continues to receive raves. Chef Alain has created a lovely open-air restaurant that turns out carefully prepared and nicely presented French food accompanied by good wines and personal attention. **Known for:** filet mignon cooked to perfection; best-in-the-Caribbean reputation; friendly beach side service. *Average main: $38* *Meads Bay Beach, Long Bay Village* *264/498–5888* *www.facebook.com/jacala-beach-restaurant* *Closed Mon. and Tues. and Aug. and Sept.*

Johnno's Beach Stop
$$ | **CARIBBEAN** | **FAMILY** | Now operating at lunch on Thursday to Sunday, Johnno's offers some of the best seafood on the island. Enjoy succulent fried, boiled, or steamed fish with sides like rice and peas, french fries or funchi (a hearty polenta). **Known for:** classic Caribbean beach bar; seafood; outpost on Prickly Pear Cay. *Average main: $20* *Sandy Ground, Sandy Ground Village* *264/497–2728* *www.facebook.com/johnnosbeachstop* *Closed Mon. to Wed. No dinner.*

Leon's at Meads Bay
$$ | **ECLECTIC** | Part of the neighboring Malliouhana Resort, this trendy beach shack has a local, laid-back atmosphere. Have lunch on the colorful benches or sit in comfortable lounge chaises under bright umbrellas while you enjoy johnnycake burgers, ceviche, and crispy snacks. **Known for:** live music on weekends; toes in the sand dining; great sunset spot. *Average main: $15* *Malliouhana Resort, Meads Bay, West End Village* *264/497–6117* *aubergeresorts.com/malliouhana/dine/leons-meads-bay* *Closed Mon. and Tues.*

Jacala Beach Restaurant, located on Meads Bay, is a great place to put your toes in the sand.

Madeariman Bar and Restaurant

$$$ | BRASSERIE | FAMILY | This casual, feet-in-the-sand bistro right on beautiful Shoal Bay East is open for breakfast, lunch, and dinner. The soups, salads, and simple grills here are served in generous portions with a bit of French flair, and the delicious pizzas are cooked in a stone oven. **Known for:** simple yet tasty food; prime location on Shoal Bay East; great stone oven pizza. *Average main: $26 Shoal Bay East, Shoal Bay Village 264/497–5750 www.madeariman.restaurant.*

Mango's Seaside Grill

$$$$ | SEAFOOD | FAMILY | Sparkling-fresh fish specialties have starring roles here. Sit in this semi-open-air restaurant on beautiful Barnes Bay and enjoy the salty breeze and sounds of the waves rolling in as you dive into light and healthy dishes like spicy grilled whole snapper and Cruzan rum–barbecued chicken. **Known for:** mango ginger crème brulee; laid-back but high-end atmosphere; fresh fish dishes. *Average main: $36 Barnes Bay 264/497–6479 www.mangos-seasidegrill.com Closed Tues. and Aug. – Oct.*

Ocean Echo

$$$$ | CARIBBEAN | FAMILY | It's nonstop every day from lunch until late at this relaxed and friendly restaurant, great for salads, burgers, grills, pasta, and fresh fish. A couple of times a week there is live music as well as the possibility of dancing with an excellent island cocktail in hand. **Known for:** beachside tables; the "Rumzie," Anguilla's rum punch; delicious pizzas and lobster salad. *Average main: $35 Meads Bay Beach, Long Bay Village 264/498–5454 www.oceanechoanguilla.com.*

Picante

$$$ | MEXICAN | FAMILY | This casual, wildly popular bright-red roadside Caribbean *taquería,* opened by a young California couple, serves huge, tasty burritos with a choice of fillings, fresh warm tortilla chips with first-rate guacamole, huge (and fresh) taco salads, seafood enchiladas, chipotle ribs, and tequila-lime chicken grilled under a brick. Passion-fruit margaritas are a must, and there are some serious tequila options. **Known for:** picnic-table seating; passion-fruit margarita; tacos. *Average main: $21 West End Rd., West End Village 264/498–1616 www.picante-restaurant-anguilla.com Closed Sun. and mid-Aug.–mid Oct. No lunch.*

Roy's Bayside Grill

$$$ | **CARIBBEAN** | **FAMILY** | Roy's is comfort food heaven, whether you crave red snapper fish-and-chips or a hamburger with all the fixings. Come any time of day for good cooking and a friendly vibe. **Known for:** grilled lobster; home-style cooking and awesome margaritas; incredible beachfront location. *Average main: $25 Road Bay, Sandy Ground Village 264/497–2470 www.roysbaysidegrill.com.*

SandBar

$$ | **ECLECTIC** | Tasty and shareable small plates, a friendly beach vibe, and gorgeous sunsets are on offer here, as are cool music, gentle prices, and potent tropical cocktails. The menu changes seasonally, but it always features tapas brought to a new level, usually traditional foods prepared in unconventional ways. **Known for:** daily happy hour; big tapas plates at reasonable prices; great sunset views. *Average main: $12 Sandy Ground Village 264/498–0171 Closed Sun. and Mon.*

Sharky's

$$$ | **CARIBBEAN** | **FAMILY** | A not-to-be-missed restaurant where Caribbean flavors steal the show, Sharky's is a result of Chef Lowell Hodge's perfectionism. He does a few things here and does them well, as a usually full house well attests ("house," by the way, is an operative word—you'll dine on the front porch of a private home). **Known for:** few menu items but all are hits; the chef's family recipes; high-end dining for a fraction of the price. *Average main: $25 Rte. 1 West End Village and Albert Hughes Dr. Just past the gas station 264/729–0059 No credit cards.*

★ Straw Hat

$$$$ | **ECLECTIC** | **FAMILY** | A charming owner, a gorgeous oceanfront location, sophisticated and original food, and friendly service are why this stylish restaurant on the beautiful Meads Bay has been in business since the mid-1990s. Whether for breakfast, lunch, late afternoon snack, or dinner, you will find appealing, tasty, and fresh choices to mix up or share. **Known for:** fairly priced cocktails; beach view; mahi and shrimp ceviche with plantain chips. *Average main: $35 Frangipani Beach Resort, Long Bay Village 264/497–8300 www.strawhat.com Closed Sept. and Oct.*

Tasty's

$$$ | **CARIBBEAN** | **FAMILY** | Satisfying everyone's taste buds since 1999, this roadside restaurant in South Hill is a well known spot for locals and visitors alike. You'll find that breakfast, lunch, tapas, or dinner at Tasty's is, well, very tasty. **Known for:** seafood salad; classic Caribbean with a creole edge; Tuesday and Friday happy hour. *Average main: $26 Main Rd., South Hill Village 264/584–2737 www.facebook.com/tastysrestaurantanguilla Closed Thurs.*

Trattoria Tramonto Restaurant

$ | **ITALIAN** | **FAMILY** | The island's beloved beachfront Italian restaurant (open for lunch only) features a serenade of soft jazz on the sound system and gently lapping waves a few feet away. Pastas are homemade and served in a dozen ways. **Known for:** beachy setting; classic Northern Italian meals next to the sea; relaxing tropical ambience. *Average main: $5 1254 Shoal Bay West, Shoal Bay Village 264/497–8819 www.trattoriatramonto.com Closed Mon. and Tues. and Aug.–Oct. No dinner.*

Aurora Anguilla Resort & Golf Club is a family-friendly resort on Rendezvous Bay.

★ **Veya and Meze at Veya**

$$$$ | **ECLECTIC** | On the suavely minimalist four-sided verandah, stylishly appointed tables glow with flickering candlelight from sea urchin–shape porcelain votive holders. Chic patrons mingle and sip mojitos to the purr of soft jazz in a lively lounge. **Known for:** live music nightly; Veya sparklers; Moroccan shrimp "cigars". *Average main: $45* ✉ *Sandy Ground Village* ☎ *264/498–8392* 🌐 *www.veyarestaurant.com* ⏲ *Closed Sun. and Sept.–mid-Oct. Closed Sat. in June–Aug. and in late Oct. No lunch.*

Hotels

Tourism on Anguilla is newer than some Caribbean islands—most development didn't begin until the early 1980s. The lack of native topography and, indeed, vegetation, and the blindingly white expanses of beach have inspired building designs of some interest; architecture buffs might have fun trying to name some of the most surprising examples. Inspiration largely comes from the Mediterranean: the Greek Islands, Morocco, and Spain, with some Miami-style art deco thrown into the mixture.

Anguilla accommodations basically fall into two categories: grand resorts and luxury resort-villas, or low-key, simple, locally owned apartments and small beachfront complexes. The former can be surprisingly expensive, the latter surprisingly reasonable. In the middle are some condo-type options, with full kitchens and multiple bedrooms, which are great for families or for longer stays. Private villa rentals are becoming more common and are increasing in number and quality of design and upkeep every season as development on the island accelerates.

A good phone chat or email exchange with the management of any property is a good idea, as units within the same complex can vary greatly in layout, accessibility, distance to the beach, and view. When calling to reserve a room, ask about special discount packages, especially in spring and summer. Most hotels include continental breakfast in the price, and many have meal-plan options. But keep in mind that Anguilla is home to dozens of excellent restaurants before you lock yourself into an expensive meal plan that you may not be able to change. All hotels charge a 10% tax, a $1 per room/per day tourism marketing levy, and—in most cases—an additional 10% service charge. A few properties include these charges in the published rates, so check carefully when evaluating prices.

PRIVATE VILLAS AND CONDOS

The tourist office publishes an annual *Anguilla Travel Planner* with informative listings of available vacation apartment rentals.

RENTAL CONTACTS

Ani Private Resorts

Little Bay 718/577–1188 www.aniprivateresorts.com.

Kishti Villa Collection

Long Bay Village 609/225-5678, 264/235–2110 www.villakishticollection.com.

HOTELS AND RESORTS

Altamer

$$$$ | **RESORT** | **FAMILY** | Architect Myron Goldfinger's geometric symphony of floor-to-ceiling windows, cantilevered walls, and curvaceous floating staircases set on a white-sand private beach is fit for any celebrity (or CEO)—as is the price tag. **Pros:** great for big groups; stunning decor and beautiful architectural design; outstanding luxury, privacy, and service. **Cons:** a minimum of 5 nights is required; expensive; a bit out of the way. *Rooms from: $4800 Rte. 1, Shoal Bay Village 800/475–9233 www.altamer.com 3 villas Free Breakfast.*

Anguilla Great House Beach Resort

$$ | **RESORT** | **FAMILY** | These traditional West Indian–style bungalows are strung along one of Anguilla's longest beaches. **Pros:** good prices; real, old-school Caribbean; right on one of the most popular beaches. **Cons:** not exquisite or luxurious, which many seek in Anguilla; looks a bit tired; very simple rooms. *Rooms from: $310 Rendezvous Bay 264/497–6061, 800/583–9247 www.anguillagreathouse.com 31 rooms No Meals.*

Aurora Anguilla Resort & Golf Club

$$$$ | **RESORT** | **FAMILY** | Formerly the Resorts and Residences by CuisinArt, this new and quite lavish resort operated by Olympus Ventures opened in late 2021. **Pros:** Greg Norman golf course; on-site restaurants, bars, and spa; gorgeous, luxurious rooms. **Cons:** takes time to go to one end of the resort to the next; beach can be rough; expensive. *Rooms from: $701 Rendezvous Bay 264/498–2000, 800/210–6444 U.S. www.auroraanguilla.com 98 rooms Free Breakfast.*

★ **Belmond Cap Juluca**

$$$$ | **RESORT** | **FAMILY** | Strung along 179 acres of breathtaking Maundays Bay, these romantic, domed villas are a long-time Anguilla favorite, thanks to a caring staff, great sports facilities, and plenty of privacy and comfort. **Pros:** great on-site restaurants; miles of talcum-soft sand; impeccable, warm service. **Cons:** comparatively high rates; sun sets on the opposite side of the resort; may be booked well in advance. *Rooms from: $875 Maunday's Bay 264/497–6666, 264/497–6779 reservations www.belmond.com/capjuluca 108 rooms Free Breakfast.*

Carimar Beach Club

$$$$ | **APARTMENT** | **FAMILY** | This horseshoe of bougainvillea-draped Mediterranean-style buildings on beautiful Meads Bay has the look of a Sun Belt condo. **Pros:** excellent beach location; great value; easy walk to restaurants and spa. **Cons:** not much privacy in the courtyard; air-conditioning only in bedrooms; no pool or restaurant. *Rooms from: $480 Meads Bay, West End Village 264/497–6881, 800/681–6956 US www.carimar.com 24 apartments No Meals.*

★ **Four Seasons Resort and Residences Anguilla**

$$$$ | **RESORT** | **FAMILY** | On a promontory over 3,200 feet of pearly sand on Barnes Bay, this showpiece wows sophisticates. **Pros:** spacious rooms; state-of-the-art luxury; cutting-edge contemporary design. **Cons:** expensive; very large resort; international rather than Caribbean feel. *Rooms from: $925 Barnes Bay, West End Village 264/201–9580 US, 264800/497–7000 www.fourseasons.com/anguilla Closed end of Aug. to Mid Oct. 180 units No Meals.*

Frangipani Beach Resort

$$$ | **RESORT** | **FAMILY** | Located on the beautiful Champagne sands of Meads Bay, this Mediterranean-style property has a welcoming and laid-back feel, and the friendly service immediately sets you at ease. **Pros:** first-rate on-site restaurant; great beach; good location for restaurant-hopping and water sports activities. **Cons:** you will not want to leave; more like a condo than a resort; some rooms lack a view. *Rooms from: $450 Meads Bay, West End Village 264/497–6442 www.frangipaniresort.com Closed Sept. and Oct. 23 rooms Free Breakfast.*

La Vue Inn

$ | **HOTEL** | **FAMILY** | Although it's not on the beach, this family-owned and-operated boutique inn sitting on a cliff in the middle of the island offers breathtaking views of Sandy Ground Village and Road Bay below. **Pros:** swimming pool and restaurant on property; stunning vistas from ocean-view rooms; a great stay without breaking the bank. **Cons:** not on the beach; minimum stay of 2 nights; no elevators. *Rooms from: $200 Back St., South Hill Village 264/476–3000, 264/497–3000 www.lavueinn.com 28 rooms No Meals.*

★ **Malliouhana, An Auberge Resort**

$$$$ | **RESORT** | This classic luxury hotel perched cliffside over beautiful Meads Bay beach is a fancifully modern yet relaxed beach paradise. **Pros:** spacious rooms and bathrooms; great location on Meads Bay; friendly and attentive service. **Cons:** car necessary to explore the island (if you want to); property takes a fair amount of walking to get around; lots of stairs and no elevators. *Rooms from: $1399 Meads Bay 264/497–6111 aubergeresorts.com/malliouhana Closed late Aug.–late Oct. 58 rooms No Meals.*

Meads Bay Beach Villas

$$$$ | **APARTMENT** | **FAMILY** | These gorgeous one-, two-, and three-bedroom villas right on Meads Bay have a cult following, so it can be hard to book them, but if you score a stay here, you'll understand why. **Pros:** private pools; large private villas; beautiful beach. **Cons:** if you like complaining, you may get bored—this is a top-notch resort; very busy resort but service still remains excellent; more condo than hotel in terms of service. *Rooms from: $700 Meads Bay Rd., West End Village 264/497–0273, 215/550–6011 Ext. 105 US www.meadsbaybeachvillas.com 4 villas No Meals.*

Quintessence

$$$$ | **HOTEL** | Walking into this 5-star Relais & Chateaux hotel is like walking into a grand mansion, with a main reception area that can only be described as a tropical gallery; the owner's collection of Haitian art is the biggest outside of Haiti. **Pros:** superb service; intimate and private; excellent on-site dining experiences. **Cons:** no kids under 12 years old; beach is a steep walk downhill and there are no elevators; only 9 suites. *Rooms from: $1250 Long Bay, Long Bay Village 264/498–8106, 800/234–7468 US Toll Free www.qhotelanguilla.com 9 suites No Meals.*

Serenity Cottages

$$ | **APARTMENT** | **FAMILY** | Despite the name, these aren't cottages but large, fully equipped, and relatively affordable one- and two-bedroom apartments (and studios) in a small complex set in a lush garden at the far end of glorious Shoal Bay Beach East. **Pros:** two convenient restaurants; quiet end of beach with snorkeling outside the door; weeklong packages. **Cons:** location requires a car and extra time to drive to the West End; more condo than hotel in terms of staff; no pool. *Rooms from: $350* *Shoal Bay Village* *264/497–3328* *www.serenity.ai* *Closed Sept.* *10 units* *No Meals.*

Shoal Bay Villas

$$$ | **APARTMENT** | **FAMILY** | In this old-style property on Shoal Bay's incredible 2-mile (3-km) beach, studios and one- and two-bedroom apartments all have balconies over the water. **Pros:** friendly and casual beachfront property; full kitchens; pool and spa on-site. **Cons:** luxury touches are lacking; you'll want a car; rather basic. *Rooms from: $420* *Shoal Bay Village* *264/497–2051, 562/366-4813 VOIP* *www.sbvillas.ai* *Closed Aug. 30–Oct. 24* *12 units* *No Meals.*

★ **Tranquility Beach**

$$$$ | **RESORT** | With modern one-, two- or three-bedroom condos right on beautiful Meads Bay, this resort, completed in 2020, is one of the island's newest luxury beachfront experiences. **Pros:** friendly and dedicated staff; excellent beach service; private hot tub. **Cons:** no swimming pool; feels more like a condominium than a resort; breakfast not included in the rate. *Rooms from: $575* *Meads Bay, West End Village* *264/462–6000* *www.tranquilitybeachanguilla.com* *15 condos* *No Meals.*

Turtle's Nest Beach Resort

$$ | **APARTMENT** | **FAMILY** | This complex of studios and one- to three-bedroom oceanfront condos is right on Meads Bay Beach, with some of the island's best restaurants a sandy stroll away. **Pros:** well-kept grounds and pool; beachfront; huge apartments. **Cons:** may be busy in high season; may need a car if you want to explore; no elevator, so fourth-floor units are a climb (but have great views). *Rooms from: $375* *Meads Bay, West End Village* *264/497–7979, 264/476–7979* *www.turtlesnestanguilla.com* *22 units* *No Meals.*

Zemi Beach House Hotel & Spa / Residences

$$$$ | **RESORT** | With two pools, two restaurants, a Rhum Room for cocktails and cigars, a tennis court, and a kids' program, there's something for everyone at this luxury resort on a gorgeous, 400-foot stretch of Shoal Bay East's white-sand beach. **Pros:** beautiful boutique property; fabulous beach location; desirable amenities. **Cons:** during busiest weeks restaurant service may be less than perfect; expensive; need a car to get around the island. *Rooms from: $695* *Shoal Bay Village* *264/584–0001* *www.zemibeach.com* *76 rooms* *No Meals.*

Nightlife

In mid- to late March, on the first full moon before Easter, reggae star and impresario Bankie Banx stages Moonsplash, a three-day music festival that showcases local and imported talent. Anguilla Day's boat races, in May, are the most important sporting event of the year. At the end of July, the Anguilla Summer Festival has boat races by day and Carnival parades, calypso competitions, and parties at night. Some years bring a jazz festival.

Most hotels and many restaurants offer live entertainment in high season and on weekends: it might include pianists, jazz combos, or traditional steel and calypso bands. Friday and Saturday, Sandy Ground is the hot spot; Wednesday and Sunday the action shifts to Shoal Bay.

Nightlife action doesn't really start until 9 and runs late into the night. Be aware that taxis are not readily available then. If you plan to take a cab back to your lodging at the end of the night, make arrangements in advance with the driver who brings you to your destination or with your hotel concierge.

Dune Preserve

LIVE MUSIC | There is live music on Wednesday, Friday, and Sunday nights at this funky driftwood-fabricated home of reggae star Bankie Banx, who often performs here. By day it's the quintessential beach bar with barbecue ribs and grilled fresh seafood. At night there's a dance floor, beach bar, small menu, and potent rum cocktails, of course. In high season there's a $20 cover. Moonsplash, an annual three-day event in March, is not to be missed. ✉ *Rendezvous Bay* ☎ *264/729–4215* 🌐 *www.bankiebanx.net/dunepreserve.*

★ Elvis' Beach Bar

BARS | Actually a boat, this popular beach bar is a great place to hear music and sip the best rum punch on Earth. You can also snack on Mexican food (try the goat tacos), play beach volleyball, or watch any happening sports event on the big TV. The bar is closed Tuesday, and there's live music occasionally. The sunsets here are spectacular and always mark the beginning of another great night. ✉ *Sandy Ground Village* ☎ *264/498–0101* 🌐 *www.elvisbeachbar.com.*

Shopping

Anguilla is by no means a shopping destination, but a couple of boutiques stock cute beachwear and accessories. Hard-core shopping enthusiasts might like a day trip to nearby St. Martin.

Well-heeled visitors sometimes organize boat or plane charters through their hotel concierge for daylong shopping excursions to St. Barth. Anguilla Air Services also offers a reasonably priced daily round-trip to St. Barth.

The island's tourist publication, *True Anguilla,* has shopping tips and is available free at the airport and in shops. For upscale designer sportswear, check out small boutiques in the larger resorts like the Four Seasons. Outstanding local artists sell their work in galleries, which often arrange studio tours (or check with the Anguilla Tourist Board).

ART AND CRAFTS

★ Anguilla Sands and Salts

CRAFTS | Gorgeous jewelry, unique souvenirs, bath salts, body scrubs, and infused sea salt are handmade with resources found in Anguilla at this charming local shop. Jewelry created with sand from the island's beaches allows you to take a piece of your favorite beach with you, while salt gathered from the island's salt ponds by the owner himself forms the salt products. The sea salts are infused with herbs like rosemary, thyme, onion, garlic, and curry. Fun themed nights include Margarita Thursday, when the back patio transforms into a hangout for locals and visitors and margaritas are served (in sea salt-rimmed glasses, of course). ✉ *South Hill, South Hill Village* ☎ *264/582–9211* 🌐 *www.anguillasands.com.*

Boutique Bijoux

JEWELRY & WATCHES | It's almost impossible to leave without buying something at this cute store in Sandy Ground; it's the place for fun handmade sterling silver jewelry, fabulous hand bags and totes, cover-ups, and handmade souvenirs. ✉ *Sandy Ground, Sandy Ground Village* ☎ *264/583–0823* 🌐 *www.facebook.com/anguilla.bijoux* ⏲ *Closed Sun.*

Devonish Art Gallery

CRAFTS | This gallery purveys the wood, stone, and clay creations of Courtney Devonish, an internationally known potter and sculptor, plus creations by his wife, Carolle, a bead artist. Works by other

Caribbean artists and regional antique maps are also available. ✉ *Lower South Hill, South Hill Village* ☎ *264/584–6019* 🌐 *www.devonishart.com.*

Hibernia Restaurant and Art Gallery

ART GALLERIES | Striking pieces are culled from the owners' travels, from contemporary Eastern European art to traditional Southeast Asian crafts. The gallery is accessible during restaurant opening hours or by appointment. ✉ *Harbor Ridge Dr., Island Harbour* ☎ *264/497–4290* 🌐 *www.hiberniarestaurant.com* ⏲ *Closed Sun. and Mon. and Aug. to Oct.*

L. Bernbaum Art Gallery

ART GALLERIES | Originally from Texas, Lynne Bernbaum has been working and living in the Caribbean for decades and exhibits around the world. Her paintings and prints are inspired by the island's natural beauty but have unusual perspectives and a hint of surrealism. The gallery is open Wednesday through Saturday 11–5 pm. ✉ *Sandy Ground Village* ☎ *264/476–5211* 🌐 *www.lynnebernbaum.com.*

Paint Studios

ART GALLERIES | **FAMILY** | This delightful gallery and art studio in Shoal Bay East not only offers beautiful pieces by local artists but also spectacular views of the turquoise waters of one of the island's best beaches. Owned and operated by Anguilla resident and artist Emily Garlick, Paint is much more than just a place where art is exhibited. There are four resident artists that use the space to work, allowing you to be a part of their creative process. Next to art events and exhibits, this studio also hosts paint classes for kids and adults, including their popular "Sip and Paint" events. ✉ *Shoal Bay East, Shoal Bay Village* ☎ *264/772–3652.*

CLOTHING

Irie Life

CRAFTS | This popular boutique sells vividly hued beach and resort wear and flip-flops, as well as attractive handicrafts, jewelry, and collectibles from all over the Caribbean. ✉ *South Hill Village* ☎ *264/497–6527* 🌐 *www.irielife.com.*

Limin' Boutique

JEWELRY & WATCHES | Visit this attractive boutique for sensational repurposed jewelry and handicrafts such as bags and totes made from old sails from Anguilla's famous racing boats, "Dune Jewelry" made from the sand from local beaches, hand-designed purses, and Mela jewelry made from natural elements found on the island. There is also a good selection of stylish beach cover-ups and hand-painted Christmas ornaments. ✉ *Tranquility Beach Resort, John Hodge Dr., Meads Bay, West End Village* ☎ *264/583–3733* 🌐 *www.liminartisangifting.com* ⏲ *Closed Sun.*

Petals Boutique

JEWELRY & WATCHES | This lovely boutique has attractive beachwear, jewelry, and accessories, as well as an assortment of local products. ✉ *Frangipani Beach Resort, Rte. 1, Long Bay Village* ☎ *264/497–6442* ⏲ *Closed Mon.*

SeaSpray Boutique and Smoothies

CRAFTS | Enjoy a rum punch or a delicious fruit smoothie while you shop for Anguillian arts and crafts, handcrafted jewelry, and charming handmade Christmas ornaments. They stock delicious locally made preserves from Anguilla's Jammin, locally made banana rum, and souvenirs. ✉ *South Hill Roundabout, The Valley* ☎ *264/235–1650* 🌐 *www.facebook.com/SeaSprayAnguilla* ⏲ *Closed Sun.*

A Day at the Boat Races

If you want a different kind of trip to Anguilla, try for a visit during Carnival, which usually starts on the first Monday in August and continues for about 10 days. Colorful parades, beauty pageants, music, delicious food, arts-and-crafts shows, fireworks, and nonstop partying are just the beginning. The music starts with sunrise jam sessions—as early as 4 am—and continues well into the night. The high point? The boat races. A national passion, it's the official national sport of Anguilla and the highlight of many other cultural events like Anguilla Day.

Anguillians from around the world return home to race old-fashioned, made-on-the-island wooden boats that have been in use on the island since the early 1800s. Similar to some of today's fastest sailboats, these are 15 to 28 feet in length and sport only a mainsail and jib on a single 25-foot mast. The sailboats have no deck, so heavy bags of sand, boulders, and sometimes even people are used as ballast. As the boats reach the finish line, the ballast—including some of the sailors—gets thrown into the water in a furious effort to win the race. Spectators line the beaches and follow the boats on foot, by car, and from even more boats. You'll have almost as much fun watching the fans as you will the races.

FOOD AND WINE

Grands Vins de France

WINE/SPIRITS | The best vino on Anguilla can be found this wine shop in South Hill. Wine aficionados will not be disappointed by the magnificent 1,300-deep collection. Wines not only from France but also from the U.S., Argentina, Italy, New Zealand, South Africa, and Spain are for sale and range from $8 to $3,000 per bottle. An expert wine consultant can assist you with choosing the right wine. ✉ *South Hill, South Hill Village* ☎ *264/497–6498, 264/235–6498* 🌐 *facebook.com/grandsvinsdefranceanguilla.*

Activities

Anguilla's expanding sports options include an excellent golf course (at the Aurora Golf Resort), designed by Greg Norman to accentuate the natural terrain and maximize the stunning ocean views over Rendezvous Bay. Players say the par-72 course is reminiscent of Pebble Beach. Guided tours are also an option; a round-the-island tour by taxi takes about 2½ hours and costs about $80 for one or two people, $10 for each additional passenger. Special-interest nature and culture tours are available.

DIVING

Anguilla boasts seven marine park; sunken wrecks; a long barrier reef; walls, canyons, and hulking boulders; varied marine life, including greenback turtles and nurse sharks; and exceptionally clear water. All make for excellent diving. **Prickly Pear Cay** is a favorite spot. **Stoney Bay Marine Park,** off the northeast end, showcases the *El Buen Consejo,* a 960-ton Spanish galleon that sank in 1772. Divers love finding all 29 cannons. Other good dive sites include **Grouper Bowl,** with exceptional hard-coral formations; **Ram's Head,** with caves, chutes, and tunnels; and **Upper Flats,** where you are sure to see stingrays.

★ SCUBA SHACK - Shoal Bay
Scuba and Watersports
BOATING | FAMILY | This highly rated PADI dive center runs daily private dives and scheduled dives for certified divers Monday through Friday from Roy's Bayside Grill in Sandy Ground. Dives with full equipment start at $180. Advanced courses, snorkeling, and sightseeing trips are also available. There's a full range of PADI courses for adults and kids; the minimum age is 10 years old. The shop sells masks, snorkels, fins, T-shirts, hats, and shirts. You can find availability and complete scheduling, secure booking, the liability release, and certification cards on their website. ✉ *Roy's Bayside Grill, Sandy Ground Village* ☎ *264/235–1482* 🌐 *www.scubashackaxa.com* ☞ *Booking and liability releases via website.*

GOLF

★ Aurora International Golf Club
GOLF | This Greg Norman course, renovated when it became part of Aurora Anguilla Resort & Golf Club, qualifies as one of the best golf courses in the Caribbean. Thirteen of its 18 holes are directly on the water, and it features sweeping sea vistas, elevation changes, and an ecologically responsible watering system of ponds and lagoons that snake through the grounds. Players including President Bill Clinton have thrilled to the spectacular vistas of St. Martin and blue sea at the tee box of the 390-yard starting hole—the Caribbean's answer to Pebble Beach. There's also a 9-hole short course. ✉ *Aurora Anguilla Resort & Golf Club, Rendezvous Bay* ☎ *800/210–6444* 🌐 *auroraanguilla.com/golf* 🎫 *$395 for 18 holes ($245 resort guests), $295 for 9 holes ($185 hotel guests)* ⛳ *18 holes, 7200 yards, par 72.*

EXCURSIONS

★ Sandy Island
BOATING | FAMILY | Spend the day swimming, lounging, eating, and snorkeling on this breathtaking cay off Sandy Ground. This tiny spit of sand is famous for its beach bar, serving local seafood and fresh fruit cocktails. They also have a great wine list and a stunning view. Take the daily sea shuttle, appropriately called *Happiness,* from the small pier in Sandy Ground to this oasis in the middle of the ocean for about $40 round-trip or book a private day-trip with one of the many charter boat companies that have Sandy Island as part of their itinerary. ✉ *Sandy Ground Village* ☎ *264/497–6534* 🌐 *www.mysandyisland.com* ☞ *Open by reservation only Sept. 1–Oct. 31.*

HORSEBACK RIDING

Seaside Stables
HORSEBACK RIDING | FAMILY | Ever dreamed of a sunset gallop (or slow clomp) on the beach? A private ocean ride in the morning or afternoon is $125 for 60 to 75 minutes. Prior riding experience is not required as the horses are very gentle. Choose from English or Western saddles. ✉ *Paradise Dr., Cove Bay* ☎ *264/235–3667* 🌐 *www.seasidestablesanguilla.com* 🎫 *$125 per ride* ☞ *No group rides.*

SEA EXCURSIONS

A number of boating options are available for airport transfers, day trips to offshore cays, day trips to St. Martin and St. Barth, or just whipping through the waves en route to a picnic spot.

Calypso Charters
BOATING | FAMILY | Book a private or semiprivate charter with Calypso on one of their eight powerboats for a trip around Anguilla, a deep-sea fishing trip, or a sea excursion to neighboring islands St. Barth and St. Martin. They offer a lovely two-hour sunset cruise leaving from Sandy Ground and you can book your airport transfer, private or otherwise, with them as well. Their local captains are some of the most experienced and know the waters around Anguilla well. ✉ *Sandy Ground Village* ☎ *264/584–8504, 264/462–8504* 🌐 *www.calypsochartersanguilla.com* 🎫 *Airport transfer: $65 per adult one-way.*

Funtime Charters

BOATING | With 11 powerboats from 32 to 48 feet, this charter and shuttle service arranges private and scheduled boat transport to the airport, including luggage services ($70 per person one way for adults); day trips to St. Barth; and other powerboat excursions, including inter-island excursions. ✉ *West End Village* ☎ *264/497–6511* 🌐 *www.funtimecharters.com.*

★ **Junior's Glass Bottom Boat**

DIVING & SNORKELING | **FAMILY** | Junior has a great reputation for showing you the underwater scenery of Anguilla, starting with reef trips on his glass bottom boat. For an underwater peek at sea turtles and stingrays without getting wet, catch a ride with him. Guided snorkeling trips and instruction are available, too; Junior is great with kids and very knowledgeable. It's best to book in advance, especially during holidays. His services are $40 per person per hour or $80 per person per hour with snorkeling included; children 5 years and under are free. ✉ *Shoal Bay Village* ☎ *264/235–1008* 🌐 *www.junior.ai.*

Surf AXA

SURFING | Surf AXA offers everything for beginner or experienced surfers, including instruction and surfboard rentals. Guided surf tours are also available here, as well as ECO land tours. Operating out of the colorful Lime Keel House in East End, which offers a Saturday dinner and a Sunday Brunch, this spot is a must for surfers, wanna-be surfers, and nature lovers. ✉ *South Hill Village* ☎ *264/583–4613* 🌐 *surfaxa.com* 🎟 *$20 board rental, $250 off shore surf tour, $80 surf lesson and $100 ECO tours* ☞ *Book via website.*

Chapter 4

ANTIGUA AND BARBUDA

Updated by
Alicia Simon

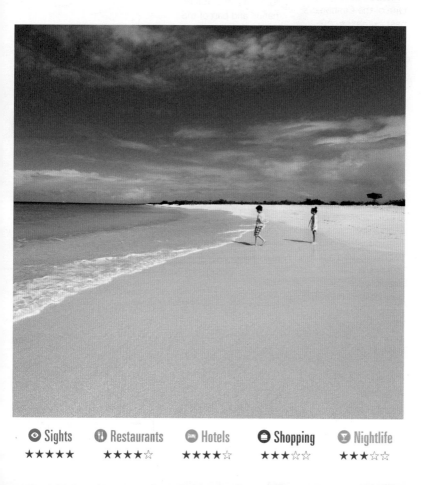

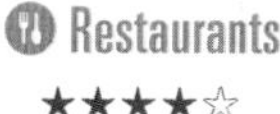

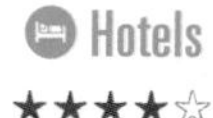

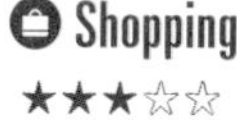

WELCOME TO ANTIGUA AND BARBUDA

TOP REASONS TO GO

★ **Beaches Galore:** So many paradisiacal beaches of every size provide a tremendous selection for islands this size.

★ **Nelson's Dockyard:** One of the Caribbean's best examples of historic preservation and a UNESCO World Heritage Site.

★ **Sailing Away:** With several natural anchorages and tiny islets to explore, Antigua is a major sailing center.

★ **Activities Galore:** Land and water sports, sights to see, and nightlife.

★ **Shopping Options:** A nice selection of shopping options, from duty-free goods to artwork from local artists and craftspeople (especially distinctive ceramics).

At 108 square miles (280 square km), Antigua is the largest of the British Leeward Islands. Its smaller sister island, Barbuda, is 62 square miles (161 square km) and lies 26 miles (42 km) to the north. Together, they form an independent nation and part of the British Commonwealth. The islands were under British control from 1667 until they achieved independence in 1981.

1 Antigua. This lush Leeward island boasts 95 miles of pristine coast spanning 365 beaches.

2 Barbuda. A flat coral atoll north of Antigua with 17 miles (27 km) of gleaming white-sand beaches.

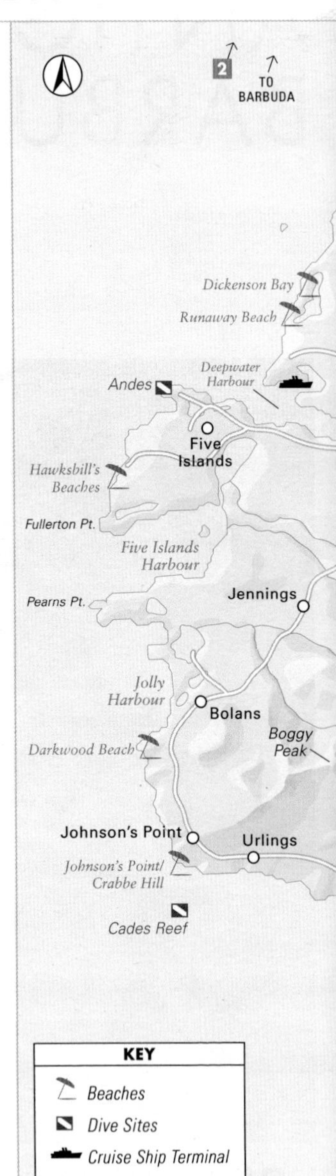

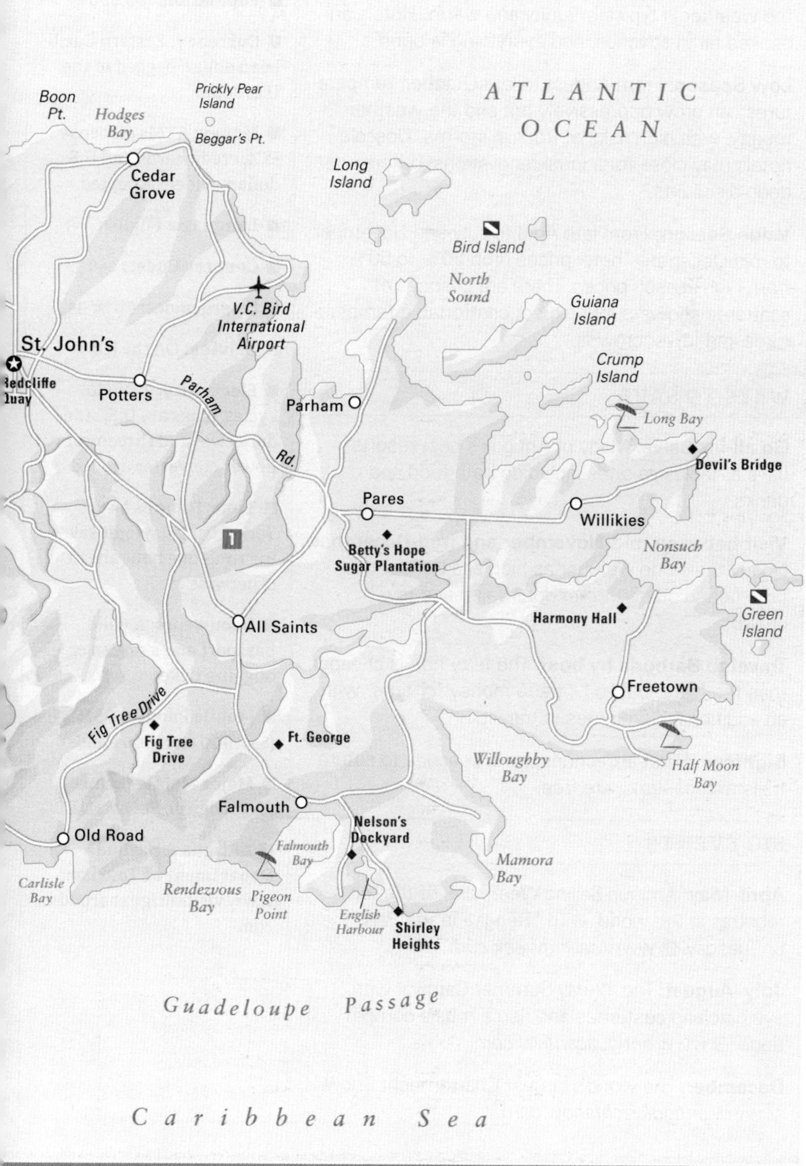
ATLANTIC OCEAN
Boon Pt.
Hodges Bay
Prickly Pear Island
Beggar's Pt.
Cedar Grove
Long Island
Bird Island
North Sound
Guiana Island
Crump Island
Long Bay
Devil's Bridge
V.C. Bird International Airport
St. John's
Redcliffe Quay
Potters
Parham Rd.
Parham
Pares
Willikies
Betty's Hope Sugar Plantation
Nonsuch Bay
Green Island
Harmony Hall
All Saints
Freetown
Fig Tree Drive
Ft. George
Willoughby Bay
Half Moon Bay
Falmouth
Nelson's Dockyard
Old Road
Falmouth Bay
Mamora Bay
Carlisle Bay
Rendezvous Bay
Pigeon Point
English Harbour
Shirley Heights
Guadeloupe Passage
Caribbean Sea

4

Antigua and Barbuda WELCOME TO ANTIGUA AND BARBUDA

ISLAND SNAPSHOT

WHEN TO GO

High Season: Mid-December through mid-April. The most fashionable and expensive time to visit, when the weather is typically sunny and warm. Hotels are booked far in advance, and everything is open.

Low Season: From August to late October, temperatures can grow oppressively hot and the weather muggy, with high risks of tropical storms. Upscale hotels may close for annual renovations; others offer deep discounts.

Value Season: From late April to July and November to mid-December, hotel prices drop 20% to 50% from high season prices. There are chances of scattered showers, but expect comfortable temperatures and fewer crowds.

WAYS TO SAVE

Go all-inclusive. Many of Antigua's best resorts have all-inclusive rates including both food and drinks.

Visit between mid-November and mid-December. Nearly the same weather as high season but this time period offers tremendous value and few crowds.

Travel to Barbuda by boat. The ferry ride is cheaper than the flight, but you'll trade money for time, with an additional 70 minutes in transit.

Sightsee. Most attractions, from beaches to nature trails to museums, are free.

BIG EVENTS

April–May: Antigua Sailing Week, one of the top regattas in the world, with "Reggae in the Park" held on Tuesday. 🌐 *www.sailingweek.com*

July–August: The 12-day Summer Carnival with eye-catching costumes and fierce music competitions. 🌐 *www.antiguacarnival.com*

December: The world's largest Charter Yacht Show. 🌐 *www.antiguayachtshow.com*

AT A GLANCE

- **Capital:** Saint John's
- **Population:** 100,000
- **Currency:** Eastern Caribbean dollar; pegged to the U.S. dollar
- **Money:** ATMs dispense EC$; credit cards and U.S. dollars widely accepted
- **Language:** English
- **Country Code:** 1 268
- **Emergencies:** 911 or 999
- **Driving:** On the left
- **Electricity:** 230v/60 cycles; plugs are U.S. standard two- and three-prong. Power converter needed
- **Time:** Same as New York during daylight saving time; one hour ahead otherwise
- **Documents:** A valid passport and a return or ongoing ticket
- **Mobile Phones:** GSM (850, 900 and 1900 bands)
- **Major Mobile Companies:** Digicel, FLOW, INET
- **Antigua & Barbuda Department of Tourism:** www.visitantiguabarbuda.com

Antigua is famous for its 365 sensuous beaches, "one for every day of the year," as locals love saying—though when the island was first developed for tourism, the unofficial count was 52 ("one for every weekend"). Either way, even longtime residents haven't combed every stretch of sand.

The island's extensive archipelago of cays and islets is what attracted the original Amerindian settlers—the Ciboney—at least 4,000 years ago. The natural environment, which is rich in marine life, flora, and fauna, has been likened to a "natural supermarket." Antigua's superior anchorages and strategic location naturally caught the attention of the colonial powers. The Dutch, French, and English waged numerous bloody battles throughout the 17th century (eradicating the remaining Arawaks and Caribs in the process), with England finally prevailing in 1667. Antigua remained under English control until achieving full independence on November 1, 1981, along with Barbuda, 26 miles (42 km) to the north.

Boats and beaches go hand in hand with hotel development, and Antigua's tourist infrastructure has mushroomed since the 1950s. Though many of its grandes dames such as Curtain Bluff remain anchors, today all types of resorts line the sand, and the island offers something for everyone, from gamboling on the sand to gambling in casinos. Environmental activists have become increasingly vocal about preservation and limiting development, and not just because green travel rakes in the green. Antigua's allure is precisely that precarious balance and subliminal tension between its unspoiled, natural beauty and its sun-sand-surf megadevelopment. And the British heritage persists, from teatime (and tee times) to fiercely contested cricket matches.

Planning

Getting Here and Around

Most Antigua hotels provide free island maps, and you should get your bearings before heading out on the road. Street names aren't listed (except in St. John's), though *some* easy-to-spot signs lead the way to major restaurants and resorts. Locals generally give directions in terms of landmarks (turn left at the yellow house, or right at the big tree). Wear a swimsuit under your clothes—one of the sights to strike your fancy might be a secluded beach.

AIR

Nonstop flights are available from Atlanta (Delta, once weekly on Saturday), Charlotte (American, once weekly on Saturday), Miami (American, twice daily), New York–JFK (American, daily; Delta, once weekly on Saturday; JetBlue, three times

Did You Know?

During the plantation days, particularly in Barbados and Antigua, it was necessary for working-class people to build tiny chattel houses. Their homes needed to be small and portable (movable property) because workers were often fired without notice and ordered off the land where they lived and worked.

a week), Newark (United, once weekly on Saturday), and Orlando (Frontier Airlines, once weekly on Saturday).

AIRPORT CONTACT V. C. Bird International Airport. *(ANU) ✉ Pavilion Dr., Osbourn ☎ 268/484–1322, 268/484–1417, 268/484–1415 🌐 www.vcbia.com.*

AIRLINE CONTACTS American Airlines. *✉ Royal Palm Plz., Friar's Hill Rd. ✣ Opposite Caribbean Union Bank, in the plaza ☎ 268/462–0950, 268/481–4699 🌐 www.aa.com.* **BMN SVG Airways.** *✉ Pavilion Dr. ☎ 268/562–8033, 268/562–7183 🌐 www.bmnsvgairways.com.* **Caribbean Airlines.** *☎ 800/523-5585, 800/920–4225 🌐 www.caribbean-airlines.com.* **Delta Airlines.** *☎ 800/221–1212, 268/562–5951 🌐 www.delta.com.* **JetBlue.** *☎ 800/538–2583 🌐 www.jetblue.com.* **LIAT.** *☎ 268/480–5600, 268/480–5601, 268/480–5602 🌐 www.liat.com.* **United Airlines.** *☎ 800/864–8331, 268/484-1312, 268/462–5355 for operations, 268/484–1311 for flight information 🌐 www.united.com.*

BOAT AND FERRY

Ferries between Antigua and Barbuda run daily, departing St. John's Harbour at the bottom of High Street by the Heritage Quay Ferry Dock.

CONTACTS Barbuda Express. *✉ High St., St. John's ☎ 268/764–2291, 268/764–8643, 268/560–7989 🌐 www.barbudaexpress.com.*

CAR

Many of the main roads have been resurfaced and repaved making for smooth driving. Some bumpy dirt stretches in remote locations and a few hilly areas that flood easily and become impassable for a day remain. Driving is on the left. To rent a car, you need a valid license and a temporary permit ($20), available through the rental agent or any police station (Coolidge Police Station is right off Airport Rd.). Costs start at about $50 per day in season, with unlimited mileage, though multiday discounts are standard. Most agencies offer automatic or standard and right- or left-hand drive. Four-wheel-drive vehicles (from $55 per day) will get you more places and are useful for those roads that remain full of potholes.

CONTACTS Avis. *☎ 268/462–2847 main office, 268/462–2849 at the airport 🌐 www.avis.com.* **Budget.** *☎ 268/561–6399, 268/736–6400 🌐 www.budget.com.* **Dollar.** *☎ 268/462–0362 office, 268/462–8802 at the airport 🌐 www.dollar.com.* **Hertz.** *☎ 268/481–4440 Sir George Walter Hwy (Airport Rd.), 268/729–4455 airport 🌐 www.hertz.com.* **Thrifty.** *☎ 268/462–9532 Sir Walter George Hwy (Airport Rd.), 268/462–8803 airport 🌐 www.thrifty.com.*

TAXI

Some cabbies may take you from St. John's to English Harbour and wait for about a half hour while you look around, for about $50 per couple.

Health and Safety

Dengue, chikungunya, and zika have all been reported throughout the Caribbean. We recommend that you protect yourself from these mosquito-borne illnesses by keeping your skin covered and/or wearing mosquito repellent. The mosquitoes that transmit these viruses are as active by day as they are by night.

Hotels and Resorts

In Antigua you're almost certain to have an excellent beach regardless of where you stay. Dickenson Bay and Five Islands Peninsula suit beachcombers who want proximity to St. John's, and Jolly Harbour offers affordable options and activities galore. English Harbour and the southwest coast have the best inns and several excellent restaurants—although many close from August until well into October; it's also the yachting crowd's hangout. Resorts elsewhere on the island are ideal for those seeking seclusion; some are so remote that all-inclusive packages or rental cars are a must. Barbuda, Antigua's sister isle, is still rebounding from the devastation of Hurricane Irma in 2017, leaving it with one posh resort, several guesthouses, and many projects said to be in the pipeline.

All-Inclusive Resorts: Most of the all-inclusives aim for a mainstream, package-tour kind of crowd—with varying degrees of success—though offerings such as Jumby Bay, Galley Bay, and Curtain Bluff are more upscale.

Luxury Resorts: A fair number of luxury resorts cater to the well-heeled in varying degrees of formality on Antigua and to a lesser extent on Barbuda.

Small Inns: A few small inns, some historic, can be found around Antigua, mostly concentrated in or near English Harbour.

Hotel reviews have been shortened. For full information, visit Fodors.com.

What It Costs in U.S. Dollars

$	$$	$$$	$$$$
RESTAURANTS			
under $12	$12–$20	$21–$30	over $30
HOTELS			
under $275	$275–$375	$376–$475	over $475

Tours

Almost all taxi drivers double as guides; an island tour with one costs about $25 an hour. Every major hotel has a cabbie on call and may be able to negotiate a discount, particularly off-season. Several operators specialize in off-road, four-wheel-drive adventures that provide a taste of island history and topography.

Scenic Tours

Scenic Tours Antigua offers value for money (around $47 for adults) with tours of historical sights and natural marvels including Nelson's Dockyard and Devil's Bridge. Six and half hour tours also dot the coastline, visiting some of the island's 365 beaches and beach bars. ✉ *St. John's* ☎ *268/720–8844, 268/780–8844* 🌐 *www.scenictoursantigua.com.*

Tropical Adventures Antigua

Four-wheel off-road adventures by Tropical Adventures Antigua, which also runs other land- and water-based excursions, enables you to fully appreciate the island's natural beauty, history, folklore, and cultural heritage as you zoom about the southwest part of Antigua. Hiking is involved, though it's not strenuous. Lunch and snorkeling are also included. Active adventurers will particularly enjoy the combo Land Rover–kayak outback ecotour. ☎ *268/480–1225* 🌐 *www.tropicalad.com* 🎟 *From $110.*

Visitor Information

CONTACTS Antigua & Barbuda Tourist Offices. ☎ *212/541–4117 in New York City, 268/463–9522 in Antigua, 305/381–6762 in Miami* 🌐 *www.ab.gov.ag.* **Barbudaful.net.** 🌐 *www.barbudaful.net.*

Weddings

No minimum residency or blood test is required. A license application fee is $40. You must have valid passports as proof of citizenship and, in the case of previous marriages, the original divorce or annulment decree. A marriage certificate registration fee is $40. The marriage officer receives $250.

Antigua

Sights

Some say Antigua has so many beaches that you could visit a different one every day for a year. Most have snow-white sand, and many are backed by lavish resorts that offer sailing, diving, windsurfing, and snorkeling. The largest of the British Leeward Islands, Antigua was the headquarters from which Lord Horatio Nelson (then a mere captain) made his forays against the French and pirates in the late 18th century. You may wish to explore English Harbour and its carefully restored Nelson's Dockyard, as well as tour old forts, historic churches, and tiny villages. Appealing aspects of the island's interior include a small tropical rain forest ideal for hiking and ziplining, ancient Amerindian archaeological digs, and restored sugar mills.

St. John's, Antigua's capital, with some 45,000 inhabitants (nearly half the island's population), lies at sea level at the inland end of a sheltered northwestern bay. Although it has seen better days, a couple of notable historic sights and some good waterfront shopping areas make it worth a visit. At the far south end of town, where Market Street forks into Valley and All Saints roads, haggling goes on every Friday and Saturday, when locals jam the **Public Market** to buy and sell fruits, vegetables, fish, and spices. Ask before you aim a camera; your subject may expect a tip. This is old-time Caribbean shopping, a jambalaya of sights, sounds, and smells.

Betty's Hope Sugar Plantation
HISTORY MUSEUM | Just outside the village of Pares, a marked dirt road leads to Antigua's first sugar plantation, founded in the 1670s. You can tour the twin windmills, various ruins, still-functional crushing machinery, and the visitor center's exhibits (often closed) on the island's sugar era. The private trust overseeing the restoration has yet to realize its ambitious, environmentally aware plans to replant indigenous crops destroyed by the extensive sugarcane plantings. Indeed, the site is somewhat neglected, with goats grazing the grounds. ✉ *Pares Village Main Rd., Pares* ☎ *268/464–2429* 🌐 *www.antiguamuseums.net* 🎟 *$2* ⏲ *Closed weekends.*

Cathedral of St. John the Divine
CHURCH | At the south gate of the Anglican Cathedral of St. John the Divine are figures of St. John the Baptist and St. John the Divine, said to have been taken from one of Napoléon's ships and brought to Antigua. The original church was built in 1681, replaced by a stone building in 1745, and destroyed by an earthquake in 1843. The present neo-baroque building dates from 1845; the parishioners had the interior completely encased in pitch pine, hoping to forestall future earthquake damage. Tombstones bear eerily eloquent testament to the colonial days. Call ahead to arrange a tour. ✉ *Between Long and Newgate Sts., St. John's* ☎ *268/462–0820* 🌐 *www.thestjohnscathedral.com.*

Devil's Bridge
NATURE SIGHT | Part of Indian Town Point National Park, this natural wonder was formed by the thrashing waves of the Atlantic Ocean against the delicate limestone of the coastline over hundreds of years. You may be tempted to cross the bridge for the thrill, but exercise caution—you do so at your own risk. If visiting during Easter, the skies over the bridge are home to hundreds of kites during the annual **Kite Festival.** ✉ *Dockyard Dr., Long Bay* 🌐 *www.nationalparksantigua.com.*

Falmouth
TOWN | This coastal town with grand views of Falmouth Harbour is said to be one of the first towns established in Antigua, and its St. Paul's Anglican Church is believed to be the nation's earliest church. The somewhat uncertain

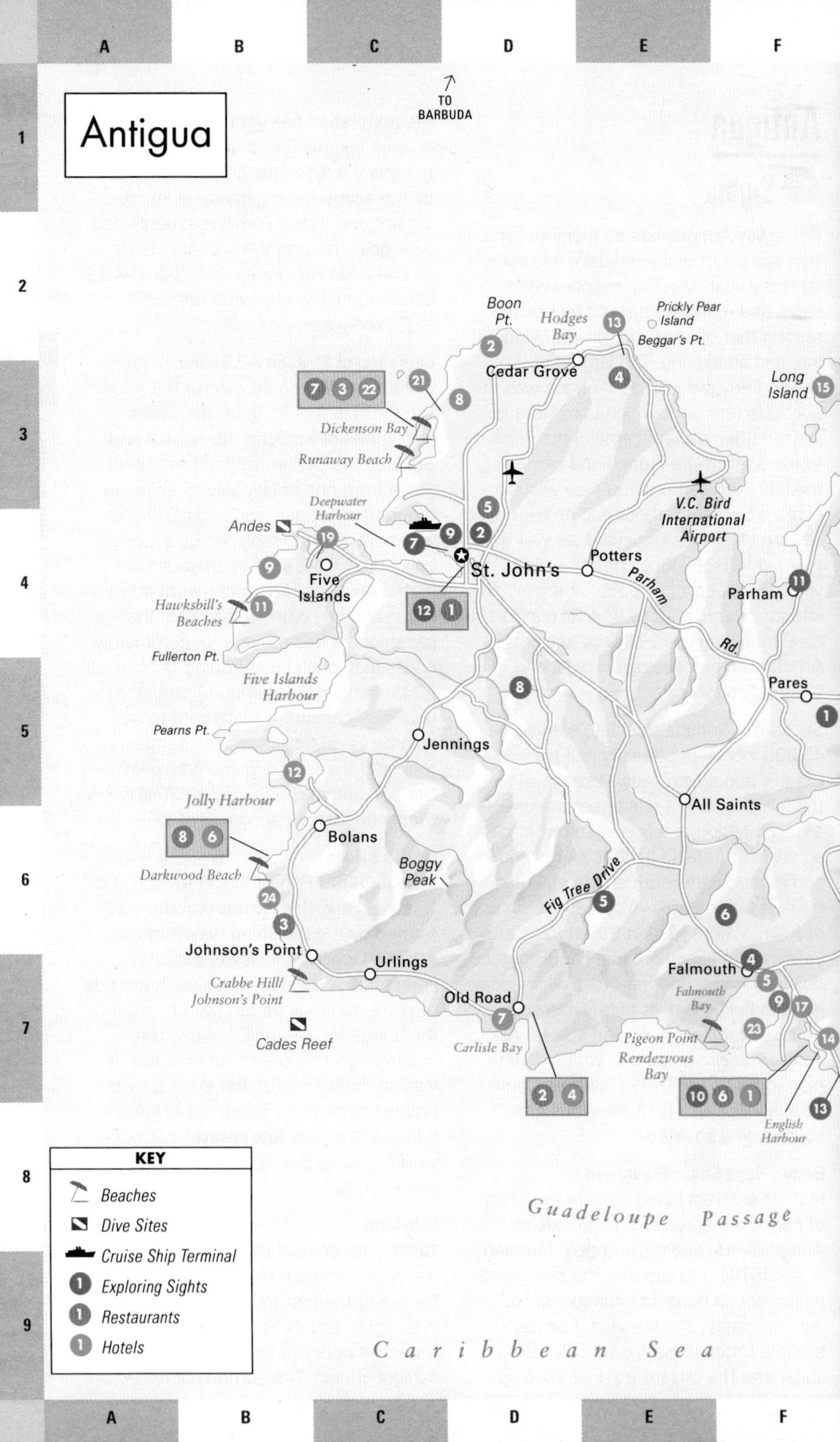

A
B
C
D
E
F
1
2
3
4
5
6
7
8
9
Antigua
TO BARBUDA
Boon Pt.
Hodges Bay
Prickly Pear Island
Beggar's Pt.
Cedar Grove
Long Island
Dickenson Bay
Runaway Beach
Deepwater Harbour
V.C. Bird International Airport
Andes
Five Islands
St. John's
Potters
Parham Rd.
Parham
Hawksbill's Beaches
Fullerton Pt.
Five Islands Harbour
Pares
Pearns Pt.
Jennings
Jolly Harbour
All Saints
Bolans
Darkwood Beach
Boggy Peak
Fig Tree Drive
Johnson's Point
Urlings
Crabbe Hill/ Johnson's Point
Falmouth
Old Road
Falmouth Bay
Cades Reef
Carlisle Bay
Pigeon Point
Rendezvous Bay
English Harbour
KEY
Beaches
Dive Sites
Cruise Ship Terminal
Exploring Sights
Restaurants
Hotels
Guadeloupe Passage
Caribbean Sea

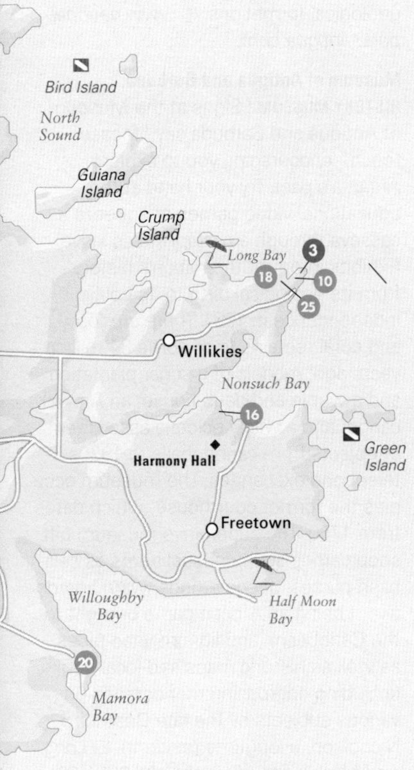

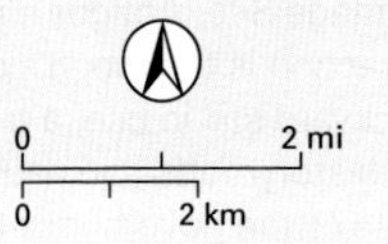

Sights

1 Betty's Hope Sugar Plantation F5
2 Cathedral of St. John the Divine D4
3 Devil's Bridge.............. I4
4 Falmouth F7
5 Fig Tree Drive............. E6
6 Ft. George................. F6
7 Heritage Quay.......... D4
8 Megaliths of Greencastle Hill D5
9 Museum of Antigua and Barbuda D4
10 Nelson's Dockyard F7
11 Parham...................... F4
12 Redcliffe Quay D4
13 Shirley Heights........... F7

Restaurants

1 Big Banana—Pizzas in Paradise D4
2 East D7
3 Jacqui O's BeachHouse at Love Beach........... B6
4 Le Bistro E3
5 Papa Zouk D4
6 PIllars Restaurant & Bar........................ F7
7 Salt Plage.................C3
8 Sheer Rocks............ B6
9 Trappas F7

Hotels

1 Admiral's Inn............. F7
2 Blue Waters Resort & Spa D2
3 Buccaneer Beach Club.........................C3
4 Carlisle Bay D7
5 Catamaran Hotel......... F7
6 Cocobay Resort B6
7 Curtain Bluff............. D7
8 Dickenson Bay Cottages D3
9 Galley Bay Resort & Spa..................... B4
10 Hammock Cove Antigua I4
11 Hawksbill by Rex Resorts.......... B4
12 HBK Villas B5
13 Hodges Bay Resort & Spa......................E2
14 Inn At English Harbour.................. F7
15 Jumby Bay Island F3
16 Nonsuch Bay Resort ... H5
17 Ocean Inn................. F7
18 Pineapple Beach Club.......................... H4
19 Royalton Antigua C4
20 St. James's Club......... G7
21 Sandals Grande Antigua Resort & Spa.............C3
22 Siboney Beach Club.....C3
23 South Point............... F7
24 Tamarind Hills........... B6
25 Verandah Resort & Spa........................I4

history in no way detracts from the township's sleepy beauty. There's also a vendors mall quizzically situated on a busy, meandering road, where visitors stop to pick up tchotchkes and witness a breathtaking view of the harbors.

Fig Tree Drive

SCENIC DRIVE | This rutted, steep road takes you through the rain forest, which is rich in mangoes, pineapples, and banana trees (*fig* is the Antiguan word for "banana"). The rain forest is the island's hilliest area—1,319-foot Boggy Peak (renamed Mt. Obama), to the west, is the highest point. At its crest, Elaine Francis sells seasonal local fruit juices—ginger, guava, sorrel, passion fruit—and homemade jams at a stall she dubs the Culture Shop. A few houses down (look for the orange windows) is the atelier of noted island artist Sallie Harker (www.sallieharker.com) whose work displays shimmering seascapes and vividly hued fish incorporating gold leaf. You'll also pass several tranquil villages with charming churches and Antigua Rainforest Canopy Tours here. ✉ *Fig Tree Dr.*

Ft. George

TOWN | East of Liberta—one of the first settlements founded by freed slaves—on Monk's Hill, this fort was built between 1689 and 1720. Among the ruins are the sites for 32 cannons, water cisterns, the base of the old flagstaff, and some of the original buildings. ✉ *Great Fort George Monk's Hill Trail, St. Paul.*

Heritage Quay

BUSINESS DISTRICT | Shopaholics head directly for Heritage Quay, an ugly multimillion-dollar complex. The two-story buildings contain stores that sell duty-free goods, sportswear, down-island imports (paintings, T-shirts, straw baskets), and local crafts. There are also restaurants, a bandstand, and a casino. Cruise-ship passengers disembark here from the 500-foot-long pier. Expect heavy shilling. ✉ *High and Thames Sts., St. John's.*

Megaliths of Greencastle Hill

NATURE SIGHT | It's an arduous climb through thick bush (a local guide is recommended) to these eerie rock slabs in the south-central part of the island. Some say the megaliths were set up by early inhabitants for their worship of the sun and moon or as devices for measuring time astronomically; others believe they're nothing more than unusual geological formations. 🌐 *www.nationalparksantigua.com.*

Museum of Antigua and Barbuda

HISTORY MUSEUM | Signs at the Museum of Antigua and Barbuda say "Please touch," encouraging you to explore Antigua's past. Try your hand at the educational video games or squeeze a cassava through a *matapi* (grass sieve). Exhibits interpret the nation's history, from its geological birth to its political independence in 1981. There are fossil and coral remains from some 34 million years ago; models of a sugar plantation and a wattle-and-daub house; an Arawak canoe; and a wildly eclectic assortment of objects from cannonballs to 1920s telephone exchanges. The museum occupies the former courthouse, which dates from 1750. The superlative museum gift shop carries such unusual items as calabash purses, seed earrings, warri boards (warri being an African game brought to the Caribbean), and lignum vitae pipes, as well as historic maps and local books (including engrossing monographs on various subjects by the late Desmond Nicholson, a longtime resident). ✉ *Long and Market Sts., St. John's* ☎ *268/462–1469, 268/462–4930* 🌐 *www.antiguamuseums.net* 🎟 *$3* 🕓 *Closed Sun.*

★ Nelson's Dockyard

MUSEUM VILLAGE | A UNESCO World Heritage Site, Antigua's most famous attraction is the world's only Georgian-era dockyard still in use, a treasure trove for history buffs and nautical nuts alike. In 1671 the governor of the Leeward Islands wrote to the Council for Foreign

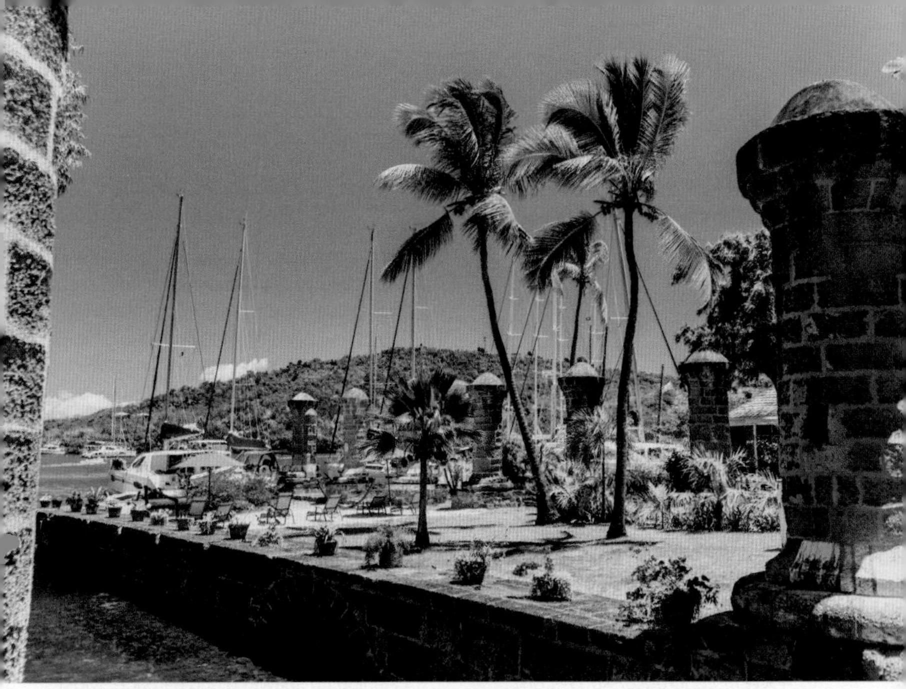

Nelson's Dockyard at English Harbour is a UNESCO World Heritage Site.

Plantations in London, pointing out the advantages of this landlocked harbor. By 1704 English Harbour was in regular use as a garrisoned station. In 1784, 26-year-old Horatio Nelson sailed in on HMS *Boreas* to serve as captain and second-in-command of the Leeward Island Station. Under him was the captain of HMS *Pegasus,* Prince William Henry, duke of Clarence, who was later crowned King William IV. The prince acted as best man when Nelson married Fannie Nisbet on Nevis in 1787.

When the Royal Navy abandoned the station at English Harbour in 1889, it fell into a state of decay, though adventuresome yachties still lived there in near-primitive conditions. The Society of the Friends of English Harbour began restoring it in 1951; it reopened with great fanfare as Nelson's Dockyard on November 14, 1961. Within the compound are crafts shops, restaurants, and two splendidly restored 18th-century hotels, the Admiral's Inn and the Copper & Lumber Store Hotel, worth peeking into. (The latter, occupying a supply store for Nelson's Caribbean fleet, is a particularly fine example of Georgian architecture, its interior courtyard evoking Old England.) The Dockyard is a hub for oceangoing yachts and serves as headquarters for the annual Boat Show in early December and the Sailing Week Regatta in late April and early May. Water taxis will ferry you between points for EC$5. The Dockyard National Park also includes serene nature trails accessing beaches, rock pools, and crumbling plantation ruins and hilltop forts.

The Dockyard Museum, in the original Naval Officer's House, presents ship models, mock-ups of English Harbour, displays on the people who worked there and typical ships that docked, silver regatta trophies, maps, prints, antique navigational instruments, and Nelson's very own telescope and tea caddy. ✉ *Dockyard Dr., English Harbour Town* ☎ *268/481–5041 for National Parks Authority, visitor's services, 268/481–5021, 268/481–5022* 🌐 *www.nationalparksantigua.com* 🎟 *$2 suggested donation.*

Parham

TOWN | This sleepy village is a splendid example of a traditional colonial settlement. St. Peter's Church, built in 1840 by English architect Thomas Weekes, is an octagonal Italianate building with unusual ribbed wooden ceiling, whose facade is richly decorated with stucco and keystone work, though it suffered considerable damage during an 1843 earthquake.

★ Redcliffe Quay

BUSINESS DISTRICT | Redcliffe Quay, at the water's edge just south of Heritage Quay, is the most appealing part of St. John's. Attractively restored (and superbly re-created) 19th-century buildings in a riot of cotton-candy colors house shops, restaurants, galleries, and boutiques are linked by courtyards and landscaped walkways. ✉ *Redcliffe St., St. John's* 🌐 *www.historicredcliffequay.com.*

Shirley Heights

VIEWPOINT | This bluff affords a spectacular view of English Harbour and Falmouth Harbour. The heights are named for Sir Thomas Shirley, the governor who fortified the harbor in 1781. At the top is Shirley Heights Lookout, a restaurant built into the remnants of the 18th-century fortifications. Most notable for its boisterous Sunday barbecues that continue into the night with live music and dancing, it serves dependable burgers, pumpkin soup, grilled meats, and rum punches.

Not far from Shirley Heights is the **Dow's Hill Interpretation Centre,** where observation platforms provide still more sensational vistas of the English Harbour area. A multimedia sound-and-light presentation on island history and culture, spotlighting lifelike figures and colorful tableaux accompanied by running commentary and music, results in a cheery, if bland, portrait of Antiguan life from Amerindian times to the present. ✉ *Dockyard Dr., Shirley Heights* ☎ *268/481–5021, 268/481–5022* 🌐 *www.nationalparksantigua.com* 🎫 *$15 (includes Shirley Heights, Nelson's Dockyard, the Blockhouse, and Dow's Hill Interpretation Centre.*

CASINOS

King's Casino

CASINO | You can find abundant slots and gaming tables at this unintentionally retro (Naugahyde seats and 1970s music on the sound system) King's Casino. The best time to go is Friday and Saturday nights, which jump with energetic karaoke competitions, live bands, and dancing. ✉ *Heritage Quay, St. John's* ☎ *268/462–1727* 🌐 *www.kingscasino.com.*

Beaches

Antigua's beaches are public, and many are lined with resorts that have watersports outfitters and beach bars. The government does a fairly good job of cleaning up seaweed and garbage. Most restaurants and bars on beaches won't charge for beach-chair rentals if you buy lunch or drinks; otherwise the going rate is $5 to $10. Access to some of the finest stretches, such as those at the Five Islands Peninsula resorts, is restricted (though, often, if you're polite, the guards will let you through); however, there are no private beaches in Antigua. Sunbathing topless is strictly illegal except on one small beach at Hawksbill by Rex Resorts. When cruise ships dock in St. John's, buses drop off loads of passengers on most of the west-coast beaches. Choose such a time to visit one of the more remote east-end beaches or take a day trip to Barbuda.

Crabbe Hill/Johnson's Point

BEACH | This series of connected, deserted beaches on the southwest coast looks out toward Montserrat, Guadeloupe, and St. Kitts. Notable beach bar–restaurants include OJ's, Jacqui O's BeachHouse, and Turner's. The water is generally placid, though not good for snorkeling. **Amenities:** food and drink. **Best for:** sunset; swimming; walking. ✣ *3 miles (5 km) south of Jolly Harbour complex, on main west-coast road.*

Darkwood Beach

BEACH | **FAMILY** | This attractive ½ mile (1 km) beach with warm, translucent waters and brown-sugar sands has everything you need for a fun and relaxing day on the beach, including a breathtaking view of Montserrat. Admired by locals and visitors, it can be quite crowded when cruise ships are in port, but desolate otherwise. Darkwood Beach Bar is your best option for a bite to eat and a cold drink; you can also rent snorkeling gear and chairs there. There are a few other food stalls along the beach. An inflatable playground is moored just off the coast—it's perfect for busying (and tiring out) tots. **Amenities:** food and drink. **Best for:** snorkeling; swimming. ✉ *2 miles (3 km) south of Jolly Harbour and roughly ½ mile (1 km) southwest of Valley Church, off Valley Rd.*

Dickenson Bay

BEACH | Along a lengthy stretch of well-kept powder-soft white sand and exceptionally calm water, you can find small and large hotels (including Siboney Beach Club and Sandals), water sports, concessions, and beachfront restaurants (Salt Plage Beach Bar & Restaurant and Ana's on the Beach are recommended). There's decent snorkeling at either point. A floating bar, Kon Tiki, drifts just off the coast, catering to the fun and buzzed crowd. **Amenities:** food and drink; water sports. **Best for:** partiers; snorkeling; swimming; walking

✣ *2 miles (3 km) northeast of St. John's, along main coast road.*

Half Moon Bay

BEACH | This ½-mile (1-km) ivory crescent is a prime snorkeling and windsurfing area. On the Atlantic side, the water can be rough at times, attracting intrepid hard-core surfers and wakeboarders. The northeastern end, where a protective reef offers spectacular snorkeling, is much calmer. A tiny bar has restrooms, snacks, and beach chairs. Half Moon is a real trek, but one of Antigua's showcase beaches. **Amenities:** food and drink. **Best for:** snorkeling; sunrise; surfing; windsurfing. ✉ *Dockyard Dr.* ✣ *on southeast coast, 1½ mile (2½ km) from Freetown.*

Pigeon Point

BEACH | Near Falmouth Harbour lie two fine white-sand beaches reasonably free of seaweed and driftwood. The leeward side is calmer, the windward side is rockier, and there are sensational views and snorkeling around the point. Several restaurants and bars are nearby, though Bumpkin's (and its potent banana coladas) and the more upscale bustling Catherine's Cafe Plage satisfy most on-site needs. **Amenities:** food and drink. **Best for:** snorkeling; swimming; walking. ✉ *Off main south-coast road, southwest of Falmouth.*

Runaway Beach

BEACH | An often unoccupied stretch of bone-white sand, this beach is still rebuilding after years of hurricane erosion, with just enough palms left for shelter. Both the water and the scene are relatively calm, the sand is reasonably well maintained, and Mystic Beach Bar (formerly Sandhaven) offers cool shade and cold beer. Horseback riding is available. Hug the lagoon past the entrance to Siboney Beach Club to get here; the Buccaneer Beach Club is the unofficial demarcation point between Dickenson and Runaway bays. **Amenities:** food and drink. **Best for:** snorkeling; swimming; walking. ✉ *Approximately 2 miles (3 km) northwest of St. John's, down main north-coast road from Dickenson Bay, St. John's.*

Restaurants

Antigua's restaurants have been given a run for their money with the advent of all-inclusive resorts. That hasn't deterred restaurateurs from opening eateries of all kinds, each new one seemingly more ambitious than the last. They seem to be opening (but sometimes closing) every few months. But several worthwhile hotel dining rooms and a few nightspots remain reliable, especially in the English/Falmouth Harbour and Dickenson Bay areas. Virtually every chef incorporates local ingredients and elements of West Indian cuisine.

Most menus list prices in both EC and U.S. dollars; if not, ask which currency the menu is using. Always double-check whether credit cards are accepted and service is included. Dinner reservations are highly recommended in high season.

What to Wear: Perhaps because of the island's British heritage, Antiguans tend to dress more formally for dinner than dwellers on many other Caribbean islands. Wraps and shorts (no beach attire) are de rigueur for lunch, except at local hangouts.

Big Banana—Pizzas in Paradise
$$ | **PIZZA** | **FAMILY** | Big Banana has modern rustic decor befitting its past as an 18th-century rum house, and it's fortunately retained its former charm and distinction as one of the most popular casual dining eateries on island. The menu includes pizza, burgers, wraps, and scrumptious down-home local food—try the catch of the day, which, when paired with flavorsome fruit crushes (the coconut is divine), is a great way to end a day of window-shopping in the quays. **Known for:** family-friendly; wide selection of pizzas; lively atmosphere. *Average main: $18 ✉ Redcliffe Quay, Redcliffe St., St. John's ☎ 268/480–6985 🌐 www.bigbanana-antigua.com ⏲ Closed Sun.*

East
$$$$ | **ASIAN FUSION** | Crossing the intricate Indonesian carved wood vestibule, you are transported to the far east with a menu that features Japanese, Balinese, Thai, and Indonesian cuisine that ferries guests on a journey through the delicate, complex flavors of the East. The luxurious dark wood furniture, flooring, and dim lighting juxtaposed against bright fuchsia chair covers, crisp white serving trays, chartreuse candleholders, and airy potted bamboo make for a romantic setting. **Known for:** romantic atmosphere; Asian fusion cuisine; couples retreat (kids can dine between 6 and 7 pm). *Average main: $32 ✉ Carlisle Bay Resort, Old Road ☎ 268/484–0000 🌐 www.carlisle-bay.com ⏲ No lunch.*

★ Jacqui O's BeachHouse at Love Beach
$$$$ | **ECLECTIC** | This Saint-Tropez inspired beachfront haven, where white floorboards seamlessly integrate with the alabaster sands of Love Beach, is also where restaurateur Lance Leonhardt, dubbed Lancelot the Lionheart, holds court. The gregarious host is as much a part of the atmosphere as the seashell chandeliers and DJ booth, which he also mans when he's not serving up exquisitely plated and crafted delights including perfectly seared blackened scallop risotto and a twist on gazpacho adding sweet black pineapple. **Known for:** Pavarotti's "Miserere" welcomes the sunset every evening; prawn ravioli; superb service and excellent wine pairings. *Average main: $35 ✉ Off Valley Rd., Crab Hill ☎ 268/562–2218 ⏲ Closed Mon.*

Le Bistro
$$$$ | **FRENCH** | This Antiguan institution has in recent years renovated with modern Mediterranean-ish digs, including cerulean blue and lime green walls and a stylish lounge area and bar. It's an inviting space for supping on classic regional fare with indigenous ingredients; order one of the daily specials—smoked marlin carpaccio with pink peppercorns, or prawns in a gossamer ginger white wine sauce laced with leeks—when possible. **Known for:** extensive wine list; authentic French cuisine; sublime desserts. *Average main: $34 ✉ Hodges Bay Rd., Hodges Bay ☎ 268/462–3881 🌐 www.lebistroantigua.com ⏲ Closed Mon. No lunch.*

Papa Zouk

$$$ | **CARIBBEAN** | According to owner Bert Kirchner, Papa Zouk is not a restaurant, but a rum shop surreptitiously disguised as a favorite seafood joint—don't miss the pan-fried snapper and garlicky gumbo (bouillabaisse). Located off the beaten path, the deliberately kitschy decor—madras tablecloths and lobster traps turned chandeliers—draws a hodgepodge of characters from locals to English Harbour yachties, actor Robert De Niro, and the man who notoriously set the bar ablaze. **Known for:** good times, but it's prudent to call ahead; mouth-watering seafood; international rums. *Average main: $24 ✉ Hilda Davis Dr., Gambles Terrace, St. John's ☎ 268/464–0795, 268/464–6044 No credit cards ⏲ Closed Sun. No lunch.*

Pillars Restaurant & Bar

$$$$ | **ECLECTIC** | "Location, location, location" is the real draw of this spot within Nelson's Dockyard, which is seamlessly integrated into the waterfront promenade with amazing views of the harbor and its namesake, the Boat House Pillars. Open for all meals—lunch is seldom crowded—a varied (and pricey) menu includes items like Thai shrimp cakes and a Mediterranean eggplant caprese sandwich. **Known for:** deliciously tart fresh lime squash; fabulous view; lounging areas. *Average main: $35 ✉ Admiral's Inn, Dockyard Dr., Nelson's Dockyard, English Harbour Town ☎ 268/460–1027 🌐 www.admiralsantigua.com.*

Salt Plage

$$$ | **ECLECTIC** | Sandwiched between Siboney Beach Club and the great blue sea, under a bamboo-accented natural-wood thatched roof grounded by multicolored stone floors, this little gem has an efficient and welcoming staff that's doting without being suffocating. The fare is simple and deftly prepared, including perfectly chewy New York–style bagels with lox in the morning, and sweet potato and butternut sauté served with coconut bouillon and crispy papadam. **Known for:** simple, imaginative menu; cabanas and beach loungers available for rent; on the beach. *Average main: $30 ✉ Siboney Beach Club, Marina Bay Rd., Dickenson Bay ☎ 268/462–0806 🌐 www.siboneybeachantigua.com.*

★ **Sheer Rocks**

$$$ | **ECLECTIC** | Comprising a series of tiered wood decks carved into the cliffside, this popular spot offers views that are every bit as sought after as the food. The menu encompasses a tapestry of creative tapas, many of which can be served in larger portions, like umami-braised beef short ribs and truffle mac-and-cheese infused with porcini stock. **Known for:** gin-and-tonic cocktail menu; swish lounging areas; sublime views. *Average main: $29 ✉ CocoBay Resort, Valley Rd. ☎ 268/562–4510, 268/464–5283 🌐 www.sheer-rocks.com.*

Trappas

$$ | **SEAFOOD** | With a bustling atmosphere and easy approach to dining, Trappas is the place where everyone knows your name. The wide-ranging prix-fixe menu (an appetizer and main will set you back about EC$100) has delectable bits, including a rich and spicy seafood chowder, sizable serving of crispy calamari, and creamy seafood pasta. **Known for:** crispy calamari and delectable seafood soup; straightforward menu with predictable pricing; fun, familiar atmosphere with doting staff. *Average main: $16 ✉ Main Rd., English Harbour Town ☎ 268/562–3534 No credit cards.*

Hotels

Scattered along Antigua's beaches and hillsides are exclusive, elegant hideaways; romantic restored inns; and all-inclusive hot spots for couples. Hammock Cove Resort, Hodges Bay Resort & Spa, and Royalton Antigua Resort and Spa have all opened in recent years, and there are several developments in the pipeline, including Callaloo Cay and Marriott's Coconut Bay Resort, but construction hadn't yet begun as of this writing.

TIP→ Check individual lodgings for restrictions (many have minimum stays during certain high-season periods). Look also for specials on the Web or from tour packagers, since hotels' quoted rack rates are often negotiable (up to 45% off in season).

★ Admiral's Inn

$ | **B&B/INN** | Nestled within the historic Nelson's Dockyard complex, this former pitch and tar store–turned–inn features the exposed, original brick stairwell as well as original timbered ceilings in the small but comfortable rooms replete with whitewashed brick walls, polished hardwood floors, sailing prints, and four-poster beds swathed in mosquito netting. **Pros:** charming restaurant setting; historic ambience yet contemporary boutique style; free shuttle to nearby beaches. **Cons:** miniscule man-made beach; no fridge or coffeemaker in rooms; occasionally noisy when yachties take over the bar. *Rooms from: $205 Dockyard Dr., English Harbour Town 268/460–1027, 268/460–1153 www.admiralsantigua.com 23 rooms No Meals.*

★ Blue Waters Resort & Spa

$$$$ | **RESORT** | A well-heeled Brit crowd goes barefoot at this swank yet understated seaside retreat, whose lobby immediately puts you in the Caribbean mindset with vast white cathedral ceilings and sand-colored walls that mimic the color of driftwood, all accented by jewel tones culled from the surroundings—a mixture of emerald green, turquoise, and sapphire with hints of indigo. **Pros:** serene spa; pomp without pretension; exquisite setting. **Cons:** long walks to main areas from some rooms; little steps along the hillside make it less accessible for the physically challenged; small beachfront. *Rooms from: $500 Boon Point, Atlantic Ave., Soldier's Bay, Weatherills 268/462–0290, 800/557–6536 www.bluewaters.net 107 units All-Inclusive.*

Buccaneer Beach Club

$ | **APARTMENT** | This simple, yet charming compound opens onto the quieter part of Dickenson Bay, yet it's merely steps from the rollicking restaurants and nightlife. **Pros:** well-equipped units with flat-screen TVs; unfussy but inviting decor; quieter part of beach. **Cons:** no beach view from rooms; hotel beach is sometimes eroded; few facilities. *Rooms from: $245 Marina Bay Rd., Dickenson Bay 268/562–6785 www.buccaneer-beach.com 18 units No Meals.*

★ Carlisle Bay

$$$$ | **RESORT** | This cosmopolitan, boutique sister property of London's trendy One Aldwych hotel daringly eschews everything faux colonial and Creole, instead providing a monochromatic, magazine-worthy look that combines cool, classy minimalism with unsnobbish warmth. **Pros:** luxurious; attentive service; family-friendly. **Cons:** no elevators; aggressively hip; pricey restaurants. *Rooms from: $1020 Old Rd., Carlisle Bay 268/484–0000, 866/502–2855 reservations only www.carlisle-bay.com Closed late Aug.–early Oct. 87 suites Free Breakfast.*

Catamaran Hotel

$ | **HOTEL** | **FAMILY** | Mere steps from the water's edge, the main building at the congenial cozy harbor front "Cat Club" evokes a plantation great house with verandahs, white columns, and hand-carved doors. **Pros:** free sailing lessons; central location; friendly staff. **Cons:** small beach (swimming not advised); dated room decor; surrounding area has limited dining and nightlife options during off-season (May–November). *Rooms from: $170 Great Fort George Monks Hill Trail, Falmouth Harbour 268/460–1036 www.catamaranantigua.com 14 rooms No Meals.*

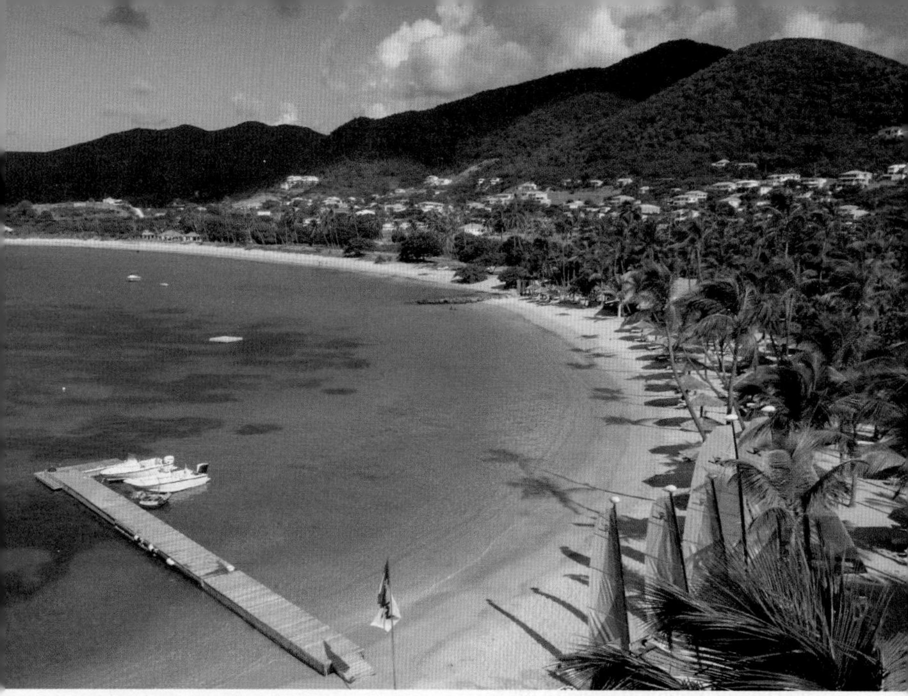

The Bay Beach in front of Curtain Bluff has calm, clear water perfect for swimming.

Cocobay Resort

$$$$ | RESORT | This healing, hillside spa hideaway aims to "eliminate all potential worries" by emphasizing simple, natural beauty and West Indian warmth—yoga classes, a boutique gym, nature hikes, and TV-free rooms further promote de-stressing. **Pros:** emphasis on local nature and culture; beautiful views; nice main pool and bar. **Cons:** mediocre food; not directly set on a beach; difficult climb for those with mobility challenges. *Rooms from: $540 ✉ Valley Rd., Valley Church, Jolly Harbour ☎ 268/562–2400, 508/506–1006 ⊕ www.cocobayresort.com 65 cottages All-Inclusive.*

★ Curtain Bluff

$$$$ | RESORT | An incomparable beachfront setting, impeccable service, superb extras (free scuba diving), effortless elegance: Curtain Bluff is that rare retreat that feels forever modern while exuding a magical timelessness. **Pros:** elegant waterfront spa; sublime food, including Italian eatery on the beach; beautiful beaches. **Cons:** some find clientele standoffish; lodgings atop bluff not ideal for those with mobility challenges; despite offering value, pricey by most standards. *Rooms from: $1265 ✉ Old Rd., Morris Bay ☎ 268/462–8400, 888/289–9898 for reservations ⊕ www.curtainbluff.com ⏲ Closed late Aug.–late Oct. 72 rooms All-Inclusive.*

Dickenson Bay Cottages

$ | APARTMENT | Lush landscaping snakes around the two-story buildings and pool at this small hillside complex, which offers excellent value for families. **Pros:** quiet, even with children on property; relatively upscale comfort at down-home prices; walking distance to Dickenson Bay dining and activities. **Cons:** distant views of the sea from a few rooms; no food options; a hike from the beach. *Rooms from: $183 ✉ Anchorage Rd., Marble Hill ☎ 268/462–4940 ⊕ www.dickensonbaycottages.com 14 units No Meals.*

★ Galley Bay Resort & Spa

$$$$ | **RESORT** | This posh, adult-only all-inclusive channels the fictional Bali H'ai (with colonial architectural flourishes) on 40 lush acres with a man-made lagoon, stunning grotto pool, a bird sanctuary laced with nature trails, and a magnificent boardwalk-lined ecru beach. **Pros:** impeccable maintenance; tranquil spa; gorgeous beach and grounds. **Cons:** surf can be too strong for weaker swimmers; only suites have tubs; some lodgings are small and lack a view. *Rooms from: $1020 ✉ Grays Farm Rd., Five Islands Village ☎ 268/462–0302, 866/203–3085 🌐 www.galleybayresort.com 98 rooms 🍽 All-Inclusive.*

Hammock Cove Antigua

$$$$ | **ALL-INCLUSIVE** | This quintessential modern Caribbean boutique hotel and carefully curated couple's retreat succeeds at balancing minimalism and extravagance with a customer-centric approach—clean, sleek lines; muted neutral tones; and vivacious pops of color and texture create an attention-grabbing design. **Pros:** room service included in the rates; sublime setting; beautiful and spacious cottages. **Cons:** not a good fit for people with disabilities; hard-to-find entrance; deafening silence. *Rooms from: $700 ✉ Devil's Bridge National Park ☎ 800/858–4618, 268/484–6550 🌐 www.hammockcoveantigua.com 41 villas 🍽 All-Inclusive.*

Hawksbill by Rex Resorts

$$ | **RESORT** | Four secluded beaches (including one clothing-optional strand) are this adults-only resort's main attraction, but you'll also find verdant grounds with landscaped walkways, plantation-style cottages trimmed with gingerbread fretwork and radiant bougainvillea, and a backdrop of jade mountains that maximize Hawksbill's old-time Caribbean feel. **Pros:** budget-friendly with online deals; sublime setting; pretty grounds. **Cons:** haphazard maintenance; not ideal for guests with disabilities; unmemorable food. *Rooms from: $298 ✉ Grays Farm Main Rd., Five Islands Village ☎ 268/462–0301 🌐 www.hawksbillbyrexresorts.com 112 rooms 🍽 All-Inclusive.*

HBK Villas

$ | **RESORT** | These duplex, two-bedroom villas ring the marina of a sprawling, 500-acre compound offering every conceivable facility from restaurants and shops to a golf course. **Pros:** plentiful recreational, dining, and nightlife choices nearby; nice beach; good value. **Cons:** you can't charge most restaurants and activities to your villa; villas tend to be lower-end; mosquitos can be a problem. *Rooms from: $190 ✉ Jolly Harbour ☎ 268/462–6166, 268/462–6168 🌐 www.hbkvillas.com 50 villas 🍽 No Meals.*

Hodges Bay Resort & Spa

$$$$ | **RESORT** | **FAMILY** | This contemporary-sculptural resort nestled inside (and under) the Hodges Bay community merges a biophilic edenlike jungle vibe with MoMA-reminiscent design in which lush gardens and creeping fig vines cover the entrance, seemingly reclaiming the property. **Pros:** ample dining and nightlife choices; smartly appointed rooms; central location. **Cons:** hilly layout presents mobility challenges; tiny beach; not all-inclusive. *Rooms from: $776 ✉ Sandy La., Hodges Bay ☎ 917/979–4300, 268/484–8000 🌐 www.hodgesbay.com 79 units 🍽 No Meals.*

Inn at English Harbour

$$$$ | **RESORT** | This genteel resort, long a favorite with Brits and the boating set, is ideal for those seeking beachfront accommodations near English Harbour's attractions, yet it suffers from a split personality: the original hilltop buildings hold the beamed, flagstone bar and dining room with scintillating harbor panoramas, while four cramped if stylishly monochrome beachfront rooms are serviceable (beware windless days and biting insects), but have easy access to the funky-elegant beach bar and the complimentary water sports.

Pros: stylish rooms; spectacular views; central English Harbour location. **Cons:** high prices; almost too quiet; tiny beach. *Rooms from: $756 Freeman's Bay, Dockyard Dr., English Harbour Town 268/460–1014 www.theinnantigua.com Closed during low season (the timing varies each year) 28 units Free Breakfast.*

★ Jumby Bay Island

$$$$ | **RESORT** | **FAMILY** | This refined resort proffers all the makings of a classic Caribbean private island hideaway, right from the stylish airport private car pickup, private launch, dockside greeting, and registration at your leisure. **Pros:** impeccable dining; isolated private island location; inventive, complimentary children's programs. **Cons:** boat ride to the mainland; jet noise occasionally disturbs the main beach; isolated private island location. *Rooms from: $1995 Burma Rd., Long Island 268/462–6000, 800/749–1802 for reservations www.jumbybay-island.com 40 rooms All-Inclusive.*

★ Nonsuch Bay Resort

$$$$ | **RESORT** | **FAMILY** | This exclusive 40-acre compound's handsome, gabled Georgian-style buildings cascade down the lushly landscaped hillside to the eponymous bay, flecked with sails; aptly, aquatic activities abound, including sailing, windsurfing, and kitesurfing. **Pros:** standout cuisine; vast water-sport offerings; fully equipped kitchens. **Cons:** hilly layout presents mobility challenges; pretty but cramped beach; remote setting requires a car. *Rooms from: $600 Hughes Point, Nonsuch Bay 268/562–8000, 888/844–2480 www.nonsuchbayresort.com 85 rooms All-Inclusive only the Escape section is all-inclusive.*

Ocean Inn

$ | **B&B/INN** | Views of English Harbour, affable management, and affordability distinguish this homey inn whose main house has six snug guest rooms (two share a bathroom); the four hillside cottages are the nicest (especially Numbers 8 and 9). **Pros:** inexpensive; short walk to restaurants; 10-minute drive to beaches. **Cons:** basic gym; tours outside clamoring for pics of the view; worn rooms need updating. *Rooms from: $110 English Harbour Town 268/463–7950 www.theoceaninn.com 6 rooms Free Breakfast.*

Pineapple Beach Club

$$ | **ALL-INCLUSIVE** | The traditional Caribbean architecture at this adults-only resort strikes a nostalgic but not particularly inspiring note, but its natural attributes are the star of the show: set on 30 unspoiled acres encompassing a pristine horseshoe-shape beach, the property has magnificent landscaping. **Pros:** stunning natural setting; attentive staff; great variety of dining options. **Cons:** sprawling property not disability-friendly; some lounging are small and lack a view; outdated surroundings. *Rooms from: $350 Long Bay 866/939–9947, 268/463–2006 www.pineapplebeachclub.com 180 rooms All-Inclusive.*

Royalton Antigua

$$$$ | **ALL-INCLUSIVE** | **FAMILY** | Rising from the ashes of the dilapidated Grand Royal Antigua Resort this modishly hip all-inclusive all but sends smoke signals to the young, chic Instagram-ready crowd. **Pros:** secluded location; excellent children's club; lively atmosphere. **Cons:** noisy pool and beach area; expensive; bustling energy can be a bit much for some. *Rooms from: $630 Deep Bay St., Five Islands Village 268/484–2000, 855/744–8371 www.royaltonresorts.com 300 rooms All-Inclusive.*

St. James's Club

$$$$ | **RESORT** | **FAMILY** | Management has diligently smartened the public spaces and exquisite landscaping at this venerable resort, taking full advantage of the peerless location straddling 100 acres on Mamora Bay. Regularly refurbished rooms are commodious and vibrantly decorated (the Royal Suite, Premium,

and Beachfront units are worth the extra cost, boasting elegantly enhanced bathrooms). **Pros:** additional adult pools offer more privacy; splendid remote location; plentiful activities. **Cons:** sprawling hilly layout not ideal for physically challenged; tour groups can overrun the resort; remote location makes a car a necessity for non-all-inclusive guests. *Rooms from: $760 Dockyard Dr., Mamora Bay 866/941–9624 www.stjamesclubantigua.com 314 rooms All-Inclusive.*

Sandals Grande Antigua Resort & Spa

$$$$ | **RESORT** | The sumptuous public spaces, lovely beach, glorious gardens, and plethora of facilities almost mask this resort's impersonal atmosphere, and renovations have added plunge pools and larger bathrooms to the rondavels (bungalows with thatched roofs). **Pros:** huge online advance booking savings; lively atmosphere; good dining options. **Cons:** uneven service; too bustling; sprawling layout. *Rooms from: $648 Dickenson Bay 888/726–3257 reservations only, 268/484–0100 www.sandals.com 373 rooms All-Inclusive Three-night minimum.*

★ **Siboney Beach Club**

$$ | **HOTEL** | Out with the old and in with new, ownership that is—this beloved property has been not just been revived but reimagined after years of renovations that include the reception building's modern Saint-Tropez–like clean lines, which stand out among the row of old haunts. **Pros:** great value; friendly service; superb location. **Cons:** no meals included; busy area; ongoing construction. *Rooms from: $345 Dickenson Bay 268/462–0806 www.siboneybeachantigua.com 30 rooms No Meals.*

South Point

$$$$ | **HOTEL** | From the slate-gray lobby with baby grand piano and stainless-steel bar to the minimal open plan of the two-level suites, South Point fashions itself as minimalist chic lodging. **Pros:** large, open-concept rooms; transcendent views of mega-yachts in the harbor; walking distance from the island's best restaurants. **Cons:** expensive; restaurant music can be heard in rooms; seasonally smelly sea. *Rooms from: $900 Yacht Club Dr., English Harbour Town 268/562–9600, 800/857–2082 U.S. reservations www.southpointantigua.com 23 rooms Free Breakfast.*

Tamarind Hills

$$$$ | **HOTEL** | **FAMILY** | Nimbly nestled into a hillside, cushioned between two famous beaches (Ffryes and Darkwood), Tamarind Hills sports a modern, architectural design that niftily juxtaposes classic Caribbean touches like richly stained greenheart wood and sun-bleached, ashen shingled roofs. **Pros:** family-friendly luxury; close to restaurants and nightlife; wide-open space indoors seamlessly transitions outdoors. **Cons:** set just off a major thoroughfare; villas can be uncomfortably close together; small, rocky man-made beach. *Rooms from: $700 Ffryes Beach Off of Valley Rd, between Ffryes Beach and Darkwood Beach 268/562–7380 www.tamarind-hills.com 14 villas No Meals.*

Verandah Resort & Spa

$$$$ | **RESORT** | **FAMILY** | Verandah's splendid hillside setting overlooks calm, reef-protected Dian Bay, and hiking trails snake around the property to Devil's Bridge National Park. **Pros:** good kids' club and facilities with own pool; gorgeous remote location; scads of amenities. **Cons:** though shuttles ply the resort, its hilly layout is problematic for the physically challenged; noise carries between adjoining units; smallish beaches. *Rooms from: $500 Long Bay 268/562–6848, 866/213–2359 reservations www.verandahresortandspa.com 185 rooms All-Inclusive.*

Nightlife

Most of Antigua's evening entertainment takes place at the resorts, which occasionally present calypso singers, steel bands, limbo dancers, and folkloric groups. Check with the tourist office for up-to-date information. In addition, a cluster of clubs and bars pulsate into the night in season around English and Falmouth harbors.

BARS

Abracadabra

BARS | The magic truly takes place after dinner at Abracadabra's Italian restaurant, as the space transforms into a disco on the covered wooden deck set in the venue's gardens. No-fuss drinks invite partygoers to a raucous night around 11 pm on weekends (an impromptu jam can occur during the week if the vibe demands). A blend of local DJs spinning reggae to rock and legendary themed parties fuse with a melting pot of guests to create the perfect vibe. For more relaxed environs there is a shack in the back playing reggae and lovers rock (think Sade). ✉ *Nelson's Dockyard, English Harbour Town* ☎ *268/460–2701* 🌐 *abracadabra-antigua.com.*

Ana's on the Beach

BARS | This enormous, multitier, mostly alfresco beach bar–cum–art gallery styles itself a restaurant-lounge. Although the ramrod chrome-finished chairs make for rigid seating, the loud music begs for earplugs, and the globe-trotting menu is too ambitious, this is nonetheless a hip, happening spot and prime Grade A meet market. Breakfast features a hodgepodge menu of local and international treats. The friendly staff is garbed in black pants and bubblegum-pink shirts (stenciled "love is in the air"), the cocktails are fairly inventive, and the rotating art on the walls—including an epoxy-painted surfboard dangling from the white beamed ceiling—displays a savvy selection of the hottest up-and-coming local artists in various media. ✉ *Dickenson Bay* ☎ *268/464–1389* 🌐 *www.anas.ag.*

Indigo on the Beach

COCKTAIL LOUNGES | Indigo on the Beach is a soigné spot, yet it's relaxed and great any time of day for creative tapas, salads, grills, and burgers. But the beautiful people turn out in force come evening to pose at the fiber-optically lighted bar, or on white lounges scattered with throw pillows. ✉ *Carlisle Bay, Old Road* ☎ *268/480–0000* 🌐 *www.carlisle-bay.com.*

Mainbrace Pub

PUBS | The Mainbrace Pub has a historic ambience, right down to its warm brick walls and hardwood accents, and is known as a beer, darts, and fish-and-chips kind of hangout for the boating set. ✉ *Copper & Lumber Store Hotel, English Harbour Town* ☎ *268/460–1058.*

★ **Shirley Heights Lookout**

GATHERING PLACES | The ruins of this timeworn military base transform into a party venue—one that its namesake, Sir Thomas Shirley, would undoubtedly frown upon. After 4:30 pm on Sunday and Thursday, strong rum punch starts to flow, steel pans stir visitors into a frenzy, and the scent of barbecue wafting through the air is irresistible. The lookout is packed full of swaying partiers by 7 pm. It's $10 to enter and be sure to wear sensible shoes. ✉ *Shirley Heights* ☎ *268/729–0636 reservations, 268/764–0389* 🌐 *www.shirleyheightslookout.com* ⏲ *Closed Mon.*

Shopping

Antigua's duty-free shops are at Heritage Quay, where cruise ships call. Bargains can be found on perfumes, liqueurs, and liquor (including English Harbour Antiguan rum), jewelry, china, and crystal. As for other local items, check out straw hats, baskets, batik, pottery, Susie's Hot Sauce, and hand-printed cotton clothing. Fine artists to look for include Gilly

Gobinet (neo-postimpressionist islandscapes), Heather Doram (exquisite, intricately woven collage wall hangings), Jan Farara, Jennifer Meranto (incomparable hand-painted black-and-white photos of Caribbean scenes), and Heike Petersen (delightful dolls and quilts).

TIP→ Many businesses in the English/Falmouth harbors are closed from June to October. Call ahead to confirm hours of operation.

BOOKS AND MAGAZINES

Best of Books

BOOKS | In an old white building in the middle of town, this quaint bookstore is said to have the "widest variety of books" in the Eastern Caribbean. The shelves are stocked with local reads, cookbooks, and children's books alongside international bestsellers. There's also a US$1 used book rack outside with beach-perfect selections. ✉ *Lower St. Mary's St., St. John's* ☎ *268/562–3198.*

CLOTHING

Exotic Antigua

OTHER SPECIALTY STORE | This shop sells everything from Indonesian blankets to Tommy Bahama resort wear. ✉ *Redcliffe Quay, St. John's* ☎ *268/562–1288.*

Noreen Phillips

WOMEN'S CLOTHING | Couturiere Noreen Phillips masterfully creates one-of-a-kind evening gowns and complementary accessories for women of "discerning tastes." The candy-colored creations showcase flattering silhouettes, luxurious fabrics, and limitless design selections. ✉ *Redcliffe Quay, St. John's* ☎ *268/462–3127.*

Sunseakers

SWIMWEAR | If by chance you forgot to pack beachwear don't despair—this shop has limitless options of designer swimsuits, beachwear, and flip-flops. ✉ *Heritage Quay, St. John's* ☎ *268/462–4523.*

DUTY-FREE GOODS

Abbott's Jewellery

DUTY-FREE | The official Rolex retailer for Antigua, Abbott's also offers an extensive collection of beautiful luxury jewelry. Just across the hall, you will find their perfumery and selection of fine crystal and china. ✉ *Heritage Quay, St. John's* ☎ *268/462–3107* 🌐 *www.abbottsjewellery.com.*

Lipstick

DUTY-FREE | Your senses will be overwhelmed by the opulence of high-end perfumes and colognes wafting through the air at this small perfumery. And, yes, they do sell lipstick from Chanel to Lancôme. ✉ *Heritage Quay, St. John's* ☎ *268/562–1133.*

HANDICRAFTS

Cedars Pottery

CRAFTS | Partners in artistry and life, acclaimed ceramists Michael Hunt and Imogen Margrie create vibrant, eclectic, functional art that includes decorative thrown tableware, earthenware vases, and the pervasive wall sconce with cutout motifs. The pair realized a decades-long dream of opening their gallery in 2018, identifiable by its stunning cobalt palisade gate and gravity-defying ample vase tilted warily against the saffron wall. Within the gates lies an indoor gallery with extensive pieces by the artists and few local artists; the expansive garden has ambitious statues seamlessly integrated within the foliage. ✉ *St. Clare Estate, Buckleys Rd., Buckleys* ☎ *268/460–5293* 🌐 *www.cedarspottery.com.*

Rhythm of Blue Gallery

CRAFTS | Nancy Nicholson co-owns Rhythm of Blue Gallery; she's renowned for her exquisite glazed and matte-finish ceramics, featuring Caribbean-pure shades, as well as her black-and-white yachting photos and flowing batik creations. You'll also find exhibitions showcasing leading regional artists working in media from batik to copper, as well as handcrafted salt scrubs and jewelry. ✉ *Dockyard Dr., English Harbour Town* ☎ *268/562–2230, 268/770–7888* 🌐 *www.rhythmofblue.com.*

Sarah Fuller Pottery

CRAFTS | The island itself is potter Sarah Fuller's muse. Within the cobalt doors of her Dutchman's Bay gallery and retail space, you'll find her signature ocean-inspired turquoise and blue ceramics, driftwood and clay wind chimes, and sconces with island-themed carvings. Call before visiting the studio. ✉ *Dutchman's Bay, Coolidge, St. John's* ☎ *268/562–1264* 🌐 *www.sarahfullerpottery.com.*

JEWELRY

Colombian Emeralds

JEWELRY & WATCHES | The Antiguan branch of the largest retailer of Colombian emeralds in the world also carries a wide variety of other gems. There are smaller outlets at the airport, Sandals Grande Antigua, and St. James's Club. ✉ *Heritage Quay, St. John's* ☎ *268/462–3462* 🌐 *www.colombianemeralds.com.*

Diamonds International

JEWELRY & WATCHES | You'll find a huge selection of loose diamonds as well as a variety of watches, rings, brooches, bracelets, and pendants at Diamonds International. Several resorts have branches. ✉ *Heritage Quay, St. John's* ☎ *268/481–1880* 🌐 *www.diamondsinternational.com.*

Goldsmitty

JEWELRY & WATCHES | Hans Smit is the Goldsmitty, an expert goldsmith who turns gold, black coral, petrified coral (which he dubs Antiguanite), and precious and semiprecious stones into one-of-a-kind works of art. ✉ *Redcliffe Quay, St. John's* ☎ *268/462–4601* 🌐 *www.goldsmitty.com.*

SHOPPING AREAS

Heritage Quay, in St. John's, has 35 shops—including many that are duty-free—that cater to the cruise-ship crowd, which docks almost at its doorstep. Outlets here include Longchamp, the Body Shop, and Sunglass Hut. There are also shops along **St. John's, St. Mary's, High,** and **Long streets.** The tangerine-and-lilac-hue four-story **Vendor's Mall** at the intersection of Redcliffe and Thames streets gathers the pushy, pesky vendors who once clogged the narrow streets. It's jammed with stalls; air-conditioned indoor shops sell some higher-price, if not higher-quality, merchandise. On the west coast the Mediterranean-style, arcaded **Jolly Harbour Marina** holds some interesting galleries and shops, as do the marinas and the main road snaking around English and Falmouth harbors.

Redcliffe Quay, on the waterfront at the south edge of St. John's, is by far the most appealing shopping area. Several restaurants and more than 30 boutiques, many with one-of-a-kind wares, are set around landscaped courtyards shaded by colorful trees.

Activities

Several all-inclusives offer day passes that permit use of all sporting facilities, from tennis courts to water-sports concessions, as well as free drinks and meals. The cost begins at $50 for singles (but can be as much as $200 for couples at Sandals), and hours generally run from 8 am to 6 pm, with extensions available until 2 am for some. Antigua has long been famed for its cricketers (such as Viv Richards and Richie Richardson); aficionados will find one of the Caribbean's finest cricket grounds right by the airport, with major test matches running January through June.

ADVENTURE TOURS

Antigua is developing its ecotourist opportunities, and several memorable offshore experiences involve more than just snorkeling. The archipelago of islets coupled with a full mangrove swamp off the northeast coast is unique in the Caribbean.

Adventure Antigua

BOATING | The enthusiastic Eli Fuller, who is knowledgeable not only about the ecosystem and geography of Antigua but also about its history and politics (his grandfather was the American consul), runs Adventure Antigua. His thorough seven-hour excursion (Eli dubs it "re-creating my childhood explorations") includes stops at Guiana Island (for lunch and guided snorkeling; turtles, barracuda, and stingrays are common sightings), Pelican Island (more snorkeling), Bird Island (hiking to vantage points to admire the soaring ospreys and frigate and red-billed tropic birds), and Hell's Gate (a striking limestone rock formation where the more intrepid may hike and swim through sunken caves and tide pools painted with pink and maroon algae). The company also offers a fun "Xtreme Circumnavigation" variation on a racing boat catering to adrenaline junkies who "feel the need for speed." It also visits Stingray City and Nelson's Dockyard, and offers a more sedate Antigua Classic Yacht sail-and-snorkel experience that explains the rich Caribbean history of boatbuilding. ☎ *268/726–6355* 🌐 *www.adventureantigua.com.*

Stingray City Antigua

WILDLIFE-WATCHING | **FAMILY** | Stingray City Antigua is a carefully reproduced "natural" environment nicknamed by staffers "the retirement home," although the 30-plus stingrays (ranging from infants to seniors) are frisky. You can stroke, feed, even hold the striking gliders—"They're like puppy dogs," one guide swears—as well as snorkel in deeper protected waters. The tour guides do a marvelous job of explaining the animals' habits, from feeding to breeding, and their predators (including man). ✉ *Seaton's Village* ☎ *268/562–7297* 🌐 *www.stingraycityantigua.com.*

BOATING

Antigua's circular geographic configuration makes boating easy, and its many lovely harbors and coves provide splendid anchorages. Experienced boaters will particularly enjoy Antigua's east coast, which is far more rugged and has several islets; be sure to get a good nautical map, as there are numerous minireefs that can be treacherous. If you're just looking for a couple of hours of wave-hopping, stick to the Dickenson Bay or Jolly Harbour area.

Nicholson Yacht Charters

BOATING | Nicholson Yacht Charters are real professionals, true pioneers in Caribbean sailing, with three generations spanning 60 years of experience. A long-established island family, they can offer you anything from a 20-foot ketch to a giant schooner. ✉ *English Harbour Town* ☎ *268/460–1530, 268/720–6750 WhatsApp* 🌐 *www.nicholsoncharters.com.*

Ondeck

BOATING | Ondeck runs skippered charters out of the Antigua Yacht Club Marina in Falmouth Harbour, terrific one- and two-day sailing workshops, and ecoadventure trips to Montserrat on a racing yacht. You can even participate in official regattas. Instructors and crew are all seasoned racers. Bareboating options and sunset cruises are also available. ☎ *268/562–6696* 🌐 *ondecksailing.com.*

Sunsail

BOATING | The possibilities are endless and custom for experienced sailors choosing to cruise their day away on the cool calm waters surrounding Antigua. Options include visiting the nation's anchorages, from Nonsuch Bay to Maiden Island on a 41-foot Monohull. A week-long journey can take you from Antigua to

Guadeloupe and back, starting at $4,800. If available, Manager Lovena and her crew offer a skippered day charter to the nation's anchorages. ☎ *268/460–2615* 🌐 *www.sunsail.com.*

DIVING

Antigua is an unsung diving destination, with plentiful undersea sights to explore, from coral canyons to sea caves. Barbuda alone features roughly 200 wrecks on its treacherous reefs. The most accessible wreck is the 1890s bark *Andes,* not far out in Deep Bay, off Five Islands Peninsula. Among the favorite sites are **Green Island, Cades Reef,** and **Bird Island** (a national park). Memorable sightings include turtles, stingrays, and barracuda darting amid basalt walls, hulking boulders, and stray 17th-century anchors and cannon. One advantage is accessibility in many spots for shore divers and snorkelers. Double-tank dives run about $90.

Dockyard Divers

SCUBA DIVING | With over 40 years of diving experience and nearly half of those off the coasts and around the reefs of the Caribbean, ex-merchant seaman Captain Tony Fincham and Dockyard Divers offer diving and snorkeling trips and private scuba instruction in some of the most sought-after dive sites on the southern coast (including Pillars of Hercules and Stingray Alley), which are suitable for both novice and experienced divers. For certified divers, two tanks will run you $99 and a five-day, two-tank dive package is a steal at $445. ✉ *Nelson's Dockyard, English Harbour Town* ☎ *268/729–3040* 🌐 *www.dockyard-divers.com.*

FISHING

Antigua's waters teem with game fish such as marlin, wahoo, and tuna. Most boat trips include equipment, lunch, and drinks. Figure at least $495 for a half day, $850 for a full day, for up to six people.

Obsession

FISHING | The 45-foot Hatteras Convertible Sportfisherman *Obsession* has top-of-the-line equipment, including an international-standard fighting chair, Rupp outriggers, and handcrafted rods. Also available is the new 55-foot Hatteras Sportfisherman, the *Double Header.* Beer and soft drinks are included in the rates. Captain Derek Biel is a seasoned sea salt, a certified I.G.F.A. Ambassador who has competed in many tournaments over the past quarter century. ☎ *268/462–3174, 954/636–4862 in the U.S.* 🌐 *www.charternet.com/charters/obsession* 💵 *$600 per half day, $1,000 for 8 hrs for six guests.*

Overdraft

FISHING | Frankie Hart, a professional fisherman who knows the waters intimately and regales clients with stories of his trade, operates *Overdraft,* a spacious, fiberglass 40-footer outfitted with the latest techno-gadgetry. He also rents the 26-foot *H2O,* a ProKat versatile enough to accommodate fly-fishing and deeper-water bay bait fishing. ✉ *English Harbour Town* ☎ *268/720–4954, 268/463–3112* 🌐 *www.antiguafishing.com* 💵 *From $495.*

GOLF

Though Antigua hardly qualifies as a duffer's delight, its two 18-hole courses offer varied layouts.

Cedar Valley Golf Club

GOLF | Finished as Antigua's first 18-hole golf course in 1977, Cedar Valley is not particularly well maintained terrain, but nonetheless offers some attractive vistas and challenges with narrow hilly fairways and numerous doglegs (hole 7 is a perfect example). The 5th hole has exceptional ocean vistas from the top of the tee, and the par-5 9th offers the trickiest design with steep slopes and swales. Carts are $42 ($22 for nine holes). An unlimited weekly golf pass costs $220. The 18 plus 1 Cafe offers free Wi-Fi. *Friar's Hill, St. John's* *268/462–0161* *www.cedarvalley.golf* *$60 ($31 for 9 holes)* *18 holes, 6157 yards, par 70.*

Jolly Harbour Golf Course

GOLF | The flat Florida-style layout of Jolly Harbour was designed by Karl Litten. It's lushly tropical with challenging trade winds. Seven lakes add to the challenge, but the facility struggles with conditioning. The 15th is the signature hole, with a sharp dogleg and long carry over two hazards. Unfortunately, despite improved maintenance, fairways are often dry and patchy, drainage is poor, and the pro shop and "19th hole" are barely adequate. Visitors can participate in regular tournaments and "meet-and-greet" events. *Jolly Harbour* *268/462–7771 ext 625* *www.jollyharbourmarina.com* *$57.50 ($97.75 including cart); $34.50 for 9 holes, $23 for cart* *18 holes, 5587 yards, par 71.*

HORSEBACK RIDING

Comparatively dry Antigua is best for beach rides, though you won't find anything wildly romantic and deserted à la *Black Stallion.*

Antigua Equestrian Center - Spring Hill Riding Club

HORSEBACK RIDING | Novice riders enjoy a scenic trek through plantations and beaches near Spring Hill Riding Club's prime English Harbour location ($65). For more advanced and adventurous riders a steep trek through illustrious Rendezvous Bay is on the menu ($125); for an additional $45, riders can join the horses for a refreshing dip in the sea after the ride. *Falmouth Harbour* *268/460–7787, 268/773–3139* *www.antiguaequestrian.com.*

SAILING AND SNORKELING

Not a sailor yourself? Consider signing up for one of the following boat tours. Each tour provides a great opportunity to enjoy the seafaring life while someone else captains the ship.

Miguel's Holiday Adventures

SAILING | Tours leave from the Hodges Bay jetty for snorkeling, rum punches, and lunch (lobster, conch, and barbecue chicken capped off with homemade cake and cocktails from the beach bar) at Prickly Pear Island. A full-scale bar was under construction as of this writing. Call ahead for the schedule. *268/772–3213 mobile* *www.pricklypearisland.com.*

Tropical Adventures

SAILING | Circumnavigate the island's illustrious coasts aboard the luxury catamaran *Excellence.* The half-day tour includes strong drinks, lunch, and a stopover at one of the island's 365 beaches. Tours also go to Barbuda and snorkeling at Cades Reef, starting at $100. *268/480–1225* *www.tropicalad.com* *From $100.*

Wadadli Cats

SAILING | Looking for a party on a boat with some snorkeling and sightseeing on the side? Hop aboard the 66-foot Wadadli Cats vessel to eat, drink, and be merry as you circumnavigate the island, snorkel on fish-packed Cades Reef, or cruise along the coast of uninhabited Bird Island on the spacious *Spirit of Antigua.* *268/462–4792* *www.wadadlicats.com* *From $95.*

WINDSURFING AND KITEBOARDING

Most major hotels offer windsurfing equipment. The best areas are Nonsuch Bay and the east coast (notably Half Moon and Willoughby bays), which is slightly less protected and has a challenging juxtaposition of sudden calms and gusts.

Kitesurf Antigua

WINDSURFING | Kitesurf Antigua's laid-back team of certified trainers ply their trade against the backdrop of Jabberwock Beach's famous trade winds. Packages suited for beginners to advanced are available, but will set you back a pretty penny (from $340 and

$750); hourly sessions start at $100 and custom packages are available.

TIP→ Booking two weeks in advance is recommended.

✉ *Jabberwock Beach* ☎ *268/720–5483* 🌐 *www.kitesurfantigua.com* 🎫 *$340, 4-hr private beginner's course.*

ZIPLINING

Antigua Rainforest Canopy Tours

ZIP LINING | Zip above the canopies of Antigua's rain forest at Antigua Rainforest Canopy Tours, a one-of-a-kind experience where young, energetic "rangers" ensure a safe and raucous time 200 to 300 feet above the ground. There's even a café for post-ride relaxation. Tours kick off on the hour between 9 am and 1 pm, but during the off-season be sure to call for their pared-down schedule. ✉ *Fig Tree Dr., Wallings* ☎ *268/562–6363* 🌐 *www.antiguarainforest.com* 🎫 *$59.*

Barbuda

In 2017, Hurricane Irma brought island-wide devastation to Barbuda, a flat, 62-square-mile (161-square-km) coral atoll—with 17 miles (27 km) of gleaming white-sand beaches (sand is the island's main export)—that is 26 miles (42 km) north of Antigua. Recovery has been slow, and most of the hotels and guesthouses have closed. The five-star boutique Barbuda Belle hotel remains, as do hopes of impending luxury developments (including the controversial Paradise Found Resort co-owned by actor Robert De Niro), redevelopment of old resorts, and the post-hurricane recovery of Barbuda on a whole. De Niro has delivered on one project with the opening of **Nobu Barbuda** on Princess Diana Beach. The legendary Japanese fusion restaurant is banking on bringing some star power to the sister isle.

Interested in Montserrat?

Trips to Antigua are often paired with an excursion to Montserrat, as it's only a 20-minute plane ride or 90-minute ferry ride (though the ferry wasn't running as of this writing). If you're interested in learning more about this tiny island southwest of Antigua, check out Fodors.com for more information.

Travelers to the tiny coral atoll will find nesting terns, turtles, and frigate birds that outnumber residents at least 10 to 1. Goats, guinea fowl, deer, and wild boar roam the roads, all fair game for local kitchens. Princess Diana Beach (aka Pink Beach) lures beachcombers, caves and sinkholes filled with rain forest or underground pools (containing rare, even unique crustacean species) attract spelunkers, and reefs and roughly 200 offshore wrecks draw divers and snorkelers. The **Frigate Bird Sanctuary,** a wide mangrove-filled lagoon, is home to an estimated 400 species of birds, including frigate birds with 8-foot wingspans, and Barbuda's sole historic ruin is an 18th-century tower. Most of Barbuda's residents live in Codrington, the island's main town.

GETTING HERE

Barbuda is reachable by boat via the *Barbuda Express* and the Island Express. The trip takes about 90 minutes and both ferries depart from St. John's Harbour at the bottom of High Street by the Heritage Quay Ferry Dock. Call or visit the websites for schedules.

CONTACTS Barbuda Express. ✉ *High St., St. John's* ☎ *268/764–2291, 268/764–8643, 268/560–7989* 🌐 *www.barbudaexpress.com.*

Sights

Frigate Bird Sanctuary

WILDLIFE REFUGE | Barbuda's unique ecosystem and well-preserved landscape make it the idyllic location for a bevy of fauna and flora. Codrington Lagoon is home to the sanctuary and (historically) around 5,000 frigate birds, however, the population is still recovering from 2017's Hurricane Irma. Tours are readily available to view these black beauties, as well as 180 other species of birds. During the breeding season, male Man O' War (birds, not jellyfish) inflate their red throat sacs and show off their impressive 8-foot wingspan. ✉ *Codrington Lagoon.*

Martello Tower

HISTORIC SIGHT | Barbuda's sole historic ruin is the 18th-century, cylindrical, 56-foot-tall tower, which was probably a lighthouse built by the Spaniards before English occupation. ✉ *off Rte. 1.*

Beaches

★ Princess Diana Beach

BEACH | You can sometimes walk miles of this classic strand without encountering another footprint. That has changed, just a little, now that Robert's De Niro's Nobu Barbuda restaurant has arrived on this pink shore. The beach has a champagne hue, with sand soft as silk; crushed coral often imparts a rosy glint in the sun, hence its unofficial name—Pink Beach. The water can be rough with a strong undertow in spots, though it's mainly protected by the reefs that make the island a diving mecca. Hire a taxi to take you here, since none of the roads are well-marked. **Amenities:** none. **Best for:** snorkeling; solitude; walking. ✣ *1 mile (2 km) from ferry and airstrip along unmarked roads.*

Hotels

Barbuda Belle

$$$$ | **RESORT** | This restorative retreat hidden away on the northern side of Barbuda inspires relaxation and rejuvenation purely through its idyllic natural environs without trading sustainability for luxury. **Pros:** utter solitude; green without trading luxury; friendly attentive staff. **Cons:** scant nightlife and activities; few guests to mingle with; isolated. $ *Rooms from: $890* ✉ *Cedar Tree Point* ☎ *268/783–4779* 🌐 *www.barbudabelle.com* *8 rooms* 🍽 *Free Breakfast.*

Chapter 5

ARUBA

Updated by
Susan Campbell

Sights	Restaurants	Hotels	Shopping	Nightlife
★★★★★	★★★★☆	★★★☆☆	★★★☆☆	★★☆☆☆

WELCOME TO ARUBA

TOP REASONS TO GO

★ **The Beaches:** Powder-soft beaches and turquoise waters or wild waves crashing rocky cliffs.

★ **The Nightlife:** An after-dark vibe for everyone and dance-till-you-drop spots, plus party buses like the Kukoo Kunuku, which rolls the revelry right into the streets, make this island really move after sunset.

★ **The Restaurants:** More than 400 restaurants with fare from around the world and local snack hideaways offer foodies much to discover.

★ **The Casinos:** Aruba's modern casinos will please both casual and serious gamblers.

★ **The Welcome:** A friendly multilingual population devoted to tourism guarantees smiles everywhere you go. "Bon bini" means "Welcome," and you'll always feel as if you are.

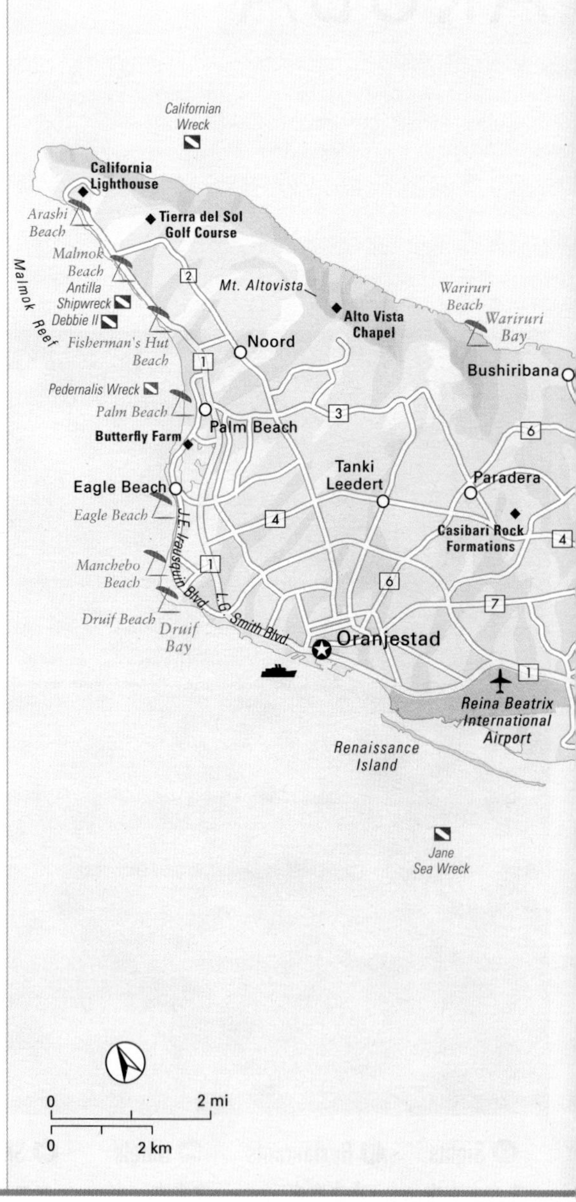

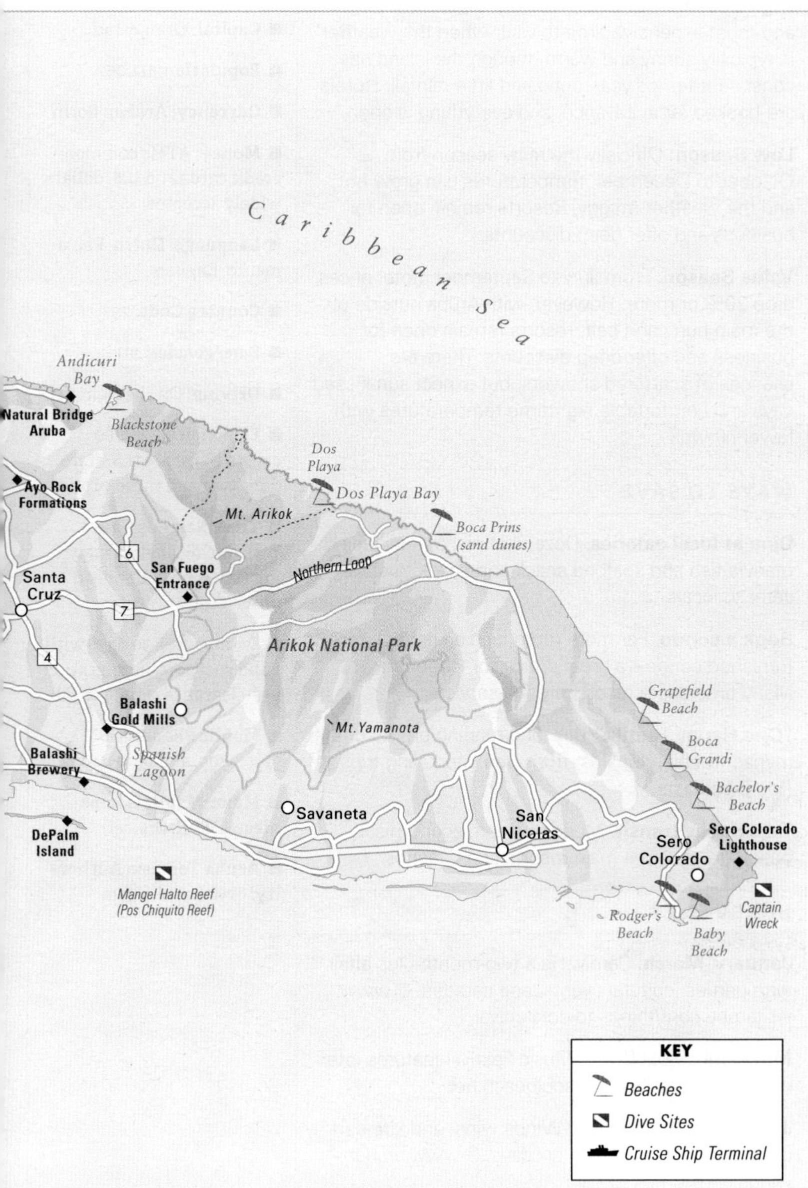
Caribbean Sea
Andicuri Bay
Natural Bridge Aruba
Blackstone Beach
Ayo Rock Formations
Dos Playa
Dos Playa Bay
Mt. Arikok
Boca Prins (sand dunes)
6
Santa Cruz
San Fuego Entrance
Northern Loop
7
4
Arikok National Park
Grapefield Beach
Balashi Gold Mills
Mt. Yamanota
Boca Grandi
Balashi Brewery
Spanish Lagoon
Bachelor's Beach
Savaneta
San Nicolas
Sero Colorado Lighthouse
Sero Colorado
DePalm Island
Mangel Halto Reef (Pos Chiquito Reef)
Rodger's Beach
Baby Beach
Captain Wreck
KEY
Beaches
Dive Sites
Cruise Ship Terminal

ISLAND SNAPSHOT

WHEN TO GO

High Season: December to May is the most popular and most expensive time to visit, when the weather is typically sunny and warm, though the island has consistent temps year-round and little rainfall. Hotels are booked far in advance, and everything is open.

Low Season: Officially the rainy season from October to December, temperatures can grow hot and the weather muggy. Resorts remain open for business and offer deep discounts.

Value Season: From July to September, hotel prices drop 20% or more. However, with Aruba outside of the main hurricane belt, resorts remain open for business and offer deep discounts. There are chances of scattered showers, but expect sun-kissed days and comfortable nighttime temperatures with fewer crowds.

WAYS TO SAVE

Dine at local eateries. Dozens of places—including many a fish and seafood shack and snack trucks—cater to locals.

Book a condo. For more room (and a kitchen), rent a furnished condo—a great option for longer stays. Many time-share resorts are full-service.

"One Happy Family." This long-running promo offers myriad freebies for kids, from free snorkeling trips to free breakfasts.

Take public transit. Modern, clean, economical buses travel to the main resorts and beaches.

BIG EVENTS

January–March: Carnival is a two-month-plus affair with parties, cultural events, and parades. 🌐 www.visitaruba.com/things-to-do/carnival

May: Aruba Soul Beach Music Festival features international artists. 🌐 www.soulbeach.net

June–July: The Aruba Hi-Winds wind- and kite-surf competitions unfold over six days. 🌐 www.arubahi-winds.com

ARUBA AT A GLANCE

- **Capital:** Oranjestad
- **Population:** 112,062
- **Currency:** Aruban florin
- **Money:** ATMs common; credit cards and U.S. dollars widely accepted
- **Language:** Dutch, Papiamento, English
- **Country Code:** 297
- **Emergencies:** 911
- **Driving:** On the right
- **Electricity:** 127v/60 cycles; plugs are U.S. standard two-and three-prong
- **Time:** Same as New York during daylight saving time; one hour ahead otherwise
- **Documents:** 30 days with valid passport; immigration pre-clearance return to U.S.
- **Mobile Phones:** GSM (900, 1800, and 1900 bands)
- **Major Mobile Companies:** SETAR, Digicel
- **Aruba Tourism Authority:** www.aruba.com

Aruba not only has beautiful beaches and world-class resorts, but also near-perfect weather: It's outside the hurricane belt, receives just 20 inches of rainfall per year, and has constant cooling trade winds. On the south coast, the action is nonstop both day and night; the rugged north coast boasts a desolate beauty that calls to those who seek solitude in nature.

Cruise ships gleam in Oranjestad Harbour, and thousands of eager tourists spill out into downtown Oranjestad. The mile-long stretch of L. G. Smith Boulevard (aka "The Strip") is lined with cafés, designer stores, restaurants, and many entertainment and dining/nightlife forums and casinos. The countryside is dotted with colorful *cunucu* (country-style houses) and stretches out into a cacti-studded rocky desert landscape that becomes Arikok National Park—a protected preserve covering 20% of the island's landmass.

As with Bonaire and Curaçao, the island was originally populated by the Caquetio, an Amerindian people related to the Arawak. After the Spanish conquered the island in 1499, Aruba was basically left alone, since it held little in the way of agricultural or mineral wealth. The Dutch took charge of the island in 1636, and things remained relatively quiet until gold was discovered in the 1800s.

Like the trademark *watapana* (divi-divi) trees that have been forced to bow to odd angles by the constant trade winds, Aruba has always adjusted to changes in the economic climate. Mining dominated the economy until the early part of the 20th century, when the mines became unprofitable. Shortly thereafter, Aruba became home to a major oil-refining operation, which was the economic mainstay until the early 1990s, when its contribution to the local economy was eclipsed by tourism. Today, after being so resolutely dedicated to attracting visitors for so many years, Aruba's national culture and tourism industry are inextricably intertwined.

There is good reason why Aruba has more repeat visitors than any other island in the Caribbean—it offers something for everyone: a pleasant climate, excellent facilities, nightlife, nature, and warm and friendly locals. The hospitality industry here is of the highest order. The U.S. dollar is accepted everywhere, and English is spoken universally.

MAJOR REGIONS

The pastel-colored houses of Dutch settlers still grace the waterfront in the capital city of **Oranjestad**. The area surrounding **Manchebo, Druif, and Eagle Beaches** is where you'll find wide beaches and the so-called low-rise hotels. High-rise hotels and casinos line **Palm Beach** in the district of **Noord**. The **Western Tip**, further north, is home to the California Lighthouse and Arashi Beach. The wild **Arikok National Park** occupies much of the island's east coast. On the west coast, the steady breezes attract windsurfers to the shallow, richly colored waters; here you'll find the towns of **Savaneta and San Nicolas.**

Planning

Getting Here and Around

Aruba's wildly sculpted landscape is replete with rocky deserts, cactus clusters, secluded coves, blue vistas, and brilliant beaches. To see the island's wild, untamed beauty, you can rent a car, take a sightseeing tour by bus, van, jeep, UTV, horseback, and even motorcycle. Or hire a cab or private tour driver, there many options from basic vans to luxury VIP vehicles. The main highways are well paved, but on the windward side (the north- and east-facing side) some roads are still a mixture of compacted dirt and stones. A four-wheel-drive vehicle is recommended to really explore the outback.

AIR

Many airlines fly nonstop to Aruba's modern **Reina Beatrix International Airport** (AUA) from several cities in North America; connections will usually be at a U.S. airport.

There are nonstop flights from Atlanta (Delta), Boston (American, JetBlue, American), Charlotte (American), Chicago (United), Fort Lauderdale (Spirit), Houston (United), Miami (American), Newark (United), New York–JFK (American, Delta, JetBlue), Philadelphia (American), and Washington, D.C.–Dulles (United). Southwest Airlines flies to Aruba from Baltimore, Orlando, and Houston as well.

AIRLINE CONTACTS American Airlines. ☎ *297/582–2700 on Aruba, 800/433–7300* 🌐 *www.aa.com.* **Delta Airlines.** ☎ *800/221–1212* 🌐 *www.delta.com.* **JetBlue.** ☎ *297/588–5388* 🌐 *www.jetblue.com.* **Southwest Airlines.** ☎ *800/435–9792* 🌐 *www.southwest.com.* **Spirit Airlines.** ☎ *801/401–2222* 🌐 *www.spiritair.com.* **Sunwing Airlines.** ✉ *Toronto* ☎ *877/786–9464* 🌐 *www.sunwing.ca.* **United Airlines.** ☎ *800/864–8331* 🌐 *www.united.com.* **Westjet.** ✉ *Toronto* ☎ *888/937–8538* 🌐 *www.westjet.com.*

BUS

Public transportation with Arubus is excellent; it's a great way to explore the different resorts and beaches along the main tourist areas or get groceries to bring back to your hotel. A modern, air-conditioned fleet of clean, well-scheduled buses travels from the Downtown Oranjestad terminal and stops at every major resort all the way to the end of Palm Beach and then all the way to Malmok and Arashi Beach. Fare is less than $5. Schedules are online.

CONTACTS Arubus. ✉ *Oranjestad* 🌐 *www.arubus.com.*

CAR

To explore the countryside and try different beaches, you should rent a car. Try to make reservations before arriving, and rent a four-wheel drive if you plan to explore the island's natural sights. For just getting to and around town, taxis are preferable, and you can use tour companies to arrange your activities.

To rent a car, a deposit of $500 (or a signed credit-card slip) is often required. Rates vary but can be between $47 and $75 a day (local agencies generally have lower rates).

International traffic signs and Dutch-style traffic signals (with an extra light for a turning lane) can be misleading if you're not used to them; use extreme caution, especially at intersections, until you grasp the rules of the road. Speed limits are rarely posted but are usually 50 mph (80 kph) in the countryside. Major highways have been recently upgraded but navigating the multitude of roundabouts can be a challenge for non locals. Gas prices average about $1 per liter (about $6 per gallon), which is reasonable by Caribbean standards, but this changes often.

CONTACTS Amigo. ✉ *Across from Arrival Terminal Airport and in Oranjestad, Schotlandstraat 56* ☎ *297/583–8833* 🌐 *www.amigocar.com.* **Aruparking.** ✉ *Wilhelminastraat 13, Oranjestad* ☎ *297/520-2323* 🌐 *www.aruparking.com.* **Avis.** ✉ *Reina Beatrix Airport* ☎ *297/582–5496 in Aruba, 800/532–1527* 🌐 *www.avis.ca/en/locations/ab/eagle-beach.* **Budget.** ✉ *Reina Beatrix Airport* ☎ *297/582–8600, 800/472–3325 in Aruba* 🌐 *www.budgetaruba.com.* **Dollar.** ✉ *Reina Beatrix Airport, Oranjestad* ☎ *297/583–0101* 🌐 *www.dollar.com.* **Hertz.** ✉ *Sabana Blanco 35, near airport, Oranjestad* ☎ *297/582–1845* 🌐 *rentacarinaruba.com.* **Thrifty.** ✉ *Reina Beatrix Airport* ☎ *297/583–4902* 🌐 *www.thriftycarrentalaruba.com.* **Tropic Car Rental.** ✉ *Reina Beatrix Airport* ☎ *297/583–7336* 🌐 *www.tropiccarrent-aruba.com.*

TAXI

There's a dispatch office at the airport; you can also flag down taxis on the street (look for license plates with a "TX" tag). Alternatively, ask at the front desk of any resort to call you a cab. Rates are fixed (i.e., there are no meters; the rates are set by the government and displayed on a chart), though you and the driver should agree on the fare before your ride begins. Add $2 to the fare after midnight and $3 on Sundays and holidays. An hour-long island tour should cost about $45 with up to four people, but agree on a fare before heading out. You can view taxi zone rates at 🌐 www.aruba.com/us/news/aruba-taxi-rates-2018—2022

CONTACT Arubas Transfer Tour & Taxi C.A.. ✉ *Reina Beatrix Airport* ☎ *297/582–2116, 297/582–2010* 🌐 *www.airportaruba.com/taxi-transportation.*

Beaches

Virtually every popular Aruba beach has resorts attached, but because nearly all beaches are public, there is never a problem with access. However, lounges, showers, and shade palapas are reserved for hotel guests.

The major beaches, which back up to the hotels along the southwestern strip, are often crowded but you can usually keep walking to find a secluded spot. Make sure you're well protected from the sun. Burning happens fast; you feel the intensity of the rays less because of the cool trade winds. Luckily, there are many covered bars and refreshment stands at every hotel and many piers with shade and bars as well. On the island's northeastern side, stronger winds make the waters too choppy for swimming and the current is unforgiving, but the vistas are great, and the terrain is wonderful for exploring. You'll often find expert kitesurfers, bodyboarders, and windsurfers enjoying the wild surf.

Health and Safety

Dengue, chikungunya, and zika have been reported throughout the Caribbean. We recommend that you protect yourself from these mosquito-borne illnesses by keeping your skin covered and/or wearing mosquito repellent. The mosquitoes that transmit these viruses are as active by day as they are at night.

For updated health and safety measures and requirements, visit www.aruba.com/us/health-happiness-code

Hotels

Hotels on the island are categorized as low-rise or high-rise and are grouped in two distinct areas along L. G. Smith and J. E. Irausquin boulevards north of Oranjestad. The low-rise properties are closer to the capital, the high-rises in a swath a little farther north. Hotel rates, with the exception of those at a few all-inclusives, generally do not include meals or even breakfast. The larger resorts are destinations unto themselves, with shopping, entertainment, and casinos. Since most hotel beaches are equally fabulous, it's the resort, rather than its location, that is a bigger factor in how you enjoy your vacation.

Boutique Resorts: You'll find a few small resorts that offer more personal service, though not always the same level of luxury as the larger places. But smaller resorts are better suited to the natural sense of Aruban hospitality you'll find all over the island.

Large Resorts: These all-encompassing vacation destinations offer myriad dining options, casinos, shops, water-sports centers, health clubs, and car-rental desks. Many large resorts are also adding all-inclusive options or are already all-inclusive now.

Time-shares: Large time-share properties offer visitors everything needed to prepare their own meals (except for food) and have a bit more living space than in a typical resort hotel room; some also have in-room laundry equipment.

Aruba also has Airbnb.

Hotel reviews have been shortened. For full information, visit Fodors.com.

What It Costs in U.S. Dollars

$	$$	$$$	$$$$
RESTAURANTS			
under $12	$12–$20	$21–$30	over $30
HOTELS			
under $275	$275–$375	$376–$475	over $475

Nightlife

Unlike many islands, Aruba's nightlife isn't confined to the touristy folkloric shows at hotels. Arubans like to party and there are lots of entertainment sectors where you'll find locals and visitors gathering in droves. The Palm Beach strip offers scads of venues and Downtown Oranjestad has really upped its party scene in the past few years.

Aruban casinos offer something for both high and low rollers; some have nightly entertainment in their lounges. Serious gamblers may want to look for the largest or the most active casinos, but many simply visit the casino closest to or in their hotel.

Restaurants

Be sure to seek out spots where you can try Aruban specialties such as *pan bati* (a mildly sweet bread that resembles a pancake) and *keshi yena* (a baked concoction of Gouda or Edam cheese, spices, and meat or seafood in a rich brown sauce). Most restaurants are more international in style. Reservations are essential for dinner in high season. The larger restaurants don't typically close any day of the week, but if they do, Monday is usually the day of choice.

What to Wear. Cover-ups, shorts, and flip-flops should be reserved for casual beach bars. Formal dress is rarely required, but it is appreciated by the locals as a sign of respect in their fancier spots, and they often dress to the nines themselves for an evening out. There's usually a warm breeze when dining outside so a sweater isn't needed, but if there's a lot of foliage around, bring insect repellent. You'll often need a light sweater or wrap when dining indoors as Arubans can really overdo it with the air-conditioning.

Shopping

The only real duty-free shopping is in the departure area of the airport. (Passengers bound for the United States should be sure to shop before proceeding through U.S. customs in Aruba.) Downtown stores do have very low sales tax though and some excellent bargains on high-end luxury items like gold, silver, and jewelry. Major credit cards are welcome everywhere, as are U.S. dollars. Aruba's souvenir and crafts stores are full of Dutch porcelains and figurines, as befits the island's heritage. Dutch cheese is a good buy, as are hand-embroidered linens and any products made from the native aloe vera plant. Local arts and crafts run toward wood carvings and earthenware emblazoned with "Aruba: One Happy Island" and the like, but there are many shops with unique Aruban items like designer wear and artwork. Don't try to bargain unless you are at a flea market: Arubans consider it rude to haggle. Best bet to get some authentic locally made souvenirs is often at the weekly outdoor arts and craft markets at the resorts or at the open air malls.

Tours

★ Aruba Downtown Trolley

GUIDED TOURS | If you'd rather ride instead of walk around the charming little capital city, then get on board one of Aruba's free eco-trolleys that loop in and around the town all day. There are four in all, leaving the port around every half hour, and you can hop on and hop off when you please to tour the main streets, back streets, and attractions. You don't need to be a cruise passenger. All trolleys have a shaded level, and two are double-decker, offering the best views and photo ops from the top. They are a great way to acquaint yourself with the lay of the land, and they move very slowly, so you can anticipate your next stop well in advance. There are nine stops in all in a figure-eight loop. Trolleys run daily until 5 pm beginning at the cruise terminal, sometimes later if there are a lot of cruise ships in port. ✉ *Aruba Cruise Terminal, Oranjestad* 🌐 *www.aruba.com/us/explore/downtown-trolley* 🎟 *Free.*

★ Aruba Walking Tours

WALKING TOURS | **FAMILY** | The daytime walking tour highlights all the cool attractions and historical sights found in Oranjestad, Aruba's charming, colorful capital; but they also have an evening tour revolving around a progressive dinner (Monday and Thursday beginning at 5:45 pm) called Fusions of the World Food Tour that stops at downtown restaurants for tapas and drinks. Day tours begin at 9 am on Monday, Wednesday, and Friday, and cover the entire downtown at a leisurely pace in about 2½ hours. Free Wi-Fi, bottled water, entrance to museums, a local food tasting, and more are all included in the price, and the guides are well-informed, fun to be with, and speak many languages in addition to English. Reservations are recommended. ✉ *Oranjestad* ✥ *Meet at Cosecha Aruba* ☎ *297/699-0995* 🌐 *www.arubawalkingtours.com* 🎟 *Day tour $39. Night tour $79.*

★ Kukoo Kunuku Party & Foodie Tours

SPECIAL-INTEREST TOURS | Best known for their wild and crazy barhopping tours aboard brightly painted red party buses, this outfit also dials it down a notch for their foodie tours like the Dinner & Nightlife Tour that includes a sunset champagne toast or the Wine On Down The Road tour, which features an

Cunucu Houses

Pastel houses surrounded by cacti fences adorn Aruba's flat, rugged *cunucu* ("country" in Papiamento). The features of these traditional houses were developed in response to the environment. Early settlers discovered that slanting roofs allowed the heat to rise, and small windows helped to keep in the cool air. Among the earliest building materials was caliche, a durable calcium carbonate substance found in the island's southeastern hills. Many houses were also built using interlocking coral rocks that didn't require mortar (this technique is no longer used, thanks to concrete). Contemporary design combines some of the basic principles of the earlier homes with touches of modernization: windows, though still narrow, have been elongated; roofs are constructed of bright tiles; pretty patios have been added; and doorways and balconies present an ornamental face to the world beyond. Cacti fences are still used to keep meandering wild goats out of gardens. Some of these houses have been beautifully restored and turned into restaurants or art venues.

onboard sommelier and stops at some of Aruba's finest dining spots for wine and tapas. They also offer a Happy Hour tour. ✉ *Oranjestad* ☎ *297/586–2010* 🌐 *www.kukookunuku.com* 🎫 *From $50.*

Visitor Information

CONTACT Aruba Tourism Authority. ✉ *L. G. Smith Blvd. 8, Oranjestad* ☎ *800/862–7822 in the U.S./international, 297/582–3777 in Aruba* 🌐 *www.aruba.com.*

Weddings

You must be over 18 and submit the appropriate documents one month in advance. Couples are required to submit birth certificates with raised seals, through the mail or in person, to Aruba's Office of the Civil Registry. They also need an *apostille*—a document proving they are free to marry—from their country of residence. Most major hotels have wedding coordinators, and there are many excellent independent wedding planners and photographers on the island.

Oranjestad

Aruba's capital is best explored by the free eco-trolley—hop on/hop off affair—and on foot. Major improvements downtown have opened up the back roads of Main Street and have created many resting spaces and pedestrian-only lanes. New small malls, restaurants, attractions, and museums can be explored there. New outdoor nightlife venues surrounding Plaza Daniel Leo have also brought the historic area to life after dark. Also worth exploring is the linear park and boardwalk and the new outdoor art spaces along the waterfront. Bikeshare stations are dotted along it, and the paved path along the sea is popular for joggers, too.

GETTING HERE AND AROUND

Traffic can get dense near Oranjestad and L. G. Smith Boulevard, especially at rush hour, though a new highway from the airport to the main resorts avoids downtown and eases the traffic gridlock; outside of the city, traffic is sparse. Route 1A travels southbound along the western coast, and 1B is simply northbound along the same road. Most rental cars have a GPS, which makes finding your way easier.

Sights

Aruba Aloe Museum & Factory

FACTORY | Aruba has the ideal conditions to grow the aloe vera plant. It's an important export, and there are aloe stores all over the island. The museum and factory tour reveal the process of extracting the serum to make many products used for beauty, health, and healing. Guided or self-guided tours are available in English, Dutch, Spanish, and Papiamento; the last tour on Sunday is at 12:30 pm. There's a store to purchase their products on-site, and they are also available online. **TIP→ Look for their reef-safe sunscreen; it's available island-wide.** ✉ *Pitastraat 115, Oranjestad* ☎ *800/952–7822* 🌐 *www.arubaaloe.com* 🎫 *Free.*

★ **De Palm Private Island**

WATER SPORTS | **FAMILY** | This delightful private island experience encompasses all ages, even toddlers, but it has numerous adult-oriented enclaves with premium seating, beach cabanas, and big luxe cabana rentals with VIP service and private bars. They also have their own flock of flamingos in a protected area. All-inclusive packages include all food and drink, access to a colorful kids' waterpark, new body-drop waterslides, banana boat rides, snorkel equipment, guided snorkel tours, and fun activities like salsa lessons. Additional add-ons include their signature Seatrek experience, an underwater air helmet walk, as well as SNUBA deep dive snorkeling, and spa services. The water taxi to the island is free, and hotel pick-up and drop-off option is available. **TIP→ The reef is home to huge neon blue ever-smiling parrotfish, so bring an underwater camera!** ✉ *De Palm Island Ferry Terminal, De Palm Island Way Z/N, Oranjestad* ☎ *297/522–4400* 🌐 *www.depalmisland.com* 🎫 *From $115 including bus; from $109 no bus.*

Fort Zoutman

MILITARY SIGHT | One of the island's oldest edifices, Aruba's historic fort was built in 1796 and played an important role in skirmishes between British and Curaçao troops in 1803. The Willem III Tower, named for the Dutch monarch of that time, was added in 1868 to serve as a lighthouse. Over time the fort has been a government office building, a police station, a prison, and a small museum (now closed). ✉ *Zoutmanstraat, Oranjestad.*

Renaissance Marketplace

STORE/MALL | **FAMILY** | The complex beside the Oranjestad marina and the park around it is the place where you're most likely to happen upon some great free entertainment, including pop-up festivals. Although there's live entertainment every night at the far end in the common area bandstand, many of the bars and cafés also have their own music. You'll also find a casino, movie theaters, and arty little shops that are open late. Occasionally, there's a big gala music festival, and every Friday night there's a local artisans market from 7–10 pm. Even if there's no planned additional activity, it's a wonderful spot to explore in the evening to experience a truly enchanting tropical night full of colorful lights and sounds along the water. ✉ *Marina, L.G. Smith Blvd. 82, Oranjestad* ☎ *297/583–6000* 🌐 *www.shoprenaissancearuba.com* 🎫 *Free.*

CASINOS

Wind Creek Crystal Casino

CASINO | Part of the Renaissance Aruba Wind Creek Resort, this glittering casino evokes Monaco's grand establishments. They have lots of modern slots, and table games like Blackjack, Roulette, Baccarat, and different types of poker. This casino is popular among cruise-ship passengers, who stroll over from the port to watch and play in tournaments and bet on sporting events. There's live entertainment Tuesday through Sunday,

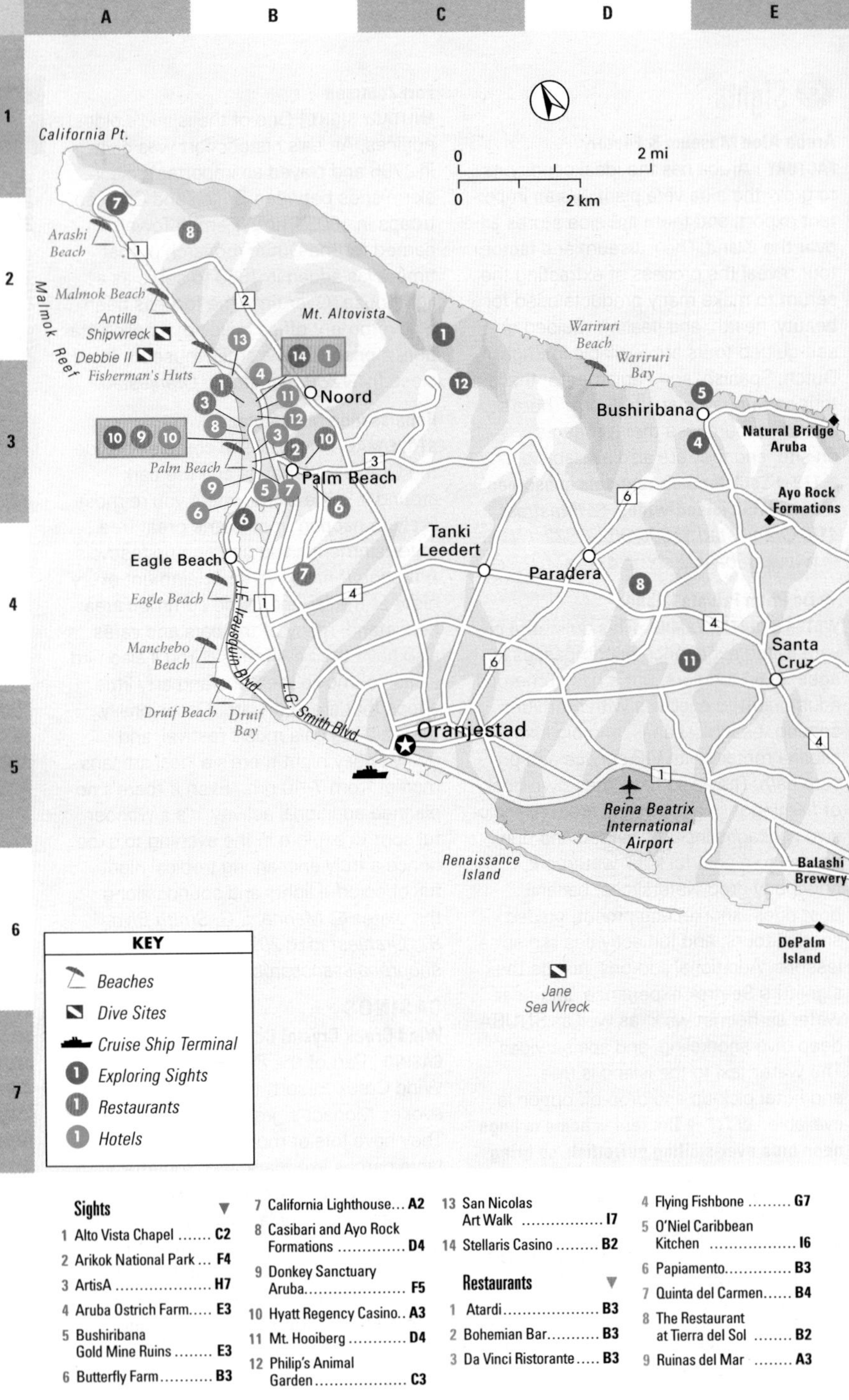

A
B
C
D
E
1
2
3
4
5
6
7
0
2 mi
0
2 km
California Pt.
Arashi Beach
Malmok Beach
Malmok Reef
Antilla Shipwreck
Debbie II
Fisherman's Huts
Mt. Altovista
Noord
Palm Beach
Eagle Beach
Manchebo Beach
Druif Beach
Druif Bay
J.E. Irausquin Blvd.
L.G. Smith Blvd.
Wariruri Beach
Wariruri Bay
Bushiribana
Natural Bridge Aruba
Ayo Rock Formations
Tanki Leedert
Paradera
Santa Cruz
Oranjestad
Reina Beatrix International Airport
Renaissance Island
Balashi Brewery
DePalm Island
Jane Sea Wreck
KEY
Beaches
Dive Sites
Cruise Ship Terminal
Exploring Sights
Restaurants
Hotels
Sights
1 Alto Vista Chapel C2
2 Arikok National Park ... F4
3 ArtisA H7
4 Aruba Ostrich Farm..... E3
5 Bushiribana Gold Mine Ruins E3
6 Butterfly Farm........... B3
7 California Lighthouse... A2
8 Casibari and Ayo Rock Formations D4
9 Donkey Sanctuary Aruba..................... F5
10 Hyatt Regency Casino.. A3
11 Mt. Hooiberg D4
12 Philip's Animal Garden.................... C3
13 San Nicolas Art Walk I7
14 Stellaris Casino B2
Restaurants
1 Atardi........................ B3
2 Bohemian Bar........... B3
3 Da Vinci Ristorante..... B3
4 Flying Fishbone G7
5 O'Niel Caribbean Kitchen I6
6 Papiamento.............. B3
7 Quinta del Carmen...... B4
8 The Restaurant at Tierra del Sol B2
9 Ruinas del Mar A3

F G H I J

Palm Beach, Noord, and Western Tip (California Dunes)

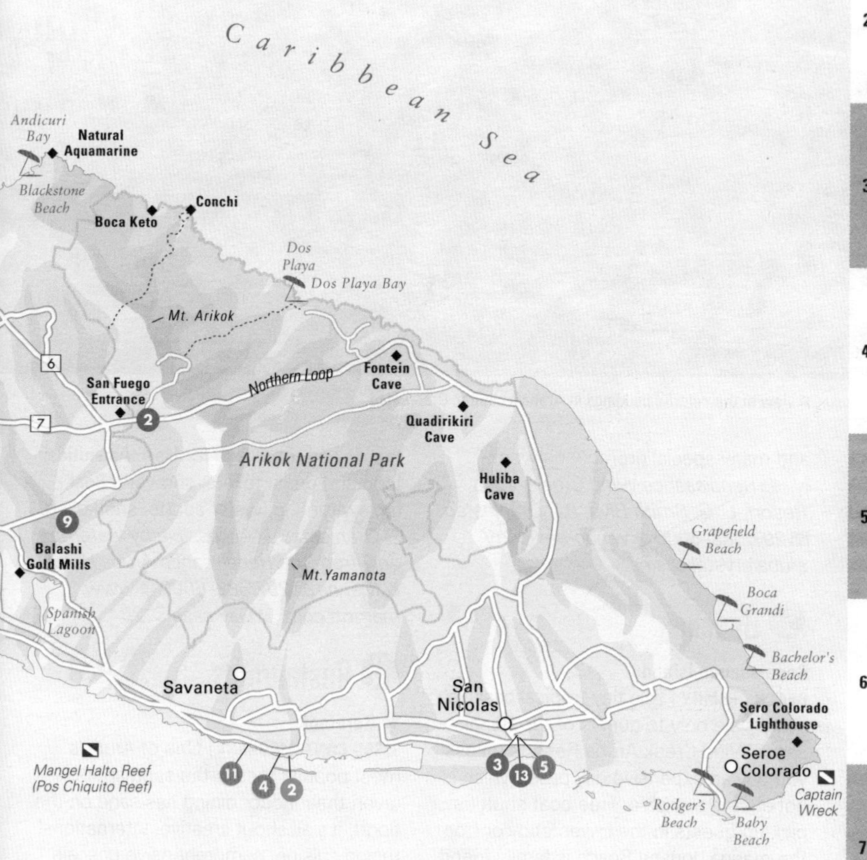

10 2 Fools And A Bull Gourmet Studio B3

11 Zeerovers................ G7

Hotels

1 Aruba Marriott Resort & Stellaris Casino....... B2

2 Aruba Ocean Villas..... G7

3 Barceló Aruba B3

4 Boardwalk Boutique Hotel Aruba B3

5 Courtyard Aruba Resort B3

6 Divi Aruba Phoenix Beach Resort........... B3

7 Hilton Aruba Caribbean Resort and Casino...... B3

8 Holiday Inn Resort-Aruba..................... B3

9 Hotel Riu Palace Aruba..................... B3

10 Hyatt Regency Aruba Resort Spa And Casino A3

11 Marriott's Aruba Ocean Club.............. B3

12 Radisson Blu Aruba B3

13 Ritz-Carlton, Aruba B2

A view of the colorful buildings in Aruba's capital, Oranjestad.

and many special promotions weekly. ✉ *Renaissance Wind Creek Aruba Resort, L. G. Smith Blvd. 82, Oranjestad* ☎ *297/583–6000* 🌐 *windcreek.com/aruba/crystal-casino.*

 Beaches

Renaissance Island

BEACH | FAMILY | This tiny tropical oasis is accessible only to guests of the Renaissance Wind Creek Aruba Resorts unless you buy an expensive day pass, which is not always available. Free boat shuttles pick up guests in the lower lobby or from the marina. Iguana Beach is family-friendly, while Flamingo Beach is limited to adults and hosts half a dozen resident flamingos. (Children may visit the flamingos for a photo op daily from 10 to 11 am but must have an adult present.) The waters are clear and full of colorful fish; swimming is in a protected area, and there's a full-service restaurant, a beach bar, and waiter service on the beach. Rent a cabana for more luxuries. If you book a spa treatment, you can spend the rest of the day on the island for free. **Amenities:** food and drink; toilets; showers. **Best for:** swimming; water sports; snorkeling. ✉ *Oranjestad* ✣ *Accessible by water taxi only from the Renaissance Aruba Hotel & Marina* ☎ *297/583–6000* 🌐 *www.marriott.com* 🎟 *Day pass $125.*

 Restaurants

★ Barefoot

$$$$ | CONTEMPORARY | One of Aruba's most popular toes-in-the-sand spots (even their indoor dining has sand on the floor), it's all about creative, international fusion cuisine, comprehensive upscale wine choices, and superb signature cocktails in an ultimate barefoot-luxury setting. The sunset views are always spectacular. **Known for:** great service and consistent quality fare; romantic toes-in-the-sand dining; creative fusions like lobster cappuccino bisque. 💲 *Average main: $35* ✉ *L. G. Smith Blvd. 1, Oranjestad* ✣ *on Surfside Beach* ☎ *297/588–9824* 🌐 *www.barefootaruba.com* ⏲ *No lunch.*

★ Cuba's Cookin'

$$$ | **CUBAN** | This red-hot landmark establishment in the heart of Renaissance Marketplace specializes in traditional Havana specialties and is the only spot on Aruba where you can enjoy an authentic Cuban sandwich for lunch. Their boast of having the best mojitos in town is a fair claim, and there's even a surprisingly good selection of gluten-free, vegetarian, and vegan fare on offer. **Known for:** hot live music and alfresco dancing seven nights a week; an impressive selection of original Cuban art; melt-in-your-mouth ropa vieja (Cuba's national skirt steak dish). *Average main: $28 ✉ Renaissance Marketplace, L. G. Smith Blvd. 82, Oranjestad ☎ 297/588–0627 🌐 www.cubascookin.com.*

★ The Dutch Pancakehouse

$$ | **DUTCH** | **FAMILY** | Dutch pancakes are unlike North American-style flapjacks since they can be both savory and sweet, offering opportunities for breakfast, lunch, and dinner, and this legendary spot in the Renaissance Marketplace is considered the absolute best place to try them. More like thin crepes, they can be covered in (or stuffed with) a multitude of ingredients, which might include meats, vegetables, and cheeses. **Known for:** consistently good-quality fare and friendly service; over 50 styles of sweet and savory Dutch-style pancakes; a surprising selection of excellent schnitzels. *Average main: $15 ✉ Renaissance Marketplace, L. G. Smith Blvd. 9, Oranjestad ☎ 297/583–7180 🌐 www.thedutchpancakehouse.com.*

El Gaucho Argentine Grill

$$$$ | **STEAKHOUSE** | **FAMILY** | Aruba's original go-to mecca for carnivores since 1977, El Gaucho is famous for meat served in mammoth portions. Though to be honest, it's not all about meat; seafood platters are something to consider as well. **Known for:** strolling musicians who create a fun and boisterous atmosphere; 16-ounce Gaucho steak; largest shish kebab on the island. *Average main: $40 ✉ Wilhelminastraat 80, Oranjestad ☎ 297/582–3677 🌐 www.elgaucho-aruba.com ⏲ Closed Mon.*

L. G. Smith's Steak & Chop House

$$$$ | **STEAKHOUSE** | A study in teak, cream, and black, this fine steak house offers some of the best beef on the island. Subdued lighting and cascading water create an elegant atmosphere, and the view over the harbor makes for an exceptional dining experience. **Known for:** 4-course beef and wine tasting menu from around the world; USDA-certified Angus beef; excellent wine list and stellar signature cocktails. *Average main: $50 ✉ Renaissance Aruba Marina Resort & Casino, L. G. Smith Blvd. 82, Oranjestad ☎ 297/523–6195 🌐 www.lgsmiths.com.*

★ Patio 15

$$ | **INTERNATIONAL** | A very exciting new addition to Downtown's backstreets, Patio 15 is set in a stunningly restored two-story heritage house with a humongous patio and outdoor event space. The food, drink, and entertainment venue has become an instant hit with both locals and visitors alike who enjoy creative craft cocktails along with intriguing tapas-sized mains like watermelon feta pizza or fried spam sliders with plantains and Madam Jeanette's hot sauce. **Known for:** neon light shows and exciting special events; weekend gathering spot with live or DJ music and large dance space; trendy tapas and oversized signature sangria by the glass. *Average main: AWG12 ✉ Weststraat 15, Oranjestad ☎ 297/588–1515 🌐 www.patio15aruba.com ⏲ Closed Mon. No lunch.*

★ Pinchos Grill & Bar

$$$$ | **ECLECTIC** | One of the most romantic settings on the island is highlighted by enchanting twinkling lights strung over the water on a pier. *Pinchos* ("skewers" in Spanish) offers a fairly extensive menu of both meat and seafood skewers in addition to more creative main courses.

Known for: excellent personalized service; romantic pier-side atmosphere; signature sangria. *Average main: $35* ✉ *L. G. Smith Blvd. 7, Oranjestad* ☎ *297/583–2666* 🌐 *www.pinchosaruba.com* ⏲ *No lunch.*

Reflexions Beach Aruba

$$$ | **INTERNATIONAL** | A sophisticated upscale spot on the water minutes from Downtown Oranjestad does its best to replicate the South Beach Miami scene with luxe cabanas and daybeds, and beach and pool service around a chic seaside bar. It can be lively at nights when there are musical events, but dinner is mostly laid-back in high style with a good selection of quality cuts of meats and fresh fish and seafood, plus a good selection of fine Champagnes. **Known for:** stunning sunsets and chic vibe; superb creative tapas and signature cocktails; great pool right on the beach. *Average main: $25* ✉ *L. G. Smith Blvd. 1A, Surfside Beach, Oranjestad* ☎ *297/582–0153* 🌐 *www.reflexionsaruba.com.*

★ **Taste My Aruba**

$$$$ | **CARIBBEAN** | Foodies in the know are beating a path to this new down-to-earth eatery housed in a beautifully restored 100-year-old heritage house to enjoy locally sourced fare, especially fresh fish and local lobster. The menu changes daily depending on the bounty, but rarely disappoints, with the driving force of repeat business due to the larger-than-life personality of owner Nathaly de Mey and the culinary skills of her talented nephew Chef Derwin Tromp. **Known for:** outstanding personal service and welcoming atmosphere; expertly prepared giant local lobster and fresh fish straight from the boat; authentic local experience and locally sourced fare. *Average main: $32* ✉ *Wilhelminastraat 57, Oranjestad* ☎ *297/588–1600* 🌐 *www.tastemyaruba.com* ⏲ *Closed Sun.*

Wilhelmina

$$$$ | **INTERNATIONAL** | Choose from a simple and elegant indoor dining area or a tropical outdoor garden oasis to sample from the creative international menu that includes choices of quality meats, homemade pastas, and fresh fish and seafood, all with suggested wine pairings from the well-regarded cellar. The menu also includes an impressive offering of avant-garde vegetarian dishes. **Known for:** exotic mains like Surinamese sea bass and Indonesian-style roast pork; creative takes on conventional dishes like a signature salad with rock lobster and scallops; excellent selection of fine wines. *Average main: $40* ✉ *Wilhelmenastraat 74, Oranjestad* ☎ *297/583–0445* 🌐 *www.wilhelminaaruba.com* ⏲ *Closed Mon. No lunch.*

Hotels

Renaissance Wind Creek Aruba Resort - Marina Hotel

$$$ | **HOTEL** | The adults-only hotel of the Wind Creek Renaissance's twin resorts offers guests a chic, waterfront urban oasis overlooking the Downtown marina with fine dining, a cool club infinity bar, and glitzy casino on site. **Pros:** beautiful private island beach with deluxe cabana rentals; in the heart of the best Downtown shopping and dining; good choice of in-hotel nightlife and restaurants and in-house casino. **Cons:** marina pool is tiny; rooms are small and have no balconies; nights can be noisy. *Rooms from: $464* ✉ *L. G. Smith Blvd. 82, Oranjestad* ☎ *297/583–6000, 800/421–8188* 🌐 *www.marriott.com/hotels/travel/auabr-renaissance-wind-creek-aruba-resort/* *296 rooms* *No Meals.*

Renaissance Wind Creek Aruba Resort - Ocean Suites

$$$$ | **RESORT** | **FAMILY** | Spacious suites attract families and groups to this downtown resort that offers its own man-made beach on the sea and free water taxi to its lovely private island minutes

away. **Pros:** steps from Downtown; private island access; spacious water circuit and stellar sea views. **Cons:** limited water sports; limited dining on-site; can be noisy at night as it's right Downtown. *Rooms from: $543 ✉ Renaissance Beach, L. G. Smith Blvd., Oranjestad ☎ 297/583–6000 🌐 www.marriott.com/hotels/hotel-rooms/auabr-renaissance-wind-creek-aruba-resort/ 259 rooms No Meals.*

Nightlife

★ Alfie's in Aruba

PUBS | Owned by a lively expat Canadian couple, this popular watering hole in the back streets of Downtown has been attracting people from all over the world to sample their hospitality and over 50 types of craft beer. Live music Thursday, Friday, and Saturday nights also attracts the crowds, and their pub food is to die for. Think seven-cheese Mac 'n' Cheese nights, crispy Nashville-style hot fried chicken with a kick, melt-in-your-mouth ribs, and mega-burgers so big you can hardly fit them in your mouth. But they haven't forgotten their homeland; authentic Quebec-style poutine and even vegan poutine are also both available there. Look for the big Canadian flag out front. *✉ Dominicanessenstraat 10, Oranjestad ☎ 297/569–5815 🌐 www.alfiesinaruba.com Closed Mon. No lunch.*

★ Bochincha Container Yard

GATHERING PLACES | An impressive new multistory entertainment complex built from old shipping containers sits right behind the Local Market. The carnival-style atmosphere and high-octane music provided by either live bands or DJs create the backdrop for an eclectic choice of international fare via food truck-style kiosks; there are also multiple bars, a wine shop, a cigar store, and a tattoo and barber shack. *✉ Rockefellerstraat 8 ✥ Behind the Local Market ☎ 297/732-0808 🌐 bochincha.com No lunch..* Alfresco Food and Drink Emporium

★ The West Deck Island Grill Beach Bar

BARS | You'll find this casual wooden deck beach bar along Linear Park facing Governor's Bay. Enjoy one of their special upside-down margaritas or incredible craft cocktails while you catch a stellar sunset and watch the cruise ships go by. After dark, the music takes it up a notch—sometimes live—and the atmosphere is fun and friendly. It's as popular with locals as it is with visitors. Great Caribbean tapas and grilled specialties are also on tap. *✉ Governor's Bay Oranjestad, L. G. Smith Blvd., Oranjestad ✥ Linear Park (next to the Queen Wilhelmina Park, adjacent to the Renaissance Suites) ☎ 297/587–2667 🌐 www.thewestdeck.com.*

Performing Arts

UNOCA

ARTS CENTERS | Although UNOCA is Aruba's national gallery, it's much more, acting as an anchor to host cultural and performance events, which are often held there. *✉ Stadionweg 21, Oranjestad ☎ 297/583–5681 🌐 unoca.aw.*

Shopping

DUTY FREE

Dufry

JEWELRY & WATCHES | No doubt you've seen this brand of duty-free stores in airports all over the world, but don't expect to see the same duty-free items like tobacco and spirits in this one, and the prices are not completely duty-free. What you will find are great bargains on cosmetics, perfumes, jewelry, and accessories from such brands as Carolina Herrera, Calvin Klein, Armani, Montblanc, and more. And there's always some kind of major sale on something of good quality going on there. There's another outlet in Royal Plaza Mall. *✉ G. F. Betico Croes 29, Oranjestad ☎ 297/582-2790 🌐 www.dufry.com Closed Sun.*

Little Switzerland

With stores in the Royal Plaza Mall and one in Paseo Herencia—these well-known outlets specialize in designer jewelry and upscale timepieces by big-name designers like TAG Heuer, David Yurman, Breitling, Roberto Coin, Chopard, Pandora, Tiffany & Co., Cartier, Movado, Omega, and John Hardy. They also own the TAG Heuer Boutique in the Renaissance Mall. ✉ *Royal Plaza Mall, L. G. Smith Blvd. 94, Oranjestad* ☎ *248/809-5560 ext. 40230* 🌐 *www.littleswitzerland.com.*

Penha

SOUVENIRS | Originating in Curaçao in 1865, Penha has branched out throughout the Caribbean and has eight stores on Aruba. The largest is right next to the Renaissance Marina Hotel. The store is particularly known for good prices on high-end perfumes, cosmetics, skincare products, eyewear, and fashions. You'll find brand names such as MAC, Lancôme, Estée Lauder, Clinique, Chanel, Dior, Montblanc, and Victoria's Secret to name just a few. There's another location in Palm Beach Plaza. ✉ *Caya G. F. Betico Croes 11/13, Oranjestad* ☎ *297/582–4160* 🌐 *www.jlpenha.com.*

ELECTRONICS

★ Boolchand's Digital World

ELECTRONICS | Family-run Boolchand's began in the 1930s and has since become a major retail institution throughout the Caribbean; they opened their first shop on Aruba in 1974. Today, their Downtown "Digital World" is your one-stop shop to get a high-tech fix at seriously low prices. Top-quality merchandise by major brands includes the latest in computers, cameras, and tech accessories, as well as quality watches and Pandora jewelry. ✉ *Havenstraat 25, Oranjestad* ☎ *297/583-0147* 🌐 *boolchand.com* 🕓 *Closed Sun.*

JEWELRY

★ Kay's Fine Jewelry

JEWELRY & WATCHES | Kay's family-run emporium is a well-known Aruba fixture on the fine-jewelry scene, and their designs have won awards. Exquisite settings featuring white and colored diamonds are their claim to fame, and they also have a fine selection of precious gems and brand-name timepieces. ✉ *Westraat 8, Oranjestad* ☎ *297/588–9978* 🌐 *www.kaysfinejewelry.com* 🕓 *Closed Sun.*

SHOPPING AREAS AND MALLS

★ Renaissance Mall

MALL | Upscale, name-brand fashion and luxury brands of perfume, cosmetics, and leather goods are what you'll find in the array of 60 stores spanning two floors in this mall located within and underneath the Renaissance Marina Resort. You'll also find specialty items like cigars and designer shoes plus high-end gold, silver, diamonds, and quality jewelry at low- or no-duty prices. Cafés and high-end dining, plus a casino and spa, round out the offerings. Shopping until 7 pm daily. ✉ *Renaissance Marina Resort, L. G. Smith Blvd. 82, Oranjestad* ☎ *297/523–6065* 🌐 *www.shoprenaissancearuba.com* 🕓 *Closed Sun.*

★ Renaissance Marketplace

MALL | **FAMILY** | The Renaissance Marketplace is more of a dining and gathering spot along the marina than a market, though they do hold a weekly local artisans' outdoor market every Friday night. It's a lively spot with a few souvenir shops and specialty stores, and locals frequent the modern cinema. But mostly it's full of eclectic dining emporiums and trendy cafés, and they have live music some weekends in their alfresco square. The Wind Creek Seaport casino is also here, and it's steps from the cruise terminal on the marina. ✉ *L. G. Smith Blvd. 82, Oranjestad* ☎ *297/583–6000* 🌐 *www.shoprenaissancearuba.com.*

Royal Plaza Mall

MALL | It's impossible to miss this gorgeous colonial-style, cotton-candy-colored building with the big gold dome gracing the front street along the marina. It's one of the most photographed in Oranjestad. Three levels of shops (both indoors and out) make up this artsy arcade full of small boutiques, cigar shops, designer clothing outlets, gift and jewelry stores, and souvenir kiosks. Great dining and bars are found within as well. ✉ *L. G. Smith Blvd. 94, Oranjestad* ☎ *297/588–0351* ⏲ *Closed Sun.*

SOUVENIRS

★ The Mask—Mopa Mopa Art

CRAFTS | These shops specialize in original masks and crafty items called mopa mopa art. Originating with the Quillacingas people of Ecuador and Colombia, the art is made from the bud of the mopa mopa tree, boiled down into a resin, colored with dyes, and applied to carved mahogany and other woods like cedar. Masks, jewelry boxes, coasters, whimsical animal figurines, and more make wonderfully unique gifts and souvenirs. The masks are also believed to ward off evil spirits. Find them in Paseo Herencia Mall, Royal Plaza Mall, Renaissance Marketplace and Alhambra Mall. You can also buy works online. ✉ *Renaissance Marketplace, L. G. Smith Blvd. 9, Oranjestad* ☎ *297/588–7297* 🌐 *www.mopamopaaruba.com* ⏲ *Closed Sun.*

Manchebo, Druif, and Eagle Beaches

Unlike the action-packed party that is Palm Beach, Eagle Beach is where you go to unwind, relax, recharge, and rejuvenate in pristine postcard-perfect settings. Once you experience it, you'll see why it's consistently rated among the top three beaches on the planet, and you'll want to go back.

Nearby, an entire village of Divi Resorts encompasses Druif Beach, while Manchebo Beach is the broadest stretch of sand on the island. It's become the spot for health and wellness retreats, and it's known to have the most eco-friendly hotel in the entire Caribbean. Unlike pond-calm Palm Beach, this region has the largest waves and sometimes very strong currents at certain areas like Punto Brabo, so take care when swimming.

Sights

★ Gloria-Movies, Entertainment, Dining & Play

PERFORMANCE VENUE | This exciting new entertainment complex was named after "Teatro Gloria," Aruba's very first movie theatre built back in 1930s, and now offers the most modern cinematic experience in the entire Caribbean. There are ten cinemas in all including IMAX and VIP Theatres and there's also a children's bouncy playground, a Starbucks, a huge food court, and stand-alone upscale dining options like P.F. Chang's and VIP Grill & Lounge. There are also special musical events with live bands or DJs. ✉ *Caya Dr. J.E.M. Arends 8, Eagle Beach* ☎ *297/523-6841* 🌐 *www.facebook.com/TheMoviesIMAXGloria.*

CASINOS

★ Alhambra Casino

CASINO | Part of the Divi family and accessible by complimentary golf cart shuttle from all of the company's resorts except for Divi Phoenix, this is a lively popular casino with a big selection of modern slots, blackjack, craps, poker, roulette, and more. Be sure to join their Player's Club—it's free and offers free slot credits, and you earn points with your card as well. The Cove restaurant serves light meals and drinks; you'll also receive free drinks on the floor when you're playing the games. Special theme nights and promotions run all week. ✉ *L. G. Smith Blvd. 47, Druif* ☎ *297/588–9000* 🌐 *www.casinoalhambra.com.*

Beaches

Druif Beach

BEACH | FAMILY | Fine white sand and calm water make this beach a great choice for sunbathing and swimming. It's the base beach for the Divi collections of all-inclusive resorts, so amenities are reserved for guests. But the locals like it, too, and often camp out here as well with their own chairs and coolers. The beach is accessible by bus, rental car, or taxi, and it's within easy walking distance to many stores for food and drinks. The new Beach Bar—owned by Divi Resorts, but not part of the all-inclusive plan—is open to the public and a superb spot to have lunch or early dinner, swim, and watch the sunset. **Amenities:** food and drink; toilets; parking (free); water sports. **Best for:** swimming; partiers. ✉ *J. E. Irausquin Blvd., Druif* ✣ *Near the Divi resorts, south of Punta Brabo.*

★ **Eagle Beach**

BEACH | Aruba's most photographed stretch of sand, Eagle Beach is not only a favorite with visitors and locals, but also of sea turtles. More sea turtles nest here than anywhere else on the island. This pristine stretch of blinding white sand and aqua surf is ranked among the best beaches in the world. Many of the hotels have facilities on or near the beach, and refreshments are never far away, but chairs and shade palapas are reserved for resort guests only. **Amenities:** food and drink; toilets; parking (no fee). **Best for:** sunsets; swimming; water sports. ✉ *J. E. Irausquin Blvd., north of Manchebo Beach, Druif.*

★ **Manchebo Beach** (*Punta Brabo*)

BEACH | Impressively wide, the white-sand shoreline in front of the Manchebo Beach Resort (technically where Eagle Beach begins) is the backdrop for the numerous yoga classes now taking place under the giant palapa since the resort began offering health and wellness retreats. This sandy stretch is the broadest on the island; in fact you can even get a workout just getting to the water! Waves can be rough and wild at certain times of the year, though, so mind the current and undertow when swimming. **Amenities:** food and drink; toilets. **Best for:** swimming; sunsets; walking.

TIP→ The Bucuti beach bar is reserved exclusively for guests of the Bucuti & Tara Beach Resort. ✉ *J. E. Irausquin Blvd., Druif* ✣ *At Manchebo Beach Resort.*

Restaurants

★ **The Chophouse**

$$$$ | INTERNATIONAL | Low-key elegance and soft piano music set the stage for this indoor enclave where meaty chops and steaks are king and classic silver service is still in vogue. The big surprise here though is the chic Omakase Japanese Sushi Bar that shares the space, and their selection of vegetarian, vegan, and gluten-free options is impressive. **Known for:** elegant old-world atmosphere combined with a modern sushi bar; predominately organic and sustainable fare; premium steaks and chops. Ⓢ *Average main: $45* ✉ *Manchebo Resort, J. E. Irausquin Blvd. 55, Druif* ☎ *297/522–3444* 🌐 *www.thechophousearuba.com* ⏲ *Sushi bar closed Sun. and Mon.*

★ **Elements**

$$$$ | CONTEMPORARY | A stellar spot with stunning seaside views, this strictly adults-only dining spot embodies the resort's global reputation for promoting green living and a healthy lifestyle. The wide-ranging menu of internationally flavored dishes includes many organic, vegan, vegetarian, and gluten-free choices that use locally sourced ingredients whenever possible. **Known for:** romantic surfside atmosphere with private prix-fixe palapa dining; authentic Aruban/Caribbean buffet; à la carte Sunday brunch. Ⓢ *Average main: $40* ✉ *Bucuti and Tara Beach Resort, L. G. Smith Blvd. 55B, Eagle Beach* ☎ *297/583–1100* 🌐 *www.elementsaruba.com* ☞ *Credit cards only, no cash.*

★ **Fusion Restaurant Wine & Piano Bar**

$$$$ | **INTERNATIONAL** | What began as a classy laid-back wine and tapas piano bar, has evolved into more of a New York-style steak lounge meets BBQ joint thanks to the popularity of the Big Green Egg BBQ trend. Once they began using this ceramic outdoor charcoal grill to offer up big hearty juicy cowboy steaks and grilled lobster tails, the aroma and smoke drew an entirely different kind of hungry and hearty crowd. **Known for:** excellent selection of wine; creative "pair and share" tapas selections; Fusion special for two (22-oz. Cowboy steak, two lobster tails, and wine). *Average main: $45 ✉ Alhambra Mall, J. E. Irausquin Blvd., Druif ☎ 297/280–9994 🌐 www.fusion-aruba.com ⏲ Closed Sun. No lunch.*

★ **Infini**

$$$$ | **FUSION** | Created in spring 2021 by legendary local chef Urvin Croes, one of the island's most innovative purveyors of ultramodern cuisine, this new chef's table experience offers infinite possibilities for the palate. The "Chef's Impression" experience is an extensive 12-course themed menu based on world flavors and seasonal, locally sourced (whenever possible) ingredients; the plating of each dish is often so exquisite you might hesitate to dig in, but don't. **Known for:** vegan or dietary restriction menus available with advance notice; chef and team personally talk you through the dining journey; wine and craft cocktail pairings for an extra charge. *Average main: $149 ✉ J.E. Irausquin Blvd. 266, Eagle Beach ☎ 297/280–8869, 297/699–3982 🌐 infiniaruba.com ⏲ Closed Mon. No lunch.*

★ **Passions on the Beach**

$$$$ | **INTERNATIONAL** | With stunning seafront sunsets and tiki torch lighting to enhance the mood, the signature restaurant of Amsterdam Manor is a favorite romantic escape for those seeking toes-in-the-sand dining. Popular with families (children under three eat free) and small groups as well, beachfront breakfasts and lunches are served, and though "reef cuisine" is their specialty, there's also meat, vegetarian, and vegan offerings. **Known for:** romantic toes-in-the-sand dining; signature seafood platters; three-course prix-fixe menu. *Average main: $45 ✉ Amsterdam Manor Beach Resort, J. E. Irausquin Blvd. 252, Eagle Beach ☎ 800/527–1118 🌐 www.passions-restaurant-aruba.com ☞ Credit or debit cards only, no cash.*

★ **Screaming Eagle Restaurant Aruba**

$$$$ | **INTERNATIONAL** | Not content to perch on its laurels being one of the most consistently highest-rated dining spots on the island, Screaming Eagle decided to reinvent itself recently to offer a more enticing alfresco experience by creating a toes-in-the sand dining experience without actually being at the beach! Thankfully, they haven't messed with the food, still serving up killer international fare indoors and out, with an extensive wine list to match. **Known for:** excellent wine cellar and multiple Wine Spectator awards; rotating menu of seasonal specialties and three-course surprise menu also available in vegetarian and vegan versions; excellent and eclectic selection of fresh fish and seafood dishes as well as top quality meats. *Average main: $45 ✉ J. E. Irausquin Blvd. 228, Eagle Beach ☎ 297/566–3050 🌐 screamingeaglearuba.com ⏲ No lunch.*

★ **Twist of Flavors**

$$$ | **INTERNATIONAL** | **FAMILY** | There's always something cool happening at this bright and lively indoor-outdoor spot on the corner of Alhambra Mall. The internationally kaleidoscopic menu includes everything from Dutch pancakes to Asian specialties to gourmet burgers to Caribbean seafood, pasta, and more … and surprisingly, they do it all very well. **Known for:** unexpected selection of international fare; specials nights like Friday's "Create your own burgers," Wednesday's

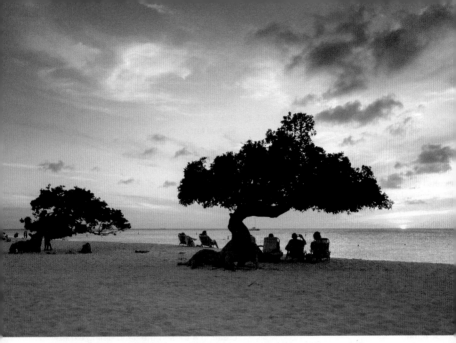

Eagle Beach is home to Aruba's iconic Fofoti tree and a great spot for sunsets and selfies.

grouper night, and Tuesday's all night early-bird special; excellent food in a fun, lively atmosphere. *Average main: $30* *Alhambra Mall, J. E. Irausquin Blvd. 47, Eagle Beach* *297/280–2518* *www.twistofflavorsaruba.weebly.com.*

★ Windows on Aruba

$$$$ | INTERNATIONAL | This stylish, modern restaurant overlooking Divi Golf Village is an elegant indoor affair offering high-end international fare for dinner a few nights a week. Their famous all-you-can-eat Royal Brunch (available weekends) includes endless mimosas, and gourmet surprises, dozens of enticing appetizers and sides, and lots of decadent desserts. **Known for:** beautiful panoramic views from floor-to-ceiling windows; upscale gourmet fare; cosmopolitan bar area and stellar service. *Average main: $55* *Divi Village Golf Resort, J. E. Irausquin Blvd. 41, Druif* *297/523–5017* *www.windowsonaruba.com* *Closed Mon. and Tues.*

Hotels

Amsterdam Manor Beach Resort

$$ | HOTEL | FAMILY | Now with the distinction of being Aruba's only pet-friendly AAA Three Diamond hotel, Amsterdam Manor was first built in 1989 as a no-frills escape to attract Dutch visitors, especially families, seeking great value just steps from famed Eagle Beach. **Pros:** bright, clean, and eco-friendly oasis; home to famous romantic restaurant Passions on the Beach; warm family-run atmosphere with superb staff and service. **Cons:** small pool; not right on the beach; WaveRunners at beach can be noisy. *Rooms from: $300* *Eagle Beach, J. E. Irausquin Blvd. 252, Eagle Beach* *297/527–1100, 800/969–2310* *www.amsterdammanor.com* *72 rooms* *No Meals* *Cashless resort.*

★ Bucuti & Tara Beach Resort

$$$$ | HOTEL | Having achieved the first carbon-neutral status in the Caribbean, and winning multiple prestigious global eco awards, this landmark adults-only luxury boutique hotel offers exquisite personal service in an extraordinary beach setting. **Pros:** eco-friendly barefoot luxury at its best; accessible management, with owners often on property; unique arrival experience with personal concierge and iPad check-in. **Cons:**; not all rooms have sea views; a little too quiet for some (no nighttime entertainment). *$ Rooms from: $585 ✉ L. G. Smith Blvd. 55B, ☎ 297/583–1100 🌐 www.bucuti.com ⇨ 104 rooms 🍽 Free Breakfast.*

★ Divi Aruba All-Inclusive
$$$$ | RESORT | The more upscale choice of Divi's sister all-inclusives, this resort is favored more by couples and honeymooners as the newer 60-room tower with its own pool and bar offers up some excellent sea views; there are four super-luxe two-bedroom oceanfront suites with whirlpool tubs. **Pros:** cosmopolitan lively vibe; on wonderful stretch of beach; eclectic choice of dining and entertainment. **Cons:** not all rooms have sea views; some older rooms are small by modern standards; reservations mandatory for the more upscale restaurants. *$ Rooms from: $640 ✉ L. G. Smith Blvd. 93, Druif ☎ 297/525–5200, 800/554–2008 🌐 www.diviaruba.com ⇨ 269 rooms 🍽 All-Inclusive ☞ 3- or 5-night minimum.*

Divi Dutch Village Resort
$$$ | RESORT | FAMILY | The non-beachfront complexes behind the Divi Aruba have spacious, freshly renovated suites that come with full kitchens. **Pros:** modern appliances and all cookware supplied; even though it's not beachfront, the beach is just steps away; supermarkets close by for easy food shopping. **Cons:** very quiet for those seeking action; no ocean views in rooms; not a beachfront property. *$ Rooms from: $384 ✉ J. E. Irausquin Blvd. 47, Oranjestad ☎ 297/583–5000 🌐 www.diviresorts.com ⇨ 123 rooms 🍽 All-Inclusive.*

Divi Village Golf & Beach Resort
$$$ | RESORT | FAMILY | All the rooms at this all-suites golf resort community across the street from Druif Beach include fully equipped kitchens, but an all-inclusive option is also available with access and shuttles to sister resorts Tamarijn, Divi Aruba, and Divi Dutch Village. **Pros:** lush and lovely grounds with freshwater lagoons and wildlife; excellent golf course; dedicated beach space with lounge chairs and shade palapas across the street. **Cons:** no ocean-view rooms; the resort is not beachfront; no suites have two beds, only one bed and a sleeper sofa. *$ Rooms from: $455 ✉ J. E. Irausquin Blvd. 93, Druif ☎ 297/583–5000 🌐 www.divivillage.com ⇨ 348 rooms 🍽 All-Inclusive ☞ 3-night minimum for all-inclusive.*

La Cabana Beach Resort & Casino
$$ | RESORT | FAMILY | A warm and friendly complex of mostly time-share units draws repeat visitors (primarily families) who enjoy the spacious accommodations equipped with everything you could possibly need for a home base away from home, including a fully equipped kitchen. **Pros:** laundry facilities on every floor; lively family-friendly atmosphere with large pool facilities; the only on-resort chapel on the island. **Cons:** limited number of shade palapas; you must cross the road to get to the beach; few rooms have sea views. *$ Rooms from: $300 ✉ J. E. Irausquin Blvd. 250, Eagle Beach ☎ 297/520–1100 🌐 www.lacabana.com ⇨ 449 rooms 🍽 No Meals.*

Manchebo Beach Resort & Spa
$$$ | RESORT | One of the original low-rise resorts built on Aruba has refreshed and reinvented itself over the past few years to become a dedicated health and wellness resort with daily complimentary seafront yoga, Pilates classes, and healthy and healing cuisine menus. **Pros:** great on-site restaurants and culinary events; all-inclusive meal plans available; on the island's broadest and most

pristine white-sand beach. **Cons:** not much in way of entertainment; rooms are on the small side; not all rooms have sea views. *Rooms from: $400* *J. E. Irausquin Blvd. 55, Manchebo Beach* *297/522–3444, 297/522–3444* *www.manchebo.com* *72 rooms* *Free Breakfast.*

★ Tamarijn Aruba All-Inclusive Beach Resort

$$$$ | **RESORT** | **FAMILY** | Having received a major multimillion-dollar refreshment in 2021, the interiors of this popular all-inclusive now almost rival the stellar sea scenes mere steps from each door and the rooms (all oceanfront) have been outfitted with new technology and modern amenities like Nespresso machines and Smart TVs; king rooms also have sofa beds. **Pros:** complimentary Sea Turtle's Kids Club; complimentary shuttle service between Divi resorts and the Alhambra Casino and Mall; children 12 and under stay and eat free. **Cons:** no room service; beach entrance to sea can be rocky (beach shoes recommended); main pool can become crowded. *Rooms from: $640* *J. E. Irausquin Blvd. 41, Punta Brabo* *297/594–7888, 800/554–2008* *www.tamarijnaruba.com* *236 rooms* *All-Inclusive* *3-night minimum.*

Shopping

★ The Shops at Alhambra Mall

SHOPPING CENTER | There's an eclectic array of shops and dining in alfresco Alhambra Mall with the casino as its focal point. Dotted with small retail stores and souvenir shops and a full-service market and deli, the mall also has multiple fast-food outlets as well as finer dining options like Fusion Wine & Piano Bar, The Brownstone Restaurant, and Twist of Flavors. There's often live music at night, and there's a small spa. Stores are open late, and the casino is open until the wee hours. *L. G. Smith Blvd. 47, Druif* *297/583–5000* *www.facebook.com/alhambrashops.*

★ Super Food Plaza

SHOPPING CENTER | This massive complex offers all kinds of extras; it's more like a small department store. Beyond a huge fresh produce section, fresh fish and seafood market, bakery, and deli section, there's also a café, a drugstore, and even a toy store on-site. It's truly a one-stop for all your needs. **TIP→ Even if you are only on island for a week, chances are good you will make more than one visit here, so first trip, stop by the customer service desk and ask for a Tourist Bonus Card to save on all kinds of products and take advantage of weekly specials.** They also deliver, and you can shop online and order curbside pick-up, too. *Bubali 141-A, Eagle Beach* *297/522–2000* *www.superfoodaruba.com.*

Palm Beach, Noord, and Western Tip (California Dunes)

The district of Noord is home to the bulk of high-rise hotels and casinos that line Palm Beach. The hotels and restaurants, ranging from haute cuisine to fast food, are densely packed into a few miles running along the beachfront, while the bulk of the nightlife takes place across the street from the hotels along J. E. Irausquin Boulevard. Also known as "The Strip", the boulevard begins with Cove Mall, a new two-story complex across from the Holiday Inn that's jam-packed with bars and restaurants including a new rooftop supper club. When other areas of Aruba are shutting down for the night, this area is guaranteed to still be buzzing with activity. Farther inland you'll find more local eateries and residential areas.

Palm Beach and Noord

Sights

Bushiribana Gold Mine Ruins

BEACH | You can view what is left of Aruba's onetime gold rush at the seaside ruins of a gold smelter; it's a great spot for photo ops. It's ironic that the Spanish left the island alone basically because they thought it was worthless; in fact, they dubbed it "isla inutil" (useless island) since they thought it had no gold or silver, but locals did find some long after the Spanish left. There is also a secret little natural pool nearby. ✉ *North Coast, Bushiribana* ✣ *Near the California Lighthouse.*

★ **Butterfly Farm**

FARM/RANCH | **FAMILY** | Hundreds of butterflies and moths from around the world flutter about this spectacular garden. Guided tours (included in the price of admission) provide an entertaining look into the life cycle of these insects, from egg to caterpillar to chrysalis to butterfly or moth. After your initial visit, you can return as often as you like for free during your vacation.

TIP→ Go early in the morning when the butterflies are most active; wear bright colors if you want them to land on you.

Early morning is also when you are most likely to see the caterpillars emerge from their cocoons and transform into butterflies or moths. Their little Nectar Café out front serves refreshing drinks and homemade popsicles. ✉ *J. E. Irausquin Blvd., across from Divi Phoenix Aruba Beach Resort, Palm Beach* ☎ *297/586–3656* 🌐 *www.thebutterflyfarm.com* 🎟 *$16 (good for return visits).*

★ **Philip's Animal Garden**

FARM/RANCH | **FAMILY** | This nonprofit exotic animal rescue and rehabilitation foundation is a wonderful, child-friendly attraction you'll find just off the beaten track up in Noord. Each guest is given a bag of treats for the animal residents, which include monkeys, peacocks, an emu, an ocelot, an alpaca, and many other types of creatures you're not likely to see elsewhere on Aruba. There's a large playground and ranch so little ones can run. It is also a stop on some tours. ✉ *Alto Vista 116, Noord* ☎ *297/593–5363* 🌐 *www.philipsanimalgarden.com* 🎟 *$10.*

CASINOS

Hyatt Regency Casino

CASINO | One of the island's smaller gaming spots, but just as glitzy, this recently enhanced casino offers 13 gaming tables, 148 slot machines, and 13 video poker machines. ✉ *Hyatt Regency Aruba Beach Resort & Casino, J. E. Irausquin Blvd. 85,* ☎ *297/586–1234* 🌐 *www.hyatt.com.*

★ **Stellaris Casino**

CASINO | This is one of the largest casinos on the island. There are 500 modern interactive slots as well as 26 tables with games like craps, roulette, poker, and blackjack. There's a state-of-the-art race and sports-betting operation. Don't forget to join the VIP Club program, where you can earn points, comps, and prizes. They offer free cocktails for gamers, and there are many special theme and entertainment nights. ✉ *Aruba Marriott Resort, L. G. Smith Blvd. 101, Palm Beach* ☎ *297/586–9000* 🌐 *www.stellariscasino.com.*

Beaches

Fisherman's Huts (*Hadicurari*)

BEACH | Beside the Ritz-Carlton, Fisherman's Huts is a windsurfer's, kiteboarder's, and now "wing-foiling" haven. Swimmers might have a hard time avoiding all the boards going by; as this is the nexus of where the lessons take place for these water sports, it's always awash in students and experts and board hobbyists. It's a gorgeous spot to just sit and watch the sails on the sea, and lately, it's become increasingly popular among paddleboarders and sea kayakers,

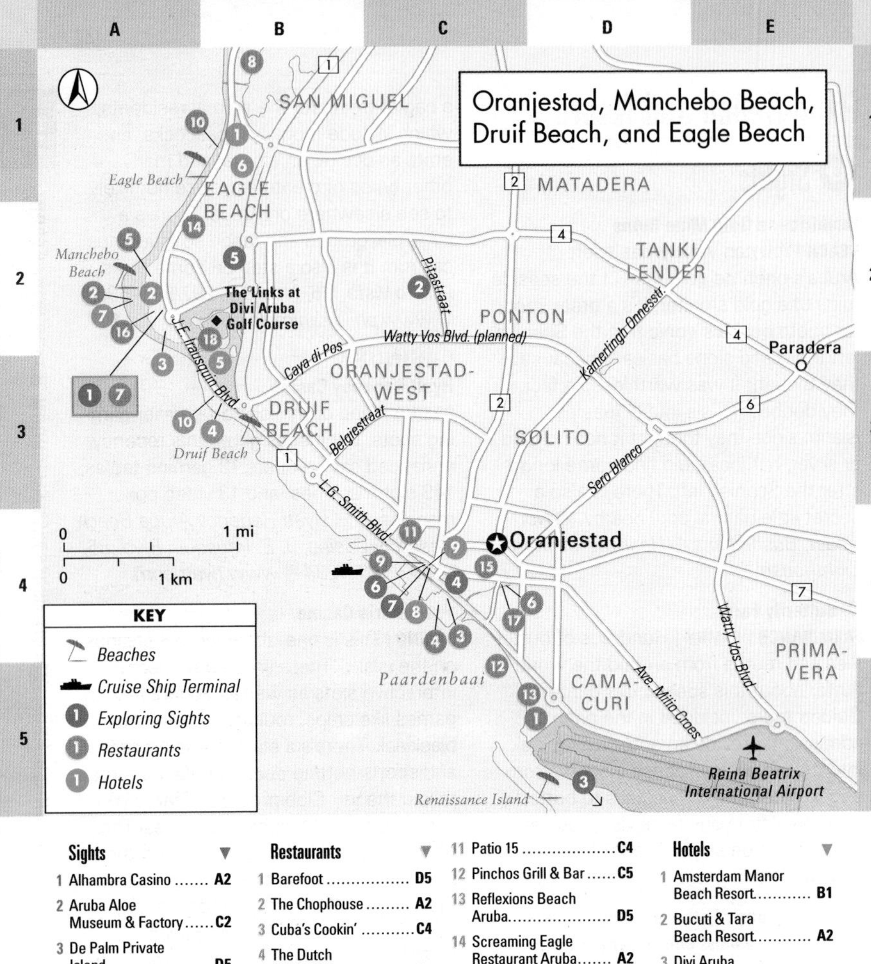

Sights

1 Alhambra Casino **A2**
2 Aruba Aloe Museum & Factory **C2**
3 De Palm Private Island..................... **D5**
4 Fort Zoutman **C4**
5 Gloria-Movies, Entertainment, Dining & Play............ **B2**
6 Renaissance Marketplace.............. **C4**
7 Wind Creek Crystal Casino............ **C4**

Restaurants

1 Barefoot **D5**
2 The Chophouse **A2**
3 Cuba's Cookin' **C4**
4 The Dutch Pancakehouse........... **C4**
5 Elements................. **A2**
6 El Gaucho Argentine Grill............ **C4**
7 Fusion Restaurant Wine & Piano Bar **A2**
8 Infini **B1**
9 L. G. Smith's Steak & Chop House............ **C4**
10 Passions on the Beach............ **B1**
11 Patio 15 .... **C4**
12 Pinchos Grill & Bar **C5**
13 Reflexions Beach Aruba..................... **D5**
14 Screaming Eagle Restaurant Aruba....... **A2**
15 Taste My Aruba **C4**
16 Twist of Flavors **A2**
17 Wilhelmina **C4**
18 Windows on Aruba..... **B2**

Hotels

1 Amsterdam Manor Beach Resort............ **B1**
2 Bucuti & Tara Beach Resort............ **A2**
3 Divi Aruba All-Inclusive **A2**
4 Divi Dutch Village Resort.................... **B3**
5 Divi Village Golf & Beach Resort **B3**
6 La Cabana Beach Resort & Casino......... **B1**
7 Manchebo Beach Resort & Spa **A2**
8 Renaissance Wind Creek Aruba Resort - Marina Hotel **C4**
9 Renaissance Wind Creek Aruba Resort - Ocean Suites............. **C4**
10 Tamarijn Aruba All-Inclusive Beach Resort........... **B3**

too. Only drinks and small snacks are available at the operator's shacks. There are no restrooms, but the Ritz lobby is nearby in a pinch. **Amenities:** food and drink; parking (free); water sports. **Best for:** windsurfing. ✉ *Palm Beach* ✣ *North of Aruba Marriott Resort.*

★ Palm Beach

BEACH | This is the island's most populated and popular beach running along the high-rise resorts, and it's crammed with every kind of water-sports activity and food-and-drink emporium imaginable. It's always crowded no matter the season, but it's a great place for people-watching, sunbathing, swimming, and partying; and there are always activities happening like paddleboarding, and even paddleboard yoga. The water is pond-calm; the sand, powder-fine. **Amenities:** food and drink; showers; toilets; water sports. **Best for:** partiers; swimming. ✉ *J. E. Irausquin Blvd. between Divi Phoenix Resort and Ritz-Carlton Aruba, Palm Beach.*

Restaurants

Atardi

$$$$ | **INTERNATIONAL** | This bopping beach bar by day turns into a toes-in-the-sand restaurant at night with tables in the sand, soft jazz music wafting through the air, and tiki torches lit to provide a lovely seaside dining oasis. The menu specializes in fresh fish and seafood, but the meat mains are also grilled to perfection. **Known for:** spectacular sunset viewing location; catch-of-the-day specialities like macadamia-nut-crusted grouper; romantic toes-in-the-sand dining. *Average main: $40* ✉ *Aruba Marriott Resort, L. G. Smith Blvd. 101, Noord* ☎ *297/520–6537* 🌐 *www.marriott.com.*

Bohemian

$$$$ | **INTERNATIONAL** | Secreted away near the Barcelo resort you'll find a hip, little laid-back tropical oasis of tiki-style huts and "bohemian" escapes with a focus on French and world cuisine, sometimes with a local Caribbean twist. It's well worth seeking out for the cool vibe and eclectic choice of fare ranging from raclette or ginger and honey duck to braised lamb or paella, with some creative vegetarian and vegan options thrown in. **Known for:** house-made foie gras and excellent charcuterie and cheese plates; early-bird three-course set menu.; fresh mussels flown in from Holland when available. *Average main: $40* ✉ *J. E. Irausquin Blvd. 83, Beside the Barcelo, Palm Beach* ☎ *297/280-8448* 🌐 *bohemianaruba.com/* ⏲ *No lunch.*

★ Da Vinci Ristorante

$$$$ | **ITALIAN** | **FAMILY** | Don't let the rustic decor fool you: this is not your average Italian resort eatery, though it's an inviting choice for large groups. Da Vinci pulls out all the stops to present a seriously upscale, authentic, and creative menu of Mediterranean favorites. **Known for:** family-friendly yet upscale atmosphere; creative Italian fare; excellent wine cellar. *Average main: $35* ✉ *Holiday Inn Resort Aruba, J. E. Irausquin Blvd. 230, Palm Beach* ☎ *297/586–3600* 🌐 *www.holidayarubaresort.com* ⏲ *Closed Sun.*

Papiamento

$$$$ | **ECLECTIC** | The Ellis family converted its 126-year-old manor into a bistro with an atmosphere that is elegant, intimate, and always romantic. You can feast in the small dining room, which is filled with antiques, or outdoors on the terrace by the pool. **Known for:** creative takes on traditional local dishes; fresh locally sourced ingredients, often from the owner's garden; one of the best places to try keshi yena, Aruba's national dish. *Average main: $35* ✉ *Washington 61, Noord* ☎ *297/586–4544* 🌐 *www.papiamentoaruba.com* ⏲ *Closed Sun. No lunch.*

★ Quinta del Carmen

$$$$ | **DUTCH** | Set in a beautifully restored 100-year-old mansion with a lovely outdoor courtyard, Quinta del Carmen's cuisine is best defined as modern Caribbean-Dutch. There are a few traditional Dutch favorites like cheese croquettes and mushrooms and cream, and the watermelon salad is sweet, salty, and perfectly refreshing, while the *sucade-lappen* (flank steak stewed in red wine and herbs) has a depth of flavor that comes from hours in the pot. **Known for:** gorgeous antique mansion setting full of avant-garde art; upscale Dutch comfort food; tapas garden for shareables. *Average main: $40* *Bubali 119, Noord* *297/587–7200* *www.quintadelcarmen.com.*

Ruinas del Mar

$$$$ | **CARIBBEAN** | This scenic spot is famous for its gorgeous circuit of waterfalls cascading around stone "ruins" that offers the ideal setting for romantic dinners and sunny breakfasts. Indoor dining affords a lagoon view while the outdoor terrace overlooks a koi pond. **Known for:** the resident black swans; romantic setting for date night; a comprehensive specialty coffee menu. *Average main: $45* *Hyatt Regency Aruba Beach Resort and Casino, J. E. Irausquin Blvd. 85, Palm Beach* *297/586–1234* *aruba.hyatt.com* *No lunch.*

2 Fools and a Bull Gourmet Studio

$$$$ | **INTERNATIONAL** | One of Aruba's very first forays into the chef's table experience, here you'll enjoy an intimate evening of culinary entertainment that plays like a fun dinner party with friends rather than something you pay for. At most, 17 guests are assembled around the U-shaped communal dinner table for a five-and-a-half course creative gourmet adventure. **Known for:** perfect wine pairings (optional); adults-only with reservations required far in advance; an intimate chef's table experience. *Average main: $130* *Palm Beach 17, Noord* *297/586–7177* *www.2foolsandabull.com* *Closed weekends.*

Hotels

Aruba Marriott Resort & Stellaris Casino

$$$$ | **RESORT** | **FAMILY** | This full-service resort offers both family-friendly amenities as well as an adults-only luxury floor that has its own pool and snazzy lounge on the ground floor. **Pros:** one of the island's best casinos; lots of water sports options right out front; adults-only oasis and adults-only floor. **Cons:** main pool can be noisy and crowded with kids; beachfront can become crowded in high season; not all rooms have sea views. *Rooms from: $599* *L. G. Smith Blvd. 101, Palm Beach* *297/586–9000, 800/223–6388* *www.marriott.com* *414 rooms* *No Meals.*

Barcelo Aruba

$$$$ | **RESORT** | **FAMILY** | This family-friendly all-inclusive offers something for everyone, with an extensive pool complex, great nightly entertainment, a dedicated kids' club, and an eclectic choice of à la carte dining. **Pros:** spacious rooms, many with good sea views; excellent location for Palm Beach water sports and shopping; Royal Club level has a dedicated dining room and lounge. **Cons:** beach in front can get very crowded; pool area can be very noisy with activities; difficult to get a shaded beach lounge if you don't go early. *Rooms from: $770* *J. E. Irausquin Blvd. 83, Palm Beach* *297/586–4500* *www.barcelo.com/en-ca/hotels/aruba/* *373 rooms* *All-Inclusive.*

★ **Boardwalk Boutique Hotel Aruba**

$$$ | **HOTEL** | What began as a tiny family-run enclave in a historic coconut plantation has since evolved into an enchanting boutique resort of Caribbean cottage-style "casitas" connected by a signature wooden boardwalk and surrounded in vibrant blooms and lush landscaped gardens. **Pros:** intimate resort with many secret oasis spots for ultimate privacy; stellar personal service and health and wellness focus; modern digital

amenities like key and concierge apps and 5G Wi-Fi. **Cons:** no on-site entertainment; not right on the beach; smokers must indulge outside of the property's security gates. *Rooms from: $450* ✉ *Bakval 20, Palm Beach* ☎ *297/586–6654* 🌐 *www.boardwalkaruba.com* *46 units* *No Meals.*

Courtyard Aruba Resort

$ | **HOTEL** | A bright, contemporary economical alternative to the high-rises on Palm Beach, this property is ideally suited for workcations or small group getaways with modern rooms outfitted with the latest technology, and an inviting pool area that includes a swim-up bar and a small spa on-site. **Pros:** walking distance to the beach; clean modern rooms; great value. **Cons:** little entertainment; not right on the sea; beach chairs do not include shade palapas. *Rooms from: $250* ✉ *J. E. Irausquin Blvd. 330, Palm Beach* ☎ *297/586-7700* 🌐 *www.marriott.com/en-us/hotels/auacy-courtyard-aruba-resort/overview/* *192 rooms* *No Meals.*

★ **Divi Aruba Phoenix Beach Resort**

$$$$ | **RESORT** | **FAMILY** | With incredible views from its high-rise tower, stunning rooms awash in tropical colors, state-of-the-art amenities, and comfortable, homey accommodations, Divi Aruba Phoenix rises above the fray on busy Palm Beach. **Pros:** great private beach away from the main Palm Beach frenzy; beautifully appointed rooms, some with whirlpool bathtubs; all units have sea views. **Cons:** no reserving shade palapas; no shuttle service to other Divi properties; no all-inclusive plan. *Rooms from: $740* ✉ *J. E. Irausquin Blvd. 75, Palm Beach* ☎ *297/586–1170* 🌐 *www.diviarubaphoenix.com* *240 rooms* *No Meals.*

Hilton Aruba Caribbean Resort and Casino

$$$$ | **HOTEL** | **FAMILY** | Sprawling over 15 acres of white sand and lush tropical gardens with a lovely water circuit winding throughout, this iconic resort is located where the first hotel debuted on Palm Beach in 1959 and was the birthplace of the famous Aruba Ariba cocktail. **Pros:** Palm Beach Club VIP program has special perks and a lounge; excellent beachfront area never feels crowded, even when at capacity; grand ballroom is ideal for big events. **Cons:** not all rooms have sea views; food and drink can be pricey; sometimes long lines at the breakfast buffets. *Rooms from: $600* ✉ *J. E. Irausquin Blvd. 81, Palm Beach* ☎ *297/586–6555* 🌐 *www.hiltonaruba.com* *357 rooms* *No Meals.*

★ **Holiday Inn Resort Aruba**

$$$ | **RESORT** | **FAMILY** | The resort's massive lemon-yellow buildings that sprawl across a prime spot on Palm Beach offer a revelation compared to what most might think a Holiday Inn stay might entail—inviting rooms, a fun vibe, and distinct sections that will appeal to those looking for quiet active fun or a family-friendly environment. **Pros:** all-inclusive plan available; right across the street from the best Palm Beach nightlife; kids stay free and enjoy an excellent kids' club. **Cons:** reception can be busy with big groups; shade palapas need to be reserved and rented; not all rooms have sea views. *Rooms from: $415* ✉ *J. E. Irausquin Blvd. 230, Palm Beach* ☎ *297/586–3600, 800/465–4329* 🌐 *www.holidayarubaresort.com* *590 rooms* *No Meals.*

Hotel Riu Palace Aruba

$$$$ | **RESORT** | **FAMILY** | This family-friendly all-inclusive is a massive complex surrounding an expansive water circuit with a choice of five restaurants and scads of free activities. **Pros:** spacious water circuit for families; nice shallow beachfront; a wide choice of entertainment and dining. **Cons:** few rooms have unobstructed sea views; few spots to escape in solitude; beach and pool area get very busy and noisy. *Rooms from: $630* ✉ *J. E. Irausquin Blvd. 79, Palm Beach* ☎ *297/586–3900* 🌐 *www.riu.com* *400 rooms* *All-Inclusive.*

Hyatt Regency Aruba Resort Spa and Casino
$$$$ | **RESORT** | **FAMILY** | Located on 12 acres of prime beachfront, the rooms and suites at this landmark resort have all been recently refreshed and welcome couples as well as families. **Pros:** luxurious adults-only beachfront pool; many rooms have spectacular ocean views; lush tropical landscaping leads down to spacious beachfront. **Cons:** not all rooms have sea views; some standard rooms are on the small side with small balconies; few rooms have full balconies. *Rooms from: $599* ✉ *J. E. Irausquin Blvd. 85, Palm Beach* ☎ *297/586–1234, 800/554–9288* 🌐 *www.hyatt.com* *359 rooms* *No Meals.*

Marriott's Aruba Ocean Club
$$$$ | **TIMESHARE** | **FAMILY** | First-rate amenities and lavishly decorated villas with balconies and full kitchens have made this timeshare an island favorite. **Pros:** excellent beach; relaxed atmosphere; feels more like a home than a hotel room. **Cons:** attracts large families, so lots of kids are about; beach can get crowded; grounds are not within view of the sea. *Rooms from: $771* ✉ *L. G. Smith Blvd. 99, Palm Beach* ☎ *297/586–9000* 🌐 *www.marriott.com* *218 rooms* *No Meals.*

★ **Radisson Blu Aruba**
$$$ | **HOTEL** | **FAMILY** | This modern, stylish high-rise behind the Palm Beach strip overlooks a gorgeous water circuit and spa. **Pros:** expansive water circuit includes an adults-only pool and a whirlpool nook; ideal for families that want space; two floors of premium penthouse suites. **Cons:** not all rooms have balconies; not all rooms have sea views; not on the beach. *Rooms from: $400* ✉ *J. E. Irausquin Blvd. #97-A, Noord* ☎ *866/856–9066* 🌐 *www.radissonhotelsamericas.com* *132 rooms* *No Meals.*

★ **Ritz-Carlton, Aruba**
$$$$ | **HOTEL** | This massive hotel sits on a broad stretch of white sand with all rooms overlooking the sea. **Pros:** stunning sunset views from rooms and the atrium lobby bar; spacious grounds so it never feels crowded; exemplary personal service. **Cons:** pricey compared to other similar properties; attracts many large groups; sheer size and design gives it a big-box feel. *Rooms from: $750* ✉ *L. G. Smith Blvd. 107, Palm Beach* ☎ *527–2222* 🌐 *www.ritzcarlton.com* *320 rooms* *No Meals.*

Nightlife

BARS AND CLUBS

★ **Bugaloe Bar & Grill**
BARS | This colorful beach bar at the tip of De Palm Pier on busy Palm Beach is hopping night and day with visitors and locals alike. Paint-spattered wooden tables and chairs on a plank floor under a massive palapa draw barefoot beachcombers in for frozen cocktails, cold beer, and casual fare where live music is king. The revelry starts as early as happy hour and continues well into the night. There are karaoke nights, salsa nights, and rotating food specials. It's also an optimal spot to catch a magical sunset over the waves. ✉ *De Palm Pier, Noord* ✣ *In between Riu and Hilton on Palm Beach* ☎ *297/586–2233* 🌐 *www.bugaloe.com.*

★ **MooMba Beach Bar**
GATHERING PLACES | As the central party spot on the busiest part of Palm Beach, this open-air bar is famous for its Sunday-night blowouts with big crowds of locals gathering to dance in the sand to live bands or DJs. The barkeeps are mixology masters, and happy hours are very popular. There are early and late drink specials every night except Sunday. The attached restaurant is also a wonderful surf-side spot for breakfast, lunch, and dinner, and there are tables in the sand for romantic dinners before partying. ✉ *J. E. Irausquin Blvd. 230, Palm Beach* ✣ *Between Holiday Inn and Marriott Surf Club* ☎ *297/586–5365* 🌐 *www.moombabeach.com.*

★ **purebeach**

BARS | A very lively happy-hour spot with its cool swim-up pool bar, purebeach is the place to be especially on Sundays for live music and dancing. They also offer some special musical events throughout the week. But day or night, they are known for killer Caribbean cocktails and creative international fare with weekly specials. There's also an oversized adult-only seafront whirlpool right beside it for romantic nights under the tropical stars with music. ✉ *Divi Phoenix Aruba Resort, J. E. Irausquin Blvd. 75, Palm Beach* ☎ *297/586–6606* 🌐 *www.purebeacharuba.com.*

Shopping

GIFTS

★ **T. H. Palm & Company**

ANTIQUES & COLLECTIBLES | With an eclectic collection of upscale and exclusive items curated from all over the world by the owner, this unique boutique offers everything from top-line fashions for men and women, including footwear, handcrafted jewelry, and accessories, to art deco items for the home and novelty gifts for pets. It's a very popular spot for locals to buy gifts as well as for visitors to buy one-of-a-kind souvenirs. A portion of all proceeds goes to the community through a special give-back program. ✉ *J. E. Irausquin Blvd. 87, Palm Beach* ☎ *297/592-7804* 🌐 *www.thpalmandcompany.com.*

JEWELRY

★ **Shiva's Gold and Gems**

JEWELRY & WATCHES | A reputable family-run business with shops throughout the Caribbean, this Palm Beach Plaza location saves shoppers from heading to Oranjestad for the type of top-quality diamonds and jewelry Downtown is famous for (though there is a location Downtown as well). Luxury watches, precious gems, gold, silver, and more are first-rate here, and this is the only store on Aruba that belongs to the Leading Jewelers of the World, which has fewer than 100 retail members. ✉ *Palm Beach Plaza, L. G. Smith 95, Palm Beach* ☎ *297/583-4011* 🌐 *www.shivasjewelers.com* ⏲ *Closed mornings and Sun.*

SHOPPING AREAS AND MALLS

Palm Beach Plaza

MALL | FAMILY | Aruba's most modern mall has three floors of shops offering fashion, tech, electronics, jewelry, souvenirs, and more. Entertainment includes glow-in-the-dark bowling, a modern video arcade, a sports bar, and the main floor indoor courtyard is often used for local festivals and events like fashion shows. Dining includes a food court and stand-alone restaurants and bars, and there are also modern air-conditioned cinemas and a spa within, as well as free Wi-Fi. ✉ *Palm Beach Plaza, L. G. Smith Blvd. 95* ☎ *297/586–0045* 🌐 *www.palmbeachplaza.com.*

★ **Paseo Herencia**

MALL | FAMILY | A gorgeous, old-fashioned colonial-style courtyard and clock tower encase souvenir and specialty shops, cinemas, dining spots, cafés, and bars. Just off Palm Beach, this low-rise alfresco mall is famous for its nightly "liquid fireworks" shows—neon-lit water fountains waltz to music in a choreographed dance. Visitors can enjoy it for free from an outdoor amphitheater where many cultural events take place, and there's an Aruban walk of fame here. There's also a fancy carousel for children. New dining outlets line the outside street entrances now, too, like Sibarita Cafe-Bar, a new picnic terrace, and some cool new food truck–style kiosks offering authentic Aruban snacks. ✉ *J. E. Irausquin Blvd. 382, Palm Beach* ☎ *297/586–6533* 🌐 *www.paseoherencia.com.*

Western Tip (California Dunes)

No trip to Aruba is complete without a visit to the California Lighthouse, and it's also worth exploring the rugged area of the island's western tip. This is the transition point between Aruba's calmer and rougher coasts. Malmok Beach and Arashi Beach are popular with locals; both are excellent spots for grabbing dramatic sunset photos.

Sights

★ Alto Vista Chapel

NOTABLE BUILDING | Meaning "high view," Alto Vista was built in 1750 as the island's first Roman Catholic Church. The simple yellow-and-orange structure stands out in bright contrast to its stark desert-like surroundings, and its elevated location affords a wonderful panoramic view of the northwest coast. Restored in 1953, it still holds regular services today and also serves as the culmination point of the annual walk of the cross at Easter. You will see small signposts guiding the faithful to the Stations of the Cross all along the winding road to its entrance. This landmark is a typical stop on most island tours. Make sure to walk out back to see the Aruba Peace Labyrinth. **TIP→ Make sure to buy coconut water from the famous coconut man out front.** ✉ *Alto Vista Rd., Noord* ✣ *Follow the rough, winding dirt road that loops around the island's northern tip, or from the hotel strip, take Palm Beach Rd. through three intersections and watch for the asphalt road to the left.*

★ California Lighthouse

LIGHTHOUSE | FAMILY | Built in 1916, the landmark lighthouse on the island's eastern tip is open to the public, and visitors can climb the spiral stairs to discover a fabulous panoramic view for a small fee. Declared a national monument in 2015, the lighthouse was built because of and named after, the merchant ship *California* that sunk nearby. There are also spectacular private catered 3-course dinner experiences for two people at the top that can be booked through Experitours; there's a choice of sunset seating or under-the-stars seating. It's one of only two lighthouse dinner experiences in the world. ✉ *2 Hudishibana, Westpunt* ☎ *297/699–0995* 🌐 *arubawalkingtours.com/california-lighthouse-exclusive-dining-experience/* 🎫 *$5.*

Beaches

★ Arashi Beach

BEACH | This is the local favorite, a half-mile stretch of gleaming white sand with rolling surf and great snorkeling. It can get busy on weekends—especially on Sunday—with local families bringing their own picnics, and visitors have discovered a cool little beach bar called Arashi Beach Shack there with great food, drinks, a lounge, and beach umbrella rentals. **Amenities:** food and drink; toilets; parking (free). **Best for:** swimming; snorkeling; walking. ✉ *Malmokweg* ✣ *West of Malmok Beach, on the west end* 🌐 *www.facebook.com/ArashiBeachShack.*

Malmok Beach (*Boca Catalina*)

BEACH | On the northwestern shore, this small, nondescript beach borders shallow waters that stretch 300 yards from shore. There are no snack or refreshment stands, but that might change soon with the addition of a new boardwalk leading from Fisherman's Huts beach (part of the Linear Park project) that is now attracting cyclists, strollers, and runners. Most of the main snorkel boat tours stop here for a dip as well as for its incredible sunsets. There is no easy access into the water from the shore; it's very rocky with sharp cliffs and steep descents. Snorkeling is best done from a boat. **Amenities:** none. **Best for:** solitude; snorkeling; sunsets. ✉ *J. E. Irausquin Blvd., Malmokweg.*

Restaurants

The Restaurant at Tierra del Sol

$$$$ | INTERNATIONAL | The main restaurant at Tierra del Sol sits next to the cliff-top pool and golf course and offers great views of the northwest coast and the California lighthouse. The atmosphere is very country club, but they have a new great new BBQ Saturday and Sunday brunch/lunch featuring ribs and chicken and comfort food sides. **Known for:** prix-fixe "all u can taste" menu with apps, tapas, and add-ons; great views and romantic candlelight alfresco dining; popular à la carte Sunday brunch. *Average main: $65* ✉ *Tierra del Sol Resort* ☎ *297/586–7800* 🌐 *www.tierradelsol.com* ⏲ *No dinner Sun. and Mon.*

Savaneta and San Nicolas

Savaneta, the island's original capital, is historically referred to as Commander's Bay since this is where the first Dutch Commanders resided. The area now has a cool off-the-radar vibe as well as some excellent local eats. Farther south, the little ex-refinery town of San Nicolas is known locally as Sunrise City due to its brilliant sunrises. Today both towns are receiving renewed interest as tourist destinations as they begin to focus more on preserving and promoting the island's history, culture, and art.

Sights

★ ArtisA

ARTS CENTER | Part art gallery, part administrative foundation, ArtisA (Art is Aruba) is responsible for the art and culture revolution in San Nicolas. The foundation displays local art for sale, hosts monthly exhibits for local artists, and is the spot to purchase tickets for the guided Aruba Mural Tours (also available online). They are now hosting art-meets-cuisine special events with local chefs' table dinners highlighting a showcase inspired by local artists within their space. ✉ *Bernard van de Veen Zeppenfeldstraat 6, San Nicolaas* ☎ *297/593–4475* 🌐 *www.artisaruba.com* ⏲ *Closed Sun.*

San Nicolas Art Walk

PUBLIC ART | In the past few years, San Nicolas has seen an extraordinary revitalization and beautification thanks to new art initiatives organized by the local artist's foundation, ArtisA (Art is Aruba). What began as a simple mural project in 2015 has since blossomed into the establishment of an annual Aruba Art Fair whose aim is to create more public art projects. The incredible murals can cover entire buildings, and every year the collection grows. You'll find mosaic art like angel wings made of seashells, glowing lionfish, 3D installations, interactive art, sculptures, and many murals everywhere. **■ TIP→ You can see the installations on a leisurely walk using the online map, or on a guided walk with Aruba Mural Tours.** ✉ *San Nicolas* 🌐 *arubamuraltours.com*

Beaches

★ Baby Beach

BEACH | FAMILY | On the island's eastern tip (near the refinery), this semicircular beach borders a placid bay of turquoise water that's just about as shallow as a wading pool—perfect for families with little ones. A small coral reef basin at the sea's edge offers superb snorkeling, but do not pass the barrier as the current is extremely strong outside the rocks. The JADS dive shop offers snorkel equipment rentals, and this is a popular place to see and swim with sea turtles, too. Rum Reef on one end is a unique adults-only bar and infinity pool overlooking the beach, and below it is a family-friendly beach and snack bar. On the other end you can rent clamshell shade tents and lounges on the beach from Big Mamma

Grill, also a family-friendly gathering spot. **Amenities:** food and drink; showers; toilets; parking (free); **Best for:** snorkeling; swimming. ✉ *Seroe Colorado.*

Boca Grandi

BEACH | This is *the* choice for the island's best kiteboarders and expert windsurfers, even more so than Fisherman's Huts. But the currents are seriously strong, so it's not safe for casual swimming. It's very picturesque, though, and a perfect spot for a picnic. It's a few minutes from San Nicolas proper; look for the big red anchor or the kites in the air. But be forewarned: the conditions are not for amateurs, and there are no lifeguards or facilities nearby should you get into trouble. **Amenities:** parking (free). **Best for:** solitude; walking; windsurfing. ✉ *San Nicolas* ✣ *Near Seagrape Grove, on the east end.*

Rodger's Beach

BEACH | **FAMILY** | Near Baby Beach on the island's eastern tip, this beautiful curving stretch of sand is only slightly marred by its proximity to the tanks and towers of the oil refinery at the bay's far side. Look for the stone stairs descending to the sand; the swimming conditions are excellent here. It's usually very quiet during the week, so you might have the beach all to yourself, but it's a local favorite on weekends. Full facilities can be found next door at JADS dive center strip on Baby Beach. **Amenities:** food and drink; toilets; parking (free). **Best for:** swimming; solitude. ✉ *Seroe Colorado* ✣ *Next to Baby Beach.*

Restaurants

★ Flying Fishbone

$$$$ | **INTERNATIONAL** | Opened in 1977, this was the first restaurant in Aruba to offer feet-in-the-water dining, and that's why the legendary landmark is so worth the trek out to Savaneta for its insanely romantic seaside setting. An international menu is designed to please all palates, but the real culinary draw is fish straight from the island's most famous local fisherman's pier located a few doors over. **Known for:** tables set right in the ocean; personal flambéed baked Alaska; "Savaneta's Seafood History" featuring the very local catch of the day. *$ Average main: $40* ✉ *Savaneta 344, Savaneta* ☎ *297/584–2506* 🌐 *www.flyingfishbone.com* ⏲ *No lunch.*

O'Niel Caribbean Kitchen

$$ | **CARIBBEAN** | **FAMILY** | Right smack in the middle of the exciting San Nicolas art walk, O'Niel's is a warm and welcoming eatery that's an ideal spot to get your Jamaican jerk on. Real deal Jamaican dishes like ackee with salt fish and oxtail with beans are menu favorites, but there are also many local Aruban specialties like goat stew and fresh local fish and seafood. **Known for:** local favorite; coconut-infused dishes like shrimp or chicken with rum and sweet chili sauce; real-deal Jamaican specialties like ackee with salt fish. *$ Average main: AWG15* ✉ *Bernard van de Veen Zeppenfeldstraat 15, San Nicolas* ☎ *297/584–8700* 🌐 *www.facebook.com/OnielCaribbeanKitchen297* ⏲ *Closed Mon.*

Zeerovers

$ | **CARIBBEAN** | **FAMILY** | With a name that means "pirates" in Dutch, this small restaurant sits right on the Savaneta pier, where the local fishermen bring in their daily catch. The menu is basic: the day's fish and other seafood fried almost as soon as it's lifted out of the boat, with sides of local staples like plantains that you can chase down with cold local beer. **Known for:** picturesque sea view and sunsets; freshest fish on the island; lively local hangout. *$ Average main: $10* ✉ *Savaneta Pier, Savaneta 270A, Savaneta* ☎ *297/584–8401* 🌐 *www.facebook.com/zeerovers* ⏲ *Closed Mon. and Tues.*

Hotels

★ Aruba Ocean Villas

$$$$ | RESORT | A secret collection of stunning adults-only luxury accommodations is tucked away in Savaneta. **Pros:** far from the tourist fray; insanely romantic setting, ideal for honeymoons; luxurious elite vibe yet friendly staff. **Cons:** no pool in common area; a car is needed; little entertainment. *Rooms from: $499* *Savaneta 356A, Savaneta* *A few doors down from the Flying Fishbone restaurant* *877/920–1381 in the U.S.* *www.arubaoceanvillas.com* *8 villas* *Free Breakfast.*

Arikok National Park and Environs

First-time visitors are often surprised to discover how desert-like the other side of Aruba becomes once away from the landscaped grounds of the resorts with their swaying palms and brightly colored blooms. The island's interior and northeast coast are arid, rocky, and wild, but they have their own unique beauty and are well worth exploring for surreal scenic vistas, romantic wave-whipped cliffs, and vast expanses of untouched wilderness.

Arikok National Park takes up approximately 20% of the island and is fiercely protected due to its fragile ecosystem; visitors must pay a park fee and abide by park rules. Within the park there are many surprises beyond cacti forests, dry riverbeds, and twisted divi-divi trees. There are cool caves like Fontein and Guadarikiri, a remote natural pool known as "Conchi," and Mt. Jamanota, the island's highest peak. Meandering goats and donkeys are common, but the park's elusive wildlife *is* easier to discover with the help of a guide. Park rangers offer free tours and man the entrances to the caves to answer questions about their history.

Surrounding the park in the interior are neighborhoods worth exploring if you want to see how the locals live, like in Santa Cruz where you should sleuth out the numerous "snacks"—small food outlets that serve great homemade fare at very low prices. **TIP→ Make sure you have cash. These spots don't take credit cards.**

There's also Paradera, a small interior neighborhood where you'll find three natural attractions—the Casibari and Ayo rock formations and Mt. Hooiberg ("The Haystack")—all worth a visit on their own.

Sights

★ Arikok National Park

NATIONAL PARK | Covering almost 20% of the island's landmass, this protected preserve of arid, cacti-studded outback has interesting nature and wildlife if you know where to look. There are close to 30 miles of hiking trails within the park zone including a trek up Mt. Jamanota, the island's highest peak. Hiking maps for all levels of hikers are free at the visitor center, and in-depth maps of the park and its attractions are also available for download online at their website. It's highly recommended to take a guided tour on foot or by vehicle, as the roads can be very rough in some places; there are plenty of excursions by ATV, UTV, Jeep safaris, and more. A guided preview of what you can expect will help you if you want to return in your own rental car as well, but keep in mind that a 4x4 vehicle is a must and all visitors must pay a park entrance fee, which helps fund the park's ecoconservation. Some trails lead to glorious seaside coastal views, but a guided tour will help you understand the significance of the region and help you find attractions like the caves on the northeastern coast. There are no facilities past the visitor center so bring plenty of water and sunscreen and wear good shoes, as the terrain is very rocky.

A new region near Spanish Lagoon has also been added recently as part of its protected area due to the importance of its freshwater canals and mangrove forests, but it is closer to Savaneta on the southwest coast, and not within the original park confines.

TIP→ You can book free guided hikes with a park ranger by phone or email, but must reserve 48 hours in advance. ✉ *San Fuego 70, Arikok National Park* ☎ *297/585–1234* 🌐 *www.arubanationalpark.org* 🎫 *$11* 🕒 *Park closes at 4 pm daily.*

Aruba Ostrich Farm

FARM/RANCH | FAMILY | Everything you ever wanted to know about the world's largest living birds can be found at this farm and ranch. There are emus, too. A large *palapa* (palm-thatched roof) houses a gift shop and restaurant that draws large bus tours, and tours of the farm are available every half hour starting at 10 am until 3 pm, seven days a week. Feeding the ostriches is fun, and you can also hold an egg in your hands. There is a full-service restaurant on-site as well as a farmer's market (check Facebook for dates), and the souvenir shop sells unique, locally made crafts and keepsakes. ✉ *Matividiri 57, Paradera* ☎ *297/585–9630* 🌐 *www.arubaostrichfarm.com* 🎫 *$14.*

Casibari and Ayo Rock Formations

NATURE SIGHT | The odd-looking massive boulders at Ayo and Casibari are a mystery as they don't match the island's geological makeup in any other spot. They seem to have just cropped up out of nowhere, but they're cool to see and Casibari is fun to climb with man-made steps and handrails and tunnels set within the weird rock formation. Kids will love this all-natural jungle gym. You are not permitted to climb Ayo, but it's still worth a visit to see the ancient pictographs in a small cave (the entrance has iron bars to protect the drawings from vandalism). ✉ *Paradera* 🌐 *www.aruba.com/us/explore/rock-formations.*

★ Donkey Sanctuary Aruba

FARM/RANCH | FAMILY | Take a free tour of the island's only donkey sanctuary where volunteers help abandoned and sometimes ill wild animals enjoy a happy forever home. This is a nonprofit organization and can always use help, whether financial or with chores. You can donate there or on their website, and you can even adopt a donkey—your donation goes to its annual feed and care. There is also a great donkey-themed gift shop. It's a great family outing for all ages. **TIP→ Bring carrots and apples for a really warm welcome from the residents.** ✉ *Bringamosa, 2-Z Santa Cruz, Santa Cruz* ☎ *297/593–2933* 🌐 *main.arubandonkey.org/portal* 🎫 *Free.*

Mt. Hooiberg

MOUNTAIN | Named for its shape (*hooiberg* means "haystack" in Dutch), this 541-foot peak lies inland just past the airport. You are bound to notice it as your plane lands. If you have the energy, you can climb the 562 steps to the top for an impressive view of Oranjestad (and Venezuela on clear days). It is the island's second-highest peak; Mt. Jamanota at 617 feet is the tallest. **TIP→ It's a very hot climb with no shade, so wear a hat, apply plenty of sunscreen, and bring water.** ✉ *Hooiberg 11, near Santa Cruz, Paradera.*

Activities

Aruba is one of the best places for the offbeat sport of beach tennis and now hosts many international tournaments on its beaches. It's also one of the best places to learn windsurfing and kiteboarding due to prime conditions just off Palm Beach. As for water sports, there is little you cannot do on Aruba, including modern thrill activities such as Jetlev, an over-water jet pack flight; the hoverboard, an air-propelled skateboard over the waves; and jet blades, ski boots on a board that lifts you over the water.

Parasailing, banana boats, wave runners, kayaking, paddleboarding, yoga on paddleboard... Aruba has it all, even a real submarine.

DAY SAILS

There is a large variety of snorkeling, dinner, sunset, and party cruises to choose from. The larger operators offer the best experience, though the smaller ones might offer the best price. Private speedboat tours with customizable snorkel stops are available via Freedom charters run by the Experitours group.

★ Jolly Pirates

SNORKELING | **FAMILY** | Aruba's unique, pirate-themed sailing adventure is a rollicking ride aboard a big, beautiful teak schooner complete with a wild and crazy swashbuckling crew and an open bar. The ships offer snorkeling tours with two or three stops and a rope-swing adventure, and the sunset cruises are also first-rate. Prepare to party hearty (it's basically impossible not to) due to their signature "pirate's poison" rum punch and infectious loud music. Snorkel trips always include the *Antilla* wreck. Departures are from Hadicurari Pier beside MooMba Beach Bar. ✉ *Hadicurari Pier, Palm Beach* ✣ *Office behind MooMba Beach Bar* ☎ *586–8107* 🌐 *www.jolly-pirates.com* 🎫 *From $38.50 (sunset sail) $58 (snorkel sail).*

Montforte III

SAILING | Take your sailing experience up a notch aboard this luxurious teak schooner that is designed to pamper. Exclusive tours take you to spots like Spanish Lagoon for snorkeling and kayaking, and around Boca Catalina for four-course dinners under the stars. Unlimited premium spirits, signature cocktails, tapas, and snacks are included in all trips, and there's sometimes live music onboard as well. Departure is from Pelican Pier. ✉ *Pelican Pier, Palm Beach* ☎ *297/583–0400* 🌐 *www.monfortecruise.com* 🎫 *From $139.*

Sailaway Tours Aruba

SAILING | At 110 feet, the *Lady Black* is a beautifully retrofitted old-fashioned wooden schooner that's also the island's largest party ship. Enjoy an open bar and a big rope hammock on the bow while you sail with one of their snorkel, sunset, or dinner cruises. The friendly crew is happy to help you try some antics on the rope swing, and you can even hop on their backs while they do flips into the water. The party can get crazy. Available for private charters as well. ✉ *Hadicurari Pier, Palm Beach* ✣ *Look for their sign to check in across from MooMba Beach Bar in front of Hadicurari Pier* ☎ *297/739–9000* 🌐 *www.sailawaytour.com* 🎫 *From $64.*

★ Tranquilo Charters Aruba

SAILING | Captain Mike Hagedoorn, a legendary Aruban sailor, handed the helm over to his son Captain Anthony a few years ago after 20 years of running the family business. Today, *The Tranquilo*—a 43-foot sailing yacht—still takes small groups of passengers to a secluded spot at a Spanish lagoon named Mike's Reef, where not many other snorkel trips venture. The lunch cruise to the south side always includes "Mom's famous Dutch pea soup," and they also do private charters for dinner sails and sailing trips around Aruba's lesser-explored coasts. Look for the red boat docked at the Renaissance Marina beside the Atlantis Submarine launch. ✉ *Renaissance Marina, Oranjestad* ☎ *297/586–1418* 🌐 *www.tranquiloaruba.com* 🎫 *From $100.*

DIVING AND SNORKELING

With visibility of up to 90 feet, the waters around Aruba are excellent for snorkeling and diving. Advanced and novice divers alike will find plenty to occupy their time, as many of the most popular sites—including some interesting shipwrecks—are found in shallow waters ranging from 30 to 60 feet. Coral reefs covered with sensuously waving sea fans and eerie giant sponge tubes attract a colorful

A bouquet of colorful reefs can be explored in the waters of Aruba.

menagerie of sea life, including gliding manta rays, curious sea turtles, shy octopuses, and grunts, groupers, and other fish. Marine preservation is a priority on Aruba, and regulations by the Conference on International Trade in Endangered Species make it unlawful to remove coral, conch, and other marine life from the water. There are many snorkeling trips for all ages with large operators and DePalm Island also has excellent snorkeling.

Scuba diving operator prices vary depending on the trip. If you want to go all the way, complete open-water certification takes at least four days worth of instruction. You can often begin instruction in a resort pool.

★ DePalm Pleasure Sail & Snorkeling

SNORKELING | **FAMILY** | The luxury catamaran *DePalm Pleasure* offers three-stop snorkel trips to the island's most popular fish-filled spots daily including the *Antilla* shipwreck. They also offer the option to try SNUBA. The romantic sunset sails are popular excursions. Buffet and open bar are included. Hotel pickup and drop-off are also included (unless within easy walking distance of their pier on Palm Beach). ✉ *Palm Beach, DePalm Pier, between the Hilton and the Riu resorts, Noord* ☎ *297/522–4400* 🌐 *depalm.com.*

Native Divers Aruba

SCUBA DIVING | A small, personal operation, Native Divers Aruba specializes in PADI open-water courses. Ten different certification options include specialties like Multilevel Diver, Search & Recovery Diver, and Underwater Naturalist. Their boat schedule is also flexible, and it's easy to tailor instruction to your specific needs. They also allow snorkelers to tag along and provide all the necessary equipment. They also do resort classes and refresher courses. ✉ *Marriott Surf Club, Palm Beach* ✣ *On the beach in front of Marriott Surf Club* ☎ *297/586–4763* 🌐 *www.nativedivers.com* 🎫 *From $100.*

FISHING

Deep-sea catches here include barracuda, kingfish, wahoo, bonito, and tuna. November to April is the catch-and-release season for sailfish and marlin. Many skippered charter boats are available for half- or full-day sails. Package prices vary but typically include tackle, bait, and refreshments. Some restaurants will cook your catch for you, like Driftwood, which also has its own charter fishing operation.

Teaser Fishing Charters Aruba

FISHING | FAMILY | The expertise of the Teaser crew is matched by a commitment to sensible fishing practices, which include catch and release and avoiding ecologically sensitive areas. The company's yacht is fully equipped, and the crew seem to have an uncanny ability to locate the best fishing spots with Captain Milton at the helm. ✉ *Renaissance Marina, Oranjestad* ☎ *297/593–9228* 🌐 *www.teaserfishingaruba.com* 🎫 *From $400 (limit 6 people).*

GOLF

The Links at Divi Aruba

GOLF | This 9-hole course was designed by Karl Litten and Lorie Viola. The par-36 flat layout stretches to 2,952 yards and features paspalum grass (best for seaside courses) and takes you past beautiful lagoons. It's a testy little course with water abounding, making accuracy more important than distance. Amenities include a golf school with professional instruction, a driving range, a practice green, and a two-story golf clubhouse with a pro shop. ✉ *Divi Village Golf & Beach Resort, J. E. Irausquin Blvd. 93, Druif* ☎ *297/581–4653* 🌐 *www.divilinks.com* 🎫 *From $96, after 3pm $79* ⛳ *9 holes, 2952 yards, par 36.*

★ Tierra del Sol

GOLF | Stretching out to 6,811 yards, this stunning course is situated on the northwest coast near the California Lighthouse and is Aruba's only 18-hole course. Designed by Robert Trent Jones Jr., Tierra del Sol combines Aruba's native beauty (cacti and rock formations, stunning views) with good greens and beautiful landscaping. Wind can also be a factor here on the rolling terrain, as are the abundant bunkers and water hazards. Greens fees include a golf cart equipped with GPS and a communications system that allows you to order drinks for your return to the clubhouse. The club also offers clinics and lessons and hosts many major tournament and gala golf events annually. ✉ *Tierra del Sol Resort, Caya di Solo 10, Malmokweg* ☎ *297/586–7800* 🌐 *www.tierradelsol.com/golf* 🎫 *From $89 for 9 holes high season* ⛳ *18 holes, 6811 yards, par 71.*

GUIDED TOURS AND MULTISPORT OUTFITTERS

Aruba Outdoor Adventures

KAYAKING | FAMILY | This small, family-run outfitter offers a unique combination of small-group (six people max) pedal-kayaking and snorkel tours along the island's southeastern coast. Mangroves and reef explorations take you around calm water near Mangel Halto, Savaneta, and Barcadera; well-informed guides explain the natural environment and help guests navigate the snorkeling portions. No kayaking experience is necessary. Pickup and drop-off are included, as well as snorkel equipment, a dry bag, snacks, and drinks. Departures are from the DePalm Island Ferry Terminal outside Oranjestad. ✉ *DePalm Island Ferry Terminal, Balashi* ☎ *297/749–6646* 🌐 *www.arubaoutdooradventures.com* 🎫 *From $80.*

★ De Palm Tours

BOATING | FAMILY | Aruba's premier tour company covers every inch of the island on land and under sea, and they even have their own submarine (*Atlantis*) and semi-submarine (*Seaworld Explorer*) and their own all-inclusive private island destination (De Palm Island), which has great snorkeling as well as Seatrek, a cool underwater air-supplied-helmet walk. Land exploration options include air-conditioned bus sightseeing tours and rough and rugged outback jaunts by jeep safari to popular attractions like the natural pool. You can also do off-road tours in a UTV (two-seater utility task vehicle) via their guided caravan trips. On the waves, their luxury catamaran *De Palm Pleasure* offers romantic sunset sails and snorkel trips that include an option to try SNUBA—deeper snorkeling with an air-supplied raft at Aruba's most famous shipwreck. De Palm also offers airport transfers and private VIP transfers. ✉ *L. G. Smith Blvd. 142, Oranjestad* ☎ *297/522–4400* 🌐 *depalm.com.*

★ Driftwood Charters

FISHING | *Driftwood* is a tournament-rigged, 35-foot yacht manned by Captain Herby, who is famous for offering deep-sea fishing charters on Aruba since the early 1990s. He is also co-owner of Driftwood Restaurant and is always happy to bring your catch to their chef for expert preparation so you can enjoy it for dinner the very same night. Charters can accommodate up to six people. ✉ *Seaport Marina, Oranjestad* ☎ *297/583–2515* 🌐 *www.driftwoodfishingcharters.com/* 🎫 *From $400.*

★ Octopus Aruba

SAILING | Octopus has been offering group and private snorkel and party sails on their catamaran for decades, but now they also offer a whole new experience with a fleet of cool "aqua donut" boats. The donuts seat up to 10 people on a comfy padded bench circling a large table; you can captain it yourself or have it crewed. Stable and easy to navigate, the aqua donut won't sink even if it's full of water. Octopus offers two very unique catered adventures aboard them—a luxury brunch and snorkel outing, and a gourmet dinner sunset cruise. It's like having your own table and floating bar on the sea, but they call it your own "private island." ✉ *Palm Beach* ✣ *Orange beach hut between the Playa Linda and Holiday Inn* ☎ *297/560–6565* 🌐 *octopusaruba.com* 🎫 *From $69.99.*

★ Red Sail Sports Aruba

BOATING | A dynamic company established in 1989, they are experts in the field of water-sports recreation. They offer excellent diving excursions and instruction, snorkel sails, sunset sails, and full dinner sails. The company also has its own sports equipment shops and you can now book many land excursions through them. ✉ *J. E. Irausquin Blvd. 348-A, Palm Beach* ☎ *297/523–1600* 🌐 *www.redsailaruba.com.*

HIKING

Aruba's arid and rugged countryside is full of flora and fauna. Arikok National Wildlife Park is an excellent place to glimpse the real Aruba; start at the visitor center to get guidance and maps, or see their website for online trails maps (www.arubanationalpark.org). The heat can be oppressive, so be sure to take it easy, wear a hat, wear plenty of sunscreen, and have lots of water handy. A guided hike will show you where to find the island's elusive but interesting wildlife in the arid outback. Entrance to the park is located at the Visitor's Centre; there's a fee for those over 17. Guides can be reserved in advance as well.

EL Tours

GUIDED TOURS | This outfit offers an eclectic range of island tours including Aruba highlights; beach hopping with snorkeling ops; a fauna tour visiting the island's best animal sanctuaries; hiking tours with a park ranger in Arikok National Park; and morning and afternoon off-roading options. Private tours are also available. The range of vehicles includes air-conditioned and open-air buses, jeeps, and UTVs. They also offer a wide range of transfer services. ✉ *Barcadera 4, Oranjestad* ☎ *297/585–6730* 🌐 *www.eltoursaruba.com* 🎫 *From $37.*

HORSEBACK RIDING

Aruba's horses are descendants of the steeds called *paso finos* brought by the Spanish. They were favored for their fine steps and smooth gait even when trotting, so riders are always assured a smooth and gentle ride. Tours can include short jaunts along a secret beach and longer rides on cacti-studded backcountry trails.

★ Rancho La Ponderosa

HORSEBACK RIDING | FAMILY | Discover the wild pristine north coast on horseback and visit secret Wariruri beach for a gallop along the sea. Small group or private tours are available mornings and afternoons, and special private packages including a picnic in nature, a photoshoot, and other special add-ons can be arranged. They only use Paso Fino horses known for their exceptionally smooth gait. Complimentary pick up and drop off is provided at major hotels. ✉ *Papaya 30, Paradera* ☎ *297/594–8884* 🌐 *horsebackridingaruba.com* 🎫 *From $105* 🕓 *Closed Sun.* ☞ *Children must be over 6 years old to ride their own horse.*

★ Rancho Loco

HORSEBACK RIDING | FAMILY | Surrounded by a lush fruit and vegetable farm, Rancho Loco is touted as the "greenest ranch in Aruba." This equestrian center also gives lessons and boards and trains horses. Their tours range from sunset jaunts on Moro Beach to Arikok Park interior treks including trips to the Natural Pool. Private rides also available. ✉ *Sombre 22-e, Santa Cruz* ☎ *297/592–6039* 🌐 *www.rancholocoaruba.com/en* ☞ *From $95.*

KAYAKING

★ Aruba Watersports Center

DIVING & SNORKELING | FAMILY | This family-run, full-service water sports outfitter is right on Palm Beach, offering a comprehensive variety of adventures including small group PADI dives and snorkeling trips, but also WaveRunners, tubing, Hobie Cat sailing, stand-up paddleboarding, kayaking, wakeboarding, and parasailing and more. Snorkeling trips aboard the *Arusun* are for small groups, and the boat goes to spots others don't, including the *Pedernales* wreck. ✉ *L. G. Smith Blvd. 81B, Palm Beach* ✣ *Between Barcelo and Hilton resorts* ☎ *297/586–6613* 🌐 *www.arubawatersportscenter.com* 🎫 *Water float rentals start at $10 per day.*

★ Clear Kayak Aruba

KAYAKING | FAMILY | This is the only Aruba outfitter that offers clear-bottom sea kayaks, and the only one offering night tours as well. By day, groups paddle through the natural mangroves at Mangel Halto with a guide who can tell you how the roots create a natural nursery for juvenile marine life; the route also passes over lots of big, healthy coral full of colorful tropical fish. A second tour begins at Arashi Beach at dusk; then, after dark, the kayaks are lit up with LED lights that attract marine life to their clear bottoms. ✉ *Savaneta 402, Savaneta* ☎ *297/566–2205* 🌐 *www.clearkayakaruba.com* 🎫 *From $65* 🕓 *Closed Mon.* ☞ *Children must be age 8 and over for day tours and 12 and over for night tours.*

SPAS

Eforea Spa

SPAS | Hilton's answer to Zen incarnate, the soothing white seafront building beckons you to enter a world of relaxing signature "journeys" in a Japanese-inspired enclave. Treatments include both the typical and avant-garde, and there are options for both women and men, as well as special seaside massages for couples. There's also a stellar water circuit and full-service beauty salon on-site. Their signature massage includes Aruban aloe and local rum. ✉ *Hilton Aruba Resort, J. E. Irausquin Blvd. 81, Palm Beach* ☎ *297/526–6052* 🌐 *www.hilton.com.*

Okeanos Spa

SPAS | The full-service spa at the Renaissance Wind Creek Aruba Resort is well equipped to help you relax to the max, but the incredible seaside palapa cove on private Renaissance Island is the best venue for a relaxing couple's massage or a signature treatment. It's accessible by free water taxi when you book a treatment, and your purchase also gains you access to the private island. Access to the island is otherwise limited to resort guests. There is a beach bar and a full-service restaurant on-site, so you can make an entire blissful day of it. ✉ *Renaissance Aruba Resort & Casino, L. G. Smith Blvd. 82, Oranjestad* ☎ *297/583–6000* 🌐 *www.marriott.com/hotels/travel/auabr-renaissance-wind-creek-aruba-resort/.*

Pure Indulgence Spa

SPAS | The Pure Indulgence spa at Divi Aruba Phoenix Resort is in keeping with the Pure Beach and Pure Ocean Divi branding. With gorgeous rooms and couple's suites, they offer Microsilk Hydrotherapy baths and premium Hansgrohe Raindance rain showers, and the facility features top-of-the-line treatments and many extras, including made in Aruba eco-friendly products. The mani-pedi loft boasts spectacular sea views, and they are well equipped to accommodate bridal parties, as well as children and teen mani-pedi parties. Seaside couple's massages are also available. ✉ *Divi Aruba Phoenix Resort, J. E. Irausquin Blvd. 75, Palm Beach* ☎ *297/586–6066* 🌐 *www.purespaaruba.com.*

ZoiA Spa

SPAS | This luxurious full-service oasis named after the Papiamento word for balance offers treatments indoor and out, and focuses on using Aruba's natural resources for rejuvenation as much as possible—ingredients like red mud, seaweed, and aloe. Their latest unique signature treatments take place right in the water in their new adults-only Trankilo pool facing the sea. "Massage den Awa" is the solo treatment, or you can do it in tandem with your partner with their "Trankilo Couples Devotion" for pure floating bliss. Their express mani-pedis are also very popular, and they offer a full range of hair care in their salon, too. ✉ *Hyatt Regency Aruba Beach Resort & Casino, J. E. Irausquin Blvd. 85, Palm Beach* ☎ *297/586–1234* 🌐 *www.hyatt.com* ⏲ *Closed Sun.*

WINDSURFING

The southwestern coast's tranquil waters and gentle trade winds make conditions ideal for windsurfing, kiteboarding, and the newer sport of wing foiling at Fishermen's Huts. It's so ideal, world champions like local Aruban Sarah-Quita Offringa have trained here; Offringa has won the women's freestyle world champion over a dozen times to date. The annual Hi-Winds Competition also attracts the world's best each year and brings out big crowds to party on this beach. Even if you're not a world champion, you'll find expert instruction and modern equipment rental for all skill levels.

★ **Aruba Active Vacations**

WINDSURFING | This major outdoor activity center includes kiteboarding, windsurfing, mountain bike tours and rentals, hobiecat sailing, and landsailing. The outfit offers instructions and rentals for all. They're located on one of Aruba's most ideal beaches for windsurfing and kiteboarding, at Fisherman's Huts. ✉ *Near Fisherman's Huts beside Ritz-Carlton Aruba, Malmokweg* ☎ *297/586–0989* 🌐 *www.aruba-active-vacations.com.*

Chapter 6

BARBADOS

Updated by
Lee Yeaman

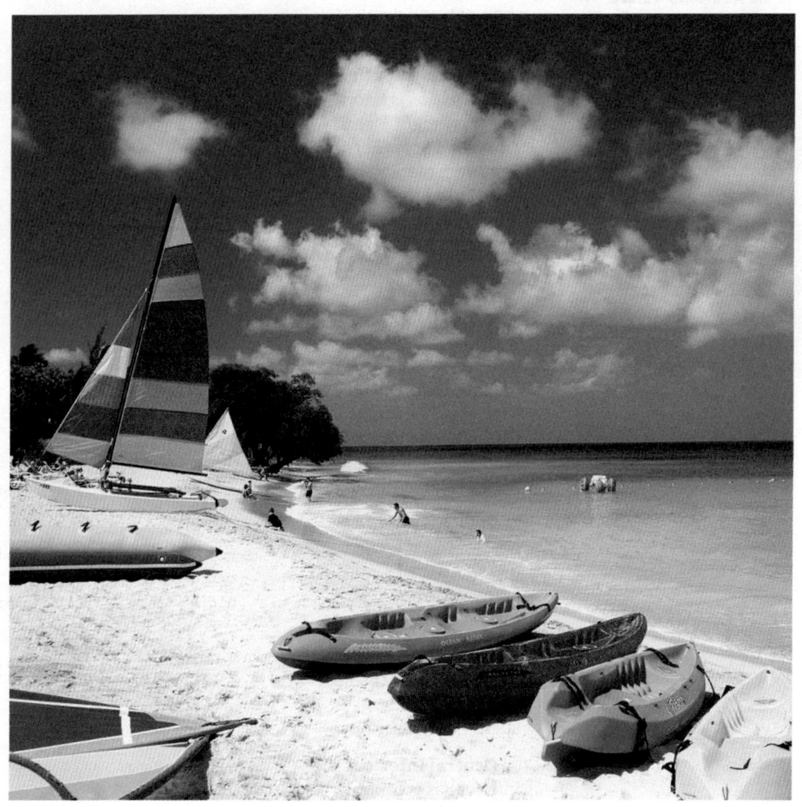

Sights ★★★★★

Restaurants ★★★★★

Hotels ★★★★★

Shopping ★★★★★

Nightlife ★★★★★

WELCOME TO BARBADOS

TOP REASONS TO GO

★ **Great Resorts:** They run the gamut—from unpretentious to ultraluxe.

★ **Great Golf:** Tee off at some of the best championship courses in the Caribbean.

★ **Restaurants Galore:** Great food ranges from street-party barbecue to world-class dining.

★ **Wide Range of Activities:** Land and water sports, historic sights, tropical gardens, and nightlife ... there's always plenty to do.

★ **Welcoming Locals:** Bajans are friendly, welcoming, helpful, and hospitable. You'll like them; they'll like you.

1 **Bridgetown and The Garrison.** A UNESCO World Heritage Site with shopping and an esplanade.

2 **Hastings, Rockley, and Worthing.** Broad beaches with reef-protected, crystal-clear waters.

3 **St. Lawrence Gap.** The southern coast buzzes with beachfront hotels and numerous places to shop, eat, and drink.

4 **Oistins and the surrounding South Point Area.** Oistins is known for its Friday night Fish Fry. The island's southernmost points are marked by historic lighthouses and broad beaches.

5 **Crane and the Southeast.** Magnificent beaches and stunning views mark this remote, mainly residential area.

6 **Holetown and Vicinity.** The center of the Platinum Coast has luxurious, sea-facing resorts and mansions.

7 **Speightstown.** The north's commercial center has shops, cafes, and many restored 19th-century buildings.

8 **East Coast.** There is no swimming, but the East Coast hosts annual surfing competitions.

9 **Central Interior.** The interior has botanical gardens, far-reaching views, and a cave to explore.

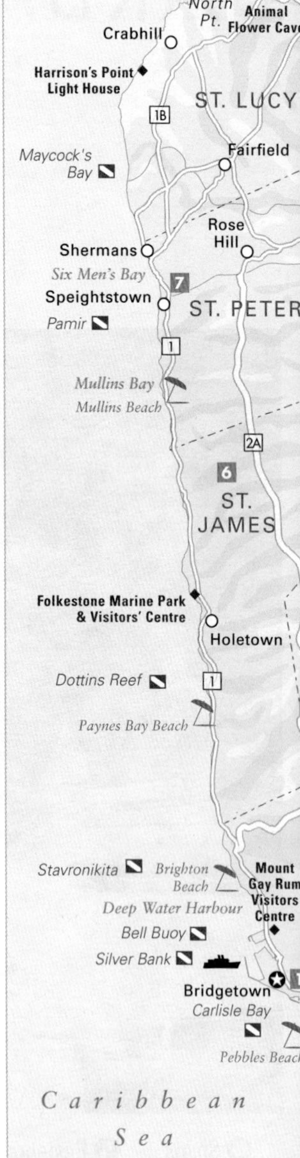

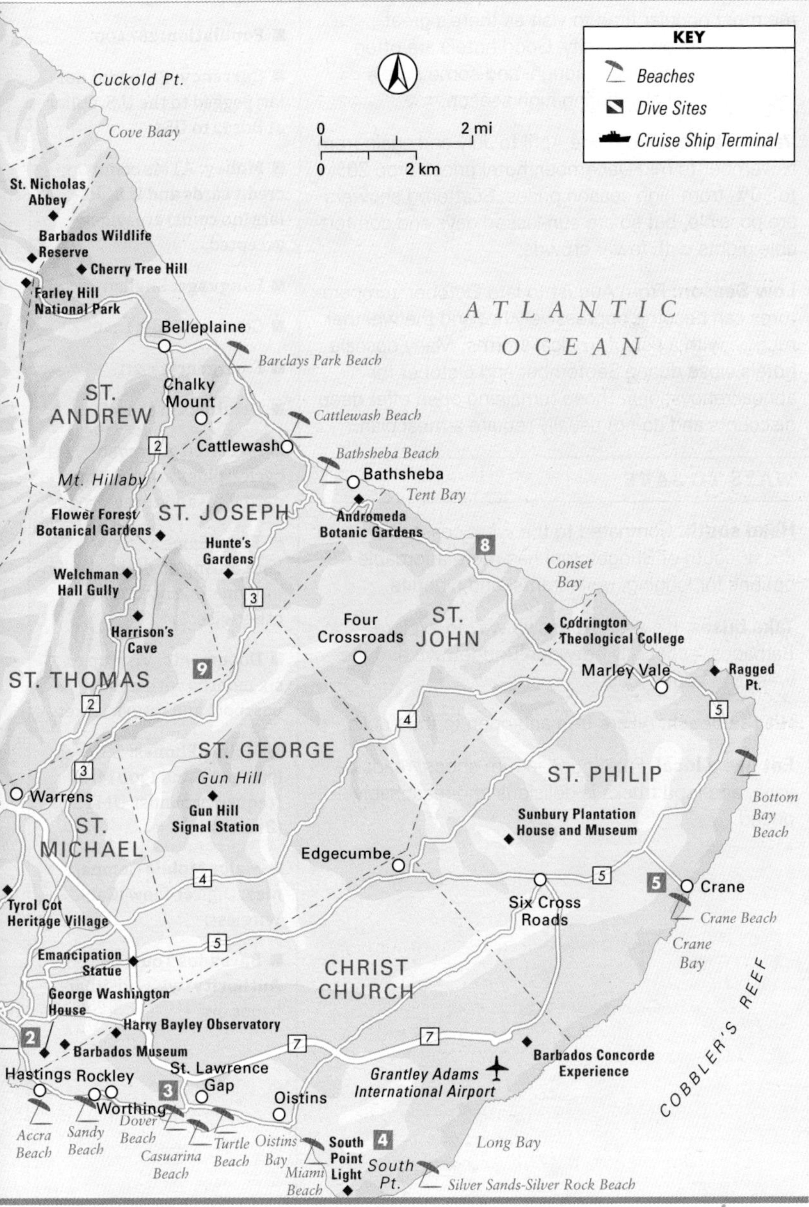
KEY
Beaches
Dive Sites
Cruise Ship Terminal
0
2 mi
0
2 km
ATLANTIC OCEAN
Cuckold Pt.
Cove Baay
St. Nicholas Abbey
Barbados Wildlife Reserve
Cherry Tree Hill
Farley Hill National Park
Belleplaine
Barclays Park Beach
ST. ANDREW
Chalky Mount
Cattlewash Beach
Cattlewash
Bathsheba Beach
Bathsheba
Tent Bay
Mt. Hillaby
Flower Forest Botanical Gardens
ST. JOSEPH
Andromeda Botanic Gardens
Hunte's Gardens
Welchman Hall Gully
Conset Bay
Harrison's Cave
Four Crossroads
ST. JOHN
Codrington Theological College
Marley Vale
Ragged Pt.
ST. THOMAS
ST. GEORGE
Gun Hill
Gun Hill Signal Station
ST. PHILIP
Warrens
ST. MICHAEL
Sunbury Plantation House and Museum
Bottom Bay Beach
Edgecumbe
Six Cross Roads
Crane
Crane Beach
Crane Bay
Tyrol Cot Heritage Village
Emancipation Statue
CHRIST CHURCH
George Washington House
Harry Bayley Observatory
Barbados Museum
COBBLER'S REEF
Barbados Concorde Experience
St. Lawrence Gap
Grantley Adams International Airport
Hastings
Rockley
Worthing
Oistins
Accra Beach
Sandy Beach
Dover Beach
Casuarina Beach
Turtle Beach
Oistins Bay
Miami Beach
South Point Light
South Pt.
Long Bay
Silver Sands-Silver Rock Beach

ISLAND SNAPSHOT

WHEN TO GO

High Season: Mid-December through mid-April is the most popular time to visit as there's great weather and low humidity. Good hotels are often booked far in advance though, and some hotels require a meal plan during high season.

Value Season: From late April to July and again from November to mid-December, hotel prices drop 20% to 50% from high-season prices. Scattered showers are possible, but so are sun-kissed days and comfortable nights with fewer crowds.

Low Season: From August to late October, temperatures can become oppressively hot and the weather muggy, with a risk of tropical storms. Many upscale hotels close during September and October for annual renovations. Those remaining open offer deep discounts and do not usually require a meal plan.

WAYS TO SAVE

Head south. Compared to the west coast, the south coast (south of Bridgetown) has more affordable options for lodging, restaurants, and nightlife.

Take buses. It's an inexpensive way to explore Barbados, especially between Bridgetown and the west and south coasts.

Hit the beach. All are free and open to the public.

Eat like a local. Fare found in rum shops, roadside vans, and food trucks is delicious and reasonably priced.

AT A GLANCE

- **Capital:** Bridgetown
- **Population:** 287,400
- **Currency:** Barbados dollar; pegged to the U.S. dollar at Bds$2 to US$1
- **Money:** ATMs common; credit cards and U.S. dollars (no coins) are widely accepted
- **Language:** English
- **Country Code:** 1 246
- **Emergencies:** 211
- **Driving:** On the left
- **Electricity:** 110v/50 cycles; plugs are U.S. standard two- and three-prong
- **Time:** Same as New York during daylight saving time; one hour ahead otherwise
- **Documents:** Visit up to six months with a valid passport and return ticket
- **Mobile Phones:** GSM (900, 1800, and 1900 MHz frequency bands); UMTS (B1 2100)
- **Major Mobile Companies:** Digicel, Flow (Cable & Wireless)
- **Barbados Tourism Authority:** www.visitbarbados.org

Isolated in the Atlantic Ocean, 108 miles (174 km) southeast of Saint Lucia, Barbados stands apart from its neighbors in the Lesser Antilles archipelago, the chain of islands that stretches in a graceful arc from the Virgin Islands to Trinidad. It's a sophisticated tropical island with a rich history, lodgings to suit every taste and pocketbook, and plenty to pique your interest both day and night.

The island's name, which means "bearded one," was given to it by the Portuguese who encountered a large number of bearded fig trees when they visited some centuries ago. An unusual name isn't the only thing that separates this island from others in the region. In terms of location, Barbados is completely surrounded by the Atlantic Ocean and is not touched by the Caribbean Sea at all. In terms of geology, instead of being the peak of a volcanic mountain range, Barbados is the top of a single, relatively flat protuberance of coral and limestone.

Many Bajans (*Bay*-juns, derived from the phonetic British pronunciation of Barbadian) live and work in and around Bridgetown, the capital city, which is situated on the southwest coast of the pear-shape island. Bridgetown, along with its surrounding Garrison, is a UNESCO World Heritage Site. In this region, broad sandy beaches and coves make up the coastline; the interior is consumed by forested hills and gullies and acre upon acre of sugarcane.

Without question, Barbados is the "most British" island in the Caribbean. British rule in Barbados carried on uninterrupted for 340 years—from the first established British settlement in 1627 until independence was granted in 1966. That's not to say that there weren't significant struggles in Barbados, as elsewhere in the Caribbean. Between the 17th- and 18th-century, British landowners' African-born slaves and other indentured servants shaped Barbados history.

Although Barbados achieved universal voting rights in 1943 and opted for full independence from the United Kingdom in 1966, British influence remains strong today in terms of local manners, attitudes, sports, customs, and politics. It's all tempered, of course, by the characteristically warm nature of the Bajan people. What's more, African and North American influences here have resulted in a truly Caribbean cocktail of arts, culture, language, and identity.

Visitor amenities are concentrated on the west coast, in St. James and St. Peter parishes (appropriately dubbed the Platinum Coast), and the south coast, in Christ Church Parish. Along the west coast—toward historic Holetown, site of the first British settlement, and north to the quaint "city" of Speightstown—are luxury beachfront resorts, luxurious private villas, and fine restaurants—all enveloped by lush gardens and tropical foliage. The trendier, more commercial south coast offers competitively priced hotels and beach resorts, and its St. Lawrence Gap area is jam-packed with restaurants and nightlife. The relatively wide-open spaces along the southeast coast are proving ripe for development, with some wonderful hotels taking up the baton for south coast luxury. For their own vacations, though, Bajans escape to the rugged east coast, where the Atlantic surf pounds the dramatic shoreline with unrelenting force.

Barbadians are warm, friendly, and hospitable people who are genuinely proud of their country and culture. Although tourism is the island's number one industry, the island has a sophisticated business community and stable government; so life here doesn't skip a beat once vacationers head home or cruise passengers return to their ship. That said, your heart may skip a beat when you think about your wonderful time in Barbados.

MAJOR REGIONS

The terrain changes dramatically from each of the island's 11 parishes to the next, and so does the pace. **Bridgetown,** the capital, is a small but busy Caribbean city in the parish of St. Michael. Just south of Bridgetown is the Garrison Historic District, which became a UNESCO World Heritage Site in 2011.

On the lively **South Coast,** the daytime hustle and bustle produce palpable energy that continues well into the night at restaurants and bars. Stretching along Highway 7 from The Garrison are the bustling commercial areas of Hastings, Rockley, and Worthing. This area, including St. Lawrence Gap, is chockablock with condos, high- and low-rise hotels, and beach parks. It also has many places to eat, drink, shop, and party. Oistins, just east of St. Lawrence Gap, is one of the island's four major towns (along with Bridgetown, Holetown, and Speightstown) and the only "town" on the south coast. It's known for its Friday night Fish Fry. Crane marks the beginning of the island's southeast coast, which extends as far as Ragged Point.

The **West Coast** extends from just north of Bridgetown, through St. James Parish and the city of Holetown, to Speightstown in St. Peter Parish. Gentle Caribbean waves lap the coastline, and leafy mahogany trees shade its stunning coves and sandy beaches. Elegant homes and luxury hotels make up much of the waterfront property in this area. Dubbed Barbados's "Platinum Coast," due to the white sand beaches, it is a direct contrast to the small villages and vast sugar plantations found throughout the **Central Interior** that reflect the island's history.

On the dramatic **East Coast,** the crashing Atlantic surf has eroded the shoreline, forming steep cliffs and exposing prehistoric rocks that look like giant mushrooms. Bathsheba and Cattlewash in St. Joseph Parish are favorite seacoast destinations for local folks on weekends and holidays. Farther north in St. Andrew's Parish, lies The Scottish District. Named after the freed indentured workers from Scotland who settled in the area. The terrain reminded them of Scotland's roaming glens. From the top of Cherry Tree Hill you can see the full length of the island's East coast and sweeping views out over the Atlantic. Part of the St. Nicholas Abbey plantation, Cherry Tree Hill was named for the large number of cherry trees that once stood here. They have since been replaced by an arch of beautiful Mahogany trees.

Planning

Getting Here and Around

AIR

You can fly nonstop to Barbados from Miami and Charlotte (American); Boston, Fort Lauderdale, and New York–JFK (JetBlue); Newark and Washington Dulles (United); Toronto (Air Canada, Westjet).

Caribbean Airlines offers connecting service from Fort Lauderdale, Miami, Orlando, and New York–JFK via Port of Spain, Trinidad, but this adds at least two hours to your flight time even in the best of circumstances and may not be the best option for most Americans. Barbados is also well connected to other Caribbean islands via LIAT airline. Grenadines Air Alliance (Mustique Airways and SVG Air) connects Barbados with St. Vincent and with Bequia, Canouan, Mustique, and Union Island in the Grenadines. Many passengers use Barbados as a transit hub, often spending the night each way. Not all airlines flying into Barbados have local numbers. If your airline doesn't have a local contact number on the island, you may have to pay for the call.

Airports and Transfers: Grantley Adams International Airport (BGI) is a stunning, relatively modern facility located in Christ Church Parish, on the south coast. The airport is about 15 minutes from most hotels situated along the south or east coast, 45 minutes from the west coast, and about 30 minutes from Bridgetown. If your hotel does not offer airport transfers, you can take a taxi or a shared van service to your resort. There is duty-free available on arrival, though limited, but the departure lounge is set up like a small mall.

AIRLINE CONTACTS American Airlines. ☎ *246/428–4170, 800/744–0006 in Barbados, 800/433–7300 in U.S.* 🌐 *www.aa.com.* **Caribbean Airlines.** ☎ *800/744–2225 in the Caribbean, 800/920–4225 in U.S.* 🌐 *www.caribbean-airlines.com.* **Grenadine Air Alliance.** ☎ *246/228–5544* 🌐 *www.grenadine-air.com.* **JetBlue.** ☎ *877/596–2413 in Barbados, 800/538–2583 in U.S.* 🌐 *www.jetblue.com.* **LIAT.** ☎ *246/434–5428 in Barbados, 888/844–5428 in the Caribbean, 268/480–5601 in U.S. (toll call)* 🌐 *www.liat.com.*

AIRPORT Grantley Adams International Airport. *(BGI)* ☎ *246/536–1300* 🌐 *www.gaia.bb.*

BUS

Bus service is efficient and inexpensive. Public buses are blue with a yellow stripe; yellow buses with a blue stripe are privately owned and operated; and private "Zed-R" vans (so called for their ZR license plate designation) are white with a maroon stripe and also privately owned and operated. All buses travel frequently along Highway 1 (between Bridgetown and Speightstown) and Highway 7 (along the south coast), as well as inland routes. The fare is Bds$3.50 for any one destination; exact change in local currency is appreciated. Buses run about every 20 minutes until midnight. Small signs on roadside poles that say "To City" or "Out of City," meaning the direction relative to Bridgetown, mark the bus stops. Flag down the bus with your hand, even if you're standing at the stop. Bridgetown terminals are at Fairchild Street for buses to the south and east and at Lower Green for buses to Speightstown via the west coast.

CAR

Barbados has busy roads, many of which are in need of repair. Traffic can be heavy on the highways, particularly around Bridgetown; Apps such as Waze are widely used. Be sure to keep a map handy, as the road system in the countryside can be very confusing. Be especially careful negotiating roundabouts (traffic circles).

Bajans drive on the left, British-style. They also flash their lights often, either to let you out at an intersection or to simply say "Hello" if they recognize you. The speed limit is 30 mph (50 kph) in the country, 20 mph (30 kph) in town. Bridgetown actually has rush hours: 7 to 9 am and 4 to 6 pm. Park only in approved parking areas; downtown parking costs Bds75¢ to Bds$1 per hour.

Car Rentals: Most car rental agencies require renters to be between 21 and either 70 or 75 years of age and have a valid driver's license and major credit card. Dozens of agencies rent cars, jeeps, or minimokes (small, open-sided vehicles). Rates range from about $75 per day for a minimoke to $100 or more per day for a four-wheel-drive vehicle and $150 or more for a luxury car (you can get a better deal if you book for a week or more) in high season. Most firms also offer discounted three-day rates, and many require at least a two-day rental in high season. The rental generally includes insurance, pickup and delivery service, maps, 24-hour emergency service, and unlimited mileage.

A local driver's permit, which costs $5 (valid for two months), is obtained through the rental agency.

CAR RENTAL CONTACTS Coconut Car Rentals. ✉ *Dayrell's Rd., Rockley* ☎ *246/262–1115.* **Courtesy Rent-A-Car.** ✉ *Grantley Adams International Airport* ☎ *246/431–4160* 🌐 *www.courtesyrentalsbb.com.* **Drive-a-Matic Car Rentals.** ✉ *CWTS Complex, Lower Estate, Warrens* ☎ *246/434–8440, 800/581–8773* 🌐 *www.carhire.tv.*

TAXI

Taxis operate 24 hours a day. They aren't metered but rates are fixed by the government. Taxis carry up to three passengers, and the fare may be shared. Sample one-way fares from Bridgetown are Bds$20 to Holetown, Bds$25 to Speightstown, Bds$20 to St. Lawrence Gap, and Bds$30 to Bathsheba. Always ask the driver to quote the price before you get in, and be sure that you both understand whether it's quoted in Bds or U.S. dollars. Drivers can also be hired for an hourly rate of about Bds$35–Bds$40 for up to three people. There are also local taxi apps such as PickUp.

Beaches

Geologically, Barbados is a coral-and-limestone island (not volcanic) with only one river and, as a result, beautiful beaches. The southern and western coastlines tend to have calmer stretches, with clear waters that are perfect for swimming and snorkeling. The east and north coasts are more dramatic, with cliffs and large waves; perfect for surfing, but dangerous for swimming.

Across the island, when the surf is too high and swimming becomes dangerous, a red flag will be hoisted on the beach. A yellow flag—or a red flag at half-staff—means swim with caution. Topless sunbathing is not allowed anywhere in Barbados.

Beaches are not private in Barbados but resorts have made access to some more difficult.

Health and Safety

Dengue, chikungunya, and zika have all been reported throughout the Caribbean. We recommend that you protect yourself from these mosquito-borne illnesses by keeping your skin covered and/or wearing mosquito repellent. The mosquitoes that transmit these viruses are as active by day as they are by night.

Crime isn't a major problem in Barbados, but take normal precautions. Lock your room, and don't leave valuables— particularly passports, tickets, and wallets— in plain sight or unattended on the beach. Use your hotel safe. For personal safety,

On the island's southeast coast, the pink sands of Crane Beach are perfect for a stroll.

avoid walking on the beach or on unlighted streets at night. Lock your rental car, and don't pick up hitchhikers. Using or trafficking in illegal drugs is strictly prohibited in Barbados. Any offense is punishable by a hefty fine, imprisonment, or both.

Hotels

Great resorts run the gamut—from unpretentious to knock-your-socks-off—in size, intimacy, amenities, and price. Many are well suited to families. Most visitors stay either in luxurious beachfront enclaves on the fashionable west coast—in St. James and St. Peter parishes, north of Bridgetown—or on the action-packed south coast with easy access to small, independent restaurants, bars, and nightclubs in and around St. Lawrence Gap. A few inns on the remote southeast and east coasts offer spectacular ocean views and tranquillity, but those on the east coast don't have swimming beaches nearby.

Families and long-term visitors may choose from a variety of condos—from busy time-share resorts to more sedate holiday complexes. Villas and villa complexes range from luxurious to simple.

In keeping with the smoke-free policy enforced throughout Barbados, smoking is restricted to open outdoor areas such as the beach. It is not permitted in hotels (neither rooms nor public areas) or in restaurants.

Prices in Barbados can be twice as high in season (December 15–April 15) as during the quieter months, although special promotions and vacation packages are often available throughout the year. Most hotels include no meals in their rates; some include breakfast, many offer a meal plan, others require you to purchase the meal plan in the high season, and a few offer all-inclusive packages.

Hotel reviews have been shortened. For full information, visit Fodors.com.

PRIVATE VILLAS AND CONDOS

Families and long-term visitors may choose from a wide variety of condos (everything from busy time-share resorts to more sedate vacation complexes). Villas and villa complexes can be luxurious, simple, or something in between. There are also a wide range of booking platforms available, including Airbnb.

Local real-estate agencies will arrange vacation rentals of privately owned villas and condos along the west coast in St. James and St. Peter. All villas and condos are fully furnished and equipped, including appropriate staff depending on the size of the villa or unit—which can range from one to eight bedrooms; the staff usually works six days a week. Most villas have TVs and other entertainment devices; all properties have telephones and Internet access. International telephone calls are usually blocked; plan on using your own mobile phone or a phone card. Vehicles generally are not included in the rates, but rental cars can be arranged for and delivered to the villa upon request. Linens and basic supplies (such as bath soap, toilet tissue, and dishwashing detergent) are normally included.

Units with one to six bedrooms and as many baths run $200 to $2,500 per night in summer and double that in winter. Rates include utilities and government taxes. The only additional cost is for groceries, staff gratuities, and extraordinary or optional requests. A security deposit is required upon booking and refunded seven days after departure less any damages or unpaid miscellaneous charges.

Apartments are available for vacation rentals in buildings or complexes that can have as few as three or four units or as many as 30 to 40 units—or even more. Prices range from $30 to $300 per night.

CONTACTS Airbnb. ☎ *855/424–7262, 415/800–5959 in U.S.* 🌐 *www.airbnb.com.* **Altman Real Estate.** ✉ *Hwy. 1, Derricks, Durants* ☎ *246/432–0840, 866/360–5292 in U.S.* 🌐 *www.altmanbarbados.com.* **Blue Sky Luxury.** ✉ *Newton House, Hwy. 1B, Battaleys* ☎ *246/622–4466, 866/404–9600 in U.S.* 🌐 *www.blueskyluxury.com.* **Island Villas.** ✉ *Trents Bldg., Holetown* ☎ *246/432–4627, 866/978–8499 in U.S.* 🌐 *www.island-villas.com.*

What It Costs in U.S. Dollars

	$	$$	$$$	$$$$
RESTAURANTS				
	under $13	$13–$20	$21–$30	over $30
HOTELS				
	under $275	$275–$375	$376–$475	over $475

Nightlife

When the sun goes down, Bajans "lime"—which can mean anything from getting together for a drink and casual chat to enjoying a full-blown "jump-up" or street party. Most resorts have nightly entertainment in season, and nightclubs often have live bands for listening and dancing. The busiest bars and dance clubs rage until 3 am. On Saturday night, some clubs—especially those with live music—charge a cover of $20 or more. Many bars and nightspots feature happy hours.

Barbados supports the rum industry with more than 1,600 "rum shops," simple bars where (mostly) men congregate to discuss the world or life in general, drink rum, and eat a cutter (sandwich). In more sophisticated establishments, you can find upscale rum cocktails made with the island's renowned Mount Gay and Cockspur brands—and no shortage of Barbados's own Banks Beer.

Restaurants

First-class restaurants and hotel dining rooms serve quite sophisticated cuisine—often prepared by chefs with international experience and rivaling the dishes served in the world's best restaurants. Most menus include seafood: dolphin (mahimahi), kingfish, snapper, and flying fish prepared every way imaginable. Flying fish is so popular that it has become an official national symbol. Shellfish also abounds, as do steak, pork, and local black-belly lamb.

Specialty dishes include *buljol* (a cold salad of pickled codfish, tomatoes, onions, sweet peppers, and celery) and *conkies* (cornmeal, coconut, pumpkin, raisins, sweet potatoes, and spices, mixed together, wrapped in a banana leaf, and steamed). *Cou-cou,* often served with steamed flying fish, is a mixture of cornmeal and okra and usually topped with a spicy creole sauce made from tomatoes, onions, and sweet peppers. Bajan-style pepper pot is a hearty stew of oxtail, beef, and other meats in a rich, spicy gravy, simmered overnight.

For lunch, restaurants often offer a traditional Bajan buffet of fried fish, baked chicken, salads, macaroni pie (macaroni and cheese), and a selection of steamed or stewed provisions (local roots and vegetables). Be cautious with the West Indian condiments—like the sun, they're hotter than you think. Typical Bajan drinks—in addition to Banks Beer and Mount Gay, Cockspur, or Malibu rum—are *falernum* (a liqueur concocted of rum, sugar, lime juice, and almond essence); *mauby* (a nonalcoholic drink made by boiling bitter bark and spices, straining the mixture, and sweetening it); and Ponche Kuba, a creamy spiced rum liqueur (Caribbean eggnog) that's especially popular around the holidays. You're sure to enjoy the fresh fruit or rum punch, as well.

WHAT TO WEAR

The dress code for dinner in Barbados is conservative, casually elegant, and, occasionally, formal—a jacket and tie for gentlemen and a cocktail dress for ladies in the fanciest restaurants, particularly during the winter holiday season. Otherwise, a collared shirt for gents and a sundress or dress slacks for ladies. Jeans, shorts, and T-shirts (either sleeveless or with slogans) are always frowned upon at dinner. Beach attire is appropriate only at the beach.

Shopping

One of the most long-lasting souvenirs to bring home from Barbados is a piece of authentic Caribbean art. The colorful flowers, quaint villages, mesmerizing seascapes, and fascinating cultural experiences and activities that are endemic to the region and familiar to visitors have been translated by local artists onto canvas and into photographs, sculpture, and other media. Gift shops and even some restaurants display local artwork for sale, but the broadest array will be found in a gallery. Typical Bajan crafts include pottery and ceramics, shell and glass art, wood carvings, handmade dolls, watercolors, and other artwork (both originals and prints).

Although many of the private homes, greathouses, and museums in Barbados are filled with priceless antiques, you'll find few for sale—mainly British antiques and some local pieces, particularly mahogany furniture. Look instead for more reasonably priced (and easier to transport) old prints and paintings.

DUTY-FREE SHOPPING

Duty-free luxury goods—china, crystal, cameras, porcelain, leather items, electronics, jewelry, perfume, and clothing—are found at Bridgetown's Broad Street department stores and their branches, at the high-end Limegrove Lifestyle Centre in Holetown, at the Bridgetown

Cruise Terminal (for passengers only), and the departure lounge at Grantley Adams International Airport. Prices are often 30% to 40% less than full retail. To buy goods at duty-free prices, you must produce your passport, immigration form, or driver's license, along with departure information (such as flight number and date) at the time of purchase—or you can have your purchases delivered free to the airport or harbor for pickup; duty-free alcohol, tobacco products, and some electronic equipment *must* be delivered to you at the airport or harbor.

GROCERIES

If you've chosen self-catering lodgings, are looking for snacks, or just want to explore a local grocery store, you'll find large, modern supermarkets at Sunset Crest in Holetown on the west coast; in Oistins, at Sargeant's Village (Sheraton Mall), and in Worthing on the south coast; and at Warrens (Highway 2, north of Bridgetown) in St. Michael. Don't be shocked by the prices: Barbados imports most food. Local, more affordable options include Cheapside Market (located in Bridgetown) and roadside vendors. Local meat can be purchased from Carmita's, and fish can be bought at the Bridgetown and Oistins fish markets.

Tours

Taxi drivers will give you a personalized tour of Barbados for about $35 to $40 per hour for up to three people. Or you can choose an overland mountain-bike journey, a 4x4 safari expedition, or a full-day bus excursion. The prices vary according to the mode of travel and the number and kind of attractions included. Ask guest services at your hotel to help you make arrangements.

Eco Adventures

GUIDED TOURS | This tour company proudly declares that they offers tours by Bajans. The 5½ hour Freedom Footprints tour explains the real story of Barbados and takes guests to interesting historical places like the Newton Slave Burial Ground, the only known burial ground in the Western Hemisphere for the enslaved on a plantation, the free villages of Bourne's Land and Sweet Bottom, and the Barbados museum. A full traditional Bajan lunch is included. 🌐 *www.ecoadventures-barbados.com.*

Island Safari

ADVENTURE TOURS | **FAMILY** | Discover all the popular attractions and scenic locations via a 4x4 jeep—including some gullies, forests, and remote areas that are inaccessible by conventional cars and buses. A full-day tour (5½ hours) includes snacks or lunch. You can also arrange your own private safari (three to six hours). ✉ *CWTS Complex, Salters Rd., Lower Estate* ☎ *246/429–5337* 🌐 *www.islandsafari.bb* 🎫 *From $98.*

SunTours Barbados

GUIDED TOURS | **FAMILY** | Whether you want to take a full-day island tour, concentrate on historic sites, focus on photography, or go as you please, SunTours is happy to accommodate your interests. Options range from a half-day tour of Bridgetown and The Garrison to a full-day island tour (including lunch and entrance fees)—or you can pay by the hour for a personalized adventure for up to four people. Vehicles vary depending on the group; the fleet includes comfortable passenger cars and SUVs, luxury cars and limos, minivans (with or without a wheelchair lift), and large tour buses. ✉ *CWTS Complex, Hwy. 4B, Lower Estate* ☎ *246/434–8430* 🎫 *From $35.*

Visitor Information

The main tourism office is north of Bridgetown in the town of Warrens, but there are also locations at the Grantley Adams International Airport and at the Cruise Ship Terminal.

CONTACTS Barbados Tourism Marketing, Inc. ✉ *1 Barbados Pl., Warrens* ☎ *246/535–3700, 212/551–4350 in U.S.* 🌐 *www.visitbarbados.org.*

Weddings

There are no minimum residency requirements to get married; however, you both need to obtain a marriage license, in person, from the Ministry of Home Affairs (☎ 246/621–0227). All fees must be paid in cash. Fees vary greatly; it's best to get in touch with a local wedding planner or your hotel for specifics. If either party is divorced or widowed, the appropriate paperwork must be presented to obtain the license.

Bridgetown and the Garrison

This bustling capital city, inscribed in 2011—along with The Garrison Historic Site—onto the UNESCO World Heritage List, is a duty-free port with a compact shopping area. The principal thoroughfare is Broad Street, which leads west from National Heroes Square. Downtown Bridgetown is easily walkable, whether you're interested in visiting historical sights, duty-free shopping, or simply having lunch and people-watching along The Careenage.

GETTING HERE AND AROUND

Several hotels offer a free shuttle service that takes guests to and from downtown Bridgetown (Monday through Saturday during business hours), and it's a short walk or quick taxi ride from the Cruise Ship Terminal. For sights and experiences located beyond the city center, you'll need to drive or take a taxi or bus.

Sights

Barbados Military Cemetery

CEMETERY | The cemetery, also referred to as Gravesend or Garrison Military Cemetery, is near the shore behind historic St. Ann's Fort. First used in 1780, when the area was pretty much marshland, the dead were placed in shallow graves or simply left on top of the ground where, within a few short days, many were absorbed into the swamp. In the early 20th century, a number of the remaining graves were dug up to provide room for oil storage tanks; salvaged headstones were placed on a cenotaph, erected in 1920–24. A "Cross of Sacrifice" was erected in 1982 to honor all the military dead; a second cenotaph, erected in 2003, honors the Barbadian merchant seamen who died in World War II. ✉ *Needham's Point, Carlisle Bay, Garrison* ↔ *Behind Hilton Barbados Resort* ☎ *246/536–2021* 🎫 *Free.*

★ **Barbados Museum & Historical Society**

HISTORY MUSEUM | **FAMILY** | The galleries of this museum, established in 1930 and located in Barbados's UNESCO World Heritage Site, are housed in a 19th-century military prison building. More than 5,000 artifacts—dating from prehistoric times through the 21st century—tell the story of the people of Barbados, revealing the island's rich history, culture, and heritage. The on-site Shilstone Memorial Library is home to rare West Indian materials, archival documents, photographs, hard-to-find books, and maps dating from the 17th century. ✉ *St. Ann's Garrison, Hwy. 7, Garrison* ☎ *246/538–0201* 🎫 *Bds$15.*

Barbados Turf Club

SPORTS VENUE | **FAMILY** | Horse racing is a big part of Bajan culture, and "going to the races" is an event for everyone. The races are administered by the Barbados Turf Club. Races take place on alternate Saturdays throughout the year at the Garrison Savannah, a 6-furlong grass

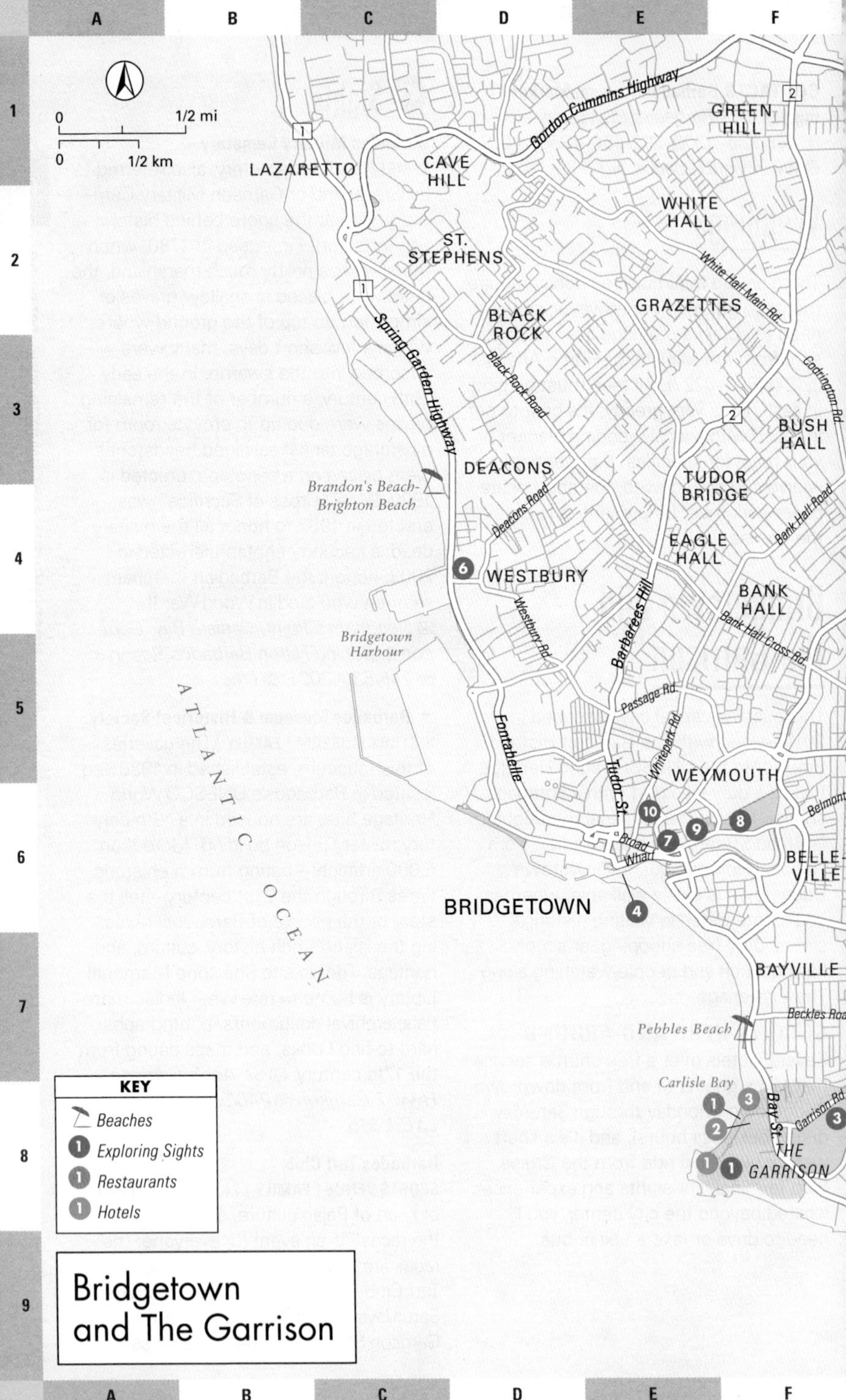

A
B
C
D
E
F
1
2
3
4
5
6
7
8
9
0
1/2 mi
1/2 km
LAZARETTO
CAVE HILL
Gordon Cummins Highway
GREEN HILL
WHITE HALL
ST. STEPHENS
White Hall Main Rd.
BLACK ROCK
GRAZETTES
Spring Garden Highway
Black Rock Road
Codrington Rd.
BUSH HALL
DEACONS
TUDOR BRIDGE
Brandon's Beach-Brighton Beach
Deacons Road
Bank Hall Road
EAGLE HALL
WESTBURY
BANK HALL
Barbarees Hill
Westbury Rd.
Bank Hall Cross Rd.
Bridgetown Harbour
ATLANTIC OCEAN
Passage Rd.
Fontabelle
Whitepark Rd.
Tudor St.
WEYMOUTH
Belmont
Broad
Wharf
BELLE-VILLE
BRIDGETOWN
BAYVILLE
Beckles Road
Pebbles Beach
Carlisle Bay
Bay St.
Garrison Rd.
THE GARRISON
KEY
Beaches
Exploring Sights
Restaurants
Hotels
Bridgetown and The Garrison

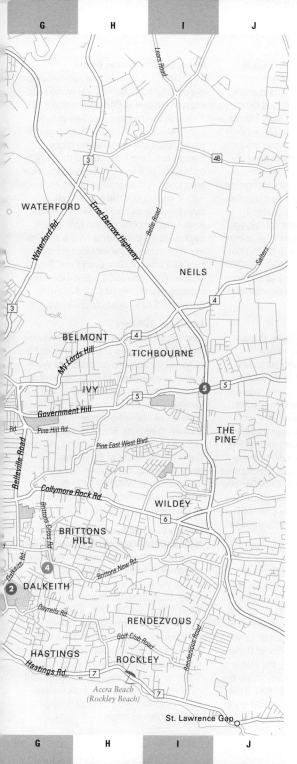

Sights

1 Barbados Military Cemetery F8
2 Barbados Museum & Historical Society G8
3 Barbados Turf Club F8
4 The Careenage E6
5 Emancipation Statue I5
6 Mount Gay Rum Visitors Centre D4
7 Parliament Buildings E6
8 Queen's Park and Queen's Park Gallery F6
9 St. Michael's Cathedral E6
10 Synagogue Historic District E6

Restaurants

1 Dippers Beach Bar F8

Hotels

1 Hilton Barbados Resort E8
2 Island Inn Hotel F8
3 Radisson Aquatica Resort Barbados F8
4 Sweetfield Manor G7

oval in Christ Church, about 3 miles (5 km) south of Bridgetown. There is also occasional night racing. Important events include the Sandy Lane Barbados Gold Cup, held in late February or early March, and the Boxing Day Races on December 26. You can watch for free on the grounds, or pay for tickets, which vary in price according to where you sit—the dress-to-the-nines boxes, the members lounge, or the grandstands (grabbing a seat up close on the grounds with a picnic is also an option). Regardless of where you sit, you can't help but get caught up in the energy and excitement of the events. ✉ *The Garrison Savannah, Garrison* ☎ *246/626–3980* 🌐 *www.barbadosturfclub.org* 🎫 *Entrance ranges from $10Bds to $100Bds for the day. Event prices vary.*

The Careenage

MARINA/PIER | In the early days, Bridgetown's natural harbor was where schooners were turned on their sides (careened) to be scraped of barnacles and repainted. Today, The Careenage serves as a marina for pleasure yachts and excursion boats, as well as a gathering place for locals and tourists alike. A boardwalk skirts the north side of The Careenage; on the south side, a lovely esplanade has pathways and benches for pedestrians and a statue of Errol Barrow, the first prime minister of Barbados. The Chamberlain Bridge and the Charles Duncan O'Neal Bridge span The Careenage. ✉ *Bridgetown.*

Emancipation Statue

PUBLIC ART | This powerful statue of a slave—whose raised hands, with broken chains hanging from each wrist, evoke both contempt and victory—is commonly referred to as the Bussa Statue. Bussa was the man who, in 1816, led the first slave rebellion on Barbados. The work of Barbadian sculptor Karl Brodhagen, the statue was erected in 1985 to commemorate the emancipation of the slaves in 1834. ✉ *St. Barnabas Roundabout, Haggatt Hall* ✣ *At intersection of ABC Hwy. and Hwy. 5.*

Mount Gay Rum Visitors Centre

DISTILLERY | On this popular tour, you learn the colorful story behind the world's oldest rum—made in Barbados since 1703. Although the modern distillery is in St. Lucy Parish, in the far north, tour guides here explain the rum-making process. Equipment, both historic and modern, is on display, and rows and rows of barrels are stored in this location. Tours conclude with a tasting and the opportunity to buy duty-free rum and gifts—and even have lunch or cocktails (no children on cocktail tour), depending on the day. The lunch or cocktail tour includes transportation. ✉ *Exmouth Gap, Brandons, Spring Garden Hwy.* ☎ *246/227–8864* 🌐 *www.mountgayrum.com* 🎫 *$20, $70 with cocktails, $75 with lunch* 🕒 *Closed Sun.*

Parliament Buildings

GOVERNMENT BUILDING | **FAMILY** | Overlooking National Heroes Square in the center of town, these Victorian buildings were constructed around 1870 to house the British Commonwealth's third-oldest parliament (after Britain itself and Bermuda). A series of stained-glass windows in the East Wing depicts British monarchs from James I to Victoria. The National Heroes Gallery & Museum of Parliament is in the West Wing. ✉ *National Heroes Sq., Trafalgar St.* ☎ *246/310–5400* 🌐 *www.barbadosparliament.com* 🎫 *Museum $10* 🕒 *Closed Tues. and Sun.*

Queen's Park and Queen's Park Gallery

NATIONAL PARK | **FAMILY** | This national park is the site of beautiful gardens, a children's playground, a sports/events field, and one of the island's two immense baobab trees. Brought to Barbados from Guinea, West Africa, around 1738, this tree has a girth of more than 60 feet. Queen's Park House, built in 1783 and the historic home of the British troop commander, now houses the Daphne Joseph Hackett Theatre, which hosts special events and exhibits, and the Queen's Park Gallery, which features work by both emerging and established artists.

The park underwent refurbishments in 2021; the most notable is the new lake that features a stunning map of Barbados. There are plans to rename the park and transform the space into a hub of Bajan arts and culture.

✉ *Queen's Park, Constitution Rd.* ☎ *246/427–2345* 🌐 *www.ncf.bb/queens-park-gallery* 🎫 *Free* 🕒 *Gallery closed Sun. and Mon.*

St. Michael's Cathedral
CHURCH | Although no one has proven it, George Washington is said to have worshipped here in 1751 during his only trip outside the United States. By then, the original structure was already nearly a century old. Destroyed or damaged twice by hurricanes, the cathedral was rebuilt in 1789 and again in 1831. Officially called "Cathedral Church of Saint Michael and All Angels," it currently seats 1,600 people and boasts the largest pipe organ in the Caribbean. ✉ *St. Michael's Row* ✣ *East of National Heroes Sq.* ☎ *246/427–0790* 🌐 *saintmichaelscathedral.bb* 🕒 *Closed Mon.*

★ Synagogue Historic District
CEMETERY | FAMILY | Providing for the spiritual needs of one of the oldest Jewish congregations in the western hemisphere, the Nidhe Israel Synagogue was formed by Sephardic Jews who arrived in 1628 from Brazil and introduced sugarcane to Barbados. The adjoining cemetery has tombstones dating from the 1630s. The original house of worship, built in 1654, was destroyed in an 1831 hurricane, rebuilt in 1833, and restored in 1986 with the assistance of the Barbados National Trust. The adjacent museum, opened in 2009 in a restored coral-stone building from 1750, documents the story of the Barbados Jewish community. A significant project in 2017 updated the grounds and restored artisans' workshops and other buildings on the newly designated Synagogue Historic Site. You can arrange an insightful, private tour of both the grounds and the museum. Friday-night services are held in winter months, but the building is open to the public year-round. Shorts are not acceptable during services but may be worn at other times. ✉ *Synagogue La.* ☎ *246/436–6869* 🌐 *synagoguehistoricdistrict.com* 🎫 *Museum, Mikva and Synagogue $25* 🕒 *Closed weekends.*

Beaches

Brandon's Beach–Brighton Beach
BEACH | FAMILY | Just north of downtown Bridgetown and within walking distance of the cruise ship terminal, the sea at this southernmost pair of west coast beaches is as calm as a lake. This is also one of the island's longest sandy stretches: you can easily walk from here all the way up to Batts Rock Beach. On hot days, particularly on weekends and holidays, you'll find locals taking a quick dip. Beach chairs and umbrellas are available for rent. **Amenities:** food and drink; lifeguard; parking (no fee); showers; toilets. **Best for:** swimming; walking. ✉ *Spring Garden Hwy.*

★ Pebbles Beach
BEACH | FAMILY | On the southern side of Carlisle Bay, just south of Bridgetown, this broad half circle of white sand is one of the island's best family-friendly beaches—and it can become crowded on weekends and holidays. The southern end of the beach wraps around the Hilton Barbados; the northern end is adjacent to the Radisson Aquatica Resort Barbados. Umbrellas and beach chairs are available to rent. Bring snorkel gear and swim out to see one of the shipwrecks. Arrive early in the morning (before 7 am) to watch race horses from Garrison Savannah taking a swim. **Amenities:** food and drink; parking; showers; toilets; water sports. **Best for:** snorkeling; swimming; walking. ✉ *Aquatic Gap, Garrison* ✣ *South of Bridgetown.*

Restaurants

Dippers Beach Bar

$$ | **CARIBBEAN** | Located on the top floor of Barbados Cruising Club, Dippers is a relaxed affair, serving food—Bajan fishcakes, chicken, macaroni pie, and its world-famous cheesy garlic bread—and music into the night. Sit on the rooftop terrace and watch the sun set as you sip a rum punch. **Known for:** beach attire is acceptable; relaxed atmosphere; great food like cheesy garlic bread. *Average main: BD$25 Barbados Cruising Club, Aquatic Gap Located on Pebbles Beach just past the Radisson Aquatica Hotel barbadoscruisingclub.org.*

There are no hotels within Bridgetown, but hotels in the Garrison neighborhood are close enough if you want to be near to the capital.

Hilton Barbados Resort

$$$$ | **HOTEL** | **FAMILY** | Beautifully situated on the sandy Needham's Point peninsula, all 350 units in this high-rise resort hotel have private balconies overlooking either the ocean or Carlisle Bay; 77 rooms on executive floors offer a private lounge and concierge services. **Pros:** accessible rooms available; great location near town and on a beautiful beach; lots of services and amenities. **Cons:** lacks island ambience; huge group/convention hotel; service and communication should be better. *Rooms from: $480 Aquatic Gap, Needham's Point, Garrison 246/426–0200 www.hiltonbarbadosresort.com 350 rooms No Meals.*

Island Inn Hotel

$$$ | **HOTEL** | Constructed in 1804 as a rum storage facility for the British Regiment, this quaint, all-inclusive boutique hotel—less than a mile from Bridgetown and steps away from beautiful Pebbles Beach on Carlisle Bay—appeals to singles, couples, and families. **Pros:** excellent all-inclusive value; friendly, accommodating, attractive atmosphere; smartly decorated rooms. **Cons:** near but not directly on the beach; rooms near the front may be noisier and don't have a patio; small pool. *Rooms from: $435 Aquatic Gap, Garrison 246/436–6393 www.islandinnbarbados.com 24 rooms All-Inclusive.*

Radisson Aquatica Resort Barbados

$$$ | **HOTEL** | Rooms in this high-rise hotel overlooking pretty Carlisle Bay, just south of Bridgetown, are modern and sleek with espresso-color furniture, sparkling white linens, and each with a desk with ergonomic chair, comfortable sitting chair and ottoman, 42-inch flat-screen TV, and the latest in-room technology. **Pros:** convenient location; excellent beach; beautiful sunsets from ocean-facing rooms. **Cons:** skip the restaurant and opt for Dippers or the Hilton; noisy air-conditioning, no room refrigerator; pool area could use more umbrellas. *Rooms from: $430 Aquatic Gap, Garrison 246/426–4000, 800/333–3333 in U.S. www.radisson.com/barbados 124 rooms No Meals.*

★ **Sweetfield Manor**

$$ | **B&B/INN** | Perched on a ridge about a mile from downtown Bridgetown, this restored plantation house (circa 1900) was once the residence of the Dutch ambassador and is now a delightful bed-and-breakfast. **Pros:** peaceful enclave, primarily for adults; inviting pool and gardens; delicious gourmet breakfast. **Cons:** rental car advised; not recommended for young children; long walk (or short car ride) to beach. *Rooms from: $300 Brittons New Rd. 246/429–8356 sweetfieldmanor.com 10 rooms Free Breakfast.*

Nightlife

While Bridgetown has a couple of popular nightspots, Baxter's Road, just south of the city center, is sometimes called "The Street That Never Sleeps." Night owls head there any night of the week for after-hours fun and food. The strip of rum shops begins to hit its stride at 11 pm, but locals usually show up around 3 am. Street vendors sell freshly made "Baxter's Road" fried chicken and other snacks all night long, but Enid's is the place to see and be seen.

Shopping

Bridgetown's **Broad Street** is the primary downtown shopping area. **The Colonnade Mall,** in the historic Colonnade Building on Broad Street, has about 40 shops that sell everything from Piaget watches to postcards; across the street, **Mall 34** has more than 20 shops where you can buy duty-free goods, souvenirs, and snacks. At the **cruise ship terminal** shopping arcade, passengers can buy both duty-free goods and Barbadian-made crafts at more than 30 boutiques and a dozen vendor carts and stalls. Allow time before boarding your plane to shop in the **airport departure lounge,** which has a dozen or more shops that sell duty-free alcohol, souvenirs, clothing, and more.

A free Bridgetown shopping shuttle serves hotels on the south and west coasts, so guests can visit downtown shops, see the sights, and perhaps have lunch. The shuttle operates Monday through Saturday, departing from the hotels at 9:30 and 11 am and returning from Bridgetown at 1:30 and 3 pm. Reserve your seat with your hotel concierge a day ahead.

Hastings, Rockley, and Worthing

Hastings, Rockley, and Worthing are, essentially, bustling commercial areas, one after the other, that stretch along Highway 7 from The Garrison Historic Area to St. Lawrence Gap. You'll find a variety of hotels, restaurants, shops, and other businesses here; the mile-long South Coast Boardwalk that's perfect for a morning run, an evening stroll, or a walk along the beachfront any time of day; a public golf course (in Rockley); and beach after beach after beach.

Beaches

Accra Beach (*Rockley Beach*)
BEACH | **FAMILY** | This popular beach, adjacent to the Accra Beach Hotel, has a broad swath of white sand with gentle surf and a lifeguard, plenty of nearby restaurants for refreshments, a playground, and beach stalls for renting chairs and equipment for snorkeling and other water sports. The South Coast Boardwalk, great for walking or running, begins here and follows the waterfront west—past private homes, restaurants, and bars—for about a mile (1½ km) to Needham's Point. **Amenities:** food and drink; lifeguards; parking (no fee); water sports. **Best for:** snorkeling; swimming; walking. ✉ *Hwy. 7, Rockley.*

Restaurants

Buzo Osteria Italiana
$$$$ | **ITALIAN** | **FAMILY** | Specialties at this lively, modern, air-conditioned restaurant include fresh pasta, thin-crust pizzas, colorful salads, and decadent desserts. Enjoy an aperitif, martini, or their specialty sorrel cocktail at the chic bar. **Known for:** extensive wine list; consistently good service; variety of pizza toppings. [$] *Average main: $40* ✉ *The Pavillion, Hastings Main Rd., Worthing* ☎ *246/629–2896* 🌐 *buzorestaurant.com.*

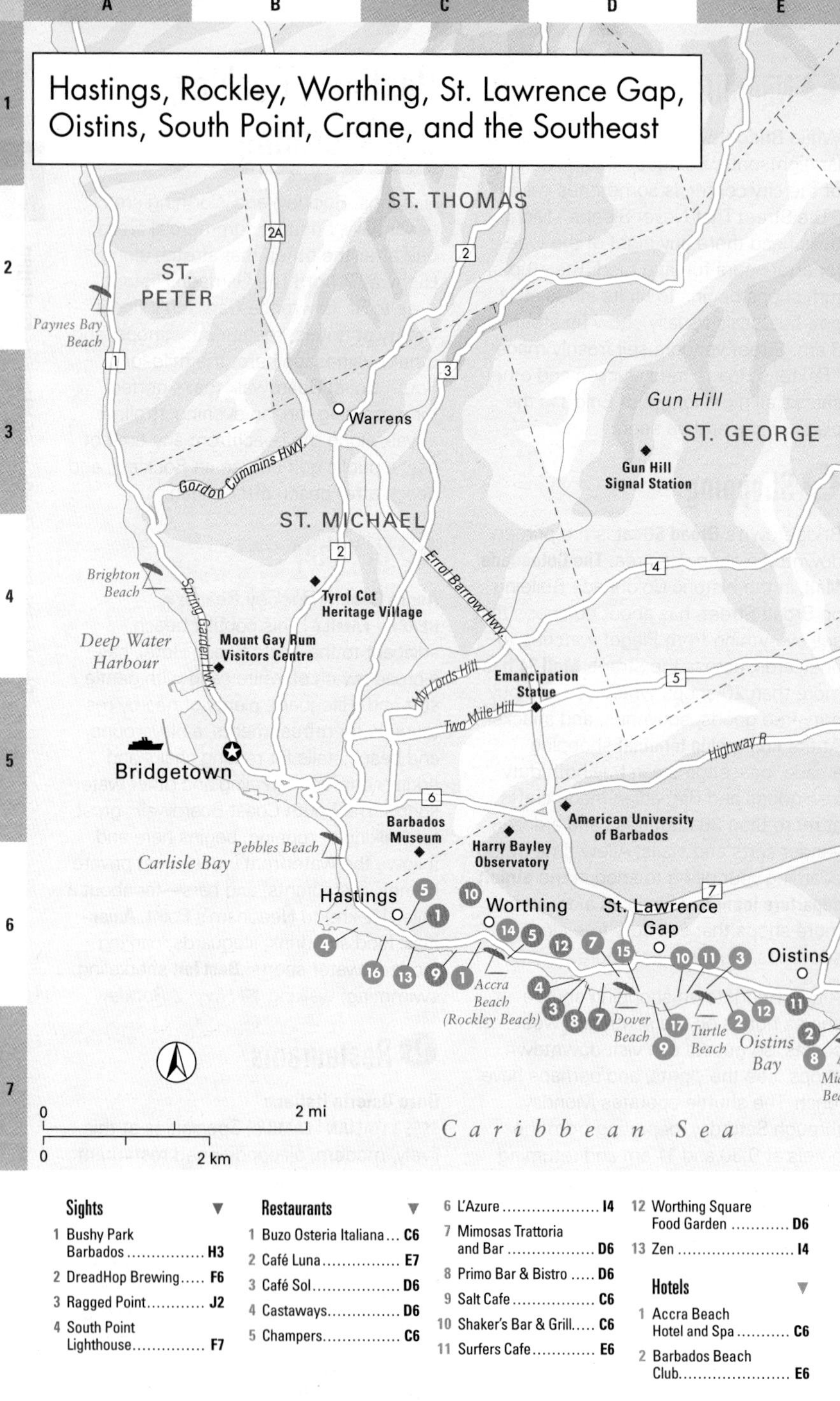
Hastings, Rockley, Worthing, St. Lawrence Gap, Oistins, South Point, Crane, and the Southeast
A
B
C
D
E
1
2
3
4
5
6
7
ST. THOMAS
ST. PETER
Paynes Bay Beach
Warrens
Gordon Cummins Hwy.
Gun Hill
ST. GEORGE
Gun Hill Signal Station
ST. MICHAEL
Errol Barrow Hwy.
Brighton Beach
Spring Garden Hwy.
Tyrol Cot Heritage Village
Deep Water Harbour
Mount Gay Rum Visitors Centre
My Lords Hill
Emancipation Statue
Two Mile Hill
Highway R
Bridgetown
American University of Barbados
Barbados Museum
Harry Bayley Observatory
Pebbles Beach
Carlisle Bay
Hastings
Worthing
St. Lawrence Gap
Oistins
Accra Beach (Rockley Beach)
Dover Beach
Turtle Beach
Oistins Bay
Miami Beach
0
2 mi
0
2 km
Caribbean Sea
Sights
1 Bushy Park Barbados H3
2 DreadHop Brewing..... F6
3 Ragged Point............ J2
4 South Point Lighthouse............... F7
Restaurants
1 Buzo Osteria Italiana... C6
2 Café Luna................ E7
3 Café Sol.................. D6
4 Castaways................ D6
5 Champers................ C6
6 L'Azure.................... I4
7 Mimosas Trattoria and Bar D6
8 Primo Bar & Bistro D6
9 Salt Cafe C6
10 Shaker's Bar & Grill..... C6
11 Surfers Cafe E6
12 Worthing Square Food Garden D6
13 Zen I4
Hotels
1 Accra Beach Hotel and Spa C6
2 Barbados Beach Club........................ E6

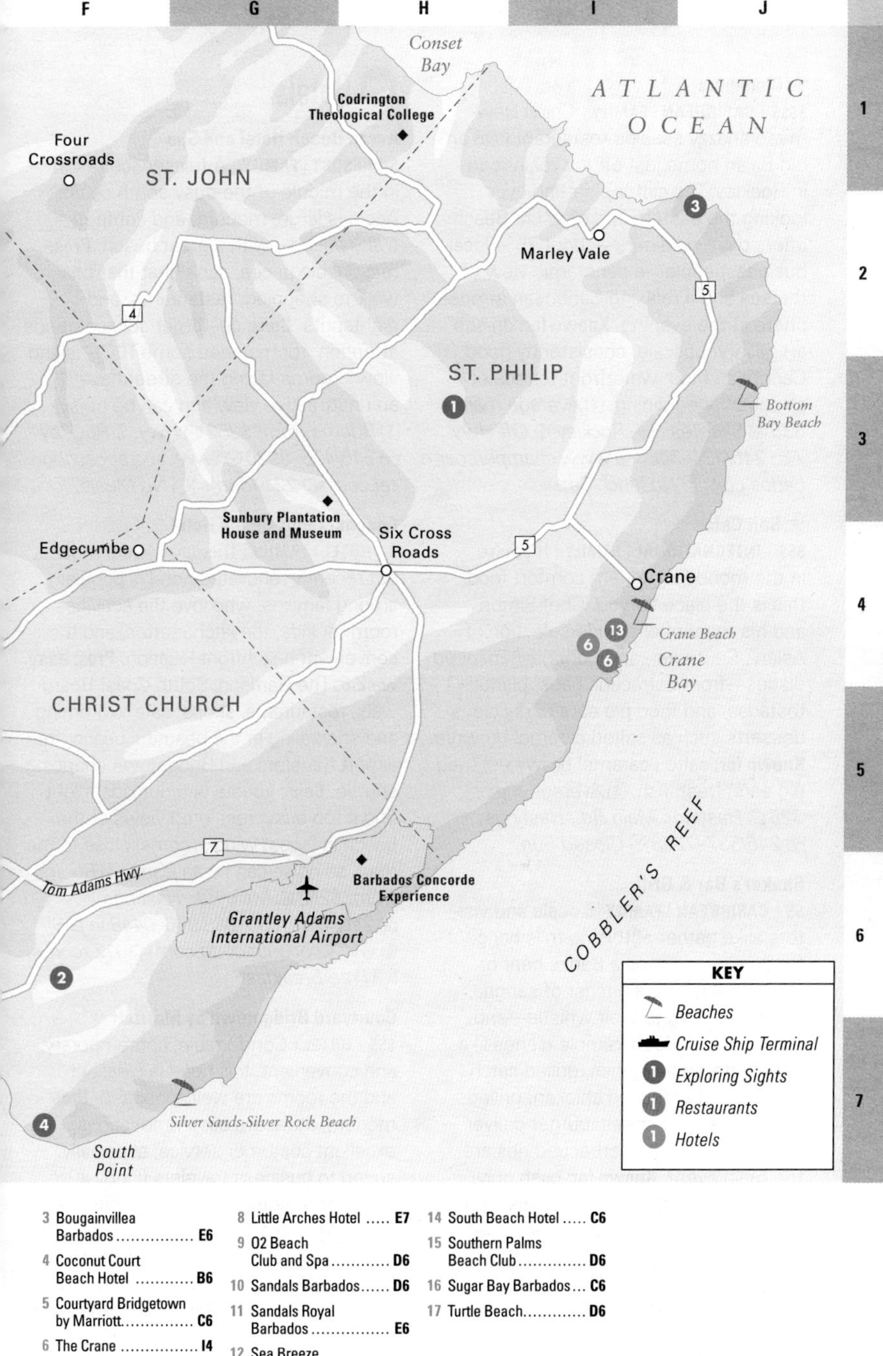

3 Bougainvillea Barbados E6
4 Coconut Court Beach Hotel B6
5 Courtyard Bridgetown by Marriott........ C6
6 The Crane I4
7 Divi Southwinds Beach Resort........ D6
8 Little Arches Hotel E7
9 O2 Beach Club and Spa D6
10 Sandals Barbados...... D6
11 Sandals Royal Barbados E6
12 Sea Breeze Beach House........ E6
13 The SoCo Hotel C6
14 South Beach Hotel C6
15 Southern Palms Beach Club D6
16 Sugar Bay Barbados... C6
17 Turtle Beach........ D6

★ Champers

$$$$ | **CARIBBEAN** | **FAMILY** | Chiryl Newman's snazzy seaside restaurant is in an old Bajan home just off the main road in Rockley. The cliff-top setting overlooking the eastern end of Accra Beach offers daytime diners—about 75% local businesspeople—a panoramic view of the sea and a relaxing Caribbean atmosphere in the evening. **Known for:** on-site art gallery; upscale, consistently good Caribbean food; waterfront terrace or air-conditioned dining. *Average main: $35 Skeetes Hill, Rockley Off Hwy. 7 246/434–3463 www.champersbarbados.com No lunch Sat.*

★ Salt Cafe

$$$ | **INTERNATIONAL** | **FAMILY** | If you're in the mood for modern comfort food, this is the place for you. Chef Simon and his team offer a wide selection of Asian-, Southern-, and Caribbean-inspired dishes—from barracuda baos, plantain tostadas, and fried pig ears to delicious desserts such as salted caramel brownie. **Known for:** salted-caramel brownies; fried pig ears; fresh fish. *Average main: $25 Hastings Main Rd., Hastings 246/537–7258 Closed Sun.*

Shaker's Bar & Grill

$$ | **CARIBBEAN** | **FAMILY** | Locals and visitors alike gather at this no-frills hangout for drinks—perhaps a Banks beer or two, a margarita, a pitcher of sangria, or whatever wets their whistle—and delicious local food. Simple dishes like beer-battered flying fish, grilled catch of the day, barbecued chicken, grilled steak, or a solid cheeseburger deliver the goods, but the barbecued ribs are the main event. **Known for:** cash only; finger-lickin' barbecued ribs; small, busy, convivial "rum shop" on a quiet side street. *Average main: $17 Browne's Gap, Rockley 246/228–8855 www.shakersbarbados.com/visit.html No credit cards.*

Hotels

Accra Beach Hotel and Spa

$ | **RESORT** | **FAMILY** | A full-service resort in the middle of the busy south coast, Accra is large, modern, and competitively priced—with a great beach. **Pros:** reasonable prices; can't beat that beach; walk to shopping, restaurants, and nightspots. **Cons:** customer service needs attention; rooms need some TLC; "island view" rooms facing the street have an unattractive view and can be noisy. *Rooms from: $252 Hwy. 7, Rockley 246/435–8920 www.accrabeachhotel.com 221 rooms No Meals.*

Coconut Court Beach Hotel

$ | **HOTEL** | **FAMILY** | This family-run, modest but recently renovated hotel is popular among families, who love the activities room for kids, the kitchenettes, and the convenient beachfront location. **Pros:** easy walk to The Garrison, South Coast Boardwalk, restaurants, shops; safe swimming and snorkeling at the beautiful beach; free airport transfers and Bridgetown shopping shuttle. **Cons:** guests without kids might find it too busy; restricted views of the beach in "west wing" rooms; close to the road, so noise can be an issue. *Rooms from: $252 Main Rd., Hastings 246/427–1655, 888/506–0448 in U.S. www.coconut-court.com 112 rooms Free Breakfast.*

Courtyard Bridgetown by Marriott

$$$ | **HOTEL** | Comfortable, contemporary, and convenient, this hotel is pleasant and the rooms are well appointed. **Pros:** modern, attractive accommodations; excellent customer service; especially suited to business travelers (lobby is great for remote work). **Cons:** limited on-site dining options; comparatively little "Caribbean resort" atmosphere; walk to beach. *Rooms from: $401 Hwy. 7, Hastings Main Rd., Garrison Set back a block from road 246/625–0000 www.marriott.com 118 rooms No Meals.*

The SoCo Hotel

$$$$ | HOTEL | Sophisticated travelers, particularly couples, love this ultramodern, adults-only boutique hotel strategically poised on the beachfront in Hastings. **Pros:** convenient location; all rooms have an ocean view; lovely beach with long boardwalk. **Cons:** morning road noise can be distracting; mixed reviews on the food; showers only, no tubs. *Rooms from: $700* *Hastings Main Rd., Hastings* *246/537–7626* *www.thesocohotel.com* *24 rooms* *All-Inclusive.*

South Beach Hotel

$$ | HOTEL | FAMILY | You enter the sleek lobby of this cool condo-style hotel, across the street from spectacular Accra Beach, via a footbridge across a double-wide lap pool that runs the length of the property. **Pros:** washer/dryer on every floor; near shopping, restaurants, and nightlife; Accra Beach is great for families. **Cons:** more Miami Beach than Caribbean style; pool, while beautiful, is a shallow lap pool; beach is across the street. *Rooms from: $312* *Main Rd., Hwy. 7, Rockley* *At Accra Beach* *246/435–8561, 888/964–0030 in U.S.* *www.southbeachbarbados.com* *49 suites* *Free Breakfast.*

Sugar Bay Barbados

$$$$ | ALL-INCLUSIVE | FAMILY | Tropical gardens and a dramatic water feature mask the proximity of the main road to this large, all-inclusive beachfront resort near the Garrison Historic Area. **Pros:** sustainable practices; great swimming and snorkeling beach and close to Garrison sights; friendly, accommodating staff. **Cons:** dining and entertainment area gets congested; limited access to specialty restaurants without a surcharge; one pool is small and larger pool is often full of kids. *Rooms from: $500* *Hastings Main Rd., Hastings* *246/622–1101* *www.sugarbaybarbados.com* *138 rooms* *All-Inclusive.*

Shopping

In Rockley, Christ Church, **Quayside Centre** has a small number of boutiques. Coconut Walk Mall and Lanterns Mall are situated in Hastings and each have a small number of independent retailers.

St. Lawrence Gap

St. Lawrence Gap, a busy section of the island's South Coast, has several beachfront hotels and resorts and many places to eat, drink, shop, and party.

Beaches

Dover Beach

BEACH | FAMILY | All along the St. Lawrence Gap waterfront, Dover Beach is one of the most popular beaches on the south coast. The sea is fairly calm, with small to medium waves, and the white-sand beach is broad and brilliant. Divi Southwinds and Ocean Two resorts, as well as several restaurants, are nearby. There's a small boardwalk, a promenade with a food court, water sports and beach chair rentals, and a playground. **Amenities:** food and drink; parking (no fee); toilets; water sports. **Best for:** snorkeling; swimming. *St. Lawrence Gap, Dover.*

Turtle Beach (*Maxwell Beach*)

BEACH | FAMILY | Stretching from Turtle Beach Resort and Sandals Barbados at the eastern end of St. Lawrence Gap to Bougainvillea Barbados on Maxwell Coast Road, this broad strand of powdery white sand is great for sunbathing, strolling, and—with low to medium surf—swimming and boogie boarding. This beach is a favorite nesting place for turtles; hence, its name. If you're lucky, you may see hundreds of tiny hatchlings emerge from the sand and make their way to the sea. Find public access and parking on Maxwell Coast Road, near Bougainvillea Barbados. **Amenities:** food and drink; parking (no fee). **Best for:** swimming; walking. ✉ *Maxwell Coast Rd., Dover.*

Restaurants

Café Sol

$$ | **MEXICAN** | **FAMILY** | Have a hankerin' for Tex-Mex food? Enjoy nachos, tacos, burritos, empanadas, fajitas, and tostadas in this Mexican bar and grill at the western entrance to busy St. Lawrence Gap. **Known for:** good, filling Mexican specialties, plus "gringo" favorites; busy, boisterous, and fun; good service despite the crowded space. *Average main: $20* ✉ *St. Lawrence Gap, Dover* ☎ *246/420–7655* *www.cafesolbarbados.com* *No lunch Mon.*

Castaways

$$$ | **CARIBBEAN** | Enjoy the breathtaking views overlooking St. Lawrence Bay—you may see sea turtles bobbing around in the shallow surf during the day—paired with a diverse menu and cocktail list. The reasonably priced menu caters to various diets and restrictions, featuring local dishes with fresh fish, as well as international dishes. **Known for:** Saturday lunch; perfect spot for sunset cocktails; early dinner locale before a night out in The Gap. *Average main: $30* ✉ *St. Lawrence Gap, Dover* ☎ *246/420–7587* *www.castawaysbb.com* *No lunch.*

Mimosas Trattoria and Bar

$$ | **ITALIAN** | **FAMILY** | Tucked away in the heart of St. Lawrence Gap, this waterfront restaurant is great for families with small children and has indoor and outdoor dining and play areas. The food is casual—think pizza, pasta, vegetarian choices, and of course, mimosas. **Known for:** colorful vibes; the best mimosas around; generous portions. *Average main: $20* ✉ *St. Lawrence Gap, Oistins, Oistins.*

★ **Primo Bar & Bistro**

$$$$ | **SEAFOOD** | This sleek, open-plan bistro has become popular for waterfront dining at its best. In addition to seafood subtly spiced with West Indian flavors, diners can opt for flavorful meat and pasta dishes or, of course, a perfectly grilled steak. **Known for:** waterside location—sunset a bonus at cocktail hour; fresh seafood; open-air dining. *Average main: $35* ✉ *St. Lawrence Gap, Dover* ☎ *246/573–7777* *www.primobarandbistro.com* *No lunch Mon.–Thurs.*

Hotels

Barbados Beach Club

$$$ | **RESORT** | **FAMILY** | Designed with families in mind, this four-story, all-inclusive hotel (with elevators) sits on a beautiful stretch of south-coast beach, and for the price of your room, you can enjoy activities ranging from beach volleyball or miniature golf to nature walks. **Pros:** wonderful for kids; great beach; promotional deals add value. **Cons:** food varies daily but is rather uninspired; meals at set times, not all day; buzz of activity not for everyone. *Rooms from: $400* ✉ *Maxwell Coast Rd., Maxwell* ☎ *246/428–9900* *www.barbadosbeachclub.com* *110 rooms* *All-Inclusive.*

Bougainvillea Barbados

$$$ | **RESORT** | **FAMILY** | Attractive seaside town houses, each with a separate entrance, wrap around the pool or face the beachfront; the suites, decorated in appealing Caribbean pastels, are huge compared with hotel suites elsewhere in this price range and have full kitchens. **Pros:** three pools, one with a swim-up bar, and lots of water sports; great for families but also appeals to couples and honeymooners; tennis court and air-conditioned fitness center. **Cons:** seven-night minimum stay in high season; sea can be a little rough for swimming; rooms are on four levels with no elevator. *Rooms from: $410* ✉ *Maxwell Coast Rd., Maxwell* ☎ *246/628–0990, 800/495–1858 in U.S.* *www.bougainvillearesort.com* *100 suites* *No Meals.*

Divi Southwinds Beach Resort
$ | **RESORT** | **FAMILY** | This all-suites resort is situated on 20 acres of lawn and gardens bisected by action-packed St. Lawrence Gap. The property south of "The Gap" wraps around a stunning half mile of Dover Beach, where 16 beach villas provide an intimate setting steps from the sand. **Pros:** kids' club; beautiful beach plus three pools; close to shopping, restaurants, and nightspots. **Cons:** service needs improvement; some rooms aching for renovations; water sports cost extra. *Rooms from: $225 ✉ St. Lawrence Main Rd., Hwy. 7, Dover ☎ 246/428–7181, 800/367–3484 🌐 www.divisouthwinds.com 133 rooms 🍴 No Meals.*

★ **O2 Beach Club and Spa**
$$$$ | **ALL-INCLUSIVE** | **FAMILY** | Formerly the Oceans Two Resort and Residence, this stunning property has undergone an amazing transformation and re-opened as the coolest VIP beach club in Barbados. **Pros:** great food and service; great for families with teenagers; adult-only pools and swim-up bar. **Cons:** not so great for younger kids; pools a little small. *Rooms from: $1000 ✉ O2 Beach Club and Spa, Dover Rd., St Lawrence Gap, Oistins 🌐 www.o2beachclubbarbados.com 130 rooms 🍴 All-Inclusive.*

Sandals Barbados
$$$$ | **RESORT** | Romance is definitely in the air at this truly magnificent (couples-only) Sandals property, which surrounds an 8-acre garden and lagoon—the longest and largest in Barbados. **Pros:** visit, dine, and play at Sandals Royal Barbados next door; great beach and beautiful garden; myriad activities, including unlimited scuba diving, windsurfing, and sailing. **Cons:** lacks Bajan authenticity; with so much to do, it's easy to forget there's a whole island to explore; fabulously expensive, so look for frequent promotional offers. *Rooms from: $811 ✉ St. Lawrence Gap, Maxwell ✣ At Maxwell Coast Rd. ☎ 246/620–3600, 888/726–3257 🌐 www.sandals.com/barbados 280 rooms 🍴 All-Inclusive.*

Sandals Royal Barbados
$$$$ | **ALL-INCLUSIVE** | Sandals's second resort on the island, opened in December 2017 adjacent to sister resort Sandals Barbados, features all concierge- and butler-level suites with all the implied pampering. **Pros:** complimentary airport shuttle service; suites are ultraluxurious, ultraromantic... ultra-ultra; with 17 possible dining options, you'll never go hungry. **Cons:** getting a taxi is always an issue at Sandals, as you're urged to use their own tour service; spa services cost extra; with so much to do on-site, you may not experience the island itself. *Rooms from: $950 ✉ Maxwell Coast Rd., Maxwell ☎ 246/620–3600, 888/726–3257 in U.S. 🌐 www.sandals.com/royal-barbados 222 suites 🍴 All-Inclusive.*

Southern Palms Beach Club
$$ | **RESORT** | **FAMILY** | This resort is pretty in pink, you might say, with its (pink) plantation-style main building opening onto an inviting pool area and 1,000 feet of white sandy beach. **Pros:** great location with nice beach; friendly and accommodating staff; hotel food and entertainment are very good, and other options are nearby. **Cons:** property is dated; beach vendors can be a nuisance (not the hotel's fault); rooms are large and clean but bathrooms are dated. *Rooms from: $325 ✉ St. Lawrence Gap, Dover ☎ 246/428–7171 🌐 www.southernpalms.net 92 rooms 🍴 No Meals.*

Turtle Beach
$$$$ | **RESORT** | **FAMILY** | Families flock to this resort, part of the Marriott portfolio, because it offers large, bright suites and enough all-included activities for everyone. **Pros:** lots of complimentary water sports; good choice for families; daily rounds of golf at Barbados Golf Club included. **Cons:** buffet meals are a little tired; pools are small relative to the number of kids in them; refrigerators are stocked only in one-bedroom suites.

Enterprise Beach's soft white sand and clear water makes it one of the most popular spots near Oistins.

Rooms from: $624 ✉ St. Lawrence Gap, Dover ⊕ At Maxwell Coast Rd. ☎ 246/428–7131, 855/687–6453 in U.S. 🌐 www.turtlebeachresortbarbados.com ⇨ 161 suites 🍴 All-Inclusive.

Nightlife

St. Lawrence Gap, the narrow waterfront byway with restaurants, bars, and hotels one right after another, is where the action is on the south coast.

Shopping

At **Chattel House Village,** a cluster of boutiques in St. Lawrence Gap, you can buy locally made crafts and other souvenirs.

Oistins and the Surrounding South Point Area

The southernmost point of Barbados is marked by one of the island's four historic lighthouses. Primarily a residential area, the broad beaches at Silver Sands and Silver Rock are a favorite gathering place of windsurfers and kitesurfers.

Oistins, an active fishing village just east of St. Lawrence Gap, is one of the island's four major towns (along with Bridgetown, Holetown, and Speightstown) and the only "town" on the south coast. Oistins is well-known for its Friday night Fish Fry. In Enterprise, a short distance east of town, there's a popular beach and delightful inn.

Sights

DreadHop Brewing

BREWERY | FAMILY | This family-owned and -managed microbrewery burst onto the scene in 2013, much to the delight of beer enthusiasts bored with the regular local options. DreadHop brewery offers nine varieties of beer on tap, from a double IPA to stout and summer ale. The breezy, lively tap room is a favorite among locals, families, and visiting brew enthusiasts, who enjoy a few pints over the weekend or at one of the popular weekly quiz nights. Bar food such as samosas, burgers, loaded fries, and roti are available. Pets are welcome but must remain outside. ✉ *Brewery La., Gibbons Industrial Park, Gibbons, Oistins* ☎ *246/622–1225* 🌐 *www.caribbeanbrewhouse.com* 🕐 *Closed Sun.–Tues.*

South Point Lighthouse

VIEWPOINT | This is the oldest of four lighthouses on Barbados. Assembled on the island in 1852, after being displayed at London's Great Exhibition the previous year, the landmark lighthouse is just east of Miami (Enterprise) Beach near the southernmost point of land on Barbados. The 89-foot tower, with its distinguishing red and white horizontal stripes, is closed to the public—but visitors may freely walk about the site, take photos, and enjoy the magnificent ocean view. ✉ *South Point, Lighthouse Dr., Atlantic Shores.*

Beaches

★ **Miami Beach** (*Enterprise Beach*)

BEACH | This lovely spot on the coast road, just east of Oistins, is a slice of pure white sand with shallow and calm water on one side, deeper water with small waves on the other, and cliffs on either side. Located in a mainly upscale residential area, the beach is mostly deserted except for weekends when folks who live nearby come for a swim. You'll find a palm-shaded parking area, snack carts, and chair rentals. It's also a hop, skip, and jump from Little Arches Hotel. **Amenities:** food and drink; parking (no fee). **Best for:** solitude; swimming. ✉ *Enterprise Beach Rd., Enterprise.*

Silver Sands–Silver Rock Beach

BEACH | FAMILY | Nestled between South Point, the southernmost tip of the island, and Inch Marlow Point, the Silver Point Hotel overlooks this long, broad strand of beautiful white sand that always has a strong breeze. That makes this beach the best in Barbados for intermediate and advanced windsurfers and, more recently, kiteboarders. There's a small playground and shaded picnic tables. **Amenities:** parking (no fee); water sports. **Best for:** solitude; swimming; walking; windsurfing. ✉ *Off Hwy. 7, Silver Sands.*

Restaurants

Café Luna

$$$$ | ECLECTIC | With a sweeping view of pretty Miami (Enterprise) Beach, the alfresco dining deck on top of the Mediterranean-style Little Arches Hotel is spectacular at lunchtime and magical in the moonlight. At dinner, the expertise of executive chef and owner Mark "Moo" de Gruchy is displayed through his classic Bajan fish stew, as well as contemporary and gluten-free "Pan-Tropical" dishes. **Known for:** focus on sustainable, locally produced ingredients; romantic cocktails and dining under the stars; mouthwatering dishes. 💲 *Average main: $32* ✉ *Little Arches Hotel, Enterprise Beach Rd., Oistins* ☎ *246/428–6172* 🌐 *www.cafelunabarbados.com.*

Surfers Cafe

$ | CARIBBEAN | FAMILY | The food at Surfer's Cafe is hearty, traditional, and Bajan—think homemade Bajan fish cakes, *buljol* (chopped salted cod, tomatoes, and chilies), or flying fish—with good-sized portions. The decor is rustic and the views are amazing; if you're lucky enough to be seated at the large table outside, you will feel as if you are on board an old-fashioned pirate ship. **Known for:** amazing views and laidback vibe; beachside dining; opens at 8 am for breakfast and food is served until 10 pm. *Average main: $10 Main Rd., Oistins, Oistins 246/435–5996.*

Hotels

Little Arches Hotel

$$ | **HOTEL** | Just east of the fishing village of Oistins, this classy boutique hotel has a distinctly Mediterranean atmosphere and a perfect vantage point overlooking the sea. **Pros:** across from Miami Beach; stylish accommodations; complimentary full breakfasts with weeklong stay. **Cons:** small pool; road traffic is sometimes distracting; fairly remote residential area. *Rooms from: $340 Enterprise Beach Rd., Oistins 246/420–4689 www.littlearches.com 10 rooms No Meals.*

Sea Breeze Beach House

$$$$ | **RESORT** | **FAMILY** | Sitting on 1000 feet of crisp white sand, the family-friendly hotel is deserving of the name as the property catches the cool trade winds blowing off the Atlantic so you never feel too hot. **Pros:** lots of activities and restaurants to choose from; great staff and service; great for families with small children. **Cons:** older children might get bored. *Rooms from: $1500 Maxwell Coast Rd., Oistins 246/428–2825 122 rooms All-Inclusive.*

Nightlife

★ Oistins Fish Fry

THEMED ENTERTAINMENT | **FAMILY** | This is the place to be on Friday evening, when this south-coast fishing village becomes a lively and convivial outdoor street party suitable for the whole family. Barbecued chicken and a variety of fish, along with all the traditional sides, are served fresh from the grill and consumed at roadside picnic tables. Servings are huge, and prices are inexpensive—about $10–$15 per plate. Recommendations include lionfish, plantain, and breadfruit. Drinks, music, and dancing add to the fun. To avoid the crowds, come any day but Friday for lunch or dinner. *Oistins Main Rd., Oistins.*

Crane and the Southeast

Crane marks the beginning of the island's southeast coast, which extends as far as Ragged Point. The coastline is marked by an expansive villa resort, another in the development stage, pretty bays, and a couple of the island's most magnificent beaches. The inland area is mostly residential—along with miles of canefields, a historic greathouse, and an occasional oil well.

Sights

Bushy Park Barbados

SPORTS VENUE | **FAMILY** | Bushy Park in Saint Philip parish is a 1.4-mile (2.2-km) FIA Grade Three motorsports course that hosts professional auto racing events, including the annual Global Rally Cross Championship. Visitors can test their skills in a variety of race cars, from go-karts to Suzuki Swift Sport race cars. The track is open to the public on days when races are not scheduled. *Gaskin 246/537–1360 www.bushyparkbarbados.com From $35 for go-karts, from $180 for driving experiences.*

Ragged Point

VIEWPOINT | This is the location of East Coast Light, one of four strategically placed lighthouses on the island. Although civilization in the form of new homes is encroaching on this once-remote spot, the view of the entire Atlantic coastline is still spectacular—and the cool ocean breeze is refreshing on a hot day. *Marley Vale Free.*

Ragged Point Lighthouse marks the easternmost point of Barbados.

Beaches

★ Bottom Bay Beach

BEACH | FAMILY | Popular for fashion and travel-industry photo shoots, Bottom Bay is the quintessential Caribbean beach. Secluded, surrounded by a coral cliff, studded with a stand of palms, and blessed with an endless ocean view, this dreamy enclave is near the southeasternmost point of the island. The Atlantic Ocean waves can be too strong for swimming, but it's the picture-perfect place for a picnic lunch on the shore. Park at the top of the cliff and follow the steps down to the beach. Note: because of the seclusion, it's not advisable for women to go to this beach alone; going with a group is much safer. **Amenities:** none. **Best for:** solitude; swimming; walking. ✉ *Hwy. 5, Apple Hall.*

★ Crane Beach

BEACH | FAMILY | This exquisite crescent of pink sand on the southeast coast was named not for the elegant, long-legged wading bird but for the crane used to haul and load cargo when this area served as a busy port. Crane Beach usually has a steady breeze and lightly rolling surf that varies in color from aqua to turquoise to lapis and is great for bodysurfing. Access to the beach is either down 98 steps or via a cliffside, glass-walled elevator on The Crane resort property. **Amenities:** food and drink; lifeguards; parking (no fee); toilets. **Best for:** swimming; walking. ✉ *Crane.*

Restaurants

★ L'Azure

$$$$ | CARIBBEAN | Perched on an oceanfront cliff overlooking Crane Beach, L'Azure is an informal breakfast and luncheon spot by day that becomes elegant after dark. Enjoy seafood chowder or a light salad or sandwich while absorbing the breathtaking panoramic view of the beach and sea beyond. **Known for:** Sunday gospel brunch; lovely setting whether day or evening; classy cuisine and service. 💲 *Average main: $32* ✉ *The Crane Resort, Crane* ☎ *246/423–6220* 🌐 *www.thecrane.com.*

★ Worthing Square Food Garden

$ | **INTERNATIONAL** | **FAMILY** | This food-truck park is a great spot to sample a wide variety of dishes for lunch or dinner. Venezuelan arepas, Italian pizzas, Jamaican jerk pork, Trinidadian roti, and Bajan classics are among the many options here. **Known for:** family friendly; casual atmosphere; affordable international and Caribbean cuisine. *Average main: $10 ✉ Worthing, Worthing ✥ Behind Cave Shepherd and gas station ☎ 246/832–6060 No credit cards.*

Zen

$$$$ | **ASIAN** | Thai and Japanese specialties reign supreme in a magnificent setting overlooking Crane Beach. The centerpiece of the sophisticated, Asian-inspired decor is a 12-seat sushi bar, where chefs prepare exotic fare before your eyes. **Known for:** modern, Asian-inspired decor; Thai or Japanese prix-fixe tasting menu—or à la carte dining; traditional Japanese-style tatami room. *Average main: $32 ✉ The Crane Resort, Crane ☎ 246/423–6220 www.thecrane.com No lunch. Closed Tues.*

Hotels

★ The Crane

$$$$ | **RESORT** | **FAMILY** | Hugging a seaside bluff on the southeast coast, The Crane incorporates the island's oldest hotel in continuous operation; the original coral-stone hotel building (1887) is the centerpiece of a luxurious, 40-acre villa complex that includes private residences, numerous pools, restaurants, bars, and even a little village. **Pros:** fabulous suites and five great restaurants; enchanting view, beach, and pools; complimentary kids' club. **Cons:** villas are considerably more expensive and more modern than historic hotel rooms; rental car recommended; remote location. *Rooms from: $550 ✉ Crane ☎ 246/423–6220, 866/978–5942 in U.S. www.thecrane.com 252 rooms No Meals.*

Holetown and Vicinity

Holetown, in St. James Parish, marks the center of the Platinum Coast—so called for the vast number of luxurious resorts and mansions that face the sea. Holetown is also where Captain John Powell and the crew of the British ship Olive Blossom landed on May 14, 1625, to claim the island for King James I (who had actually died of a stroke seven weeks earlier).

Sights

Folkestone Marine Park and Museum

BEACH | **FAMILY** | Facilities at this family-oriented marine park include a playground, basketball court, picnic area, and a beach with lifeguards. There's also an underwater snorkeling trail (equipment rental, $10 for the day) around Dottins Reef, just off the beach in the 2.2-mile (3½-km) protected marine reserve. Nonswimmers can opt for a glass-bottom boat tour. The ship *Stavronikita*, deliberately sunk in 120 feet of water about a half mile from shore, is home to myriad fish and a popular dive site. *✉ Hwy. 1, Church Point, Holetown ☎ 246/422–2314 Museum exhibits $1.*

Beaches

Paynes Bay Beach

BEACH | The stretch of beach just south of Sandy Lane is lined with luxury hotels—Tamarind, The House, and Treasure Beach among them. This is where Jay Z proposed to Beyoncé and is known for celeb spotting if that's your thing. It's a very pretty area, with plenty of beach to go around, calm water, and good snorkeling. Public access is available at several locations along Highway 1, though parking is limited. Amenities: food and drink. Best for: snorkeling; sunset; swimming; walking. *✉ Hwy. 1.*

Coral-stone cottages are scattered around Coral Reef Club's 12-acres of gardens.

Restaurants

★ La Cabane

$$$$ | MEDITERRANEAN | FAMILY | The chef and his brigade whip up a Mediterranean-inspired, organic, farm to table menu at this relaxed, beachfront spot that's popular with locals and visitors. Mains such as roasted pork or whole fish are paired with seasonal vegetables and delicious hand-cut fries. **Known for:** shoes are optional; delightful beachfront atmosphere; farm to table menu. *Average main: $40 ✉ Batts Rock Beach ☎ 246/256–2131 🌐 www.lacabanebarbados.com.*

★ Lone Star

$$$$ | MODERN EUROPEAN | FAMILY | At the tiny but chic Lone Star Hotel, a short drive north of Holetown, the finest local ingredients are turned into gastronomic delights. Lunchtime brings tasty salads, sandwiches, and wood-fired pizzas, served in the oceanfront bar; after sunset, the casual daytime atmosphere turns trendy. **Known for:** sunset cocktails in the lounge; lovely setting overlooking the sea; breakfast on the boardwalk. *Average main: $45 ✉ Lone Star Hotel, Hwy. 1, Mount Standfast ☎ 246/629–0599 🌐 www.thelonestar.com.*

The Mews

$$$$ | INTERNATIONAL | Once the private home of actress Minnie Driver's dad, the front room is now an inviting bar; an interior courtyard is an intimate, open-air dining area; and the second floor is a maze of small dining rooms and balconies. But it's the food—classic, bistro, or tapas—that draws the visitors. **Known for:** becomes a cozy bar and party spot after dinner; eclectic menu; unique atmosphere. *Average main: $35 ✉ 2nd St., Holetown ☎ 246/432–1122 🌐 www.themewsbarbados.com.*

QP Bistro at The Cliff

$$$$ | **ITALIAN** | On the former site of the renowned Cliff Beach Club, the new bistro is helmed by Michelin-starred executive chef Antonio Mellino. The Italian-inspired menu features pizzas, salads, and classic pasta dishes like fettuccine bolognese and homemade egg pappardelle with seafood; desserts vary daily. **Known for:** beautiful surroundings; ocean views; fine dining experience. *Average main: $100* *Hwy. 1, Derricks* *246/432–0797* *www.qpbistro.com.*

★ Sea Shed

$$$$ | **INTERNATIONAL** | **FAMILY** | This trendy, bustling restaurant is a favorite west-coast dining spot of local professionals, families, and visitors. Mediterranean and Caribbean flavors enliven inventive thin-crust pizzas and tasty salads; the dinner menu also includes fresh seafood and vegetarian selections. **Known for:** family-friendly, kids can play on the beach; lively, bustling atmosphere; casual chic dining on the beach. *Average main: $40* *Mullins Beach, Mullins* *246/572–5111* *www.seashedbarbados.com.*

★ The Tides

$$$$ | **MODERN EUROPEAN** | Perhaps the most intriguing feature of this stunning setting—besides the sound of waves crashing onto the shore just feet away—is the row of huge tree trunks growing right through the dining room. The food is equally dramatic as a contemporary twist is given to fresh seafood, fillet of beef, rack of lamb, and other top-of-the-line main courses by adding inspired sauces and delicate vegetables and garnishes. **Known for:** the cozy lounge and on-site art gallery; long considered one of the island's best restaurants; vegetarian and children's menus. *Average main: $45* *Balmore House, Hwy. 1, Holetown* *246/432–8356* *www.tidesbarbados.com.*

Hotels

The Club, Barbados Resort & Spa

$$$$ | **RESORT** | This is one of the island's few adults-only (age 16 and up) all-inclusive resorts and the only one on the west coast; only spa and salon services and room service cost extra. **Pros:** waterskiing included; intimate adults-only atmosphere; walk to beaches. **Cons:** three-night stay required in high season; not fully accessible to people with disabilities; beach erodes to almost nothing after fall storms, but the sandy beach deck is a good substitute. *Rooms from: $890* *Hwy. 1, Vauxhall, Holetown* *246/432–7840, 866/830–1617* *www.theclubbarbados.com* *158 rooms* *All-Inclusive.*

★ Colony Club

$$$$ | **RESORT** | The signature hotel of seven Elegant Hotel properties on Barbados is certainly elegant, but with a quiet, friendly, understated style primarily targeted to adults. **Pros:** complimentary motorized and nonmotorized water sports; swim-up rooms and bar; Bait-to-Plate fishing trip with the chef. **Cons:** beach comes and goes, depending on storms; kid-friendly activities only during summer and holidays; pricey but often has good promotional offers. *Rooms from: $1040* *Hwy. 1, Porters* *246/422–2335, 855/805–6646* *eleganthotels.com/colony-club* *96 rooms* *Free Breakfast.*

★ Coral Reef Club

$$$$ | **RESORT** | This upscale resort, with pristine coral-stone cottages scattered over 12 acres of flower-filled gardens, offers elegance in a welcoming, informal atmosphere. **Pros:** beautiful suites with huge verandahs; delightful appearance and atmosphere; delicious dining. **Cons:** no kids mid-January through February; narrow beach sometimes disappears, depending on fall weather; few room TVs. *Rooms from: $915* *Hwy. 1, Porters* *246/422–2372* *www.coralreefbarbados.com* *Closed mid-May–mid-July and Sept.* *88 rooms* *Free Breakfast.*

Every unit at the Fairmont Royal Pavilion has uninterrupted sea views from a broad balcony or patio.

Crystal Cove Hotel

$$$$ | RESORT | FAMILY | This seaside colony of attached duplex cottages, whitewashed and trimmed in perky pastels, appeals to both couples and families. **Pros:** all water sports, including waterskiing and banana boat or tube rides, are complimentary; kids' club with activities all day and babysitting service at night; exchange dining program with sister resorts on the west coast. **Cons:** quality and variety of culinary offerings could use improvement; lots of stairs make it difficult for physically challenged visitors; few activities immediately outside the resort, although it's not far from Bridgetown. *Rooms from: $1130 Hwy. 1, Appleby 246/419–2800, 855/258–0902 in U.S. eleganthotels.com/crystal-cove 88 rooms All-Inclusive.*

Fairmont Royal Pavilion

$$$$ | RESORT | FAMILY | Every unit in this luxurious resort has immediate access to 11 acres of tropical gardens and an uninterrupted sea view from a broad balcony or patio. **Pros:**; top-notch service—everyone remembers your name; excellent dining; swimming with turtles included. **Cons:** breakfast buffet needs inspiration; small bathrooms; dining—and everything else—is expensive. *Rooms from: $1120 Hwy. 1, Porters 246/422–5555, 866/540–4485 www.fairmont.com/barbados Closed Oct.–mid-Nov. 73 rooms Free Breakfast.*

★ The House

$$$$ | HOTEL | Privacy, luxury, and service are hallmarks of this intimate, adults-only sanctuary adjacent to sister resort Tamarind. **Pros:** complimentary half-hour massage; pure relaxation in stylish surroundings; privacy assured. **Cons:** not enough sunbeds in pool area; unable to walk anywhere; small pool and narrow beach. *Rooms from: $1185 Hwy. 1, Paynes Bay 246/432–5525, 855/220–8459 in U.S. www.eleganthotels/the-house.com 34 rooms Free Breakfast.*

Lone Star Hotel

$$$$ | HOTEL | FAMILY | A 1940s-era service station just north of Holetown was transformed into a sleek beachfront boutique hotel that—fortunately or unfortunately—has since been discovered by celebrities. **Pros:** family friendly; on a beautiful beach, great for walking; close to Holetown and west coast activities. **Cons:** close to road, so early morning traffic can be noisy; no pool; no activities except for the beach. *Rooms from: $705 Hwy. 1, Mount Standfast 246/629–0600 www.thelonestar.com 6 rooms No Meals.*

Mango Bay
$$$$ | **RESORT** | **FAMILY** | This beachfront resort in the heart of Holetown is within walking distance of shops, restaurants, nightspots, historic sights, and the public bus to Bridgetown and Speightstown. **Pros:** accommodating staff; the Holetown location; food is good, but there's only one restaurant. **Cons:** noise can be an issue for rooms facing the bar area or that back up to the street; vendors on the beach can be annoying; small pool. *Rooms from: $680 2nd St., Holetown 246/626–1384 www.mangobaybarbados.com 76 rooms All-Inclusive.*

★ The Sandpiper Hotel
$$$$ | **RESORT** | **FAMILY** | An intimate vibe and (practically) private beach keep guests coming back to this family-oriented hideaway, with accommodations spread throughout 7 acres of gardens. **Pros:** Tree Top suites are fabulous—but pricey; private and sophisticated; dining, spa, and tennis privileges at nearby Coral Reef Club. **Cons:** few room TVs; book far in advance, as hotel is small and popular (75% repeat guests); beach is small, typical of west coast beaches. *Rooms from: $915 Hwy. 1, Folkestone, Holetown 246/422–2251 www.sandpiperbarbados.com 50 rooms Free Breakfast.*

★ Sandy Lane Hotel and Golf Club
$$$$ | **RESORT** | **FAMILY** | Few places in the Caribbean compare to Sandy Lane's luxurious facilities and ultrapampering service—or to its astronomical prices. **Pros:** great golf; cream of the crop; excellent dining and amazing spa. **Cons:** though lovely, beach can feel crowded; although you don't need to dress up to walk through the lobby, you'll feel that you should; over-the-top for most mortals. *Rooms from: $1800 Hwy. 1, Paynes Bay, Holetown 1½ miles (2 km) south of town 246/444–2000, 866/444–4080 in U.S. www.sandylane.com 113 rooms Free Breakfast.*

Tamarind
$$$$ | **RESORT** | **FAMILY** | This sleek Mediterranean-style resort, which sprawls along 750 feet of prime west-coast beachfront south of Holetown, is large enough to cater to active families and sophisticated couples, including honeymooners. **Pros:** lots of complimentary water sports, including waterskiing and banana boat rides; very big resort, yet layout affords privacy; right on superb Paynes Bay beach. **Cons:** rooms on the road side of the property prone to traffic noise; uninspired buffet breakfast; some rooms could use a little TLC. *Rooms from: $855 Hwy. 1, Paynes Bay 246/432–1332, 855/326–5189 in U.S. eleganthotels.com/tamarind 104 rooms Free Breakfast.*

Treasure Beach
$$$$ | **HOTEL** | Quiet, upscale, and intimate, this adults-only boutique hotel a couple of miles south of Holetown was gutted and completely refurbished in late 2017. **Pros:** complimentary Chef's Table dinner with a five-night stay; cozy retreat; complimentary art gallery tour. **Cons:** no kids allowed; offshore turtle swimming attracts boatloads of tourists; narrow beach. *Rooms from: $939 Hwy. 1, Paynes Bay 246/419–4200, 888/996–9947 in U.S. eleganthotels.com/treasure-beach 35 rooms Free Breakfast.*

Waves Hotel & Spa
$$$$ | **HOTEL** | **FAMILY** | The main part of this hotel—lobby, most guest rooms, restaurant, snack bar, bar and lounge, and a pool—is perched on a cliff overlooking a sandy beach. **Pros:** motorized water sports (and instruction) are included; relaxed atmosphere for both couples and

families; friendly, accommodating staff. **Cons:** pools are small; no connecting rooms for families with kids; adults-only rooms are across the street from the beach. *Rooms from: $636* *Hwy. 1* *246/424–7571, 855/465–8885 in U.S.* *eleganthotels.com/waves* *70 rooms* *All-Inclusive.*

Nightlife

Holetown's restaurants and clubs on 1st and 2nd streets are giving "The Gap" a run for its money. Along with a half dozen or so restaurants that offer fare ranging from ribs or pizza to elegant cuisine, a handful of nightspots and night "experiences" have cropped up recently.

Shopping

Holetown has the upscale **Limegrove Lifestyle Centre,** a stylish shopping mall with high-end designer boutiques, as well as **Chattel House Village,** small shops in colorful cottages with local products, fashions, beachwear, and souvenirs. Also in Holetown, **Sunset Crest Mall** has two branches of the Cave Shepherd department store, a bank, a pharmacy, and several small shops; at **West Coast Mall,** you can buy duty-free goods, island wear, and groceries.

Speightstown

The west coast extends from just north of Bridgetown, through St. James Parish, to Speightstown in St. Peter Parish. Speightstown, the north's commercial center and once a thriving port city, now relies on its local shops and informal restaurants. Many of Speightstown's 19th-century buildings, with traditional overhanging balconies, have been restored. The island's northernmost reaches, St. Peter and St. Lucy parishes, have a varied topography and are lovely to explore.

Beaches

★ Heywoods Beach

BEACH | FAMILY | Unlike other west coast beaches, Heywoods is quiet and unspoiled. The long stretch of crisp white sand is wide and never busy, and the water is calm and ideal for snorkeling and swimming. The entrance to the sea is a gentle slope making it ideal for kids. There are no amenities here for snacks so take a picnic. **Amenities:** none. **Best for:** sunset; swimming; snorkeling; walking. *Heywoods Beach, Heywoods.*

Mullins Beach

BEACH | FAMILY | Home to The Royal Westmoreland Beach Club and The Sea Shed restaurant, this popular beach is often crowded and it can be difficult to find good real estate. There are beach chairs, umbrellas, and Jet skis for rent though, and a burger vendor and small bar in between the beach club and Sea Shed that are locally run and are less expensive options. The entry to the sea is rocky and the beach is very bad for sand flies. Parking can be found in the adjacent residential streets. **Amenities:** food. **Best for:** sunset; swimming; walking. *Hwy. 1B, Mullins.*

Restaurants

The Fish Pot

$$$$ | CARIBBEAN | Bright and cheery by day and relaxed and cozy by night, The Fish Pot offers a tasty dining experience in a setting that's classier than its name might suggest. Just north of Speightstown and the little fishing village of Six Men's Bay, this attractive restaurant serves internationally inspired, modern Caribbean cuisine. Gaze seaward through windows framed with pale-green louvered shutters while you dine. **Known for:** seaside locale; modern Caribbean cuisine; laid-back ambience. *Average main: $35* *Little Good Harbour Hotel, Hwy. 1B* *246/439–3000* *www.littlegoodharbourbarbados.com.*

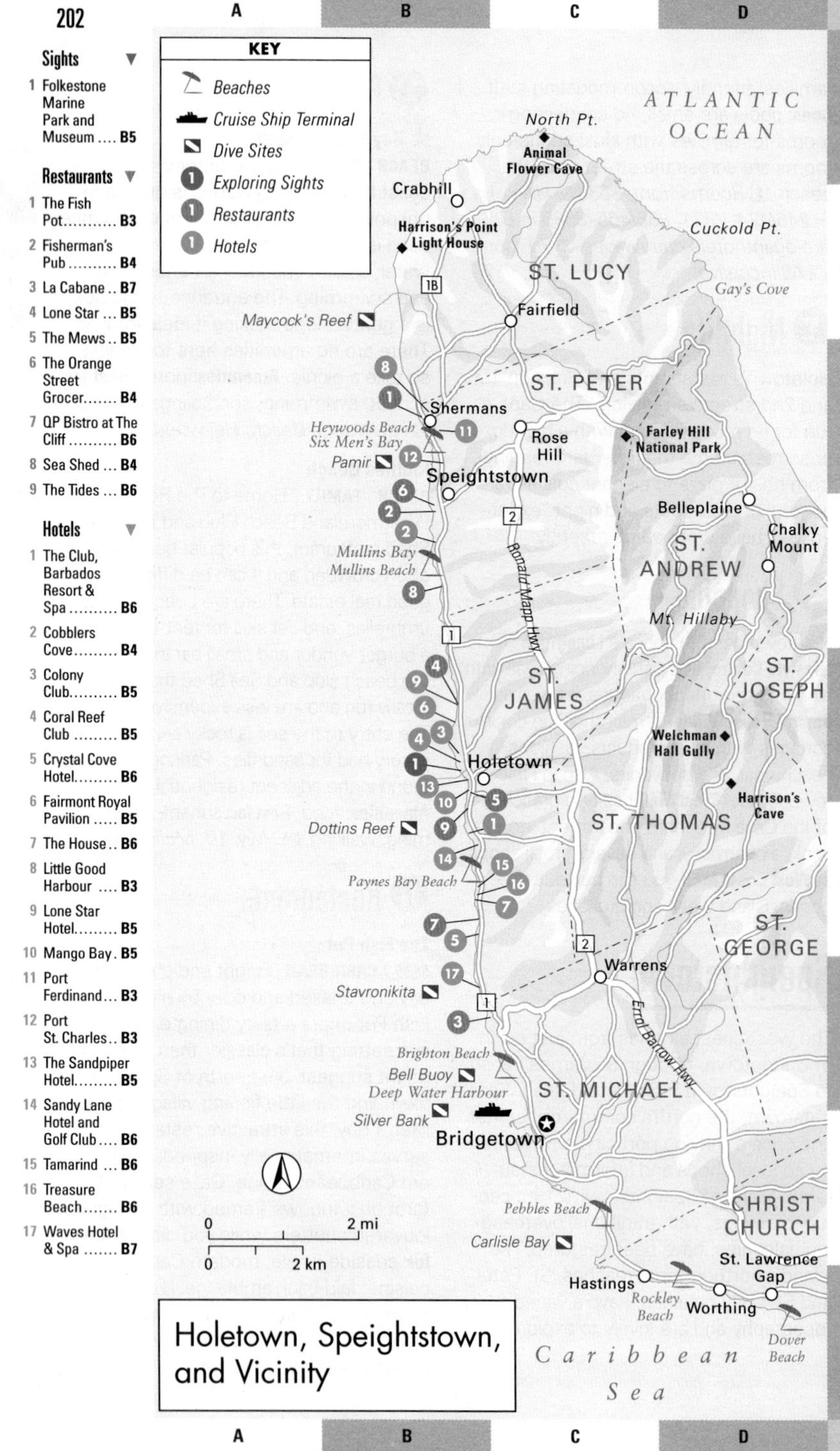
Sights
1 Folkestone Marine Park and Museum B5
Restaurants
1 The Fish Pot.......... B3
2 Fisherman's Pub B4
3 La Cabane .. B7
4 Lone Star ... B5
5 The Mews .. B5
6 The Orange Street Grocer....... B4
7 QP Bistro at The Cliff B6
8 Sea Shed ... B4
9 The Tides ... B6
Hotels
1 The Club, Barbados Resort & Spa B6
2 Cobblers Cove......... B4
3 Colony Club.......... B5
4 Coral Reef Club B5
5 Crystal Cove Hotel......... B6
6 Fairmont Royal Pavilion B5
7 The House .. B6
8 Little Good Harbour B3
9 Lone Star Hotel......... B5
10 Mango Bay . B5
11 Port Ferdinand... B3
12 Port St. Charles .. B3
13 The Sandpiper Hotel......... B5
14 Sandy Lane Hotel and Golf Club B6
15 Tamarind ... B6
16 Treasure Beach....... B6
17 Waves Hotel & Spa B7
KEY
Beaches
Cruise Ship Terminal
Dive Sites
Exploring Sights
Restaurants
Hotels
A
B
C
D
1
2
3
4
5
6
7
8
9
ATLANTIC OCEAN
North Pt.
Animal Flower Cave
Crabhill
Harrison's Point Light House
Cuckold Pt.
ST. LUCY
Gay's Cove
1B
Fairfield
Maycock's Reef
ST. PETER
Shermans
Heywoods Beach
Six Men's Bay
Pamir
Rose Hill
Farley Hill National Park
Speightstown
Belleplaine
2
Ronald Mapp Hwy
Chalky Mount
ST. ANDREW
Mullins Bay
Mullins Beach
Mt. Hillaby
1
ST. JAMES
ST. JOSEPH
Welchman Hall Gully
Holetown
Harrison's Cave
ST. THOMAS
Dottins Reef
Paynes Bay Beach
ST. GEORGE
2
Warrens
Stavronikita
1
Errol Barrow Hwy
Brighton Beach
Bell Buoy
Deep Water Harbour
ST. MICHAEL
Silver Bank
Bridgetown
Pebbles Beach
CHRIST CHURCH
0
2 mi
0
2 km
Carlisle Bay
St. Lawrence Gap
Hastings
Rockley Beach
Worthing
Dover Beach
Caribbean Sea
Holetown, Speightstown, and Vicinity

Fisherman's Pub

$$ | **CARIBBEAN** | **FAMILY** | As local as local gets, this open-air, waterfront beach bar (a former rum shop) is built on stilts a stone's throw from the Speightstown fish market. For years, fishermen and other locals have come here for the inexpensive, authentic Bajan lunch buffet. **Known for:** right on the waterfront; truly local food in a truly local (family-owned) environment; fill up for a few bucks. *Average main: $12 Queen's St., Speightstown 246/422–2703 Closed Sun. Apr.–Oct.*

The Orange Street Grocer

$$ | **CAFÉ** | An eclectic deli bistro serving farm-to-plate-inspired food, the menu at Orange Street Grocer includes fresh salads, baguettes, wraps, healthy bowls, and wood-fired pizza. They are open for breakfast and lunch, but stay open later on Friday and Saturday for dinner service. **Known for:** the best brunch around; farm-fresh ingredients; house-made food. *Average main: $15 Queens St., Speightstown www.theorangestreetgrocer.com No dinner Sun.–Thurs.*

Hotels

★ Cobblers Cove

$$$$ | **RESORT** | Flanked by tropical gardens on one side and the sea on the other, this English country–style resort has 10 two-story cottages, each with four elegant suites that include a bedroom, a comfy sitting room with sofa bed, a small library, and a wall of louvered shutters that open wide to a patio. **Pros:** amazing penthouse suites; peaceful and quiet; complimentary excursion to swim with the turtles. **Cons:** only bedrooms and some sitting rooms have air-conditioning; no room TVs; small beach. *Rooms from: $658 Road View, Hwy. 1B, Speightstown 246/422–2291 www.cobblerscove.com 42 suites Free Breakfast.*

Little Good Harbour

$$$ | **HOTEL** | **FAMILY** | A cluster of spacious self-catering cottages, built in updated chattel-house style with gingerbread balconies, overlooks a narrow strip of beach north of Speightstown—just beyond the fishing community of Six Men's Bay. This little enclave, with one-, two-, and three-bedroom (mostly) duplex suites, is a perfect choice for self-sufficient travelers who don't need the hand-holding that resorts provide and who relish the chance to experience a delightful slice of Bajan village life. **Pros:** good choice for families; spacious units with fully equipped kitchens; laid-back atmosphere. **Cons:** remote location; air-conditioning in bedrooms only; tiny beach across a busy road. *Rooms from: $450 Hwy. 1B 246/439–3000 www.littlegoodharbourbarbados.com Closed Sept. 20 suites No Meals.*

Port Ferdinand

$$$$ | **APARTMENT** | **FAMILY** | At this luxurious lifestyle resort surrounding a human-made waterway, residents can dock their megayachts at the back door and rest their heads in breathtaking one-, two-, and three-bedroom units with high-end furnishings, wall-to-wall windows that take in the view, full kitchens, en suite bathrooms, and lots of space for either relaxing or entertaining. **Pros:** elevator access from lobby to upper floors and dock level; indoor and outdoor kids activities; spacious units with designer furnishings. **Cons:** kids need to be well-behaved given the high-end furnishings and dock access; more like condo living than a resort experience. *Rooms from: $735 Hwy. 1B, Retreat, Six Men's Bay, Heywoods 246/272–2000, 855/346–8662 in U.S. www.portferdinand.com No credit cards 46 suites No Meals.*

Port St. Charles

$$$$ | **HOUSE** | **FAMILY** | A luxury residential marina development near historic Speightstown, Port St. Charles is a great choice for boating enthusiasts who either arrive on their own yacht or plan to charter one during their stay. **Pros:** free water taxi around the property; a boater's dream; well-appointed units with beautiful views. **Cons:** the number of units available for short-term stays varies; minimum 14-night stay for some units in high season; far removed from many activities and restaurants. *$ Rooms from: $535 ✉ Hwy. 1B, Heywoods ☎ 246/419–1000 ⊕ www.portstcharles.com 156 suites No Meals.*

East Coast

On the east coast, the crashing Atlantic surf has eroded the shoreline, forming steep cliffs and exposing prehistoric rocks that look like giant mushrooms. Bathsheba and Cattlewash are favorite seacoast destinations for local folks on weekends and holidays. In the central interior, narrow roads weave through tiny villages and along and between the ridges. The landscape is covered with tropical vegetation and is rife with fascinating caves and gullies. Between the sweeping views out over the Atlantic and the tiny fishing towns along the northwestern coast are forest and farm, moor and mountain. Most guides include a loop through the far north on a daylong tour of the east coast—it's a beautiful drive.

Sights

★ Andromeda Botanic Gardens

GARDEN | **FAMILY** | More than 600 beautiful and unusual plant specimens from around the world are cultivated in 6 acres of gardens nestled among streams, ponds, and rocky outcroppings overlooking the sea above the Bathsheba coastline near Tent Bay. The gardens were created in 1954 with flowering plants collected by the late horticulturist Iris Bannochie (1914–88). They're now administered by the Barbados National Trust. The Gallery Shop features local art, photography, and crafts. The Garden Café serves sandwiches, salads from the gardens, desserts, and drinks. Entrance fees include unlimited return visits within 3 weeks. *✉ Bathsheba ☎ 246/433–9384 ⊕ www.andromedabarbados.com Bds$30.*

★ Animal Flower Cave

CAVE | **FAMILY** | Small sea anemones, or sea worms, resemble flowers when they open their tiny tentacles. They live in small pools in this sea cave at the island's very northern tip. The cave itself, discovered in 1750, has a coral floor that ranges from 126,000 to 500,000 years old, according to geological estimates. Coral steps lead through an opening in the "roof" into the cave. Bring your bathing suit. Depending on that day's sea swells, you can swim in the naturally formed pool—and the view of breaking waves from inside the cave is magnificent. Steep stairs, uneven surfaces, and rocks make this an unwise choice for anyone with walking difficulties. The Restaurant, perched at the top of the cliff, opens daily for lunch. The property has a playground, as well as lots of pet goats and sheep wandering around.

TIP→ The far north is an alternative route to the east coast, and this is a great place to stop for an adventure and refreshments. *✉ North Point, Conneltown ☎ 246/439–8797 ⊕ www.animalflowercave.com $12.*

★ Barbados Wildlife Reserve

This reserve at the top of Farley Hill is the habitat of herons, innumerable land turtles, screeching peacocks, shy deer, elusive green monkeys, brilliantly colored parrots (in a large walk-in aviary), snakes, and a caiman. Except for the snakes and the caiman, the animals run or fly freely—so step carefully and keep your hands to yourself. Feeding times (10 am and 2 pm) are your best chances to glimpse green monkeys.

■ TIP→ Admission to the reserve also includes admission to nearby Grenade Hall Signal Station (a 19th-century lookout tower) and Forest. ✉ *Hwy. 2* ✣ *Across from Farley Hill National Park* ☎ *246/422–8826* 🌐 *www.barbadoswildlifereserve.com* 🎫 *$15* ☞ *Cash only.*

Barclays Park

CITY PARK | FAMILY | Straddling the Ermy Bourne Highway on the east coast, just north of Bathsheba, this 50-acre public park was gifted to Barbados by Barclays Bank (now First Caribbean International Bank) after independence was declared in 1966. Pack a picnic lunch, run around, and enjoy the gorgeous ocean view. ✉ *Ermy Bourne Hwy., Cattlewash.*

★ Cherry Tree Hill

VIEWPOINT | The cherry trees for which this spot was named have long since disappeared, but the view from Cherry Tree Hill, just east of St. Nicholas Abbey greathouse, is still one of the most spectacular in Barbados. Although only about 850 feet above sea level, it is one of the highest points on the island and affords a broad view of the rugged east coast and the entire Scotland District—so named because its rolling hills resemble the moors of Scotland. Today, when approaching from the west, you drive through a majestic stand of mature, leafy mahogany trees. Stop at the crest of the hill for a stunning panoramic view. ✉ *Cherry Tree Hill Rd., Moore Hill.*

Codrington Theological College

COLLEGE | An impressive stand of cabbage-palm trees lines the road leading to the coral-stone buildings and serene grounds of Codrington College, the oldest Anglican theological seminary in the western hemisphere, opened in 1745 on a cliff overlooking Conset Bay. The college's benefactor was Christopher Codrington III (1668–1710), a former governor-general of the Leeward Islands, whose antislavery views were unpopular in the plantocracy of the times. You can visit the chapel, stroll the grounds, gaze at the duck pond, enjoy the view, and even have a picnic. ✉ *Sargeant St., Codrington College* ☎ *246/416–8051* 🌐 *www.codrington.org* 🎫 *Donations welcome.*

Chalky Mount

This tiny east-coast village is perched high in the clay-yielding hills that have supplied local potters for about 300 years. A few working potteries are open daily to visitors, who can watch as artisans create bowls, vases, candleholders, and decorative objects—which are, of course, for sale.

Farley Hill National Park

VIEWPOINT | FAMILY | At this national park in northern St. Peter, across from the Barbados Wildlife Reserve, gardens and lawns—along with an avenue of towering palms and gigantic mahogany, whitewood, and casuarina trees—surround the imposing ruins of a plantation greathouse built by Sir Graham Briggs in 1861 to entertain royal visitors from England. Partially rebuilt for the filming of *Island in the Sun,* the classic 1957 film starring Harry Belafonte and Dorothy Dandridge, the structure was destroyed by fire in 1965. Behind the estate is a sweeping view of the region called Scotland for its rugged landscape. The park has a playground and is also the site of festivals and musical events. ✉ *Hwy. 2* ☎ *246/422–3555* 🎫 *Bds$6 per car, pedestrians free.*

Morgan Lewis Windmill

WINDMILL | Built in 1727 of boulders "cemented" in place with a mixture of egg whites and coral dust, the mill was operational until 1945. Today it's the only remaining windmill in Barbados with its wheelhouse and sails intact. The mill was donated to the Barbados National Trust in 1962 and eventually restored to original working specifications in 1998 by millwrights from the United

Kingdom. ✥ *Southeast of Cherry Tree Hill* ☎ *246/426–2421* 🌐 *www.barbadosnationaltrust.org* 🎫 *Bds$10 guided tour; Bds$5 mill entrance* ⏲ *Closed Sun.*

St. Nicholas Abbey

HISTORIC HOME | The island's oldest greathouse (circa 1650) was named after the original British owner's hometown, St. Nicholas Parish, near Bristol, and Bath Abbey nearby. Its stone-and-wood architecture makes it one of only three original Jacobean-style houses still standing in the western hemisphere. Behind the greathouse and its lush tropical garden is a rum distillery that produces award-winning rum with a 19th-century steam press; rum tasting tours are available. It is the only estate-distilled rum in the world (this is the process of growing cane, distilling, and bottling, all done on the same premises). The St. Nicholas Abbey Heritage Railway, introduced in 2018, takes visitors on an hour-long steam train ride through the property. Unfortunately, this well-curated attraction doesn't fully acknowledge or memorialize the tragedy of slavery and the lives of the enslaved people that would have also called this site home. ✉ *Cherry Tree Hill Rd., Moore Hill* ☎ *246/422–5357* 🌐 *www.stnicholasabbey.com* 🎫 *$23* ⏲ *Closed Sat.*

Beaches

Be cautioned: While you might see surfers at Bathsheba Soup Bowl, swimming at east-coast beaches is treacherous, even for strong swimmers, and is *not* recommended. Waves are high, the bottom tends to be rocky, the currents are unpredictable, and the undertow is dangerously strong.

Bathsheba Beach

BEACH | **FAMILY** | Although unsafe for swimming, the miles of untouched sand along the East Coast Road in St. Joseph Parish are great for beachcombing and wading. Expert surfers from around the world converge on Bathsheba Soup Bowl, at the south end of the beach, each November for the Barbados Independence Pro competition. **Amenities:** none. **Best for:** solitude; sunrise; surfing; walking. ✉ *East Coast Rd., Bathsheba.*

★ Cattlewash Beach

BEACH | **FAMILY** | Swimming is unwise at this windswept beach with pounding surf, which follows the Atlantic Ocean coastline in St. Andrew, but you can take a dip, wade, and play in the tidal pools. Barclays Park, a 50-acre public park up the road, has a shaded picnic area. **Amenities:** none. **Best for:** solitude; sunrise; walking. ✉ *Ermy Bourne Hwy., Cattlewash.*

Restaurants

The Atlantis

$$$ | **CARIBBEAN** | **FAMILY** | For decades, an alfresco lunch on the Atlantis deck overlooking the ocean has been a favorite of both visitors and Bajans. A pleasant atmosphere and good food have always been the draw, with a casually elegant dining room and a top-notch menu that focuses on local produce, seafood, and meats. **Known for:** West Indian buffet luncheon on Wednesday and Sunday and kids' menu every day; best place for lunch when touring the east coast; stunning ocean views from your table. [$] *Average main: $29* ✉ *The Atlantis Historic Inn, Tent Bay* ☎ *246/433–9445* 🌐 *www.atlantishotelbarbados.com.*

Round House

$$$ | **CARIBBEAN** | **FAMILY** | Owners Robert and Gail Manley oversee the menu for guests staying in their historic (1832) manse-turned-inn, as well as tourists enjoying the east coast and Bajans dining out. The lunch menu—served on a deck overlooking the Atlantic Ocean—includes house-made soups and quiches, sandwiches, salads, and pasta. **Known for:** Friday night barbecue dinner, biweekly in high season, with live music; casual alfresco dining overlooking smashing ocean surf; good spot for lunch, served all afternoon,

when touring the east coast. *Average main: $26 Bathsheba 246/433–9678 www.roundhousebarbados.com Closed Mon. and Tues. No dinner.*

Hotels

The Atlantis Historic Inn

$$ | **B&B/INN** | Renowned for its spectacular oceanfront location, this hotel has been a fixture on the rugged east coast for more than a century. **Pros:** popular restaurant; historical and modern blend beautifully; spectacular oceanfront location. **Cons:** remote location, so rental car is advised; no beach for swimming, but there is a pool; for oceanfront rooms, smashing waves can be noisy at night. *Rooms from: $281 Tent Bay 246/433–9445 www.atlantishotelbarbados.com 9 rooms Free Breakfast.*

★ ECO Lifestyle + Lodge

$ | **B&B/INN** | This sustainable boutique hotel is inspired by its natural surroundings—a cliff overlooking the sea that's thick with palm trees and other tropical foliage. **Pros:** yoga, massage, and meditation in the Zen Gully; peaceful and relaxing; farm-to-table menu in the small restaurant. **Cons:** no TV or in-room telephone; some rooms have no air-conditioning; remote location. *Rooms from: $219 Tent Bay 246/433–9450 www.ecolifestylelodge.com 10 rooms Free Breakfast.*

Round House Inn

$ | **B&B/INN** | It's hard to tell which is more appealing: the view of the rugged coastline or the magnificent historic (1832) manse strategically perched on the cliff to take advantage of the view. **Pros:** quiet and peaceful—bring a good book; fabulous ocean views; small and intimate. **Cons:** few on-site activities; no TV (if you care); really remote location. *Rooms from: $175 Bathsheba 246/433–9079 www.roundhousebarbados.com 4 rooms Free Breakfast.*

Central Interior

The central interior of Barbados is dotted with small villages and covered with miles and miles of sugarcane. It's also marked by the island's unique cave system, a forested gully, magnificent gardens, and an amazing view of the entire south coast. Whether traveling around the south, east, or west coast, be sure to incorporate this area into your tour.

Sights

★ Coco Hill Forest

FOREST | **FAMILY** | This lush, 52-acre tropical forest is ideal for nature walks, hiking, and forest bathing, or if you need a break from the beach. The view over the island's east coast is simply breathtaking. Hiking trails are approximately 1½ miles long and should take 1½ hours to complete.

TIP→ Hire a guide to share details on the hundreds of tree, plant, and herb species, as well as the history of agriculture in Barbados and the project's mission to regenerate the soils.

Check their Facebook page for the latest tour details. *Richmond Rd., Melvin Hill, Bathsheba 246/235–4926 www.facebook.com/cocohillforest $10 Closed Mon. and Tues.*

Flower Forest Botanical Gardens

GARDEN | **FAMILY** | It's a treat to meander among fragrant flowering bushes, canna and ginger lilies, puffball trees, and more than 100 other species of tropical flora in a cool, tranquil forest of flowers and other plants. A ½-mile (1-km) path winds through the 53.6-acre grounds, a former sugar plantation; it takes about 30 to 45 minutes to follow the path, or you can wander freely for as long as you wish. Benches throughout provide places to pause and reflect. There's also a snack bar, a gift shop, and a beautiful view of Mt. Hillaby, at 1,100 feet the island's highest point. *Hwy. 2, Richmond*

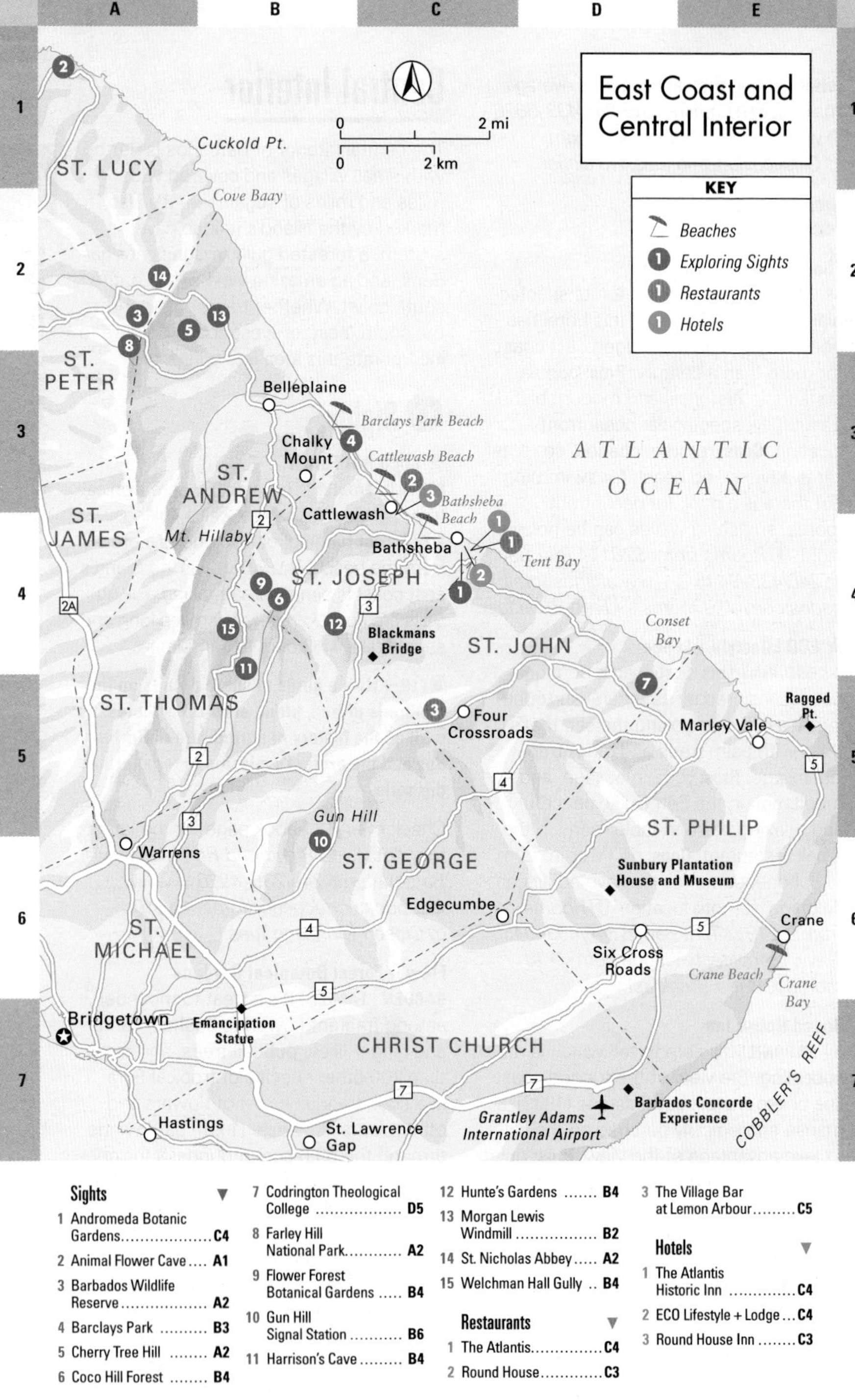
East Coast and Central Interior
KEY
Beaches
Exploring Sights
Restaurants
Hotels
0
2 mi
0
2 km
A
B
C
D
E
1
2
3
4
5
6
7
Cuckold Pt.
ST. LUCY
Cove Baay
ST. PETER
Belleplaine
Barclays Park Beach
Chalky Mount
Cattlewash Beach
ST. ANDREW
Cattlewash
Bathsheba Beach
ST. JAMES
Mt. Hillaby
Bathsheba
Tent Bay
ATLANTIC OCEAN
ST. JOSEPH
Conset Bay
Blackmans Bridge
ST. JOHN
ST. THOMAS
Four Crossroads
Ragged Pt.
Marley Vale
Gun Hill
ST. PHILIP
Warrens
ST. GEORGE
Sunbury Plantation House and Museum
Edgecumbe
ST. MICHAEL
Six Cross Roads
Crane
Crane Beach
Crane Bay
Bridgetown
Emancipation Statue
CHRIST CHURCH
COBBLER'S REEF
Barbados Concorde Experience
Grantley Adams International Airport
Hastings
St. Lawrence Gap
Sights
1 Andromeda Botanic Gardens C4
2 Animal Flower Cave A1
3 Barbados Wildlife Reserve A2
4 Barclays Park B3
5 Cherry Tree Hill A2
6 Coco Hill Forest B4
7 Codrington Theological College D5
8 Farley Hill National Park A2
9 Flower Forest Botanical Gardens B4
10 Gun Hill Signal Station B6
11 Harrison's Cave B4
12 Hunte's Gardens B4
13 Morgan Lewis Windmill B2
14 St. Nicholas Abbey A2
15 Welchman Hall Gully B4
Restaurants
1 The Atlantis C4
2 Round House C3
3 The Village Bar at Lemon Arbour C5
Hotels
1 The Atlantis Historic Inn C4
2 ECO Lifestyle + Lodge C4
3 Round House Inn C3

☎ *246/433–8152* 🌐 *www.flowerforestbarbados.com* 🎫 *$15.*

Gun Hill Signal Station

MILITARY SIGHT | FAMILY | The 360-degree view from Gun Hill, at 700 feet, was of strategic importance to the 18th-century British army. Using lanterns and semaphore, soldiers here could communicate with their counterparts at the south coast's Garrison and the north's Grenade Hill about approaching ships, civil disorders, storms, or other emergencies. Time moved slowly in those days, and Captain Henry Wilkinson whiled away his off-duty hours by carving a huge lion from a single rock—on the hillside below the tower. Come for a short history lesson but mainly for the view; it's so gorgeous that military invalids were sent here to convalesce. There's a small café for refreshments. ✉ *Fusilier Rd., Gun Hill* ☎ *246/429–1358* 🌐 *www.barbadosnationaltrust.org/project/gunhill* 🎫 *$6.*

★ Harrison's Cave

CAVE | FAMILY | This limestone cavern, complete with stalactites, stalagmites, subterranean streams, and a 40-foot underground waterfall, is a rare find in the Caribbean—and one of Barbados's most popular attractions. Tours include a nine-minute video and an hour-long underground journey via electric tram. The visitor center has interactive displays, life-size models and sculptures, a souvenir shop, a restaurant, and elevator access to the tram for people with disabilities. Tram tours fill up fast, so book ahead. More intrepid visitors may like the 1½-hour walk-in tour or 4-hour eco-adventure tour, exploring nature trails and some of the cave's natural passages. ✉ *Allen View, Welchman Hall* ✣ *Off Hwy. 2* ☎ *246/417–3700* 🌐 *www.harrisonscave.com* 🎫 *Tours from $57.*

★ Hunte's Gardens

GARDEN | Horticulturist Anthony Hunte spent two years converting an overgrown sinkhole (caused by the collapse of a limestone cave) into an extraordinary garden environment. Trails lead up, down, and around 10 acres of dense foliage—everything from pots of flowering plants and great swaths of thick ground cover to robust vines, exotic tropical flowers, and majestic 100-year-old cabbage palms reaching for the sun. Benches and chairs, strategically placed among the greenery, afford perfect (and fairly private) vantage points, while classical music plays overhead. Hunte lives on the property and welcomes visitors to his verandah for a glass of juice or rum punch. Just ask, and he'll be happy to tell you the fascinating story of how the gardens evolved. ✉ *Hwy. 3A, Coffee Gully, Castle Grant* ☎ *246/433–3333* 🌐 *www.huntesgardensbarbados.com* 🎫 *$20.*

Welchman Hall Gully

TRAIL | FAMILY | This 1½-mile-long (2-km-long) natural gully is really a collapsed limestone cavern, once part of the same underground network as Harrison's Cave. The Barbados National Trust protects the peace and quiet here, making it a beautiful place to hike past acres of labeled flowers and stands of enormous trees. You can see some interesting birds and troops of native green monkeys. There are some scheduled, free, guided tours, and a guide can be arranged with 24 hours' notice. Otherwise, the 30- to 45-minute walk is self-guided. ✉ *Welchman Hall* ☎ *246/438–6671* 🌐 *www.welchmanhallgullybarbados.com* 🎫 *$14* ☞ *Cash only.*

Restaurants

★ The Village Bar at Lemon Arbour

$ | CARIBBEAN | Commonly known as Lemon Arbour, this is the place to be on a Saturday afternoon, as Bajans from all walks of life descend on this family-run restaurant and bar overlooking the countryside. Try some "pudding and souse"—a local dish combining steamed sweet potato (the pudding) and pickled pork (souse)—it tastes better than it sounds! **Known for:** great people watching (it can get quite lively); pudding and souse, and other Bajan dishes; relaxed and lively atmosphere. $ *Average main: $10* ✉ *Lemon Arbour* ☎ *246/433–3162* ⌚ *Closed Sun.*

Activities

Cricket, football (soccer), polo, and rugby are extremely popular sports in Barbados for participants and spectators alike, with local, regional, and international matches held throughout the year. Contact Barbados Tourism Marketing, Inc., or check newspapers for information.

DIVING AND SNORKELING

More than two-dozen dive sites lie along the west coast between Maycocks Bay and Bridgetown and off the south coast as far as the St. Lawrence Gap. Certified divers can explore flat coral reefs and see dramatic sea fans, huge barrel sponges, and more than 50 varieties of fish. Divers regularly explore nine sunken wrecks, and at least 10 more are accessible to experts. Underwater visibility is generally 80 to 90 feet. The calm waters along the west coast are also ideal for snorkeling. The marine reserve, a stretch of protected reef between Sandy Lane and the Colony Club, contains beautiful coral formations accessible from the beach.

DIVE SITES

On the west coast, **Bell Buoy** is a large, dome-shape reef where huge brown coral tree forests and schools of fish delight all categories of divers at depths of 20 to 60 feet. At **Dottins Reef,** off Holetown, you can see schooling fish, barracudas, and turtles at depths of 40 to 60 feet. **Maycocks Bay,** on the northwest coast, is particularly enticing; large coral reefs are separated by corridors of white sand, and visibility is often 100 feet or more. The 165-foot freighter *Pamir* lies in 60 feet of water off Six Men's Bay; it's still intact, and you can peer through its portholes at dozens of varieties of tropical fish. **Silver Bank** is a healthy coral reef with beautiful fish and sea fans; you may get a glimpse of the *Atlantis* submarine at 60 to 80 feet. Not to be missed, the *Stavronikita* is a scuttled Greek freighter at about 135 feet; hundreds of butterfly fish hang out around its mast, and the thin rays of sunlight filtering down through the water make exploring the huge ship a wonderfully eerie experience.

Farther south, **Carlisle Bay** is a natural harbor and marine park just below Bridgetown. Here you can retrieve empty bottles thrown overboard by generations of sailors and see cannons and cannonballs, anchors, and six shipwrecks (*Berwyn, Fox, CTrek, Eilon,* the barge *Cornwallis,* and *Bajan Queen*) lying in 25 to 60 feet of water, all close enough to visit on the same dive. The *Bajan Queen,* a cruise vessel that sank in 2002, is the island's newest wreck.

Dive shops provide a two-hour beginner's "resort" course (about $100) followed by a shallow dive, or a weeklong certification course (about $450). Once you're certified, a one-tank dive costs $70 to $80; a two-tank dive runs $120 to $125. All equipment is supplied, and you can purchase multidive packages. Gear for snorkeling is available (free or for a small rental fee) from most hotels. Snorkelers can usually accompany dive trips for $30 for a one- or two-hour trip. Most dive shops have relationships with hotels and offer dive packages to hotel guests, including round-trip transfers.

★ Barbados Blue

DIVING & SNORKELING | FAMILY | Located within the Hilton Barbados hotel complex at Needham's Point, Barbados Blue offers daily scuba and snorkeling trips to Carlisle Bay Marine Park—think shipwrecks and hawksbill turtles—as well as private boat charters and PADI classes. Scuba and snorkeling gear are available to rent, along with underwater digital cameras, and hotel pickup can be arranged. Added bonuses: the facility is 100% eco-aware, it's the only dive operator with two marine biologists on staff, and your money directly benefits the marine park and a coral restoration project. ✉ *Hilton Barbados, Aquatic Gap, Garrison* ☎ *246/434–5764, 800/929–7154 in U.S.* 🌐 *www.divebarbadosblue.com* 🎫 *Prices vary.*

Dive Hightide Watersports

SCUBA DIVING | FAMILY | On the west coast, Dive Hightide Watersports offers three dive trips daily—one- and two-tank dives and night reef–wreck–drift dives—for up to eight divers, along with PADI instruction, equipment rental, and free transportation. ✉ *Coral Reef Club, Hwy. 1, Holetown* ☎ *246/432–0931, 800/970–0016, 800/513–5763* 🌐 *www.divehightide.com.*

Dive Shop, Ltd

SCUBA DIVING | FAMILY | Next to the marine park on Carlisle Bay, just south of Bridgetown, the island's oldest dive shop offers daily reef and wreck dives, plus beginner classes, certification courses, and underwater photography instruction. Underwater cameras are available for rent. Free transfers are provided between your hotel and the dive shop. ✉ *Amey's Alley, Upper Bay St., Garrison* ✣ *Next to Nautilus Beach Apts.* ☎ *246/426–9947* 🌐 *www.divebds.com.*

★ Trident Freedivers

DIVING & SNORKELING | FAMILY | Barbadian Freediving record holder Johanna Loch-Allen offers freediving tours and certification, as well as spearfishing tours and underwater photoshoots. Whether you're a beginner or a more advanced freediver, Johanna shows you the best spots on the island. A popular tour includes spearing the invasive lionfish from the reefs around Barbados, followed by ice cold beers and a barbecue on the beach. If you're feeling really fancy, you can have fresh lionfish ceviche prepared on the spot. ✉ *Barbados Freedivers, Hastings* ☎ *246/234–7778* 🌐 *www.freedivebarbados.com.*

FISHING

Fishing is a year-round activity in Barbados, but prime time is January through April, when game fish are in season. Whether you're a serious deep-sea fisher looking for marlin, sailfish, tuna, and other billfish or you prefer angling in calm coastal waters where wahoo, barracuda, and other smaller fish reside, you can choose from a variety of half- or full-day charter trips departing from Careenage in Bridgetown. Expect to pay $175 per person for a shared half-day charter; for a private charter, expect to pay $500 to $600 per boat for a four-hour half-day or $950 to $1,000 for an eight-hour full-day charter. Spectators who don't fish are welcome for $50 per person.

Billfisher Deepsea Fishing

FISHING | *Billfisher III*, a 40-foot Viking Sport Fisherman, accommodates up to six passengers with three fishing chairs and five rods. Captain Ralphie White's full-day charters include a full lunch; all trips include drinks and transportation to and from the boat. ✉ *Bridge House Wharf, Cavans La., The Careenage, Bridgetown* ☎ *246/431–0741* 🌐 *www.greatadventuresbarbados.com.*

Cannon Charters

FISHING | *Cannon II*, a 42-foot Hatteras Sport Fisherman, has three chairs and five rods and accommodates six passengers. Drinks and snacks are complimentary, and lunch is served on full-day charters. ✉ *The Careenage, Bridgetown* ☎ *246/424–6107* 🌐 *www.fishingbarbados.com.*

High Seas Fishing Charters

FISHING | *Ocean Hunter*, a 42-foot custom-built sportfishing boat, has an extended cockpit that easily accommodates six people. Choose a four-, six-, or eight-hour charter. All tackle and bait are supplied, as well as drinks and snacks. Charter rates include hotel transfers. ✉ *The Careenage* ☎ *246/233–2598* 🌐 *www.sportfishingbarbados.com.*

GOLF

Barbadians love golf, and golfers love Barbados. Courses open to visitors are listed below.

Barbados Golf Club

GOLF | The first public golf course on Barbados, an 18-hole championship course (two returning 9s), was redesigned in 2000 by golf course architect Ron Kirby. The course has hosted numerous competitions, including the European Senior tour in 2003. Several hotels offer preferential tee-time reservations and reduced rates. Cart, trolley, club, and shoe rentals are all available. ✉ *Hwy. 7, Durants* ☎ *246/538–4653* 🌐 *www.barbadosgolfclub.com* 🎫 *$105 for 18 holes; $65 for 9 holes; 3-, 5-, and 7-day passes $255, $400, $525, respectively* 🏌 *18 holes (2 returning 9s), 6805 yds, par 72.*

★ Country Club at Sandy Lane

GOLF | At this prestigious club, golfers can play the Old Nine or either of two 18-hole championship courses: the Tom Fazio–designed Country Club Course and the spectacular Green Monkey Course, which is reserved for hotel guests and club members. The layouts offer a limestone-quarry setting (Green Monkey), a modern style with lakes (Country Club), and traditional small greens and narrow fairways (Old Nine). Golfers can use the driving range for free. The Country Club Restaurant and Bar, overlooking the 18th hole, is open to the public. Caddies, trolleys, clubs, and shoes are available for rent, as are GPS-equipped carts that alert you to upcoming hazards, give tips on how to play holes, and let you order refreshments. ✉ *Sandy Lane Hotel, Hwy. 1* ☎ *246/444–2000, 866/444–4080 in U.S.* 🌐 *www.sandylane.com/golf* 🎫 *Country Club: $240 for 18 holes ($200 hotel guests); $150 for 9 holes ($130 for guests); 7-day pass $1350 ($1250 for guests). Green Monkey: $390 for 18 holes (guests only). Old Nine: $90 for 9 holes ($75 guests); 7-day pass $560 ($450 guests)* 🏌 *Green Monkey: 18 holes, 7343 yds, par 72; Country Club: 18 holes, 7060 yds, par 72; Old Nine: 9 holes, 3345 yds, par 36.*

HIKING

Hilly but not mountainous, the northern interior and the east coast are ideal for hiking.

★ Barbados Hiking Association

HIKING & WALKING | **FAMILY** | Free walks sponsored by the Barbados National Trust and the Barbados Hiking Association are conducted year-round and are a great way to see the island. Experienced guides group you with others of similar ability on "Stop and Stare" walks, 5 to 6 miles (8 to 10 km); medium hikes, 8 to 10 miles (13 to 16 km); medium-fast hikes, 10 to 12 miles (16 to 19 km); or really fast hikes, 12 to 14 miles (19 to 23 km). Wear loose clothes, sensible shoes, sunscreen, and a hat, and bring a camera and water. Routes and locations change, but each hike is a loop, finishing where it began. Check newspapers, call the Trust, or check the Association's Facebook page for schedules and meeting places. ✉ *Barbados National Trust, Wildey House, Errol Barrow Hwy., Wildey* ☎ *246/426–2421* 🌐 *www.facebook.com/groups/hikebarbados/.*

Hike Barbados

HIKING & WALKING | **FAMILY** | Stephen Mendes offers private, customized, guided hikes in Barbados. He caters to parties of any size for a fixed price regardless of numbers. If your party size is three or less he will even pick you up and drop you off afterwards. He offers, 2-, 4-, 6-, or 8-mile scenic tourist hikes around the island. ✉ *Doverdale, Nelson Road, Navy Gardens, Dover* ☎ *246/4304818 Whatsapp* ✉ *hikebarbados@yahoo.com* 🌐 *https://hikebarbados.com* 🎫 *Payment on arrival. No deposit required. No cancellation fees. 2–4 miles $220; 2–6 miles $250; 6–8 miles $275; 8–10 miles $325 (fixed price for any group size).*

HORSE RACING

Barbados Turf Club

SPORTS VENUE | FAMILY | Horse racing is a big part of Bajan culture, and "going to the races" is an event for everyone. The races are administered by the Barbados Turf Club. Races take place on alternate Saturdays throughout the year at the Garrison Savannah, a 6-furlong grass oval in Christ Church, about 3 miles (5 km) south of Bridgetown. There is also occasional night racing. Important events include the Sandy Lane Barbados Gold Cup, held in late February or early March, and the Boxing Day Races on December 26. You can watch for free on the grounds, or pay for tickets, which vary in price according to where you sit—the dress-to-the-nines boxes, the members lounge, or the grandstands (grabbing a seat up close on the grounds with a picnic is also an option). Regardless of where you sit, you can't help but get caught up in the energy and excitement of the events. ✉ *The Garrison Savannah, Garrison* ☎ *246/626–3980* 🌐 *www.barbadosturfclub.org* 🎟 *Entrance ranges from $10Bds to $100Bds for the day. Event prices vary.*

SEA EXCURSIONS

Minisubmarine voyages are enormously popular with families and those who enjoy watching fish but don't wish to get wet. Party boats depart from Bridgetown's Deep Water Harbour for sightseeing and snorkeling or romantic sunset cruises. Prices are $70 to $125 per person for four- or five-hour daytime cruises and $60 to $85 for three- or four-hour sunset cruises, depending on the type of refreshments and entertainment included; transportation to and from the dock is provided. For an excursion that may be less splashy in terms of a party atmosphere—but is definitely splashier in terms of the actual experience—turtle tours allow participants to swim with and feed a resident group of hawksbill and leatherback sea turtles.

Atlantis Submarine

BOATING | FAMILY | This 50-foot, 48-passenger submarine turns the Caribbean into a giant aquarium. The two-hour voyage takes in wrecks and reefs as deep as 150 feet. Children love the adventure, but they must be at least 3 feet tall. ✉ *Shallow Draught, Bridgetown* ☎ *246/436–8929* 🌐 *www.barbados.atlantissubmarines.com* 🎟 *From $112.*

Cool Runnings Catamaran Cruises

BOATING | FAMILY | Captain Robert Povey, owner of *Cool Runnings* catamaran, skippers a five-hour lunch cruise with stops to swim with the fishes, snorkel with sea turtles, and explore a shallow shipwreck. A four-hour sunset cruise includes swimming, snorkeling, and exploring underwater as the sun sinks. Delicious meals with wine, along with an open bar, are part of all cruises. ✉ *Carlisle House, Carlisle Wharf, Hincks St., Bridgetown* ☎ *246/436–0911* 🌐 *www.coolrunnings-barbados.com* 🎟 *Lunch cruise $100, sunset cruise $90.*

★ Tiami Catamaran Cruises

BOATING | FAMILY | Tiami operates five catamaran party boats for luncheon cruises to a secluded bay for swimming with turtles or for romantic sunset and moonlight cruises. Daytime cruises include buffet lunch, open bar, and three swim/snorkel stops. Evening cruises include a swim/snorkel stop as the sun goes down, buffet dinner, and cocktails.

TIP→ Round-trip hotel transfers are complimentary for all cruises. ✉ *Shallow Draught, Bridgetown* ☎ *246/430–0900* 🌐 *www.tiamicatamarancruises.com* 🎟 *Lunch cruises from $100, sunset cruises from $90.*

SURFING

The best surfing is at Bathsheba Soup Bowl on the east coast; the Barbados Independence SurfPro championship (an international competition) is held here every November. But the water on the windward (Atlantic Ocean) side of the island is safe only for the most experienced surfers. Surfers also congregate at Surfer's Point, at the southern tip of Barbados near Inch Marlow, where the Atlantic Ocean meets the Caribbean Sea.

Zed's Surfing Adventures

SURFING | **FAMILY** | This outfit rents surfboards, provides lessons, and offers surf tours including equipment, guide, and transportation to surf breaks appropriate for your experience. Two-hour group lessons are held regularly; a six-hour package includes three lessons and a week's board rental. Surfboard rentals for experienced surfers and private lessons are always available. ✉ *Surfer's Point, Inch Marlowe* ☎ *246/428–7873* 🌐 *www.zedssurftravel.com* 🎫 *From $60 for lessons, from $30 2-hour board rental, $40 for full day rental.*

Barry's Surf Barbados

SURFING | Barry's surf school offers lessons in small groups, with a maximum four people per group. They are located in a great location in Oistin's with two surf breaks out front. Surf lessons include a rash vest and board rental for the rest of the day so you can carry on practicing what you have learned. Friendly instructors will help to get you started. Barry's also offers equipment and Jimmy Jeep rentals to let you travel around the island with your board. ✉ *Barry's Surf Barbados, Oistin's, Oistins* 🎫 *Lessons start from $75 including full-day board and rash vest rental. Equipment rental starts at $30 per day or $150 per week.*

WINDSURFING AND KITEBOARDING

Barbados is one of the prime locations in the world for windsurfing—and, increasingly, for kiteboarding. Winds are strongest November through April at the island's southern tip, at Silver Sands–Silver Rock Beach, which is where the Barbados Windsurfing Championships are held in mid-January. Use of windsurfing boards and equipment, as well as instruction, are often among the amenities included at larger hotels, and some also rent to nonguests. Kiteboarding is a more difficult sport that requires several hours of instruction to reach proficiency; Silver Sands is about the only location where you'll find kiteboarding equipment and instruction. Stand-up paddling has also become increasingly popular, and most surf shops (and many resorts) offer paddling equipment and instruction.

deAction Surf Shop

WINDSURFING | Directly on Silver Sands–Silver Rock Beach, Brian "Irie Man" Talma's shop stocks a range of rental surfing equipment and offers beginner windsurfing, kiteboarding, surfing, and stand-up paddling lessons. Conditions are ideal, with waves off the outer reef and flat water in the inner lagoon. Kiteboarding, which isn't easy, generally involves six hours of instruction broken up into two or three sessions: from flying a small kite to getting the body dragged with a big kite to finally getting up on the board. All equipment is provided. ✉ *Silver Sands–Silver Rock Beach, Silver Sands* ☎ *246/428–2027* 🌐 *www.briantalma.com.*

★ **Paddle Barbados**

WATER SPORTS | **FAMILY** | Paddle Barbados offers instruction, rentals, stand-up paddle yoga sessions, and tours around the harbor. A quick lesson will get you up on the board and paddling away in about 10 minutes. ✉ *Barbados Cruising Club, Aquatic Gap, Garrison* ☎ *246/249–2787* 🌐 *www.paddlebarbados.com* 🎫 *Rentals from $15 for two hours. Lessons from $15.*

Chapter 7

BONAIRE

Updated by
Susan Campbell

Sights ★★★★☆ | Restaurants ★★★☆☆ | Hotels ★★★☆☆ | Shopping ★★★☆☆ | Nightlife ★★★☆☆

WELCOME TO BONAIRE

TOP REASONS TO GO

★ **The Diving:** As locals say, you come here to dive, eat, dive, sleep, and dive.

★ **The Snorkeling:** You don't have to be a certified diver to appreciate Bonaire's reefs; snorkelers can see much of the beauty just below the surface of the water.

★ **The Quiet:** Visitors came to enjoy the tranquility of the island long before they started exploring diving.

★ **The Dining:** Dining options are surprisingly good and varied for such a small island.

★ **The Windsurfing:** This is one of the best places in the world to learn to windsurf.

★ **The Smiles:** Bonaireans are genuinely friendly, offering salutations to friends and strangers alike.

The landscape of Bonaire is peppered with acres of cactus and aloe plants. This is an arid climate with a stark beauty. Divers come to explore some of the best sites this side of Australia's Great Barrier Reef. Above the water are more than 15,000 flamingos—the biggest flock in the Western Hemisphere. With just over 21,000 people, this unspoiled island (112 square miles [290 square km]) has a small-town atmosphere. Kralendijk, the capital, has just over 3,000 inhabitants. The entire coastline—from the high-water tidemark to a depth of 200 feet—is protected as part of the Bonaire Marine Park, making it one of the Western Hemisphere's best diving destinations.

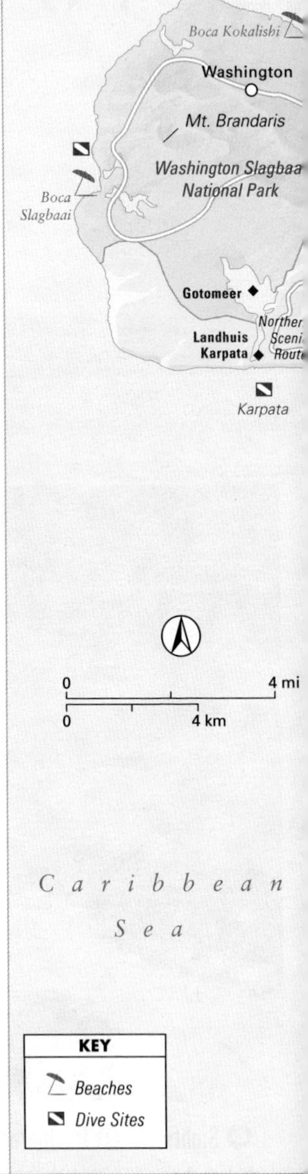

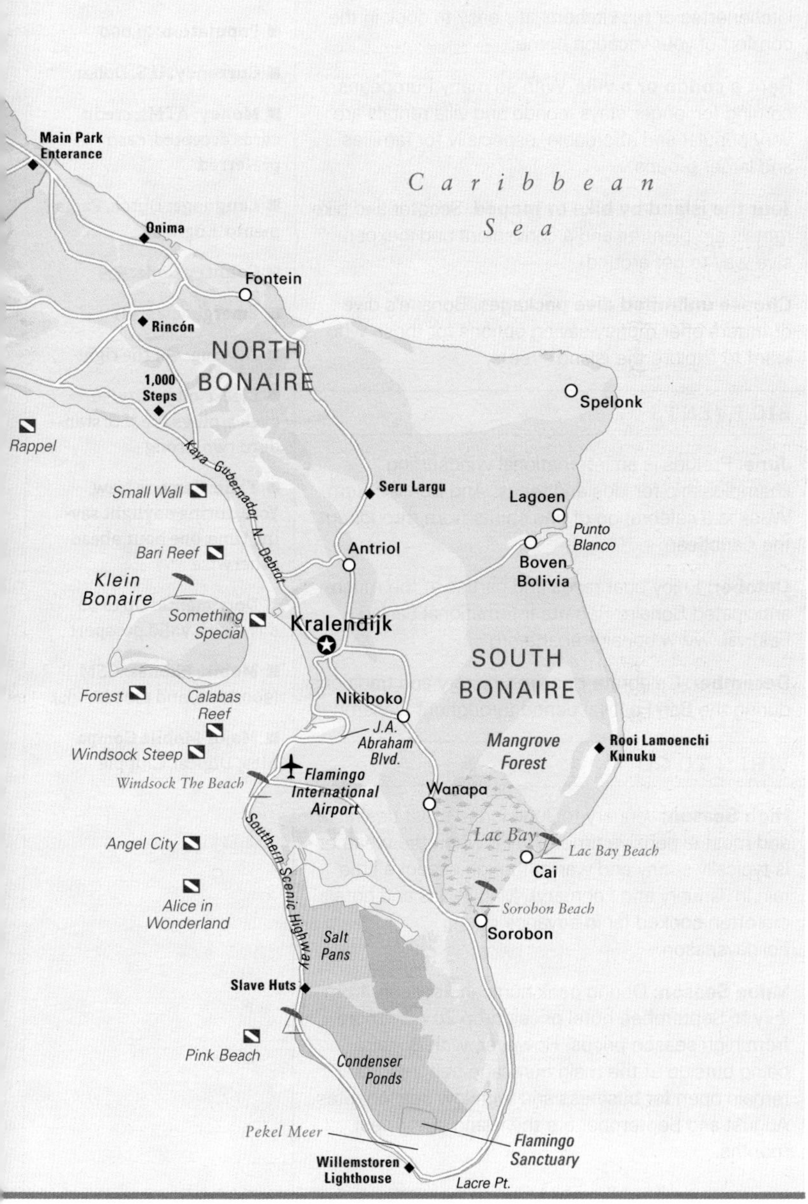

Caribbean Sea
Main Park Enterance
Onima
Fontein
Rincón
NORTH BONAIRE
1,000 Steps
Rappel
Kaya Gubernador N. Debrot
Spelonk
Small Wall
Seru Largu
Lagoen
Punto Blanco
Antriol
Boven Bolivia
Bari Reef
Klein Bonaire
Something Special
Kralendijk
SOUTH BONAIRE
Forest
Calabas Reef
Nikiboko
J.A. Abraham Blvd.
Windsock Steep
Mangrove Forest
Rooi Lamoenchi Kunuku
Flamingo International Airport
Windsock The Beach
Wanapa
Southern Scenic Highway
Lac Bay
Lac Bay Beach
Angel City
Cai
Alice in Wonderland
Sorobon Beach
Sorobon
Salt Pans
Slave Huts
Pink Beach
Condenser Ponds
Pekel Meer
Flamingo Sanctuary
Willemstoren Lighthouse
Lacre Pt.

ISLAND SNAPSHOT

WAYS TO SAVE

Self-cater. With many accommodations including kitchenettes or full kitchens, it's easy to cook in the comfort of your vacation home.

Rent a condo or a villa. With so many Europeans coming for longer stays, condo and villa rentals are very popular and affordable, especially for families and larger groups.

Tour the island by bike or moped. Scooter and bike rentals are plentiful and a convenient and inexpensive way to get around.

Choose unlimited dive packages. Bonaire's dive outfitters offer money-saving options for those who want to explore the island's reefs.

BIG EVENTS

June: ProKids is an international windsurfing championship for kids and teens. And Bonaire Rum Week is a celebration of fine spirits from throughout the Caribbean.

October: Enjoy boat races and parties at the much-anticipated Bonaire Regatta International Sailing Festival. www.bonaireregatta.org

December: Celebrate Bonaire's history and traditions during the Bari Festival period throughout December.

WHEN TO GO

High Season: January to June is the most desirable and most expensive time to visit, when the weather is typically sunny and warm (though expect a little rain in January and February). Many villas and hotels are often booked far in advance during holidayseason.

Value Season: During peak hurricane season, from July to September, hotel prices drop 20% or more from high season prices. However, with Bonaire being outside of the main hurricane belt, resorts remain open for business and with low season rates. August and September are the island's warmest months.

AT A GLANCE

- **Capital:** Kralendijk
- **Population:** 21,000
- **Currency:** U.S. Dollar
- **Money:** ATMs; credit cards accepted, cash preferred
- **Language:** Dutch, Papiamento, English
- **Country Code:** 599
- **Emergencies:** 911
- **Driving:** On the right
- **Electricity:** 127v/50 cycles; plugs are U.S. standard two-prong
- **Time:** Same as New York during daylight saving time; one hour ahead otherwise
- **Documents:** Up to 90 days with valid passport
- **Mobile Phones:** GSM (900, 1800, and 1900 bands)
- **Major Mobile Companies:** Digicel, Chippie

Bonaire is one of the best destinations in the Caribbean for shore diving. The dry climate and coral composition of the island mean that there's little soil runoff, allowing near-perfect visibility in the coastal waters. Although tourism, particularly diving tourism, is the backbone of the economy here, authorities strive to keep the booming hotel industry from damaging the precious ecosystem. Thankfully, most visitors come to Bonaire for the natural beauty, preventing the island from becoming overly developed and commercialized.

Locals are serious about conserving Bonaire's natural beauty. All the coastal waters of the island were turned into a national park in 1979, and in 1999 Bonaire purchased the 1,500-acre privately owned outlying island of Klein Bonaire to prevent unwanted development. Anyone diving around the island must purchase a one-year permit, and park rangers patrol the waters, handing out hefty fines to people who violate park rules. Spearfishing, removing coral, and even walking on coral are just some of the restricted activities. These rules have resulted in a pristine marine environment that makes for a supremely satisfying dive experience. Damage to the reefs caused by rare passing hurricanes is usually quickly repaired by the healthy ecosystem. Even the license plates in Bonaire declare it a diver's paradise.

Bonaire also offers a variety of experiences above the surface to those willing to explore its 112 square miles (290 square km). The southern salt flats give an interesting glimpse into the island's economic history. Washington–Slagbaai National Park, in the north, has the island's highest peak (784 feet) and is a haven for some of the thousands of flamingos that make Bonaire their home. The near-perfect climate also makes Bonaire the ideal destination for soaking in some sun.

Although many islanders claim that the name Bonaire comes from the French for "good air," this explanation is unlikely as the island was never colonized by the French. It was first inhabited by an Amerindian people (related to the Arawaks) called the Caquetios. Alonso de Ojeda and Amerigo Vespucci landed here in 1499 and claimed it for Spain. It seems likely that they adopted the Amerindian name for the island, which probably sounded very much like Bonaire and meant "low country." Because the Spanish found little use for the island except as a penal colony, the original inhabitants were shipped off to work on the plantations of Hispaniola, and Bonaire remained largely undeveloped. When the Dutch seized the islands of Aruba, Bonaire, and Curaçao in 1633, they developed Bonaire's salt industry, which still helps fuel the economy.

Most of the 21,000 inhabitants live in and around the capital, Kralendijk. Part of the BES Islands, Bonaire, St. Eustatius, and Saba were made special municipalities of the Netherlands in 2010. Before this change Bonaire was governed from neighboring Curaçao.

Planning

Getting Here and Around

AIR

Bonaire International Airport—better known as Flamingo Airport as its terminal is painted bright pink in tribute to the island's famous resident flamingo colony—though small, is quite modern. Beyond security, you'll find food and drink amenities, air-conditioned waiting areas, and a few duty-free shops. It's just over five minutes from downtown Kralendijk, and a short drive to most of the island's major resorts. Car rental and taxi transportation are available in front of the terminal. From the United States, direct flights are available with United Airlines from Newark and Houston, Delta from Atlanta, and American from Miami. You can also fly here via Aruba or Curacao, which have more options, connecting with regional carriers—Aruba Airlines, EZ Air, Divi Divi Air, and Winair offer frequent inter-island flights.

AIRLINE CONTACTS Aruba Airlines. ☎ *5999/735–0339* 🌐 *www.arubaairlines.com.* **EZ Air.** ☎ *5999/560–1900* 🌐 *www.flyezair.net.* **Divi Divi Air.** ✉ *Flamingo Airport* ☎ *599/717–2121* 🌐 *www.flydivi.com.* **Winair.** ✉ *Flamingo Airport* ☎ *721/545–4237* 🌐 *www.fly-winair.sx.*

AIRPORT Bonaire International Airport. *(BON, Flamingo Airport)* ✉ *EEG Blvd.* ☎ *599/717–5600* 🌐 *www.bonaireinternationalairport.com.*

BIKE AND MOPED

Scooters are a fun way to get around the island by day. Rates are about $25 per day for a one-seater and up to $35 for a deluxe two-seater. A valid driver's license and cash deposit or credit card are required.

CONTACTS Bonaire Motorcycle Shop. ✉ *Kaya Grandi 64, Kralendijk* ☎ *599/717–7790* 🌐 *www.motorcycleshopbonaire.com.* **Bonaire Scooter Rental.** ✉ *Kaya Grandi 72, Kralendijk* ☎ *599/796–2000* 🌐 *www.scootersbonaire.com.*

CAR

The best way to get around Bonaire is by rental car, as there's no public transportation. And if you plan on shore diving a lot, several outfits rent pickup trucks that are more suitable for hauling your gear around. Though the minimum age for car rental is 21 years, there is often a surcharge for those under 25, and some agencies will not rent to anyone under 30. You'll need a valid driver's license and a credit card. There's a 6% sales tax on rental fees and a government tax of $4 per day, and gas prices are typically double of those in the US. Traffic is to the right, and there's not a single traffic light on the island. Be on the lookout for meandering wild donkeys and goats—they don't know the rules of the road.

CONTACTS Avis. ✉ *Flamingo Airport, Kralendijk* ☎ *599/717–5795* 🌐 *www.avis-bonaire.com.* **Bonaire Rent a Car.** ✉ *Kaya International 1, Kralendijk* ☎ *599/786–6090* 🌐 *www.bonairerentacar.com.* **Budget.** ✉ *Kaya Industria 10, Kralendijk* ☎ *599/717–4700* 🌐 *www.bonaire-budget-car.com.* **Island Car Rentals.** ✉ *Opposite Flamingo Airport, Kaya Internationaal 130, Kralendijk* ☎ *599/717–2100* 🌐 *www.island-carrentalsbonaire.com.* **Voyager Bonaire Car Rental.** ✉ *Kaya Industria 4* ☎ *599/717–4123* 🌐 *www.voyagerbonaire.com.*

TAXI

Taxis are unmetered; fixed rates are controlled by the government. From most hotels into town it costs $10–$20. Fares increase from 7 pm to midnight by 25% and from midnight to 6 am by 50%. Drivers will conduct half-day tours; they start around $25 per person for up two hours. Airport taxi rates depend on distance and number in the party. Most fares are $10–$20 one-way.

CONTACTS Airport Taxi Stand. ☎ *599/717–8100.* **Taxi Central Dispatch.** ☎ *599/717–8100* 🌐 *www.bonairetaxi.net.*

Health and Safety

Dengue, chikungunya, and zika have all been reported throughout the Caribbean. We recommend that you protect yourself from these mosquito-borne illnesses by keeping your skin covered and/or wearing mosquito repellent. The mosquitoes that transmit these viruses are as active by day as they are by night.

Hotels and Resorts

Alongside the numerous basic lodges that primarily cater to divers, you'll find a few larger, full-service resorts—most of which are clustered around Kralendijk and the best of which are on decent (albeit mostly man-made) beaches. The island's self-catering accommodations are great for families and budget travelers. There are also luxe villa rentals for those seeking more personal and upscale accommodations.

Bonaire has a growing number of Airbnb rentals, too.

Hotel reviews have been shortened. For full information, visit Fodors.com.

CONTACTS Sun Rentals Bonaire. ☎ *599/717–6130* 🌐 *www.sunrentalsbonaire.com.*

What It Costs in U.S. Dollars

	$	$$	$$$	$$$$
RESTAURANTS				
	under $12	$12–$20	$21–$30	over $30
HOTELS				
	under $275	$275–$375	$376–$475	over $475

Weddings

One person must apply for temporary residency. Official witnesses must also apply for residency, but most wedding coordinators can arrange for local witnesses. After the marriage, an *apostille* (official seal) must be placed on the marriage license and certificate. Blood tests are not required and there's no specific residency period. Hiring a local professional wedding planner can really help you navigate the steps more easily, and they can even help you plan the rest of your holiday.

CONTACTS Bonaire Wedding Co.. ✉ *Kaya Hobo 1, Kralendijk* ☎ *599/701–7373* 🌐 *www.weddingbonaire.com.*

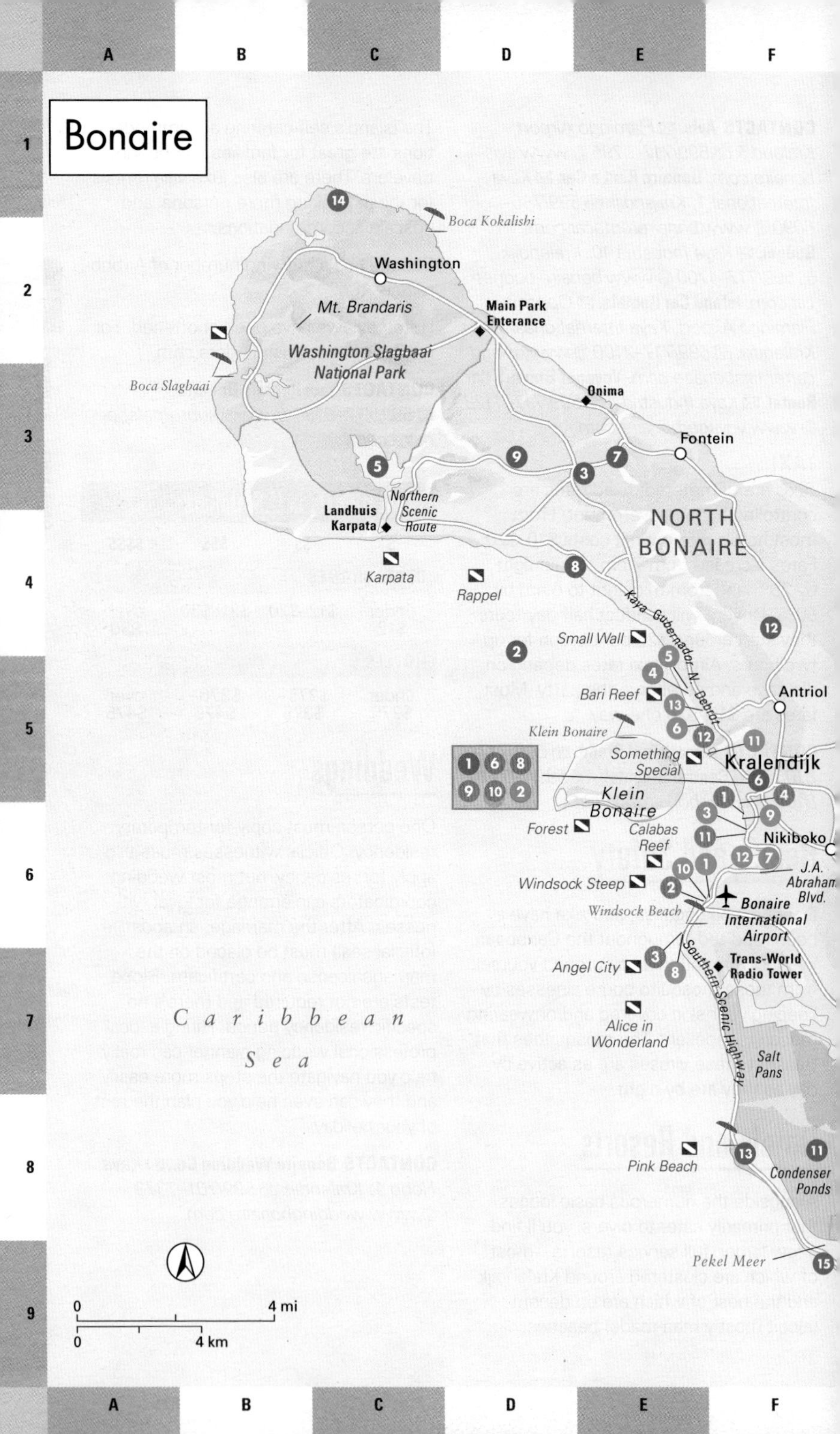

A
B
C
D
E
F
1
2
3
4
5
6
7
8
9
Bonaire
Boca Kokalishi
Washington
Mt. Brandaris
Main Park Enterance
Washington Slagbaai National Park
Boca Slagbaai
Onima
Fontein
Northern Scenic Route
Landhuis Karpata
NORTH BONAIRE
Karpata
Rappel
Kaya Gubernador N. Debrot
Small Wall
Bari Reef
Antriol
Klein Bonaire
Something Special
Kralendijk
Klein Bonaire
Forest
Calabas Reef
Nikiboko
J.A. Abraham Blvd.
Windsock Steep
Windsock Beach
Bonaire International Airport
Trans-World Radio Tower
Angel City
Southern Scenic Highway
Alice in Wonderland
Caribbean Sea
Salt Pans
Pink Beach
Condenser Ponds
Pekel Meer
0
4 mi
0
4 km

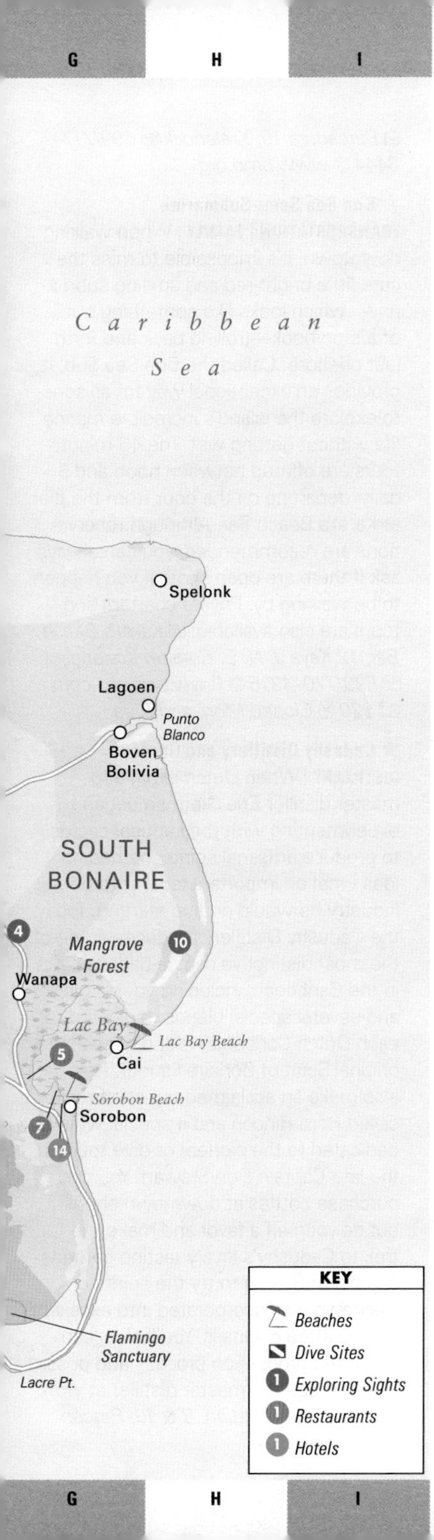

Sights

1 Bon Sea Semi-Submarine F5
2 Bonaire Marine Park ... D4
3 Cadushy Distillery and Gardens E3
4 Flamingo Adventure Golf G6
5 Gotomeer C3
6 Kralendijk F5
7 Mangazina di Rei Cultural Park E3
8 1,000 Steps E4
9 Rincón D3
10 Rooi Lamoenchi Kunuku H6
11 Salt Pans F8
12 Seru Largu F4
13 Slave Huts F8
14 Washington Slagbaai National Park C1
15 Willemstoren Lighthouse F9

Restaurants

1 At Sea F6
2 Boudoir E6
3 Brass Boer E7
4 Capriccio F6
5 Foodies G7
6 Grandi Restaurant F5
7 Hang Out Beach Bar ... G7
8 Hofi Restaurant F5
9 It Rains Fishes F5
10 Mona Lisa Bar & Restaurant F5
11 Sebastian Restaurant on the Sea F6
12 Spice Beach Club F5

Hotels

1 Bellafonte Luxury Oceanfront Hotel E6
2 Bonaire Oceanfront Apartments F5
3 Bruce Bowker's Carib Inn F6
4 Buddy Dive Resort E5
5 Captain Don's Habitat ... E5
6 Chogogo Dive & Beach Resort E5
7 Courtyard Bonaire Dive Resort F6
8 Delfins Beach Resort E7
9 Divi Flamingo Beach Resort F6
10 Grand Windsock Resort E6
11 Harbour Village Beach Club F5
12 Plaza Beach & Dive Resort Bonaire F6
13 Sand Dollar Condominium Resort E5
14 Sorobon Beach Resort G7

Bonaire

Sights

Two routes, north and south from Kralendijk, the island's small capital, are possible on the 24-mile-long (39-km-long) island; either route will take from a few hours to a full day, depending on whether you stop to snorkel, swim, dive, or lounge. Those pressed for time will find that it's easy to explore the entire island in a day if stops are kept to a minimum. Note that Bonaire's National Parks Foundation requires all nondivers (including swimmers, snorkelers, kite- and windsurfers, and paddleboarders) to pay a $25 annual Nature Fee to enter the water anywhere around the island (divers pay $45). The fee can be paid at most dive shops, hotel front desks, the tourism office, and tour operators. Washington Slagbaai National Park charges $3 to enter the visitor center.

★ Bonaire Marine Park

NATIONAL PARK | The Bonaire Marine Park, founded in 1979 to protect the island's most precious natural resource, covers an area of less than 700 acres and includes all the waters around the island from the high-water mark to the 60-meter depth. Because it has so zealously protected its marine environment, Bonaire offers an amazing diversity of underwater life. Turtles, rays, and fish of every imaginable color abound in the pristine waters of the park. Several well-enforced rules include: (1) pay the annual Nature Fee, and attach the yellow tag you receive to an item of scuba gear; (2) no spearfishing; (3) no dropping anchor; and (4) no touching, stepping on, or collecting coral. Checkout dives—dives you do first with a master before going out on your own—are required, and you can arrange them through any dive shop. All dive operations offer classes in free buoyancy control, advanced buoyancy control, and photographic buoyancy control. ✉ *Barcadera 10, Kralendijk* ☎ *599/717–8444* 🌐 *www.bmp.org.*

★ Bon Sea Semi-Submarine

TRANSPORTATION | **FAMILY** | When walking downtown, it's impossible to miss the cute little bright-red and smiling submarine—which looks like something out of a storybook—trolling back and forth just offshore. Called the Bon Sea Sub, it provides an exceptional way for all ages to explore the island's incredible marine life without getting wet. The 45-minute tours are offered between noon and 5 daily, departing on the hour from the pier at Karel's Beach Bar. Although reservations are recommended, you can always ask if there are open spots if you happen to be walking by. Private charters and tours are also available. ✉ *Karel's Beach Bar, 12 Kaya J. N. E. Craane, Kralendijk* ☎ *599/770–4216* 🌐 *www.bon-sea.com* 🎫 *$20* 🕑 *Closed Mon. and Tues.*

★ Cadushy Distillery and Gardens

DISTILLERY | When Dutch expat and master distiller Eric Gietman began experimenting with the kadushi cactus to produce artisanal spirits, he had no idea what an important local cottage industry he would end up starting. Today, the Cadushy Distillery produces some of the most distinctive cactus-based spirits in the Caribbean, including vodka, gin, and several special blends dedicated to each Dutch Caribbean Island as well the original Spirit of Bonaire liqueur. They also make an acclaimed top-shelf rum called Rom Rincón and a special whiskey dedicated to the pioneer of dive tourism, the late Captain Don Stewart. You can purchase bottles at downtown shops, but do yourself a favor and make the trek to Cadushy's lovely tasting gardens and bar in Rincon to try the spirits on their own and incorporated into excellent hand-crafted cocktails. You'll also learn about the production process and possibly even see the master distiller at work. ✉ *Kaya C. D. Crestian, 8 & 10, Rincón*

☎ *599/701–7011* 🌐 *www.cadushy.com* 🎫 *Free* 🕒 *Closed Sun.*

Flamingo Adventure Golf

GOLF COURSE | **FAMILY** | While driving toward Sorobon from downtown, you will no doubt suddenly come upon things like the Eiffel Tower, Statue of Liberty, King Kong, and a pirate ship. Don't worry. You're not hallucinating. Rather, you've just stumbled upon Bonaire's big, quirky, miniature-golf complex—and it's not only for kids. In addition to delicious snacks like Dutch pancakes, it also has a great bar with killer cocktails and two hot tubs in which you can soak for an extra fee. ✉ *Kaminda Lac, Kralendijk* ☎ *599/786–7857* 🌐 *www.flamingoadventuregolfbonaire.com* 🕒 *Closed Mon.*

Gotomeer

WILDLIFE REFUGE | **FAMILY** | Bonaire is one of the few places in the world where pink flamingos nest and this saltwater lagoon near the island's northern end is one of their favorite places to hang out; there are about 15,000 of them in Bonaire (almost as many as the number of human residents). January to June is the best time to see these shy, spindly-leg creatures as they stick around to tend to their gray-plumed babies. Take the paved road along the lagoon to the parking and observation area for great views of the lagoon and Washington Slagbaai National Park. ✉ *Kaminda Goto, Rincón.*

Kralendijk

TOWN | Bonaire's small, tidy capital city (population just over 3,000) is five minutes from the airport. The main drag, J. A. Abraham Boulevard, turns into Kaya Grandi in the center of town. Along it are most of the island's major stores, boutiques, and restaurants and some new hotel and apartment complexes. Across Kaya Grandi, opposite Littman's jewelry store, is Kaya L. D. Gerharts, with several small supermarkets, a handful of snack shops, and some of the better restaurants. Walk down the narrow waterfront avenue called Kaya C. E. B. Hellmund, which leads straight to the North and South piers. In the center of town, the Harbourside Mall has chic boutiques. Along this route is Ft. Orange, with its cannons. From December through April, when cruise ships dock in the harbor, they're greeted by a pop-up open-air market of locally made goods and representatives from tour operators eager to sweep passengers off to explore the island's many different diversions. The diminutive ocher-and-white structure that looks like a tiny Greek temple is the produce market, where you can find plenty of fresh produce. Pick up the brochure *Walking and Shopping in Kralendijk* from the tourist office for a map and complete list of all the monuments and sights in the town. ✉ *Kralendijk.*

★ Mangazina di Rei Cultural Park

HISTORY MUSEUM | **FAMILY** | Built around the second-oldest stone structure on Bonaire, this cultural park a few miles before Rincón provides a fascinating insight into the island's history. The museum commands an excellent view of the surrounding countryside and contains artifacts tracing the often hard lives of the early settlers. Numerous structures built around the museum illustrate how living conditions have changed over the years. The park is usually filled with island schoolkids learning how to use traditional musical instruments and how to cook local foods. The last Saturday of each month features a cultural market. Enjoy local food and purchase crafts while listening to island music. Arrive early for the best selection of treats. ✉ *Kaya Rincón z/n, Rincón* ☎ *599/786–2101* 🌐 *www.mangazinadirei.org* 🎫 *$10* 🕒 *Closed Sat.–Mon.*

1,000 Steps

VIEWPOINT | Directly across the road from the Radio Nederland towers on the main road north, you'll see a short yellow marker that points to the location of these limestone stairs carved right out of the cliff. They lead to a lovely coral beach and protected cove where you can snorkel and dive. Although there are really only 67 steps, it feels like there are 1,000 of them when you walk back up carrying scuba gear. ✉ *Queen's Hwy., Rincón.*

★ Rincón

TOWN | The island's original Spanish settlement, Rincón is where slaves brought from Africa to work the plantations and salt fields lived. Today it's a well-kept cluster of pastel cottages and 19th-century buildings that constitute Bonaire's oldest village. There are several local eateries and bars in town, and it's also home to renowned Cadushy Distillery. Dia di Rincón (Rincón Day) is an annual festival and holiday held April 30. This massive street party features local food, music, and revelry. Arrive early if traveling with children. By nighttime, it's a lively boisterous party vibe. ✉ *Rincón.*

★ Rooi Lamoenchi Kunuku

MUSEUM VILLAGE | **FAMILY** | Owner Ellen Herrera restored her family's homestead north of Lac Bay, in the Bonairean *kadushi* (cactus) wilderness, to educate tourists and residents about the history and tradition of authentic kunuku living and to show the unspoiled terrain during two daily tours (you must make an appointment in advance). Tours take a couple of hours. ✉ *Kaya Suiza 23* ☎ *599/717–8489* 🌐 *www.facebook.com/rooilamoenchikunukuparkbonaire* 🎫 *$21.*

Salt Pans

FACTORY | Rising like mountains of snow, Bonaire's salt pans are hard to miss. Harvested once a year, the "ponds" are owned by Cargill, Inc., which has reactivated the 19th-century salt industry with great success (one reason for that success is that the ocean on this part of the island is higher than the land, which makes irrigation a snap). Keep a lookout for the three 30-foot obelisks (white, blue, and red) that were used to guide the trade boats coming to pick up the salt. Look also in the distance across the pans to the abandoned solar saltworks that's now a designated flamingo sanctuary. With the naked eye you might be able to make out a pink-orange haze just on the horizon; with binoculars you will see a sea of bobbing pink bodies. The sanctuary is completely protected, and no entrance is allowed (flamingos are extremely sensitive to disturbances of any kind). ✉ *South Bonaire.*

Seru Largu

VIEWPOINT | Just off the main road, this spot, at 394 feet in elevation, is one of the highest on the island. A paved but narrow and twisting road leads to a magnificent daytime view of Kralendijk's rooftops and the island of Klein Bonaire. A large cross and figure of Christ stand guard at the peak, with an inscription reading *ayera* (yesterday), *awe* (today), and *semper* (always). Many locals make their daily hike up the hill for a vigorous workout. ✉ *Rincón.*

Slave Huts

RUINS | The salt industry's history is revealed in Rode Pan, the site of two groups of tiny slave huts. The white huts are on the right side of the road, opposite the salt flats; the second grouping, called the red slave huts, stretches across the road toward the island's southern tip. During the 19th century, enslaved people worked the salt pans by day and slept in the cramped huts. Each Friday afternoon they walked many hours to Rincón to spend the weekend with their families, returning each Sunday. The Red Slave area is a popular dive spot during low wind and calm seas. When the wind is strong and waves prevail, the local windsurf posse heads to Red Slave to catch the swell. ✉ *South Bonaire.*

★ Washington Slagbaai National Park

NATIONAL PARK | **FAMILY** | Once a plantation producing divi-divi trees (the pods were used for tanning animal skins), aloe (used for medicinal lotions), charcoal, and goats, the park is now a model of conservation. It's easy to tour the 13,500-acre tropical desert terrain on the dirt roads. A truck or jeep is recommended for clearance along the rutted roads. As befits a wilderness sanctuary, the well-marked, rugged routes force you to drive slowly enough to appreciate the animal life and the terrain. (Think twice about coming here if it has rained recently—the mud you may encounter will be more than inconvenient.) If you're planning to hike, bring a picnic lunch, camera, sunscreen, and plenty of water. There are two routes: the long one (22 miles [35½ km]) is marked by yellow arrows, the short one (15 miles [24 km]) by green arrows. Goats and donkeys may dart across the road, and you may catch sight of large iguanas camouflaged in the shrubbery.

Bird-watchers are really in their element here. Right inside the park's gate, flamingos roost on the salt pan known as Salina Mathijs, and exotic parakeets congregate at the base of 784-foot Mt. Brandaris, Bonaire's highest peak. Some 130 species of birds fly in and out of the shrubbery. Keep your eyes open and your binoculars at hand. Swimming, snorkeling, and scuba diving are permitted, but you're asked not to frighten the animals or remove anything from the grounds. Absolutely no hunting, fishing, or camping is allowed. A useful guide to the park is sold in the visitor center. To get here, take the secondary road north from the town of Rincón. To enter, you'll need a photo ID and proof that you've paid the Bonaire National Parks Foundation's annual Nature Fee. ✉ *Washington Slagbaai National Park* ☎ *599/717–8444* 🌐 *www.stinapabonaire.org/washington-slagbaai* 🎫 *Park: Annual Nature Fee proof of purchase ($25 nondivers, $45 divers). Visitor Center: $3.*

Willemstoren Lighthouse

LIGHTHOUSE | Bonaire's first lighthouse was built in 1837 and is now automated (but closed to visitors). Take some time to explore the beach and notice how the waves, driven by the trade winds, play a crashing symphony against the rocks. Locals stop here to collect pieces of driftwood in spectacular shapes and to build fanciful pyramids from objects that have washed ashore. ✉ *South Bonaire.*

 Beaches

Although most of Bonaire's charms are underwater, there are a few beautiful beaches. Don't expect long strands of white sand, but many dive and snorkel sites have suitable entries for swimmers. Bonaire's pristine water and protected reefs (remember that it's unlawful to touch or stand on coral) offer stunning settings for sunrise or sunset viewing. Several hotels have lovely beaches that are accessible to nonguests for a nominal fee. Before heading to the beach and entering the waters, be sure to pay the Bonaire National Parks Foundation's requisite Nature Fee ($25 nondivers, $45 divers). For the best beach experience, grab a water taxi to Klein Bonaire. Beach booties—or water shoes—are highly recommended everywhere, as the entrance to the water is often rocky.

Boca Slagbaai

BEACH | Inside Washington Slagbaai National Park, this popular snorkel and dive site has interesting offshore coral gardens that are good for snorkeling. Bring scuba boots or canvas sandals to walk into the water, because the beach is rough on bare feet. The gentle surf makes it an ideal place for swimming and picnicking. Sunday is a lively time, when locals come to picnic. **Amenities:** parking; water sports. **Best for:** snorkeling; solitude; swimming; walking. ✉ *Off main park road, Washington Slagbaai National Park.*

Klein Bonaire

BEACH | **FAMILY** | Just a water-taxi hop across from Kralendijk, this little island offers picture-perfect white-sand beaches. Klein Bonaire is one of Bonaire's most popular snorkel spots. Local boat tours frequent the island in hopes of spotting turtles. The area is protected, so absolutely no development has been allowed.

Make sure to pack everything before heading to the island, including water and an umbrella to hide under because there are no refreshment stands or changing facilities, and there's almost no shade either. Boats leave from the Pier, across from It Rains Fishes restaurant—you can reserve online or hop on and pay (the round-trip water taxi fare is $20). **Amenities:** none. **Best for:** snorkeling; solitude; swimming; sunbathing. ☎ *599/717–1133* 🌐 *www.watertaxikleinbonaire.com.*

Sorobon Beach

BEACH | **FAMILY** | One of Bonaire's most beautiful beaches is also *the* place to windsurf. The sand is powdery white, and the gin-clear water is shallow, allowing swimmers to walk up to the reef on a calm-breeze day. You can also rent a stand-up paddleboard and cruise the shallows looking for turtles; the snorkeling here is amazing, too. Keep in mind, though, that all sea life is protected, so no touching or removing shells or creatures. On-site operators offer equipment rentals and expert instructions for lessons for windsurfing and wing foiling. Two restaurants offer diverse menus, including tropical drinks. The public beach area near the marina has restrooms and huts for shade. **Amenities:** food and drink; parking; showers; toilets; water sports. **Best for:** snorkeling; paddleboarding; windsurfing. ✉ *Kaya IR. Randolph Statius van Eps, Sorobon Beach, Sorobon* ✥ *Take E.E.G. Blvd. south from Kralendijk to Kaya IR. Randolph Statius van Eps.*

Windsock Beach

BEACH | Near the airport (just off E.E.G. Boulevard), this pretty little spot by the Grand Windsock resort looks out toward the north side of the island and has about 200 yards of white sand along a rocky shoreline. It's a popular dive and snorkel site, and swimming conditions are good. You can dine at Grand Windsock Bonaire's restaurant and bar, or picking up tasty bites at the Kite City Food Truck. **Amenities:** food and drink. **Best for:** snorkeling; swimming. ✉ *Off E.E.G. Blvd.* 🌐 *www.grandwindsockbonaire.com.*

 Restaurants

Dining on Bonaire is a delight as you can find everything from Caribbean to South American and Asian cuisines. Note that many restaurants serve only dinner, and only a few establishments outside hotels are open for breakfast. Stylish and sophisticated new spots continue to pop up all around the island, not just at the main resorts but also downtown and off the beaten path, such as Foodies across from Lac Bay.

★ At Sea

$$$ | **INTERNATIONAL** | Chef Jeroen and his wife Tiffany have created a seaside dining oasis that offers a leisurely, relaxed experience and some of the island's most creative seafood, steak, and vegetarian dishes and utilizing both locally and globally sourced ingredients. Choose from enticing small plates like ceviche lionfish or truffle risotto, or opt for a multicourse feast with optional wine pairings. **Known for:** terrific service; four- to six-course chef's surprise menus; creative small plates. 💲 *Average main: $30* ✉ *Kaya Hellmund 25, Kralendijk* ☎ *599/701–0134* 🌐 *www.atseabonaire.com* 🕒 *Closed Sun. and Mon.*

Boudoir

$$ | **ECLECTIC** | An excellent patio eatery at the Royal Palm Mall offers a excellent breakfasts and an eclectic range of soups, salads, sandwiches, and burgers for lunch. The vibe shifts at night, when the restaurant morphs into "Avocados," with a special menu devoted to these creamy, nutty-tasting delicacies. **Known for:** avocado specialties; Sunday brunch; unfussy ambience. 💲 *Average main: $12* ✉ *Kaya Grandi 26 F/G, Kralendijk* ☎ *599/717–4321* 🌐 *www.bonaireboudoir.com.*

★ Brass Boer

$$$$ | **CONTEMPORARY** | Owners of the critically acclaimed De Librije restaurant in the Netherlands and longtime Bonaire visitors, Dutch master chef Jonnie Boer and his wife, Therese, operate this hip restaurant in Delfins Beach Resort. Enjoy some of the island's most exciting and creative fusion fare (miso-cured monkfish, sweetbreads with peanut, coconut, and pineapple)—prepared in an open kitchen—in a gorgeous seaside setting with glassed-in banquettes. **Known for:** extensive upscale wine list; shareable small plates; avant-garde cuisine. *Average main: $35 Delfins Beach Resort, 44 Punt Vierkant, Kralendijk 599/717–5050 www.brassboer.com Closed Sun.*

★ Capriccio

$$$ | **ITALIAN** | This splendid, family-run Italian eatery offers casual à la carte dining on a terrace or meals in a more romantic setting in a tonier, air-conditioned dining room. Choose from 50 regular offerings—including thin-crust prosciutto pizzas, caprese salads, linguini with scallops, and red wine–braised lamb shank—or go for the five-course prix-fixe menu. **Known for:** homemade pasta, bread, and pizza; authentic Italian specialties, including seasonal panettone; extensive wine cellar. *Average main: $25 Kaya Hellmund 5, Kralendijk 599/717–7230 www.capricciobonaire.com Closed Mon. & Tues. No lunch weekends.*

★ Foodies

$$$ | **INTERNATIONAL** | This aptly named, eclectic eatery serves everything from pasta and risotto to ribs and skewers to schnitzels and shareables in a labyrinth of dining nooks, decks, and gardens. At lunch, it attracts hungry crowds with inventive burgers and sandwiches; at night, two bars draw folks for cocktails and tapas, and the chef's surprise dinners pack in those looking for a full meal. **Known for:** stellar selection of wines by the glass; three-course chef's surprise and special-of-the-day menus; killer bay views from the front terrace. *Average main: $30 Kaminda Sorobon 106, Sorobon 599/717–5369 www.foodiesbonaire.com Closed Mon. and Tues.*

Grandi Restaurant

$$ | **ITALIAN** | Though "grandi" means "big" in Papiamento, this tiny spot is quite the opposite—the trendy downtown hideaway opened in 2022 and specializes in authentic, artfully plated Italian fare with some fusion accents, and always a fresh catch of the day, oysters on the half shell, and a well-curated antipasto selection. Try the chef's surprise small-plate menu, which you can pair with wines. **Known for:** creative small plates; superb charcuterie plates; great wine and Champagne menu. *Average main: $20 Kaya Grandi 7, Kralendijk 599/786–7777 www.restaurantgrandi.com Closed weekends.*

★ Hang Out Beach Bar

$$ | **CARIBBEAN** | Overlooking Lac Bay, the training ground for the famous Bonaire Windsurf Team, this breezy bar offers libations and tasty sandwiches, salads, and daily specials in a lively surfside setting until 6 pm most days, with the exception of Thursday, when there's a famous barbecue and live music well into the evening, and Sunday. Lounge beds, sofas in the sand, and lots of shady nooks make this a wonderful place to chill and party on the beach. **Known for:** live music; great sangria and craft cocktails; Thursday-night barbecues. *Average main: $15 Kaminda Sorobon 12, Kralendijk www.hangoutbeachbar.com No dinner Mon.–Wed., Fri., and Sat.*

Hofi Restaurant

$$ | **INTERNATIONAL** | Opened in 2021, this enchanting little secret garden enclave is the ideal spot to unwind after a day by the sea with high-end cocktails, gourmet tapas, and other shareables. Look for the oil lanterns outside a golden gate near famous Gio's Gelateria to discover creative takes on classic meat and

seafood dishes; fans of plant-based fare enjoy such meatless dishes as vegan tartare and beetroot tartelette. **Known for:** top-notch service; creative bites; excellent cocktails using high-end spirits. *Average main: $20 Kaya Grandi 32B, Kralendijk 599/786–6329 www.hofirestaurant.com Closed Tues. and Wed. No lunch.*

★ It Rains Fishes
$$$$ | **ECLECTIC** | This urban-chic establishment housed in a century-old traditional home with a magical seafront setting provides impeccable service and a creative, diverse menu that emphasizes grilled local fish—the restaurant even has its own little seafood market just outside. Open for lunch weekdays with a diverse menu of Dutch-style sandwiches, wraps, burgers, and fish and chips, too, it's a wonderful downtown spot for watching the boats on the water. **Known for:** three-course chef's menus; catch-of-the-day with creative preparations; creative seafood. *Average main: $35 Kaya Jan N.E. Craane 24, Kralendijk 599/717–8780 www.itrainsfishesbonaire.com Closed Sun. No lunch Sat.*

Mona Lisa Bar & Restaurant
$$$$ | **EUROPEAN** | Popular with both locals and visitors, this little dining spot in the town center features continental, Caribbean, and Indonesian fare, which you can enjoy indoors or outside. Popular items include the Wiener schnitzel and the fresh fish dishes. **Known for:** Indonesian saté; house-made desserts like passion fruit cheesecake; wahoo with saffron sauce. *Average main: $38 Kaya Grandi 15, Kralendijk 599/717–8718 Closed weekends. No lunch.*

Sebastian's Restaurant on the Sea
$$$ | **SEAFOOD** | Reserve in advance for a sunset dining experience at this chic, romantic, waterfront spot (the pier table, which seats up to 25 people, is one of Bonaire's most sought after). Chef Sebastian has created his own niche, with an eclectic menu of international dishes prepared with a Mediterranean flair. **Known for:** Sunday Italian nights (pasta and house-made pizza at great prices); Wednesday "Kitchen Nights" for chef's surprise four-course menus; daily fresh-fish specials. *Average main: $30 J.A. Abraham Blvd. 60, Kralendijk 599/717–1697 www.sebastiansrestaurantbonaire.com.*

Spice Beach Club
$$$ | **CARIBBEAN** | At this seaside eatery specializing in Caribbean-inspired tapas, the flavors are bold, the plating is artistic, and the water's-edge tables are illuminated by torches. After dinner, head to the neighboring beach bar to enjoy a lively vibe and DJ entertainment. **Known for:** creative international fare; private cabana dinners for two by firepits; rocking beach bar happy hours and later-night entertainment. *Average main: $25 Kaya Gobernador Nicolaas Debrot 73, Kralendijk 599/717–8060 www.spicebonaire.com.*

Hotels

Historically, most of Bonaire's hotels and resorts catered to divers and provided few creature comforts. But today's accommodation scene has evolved to embrace many different types of travelers—including those seeking luxury—and there's a good cross-section of brand-new resorts for family-friendly holidays, a handful of cool new little boutique hotels, and trendy modern complexes with a wide assortment of all-inclusive and European-plan options for all budgets and travel styles. You'll find plenty of fully equipped condos and apartments for extended stays, including a few Airbnbs. A popular trend is renting villas, and the prices for these large multistory stand-alone houses with their own pools and luxury amenities are typically much lower than elsewhere in the Caribbean. Sun Rentals Bonaire (www.sunrentalsbonaire.com) has a portfolio of over 30 rentals, including some that can sleep up to 10 people.

If you're self-catering, note that there are two surprisingly large modern supermarkets with an excellent selection of Dutch foods as well as a few local mom-and-pop shops for more local Caribbean products. Some resorts offer grocery delivery, too.

Bellafonte Luxury Oceanfront Hotel

$ | **HOTEL** | The quintessentially Caribbean Bellafonte has breathtaking ocean views, close proximity to dining spots, and uncluttered, contemporary guest quarters with teak furnishings, steel accents, and modern amenities. **Pros:** small infinity dipping pool overlooking the sea; diving straight from the hotel pier; upper rooms have excellent views. **Cons:** not directly on a beach (but has direct water access from a private pier); not all rooms have ocean views; no on-site restaurant. *Rooms from: $225 ✉ E. E. G. Blvd. 10, Belnem ☎ 599/717–3333 🌐 www.bellafontebonaire.com 22 units No Meals.*

★ Bonaire Oceanfront Apartments

$ | **HOTEL** | This small, homey, family-run oceanfront complex—within easy walking distance of everything so no car is required—is a practical base for those coming to dive or explore on a budget. **Pros:** free high-speed Internet; great location right downtown; on-site dive shop (tanks and lockers available 24/7). **Cons:** no on-site dining; can be a little noisy at times; basic amenities. *Rooms from: $99 ✉ Kaya Grandi 65, Kralendijk ☎ 599/717–6130 🌐 www.sunrentalsbonaire.com/listings/bonaire-oceanfront-apartments 13 rooms No Meals.*

Bruce Bowker's Carib Inn

$ | **B&B/INN** | The cozy rooms and the personal touches of late owner–dive-instructor legend Bruce Bowker are why this resort consistently boasts the highest return-visitor ratio on the island (there is a minimum three-night stay). **Pros:** Wi-Fi throughout; intimate and friendly; excellent dive courses. **Cons:** tiny pool; nondivers will find little to entertain them; some accommodations are rather spartan. *Rooms from: $139 ✉ J. A. Abraham Blvd. 46, Kralendijk ☎ 599/717–8819 🌐 www.caribinn.com 11 units No Meals.*

Buddy Dive Resort

$ | **RESORT** | **FAMILY** | Well-equipped rooms with private balconies or patios, a nicely landscaped compound, and excellent dive and drive-and-dive packages and amenities keep guests coming back to this large resort. **Pros:** great snorkeling and swimming from the man-made beach; dive shop and on-site tank-filling station; open-air restaurant with fantastic ocean views. **Cons:** not all rooms have sea views; room amenities vary depending on location; complex can feel like a maze. *Rooms from: $139 ✉ Kaya Gobernador N. Debrot 85, Kralendijk ☎ 599/717–5080, 866/462–8339 🌐 www.buddydive.com 78 units No Meals.*

Captain Don's Habitat

$ | **HOTEL** | Bonaire's very first hotel catering to divers remains a favorite even four decades later with a PADI and SDI (Suba Diving International) Center offering more than 20 specialty courses; mesmerizing reef formations 90 feet from shore; and beautifully renovated accommodations that include oceanfront rooms and suites, luxurious three-bedroom villas, and a few cottages. **Pros:** popular bar and restaurant; full-service spa; historic and ecofriendly. **Cons:** not all rooms have ocean views; no beach; little for nondivers to do. *Rooms from: $169 ✉ Kaya Gobernador N. Debrot 113, Kralendijk ☎ 599/717–8290, 800/327–6709 🌐 www.habitatbonaire.com 46 units No Meals.*

Chogogo Dive & Beach Resort

$ | **RESORT** | **FAMILY** | This full-service resort opened in 2021 just steps from downtown, offering its own beach, a large pool, and the island's only lazy river ride, which snakes its way around the fresh studios, villas, and apartment-style accommodations. **Pros:** ecofriendly design and electric-car rentals; walking distance to town; lots of diversions, beyond diving, for families. **Cons:** not all rooms have ocean views; day passes for the public can lead to crowded grounds; modern design lacks local color. *Rooms from: $193 75B Kaya Gobernador N Debrot 599/788–9985 www.chogogobonaire.com 189 rooms No Meals.*

Courtyard Bonaire Dive Resort
$ | **HOTEL** | **FAMILY** | Although this Marriott chain property is a bit out of character for Bonaire, it has been painted in eye-popping Caribbean colors that match the tropical vibe; it has modern, well-equipped rooms with nautical themes; and it makes a practical base for families on a budget and business travelers. **Pros:** large pool and water circuit; high-tech amenities; on-site dive center and gym. **Cons:** impersonal prefabricated feel; top-floor rooms have tiny French balconies; located canal-side rather than seaside. *Rooms from: $235 Kaya International 2, Kralendijk 599/715–2222 www.marriott.com 115 rooms No Meals.*

★ **Delfins Beach Resort**
$ | **RESORT** | This lavish oasis of accommodations exudes barefoot luxury at its best, with well-equipped and chic modern suites, high-end villas options, some with their own plunge pools and spacious penthouse suites all cresting a lovely little beach surrounded by a spectacular water feature. **Pros:** first-rate on-site dive operation; upscale yet fun and friendly vibe; community spirit. **Cons:** you need a car to go to town; need beach shoes on rocky waterfront; not all rooms are full sea view. *Rooms from: $270 44 Punt Vierkant, Kralendijk 599/715–5000 www.delfinsbeachresort.com 148 units No Meals.*

★ **Divi Flamingo Beach Resort**
$ | **RESORT** | **FAMILY** | One of the island's oldest complexes and original dive resorts has kept up with the times by regularly refurbishing the grounds, rooms, facilities, and water circuits—most recently they've redone their studios, which are perfect for divers. **Pros:** the Caribbean's only "barefoot" casino; short walk to downtown; family-friendly vibe with great shallow snorkeling on-site. **Cons:** options for all-inclusive dining are somewhat limited; beach is tiny; some rooms are very small. *Rooms from: $225 J. A. Abraham Blvd. 40, Kralendijk 599/717–8285, 800/367–3484 www.diviflamingo.com 129 rooms All-Inclusive.*

Grand Windsock Resort
$$ | **RESORT** | **FAMILY** | A sprawling collection of new luxury villas and apartment rentals surrounds their own private pool and flanks one of the best snorkeling areas on the island across the street; in fact, you'll rarely pass this little beach by the road without seeing a few dozen snorkel tops floating around the bay. **Pros:** lots of modern amenities, including on-site laundry facilities; there's more of a community feel than a resort; great oceanfront dining and bar. **Cons:** car needed to get to downtown shopping; monochrome design lacks local color; pool can be noisy with kids. *Rooms from: $260 EEG Blvd. 3, Kralendijk 599/717–5363 www.grandwindsock-bonaire.com 72 units No Meals.*

★ **Harbour Village Beach Club**
$$ | **HOTEL** | This upscale enclave is one of Bonaire's best luxury accommodations, especially if you opt for one of the one-bedroom beachfront villas, which are lavishly appointed and have outlandishly large marble bathrooms. **Pros:** convenient to downtown; private beach; upscale amenities. **Cons:** faces a busy marina; not all rooms are oceanfront; standard rooms are a bit small. *Rooms from: $350 Kaya Gobernador N. Debrot 71, Kralendijk 599/717–7500, 800/424–0004 www.harbourvillage.com 60 units No Meals.*

The Donkeys of Bonaire

Visitors to Bonaire are often startled by the sight of donkeys lazily roaming about the island. In fact, these little equines are an integral part of Bonaire's history as well as its modern landscape.

Bonaire has no large indigenous mammals. Donkeys were imported to the island in the 1500s to serve the needs of Spanish colonists. They provided an effective means of transport and continued to be used for that purpose for the salt industry that eventually developed. With their minimal water requirements and ability to eat just about any vegetation, the animals proved well adapted to the arid environment. Later, when the salt industry became more mechanized and other forms of transport were introduced, the donkeys were left to wander. With no predators to deal with and little competition for the scrub and cacti that cover the island, the donkeys have survived, and their numbers have even increased over the years.

Today there are not as many wild donkeys as there once were, but those still around charm tourists. Islanders often have a more tarnished view. Roaming about in search of food, donkeys often push through fences and munch and stomp through ornamental plants. However, Bonaire's relationship with the ubiquitous quadrupeds seems destined to remain close for the foreseeable future, and many have been moved to Donkey Sanctuary Bonaire (www.donkeysanctuary.org), which is free to visit (bring apples and carrots to make fast friends).

★ Plaza Beach & Dive Resort Bonaire
$$ | **RESORT** | **FAMILY** | One of the island's first resorts has since been overtaken by the Van Der Valk organization, which has completely refreshed and renovated this sprawling, all-inclusive, family-friendly oasis. **Pros:** lots of activities and entertainment for all ages; excellent beach and water feature; well-maintained. **Cons:** pool and beach area can get noisy with families; most restaurants are buffet-style; not all rooms are beachfront. *Rooms from: $300* *J. A. Abraham Blvd. 80, Kralendijk* *599/717–2500, 855/242–8899 in U.S.* *www.plazaresortbonaire.com* *126 units* *All-Inclusive.*

Sand Dollar Condominium Resort
$ | **RESORT** | **FAMILY** | This complex has family-friendly condos (from studio to three-bedroom units), each of which is individually owned and decorated for a comfortable, lived-in feeling and contain fully equipped kitchens. **Pros:** on-site grocery, ATM, and dining options; all units have great ocean views; well-designed for families. **Cons:** not all units are wheelchair-accessible; residential vibe might not appeal to some; three-night minimum stay. *Rooms from: $190* *Kaya Gobernador N. Debrot 79, Kralendijk* *599/717–8738, 800/288–4773* *www.sanddollarbonaire.com* *50 condos* *No Meals.*

Sorobon Beach Resort
$ | **RESORT** | **FAMILY** | With a focus on health and wellness offerings, Sorobon—on lovely, shallow Lac Bay—offers a plethora of activities (yoga, windsurfing, kiteboarding) for all ages. **Pros:** on-site wellness and yoga center; excellent beach bar and two restaurants; stunning beachfront ideal for wellness and windsurfing. **Cons:** extra charge for daytime air-conditioning; no TVs in rooms; 15 minutes to town for shopping and restaurants. *Rooms from: $250* *Sorobon Beach, Sorobon*

Pool at the Harbour Village Beach Club

☎ 599/717–8080 🌐 www.sorobon-beachresort.com 40 units 🍽 Free Breakfast.

Nightlife

Bonaire doesn't have a big reputation for nightlife, as many visitors spend their nights diving, but if you're seeking after-dark revelry, just follow your ears around the small downtown in search of live music and DJ-driven beats. Most of the main resorts have their own rotating entertainment, and there are a few far-flung haunts with special music nights, such as Foodies and Hang-Out Beach Bar.

Carnaval, generally held in February, is the usual nonstop parade of steel bands, floats, and wild costumes, albeit on a much smaller scale than on some other islands. It culminates in the ceremonial burning in effigy of King Momo, representing the spirit of debauchery.

Cuba Compagnie Bonaire

LIVE MUSIC | In a historic, traditional Dutch Antillean structure, this trendy club has a vibrant music scene, including a Thursday Latin Dance Night. The beverages of choice are the house mojito and cuba libre; an extensive international menu is ever changing but always sensational. The patio tables overlooking the waterfront district are perfect for sunsets and people-watching. ✉ *Kaya Grandi 1, Kralendijk* ☎ *599/787–7420* 🌐 *www.cubacompagniebonaire.nl.*

★ Karel's Beach Bar

BARS | This legendary "beach bar" is one of the island's first hangouts, but it is really on its own pier in the heart of downtown and serves breakfast, lunch, and dinner with great views of the cruise port. Lively happy hours and musical theme nights and revelry make it a favorite after-dark. Check the Facebook page for special events. ✉ *Kaya J. N. E. Craane 12, Kralendijk* ☎ *599/717–8434* 🌐 *www.karelsbeachbar.com.*

★ Little Havana

BARS | Little Havana is the place to mix and mingle with locals and other visitors while listening to DJs or jazz and other jam sessions. Prepare to get up close and personal with modelesque blondes, handsome Antilleans, and oldsters alike. The place gets so packed, crowds spill into the streets, drinking into the wee hours. Happy hour is a favorite, but the witching hours are from 11 pm until 2 am. The bartenders mix up the island's best caipirinhas, and the cigar humidor is stocked with selections from Cuba and the Dominican Republic. ✉ *Kaya Bonaire 4, Kralendijk* ☎ *599/770–1787* 🌐 *www.littlehavanabonaire.com.*

Shopping

You can get to know all of the shops in Kralendijk in an hour or so. Most are on Kaya Grandi and adjacent streets. Harbourside Mall is a pleasant, open-air establishment with several fine air-conditioned shops. Look for shops that specialize in products made from Bonaire's famous sea salt and stores that stock locally made Cadushy spirits. If you're seeking local arts, crafts, and other products, visit the Bonaire Arts and Crafts Cruise Market, which pops up with stalls from more than 40 artisans whenever there's a large ship in port. There are also a few duty-free shops in the airport.

Don't take home items made from tortoiseshell; they aren't allowed into the United States. Remember, too, that it's forbidden to take sea fans, coral, conch shells, and all other forms of marine life off the island.

Activities

DIVING AND SNORKELING

Bonaire has some of the best reef diving this side of Australia's Great Barrier Reef. It takes only five to 25 minutes to reach many sites, the current is usually mild, and although some reefs have sudden, steep drops, most begin just offshore and slope gently downward at a 45-degree angle. General visibility runs 60 to 100 feet. You can see several varieties of coral: knobby-brain, giant-brain, elkhorn, staghorn, mountainous star, gorgonian, and black. You can also encounter schools of parrotfish, surgeonfish, angelfish, eel, snapper, and grouper. Shore diving is excellent just about everywhere on the leeward side, which—along with the west side of Klein Bonaire—also has some of the best snorkeling spots. There are sites suitable for every skill level; they're clearly marked by yellow stones on the roadside.

Divers must pay a Bonaire National Park Foundation's Nature Fee of $45. It's good for one year and allows access not only to the waters around the island but also to Washington Slagbaai National Park. The fee can be paid at most dive shops, the tourism office in Kralendijk, at all STINAPA (National Parks Foundation) offices, and the activity desks of most hotels. Every cent of this fee goes toward the care and management of the park and is money well spent, as islanders and most visitors will tell you. Bonaire takes the ecoprotection of their island very seriously, so as they saying goes, "Leave only footprints and take only photographs."

DAY SAILS AND SNORKELING TRIPS

Blue Bay Bonaire

SAILING | **FAMILY** | Blue Bay offers a wide range of sailing, snorkeling, sunset, and barbecue cruises as well as custom tours. They also rent three motorboats, which hold up to six passengers, and can include wakeboarding equipment on request. ✉ *Plaza Resort, J. A. Abraham*

A Bonaire diver shows off her photographic buoyancy control.

Blvd., Kralendijk ☎ *599/701–5500* 🌐 *www.bluebaybonaire.com* 🎫 *From $60.*

★ Epic Tours

SAILING | FAMILY | Choose from a range of small group sailing tours aboard a sleek, modern 44-foot or 40-foot catamaran. They also do special luxury brunches and chill and grill barbecues. Epic also operates the regularly scheduled water taxis from downtown to stunning No Name Beach on uninhabited Klein Bonaire. ✉ *Club Nautica, Kaya J. N. E. Craane 24, Kralendijk* ☎ *599/717–1133* 🌐 *www.epictoursbonaire.com* 🎫 *From $85.*

Woodwind

SAILING | The *Woodwind* is a 42-foot trimaran offering charter sailing and snorkeling trips of four or five hours, with up to 18 passengers. It departs from the dock at the Divi Flamingo Beach Resort. Many patrons report seeing sea turtles on these cruises. ☎ *599/786–7055* 🌐 *www.woodwindbonaire.com* 🎫 *From $85.*

DIVE SITES

The *Guide to the Bonaire Marine Park* lists 86 dive sites (including 16 shore-dive-only and 35 boat-dive-only sites). Another fine reference book is the *Diving and Snorkeling Guide to Bonaire,* by Jerry Schnabel and Suzi Swygert. Guides associated with the various dive centers can give you more complete directions. With so many sites, there is something for every level of diver. Bonaire Tourism's website also provides updates maps and diving information. Below are a few of the better-known spots.

Angel City

SCUBA DIVING | Take the trail down to the shore adjacent to the Radio Nederland tower station; dive in and swim south to Angel City, one of the shallowest and most popular sites in a two-reef complex that includes Alice in Wonderland. The boulder-size green-and-tan coral heads are home to black margates, Spanish hogfish, gray snappers, stingrays, horse-eye jacks, and large purple tube sponges.

Bari Reef

SCUBA DIVING | The entrance to one of Bonaire's most diverse reefs is walking distance from downtown. More than 300 species of marine life have been spotted there.

Bruce's Rappel

SCUBA DIVING | Locals call this spectacular site "Boca di Tota," but the official name is dedicated to the late and legendary Bruce Bowker (original owner of Bruce Bowker's Carib Inn), a true pioneer of diving instruction on Bonaire. The shore is a sheer cliff, and the lush coral growth is the habitat of some unusual varieties of marine life, including occasional orange seahorses, squid, spiny lobsters, and spotted trunkfish.

Calabas Reef

SCUBA DIVING | Off the shores of the Divi Flamingo Beach Resort, the island's busiest dive site is replete with Christmas-tree worms, sponges, and fire coral adhering to a ship's hull. Fish life is frenzied, with the occasional octopus, sea turtle, and even seahorse putting in an appearance.

Forest

SCUBA DIVING | This diverse site off the southwest coast of Klein Bonaire is easily accessed via a dive shop boat trip. Named for the abundant black-coral forests found here, the site is best known for massive purple stovepipes, gorgonian fans, and plumes, as well as some amazing turtles.

Salt Pier

DIVING & SNORKELING | The Cargill Salt Pier has a relatively easy entry and is one of Bonaire's most popular dive sites. Turtles are often found swimming close to shore, and large colorful schools of fish gather around the pylons of the pier making this a can't miss spot. Note: no diving is allowed when ships are at the pier.

Small Wall

SCUBA DIVING | One of Bonaire's three complete vertical wall dives (and one of its most popular night-diving spots) is near Barcadera Beach. Because the access to this site is on private property, this is usually a boat-diving site. The 60-foot wall is frequented by squid, turtles, tarpon, and barracuda and has dense hard and soft coral formations; it also allows for excellent snorkeling.

Something Special

SCUBA DIVING | This easy-to-access shore diving area is just south of the marina entrance at Harbour Village Beach Club and is famous for its garden eels. They wave about from the relatively shallow sand terrace looking like long grass in a breeze. Beware of boat traffic, as it is close to the marina.

Windsock

SCUBA DIVING | This excellent shore-dive site (from 20 to 80 feet) is also a popular place for snorkeling. It's in front of the small beach opposite the airport runway, with an entrance that's relatively easy to access. The current is moderate, the elkhorn coral profuse; you might also see angelfish and rays.

DIVE OPERATORS

Many of the island's dive shops are located at and/or are affiliated with dive resorts. Many also offer PADI and NAUI certification courses and SSI, as well as underwater photography and videography courses. Some shops are also qualified to certify dive instructors. Full certification courses cost approximately $385; open-water refresher courses run about $240; a one-tank boat dive with unlimited shore diving costs about $40; a two-tank boat dive with unlimited shore diving is about $65. As for equipment, renting a mask, fin, and snorkel costs about $12 altogether; for a BC (buoyancy compensator) and regulator, expect to pay about $20.

Most dive shops on Bonaire offer a complete range of snorkel gear for rent and will provide beginner training; some dive operations also offer guided snorkeling and night snorkeling. The cost for a guided snorkel session is about $50 and includes slide presentations, transportation to the site, and a tour. Gear rental runs about $10 per 24-hour period.

Bonaire Scuba

DIVING & SNORKELING | Certified since 2000 and diving around Bonaire since 2013, PADI Dive instructor Larry Stern provides highly customizable courses and friendly service for all skill levels. He specializes in private guided shore dives with small groups of one to four people and offers complimentary transportation and daily or weekly equipment rentals. ☎ *599/777–3483* 🌐 *www.bonairescuba.com.*

Bruce Bowker's Carib Inn Dive Center

SCUBA DIVING | Carib Inn offers a homey, casual, and laid-back dive experience, originally spearheaded by the late Bruce Bowker, a legend of Bonaire diving history. The excellent retail shop stocks all your dive needs, including regulators, skins, and snorkel gear. This full-service dive center is a one-stop shop for those in the know. It's rustic with no frills but has a loyal following. ✉ *J.A. Abraham Blvd. 46, Kralendijk* ☎ *599/717–8819* 🌐 *www.caribinn.com.*

★ Captain Don's Habitat Dive Shop

SCUBA DIVING | This company—founded by the late, great underwater environmentalist Captain Don Stewart—has a high repeat rate for a reason. In addition to being a full-service lodging and conference facility, it's a PADI Five Star Gold Palm Resort with an SDI 5-Star Professional Development Center. They offer boat dives from their pier three times a day, and offer special rates for resort guests. ✉ *Kaya Gobernador N. Debrot 113, Kralendijk* ☎ *599/717–8290* 🌐 *www.habitatbonaire.com.*

★ Dive Friends Bonaire

SCUBA DIVING | Dive Friends is an award-winning full-service PADI Five Star IDC Dive Center, catering to everyone from beginners to technical divers. It has eight full-service locations for convenient shore diving, boat diving, and training, as well as five retail shops for dive gear, clothing, and souvenirs, and underwater photography courses and photo equipment rentals are available. Dive Friends is also the proud organizer of quarterly reef cleanups, whose volunteers include both locals and visitors. ✉ *Playa Lechi 24, Kralendijk* ☎ *599/780–2572* 🌐 *www.dive-friends-bonaire.com.*

Divi Dive Bonaire

SCUBA DIVING | Divi Flamingo Beach Resort's dive operations are helmed by Dive Master Pascal Van Empelen, who oversees five dive boats, a full-service modern dive shop, and multiple dive courses and lessons. Boat dives are offered daily, as are courses in the Reef Renewal Project, which consists of assembling a coral nursery on the resort's own reef. Divi Dive is a full-service PADI Gold Palm Resort dive center with options for everyone, from beginners to advanced dive enthusiasts. ✉ *Divi Flamingo Resort & Casino, J. A. Abraham Blvd. 40, Kralendijk* ☎ *800/367–3484, 599/717-8285 Ext. 1* 🌐 *dividive.com.*

Toucan Diving

SCUBA DIVING | This full-service PADI Five Star dive center at the Plaza Beach Resort has its own reef, the 18th Palm, which is an excellent shore dive. You can experience it on private tours and guided night dives. The company also offers day and night boat dives to other parts of the island and a full complement of courses for all ages and skill levels. ✉ *Plaza Beach Resort Bonaire, J. A. Abraham Blvd. 80, Kralendijk* ☎ *599/717–2500* 🌐 *www.toucandiving.com.*

★ VIP Diving

DIVING & SNORKELING | Bonaire's most personalized and upscale dive operator works with groups of no more than four to ensure that each dive is a special, customized adventure. Look into the "Mindful Diver" yoga experience, or consider augmenting your outing with a "dive butler" to cater to your every need. They are also a Green Star Awarded outfit by PADI and pioneers in UV-light night diving, which is a surreal experience. ✉ *J. A. Abraham Blvd. 77, Kralendijk* ☎ *599/701–7701* 🌐 *www.vipdiving.com.*

Wannadive

SCUBA DIVING | This is a casual, efficient dive company with two island locations. In addition to working with divers of all skill levels and interests—beginner to professional, recreational to technical—they have a large inventory of rental dive and snorkel equipment, offer repair services, and run daily boat-dive trips to Klein Bonaire. ✉ *Kaya Gobernador N. Debrot 73, Kralendijk* ☎ *599/717–8884* 🌐 *www.wannadive.com.*

FISHING

Le Grand Bleu

FISHING | This outfit has a wide range of deep-sea fishing options and offers hotel pick-up service. ✉ *Kralendijk* ☎ *599/795–1139* 🌐 *www.fishingbonaire.com.*

Piscatur Charters

FISHING | Captain Chris is the man for all of your fishing needs. His company offers light-tackle angler reef fishing for jackfish, barracuda, and snapper. You can charter the 42-foot Sport Fisherman *Piscatur,* which carries up to six people. Captain Chris will also organize bonefishing tours. ✉ *Kaya H. J. Pop 3, Kralendijk* ☎ *599/717–8774* 🌐 *www.piscatur.com.*

GOLF

★ Piedra So

GOLF | Bonaire's unique 18-hole, ocean-front par 72 golf course was designed to seamlessly blend in with nature with artificial grass only at the putting greens and the rest of the area set in among the red earth, coarse sand, and cacti of the scrubby semi-desert landscape. Even most pro golfers will be challenged with these conditions and wild donkeys meandering on to the course can also add unusual hazards. But the vibe is fun and friendly, and the on-site golf school provides lessons by PGA pro golfer Florus Josten. ✉ *Kralendijk* ☎ *599/785–3232* 🌐 *www.piedraso.com* 💳 *From $25.* 🏌 *18 holes, 6143 yards, par 72.*

GUIDED TOURS

★ Bonaire Tours & Vacations

GUIDED TOURS | This is one of the island's premier tour companies, and though it caters primarily to a cruise ship clientele, it also offers transfers and private VIP tours and experiences to the general public. ✉ *Kaya Gobernador N. Debrot, Kralendijk* ☎ *599/717–8778* 🌐 *www.bonairetoursandvacations.com.*

★ Tropical Travel

GUIDED TOURS | This full-service tour company for the cruise ship and tourism sector has a fleet of large buses and small vans that whisk guests off for day excursions, touring the island's many attractions, including the national park. You can also book sail and snorkel tours, ecotours via tuktuk, and glass-bottom kayak experiences as well as landsailing (blokarting) adventures on one of the longest tracks in the world. Scooter and bike rentals are also available. ✉ *Plaza Beach Resort Bonaire, J. A. Abraham Blvd. 80, Kralendijk* ☎ *599/701–1232* 🌐 *www.tropicaltravelbonaire.com.*

HORSEBACK RIDING

★ Horse Ranch Bonaire

HORSEBACK RIDING | **FAMILY** | For the chance to cross horseback riding directly into the sea off your bucket list, book an epic ride with this friendly, full-service, family-run ranch. Most of the horses are Paso Finos, which are known for their smooth gait, and groups are kept to no more than six riders to maximize enjoyment. Although you must be over 10 to ride, little ones can enjoy a pony ride or visit the cute creatures in the petting zoo. Advance reservations are required. ✉ *Kaminda Warahama 40, Tera Korá* ☎ *599/786–2094* 🌐 *www.horseranchbonaire.com* 💳 *From $135.*

KAYAKING

Mangrove Info Center Kayak Excursions

KAYAKING | The center's guided mangrove tours—in double or single kayaks—are suited to ages 5 and up. The trips last an hour or, with snorkeling included, two hours. Participants are encouraged to bring their own snorkel gear (except for fins, which aren't permitted in this fragile, protected area), but gear can also be provided with advance notice. Reservations are recommended, and payment is cash only. ✉ *Kaminda Lac 141, on road to Lac Cai, Sorobon* ☎ *599/780–5353* 🌐 *www.mangrovecenter.com* 🎟 *From $30.*

LANDSAILING

★ Bonaire Landsailing Adventures

LOCAL SPORTS | Sail on dry land in a cool "blokart"—a landsailing vehicle built in New Zealand, which is where this sport originated. This outfit provides all the instruction you need for an exciting trek along one of the longest tracks in the world, and the island's steady trade winds provide the ideal conditions. It's an easy activity to learn, and it's great for family adventures. Participants must be over 7 years old to power their own vehicle, but the company also has double blokarts in which adults can drive with a smaller child. They also offer a cool seven-hour combo tour that includes spelunking and snorkeling in Bonaire's unique ancient caves. ☎ *599/786–1572* 🌐 *www.landsailingadventures.com.*

WINDSURFING

With gin-clear water and steady onshore trade winds, Bonaire is considered one of the world's best places for windsurfing, particularly in Lac Bay, a protected cove on the east coast. Pros travel here to train with the top-rated Team Bonaire; novice sailors come to hone their skills, and the shallow calm waters encourage parents to bring their little ones out to learn the sport, too. The island's windsurfing companies are headquartered on Sorobon Beach.

Bonaire Windsurf Place

WINDSURFING | Commonly referred to as "The Place," this shop rents the latest Hot Sails Maui, Starboard, and RRD equipment. The service is personal and efficient. Note that the windsurf launch can be quite congested on cruise ship days as the shop rents loungers, thus attracting a lot of beachgoers. There is also a beach hut for snacks and drinks, a surf shop, and massage on the beach offered by their small spa. ✉ *Sorobon* ☎ *599/717–2288* 🌐 *www.bonairewindsurfplace.com.*

★ Frans Paradise

WINDSURFING | Windsurfing legends and brothers Taty and Everon (Tonky) Frans opened this school on the very beach where they learned to harness the wind at an early age. Even novices should have no problem learning how to master the board with the expert instruction from these world champions, and the shallow waters and calm conditions of Lac Bay are ideal. Both windsurfing and windfoiling lessons for all ages are offered. ✉ *Sorobon* ☎ *599/785–0514* 🌐 *www.fransparadise.com.*

★ Jibe City

WINDSURFING | Situated on Lac Bay, this is Bonaire's premiere windsurf center, with rentals by the day or the week and a crew of dedicated staff who cater to all levels. They have rigged-and-ready, state-of-the-art gear and frequent windsurf clinics for kids, plus windfoiling instruction, yoga classes, and SUP and kayak rentals. This is also the site of Hang Out Beach Bar with its famous Thursday night barbecues, and you'll often see members of Team Bonaire hanging out here and training for international events. ✉ *Sorobon* ☎ *599/717–5233* 🌐 *www.jibecity.com.*

Chapter 8

BRITISH VIRGIN ISLANDS

Updated by
Robert Curley

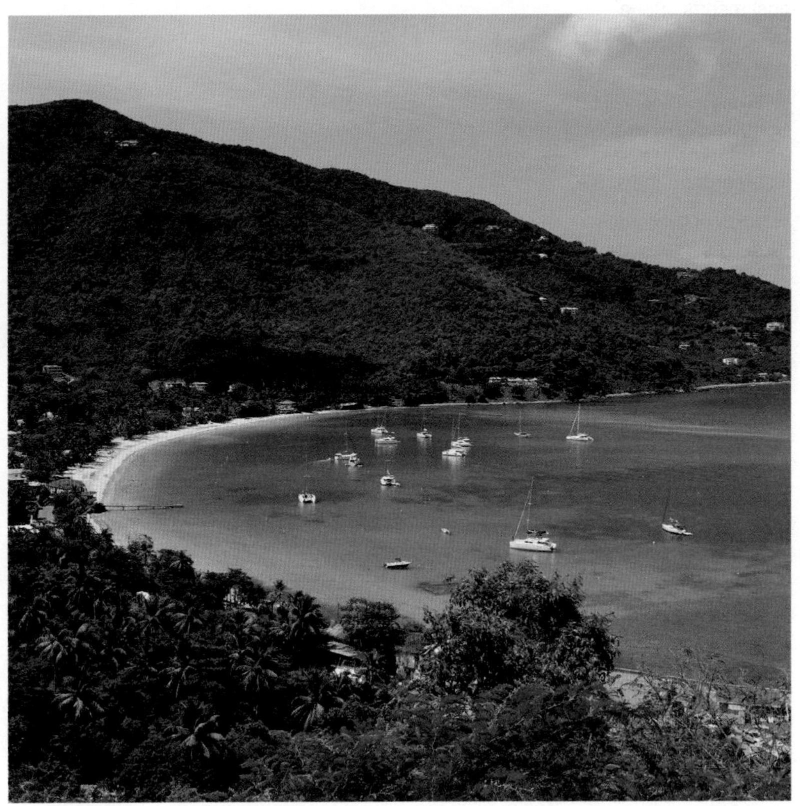

Sights	Restaurants	Hotels	Shopping	Nightlife
★★★★★	★★★★☆	★★★☆☆	★★★☆☆	★★★☆☆

WELCOME TO BRITISH VIRGIN ISLANDS

TOP REASONS TO GO

★ **The Perfect Place to Sail:** With more than 60 islands in the chain, sailors can drop anchor at a different, perfect beach every day.

★ **Low-Key Resorts:** Laid-back (but luxurious) resorts offer a full-scale retreat from your everyday life.

★ **Diving and Snorkeling:** Both are great, and vibrant reefs are often just feet from the shore.

★ **Jost Van Dyke:** Your trip isn't complete until you've chilled at the casual beach bars here.

★ **Few Crowds:** There's little mass tourism; the farther you get from Tortola, the quieter things become.

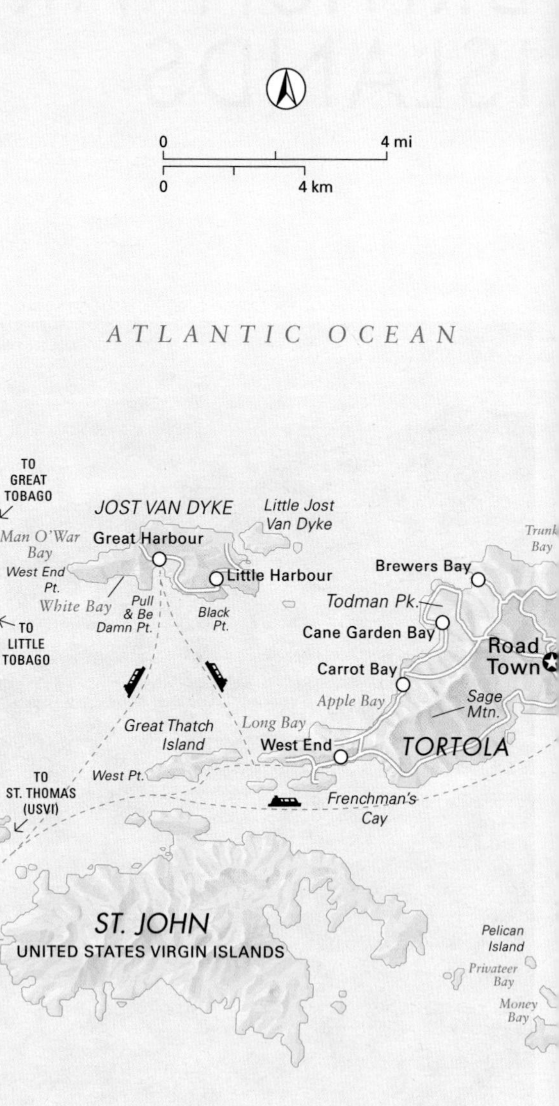

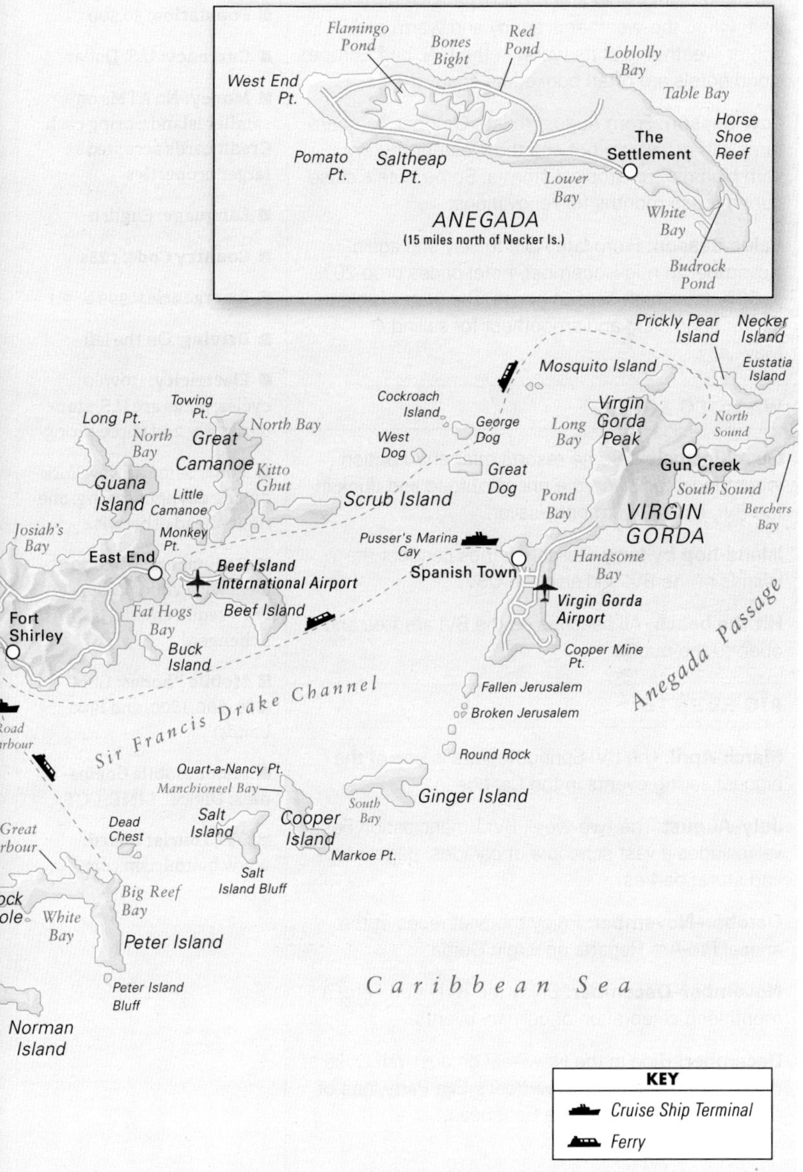
Flamingo Pond
Bones Bight
Red Pond
Loblolly Bay
Table Bay
West End Pt.
Horse Shoe Reef
The Settlement
Pomato Pt.
Saltheap Pt.
Lower Bay
White Bay
ANEGADA
(15 miles north of Necker Is.)
Budrock Pond
Prickly Pear Island
Necker Island
Eustatia Island
Mosquito Island
Cockroach Island
Towing Pt.
Long Pt.
North Bay
North Bay
Great Camanoe
Kitto Ghut
George Dog
West Dog
Great Dog
Long Bay
Virgin Gorda Peak
North Sound
Gun Creek
South Sound
Guana Island
Little Camanoe
Scrub Island
Pond Bay
VIRGIN GORDA
Berchers Bay
Josiah's Bay
Monkey Pt.
Pusser's Marina Cay
East End
Beef Island International Airport
Spanish Town
Handsome Bay
Fort Shirley
Fat Hogs Bay
Beef Island
Virgin Gorda Airport
Anegada Passage
Buck Island
Copper Mine Pt.
Fallen Jerusalem
Broken Jerusalem
Sir Francis Drake Channel
Road Harbour
Round Rock
Quart-a-Nancy Pt.
Manchioneel Bay
Ginger Island
South Bay
Great Harbour
Dead Chest
Salt Island
Cooper Island
Markoe Pt.
Salt Island Bluff
Big Reef Bay
White Bay
Peter Island
Peter Island Bluff
Caribbean Sea
Norman Island
KEY
Cruise Ship Terminal
Ferry

ISLAND SNAPSHOT

WHEN TO GO

High Season: Mid-December through mid-April is the most fashionable and most expensive time to visit, when the weather is sunny and warm and winter weather is at its worst in the U.S. and Europe. Good hotels are often booked far in advance.

Low Season: From August to late October, temperatures can grow very hot and the weather muggy, with high risks of tropical storms. Some hotels close during these months for renovations.

Value Season: From late April to July and again November to mid-December, hotel prices drop 20% to 50% from high-season prices. The water is clearest for snorkeling and smoothest for sailing in May–July.

WAYS TO SAVE

Go all-inclusive. Some resorts offer an AI option when booking. Given the prices of food and drink in the BVI, it can be a money-saver.

Island-hop by ferry. Reliable ferries connect the islands of the BVI and also the USVI.

Hit the beach. All beaches on the BVI are free and open to the public.

BIG EVENTS

March-April: The BVI Spring Regatta is one of the biggest sailing events in the Caribbean.

July–August: The two-week BVI Emancipation Festival includes a vast schedule of parades, pageants, and street parties.

October–November: Enjoy the boat races at the annual Pro-Am Regatta on Virgin Gorda.

November–December: Enjoy the BVI Food Fete, a monthlong celebration of culinary events.

December: Ring in the New Year on Jost Van Dyke at Foxy's Old Year's Night New Year's Eve Party, one of the top celebrations in the Caribbean.

AT A GLANCE

- **Capital:** Road Town
- **Population:** 30,500
- **Currency:** U.S. Dollar
- **Money:** No ATMs on smaller islands; bring cash. Credit cards accepted at larger properties
- **Language:** English
- **Country Code:** 1 284
- **Emergencies:** 999 or 911
- **Driving:** On the left
- **Electricity:** 110v/60 cycles; plugs are U.S. standard two- and three-prong
- **Time:** Same as New York during daylight saving; one hour ahead otherwise
- **Documents:** Up to 30 days with valid passport with requirements (ASEAN, Schengen)
- **Mobile Phones:** GSM (850, 900, 1800, and 1900 bands)
- **Major Mobile Companies:** Digicel, LIME, CCT
- **BVI Tourist Board:** www.bvitourism.com

Once a sleepy collection of about 60 islands and cays, some of the British Virgin Islands now see large cruise ships. Shoppers sometimes crowd the downtown area of Road Town on Tortola, and traffic occasionally comes to a standstill. Even the second-largest island, Virgin Gorda, gets its share of smaller ships anchored off the main village of Spanish Town. Despite the growth in the territory's tourism industry, it's still easy to escape the hubbub. Even hotels outside Road Town usually provide a quiet oasis, and those on the other islands can be downright serene.

Each island has a different flavor. Want access to lots of restaurants and shopping? Make Tortola your choice. The largest of the BVI, it covers 21.5 square miles (55.7 square km) and sits only a mile from St. John in the United States Virgin Islands (USVI). If you want to kick back at a small hotel or posh resort, try Virgin Gorda. Sitting nearly at the end of the chain, the 8-square-mile (21-square-km) island offers stellar beaches and a laid-back atmosphere. If you really want to get away from it all, the outermost islands, including Anegada and Jost Van Dyke, will fill the bill. Some of the smallest—Norman, Peter, Cooper, and Necker—are home to just one resort or restaurant. Others remain uninhabited specks on the horizon.

Visitors have long come to the BVI, starting with the Arawaks, who came over from South America and settled in these islands around 100 BC. Christopher Columbus dropped anchor in 1493 and called the islands Las Once Mil Virgines—the 11,000 Virgins—in honor of the 11,000 virgin companions of St. Ursula, martyred in the 4th century AD. Pirates and buccaneers followed, and then came the British, who farmed the islands until slavery was abolished in 1834. The BVI are still politically tied to Britain, so the queen appoints a royal governor, but residents elect a local House of Assembly. Financial services and tourism share top billing in the territory's economy, but the majority of the islands' jobs are tourism-related. Despite the growth, you can usually find an uncrowded beach and a welcoming smile.

Planning

Getting Here and Around

AIR

There's frequent service among several airlines to either Tortola or Virgin Gorda via San Juan and St. Thomas, and occasional flight from a few other Caribbean locales, such as Antigua, Sint Maarten, and Santo Domingo. Inter-island flights within the BVI are also available. Prices and connections for international are often better through St. Thomas, even with the added cost of taking the ferry over from Charlotte Amalie. If you have seven or more people in your party, you can also charter a plane from St. Thomas or San Juan.

AIRPORTS

Tortola (EIS), Virgin Gorda (VIJ), and Anegada (NGD).

AIRPORT TRANSFERS Mahogany Car Rentals. ✉ *Spanish Town* ☎ *284/495–5469, 284/545–0058, 284/540–2309* 🌐 *www.mahoganycarrentalsbvi.com.*

BOAT AND FERRY

Frequent daily ferries connect Tortola with St. Thomas (both Charlotte Amalie and Red Hook) and St. John. Ferries also link Tortola with Jost Van Dyke and Virgin Gorda as well as several resorts. Tortola has two ferry terminals, at West End and Road Town. Some resorts use the dock at Trellis Bay for their private ferries. Schedules vary, and not all companies make daily trips. All Red Hook–bound ferries stop in Cruz Bay to clear customs and immigration.

Ferries also connect Virgin Gorda with St. Thomas (both Charlotte Amalie and Red Hook) and St. John, but not daily. Ferries to Virgin Gorda land in Spanish Town. Schedules vary by day, and not all companies make daily trips.

The BVI Tourist Board website 🌐 *www.bvitourism.com/inter-island-ferries* has links to all the ferry companies, and these sites are the best sources for ever-changing routes and schedules.

CONTACTS Foxy's Charters. ✉ *Great Harbour* ☎ *284/346–0356* 🌐 *www.foxyscharters.com.* **Inter-Island Boat Service.** ☎ *340/776–6597* 🌐 *www.interislandboatservices.com.*

CAR

Driving in the BVI is on the left, British-style, but your car will always have its steering wheel on the left, as in the United States. Your valid U.S. license will also do for driving in the BVI. The minimum age to rent a car is 25. Most agencies offer both four-wheel-drive vehicles and conventional cars (often compacts). Tortola, Virgin Gorda, Jost Van Dyke, and Anegada have car-rental agencies.

TAXI

Taxi rates are set by destination in the BVI; charges are per person but discounts apply for groups of three or more. The taxi number is always on the license plate. There is a Taxi Tariff with set rates for various itineraries: ask your taxi driver, or see 🌐 *www.bvitourism.com/taxis.*

Health and Safety

Dengue, chikungunya, and zika have all been reported throughout the Caribbean from time to time; check the U.S. Centers for Disease Control and Prevention website for current alerts. We recommend that you protect yourself from these mosquito-borne illnesses by keeping your skin covered and/or wearing mosquito repellent. The mosquitoes that transmit these viruses are as active by day as they are by night. The crime rate in the BVI is low; criminals rarely target visitors, but when they do it's typically for theft and other petty crimes.

Hotels and Resorts

Pick your island carefully, because each is different, as are the logistics of getting there. **Tortola** gives you the widest choice of restaurants, shopping, and resorts. **Virgin Gorda** has fewer off-resort places to eat and shop, but the resorts themselves are often better, and the beaches are wonderful. **Anegada** is remote and better suited for divers. **Jost Van Dyke** has some classic Caribbean beach bars, along with fairly basic accommodations.

Private-island resorts. When you want to be pampered or just to bask in isolation for a few days consider a private-island resort, reached only by ferry. Some are high-priced and exclusive, while others offer solitude at a price comparable to those charged by mainland resorts.

Resorts. The largest resort in the British Virgin Islands has 80-some rooms, and most have considerably fewer. Luxury here is more about personal service than over-the-top amenities.

Yacht charter. To enjoy everything the BVI have to offer, drop anchor where and when you want.

Villas and condos. A good option for families, you'll find these accommodations in abundance.

Hotel reviews have been shortened. For full information, visit Fodors.com.

What It Costs in U.S. Dollars

$	$$	$$$	$$$$
RESTAURANTS			
under $12	$12–$20	$21–$30	over $30
HOTELS			
under $275	$275–$375	$376–$475	over $475

PRIVATE VILLAS

Those craving seclusion would do well at a villa. Most have full kitchens and maid service. Prices per week in winter run from around $2,000 for a one- or two-bedroom villa up to $10,000 for a five-room beachfront villa. Rates in summer are substantially less. On Virgin Gorda a villa in the North Sound area means you can pretty much stay put at night unless you want to make the drive on its narrow roads. If you opt for a spot near The Baths, it's an easier drive to town.

Villas Virgin Gorda
This management company's dozen-plus properties stretch from The Baths to the Nail Bay area. Several budget properties are included among the pricier offerings. Most houses have private pools, and a few are right on the beach. ☎ *284/540–8002* 🌐 *www.villasvirgingorda.com.*

Virgin Gorda Villa Rentals
This company's 20-plus properties are all near Leverick Bay Resort and Mahoe Bay, so they are perfect for those who want to be close to activities. Many of the accommodations—from one to six or more bedrooms—have private swimming pools and air-conditioning, at least in the bedrooms. All have full kitchens, are well maintained, and have spectacular views. ✉ *Mahoe Bay* ☎ *284/542–4014, 284/542–4011* 🌐 *www.vgvirgingordavilla-rentals.com.*

Visitor Information

CONTACTS BVI Tourist Board. ☎ *212/563–3117, 800/835–8530 in the U.S.* 🌐 *www.bvitourism.com.*

Weddings

You must apply in person for your license on weekdays at the attorney general's office in Wickham's Cay, Road Town, Tortola. The license costs $220 if you're in the country less than 15 days, or $120 if you've been in the BVI for longer. Processing takes a full business day. If you plan to be married in a church, announcements (called *banns* locally) must be published for three consecutive Sundays in the church bulletin. Only the registrar or clergy can perform ceremonies. The registrar charges $340 at the office and $220 at another location. No blood test is required.

CONTACTS Island Style Weddings. ☎ *340/774–1484* 🌐 *www.islandstyleweddings.com.*

Tortola

Once a sleepy backwater, Tortola is busier these days, particularly when several cruise ships tie up at the Road Town dock. Passengers crowd the streets and shops, and open-air jitneys filled with cruise-ship passengers create bottlenecks on downtown streets. That said, most folks visit Tortola to relax on its deserted sands or linger over lunch at one of its many delightful restaurants. Beaches, like the popular strand at Cane Garden Bay, are never more than a few miles away, and the steep green hills that form Tortola's spine are fanned by gentle trade winds. The neighboring islands glimmer like emeralds in a sea of sapphire. It can be a world far removed from the hustle of modern life, but Tortola simply can't compare with Virgin Gorda in terms of beautiful beaches—or luxury resorts, for that matter.

Initially settled by the indigenous Taíno people, Tortola saw a string of visitors over the years. Christopher Columbus sailed by in 1493 on his second voyage to the New World, and ships from Spain, Holland, and France made periodic visits about a century later. Sir Francis Drake arrived in 1595, leaving his name on the passage between Tortola and St. John. Pirates and buccaneers followed, with the British finally laying claim to the island in the late 1600s. In 1741, John Pickering became the first lieutenant governor of Tortola, and the seat of the British government moved from Virgin Gorda to Tortola. As the agrarian economy continued to grow, enslaved people were forced here from Africa. The slave trade was abolished in 1807, but enslaved people in Tortola and the rest of the BVI did not gain their freedom until August 1, 1834, when the Emancipation Proclamation was read at Sunday Morning Well in Road Town. That date is celebrated every year with the island's annual Carnival.

Visitors have a choice of accommodations, but most fall into the small and smaller-still categories. When driving, note that Tortola's main roads are well paved for the most part, but there are exceptionally steep hills and sharp curves.

Around Road Town

The bustling capital of the BVI looks out over Road Harbour. It takes only an hour or so to stroll the streets of downtown and the waterfront, checking out the traditional West Indian buildings painted in pastel colors and with corrugated-tin roofs, bright shutters, and delicate fretwork trim. Shops and restaurants are clustered around the dock for the ferry and in Tortola Pier Park, where cruise ships disembark. Or just choose a seat on one of the benches in Sir Olva

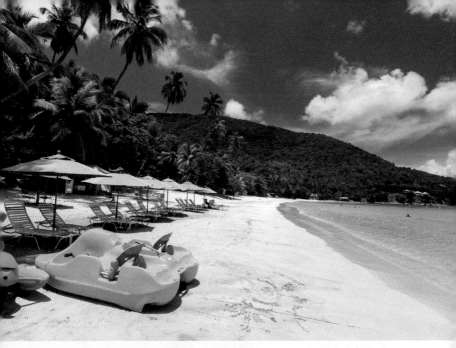

Tortola's clear water is inviting for water sports.

Georges Square, on Waterfront Drive and watch the people come and go.

Sights

Fort Burt

HOTEL | The most intact historic fort on Tortola (that's not saying much, however) was raised by the Dutch in the early 17th century to safeguard Road Harbour, then rebuilt by the British. It sits on a hill at the western edge of Road Town and is now the site of a small hotel (also named Fort Burt). The foundations and magazine remain, and the structure offers a commanding view of the harbor. ✉ *Waterfront Dr., Road Town* ☎ *284/494–2587* 🌐 *www.fortburt.com* 🎫 *Free.*

Her Majesty's Prison Museum

JAIL/PRISON | Road Town's formidable prison was constructed in the mid-19th century and went on to hold prisoners in relatively primitive conditions for more than a century before closing in 2007. The prisoners confined to the humid barred cells were lucky compared to those who were hung in a creepy chamber, where the gallows claimed its last victim in the 1970s. Informative, docent-led tours offer insights into island history and the administration of justice from the colonial period into the early 21st century. ✉ *Main St., Road Town* ☎ *284/494–3132* 🎫 *$5* ⏲ *Closed weekends.*

J.R. O'Neal Botanic Gardens

GARDEN | This 3-acre showcase of plant life has sections devoted to prickly cacti and succulents, hothouses for ferns and orchids, gardens of medicinal herbs, and plants and trees indigenous to the seashore. A boulevard of royal palms was previously one of the most prominent features, but a number of these were felled in the 2017 hurricane. Otherwise, the gardens have recovered quite nicely. ✉ *Botanic Station, Road Town* ☎ *284/393-9284* 🌐 *www.bvinpt.org/jr-o-neal-botanical* 🎫 *$3* ⏲ *Closed weekends.*

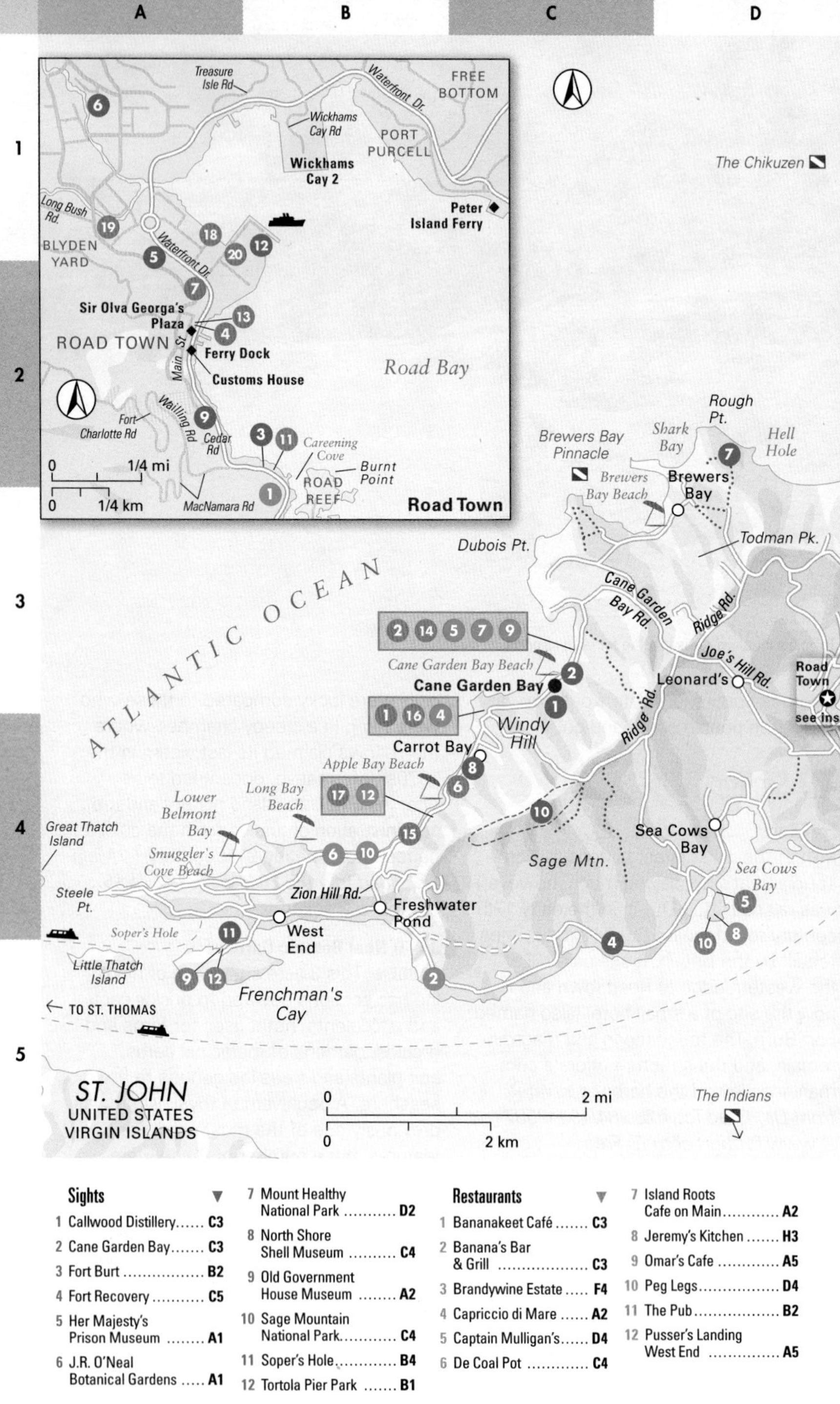
A
B
C
D
1
2
3
4
5
Treasure Isle Rd
Waterfront Dr.
FREE BOTTOM
Wickhams Cay Rd
PORT PURCELL
Wickhams Cay 2
Peter Island Ferry
Long Bush Rd.
BLYDEN YARD
Waterfront Dr.
Sir Olva Georga's Plaza
ROAD TOWN
Main St.
Ferry Dock
Customs House
Road Bay
Fort Charlotte Rd
Wailling Rd
Cedar Rd
Careening Cove
Burnt Point
ROAD REEF
MacNamara Rd
0 1/4 mi
0 1/4 km
Road Town
The Chikuzen
Rough Pt.
Shark Bay
Hell Hole
Brewers Bay Pinnacle
Brewers Bay Beach
Brewers Bay
Todman Pk.
Dubois Pt.
ATLANTIC OCEAN
Cane Garden Bay Rd.
Ridge Rd.
Joe's Hill Rd.
Road Town see inset
Cane Garden Bay Beach
Cane Garden Bay
Leonard's
Windy Hill
Carrot Bay
Ridge Rd.
Apple Bay Beach
Long Bay Beach
Lower Belmont Bay
Great Thatch Island
Smuggler's Cove Beach
Sage Mtn.
Sea Cows Bay
Sea Cows Bay
Steele Pt.
Zion Hill Rd.
Freshwater Pond
Soper's Hole
West End
Little Thatch Island
Frenchman's Cay
TO ST. THOMAS
ST. JOHN
UNITED STATES VIRGIN ISLANDS
0 2 mi
0 2 km
The Indians
Sights
1 Callwood Distillery...... C3
2 Cane Garden Bay....... C3
3 Fort Burt B2
4 Fort Recovery C5
5 Her Majesty's Prison Museum A1
6 J.R. O'Neal Botanical Gardens A1
7 Mount Healthy National Park D2
8 North Shore Shell Museum C4
9 Old Government House Museum A2
10 Sage Mountain National Park............ C4
11 Soper's Hole............. B4
12 Tortola Pier Park B1
Restaurants
1 Bananakeet Café C3
2 Banana's Bar & Grill C3
3 Brandywine Estate F4
4 Capriccio di Mare A2
5 Captain Mulligan's..... D4
6 De Coal Pot C4
7 Island Roots Cafe on Main............ A2
8 Jeremy's Kitchen H3
9 Omar's Cafe A5
10 Peg Legs.................. D4
11 The Pub.................. B2
12 Pusser's Landing West End A5

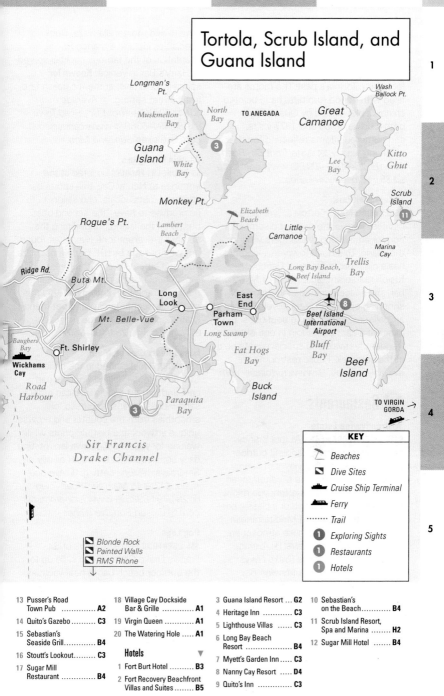

Tortola, Scrub Island, and Guana Island

13 Pusser's Road Town Pub **A2**
14 Quito's Gazebo **C3**
15 Sebastian's Seaside Grill............. **B4**
16 Stoutt's Lookout......... **C3**
17 Sugar Mill Restaurant **B4**
18 Village Cay Dockside Bar & Grille **A1**
19 Virgin Queen **A1**
20 The Watering Hole **A1**

Hotels

1 Fort Burt Hotel **B3**
2 Fort Recovery Beachfront Villas and Suites **B5**
3 Guana Island Resort ... **G2**
4 Heritage Inn **C3**
5 Lighthouse Villas **C3**
6 Long Bay Beach Resort **B4**
7 Myett's Garden Inn **C3**
8 Nanny Cay Resort **D4**
9 Quito's Inn **C3**
10 Sebastian's on the Beach............ **B4**
11 Scrub Island Resort, Spa and Marina **H2**
12 Sugar Mill Hotel **B4**

★ Old Government House Museum

HISTORIC HOME | The official government residence until 1997, this gracious building now displays a nice collection of artifacts from Tortola's past. The rooms are filled with period furniture, hand-painted china, books signed by Queen Elizabeth II on her 1966 and 1977 visits, and numerous items reflecting Tortola's seafaring legacy. ✉ *Waterfront Dr., Road Town* ☎ *284/494–4091* 🌐 *www.oghm.org* 🎟 *$5* ⏲ *Closed weekends.*

Tortola Pier Park

PEDESTRIAN MALL | Tortola's Cyril B. Romney Pier Park is the point of disembarkation for cruise ship passengers visiting the island. This Road Town development has a cigar bar, pizza joint, Caribbean fusion restaurant, an outpost of Myett's bar, and an ice cream parlor. Diverse shopping options include jewelry stores, art galleries, and clothing boutiques. You can rent a car here or join in one of the frequent festivals and special events held at the complex. Public restrooms are available as well. 🌐 *www.tortolapier.com.*

 Restaurants

★ Brandywine Estate

$$$$ | **MEDITERRANEAN** | At this Brandywine Bay restaurant, candlelit outdoor tables have sweeping views of nearby islands. The menu has a Mediterranean bistro flair but changes often; you might find grilled local king fish or a classic paella. **Known for:** extensive Mediterranean tapas selection; gardenlike atmosphere; stunning Caribbean views. 💲 *Average main: $36* ✉ *Sir Francis Drake Hwy., east of Road Town, Brandywine Bay* ☎ *284/495–2301* 🌐 *www.brandywine.vg* ⏲ *Closed Mon. and Tues.*

★ Capriccio di Mare

$$ | **ITALIAN** | Stop by this casual, authentic Italian outdoor café—look for the turquoise Vespa out front—for an espresso, gelato, a fresh pastry, a bowl of perfectly cooked pasta, or a crispy tomato-and-mozzarella pizza. Drink specialties include a mango Bellini, an adaptation of the famous cocktail served at Harry's Bar in Venice. **Known for:** specialty cocktails; authentic Italian fare; lively street setting. 💲 *Average main: $16* ✉ *196 Waterfront Dr., Road Town* ☎ *284/494–5369* 🌐 *www.capricciobvi.com* ⏲ *Closed Sun. and Mon.*

Captain Mulligan's

$$ | **BURGER** | **FAMILY** | Located at the entrance to Nanny Cay, this sports bar attracts expats, locals, and sailors with its promise to have "the second-best burger on the island," underlining the eatery's irreverent tone (we never found out who has the best!). Hot wings, pizza, ribs, and burgers are on the menu, and most people come to watch the game on the big-screen TVs. **Known for:** BBQ ribs; sports bar scene; family- and pet-friendly atmosphere. 💲 *Average main: $18* ✉ *Nanny Cay* ☎ *284/494–0602.*

Island Roots Cafe on Main

$ | **CARIBBEAN** | Located in the historic Customs House, Island Roots is part café and part art gallery. You can order sandwiches, salads, espresso, or smoothies from the counter and browse unique artwork and historic prints while waiting for your meal. **Known for:** rotating daily soup specials; breakfast all day on Saturdays; historic setting. 💲 *Average main: $12* ✉ *15 Main St., Road Town* ☎ *284/494-8985* 🌐 *www.islandrootsbvi.com* ⏲ *Closed Sun. No dinner.*

Peg Legs

$$$ | **SEAFOOD** | Take in views of Sir Francis Drake Channel and sidle up to the outdoor beach bar to hear yachties swap sea stories at this mariner-friendly eatery. Menu offerings range from burgers and pizzas to daily fresh seafood. **Known for:** Spring Regatta after-parties; people-watching; great views. 💲 *Average main: $29* ✉ *Nanny Cay* ☎ *284/494–0028* 🌐 *nannycay.com.*

The Pub

$$$ | **ECLECTIC** | Hamburgers, salads, and sandwiches are typical lunch offerings at this Road Town eatery, along with classic British fare such as shepherd's pie and fish and chips. In the evening you can get your Anegada lobster grilled or jerked. **Known for:** live entertainment Thursday and Friday; billiards and bar games; tasty pub classics. *Average main: $21 ✉ Columbus Centre, Waterfront Dr., Road Town ☎ 284/345–1122.*

Pusser's Road Town Pub

$$ | **ECLECTIC** | **FAMILY** | Almost everyone who visits Tortola stops here at least once to have a bite and to sample the famous Painkiller, made with Pusser's Royal Navy rum, pineapple and orange juices, and cream of coconut. The predictable menu includes pizza, shepherd's pie, fish-and-chips, burgers, and occasional seafood specials. **Known for:** reliably good comfort fare; popular happy hour; Pusser's rum. *Average main: $22 ✉ Waterfront Dr., Road Town ☎ 284/494–3897 🌐 www.pussers.com.*

Village Cay Dockside Bar & Grille

$$$ | **ECLECTIC** | Docked sailboats stretch nearly as far as the eye can see at this busy Road Town marina restaurant. The alfresco dining and convivial atmosphere make it popular with both locals and visitors. **Known for:** outdoor dining; lunch buffet; happy hour. *Average main: $24 ✉ Wickham's Cay I, Road Town ☎ 284/494–2771 🌐 www.villagecaybvi.com.*

Virgin Queen

$$$ | **ECLECTIC** | The sailing and rugby crowds head here to play darts, drink beer, and eat Queen's Combo pizza—a crusty, cheesy pie topped with sausage, onions, green peppers, and mushrooms. Also on the menu is excellent West Indian and English fare: barbecued ribs with beans and rice, curry chicken, bangers and mash, shepherd's pie, and grilled sirloin steak. **Known for:** local bar scene; pizza; West Indian and English fare. *Average main: $21 ✉ Flemming St., Road Town ☎ 284/494–2310 ⊙ Closed Sun.*

The Watering Hole

$$ | **MODERN BRITISH** | Quietly tucked into a corner on Road Town's waterfront, the Watering Hole is an oasis amidst the jungle of concrete government buildings and banks in downtown Road Town. South African wine and local and imported beer—along with coffee, Wi-Fi, and light fare like pizza, sandwiches, wraps and tacos—make this a popular lunch spot for Road Town professionals and charter-yacht crews. **Known for:** good nightly specials; South African wines; breakfast. *Average main: $18 ✉ Road Town ✣ Wickham's Cay ☎ 284/346–5950 🌐 www.facebook.com/wateringholebvi ⊙ Closed Sun.*

Hotels

Fort Burt Hotel

$ | **HOTEL** | This hotel's biggest claim to fame is that it was built atop the ruins of a historic fort dating back at least to the 18th century and perhaps earlier: it was raised by the Dutch, later improved by the English, and boasts some of the best views in Road Town along with a small, pleasant swimming pool. **Pros:** views of Road Town and harbor; budget-friendly rates; on the ruins of historic Fort Burt. **Cons:** faded property could use a facelift; very basic; no beach. *Rooms from: $99 ✉ Waterfront Drive, Fisher Estate, Road Town ☎ 284/494–2587 🌐 www.fortburt.com 16 rooms No Meals.*

Nanny Cay Resort

$ | **HOTEL** | This quiet oasis is far enough from Road Town to give it a secluded feel but close enough to make shops and restaurants convenient. **Pros:** nearby shops and restaurants; pleasant rooms; marina atmosphere. **Cons:** busy location; not a lot of frills in the rooms; need car to get around. *Rooms from: $200 ✉ Waterfront Dr., Nanny Cay ☎ 284/394–2512 🌐 www.nannycay.com 52 rooms No Meals.*

Brightly colored houses populate the hills of Tortola.

Nightlife

The Pub

BARS | At this popular watering hole there are pool tables and a happy hour from 5 to 7; take your drinks onto the patio out back facing the marina. ✉ *Waterfront St., Road Town* ☎ *284/345–1122, 284/494-6711.*

Pusser's Road Town Pub

BARS | Try Pusser's famous mixed drink, the Painkiller, and snack on the excellent pizza. The tin Painkiller cup is a must-have BVI souvenir. ✉ *Waterfront St., Road Town* ☎ *284/494–3897* 🌐 *www.pussers.com.*

Shopping

Many shops and boutiques are clustered along and just off Road Town's **Main Street.** You can shop in Road Town's **Wickham's Cay I** adjacent to the marina. The **Crafts Alive Market** on the Road Town waterfront is a collection of colorful West Indian–style buildings with shops that carry items made in the BVI. You might find pretty baskets or interesting pottery or perhaps a bottle of home-brewed hot sauce. **Tortola Pier Park,** where cruises ships dock, provides another retail option.

Allamanda Gallery

ART GALLERIES | Photography by the gallery's owner, Amanda Baker, as well as books, gifts, and cards are on display and available to purchase at this shop in the Moorings marina village. A second location is at Soper's Hole on Virgin Gorda. ✉ *Moorings Marina, Wickham's Cay II, Road Town* ☎ *284/494–6680, 284/541–8873* 🌐 *www.theallamandagallery.com* ⏲ *Closed Sun.*

Arawak Surf

MIXED CLOTHING | This boutique carries batik sundresses, sportswear, swimwear, and resort wear for men and women. There's also a selection of furniture and children's clothing and books. Look for brands like Reef and Havaianas for sandals, sunglasses by Peppers and Izipizi, and clothing by Hurley and Quicksilver. A second location is in Leverick Bay. ✉ *Nanny Cay Marina, Nanny Cay* ☎ *284/494–5240* 🌐 *www.arawakvi.com.*

Latitude 18°

MIXED CLOTHING | This store sells Maui Jim, Ray-Ban, and Oakley sunglasses; Freestyle watches; and a fine collection of beach towels, sandals, Crocs, sundresses, and sarongs. ✉ *Waterfront Dr., Road Town* ☎ *284/494–7807* 🌐 *www.latitude18.com.*

Pusser's Company Store

GENERAL STORE | The Road Town Pusser's sells nautical memorabilia, clothing for both men and women, handsome decorative bottles of Pusser's rum, and gift items bearing Pusser's iconic logo. ✉ *Main St. at Waterfront Rd., Road Town* ☎ *284/494–2467, 800/787–7377* 🌐 *www.pussers.com.*

RiteWay

SUPERMARKET | This supermarket has fresh produce, deli, prepared foods, meats, bakery, and all the grocery items you'll need for your villa or yacht. You can shop for yourself or set up a provisioning order. You'll find RiteWay locations all over Tortola, and there's also one on Virgin Gorda. ✉ *Waterfront Dr. at Pasea Estate, Road Town* ☎ *384/347–1188* 🌐 *www.rtwbvi.com.*

West End

Sights

Fort Recovery

MILITARY SIGHT | An unrestored but largely intact 17th-century Dutch fort sits amid a profusion of tropical greenery on the grounds of the Fort Recovery Beachfront Villas and Suites. The most interesting thing to see here are the remains of a martello tower, a type of fortification used to make up for the site's lack of elevation; it's rarely found in the Caribbean. There are no guided tours, but you're welcome to stop by and poke around. ✉ *Waterfront Dr., Pockwood Pond, Road Town* ☎ *284/541–0955, 518/435-5436* 🌐 *www.fortrecovery.com* 🎫 *Free.*

Soper's Hole

TOWN | On this little island connected by a causeway to Tortola's western end, you can find a marina and a captivating complex of pastel West Indian–style buildings with shady balconies, shuttered windows, and gingerbread trim that house art galleries, boutiques, and restaurants, including the popular Pusser's Landing West End and two Omar's restaurants (Omar's Fusion and Omar's Cafe). ✉ *Soper's Hole.*

Beaches

Smuggler's Cove Beach

BEACH | A beautiful, palm-fringed beach, Smuggler's Cove is down a pothole-filled dirt road. After bouncing your way down (a four-wheel-drive rental is highly recommended), you'll feel as if you've found a hidden piece of the island. You probably won't be alone on weekends, though, when the beach attracts snorkelers and sunbathers. There's a fine view of Jost Van Dyke. The popular Nigel's Boom Boom Beach Bar has grilled food and the requisite Painkillers; the extremely informal Patricia's beach bar is next door. Follow Long Bay Road past Long Bay Beach Club, keeping to the roads nearest the water until you reach the beach. It's about a mile past the resort. **Amenities:** food and drink, parking. **Best for:** snorkeling; swimming. ✉ *Long Bay Rd., Long Bay.*

Restaurants

★ Omar's Cafe

$$ | **CARIBBEAN** | This pretty pastel Soper's Hole eatery serves the best breakfast on Tortola. Omelets, French toast, waffles, espresso, cappuccino, smoothies, and excellent bagels are served at a breezy counter–dining room combo, but the best seats are out back by the marina. **Known for:** friendly crowd; great breakfasts; omelets, smoothies, and bagels. *Average main: $14* ✉ *Soper's Hole Marina, Soper's Hole* ☎ *345–4771* 🌐 *www.omarscafebvi.com* ⏲ *No dinner.*

Pusser's Landing West End
$$ | **AMERICAN** | Yachties navigate their way to the Soper's Hole boardwalk location of this locally renowned restaurant chainlet, guided by the big red Pusser's sign facing the water. From late morning to well into the evening, you can belly up to the outdoor mahogany bar or sit downstairs for sandwiches, fish and chips, and wings. **Known for:** outdoor deck; happy hour; pub fare. *Average main: $19* ✉ *Soper's Hole* ☎ *284/495–4554* 🌐 *www.pussers.com.*

Hotels

★ Fort Recovery Beachfront Villas and Suites
$$ | **RESORT** | **FAMILY** | This small but special property stands out because of its friendly service and opportunities for socializing with fellow guests, and all of its rooms have good views across the water toward St. John. **Pros:** historic site; beautiful beach; spacious units. **Cons:** not as posh as some locations; isolated location; need car to get around. *Rooms from: $345* ✉ *Waterfront Dr., Soper's Hole* ☎ *284/541–0955, 855/349–3355* 🌐 *www.fortrecovery.com* *24 villas* *No Meals.*

East End

Beaches

Lambert Beach
BEACH | Home to a Wyndham resort, Lambert Beach is a palm-lined, wide, sandy beach with parking along its steep downhill access road. The main attraction here is peace and quiet, but there is a bar and restaurant at the hotel. Turn at the sign for the Wyndham Lambert resort. **Amenities:** food and drink; parking; toilets. **Best for:** solitude; swimming. ✉ *Lambert Rd., off Ridge Rd., East End.*

Long Bay Beach, Beef Island
BEACH | If this beach wasn't located right next to the airport, it probably would show up on lists of the Caribbean's most beautiful strands. Long Bay on Beef Island has superlative scenery: the beach stretches seemingly forever, and you can catch a glimpse of Little Camanoe and Great Camanoe islands. Just keep your eyes out to sea and not on the runway behind you. If you walk around the bend to the right, you can see little Marina Cay and Scrub Island. Swim out to wherever you see a dark patch for some nice snorkeling. Turn left shortly after crossing the bridge to Beef Island. **Amenities:** food and drink; toilets. **Best for:** snorkeling; swimming. ✉ *Beef Island Rd.*

Restaurants

Jeremy's Kitchen
$$ | **AMERICAN** | Situated on Trellis Bay's beachfront, brightly painted Jeremy's Kitchen is the ideal spot to enjoy a leisurely breakfast or lunch while people-watching. Omelets, croque madame and monsieur sandwiches, and eggs Benedict are breakfast favorites, while pasta, curries, roti, and quesadillas round out the lunch and dinner options. "Jeremy's Awesome Sandwich" fits a choice of meats and seafood between slices of seven-grain bread with grilled cheese, vegetables, and mango relish. **Known for:** beachfront dining; "Jeremy's Awesome Sandwich"; laid-back island vibes. *Average main: $13* ✉ *Trellis Bay* ☎ *284/345–5177* 🌐 *www.jeremyskitchen.com.*

North Shore

 Sights

Callwood Distillery

DISTILLERY | Nobody is really sure how long rum has been made at the Callwood Distillery, but it's been at least 200 years, and one thing is certain: it houses the longest continuously operated copper pot still in the Caribbean. Located on a side street in Cane Garden Bay, the ancient distillery offers tours and tastings of its uniquely flavored rums, made directly from the juice of pressed sugar cane, not molasses or refined sugar. For a true taste of the BVI, it doesn't get more authentic than Callwood's barrel-aged spirits. ✉ *Cane Garden Bay, Cane Garden Bay* ☎ *284/495–9383* 🌐 *www.callwood-cane-rum.myshopify.com* 🎫 *Tours $5, tastings $1* ⏲ *Closed Sun. except when cruise ships are in port.*

★ Cane Garden Bay

TOWN | Once a sleepy village, Cane Garden Bay has become one of Tortola's most popular destinations. Stay at a small hotel or guesthouse here, or stop by for lunch, dinner, or drinks at a seaside restaurant, or popular nightspots like Quito's and Myett's. You can find a few small stores selling clothing and basics such as sunscreen, and one of Tortola's most popular beaches is at your feet. Myett's offers hotel rooms almost directly on the beach, while the newer Quito's Inn has smartly appointed rooms. The roads in and out of this area are dauntingly steep, so use caution when driving. ✉ *Cane Garden Bay.*

North Shore Shell Museum

OTHER MUSEUM | Egbert Donovan, the "shell man" of Carrot Bay, entertains passing buses full of tourists with tunes on his guitar and welcomes those who tarry longer to visit his museum crammed with thousands of sea shells, gathered over the course of almost 30 years from the nearby waters and shoreline. Donovan's shell-gathering boat was a victim of Hurricane Irma, so now he spends more time showing off his shells and serving bush tea and turtle soup to visitors. ✉ *Carrot Bay, Cane Garden Bay* ☎ *284/343–7581* 🎫 *Free.*

 Beaches

Apple Bay Beach

BEACH | Along with nearby Little Apple Bay and Capoon's Bay, this is your spot if you want to surf—although the white, sandy beach itself is narrow. Sebastian's, a casual hotel, caters to those in search of the perfect wave. Otherwise, there's nothing else in the way of amenities. Good waves are never a sure thing, but you're more apt to find them in January and February. If you're swimming and the waves are up, take care not to get dashed on the rocks. **Amenities:** none. **Best for:** surfing; swimming. ✉ *North Shore Rd. at Zion Hill Rd., Apple Bay.*

Brewers Bay Beach

BEACH | This beach is easy to find, but the steep, twisting roads leading down to it can be a bit daunting. An old sugar mill and the ruins of a rum distillery are off the beach along the road. Nicole's Beach Bar provides Painkiller cocktails to thirsty sunbathers. You can actually reach the beach from either Brewers Bay Road East or Brewers Bay Road West. **Amenities:** food and drink. **Best for:** snorkeling; swimming. ✉ *Brewers Bay Rd. E, off Cane Garden Bay Rd., Brewers Bay.*

★ Cane Garden Bay Beach

BEACH | This silky stretch of sand boasts exceptionally calm crystalline waters—except when storms at sea turn the water murky. Snorkeling is good along the edges. Casual guesthouses, restaurants, bars, and shops are steps from the beach in the village of the same name. The beach is a laid-back, even somewhat funky place to put down your towel. It's the closest beach to Road Town and one of the BVI's best-known anchorages.

Unfortunately, it can be very crowded with day-trippers when cruise ships dock in Road Town. Water-sports shops rent equipment. **Amenities:** food and drink; toilets; water sports. **Best for:** snorkeling; swimming; partiers. ✉ *Cane Garden Bay Rd., off Ridge Rd., Cane Garden Bay.*

Long Bay Beach
BEACH | This beach is a stunning, mile-long stretch of white sand; have your camera ready to snap the breathtaking approach. The entire beach is open to the public and is often used by people staying in villas in the Long Bay/Belmont area and at the Long Bay Beach Resort. The water isn't as calm here as at Cane Garden or Brewers Bay, but it's still swimmable. Turn left at Zion Hill Road; then travel about half a mile. **Amenities:** none. **Best for:** swimming. ✉ *Long Bay Rd., Long Bay.*

Restaurants

Banana's Bar & Grill
$$$ | **ECLECTIC** | Blessedly cool air-conditioning greets diners on muggy Caribbean evenings at this upscale Cane Garden Bay restaurant, which is equally happy to serve you light pizza, burger, and roti fare or fancier dishes like sautéed Anegada conch and short ribs in a red wine reduction. **Known for:** air-conditioning; good wine selection; inventive seafood. *Average main: $23* ✉ *Cane Garden Bay* ☎ *284/495-9053, 284/440-3252* *Closed Mon.*

★ **Bananakeet Café**
$$$$ | **ECLECTIC** | The sunset sea-and-mountain views are stunning at this poolside restaurant at the Heritage Inn, so arrive early for the predinner happy hour. Caribbean fusion best describes the fare, with an emphasis on steaks, seafood, and pasta, including shrimp swimming in ginger butter sauce and pork tenderloin marinated in rum. **Known for:** good wine and cocktail list; sunset happy hour; panoramic views. *Average main: $36* ✉ *Heritage Inn, North Coast Rd., Great Carrot Bay* ☎ *284/494–5842* 🌐 *www.heritageinnbvi.com* *No lunch.*

De Coal Pot
$$$ | **CARIBBEAN** | Say hi to Paco the Parrot as you enter this inviting Carrot Bay restaurant, which has dining on two levels with views out to sea. Paco may or may not reply, but expect a warm welcome from owner Evelyn Dawson and her staff, who serve up favorites like jerk pork chops and Guyanese-spiced curry grouper and red snapper as well as roti, conch fritters, and other simpler fare. **Known for:** friendly staff; flavorful Caribbean cuisine; tropical cocktails. *Average main: $27* ✉ *Great Carrot Bay* ☎ *284/545–6510* 🌐 *www/decoalpotbvi.com* *Closed Sun.*

★ **Quito's Gazebo**
$$$ | **CARIBBEAN** | This beachside bar and restaurant is owned and operated by island native Quito Rymer, a multitalented recording star, which explains why there's live music nearly every night of the week. The menu is Caribbean, with an emphasis on fresh fish—try the conch fritters or the jerk chicken. **Known for:** casual picnic table dining; live music; lighter options like burgers and fish tacos. *Average main: $21* ✉ *Cane Garden Bay* ☎ *284/495–4837* 🌐 *www.quitosbvi.com.*

Sebastian's Seaside Grill
$$$ | **ECLECTIC** | The waves practically lap at your feet at this friendly beachfront restaurant on Tortola's North Shore, a perfect spot to stop for lunch on your around-the-island tour. The dinner menu emphasizes seafood—especially lobster and local fish—but you can also find pasta dishes, barbecued chicken, and New York strip steak. **Known for:** weekend brunch; surfer vibe; live entertainment at night. *Average main: $29* ✉ *Sebastian's on the Beach, North Coast Rd., Apple Bay* ☎ *284/544–4212* 🌐 *www.sebastians-bvi.com.*

Stoutt's Lookout

$$ | **BURGER** | Fish burgers and long-distance views are on the menu in the reggae-colored Stoutt's Lookout, the domain of gregarious owner Prince Stoutt. Burgers and barbecue ribs round out the lunch menu, all best washed down with a punch made with local Callwood rum and pineapple, guava, and orange juice. **Known for:** Callwood rum punch; views of Cane Garden Bay; burgers. *Average main: $12 Cane Garden Bay, Cane Garden Bay At the intersection of Windy Hill and Ridge Rd. 284/442–0432.*

★ **Sugar Mill Restaurant**

$$$$ | **CONTEMPORARY** | Candles gleam and the background music is peaceful in this romantic restaurant inside a 17th-century sugar mill. Well-prepared selections on the à la carte menu, which changes nightly, include pasta and vegetarian entrées, but the best deal is the three-course prix-fixe menu. **Known for:** inventive Caribbean cuisine; memorable historic setting; banana flambé. *Average main: $49 Sugar Mill Hotel, North Coast Rd., Apple Bay 284/344–8612 www.sugarmillhotel.com No lunch.*

Hotels

Heritage Inn

$ | **B&B/INN** | The gorgeous sea and mountain views are the stars at this small hotel perched on the edge of Windy Hill, offering modest rooms but pleasant rooms with splashes of turquoise accenting a white background. **Pros:** room has kitchenette, but there's also a great restaurant; stunning views; fun vibe. **Cons:** not on beach; close to road; need car to get around. *Rooms from: $225 North Coast Rd., Great Carrot Bay 284/494–5842 www.heritageinn.vg 7 rooms No Meals.*

Lighthouse Villas

$ | **B&B/INN** | Just uphill from the beach, the Lighthouse Villas offer spacious accommodations with shaded balconies overlooking Cane Garden Bay. The six studio efficiency villas are bright and cheerfully decorated in traditional Caribbean style, all set in a single building with a small garden pool deck that's good for a cooling dip or socializing with other guests. **Pros:** full kitchens in unit; close to restaurants, bars, and beach; rooms have A/C. **Cons:** small pool; basic decor; 50 percent deposit required at reservation. *Rooms from: $150 Cane Garden Bay, Cane Garden Bay 284/494–5482 www.lighthousevillasbvi.com 6 rooms No Meals.*

Long Bay Beach Resort

$$$$ | **RESORT** | Reopened and completely reinvented in 2022 by new owners following devastation by Hurricane Irma, this chic and ultra-posh resort on one of the island's most gorgeous stretches of beach features airy accommodations with private verandahs, urbane design-driven decor, stylish 1748 Restaurant and Johnny's Beach Bar, and a slew of pleasurable amenities, from massages on the beach to cabanas and daybeds. **Pros:** numerous activities; stunning location; sleek, urbane decor. **Cons:** on the spendy side; no meals included; need car to get around. *Rooms from: $495 Long Bay Rd., Long Bay 284/345–3773 www.longbay.com 20 suites No Meals.*

Myett's Garden Inn

$$ | **HOTEL** | Tucked away in a beachfront garden, this tiny hotel puts you right in the middle of Cane Garden Bay's busy hustle and bustle, and its adjacent restaurant is one of the area's hot spots. **Pros:** shops nearby; beautiful beach; good restaurant. **Cons:** few common amenities; need a car to venture out; busy location. *Rooms from: $175 Cane Garden Bay*

☎ 284/495–9649 🌐 www.myetts.com 🛏 11 units 🍽 No Meals.

★ **Quito's Inn**

$$ | **HOTEL** | It's hard to tell whether you're in Cane Garden Bay or Miami's South Beach when you walk into this stylish mid-rise—itself a BVI rarity—just off the beach and across the street from the more established Quito's Gazebo restaurant. **Pros:** beautiful modern design; luxury rooms with lofty ocean views and kitchenettes; private pool and bar area. **Cons:** need a car to get around; restaurant is across the street; close but not directly beach. 💲 *Rooms from: $340* ✉ *Cane Garden Bay* ☎ *284/495–4837* 🌐 *www.quitosbvi.com* 🛏 *21 rooms* 🍽 *No Meals.*

Sebastian's on the Beach

$ | **HOTEL** | Sitting on the island's north coast, Sebastian's has a casual beach vibe and rooms that vary in amenities and price, all of them attractively remodeled following Hurricane Irma, with the 12 oceanfront rooms a bit more up-to-date than those that the hotel calls "beach rear." These less expensive rooms are across the street from the ocean and lack views. **Pros:** beachfront rooms; nice beach; good restaurants. **Cons:** need car to get around; some rooms nicer than others; on busy road. 💲 *Rooms from: $164* ✉ *North Coast Rd., Apple Bay* ☎ *284/495–4206, 284/544–4212* 🌐 *www.sebastiansbvi.com* 🛏 *42 units* 🍽 *No Meals.*

★ **Sugar Mill Hotel**

$$ | **RESORT** | Though it's not a sprawling resort, this renowned historic property has a Caribbean cachet that's hard to beat, thanks to its lovely gardens, prime North Shore location just across from the sand, and its iconic restaurants, which are set in a 400-year-old sugar mill and on the beach, respectively. **Pros:** blissful views; lovely rooms; outstanding restaurants. **Cons:** need car to get around; small beach; on busy road. 💲 *Rooms from: $349* ✉ *North Coast Rd., Apple Bay* ☎ *284/344–8612* 🌐 *www.sugarmillhotel.com* 🛏 *22 units* 🍽 *Free Breakfast.*

Nightlife

★ **Myett's Garden & Grille Restaurant**

BARS | Local bands play at this popular spot on the beach, which has live music several nights a week and a popular happy hour. ✉ *Cane Garden Bay* ☎ *284/495–9649* 🌐 *www.myetts.com.*

Quito's Gazebo

BARS | This bar founded by BVI recording star Quito Rymer has live bands performing on Wednesday, Friday, and Saturday, just in time for dinner or sunset cocktails. ✉ *Cane Garden Bay* ☎ *284/495–4837* 🌐 *www.quitosltd.com.*

Mid-Island

Sights

Mount Healthy National Park

RUINS | The remains of an 18th-century sugar plantation can be seen here. The windmill structure, the last one standing in the BVI, has been restored, and you can also see the ruins of a factory with boiling houses, storage areas, stables, a hospital, and many dwellings. It's a nice place to picnic and reflect on the island's history. ✉ *Ridge Rd., Todman Peak* ☎ *284/393–9284* 🌐 *www.bvinpt.org* 🎫 *Free.*

Sage Mountain National Park

NATIONAL PARK | At 1,716 feet, Sage Mountain is the highest peak in the BVI. From the parking area, a trail leads you in a loop not only to the peak itself (and extraordinary views) but also to a small rain forest that is sometimes shrouded in mist. There are a dozen hiking trails total in the park. Most of the forest was cut down over the centuries for timber, to create pastureland, or for growing sugarcane, cotton, and other crops. In 1964, this 127-acre park was established to preserve what remained. Up here you can see mahogany trees, white cedars, mountain guavas, elephant-ear vines, mamey trees, and giant bullet woods, plus birds like mountain

American or British?

Yes, the Union Jack flutters overhead in the tropical breeze, schools operate on the British system, place-names have British spellings, Queen Elizabeth II appoints the governor—and the Queen's picture hangs on many walls. Indeed, residents celebrate the Queen's birthday every June with a public ceremony. You can overhear that charming English accent from a good handful of expats when you're lunching at Road Town restaurants, and you can buy "biscuits"—what Americans call cookies—in the supermarkets.

But you can pay for your lunch and the biscuits with American money, because the U.S. dollar is legal tender here. The unusual circumstance is a matter of geography. The practice started in the mid-20th century, when BVI residents went to work in the nearby USVI. On trips home, they brought their U.S. dollars with them. Soon they abandoned the barter system, and in 1959 the U.S. dollar became the official form of money. Interestingly, the government sells stamps (for use only in the BVI) that often carry pictures of Queen Elizabeth II and other royalty with the monetary value in U.S. dollars and cents.

The American influence continued to grow when Americans began to open businesses in the BVI because they preferred its quiet to the hustle and bustle of St. Thomas. Inevitably, cable and satellite TV's U.S.-based programming, along with Hollywood-made movies, further influenced life in the BVI. And most goods are shipped from St. Thomas in the USVI, meaning you can find more American products than British ones on the supermarket shelves.

But don't get too carried away with either association; at heart, the BVI's culture is neither British or American—but purely West Indian.

doves and thrushes. Take a taxi from Road Town or drive up Joe's Hill Road and make a left onto Ridge Road toward Chalwell and Doty villages. The road dead-ends at the park. ✉ *Ridge Rd., Sage Mountain* ☎ *284/393–9284* 🌐 *www.bvinpt.org* 🎫 *$3.*

Activities

DIVING AND SNORKELING

Clear waters and numerous reefs afford some wonderful opportunities for underwater exploration. In some spots visibility reaches 100 feet, but colorful reefs teeming with fish are often just a few feet below the sea surface. The BVI's system of marine parks means the underwater life visible through your mask will stay protected.

There are several popular dive spots around the islands. **Alice in Wonderland** is a deep dive south of Ginger Island with a wall that slopes gently from 15 feet to 100 feet. It's an area overrun with huge mushroom-shape coral, hence its name. Crabs, lobsters, and shimmering fan corals make their homes in the tunnels, ledges, and overhangs of **Blonde Rock,** a pinnacle that goes from 15 feet below the surface to 60 feet deep. It's between Dead Chest and Salt Island. When the currents aren't too strong, **Brewers Bay Pinnacle** (20 to 90 feet down) teems with sea life. At the **Indians,** near Pelican Island, colorful coral decorates canyons and grottoes created by four large, jagged pinnacles that rise 50 feet from the ocean floor. The **Painted Walls** is a shallow dive site where coral and sponges create a kaleidoscope of colors on the walls of four long gullies. It's northeast of Dead Chest.

The *Chikuzen,* sunk northwest of Brewers Bay in 1981, is a 246-foot vessel in 75 feet of water; it's home to thousands of fish, colorful corals, and big rays. In 1867 the RMS *Rhone,* a 310-foot royal mail steamer, split in two when it sank in a devastating hurricane. It's so well-preserved that it was used as an underwater prop in the 1977 movie *The Deep.* You can see the crow's nest and bowsprit, the cargo hold in the bow, and the engine and enormous propeller shaft in the stern. The ship's four parts are at various depths, from 30 to 80 feet. Get yourself some snorkeling gear and hop aboard a dive boat to this wreck near Salt Island (across the channel from Road Town). Every dive outfit in the BVI runs scuba and snorkel tours to this part of the BVI National Parks Trust; if you have time for only one trip, make it this one. Rates start at around $95 for a one-tank dive and $130 for a two-tank dive.

Blue Water Divers

SCUBA DIVING | Located in the Nanny Cay marina, this first-rate company teaches resort, open-water, rescue, and advanced diving courses, and also makes daily dive trips, including to the fabled *RMS Rhone* wreck. Rates include all equipment as well as instruction. Reserve two days in advance. ✉ *Nanny Cay Marina, Nanny Cay* ☎ *284/494–2847, 284/340–4311* 🌐 *www.bluewaterdiversbvi.com.*

FISHING

Most of the boats that take you deep-sea fishing for blue marlin, white marlin, wahoo, tuna, and dolphinfish (mahimahi) leave from nearby St. Thomas, but local anglers like to fish the shallower water for bonefish. Guided fly-fishing wading trips are $445 for a half-day.

Jack Trout Fly Fishing

FISHING | Wade into the shallow waters of Tortola in pursuit of bonefish and tarpon. A half-day wading trip is $445 for up to two people; full-day is $575. Lunch, drinks, and gear are included. ✉ *Nanny Cay Marina, Nanny Cay* ☎ *530/926–4540* 🌐 *www.jacktrout.com.*

HIKING

Sage Mountain National Park attracts hikers who enjoy the quiet trails that crisscross the island's loftiest peak. There are some lovely views and the chance to see rare species that grow only at higher elevations. You can also hike to some dramatic coastal headlands and "caves" formed by tumbled boulders at Shark Bay.

SAILING

The BVI are among the world's most popular sailing destinations. They're clustered together and surrounded by calm waters, so it's fairly easy to sail from one anchorage to the next. Most of the Caribbean's biggest sailboat charter companies have operations in Tortola. If you know how to sail, you can charter a bareboat (perhaps for your entire vacation); if you're unschooled, you can hire a boat with a captain. Prices vary depending on the type and size of the boat you wish to charter. In season, a weekly charter runs from $2,500 to $35,000 or more. Book early to make sure you get the boat that fits you best. Most of Tortola's marinas have hotels, which give you a convenient place to spend the nights before and after your charter.

If a day sail to some secluded anchorage is more your cup of tea, the BVI have numerous boats of various sizes and styles that leave from many points around Tortola. Prices start at around $135 per person for a full-day sail, including drinks and snorkeling equipment.

Aristocat Charters

SAILING | This company's 45-foot catamarans, *Sugar Rush* and *Sweet Escape*, set off for sailing and snorkeling trips to Jost Van Dyke, Norman Island, Cooper Island, and other small islands, as well as The Baths. Day-sailing charters run from Soper's Hole (Frenchman's Cay), West End, and the Village Cay Marina in Road Town. ✉ *Road Town* ☎ *284/499–1249* 🌐 *www.aristocatcharters.com.*

The Catamaran Company

SAILING | The catamarans available for charter come with or without a captain; sailing cats range in length from 35 to 52 feet, with three to five double cabins. ✉ *Hodges Creek Marina, East End* ☎ *284/544–6661, 800/262–0308* 🌐 *www.catamarans.com.*

Island Surf and Sail

WATER SPORTS | Based in Soper's Hole, Island Surf and Sail rents kayaks, paddleboards, SUP boards, surfboards, fishing equipment, snorkeling equipment, various water toys, and—amusingly—guitars. The company also offers private sailing day trips and dive instruction. ✉ *Soper's Hole Marina, Soper's Hole* ☎ *284/345—0123* 🌐 *www.bviwatertoys.com.*

Island Time Power Boat Rentals

BOATING | Island Time rents a small fleet of open sportfishing boats (23 to 30 feet) for $255 for a six-passenger inflatable to $630 per day for a 28-foot Cobia that can carry eight. ✉ *Nanny Cay Marina, Nanny Cay* ☎ *284/495–9993* 🌐 *www.islandtime-bvi.com.*

The Moorings

BOATING | One of the world's best bareboat operations, the Moorings has a large fleet of both monohull boats and catamarans (sail and power, or power only). Catamarans, the most popular option, range in size from 36 to 50 feet and have three to five cabins. Hire a captain or sail the boat yourself for a week or more of island hopping in the U.S. and British Virgin Islands. The Moorings base in Road Town has extensive facilities, including provisioning, a restaurant, and a hotel. ✉ *Wickham's Cay II, Road Town* ☎ *888/416-0814* 🌐 *www.moorings.com.*

Regency Yacht Vacations

BOATING | If you prefer a powerboat, call Regency Yacht Vacations. It handles captain and full-crew sail and powerboat charters, as well as sail and powered catamarans and everything up to megayachts. The range of vessels is impressive: you can spend about $16,000 for a week on a catamaran with a crew of two or more than half a million bucks to take 12 guests along for a cruise on the three-mast megayacht *Maltese Falcon.* ✉ *Wickham's Cay I, Road Town* ☎ *800/524–7676* 🌐 *www.yachtfleet.com.*

Sunsail

SAILING | A full fleet of boats, including catamarans and monohull sailboats, can be chartered with or without a captain. Prices start at around $2,800 for a week's bareboat sail. ✉ *Wickham's Cay II, Road Town* ☎ *866/514–9778* 🌐 *www.sunsail.com.*

Voyage Charters

SAILING | Voyage has a variety of sailboats for charter, with or without a captain and crew. Their fleet includes electric-powered 48-foot sailing catamarans as well as conventional sailing and power cats. ✉ *Soper's Hole Marina* ☎ *443/569–7007, 888/869–2436* 🌐 *www.voyagecharters.com.*

SURFING

Surfing is big on Tortola's north shore, particularly when the winter swells come into Cane Garden, Josiah's, Apple Bays, and Smuggler's Cove. Rent surfboards for $40–$50 for a full day from Island Surf and Sail in Soper's Hole.

WINDSURFING

Steady trade winds make windsurfing a breeze. Three of the best spots for sailboarding are Nanny Cay, Slaney Point, and Trellis Bay on Beef Island. Rates for sailboards start at about $40 a day.

Island Surf and Sail

WINDSURFING | This company in Soper's Hole rents kayaks, standup paddleboards, surfboard, snorkel gear, and other beach and water toys. ✉ *Soper's Hole* ☎ *284/494–0123* 🌐 *www.bviwatertoys.com.*

Side Trips from Tortola

Scrub Island

This 250-acre island, a short ferry ride from Trellis Bay near Tortola's Beef Island Airport, was once occupied by Taíno and Arawak peoples and later the site of a colonial copper mine. Unoccupied for years, the island was developed into a luxury resort with a marina, spa, and posh villas in the 2010s.

Hotels

★ Scrub Island Resort, Spa and Marina

$$$$ | **RESORT** | Part of Marriott's Autograph Collection, this swanky resort is on a 250-acre island just off the east end of Tortola and provides a posh getaway for relaxing around the pool or beach, enjoying a water-sports excursion or two, and being pampered in the plush spa. **Pros:** full-service marina; lots of activities; very good spa. **Cons:** only reachable by boat; only a few dining options; expensive. *Rooms from: $854* ☎ *877/890–7444, 284/394–3440* 🌐 *www.scrubisland.com* *63 units* *No Meals.*

Virgin Gorda

Virgin Gorda, or "Fat Virgin," received its name from Christopher Columbus. The explorer envisioned the island as a pregnant woman in a languid recline, with Gorda Peak being her big belly and the boulders of The Baths her toes. Different in topography from Tortola, with its arid landscape covered with scrub brush and cactus, Virgin Gorda has a slower pace of life, too.

One of the most efficient ways to see Virgin Gorda is by boat. There are few roads, and most byways don't follow the scalloped shoreline. The main route sticks resolutely to the center of the island, linking The Baths on the southern tip with Gun Creek and Leverick Bay at North Sound. The craggy coast, cut through with grottoes and fringed by palms and boulders, has a primitive beauty. If you drive, you can hit all the sights in one day. The best plan is to explore the area near your hotel (either Spanish Town or North Sound) first, then take a day to drive to the other end. Stop to climb Gorda Peak, which is in the island's center. There are few signs, so come prepared with a map.

Villas are scattered all over Virgin Gorda, but hotels are centered in and around The Valley, Nail Bay, and in the North Sound area. Except for Leverick Bay Resort, the hotels in North Sound are reached only by boat.

Virgin Gorda is not a place you come to for nightlife, but that doesn't mean the island is totally dead after dark. A few bars and restaurants in Spanish Town and Leverick Bay have live music, and boaters make their way to the Bitter End Yacht Club for dinner and drinks, too.

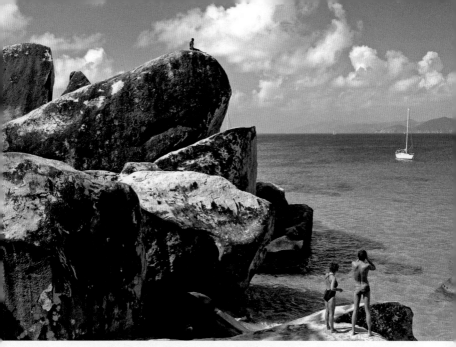

Massive granite boulders are a sight to behold at the Baths National Park.

The Valley

Sights

★ The Baths National Park

BEACH | **FAMILY** | At Virgin Gorda's most celebrated sight, giant boulders are scattered about the beach and in the water. Some are almost as large as houses and form remarkable grottoes. Climb between these rocks to swim in the many placid pools. Snorkelers and divers will find even more tumbled boulders below the surface. Early morning and late afternoon are the best times to visit if you want to avoid crowds. If it's privacy you crave, follow the shore northward to quieter bays—Spring Bay, the Crawl, Little Trunk, and Valley Trunk—or head south to Devil's Bay. ✉ *Off Tower Rd., Spanish Town* ☎ *284/494–2069* 🌐 *www.bvitourism.com* 🎫 *$3.*

Copper Mine National Park

RUINS | A tall stone shaft silhouetted against the sky, a small stone structure that overlooks the sea, and a deep cistern are part of what was once a copper mine, now in ruins. Established 400 years ago, it was worked first by the Spanish, then by the English until the early 20th century. There's not too much in the way of interpretive signs at the site, but the location is beautiful. ✉ *Copper Mine Rd., Spanish Town* 🎫 *Free.*

Spanish Town

TOWN | Virgin Gorda's peaceful main settlement, on the island's southern wing, is so tiny that it barely qualifies as a town at all. In the part of the island known as "The Valley," Spanish Town has a marina, some shops, a few restaurants and bars, and a couple of car-rental agencies. Just north of town is the ferry terminal. ✉ *Spanish Town.*

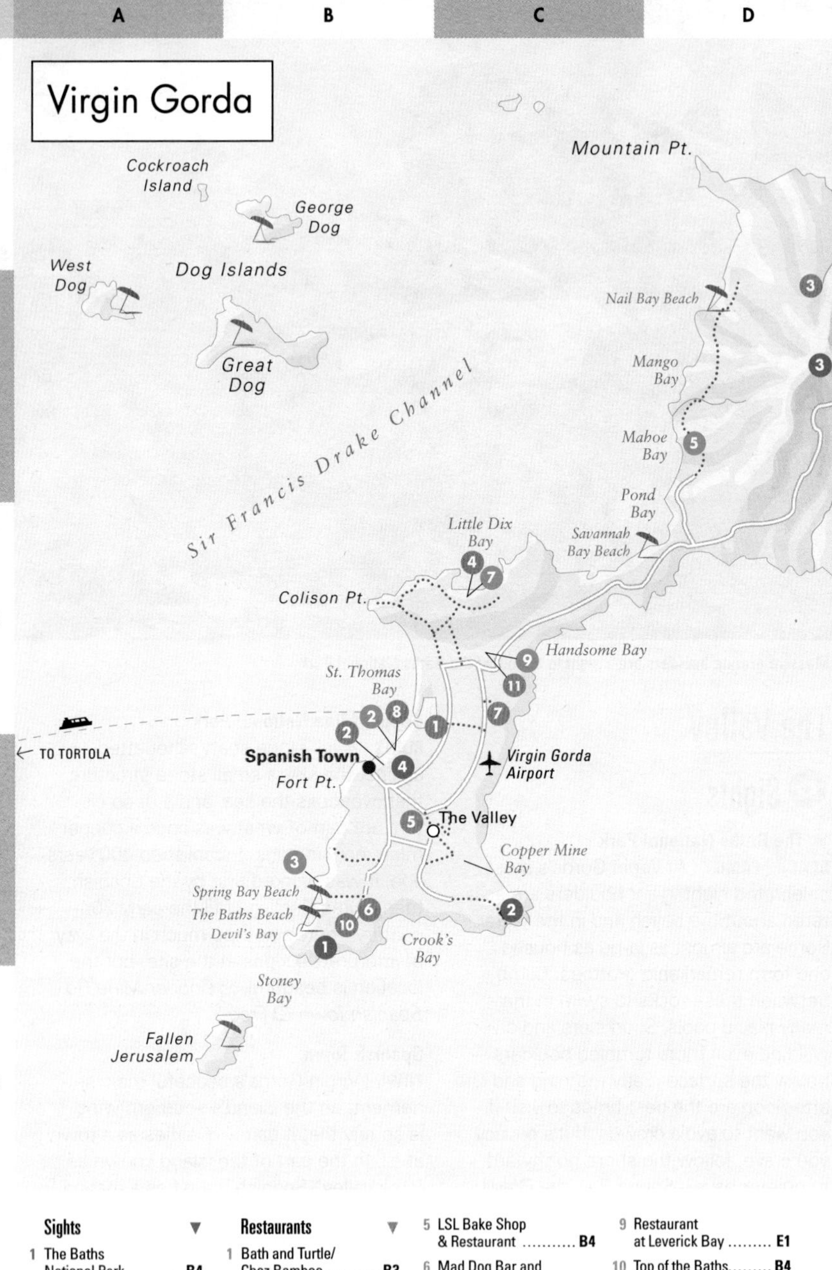

Sights

1 The Baths National Park **B4**
2 Copper Mine National Park **C4**
3 Gorda Peak National Park............ **D2**
4 Spanish Town........... **B4**

Restaurants

1 Bath and Turtle/ Chez Bamboo **B3**
2 CocoMaya............... **B4**
3 Hog Heaven **D2**
4 Little Dix Bay Pavilion **C3**
5 LSL Bake Shop & Restaurant **B4**
6 Mad Dog Bar and Restaurant **B4**
7 Mermaids and Pirates **C3**
8 The Reef Restaurant at Fischer's Cove........ **B4**
9 Restaurant at Leverick Bay **E1**
10 Top of the Baths......... **B4**
11 The Village Cafe & Restaurant **C3**

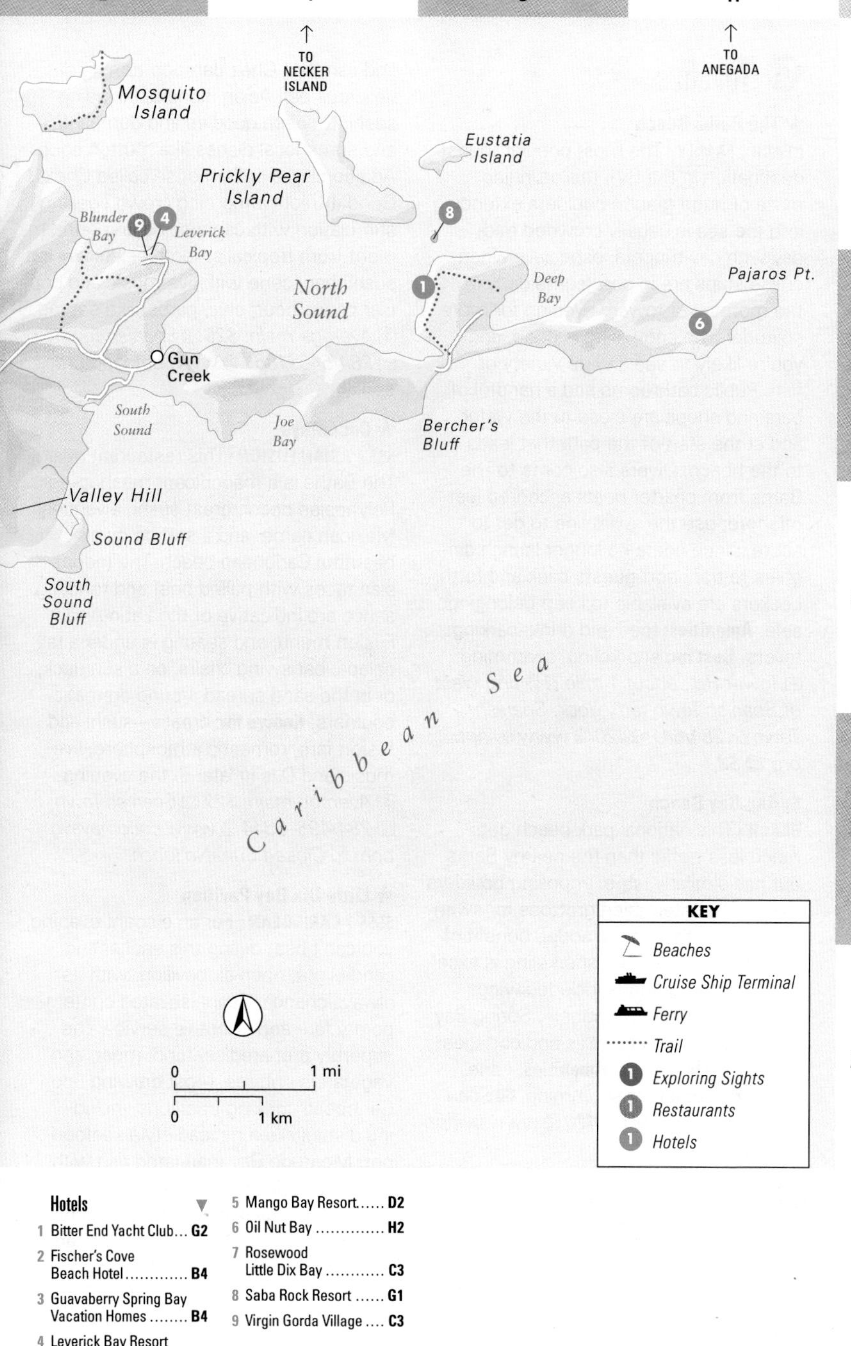

Hotels

1 Bitter End Yacht Club... **G2**
2 Fischer's Cove Beach Hotel............ **B4**
3 Guavaberry Spring Bay Vacation Homes........ **B4**
4 Leverick Bay Resort and Marina.............. **E1**
5 Mango Bay Resort...... **D2**
6 Oil Nut Bay.............. **H2**
7 Rosewood Little Dix Bay............ **C3**
8 Saba Rock Resort...... **G1**
9 Virgin Gorda Village.... **C3**

Beaches

★ The Baths Beach

BEACH | FAMILY | The most popular tourist destination in the BVI, this stunning maze of huge granite boulders extending into the sea is usually crowded midday with day-trippers, especially when cruise ships are in port (come early in the morning or toward evening for more solitude). The snorkeling is good, and you're likely to see a wide variety of fish. Public bathrooms and a handful of bars and shops are close to the water and at the start of the path that leads to the beach. Divers also come to The Baths from charter boats anchored just offshore; use the swim line to get to shore, since boats no longer launch dinghies to transport guests back and forth. Lockers are available to keep belongings safe. **Amenities:** food and drink; parking; toilets. **Best for:** snorkeling; swimming. ✉ *Tower Rd., about 1 mile (1½ km) west of Spanish Town ferry dock, Spanish Town* ☎ *284/541–2420* 🌐 *www.bvinpt.org* 🎫 *$3.*

Spring Bay Beach

BEACH | This national park beach gets much less traffic than the nearby Baths but has similarly large, imposing boulders that create interesting grottoes for swimming. Plus, there's the added benefit of no admission fee. The snorkeling is excellent, and the grounds include swings and picnic tables. Guavaberry Spring Bay Vacation Homes has villas and cottages right near the beach. **Amenities:** none. **Best for:** snorkeling; swimming. ✉ *Spanish Town* ☎ *284/541–2420* 🌐 *www.bvinpt.org* 🎫 *Free.*

Restaurants

Bath and Turtle/Chez Bamboo

$$$ | ECLECTIC | These two friendly restaurants share the same lovely hideaway and serve tasty meals all day between them, with informal Bath and Turtle your go-to for breakfast and lunch fare and candlelit Chez Bamboo turning out delicious pan-Asian dinners, including sushi, Chinese noodles and dumpling, and some local dishes like mutton soup. Additionally, a coffeehouse called Chez B Grind attracts a morning crowd seeking stimulation with cappuccino and refreshment from tropical smoothies. **Known for:** sushi; bar scene with live music and popular happy hour; chic, gardenlike setting. $ *Average main: $26* ✉ *Spanish Town* ☎ *284/545–1861* 🌐 *www.bathandturtle.com.*

★ CocoMaya

$$$ | ASIAN FUSION | This restaurant near The Baths is a magnificent mashup—Polynesian decor, great sushi, a vaguely Mexican name, and a setting on a beautiful Caribbean beach. The Indonesian tacos with pulled beef and rendang sauce are indicative of the Latin-Asian Fusion menu, and seating is under a tall palapa, bar swing chairs, on a sun deck, or in the sand spread around dramatic boulders. **Known for:** creative sushi and fusion fare; romantic atmosphere; live music and DJs in later in the evening. $ *Average main: $27* ✉ *Spanish Town* ☎ *284/495–6344* 🌐 *www.cocomayavg.com* ⏲ *Closed Sun. No lunch.*

★ Little Dix Bay Pavilion

$$$$ | CARIBBEAN | For an elegant evening, you can't beat dining this enchanting, candlelight, open-air pavilion, with its always-changing sophisticated contemporary fare and attentive service. The superbly prepared seafood, meat, and vegetarian entrées, most drawing upon Caribbean cooking traditions, including dishes like a Trinidad-style seafood pot, Montego Bay marinated fish with Jamaican spices, and tandoori-marinated lamb chops. **Known for:** excellent service; refined atmosphere; stellar Caribbean-influenced cuisine. $ *Average main: $45* ✉ *Little Dix Bay Resort, off Little Rd., Spanish Town* ☎ *284/495–5555* 🌐 *www.rosewoodhotels.com.*

LSL Bake Shop & Restaurant
$$ | **ECLECTIC** | Along the road to The Baths, this small restaurant with pedestrian decor is a local favorite for fresh bread, cakes and pastries, and informal dining. You can always find fresh fish on the menu, accompanied by traditional local sides like peas and rice. **Known for:** fresh-baked cakes; Friday-night barbecues; local fish. *Average main: $16* ✉ *Tower Rd., Spanish Town* ☎ *284/495–5151, 284/340–5151* 🌐 *www.lslbakeshop.com.*

Mad Dog Bar and Restaurant
$$ | **ECLECTIC** | Visitors to The Baths can forgo the beach's snack bar for more satisfying fare—burgers, conch fritters, smoothies, rum punches—at this porch-wrapped restaurant near the park entrance. Ask about the house-made pastries and cakes, which are often available. **Known for:** right by The Baths; cold drinks; conch fritters. *Average main: $13* ✉ *Baths Hill* ☎ *284/544–2681* 🌐 *www.mad-dog-bar-restaurant.business.site* *No dinner.*

Mermaids and Pirates
$$ | **CARIBBEAN** | Freestanding shops selling gifts, ice cream, and bakery items give this casual roadside bar and restaurant the feel of a little village. Crowds gather on game days to watch sports under a covered patio or inside the air-conditioned dining room, while feasting on basic breakfasts and exceptionally good and authentic Caribbean lunch and dinner fare. **Known for:** stewed mutton; sports bar with wagering; grilled local fish with fungi (a traditional hot cornmeal dish). *Average main: $15* ✉ *Spanish Town* ☎ *284/345–1728.*

The Reef Restaurant at Fischer's Cove
$$$ | **CARIBBEAN** | Dine seaside at this alfresco restaurant that's open to the breezes and features occasional live music. If pumpkin soup is on the menu, give it a try for a true taste of the Caribbean, although you can also get burgers, pizza, and salads at lunch, and local fish and conch fritters. **Known for:** Saturday-night pig roasts; friendly staff; great views. *Average main: $26* ✉ *Lee Rd., Spanish Town* ☎ *284/495–5253* 🌐 *www.fischerscove.com.*

Top of the Baths
$$$ | **ECLECTIC** | **FAMILY** | At the entrance to The Baths, this popular restaurant has tables on an outdoor terrace or in an open-air pavilion; all have stunning views of the Sir Francis Drake Channel. The restaurant starts serving early for breakfast; for lunch, hamburgers, coconut chicken sandwiches, fish-and-chips, and sushi are among the offerings. **Known for:** key lime pie; great location with a swimming pool; stunning views. *Average main: $23* ✉ *Spanish Town* ☎ *284/495–5497* 🌐 *www.topofthebaths.com.*

The Village Cafe & Restaurant
$$$ | **ECLECTIC** | Meals are served poolside under the shade of umbrellas at this casual eatery at the Virgin Gorda Village condo complex. The lunch menu includes salads, pizzas, rotis, and burgers, but the lobster wrap is a must-have. **Known for:** fish-and-chips with Cajun spices; lobster tacos; casual lunch. *Average main: $26* ✉ *Virgin Gorda Village, North Sound Rd., Spanish Town* ☎ *284/343–8092, 284/545–0283, 284/495–5350* 🌐 *www.virgingordavillage.com* *Closed Mon.*

Hotels

Fischer's Cove Beach Hotel
$ | **RESORT** | Post-storm renovations have reopened six of this beachfront hotel's standard rooms and studios, with rebuilds of the cottages and oceanfront rooms planned. **Pros:** good restaurant; beachfront location; budget price. **Cons:** no air-conditioning in some rooms; no meals included; basic units. *Rooms from: $155* ✉ *Lee Rd., Spanish Town* ☎ *284/495–5253* 🌐 *www.fischerscove.com* *6 units* *No Meals.*

Guavaberry Spring Bay Vacation Homes
$ | **HOTEL** | Rambling back from the beach, these hexagonal one-, two-, and three-bedroom villas give you all the comforts of home—and the resort's own stretch of striking, boulder-fringed beach is a short walk minutes away. **Pros:** scenic outdoor decks with ocean views; short walk to The Baths (and excellent snorkeling); easy drive to town. **Cons:** credit cards not accepted; extra charge for air-conditioning; few amenities. *Rooms from: $185 ✉ Tower Rd., Spanish Town ☎ 284/544–7186 🌐 www.guavaberryspringbay.com No credit cards 19 units No Meals.*

★ **Rosewood Little Dix Bay**
$$$$ | **RESORT** | **FAMILY** | This swanky laid-back resort offers a gorgeous crescent of sand, plenty of activities, excellent restaurants, and sleek rooms, suites, and villas with bright, clean mid-century modern furniture and a casual feel that match the resort's "barefoot luxury" ethos. **Pros:** outstanding amenities; relaxed sophistication; gorgeous grounds. **Cons:** insular though not isolated; very spread out; expensive. *Rooms from: $850 ✉ Off Little Rd., Spanish Town ☎ 284/495–5555 🌐 www.rosewoodhotels.com 80 rooms No Meals.*

Virgin Gorda Village
$ | **HOTEL** | All the one- through four-bedroom condos in this upscale complex a few minutes' drive from Spanish Town have at least partial ocean views, and the location is ideal—close enough so that you can easily pop out to dinner, but far enough to make you feel as if you're more isolated than you really are. **Pros:** modern, updated units; close to Spanish Town; lovely pool. **Cons:** some noisy roosters nearby; on a busy street; no beach. *Rooms from: $210 ✉ North Sound Rd. ☎ 284/495–5544, 284/495–5986 🌐 www.virgingordavillage.com 30 condos No Meals.*

Nightlife

Bath and Turtle/Chez Bamboo
BARS | During high season, the Bath and Turtle (and the adjacent Chez Bamboo) is one of the liveliest spots on Virgin Gorda, hosting DJs and live music several nights a week. *✉ Lee Rd., Spanish Town ☎ 284/495–5752 🌐 www.bathturtle.com.*

The Rum Room
BARS | The Rum Room at Little Dix Bay presents live entertainment several nights a week in season. *✉ Little Dix Bay Resort, Little Rd., Spanish Town ☎ 284/495–5555 🌐 www.littledixbay.com.*

Shopping

The Beach House at Little Dix Bay Resort
GENERAL STORE | This tony hotel shop has the latest in resort wear for men and women, as well as jewelry, books, housewares, and expensive T-shirts. *✉ Little Dix Bay Resort, Little Rd., Spanish Town ☎ 284/495–5555 🌐 www.littledixbay.com.*

RiteWay Virgin Gorda
WINE/SPIRITS | The store isn't much to look at, inside or out, but it has the best wine prices on Virgin Gorda, along with the usual basic supermarket items. *✉ Long Rd., Spanish Town ☎ 284/340–2263 🌐 www.riteway.vg.*

Rosy's Supermarket
SUPERMARKET | This store carries the basics plus an interesting selection of ready-to-cook meals, such as whole seasoned chickens. *✉ Rhymer Rd., Spanish Town ☎ 284/495–5245 🌐 www.rosysvg.com.*

North Sound

Restaurants

★ Hog Heaven

$$$ | BARBECUE | FAMILY | The million-dollar view is the thing at this simple wooden restaurant perched on a hillside overlooking the North Sound. If the scenery alone isn't enough to make you feel as if you're ready to be singing with the angels, this barbecue joint's succulent pork, local fish, and conch in butter sauce will help. **Known for:** rum drinks; spectacular views; barbecue. *$ Average main: $22 ✉ North Sound ☎ 284/547–5964.*

Restaurant at Leverick Bay

$$$$ | ECLECTIC | Chef Stanley Ramotar's gourmet menu at this marina restaurant draws cruise ship passengers on tour as well as hotel guests, locals, and mariners. Anegada lobster is a perennial favorite along with rack of lamb and filet mignon. **Known for:** Anegada lobster; Friday-night beach barbecue party; happy hour with live music. *$ Average main: $38 ✉ Leverick Bay Resort & Marina, Leverick Bay Rd., Leverick Bay ☎ 284/541–8879, 284/346–7241 🌐 www.leverickbayvg.com ⏲ Closed Fri.*

Hotels

★ Bitter End Yacht Club

$$$$ | RESORT | FAMILY | Sailing's the thing at this busy marina in the nautically inclined North Sound, where the long-popular hotel has been recently rebuilt with new Marina Villas that feature a sail-loft vibe and shoreline decks, plus several overwater bungalows. **Pros:** beautiful newly designed rooms and restaurant; lots of water sports; good diving opportunities. **Cons:** limited activities unless you love the water; still some ongoing renovations as of this writing; expensive. *$ Rooms from: $750 ✉ North Sound ☎ 800/872–2392, 284/393–2745 🌐 www.beyc.com 🛏 2 rooms 🍽 No Meals.*

Leverick Bay Resort and Marina

$ | RESORT | With its colorful buildings and bustling marina, Leverick Bay is a good choice for visitors who want easy access to water-sports activities and who don't mind that the beach is quite small. **Pros:** fun location; good restaurant; small grocery store. **Cons:** basic rooms; no laundry in units; 15-minute drive to town. *$ Rooms from: $125 ✉ Off Leverick Bay Rd., Leverick Bay ☎ 284/542–4011, 284/542–4014 🌐 www.leverickbayvg.com 🛏 14 rooms 🍽 No Meals.*

Oil Nut Bay

$$$$ | APARTMENT | FAMILY | Although this compound of one- to six-bedroom villas (with more on the way) isn't a private island resort, it's so far from anything else on the remote east end of Virgin Gorda that it may as well be. **Pros:** private and exclusive; impressive array of amenities; kid-friendly features. **Cons:** can only get here by boat or helicopter; extremely high rates; far from dining and shopping elsewhere on the island. *$ Rooms from: $1050 ✉ North Sound ☎ 284/393–1000, 866/681–0587 🌐 www.oilnutbay.com 🛏 35 units 🍽 No Meals.*

Saba Rock Resort

$$$$ | RESORT | Reachable only by ferry or by private yacht, this resort on its own tiny cay is perfect for folks who enjoy seclusion and also mixing and mingling with the sailors who drop anchor for the night. **Pros:** good diving nearby; convivial atmosphere; convenient transportation. **Cons:** on a very small island; isolated location; tiny beach. *$ Rooms from: $550 ✉ North Sound ☎ 284/393–9220 🌐 www.sabarock.com 🛏 7 units 🍽 No Meals.*

Nightlife

Leverick Bay Resort

BARS | This marina resort's restaurant and Jumbie's Beach Bar has a nightly happy hour with a pirate-themed musical performance on Monday, Tuesday, and Wednesday, and hosts bands several other nights a week. Things really get going at the Friday night beach barbecue, which features moko jumbie stilt-walkers, fire dancers, and a DJ. ✉ *Leverick Bay Resort & Marina, Leverick Bay Rd., Leverick Bay* ☎ *284/541–8879, 284/346–7241, 284/340–3005* 🌐 *www.leverickbayvg.com.*

Shopping

Chef's Pantry

FOOD | This store in Leverick Bay has the fixings for an impromptu party in your villa or to provision your boat—fresh seafood, specialty meats, imported cheeses, daily baked breads and pastries, and an impressive wine and spirits selection. ✉ *Leverick Bay Marina, Leverick Bay Rd., Leverick Bay* ☎ *284/541–2881* 🌐 *www.leverickbayvg.com.*

Pusser's Company Store

GENERAL STORE | A trademark line of sportswear, rum products, and gift items is available here. ✉ *Leverick Bay Marina, Leverick Bay Rd., Leverick Bay* ☎ *284/495–5423, 284/495–6952* 🌐 *www.pussers.com.*

Northwest Shore

Sights

Gorda Peak National Park

NATIONAL PARK | There are two trails at this 260-acre park, which contains the island's highest point, at 1,359 feet. Signs on North Sound Road mark both entrances. It's a short but steep 30- to 50-minute hike (depending on which trail you take) through a rare Caribbean dry forest to a small clearing, where you can enjoy some high-level views. ✉ *North Sound Rd., Gorda Peak* ☎ *284/541–2420* 🌐 *www.bvinpt.org* 🎫 *Free.*

Beaches

Fallen Jerusalem Island and the Dog Islands

BEACH | You can easily reach these quaintly named islands by boat, which you can rent in either Tortola or Virgin Gorda; they're also a popular destination for dive and snorkeling charter boats. Fallen Jerusalem and the Dogs are part of the National Parks Trust of the Virgin Islands, and their seductive beaches and unparalleled snorkeling display the BVI at their hedonistic best. Fallen Jerusalem has two small beaches for a Robinson Crusoe experience. **Amenities:** none. **Best for:** solitude; snorkeling. ☎ *284/541–2420* 🌐 *www.bvinpt.org* 🎫 *Free.*

Nail Bay Beach

BEACH | At the island's north tip, the three beaches on Nail Bay are ideal for snorkeling. Mountain Trunk Bay is perfect for beginners, and Nail Bay and Long Bay beaches have coral caverns just offshore. The Sugarcane Restaurant at the nearby Nail Bay Sports Club serves lunch and dinner. **Amenities:** food and drink. **Best for:** snorkeling; swimming. ✉ *Nail Bay Resort, off Plum Tree Bay Rd., Nail Bay* 🎫 *Free.*

Savannah Bay Beach

BEACH | This is a wonderfully private beach close to Spanish Town. It may not always be completely deserted, but you can find a spot to yourself on this long stretch of soft white sand in front of the tall dunes. Bring your own mask, fins, and snorkel, as there are no facilities. Nearby villas are available through rental property agencies. The view from atop the dunes is a photographer's delight. **Amenities:** none. **Best for:** solitude; snorkeling; swimming. ✉ *Off N. Sound Rd., ¾ mile (1¼ km) east of Spanish Town ferry dock, Savannah Bay* 🎫 *Free.*

Hotels

Mango Bay Resort

$ | **RESORT** | Facing west to capture sunsets, this collection of whitewashed contemporary condos and villas will make you feel right at home. **Pros:** homes come with floats, kayaks, and snorkeling equipment; nice beach; lively location that's an easy drive from restaurants. **Cons:** need car to get around; some units have lackluster views; drab decor. *$ Rooms from: $260 ✉ Plum Tree Bay Rd., Pond Bay ☎ 284/340–8804 🌐 www.mangobayresort.com 17 units No Meals.*

Activities

DIVING AND SNORKELING

There are some terrific snorkel and dive sites off Virgin Gorda, including areas around The Baths, the North Sound, and the Dogs. The Chimney at Great Dog Island has a coral archway and canyon covered with a wide variety of sponges. At Joe's Cave, an underwater cavern on West Dog Island, huge groupers, eagle rays, and other colorful fish accompany divers as they swim. At some sites you can see 100 feet down, but divers who don't want to go that deep and snorkelers will find plenty to look at just below the surface.

Dive BVI

SCUBA DIVING | In addition to day trips, Dive BVI also offers expert scuba instruction and certification. The Yacht Harbour location is housed in a shipping container; there's a fancier location at the Scrub Island resort. Charter boats can also be met for rendezvous dives at various locations in the BVI. *✉ Virgin Gorda Yacht Harbour, Lee Rd., Spanish Town ☎ 284/541–9818 Yacht Harbour, 284/340–0829 Scrub Island 🌐 www.divebvi.com.*

Sunchaser Scuba

SCUBA DIVING | Resort, advanced, and rescue courses are all available here along with dive charters to northern BVI sites like the Dog Islands, the *RMS Rhone*, and other destinations—all 15 to 45 minutes away from their base at the Bitter End Yacht Club. *✉ Bitter End Yacht Club, North Sound ☎ 284/344–2766 🌐 www.sunchaserscuba.com.*

SAILING AND BOATING

Double D Charters

BOATING | If you just want to sit back, relax, and let the captain take the helm, choose a sailing or power yacht from Double "D" Charters. Rates start at $300 for a day trip to Cooper Island, Norman Island, Jost Van Dyke, or Anegada. Private full-day cruises or sails for up to eight people run from $1,100. *✉ Virgin Gorda Yacht Harbour, Lee Rd., Spanish Town ☎ 284/499–2479 🌐 www.doubled-bvi.com.*

Jost Van Dyke

Named after an early Dutch settler, Jost Van Dyke is a small island northwest of Tortola. It's also a place to *truly* get away from it all. Mountainous and lush, the 4-mile-long (6½-km-long) island—with fewer than 200 full-time residents—has a few small hotels, some rental houses and villas, a campground, a couple of shops, a handful of cars, and a single road. There are no banks or ATMs on the island, and some restaurants and shops accept only cash. It's a good idea to buy groceries on St. Thomas or Tortola before arriving if you're staying for a few days. Life definitely rolls along on "island time," especially during the off-season from August to November, when finding a restaurant open for dinner can be a challenge. Water conservation is encouraged, as the source is rainwater collected in cisterns. Many lodgings will ask you to follow the Caribbean golden rule: "In the land of sun and fun, we never flush for number one." Jost is one of the Caribbean's most popular anchorages, and there are a disproportionately large number of informal bars and restaurants, which have helped earn Jost its reputation as the "party island" of the BVI.

Beaches

★ Great Harbour Beach

BEACH | FAMILY | Great Harbour has an authentic Caribbean feel that's not just for tourists. Small bars and restaurants line the sandy strip of beach that serves as the community's main street. While the island's main settlement may not have the unspoiled natural beauty of some popular beaches, it holds a quaint charm. There are a few areas suited to swimming, with calm, shallow water perfect for children; however, the attraction here is more about the beach scene than the actual beach. Ali Baba and SeaCrest Inn have rooms on the bay. Bring your bug spray for sand flies in the early evenings. **Amenities:** food and drink; toilets. **Best for:** walking; swimming. ✉ *Great Harbour.*

Sandy Cay

BEACH | Just offshore, the little islet known as Sandy Cay is a gleaming sliver of white sand with marvelous snorkeling and an inland nature trail. Previously part of the private estate of the late philanthropist and conservationist Laurance Rockefeller, the Cay is now a protected area. You can hire any boatman on Jost Van Dyke to take you out; just be sure to agree on a price and a time to be picked up again. Jost Van Dyke Scuba also runs snorkel trips to the island. As this is a national park, visitors are asked to "take only photos and leave only footprints." Nevertheless, it's become an increasingly popular location for weddings, which require approval from the BVI National Parks Trust. Experienced boaters can rent a boat or dinghy to go here, but be aware that winter swells can make beach landings treacherous. **Amenities:** none. **Best for:** snorkeling; swimming; walking.

★ White Bay Beach

BEACH | FAMILY | On the south shore of Jost Van Dyke and the "next bay over" from Great Harbour, this long stretch of picturesque white sand is especially popular with boaters who come ashore for a libation at one of the many beach bars that offer refuge from the sun. Despite the sometimes rowdy bar scene, the beach is large enough to find a quiet spot, particularly late in the day when most of the day-trippers disappear and the beach becomes serene. There are a few small hotels with rooms just behind the beach or a short walk uphill. Swimmers and snorkelers should be cautious of boat traffic in the anchorage. **Amenities:** food and drink; toilets. **Best for:** partiers; swimming; walking. ✉ *White Bay.*

Restaurants

Restaurants on Jost Van Dyke are informal (some serve meals family-style at long tables) and often charming. The island is a favorite charter-boat stop, and you're bound to hear people exchanging stories about the previous night's anchoring adventures. Most restaurants don't take reservations (but for those that do, they are usually required, especially for dinner and most especially in the offseason). In all cases, dress is casual.

Abe's by the Sea

$$$$ | ECLECTIC | Many sailors who cruise into this quiet bay come so they can dock right at this open-air eatery to enjoy the conch, lobster, and other fresh catches, always with peas and rice and coleslaw on the side. Chicken and ribs round out the menu, and affable owners Abe Coakley and his wife, Eunicy, add a pinch of hospitality that makes a meal into a memorable evening. **Known for:** warm hospitality; fresh seafood; outdoor dining. $ *Average main: $40* ✉ *Little Harbour* ☎ *284/541–1087, 284/496–8429* ✎ *abesbythesea@hotmail.com.*

Boats line the shores of Jost Van Dyke.

Ali Baba's

$$$ | **SEAFOOD** | Lobster is the main attraction at this beach bar with a sandy floor, which is just some 20 feet from the sea. Grilled local fish—including swordfish, kingfish, and wahoo—are caught fresh daily, and the BabaQ ribs are the house specialty. **Known for:** potent rum punch; chicken roti; barbecue ribs. *Average main: $30 Great Harbour 284/495–9280 www.alibabasrestaurantandbarbvi.com No credit cards.*

Coco Loco's Beach Bar Restaurant

$$ | **ECLECTIC** | Sign your name on the wall and then sit down for pizza, tacos, burgers, or local treats like conch fritters or roti at this unassuming beach bar on White Bay. The drinks selection includes a heady Uncle Wendell's Rum Punch, in addition to the usual Bushwackers and Painkillers (the latter can be made in the traditional fashion or in a vanilla version). **Known for:** laid-back vibe; stone-oven pizza; strong cocktails. *Average main: $16 White Bay 284/546-2967.*

Cool Breeze Sports Bar & Restaurant

$$$ | **BARBECUE** | This brightly colored eatery with a pool table and big-screen TVs for watching sports is frequented by locals and visitors. Expect a range of dinner options, including fresh grilled lobster, barbecue chicken and ribs, and vegetarian dishes. **Known for:** live sports on TV; local scene; Caribbean-style barbecue. *Average main: $29 Great Harbour 284/440–0302, 284/496–0855 www.coolbreezejvd.com No credit cards.*

★ Foxy's Taboo

$$ | **MEDITERRANEAN** | **FAMILY** | It's well worth the winding, hilly drive or sometimes rough sail to get to Taboo, where there's a sophisticated menu and friendly staff with a welcoming attitude. Kebabs, hummus, and veggie-stuffed pitas stand alongside eggplant cheesecake on the Mediterranean-inspired menu. **Known for:** friendly staff; Mediterranean fare with flair; scenic views. *Average main: $15 East End 284/442–3074 www.foxysbvi.com.*

Foxy's Tamarind Bar and Restaurant
$$$ | **ECLECTIC** | **FAMILY** | The big draw here is the owner, Foxy Callwood, a famed calypso singer who will serenade you with funny songs as you fork into grilled chicken, burgers, barbecue ribs, and lobster. Check out the pennants, postcards, and weathered T-shirts that adorn every inch of the walls and ceiling of this large, two-story beach bar; they've been left by previous visitors who are mostly either day-trippers from elsewhere in the Virgin Islands or yacht owners. **Known for:** happy hour and locally brewed beer; Foxy, a Virgin Islands icon; live music and performances. *Average main: $35* ✉ *Great Harbour* ☎ *284/442–3074* 🌐 *foxysbar.com.*

Gertrude's Beach Bar and Restaurant
$$ | **BURGER** | A casual bar and West Indian restaurant right on White Bay Beach, Gertrude's makes guests feel at home with burgers, conch fritters, and rotis. Ask the bartender to mix you a drink, or you can pour your own. **Known for:** conch fritters and burgers; beachfront setting; giant Adirondack chair. *Average main: $20* ✉ *White Bay* ☎ *284/495–9104.*

Harris' Place
$$$$ | **ECLECTIC** | **FAMILY** | Owner Cynthia Harris is as famous for her friendliness as she is for her food. Lobster in a garlic butter sauce, and other freshly caught seafood, as well as pork, chicken, and ribs, are on the menu. **Known for:** housemade key lime pie; fresh seafood; live music. *Average main: $45* ✉ *Little Harbour* ☎ *284/344–8816* 🌐 *www.harrisplacejvd.com* ⏲ *Closed Tues.*

★ **Hendo's Hideout**
$$$ | **AMERICAN** | **FAMILY** | This upscale but family-friendly beach bar at White Bay beach features a handsome wood bar, lounge area, and hammocks nestled in among the palm trees, making you feel as if you're at a small resort. The pulled pork tacos are excellent, and bottomless mimosas are served with Sunday brunch. **Known for:** lobster ravioli; beachside dining; family-friendly atmosphere. *Average main: $30* ✉ *White Bay* ☎ *284/340–0074* 🌐 *www.hendoshideout.com* ⏲ *No dinner Mon.–Tues.*

Ivan's Stress Free Bar
$$$$ | **CARIBBEAN** | There's not much stress at any time in the BVI (hurricane season excepted), but Ivan's Stress Free Punch takes "liming" to an even more chill level. Tamarind wings put a local twist on the appetizer menu, and the Wednesday night barbecue offers a choice of ribs, chicken, fresh fish, conch, and lobster. **Known for:** quiet spot on the beach; strong punch; Wednesday-night barbecues. *Average main: $35* ✉ *White Bay* ☎ *284/513–1095.*

Seddy's One Love Bar and Grill
$$$ | **ECLECTIC** | Top dishes at this beachfront eatery include seafood freshly caught by owner Seddy, who also may come to your table and perform magic tricks. Local lobster finds its way into nachos and quesadillas, and the Food Network's Alton Brown once sought out this beachfront eatery and featured its stewed conch on a flavor-finding trip. **Known for:** year-round Christmas tree out front; beachy decor; Bushwacker cocktails. *Average main: $28* ✉ *White Bay* ☎ *937/470–8523* 🌐 *www.seddysonelovebarandgrill.com.*

★ **Soggy Dollar Bar**
$$ | **CARIBBEAN** | Caribbean-style, casual beach fare rules at this must-stop destination for BVI boaters, whose habit of wading ashore for a drink gives the bar its distinctive name. Don't miss the Painkiller cocktail, the semi-official drink of the BVI, invented here. **Known for:** wading ashore from your boat—that's where the name comes from; the Painkiller cocktail was invented here; lively beach party. *Average main: $15* ✉ *White Bay* ☎ *284/495–9888* 🌐 *www.soggydollar.com.*

Sydney's Peace and Love
$$$$ | **CARIBBEAN** | At this open-air terrace eatery on the water's edge, you can find great local lobster and fish, as well as barbecue chicken and ribs with all the fixings, including peas and rice, corn, coleslaw, and potato salad. A popular pig roast happens on Monday and Saturday nights. **Known for:** jukebox; local flair; fresh lobster. *Average main: $35 ✉ Little Harbour ☎ 284/344–2160.*

The Tipsy Shark
$$ | **CARIBBEAN** | The roof deck at this Great Harbour restaurant is so perfect it makes you wonder why it's the first one that any eatery on the beach has built. The elevated view of yachts bobbing on mooring balls is lovely day or night, and brother-sister owners Renee and Randy Singh sprinkle Guyanese and South Asian cooking influences on the catch of the day, which can be topped with a Creole, caper, or coconut cream sauce. **Known for:** friendly service; cocktails made with house-produced sugar cane; curry and Creole dishes. *Average main: $14 ✉ Little Harbour ☎ 284/343–6866.*

Hotels

Ali Baba's Heavenly Rooms
$ | **B&B/INN** | Just above Ali Baba's restaurant, owner Wayson "Baba" Hatchett offers seven simple but attractive rooms—three renovated after the 2017 hurricane, the other four brand-new—steps from the beach, each equipped with queen beds, air-conditioning, a private bath, and a porch with water views. **Pros:** private bath; convenient location; air-conditioning. **Cons:** basic decor; small; noisy area of Great Harbour. *Rooms from: $130 ✉ Great Harbour ☎ 284/495–9280 🌐 www.alibabasrestaurantandbarbvi.com 7 rooms No Meals.*

Ivan's Stress Free Guest House
$ | **B&B/INN** | It's a bit of an uphill climb to get to Ivan Chinnery's simple but comfortable guesthouses, but you'll appreciate the distance on nights when the beach party gets rocking down on the shore, including at Ivan's Stress Free Bar. Three of the four rooms have kitchens; all have air-conditioning, TVs, and private baths. **Pros:** kitchen units; close to beach; affordable rates. **Cons:** limited amenties; basic decor; uphill walk to room. *Rooms from: $55 ✉ White Bay ☎ 340/513–1095, 284/547–3375 🌐 www.ivansstressfreeguesthouse.com 7 units No Meals.*

Perfect Pineapple Guest Houses
$ | **B&B/INN** | One-bedroom suites, as well as one- and two-bedroom guesthouses, all come equipped with private bath, air-conditioning, stove, satellite TV, and refrigerator. **Pros:** owner's taxi service can get you around the island; steps from popular White Bay beach; friendly owners. **Cons:** no restaurant; in need of updating; basic furnishings. *Rooms from: $170 ✉ White Bay ☎ 340/514–0713, 284/543–3815 🌐 www.perfectpineapple.com 6 rooms No Meals.*

★ White Bay Villas and Seaside Cottages
$$$ | **HOTEL** | **FAMILY** | Beautiful views and friendly staff keep guests coming back to these hilltop one- to three-bedroom villas and cottages, the nicest accommodations on the island. **Pros:** friendly staff; incredible views; full kitchens. **Cons:** steep access roads; rental car recommended; 10- to 15-minute walk to White Bay and Great Harbour's restaurants and beaches. *Rooms from: $389 ✉ White Bay ☎ 340/201–4976, 284/541–1900, 800/778–8066 🌐 www.jostvandyke.com 20 units No Meals.*

Nightlife

Jost Van Dyke is the most happening place to go bar-hopping in the BVI, so much so that it is an all-day enterprise for some. In fact, yachties will sail over just to have a few drinks. All the spots are easy to find, clustered in three general locations: Great Harbour, White Bay, and

Little Harbour. On the Great Harbour side you can find Foxy's, Corsairs (which had been closed during the pandemic as of this writing), and Ali Baba's; on the White Bay side are the One Love Bar and Grill, Hendo's Hideout, and the Soggy Dollar Bar, where legend has it the famous Painkiller was first concocted; and in Little Harbour are Harris' Place, Sydney's Peace and Love, and Abe's by the Sea. Foxy's Taboo has Diamond Cay—home to Jost's famous Bubbly Pool—all to itself, but just across the shallow bay is the B-Line, the most off-the-beaten path beach bar on the island. If you can't make it to Jost Van Dyke, you can have a Painkiller at almost any bar in the BVI. Once the sun goes down the atmosphere cools considerably, but the beat goes on at Foxy's.

Activities

JVD Scuba and BVI Eco-Tours

SCUBA DIVING | Check out the undersea world around the island with dive master Colin Aldridge. One of the most impressive dives in the area is off the north coast of Little Jost Van Dyke. Here you can find the Twin Towers: a pair of rock formations rising an impressive 90 feet. A one-tank dive costs $90, a two-tank dive $135, and a four-hour beginner course is $150 plus the cost of equipment. Colin and crew also offer trips to Sandy Cay and Sandy Spit, Norman Island, Virgin Gorda (The Baths), and other dive sites in the northwest British Virgin Islands. You can also rent snorkel equipment, dive gear, stand-up paddleboards, and kayaks here. ✉ *Great Harbour* ☎ *284/443–2222, 757/287–2731 U.S. phone* 🌐 *jostvandyke-scuba.com.*

Ocean Spa

SPAS | When life gives you hurricanes, turn the debris into a spa. That's what Jost Van Dyke resident Dale Mapp did following 2017's Hurricane Irma, salvaging various pieces of flotsam and jetsam and turning them into a floating spa permanently anchored in the waters of White Bay. The spa has two treatment rooms with sections of see-through flooring and windows open to allow in cooling breezes. Services include a variety of massages, including a romantic moonlight couples treatment followed by champagne. ✉ *White Bay* ☎ *284/341–3782* 🌐 *www.theoceanspabvi.com.*

Paradise Jeep Rentals

FOUR-WHEELING | This reliable company offers the ideal vehicles to tackle Jost Van Dyke's steep, winding roads. Even though Jost is a relatively small island, you really need to be in shape to walk from one bay to the next. This outfit rents two-door Suzuki Jimmys for $65 per day, four-door Grand Vitaras for $75, and eight-seat Kia Mojaves for $90. Discounts are available for rentals of six or more days. It's next to the fire station in Great Harbour. Reservations are a must. ✉ *Great Harbour* ☎ *284/547–1040.*

Anegada

Anegada lies low on the horizon about 14 miles (22½ km) north of Virgin Gorda. Unlike the hilly volcanic islands typical elsewhere in the BVI, Anegada is a flat coral-and-limestone atoll. Nine miles (14 km) long and 2 miles (3 km) wide, the island rises no more than 28 feet above sea level. In fact, by the time you're able to see it, you may have run your boat onto a reef. (More than 300 captains unfamiliar with the waters have done so since exploration days.) Although the reefs are a sailor's nightmare, they—and the shipwrecks they've caused—are a scuba diver's dream. Snorkeling, especially in the waters around Loblolly Bay on the North Shore, is a transcendent experience. You can float in shallow, calm water just a few feet from shore and see one coral formation after another, each shimmering with a rainbow of colorful fish. Many local captains are happy to take visitors out fishing for bonefish.

Such watery pleasures are complemented by ever-so-fine, ever-so-white sand (the northern and western shores have long stretches of the stuff) and the occasional beach bar (stop in for burgers, local lobster, or a frosty beer). The island's 300 or so people live primarily in a small south-side village called the Settlement, which has two grocery stores, a bakery, and a general store.

TIP→ Note that the island has no banks or ATMs, and that many restaurants and shops take only cash.

Sights

Conch Shell Mounds

BEACH | The vanished indigenous residents of Anegada left their mark on the low-lying island by creating piles of thousands of conch shells that remain visible today. More modern fisherman also have created large piles of pink, sun-bleached conch shells in the shallow emerald waters off the island's southeast tip, creating an artificial island that can be visited (in combination with snorkeling and a look at Anegada's resident flamingos, which tend to congregate in nearby waters) on a tour with Kelly's Land and Sea Tours. ✉ *East End* ☎ *284/496–0961* *kelvin.faulkner91@gmail.com* *$40 for two-hour snorkeling visit with Kelly's.*

Faulkner House Museum

HISTORIC HOME | Theodolph Halburn Faulkner, a native of tiny Anegada, played an outsized role in winning freedom and democracy for the people of the British Virgin Islands, leading a 1949 march of more than 1,500 people to Road Town to demand a constitution and legislative representation. Faulkner's modest home in The Settlement—the first built of concrete on the island—is preserved as a museum detailing this history and offering a window into life on Anegada as it was in the middle of the previous century. ✉ *The Settlement* ☎ *284/499–1496* *Free* *Closed weekends.*

Restaurants

★ Anegada Reef Hotel Restaurant

$$$$ | SEAFOOD | Seasoned yachties gather here nightly to share tales of the high seas; the open-air bar is the busiest on the island. Dinner is by candlelight under the stars and always includes famous Anegada lobster, steaks, and succulent baby back ribs—all prepared on a large grill by a little open-air bar. **Known for:** open-air bar; grilled lobster; fun atmosphere. *Average main: $38* ✉ *Setting Point* ☎ *284/495–8002* *www.anegada-reef.com.*

Big Bamboo

$$$ | SEAFOOD | FAMILY | This beachfront bar and restaurant tucked among seagrape trees at famous Loblolly Bay is the island's most popular destination for lunch. After you've polished off a plate of succulent Anegada lobster, barbecue chicken, or fresh fish, you can spend the afternoon on the beach, where the snorkeling is excellent and the view close to perfection, or browsing through the gift shop. **Known for:** frozen drinks; spectacular beach; free shuttle from ferry. *Average main: $22* ✉ *Loblolly Bay* ☎ *284/499–1680, 284/344–6251* *www.bigbambooanegada.com.*

★ Neptune's Treasure

$$$$ | SEAFOOD | FAMILY | The owners, the Soares family, have lived on the island for more than half a century, and catch, cook, and serve the seafood at this homey bar and restaurant a short distance from Setting Point. The fresh lobster, swordfish, tuna, and mahimahi are all delicious. **Known for:** locally harvested seafood; authentic local feel; fresh baked goods. *Average main: $32* ✉ *Pomato Point* ☎ *284/345–5436* *www.neptunestreasure.com.*

Potter's By the Sea

$$$$ | SEAFOOD | Friendly staff and a lively atmosphere just a few steps from the dock complement freshly grilled lobster and other seafood selections such as

Anegada's vanished indigenous residents left behind conch shell mounds.

snapper and grouper. Potter's also offers a beach shuttle, free Wi-Fi, moorings and a dingy dock, and live music (ask about the schedule when you call ahead for dinner reservations). **Known for:** local seafood; local vibe; waterfront dining. *Average main: $50 ✉ Setting Point ☎ 284/341–9769 🌐 pottersanegada.com.*

Sid's Pomato Point Restaurant

$$$ | **SEAFOOD** | This relaxed restaurant and bar sits on one of the best beaches on the island and enjoys Anegada's most dramatic sunset views. Entrées include tacos, ribs, steaks, and freshly caught seafood, including local lobster and conch. **Known for:** beautiful beach location; historic artifacts on display; sunset views. *Average main: $30 ✉ Pomato Point ☎ 284/441–5565.*

Tipsy Beach Bar

$$$$ | **SEAFOOD** | Anegada Ann, the owner of the bright and cheery Ann's Guest Houses, runs this bar on the beach named for the cow bones that once washed up on shore. This wiggle-your-toes-in-the-sand eatery on the northern shore is a fun place to watch the antics of surfers and kiteboarders skidding across the bay, while tucking into stewed conch, curried lobster, or quesadillas and tacos. **Known for:** bright and friendly atmosphere; snorkeling on-site; beach vibes. *Average main: $36 ✉ Cow Wreck Bay ☎ 284/440–4149, 954/516–8957 🌐 www.cowwreckbeachbvi.com.*

★ The Wonky Dog

$$$$ | **SEAFOOD** | The laid-back, low-key vibe of this Setting Point bar and restaurant is infectious. Lobster served on a seaside rooftop pairs with draft beer and craft cocktails, but the menu is surprisingly diverse, offering everything from braised lamb shanks to cauliflower steak. **Known for:** lobster; friendly atmosphere; live music. *Average main: $59 ✉ Setting Point ☎ 284/547–0539, 284/441–0539, 284/344–1265 🌐 www.thewonkydog.com.*

Hotels

Anegada Beach Club

$ | **RESORT** | This is a laid-back beach club setting with well-equipped hotel rooms and luxury "palapa retreats" overlooking the dunes. **Pros:** plenty of outdoor activities; option to adjoin king and junior suites is handy for families; bar and restaurant on-site. **Cons:** small pool; pricey; remote location. *Rooms from: $235* *Keel Point* *284/346–4005* *www.anegadabeachclub.com* *23 units* *No Meals.*

Anegada Reef Hotel

$ | **HOTEL** | Head here if you want to bunk in comfortable lodging near Anegada's most popular anchorage; this venerable hotel, a destination for more than 40 years, still feels like the nerve center for the island. **Pros:** rents cars and arranges tours; everything you need is nearby; nice sunsets. **Cons:** often a party atmosphere at the bar; no beach; simple rooms. *Rooms from: $195* *Setting Point* *284/495–8002* *www.anegadareef.com* *20 rooms* *No Meals.*

Ann's Guest Houses at Cow Wreck Beach

$ | **B&B/INN** | Brightly painted, furnished one- or two-bedroom villas with full kitchens are within steps of Cow Wreck Beach and the Tipsy beach bar and restaurant, which has equally vivid sun shelters and picnic tables. **Pros:** fun restaurant; secluded location; great snorkeling. **Cons:** need a car to get around, but vehicle-rental service is available; location too remote for some; the island's free-roaming livestock sometimes leave "presents" behind. *Rooms from: $200* *Cow Wreck Bay* *284/440–4149, 954/516–8957* *www.cowwreckbeachbvi.com* *7 units* *No Meals.*

Neptune's Treasure

$ | **B&B/INN** | **FAMILY** | Basic waterfront rooms with simple furnishings and lovely views of the ocean are the hallmark of this family-owned guesthouse. **Pros:** good restaurant; waterfront property with nice sunset views; run by a family full of tales of the island. **Cons:** no pool; narrow beach; simple rooms. *Rooms from: $150* *Pomato Point* *284/345–5436* *www.neptunestreasure.com* *10 rooms* *No Meals.*

Activities

Danny's Bonefishing

FISHING | Danny Vanterpool offers half-, three-quarter-, and full-day bonefishing excursions around Anegada. The cost is $400 for a half day (four hours) and $600 for a three-quarter-day (six hour) fishing trip for up to two people. Meet the boat at Setting Point. *Setting Point* *284/441–6334, 284/344–1226* *www.dannysbonefishing.com.*

Mini Moke Rentals

FISHING | Anegada's calm weather, compact size, and gentle terrain make it perfect for exploring by open-topped vehicle. This company based at the Anegada Reef Hotel will rent you a Jeep-like Mini Moke that you can motor around in for the day in search of hidden beaches and friendly bars. *Anegada Reef Hotel, Setting Point* *284/441–0799, 284/495–8002* *www.anegadareef.com.*

Cooper Island

This small, hilly island on the south side of the Sir Francis Drake Channel, about 8 miles (13 km) from Road Town, Tortola, is popular with the charter-boat crowd. There are no paved roads (which doesn't really matter, as there aren't any cars), but you can find a beach restaurant, rum bar, brewery, coffee shop, a casual hotel, a few houses (some are available for rent), and great snorkeling at the south end of Manchioneel Bay.

Hotels

★ Cooper Island Beach Club

$ | **RESORT** | Relaxation is the focus at this small resort, but folks who want to simply swim, snorkel, or chill on the beach can also feel right at home in eight comfortable rooms with attractive recycled furniture, tile floors, and lovely sea views. **Pros:** excellent brewery and rum bar; laid-back vibe; easy access to diving, snorkeling, and other water sports. **Cons:** minimal nightlife; island beyond the resort is not accessible; rooms have no air-conditioning. *Rooms from: $265* ✉ *Manchioneel Bay* ☎ *284/543–2266, 800/542–4624* 🌐 *www.cooperisland-beachclub.com* *8 rooms* *Free Breakfast.*

Guana Island

Guana Island sits off Tortola's northeast coast. Sailors often drop anchor at one of the private island's bays for a day of snorkeling and sunning. The island is a designated wildlife sanctuary, and scientists often come here to study its flora and fauna. It's home to a back-to-nature resort that offers few activities other than relaxation. Unless you're a hotel guest or a sailor, there's no easy way to get here.

Hotels

★ Guana Island Resort

$$$$ | **RESORT** | This charming resort is perfect for those wanting to hike, snorkel, swim, and relax at the beach in comfort. **Pros:** good for nature lovers; secluded feel; lovely grounds. **Cons:** minimal nightlife; no TVs or radios in rooms; very expensive. *Rooms from: $890* ☎ *800/544–8262* 🌐 *www.guana.com* *21 rooms* *All-Inclusive.*

Norman Island

This uninhabited island is the supposed setting for Robert Louis Stevenson's *Treasure Island.* The famed caves at Treasure Point are popular with day sailors and powerboaters. If you land ashore at the island's main anchorage, you can find the casual Pirate's Bight Bar & Restaurant and The Club for fine dining. Behind the buildings is a trail that winds up the hillside and reaches a peak with a fantastic view of the Sir Francis Drake Channel to the north. The island boasts nearly 12 miles (20 km) of hiking trails. Call Pirate's Bight for information on ferry service to accommodate day-trippers.

Restaurants

Pirate's Bight

$$$$ | **SEAFOOD** | This breezy, open-air dining establishment boasts quirky beach-bar eccentricities (a cannon is fired at sunset and bar partrons play games like "Giant Jenga"), all while maintaining a slightly refined feeling. The owners offer ferry service from Hannah Bay on Tortola, giving the restaurant the feel of a casual day resort, with resort prices for the food to match. **Known for:** live entertainment; beach club setting; fun atmosphere. *Average main: $39* ✉ *The Bight* ☎ *284/443–1305* 🌐 *www.pirates-bight.com.*

Willy T

$$ | **ECLECTIC** | *Willy T* is a floating bar and restaurant that's anchored in Pirate's Bight. The current boat is new; its predecessor, sunk in 2017's Hurricane Irma, lies nearby at the bottom of the Bight and is now a dive site, complete with skeleton crew. **Known for:** party atmosphere; conch fritters; West Indian roti. *Average main: $18* ☎ *284/340-8603 for boaters, use VHF Channels 16/74* 🌐 *willy-t.com.*

Chapter 9

CAYMAN ISLANDS

Updated by
Sara Liss

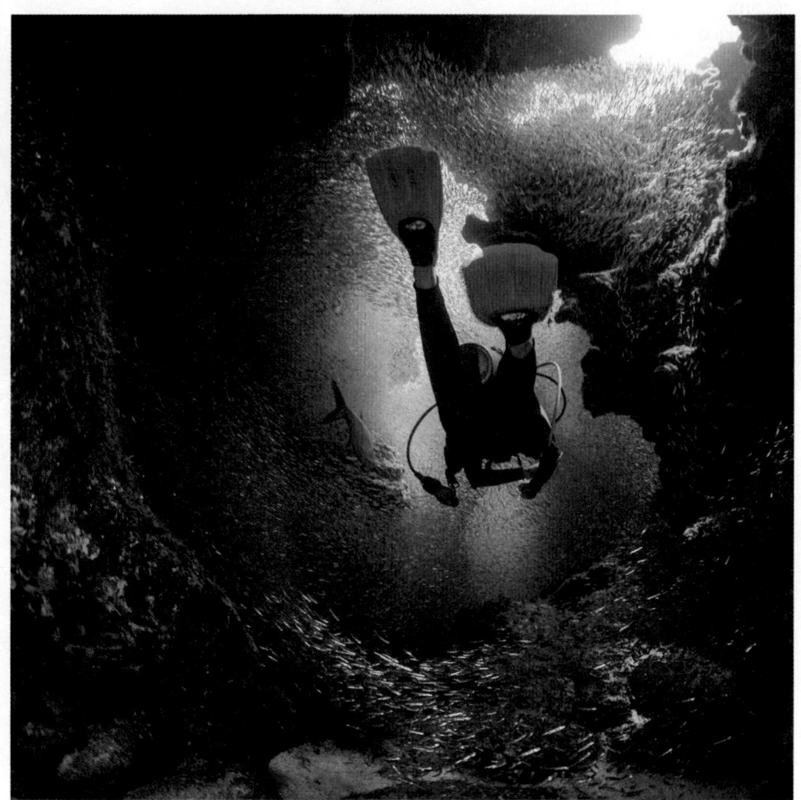

Sights	Restaurants	Hotels	Shopping	Nightlife
★★★★★	★★★★☆	★★★☆☆	★★★☆☆	★★☆☆☆

WELCOME TO CAYMAN ISLANDS

TOP REASONS TO GO

★ **Diving:** Underwater visibility is among the best in the Caribbean, and nearby reefs are healthy.

★ **Safety and Comfort:** With no panhandlers, little crime, and top-notch accommodations, it's an easy place to vacation.

★ **Dining Scene:** The cosmopolitan population extends to the varied dining scene, from Italian to Indian.

★ **Fabulous Snorkeling:** A snorkeling trip to Stingray City is an experience you'll always remember.

★ **Beaches:** Grand Cayman's Seven Mile Beach is one of the Caribbean's best sandy beaches.

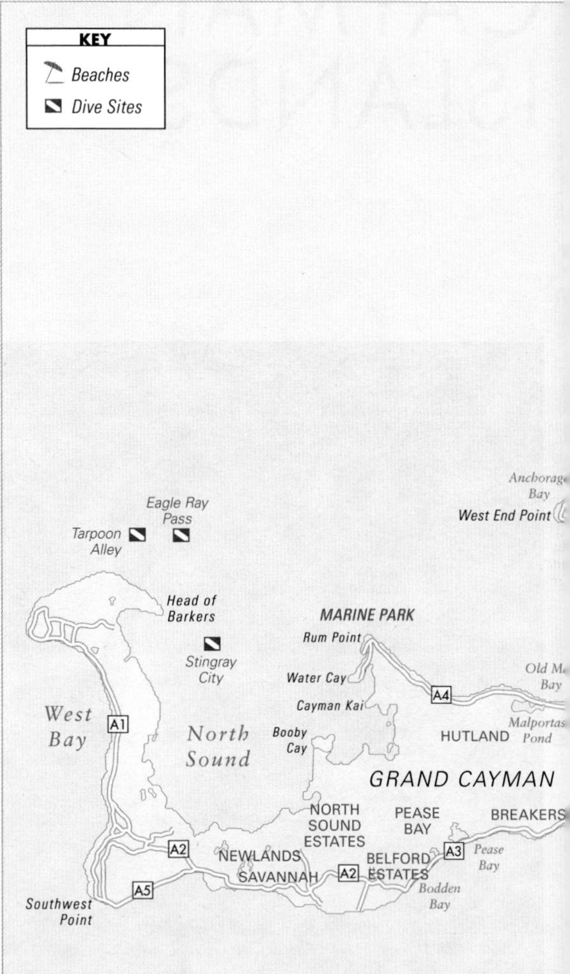

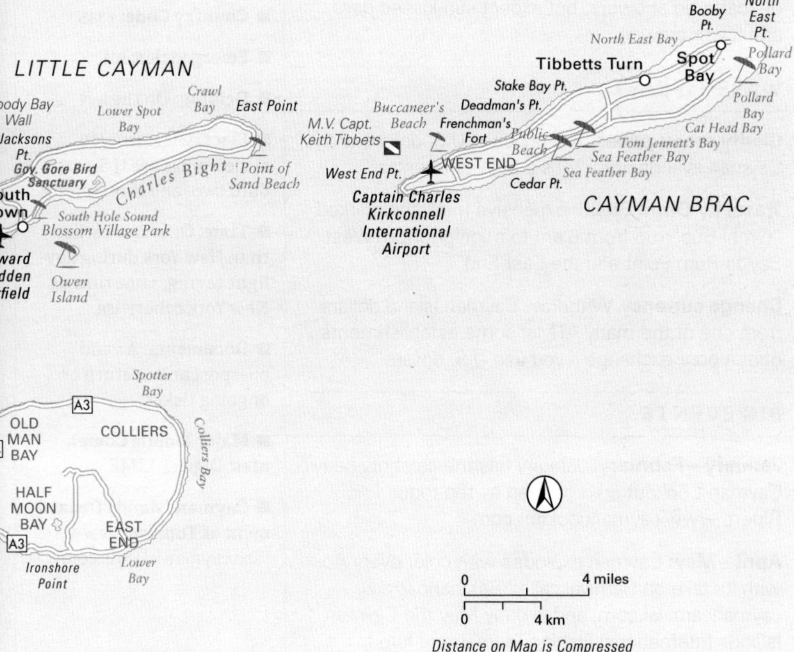
Caribbean Sea
LITTLE CAYMAN
Crawl Bay
East Point
Lower Spot Bay
Jacksons Pt.
Gov. Gore Bird Sanctuary
Charles Bight
Point of Sand Beach
South Hole Sound
Blossom Village Park
Owen Island
Buccaneer's Beach
M.V. Capt. Keith Tibbets
Frenchman's Fort
Deadman's Pt.
Stake Bay Pt.
Tibbetts Turn
North East Bay
Booby Pt.
North East Pt.
Spot Bay
Pollard Bay
Pollard Bay
Cat Head Bay
Tom Jennett's Bay
Sea Feather Bay
Sea Feather Bay
Public Beach
WEST END
West End Pt.
Cedar Pt.
Captain Charles Kirkconnell International Airport
CAYMAN BRAC
Spotter Bay
A3
OLD MAN BAY
COLLIERS
Colliers Bay
HALF MOON BAY
EAST END
A3
Ironshore Point
Lower Bay
0
4 miles
0
4 km
Distance on Map is Compressed
Scale is Approximate
Caribbean Sea

ISLAND SNAPSHOT

WHEN TO GO

High Season: Mid-December through mid-April is the most popular, and most expensive, time to visit. Good hotels book up, so plan ahead.

Low Season: From August to late October, temperatures get hot and the weather muggy, with high risks of tropical storms. Many upscale hotels close for annual renovations or offer deep discounts.

Value Season: From late April to July and again November to mid-December, hotel prices drop 20% to 50% from high-season prices. There are chances of scattered showers, but expect sun-kissed days and fewer crowds.

WAYS TO SAVE

Clarify menu prices. Are prices in U.S. dollars or the Cayman Islands dollar? It's a 25% difference.

Travel by Omni Bus. Inexpensive minivans marked "Omni Bus" run from 6 am to midnight from West Bay to Rum Point and the East End.

Change currency. Withdraw Cayman Island dollars from one of the many ATMs; some establishments offer a poor exchange if you use U.S. dollars.

BIG EVENTS

January—February: January has the celebrity-heavy Cayman Cookout co-organized by top toque Eric Ripert. www.caymancookout.com

April—May: Cayman explodes with color every April with its take on Carnival called Batabano www.caymancarnival.com, and in early May the Cayman Islands International Fishing Tournament lures anglers from around the world. www.fishcayman.com

November: Pirates Week Festival is a massive 11-day party, featuring parades, costume competitions, street dances, fireworks, and more. www.piratesweekfestival.com

AT A GLANCE

- **Capital:** George Town
- **Population:** 65,700
- **Currency:** Cayman Islands dollar
- **Money:** ATMs common; credit cards accepted in most places on Grand Cayman
- **Language:** English
- **Country Code:** 1 345
- **Emergencies:** 911
- **Driving:** On the left
- **Electricity:** 120v/60 cycles; plugs are U.S. standard two- and three-prong
- **Time:** One hour earlier than New York during daylight saving; same time as New York otherwise
- **Documents:** A valid passport and a return or ongoing ticket
- **Major Mobile Companies:** Digicel, LIME
- **Cayman Islands Department of Tourism:** www.visitcaymanislands.com

This British Overseas Territory, which consists of Grand Cayman, smaller Cayman Brac, and Little Cayman, is one of the Caribbean's most popular destinations, particularly among Americans, who have become homeowners and constant visitors. The island's extensive array of banks also draws travelers from around the globe.

Columbus is said to have sighted the islands in 1503 and dubbed them *"Las Tortugas"* after seeing so many turtles in the sea. The name was later changed to Cayman, referring to the caiman crocodiles that once roamed the islands. The Cayman Islands remained largely uninhabited until the late 1600s, when England seized them and Jamaica from Spain. Emigrants from England, Holland, Spain, and France arrived, as did refugees from the Spanish Inquisition and deserters from Oliver Cromwell's army in Jamaica; many brought enslaved people with them as well. The Cayman Islands' caves and coves were also perfect hideouts for the likes of Blackbeard, Sir Henry Morgan, and other pirates out to plunder Spanish galleons. Many ships fell afoul of the reefs surrounding the islands, often with the help of Caymanians, who lured vessels to shore with beacon fires.

Today's Cayman Islands are seasoned with suburban prosperity (particularly Grand Cayman) and stuffed with crowds (the hotels that line the famed Seven Mile Beach are often full, even in the slow summer season). Most Cayman Islanders live on Grand Cayman, where the cost of living is at least 20% higher than in the United States, but the crime rate is very low. Add political and economic stability to the mix, and you have a fine island recipe indeed.

Planning

Getting Here and Around

AIR

Grand Cayman's Owen Roberts International Airport completed a $67 million expansion in 2019, roughly tripling the size of the airport facilities. You can fly nonstop to Grand Cayman from Atlanta (Delta), Charlotte (American Airlines daily), Chicago (United), Denver (Cayman Airways), Fort Lauderdale (JetBlue, Southwest), Houston (United), Miami (American, Cayman Airways), New York–JFK (Cayman Airways, JetBlue), Newark (United), Philadelphia (American Airlines), Tampa (Cayman Airways), and Washington, D.C. (United).

Almost all nonstop air service is to Grand Cayman, with connecting flights on Cayman Airways Express to Cayman Brac and Little Cayman on a small propeller plane; there's also interisland charter-only service on Island Air. Once-weekly nonstops on Cayman Airways link Miami with Cayman Brac.

AIRLINE CONTACTS American Airlines. ☎ *345/949–0666* 🌐 *www.aa.com.* **Cayman Airways.** ☎ *345/949–2311* 🌐 *www.caymanairways.com.* **Delta.** ☎ *345/945–8430* 🌐 *www.delta.com.* **Island Air.** ✉ *100 Roberts Dr., George Town* ☎ *345/949–5252* 🌐 *www.islandair.ky.*

AIRPORTS Edward Bodden Airfield. (*LYB*) ✉ *Guy Banks Rd., Blossom Village* ☎ *345/948–0021* 🌐 *www.caymanairports.com.* **Sir Captain Charles Kirkconnell International Airport.** (*CYB*) ✉ *Church Cl, West End.* **Owen Roberts International Airport.** (*GCM*) ✉ *298 Owen Roberts* ☎ *345/943–7070* 🌐 *www.caymanairports.com.*

BIKE AND SCOOTER

When renting a motor scooter or bicycle, remember to drive on the left and wear sunblock and a helmet. Bicycles ($15 a day) and scooters ($35 to $40 a day) can be rented in George Town. On Cayman Brac or Little Cayman your hotel can make arrangements (most offer complimentary bicycles for local sightseeing).

CONTACTS Scooten! Scooters!. ✉ *Blossom Village* ☎ *345/916–4971* 🌐 *www.scootenscooters.com.*

BUS

On Grand Cayman, bus service—consisting of minivans marked "Omni Bus"—is efficient, inexpensive, and plentiful, running from 6 am to midnight (depending on route) roughly every 15 minutes in the Seven Mile Beach area and George Town, with fares from CI$1.50 to CI$3.

CONTACTS Bus Information Hotline. ☎ *345/945–5100* 🌐 *thebusschedule.com/EN/ky.*

CAR

Driving is easy on Grand Cayman, but there can be considerable traffic, especially during rush hour. One major road circumnavigates most of the island. Driving is on the left, British-style, and there are roundabouts. Speed limits are 30 mph (50 kph) in the country, 20 mph (30 kph) in town. There's much less traffic on Cayman Brac and even less on Little Cayman. Gas is expensive.

Car Rentals: You'll need a valid driver's license and a credit card to rent a car. Most agencies require renters to be between 21 and 70, though some require you to be 25. If you are over 75, you must have a certified doctor's note attesting to your ability. A local driver's permit, which costs $20, is obtained through the rental agencies, many of which offer complimentary pickup and drop-off along Seven Mile Beach. Rates can be expensive (from $45 to $95 per day), but usually include insurance.

CAR RENTAL CONTACTS (GRAND CAYMAN) Hertz Cayman. ☎ *800/654–3131, 345/943–4378 toll-free, 345/943–4378* 🌐 *www.hertzcayman.com.* **Andy's Rent a Car.** ☎ *345/949–8111, 345/949–8111 toll-free* 🌐 *www.andys.ky.* **Avis.** ✉ *George Town* ☎ *345/949–2468* 🌐 *www.aviscayman.com.* **Budget.** ✉ *George Town* ☎ *345/949–5605* 🌐 *www.budgetcayman.com.* **Cayman Auto Rentals.** ✉ *N. Church St., George Town* ☎ *345/949–1013* 🌐 *www.caymanautorentals.com.ky.* **Thrifty Car Rental.** ☎ *345/949–4790,* 🌐 *www.thrifty.com.*

CAR RENTAL CONTACTS (CAYMAN BRAC) B&S Motor Ventures. ✉ *126 Channel Rd.* ⊕ *Within walking distance of Cayman Brac Beach Resort, Brac Caribbean Beach Villas, and Carib Sands* ☎ *345/948–1646* 🌐 *www.bandsmv.com.* **CB Rent-a-Car.** ✉ *West End Rd.* ☎ *345/948–2424* 🌐 *www.cbrent-a-car.com.* **Four D's Car Rental.** ✉ *Kidco Bldg., Bert Marson Dr.* ☎ *345/948–1599, 345/948–0459.*

CAR RENTAL CONTACTS (LITTLE CAYMAN) Little Cayman Car Rentals. ✉ *898 Guy Banks Rd., Blossom Village* ☎ *345/948–1000* ✎ *rentals@littlecaymancarrentals.com* 🌐 *www.littlecaymancarrentals.com.*

TAXI

On Grand Cayman, taxis operate 24 hours a day; if you anticipate a late night, however, make pickup arrangements in advance. You generally cannot hail a taxi on the street except occasionally in George Town. Fares are metered, and are not cheap, but basic fares include as many as three passengers. Taxis are scarcer on the Sister Islands; rates are fixed and fairly prohibitive. Your hotel can recommend drivers.

Beaches

Limestone, coral, shells, water, and wind collaborated to fashion the Cayman Islands beaches. It's a classic example of the interaction between geology and marine biology. Most of the beaches in Cayman, especially on Grand and Little Cayman, resemble powdered ivory. A few, including those on Cayman Brac, are more dramatic, a mix of fine beige sand and rugged rocky "ironshore," which often signals the healthiest reefs and best snorkeling.

Health and Safety

Dengue, chikungunya, and zika have all been reported throughout the Caribbean at one time. Though they're not widespread, we still recommend that you protect yourself from these mosquito-borne illnesses by keeping your skin covered and/or wearing mosquito repellent.

Hotels and Resorts

You'll find no big all-inclusive resorts on Grand Cayman (though the Reef Resort offers an optional all-inclusive plan to its guests), which draws the bulk of Cayman Island visitors. Very few hotels offer a meal plan other than breakfast. Parking is always free at island hotels and resorts. Although the island has several resorts (mostly along Seven Mile Beach), the majority of accommodations are vacation rentals, and these are scattered throughout the island. Some of the condo complexes even offer resort-style amenities. Most resorts are on or near Seven Mile Beach, but a few are north in the West Bay Area, near Rum Point, or on the quiet East End. They may be some distance from the beach and short on style and facilities, but the island's guesthouses offer rock-bottom prices and clean simple rooms.

Both Little Cayman and Cayman Brac are more geared toward serving the needs of divers, who make up the majority of visitors. Beaches on the Sister Islands, as they are called, don't measure up (literally) to Grand Cayman's Seven Mile Beach. The smaller islands are cheaper than Grand Cayman, but with the extra cost of transportation, the overall savings are minimized.

Resorts: Grand Cayman has plenty of medium-size resorts. Little Cayman has a mix of small resorts and condos, most appealing to divers.

Condos and Villas: Grand Cayman has a wide range of condos and villas, many in resortlike compounds on or near Seven Mile Beach and the Cayman Kai area. There are even a few small guesthouses for budget-minded visitors. Cayman Brac has mostly intimate resorts and family-run inns.

Hotel reviews have been shortened. For full information, visit Fodors.com.

CONTACTS Cayman Island Vacations. ☎ *813/854–1201, 888/208–8935* 🌐 *www.caymanvacation.com.* **Cayman Villas.** ✉ *177 Owen Roberts Dr., George Town* ☎ *800/235–5888, 345/945–4144* 🌐 *www.caymanvillas.com.* **Grand Cayman Villas.** ✉ *846 Frank Sound Rd., George Town* ☎ *866/358–8455, 345/946–9524* 🌐 *www.grandcaymanvillas.net.* **Wimco.** ☎ *888/997–3970, 800/449–1553* 🌐 *www.wimco.com.*

What It Costs in U.S. Dollars

	$	$$	$$$	$$$$
RESTAURANTS	under $12	$12–$20	$21–$30	over $30
HOTELS	under $275	$275–$375	$376–$475	over $475

Nightlife

Grand Cayman nightlife is surprisingly good for such a quiet-seeming island. Check the Friday edition of the *Caymanian Compass* for listings of music, movies, theater, and other entertainment. Bars are open during evening hours until 1 am, and clubs are generally open from 10 pm until 3 am, but none may serve liquor after midnight on Saturday and none can offer dancing on Sunday. Competition is fierce between Grand Cayman's many bars and restaurants. In addition to entertainment (fish feeding to fire eating), even upscale joints host happy hours offering free hors d'oeuvres and/or drinks.

Restaurants

Despite its small size, comparative geographic isolation, and British colonial trappings, Grand Cayman offers a smorgasbord of gastronomic goodies. With more than 100 eateries, something should suit and sate every palate and pocketbook (factoring in the fast-food franchises sweeping the islandscape like tumbleweed, and stands dispensing local specialties). The term *melting pot* describes both the majority of menus.

Prices are about 25% more than those in a major U.S. city. Many restaurants add a 10% to 15% service charge to the bill; be sure to check before leaving a tip. Alcohol with your meal can send the tab skyrocketing. Buy liquor duty-free before you leave the airport and enjoy a cocktail or nightcap from the comfort of your room or balcony. Cayman customs limits you to two bottles per person. You should make reservations at all but the most casual places, particularly during the high season. Note that many bars offer fine fare (and many eateries have hip, hopping bar scenes).

What to Wear: Grand Cayman dining is casual (shorts are okay, but *not* beachwear and tank tops). Mosquitoes can be pesky when you're dining outdoors, especially at sunset, so plan ahead or ask for repellent. Winter can be chilly enough to warrant a light sweater.

Shopping

On Grand Cayman the good news is that there's no sales tax *and* there's plenty of duty-free merchandise. Locally made items to watch for include woven mats, baskets, jewelry made of a marblelike stone called Caymanite (from the cliffs of Cayman Brac), and authentic sunken treasure, though the latter is never cheap. In addition, there are several noteworthy local artists, some of whose atelier–homes double as galleries, such as Al Ebanks, Horacio Esteban, and Luelan Bodden. Unique items include Cayman sea salt and luxury bath salts (solar harvested in an ecologically sensitive manner) and Tortuga rum and rum cakes. Seven Fathoms is the first working distillery actually in Cayman itself, its award-winning rums aged underwater (hence the name). Cigar lovers, take note: some shops carry famed Cuban brands, but you must enjoy them on the island; bringing them back to the United States is illegal.

Although you can find black-coral products in Grand Cayman, they're controversial. Most of the coral sold here comes from Belize and Honduras; Cayman Islands' marine law prohibits the removal of live coral from its own sea, so most of it has been taken illegally. Black coral grows at a very slow rate (3 inches every 10 years) and is an endangered species. Buy other products instead.

There are modern, U.S.-style supermarkets for groceries (some with full-service pharmacies) on Grand Cayman. The biggest difference you'll find between these and supermarkets on the mainland is in the prices, which are about 25% to 30% more than at home.

Visitor Information

CONTACTS Cayman Islands Department of Tourism. ✉ *George Town* ☎ *212/889–9009 in New York City, 877/422–9626 in U.S., 345/949–0623 in Cayman Islands* 🌐 *www.visitcaymanislands.com.*

Weddings

Getting married in the Cayman Islands is a breeze. Documentation can be prepared ahead of time or in one day while on the island. There's no on-island waiting period. Larger resorts have on-site wedding coordinators.

Grand Cayman—West Section

Grand Cayman has long been known for two offshore activities: banking and scuba diving. With 296 banks, the capital, George Town, is relatively modern and usually bustles with activity, but never more so than when two to seven cruise ships are docked in the harbor, an increasingly common occurrence. Accountants in business clothes join thousands of vacationers in their tropical togs, jostling for tables at lunch. When they're not mingling in the myriad shops or getting pampered and pummeled in spas, vacationers delve into sparkling waters to snorkel and dive; increasingly, couples come to be married, or at least to enjoy their honeymoon. There is a lot of traffic, so check with a local to plan driving time. It can take 45 minutes during rush hours to go 8 miles (13 km).

George Town

The historic capital of George Town, on the southwest corner of Grand Cayman, is easy to explore on foot. If you're a shopper, you can spend days here; otherwise, an hour will suffice for a tour of the downtown area. To see the rest of the island, rent a car or scooter or take a guided tour. The portion of the island called West Bay is noted for its jumble of neighborhoods and a few attractions. When traffic is heavy, it's about a half hour to West Bay from George Town, but the bypass road that runs parallel to West Bay Road has made the journey easier. The less-developed East End has natural attractions from blowholes to botanical gardens, as well as the remains of the island's original settlements. Plan at least 45 minutes for the drive out from George Town (more during rush hours). You need a day to explore the entire island—including a stop at a beach for a picnic or swim.

Sights

Begin exploring the capital by strolling along the waterfront Harbour Drive to **Elmslie Memorial United Church,** named after the first Presbyterian missionary to serve in Cayman. Its vaulted ceiling, wooden arches, and sedate nave reflect the religious nature of island residents. In front of the court building, in the center of town, names of influential Caymanians are inscribed on the **Wall of History,** which commemorates the islands' quincentennial in 2003. Across the street is the **Cayman Islands Legislative Assembly Building,** next door to the **1919 Peace Memorial Building.** In the middle of the financial district is the **General Post Office,** built in 1939. Let the kids pet the big blue iguana statues.

★ **Cayman Islands National Museum**

OTHER MUSEUM | FAMILY | Built in 1833, the historically significant clapboard home of the national museum has had several different incarnations over the years, serving as courthouse, jail, post office, and dance hall. It features an ongoing archaeological excavation of the Old Gaol and excellent 3-D bathymetric displays, murals, dioramas, and videos that illustrate local geology, flora and fauna, and island history. The first floor focuses on natural history, including a microcosm of Cayman ecosystems, from beaches to dry woodlands and swamps, and offers such interactive elements as a simulated sub. Upstairs, the cultural exhibit features renovated murals, video history reenactments, and 3-D back panels in display cases holding thousands of artifacts ranging from a 14-foot catboat with animatronic captain to old coins and rare documents. These paint a portrait of daily life and past industries, such as shipbuilding and turtling, and stress Caymanians' resilience when they had little contact with the outside world. There are also temporary exhibits focusing on aspects of Caymanian culture, a local art collection, and interactive displays for kids. ✉ *3 Harbour Dr., George Town* ☎ *345/949–8368* 🌐 *www.museum.ky* 🎫 *$8* 🕒 *Closed Sun.*

Cayman Spirits/Seven Fathoms Rum

DISTILLERY | Surprisingly, this growing company, established in 2008, is Cayman's first distillery. It's garnered medals in prestigious international competitions for its artisanal small-batch rums (and is now making a splash with its smooth Gun Bay vodka as well). You can stop by for a tasting and self-guided tour (a more intensive, extensive guided tour costs $15) to learn how the rum is aged at 7 fathoms (42 feet) deep; supposedly the natural motion of the currents maximizes the rum's contact with the oak, extracting its rich flavors and enhancing complexity. ✉ *68 Bronze Rd., George Town* ☎ *345/925–5379, 345/926–8186* 🌐 *www.caymanspirits.com.*

★ **National Gallery of the Cayman Islands**

ART MUSEUM | A worthy nonprofit, this museum displays and promotes Caymanian artists and craftspeople, both established and grassroots. The gallery coordinates first-rate outreach programs for everyone from infants to inmates. It usually mounts six major exhibitions a year, including three large-scale retrospectives or thematic shows, and multimedia installations. Director Natalie Urquhart also brings in international shows that somehow relate to the island, often inviting local artists for stimulating dialogue. The gallery hosts public slide shows, a lunchtime lecture series in conjunction with current exhibits, Art Flix (video presentations on art history, introduced with a short lecture and followed by a discussion led by curators or artists), and a CineClub (movie night). The gallery has also developed an Artist Trail Map with the Department of Tourism and can facilitate studio tours. There's an excellent shop and an Art Café. ✉ *Esterly Tibbetts Hwy. at Harquail Bypass, Seven Mile Beach* ☎ *345/945–8111* 🌐 *www.nationalgallery.org.ky* 🎫 *Free* 🕒 *Closed Sun.*

★ **National Trust for the Cayman Islands**

VISITOR CENTER | This office provides a map of historic and natural attractions, books and guides to Cayman, and information on its website about everything from iguanas to schoolhouses. The expanded gift shop provides one-stop souvenir shopping, from hair clips to logwood carvings to coconut soaps, all made on the island. Regularly scheduled activities range from boat tours through the forests of the Central Mangrove Wetlands, to cooking classes with local chefs, to morning walking tours of historic George Town. The office is walkable from George Town, but be aware that it's a 20-minute hike from downtown, often in the heat. ✉ *Dart Park, 558 S. Church St., George Town* ☎ *345/749–1121* 🌐 *www.nationaltrust.org.ky.*

Beaches

Smith's Cove

BEACH | South of the Grand Old House, this tiny but popular protected swimming and snorkeling spot makes a wonderful beach wedding location. The bottom drops off quickly enough to allow you to swim and play close to shore. Although slightly rocky (its pitted limestone boulders resemble Moore sculptures), there's little debris and few coral heads, plenty of shade, picnic tables, restrooms, and parking. Surfers will find decent swells just to the south. Note the curious obelisk cenotaph "In memory of James Samuel Webster and his wife Arabella Antoinette (née Eden)," with assorted quotes from Confucius to John Donne. **Amenities:** parking (no fee); toilets. **Best for:** snorkeling; sunset; swimming. ✉ *Off S. Church St., George Town.*

Spotts Beach

BEACH | On weekends families often barbecue at this idyllic spot caught between ironshore cliffs and a barrier reef (with fine snorkeling). You might even see some wild turtles swimming here. Follow South Church Street through South Sound past Red Bay; at a little cemetery there's a turnoff to the beach with a car park. **Amenities:** none. **Best for:** snorkeling; solitude; sunrise; walking. ✉ *Shamrock Rd., Spotts, George Town* ✣ *1 mile east of East-West Arterial Rd. intersection.*

Restaurants

★ The Brasserie

$$$ | **ECLECTIC** | Actuaries, bankers, and CEOs frequent this contemporary throwback to a colonial country club for lunch and "attitude adjustment" happy hours for creative cocktails and complimentary canapés. Inviting fusion farm/sea-to-table cuisine, emphasizing local ingredients whenever possible (the restaurant has its own boat and garden), includes terrific bar tapas. **Known for:** power-broker hangout; locavore's delight; creative small plates. [$] *Average main: $29* ✉ *171 Elgin Ave., Cricket Sq., George Town* ☎ *345/945–1815* 🌐 *www.brasseriecayman.com* ⏲ *Closed weekends.*

Casanova Restaurant by the Sea

$$$ | **ITALIAN** | Owner Tony Crescente and younger brother, maitre d' Carlo, offer a simpatico dining experience, practically exhorting you to *mangia* and sending you off with a chorus of ciaos. There's some decorative *formaggio* (cheese): murals of grape clusters and cavorting cherubs, paintings of the Amalfi Coast, and *una finestra sul mare* ("window to the sea") stenciled redundantly over arches opening onto the harbor. **Known for:** particularly fine sauces; sensational harbor views; simpatico service. [$] *Average main: $30* ✉ *65 N. Church St., George Town* ☎ *345/949–7633* 🌐 *www.casanova.ky.*

Champion House II

$$ | **CARIBBEAN** | Ads trumpet that this restaurant overlooking a garden with a cheery tropical motif is "where the islanders dine"; indeed they have since the Robinson family started selling takeout from its kitchen in 1965. The West Indies breakfast, themed lunch, and Taste of Cayman dinner buffets are legendary spreads. **Known for:** traditional local and Asian dishes; lavish buffets; varied menu. [$] *Average main: $20* ✉ *43 Eastern Ave., George Town* ☎ *345/949–7882, 345/916–5736* 🌐 *www.championhouse.ky* ⏲ *Closed Sat. No dinner Sun.*

Da Fish Shack

$$$ | **SEAFOOD** | This classic clapboard seaside shanty couldn't be homier: constructed from an old fishing vessel, the structure is an authentic representation of original Caymanian architecture. The deck is perfectly placed to savor the breezes and water views, and the chill Caribbean vibe makes it feel as if you're having the freshest seafood at a friend's home. **Known for:** mellow ambience; terrific harbor views; delectable fish tacos. [$] *Average main: $25* ✉ *127 N. Church St., George Town* ☎ *345/947–8126.*

★ Grand Old House

$$$$ | EUROPEAN | Built in 1908 as the Petra Plantation House and transformed into the island's first upscale establishment decades ago, this grande dame evokes bygone grandeur sans pretension. Outside, hundreds of sparkling lights adorning the gazebos compete with the starry sky. **Known for:** classic continental fare with island twists; elegant historic setting; comparatively affordable waterside tapas bar. *Average main: $48* *648 S. Church St., George Town* *345/949–9333* *www.grandoldhouse.com* *Closed Sept. and Sun. in low season. No lunch weekends.*

Guy Harvey's Boathouse Grill

$$$$ | SEAFOOD | This stylish upstairs bistro has mahogany furnishings, ship's lanterns, porthole windows, fishing rods, and Harvey's action-packed marine art. Seasonally changing dishes are peppered with Caribbean influences and the seafood is carefully chosen to exclude overexploited and threatened species. **Known for:** luscious lobster bisque; affordable nightly specials; terrific tapas. *Average main: $40* *Aquaworld Duty-Free Mall, 66 S. Church St., George Town* *345/946-9000* *boathousecayman.com.*

Lobster Pot

$$$$ | SEAFOOD | The nondescript building belies the lovely marine-motif decor and luscious seafood at this second-story restaurant overlooking the harbor. Enjoy lobster prepared several ways (all à la sticker shock) along with reasonably priced wine, which you can sample by the glass in the cozy bar. **Known for:** predictably fine lobster, especially the Friday special lobster burger; scintillating harbor views; strong selection of wines by the glass. *Average main: $53* *245 N. Church St., George Town* *345/949–2736* *www.lobsterpot.ky* *No lunch weekends.*

MacDonald's

$ | CARIBBEAN | One of the locals' favorite burger joints—not a fast-food outlet—MacDonald's does a brisk lunch business in stick-to-your ribs basics like rotisserie chicken and escoveitch fish. The decor features yellows and pinks, with appetizing posters of food and a large cartoon chicken mounted on the wall—all an afterthought, really, to the politicos, housewives in curlers, and gossipmongers. **Known for:** juicy rotisserie chicken; popular islander hangout; perennial local pick for best burger. *Average main: $11* *99 Shedden Rd., George Town* *345/949–4640* *www.facebook.com/macdonaldscayman.*

Coffee and Quick Bites

Coffee Point Cayman

$ | ECLECTIC | FAMILY | On the surprisingly large, eclectic Asian-tinged menu using ultrafresh ingredients, standouts include homemade carrot cake, mango smoothies, cranberry-Brie-pecan salad, and rosemary-roasted portobello and pesto chicken panini. The espresso martini will perk up anyone wanting a pick-me-up. **Known for:** colorful local art; creative beverages (alcoholic and non); delectable sandwiches. *Average main: $10* *Pasadora Pl. at Smith Rd., George Town* *345/946–1956, 345/814–0157* *coffeepoint.ky.*

Hotels

Sunset House

$$ | HOTEL | This amiable seaside dive-oriented resort is on the ironshore south of George Town, close enough for a short trip to stores and restaurants yet far enough to feel secluded. **Pros:** fun international clientele; great shore diving and dive shop; lively bar scene. **Cons:** no real swimming beach; spotty Wi-Fi signal; five-night minimum stay required in high season. *Rooms from: $319* *390 S. Church St., George Town*

345/949–7111, 800/854–4767 www.sunsethouse.com 36 units Free Breakfast 5-night minimum in winter.

BARS AND MUSIC CLUBS

Cayman Cabana

BARS | The popular restaurant and bar, adorned with wild murals, fab old-timer photos, and surfboards doubling as signs, offers a classic Cayman sight: fishers anchor their boats right offshore and display their catch right outside (condo and villa renters, head here if you're in the market for fresh fish). The capable kitchen specializes in classic Caymanian cuisine; farm-to-table Thursdays are justifiably popular. This is also a prime pyrotechnic sunset- and cruise ship-watching spot, where locals laze in locally carved chairs, sipping house microbrews on the vast thatch-shaded, tiered deck. Stop by the Swanky Shack by the entrance for souvenir T-shirts and island gossip. *N. Church St., George Town 345/949–3080, 345/938–1345 www.caymancabanarestaurant.com.*

Hard Rock Café

THEMED ENTERTAINMENT | Grand Cayman's Hard Rock replicates its 137-odd brethren around the world, especially on the weekends, only with more specialty drinks (try the Orangelicious margarita with Monin pomegranate and blood-orange juices) to complement its extensive burger selection. A 1960 pink Cadillac, a Madonna bullet bra, and rotating memorabilia (gold records, costumes, guitars, and autographed photos from Elton John, Korn, John Lennon, U2, and *NSYNC) are the decor. *43 S. Church St., George Town 345/947–2020 www.hardrock.com.*

My Bar

BARS | Perched on the water's edge, this bar has great sunset views. The leviathan open-sided cabana is drenched in Rasta colors and crowned by an intricate South Seas–style thatched roof with about 36,000 palm fronds. Christmas lights and the occasional customer dangle from the rafters. They offer great grub, and the crowd is a mischievous mix of locals, expats, and tourists. *Sunset House, S. Church St., George Town 345/949–7111 www.sunsethouse.com.*

The Office Lounge

BARS | This is indeed a preferred hangout for the diverse after-work crowd, which packs both the cozy club space (adorned with customers' ties) and breezy patio, absorbing the high-octane cocktails and nightly musical mix (from country to salsa, karaoke to live bands). Happy hours are joyous indeed with CI$5 martini specials. It's invariably lively—a favorite spot for birthday, office, and bachelor and bachelorette parties and a prime place to eavesdrop on local gossip. *99 Shedden Rd., George Town 345/945–5212 www.facebook.com/theofficeloungecayman.*

Rackam's Waterfront Pub and Restaurant

BARS | Both fishermen and financiers savor sensational sunsets and joyous happy hours, then watch tarpon feeding at this open-air, marine-theme bar on a jetty. Boaters and snorkelers, before and after checking out the wreck of *The Cali*, cruise up the ladder for drinks, while anglers leave their catch on ice. There's complimentary snacks on Friday and pub fare at fair prices until midnight. *93 N. Church St., George Town 345/945–3860 www.rackams.com.*

★ **South West Collective**

BARS | A celebration of all things mixology, South West Collective occupies a prime second-floor spot with a patio and enormous picture windows overlooking the harbor. The convivial hangout offers board games, live music on Friday (and DJs spinning genuine vinyl), and a trendy but unpretentious ambience. The pub fare comes at fair prices, whether lunch or such bar bites as smoked oyster dip goosed with lemon and capers or spiced beef patties with rum barbecue sauce.

But the drinks are the thing, from loose-leaf teas to global artisan beers, house-made sangria or kombucha smoothies to craft cocktails (as well as the house moonshine). ✉ *Harbour Place, S. Church St., Level 2, George Town* ☎ *345/946–3004* 🌐 *www.southwestcollectivecayman.com* ⏲ *Closed Sun.*

Performing Arts

Harquail Theatre

ARTS CENTERS | This state-of-the-art facility seats 330 for theatrical performances, concerts, dance recitals, fashion shows, beauty pageants, art exhibits, and poetry readings sponsored by the Cayman National Cultural Foundation. ✉ *17 Harquail Dr., Seven Mile Beach* ☎ *345/949–5477* 🌐 *www.artscayman.org/harquail-theatre.*

Shopping

ART GALLERIES

Artifacts

ART GALLERIES | On the George Town waterfront, Artifacts sells Spanish pieces of eight, doubloons, and Halcyon Days enamels (hand-painted collectible pillboxes made in England), as well as antique maps and other collectibles. ✉ *Cayside Courtyard, Harbour Dr., George Town* ☎ *345/949–2442* 🌐 *www.artifacts.com.ky.*

Cathy Church's Underwater Photo Centre and Gallery

ART GALLERIES | The store has a collection of the acclaimed underwater shutterbug's spectacular color and limited-edition black-and-white underwater photos as well as the latest marine camera equipment. Cathy will autograph her latest coffee-table book, talk about her globe-trotting adventures, and schedule private underwater photography instruction on her dive boat, with graphics-oriented computers to critique your work. She also does wedding photography, above and underwater. ✉ *390 S. Church St., George Town* ☎ *345/949–7415* 🌐 *www.cathychurch.com.*

★ **Guy Harvey's Gallery and Shoppe**

ART GALLERIES | World-renowned marine biologist, conservationist, and artist Guy Harvey showcases his aquatic-inspired, action-packed art in every conceivable medium, from tableware to sportswear (even logo soccer balls and Zippos). The soaring, two-story 4,000-square-foot space is almost more theme park than store, with monitors playing sport-fishing videos, wood floors inlaid with tile duplicating rippling water, dangling catboats "attacked" by shark models, and life-size murals honoring such classics as Hemingway's *The Old Man and the Sea.* Original paintings, sculpture, and drawings are expensive, but there's something (tile art, prints, lithographs, and photos) in most price ranges. ✉ *49 S. Church St., George Town* ☎ *345/943–4891* 🌐 *www.guyharvey.com* ⏲ *Closed Sun.*

Pure Art

ART GALLERIES | About 1½ miles (2½ km) south of George Town, Pure Art purveys wit, warmth, and whimsy from the wildly colored front steps. Its warren of rooms resembles a garage sale run amok or a quirky grandmother's attic spilling over with unexpected finds, from foodstuffs to functional and wearable art. ✉ *S. Church St. and Denham-Thompson Way, George Town* ☎ *345/949–9133* 🌐 *www.pureart.ky.*

CIGARS

Given Cayman's proximity to Cuba, the tempting panatelas and robustos are readily available at reasonable prices. They are no longer considered contraband in the United States.

Churchill's Cigars

TOBACCO | A statue points the way into this tobacco emporium, which sells the island's largest selection of authentic Cubanos (and other imports), including such names as Upmann, Romeo y Julieta, and Cohiba, displayed in the dark, clubby surroundings. The enthusiastic staff will advise on drink pairings (bold older rum for a Montecristo No. 2, cognac for smaller Partagas Shorts, a single-malt scotch such as Glenmorangie for the Bolivar Belicoso Fino). There's a small airport branch as well. ✉ *Island Plaza, Harbour Dr., George Town* ☎ *345/945–6141* 🌐 *www.churchillscigarscayman.com.*

CLOTHING

Blue Wave

MIXED CLOTHING | Blue Wave and Waterman surf and clothing shops have same owners (Waterman is in Seven Mile Beach). At the George Town shop you'll find brands like Billabong, Quicksilver, and Olukai, plus essentials like sandals, sunglasses, and surfboards. ✉ *10 Shedden Rd., George Town* ☎ *345/949–8166* 🌐 *www.watermancayman.ky.*

FOODSTUFFS

Hurley's Marketplace

MARKET | Hurley's is open Monday–Saturday 7 am–11 pm. It's well-known for its hot take-out dinner specials. ✉ *Grand Harbour Shopping Centre, 1053 Crewe Rd., Red Bay Estate* ☎ *345/947–8488* 🌐 *www.hurleys.ky.*

Kirk Supermarket and Pharmacy

MARKET | This store is open Monday–Saturday 6:30 am–9:30 pm and is a particularly good source for traditional Caymanian fast food (oxtail, curried goat) and beverages at the juice bar. It also carries the largest selection of organic and special dietary products; the pharmacy (Monday–Saturday 8 am–9 pm) stocks homeopathic and herbal remedies. ✉ *413 Eastern Ave., near intersection with West Bay Rd., George Town* ☎ *345/949–7022* 🌐 *www.kirkmarket.ky* ⏲ *Closed Sun.*

Tortuga Rum Company

FOOD | This company bakes, then vacuum-seals more than 10,000 of its world-famous rum cakes daily, adhering to the original, "secret" century-old recipe. There are eight flavors, from banana to Blue Mountain coffee, as well as several varieties of candy, from taffy to truffles. The 12-year-old rum, blended from private stock though actually distilled in Guyana, is a connoisseur's delight for after-dinner sipping. You can buy a fresh rum cake at the airport on the way home at the same prices as at the factory store. ✉ *Industrial Park, N. Sound Rd., George Town* ☎ *345/943–7663* 🌐 *www.tortugarumcakes.com.*

JEWELRY

Although you can find black-coral products in Grand Cayman, they're controversial. Most of the coral sold here comes from Belize and Honduras; Cayman Islands' marine law prohibits the removal of live coral from its own sea. Black coral grows at a glacial rate (3 inches per decade) and is an endangered species. Cayman, however, is famed for artisans working with the material; shops are recommended, but let your conscience dictate your purchases.

Island Jewellers

JEWELRY & WATCHES | Locals appreciate Island Jewellers for its affordable line of watches, especially top-notch Swiss brands, from Movado to Marvin to Maurice Lacroix, and selection of stunning diamonds and jewelry. There's another branch with similar inventory in the Flagship Building. ✉ *Island Plaza, Cardinal Ave., George Town* ☎ *345/946–2333* 🌐 *www.islandjewellers.com.*

Magnum Jewelers

JEWELRY & WATCHES | Befitting its name, Magnum Jewelers traffics in high-caliber pieces by the elite likes of Girard-Perregeaux and Harry Winston for a high-powered clientele. A talented team source distinctive contemporary watches and bijoux (especially increasingly rare colored diamonds) for their equally glittery celebrity clientele, who appreciate a bargain like the rest of us. Smaller spenders might appreciate whimsical items such as pendants with hand-painted enamel sandals or crystal-encrusted purses. ✉ *Cardinal Plaza, Cardinal Ave., George Town* ☎ *345/946–9199* 🌐 *www.magnumjewelers.com.*

MALLS AND SHOPPING CENTERS

Bayshore Mall

MALL | Optimally located downtown and one of the leading shopaholics' targets (you can't miss the cotton-candy colors), this mall contains a Kirk Freeport department-store branch (Tag Heuer to Herend porcelain, Mikimoto to Mont Blanc), swank Lalique and Lladró boutiques, La Parfumerie (which often offers makeovers and carries 450 beauty brands), and other usual luxury culprits. ✉ *S. Church St., George Town.*

Cayside Courtyard

SHOPPING CENTER | This small courtyard shopping center is noted for its specialty jewelers and antiques dealers. ✉ *Harbour Dr., George Town.*

Duty Free Plaza

MALL | This mall caters to more casual shoppers with the T-shirt Factory, Island Treasures, Havana Cigars, Blackbeard's Rumcake Bakery, and the Surf Shop. It also contains a kid-pleasing 12,000-gallon saltwater aquarium with sharks, eels, and stingrays. ✉ *S. Church St., George Town.*

Island Plaza

SHOPPING CENTER | Here you'll find 15 duty- and tax-free stores, including Swarovski Boutique, Island Jewellers, and Churchill's Cigars (with bars like Margaritaville to de-stress in after binge shopping). ✉ *Harbour Dr., George Town.*

Kirk Freeport Plaza

SHOPPING CENTER | This downtown shopping center, home to the Kirk Freeport flagship department store, is ground zero for couture; it's also known for its boutiques selling fine watches and jewelry, china, crystal, leather, perfumes, and cosmetics, from Baccarat to Bulgari, Raymond Weil to Waterford and Wedgwood (the last two share their own autonomous boutique). Just keep walking—there's plenty of eye-catching, mind-boggling consumerism in all directions: Boucheron, Cartier (with its own miniboutique), Chanel, Clinique, Christian Dior, Clarins, Estée Lauder, Fendi, Guerlain, Lancôme, Yves Saint Laurent, Issey Miyake, Jean Paul Gaultier, Nina Ricci, Rolex, Rosenthal and Royal Doulton china, and more. ✉ *Cardinal Ave., George Town.*

Landmark

SHOPPING CENTER | Stores in the Landmark sell perfumes, treasure coins, and upscale beachwear; Breezes Bistro restaurant is upstairs. ✉ *Harbour Dr., George Town.*

West Bay

Sights

Cayman Turtle Centre

AQUARIUM | **FAMILY** | Cayman's premier attraction has been transformed into a marine theme park with souvenir shops and restaurants. The turtles remain a central attraction, and you can tour ponds in the original breeding and research facility with thousands in various stages of growth, some up to 600 pounds and more than 70 years old. Four areas—three aquatic and one dry—cover 23 acres; different-color bracelets determine access (the steep all-area admission includes snorkeling gear and waterslides). The park helps promote conservation, encouraging interaction (a tidal pool houses invertebrates such as starfish and crabs) and observation. Animal Program events include Keeper Talks, where you might feed birds or iguanas, and biologists' conservation programs. The freshwater **Breaker's Lagoon,** replete with cascades plunging over moss-carpeted rocks, evokes Cayman Brac. The saltwater **Boatswain's Lagoon,** replicating all the Cayman Islands and the Trench, teems with 14,000 denizens of the deep milling about a cannily designed synthetic reef. (You can snorkel here—lessons and guided tours are available.) Both lagoons have

Grand Cayman's Seven Mile Beach is home to most of the island's restaurants, resorts, and shopping centers.

underwater 4-inch-thick acrylic panels that look directly into **Predator Reef,** home to six brown sharks, four nurse sharks, and other predatory fish such as tarpons, eels, and jacks, which can also be viewed from terra (or "terror," as one guide jokes) firma. Look for feeding times. The free-flight **Aviary**, designed by consultants from Disney's Animal Kingdom, is a riot of color and noise with feathered friends representing the entire Caribbean basin; it doubles as a rehabilitation center for Cayman Wildlife and Rescue. A winding interpretive nature trail culminates in the **Blue Hole**, a collapsed cave once filled with water. Audio tours are available with different focuses, from butterflies to bush medicine. The last stop is the living museum, **Cayman Street**, with facades duplicating vernacular architecture. ✉ *786 N.W. Point Rd., West Bay* ☎ *345/949–3894* 🌐 *www.turtle.ky* 🎫 *$45 all-access, $18 Turtle Farm only.*

Beaches

Barkers

BEACH | Secluded, spectacular beaches are accessed via a dirt road just past Papagallo restaurant. There are no facilities (that's the point!), but some palms offer shade. Unfortunately, the shallow water and rocky bottom discourage swimming, and it can be cluttered at times with seaweed and debris. You may also encounter wild chickens (their forebears released by owners fleeing Hurricane Ivan in 2004). Kitesurfers occasionally come here for the gusts; it's also popular for horseback riding. **Amenities:** none. **Best for:** solitude; walking; windsurfing. ✉ *Conch Point Rd., Barkers, West Bay.*

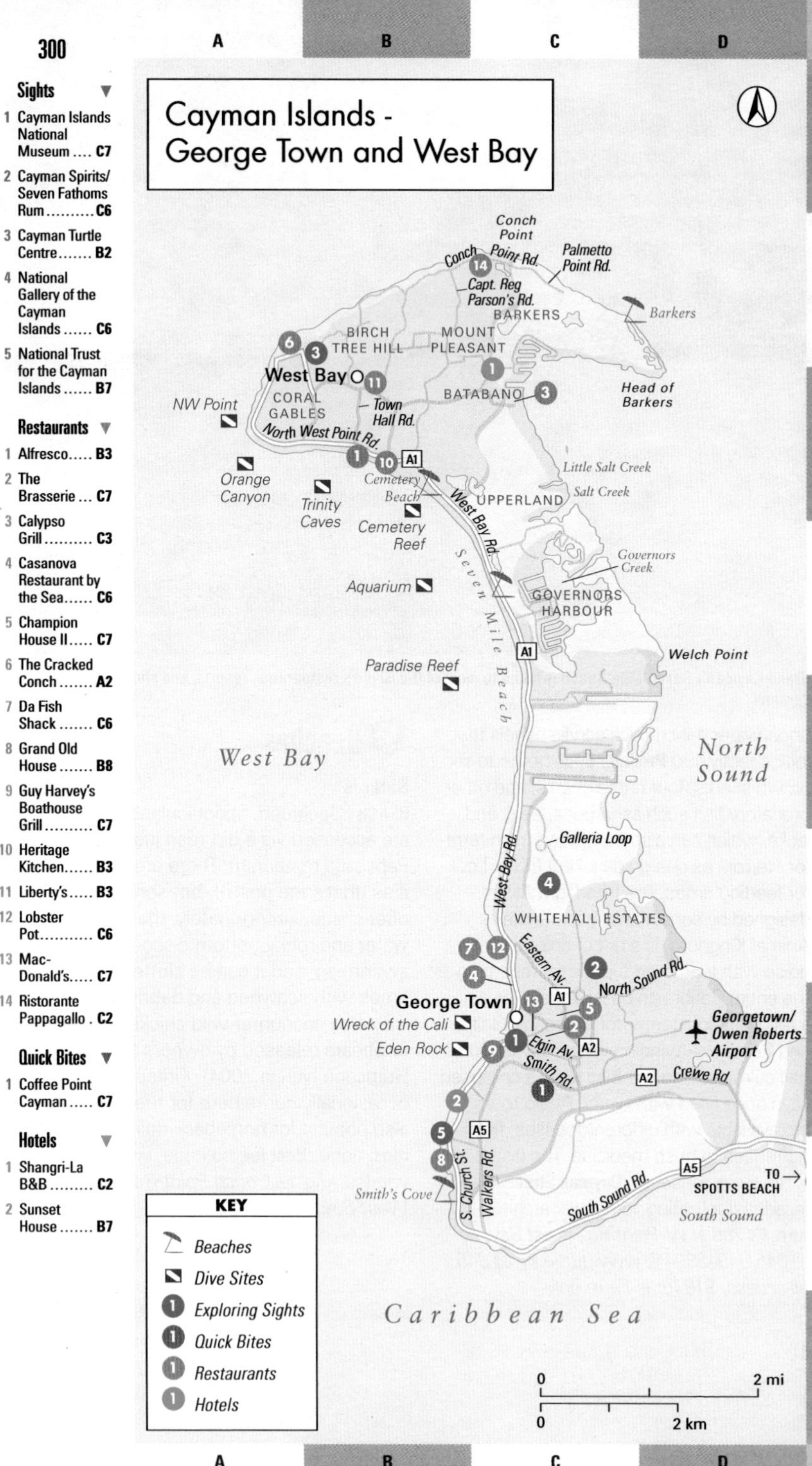
A
B
C
D
1
2
3
4
5
6
7
8
9
Sights
1 Cayman Islands National Museum C7
2 Cayman Spirits/ Seven Fathoms Rum C6
3 Cayman Turtle Centre B2
4 National Gallery of the Cayman Islands C6
5 National Trust for the Cayman Islands B7
Restaurants
1 Alfresco B3
2 The Brasserie ... C7
3 Calypso Grill C3
4 Casanova Restaurant by the Sea C6
5 Champion House II C7
6 The Cracked Conch A2
7 Da Fish Shack C6
8 Grand Old House B8
9 Guy Harvey's Boathouse Grill C7
10 Heritage Kitchen B3
11 Liberty's B3
12 Lobster Pot C6
13 Mac-Donald's C7
14 Ristorante Pappagallo . C2
Quick Bites
1 Coffee Point Cayman C7
Hotels
1 Shangri-La B&B C2
2 Sunset House B7
Cayman Islands - George Town and West Bay
Conch Point
Conch Point Rd.
Palmetto Point Rd.
Capt. Reg Parson's Rd.
BARKERS
Barkers
BIRCH TREE HILL
MOUNT PLEASANT
West Bay
CORAL GABLES
Town Hall Rd.
BATABANO
Head of Barkers
NW Point
North West Point Rd.
A1
Orange Canyon
Trinity Caves
Cemetery Beach
Cemetery Reef
West Bay Rd.
UPPERLAND
Little Salt Creek
Salt Creek
Governors Creek
GOVERNORS HARBOUR
Seven Mile Beach
Aquarium
Paradise Reef
Welch Point
West Bay
North Sound
Galleria Loop
WHITEHALL ESTATES
Eastern Av.
North Sound Rd.
George Town
Wreck of the Cali
Eden Rock
Elgin Av.
A2
Smith Rd.
Georgetown/ Owen Roberts Airport
Crewe Rd
A5
S. Church St.
Walkers Rd.
Smith's Cove
South Sound Rd.
TO → SPOTTS BEACH
South Sound
Caribbean Sea
KEY
Beaches
Dive Sites
Exploring Sights
Quick Bites
Restaurants
Hotels
0
2 mi
0
2 km

Restaurants

Alfresco

$$$ | **CARIBBEAN** | This popular locals' insider spot (though celeb sightings have run from Shaq to Sly Stallone), straddling the unofficial "border" between Seven Mile Beach and West Bay, resembles a little neighborhood diner transported to the ocean. Enjoy equally fresh sea breezes and food on the waterfront wood deck under one of the mismatched umbrellas. **Known for:** warm welcome; breezy patio overlooking Caribbean; delicious local food. *Average main: $25* *53 Town Hall Rd., West Bay* *345/947–2525* *www.alfrescobythesea.com.*

Calypso Grill

$$$$ | **ECLECTIC** | Shack-chic describes this inviting split-level eatery; the interior feels like a Caribbean painting, while the outdoor deck, with a view of frigate birds circling fishing boats, is a Winslow Homer. The menu emphasizes fish hauled in at the adjacent dock, fresh and rarely overcooked. **Known for:** superb seafood; wonderfully colorful decor; entrancing views of North Sound. *Average main: $44* *Morgan's Harbour, West Bay* *345/949–3948* *www.calypsogrillcayman.com* *Closed Mon.*

The Cracked Conch

$$$$ | **ECLECTIC** | This island institution effortlessly blends upscale and down-home as the capable chefs reinvent familiar dishes to create such delectables as crispy calamari with cardamom-marinated carrots, saffron aioli, chili jam, and chipotle sauce. The interior gleams from the elaborate light-and-water sculpture at the gorgeous mosaic-and-mahogany entrance Bubble Bar to the plush booths with subtly embedded lighting. **Known for:** sensational views; creative dishes fusing local ingredients and Continental classics; lively waterside bar section with specials. *Average main: $45* *857 N.W. Point Rd., West Bay* *345/945–5217* *www.crackedconch.com.ky/crackedconch* *Closed Sept. and Sun.–Mon.*

Heritage Kitchen

$$ | **CARIBBEAN** | West Bay's popular family-run restaurant serves up legendary raconteur Tunny Powell's fish tea, coconut grouper, barbecue ribs, and fish fry—with a generous portion of local lore and sterling sea views. The colorfully painted, gingerbread-trim lean-to is easy to miss from the main road, so look for it when you're in the area. Just go early because it's only open until 6 pm. **Known for:** lovely sea views; to-die-for Cayman classics such as fish tea; terrific place for island gossip and lore. *Average main: $15* *Heritage Sq., Just off Boggy Sand Rd., West Bay* *345/916–0444* *www.heritagekitchencayman.com* *Closed Mon. and Tues. No dinner.*

Liberty's

$$ | **CARIBBEAN** | Just follow the boisterous laughter and pulsating Caribbean tunes to this hard-to-find mint-green Caymanian cottage, where you feel like you've been invited to a family reunion. The Sunday Caribbean buffet attracts hordes of hungry church goers (call ahead to ensure they're open that week), but every day offers authentic turtle steak, oxtail, jerk, and delectable fried snapper with sassy salsas that liberate your taste buds from the humdrum. **Known for:** warm staff and clientele; extravagant Sunday buffet; good authentic local food. *Average main: $18* *140 Reverend Blackman Rd., West Bay* *345/949–3226.*

Ristorante Pappagallo

$$$$ | **ITALIAN** | Pappagallo, Italian for "parrot," hauntingly perches on the edge of a lagoon in a 14-acre bird sanctuary. Inside, riotously colored macaws, cockatoos, and parrots perch on swings behind plate glass, but Italian-born Chef Alex Menegon's food is definitely not for the birds, especially his sublime risotto, pastas, and oh-so-yummy osso buco. **Known for:** smart food and wine/cocktail

pairings; marvelously romantic "jungle" setting; delectable Italian fare. *Average main: $40* ✉ *Barkers, 444B Conch Point Rd., West Bay* ☎ *345/949–1119* 🌐 *www.pappagallo.ky* ⏲ *No lunch.*

Hotels

Shangri-La B&B

$ | **B&B/INN** | Understated good taste informs every aspect of this lavish lakeside retreat, from the waterfall pool and hot tub to a screened-in patio overlooking the bird-filled lagoon to the carved hardwood furnishings, tatted linens, and ornately embroidered pillows, and scrumptious breakfasts (to-die-for bread-and-butter pudding and sticky toffee souffle). **Pros:** rental bikes free; elegant decor; Wi-Fi included. **Cons:** hard to find; not on the beach; rental car necessary. *Rooms from: $260* ✉ *1 Sticky Toffee La., West Bay* ☎ *345/526–1170* 🌐 *www.shangrilabandb.com* *7 rooms, 1 apartment* *Free Breakfast.*

Nightlife

BARS AND LOUNGES

★ **Macabuca Oceanside Tiki Bar**

BARS | This classic beach bar has a huge deck over the water, thatched roof, amazing mosaic murals of waves, spectacular sunsets (and sunset-color libations), and tiki torches illuminating the reef fish come evening. *Macabuca* means "What does it matter?" in the Indigenous Antillean Taíno language, perfectly encapsulating the mellow vibe. Big-screen TVs, live bands and DJs on weekends, excellent pub grub, and daily specials (CI$9 jerk dishes weekends; Monday all-night happy hour, DJ, and CI$17 all-you-can-eat barbecue) lure everyone from well-heeled loafers to barefoot bodysurfers animatedly discussing current events. ✉ *857 N.W. Point Rd., West Bay* ☎ *345/945–5217* 🌐 *www.crackedconch.com.ky.*

Seven Mile Beach

Sights

Camana Bay Observation Tower

VIEWPOINT | **FAMILY** | This 75-foot structure provides striking 360-degree panoramas of otherwise flat Grand Cayman, sweeping from George Town and Seven Mile Beach to the North Sound. The double-helix staircase is impressive in its own right. Running alongside the steps (an elevator is also available), a floor-to-ceiling mosaic replicates the look and feel of a dive from seabed to surface. Constructed of tiles in 114 different colors, it's one of the world's largest marine-theme mosaics. Benches and lookout points let you take in the views as you ascend. Afterward you can enjoy 500-acre Camana Bay's gardens, waterfront boardwalk, and pedestrian paths lined with shops and restaurants, or frequent live entertainment. ✉ *Between Seven Mile Beach and North Sound, Camana Bay* ✣ *2 miles (3 km) north of George Town* ☎ *345/640–3500* 🌐 *www.camanabay.com* *Free.*

Beaches

Cemetery Beach

BEACH | A narrow, sandy driveway takes you past the small cemetery to a perfect strand just past the northern end of Seven Mile Beach. The dock here is primarily used by dive boats during winter storms. You can walk in either direction. The sand is talcum-soft and clean, the water calm and clear (though local surfers take advantage of occasional small reef breaks), and the bottom somewhat rocky and dotted with sea urchins, so wear reef shoes if wading. You'll definitely find fewer crowds. **Amenities:** none. **Best for:** snorkeling; solitude; surfing. ✉ *West Bay Rd., Seven Mile Beach.*

★ **Seven Mile Beach**

BEACH | Grand Cayman's west coast is dominated by this famous beach—actually a 5½-mile (10-km) expanse of powdery white sand overseeing lapis water stippled with a rainbow of parasails and kayaks. Free of litter and pesky peddlers, it's an unspoiled (though often crowded) environment. Most of the island's resorts, restaurants, and shopping centers sit along this strip. The public beach toward the north end offers chairs for rent ($10 for the day, including a beverage), a playground, water toys aplenty, beach bars, restrooms, and showers. The best snorkeling is at either end, by the Marriott and Treasure Island or off Cemetery Beach, to the north in West Bay. You can park at the hotels or the malls along West Bay Road, but a dedicated parking lot for day-trippers is at Public Beach. **Amenities:** food and drink; showers; toilets; water sports. **Best for:** partiers; snorkeling. ✉ *West Bay Rd., Seven Mile Beach.*

Restaurants

★ **Abacus**

$$$$ | **ECLECTIC** | This handsome Camana Bay hangout, once more notable for its stunning decor (witness the smoked glass-and-cast-iron chandeliers), has been transformed into a foodie mecca by Executive Chef Will O'Hara. His farm-to-table "contemporary Caribbean cuisine" and solid relationships with local purveyors, farmers, and fishermen attest to his success. **Known for:** fine cocktails; locavore leanings; wildly popular happy hours. $ *Average main: $39* ✉ *45 Market St., Camana Bay* ☎ *345/623–8282* 🌐 *www.abacus.ky* ⏲ *Closed Sun.*

★ **Agua**

$$$$ | **ITALIAN** | This quietly hip spot plays up an aquatic theme with indigo glass fixtures, black-and-white photos of bridges and waterfalls, and cobalt-and-white walls that subtly mimic foamy waves. Its young, international chefs emphasize seafood, preparing regional dishes from around the globe with a Caymanian slant, albeit emphasizing Peruvian and Italian specialties from *tiraditos* to *tiramisu*. **Known for:** superlative ceviches; sensational service; winning wine list and creative cocktails. $ *Average main: $31* ✉ *Camana Bay, 47 Forum La., Seven Mile Beach* ☎ *345/949–2482* 🌐 *www.agua.ky.*

Al La Kebab

$$ | **MIDDLE EASTERN** | Food romps from Malaysia through the Mediterranean to Mexico—spicy chicken tikka, Thai chicken-lemongrass soup, and tzatziki as well as unusual salads and creative sides—at this eatery. The chef-owner calls it a building-block menu; you can modify the bread and sauce—a dozen varieties, including several curries, peanut satay, jerk mayo, mango *raita* (yogurt, tomatoes, chutney), tahini, teriyaki, garlic cream, even gravy like Mom used to make. **Known for:** bargain prices; fun late-night hangout—open until 4 am weeknights, 3 am weekends; impressive variety of sauces. $ *Average main: $12* ✉ *Marquee Plaza, West Bay Rd. at Lawrence Blvd., Seven Mile Beach* ☎ *345/943–4343* 🌐 *www.kebab.ky.*

★ **Bàcaro**

$$$ | **ITALIAN** | Bàcaro (likely derived from Bacchus, Roman god of wine) is the Venetian slang term for a gastropub, dispensing upscale versions of downhome *cichetti* (the city's beloved take on tapas). This dazzling yacht club eatery, boasting gorgeous views of the marina and modish decor (terrific terrace, wonderful black-and-white fishing photos, ropes hung from the ceiling to suggest both keels and sails), delivers on the name's promise thanks to the artistry of Venetian-born head chef–owner Federico Destro, late of Luca. **Known for:** refined yet chill atmosphere; fabulous small plates; comparatively inexpensive and superb-tasting express lunch menus. $ *Average main: $28* ✉ *Cayman Islands Yacht Club, Yacht Dr., Governor's Creek, Seven Mile Beach* ☎ *345/749–4800* 🌐 *www.bacaro.ky.*

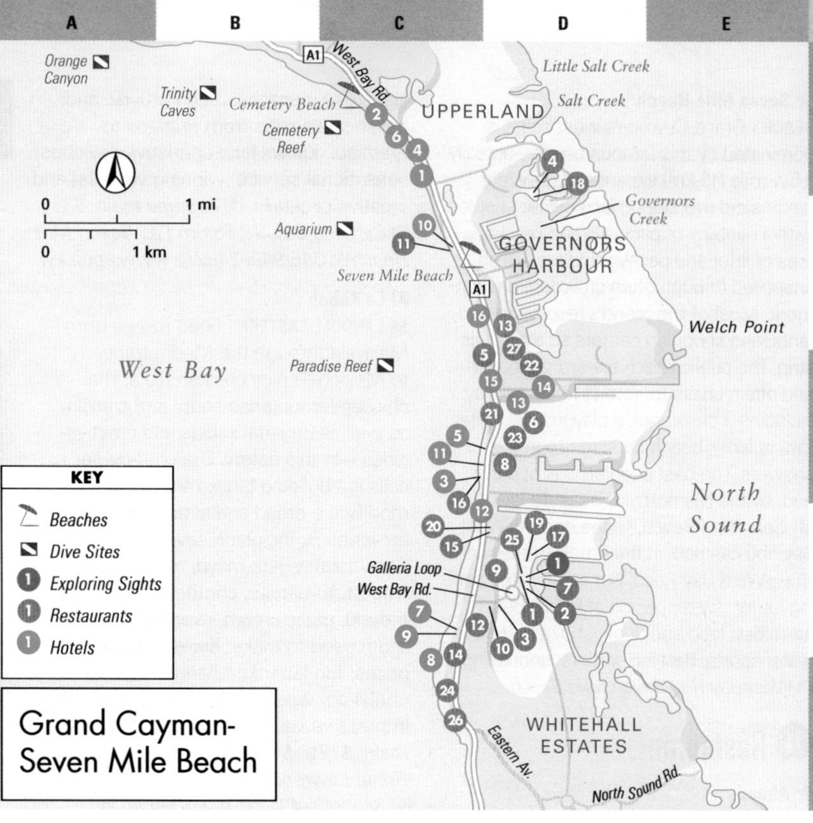

Sights

1 Camana Bay Observation Tower D4

Restaurants

1 Abacus D4
2 Agua...................... D4
3 Al La Kebab.............. D4
4 Bàcaro D1
5 Beach House............ D3
6 Blue by Eric Ripert D3
7 The Brooklyn D4
8 Casa 43 Mexican Kitchen and Tequila Bar D3
9 Chicken! Chicken! D4
10 Cimboco D4
11 Coccoloba C2
12 Craft F&B Co. C4
13 Eats Cafe D2
14 Icoa Fine Foods C4
15 Lone Star Bar and Grill...................C4
16 Luca C3
17 Mizu D4
18 Morgan's Seafood Restaurant D1
19 Pani Indian Kitchen..... D3
20 Ragazzi....................C4
21 Seven D3
22 Sunshine Grill D3
23 Taikun D3
24 Thai Orchid C5
25 The Waterfront Urban Diner D4
26 The Wharf C5
27 Yoshi Sushi D2

Hotels

1 The Anchorage C1
2 Aqua Bay Club C1
3 Caribbean Club C3
4 Christopher Columbus Condos....................C1
5 Coral Stone Club Condos....................C3
6 Discovery Point Club C1
7 Grand Cayman Marriott Beach Resort.............C4
8 The Grandview Condos....................C4
9 Hampton by Hilton Grand Cayman C4
10 Kimpton Seafire Resort & Spa C2
11 The Meridian.............C3
12 Palm Heights D4
13 The Ritz-Carlton Grand Cayman D3
14 Sunshine Suites Resort D3
15 Villas of the Galleon D3
16 The Westin Grand Cayman Seven Mile Beach Resort & Spa C2

Beach House

$$$ | **SEAFOOD** | This refined eatery glamorously channels South Beach and Santa Monica, with a sleek black bar, an earthy color scheme, and sparkly ecru curtains dividing dining spaces. Executive chef Sandy Tuason (who apprenticed with the Roux brothers, Daniel Boulud, and David Burke) masterfully adapts Mediterranean and Asian influences to local traditions and ingredients to create a "coastal cuisine" menu that offers mostly small plates and large plates to be shared family-style. **Known for:** elegant yet unstuffy atmosphere; superb seafood, especially the charcuterie and salt-baked fish; well-considered if pricey wine list. *Average main: $30* *Westin Grand Cayman Seven Mile Beach Resort & Spa, West Bay Rd., Seven Mile Beach* *345/945–3800* *www.westingrand-cayman.com* *No lunch.*

★ **Blue by Eric Ripert**

$$$$ | **SEAFOOD** | Celebrity chef Eric Ripert's trademark ethereal seafood, flawless but not fawning service, swish setting, and soothing, unpretentious sophistication make this one of the Caribbean's finest restaurants. Choose from six- and seven-course tasting menus (with or without wine pairing); there are also trendy "almost raw" and "barely touched" options. **Known for:** brilliantly fuses modern French recipes and local ingredients; stratospheric prices but worth it; stellar service. *Average main: $150* *Ritz-Carlton Grand Cayman, West Bay Rd., Seven Mile Beach* *345/943–9000* *www.ritzcarlton.com* *Closed Sun. and Mon. and Sept.–mid-Nov. No lunch.*

The Brooklyn

$$$ | **ECLECTIC** | The industrial chic setting of this wildly popular pizza and pasta joint cleverly recalls similar Brooklyn eateries in DUMBO and Williamsburg with natural wood tables for family-style dining, exposed piping, oversize metal lighting fixtures, and distressed floors. The food proves equally trendy and appealing with starters like the bountiful butcher's board of artisanal cheeses and charcuterie and creative pizzas like the jerk chicken or the Nutella S'mores 'za for dessert. **Known for:** casually hip ambience; creative pizzas; killer craft cocktails. *Average main: $23* *The Crescent, Camana Bay* *345/640–0005* *www.thebrooklyncayman.com* *No credit cards.*

★ **Casa 43 Mexican Kitchen and Tequila Bar**

$$ | **MEXICAN** | Mariachi music, sombreros, and intricate Talavera tile work set the tone at this authentic and innovative Mexican eatery tucked away off West Bay Road. Start with the savory ceviches (winners include Caribbean shrimp, Peruvian-style red snapper, and tuna Chino-Latino in soy with sesame, chile, mint, and cilantro). **Known for:** fantastically low prices by Cayman standards; tremendous tacos and tortas; simpatico staff and clientele. *Average main: $19* *Canal Point Dr., West Bay Rd., Seven Mile Beach* *Behind Copper Falls Steakhouse* *345/949–4343* *www.casa43.ky* *No lunch Sun.*

Chicken! Chicken!

$$ | **CARIBBEAN** | **FAMILY** | Devotees would probably award four exclamation points to the marvelously moist chicken, slow-roasted on a hardwood open-hearth rotisserie. Most customers grab takeout, but the decor is appealing for a fast-food joint; the clever interior replicates an old-time Cayman cottage. **Known for:** low low prices; chicken, chicken, and chicken; fantastic side dishes. *Average main: $12* *West Shore Centre, West Bay Rd., Seven Mile Beach* *345/945–2290* *www.chicken2.com.*

Cimboco

$$ | **ECLECTIC** | **FAMILY** | This animated space celebrates all things fun and Caribbean with pastel walls; cobalt glass fixtures; National Archive photographs and old newspapers about the spot's namesake, *Cimboco,* the first motorized sailing ship built in Cayman (in 1927); and

flames dancing up the exhibition kitchen's huge wood-burning oven. Everything from breads (superlative bruschetta and jalapeño corn bread) to ice creams is made from scratch. **Known for:** clever riffs on staples like pizza with local ingredients; fun, boldly colored decor; fair prices and hefty servings. *Average main: $19 Marquee Plaza, West Bay Rd. at Harquail Bypass, Seven Mile Beach 345/947–2782 www.cimboco.com.*

★ Coccoloba

$$$ | **MEXICAN FUSION** | Despite the deceptively chill vibe at this open-air setup replete with thatching and colorful hand-painted tiles and plates, the fare is haute south-of-the-border. You won't sample finer *chicharrones* (in tangy tequila barbecue sauce), fish tacos, or *elote* (corn off the cob with cotija cheese, cilantro, lime, and chipotle aioli) outside the Yucatan, while the intensely flavored flatiron steak with mole jus and chimichurri might make even dedicated vegetarians think twice. **Known for:** knowledgeable, friendly bartenders; killer sunset views; innovative Mexican street cuisine. *Average main: $26 Kimpton Seafire Resort & Spa, 60 Tanager Way, Seven Mile Beach 345/746–0000, 345/746–4111 www.coccolobacaymanislands.com.*

★ Craft F&B Co.

$$$ | **ECLECTIC** | Arguably Cayman's first true gastropub, Craft impresses with gorgeous post-industrial decor (contrasting warm white exposed brick with gray piping) and contemporary rustic cuisine that defies labels. The kitchen dubs it "familiar food with a twist" as the globe-trotting menu changes monthly and the executive chef takes sabbaticals, traveling the world for inspiration. **Known for:** sell their own house-made condiments; hip but not tragically trendy; fantastic nightly specials like "Melting Pot" Wednesday (fondue) and a raw bar on Thursday. *Average main: $24 Marquee Plaza, 489 West Bay Rd., Seven Mile Beach 345/640–0004 www.craftcayman.com.*

Eats Cafe

$$ | **ECLECTIC** | **FAMILY** | This busy and eclectic eatery has a vast menu (Cajun to Chinese), including smashing breakfasts and 10 kinds of burgers (fish and veggie versions are available). The decor is dramatic—crimson booths and walls, flat-screen TVs lining the counter, steel pendant lamps, an exhibition kitchen, gigantic flower paintings, and Andy Warhol reproductions. **Known for:** extensive "Greek diner" one-from-column-A menu; fun buzzy vibe; reasonable prices. *Average main: $19 Falls Plaza, West Bay Rd., Seven Mile Beach 345/943–3287 www.eats.ky.*

Icoa Fine Foods

$$$ | **ECLECTIC** | Icoa, the goddess of water, worshipped by the indigenous people of Venezuela's Paria Peninsula, was renowned for her exceptional beauty and alluring perfume. Innovative Dutch chef Jurgen Wevers crafts food that likewise stimulates the senses with cutting-edge cuisine, trotting from Thailand to Tunisia to Tampico, taking center stage. **Known for:** appealing adjacent wine bar; cool Cubist- and Constructivist-inspired artworks; fab Asian street food grazing menu. *Average main: $25 9–11 Seven Mile Shops, West Bay Rd., Seven Mile Beach 345/945–1915 www.icoa.ky Closed Sun. No dinner Mon.*

Lone Star Bar and Grill

$$ | **AMERICAN** | This temple to sports and the cowboy lifestyle serves a Texas-size welcome and portions. If it can be barbecued, deep-fried, jerked, pulled, or nacho-ized, it's probably on the menu. **Known for:** excellent ribs; raucous spirited atmosphere; bountiful nightly specials. *Average main: $20 688 W. Bay Rd., Seven Mile Beach 345/945–5175 www.facebook.com/lonestarbgcayman.*

★ Luca

$$$$ | **ITALIAN** | At this smart beachfront trattoria, everything has been handpicked: a wine wall of more than 3,000 international bottles; Murano glass

fixtures; arty blown-up photographs; leather banquettes; and a curving onyx-top bar. Chef Roman Kleinrath presents a more conventional, classic menu than his predecessor but still delights in unorthodox pairings like Hudson Valley foie gras with pickled figs, raspberry balsamic puree, and Port reduction. **Known for:** fabulous if expensive wine list; sleek, sophisticated decor; lovely pastas. *Average main: $42 Caribbean Club, 871 W. Bay Rd., Seven Mile Beach 345/623–4550 luca.ky Closed Mon. in Sept. and Oct. No lunch Sat.*

Mizu

$$$ | ASIAN | It's a toss-up as to which is sexier at this pan-Pacific bistro: the sleek decor or the glistening, artfully presented food. The first, courtesy of Hong Kong designer Kitty Chan, is as sensuous as a 21st-century opium den with a back-lit dragon, contemporary Buddhas, glowing granite bar, wildly hued throw pillows, and enormous mirrors. **Known for:** surprisingly authentic Asian fare; ultrahip decor and staff; huge portions ideal for sharing. *Average main: $27 The Crescent, Camana Bay 345/640–0001 www.mizucayman.com.*

★ **Morgan's Seafood Restaurant**

$$$$ | ECLECTIC | Energetic, effervescent Janie Schweiger patrols the front while husband Richard rules the kitchen at this simpatico marina spot where the menu dances just as deftly from Asia dishes like Thai seafood curry to items like chicken schnitzel that highlight the chef's Austrian upbringing. Locals and fishermen literally cruise into the adjacent dock for refueling of all sorts. **Known for:** glorious patio seating overlooking the marina and Governor's Creek; delightful husband–wife owners; fun peripatetic menu. *Average main: $39 Governor's Creek, Cayman Islands Yacht Club, Seven Mile Beach 345/946–7049 www.morganscayman.com Closed Tues. and Oct.*

Pani Indian Kitchen

$$$ | INDIAN | In every respect, from the decor to the cuisine, Pani is a joyous celebration of street food from around the subcontinent, with haute gloss. The space breathtakingly creates an Indian street bazaar indoors: bamboo-and-burlap awnings, billowing multihue fabric, representations of such deities as Ganesha, a wall of dyed tea bags, and huge brass tandoori urns in the open kitchen. **Known for:** delightful decor including an entire wall of dyed tea bags; wonderfully flavorful options for vegetarians; fantastic bargain lunch menu. *Average main: $23 The Crescent, Camana Bay 345/640–0007 www.panicayman.com.*

★ **Ragazzi**

$$$ | ITALIAN | FAMILY | The name means "good buddies," and this strip-mall jewel percolates with conversation and good strong espresso. The airy space is convivial—blond woods, periwinkle walls and columns, and handsome artworks of beach scenes, sailboats, and palm trees—and the antipasto alone is worth a visit, as are homemade breadsticks and focaccia, carpaccio, and insalata Caprese. **Known for:** thoughtful wine list showcasing lesser-known regions; reasonable prices by Cayman standards; scrumptious authentic pizzas and pastas. *Average main: $27 Buckingham Square, West Bay Rd., Seven Mile Beach 345/945–3484 www.ragazzi.ky.*

★ **Seven**

$$$$ | STEAKHOUSE | The Ritz-Carlton's all-purpose dining room, which features tall potted palms, soaring ceilings, a black-and-beige color scheme, and twin wine walls bracketing a trendy family-style table, transforms from a bustling breakfast buffet to an elegant evening eatery. Sinatra and Ella keep a sultry beat while the kitchen jazzes standard meat-and-potatoes dishes with inventive seasonings and eye-catching presentations. **Known for:** terrific happy hour cocktail and bar bite bargains;

magnificent steaks; creative sides like lobster-twice-baked mashed potatoes. 💲 *Average main: $53* ✉ *Ritz-Carlton Grand Cayman, West Bay Rd., Seven Mile Beach* ☎ *345/943–9000* 🌐 *www.ritzcarlton.com* ⏲ *No lunch.*

Sunshine Grill

$$ | **CARIBBEAN** | **FAMILY** | This cheerful, cherished locals' secret serves haute comfort food—great burgers, wahoo-mushrooms bites, and fabulous fish tacos—that elevates pub grub to an art form at bargain prices. Even the chattel-style poolside building, painted a delectable lemon with lime shutters, multihue interior columns, and orange and blueberry accents, whets the appetite. **Known for:** one of locals' top choices for burgers; warm family-friendly atmosphere and staff; fantastic affordable dinner specials. 💲 *Average main: $20* ✉ *Sunshine Suites Resort, 1465 Esterley Tibbetts Hwy., Seven Mile Beach* ☎ *345/949–3000, 345/946–5848* 🌐 *www.sunshinesuites.com.*

★ Taikun

$$$ | **JAPANESE** | **FAMILY** | Taikun is an archaic Japanese term of esteem, loosely translated as "Supreme Commander." It's an appropriate designation for this sensuous sushi spot, clad in black with crimson and gray accents and dominated by a buzzy communal table. Start with one of the terrific cocktails or indulge in the superlative sake flights, which can be optimally paired with your sushi. **Known for:** simply sensational sushi; attention to detail include grating wasabi at table; refined yet relaxed ambience. 💲 *Average main: $27* ✉ *Ritz-Carlton Grand Cayman, West Bay Rd., Seven Mile Beach* ☎ *345/943–9000* 🌐 *www.ritzcarlton.com/GrandCayman* ⏲ *No lunch.*

Thai Orchid

$$$ | **THAI** | East meets West at this elegant eatery, and the combination makes for a tasty meal. The Thai chefs turn out splendid classics like *yum nuer* (sliced chargrilled strip loin tossed with green salad in lime dressing), and seafood lovers can opt for the fresh sushi, and plentiful vegetarian options include curries perfumed with lemongrass. **Known for:** good selection of vegetarian dishes; bargain buffets; congenial waitstaff. 💲 *Average main: $28* ✉ *Queen's Court, West Bay Rd., Seven Mile Beach* ☎ *345/949–7955* 🌐 *www.thaiorchid.ky.*

The Waterfront Urban Diner

$$ | **DINER** | **FAMILY** | Ultra-contemporary design with industrial elements (exposed piping, raw timber, tugboat salvage) is a counterpoint to the down-home fare at this bustling glorified diner, whose choice seats are on the patio. Comfort food aficionados can launch into the splendid chicken and waffles, meat loaf, and poutine. **Known for:** fun for families; pleasant outdoor seating area; comfort food like poutine and a killer cinnamon roll. 💲 *Average main: $19* ✉ *The Crescent, Camana Bay* ☎ *345/640–0002* 🌐 *www.waterfrontcayman.com.*

The Wharf

$$$$ | **SEAFOOD** | The popularity of this large restaurant often leads to impersonal service and mediocre food; stick to such standards as conch fritters with spicy red pepper remoulade, and avoid anything sounding too pretentious. The location, a series of elevated decks and Victorian-style gazebos in blue and white hugging the sea, is enviable and helps to explain its enduring appeal; (wedding parties have their own pavilion, but celebrations of all sorts can overrun the place, including Salsa Tuesdays with lessons). **Known for:** delectable desserts; stunning seaside location; fun evening entertainment including tarpon feedings. 💲 *Average main: $44* ✉ *43 W. Bay Rd., George Town* ☎ *345/949–2231* 🌐 *www.wharf.ky* ⏲ *No lunch.*

Yoshi Sushi

$$$ | **JAPANESE** | This modish locals' lair serves superlative sushi. The main room's scarlet cushions, cherry blown-glass pendant lamps, leather-and-bamboo

accents, orchids, and maroon walls create an exciting vibe. **Known for:** cool vibe; innovative rolls and sushi "pizzas"; excellent cocktails. *$ Average main: $23 ✉ Falls Plaza, West Bay Rd., Seven Mile Beach ☎ 345/943–9674 🌐 www.eats.ky/yoshisushi.html.*

Hotels

The Anchorage

$$ | APARTMENT | These two-bedroom condos are cramped compared with otherwise newer compounds, but fully equipped, modernized, scrupulously clean, and—most important—affordable (at least for garden-view apartments). **Pros:** great pool at the edge of the Caribbean; incredible sweeping panoramas from George Town to West Bay from higher units; nice beach and snorkeling. **Cons:** steep surcharge for oceanview units; boxy apartments; a bit isolated from action. *$ Rooms from: $370 ✉ 1989 W. Bay Rd., Seven Mile Beach ☎ 345/945–4088 🌐 www.theanchorage-cayman.com ⇨ 15 units 🍽 No Meals.*

Aqua Bay Club

$$$$ | APARTMENT | One of the older condo complexes, ABC is scrupulously maintained, quiet, and affordable. **Pros:** free Wi-Fi and loaner cell phone for local calls; great snorkeling very close to Cemetery Reef; friendly staff. **Cons:** well-maintained but slightly dowdy; no elevator; beach can be rocky. *$ Rooms from: $600 ✉ West Bay Rd., Seven Mile Beach ☎ 345/945–4728, 800/618–1229 🌐 www.aquabayclub.com ⇨ 21 units 🍽 No Meals.*

★ Caribbean Club

$$$$ | APARTMENT | This gleaming boutique facility has a striking lobby with aquariums, infinity pool, and contemporary trattoria, Luca. **Pros:** service on the beach; luxurious, high-tech facilities beyond the typical apartment complex; trendy Italian restaurant. **Cons:** daily mad dash to claim the free, first-come cabanas; though families are welcome, they may find it imposing; poor bedroom reading lights. *$ Rooms from: $1256 ✉ 871 W. Bay Rd., Seven Mile Beach ☎ 345/623–4500, 800/941–1126 🌐 www.caribclub.com ⇨ 37 condos 🍽 No Meals.*

Christopher Columbus Condos

$$$ | APARTMENT | FAMILY | With its two- and three-bedroom condos, this enduring favorite on the peaceful northern end of Seven Mile Beach is a find for families. **Pros:** complimentary Wi-Fi; excellent snorkeling and fine beach; great value. **Cons:** top floors have difficult access for physically challenged; often overrun by families during holidays and summer; car needed. *$ Rooms from: $440 ✉ 2013 W. Bay Rd., Seven Mile Beach ☎ 345/945–4354, 866/311–5231 🌐 www.christophercolumbuscondos.com ⇨ 30 condos 🍽 No Meals.*

Coral Stone Club Condos

$$$$ | APARTMENT | In the shadow of the Ritz-Carlton, this exclusive enclave still shines by offering understated barefoot luxury, stellar service, and huge three-bedroom condos. **Pros:** free airport transfers; large ratio of beach and pool space to guests; walking distance to restaurants and shops. **Cons:** occasionally spotty maintenance in low season; Ritz-Carlton guests sometimes wander over to poach beach space; expensive in high season. *$ Rooms from: $1025 ✉ 985 W. Bay Rd., Seven Mile Beach ☎ 345/945–5820, 888/927–2322 🌐 www.coralstoneclub.com ⇨ 30 condos 🍽 No Meals.*

Discovery Point Club

$$$$ | APARTMENT | FAMILY | This older but upgraded complex of all oceanfront suites sits at the north end of Seven Mile Beach, 6 miles (9½ km) from George Town, with fabulous snorkeling in the protected waters of nearby Cemetery Reef. **Pros:** complimentary Internet; caring staff; family-friendly. **Cons:** no elevator; beach entry rocky in spots; car needed. *$ Rooms from: $675 ✉ 2043 W. Bay*

Shaded beach loungers at the Ritz-Carlton, Grand Cayman

Rd., Seven Mile Beach ☎ 345/945–4724, 866/384–9980 ⊕ www.discoverypoint-club.com ⇌ 37 condos ǀ◎ǀ No Meals.

Grand Cayman Marriott Beach Resort
$$$$ | RESORT | FAMILY | The soaring, stylish marble lobby (with exquisite art glass, majestic stingray bas relief sculpture), sets the "Beach House" tone for this bustling property. **Pros:** convenient to both George Town and Seven Mile Beach; good snorkeling and water sports; free bike and kayak rentals. **Cons:** $60 resort fee; pool and bar often noisy late; narrowest section of Seven Mile Beach. *[$] Rooms from: $599 ✉ 389 W. Bay Rd., Seven Mile Beach ☎ 345/949–0088, 800/223–6388 ⊕ www.marriottgrandcayman.com ⇌ 295 rooms ǀ◎ǀ No Meals.*

The Grandview Condos
$$$$ | APARTMENT | FAMILY | Grand view, indeed: all 69 two- and three-bedroom units (sadly only 20 are generally in the rental pool) look smack onto the Caribbean and the beach past splendidly maintained gardens. **Pros:** nice pool and hot tub; affable helpful staff including wine concierge; free Wi-Fi (when it's available). **Cons:** not all units have strong access to the free Wi-Fi signal; some units a tad worn though meticulously maintained; the long beach can be rocky. *[$] Rooms from: $605 ✉ 95 Snooze La., Seven Mile Beach ☎ 345/945–4511, 866/977–6766 ⊕ www.grandcaymanvillas.net/vrp/complex/grandview-condos ⇌ 69 condos ǀ◎ǀ No Meals ☞ 5-night minimum high season.*

Hampton by Hilton Grand Cayman
$ | HOTEL | FAMILY | What was once a no-frills hotel has transformed to a breezy Hilton property with an ideal location, next to the Marriott and near numerous shops, restaurants, and bars. **Pros:** fun, young-ish crowd; affordable; shuttle to nearby beaches, parks, and clubs. **Cons:** kitchenettes are basic; no balconies; rooms nearly a block from the beach with no sea views. *[$] Rooms from: $258 ✉ 22 Piper Way at West Bay Rd., George Town ☎ 345/945–7300, 844/229–6267 ⊕ www.caymancomfort.com ⇌ 108 suites ǀ◎ǀ Free Breakfast.*

★ Kimpton Seafire Resort & Spa

$$$$ | **RESORT** | **FAMILY** | Everything about the Seafire displays the Kimpton trademark blend of elegance with a touch of funk, artfully adapted to the tropics. **Pros:** trademark complimentary extras like evening wine tasting; sophisticated without pretension; fabulous service. **Cons:** not ideal for guests with mobility issues; long walk from some rooms to public spaces; high $80 resort fee. *Rooms from: $775 ✉ 60 Tanager Way, Seven Mile Beach ☎ 345/746–0000, 855/546–7866, 888/246–4412 toll-free reservations 🌐 www.seafireresortandspa.com 266 rooms No Meals.*

The Meridian

$$$$ | **APARTMENT** | The lavish landscaping and neo-Edwardian architecture with gables, Palladian windows, and grillwork balconies set an understated opulent tone that carries over to the interior—curved enclosed patios larger than many apartments, traditional decor favoring hardwood furnishings, four-poster beds, carved-wood chandeliers, and antique maps. **Pros:** gorgeous beachfront; restaurants and supermarket right across the street; meticulously maintained. **Cons:** pool and beach can get crowded; undeniably elegant but extremely pricey; some find it a little too popular with families. *Rooms from: $1025 ✉ 917 W. Bay Rd., Seven Mile Beach ☎ 345/945–4002 🌐 www.meridian.ky 32 condos No Meals.*

★ Palm Heights

$$ | **HOTEL** | The hottest boutique hotel on Seven Mile Beach gives off the vibe of a billionaire best friend's home rather than a typical Caribbean resort, and it's a refreshing change of pace. **Pros:** all rooms have ocean views; beautiful design; large pool. **Cons:** slow service; some rooms are small; pricey rates. *Rooms from: $349 ✉ 747 W. Bay Rd., Seven Mile Beach ☎ 203/301–1718, 646/809–7256 🌐 palmheights.com 53 suites No Meals.*

★ The Ritz-Carlton Grand Cayman

$$$$ | **RESORT** | **FAMILY** | This 144-acre, exquisitely manicured resort, offers unparalleled luxury and service infused with a sense of place, with works by local artists and craftspeople. **Pros:** fine beachfront; exemplary service; exceptional facilities with complimentary extras. **Cons:** long walk to beach (over an interior bridge) from most rooms; sprawling with a confusing layout; annoyingly high ($80) resort fee. *Rooms from: $1179 ✉ West Bay Rd., Seven Mile Beach ☎ 345/943–9000 🌐 www.ritzcarlton.com 389 rooms No Meals.*

Sunshine Suites Resort

$$ | **HOTEL** | **FAMILY** | This friendly, all-suites hotel is an impeccably clean money saver, and though the somewhat boxy but brightly designed rooms lack balconies, patios, or even views, each has a complete kitchen, pillow-top mattress, flat-screen TV, and free Wi-Fi (laptops can be rented). **Pros:** free access to business center and to nearby World Gym; cheerful staff; rocking little restaurant. **Cons:** annoying $35 resort fee; not on the beach; poor views. *Rooms from: $364 ✉ 1465 Esterley Tibbetts Hwy., off West Bay Rd., Seven Mile Beach ☎ 345/949–3000, 877/786–1110 🌐 www.sunshinesuites.com 131 suites Free Breakfast.*

Villas of the Galleon

$$$$ | **APARTMENT** | **FAMILY** | On the beachfront, snuggled between the Ritz-Carlton and Westin, Galleon's villas are just steps away from groceries, restaurants, nightlife, and water sports. **Pros:** free DSL and local calls; affable management; central location with glorious beach. **Cons:** one-bedroom units do not have a washer/dryer; slightly boxy room configuration; no pool. *Rooms from: $500 ✉ West Bay Rd., Seven Mile Beach ☎ 345/945–4433, 866/665–4696 🌐 www.villasofthegalleon.com 74 condos No Meals.*

★ The Westin Grand Cayman Seven Mile Beach Resort & Spa

$$$$ | **RESORT** | **FAMILY** | The handsomely designed, well-equipped Westin offers something for everyone, from conventioneers to honeymooners to families, not to mention what the hospitality industry calls "location location location." You can walk a perfect beach or luxuriate in a cabana, enjoy the sumptuous spa, sweat in the state-of-the-art fitness club, get wet with a Red Sail Sports branch, dine at the estimable Beach House, lounge in Grand Cayman's largest freshwater pool (with an ocean view to boot), or loll in the suave piano lounge after dark. **Pros:** better-than-advertised ocean views; terrific children's programs; superb beach (the largest resort stretch at 800 feet). **Cons:** darned expensive if you can't find an online discount; daily $65 resort fee; occasionally bustling and impersonal when large groups book. *Rooms from: $859* ✉ *West Bay Rd., Seven Mile Beach* ☎ *345/945–3800, 800/937–8461* 🌐 *www.westingrandcayman.com* *347 rooms* *No Meals.*

Nightlife

BARS AND MUSIC CLUBS

The Attic

BARS | This chic sports bar has three billiard tables, classic arcade games (Space Invaders, Donkey Kong), air hockey, and large-screen TVs (nab a private booth with its own flat-panel job). Events are daily happy hours, trivia nights, and the Caribbean's reputedly largest Bloody Mary bar on Sunday. Along with sister "O" Bar, it's ground zero for the Wednesday Night Drinking Club. For a $25 initiation (with T-shirt and personalized leather wristband, toga optional) and $10 weekly activity fee, you're shuttled by bus to three different bars, with free shots and drink specials. ✉ *Queen's Court, 2nd fl., West Bay Rd., Seven Mile Beach* ☎ *345/949–7665, 345/947–5691.*

Coconut Joe's

BARS | You can sit at the bar or swing under a century-old poinciana tree and watch the traffic go by. There are murals of apes everywhere, from gorillas doing shots to a baboon in basketball uniform (in keeping with management's facetious suggestion that you attract your server's attention by pounding your chest while screeching and scratching yourself). Friday swings with DJs and free happy hour munchies. Popular for breakfast. ✉ *West Bay Rd., Seven Mile Beach* ✣ *Across from Hampton by Hilton and Marriott* ☎ *345/943–5637.*

Fidel Murphy's Irish Pub

PUBS | Thanks to the unusual logo (a stogie-smoking Castro surrounded by shamrocks) and congenial Irish wit and whimsy, you half expect to find Raúl and Gerry Adams harping on U.S. and U.K. policy over a Harp. The Edwardian decor of etched glass, hardwood, and brass is prefabricated (constructed in Ireland, disassembled, and shipped), but everything else is genuine: the warm welcome, the ales and cider on tap, and the proper Irish stew (the kitchen also turns out conch fritters and lamb vindaloo). Sunday means all-you-can-eat extravaganzas (fish-and-chips, carvery) at rock-bottom prices. Trivia nights, happy hours, and live music lure regulars during the week. Weekends welcome live, televised Gaelic soccer, rugby, and hurling, followed by karaoke and *craic* (if you go, you'll learn the definition). ✉ *Queen's Court, West Bay Rd., Seven Mile Beach* ☎ *345/949–5189* 🌐 *www.fidelmurphys.com.*

Legendz

BARS | This sports bar has a clubby, retro feel—Marilyn Monroe and Frank Sinatra photos channel glamour days, while scarlet booths and bubble chandeliers add oomph. Good luck wrestling a spot at the bar for pay-per-view and major sporting events, but 10 TVs, including two 6-by-8-foot screens, broadcast to every corner. Also an entertainment venue, Legendz books local bands, stand-up comics, and island DJs, and serves grilled fare at reasonable prices. ✉ *Falls Centre, West Bay Rd., Seven Mile Beach* ☎ *345/943–3287* 🌐 *www.eats.ky/legendz.html.*

Lone Star Bar and Grill

BARS | Calling itself Cayman's top dive (some might call it a shrine to Texas and alcohol), this bar is defined by its vast sports memorabilia collection, nearly 30 big-screen TVs tuned to different events, and excellent margaritas. Trivia and Rock 'n' Roll Bingo nights lasso locals. ✉ *686 W. Bay Rd., Seven Mile Beach* ☎ *345/945–5175* 🌐 *www.lonestarcayman.com.*

The Wharf

BARS | Dance near the water to mellow music on Saturday evening; when there's a wedding reception in the pavilion, the crashing surf and twinkling candles bathe the proceedings in an almost Gatsby-esque glow. For something less sedate, try salsa lessons and dancing on Tuesday after dinner; most Fridays morph into a wild 1970s disco night (after the free hors d'oeuvres served during happy hour). The legendary Barefoot Man (think a Jimmy Buffett–style expat) performs Saturday. The stunning seaside setting on tiered decks compensates for often undistinguished food and service. The Ports of Call bar is a splendid place for sunset, and tarpon feeding off the deck happens nightly at 7 and 9. ✉ *43 West Bay Rd., George Town* ☎ *345/949–2231* 🌐 *www.wharf.ky.*

CIGAR AND WINE LOUNGES

★ The Bar at Ave

BARS | It's easy to overlook this bar at the entrance to the Kimpton Seafire's main restaurant unless you're waiting for your table, but that would be a mistake. It's not the decor, which is surprisingly sterile despite the handsome driftwood sculpture hanging from the cathedral ceiling. Rather it's the gregarious mixologists who hold court, inventing cocktails on the spot based on your personality and preferences. You can also order dinner from the extensive regular Ave menu, including such standouts as crispy octopus with warm potato and white bean salad or cavatelli with rabbit ragù. ✉ *Kimpton Seafire, 60 Tanager Way, Seven Mile Beach* ☎ *345/746–4111* 🌐 *www.seafireresortandspa.com.*

Silver Palm Lounge

PIANO BARS | The Silver Palm drips with cash and cachet, with a model waitstaff and chic clientele. There's an old-fashioned, leather-clad bar and another section that replicates a classic English country library (perfect for civilized, proper afternoon tea or a pre- or post-dinner Champagne or single malt). Also on tap: fab cocktails, including specialty martinis (the Silver Palm cosmopolitan is a winner—Ketel One citron, triple sec, a squeeze of fresh lime juice, and a splash of cranberry topped off with Moët Champagne); pages of wines by the glass; and an impressive list of cigars, cognacs, and aged rums. ✉ *Ritz-Carlton Grand Cayman, West Bay Rd., Seven Mile Beach* ☎ *345/943–9000* 🌐 *www.ritzcarlton.com/GrandCayman.*

★ West Indies Wine Company

WINE BARS | At this ultra-contemporary wine store, purchasing tasting cards allows you to sample any of the 80-odd wines and spirits, available by the sip or half or full glass via the argon-enhanced "intelligent dispensing system." Selections traverse a vast canny range of prices, regions, styles, and terroirs. The enterprising owners struck a deal with neighboring restaurants and gourmet shops to provide appetizers or cheese and charcuterie plates, best savored alfresco at the tables in front of the handsome space. Small wonder savvy locals congregate here after work or a movie at the nearby cineplex. ✉ *Corner of Market St. and the Paseo, Camana Bay* ☎ *345/640–9492* 🌐 *www.wiwc.ky.*

Shopping

ART GALLERIES

Ritz-Carlton Gallery

ART GALLERIES | This gallery more than fulfilled one of the resort's conditions upon securing rights to build, which was to commission local arts and artisans to help decorate the public spaces. The corridor-cum-bridge spanning West Bay Road became a gallery where Chris Christian of Cayman Traditional Arts curates quarterly exhibitions of Cayman's finest (there are also theme shows devoted to photography and local kids' art). Each piece is for sale; CTA or the hotel will mediate in the negotiations between artist and buyer at a favorable commission. ✉ *Ritz-Carlton Grand Cayman, West Bay Rd., Seven Mile Beach* ☎ *345/943–9000, 345/926–0119.*

BOOKS

Next Chapter

BOOKS | **FAMILY** | Formerly the Books and Books store, this sprawling bookstore is a literary haven with two entire rooms devoted to kids with toys, educational games, and books from toddler to YA; twice-weekly story and craft time keep them occupied while parents browse. Starbucks is also next door. ✉ *45 Market St., Camana Bay* ☎ *345/640–2665* 🌐 *www.nextchapter.ky.*

JEWELRY

★ Balaclava Jewellers

JEWELRY & WATCHES | This shop is the domain of Martina and Philip Cadien, who studied at Germany's prestigious Pforzheim Goldsmithing School. The showroom sparkles appropriately, with breathtaking handcrafted pieces—usually naturally colored diamonds set in platinum or 18K white, yellow, and rose gold—framed and lovingly, almost sensuously lit. Although there are simpler strands, this is a place where flash holds sway; the prices take your breath away, but the gaudy gems are flawless. ✉ *Governors Square, 23 Lime Tree Bay Ave., Seven Mile Beach* ☎ *345/945–5788* 🌐 *www.balaclava-jewellers.com* ⏲ *Closed Sun.*

MALLS AND SHOPPING CENTERS

Galleria Plaza

SHOPPING CENTER | Nicknamed Blue Plaza for its azure hue, Galleria Plaza features several galleries and exotic home-accessories stores dealing in rugs or Indonesian furnishings, as well as more moderate souvenir shops hawking T-shirts and swimwear. ✉ *West Bay Rd., Seven Mile Beach.*

The Strand Shopping Centre

SHOPPING CENTER | This mall has branches of Tortuga Rum and Blackbeard's Liquor, Polo Ralph Lauren, and another Kirk Freeport (this location is particularly noteworthy for china and crystal, from Kosta Boda to Baccarat, as well as a second La Parfumerie). You'll also find ATMs galore so you can withdraw cash. ✉ *West Bay Rd., Seven Mile Beach.*

West Shore Shopping Centre

SHOPPING CENTER | Dubbed Pink Plaza for reasons that become obvious upon approach, West Shore offers upscale boutiques and galleries (tenants range from Chicken Chicken to Treasure Tee). ✉ *West Bay Rd., Seven Mile Beach.*

Grand Cayman—The Eastern Districts

North Side

Sights

★ Queen Elizabeth II Botanic Park

NATURE PRESERVE | **FAMILY** | This 65-acre wilderness preserve showcases a wide range of indigenous and nonindigenous tropical vegetation, approximately 2,000 species in total. Splendid sections include numerous water features from limpid lily ponds to cascades; a Heritage

Garden with a traditional cottage and "caboose" (outside kitchen) that includes crops that might have been planted on Cayman a century ago; and a Floral Colour Garden arranged by color, the walkway wandering through sections of pink, red, orange, yellow, white, blue, mauve, lavender, and purple. A 2-acre lake and adjacent wetlands include three islets that provide a habitat and breeding ground for native birds just as showy as the floral displays: green herons, black-necked stilts, American coots, blue-winged teal, cattle egrets, and rare West Indian whistling ducks. The nearly mile-long Woodland Trail encompasses every Cayman ecosystem from wetland to cactus thicket, buttonwood swamp to lofty woodland with imposing mahogany trees. You'll encounter birds, lizards, turtles, and agoutis, but the park's star residents are the protected endemic blue iguanas, found only in Grand Cayman. The world's most endangered iguana, they're the focus of the National Trust's Blue Iguana Recovery Program, a captive breeding and reintroduction facility. This section of the park is usually closed to the public, though released "blue dragons" hang out in the vicinity. The Trust conducts 90-minute behind-the-scenes safaris Monday through Saturday at 11 am for $30. ✉ *367 Botanic Rd., North Side* ☎ *345/947–9462* 🌐 *www.botanic-park.ky* 🎫 *CI$10.*

Beaches

Old Man Bay

BEACH | The North Side features plenty of hidden coves and pristine stretches of perfect sand, where you'll be disturbed only by seabirds dive-bombing for lunch and the occasional lone fishers casting nets for sprats, then dumping them into buckets. Over the Edge restaurant is less than 1 mile (1½ km) west. Otherwise, it's fairly undeveloped for miles, save for the occasional private home. Snorkeling is spectacular when waters are calm. **Amenities:** food and drink. **Best for:** snorkeling; solitude; walking. ✉ *Queen's Hwy., Old Man Bay, North Side* ✥ *Just off Frank Sound Rd.*

Rum Point Beach

BEACH | This North Sound beach has hammocks slung in towering casuarina trees, picnic tables, casual and "fancier" dining options, a well-stocked shop for seaworthy sundries, and Red Sail Sports, which offers various water sports and boats to explore Stingray City. The barrier reef ensures safe snorkeling and soft sand. The bottom remains shallow for a long way from shore, but it's littered with small coral heads, so be careful. The Wreck is an ultracasual hangout serving outstanding pub grub from fish-and-chips to wings, as well as lethal Mudslide cocktails. Just around the bend, another quintessential beach hangout, Kaibo, rocks during the day. **Amenities:** food and drink; parking (no fee); showers; toilets; water sports. **Best for:** partiers; snorkeling. ✉ *Rum Point, North Side.*

Water Cay

BEACH | If you want an isolated, unspoiled beach, bear left at Rum Point, on the North Side, and follow the road to the end. When you pass a porte cochere for an abandoned condo development, you'll see the soft, sandy beach. Wade out knee deep and look for the large, flame-hue starfish. (Don't touch—just look.) Locals also call it Starfish or Ivory Point. **Amenities:** none. **Best for:** solitude; swimming. ✉ *North Side.*

Restaurants

Kaibo Beach Bar and Grill

$$$ | **CARIBBEAN** | Overlooking the North Sound, this beach hangout rocks during the day (fantastic lunches that cost half the price of dinner, festive atmosphere including impromptu volleyball tourneys, and free Wi-Fi) and serves murderous margaritas and mudslides well into the evening to boisterous yachties, locals, sports buffs, and expats. Enjoy smoked mahimahi pâté, brick-oven pizzas, hefty burgers, and wondrous wraps, either on the multitier seafood platter with Christmas lights or in hammocks and thatched cabanas amid the palms. **Known for:** top-notch pub grub; boisterous crowd; fun beach events. *Average main: $21 ✉ 585 Water Cay Rd., Rum Point, North Side ☎ 345/947–9975 🌐 www.kaibo.ky ⏲ Closed Mon. and Tues.*

Over the Edge

$$$ | **CARIBBEAN** | This fun, funky seaside spot brims with character and characters (a soused regular might welcome you by reciting "the daily lunch special: chilled barley soup ... That's beer"). **Known for:** appealing semi-enclosed patio; delectable local fare; island insiders' hangout. *Average main: $24 ✉ 312 North Side Rd., Old Man Bay, North Side ☎ 345/947–9568.*

Bodden Town

In the island's original south-shore capital you can find an old **cemetery** on the shore side of the road. Graves with A-frame structures are said to contain the remains of pirates. There are also the ruins of a fort and a wall erected by enslaved people in the 19th century. The National Trust runs tours of the restored 1840s **Mission House.**

Sights

Mission House

HISTORIC HOME | This classic gabled two-story Caymanian home on wooden posts, with wattle-and-daub accents, dates to the 1840s and was restored by the National Trust. The building earned its sobriquet thanks to early missionaries, teachers, and families who lived here while helping establish the Presbyterian ministry and school in Bodden Town. Shards of 19th-century glass and ceramics found on-site and period furnishings are on display. The posted opening hours are irregular, especially during the off-season; tours are by appointment only. *✉ 63 Gun Square Rd., Bodden Town ☎ 345/749–1132 🌐 www.nationaltrust.org.ky 🎟 CI$8.*

★ **Pedro St. James Castle**

HISTORIC HOME | Built in 1780, the greathouse is Cayman's oldest stone structure and the island's only remaining late-18th-century residence. In its capacity as courthouse and jail, it was the birthplace of Caymanian democracy, where in December 1831 the first elected parliament was organized and in 1835 the Slavery Abolition Act signed. The structure still has original or historically accurate replicas of sweeping verandahs, mahogany floors, rough-hewn wide-beam ceilings, outside louvers, stone and oxblood- or mustard-color limewashed walls, brass fixtures, and Georgian furnishings (from tea caddies to canopy beds to commodes). Paying obsessive attention to detail, the curators even fill glasses with faux wine. The mini-museum also includes a hodgepodge of displays from emancipation to old stamps. The buildings are surrounded by 8 acres of natural parks and woodlands. You can stroll through landscaping of native Caymanian flora and experience one of the most spectacular views on the island from atop the dramatic Great Pedro Bluff. First watch the impressive multimedia show, on the hour, complete with smoking pots, misting rains, and two screens. The poignant Hurricane Ivan Memorial outside uses text, images, and symbols to represent important aspects of the 2004 disaster. A branch of Cayman Spirits brings history further to life with rum tastings. *✉ 305 Pedro Castle Rd., Savannah, Bodden Town ☎ 345/947–3329 🌐 www.pedrostjames.ky 🎟 CI$10.*

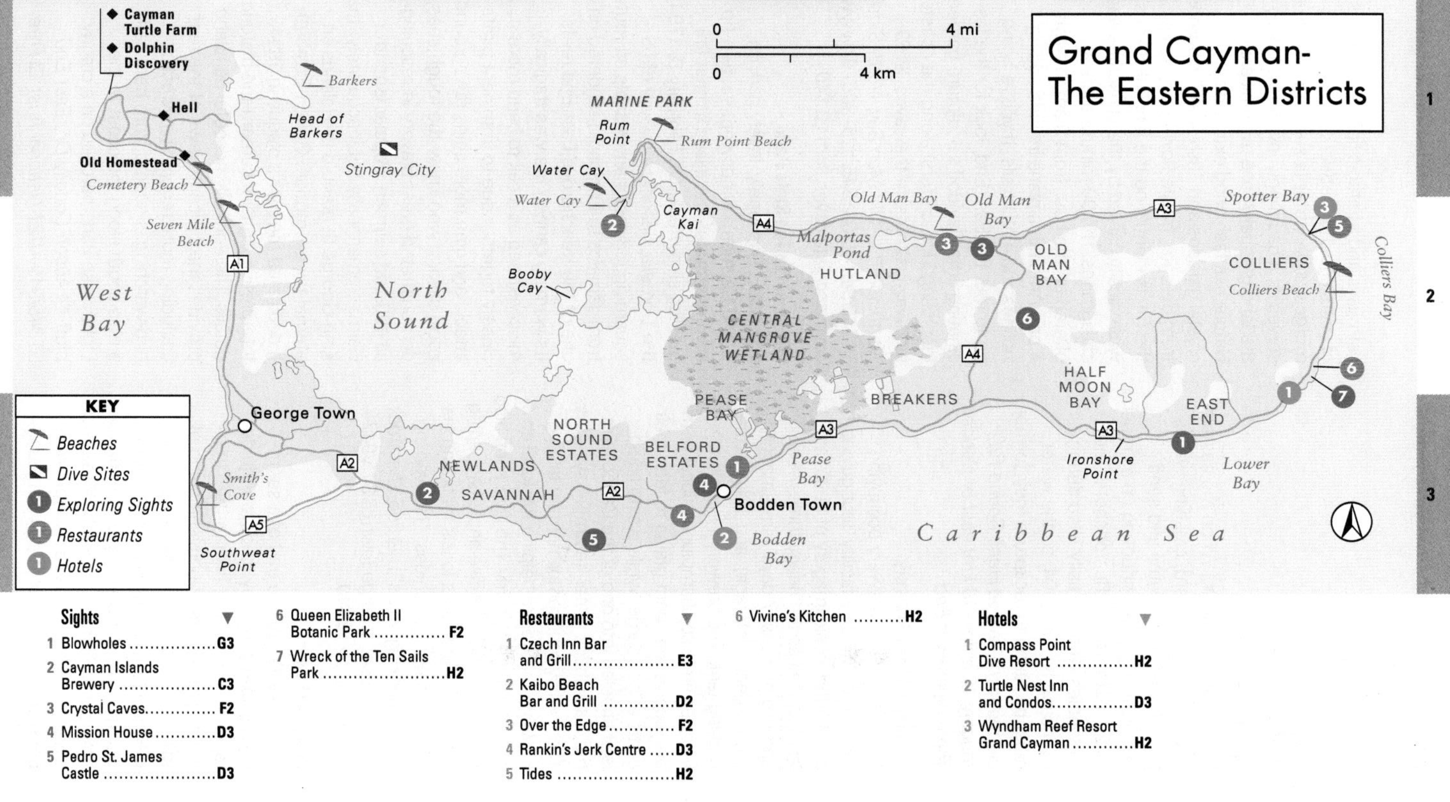

Grand Cayman-
The Eastern Districts
A
B
C
D
E
F
G
H
1
2
3
0
4 mi
0
4 km
KEY
Beaches
Dive Sites
Exploring Sights
Restaurants
Hotels
Cayman Turtle Farm
Dolphin Discovery
Hell
Old Homestead
Cemetery Beach
Seven Mile Beach
Barkers
Head of Barkers
Stingray City
West Bay
North Sound
George Town
Smith's Cove
Southwest Point
A1
A2
A3
A4
A5
MARINE PARK
Rum Point
Rum Point Beach
Water Cay
Water Cay
Cayman Kai
Booby Cay
NEWLANDS
SAVANNAH
NORTH SOUND ESTATES
BELFORD ESTATES
PEASE BAY
CENTRAL MANGROVE WETLAND
Malportas Pond
HUTLAND
Old Man Bay
Old Man Bay
OLD MAN BAY
BREAKERS
Pease Bay
Bodden Town
Bodden Bay
HALF MOON BAY
Ironshore Point
EAST END
Lower Bay
Spotter Bay
COLLIERS
Colliers Beach
Colliers Bay
Caribbean Sea
Sights
1 Blowholes G3
2 Cayman Islands Brewery C3
3 Crystal Caves F2
4 Mission House D3
5 Pedro St. James Castle D3
6 Queen Elizabeth II Botanic Park F2
7 Wreck of the Ten Sails Park H2
Restaurants
1 Czech Inn Bar and Grill E3
2 Kaibo Beach Bar and Grill D2
3 Over the Edge F2
4 Rankin's Jerk Centre D3
5 Tides H2
6 Vivine's Kitchen H2
Hotels
1 Compass Point Dive Resort H2
2 Turtle Nest Inn and Condos D3
3 Wyndham Reef Resort Grand Cayman H2

East End

 Sights

Blowholes

NATURE SIGHT | FAMILY | When the easterly trade winds blow hard, crashing waves force water into caverns and send impressive geysers shooting up as much as 20 feet through the ironshore. The blowholes were partially filled during Hurricane Ivan in 2004, so the water must be rough to recapture their former elemental drama. ✉ *Frank Sound Rd., roughly 10 miles (16 km) east of Bodden Town, near East End.*

Cayman Islands Brewery

BREWERY | In this brewery occupying the former Stingray facility, tour guides explain the iconic imagery of bottle and label as well as the nearly three-week brewing process: 7 days' fermentation, 10 days' lagering (storage), and 1 day in the bottling tank. The brewery's ecofriendly features are also championed: local farmers receive the spent grains to feed their cattle at no charge, while waste liquid is channeled into one of the Caribbean's most advanced water-treatment systems. Then, enjoy your complimentary tasting knowing that you're helping the local environment and economy. The little shop also offers cute merchandise and a happening happy hour that lures locals for liming (as a sign prominently chides: "No working during drinking hours"). ✉ *366 Shamrock Rd., Prospect, George Town* ☎ *345/947–6699* 🌐 *cib.ky* 🎟 *$10.*

★ Crystal Caves

CAVE | FAMILY | At the end of a seemingly endless, bumpy road, your guide takes you on a short hike to the "treehouse" refreshment-souvenir stand of this Grand Cayman locale. A viewing platform provides breathtaking vistas of a ginormous banyan tree framing the first cave entrance. Currently, three large caverns in the extensive network have been opened and outfitted with wood pathways and strategic lighting. Millions of years ago, the network was submerged underwater (a subterranean lake serves as a hauntingly lovely reminder); the land gradually rose over millennia. Nature has fashioned extraordinary crystal gardens and "fish-scale" columns from delicate, fragile flowstone; part of the fun is identifying the fanciful shapes whimsically carved by the stalactites and stalagmites. The 90-minute tours are offered on the hour from 9 am through 4 pm. Ambitious plans include adding ziplines and 4WD trails. If you're going on to tour the East End, look for the fascinating little Davidoff's sculpture garden (depicting local critters) along the coastal highway just outside the caves. ✉ *69 Northside Rd., Old Man Bay, North Side* ☎ *345/949–2283, 345/925–3001* 🌐 *www.caymancrystalcaves.com* 🎟 *$40.*

Wreck of the Ten Sails Park

CITY PARK | This lonely, lovely park on Grand Cayman's windswept eastern tip commemorates the island's most (in)famous shipwreck. On February 8, 1794, the *Cordelia,* heading a convoy of 58 square-rigged merchant vessels en route from Jamaica to England, foundered on one of the treacherous East End reefs. Its warning cannon fire was tragically misconstrued as a call to band more closely together due to imminent pirate attack, and nine more ships ran aground. Local sailors, who knew the rough seas, demonstrated great bravery in rescuing all 400-odd seamen. Popular legend claims (romantically but inaccurately) that King George III granted the islands an eternal tax exemption. Queen Elizabeth II dedicated the park's plaque in 1994. Interpretive signs document the historic details. The ironically peaceful headland provides magnificent views of the reef (including more recent shipwrecks); bird-watching is superb from here half a mile south along the coast to the Lighthouse Park, perched on a craggy bluff. ✉ *Austin Conolly Dr., East End* ☎ *345/949–0121 National Trust* 🎟 *Free.*

Book a tour to see the Crystal Caves, an extensive network of caves that contain colorful stalactites and stalagmites.

Beaches

Colliers Beach

BEACH | Just drive along and look for any sandy beach, park your car, and enjoy a stroll. The vanilla-hue stretch at Colliers Bay, by the Reef and Morritt's resorts (which offer water sports), is a good, clean one with superior snorkeling. **Amenities:** food and drink; water sports. **Best for:** snorkeling; solitude; sunrise; walking. ✉ *Queen's Hwy., Colliers, East End.*

Restaurants

Czech Inn Bar and Grill

$ | **CARIBBEAN** | A popular roadside grill offering Czech foods, steaks, and jerk chicken from chef Jiri Zitterbart is tucked away in Pease Bay, Bodden Town. This ramshackle bar has grown somewhat of a devoted following in a short time. **Known for:** great lobster; classic Caymanian dishes; terrific takeout. [$] *Average main: $10* ✉ *563 Bodden Town Rd., Bodden Town* ☎ *345/939–3474.*

Rankin's Jerk Centre

$$ | **CARIBBEAN** | A faux cow and pig greet you, and you can savor Miss Rankin's scrumptious turtle stew, lobster curry, and jerk dishes in her alluring garden. Don't miss her homemade bread pudding for dessert. **Known for:** great place to meet locals; pretty garden seating; traditional Caymanian fare. [$] *Average main: $12* ✉ *3032 Shamrock Rd., Bodden Town* ☎ *345/947–3155* ⏲ *Closed Sun.*

Tides

$$$$ | **ECLECTIC** | The Wyndham Reef Resort's all-purpose dining room (formerly known as Pelican's Reef) converts into a refined space come evening, its marine murals and nautical paraphernalia (rigging, fish nets) illuminated by candles, with clever partitioning by framed sails to enhance its intimacy. Most of the kitchen hails from the Caribbean, but even the buffets merrily marry culinary influences from India to Italy; they'll infuse hummus with saffron and spike spring rolls with wasabi. **Known for:** marine decor; Barefoot Man performances; bountiful

buffets. 💲 *Average main: $40* ✉ *Wyndham Reef Resort Grand Cayman, 2221 Queen's Hwy., Colliers* ☎ *345/947–3100, 345/516–0218* 🌐 *www.wyndhamcayman.com* ⏲ *No lunch.*

Vivine's Kitchen
$$ | **CARIBBEAN** | Cars practically block the road at this unprepossessing hot spot for classic Caymanian food—literally Vivine and Ray Watler's home. Prime seating is in the waterfront courtyard, serenaded by rustling seagrape leaves, crashing surf, and screeching gulls. **Known for:** good prices for giant portions; authentic Caymanian food; typical island hospitality. 💲 *Average main: $17* ✉ *Austin Dr., Gun Bay, East End* ☎ *345/947–7435* 💳 *No credit cards.*

Hotels

Compass Point Dive Resort
$$ | **RESORT** | This tranquil, congenial getaway run by the admirable Ocean Frontiers scuba operation would steer even nondivers in the right direction, from the powder-blue buildings elevated on stilts with white columns and trim to the interiors' contrasting granite accents and sparkling white-tile floors with luscious lemon, tomato, and peach walls and vivid marine photos. **Pros:** good value, especially packages; top-notch dive operation; free bike/kayak use. **Cons:** poky beaches with poor swim access; conservation is admirable but air-conditioning can't go too low; isolated location requires a car. 💲 *Rooms from: $299* ✉ *346 Austin Conolly Dr., Gun Bay, East End* ☎ *345/947–7500, 800/348–6096, 345/947–0000* 🌐 *www.compasspointdiveresort.com* *29 condos* *No Meals.*

Turtle Nest Inn and Condos
$ | **B&B/INN** | This affordable, intimate, Mediterranean-style seaside inn has roomy one-bedroom apartments and a pool overlooking a narrow beach with good snorkeling. **Pros:** caring staff; wonderful snorkeling; thoughtful extras like a car rental, free Wi-Fi, use of a mobile phone, and cheap equipment rentals. **Cons:** road noise in back rooms; ground-floor room views slightly obscured by palms; car necessary. 💲 *Rooms from: $199* ✉ *166 Bodden Town Rd., Bodden Town* ☎ *345/947–8665* 🌐 *www.turtlenestinn.com, www.turtlenestcondos.com* *18 units* *No Meals.*

Wyndham Reef Resort Grand Cayman
$$ | **RESORT** | **FAMILY** | Casual elegance prevails throughout this exceedingly well-run time-share property, which straddles a 600-foot beach on the less hectic East End. Each villa has a roomy terrace facing the sea; two-bedroom units can be partitioned, but even the studio has Wi-Fi, microwave, and fridge. **Pros:**; romantically remote; all-inclusive packages and online discounts available; enthusiastic staff (including a crackerjack wedding coordinator). **Cons:** glorious beach but often a seaweed problem; few dining options nearby; remote. 💲 *Rooms from: $349* ✉ *2221 Queen's Hwy., Colliers, East End* ☎ *345/947–3100, 888/232–0541* 🌐 *www.wyndhamcayman.com* *152 suites* *No Meals.*

Nightlife

BARS AND MUSIC CLUBS

The Beach Bar
BARS | This spot draws an eclectic group of dive masters, expats, honeymooners, and mingling singles. The knockout, colorful cocktails pack quite a punch, making the sunset last for hours. The bar dialogue is entertainment enough, but don't miss local legend, country-calypsonian Barefoot Man, when he plays "upstairs" at Tides—he's to Cayman what Jimmy Buffett is to Key West. ✉ *Wyndham Reef Resort Grand Cayman, 2221 Queen's Hwy., Colliers, East End* ☎ *345/947–3100* 🌐 *www.wyndhamcayman.com.*

Eat Like a Local

Caymanian cuisine evolved from whatever could be coaxed from the sea and eked out from the poor, porous soil. Farmers cultivated carb-rich crops that could remain fresh without refrigeration and furnish energy for the heavy labor typical of islanders' hardscrabble existence. Hence pumpkins, coconuts, plantains, breadfruit, sweet potatoes, yams, and other "provisions" (root vegetables) became staple ingredients. Turtle (now farm-raised), the traditional specialty, can be served in soup or stew and as a steak. Conch, the meat of a large pink mollusk, is prepared in stews, chowders, fritters, and pan-fried (cracked). Fish—including snapper, tuna, wahoo, grouper, and marlin—is served baked, broiled, steamed, or "Cayman-style," as an *escoveitch* (pan-fried with peppers, onions, and tomatoes).

Rundown is another classic: fish (marinated with fresh lime juice, scallions, and fiery Scotch bonnet peppers) is steamed in coconut milk with breadfruit, pumpkin dumplings, and/or cassava. Fish tea boils and bubbles similar ingredients for hours—even days—until it thickens into gravy. The traditional dessert, heavy cake, earned its name because excluding scarce flour and eggs made it incredibly dense: coconut, sugar, spices, and butter are boiled, mixed with seasonal binders (cassava, yam, pumpkin), and baked.

Jamaican influence is seen in oxtail, goat stew, jerk chicken and pork, salt cod, and ackee (a red tree fruit resembling scrambled eggs in flavor and texture when cooked), and *manish* water—a lusty goat-head stew with garlic, thyme, scallion, green banana (i.e., plantain), yam, potato, and other tubers.

Aspiring Anthony Bourdains should seek out roadside vans, huts, kiosks, and stalls dishing out unfamiliar grub that might unnerve wannabe *Survivor* contestants. They offer authentic fare at very fair prices, with main dish and heaping helpings of sides costing less than CI$10. If you thought Mickey D's special sauce or Coke were secret formulas, try prying prized recipes handed down for generations from these islanders.

Bodden Town's jerk emporia are generally considered the best.

★ South Coast Bar and Grill

BARS | This delightful seaside slice of old Cayman—grizzled regulars slamming down dominoes, fabulous sea views, old model cars, Friday-night dances to local legend Lammie, karaoke Saturday with Elvis impersonator Errol Dunbar, and reasonably priced red conch chowder and jerk chicken sausage—is also a big politico hangout. Fascinating photos, some historical, show local scenes and personalities. The juke jives, from Creedence Clearwater Revival to Mighty Sparrow. ✉ *2035 Bodden Town Rd., Breakers, East End* ☎ *345/947–2517* 🌐 *www.southcoastbar.com.*

Performing Arts

Lions Centre

ARTS CENTERS | The center hosts events throughout the year: Battle of the Bands competitions, concerts by top names on the Caribbean and international music scene such as Maxi Priest, stage productions, pageants, and sporting events. ✉ *905 Crewe Rd., Red Bay Estate, George Town* ☎ *345/945–4667, 345/949–7211.*

Prospect Playhouse

THEATER | A thrust proscenium stage allows the Cayman Drama Society and its partner arts organizations to mount comedies, musicals, and dramas (original and revival) year-round. ✉ *223B Shamrock Rd., Prospect, George Town* ☎ *345/947–1998, 345/949–5054* 🌐 *www.cds.ky.*

Activities

BIRD-WATCHING

Silver Thatch Tours

BIRD WATCHING | Geddes Hislop, who knows his birds and his island (though he's Trinidadian by birth), runs customizable five-hour natural and historic heritage tours ($50 an hour up to four people), including the Queen Elizabeth II Botanic Park's nature trail and lake and other prime birding spots. Serious birders leave at dawn. Prearranged tours include a guide, pickup and return transport, and refreshments—a great excuse to discuss herbal medicinal folklore. ☎ *345/925–7401* 🌐 *birdingpal.org/Cayman.htm.*

DIVING

One of the world's leading dive destinations, Grand Cayman's dramatic underwater topography features plunging walls, soaring skyscraper pinnacles, grottoes, arches, swim-throughs adorned with vibrant sponges, coral-encrusted caverns, and canyons patrolled by Lilliputian grunts to gargantuan groupers, hammerheads to hawksbill turtles.

There are more than 200 pristine dive sites, many less than half a mile from land and easily accessible, including wreck, wall, and shore options. Add exceptional visibility from 80 to 150 feet and calm, current-free water at a constant bathlike 80°F. Cayman is serious about conservation, with Marine Park, Replenishment, and Environmental Park zones and stringently enforced laws to protect the fragile, endangered marine environment (fines of up to $500,000 and a year in prison are the price for damaging living coral, which can take years to regrow). Most boats use biodegradable cleansers and environmentally friendly drinking cups; moorings at popular sites prevent coral and sponge damage caused by continual anchoring, and diving with gloves is prohibited to reduce the temptation to touch.

Pristine clear water, breathtaking coral formations, and plentiful marine life mark the **North Wall**—a world-renowned dive area along the North Side of Grand Cayman. **Trinity Caves,** in West Bay, is a deep dive with numerous canyons starting at about 60 feet and sloping to the wall at 130 feet. The South Side is the deepest, its wall starting 80 feet deep before plummeting, though its shallows offer a lovely labyrinth of caverns and tunnels in such sites as Japanese Gardens. The less visited, virgin East End is less varied geographically beyond the magnificent Ironshore Caves and Babylon Hanging Gardens ("trees" of black coral plunging 100 feet) but teems with "Swiss cheese" swim-throughs and exotic life in such renowned gathering spots as the Maze.

Shore-entry snorkeling spots include **Cemetery Reef,** north of Seven Mile Beach, and the reef-protected shallows of the **north and south coasts.** Ask for directions to the shallow wreck of the *Cali* in the George Town harbor area; there are several places to enter the water, including a ladder at Rackam's Pub. Among the wreckage you'll find the winch and lots of friendly fish.

★ Stingray City

SCUBA DIVING | Most dive operators offer scuba trips to Stingray City in the North Sound. Widely considered the best 12-foot dive in the world, it's a must-see for adventurous souls. Here dozens of stingrays congregate—tame enough to suction squid from your outstretched palm. You can stand in 3 feet of water at

Stingray City Sandbar as the gentle stingrays glide around your legs looking for a handout. Don't worry—these stingrays are so acclimated to tourist encounters that they pose no danger; the experience is often a highlight of a Grand Cayman trip. ✉ *Near West Bay, North Sound.*

Turtle Reef

SCUBA DIVING | The reef begins 20 feet out and gradually descends to a 60-foot miniwall pulsing with sea life and corals of every variety. From there it's just another 15 feet to the dramatic main wall. Ladders provide easy entrance to a shallow cover perfect for predive checks, and because the area isn't buoyed for boats, it's quite pristine. ✉ *West Bay.*

DIVE OPERATORS

As one of the Caribbean's top diving destinations, Grand Cayman is blessed with many top-notch dive operations offering diving, instruction, and equipment for sale and rent. A single-tank boat dive averages $85, a two-tank dive about $115 (discounts for multidive packages). Snorkel-equipment rental is about $15 a day. Divers are required to be certified and possess a C-card. If you're getting certified, save time by starting the book and pool work at home and finishing the open-water portion in warm, clear Cayman waters. Certifying agencies offer a referral service.

Strict marine-protection laws prohibit taking marine life from many areas.

Ambassador Divers

SCUBA DIVING | This on-call (around the clock), guided scuba-diving operation offers trips for two to eight persons. Co-owner Jason Washington's favorite spots include sites on the West Side and South and North Wall. Ambassador offers three boats: a 28-foot custom Parker (maximum six divers), a 46-foot completely custom overhauled boat, and a 26-footer primarily for snorkeling. Divers can be picked up from their lodgings. A two-tank boat dive is $115. ✉ *Palm Heights Hotel, 747 W. Bay Rd., Seven Mile Beach* ☎ *345/949–4530, 844/507–0441 toll-free* 🌐 *www.ambassadordivers.com.*

Cayman Aggressor IV

SCUBA DIVING | This 110-foot live-aboard dive boat offers one-week cruises for divers who want to get serious bottom time, as many as five dives daily. Nine staterooms with bathrooms en suite sleep 18. The fresh food is basic but bountiful (three meals, two in-between snacks), and the crew offers a great mix of diving, especially when weather allows the crossing to Little Cayman. Digital photography and video courses are also offered (there's an E-6 film-processing lab aboard) as well as nitrox certification. The price is $3,095 to $3,495 double occupancy for the week. ☎ *345/949–5551, 800/348–2628* 🌐 *www.aggressor.com.*

Deep Blue Divers

SCUBA DIVING | **FAMILY** | Two custom-designed 27-foot outward-driven Dusky boats ensure a smooth, speedy ride and can access sites that much larger boats can't. They accept a maximum of eight guests, under the watchful eyes of Nick Buckley, who jokes that diving is "relaxing under pressure." Personalized valet attention and flexibility bring a high repeat clientele; Nick's particularly good with kids and has taught three generations of families. He's often asked by happy customers to join them on dive trips around the world. He and his crew delight in telling stories about Cayman culture and history, including pirate tales and often hilarious anecdotes about life in the Cayman Islands. He offers underwater photo–video services and a range of PADI-certified courses; beach pickup is included. ✉ *245 N. Church St., George Town* ☎ *345/916–1293* 🌐 *www.deepbluediverscayman.com.*

Diving at one of the Cayman Islands' famous coral reefs

★ **DiveTech**

SCUBA DIVING | FAMILY | With comfortable boats and quick access to West Bay, DiveTech offers shore diving at its northwest-coast location, providing loads of interesting creatures, a miniwall, and the North Wall. Technical training (a specialty of owner NJo M Mikutowicz) is unparalleled, and the company offers good, personable service as well as the latest gadgetry such as underwater DPV scooters and rebreathing equipment. They even mix their own gases. Options include extended cross-training Ranger packages, Dive and Art workshop weeks, photography sessions with Tony Land, deep diving, free diving, search and recovery, stingray interaction, reef awareness, and underwater naturalist. Snorkel and diving programs are available for children eight and up, SASY (supplied-air snorkeling, with the unit on a personal flotation device) for five and up. Multiday discounts are a bonus. ✉ *Lighthouse Point, 571 N.W. Point Rd., West Bay* ✣ *Near Boatswain's Beach* ☎ *345/949–1700, 877/946–5658 Holiday Inn branch* 🌐 *www.divetech.com.*

Eden Rock Diving Center

SCUBA DIVING | South of George Town, this outfit provides easy access to Eden Rock and Devil's Grotto. It features full equipment rental, lockers, shower facilities, and a full range of PADI courses from a helpful, cheerful staff on its Pro 42 jet boat. ✉ *124 S. Church St., George Town* ☎ *345/949–7243* 🌐 *www.edenrockdive.com.*

★ **Indigo Divers**

SCUBA DIVING | This full-service, mobile PADI teaching facility specializes in exclusive guided dives from its 28-foot Sea Ray Bow Rider or 32-foot Stamas, the *Cats Meow* and the *Cats Whiskers.* Comfort and safety are paramount. Luxury transfers are included, and the boat is stocked with goodies like fresh fruit and homemade cookies. Captain Chris Alpers has impeccable credentials: a licensed U.S. Coast Guard captain, PADI master scuba diver trainer, and Cayman Islands Marine Park officer. Katie Alpers specializes in wreck, DPV, dry suit, boat, and deep diving, but her primary role is videographer. She edits superlative DVDs of the adventures with music and titles. They guarantee a maximum of six divers. The individual attention is pricier; the larger the group, the more you save. ✉ *Seven Mile Beach* ☎ *345/946–7279, 345/525–3932* 🌐 *www.indigodivers.com.*

★ Ocean Frontiers

SCUBA DIVING | This excellent eco-centric operation offers friendly small-group diving and a technical training facility, exploring the less trammeled, trafficked East End. The company provides valet service, personalized attention, a complimentary courtesy shuttle, and an emphasis on green initiatives and specialized diving, including unguided computer, technical, nitrox instructor, underwater naturalist, and cave diving for advanced participants. You can even participate in lionfish culls. There's a wonderful Skills Review and Tune-Up course so beginners or rusty divers won't feel over their heads. Special touches include hot chocolate and house-made muffins on night dives; the owner, Steve, will arrange for a minister to conduct weddings in full face masks. ✉ *Compass Point, 346 Austin Connelly Dr., East End* ☎ *345/640–7500, 800/348–6096 toll-free, 345/947–0000, 954/727–5312 Vonage toll-free in U.S.* 🌐 *www.oceanfrontiers.com.*

Red Sail Sports

SCUBA DIVING | **FAMILY** | Daily trips leave from most major hotels, and dives are often run as guided tours, good for beginners. If you're experienced and your air lasts long, ask the captain if you must come up with the group (when the first person runs low on air). Kids' options (ages 5 to 15) include SASY and Bubblemakers. The company also operates Stingray City tours, dinner and sunset sails, and water sports from Wave Runners to windsurfing. ☎ *345/949–8745, 345/623–5965, 877/506–6368* 🌐 *www.redsailcayman.com.*

Sundivers at Cracked Conch Macabuca

SCUBA DIVING | Owned by Ollen Miller, one of Cayman's first dive masters, the on-site dive shop at the Cracked Conch restaurant, next to Boatswain's Beach, offers competitive rates for air, lessons, and rentals; shore access to Turtle Reef; and such amenities as showers, rinse tanks, and storage. They are closed on Tuesday. ✉ *Cracked Conch, N.W. Point Rd., West Bay* ☎ *345/949–6606* 🌐 *www.crackedconch.com.ky/sun-divers.*

Sunset Divers

SCUBA DIVING | At a hostelry that caters to the scuba set, this full-service PADI teaching facility has great shore diving and seven dive boats that hit all sides of the island. Divers can be independent on boats as long as they abide by maximum time and depth standards. Instruction (in five languages, thanks to the international staff) and stay-dive packages are comparatively inexpensive. Though the company is not directly affiliated with acclaimed underwater shutterbug Cathy Church (whose shop is also at the hotel), she often works with the instructors on special courses. ✉ *Sunset House, 390 S. Church St., George Town* ☎ *345/949–7111, 800/854–4767* 🌐 *www.sunsethouse.com.*

FISHING

If you enjoy action fishing, Cayman waters have plenty to offer. Experienced, knowledgeable local captains charter boats with top-of-the-line equipment, bait, ice, and often lunch included in the price (usually $700 to $950 per half day, $1,200 to $1,600 for a full day). Options include deep-sea, reef, bone, tarpon, light-tackle, and fly-fishing. June and July are good all-around months for blue marlin, yellow- and blackfin tuna, dolphinfish, and bonefish. Bonefish have a second season in the winter months, along with wahoo and skipjack tuna.

Bayside Watersports

FISHING | Longtime fisherman Captain Eugene Ebanks established Bayside Watersports in 1974. The family-run West Bay–based company operates two first-class fishing boats, ranging from 31 feet (*Lil Hooker*) to 53 feet (the *Happy Hooker,* which sleeps six for overnight charters farther afield). The tradition began with the original *Hooker,* named after the Moldcraft Hooker lure and whose team, led by son Al Ebanks, caught a 189.4-pound yellowfin tuna in 1989 that still stands as the island record. They do reef-, tarpon-, and bonefishing trips, but their real specialty is deep-water fishing, such as at 12-Mile Bank, a 3-mile (5-km) strip 90 minutes west of Grand Cayman, where leviathan fighters congregate around the submerged peak of an underwater mountain. ✉ *Morgan's Harbour, West Bay* ☎ *345/928–2482* 🌐 *www.baysidewatersports.com.*

Oh Boy Charters

FISHING | Charters include a 60-foot yacht with complete amenities (for day and overnight trips, sunset and dinner cruises) and a 34-foot Crusader. Charles and Alvin Ebanks—sons of Caymanian marine royalty, the indomitable Captain Marvin Ebanks—jokingly claim they've been playing in and plying the waters for a century and tell tales (tall and otherwise) of their father reeling them in for fishing expeditions. No more than eight passengers on the deep-sea boats ensures the personal touch (snorkeling on the 60-footer accommodates more people). Guests always receive a good selection of their catch; if you prefer others to do the cooking, go night fishing (including catch-and-release shark safaris), which includes dinner. ☎ *345/949–6341, 345/926–0898* 🌐 *www.ohboycharters.com.*

R&M Fly Shop and Charters

FISHING | **FAMILY** | Captain Ronald Ebanks is arguably the island's most knowledgeable fly-fishing guide, with more than 20 years' experience in Cayman and Scotland. He also runs light-tackle trips on a 25-foot Robalo and 21-foot Sea Cat. Everyone from beginners—even children—to experienced casters enjoy and learn, whether wading or poling from a 17-foot Stratos Flats boat or his new sleek 17-foot Hobie Pro Angler kayaks. Free transfers are included. Captain Ronald even ties his own flies (he'll show you how). ☎ *345/947–3146, 345/916–5753 mobile* 🌐 *www.flyfishgrandcayman.com.*

GOLF

North Sound Golf Club

GOLF | Formerly the Links at Safehaven, this is Cayman's only 18-hole golf course and infamous among duffers for its strong wind gusts. Roy Case factored the wind into his design, which incorporates lots of looming water and sand bunkers. The handsome setting features many mature mahogany and silver thatch trees where iguanas lurk. Wear shorts at least 14 inches long (15 inches for women) and collared shirts. Greens fees change seasonally, and there are twilight and walking discounts (though carts are recommended), a fine pro shop, and an open-air bar with large-screen TVs. ✉ *557 Safehaven Dr., Seven Mile Beach* ✣ *Off West Bay Rd.* ☎ *345/947–4653* 🌐 *www.northsoundclub.com* 🎫 *$175 for 18 holes, $110 for 9 holes, including cart; twilight rates* 🏌 *18 holes, 6605 yards, par 71.*

Ritz-Carlton Golf Club

GOLF | Designed by Greg Norman in 2006 and built on undulating terrain near mangroves, this lovely course, formerly dubbed Blue Tip, is now open to non-Ritz-Carlton guests as well. Five of the holes are par-4s, and two are par-5s, including a 600-yarder, so there is plenty of muscle to the layout. Abundant water hazards, tricky winds, and sudden shifts in elevation challenge most duffers. No jeans are allowed, and you must wear collared golf shirts. Club rentals are available at the golf shop. ✉ *Ritz-Carlton Grand Cayman, West Bay Rd., Seven Mile Beach* ☎ *345/943–9000, 345/815–6500* 🌐 *www.ritzcarlton.com* 🎫 *$195 for 18 holes, $125 for 9 holes; twilight discounts* ⛳ *9 holes, 3515 yards, par 36.*

GUIDED TOURS

Taxi drivers give personalized tours of Grand Cayman for about $25 per hour for up to three people. Hotels also arrange helicopter rides, horseback or mountain-bike journeys, 4x4 safari expeditions, and full-day bus excursions.

Costs and itineraries are about the same regardless of the tour operator. Half-day tours average $40 to $50 a person and generally include a visit to the Turtle Farm at Boatswain's Beach aquatic park in West Bay, as well as shopping downtown. Full-day tours ($75 to $100 per person) add lunch, a visit to Bodden Town (the first settlement), and the East End, with stops at the Queen Elizabeth II Botanic Park, blowholes (if the waves are high) on the ironshore, and the site of the wreck of the *Ten Sails* (not the wreck itself—just the site). The pirate graves in Bodden Town were destroyed during Hurricane Ivan in 2004, and the blowholes were partially filled. As you can tell, land tours here are low-key. Children under 12 often receive discounts.

Eco Rides Cayman

BIKING | Green excursions that don't cost too many greenbacks are the house specialty, winding through the serene East End. The five routes ($70–$100) run from a scenic coastal route hugging the littoral without stopping, to a "cave trek" and "inland escape" that showcases natural topography—caverns, blowholes, and local farms. Hybrid rentals ($40/day) are available upon request. ✉ *2708 Seaview Dr., East End* ☎ *345/922–0754* 🌐 *www.ecoridescayman.ky.*

Webster's Tours

GUIDED TOURS | This family-run outfit, with many drivers who have been with the company for years, gladly customizes tours according to your interests, with a variety of vehicles at their disposal. The staffers are unfailingly cordial, punctual, and knowledgeable. ☎ *345/945–1433* 🌐 *www.websters.ky.*

HIKING

Mastic Trail

TRAIL | This significant trail, used in the 1800s as the only direct path to the North Side, is a rugged 2-mile (3-km) slash through 776 dense acres of woodlands, black mangrove swamps, savanna, agricultural remnants, and ancient rock formations. It encompasses more than 700 species of flora and fauna, including Cayman's largest remaining contiguous ancient forest of mastic trees (one of the heavily deforested Caribbean's last examples). A comfortable walk depends on weather—winter is better because it's drier, though flowering plants such as the banana orchid blaze in summer. Call the National Trust to determine suitability and to book a guide ($65.50); 3.5-hour tours run Tuesday through Friday morning by appointment. Or walk on the wild side with a $5 guidebook covering the ecosystems, endemic wildlife, seasonal changes, poisonous plants, and folkloric uses of flora. The trip takes about three hours. ✉ *Frank Sound Rd., East End* ⊕ *Entrance by fire station at botanic park, Breakers* ☎ *345/749–1121, 345/749–1124 for guide reservations* 🌐 *www.nationaltrust.org.ky.*

HORSEBACK RIDING

Horseback in Paradise

HORSEBACK RIDING | Gregarious Nicki Eldemire loves telling stories about horse training and life on Cayman. She leads guided tours through Barkers National Park on the West End: an unspoiled peninsular area filled with enthralling plant and animal life along the beaches and wetlands. The steeper price (starting at $90) includes transportation, but it's a private, exclusive experience with no more than four riders per group. And the mounts—mostly Arabians, Paints, and Quarter Horses are magnificent. ✉ *Barkers National Park, Conch Point, West Bay* ☎ *345/945–5839, 345/916–3530* 🌐 *www.caymanhorseriding.com.*

Mary's Stables and Equestrian Center

HORSEBACK RIDING | The top-notch training facility for the Cayman national equestrian team offers classic English riding lessons (dressage and jumping are options) in three arenas and allows you to help groom the horses. ✉ *Half Way Pond, George Town* ☎ *345/949–7360, 345/516–1751* 🌐 *www.equestriancenter.ky.*

Pampered Ponies

HORSEBACK RIDING | **FAMILY** | Offering "the ultimate tanning machine"—horses walking, trotting, and cantering along the beach—the stable leads private tours and guided trips, including sunset, moonlight, and bareback swim rides along the uninhabited beach from Conch Point to Morgan's Harbour on the north tip beyond West Bay. The charge is US$130 per person for the bareback swim, and US$115 for the basic trek. ✉ *355 Conch Point Rd., West Bay* ☎ *345/945–2262, 345/916–2540* 🌐 *www.ponies.ky.*

KAYAKING

★ Cayman Kayaks

KAYAKING | **FAMILY** | Even beginners find the tours easy (the guides dub it low-impact aerobics), and the sit-on-top tandem kayaks are stable and comfortable. The Bio Bay tour involves more strenuous paddling, but the underwater light show is magical as millions of bioluminescent microorganisms called dinoflagellates glow like fireflies when disturbed. It runs only on moonless nights and books well in advance. Passionate environmentalists, owners Tom and Lisha Watling, devised a way to limit exposure of harmful repellent and sunscreen: they designed a "black box" electric boat with a viewing hole at the bottom, as well as high walls that focus your glimpse of the stars above. Tours ($59–$69 with some kids' and group discounts) depart from different locations, most from the public access jetty to the left of Rum Point. They've temporarily discontinued the mangrove wetlands tour, but it's a splendid learning experience when it runs, providing an absorbing discussion of indigenous animals (including a mesmerizing stop at a gently pulsing, nonstinging Cassiopeia jellyfish pond) and plants, the effects of hurricanes, and conservation efforts. ✉ *Rum Point Club, North Side, Rum Point* ☎ *345/746–3249, 345/926–4467* 🌐 *www.caymankayaks.com.*

SAILING

Sail Cayman

SAILING | Neil Galway, an experienced RYA Yacht Master, runs Sail Cayman, offering 30-foot Gemini RIB ecotours and two seaworthy sailboats including the 47-foot Beneteau, *Splendour in the Wind,* for full-day or half-day private sailing or snorkeling. Though not bareboating, it is hands-on: you can crew and even captain if you enjoy sailing. Neil personalizes the cruise to suit any family or group, including Bio Bay night snorkeling, accommodating a maximum of 12–15 passengers. A half day runs $800, a full day $1,400 and up, which includes a deli-style lunch; if you have a large group, it's little more than the price for crowded excursions with twice as many strangers. ✉ *Yacht Club docks B-48, D-15, and D-17, Seven Mile Beach* ☎ *345/916–4333* 🌐 *www.sailcayman.com.*

SEA EXCURSIONS

The most impressive sights in the Cayman Islands are on and underwater, and several submarines, semisubmersibles, glass-bottom boats, and Jules Verne–like contraptions allow you to see these wonders without getting your feet wet. Sunset sails, dinner cruises, and other theme (dance, booze, pirate) cruises are available from $30 to $90 per person.

A group of stingrays patrols the shallows of Grand Cayman.

Nautilus

BOATING | On this semi-submersible you can sit above deck or venture below, where you can view the reefs and marine life through a sturdy glass hull. A one-hour undersea tour is $60. Watch divers feed the fish, or take the Captain's Nemo's Tour that includes snorkeling; a catamaran cruise to Stingray City and land-sea tours are also offered. ✉ *93 N. Church St., George Town* ⊕ *Inside Rackam's* ☎ *345/945–1355* 🌐 *www.facebook.com/nautiluscayman.*

Sea Trek

BOATING | **FAMILY** | Helmet diving lets you walk and breathe 26 feet underwater for an hour—without getting your hair wet. No training or even swimming ability is required (ages eight and up), and you can wear glasses. Guides give a thorough safety briefing, and a sophisticated system of compressors and cylinders provides triple the amount of air necessary for normal breathing while a safety diver program ensures four levels of backup. The result at near-zero gravity resembles an exhilarating moonwalk ($89). ✉ *Cayman Cabana, 53 N. Church St., George Town* ☎ *345/949–0008* 🌐 *www.seatrekcayman.com, www.snubacayman.com.*

SNORKELING

SNORKELING SITES

★ Stingray City Sandbar

SNORKELING | This site (as opposed to Stingray City, a popular 12-foot dive) is the island's stellar snorkeling attraction. Dozens of boats head here several times daily. It's less crowded on days with fewer cruise ships in port. ✉ *North Sound.*

Wreck of the Cali

SNORKELING | You can still identify the engines and winches of this old sailing freighter, which settled about 20 feet down. The sponges are particularly vivid, and tropical fish, shrimp, and lobster abound. Many operators based in George Town and Seven Mile Beach come here. ✉ *93 N. Church St., George Town* ⊕ *About 50 yards out from Rackam's Waterfront Pub.*

SNORKELING OPERATORS

Captain Marvin's

SNORKELING | Multistop North Sound snorkeling trips, as well as fishing charters and land tours, are offered by the indomitable, irrepressible Captain Marvin. One of the first regular Stingray City operators (in business since 1951), he is still going strong in his nineties, though he rarely takes the boats out himself. Full-day trips include lunch and conch dives November–April, when the crew prepares marinated conch as the appetizer; other excursions include the Crystal Caves. The half-day (three hours) tour is the best deal; though large groups can be a drawback. Reservations can be made only from 10 to 3 on weekdays or via the website. Cash payments usually receive a discount. ✉ *Cayman Islands Yacht Club, Seven Mile Beach* ☎ *345/945–7306, 345/945–6975* 🌐 *www.captainmarvins.com.*

Ebanks Watersports

SNORKELING | **FAMILY** | This outfit is run by a large family long known for its aquatic activities. Shawn Ebanks offers a range of water sports, including private charters, scuba diving, fishing, and his popular Sea-Doo wave-runner snorkel tours ($150 for single riders, $200 for two). The crew is friendly, experienced, and particularly adept at holding stingrays for the ultimate photo op; they'll even teach you how to pick one up. Two custom-fitted boats (a 45-foot Garcia and a trim 23-footer) include GPS navigation, VHS radio, freshwater shower, and other necessities. ✉ *164 Yacht Dr., Dock C, West Bay* ☎ *345/925–5273, 345/916–1631, 727/440—5200* 🌐 *www.ebankswatersports.com.*

Fantasea Tours

SNORKELING | **FAMILY** | Captain Dexter Ebanks runs tours on his 38-foot trimaran, *Don't Even Ask,* usually departing from the Cayman Islands Yacht Club ($40 including transfers, $30 children under 12). Tours are not too crowded (22 people max) and Ebanks is particularly helpful with first-timers. Like many captains, he has pet names for the rays (ask him to find Lucy, whom he "adopted") and rattles off factoids during an entertaining, nonstop narration. It's a laid-back trip, with Bob Marley and Norah Jones playing, fresh fruit and rum punch on tap. ✉ *West Bay Rd., Seven Mile Beach* ☎ *345/916–0754* 🌐 *dextersfantaseatours.com.*

Red Sail Sports

SNORKELING | **FAMILY** | Luxurious 62- and 65-foot catamarans (the *Spirits of Cayman, Poseidon, Calypso,* and *Ppalu)* often carry large groups on Stingray City, sunset, and evening sails ($45–$90) including dinner in winter. Although the service may not be personal, it's efficient. A glass-bottom boat takes passengers to Stingray City/Sandbar and nearby coral reefs. Trips run from several hotels, including the Westin and Morritt's, in addition to the Rum Point headquarters. ✉ *Rum Point, North Side* ☎ *345/949–8745, 345/623–5965, 877/506–6368* 🌐 *www.redsailcayman.com.*

SQUASH AND TENNIS

The Courts

TENNIS | Originally a collaboration between Ritz-Carlton Grand Cayman and tennis coach Nick Bollettieri (former mentor of Andre Agassi, Monica Seles, Maria Sharapova, Jim Courier, and the Williams sisters at his legendary Florida academy), the club offers three French-style red clay courts and two Wimbledon-worthy grass courts. The now-independent pros give private lessons ($125); court rental is $40 per hour. ✉ *West Bay Rd., Seven Mile Beach* ☎ *345/943–9000.*

WIND- AND KITESURFING

The East End's reef-protected shallows extend for miles, offering ideal blustery conditions (15 to 35 mph in winter, 6- to 10-knot southerlies in summer) for windsurfing and kiteboarding. Boarders claim only rank amateurs will "tea-bag" (kite-speak for skidding in and out of the water) in those "nuking" winds. They also rarely "Hindenburg" (stall because of a lack of breeze) off West Bay's Palmetto Point and Conch Point.

Cayman Windsurfing with Red Sail Sports at Morritt's

WINDSURFING | This company offers a full range of top-flight equipment as well as lessons. Rentals on top-of-the-line, regularly updated equipment start at $40 per hour. ✉ *Morritt's Tortuga Resort, Colliers, East End* ☎ *345/947–2097* 🌐 *www.tortugadivers.com.*

Kitesurf Cayman

WINDSURFING | Here you can take full advantage of the gusty conditions at Barkers Beach. Head instructor Jhon Mora is a member of the Colombian National Kitesurfing Team; lessons, including tricks such as loops and rolls, are geared toward experienced boarders. They also offer hydrofoil lessons ($300 for 1 lesson, or $100/day rental). Group rates are $150 for two hours (private introductory courses are $280); hotel transfers are free with prebooked lessons. ✉ *Barkers, West Bay* ✥ *Near Papagallo's Restaurant* ☎ *345/916–5483* 🌐 *www.kitesurfcayman.com.*

Cayman Brac

Cayman Brac is named for its most distinctive feature, a rugged limestone bluff (*brac* in Gaelic) that runs up the center of the 12-mile (19-km) island, pocked with caves and culminating in a sheer 140-foot cliff at its eastern end. The Brac, 89 miles (143 km) northeast of Grand Cayman, is a splendidly serene destination for ecoenthusiasts, offering world-class birding, scuba diving, bonefishing in the shallows or light-tackle and deep-sea angling, hiking, spelunking, and rock climbing. With only 1,800 residents—they call themselves Brackers—the island has the feel and easy pace of a small town. Brackers are known for their friendly attitude toward visitors, so it's easy to strike up a conversation. Locals wave on passing and might invite you home for a traditional rundown (a thick, sultry fish stew) and storytelling, usually about the sea, turtle schooners, and the great hurricane of 1932 (when the caves offered shelter). Brackers are as calm and peaceful as their island is rugged, having been violently sculpted by sea and wind.

Sights

★ Brac Parrot Reserve

NATURE PRESERVE | The likeliest place to spot the endangered Cayman Brac parrot—and other indigenous and migratory birds—is along this National Trust hiking trail off Major Donald Drive, aka Lighthouse Road. Prime time is early morning or late afternoon; most of the day they're camouflaged by trees, earning them the moniker "stealth parrot." The loop trail incorporates part of a path the Brackers used in olden days to cross the bluff to reach their provision grounds on the south shore or to gather coconuts, once a major export crop. It passes through several types of terrain: old farmland under grass and native trees from mango to mahogany unusually mixed with orchids and cacti. Wear sturdy shoes, as the terrain is rocky, uneven, and occasionally rough. The 6-mile (10-km) gravel road continues to the lighthouse at the bluff's eastern end, where there's an astonishing view from atop the cliff to the open ocean—the best place to watch the sunrise. ✉ *Lighthouse Rd., Tibbetts Turn* ✥ *½ mile (1 km) south of town* ☎ *345/948–0319* 🌐 *nationaltrust.org.ky/our-work/environmental/brac-parrot-reserve* 🎫 *Free.*

Cayman Brac Museum

HISTORY MUSEUM | A diverse, well-displayed collection of historic Bracker implements ranges from dental pliers to pistols to pottery. A meticulously crafted scale model of the Caymanian catboat *Alsons* has pride of place. The front room

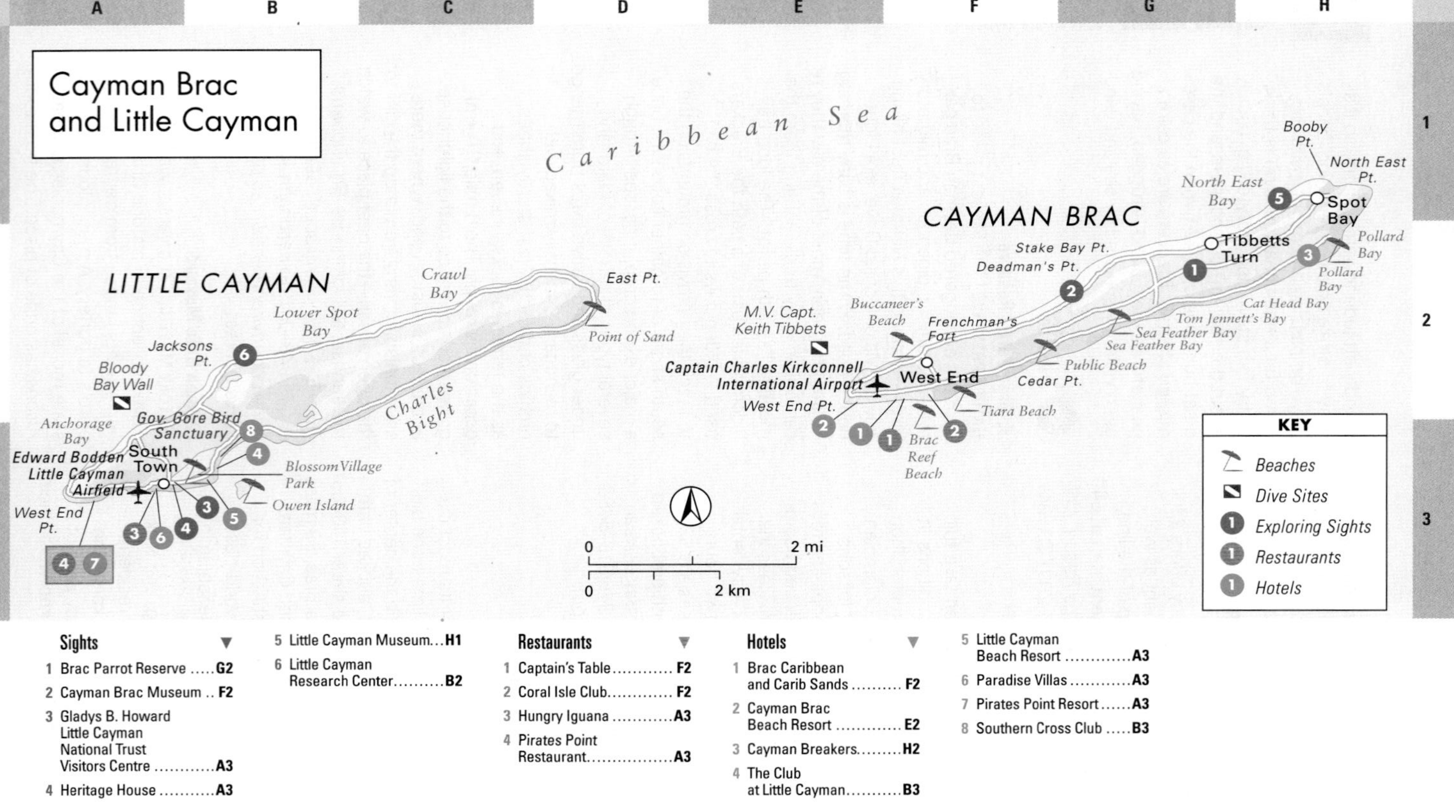

Cayman Brac
and Little Cayman
A
B
C
D
E
F
G
H
1
2
3
Caribbean Sea
LITTLE CAYMAN
CAYMAN BRAC
Crawl Bay
East Pt.
Lower Spot Bay
Point of Sand
Jacksons Pt.
Bloody Bay Wall
Anchorage Bay
Gov. Gore Bird Sanctuary
Edward Bodden Little Cayman Airfield
South Town
Charles Bight
Blossom Village Park
Owen Island
West End Pt.
M.V. Capt. Keith Tibbets
Captain Charles Kirkconnell International Airport
West End Pt.
Buccaneer's Beach
Frenchman's Fort
West End
Brac Reef Beach
Tiara Beach
Cedar Pt.
Public Beach
Deadman's Pt.
Stake Bay Pt.
Sea Feather Bay
Sea Feather Bay
Tom Jennett's Bay
Cat Head Bay
Tibbetts Turn
North East Bay
Booby Pt.
North East Pt.
Spot Bay
Pollard Bay
Pollard Bay
0
2 mi
0
2 km
KEY
Beaches
Dive Sites
Exploring Sights
Restaurants
Hotels
Sights
1 Brac Parrot Reserve G2
2 Cayman Brac Museum .. F2
3 Gladys B. Howard Little Cayman National Trust Visitors Centre A3
4 Heritage House A3
5 Little Cayman Museum... H1
6 Little Cayman Research Center.......... B2
Restaurants
1 Captain's Table............ F2
2 Coral Isle Club............. F2
3 Hungry Iguana A3
4 Pirates Point Restaurant................. A3
Hotels
1 Brac Caribbean and Carib Sands F2
2 Cayman Brac Beach Resort E2
3 Cayman Breakers......... H2
4 The Club at Little Cayman........... B3
5 Little Cayman Beach Resort A3
6 Paradise Villas A3
7 Pirates Point Resort...... A3
8 Southern Cross Club B3

reconstructs the Customs, Treasury, bank, and post office as they looked decades ago. Permanent exhibits include those on the 1932 hurricane, turtling, shipbuilding, and old-time home life. The back room hosts rotating exhibits such as one on herbal folk medicine. ✉ *Old Government Administration Bldg., 279 Stake Bay Rd., Stake Bay* ☎ *345/948–2222, 345/244–4446* 🎫 *Free.*

Heritage House

HISTORIC HOME | An acre of beautifully landscaped grounds dotted with thatched gazebos and fountains includes an old-fashioned well and tannery as well as Cola Cave (used to shelter the former estate owners during hurricanes), with informational panels. The main building, though new, replicates a traditional house; the interior has a few displays and videos depicting Brac history, but the most fascinating element is watching local artists at work. It's a great resource for books on natural history and Caymanian crafts. Daily slide shows, various cultural events, and talks by visiting naturalists are often scheduled. Call before visiting to make sure that the house is open. ✉ *218 N.E. Bay Rd., Spot Bay* ☎ *345/948–0563* 🎫 *Free.*

Beaches

Much of the Brac's coastline is ironshore, though there are several pretty sand beaches, mostly along the southwest coast (where swimmers also find extensive beds of turtle grass, which creates less than ideal conditions for snorkeling). In addition to the hotel beaches, where everyone is welcome, there is a public beach with good access to the reef; it's well marked on tourist maps. The north-coast beaches, predominantly rocky ironshore, offer excellent snorkeling.

Buccaneer's Beach

BEACH | Just north of the airport, the rocky stretch is somewhat rough, but the snorkeling is sublime; you'll recognize the area when you see the 1860 windlass (winch) of the SS *Kersearge* in the ironshore. **Amenities:** none. **Best for:** snorkeling. ✉ *Georgiana Dr., West End* ⊕ *Just before North Side Rd. E.*

Pollard Bay

BEACH | The beach by Cayman Breakers is fairly wide for this eastern stretch of the island. Start clambering east underneath the imposing bluff, past the end of the paved road, to strikingly beautiful deserted stretches accessible only on foot. The water here starts churning like a washing machine and becomes progressively rockier, littered with driftwood. Locals search for whelks here. Steps by the Breakers lead to shore dive sites. Flocks of seabirds darken the sun for seconds at a time, while blowholes spout as if answering migrant humpback whales. Don't go beyond the gargantuan rock called First Cay—the sudden swells can be hazardous—unless you're a serious rock climber. **Amenities:** none. **Best for:** solitude; walking. ✉ *South Side Rd. E, East End.*

Public Beach

BEACH | Roughly 2 miles (3 km) east of the Brac Reef and Carib Sands/Brac Caribbean resorts, just past the wetlands (the unsightly gate is visible from the road; if you hit the Bat Cave you've passed it), lie a series of strands culminating in this beach, relatively deserted despite its name. The surf is calm and the crystalline water fairly protected for swimming. There are picnic tables and showers in uncertain condition. Snorkeling is quite good. **Amenities:** showers. **Best for:** snorkeling. ✉ *South Side Rd. W.*

Sea Feather Bay

BEACH | The central section of the south coast features several lengthy ribbons of soft ecru sand, only occasionally maintained, with little shade aside from the odd coconut palm, no facilities, and blissful privacy (aside from some villas). **Amenities:** none. **Best for:** solitude; swimming, walking. ✉ *South Side Rd., just west of Ashton Reid Dr., Sea Feather Bay.*

 Restaurants

Captain's Table

$$ | **EUROPEAN** | This weathered, powder-blue, wooden building wouldn't be out of place on some remote New England shore, except perhaps for the garish pirate at the entrance. The nautical yo-ho-hokum continues inside—painted oars, model sailboats, and droll touches like a skeleton with a chef's toque—but fortunately the kitchen isn't lost at sea, despite voyaging from India to Italy. **Known for:** nautical decor; "honey-stung" chicken; shoot the breeze with locals and dive crew. Ⓢ *Average main: $19* ✉ *Brac Caribbean, 165 South Side Rd.* ☎ *345/948–1418.*

Coral Isle Club

$$ | **CARIBBEAN** | This seaside eatery daubed in a virtual rainbow of blues from turquoise to teal serves up fine local food, emphasizing fresh seafood and, on weekends, mouth- and eye-watering barbecue. The lusciously painted outdoor bar offers equally colorful sunsets, cocktails, and characters (one regular swears, "If I were any better, I'd be dangerous," before buying another round). **Known for:** weekend entertainment; fun local clientele; mouthwatering barbecue. Ⓢ *Average main: $18* ✉ *Off South Side Rd., West End* ☎ *345/948–2500.*

Cayman Brac has several hotels, resorts, and apartments. Several private villas on Cayman Brac can also be rented, most of them basic but well maintained, ranging from one to four bedrooms. Most resorts offer optional meal plans, but there are several restaurants, some of which provide free transport from your hotel. Most restaurants serve island fare (local seafood, chicken, and curries). On Friday and Saturday nights the spicy scent of jerk chicken fills the air; several roadside stands sell takeout.

PRIVATE VILLAS AND CONDOS

Brac Caribbean and Carib Sands

$ | **RESORT** | These neighboring, beachfront sister complexes offer condos with one to four bedrooms, all individually owned and decorated. **Pros:** reasonably priced for beachfront property; lively restaurant-bar; weekly discounts excellent value for families. **Cons:** Wi-Fi dodgy; limited staff; narrow unmaintained beach. Ⓢ *Rooms from: $190* ✉ *Bert Marson Dr.* ☎ *345/948–2265, 866/843–2722, 345/948–1121, 864/498–4206 toll-free* 🌐 *www.braccaribbean.ky, www.caribsands.com* *65 condos* 🍴 *No Meals.*

Cayman Brac Beach Resort

$$ | **RESORT** | Popular with divers, this well-run ecofriendly resort features a beautiful sandy beach shaded by seagrape trees slung with hammocks and a sizable free-form pool. **Pros:** free Wi-Fi; great dive outfit; coin-operated laundry on-site. **Cons:** rates include breakfast and dinner, but mandatory airport transfer of $20 per person extra; view often obscured from ground-floor units; noise from planes. Ⓢ *Rooms from: $340* ✉ *West End* ☎ *345/948–1323, 727/308–7474 for reservations in Florida, 855/484–0808* 🌐 *www.caymanbracbeachresort.com* *40 rooms* 🍴 *Free Breakfast.*

Cayman Breakers

$ | **APARTMENT** | This attractive, pink-brick, colonnaded condo development sitting between the bluff and the southeast coastal ironshore caters to climbers, who scale the bluff's sheer face, as well as divers, who appreciate the good shore diving right off the property. **Pros:** very attentive managers who live on-site; spectacular views; thoughtful extras like complimentary bikes, jigsaw puzzles, and climbing-route guides. **Cons:** some units slightly musty and faded; gorgeous beach is rocky with rough surf; nearest grocery is a 15-minute drive. *$ Rooms from: $175 ✉ The Moorings, 1902 South Side Rd. E, near East End ☎ 345/948–1463, 345/927–8826 26 condos No Meals ☞ 3-night minimum stay.*

Nightlife

Divers are notoriously early risers, but a few bars keep things hopping if not quite happening, especially on weekends, when local bands (or "imports" from Grand Cayman) often perform. Quaintly reminiscent of *Footloose* (without the hellfire and brimstone), watering holes are required to obtain music and dancing permits. Various community events including talent shows, recitals, concerts, and other stage presentations at the Aston Rutty Centre provide the rest of the island's nightlife.

Barracuda's Bar

BARS | New Yorker Terry Chesnard built his dream bar from scratch, endowing it with an almost 1960s Rat Pack ambiance. Nearly everything is handcrafted, from the elegant bar itself to the blown-glass light fixtures to the drinks. Try the Barracuda shot special "if you dare," or the cocktails, though Terry takes the greatest pride in his top-of-the-line espresso machine. The kitchen elevates pub grub to an art form with pizzas, Reubens, and French melts. Locals flock here for free pasta Friday, karaoke Wednesday, and live music on Thursday. You might walk in on a hotly contested darts, shuffleboard, or dominoes tournament, but the vibe is otherwise mellow at this charming time-warp hangout. *✉ 20 West End Rd., Creek ☎ 345/948–8511.*

La Esperanza

BARS | Known islandwide as Bussy's after the larger-than-life owner, La Esperanza overflows with drinks and good cheer. On weekends, seemingly half the island can be found here, when Bussy fires up the grill and hosts a huge beach jerk barbecue (he'll occasionally give impromptu jerk lessons). Shoot pool in the colorful lounge, or pass time at the alfresco bar or the covered pier jutting into the Caribbean. Drink in the sunset views (and cocktails in matching colors), and if available, try the luscious key lime pie made by Bussy's wife, Velma. The music, heavy on the reggae with the occasional salsa tune thrown in, blares, encouraging everyone to sway along. *✉ The Creek, Stake Bay ☎ 345/948–0591.*

Tipsy Turtle Pub

PUBS | This pub overflows with good cheer and strong drinks. The mudslides are particularly potent, and there are usually some good Cubanos. The alfresco, split-level bar (great water views from the top) serves excellent pub grub (jerk chicken pizza, Caesar salad wrap, portobello-and-Swiss cheeseburger, messy and marvelous spare ribs, tempura shrimp) for around $10 a dish. It's the kind of casual congenial hangout where almost everyone ends up buying a round at some point. Stop by for Tuesday bingo, Wednesday karaoke, or Friday barbecue with live music, which attracts large, enthusiastic crowds. *✉ Cayman Brac Beach Resort, West End ☎ 345/948–1323.*

Shopping

Shopping is limited on the Brac; there are few small stores, though many local ladies sell their wares from home. You'll also find boutiques at the Brac Reef Beach Resort. The prize craft specialties are woven thatch items (Annalise Ebanks is arguably the island's master) and Caymanite jewelry.

★ NIM Things

JEWELRY & WATCHES | Artist and raconteur Tenson Scott fashions exquisite jewelry from Caymanite (he climbs down from the lighthouse without ropes to chisel the stone), triton shells, sea eggs, and more unusual materials—hence the name, which stands for Native Island Made. His wife, Starrie, creates delicate works from sea urchins, hardening the shell with epoxy: cute turtles, bud vases, and planters decorated with minuscule shells. ✉ *N.E. Bay Rd., Spot Bay* ☎ *345/948–0461, 345/939–5306.*

Treasure Chest

MIXED CLOTHING | The shop carries simple resort wear, T-shirts, bonnets, handbags (usually with the Brac logo), and black coral and Caymanite jewelry, as well as a small selection of books, including pamphlets on local birds and fish. ✉ *Tibbetts Sq., West End* ☎ *345/948–1333.*

Activities

DIVING AND SNORKELING

Cayman Brac's waters are celebrated for their rich diversity of sea life, from hammerhead and reef sharks to stingrays to sea horses. Divers and snorkelers alike will find towering coral heads, impressive walls, and fascinating wrecks. The snorkeling off the **north coast** is spectacular, particularly at West End, where coral formations close to shore attract all kinds of critters. The walls feature remarkable topography with natural gullies, caves, and fissures blanketed with Technicolor sponges, black coral, gorgonians, and sea fans. Some of the famed sites are the West Chute, Cemetery Wall, Airport Wall, and Garden Eel Wall. The South Wall is a wonderland of sheer drop-offs carved with a maze of vertical swim-throughs, tunnels, arches, and grottoes that divers nickname Cayman's Grand Canyon. Notable sites include Anchor Wall, Rock Monster Chimney, and the Wilderness. Many fish have colonized the 330-foot MV *Capt. Keith Tibbetts,* a Russian frigate—now broken in two—that was deliberately scuttled within swimming distance of the northwest shore. An artist named Foots has created an amazing underwater Atlantis off Radar Reef. The island's two dive operators offer scuba and snorkel training and PADI certification.

Brac Scuba Shack

DIVING & SNORKELING | Partners Martin van der Touw, wife Liesel, and Steve Reese form a tremendous troika at this PADI outfit, whose selling points include small groups (10 divers max on the custom Newton 36), flexible departures, valet service, and computer profiles. The 30-foot central console *Big Blue* takes no more than five divers and does double-duty for deep-sea fishing. Courses range from Discover Scuba through Divemaster Training, as well as such specialties as wreck, nitrox, and night diving. Rates are par for the course ($110 for two-tank dives), but multiday discounts are available. ✉ *West End* ☎ *345/948–8472, 345/925–3215 mobile* 🌐 *www.bracscubashack.com.*

Reef Divers

SCUBA DIVING | Pluses here include five Newton boats from 42 to 46 feet, valet service, and enthusiastic, experienced staff; slightly higher rates reflect the extras. Certified divers can purchase à la carte dive packages even if they aren't hotel guests. They also arrange snorkeling tours. ✉ *Cayman Brac Beach Resort, West End* ☎ *800/327–3835, 345/948–1323* 🌐 *www.caymanbracbeachresort.com.*

FISHING

Robin Walton

FISHING | This experienced guide has been fishing the waters commercially for years and knows the best times and secret spots where mahimahi, wahoo, marlin, grouper, and tuna hang out. His 21-foot Bayliner Trophy, *TLC,* is equipped with GPS tracking, he quips, "because I'm lazy." He takes you to truly wonderful sites, since he doesn't like the dive-boat traffic. The maximum is four anglers, though he can fit up to eight comfortably for snorkeling. His rates are also fairly reasonable ($125 per hour) because you subsidize his income with your catch, though he generally allots 50% "or whatever you can manage" to his guests, most of whom cook at their rentals. ✉ *Stake Bay* ☎ *345/948–2382, 345/925–2382.*

HIKING

Brac Tourism Office

HIKING & WALKING | Free printed guides to the Brac's many heritage and nature trails can be obtained here (and from the airport and hotels). Traditional routes across the bluff have been marked, as are trailheads along the road. It's safe to hike on your own, though some trails are fairly hard going (wear light hiking boots) and others could be better maintained. ✉ *West End Community Park, west of airport* ☎ *345/948–1649* 🌐 *www.itsyourstoexplore.com.*

Christopher Columbus Gardens

HIKING & WALKING | For those who prefer less-strenuous walking, these gardens have easy trails and boardwalks. The park showcases the unique natural flora and features of the bluff, including two cave mouths. This is a peaceful spot dotted with gazebos and wooden bridges comprising several ecosystems from cacti to mahogany trees. ✉ *Ashton Reid Dr. (Bluff Rd.), just north of Ashton Rutty Centre.*

Sister Islands District Administration

HIKING & WALKING | The administration arranges free, government-sponsored, guided nature and cultural tours with trained local guides. Options include the Parrot Reserve, nature trails, wetlands, Lighthouse/Bluff View, caving, birding, and heritage sites. ☎ *345/948–2222.*

ROCK CLIMBING

If you are experienced and like dangling from ropes 140 feet above a churning sea, the Brac rocks. Ropes and safety gear cannot be rented on the island—you need to bring your own. Through the years, climbers have attached permanent titanium bolts to the **bluff** face, creating some 40 exotic, challenging routes that lure the international climbing community. The Cayman Breakers condo complex has route maps and descriptions.

Rock Iguana

ROCK CLIMBING | This company, run by world-class climbers, operates out of a mobile van, taking aficionados and amateurs alike to the Brac's best sites. They offer both instruction and top-notch gear (they've also been upgrading the bolts around the island). Rock Iguana can accommodate most requests, whether your thrill is rappelling down a sheer rock face or squeezing through barely accessible caverns carved into the bluff. Tours begin at $145 per person; instruction for all levels is $450 for two intense days. ☎ *345/936–2722* 🌐 *climb.ky.*

SPELUNKING

If you plan to explore Cayman Brac's caves, wear good sneakers or hiking shoes, as some paths are steep and rocky and some cave entrances are reachable only by ladders. **Peter's Cave** offers a stunning aerial view of the northeastern community of Spot Bay. **Great Cave,** at the island's southeast end, has numerous chambers and photogenic ocean views. In **Bat Cave** you may see bats hanging from the ceiling (try not to disturb them). **Rebecca's Cave** houses the grave site of a 17-month-old child who died during the horrific hurricane of 1932.

Little Cayman

The smallest, most tranquil of the Cayman Islands, Little Cayman has a full-time population of only 170, most of whom work in tourism. This 12-square-mile (31-square-km) island is still unspoiled and has only a sand-sealed airstrip, no official terminal building, and few vehicles. The speed limit remains 25 mph (40 kph), as no one is in a hurry. In fact, the island's iguanas use roads more than residents; signs created by local artists read "Iguanas Have the Right of Way." With little commercial development, the island beckons ecotourists who seek wildlife encounters, not urban wildlife. It's probably best known for its spectacular diving on Bloody Bay Wall and adjacent Jackson Marine Park. The ravishing reefs and plummeting walls encircling the island teem with more than 500 species of fish and more than 150 kinds of coral. Fly-, lake-, and deep-sea fishing are also popular, as are snorkeling, kayaking, cycling, and hiking. And the island's certainly for the birds. The National Trust Booby Pond Nature Reserve is a designated wetland, protecting around 20,000 red-footed boobies, the Western Hemisphere's largest colony. It's just one of many spots for avian aerial acrobatics. Pristine wetlands, secluded beaches, unspoiled tropical wilderness, mangrove swamps, lagoons, bejeweled coral reefs: Little Cayman practically redefines *escape*. Yet aficionados appreciate that the low-key lifestyle doesn't mean sacrificing high-tech amenities, and some resorts cater to a wealthy yet unpretentious crowd.

Sights

★ Gladys B. Howard Little Cayman National Trust Visitors Centre

VISITOR CENTER | This traditional Caymanian cottage overlooks the Booby Pond Nature Reserve; telescopes on the breezy second-floor deck permit close-up views of their markings and nests, as well as other feathered friends. Inside are shell collections; panels and dioramas discussing endemic reptiles; models "in flight"; and diagrams on the growth and life span of red-footed boobies, frigate birds, egrets, and other island "residents." The shop sells exquisite jewelry made from Caymanite and spider-crab shells, extraordinary duck decoys and driftwood carvings, and great books on history, ornithology, and geology. ✉ *Blossom Village* ☎ *345/623–1107* 🌐 *www.nationaltrust.org.ky/little-cayman.*

Little Cayman Museum

HISTORY MUSEUM | This gorgeously laid out and curated museum displays relics and artifacts, including one wing devoted to maritime memorabilia and another to superlative avian and marine photographs, which provide a good overview of this tiny island's history and heritage. ✉ *Guy Banks Rd., across from Booby Pond Nature Reserve, Blossom Village* ☎ *345/925–7625, 345/323–7166* 🌐 *www.littlecaymanmuseum.org* 🎟 *Free* 🕑 *Closed Sun.*

Little Cayman Research Center

COLLEGE | Near the Jackson Point Bloody Bay Marine Park reserve, this vital research center supports visiting students and researchers, with a long list of projects studying the biodiversity, human impact, reef health, and ocean ecosystem of Little Cayman. Reefs this unspoiled are usually far less accessible; the National Oceanic and Atmospheric Administration awarded it one of 16 monitoring stations worldwide. The center also solicits funding through the parent U.S. nonprofit organization Central Caribbean Marine Institute; if you value the health of our reefs, show your support on the website. Former chairman Peter Hillenbrand proudly calls it the "Ritz-Carlton of marine research facilities, which often are little more than pitched tents on a beach." Tours explain the center's mission and ecosensitive design (including Peter's Potty, an off-the-grid bathroom facility using compostable toilets that recycle fertilizer into gray water for the gardens); sometimes you'll get a peek at the upstairs functional wet labs and dormitories. To make it layperson-friendlier, scientists occasionally give talks and presentations. The Dive with a Researcher program (where you actually help survey and assess environmental impact and ecosystem health, depending on that week's focus) is hugely popular. ✉ *North Side* ☎ *345/948–1094* 🌐 *www.reefresearch.org.*

 Beaches

The southwest part of the island seems like one giant beach; this is where virtually all the resorts sit, serenely facing Preston Bay and South Hole Sound. But there are several other unspoiled, usually deserted strands that beckon beachcombers, all the sand having the same delicate hue of Cristal Champagne and just as apt to make you feel giddy.

Blossom Village Park

BEACH | Developed by the local chapter of the National Trust, the site of the first, albeit temporary, Cayman Islands settlement, in the 1660s, is lined with traditional cottages. Bricks are dedicated to old-time residents and longtime repeat guests. There are picnic tables, a playground, and a dock. The beach is small but has plenty of shade trees, good snorkeling, and calm water. **Amenities:** none. **Best for:** snorkeling; swimming.

★ Owen Island

BEACH | This private, forested island can be reached by rowboat, kayak, or an ambitious 200-yard swim. Anyone is welcome to come across and enjoy the deserted beaches and excellent snorkeling as well as fly-fishing. Nudity is forbidden as "idle and disorderly" in the Cayman Islands, though that doesn't always stop skinny-dippers (who may not realize they can be seen quite easily from shore). **Amenities:** none. **Best for:** fishing; snorkeling; solitude; swimming.

★ Point of Sand

BEACH | Stretching over a mile on the island's easternmost point, this secluded beach is great for wading, shell collecting, and snorkeling. On a clear day you can see 7 miles (11 km) to Cayman Brac. The beach serves as a green- and loggerhead turtle nesting site in spring, and a mosaic of coral gardens blooms just offshore. It's magical, especially at moonrise, when it earns its nickname, Lovers' Beach. There's a palapa for shade but no facilities. The current can be strong, so watch the kids carefully. **Amenities:** none. **Best for:** snorkeling; solitude; sunset; walking.

 Restaurants

Hungry Iguana

$$$ | ECLECTIC | The closest thing to a genuine sports bar and nightclub on Little Cayman, the Iggy caters to the aquatically minded set with a marine mural, wood-plank floors, mounted trophy sailfish, lots of fishing caps, and yummy fresh seafood. Conch fritters are near definitive, while lionfish fingers—when available—with jerk mayo are mouth- and eye-watering. **Known for:** surprisingly decent Indian dishes; boisterous atmosphere by Little Cayman standards; fun, (reasonably) cheap theme nights. 💲 *Average main: $26* ✉ *Paradise Villas, Guy Banks Rd., Blossom Village* ☎ *345/948–0007* 🌐 *www.paradisevillas.com* ⏲ *No dinner Sun.*

★ Pirates Point Restaurant

$$$$ | ECLECTIC | Susan Howard continues the tradition of her mother (the beloved late, irrepressible Gladys Howard), offering Texas-style and Texas-size hospitality at her ravishing little resort. Guests have first privilege, but the kitchen can usually accommodate an extra couple or two; advance reservations are both a must and a courtesy on this island, where nearly everything is imported at great cost and effort. **Known for:** popular sushi nights with ultrafresh fish; jovial atmosphere; fine dining. *Average main: $40 Pirates Point Resort, Preston Bay 345/948–1010 www.piratespointresort.com Closed Sept.–mid-Oct. No lunch.*

Hotels

Accommodations are mostly in small lodges, many of which offer meal and dive packages. The meal packages are a good idea; the chefs in most places create wonderful dishes with often limited resources.

The Club at Little Cayman

$$ | **APARTMENT** | These ultramodern, luxurious, three-bedroom condos are Little Cayman's nicest units, though only five are usually included in the rental pool. **Pros:** hot tub; luxurious digs; lovely beach. **Cons:** handsome but heavy old-fashioned decor; rear guest bedrooms dark and somewhat cramped; housekeeping not included (mandatory fee). *Rooms from: $311 South Hole Sound 345/948–1033, 727/323–8727, 888/756–7400 www.theclubatlittlecayman.com 8 condos No Meals.*

Little Cayman Beach Resort

$$$ | **RESORT** | **FAMILY** | This two-story hotel, the island's largest, offers modern facilities in a boutique setting. **Pros:** great bone- and deep-sea fishing; rates include breakfast and dinner; glorious LED-lit pool. **Cons:** bike rental fee; tiny patios; less intimate than other resorts. *Rooms from: $434 Blossom Village 345/948–1033, 855/485–0022 toll-free www.littlecayman.com 40 rooms Free Breakfast.*

Paradise Villas

$ | **APARTMENT** | Cozy, sunny, one-bedroom units with beachfront terraces and hammocks are simply but immaculately appointed with rattan furnishings, marine artwork, painted driftwood, and bright abstract fabrics. **Pros:** complimentary bike rentals; friendly staff; good value, especially online deals and dive packages. **Cons:** off-site dive shop; small bike rental fee; poky beach. *Rooms from: $229 South Hole Sound 345/948–0001, 877/322–9626 www.paradisevillas.com Closed mid-Sept.–late Oct. 12 villas No Meals.*

★ Pirates Point Resort

$$$$ | **RESORT** | Comfortable rooms and fine cuisine make this hideaway nestled between seagrape and casuarina pines on a sweep of sand one of Little Cayman's best properties. **Pros:** dynamic dive program; fabulous food; fantastic beach. **Cons:** still some units without air-conditioning; occasional Internet problems; tasteful rooms are fairly spare. *Rooms from: $520 Pirates Point 345/948–1010 www.piratespointresort.com Closed Sept.–mid-Oct. 11 rooms All-Inclusive.*

★ Southern Cross Club

$$$$ | **RESORT** | Little Cayman's first resort was founded in the 1950s as a private fishing club by the CEO of Sears-Roebuck and the CFO of General Motors, and its focus is still on fishing and diving in a barefoot luxury environment. **Pros:** international staff tells of globe-trotting exploits; free use of kayaks and snorkel gear; splendiferous beach. **Cons:** rooms include all meals but not drinks; Wi-Fi not available in some rooms and spotty elsewhere; not child-friendly (though families can rent a cottage). *Rooms from: $798 South Hole Sound 345/948–1099, 800/899–2582 www.southerncrossclub.com Closed mid-Sept.–mid-Oct. 13 units Free Breakfast.*

Activities

BIRD-WATCHING

Little Cayman offers bountiful bird-watching, with more than 200 indigenous and migrant species on vibrant display, including red-footed boobies, frigate birds, and West Indian whistling ducks. Unspoiled wetland blankets more than 40% of the island, and elevated viewing platforms (carefully crafted from local wood to blend harmoniously with the environment) permit undisturbed observation—but then, it's hard to find an area that doesn't host flocks of warblers and waterfowl. Brochures with maps are available at the hotels for self-guided bird-watching tours.

★ Booby Pond Nature Reserve

NATURE PRESERVE | The reserve is home to 20,000 red-footed boobies (the Western Hemisphere's largest colony) and Cayman's only breeding colony of magnificent frigate (man-of-war) birds. Other sightings include the near-threatened West Indian whistling duck and vitelline warbler. The RAMSAR Convention, an international treaty for wetland conservation, designated the reserve a wetland of global significance. Near the airport, the sanctuary also has a gift shop and reading library. ✉ *Next to National Trust, Blossom Village.*

National Trust

BIRD WATCHING | The National Trust for the Cayman Islands was established in 1987 with the purpose of preserving natural environments and places of historic significance for present and future generations of the Cayman Islands. 🌐 *www.itsyourstoexplore.com, www.nationaltrust.org.ky.*

DIVING AND SNORKELING

A gaudy, voluptuous tumble of marine life—lumbering grouper to fleet guppies, massive manta rays to miniature wrasse, sharks to stingrays, blue chromis to Bermuda chubs, puffers to parrot fish—parades its finery through the pyrotechnic coral reefs like a watery Main Street on Saturday night. Gaping gorges, vaulting pinnacles, plunging walls, chutes, arches, and vertical chimneys create a virtual underwater city, festooned with fiery sponges and sensuously waving gorgonians draped like come-hither courtesans over limestone settees.

Expect to pay around $105–$110 for a two-tank boat dive and $25–$30 for a snorkeling trip. The island is small and susceptible to wind, so itineraries can change like a sudden gust.

DIVE AND SNORKEL SITES

Snorkelers will delight in taking Nancy's Cup of Tea or "scaling" Mike's Mountain, as well as enjoying Eagle Ray Roundup, Three Fathom Wall, and Owen Island. The areas around the East End are difficult to access from shore because of the jagged ironshore (boats are often preferable) but are worthwhile: Mary's Bay, Snipe Point, and Lighthouse Reef (which has stunning Brac vistas).

Among the many superlative dive sites are the Great Wall, the Meadows, the Zoo, Coconut Walk Wall, School Bus Stop, Sarah's Set, Black Hole, Mixing Bowl, Charlie's Chimneys, and Blacktip Boulevard.

★ Bloody Bay Wall

NATURE SIGHT | This beach, named for being the site of a spectacular 17th-century sea battle, was declared one of the world's top three dive sites by the *maîtres* Jacques and Philippe Cousteau. Part of a protected marine reserve, it plunges dramatically from 18 to 6,000 feet, with a series of staggeringly beautiful drop-offs and remarkable visibility. Snorkelers who are strong swimmers can access the edge from shore, gliding among shimmering silver curtains of minnows, jacks, and bonefish. The creatures are amazingly friendly, including Jerry the Grouper, whom dive masters joke is a representative of the Cayman Islands Department of Tourism.

★ Jackson Wall

REEF | Adjacent to Bloody Bay, Jackson Wall and reef are nearly as stunning. Conditions are variable, the water now glassy, now turbulent, so snorkelers must be strong swimmers. It's renowned for Swiss-cheese-like swim-throughs; though it's not as precipitous as Bloody Bay, the more rugged bottom results in astonishing rock formations whose tunnels and crevices hold pyrotechnic marine life.

RECOMMENDED DIVE OPERATORS

Little Cayman Divers

SCUBA DIVING | This is a personable, experienced outfit that often customizes trips on its 42-foot Newton *Sea-esta.* ✉ *Conch Club, Blossom Village* ☎ *345/938–1026* 🌐 *www.littlecaymandivers.com.*

Pirates Point Dive Resort

SCUBA DIVING | This popular resort has fully outfitted 42-foot Newtons with dive masters who excel at finding odd and rare creatures, and encourage computer diving so you can stay down longer. ✉ *Pirates Point Resort* ☎ *345/948–1010* 🌐 *www.piratespointresort.com.*

Reef Divers

SCUBA DIVING | Little Cayman Beach Resort's outfitter offers valet service and a full complement of courses, with nitrox a specialty. The custom Newton boats include AEDs (defibrillators) and padded camera tables for protection. ✉ *Little Cayman Beach Resort, Blossom Village* ☎ *345/948–1033* 🌐 *www.littlecayman.com.*

Southern Cross Club

SCUBA DIVING | Each boat has its own dock and takes 12 divers max. The outfit has good specialty courses and mandates computer diving. ✉ *Southern Cross Club, 73 Guy Banks Rd., South Hole Sound* ☎ *345/948–1099, 800/899–2582* 🌐 *www.southerncrossclub.com.*

FISHING

Bloody Bay is celebrated equally for fishing and diving, and the flats and shallows including South Hole Sound Lagoon across from Owen Island, Tarpon Lake, and the Charles Bight Rosetta Flats offer phenomenal light-tackle and fly-fishing action: large tarpon, small bonefish, and permit (related to pompano) up to 35 pounds. Superior deep-sea fishing, right offshore, yields game fish such as blue marlin, dolphinfish, wahoo, tuna, and barracuda.

MAM's Tours

FISHING | This reliable company is run by energetic local Maxine McCoy Moore, who comes from fishing royalty of sorts (she, her mum, dad, and five brothers ran McCoy's Diving and Fishing Resort). Deep-sea fishing costs $125 per hour for up to four people; those angling for tarpon and bonefish pay $50 per hour ($75 per couple). Maxine also runs snorkeling trips to Owen Island and will take you conching in season. She's spending more time on Cayman Brac, so call in advance to ensure she'll be on island. ✉ *65 Mahogany Bay, Candle Rd., West End* ☎ *345/948–0104, 345/917–4582.*

★ Southern Cross Club

FISHING | This Caribbean chic resort across from Owen Island offers light-tackle and deep-sea fishing trips with a knowledgeable, enthusiastic staff (book in advance, even as a hotel guest). There's even a skiff with a poling tower to spot the more elusive fish. ✉ *Southern Cross Club, 73 Guy Banks Dr., South Hole Sound* ☎ *345/948–1099, 800/899–2582* 🌐 *www.southerncrossclub.com.*

HIKING

Flat Little Cayman is better suited to biking, but there are a few jaunts, notably the **Salt Rocks Nature Trail,** where you pass ancient mule pens, abandoned phosphate mines, and the rusting tracks of the original narrow-gauge railway, now alive with a profusion of flowering cacti and scrub brush.

Chapter 10

CURAÇAO

Updated by
Susan Campbell

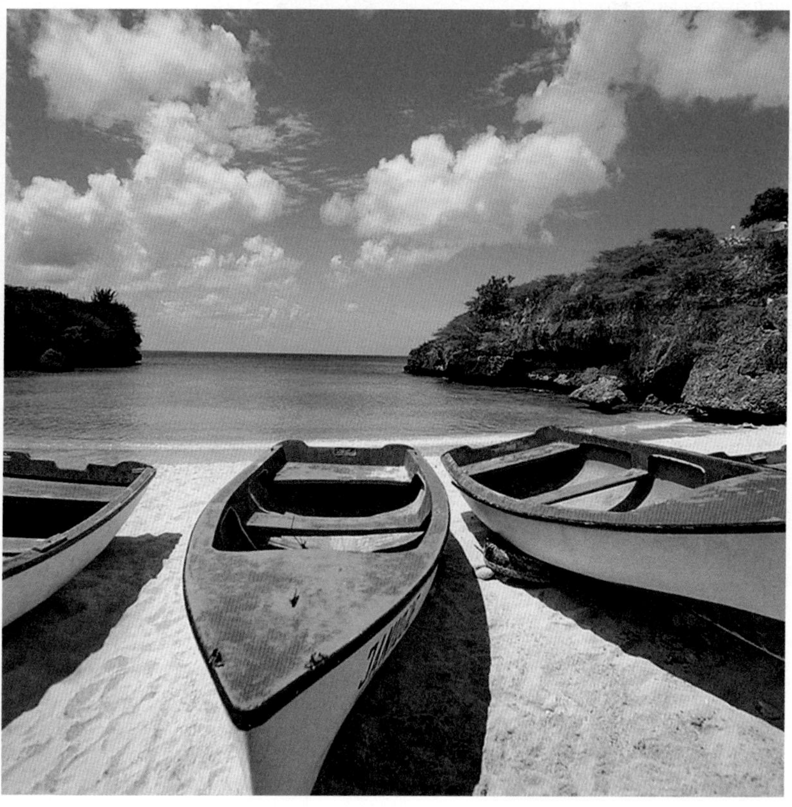

Sights	Restaurants	Hotels	Shopping	Nightlife
★★★☆☆	★★★★☆	★★★★☆	★★☆☆☆	★★☆☆☆

WELCOME TO CURAÇAO

TOP REASONS TO GO

★ **Below the Belt:** Curaçao sits below the hurricane belt, so the weather is almost always alluring, even during the off-season.

★ **Carnival:** Curaçao's biggest party draws an increasingly large crowd.

★ **Culture:** The island's cultural diversity is reflected in the good food from many different cultures.

★ **History You Can See:** Striking architecture and fascinating historic sights give you something to see when you're not shopping or sunning on the charming beaches.

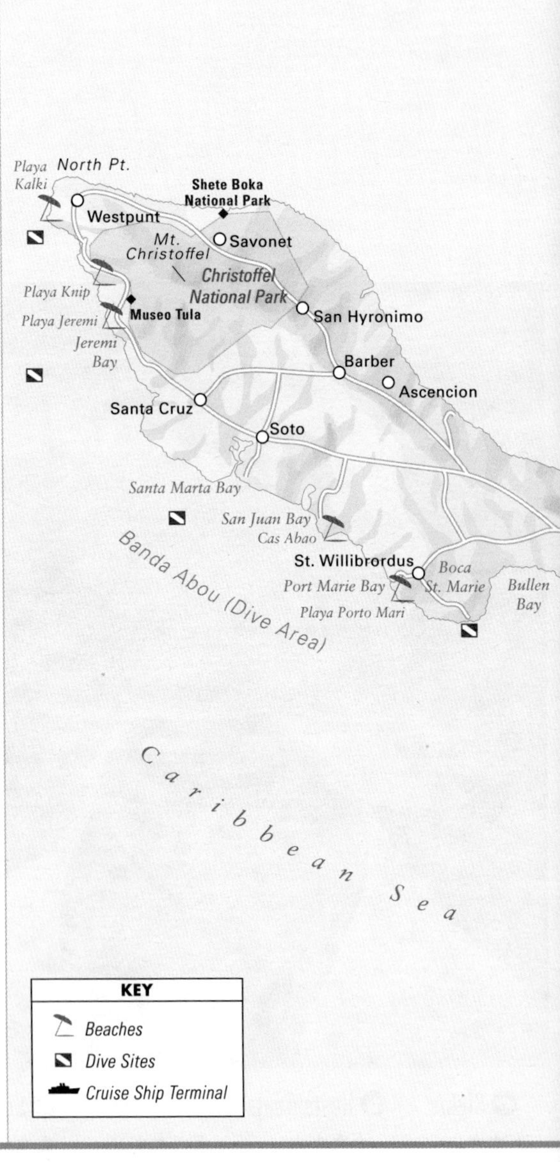

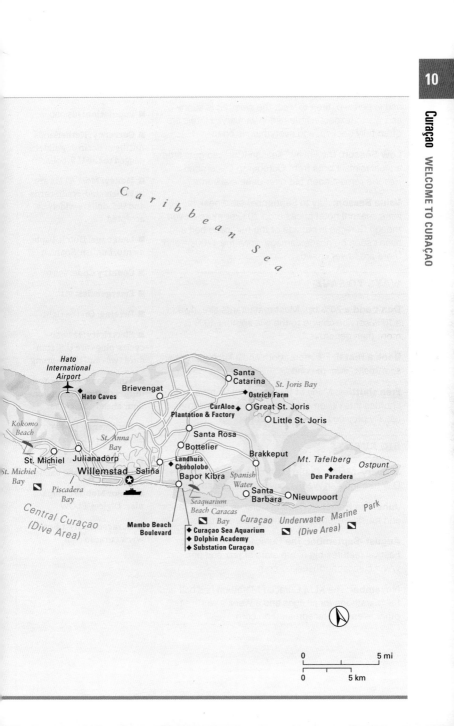

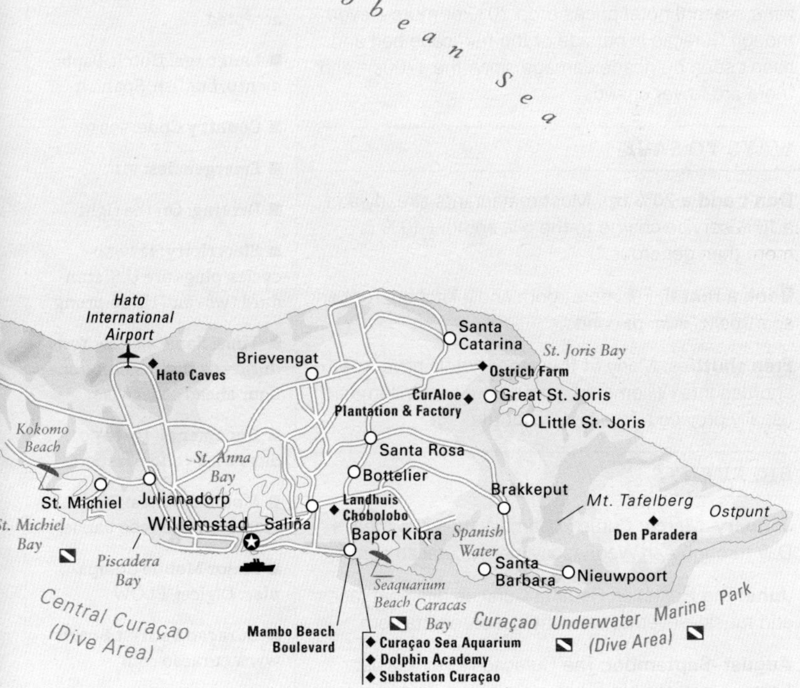
Caribbean Sea
Hato International Airport
Hato Caves
Brievengat
Santa Catarina
St. Joris Bay
Ostrich Farm
CurAloe Plantation & Factory
Great St. Joris
Little St. Joris
Kokomo Beach
St. Anna Bay
Santa Rosa
Bottelier
Brakkeput
Mt. Tafelberg
Ostpunt
St. Michiel
Julianadorp
Landhuis Chobolobo
Den Paradera
St. Michiel Bay
Willemstad
Saliña
Bapor Kibra
Spanish Water
Piscadera Bay
Santa Barbara
Nieuwpoort
Seaquarium Beach
Caracas Bay
Central Curaçao (Dive Area)
Mambo Beach Boulevard
Curaçao Sea Aquarium
Dolphin Academy
Substation Curaçao
Curaçao Underwater Marine Park (Dive Area)
0
5 mi
0
5 km

ISLAND SNAPSHOT

WHEN TO GO

High Season: January to June is the most popular, and expensive, time to visit; the weather is sunny and warm (expect a little rain in January). Hotels are often fully booked, and everything is open.

Low Season: The "rainy" season (Curaçao gets little annual rainfall) lasts from October to December. Resorts remain open but offer deep discounts.

Value Season: July to September (also peak hurricane season) hotel prices drop 20% or more—even though Curaçao is outside of the hurricane belt and hasn't seen hurricane damage since the 1700s—and there are fewer crowds.

WAYS TO SAVE

Don't add a 20% tip. Most restaurants already add a 10% service charge to the bill; another 10% is more than generous.

Book a rental. For more room and a kitchen, rent an apartment, villa, or condo.

Free shuttles. Many of the larger hotels have free shuttles into Willemstad; some hotels in Willemstad usually provide a free beach shuttle.

BIG EVENTS

January–March: Curaçao Carnival runs New Year's Day through Ash Wednesday. www.curacao.com

June: The Heineken Regatta Curaçao has boat races and musical events. www.heinekenregatta.com

August–September: The Curaçao North Sea Jazz Festival features big-name stars of jazz and pop. www.curacaonorthseajazz.com

November: The KLM Curaçao Marathon has half and full marathons for all ages and a week's worth of other events. curacaomarathon.com

AT A GLANCE

- **Capital:** Willemstad
- **Population:** 165,000
- **Currency:** Netherlands Antillean florin or guilder; pegged to the U.S. dollar
- **Money:** Most ATMs are in Willemstad; credit cards and U.S. dollars widely accepted
- **Language:** Dutch, Papiamentu, English, Spanish
- **Country Code:** 599 9
- **Emergencies:** 911
- **Driving:** On the right
- **Electricity:** 127v/50 cycles; plugs are U.S. standard two- and three-prong
- **Time:** Same as New York during daylight saving; one hour ahead otherwise
- **Documents:** Up to 90 days with valid passport
- **Mobile Phones:** GSM (900, 1800 and 1900 bands)
- **Major Mobile Companies:** Digicel, FLOW
- **Curaçao Tourist Board:** www.curacao.com

Curaçao is the most colorful and culture-rich of the Dutch Caribbean triumvirate of tropical islands called the ABCs (Aruba, Bonaire, and Curaçao). Fringed with 38 beaches and ringed with coral walls full of resplendent marine life, Curaçao is a haven for snorkelers and divers with first-rate facilities for both and a wide range of cosmopolitan hotels that welcome all. From the UNESCO World Heritage harbor city to the arid interior dotted with farm houses to the surf-pounded cliffs overlooking endless seas, there is something to satisfy every kind of traveler.

The UNESCO World Heritage city of Willemstad is divided by a deep natural harbor making it a perfect crossroads for trade, and a valuable destination for maritime powers that once ruled the high seas. It has changed hands many times over the centuries in a constant tug-of-war between the Dutch, the French, and the Spanish; even the Americans once had a brief foothold there. Today, it still attracts voyagers from all over the globe, but their designs on the historic city are purely recreational, as tourism is slated to become an increasingly important driver of the economy.

Curaçao is continually awash in colorful celebrations; from the long-lasting Carnival to a multitude of live music events like the Curaçao North Sea Jazz Festival, there is always something additionally special to enjoy beyond the unique architecture and beautiful beaches.

The Handelskade—the long row of candy-colored buildings lining Santa Anna Bay—is the signature postcard shot one will see in reference to this island. Local lore has it that in the 1800s, the governor claimed he suffered from migraines and blamed the glare from the sun's reflection off the then-white structures. To alleviate the problem, he ordered the facades painted in colors. (It's also rumored he might have had an interest in the local paint company!) But there's so much more to Willemstad for history buffs and culture seekers than brightly colored buildings. The ancient neighborhoods are alive with history and interesting stories, with many of the colonial structures that house museums and heritage sites like the Maritime Museum. Restored forts now house entertainment complexes and resorts, and recently transformed neighborhoods like Pietermaai also invite visitors to take a walk through then-and-now contrasts sitting side by side in real time.

Though first inhabited by the Arawak people, Curaçao was "discovered" by Alonzo de Ojeda (a lieutenant of Columbus) in 1499. The first Spanish settlers arrived in 1527. In 1634 the Dutch came via the Netherlands West Indies Company. Eight years later Peter Stuyvesant began his rule as governor (in 1647, Stuyvesant became governor of New Amsterdam, which later became New York). Twelve Jewish families arrived in Curaçao from Amsterdam in 1651, and by 1732 a synagogue had been built; the present structure is the oldest synagogue in continuous use in the Western Hemisphere. Over the years the city built fortresses to defend against French and British invasions—the standing ramparts now house restaurants and hotels. The Dutch claim to Curaçao was recognized in 1815 by the Treaty of Paris. From 1954 through 2006, Curaçao was the seat of government of the Netherlands Antilles, a group of islands under the umbrella of the Kingdom of the Netherlands. In 2010, after discussions with the Netherlands, Curaçao's island council granted the territory autonomy (the same status Aruba attained in 1986).

Today Curaçao's population derives from nearly 60 nationalities—an exuberant mix of Latin, European, and African roots speaking a Babel of tongues—resulting in superb restaurants and a flourishing cultural scene. Although Dutch is the official language, Papiamentu is the preferred choice for communication among the locals. English and Spanish are also widely spoken. The island, like its Dutch settlers, is known for its religious tolerance, and Curaçao is one of the most LGBTQ+-friendly islands in the Caribbean.

Planning

Getting Here and Around

AIR

Curaçao is becoming easier to get to by air as major North American airlines are adding more direct or one-stop connection flights. JetBlue has nonstop service from New York, and Aruba Airlines and American Airlines have nonstop service from Miami. American Airlines also offers service from San Juan, Puerto Rico. Air Canada, Sunwing, and WestJet offer seasonal nonstop flights from Toronto, Canada. KLM offers frequent nonstop flights from Amsterdam. Regional airlines with service between Curaçao and Aruba and Bonaire are Winair, Divi Divi Air, EZ Air, and Aruba Airlines.

Curaçao International Airport (CUR) is about 12 miles from downtown Willemstad's harbor area; the drive is roughly 15 minutes, depending on traffic. The airport has car-rental facilities, duty-free shops, and restaurants.

AIRLINE CONTACTS Aruba Airlines. ☎ *5999/735–0339* 🌐 *www.arubaairlines.com.* **Divi Divi Air.** ☎ *5999/839–1515* 🌐 *www.flydivi.com.* **EZ Air.** ☎ *5999/560–1900* 🌐 *www.flyezair.net.* **WestJet.** ☎ *888/937–8538* 🌐 *www.westjet.com/en-ca.* **Winair.** ☎ *5999/839–1172* 🌐 *www.fly-winair.sx.*

AIRPORT Curaçao International Airport. ☎ *5999/839–1000* 🌐 *www.curacao-airport.com.*

CAR

Some of the larger hotels have free shuttles into Willemstad, or you can take a quick, cheap taxi ride; some hotels in Willemstad usually provide a free beach shuttle, so it's possible to get by without a car. But if you want to really see the island contrasts, a rental car is necessary. If you're planning to do country driving or rough it through Christoffel National Park, a four-wheel-drive vehicle is best. All you need is a valid driver's license. Driving in Curaçao is on the right-hand side of the road; right turns on red are prohibited. Seat belts are required, and motorcyclists must wear helmets. Children under age four must be in child safety seats.

Car Rental: Alamo, Avis, Budget, Hertz, and National Car Rental have locations at the airport and around the island. In addition to renting a car at the airport, you can have one delivered free to your hotel. Rates range from $40 to $85 a day depending on the vehicle. Add 5% tax and optional daily insurance.

CONTACTS Alamo. ✉ *Franklin D. Rooseveltweg 449* ☎ *5999/869–4433* 🌐 *www.alamo-curacao.com.* **Payless Car Rental.** ☎ *5999/839–1500* 🌐 *www.paylesscar.com.* **Autolease Curacao.** ☎ *5999/868–3466* 🌐 *www.autoleasecuracao.com.* **Hertz.** ✉ *Curaçao International Airport* ☎ *5999/888–0088* 🌐 *www.hertz.com.* **National Car Rental.** ☎ *5999/869–4433* 🌐 *www.nationalcar.com.*

TAXI

Taxis are readily available at airport stands and at hotels in Punda, and in Otrobanda; a new service called 24/7 Taxi, which operates like Uber, is available as an app. Fares from the airport to Willemstad and the nearby beach hotels run about $20 to $35, and those to hotels at the island's western end about $45 to $60 (be sure to agree on the rate before setting off). The government-approved rates, which do not include waiting time, can be found in a brochure called "Taxi Tariff Guide," available at the airport, hotels, cruise-ship terminals, and the tourist board. Rates are for up to four passengers. There's a 25% surcharge after 11 pm. Note: If you call a taxi and then decide you do not want it, you will still have to pay a fee, typically $10.

CONTACTS 24-7 Taxi Curaçao. ✉ *Scharlooweg 19, Willemstad* ☎ *5999/844–9247* 🌐 *247taxi.cw.*

Beaches

Curaçao's 38 beautiful beaches run the gamut from isolated scenic small-cove escapes to party-hearty, full-service entertainment venues, and include family-friendly gentle surf spots and wild and rugged cliff-ringed white-sand pockets. Klein Curaçao—the uninhabited satellite sister island only accessible by boat—also has some stellar stretches of sand. Coral beaches along the southeast coast tend to be rocky in the shallow water (wear reef shoes) but they are typically the best spots to snorkel or dive—for where there are rocks, there are usually fish! The west side has more stretches of smooth sand at the shoreline. Exploring the beaches away from the hotels is a perfect way to soak up the island's character, and some have become attractions in their own right, famous for special events and parties like Kokomo. There are snack bars and restrooms on most beaches, and some will have entrance fees or charge for loungers, while others are open to the public with few facilities but are popular with locals who bring their own picnics and outdoor grills on weekends. Some tour companies are now offering half- or full-day beach tours, so you can set foot on a lot of them to discover where you might like to return to spend more time. Note that entrance fees are subject to change. There are a few urban private beaches around Willemstad belonging to the resorts. Some resorts offer day passes for access to their facilities and beach.

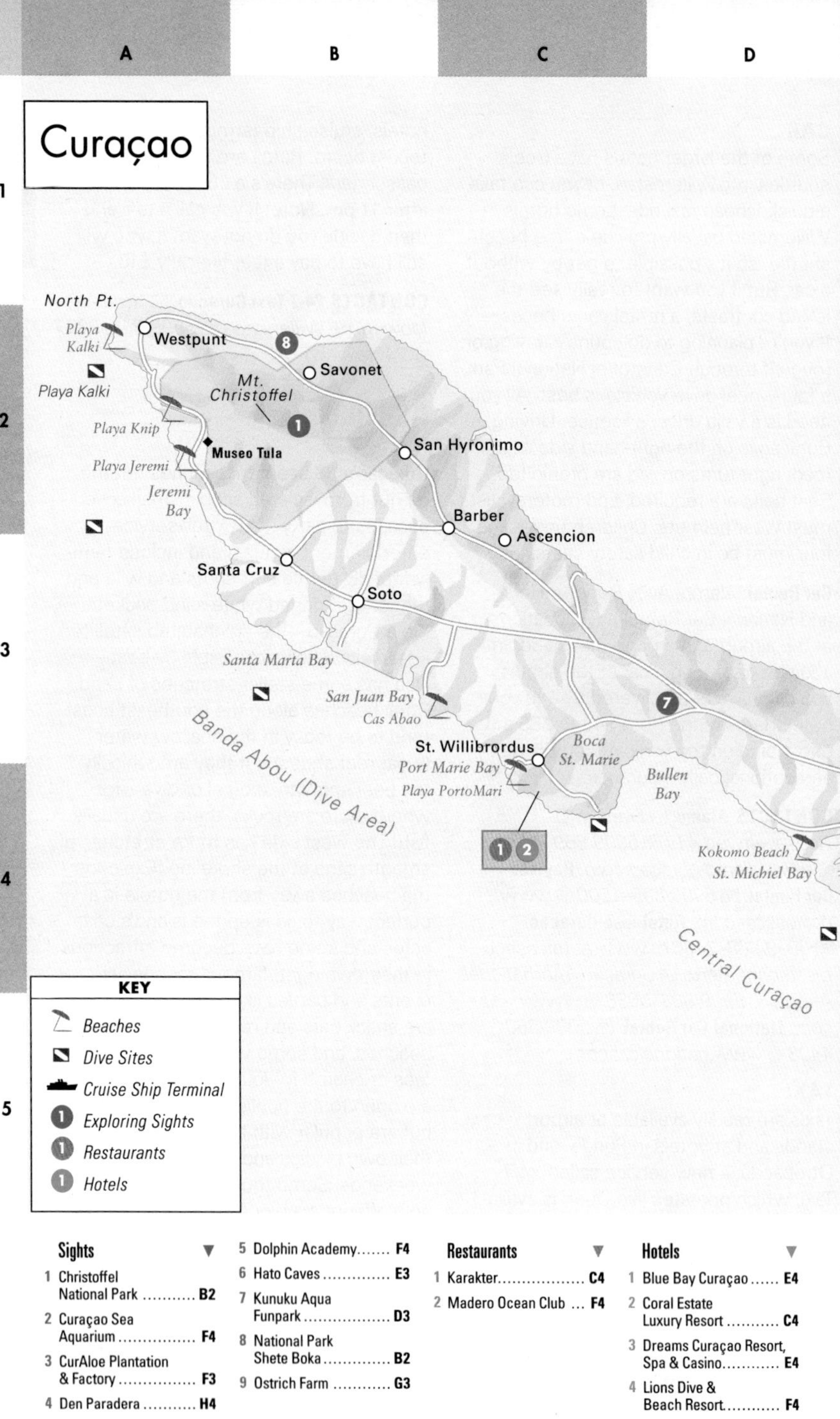

Sights

1 Christoffel National Park **B2**
2 Curaçao Sea Aquarium **F4**
3 CurAloe Plantation & Factory **F3**
4 Den Paradera **H4**
5 Dolphin Academy....... **F4**
6 Hato Caves **E3**
7 Kunuku Aqua Funpark **D3**
8 National Park Shete Boka **B2**
9 Ostrich Farm **G3**

Restaurants

1 Karakter.................. **C4**
2 Madero Ocean Club ... **F4**

Hotels

1 Blue Bay Curaçao **E4**
2 Coral Estate Luxury Resort **C4**
3 Dreams Curaçao Resort, Spa & Casino............ **E4**
4 Lions Dive & Beach Resort........... **F4**

1

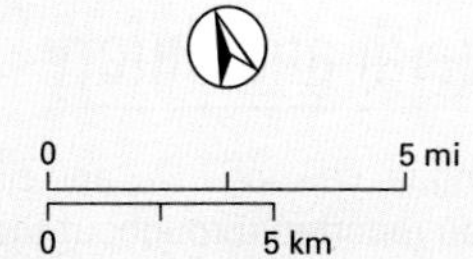

2

3

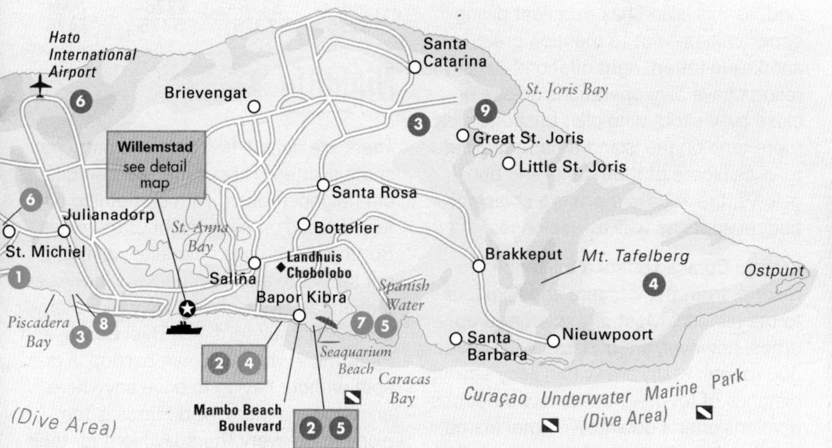

4

5

5 Livingstone Jan Thiel Beach Resort........... **F4**

6 Mondi Lodge **D4**

7 Papagayo Beach Hotel & Papagayo Beach Resort **F4**

8 Zoëtry Curaçao Resort & Spa **E4**

Health and Safety

Dengue, chikungunya, and zika have all been reported throughout the Caribbean. We recommend that you protect yourself from these mosquito-borne illnesses by keeping your skin covered and/or wearing mosquito repellent, especially at dusk. Curacao's Tourism Board website (🌐 www.curacao.com) is best to visit for up-to-date health and safety advisories.

Hotels and Resorts

Resort development was once concentrated around Willemstad, but pocket communities and resorts have cropped up far from the capital in recent years. And, as this island has excellent diving opportunities—not to mention great snorkeling (often, right offshore)—many resorts have dive operations on-site or close by. Visitors who plan to spend a bit more time on the island tend to gravitate to villas (some of them luxe) and bungalows; these days there is a choice of budget spots as well as ecolodges.

Resorts: Curaçao offers a full range of resorts, from the intimate and luxurious to the historic. Most of the larger properties, however, are midsize, with 200 to 300 rooms. Many are within easy striking distance of town—indeed, few other destinations offer a downtown hotel (namely, the Renaissance) complete with a saltwater infinity pool and palm-lined beach. Still, some resorts and petit resorts are secreted away in neighborhoods such as Jan Thiel and Pietermaai. And in Santa Barbara, a massive Sandals Royal adult-only all-inclusive is planned to open in summer of 2022 with an inventory of 350 rooms and suites.

Villas and Rentals. Villa and bungalow rentals are especially popular with divers and European visitors and are generally good options for large groups or longer stays. Coral Estates (www.coralestaterentals.com) has gorgeous villa homes to rent. The Curaçao Tourist Board (www.curacao.com) has a complete list of rental apartments, villas, and bungalows on its website.

Hotel reviews have been shortened. For full information, visit Fodors.com.

What It Costs in U.S. Dollars

$	$$	$$$	$$$$
RESTAURANTS			
under $12	$12–$20	$21–$30	over $30
HOTELS			
under $275	$275–$375	$376–$475	over $475

Nightlife

There are quite a few bars and party hot spots scattered about the island in different neighborhoods, with something different going on every night of the week. But there is no one "nightlife" district per se. There are main pockets, however, that are always nightlife-lively, like Mambo Beach Boulevard, Jan Thiel Beach, and Pietermaai where you can bar-hop in one spot without having to drive anywhere once you are there. And Punda is the place to be every Thursday night for their special "Punda Vibes Celebration" with music and dancing in the streets and fireworks over the famous floating bridge. On the far west end, Kokomo Beach is where the party is always happening, and Otrobanda has hot spots like Bario with its Friday happy hours. Most of the larger resorts have some kind of nightly entertainment on-site for their guests as well, including casinos.

Restaurants

Curaçao's culinary scene has become seriously cosmopolitan in the past few years. Though you can still find places to get traditional, local dishes like *keshi yena* (seasoned meat wrapped in cheese and baked) and goat stew, the emerging generation of chefs has really raised the bar—think Caribbean meets international with a side of nouvelle cuisine or farm-to-fork organic offerings. All the factors combine for a cornucopia of tastes and flavors that meet world-class standards. It's available in a range of locations as eclectic as the fare, from toes-in-the-sand surf-side spots and family-friendly air-conditioned emporiums to lush countryside gardens and unique historic sites like forts and farm houses.

Another popular dining trend on the island if for local chefs to host dinners in their own homes. Options range from the enchanting backyard setting of **Tableu Food Garden** in Willemstad, where small private groups can share Mediterranean-inspired fare to **Mojoi Holisitic's** tropical balcony studio, where you can learn about health and wellness cooking and attend special foodie events. And the new **Vittle Art** ancestral cooking workshop and dinner in the kunuku (countryside) is as immersive as it gets.

For authentic local-style lunches drop by the Old Market in Punda; or after the nightclubs, seek out one of the late-night snack trucks (*truki pan*) for cheap, yet satisfying, eats. Many beach bars also have fabulous fare for less than you'd expect to pay. But for the most part, fine dining will cost you what it's typically worth, especially since almost every kind of food on this island needs to be imported from elsewhere.

WHAT TO WEAR

Dress in restaurants is almost always casual (though beachwear isn't acceptable). Some of the resort dining rooms and more elegant restaurants expect the kind of classier attire that reflects their design, and locals often dress to the nines when going out for a fancy dinner or special occasion and it is appreciated when visitors do, too.

Shopping

From Dutch classics like embroidered linens, Delft earthenware, and cheeses, to local artwork and handicrafts, shopping in Willemstad can turn up some fun finds. But don't expect major bargains on watches, jewelry, or electronics; Willemstad is not a duty-free port (the few establishments that claim to be "duty-free" are simply absorbing the cost of some or all of the tax rather than passing it on to consumers). However, if you come prepared with some comparison prices, you might still dig up some good deals. There are new complexes out of downtown now for ultimate retail therapy—Mambo Beach Boulevard has an eclectic collection of trendy shops at the Sea Aquarium Park, and the Sambil megamall—a massive multilevel shopping and entertainment complex in Veeris Commercial Park—has hundreds of modern stores and trendy boutiques.Willemstad's Punda district is a treat for pedestrians, with most shops concentrated within an area of about six blocks. Closed to traffic, Heerenstraat and Gomezplein are pedestrian malls covered with pink inlaid bricks. Other major shopping streets are Breedestraat and Madurostraat. Here you can find jewelry, cosmetics, perfumes, luggage, and linens—and no shortage of trinkets and souvenirs. The Renaissance Mall right next to Rif Fort has the best selection of high-end designer clothes, accessories, and jewelry retailers and plenty of indoor parking.

Tours

Curacao Green Wheels
SELF-GUIDED TOURS | This new outfit rents sturdy, fat-tired electric scooters to provide an ecofriendly urban touring option. Their motto of "Rent smart, rent green" plays well with those seeking to help keep Curaçao's environment pristine. Single and double seater models come in a range of bright, fun colors and require little instruction for first-timers. You can rent by the day or the week, and pick-up and drop-off is available. ✉ *Architectenweg 5G, Willemstad* ☎ *5999/679–9867* 🌐 *www.curacaogreenwheels.com* 🎫 *$35 per day.*

Step By Step Curacao
GUIDED TOURS | This company offers cool stand-up electric scooters for guided tours of Willemstad's best attractions. Easy to ride on due to the fat tires, these scooters provide a great ecofriendly way to explore the island. Tours last two hours and depart from the Pirate Bay complex in Piscadera Bay. ✉ *Piratebay Piskaderabay, Willemstad* ☎ *5999/692–6404* 🌐 *stepbystepcuracao.com* 🎫 *$35* ⏲ *Closed Sun.*

Visitor Information

CONTACTS Curaçao Tourist Board. ✉ *Pietermaai 19, Pietermaai* ☎ *5999/461–8200* 🌐 *www.curacao.com.*

Willemstad

Dutch settlers came here in the 1630s, about the same time they sailed through the Verrazano Narrows to Manhattan, bringing with them original red-tile roofs, first used on the trade ships as ballast and later incorporated into Willemstad's architecture. Many of the original colonial structures remain, but this historic city is constantly reinventing itself. In addition, the government monument foundation is kept busy restoring buildings, which are susceptible to degradation by the so-called "wall cancer" caused by salty air.

The downtown core is divided into two districts: Punda (meaning "the point") and Otrobanda (meaning "the other side"). They are separated by the Santa Anna Bay waters of the harbor entrance. You can cross from one side to the other by car over the Juliana Bridge, on foot over the Queen Emma pontoon bridge (locally called "the Swinging Old Lady"), or via a free ferry, which runs when the pontoon bridge is swung open for passing ships. Some major hotels outside Willemstad offer shuttle service into town once or twice daily. Shuttles coming from the Punda side leave you near the main entrance to Ft. Amsterdam. Those coming from the Otrobanda side leave you at Rif Fort (from which it's a short walk north to the foot of the pontoon bridge).

East and south of Santa Anna Bay, **Punda** is crammed with shops, restaurants, monuments, markets, and a museum that traces the area's colorful history. Adjacent to it is the historic district of **Pietermaai,** which has morphed from a decrepit neighborhood into a colorful seat of culture. New boutique hotels, fine-dining restaurants, and trendy cafés have taken hold in restored mansions. The district even has its own security force and designated community organization, which hosts many special events and artistic projects.

The Wilhelmina Drawbridge connects Punda to the **Scharloo** district, where a tight-knit Jewish community made up of early merchants and bankers built their stately homes. Some of the neighborhood has been restored as part of the city's UNESCO World Heritage Site development; the architecture along Scharlooweg (much of it from the 17th century) is particularly magnificent. This district is also home to the island's most photographed building: a light-green mansion dubbed the "Wedding Cake House" as it looks like it's been frosted with white icing. But even this architectural confection is being eclipsed by all the spectacular street art that has popped up recently, transforming the neighborhood into a bohemian enclave that's well worth exploring.

Across the bay from Punda and stretching west and north, **Otrobanda** has lots of narrow, winding streets lined with private homes that are notable for their picturesque gables and other Dutch-influenced design elements. This neighborhood was created to accommodate the overflow of residents when the walled city of Punda became too crowded. Today, it's where you'll find the cruise terminal and the famous Rif Fort—a beautifully restored fort that now houses eateries, shops, and a museum. The "barios" of this area are in the process of becoming a new outdoor art district with new galleries, trendy cafés, and boutique stays.

Sights

★ Art Cave Francis Sling

ART GALLERY | Local artist Francis Sling is a man of many talents—painter, outdoor muralist, sculptor, musician, and poet. He documents his creative journeys in videos and online multimedia presentations to help you follow his process; his most famous installation in Scharloo was the building-wide mural he created on his own home. His passion to bring more creativity to his neighborhood also spawned local group *Street Art Skalo* who is now turning the bario into a little Wynwood (Miami) with their own outdoor art—the group was invited to the Miami art festival to create their own mural tribute to their island home. You'll recognize Sling's inimitable style popping up all over Curacao, but now he has a permanent gallery where you can purchase his art, and if you're lucky, watch the artist at work. ✉ *34-54 Bargestraat, Willemstad* ☎ *5999/518–6699* 🌐 *clubd-chef.com* 🕘 *Closed Sun.–Wed.*

★ Cathedral of Thorns

ARTS CENTER | This surreal building-size art installation was painstakingly (literally) created out of thorns. Envisioned by award-winning local artist Herman van Bergen, the sight is now open to the public who can wander through its maze of rooms. Each section is dedicated to a world religion, and nooks and crannies contain a rotating series of art objects by guest artists. It's on the grounds of Landhuis Bloemhof (a museum, art gallery, and historic plantation), but it can be visited on its own, and they often hold special cultural events there. It's an incredible sight when illuminated at night, but just as impressive to see up close during the day. **TIP→ Wear sturdy shoes, errant thorns can pierce your flip-flops!** ✉ *Landhuis Bloemhof, Willemstad* ☎ *5999/526–6349* 🌐 *cathedralofthorns.com* 🎫 *$10* 🕘 *Closed Sun.–Mon.* ☞ *You can request a personal tour with the artist in advance; he is on-site Wednesday mornings.*

Children's Museum Curacao

CITY PARK | **FAMILY** | This museum's hands-on, interactive, and multisensory exhibits—indoors and out—cover several educational themes, including nature, language, culture, and arts. Special seasonal events are held throughout the year. **TIP→ School groups often visit in the mornings, so plan your visit post-lunch for better access to the experiences.** ✉ *Rooi Catootje 1, Rozenweg, Willemstad* ☎ *5999/737–5261* 🌐 *www.childrensmuseumcuracao.org* 🎫 *$5* 🕘 *Closed Mon. and Tues.*

The Curaçao Museum (Het Curacaosch Museum)

HISTORY MUSEUM | Housed in a restored 1853 plantation house that later served as a military hospital, this small museum is filled with artifacts, paintings, and antiques that trace island history. This is also a venue for domestic and

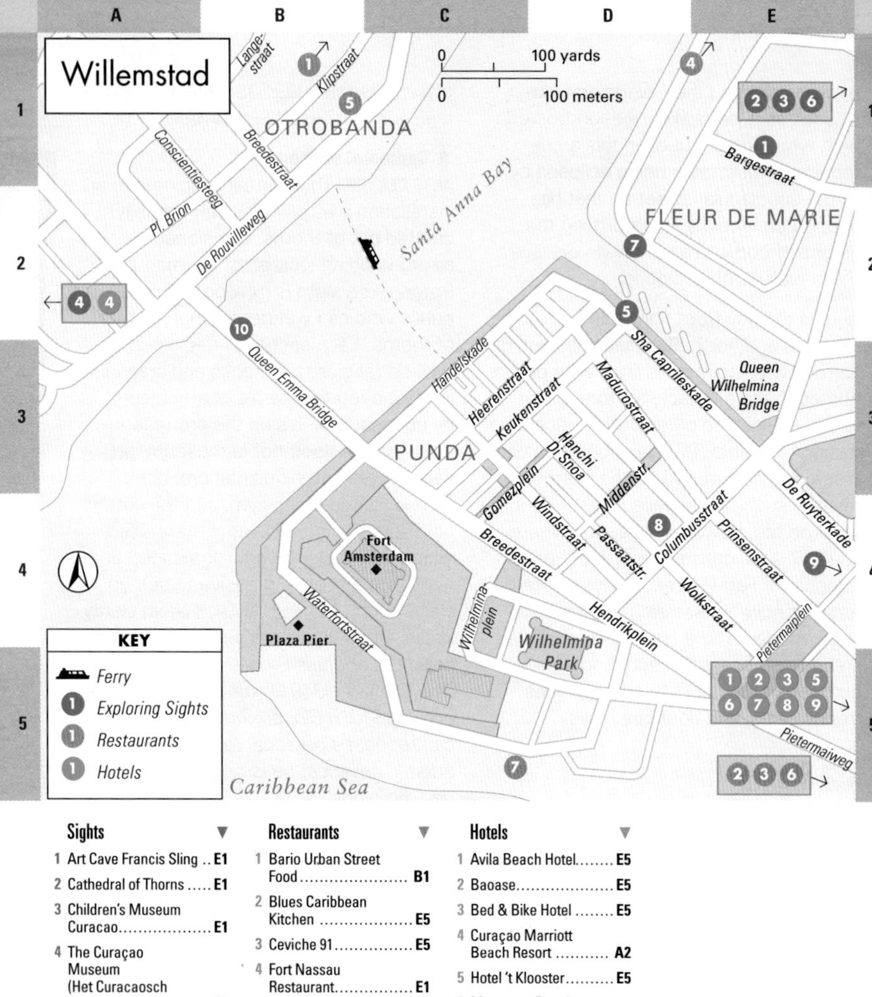

Sights

1 Art Cave Francis Sling .. **E1**
2 Cathedral of Thorns **E1**
3 Children's Museum Curacao.................. **E1**
4 The Curaçao Museum (Het Curacaosch Museum) **A2**
5 Floating Market......... **D2**
6 Landhuis Chobolobo..... **E1**
7 Maritime Museum **D2**
8 Mikvé Israel-Emanuel Synagogue **D4**
9 Plasa Bieuw (Old Market) **E4**
10 Queen Emma Bridge ... **B2**

Restaurants

1 Bario Urban Street Food **B1**
2 Blues Caribbean Kitchen **E5**
3 Ceviche 91................ **E5**
4 Fort Nassau Restaurant................ **E1**
5 Gouverneur de Rouville Restaurant & Café...... **B1**
6 Kome...................... **E5**
7 Scampi's Restaurant **C5**

Hotels

1 Avila Beach Hotel........ **E5**
2 Baoase.................... **E5**
3 Bed & Bike Hotel **E5**
4 Curaçao Marriott Beach Resort **A2**
5 Hotel 't Klooster.......... **E5**
6 Mangrove Beach Corendon Curacao All-Inclusive Resort..... **E5**
7 Renaissance Windcreek Curaçao Resort.......... **E5**
8 Scuba Lodge and Suites **E5**
9 Sunscape Curaçao Resort, Spa & Casino **E5**

international art exhibitions, and there's a sculpture garden that features work by local artists. ✉ *V. Leeuwenhoekstraat z/n, Otrobanda* ☎ *5999/462–3873* 🌐 *hetcuracaosch.museum/* 🎟 *Free* ⏲ *Closed Sun. and Mon.*

Floating Market

MARKET | Originally called the floating market because it was made up of dozens of Venezuelan schooners, the market has morphed into a more stationary local farmer's market with the majority of stalls crammed tightly together on terra firma. Though there are still some South American fishing boats selling the catch for the day, most of the wares are fresh fruit and produce and the vibe is lively and fun. Get there early morning for the best and freshest finds. ✉ *Sha Caprileskade, Punda.*

★ Landhuis Chobolobo

DISTILLERY | The famed blue Curaçao liqueur, which is made from the peels of bitter laraha oranges, originated at this distillery. The family-run operation, located on a heritage estate that dates from the 1800s, offers a choice of guided tours that include tastings, cocktails, and even mixology lessons. Free self-guided tours also include samples. ✉ *Landhuis Chobolobo, Saliña* ☎ *5999/461–3526* 🌐 *www.chobolobo.com* 🎟 *From $15* ⏲ *Closed weekends.*

★ Maritime Museum

HISTORY MUSEUM | Designed to resemble the interior of a ship, this museum contains more than 500 years of maritime and island history with model ships, historic maps, nautical charts, navigational equipment, and more. Exhibit topics include the development of Willemstad as a trading city, Curaçao's role as a contraband hub, *De Alphen* (a Dutch freighter that exploded and sank in St. Anna Bay in 1778 and was excavated in 1984), the slave trade, the development of steam navigation, and the role of the Dutch navy on the island. The museum also offers themed guided tours, including a popular ferry excursion through Curaçao's harbor. ✉ *Van der Brandhofstraat 7, Punda* ☎ *5999/465–2327* 🌐 *www.curacaomaritime.com* 🎟 *Museum $10. Harbor tour $21.* ⏲ *Closed Sun.–Tues. and Thurs.–Fri.* ✍ *Mandatory for harbor cruises.*

Mikvé Israel-Emanuel Synagogue

RELIGIOUS BUILDING | The Western Hemisphere's oldest temple in continuous use is one of Curaçao's most important sights and draws thousands of visitors per year. The synagogue was dedicated in 1732 by a Jewish community that had grown from the original 12 families who came from Amsterdam in 1651 and included Jews who fled persecution by the Inquisition in Portugal and Spain. White sand covers the synagogue floor for two symbolic reasons: a remembrance of the 40 years Jews spent wandering the desert, and a re-creation of the sand used by secret Jews, or *conversos,* to muffle sounds from their houses of worship during the Inquisition. The Jewish Cultural Museum, in the back of the temple, displays antiques and artifacts from around the world. Many of the objects are used in the synagogue, making it a "living" museum. ✉ *Hanchi Snoa 29, Punda* ☎ *5999/461–1067* 🌐 *www.snoa.com* 🎟 *$10; donations also accepted* ⏲ *Closed weekends.*

Plasa Bieuw (Old Market)

(*Marsche Bieuw*)

MARKET | The Old Market is a popular lunch stop for locals working downtown. Visitors also appreciate the hearty, simple authentic fare and good prices. Enjoy such Curaçaoan specialties as *funchi* (polenta), goat stew, fried fish, stewed okra, fried plantains, and rice and peas—all prepared right in front of your eyes in open kitchens by local cooks. ✉ *De Ruyterkade, Punda* 🌐 *www.curacao.com.*

★ Queen Emma Bridge

BRIDGE | Affectionately called "the Swinging Old Lady," this bridge, which is beautifully lit at night, crosses Santa Anna Bay, connecting the two sides of

A daring, mast-eye view of the Handelskade in Punda.

Willemstad (Punda and Otrobanda). The bridge swings open at least 30 times a day to allow passage of ships to and from the sea. The original bridge, built in 1888, was the brainchild of the American consul Leonard Burlington Smith, who made a mint off the tolls he charged for using it: $0.02 per person for those wearing shoes, free to those crossing barefoot. (Although he meant to help the poor, the rich often saved money by crossing barefoot, and the poor would often borrow shoes to cross because they were too proud to admit they could not afford the toll!) Today it's free to everyone. The bridge was dismantled and completely repaired and restored in 2005 and also restored further in 2015. ✉ *Willemstad* 🌐 *www.curacao.com.*

Restaurants

★ Bario Urban Street Food

$$ | **INTERNATIONAL** | This urban street food complex and bar is a perfect fit for the new creative vibe overtaking this historic neighborhood (bario) with all its new outdoor art and cultural attractions. Part of the Bario Boutique Hotel, it's a destination in its own right for trendy fusions of local and international eats served from kiosks made out of old shipping containers. **Known for:** dedicated vegetarian and vegan kiosk; creative dishes made from lionfish; authentic local street food and cakes. [$] *Average main: $15* ✉ *de Rouvilleweg 100, Otrobanda* ☎ *5999/524–6086* 🌐 *bariostreetfood.com* ⏲ *Closed Mon. and Tues.*

★ Blues Caribbean Kitchen

$$$$ | **CONTEMPORARY** | Jutting out over the ocean at the Avila Beach Hotel, this legendary perch is famous for its sea views, its hearty Caribbean-focused dinner fare, and its Thursday night live jazz and blues shows. If you dine out on the deck Thursdays, you might see the Punda Vibe's fireworks over the water in the distance. **Known for:** chef's special weekly three-course surprise menu; authentic local and Caribbean inspired fare; whole fresh fish and seafood platter for two. [$] *Average main: $50* ✉ *Avila*

Beach Hotel, Penstraat 130, Pietermaai ☎ 5999/788–1949 🌐 www.bluescuracao.com ⏲ No lunch. Closed Tues. and Wed.

★ Ceviche 91

$$$ | INTERNATIONAL | This exciting new gastropub at the famous Rif Fort complex is an indoor and outdoor oasis dedicated almost exclusively to creative takes and combos of every kind of ceviche imaginable including vegan ceviche. Open 7 days a week for lunch and dinner, it's the new trendy spot downtown to see and be seen for visitors and locals alike. **Known for:** creative and beautifully plated fusion fare centered around ceviche; interesting non-ceviche specials; great harbor views especially at night. *$ Average main: Nafl.36 ✉ Renaissance Mall and Rif Fort, Rif Fort 701 (fourth floor), Willemstad ☎ 5999/841–4404 🌐 ceviche91curacao.everyorder.io/.*

★ Fort Nassau Restaurant

$$$$ | EUROPEAN | Located in an 18th-century bastion of defense that affords sparkling harbor views, this is one of the island's classic, don't-miss restaurants. The diverse menu spans land and sea with local and international specialties for dinner and creative cuisine for lunch; if you book an early dinner on the deck you'll be treated to spectacular sunset views over the water. **Known for:** an excellent wine list; seasonally inspired prix-fixe tasting menus that change monthly; Caribbean bouillabaisse. *$ Average main: $45 ✉ Schottegatweg 82, near Juliana Bridge, Otrobanda ☎ 5999/461–3450 🌐 www.fortnassau.com ⏲ No lunch weekends.*

★ Gouverneur de Rouville Restaurant & Café

$$$ | ECLECTIC | Dine on the verandah of a restored 19th-century Dutch mansion overlooking Santa Anna Bay. Consistently good local and international fish, chicken, and beef dishes attract locals and visitors alike (reserve ahead if you want a table with a harbor view); be sure to stick around after dinner for live music at the bar, which stays open late. **Known for:** legendary Cuban banana soup; "Green egg" barbecue specials; authentic stobas (stews) and keshi yena (cheese stuffed with meat). *$ Average main: $25 ✉ De Rouvilleweg 9, Otrobanda ☎ 5999/462–5999 🌐 www.de-gouverneur.com.*

★ Kome

$$$$ | CONTEMPORARY | Recently redecorated with an awe-inspiring mural by famed local artist Francis Sling, Kome serves up creative fusion fare. The menu is divided into small (*chiki*) and big (*grandi*) plates, with dishes ranging from grilled octopus and chicken and waffles to Cuban ropa vieja. **Known for:** creative Saturday brunch; superb sangrias and signature drinks; extensive tapas and copas menu every Wednesday night. *$ Average main: $45 ✉ Johan van Walbeeckplein 6, Pietermaai ☎ 5999/465–0413 🌐 www.komecuracao.com ⏲ Closed Sun. and Mon.*

Scampi's Restaurant

$$$ | SEAFOOD | Part of the Waterfort Terrace, this open-air dining spot serves an interesting selection of steak and seafood dishes, including some with Asian twists or Latin American heat (there's also a children's menu). The setting can be very romantic in the evening thanks to stellar views of the sun setting over the port and a roster of signature cocktails like Coastal Kiss and Fancy Scampis. **Known for:** fresh catch of the day and sometimes fresh lobster; Scampi's mix: BBQ ribs, chicken, and shrimp; great harbor views and rotating lunch specials. *$ Average main: $25 ✉ Waterfort Terrace, Waterfortstraat 41-42, Punda ☎ 5999/465–0769 🌐 www.facebook.com/skampiscuracao ⏲ Closed Sun.*

Hotels

★ Avila Beach Hotel

$$ | HOTEL | This beautifully restored, seafront, colonial estate—where the Dutch royal family stays on visits—has state-of-the-art amenities, modern luxury, and a lively, contemporary vibe that keep it from ever feeling dated. **Pros:** gorgeous location with calm protected waters that offer great snorkeling; superb on-site dining and entertainment; wonderful staff. **Cons:** limited number of rooms for people with disabilities; not all rooms are ocean view; main beach can become crowded. *Rooms from: $305 130 Penstraat, Punda 5999/788–1949 www.avilabeachhotel.com 165 rooms, 11 apartments. No Meals.*

Bed & Bike Hotel
$ | **HOTEL** | As the name implies, rates at this cool, flame-orange, two-story hostel–hotel include the free use of bikes—very handy for touring the surrounding and thoroughly hip Pietermaai district. **Pros:** ideal location for dining, nightlife, shopping, and downtown exploration; private rooms have smart TVs and en suite baths; high-tech amenities and an on-site café. **Cons:** communal kitchenettes can get busy; shared rooms can be noisy at night; communal bathrooms with hostel rooms. *Rooms from: $82 Ansinghstraat #1, Pietermaai 5999/843–7373 www.bedandbikecuracao.com 24 rooms No Meals.*

★ Baoase
$$$$ | **RESORT** | Spacious villas, the ultimate in luxury, and top-notch service are the norm at this Balinese-inspired escape, where anything is possible—from private butlers and chefs to in-room spa treatments. **Pros:** unsurpassed luxury; beautiful landscaping and exceptional decor; every villa accesses a swim-out water circuit or has its own private pool. **Cons:** limited dining on-site; day passes are available to the beach so it can get crowded; lacks some of the amenities of a larger resort. *Rooms from: $575 Winterswijkstraat 2, Willemstad 888/409–3506 www.baoase.com 23 villas Free Breakfast.*

★ Curaçao Marriott Beach Resort
$$ | **RESORT** | A $40 million renovation transformed this legendary seafront Dutch colonial-style plantation property into a gorgeous new accommodation option. **Pros:** excellent cheerful and helpful staff; spacious grounds with lush gardens; ideal for groups and conventions with lots of meeting spaces and two large on-site ballrooms. **Cons:** not enough shade palapas or umbrella chairs; beach entrance can be rocky (reef shoes recommended); few organized activities on-site. *Rooms from: $322 John F. Kennedy Boulevard 3, Piscadera Bay, Willemstad 5999/736–8800 www.marriott.com 336 rooms No Meals.*

Hotel 't Klooster
$ | **HOTEL** | The exterior of this bright-yellow former monastery (*klooster* means "cloister") is more impressive than the hotel within, though stained-glass windows and a lovely courtyard with a plunge pool are bright spots amid the otherwise spartan interior. **Pros:** great on-site restaurant and close to other dining and nightlife options; historic charm; reasonable price. **Cons:** few amenities; can be noisy; small rooms. *Rooms from: $152 Veerstraat 12, Pietermaai 5999/698–2560 www.hotelklooster.com 24 rooms No Meals.*

★ Mangrove Beach Corendon Curacao All-Inclusive Resort
$$$$ | **ALL-INCLUSIVE** | **FAMILY** | Opened in summer 2021, this sprawling family-friendly all-inclusive complex is set on its own beach very close to downtown. **Pros:** eclectic choice of high-end and casual dining with 11 distinct outlets; an on-site dedicated dive operator; well configured for families with connecting rooms and multiple beds in some rooms. **Cons:** it's a coral beach so entry can be rocky (wear water shoes); main pool can be very noisy with children; extra charge for private pool and beach cabanas. *Rooms from: $525 31 Pater Euwensweg, Willemstad 5999/434–0650 www.hilton.com 399 rooms All-Inclusive.*

Renaissance Windcreek Curaçao Resort
$ | **RESORT** | **FAMILY** | The four gabled buildings of this downtown Willemstad resort—in the historic Rif Fort amid an entertainment complex of high-end shops, restaurants, and the large Carnaval Casino—are painted in colors that mirror those of Punda across the harbor. **Pros:** exceptionally helpful staff; every amenity imaginable (including a spectacular pool area); walking distance to all the attractions of both Otrobanda and Punda. **Cons:** few rooms have full balconies; better suited to couples and business travelers than families; Rif Fort area can get overcrowded with visitors. *Rooms from: $229* ✉ *Pater Euwensweg, Otrobanda* ☎ *5999/435–5000* 🌐 *www.renaissancecuracao.com* *237 rooms* *Free Breakfast.*

Scuba Lodge and Suites
$ | **HOTEL** | Casual chic meets bohemian boutique at this seaside resort consisting of five, brightly painted, renovated heritage homes; a small beach and surf-side pool; a PADI dive center; and a surprising location in the residential Pietermaai district. **Pros:** expert dive instruction; cheerful, homey vibe; great staff. **Cons:** few amenities; beach isn't swimmable; far from shopping. *Rooms from: $179* ✉ *Kaya Wilson (Papa) Godett 104, Pietermaai* ☎ *5999/465–2575* 🌐 *www.scubalodge.com* *39 units* *No Meals.*

★ **Sunscape Curaçao Resort, Spa & Casino**
$$ | **RESORT** | **FAMILY** | This family-friendly resort has a house reef, dive operation, spa, casino, and dedicated kids' and teens' clubs. **Pros:** upgraded amenities if you opt for the Sun Club level; ample distractions for the whole family; near the massive Curaçao Sea Aquarium complex. **Cons:** no adults-only escape in the water circuits; no-reservations dining can also mean long waits at prime times; beach gets very busy. *Rooms from: $329* ✉ *Martin Luther King Blvd. 78, Willemstad* ☎ *5999/736–7888, 866/SUNSCAPE* 🌐 *www.sunscaperesorts.com/curacao* *341 rooms* *All-Inclusive.*

Nightlife

De Heeren
GATHERING PLACES | This is a great spot to grab a locally brewed Amstel Bright and meet a happy blend of tourists and transplanted Dutch locals. Live music DJs keep it hopping after dinner. ✉ *Zuikertuintjeweg, Willemstad* ☎ *5999/736–0491* 🌐 *deheerencuracao.com* *Closed Sun.*

★ **Mundo Bizarro**
GATHERING PLACES | As the name suggests, the décor here is a hodgepodge of paraphernalia with no rhyme or reason but a lot of creativity. Locals and visitors alike flock here for an unparalleled offbeat atmosphere, super signature cocktails, great happy hours, and live-music every Thursday and Saturday. This venue also serves breakfast, lunch, and dinner. Salsa dancing is also big here. ✉ *Nieuwestraat 12, Pietermaai* ☎ *5999/461–6767* 🌐 *www.mundobizarrocuracao.com.*

★ **Punda Thursday Vibes**
THEMED ENTERTAINMENT | **FAMILY** | This Thursday-night Punda festival takes place in the area around the Queen Emma Bridge, as well as nearby backstreets, alleys, and the Gomezplein square. Happy-hour celebrations begin as early as 4 pm in the resident bars, but things really kick into high gear around 6 pm, when musicians, dancers, arts-and-crafts kiosks, food stalls, pop-up bars, and even a temporary children's playground transform the entire neighborhood into a fabulous alfresco party. Stores in the area also stay open late. The magical evening culminates at around 8 pm, with a fireworks display over the harbor. ✉ *Punda Harborfront, Punda* ☎ *5999/461–8244* 🌐 *www.pundavibescuracao.com.*

Saint Tropez Ocean Club
GATHERING PLACES | Part of the Saint Tropez Suites resort in Pietermaai, this unique day club is where French

Riviera–style meets Dutch Caribbean cool. A gorgeous infinity pool crests a rocky coast with crashing waves and is surrounded by plush daybeds, private cabanas, and loungers. A trendy bar and open-air dining spot serves small bites and full lunch, and there's also surf-side bottle service and tapas by the pool. Access is free to resort guests, and some neighboring hotels also have complimentary access; others must buy a pass. At night, it morphs into a cool open-air lounge and dinner spot often featuring hot DJs and special events. ✉ *Pietermaai 152, Pietermaai* ☎ *5999/461–7727* 🌐 *www.sainttropezcuracao.com.*

Shopping

★ Chichi Shop Punda

SOUVENIRS | You'll see the striking, colorful Chichi characters all around the island, as everything from key chains and other iconic Curaçao souvenirs to larger-than-life sculptures. If you're looking for one-stop shopping and don't want to travel to Serena's Art Factory—where the brand originates—head to this store tucked away on an alley near Gomezplein. The outlet is open late during Punda Thursday Vibes. ✉ *Gomezplein, Windstraat #15, Punda* ☎ *5999/738–0648* 🌐 *chichi-curacao.com* ⏲ *Closed Sun. and Mon.*

Freeport Jewelers

ANTIQUES & COLLECTIBLES | The Freeport Jeweler's Group consists of seven stores (including a Swarovski Boutique) around the island selling high-end brands of jewelry, watches, and collectibles. Willemstad locations are in Punda, Otrobanda, and the Zuikertuin Mall. ✉ *Punda* ☎ *800/617–0766* 🌐 *www.freeportjewelers.com.*

★ Gallery Alma Blou

ART GALLERIES | Curaçao's oldest established gallery, located in Landhuis Habaai, hosts rotating exhibits of works by top local artists. Browse for shimmering landscapes, dazzling photographs, ceramics, or even African-inspired carnival masks. A separate gift shop sells artsy souvenirs. ✉ *Frater Radulphusweg 4, Otrobanda* ☎ *5999/462–8896* 🌐 *www.galleryalmablou.com* ⏲ *Closed Sun. and Mon.*

Penha Curaçao

SOUVENIRS | Founded in 1865 and still run by the Penha family, this landmark store—situated in a UNESCO property that's one of the island's most photographed—specializes in duty-free items, including French perfumes, cosmetics, clothing, eyewear, watches, and high-end lingerie and accessories. There are several other Penha outlets across island, including at the airport. ✉ *Heerenstraat 1, Punda* ☎ *5999/461–2266* 🌐 *www.jlpenha.com* ⏲ *Closed Sun.*

Activities

DIVING AND SNORKELING

Many resorts have dive operators on-site or nearby that offer equipment rental (including snorkeling gear), guided excursions, and instruction—everything from introductory courses done in resort pools to full PADI certification. In the case of the latter, carve out at least four or five days of your vacation for instruction and practice and at least one open-water dive.

The Curaçao Underwater Marine Park includes almost a third of the island's southern diving waters. Scuba divers and snorkelers can enjoy more than 12½ miles (20 km) of protected reefs and shores, with normal visibility from 60 to 150 feet. With water temperatures ranging from 75°F to 82°F (24°C to 28°C), wet suits are generally unnecessary. No coral collecting, spearfishing, or littering is allowed. Some of the most popular dive sites are the Mushroom Forest, the wreck of the *Superior Producer*, and the Blue Room secret cave at Westpunt. Snorkelers and divers also enjoy the little

Curaçao is a great place to snorkel or scuba dive through coral reefs.

sunken tugboat at Spanish Water. Wall diving is good around the Sea Aquarium Park and they also offer open-water dives with dolphins. You can also "dive" there without getting wet by taking a cool submersible mini-sub ride down 1,000 feet via Curasub or an underwater tour from the same dock with the new U-Boat Worx.

The north coast—where conditions are dangerously rough—is not recommended for diving.

★ Dive Curacao

DIVING & SNORKELING | For experienced and wannabe divers alike, this excellent, comprehensive portal is the best one-stop resource for all things dive-related—from sites and operators to festivals and vacation packages. It also offers information on environmental events where you can volunteer to help with things like reef cleanups and marine-life-conservation or coral-restoration projects. 🌐 *www.divecuracao.info.*

GUIDED TOURS

Most of the major tour operators have pickups at the major hotels and offer tours in several languages including English (be sure to mention your preferred language when booking). Offerings have expanded beyond simple island tours in air-conditioned motor coaches to include themes such as beach-hopping, nightlife, culture, culinary, or history—some in combinations covering more than one theme. Ecofriendly modes like walking tours, electric bike tours, and tuk-tuk tours are gaining traction, while adrenaline junkies can opt for ATV, jeep safaris, and even Jet-ski tours of the island.

Art Tours Curacao

BICYCLE TOURS | Join local artist Avantia Damberg on one of several cool tours that showcase all the new outdoor art secreted around the Punda, Otrobanda, and Scharloo neighborhoods. The leisurely tours are typically conducted on weekends and last from 90 to 120 minutes. You can also book a unique bike-and-art outing or a private tour. Avantia discusses the works, the neighborhood history, and the creators who are turning these old streets and alleys into vibrant new cultural scenes. It's a wonderful way to get to know downtown better. Don't forget your camera. ☎ *5999/512–8265* 🌐 *www.facebook.com/arttourscuracao* 🎫 *$10* ⏲ *Closed weekdays.*

Atlantis Adventures Trolley Tour

GUIDED TOURS | **FAMILY** | A novel way to explore the historic city of Willemstad is via the Trolley Train, which is as brightly colored in pastel hues as the Handelskade buildings. The one-hour tour begins and ends at Fort Amsterdam and winds through the neighborhoods of Punda, Scharloo, and Pietermaai with many points of local color and interest throughout. It's only offered Thursdays at 10 am. ✉ *Punda* ☎ *5999/514–4040* 🌐 *curacao-tours.com* 🎫 *$29.*

★ **Free Walking Tours**

WALKING TOURS | Well-informed local guides take groups around the downtown sights from a meeting point at the Rif Fort. Tours are free, but tips are much appreciated. They can only accommodate a maximum of 20 people per tour, so if you are a larger group, make sure to call or book online ahead. Tours are typically two hours; bring sunscreen, water, hats, sunglasses, etc., as the walking can get hot. Check their website for English tour days as different days are in different languages. You can also book private tours, and they are now offering some specialized themed tours as well like wine tasting, rum stops, and cocktail making, which are not free. ✉ *Rif Fort or* ☎ *5999/695-4209* 🌐 *www.freewalkingtourscuracao.com* 🎫 *Free.*

East End

Even urban areas just east of sprawling Willemstad's core can be considered part of the island's east end. Adjacent to the downtown area is the Bapor Kibra district, which got its name (it literally means "broken ship") owing to a shipwreck just off its shore. Today, it's home to the Sea Aquarium and the famous Mambo Beach. Beyond it are Jan Thiel—where a man-made beach and a marina attract partiers and yachties—Spanish Waters, and the self-contained Santa Barbara community.

In more rural areas farther east, you'll find interesting attractions such as the Ostrich Farm, Serena's Art Factory—home of the Chichi, Curacao's most iconic souvenir—and secluded St. Joris Bay, where the island's best kiteboarders practice. Roads are rougher and amenities are fewer out this way, so bring water and snacks when exploring. The addition of a Sandals Royal in 2022 beside the Old Quarry Golf Course has brought more attention to this part of the island.

Sights

★ **Curaçao Sea Aquarium**

AQAURIUM | Located in Sea Aquarium Park—along with the independently operated Animal Encounters, Dolphin Academy, and Substation Curaçao—the island's original and largest marine attraction is entertaining and educational for all ages. Admission allows access to more than 40 saltwater tanks full of sea life; dolphin and sea lion shows; shark-feeding sessions; and opportunities to interact with stingrays, sea turtles, and flamingoes. For extra fees, you can also swim and snorkel with dolphins or get up close to sea lions under the supervision of a trainer as part of the Sea Lion Encounter program. Don't miss the cool new Ocean Lens underwater observatory. A snack bar and souvenir shop are also on-site. ✉ *Seaquarium Beach, Bapor Kibra* ☎ *5999/461–6666* 🌐 *www.csapark.com* 🎫 *Starting at $15* ⏲ *Closed Mon.*

CurAloe Plantation & Factory

FACTORY | The island's successful CurAloe line of products is sold in shops throughout Curaçao. On a visit to the company's plantation (admission is free), you can see more than 100,000 plant specimens, learn about aloe's myriad cosmetic and medicinal applications, and sample and purchase products. Informative videos tell the story; a helpful staff answers questions. ✉ *Kaminda Mitologia, Groot St. Joris, Willemstad* ☎ *5999/767–5577* 🌐 *www.ecocityprojects.com.*

Den Paradera

GARDEN | Dazzle your senses at this organic herb garden, where traditional folk medicines used to treat everything from stomach ulcers to diabetes are grown. Owner Dinah Veeris is a renowned expert and author in the field of herbs and plants. The kitchen is a factory of sorts used to turn homegrown plants like cactus, aloe vera, and calabash into homemade body- and skin-care products like shampoos, ointments, and oils—all for sale at the gift shop. Reservations are essential for guided tours in English, Monday through Friday at 9:30 and 10:30 am, but you can take a self-guided tour with a brochure any time of day. ✉ *Seru Grandi 105A, Morgenster* ☎ *5999/767–5608* 🌐 *www.dinahveeris.com* 🎟 *$8 self-guided tour; $9 guided.*

★ **Dolphin Academy**

COLLEGE | **FAMILY** | The Dolphin Academy—in the same location as but run independently from the Curaçao Sea Aquarium and Animal Encounters—specializes in up close interactions with its friendly, ever-smiling, namesake mammals. The trainers are extremely professional and knowledgeable, and the well-cared-for dolphins thrive in a spacious, natural, saltwater lagoon. Options include shallow-water encounters or swims, free-dive or snorkeling sessions, and lagoon or open-water scuba dives (with Ocean Encounter dive operators). There are also special packages for stays at the nearby Dolphin Suites hotel complex, which is well-equipped for people with disabilities. ✉ *Seaquarium Beach, Bapor Kibra* ☎ *5999/465–8900* 🌐 *www.dolphin-academy.com* 🎟 *From $99 (includes admission to Sea Aquarium).*

Ostrich Farm

FARM/RANCH | **FAMILY** | Though ostriches are not native to Curaçao, the island is home to one of the largest ostrich farms outside of Africa. Guided safari tours depart every hour. You'll learn about the bird's development from egg to maturity. Kids and adults alike will enjoy the chance to hold an egg, stroke a day-old chick, and sit atop an ostrich for a memorable photo. At the Restaurant Zambezi you can sample ostrich meat specialties and other African dishes. A combo safari and tour of the farm, which includes lunch or dinner, is also available, as are quad tours that cover more of the countryside. The Special African Nights package includes a visit to the aloe farm, ostrich facility tour, and three-course dinner with pickup and drop-off at your hotel. The souvenir shop sells crafts made by local artisans. ✉ *Groot St. Joris* ☎ *5999/747–2777* 🌐 *curacaoostrichfarm.com* 🎟 *$18.*

Restaurants

★ **Madero Ocean Club**

$$$ | **INTERNATIONAL** | On a fabulous beach protected by man-made breakwaters, the stylish anchor of the Mambo Beach Boulevard complex offers first-rate fare at lunch and dinner. It also has a great beach bar, a massive pool and surf-side lounge, and daybed rentals. **Known for:** exciting entertainment; premium beach cabanas; eclectic tapas and shareables. 💲 *Average main: $30* ✉ *Mambo Beach Blvd., Bapor Kibra* ☎ *5999/697–7104* 🌐 *maderooceanclub.com.*

Hotels

Lions Dive & Beach Resort

$$ | RESORT | FAMILY | The first dedicated divers' hotel beside the Sea Aquarium has morphed from a spartan lodging into a full-service boutique retreat for all kinds of guests, including families with seriously upgraded rooms, amenities, and new restaurants. **Pros:** multiple meal plan options; on a happening beach and ideal for dive enthusiasts; Olympic-length pool and sports programs for all ages. **Cons:** can be very noisy on weekends due to nightlife on Mambo Beach; not all rooms are sea view; beach can get busy. *Rooms from: $275 Mambo Beach, Bapor Kibra 5999/434–8888 www.lionsdive.com/en 113 rooms Free Breakfast.*

Livingstone Jan Thiel Beach Resort

$ | RESORT | FAMILY | A favorite of divers, this resort offers options for guests with different budgets as well as a great location just steps from Jan Thiel Beach and a village with shops, restaurants, nightspots, a spa, and a casino. **Pros:** one of the largest pools on the island; cheery, family-friendly vibe; expert on-site diving instruction. **Cons:** far from downtown; few units have sea views; basic rooms have few amenities. *Rooms from: $250 Jan Thiel, Kaya Adriàtiko 20-26, Jan Thiel 5999/747–0332 www.janthielresort.com 204 units No Meals.*

Papagayo Beach Hotel & Papagayo Beach Resort

$ | RESORT | Set on the man-made beach in Jan Thiel, this sprawling, self-contained resort community offers a choice of two distinctly different stays: Papagayo Hotel, a sleek, modern, almost minimalist enclave of 155 rooms, and Papagayo Resort, a collection of 80 luxury villas with their own private pool across the street. **Pros:** fresh and modern structures; good range of options for all budgets; lots of amenities and facilities all in one spot. **Cons:** traffic to and from downtown can be an issue; not all rooms have sea views; neighboring public beach has crowds of children/families on weekends. *Rooms from: $185 Kaya Adriátiko, Jan Thiel 5999/747–4333 www.papagayo.com 235 units No Meals.*

Nightlife

★ Jan Thiel Beach

GATHERING PLACES | A favorite party and hang-out oasis for locals and Dutch visitors, Jan Thiel Beach is crammed with sun-lounging beautiful people by day and die-hard partiers by night. And there's lots to keep them sated and entertained day and night with five beach bar/restaurants of different themes all side by side, or steps from each other, and each with their own music or DJ nights. Pastimes include great swimming and snorkeling on their house reef and lively games of beach tennis and volleyball. *Jan Thiel Beach, Jan Thiel 5999/747–0633 www.janthielbeach.com.*

★ Mambo Beach Boulevard

GATHERING PLACES | FAMILY | There's something for sunbathers, swimmers, shoppers, partiers, and foodies of all ages at Mambo Beach Boulevard's two-story seafront complex beside the Sea Aquarium Beach and Park. There's also an amusement park–style ride and a roster of special events throughout the year. This is also *the* place where locals and visitors alike let loose on weekend nights and where they sunbathe and swim during the day. *Bapor Kibra 5999/461–0616 www.mambobeach.com.*

Wet & Wild Beach Club

GATHERING PLACES | There's never a dull moment at this popular and legendary surfside party spot (the name speaks for itself) below Mambo Beach Boulevard. Friday and Sunday see their biggest party blow-out events, but it's always lively at happy hour all week, too. *Seaquarium Beach, Bapor Kibra 5999/465–1200 www.wetandwildcuracao.com No cash.*

Shopping

★ Serena's Art Factory

ART GALLERIES | You might have noticed brightly painted sculptures of colorful Caribbean women in many public places around the island, not to mention miniature versions of them for sale as souvenirs. These are Chichis®—created by the artist Serena Janet Israel and unique to Curaçao. *Chichi* means "big sister" in the local lingo, and the figures are meant to exude the warmth of matronly Caribbean women; new characters, including a man and a child, have also been created. Serena has trained many local female artists to paint them, and you're also welcome to paint your own for a one-of-a-kind souvenir at Serena's Art Factory near the Ostrich Farm. Walk-in workshops are offered twice weekly and private workshops are available on demand. A stand-alone shop in Willemstad's Punda district also sells Chichi items and offers occasional workshops. There's a $12 participation fee for walk-in workshops (Tuesday and Saturday 9 am-noon) plus the cost of materials. ✉ *Jan Louis 87a* ☎ *5999/738–0648* 🌐 *www.chichi-curacao.com.*

ATVS AND SCOOTERS

Eric's ATV Adventures

FOUR-WHEELING | Hit the road in rugged style behind the wheel of an all-terrain vehicle with Eric's ATV Adventures. All you need for a guided tour of the countryside is a regular driver's license. If you're 10 or older, you can ride as a passenger in the back seat. Helmets and goggles are provided. They also do snorkel and ATV combo tours, and they also have a new, cool party bike bus contraption that's like a bar on wheels for groups called a "bierfiets" (beer bike) in Dutch. ✉ *Bapor Kibra z/n, Jan Thiel* ☎ *5999/461–0071* 🌐 *www.curacao-atv.com* 🎫 *From $152.*

BIKING

Wanna Bike Curaçao

BIKING | **FAMILY** | The island's premier biking outfit, Wanna Bike offers mountain bike tours all over Curaçao with professional guides and top equipment. They are also the founders of the Mountain Bike Kids Club and organize many mountain bike clinics throughout the year. Their sister company "Wanna Go Outdoors" organizes corporate retreats and team-building events centered around biking and ecoadventures. ✉ *Jan Thiel Beach z/n, Jan Thiel, Willemstad* ☎ *5999/527–3720* 🌐 *www.wannabike.com* 🎫 *Tours from $55.*

DIVING AND SNORKELING

★ Ocean Encounters

SCUBA DIVING | Curaçao's largest dive operator offers a vast roster of scheduled shore and boat dives, packages, certified PADI instruction, and snorkeling opportunities. They cover the island's most popular dive sites, including the wreck of the adorable little *Superior Producer* tugboat—where barracudas hang out—and the renowned Mushroom Forest. In addition, Ocean Encounters runs the unique Animal Encounters experience at the Sea Aquarium, with whom they also partner to sponsor a children's sea camp each July. Be sure to inquire about the outfit's Sleep & Dive packages at Lion's Dive, Sunscape Resort, Dolphin Suites, and Avila Beach Hotel. ✉ *Sea Aquarium Park, Bapor Kibra* ☎ *5999/461–8131* 🌐 *www.oceanencounters.com/en.*

GOLF

★ Old Quarry Golf Course

GOLF | This lush course designed by Pete Dye has incredible vistas on the sheltered bay known as Spanish Waters. The course features a breathtaking mixture of ocean views and various forms of desert cactus, along with Dye's dramatic bunkering. The 6,920-yard layout is the best and toughest on the island. Green fees feature multiple play packages, and you can rent carts, clubs, and shoes. There is a full range of facilities, and players can celebrate their triumphs or drown their sorrows at the course's unofficial clubhouse Boca 19 – a full-service bar and restaurant in the marina just off the 18th hole. ✉ *Santa Barbara Plantation, Porta Blancu, Nieuwpoort* ☎ *5999/840–6886* 🌐 *www.oldquarrygolfcuracao.com* 🏌 *18 holes, 6920 yards, par 72* ☞ *Sunset rates start at $100. They also offered reduced rates to guests of many of the island's large resorts.*

SEA EXCURSIONS

Mermaid

CRUISE EXCURSIONS | The *Mermaid* is a 66-foot motor yacht that carries up to 60 people to deserted island Klein Curaçao five times a week. A buffet lunch, beer, and soft drinks are provided at the boat's exclusive beach house, which has picnic tables, shade huts, and other facilities. All trips depart from Fisherman's Harbour in Spanish Waters near Jan Thiel. Scuba diving is included but you need to be an experienced and licensed diver and bring your own diving equipment. ✉ *Fisherman's Pier, Jan Thiel* ☎ *5999/560–1530* 🌐 *www.mermaidboattrips.com* 🎟 *From $130* ⏲ *Closed Mon. and Sun.*

★ Miss Ann Boat Trips

CRUISE EXCURSIONS | Curacao's most popular trip to uninhabited island Klein Curacao is aboard Miss Ann's new luxury yacht *Serendipity* and their new beach club on the island provides guests with the ultimate in shade, food, and drinks as well as showers and a small massage area. They also have a small dive school there and snorkel tours seeking sea turtles are part of their day trip itinerary. The trip to the island takes about one hour. They also have other crafts for different trips including three motor yachts and 14 kayaks. ✉ *Spanish Waters, 232A Jan Sofat* ☎ *5999/767–1579* 🌐 *www.missannboattrips.com* 🎟 *All-inclusive Klein Curacao day trips start at $125.*

★ Substation Curaçao

GUIDED TOURS | Substation Curaçao offers truly unique experiences: the chance to board the five-person *Curasub* for an odyssey 450 to 1,000 feet below the waves to view colorful fish, coral walls, and shipwrecks. The submarine, which is also used by international oceanic organizations for marine research, is the same kind as that used by director James Cameron to film many underwater scenes in *Titanic.* There is no change of pressure, so anyone can enjoy going to depths that even divers can't reach. They offer four tours ranging from one hour and 450 ft. below to a shipwreck, a 1,000 ft. below dive that goes deep to the bottom of the sea, and a combo of the two that goes everywhere they can in two hours. *A Curasub* tour should be on every sea lover's bucket list. ✉ *Curacao Sea Aquarium, Bapor Kibra* ☎ *5999/465–2051* 🌐 *www.substation-curacao.com* 🎟 *From $350* ⏲ *Closed Sun. and Mon.* ☞ *No children under 8.*

West End

Interesting destinations just west of Willemstad's downtown include Piscadera Bay—home to the rollicking Pirate Bay Beach and its Aquafari attraction—and Coral Estates, a gated community with a spectacular cliffside spa. Driving farther west, particularly inland, takes you into an arid outback where the rough, cacti-studded landscape is more like what you'd expect in an Arizona desert than on a Caribbean Island. Wild donkeys and goats might wander onto the road, so use caution on curvy stretches, and be sure to bring plenty of water.

Many stellar attractions are secreted away in the west end's *kunuku* (countryside). Having good maps and clear directions will keep you from missing spectacular beaches like Cas Abao, intriguing cultural sights such as the art studio at Landhuis Jan Kok, and natural wonders like the wild flamingo colony at Salina St. Marie. And keep an eye out for the Williwood sign that mimics the famous Hollywood sign to find the island's most famous landmark spot for goat burgers. This end of the island is also home to Christoffel and Shete Boka national parks, two preserves very much worth exploring.

Sights

★ Christoffel National Park

NATIONAL PARK | The 1,239-foot Mt. Christoffel, Curaçao's highest peak, is at the center of this 4,450-acre garden and wildlife preserve under the protection of Caribbean Research and Management of Biodiversity (CARMABI). They offer many forms of touring the natural preserve, including guided hikes, jeep safaris, mountain biking, deer-watching (the island's elusive white-tailed deer are very shy), animal presentations, cave explorations, and special activities like full-moon nature walks. Visitors can also hike the mountain on their own. The exhilarating climb takes about two hours for a reasonably fit person. On a clear day, the panoramic view from the peak stretches to the mountain ranges of Venezuela. CARMABI recommends an early start as it gets very hot later in the day. Throughout the park are six hiking trails and a 20-mile (32-km) network of driving trails (use heavy-treaded tires if you wish to explore the unpaved stretches). The old Savonet plantation house there (one of the island's first plantations) now serves as a modern museum with exhibits retracing the region's history as far back as the original Indian inhabitants.

■ TIP→ There's a separate entrance fee to the museum but you can also get a combination pass that includes the park and museum for less. ✉ *Christoffel Park, Savonet* ☎ *5999/462–4242 for info and tour reservations* 🌐 *www.christoffelpark.org* 🎫 *$15.*

Hato Caves

CAVE | Stalactites and stalagmites form striking shapes in these 300,000-year-old caves. Hidden lighting adds to the dramatic effect. Indians who used the caves for shelter left petroglyphs about 1,500 years ago. More recently, slaves who escaped from nearby plantations used the caves as a hideaway. Hour-long guided tours wind down to the pools in various chambers. An Indian Trail walking path and cactus garden enlighten visitors about local vegetation. The space is also available for special events. Located just four minutes from Hato International Airport. ✉ *Rooseveltweg z/n, Hato* ☎ *5999/868–0379* 🌐 *curacaohatocaves.com* 🎫 *$10* ☞ *Last tour is at 3 pm.*

Kunuku Aqua Funpark

WATER PARK | FAMILY | You'll find this wet and wild waterpark between the towns of St. Willibrordus and Julianadorp on the west end of the island. It's a massive water circuit of pools, and slides, and water rides that are the heart of the Kunuku Aqua Resort, a sprawling community of all-inclusive stays. The water park has become a family-fun day trip destination for locals and visitors alike since they now offer day passes and the admission price includes tokens for food and drink on site. ✉ *Kunuku Aqua Resort, Weg naar St. Willibrordus 36, Kashutuin* ☎ *5999/864–4455* 🌐 *kunukuresort.com/en/daypass/* 🎫 *$38.*

National Park Shete Boka

VIEWPOINT | Shete Boka means "seven inlets" in Papiamentu, and this national park by the sea is well worth exploring. The rugged coastline with scenic inlets is dramatic and wild—the incessantly crashing waves have sculptured the coral rock into fascinating natural works art. The most impressive is Boka Tabla, where you can descend a natural rock stairway (take care, it's very slippery) to view an arched opening that looks out on the sea like a giant eye. Boka Pistol is also spectacular—jetting up into towering

Did You Know?

Three species of cacti can be found in Christoffel National Park. They grow very slowly—larger ones can be several hundred years old—and produce flowers that open for only one night during the dry season.

plumes of spray, often leaving rainbows lingering in the mist. And if you look closely as you walk upon the volcanic rock landscape, you will see coral fossil formations below your feet that are thousands of years old. This is also a popular nesting region for sea turtles. There are two hiking trails; you can purchase a map of them at park's entrance. (Note: you are required to leave the park by 4:30 pm.) ✉ *Westpunt Hwy., just past village center, Dorp Soto* ☎ *5999/864–0444* 🌐 *www.shetebokapark.org/* 🎫 *$10.*

 Beaches

Cas Abao

BEACH | FAMILY | This white-sand gem has the brightest blue water in Curaçao, a treat for swimmers, snorkelers, and sunbathers alike. Full services include a beach bar and restaurant, lockers, changing rooms on-site, and even full massages surfside are available. It can become crowded on weekends, especially Sunday, when local families descend in droves. You can rent beach chairs, paddle boats, kayaks, and snorkeling and diving gear. The beach is open from 8 am to 6 pm. **Amenities:** food and drink; lifeguards; parking; showers; toilets; water sports. **Best for:** partiers; snorkeling; swimming. ✉ *West of St. Willibrordus, about 3 miles (5 km) off Weg Naar Santa Cruz* ✣ *Turn off Westpunt Hwy. at the junction onto Weg Naar Santa Cruz; follow until the turnoff for Cas Abao, and then drive along the winding country road for about 10 mins to the beach* ☎ *5999/736–6363* 🌐 *www.casabaobeach.com.*

Kokomo Beach

BEACH | FAMILY | By day the beach at Vaersenbaai—better known as "Kokomo" after its on-site restaurant-bar—is a quiet, family-friendly, public beach with lots of free lounges, shady spots, and facilities (including a dive operator). But once the sun starts to set, it's another story. This beach is renowned for its live music and partiers; its Tuesday through Saturday happy hours featuring live music, cocktails, and tapas; and its Sunday happy hours with DJ dance parties. **Amenities:** food and drink; parking (free); toilets. **Best for:** partiers; snorkeling; swimming. ✉ *Vaersenbaai* ☎ *6999/868–0908* 🌐 *www.facebook.com/kokomocuracao* 🎫 *Free.*

Playa Jeremi

BEACH | No snack bar, no dive shop, no facilities, no fee—in fact, there's nothing but sheer natural beauty. Though the beach is sandy, there are rocky patches, so barefoot visitors should exercise care. There are a few chairs and shade umbrellas for rent and daredevils like to jump off the cliffs. Development is planned for this beach, so have a look before it's too late. **Amenities:** none. **Best for:** picnics, snorkeling; solitude; swimming. ✉ *Off Weg Naar Santa Cruz, west of Lagun.*

Playa Kalki

BEACH | This beach is at the western tip of the island right under Kura Hulanda Lodge. Sunbathers may find the narrow and rocky beach less than ideal and there is a long steep staircase down to the sand, but go to GoWest Diving there for snorkel and dive trips to the Blue Room, a cool underwater cave. **Amenities:** food and drink; parking; toilets; water sports. **Best for:** snorkeling; solitude; swimming. ✉ *Near Jaanchi's, Westpunt.*

Playa Knip

BEACH | FAMILY | Two protected coves offer crystal-clear turquoise waters. Big (Groot) Knip, also known as Playa Kenepa, is an expanse of alluring white sand, perfect for swimming and snorkeling. You can rent beach chairs and hang out under the *palapas* (thatch-roof shelters) or cool off with ice cream at the snack bar. This spot is also famous for cliff jumping by locals and adventurous visitors. There are restrooms here but no showers. It's particularly crowded on Sunday and school holidays. Just up the road, also in a protected cove, sister beach Little (Klein) Knip is a charmer, too, with picnic tables and palapas. There's no fee for these beaches. **Amenities:** food and drink; lifeguards; parking; toilets; water sports. **Best for:** snorkeling; sunrise; sunset; swimming. ✉ *Just east of Westpunt, Banda Abou.*

★ Playa PortoMari

BEACH | FAMILY | Set beneath an historic plantation site, you'll find calm, clear water and a long stretch of white sand and full facilities on this beach. A decent bar and restaurant, well-kept showers, changing facilities, and restrooms are all on-site; a nature trail is nearby. The double coral reef (explore one, swim past it, explore another) is a special feature that makes this spot popular with snorkelers and divers. It's also known as home for visiting wild pigs occasionally. **Amenities:** food and drink; lifeguards; parking; showers; toilets. **Best for:** partiers; snorkeling; swimming; walking. ✉ *Off Willibrordus Rd.* ✥ *From Willemstad, drive west on Westpunt Hwy. for 4 miles (7 km); turn left onto Willibrordus Rd. at the PortoMari billboard, and then drive 3 miles (5 km) until you see a large church; follow signs on the winding dirt road to the beach* ☎ *5999/864–7558* 🌐 *www.playaportomari.com* 🎫 *$3 per person.* ⏲ *Closes at 6:30 pm.*

Restaurants

Karakter

$$$ | INTERNATIONAL | The beachfront Karakter restaurant, which has killer sea views and is the nexus of surf-side revelry with live music on weekends, is particularly popular with the Coral Estate villas crowd (indeed, nonguests must present ID to enter the gated community and dine here). Lounges, patio tables, and nighttime tiki torches set the enchanting dining scene; friendly barkeeps make you feel right at home. **Known for:** great tapas and signature cocktails; breakfast with a view; romantic sunset dining. 💲 *Average main: $25* ✉ *Coral Estate, Willibrordus, Coral Estate Rif St. Marie* ☎ *5999/864–2233* 🌐 *www.karaktercuracao.com.*

Hotels

Blue Bay Curaçao

$ | HOTEL | FAMILY | Set in a storied plantation estate and on a beautiful beach, Blue Bay's accommodations range from luxury apartment–style rooms to standalone villas and bungalows—hillside or beachfront. **Pros:** ideal for golfers, divers, and families; spacious units; on-site dive operator. **Cons:** not all rooms are ocean view; little nightlife; a bit isolated, so a car is absolutely necessary. 💲 *Rooms from: $221* ✉ *Landhuis Blauw z/n, Willemstad* ☎ *5999/888–8800* 🌐 *www.bluebay-curacao.com* 🛏 *120 units* 🍽 *No Meals.*

Coral Estate Luxury Resort

$ | RESORT | Atop cliffs within the chic gated community of Coral Estates, this resort enclave is replete with killer sea views, trendy restaurants and bars, a beautiful beach, fabulous infinity pools, an upscale spa, and a first-rate dive operator. **Pros:** top-notch spa; stunning sea views from the cliff-top infinity pool; great snorkeling on-site and fabulous diving nearby. **Cons:** long drive to town so a rental car is a must; lanai villas have no sea views; steep stairs down to the beach. 💲 *Rooms from: $119* ✉ *Coral Estates, Rif St. Marie, Willibrordus* ☎ *5999/724–3810* 🌐 *coralestateluxuryresort.com* 🛏 *62 units* 🍽 *No Meals.*

Dreams Curaçao Resort, Spa & Casino

$$ | RESORT | Formerly the Hilton Curacao, a $15 million renovation transformed this landmark Piscadera Bay seafront property into a premiere upscale family-friendly all-inclusive. **Pros:** high-end spa and glitzy casino on-site; excellent supervised kids' club; two private beaches. **Cons:** far from downtown shopping; not all rooms are ocean view; no reservations for dining can mean waits at prime meal times. 💲 *Rooms from: $371* ✉ *Piscadera Bay*

You can cliff dive at Little Klein Knip, one of the island's prettiest, but smallest beaches.

www.dreamsresorts.com 197 rooms All-Inclusive.

Mondi Lodge

$ | **B&B/INN** | Tucked away in the *mondi* (countryside) surrounded by nature, this charming, family-run ecolodge has five thatched, palapa-style, one- and two-bedroom cottages and one romantic treehouse, perfect for those seeking a soul-soothing stay. **Pros:** close to major supermarket so you can cook your own food; gorgeous grounds full of bright blooms and greenery; very Zen vibe with friendly owner on-site. **Cons:** nature can be surprisingly noisy at night; rental car is needed; not near a beach. *Rooms from: $167 St. Michiel, Klein St. Michiel 1 Willemstad See their website or call for clear directions 599/686–7977 mondilodge.com 6 units Free Breakfast.*

★ Zoëtry Curaçao Resort & Spa

$$$$ | **ALL-INCLUSIVE** | The latest property from the AMR collection to land on Curacao is their highest-end brand with its signature Zoëtry style of intimate, boutique luxury. **Pros:** gourmet fare available for all dietary restrictions including gluten-free and vegan; sophisticated vibe with high tech modern amenities and lush gardens; 24/7 room service, complimentary laundry service and free international calling. **Cons:** not designated as adults-only which would make it more of a romantic escape; little on site entertainment; no sea views or beach. *Rooms from: $560 Piscadera Bay 5999/462–5000 www.amrcollection.com 72 rooms All-Inclusive.*

Shopping

★ Sambil Mall

SHOPPING COMPLEX | Situated in Veeris, this massive, multilevel, indoor complex has hundreds of stores, a food court, upscale and casual dining enclaves, a Carrefour Market grocery store, a high-tech cinema, and state-of-the-art bowling alleys. With lots of special events, this is an ideal spot for families seeking respite from the sun for a few hours at their special Kidi's Park (an indoor play space for kids).

✉ *Verris Commercial Park, Nst Block No. 5, Willemstad* ☎ *5999/735–3131* 🌐 *www.sambil.cw.*

Activities

DIVING AND SNORKELING

Divers Republic

DIVING & SNORKELING | **FAMILY** | Divers Republic provides a highly personalized experience with professional PADI divemasters. They offer instruction and a large range of dives at the island's best spots, as well as a Bubblemaker program for children. They also offer night snorkeling and wreck safaris. ✉ *Coral Estates Rif Marie* ☎ *5999/520–3989* 🌐 *diversrepublic.org* 💵 *Intro to dive from $85.*

GOLF

Blue Bay Golf

GOLF | Part of the Blue Bay Hotel, an ex-plantation house turned resort, this course is famous for its incredible sea views. Designed by Rocky Roquemore, it measures 6,735 yards from the tips and beckons experts and novices alike. You will be sure to enjoy the par-3 5th, which plays across and is guarded by the sea along the entire left-hand side. You can rent carts, clubs, and shoes, and if you'd like to drive your game to a new level, take a lesson from the house pro. With Pay & Play, no membership is required. Bus reservations are a must. Rates vary depending on time of day and high or low season. ✉ *Blue Bay Hotel, St. Michiel* ☎ *5999/888–8800* 🌐 *www.bluebay-curacao.com/activities/golf* 🏌 *18 holes, 6735 yards, par 72* ☞ *Nine holes from $85.*

GUIDED TOURS

Yellow Adventures Curacao

GUIDED TOURS | Part of the Yellow Group company that offers a full range of tourism services on the island, this operator offers a wide range of tours by motorcoach and boat that include many of Curaçao's best attractions and activities. Choose half- and full-day tours to beaches or historical sights, or horseback riding, diving, or snorkeling opportunities. Or discover the rugged interior by Yellow Jeep Safari that takes you throughout Christoffel National Park and its many hidden scenic wonders. ✉ *Curaçao Marriott Beach Resort, Piscadera Bay* ☎ *5999/524–6062* 🌐 *www.tourism-curacao.com.*

SEA EXCURSIONS

★ **Aquafari**

WATERSPORTS | You don't have to snorkel or dive to discover Curaçao's spectacular world of coral reefs and tropical fish. Go 30 feet deep on Aquafari's unique, ecofriendly, underwater scooter, complete with an air-supplied helmet that allows you to breathe as you normally would. After a safety briefing, the instructors, who are themselves divers, accompany you on one of the island's coolest underwater adventures and take photos of your journey for purchase. The experience, including the topside briefing, takes approximately 1½ hours, with 45 minutes underwater. They also offer a new 3-hour boat sunset cruise with live music aboard their new craft called the "Eywã." ✉ *Piscaderaweg, Pirate Bay Beach, Willemstad* ☎ *5999/513–2625* 🌐 *aquafari.net* 💵 *$115* ☞ *Minimum age 10, minimum height 4 feet, maximum weight 275 pounds.*

SPAS

8 The Experience

SPAS | Many resorts have on-site spas, but this oasis of pampering is definitely worth the short trip out to the Coral Estates area. The views from its cliffside whirlpools, open-air treatment rooms, and meditation pool are incredible. A wet room accommodates body wraps and scrubs, while a sauna and aroma-infused steam room cleanse. There's even an igloo room! Full beauty services and a diverse range of spa treatments plus special health-oriented events and classes like yoga are offered as well. ✉ *La Puerta Business Center, Coral Estates, Coral Estate Rif St. Marie* ☎ *5999/735–2388* 🌐 *8curacao.com* 🕓 *Closed Tues.*

Chapter 11

DOMINICAN REPUBLIC

Updated by
Mechi Annaís Estévez Cruz

Sights
★★★★★

Restaurants
★★★★☆

Hotels
★★★★☆

Shopping
★★★★☆

Nightlife
★★★★☆

WELCOME TO DOMINICAN REPUBLIC

TOP REASONS TO GO

★ **Great Beaches:** There are some 1,000 miles of excellent beaches, many of which are white and powdery.

★ **Great Value:** You'll find the best-value all-inclusive resorts in the Caribbean here.

★ **Myriad Outdoor Sports:** Every imaginable activity—world-class golf, horseback riding, white-water rafting, surfing, diving, windsurfing—is available here.

★ **Happening Nightlife:** In the bigger cities, enjoy the vibrant and varied offerings at trendy bars and discos.

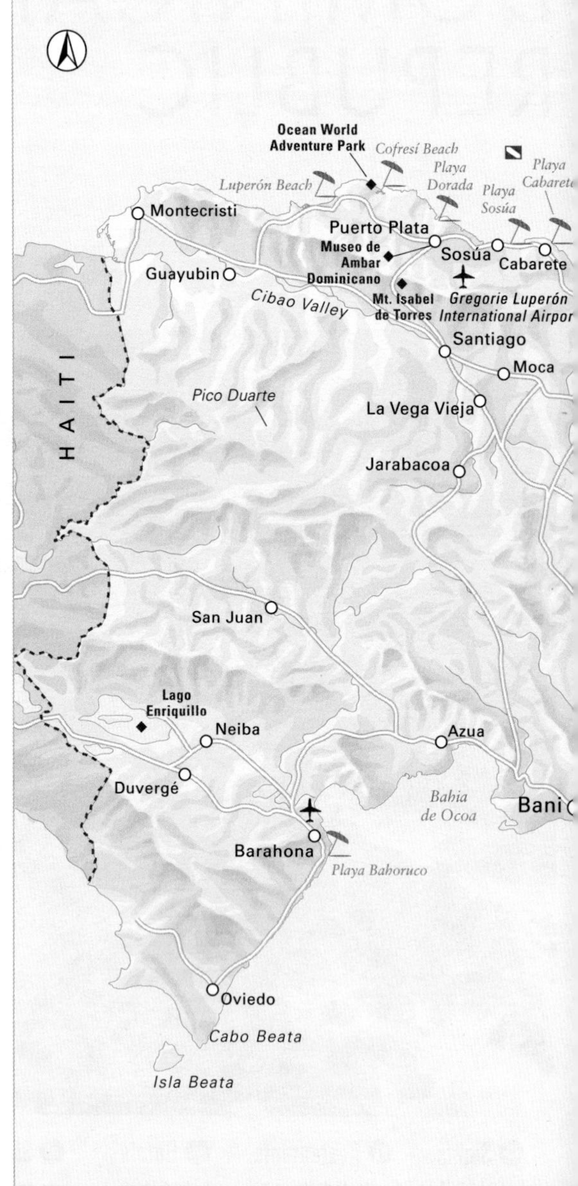

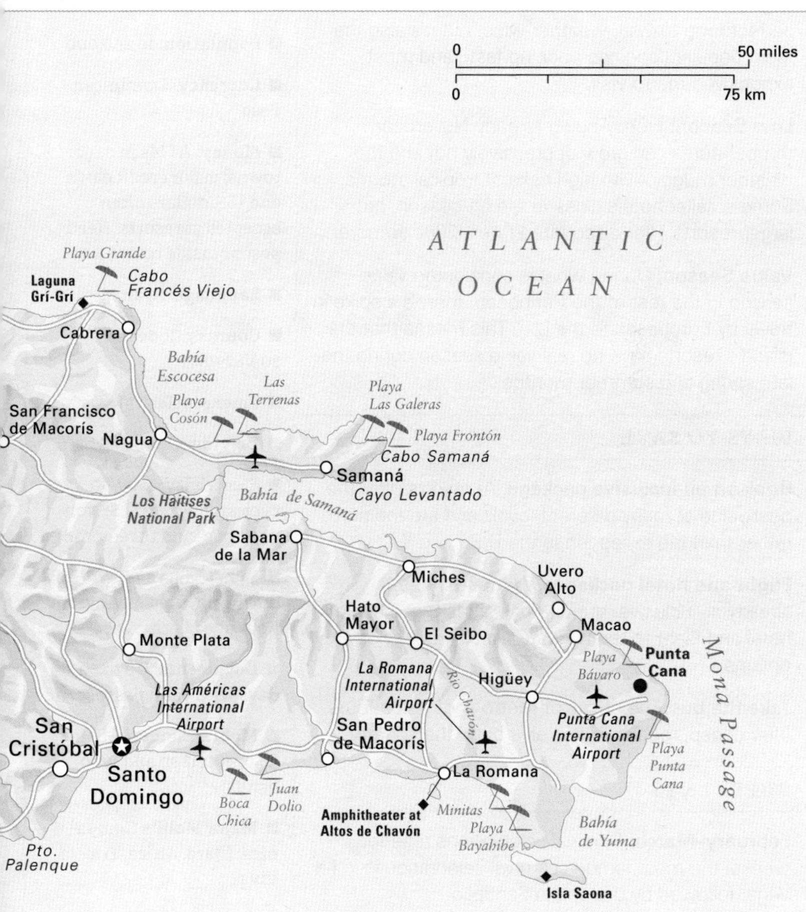
0
50 miles
0
75 km
ATLANTIC
OCEAN
Playa Grande
Laguna
Grí-Grí
Cabo
Francés Viejo
Cabrera
Bahía
Escocesa
Las
Terrenas
Playa
Cosón
Playa
Las Galeras
Playa Frontón
Cabo Samaná
San Francisco
de Macorís
Nagua
Samaná
Cayo Levantado
Bahía de Samaná
Los Haitises
National Park
Sabana
de la Mar
Miches
Uvero
Alto
Hato
Mayor
El Seibo
Macao
Monte Plata
La Romana
International
Airport
Río Chavón
Higüey
Playa
Bávaro
Punta
Cana
Mona Passage
Las Américas
International
Airport
Punta Cana
International
Airport
San Pedro
de Macorís
San
Cristóbal
Santo
Domingo
La Romana
Playa
Punta
Cana
Boca
Chica
Juan
Dolio
Amphitheater at
Altos de Chavón
Minitas
Playa
Bayahibe
Bahía
de Yuma
Isla Saona
Pto.
Palenque
Caribbean Sea
KEY
Beaches
Dive Sites

ISLAND SNAPSHOT

WHEN TO GO

High Season: December through May is really the perfect time to visit, weather wise, but it's also the most popular (lodgings book up fast), and most expensive time to visit.

Low Season: From August to early November, temperatures can grow oppressively hot and the weather muggy, with high risks of tropical storms. Some smaller hotels close in the off-season, but larger resorts offer discounted rates (20% or more).

Value Season: During what is considered value season in the rest of the Caribbean, there's a spike in travel by Europeans to the D.R. This means that the island's resorts have no real value season during the late spring and summer months.

WAYS TO SAVE

Book an all-inclusive package. AI resorts offer the best value at many different levels and are the norm rather than the exception in the D.R.

Flight and hotel packages. With most hotels already all-inclusive, grander packages that include hotel and flight to the D.R. are usually money-saving options.

Take the bus. The buses of Metro and Caribe Tours offer cheap, regular routes all around the country.

BIG EVENTS

February–March: Carnival celebrations rage for weeks; the most famous carnival celebration is in La Vega, followed by the one in Santiago.

August: Celebrate independence from Spain on August 16 in Santiago and Santo Domingo.

October: Dance and sing in Puerto Plata at the annual Merengue music festival.

November: The Dominican Republic Jazz Festival (🌐 *www.drjazzfestival.com*) is an annual event in Cabarete.

AT A GLANCE

- **Capital:** Santo Domingo
- **Population:** 10,850,000
- **Currency:** Dominican Peso
- **Money:** ATMs in major towns; major credit cards and U.S. dollars often accepted at resorts. Need pesos outside resort areas.
- **Language:** Spanish
- **Country Code:** 1 809/829/849
- **Emergencies:** 911
- **Driving:** On the right
- **Electricity:** 120v/60 cycles; plugs are U.S. standard two- and three-prong
- **Time:** Same as New York during daylight saving; one hour ahead otherwise
- **Documents:** Up to 60 days with valid passport
- **Mobile Phones:** GSM (850, 900, 1800 and 1900 bands)
- **Major Mobile Companies:** Claro, Altice, Tricom, Viva
- **Dominican Republic Tourist Office:** www.godominicanrepublic.com

Bathed by the Atlantic Ocean to the north and the Caribbean Sea to the south, the Dominican Republic is graced with 1,000 miles (1,600 km) of gorgeous beaches studded with coconut palms and sands ranging from pearl-white to golden brown to volcanic black. The island covers the eastern two-thirds of the island of Hispaniola (Haiti covers the other third).

At 18,765 square miles (48,730 square km), it's the second-largest Caribbean country (only Cuba is larger), and with more than 8.5 million people, the second-most-populous country, too. Sounds of the national language, Spanish, fill the air, which averages a balmy 82°F year-round.

The Dominican Republic's tourism board boasts that the D.R. has it all—and it does. Here, travelers can leave behind stuffy schedules and relax into a slower-paced culture that prioritizes family and joy. They can enjoy pristine virgin beaches, bustling modern and historic cities, villages with colorful bougainvillea-filled fences nestled in mountains, brown rivers with white-water rapids, and untouched rain forests full of wild orchids. Lovers of wildlife will relish seeing indigenous species such as the crocodile and the green cockatoo, symbol of the island. Bird-watchers, take note: 32 endemic species are flying around here.

Accommodations offer a remarkable range—including surfers' camps, exclusive boutique hotels, and megaresorts. Trendy restaurants, art galleries, boutique hotels, and late-night clubs help make Santo Domingo a superb urban vacation destination. Prices at all-inclusive resorts have been slowly increasing since the early aughts; however, a vacation in the D.R. can still be a relative bargain. Even the new boutique hotels are still well priced for the Caribbean. Nevertheless, government taxes on hotels and restaurants are 18%, and most non-AI hotels charge an additional 10% service charge. This 28% is obviously a major budget item. When making a reservation, inquire if the rates quoted include this 28%; sometimes they do, especially with the smaller properties.

Planning

Getting Here and Around

AIR

You can fly nonstop to the Dominican Republic from major U.S. cities including Atlanta, Boston, Charlotte, Chicago–O'Hare, Dallas–Ft. Worth, Detroit, Fort Lauderdale, Miami, Minneapolis, New York–JFK, Newark, Orlando, Philadelphia, and Washington Dulles. However, not all airlines fly to all the destinations in the D.R., and some flights connect in San Juan or airports throughout the United States. Many visitors fly nonstop on charter flights direct from the U.S. East Coast and Midwest, particularly into Punta Cana; these charters are part of a package and can be booked only through a travel agent.

Air Antilles Express flies to Santo Domingo and Punta Cana from several Caribbean destinations. Air Caraïbes flies to Santo Domingo from the French Antilles. Alas, there are no regularly scheduled domestic flights, just charters.

Airport Transfers: If you book a package through a travel agent or vacation provider, your airport transfer will almost certainly be included. If you book independently, you will have to take a taxi, rent a car, or hire a private driver-guide. offers drivers and private transfers in addition to scheduling domestic airline flights and excursions.

AIRPORTS Cibao International Airport. *(STI)* ✉ *Av. Victor M. Espaillat, Licey al Medio, Santiago* 🌐 *www.aeropuertocibao.com.do.* **El Catey International Airport.** *(AZS)* ✉ *Samaná.* **Gregorio Luperón International Airport.** *(POP)* ✉ *Rte. 5, Puerto Plata* 🌐 *www.puerto-plata-airport.com.* **La Isabella International Airport.** *(JBQ)* ✉ *Av. Pdte. Antonio Guzmán Fernández, Santo Domingo.* **La Romana/Casa de Campo International Airport.** *(LRM)* ✉ *La Romana* 🌐 *romanaairport.com.* **Las Américas International Airport.** *(SDQ)* ✉ *Ruta 66 Salida Del Aeropuerto Las Americas, Santo Domingo.* **Punta Cana International Airport.** *(PUJ)* ✉ *Punta Cana* 🌐 *www.puntacanainternationalairport.com.*

INTERNATIONAL AIRLINES Air Antilles Express. ☎ *809/688–6661 air ticket agency, 809/560–0168 call center/agency* 🌐 *www.flyairantilles.com.* **Air Caraïbes.** ☎ *809/621–8888 general services, 0590/82–47–00 in Guadeloupe, 0820/83–58–35* 🌐 *www.aircaraibes.com.*

DOMESTIC CHARTER AIRLINES Air Century. ✉ *La Isabella International Dr. Joaquin Balaguer, Av. Presidente Antonio Guzmán Fernández, Santo Domingo* ☎ *809/826–4333 charters, 305/677–9641 in U.S.* 🌐 *www.aircentury.com.* **DominicanShuttles.com.** ✉ *Torre Empresarial Forum, Av. 27 de Febrero at Av. Privada, Santo Domingo* ☎ *809/931–4073, 829/410–3326* 🌐 *www.dominicanshuttles.com.* **Helidosa Helicopters.** ✉ *Punta Cana International Airport, Punta Cana* ☎ *809/552–6069* 🌐 *www.helidosa.com.*

BUS

Privately owned buses are the cheapest way to get around the country. For example, one-way bus fare from Santo Domingo to Puerto Plata, a trip that takes 3½ hours on Caribe Tours, less on Metro Buses, a more deluxe operation, costs a fraction of what you'd pay for a taxi or rental car. Both bus lines go to Sosua, too, which takes another 15–20 minutes. There is no service to Cabarete, but taxis meet the bus and drivers are eager to take you. These bus companies make regular runs to Santiago, Puerto Plata, and other destinations from Santo Domingo. Be forewarned that air-conditioning can be frigid, and there might be a movie, possibly an American one or not. Some buses will have a restroom, but definitely BYO toilet paper. Be at the terminal 30 minutes prior to the scheduled departure if you have a ticket. (Metro Bus now suggests an hour without a ticket.)

Frequent service from Santo Domingo to the town of La Romana is provided by Express Bus, leaving every hour on the hour from 5 am to 9 pm; however, there's no office and no phone. Buses depart from Parque Enriquillo in the Zona Colonial. A ticket taker will take your money (in pesos) just before departure, charging double if you have large luggage. Travel time is about 1¾ hours, and as these are usually small, second-class buses, without air-conditioning, that make many stops, it is a rough ride—let it be your last choice. Once in La Romana, you can take a taxi to your resort. Espreso Baváro buses depart from Plaza Los Girasoles at Avenida Máximo Gómez at Juan Sánchez Ruiz; the buses are said to be first-class, but are not. What they are is cheap. They do make a stop in La Romana. If you're going to one of the Punta Cana resorts, you get off at the stop before the last and take a cab waiting at the taxi stand. Depending on which resort you are going to, that charge could be ten times as much as your bus ticket.

BUS CONTACTS Caribe Tours. ✉ *Av. 27 de Febrero at Leopoldo Navarro, Ensanches Miraflores* ☎ *809/221–4422* 🌐 *www.caribetours.com.do.* **Espreso Santo Domingo Baváro.** ✉ *Plaza Los Girasoles, Av. Máximo Gómez at Juan Sánchez Ramirez, Santo Domingo* ☎ *809/682–9670 in Santo Domingo, 809/552–1678 in Bávaro* 🌐 *www.expresobavaro.com.* **Metro Buses.** ✉ *Av. Winston Churchill at Calle Francisco Prats Ramirez Piantini, Santo Domingo* ☎ *809/582–9111 in Santiago, 809/227–0101 in Santo Domingo, 809/586–6062 in Puerto Plata, 809/571–1324 in Sosua* 🌐 *www.metroserviciosturisticos.com.*

CAR

Driving in the D.R. can be a harrowing and expensive experience; we don't recommend that the typical vacationer rent a car. It's best if you don't drive outside the major cities at night. If you must, use extreme caution, especially on narrow, unlighted mountain roads.

Driving to the Samaná Peninsula from Las Américas Airport or Santo Domingo has been made significantly easier with the new toll road, which has the time down to about two hours. Once in the city of Samaná or particularly Las Galeras, driving is not too arduous and especially if you don't book into an all-inclusive, you might want a car for sightseeing and to drive to Las Terrenas. There the traffic and one-way streets make it more stressful, but if you're staying on Playa Coson, you may want a car to go into town for some meals. Taxis are expensive for that—as much as US$60 round-trip.

The Coral Highway (Autopista del Coral), which begins between Las Américas Airport and the city, has shortened the drive time to La Romana to less than an hour. On the other end, it begins at Punta Cana's airport and takes just 45 minutes to La Romana, less to Bayahibe.

Local agencies exist, but it is highly advisable to rent only from internationally known companies. U.S. citizens should really consider only U.S.–based chains, so that if you have a problem you have easier recourse. Major agencies are in most of the island's airports. At Las Américas International Airport, most agencies are open 7 am–11 pm.

CAR RENTAL CONTACTS Avis. ☎ *809/549-0469 at Las Américas International Airport and Punta Cana Airport., 800/331–1212 in U.S..* **Budget.** ✉ *Punta Cana International Airport* ☎ *800/472–3325 for reservations outside U.S., 800/214–6094 customer service, 809/466–2028 at Punta Cana International Airport, 809/586–0413 at Gregorio Luperón International Airport, 809/549–0351 at Las Américas International Airport* 🌐 *www.budget.com.* **Europcar.** ☎ *809/549–0942 at Las Américas Airport, 809/686–2861 at Punta Cana International Airport* 🌐 *www.europcar.com.* **National.** ✉ *Casa de Campo* ☎ *809/523–8191 at Casa de Campo* 🌐 *www.nationalcar.com.*

TAXI

Wherever you are, hotel taxis are generally the best and safest option, although they can be expensive. Carry small bills; drivers rarely have change; some destinations have rather high minimum fares. Always let your hotel or restaurant call a taxi for you. Don't use "street" taxis, which are often in poor repair and can be a security risk. Recommendable radio-taxi companies in Santo Domingo are Tecni-Taxi (which also operates in Puerto Plata) and Apolo. Most taxis will also carry you out of town and will have rate charts for major destinations; just be aware that these private taxi transfers can be expensive (well over US$100) for a destination that's less than an hour away and more for destinations farther afield.

DominicanShuttles provides safe and reliable long-distance private taxi service, but trips must be arranged in advance online (as little as 24 hours or as much as weeks in advance in the case of a long-distance airport transfer). For English-speaking taxi service in Santo Domingo or long distance transfers, call Mike Tours.

CONTACTS Apolo Taxi. ✉ *Santo Domingo* ☎ *809/537–0000, 809/537–1245 for high-end cars or SUVs* 🌐 *www.apolotaxi.com.* **DominicanShuttles.** 🌐 *www.dominicanshuttles.com.* **Mike Tours.** ☎ *827/230–6742.* **Taxi-Cabarete.** ✉ *Cabarete* ☎ *809/571–0767 in Cabarete.* **Taxi-Queen Santiago.** ✉ *Santiago* ☎ *809/570–0000 in Santiago.* **Taxi-Sosúa.** ✉ *Sosúa* ☎ *809/571–3097 in Sosúa.* **Tecni-Taxi.** ☎ *809/567–2010 in Santo Domingo, 809/320–7621 in Puerto Plata.*

Health and Safety

TIP→ Never drink tap water in the D.R. (look for a hotel or restaurant that has earned an H for food-service hygiene or that has a Crystal America certification).

Dengue, chikungunya, and zika have all been reported in the Dominican Republic. We recommend that you protect yourself from these mosquito-borne illnesses by keeping your skin covered and/or wearing mosquito repellent. The mosquitoes that transmit these viruses are as active by day as they are at night.

Although crime rates in the D.R. can be high, violent crime is rare against tourists. Nevertheless, petty theft, pickpocketing, and purse snatching are an increasing concern, particularly in Santo Domingo. Pay attention, especially when leaving a bank or casino. Take hotel-recommended taxis at night.

Restaurants

The island's culinary repertoire includes Spanish, Italian, Middle Eastern, Indian, Japanese, and *nueva cocina dominicana* (contemporary Dominican cuisine). If Caribbean seafood is on the menu, it's bound to be fresh. The dining scene in Santo Domingo is the best in the country and probably offers as fine a selection of restaurants as you will find in most Caribbean destinations. Keep in mind that the touristy restaurants, such as those in the Zona Colonial, with mediocre fare and just-okay service, are becoming more and more costly, while the few fine-dining options here have lowered some of their prices. For example, La Residence now offers a daily prix-fixe chef's menu with three courses. Or you can order two generous appetizers for even less. You will have caring service and be sequestered in luxe surroundings away from the tourist hustle. Know that *capitaleños* (residents of Santo Domingo) dress for dinner and dine late. The crowds pick up after 9:30 pm.

What to Wear: In resort areas, shorts and bathing suits under beach wraps are usually (but not always) acceptable at breakfast and lunch. For dinner, long pants, skirts, and collared shirts are the norm. Restaurants tend to be more formal in Santo Domingo. Ties aren't required anywhere and now jackets are seldom mandatory in even the finer establishments.

Hotels and Resorts

All-inclusives: All-inclusive resorts predominate in Punta Cana and some other areas, and some of them are quite luxurious.

Condos: In places like Playa Dorada, apart-hotels and classy condos are now popular.

Small Hotels: Sosúa and Cabarete still have a few charming independent inns and small resorts.

Hotel reviews have been shortened. For full information, visit Fodors.com.

The Dominican Republic has the largest hotel inventory (at this writing some nearly 84,000 rooms) in the Caribbean and draws large numbers of stateside visitors. Surfers can still find digs for $25 a night in Cabarete, and the new generation of luxurious all-inclusives in Punta Cana and Uvero Alto is simply incredible.

Santo Domingo properties generally base their tariffs on the European Plan (no meals)—though many include breakfast—and maintain the same room rates year-round. Beach resorts have high winter rates, with prices reduced for the shoulder seasons of late spring and early fall (summer has become another strong season). All-inclusives dominate in Punta Cana. Cabarete was a stronghold of the small inn, but it does have all-inclusives. Villa rentals are gaining in popularity all over the island, particularly in Cabarete and the Cabrera area.

During your stay your patience may be tested at times, particularly at all-inclusives. The nodding in and out of the electricity is one annoyance, and sometimes the *plantas* (generators) either don't kick in or wheeze and hiss from age.

What It Costs in U.S. Dollars

$	$$	$$$	$$$$
RESTAURANTS			
under $12	$12–$20	$21–$30	over $30
HOTELS			
under $275	$275–$375	$376–$475	over $475

Nightlife

Santo Domingo's nightlife is vast and ever changing. Check with the concierges and locals. However clubs and bars must close at midnight during the week, and 2 am on Friday and Saturday nights. There are some exceptions to the latter, primarily clubs and casinos in hotels. Sadly, the pandemic has put some clubs out of business. Some clubs are now pushing the envelope and staying open until 3, but they do get in trouble with the authorities when caught, and you probably don't want to be there then.

Dancing is as much a part of the culture here as eating and drinking. As in other Latin countries, after dinner it's not a question of *whether* people will go dancing but *where* they'll go. Move with the rhythm of the merengue and the pulsing beat of salsa. Among the young, the word is that there's no better place to party in the Caribbean than Santo Domingo. Almost every resort in Puerto Plata and Punta Cana has live entertainment, dancing, or both.

The action can heat up—and the island does have casinos—but gambling in the Dominican Republic is more a sideline than a raison d'être. Most casinos are in the larger hotels of Santo Domingo, with a couple on the North Coast, plus many more in Punta Cana. All offer slot machines, blackjack, craps, and roulette and are generally open daily from 3 pm to 4 am, the exception being those in Santo Domingo, which, for now, must close at midnight (2 am on Friday and Saturday). You must be 18 to enter.

Shopping

Cigars continue to be the hottest commodity coming out of the D.R. Many exquisite, hand-wrapped smokes come from the island's rich Cibao Valley, and Fuente Cigars—handmade in Santiago—are highly prized. Only reputable cigar shops sell the real thing, and many you will see sold on the street are fakes. You can also buy and enjoy Cuban cigars here, but they still can't be brought back to the United States unless you purchase them in Cuba. Dominican rum and coffee are also good buys. *Mamajuana* is a popular herbal liqueur sold almost everywhere. The D.R. is the homeland of late designer Oscar de la Renta, and you may want to stop at the chic shops that carry his label's creations. La Vega is famous for its *diablos cajuelos* (devil masks), which are worn during Carnival. Look also for the delicate, faceless ceramic figurines that symbolize Dominican culture.

Though locally crafted products are often of a high caliber (and very affordable), expect to pay hundreds of dollars for designer jewelry made of amber and larimar. Larimar—a semiprecious stone the color of the Caribbean Sea—is found on the D.R.'s south coast in the hills above the city of Barahona. Prices vary according to the stone's hue and category, AAA being the highest. Amber has been mined extensively between Puerto Plata and Santiago. A fossilization of resin from a prehistoric pine tree, it sometimes encases ancient animal and plant life, from leaves to spiders to tiny lizards. Beware of fakes, which are especially prevalent in street stalls. A reputable dealer can show you how to tell the difference between real larimar and amber and imitations.

The pandemic has hit a lot communities in the Dominican Republic hard. Haggling is becoming less common and you risk offending locals this way. Vendors face fierce competition in a very small market, so they're tenacious. Unless you really plan to buy, don't even stop to look.

Visitor Information

CONTACTS Dominican Republic Tourist Office. ☎ *212/588–1012 in New York City, 305/358–2899 in Miami* 🌐 *www.godominicanrepublic.com.*

Weddings

There are no residency requirements. Blood tests are not mandatory. Original birth certificates and passports are required. Divorce certificates and proof that the bride and groom are single must be stamped by the Dominican Consulate. Documents must be submitted two weeks before the wedding and translated into Spanish. Many couples are opting to marry in the United States, then hold a ceremony at the resort of their choice followed by a reception.

Santo Domingo

Since many visitors to Santo Domingo base themselves in the historic Zona Colonial (and because this is where the vast majority of the interesting sights are located), most exploration in the city is done on foot. At night, however, you'll always want to take a taxi, particularly to outlying areas. Some hotels are now being built in the newer parts of Santo Domingo, such as Piantini, which can't be navigated on foot.

Parque Independencia separates the old city from modern Santo Domingo, a sprawling, noisy city with a population of over three million. The 12 cobblestone blocks of Santo Domingo's **Zona Colonial** contain most of the major sights in town. It's one of the most well-preserved historic districts in the Caribbean and is best explored on foot. The Zona ends at the seafront, called the Malecón.

Zona Colonial

Sights

Spanish colonization in the Americas began in Santo Domingo's 12-block Zona Colonial. Tourist brochures claim that "history comes alive here"—a surprisingly truthful statement. Almost every Thursday to Sunday night at 8:30 a typical "folkloric show" is staged at Parque Colón and Plaza de España. During the Christmas holidays there is an artisans' fair and live-music concerts take place.

Fun horse-and-carriage rides throughout the Zona are available year-round, though the commentary will likely be in Spanish. You can also negotiate to use them as a taxi, say, to go down to the Malecón. The drivers usually hang out in front of the Hostal Nicolas de Ovando. You can get a free walking-tour map and brochures in English at the Secretaria de Estado de Turismo office at Parque Colón (Columbus Park), where you may be approached by freelance, English-speaking guides who will want to make it all come alive for you. They'll work enthusiastically for $25 an hour for four people.

Most major reconstruction projects in the Zona Colonial have finally come to an end. Unfortunately, the Zona is not as safe as it once was—particularly at night and during festivals—and there's a strong police presence now. Don't walk on the streets with little pedestrian traffic and low lighting, and don't carry a lot of cash or your passport (leave them in the hotel safe).

Alcázar de Colón

HISTORIC HOME | The castle of Don Diego Colón, built in 1517, was the home to generations of the Christopher Columbus family. The Renaissance-style structure, with its balustrade and double row of arches, has strong Moorish, Gothic, and Isabelline influences. The 22 rooms are furnished in a style to which the viceroy of the island would have been accustomed—right down to the dishes and the viceregal shaving mug. The mansion's 40-inch-thick coral-limestone walls make air-conditioning impossible. Bilingual guides are on hand for tours peppered with fascinating anecdotes, like once-upon-a-time weddings. Audio tours (about 25 minutes) are available in English. ✉ *Plaza de España, Calle Atarazana 2, Zona Colonial* ☎ *809/960–9371* 🎟 *RD$100* ⏲ *Closed Mon.*

Basílica Catedral Menor Santa María de la Encarnación

CHURCH | The coral-limestone facade of the first cathedral in the New World (Catedral Primada de América) towers over the south side of the Parque Colón. Spanish workmen began building the cathedral in 1514, but left to search for gold in Mexico. The church was finally finished in 1540. Its facade is composed of architectural elements from the late Gothic to the lavish Plateresque style. Inside, the high altar is made of hammered silver. A museum houses the cathedral's treasures; it's in the former jail, a yellow building just across the street. Mass times vary, so check before going there the day before. ✉ *Calle Arzobispo Meriño, Parque Colón, Zona Colonial* ☎ *809/682–3848* 🎟 *Free.*

Calle Las Damas

STREET | "Ladies Street" was named after the elegant ladies of the court: in the Spanish tradition, they promenaded in the evening. Here you can see a sundial dating from 1753 and the Casa de los Jesuitas, which houses a fine research library for colonial history as well as the

Institute for Hispanic Culture; admission is free, and it's open weekdays from 8 to 4:30. The boutique Hodelpa Nicolás de Ovando is on this street, across from the French Embassy. If you follow the street going toward the Malecón, you will pass a picturesque alley, fronted by a wrought-iron gate, where there are perfectly maintained colonial structures owned by the Catholic Church. ✉ *Calle Las Damas, Zona Colonial.*

Iglesia Santa Bárbara

RELIGIOUS BUILDING | This combination church and fortress, the only one of its kind in Santo Domingo, was completed in 1562. It is a fine example of colonial Spanish architecture, and not as touristic as the cathedrals. Mass is held on Tuesday and Thursday evenings from 6 to 7, and on Sunday mornings from 8 to 9 and 10 to 11. The site is open every day but the church is open to the public only on days mass is held. ✉ *Av. Mella, between Calle Isabel la Católica and Calle Arzobispo Meriño, Zona Colonial* ☎ *809/682–3307* 🎫 *Free* 🕘 *Closed Mon., Wed., Fri., and Sat.*

Monasterio de San Francisco

OTHER ATTRACTION | Constructed between 1512 and 1544, the St. Francis Monastery contained the Franciscan order's church, convent, and hospital. Sir Francis Drake's demolition squad significantly damaged the building in 1586, and in 1673 an earthquake nearly finished the job. Still, when it's floodlit at night, the eerie ruins are dramatic indeed. There's live music every Sunday night from 6 to 10 pm. The scene is like an old-fashioned block party. Zone residents mingle with expats and tourists, who snap pictures of the octogenarians dancing merengue and bachata. Others who come are content to just sit in white plastic chairs, swaying and clapping. It's nice. ✉ *Calle Juan Isidro Pérez, Zona Colonial.*

Pantheon de la Patria

CHURCH | The neoclassical facade of the National Pantheon towers over Calle Las Damas, and its interior is just as impressive. Guarded daily by a presidential honor guard, this former 18th-century Jesuit church became the country's national mausoleum in 1956. It houses the remains of Dominican heroes, such as Gregorio Luperón, Salomé Ureña, José Núñez de Cáceres, Concepción Bona, Emilio Prud'Homme, Juan Sánchez Ramírez, and María Trinidad Sánchez, among others. Explore its striking baroque interior, with a ceiling mural depicting the ascension to heaven and the Last Judgment and an eternal flame burning beneath it. ✉ *Calle Las Damas, near Calle de Las Mercedes, Zona Colonial* ☎ *809/689–6010* 🎫 *Free.*

Parque Colón

CITY PARK | The huge statue of Christopher Columbus in the park named after him dates from 1897 and is the work of sculptor Ernesto Gilbert. At the far end, the Catedral Primada de América is a landmark and most worthy of a visit. Like all the parks in the Zona Colonial, this one is quite a social gathering place, as is the sidewalk café across from it. ✉ *El Conde at Calle Arzobispo Meriño, Zona Colonial.*

Plaza de España

PLAZA/SQUARE | This wide esplanade, which goes past the Casas de Reales in front of Don Diego Columbus's former palace, Alcázar de Colón, is the area in the Zona Colonial where national holidays are celebrated. It's bordered by what once were the ramparts of the original walled city. People enjoy the views of the Ozama River from here and watch the cruise-ship activity below at the terminal. Lovers stroll by night, sharing a kiss under the gas lamps. When many people talk about the Plaza de España, they often refer to the half-dozen restaurants in a row, which are on the upper level of these 16th- and 17th-century warehouses. The popular tables are on their outdoor decks. On certain weekends, cultural performances are held on a stage across from the Plaza.

■ **TIP→ Make dinner reservations on those nights and you'll have a special Santo Domingo experience.** ✉ *Calle La Atarazana, Zona Colonial.*

Restaurants

Mesón De Bari

$$ | **CARIBBEAN** | For some 45 years, this popular restaurant, where baseball is invariably on the TV at the bar, has been feeding the local Zoners what their grandmothers used to make. It's still a hangout for artists, baseball players, politicians, businesspeople, tourists, and even unaccompanied gringas, who feel comfortable here. **Known for:** authentic Dominican specialties; old-timey local ambience; stewed, sweet orange peels. $ *Average main: $16* ✉ *Calle Hostos 302, corner of Calle Salomé Ureña, Zona Colonial* ☎ *809/689–5546.*

MIX

$$ | **INTERNATIONAL** | **FAMILY** | Mix, match, and *compartir* (share) is the thought behind this trendy restaurant in an apartment tower that is still packing in the well-heeled capitaleños. It's a place with a fun atmosphere best enjoyed with a group, though you might want your very own tamarind-grilled chicken salad. **Known for:** churrasco; grazing and sharing among families; edamame can be requested instead of bread service. $ *Average main: $18* ✉ *Torre Washington, Gustavo Mejia Ricart 69, Local 102, Ensanche Serralles* ☎ *809/472–0100* 🌐 *www.mix.com.do.*

★ **Naca'n**

$$$$ | **MODERN AMERICAN** | Located in a historic building that has been meticulously restored to its 1914 glory, this elegant restaurant feels old-fashioned without being stuffy. American classics meet local ingredients in familiar but brilliantly executed dishes served by waiters in pin-striped uniforms and white gloves. **Known for:** old-timey vibes; elegant classics like wedge salad; imported prime cuts of beef. $ *Average main: $50* ✉ *Zona Colonial, Calle Isabel La Católica at Calle Mercedes* ☎ *829/954–8908* 🌐 *www.nacandr.com.*

Pat'e Palo European Brasserie

$$$ | **INTERNATIONAL** | Ideally located on Plaza de España across from the Alcázar de Colón, this restaurant has a good claim to being the first tavern in the New World (the building itself is 500 years old) and capitalizes on its historic heritage. The terrace is perfect for watching free cultural performances across from the plaza while dining alfresco from the contemporary, gastro-fusion menu. **Known for:** impressive wine list; gourmet dining; shrimp in coconut curry sauce. $ *Average main: $26* ✉ *Calle Atarazana 25, Plaza de España, Zona Colonial* ☎ *809/687–8089* 🌐 *www.patepalo.com.*

On the Menu

Among the best Dominican specialties are *queso frito* (fried cheese), *sancocho* (a thick stew of meats and chicken, served with rice and avocado slices), *pastelón* (a casserole made of mashed ripe plantains, ground meat, and topped with cheese), *pescado al coco* (fish in coconut sauce), and *tostones* (fried green plantains). Presidente is the best-known local beer, but Bohemia offers a fuller tasting option. Brugal rum is popular with the Dominicans; Barceló *añejo* (aged) rum is as smooth as cognac; and Barceló Imperial has become a mainstay, too.

Hotels

★ Billini Hotel

$ | **HOTEL** | A wonderful addition to this charmed neighborhood, this boutique hotel was created from a collection of buildings that date back to the 1700s; in its former lives, it has been an ecclesiastical library, an ammunitions depot, and a private school, but its identity as Padre Billini's library was the inspiration for the hotel today. **Pros:** special promotions and discounts found on the website; blackout drapes, monogrammed linens and towels; location in one of the best neighborhoods in the Colonial Zone. **Cons:** rooms are beautiful but strictly modern in design; some aspects of the hotel are cramped; local residents can sometimes overwhelm the pool area. *Rooms from: $250 ✉ Calle Padre Billini 258, Santo Domingo ☎ 809/338–4040 🌐 www.billinihotel.com 24 rooms Free Breakfast.*

★ Casas del XVI

$$$ | **B&B/INN** | This unique hotel concept comprises six former colonial residences that date back to the 16th century (hence the name) that have been restored and modernized by celebrity designer Patricia Reid; each house has its own allure. **Pros:** excellent deals help mitigate the high price tag; designs are magnificent; pampering service. **Cons:** no in-room phone; guests don't intermingle much; you must generally call for service. *Rooms from: $399 ✉ Calle Padre Billini 252, corner 19 de Marzo, Zona Colonial ☎ 809/688–4061 🌐 www.casasdelxvi.com 21 rooms Free Breakfast.*

Fixie Lofts

$ | **APARTMENT** | **FAMILY** | This 16th-century villa, once the first colonial hospital of the Americas, has been restored in ways that honor and highlight the 500-year-old brick and original arches. **Pros:** bespoke furnishings made by local artisans; on-site pool and garden; free bicycles for those who rent for more than a week. **Cons:** the street can be noisy (but most rooms face the courtyard); no food on site, although the owners provide recommendations; no TV or phones in rooms. *Rooms from: $125 ✉ Calle Arzobispo Meriño 314 ☎ 849/212–9824 🌐 www.fixielofts.com 7 lofts No Meals.*

★ Hodelpa Nicolás de Ovando

$ | **HOTEL** | This historic boutique hotel now owned by Hodelpa Hotels was sculpted from the residence of the first governor of the Americas, and it just might be the best thing to happen in the Zona Colonial since Diego Columbus's palace was finished in 1517. **Pros:** lavish breakfast buffet; beautifully restored historic section; a safe haven with tight security. **Cons:** no happy hour scene; some rooms could be larger; breakfast is no longer included in rates. *Rooms from: $138 ✉ Calle Las Damas, Zona Colonial ✣ Across the street from the French Embassy ☎ 809/685–9955, 800/763–4835, 809/685–9955 reservations 🌐 www.hodelpa.com 101 rooms No Meals.*

Hotel Villa Colonial

$ | **B&B/INN** | Owner Lionel Biseau turned this circa-1920s town house into a lovely boutique hotel, keeping as much of the original structure as possible, including a second-floor verandah and old-timey, patterned tile floors. **Pros:** stylish breakfast room and bar overlooking the petite pool; low rates make this an exceptional value; near the tourist area but on quiet street with rooms facing an inner courtyard. **Cons:** Wi-Fi can be intermittent—best in first-floor rooms—which are the better ones; not haute luxury; the small street sign is easy to miss and reads only "Villa Colonial." *Rooms from: $85 ✉ Calle Sanchez 157, between Calles Padre Billini and Arzobispo Noel, Zona Colonial ☎ 809/221–1049, 809/849–3104 mobile 🌐 www.villacolonial.net 11 rooms Free Breakfast.*

Nightlife

El Sartén

DANCE CLUBS | The crowd here covers all walks of Dominican life, from old men playing dominoes on the plastic tables on up to a wealthy and well-dressed group stopping by after an art opening. It's as funky and real a slice of life as it was before the neighborhood became so gentrified. When the traditional dancing begins, you'll see all ages moving to the Cuban beat, with many seriously proficient in their merengue moves. ✉ *Calle Hostos 153, Zona Colonial* ☎ *809/369-8518* ⊙ *Closed Mon. and Tues.*

Shopping

La Leyenda del Cigarro, S.R.L.

TOBACCO | This shop along El Conde in the Zona Colonial makes and sells its own branded premium cigars to clients worldwide and anyone who happens to walk into the cozy store. Enjoy the leather couch in the seating area, and let owner Julio Vilchez Rosso or a member of his personable staff regale you with the history of cigar making in the Dominican Republic and learn what makes a good cigar a good cigar. This store is perfect for the experienced connoisseur or those who'd like to become one. ✉ *Calle El Conde 161, Zona Colonial* ☎ *809/682–9932, 829/642–5509.*

L'ile Au Tresor

JEWELRY & WATCHES | The owner, Patrick Le Clercq, has some of the most attractive and creative designer pieces in native larimar and amber. If you have never bought any of these lovely stones because of cheesy settings or high prices, take a look here. His innovative custom work, in sterling or gold, can be done in 48 hours. Some staff do not speak English but can call Patrick if he's not there. ✉ *Calle Isabela la Católica 17, Zona Colonial* ☎ *829/915–1413* ⊙ *Closed Sun.*

Piantini

A surprising number of luxury hotels and trendy restaurants have opened in the city's main business district. While it's a great place to dine and stay, it's not within walking distance of any sights, so you'll need taxis to get around.

Restaurants

La Dolcerie Café Bistro

$$ | **ECLECTIC** | This cutesy, kid-friendly restaurant/bakery looks like a French café where chic patrons do lunch. It's buzzing for all three meals (it's the "in" brunch place for residents of this fashionable Piantini neighborhood), and happily, it's moderately priced, even for apps the size of mains, and generous dishes such as one of the croque madames (perhaps with pulled pork added) or eggs Benedict. **Known for:** upscale neighborhood with moderate pricing; house-made pastries; family-friendly. $ *Average main: $17* ✉ *Rafael Augusto Sanchez 20, Ensanche Piantini* ☎ *809/338–0814.*

★ **Sophia's Bar & Grill (SBG)**

$$$ | **ECLECTIC** | This formerly old-fashioned and elegant restaurant has morphed into something much more contemporary, but has still retained many of its old-world touches. Each bite is a sensory explosion; a sushi bar complements the grill menu, which offers both fish and foie gras. **Known for:** contemporary, eclectic menu; high-end neighborhood fine dining; twenty- and thirtysomething social scene. $ *Average main: $25* ✉ *Paseo de los Locutores 9, Ensanche Piantini* ☎ *809/620–1001.*

Hotels

Embassy Suites by Hilton Santo Domingo

$ | **HOTEL** | **FAMILY** | This is the capital's new contemporary landmark, sitting atop the Centro Commercial and offering flagship-quality accommodations for reasonable prices. **Pros:** everything still has a nearly new feel; the infinity pool is particularly magical for night swims; front desk service attentive. **Cons:** happy hour can be overwhelming; service can be inconsistent; the restaurant is disappointing. *Rooms from: $229* *32 Tiradentes Ave., Ensanche Naco* *809/685–0001* *www.santodomingo.embassysuites.com* *180 suites* *Free Breakfast.*

★ JW Marriott Santo Domingo

$$ | **HOTEL** | Simply put, this property belonging to Marriott's luxury brand is a charmer and may be the best hotel in the capital, with stunning lobby decor, a great restaurant, and a wonderful pool area. **Pros:** variety of English TV channels and high-tech amenities; classy atmosphere throughout; warm and efficient staff. **Cons:** this neighborhood has heavy traffic; the lobby can feel cramped because of its size and the number of visitors; some rooms are narrow and small. *Rooms from: $350* *Av. Winston Churchill No. 93, Ensanche Piantini* *809/807–1717* *www.jwmarriottsantodomingo.com* *150 rooms* *No Meals.*

Nightlife

Arturo Fuente Cigar Club

BARS | This is the cigar club that other cigar bars look up to, a classy, sceney bar and salon elegant enough that you don't need to be a smoker to enjoy it. A high-tech ventilation system keeps the room from being unpleasantly smoky. And, of course, Fuente cigars are among the best, pairing well with the finest aged rums or cognacs from the bar. This club is populated by well-heeled capitaleños, and has a semi-formal dress code, so dress the part or you may be turned away. *27 de Febrero Av. 211, Santo Domingo* *809/683–2771.*

Wine Tasting Room at El Catador

WINE BARS | This avant-garde wine bar and wine store was created by the major wine distributor El Catador. Cushy leather armchairs and hardwood floors help create a clubby atmosphere. If you want to eat, there's a good menu of tapas. You will want to buy one of the 500 bottles of wine from around the wine-making world. Generally there are a dozen wines for tasting, but there are no samplings during the busy Christmas holidays. *Calle Jose Brea Péna 43, Corner Evaristo Morales, Ensanche Piantini* *809/540–1644* *www.elcatador.com.do.*

Shopping

Acropolis Center

SHOPPING CENTER | Located at the intersection of Avenida Winston Churchill and Calle Rafael Augusto Sanchez in the Piantini district, Acropolis Center has become a favorite shopping arena for the young fashionistas and hip capitaleños (residents of Santo Domingo). Stores such as Lacoste, Kenneth Cole, United Colors of Benetton, and Barone have today's look and style. Prices, however, are generally more than what you would pay in the States. There are also several U.S. chain restaurants like Outback and Hooters, not to mention banks, a pharmacy, bars, and a Caribbean Cinema showing the latest Hollywood movies. *Av. Winston Churchill and Calle Rafael Augusto Sánchez, Ensanche Piantini* *www.acropoliscenter.com.*

Casa Virginia

DEPARTMENT STORE | One of the Dominican Republic's leading department stores, Casa Virginia was founded in 1945. The store is stocked mostly with high-end designer clothing (including a Jenny Polanco department) and fashion finds, but also has avant Italian jewelry, some moderately priced gift items, and a line of high-end men's watches. *Ágora Mall, Third Level, Av. John F. Kennedy esq. Av. Abraham Lincoln*

☎ *809/566–4000* 🌐 *casavirginia.com* ⏲ *Closed Sun.*

Galería de Arte Nader

ART GALLERIES | Top Dominican artists in various mediums are on display here. The gallery staff is well-known in Miami and New York, and works with Sotheby's. ✉ *Calle Pablo Neruda casi Calle Rafael Augusto Sánchez 22, Ensanche Piantini* ☎ *809/544–0878* ⏲ *Closed Sun.*

Lyle O. Reitzel Arte Contemporaneo

ART GALLERIES | This edgy gallery showcases mainly Latin artists from Mexico, South America, and Spain, and some of the most controversial Dominican visionaries. Specializing in contemporary art, it's been in business since 1995. Their rotating collection can include the new, the strange, and the daring. ✉ *Gustavo Mejia Ricart, Torre Piantini Suites 1 and 2 A, Ensanche Piantini* ☎ *809/227–8361* 🌐 *lyleoreitzel.com* ⏲ *Closed Sat. and Sun.*

Gazcue

Santo Domingo's seafront Malecón is lined with large convention hotels that are popular for business travelers and groups. While it's a popular place to stay, it's not within easy walking distance of the Zona Colonial, where most of the city's historic sights are located. Always take a taxi at night; it's not safe to walk here after dark.

Restaurants

Adrian Tropical

$$ | **CARIBBEAN** | Hotel concierges still recommend this Malecón institution for Dominican food (it's now a local chain of four), although it has been branded as fast food. It's touristy, yes, but Dominicans still make up the majority of customers. **Known for:** authentic local food; close to Malecón hotels; prices are reasonable. $ *Average main: $13* ✉ *Av. George Washington 2, Gazcue* ✣ *Across from the Renaissance Jaragua* ☎ *809/565–9236* 🌐 *www.adriantropical.com.*

Hotels

Catalonia Santo Domingo

$ | **HOTEL** | A contemporary landmark on the seafront, the former Hilton Santo Domingo property manages to please business people, convention attendees, and leisure travelers (the pool has sea views). **Pros:** the executive-level lounge and corner executive rooms; the lobby is both colorful and tasteful; totally soundproof rooms. **Cons:** unrenovated rooms are tired; Malecón neighborhood is sketchy by night; little about the property is authentically Dominican. $ *Rooms from: $133* ✉ *Av. George Washington 500, Gazcue* ☎ *809/685–0000* 🌐 *www.hoteles-catalonia.es* *229 rooms* *No Meals.*

Crowne Plaza Santo Domingo

$ | **HOTEL** | Leisure-minded guests may find little reason to leave this stylish 15-story hotel, especially with the second-story outdoor pool and Jacuzzi that overlook the Caribbean. **Pros:** excellent service throughout, particularly at the front desk; on-site convenience store and beauty salon; Malecón address is one of closest to Colonial Zone. **Cons:** this busy hotel can get noisy late into the evening; geared for large convention groups; maintenance is lax and rooms are tired-looking. $ *Rooms from: $220* ✉ *Av. George Washington 218, Gazcue* ☎ *809/221–0000* 🌐 *www.ihg.com/crowneplaza* *196 rooms* *No Meals.*

Courtyard by Marriott Santo Domingo

$ | **HOTEL** | Renovation in 2022 has taken what was once an aging hotel and turned it into a familiar, affordable, and more contemporary space. **Pros:** handy location for baseball games at Quisqueya Stadium; property feels new after renovation; ornate swimming pool. **Cons:** Wi-Fi is free for Marriott members only; not a luxury property; neighborhood isn't so exciting for tourists. $ *Rooms from: $170* ✉ *Maximo Gomez Av. 50-A, La Esperilla* ☎ *809/807–7727* 🌐 *www.marriott.com* *143 rooms* *No Meals.*

Sights

1 Alcázar de Colón........ **D2**

2 Basílica Catedral Menor Santa María de la Encarnación.............. **C3**

3 Calle Las Damas........ **D3**

4 Iglesia Santa Bárbara... **C1**

5 Monasterio de San Francisco............ **C2**

6 Pantheon de la Patria ... **C2**

7 Parque Colón............. **C3**

8 Plaza de España **C2**

Restaurants

1 Adrian Tropical.......... **A5**

2 La Dolcerie Café Bistro............... **A2**

3 Mesón De Bari........... **C3**

4 MIX **A2**

5 Naca'n **C2**

6 Pat'e Palo European Brasserie **C2**

7 Sophia's Bar & Grill (SBG)............. **A2**

Hotels

1 Billini Hotel **C4**

2 Casas del XVI **C4**

3 Catalonia Santo Domingo.......... **A5**

4 Courtyard by Marriott Santo Domingo.......... **A3**

5 Crowne Plaza Santo Domingo.......... **A5**

6 Embassy Suites by Hilton Santo Domingo.......... **A2**

7 Fixie Lofts................. **C2**

8 Hodelpa Nicolás de Ovando............... **D2**

9 Hotel Villa Colonial...... **B4**

10 JW Marriott Santo Domingo.......... **A2**

11 Renaissance Santo Domingo Jaragua Hotel & Casino **A5**

Renaissance Santo Domingo Jaragua Hotel & Casino
$ | **HOTEL** | This jaw-dropping oceanfront hotel stuns with its dreamy pool, contemporary decor, large guest rooms, and its casino, the largest in the Caribbean. **Pros:** room service is very good; security is tight and solo female travelers feel safe; large fitness center and spa. **Cons:** more of a business hotel than a leisure hotel; service in restaurants can be slow; can be a bit noisy at times. *Rooms from: $162 ✉ Av. George Washington 367, Gazcue ☎ 809/221–2222 🌐 www.marriott.com 300 rooms No Meals.*

Nightlife

Diamante Casino
THEMED ENTERTAINMENT | The action includes some 50 slot machines and 16 gaming tables. You can also play a couple of hands of blackjack, shoot craps, or take a spin at the roulette wheel. There's action here from 9 am to 5 am. Diamante's disco, Trio, is a hot ticket, too. Security runs a tight ship. *✉ Sheraton Santo Domingo, Av. George Washington 365 ✥ Adjacent to the Sheraton Santo Domingo ☎ 809/682–2103.*

Renaissance Santo Domingo Jaragua Casino
THEMED ENTERTAINMENT | This Malecón casino is the largest in the capital with more than 50 slot machines, baccarat, roulette, craps, blackjack, and Pai Gow poker tables. *✉ Renaissance Santo Domingo Jaragua Hotel & Casino, Av. George Washington 367, Gazcue ☎ 809/221–1435 🌐 www.marriott.com.*

The Southwest

120 miles (209 km) southwest of Santo Domingo.

As you drive into the mountains southwest of Santo Domingo you enter another world. The major city in this region is Barahona. This area is known for its larimar mines and for a few beautiful boutique resorts up on the mountains and on the alluring, undeveloped beaches south of Barahona.

Hotels

★ Casa Bonita Tropical Lodge
$$ | **B&B/INN** | **FAMILY** | This boutique property southwest of Santo Domingo, formerly a family estate, has style normally associated with urban hotels and views that take in mountains and the sea. **Pros:** a truly relaxing retreat; concierge can arrange private transfers from around the country; suites come with many extra amenities. **Cons:** not much to do in surrounding areas; it's much cooler here than in Santo Domingo; only one restaurant with few nearby choices. *Rooms from: $370 ✉ Km. 17 Carretera de La Costa, Bahoruco ☎ 809/476–5059, 809/540–5908 reservations, 800/961–5133 🌐 casabonitadr.com 5 suites and a villa Free Breakfast.*

The Southeast Coast

Las Américas Highway runs east along the coast from Santo Domingo to La Romana. Midway are well-established beach resorts such as Juan Dolio, and inland, Sammy Sosa's hometown, San Pedro de Macorís. Much farther east are

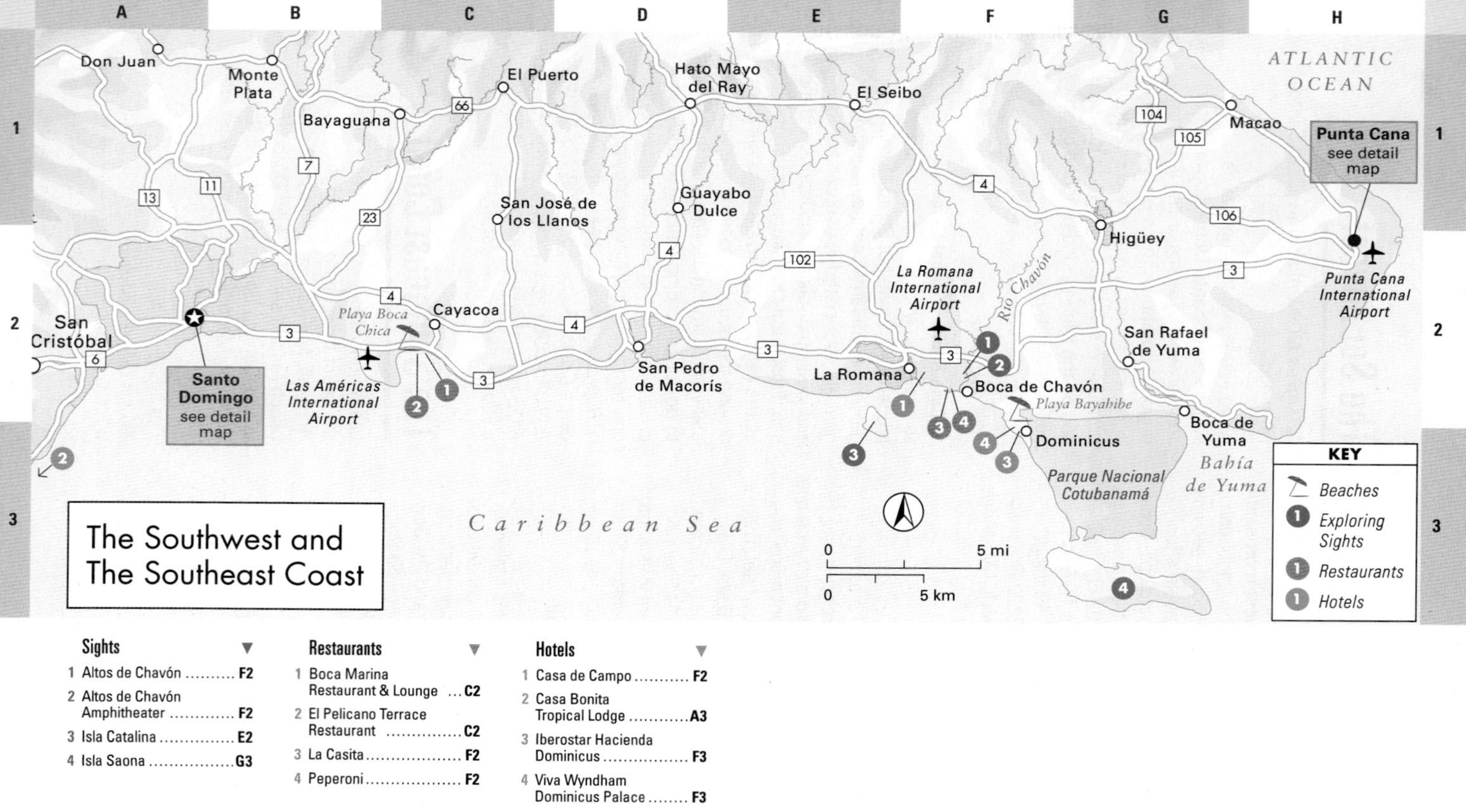

The Southwest and The Southeast Coast

Sights

1 Altos de Chavón F2
2 Altos de Chavón Amphitheater F2
3 Isla Catalina E2
4 Isla Saona G3

Restaurants

1 Boca Marina Restaurant & Lounge ... C2
2 El Pelicano Terrace Restaurant C2
3 La Casita F2
4 Peperoni F2

Hotels

1 Casa de Campo F2
2 Casa Bonita Tropical Lodge A3
3 Iberostar Hacienda Dominicus F3
4 Viva Wyndham Dominicus Palace F3

Punta Cana and Bávaro, glorious beaches on the sunrise side of the island. At the end of the highway lies the luxurious Casa de Campo resort (along with its marina and shopping village, Altos de Chavón) and its airport, both in La Romana. There are some gems among the small number of resorts in Bayahibe and Dominicus Americus. But Bayahibe Bay, all juxtaposed with fishing villages, is idyllic and truly memorable.

Boca Chica

21 miles (34 km) east of Santo Domingo, 8 miles (13 km) east of Las Américas International Airport.

The Boca Chica resort area is immediately east of Las Américas International Airport. A seasoned destination, Boca Chica is popular mainly with Dominicans and Europeans. Since it's the best beach area near Santo Domingo, it had long been popular with *capitaleños* (residents of Santo Domingo) who considered this a chic place to sun and frolic on the light sand beach, their children splashing safely in the calmest of water. These days the town is more boisterous and raunchy, and after 7 pm the city shuts down the main drag, Avenida Duarte, to vehicular traffic. While there is still some daylight, it can be fun to have a cold beer at one of the makeshift bars, and rows of food stands sell cheap Dominican dishes, the best of which are fried fish (usually bones in), served Boca Chica–style with a criolla onion sauce, and *tostones* (fried green plantains).

Beaches

Playa Boca Chica
BEACH | FAMILY | You can walk far out into warm, calm, clear waters protected by coral reefs here. On weekends, the strip with the mid-rise resorts is busy, drawing mainly Dominican families and some Europeans. But midweek is better, when the beaches are less crowded. Expect a parade of roving vendors of jewelry and sunglasses, plus hair braiders, seafood cookers, ice-cream men, and masseuses. The best section of the public beach is in front of Don Emilio's (the blue hotel), which has a restaurant, bar, decent bathrooms, and parking. It's recommended you go to one of the nicer waterfront restaurants—Boca Marina Restaurant & Lounge, El Pelicano, Neptuno's Club—and skip the public beach altogether. **Amenities:** food and drink; parking; toilets. **Best for:** partiers; sunset; swimming; walking. ✉ *Autopista Las Américas, Boca Chica* ✣ *21 miles (34 km) east of Santo Domingo.*

Restaurants

Boca Marina Restaurant & Lounge
$$$$ | SEAFOOD | This remarkable Italian-Dominican seafood restaurant continues to be the "in" spot for the young, fun, and moneyed locals as well as in-the-know visitors. The best all-over experience of the Boca beach restaurants, it extends onto a pier with palapas and lots of white draping. **Known for:** swimming off the deck (showers available for aprés swim); creative and classic preparations of delectable; portobello mushroom au gratin. **$** *Average main: $40* ✉ *Prolongación Duarte 12A, Boca Chica* ☎ *809/523–6702* 🌐 *www.bocamarina.com.do.*

El Pelicano Terrace Restaurant
$$ | SEAFOOD | FAMILY | Pelicano has an enviable deck with chaise longues and even Balinese sun beds both right in the clear water and on the beach. The least expensive of the Boca Chica trio of waterfront restaurants, and the only one with a beach, the fairly simple menu features good bets like lobster bisque and any fresh fish on the *plancha* (grill). **Known for:** ideal layover spot—it's only 15 minutes from Las Américas Airport; fresh ceviche; the tender fillet and garlicky whole red snapper. **$** *Average main:*

$19 ✉ *1 Calle Duarte, at Caracol, in front of Be Live Hamaca Suites, Boca Chica* ☎ *809/523–6500.*

La Romana

48 miles (78 km) east of Juan Dolio.

La Romana has a central park, an interesting market, a couple of good restaurants, banks and small businesses, a public beach, and Jumbo, a major supermarket. It is, at least, a real slice of Dominican life. Casa de Campo is just outside La Romana, and other resorts are found in the vicinity of nearby Bayahibe. Although there are now more resorts in the area, this 7,000-acre luxury enclave put the town on the map. Casa de Campo Marina, with its Mediterranean design and impressive yacht club and villa complex, is as fine a marina facility as can be found anywhere; the shops and restaurants at the marina are a big draw for all tourists to the area.

Sights

★ Altos de Chavón

TOWN | This replica 16th-century Mediterranean village sits on a bluff overlooking the Río Chavón, on the grounds of Casa de Campo but about 3 miles (5 km) east of the main facilities. There are cobblestone streets lined with lanterns, wrought-iron balconies, wooden shutters, courtyards swathed with bougainvillea, and Iglesia St. Stanislaus, the romantic setting for many a Casa de Campo wedding. More than a museum piece, this village is a place where artists live, work, and play. You can visit the ateliers and see the talented artisans making pottery, tapestry, and serigraphic art. The artists sell their finished wares at the Art Studios Boutique. The village also has an amber museum, an archaeological museum, a handful of restaurants, and a number of unique shops. Strolling musicians enliven the rustic ambience of ceramic tiles and cobblestone terrace, but there are now more bars and nightclubs geared to Casa de Campo's guests. Big names, including Elton John, perform at the amphitheater. Christmastime is sheer magic, with lights, music concerts, a giant Christmas tree, and a cameo appearance by Santa. ✉ *Casa de Campo, La Romana* 🌐 *www.casadecampo.com.do.*

Altos de Chavón Amphitheater

PERFORMANCE VENUE | A 5,000-seat, Grecian-style amphitheater features concerts and celebrity performances by such singers as Elton John, Julio Iglesias, his son Enrique, Sting, and the Pet Shop Boys, who all share the amphitheater's schedule of events. Show dates vary to coincide with cruise-ship arrivals, usually Sunday and Monday nights. You can combine the show with dinner at one of the village's restaurants. ✉ *Casa de Campo, La Romana* ☎ *809/523–3333 ext. 8522.*

Restaurants

La Casita

$$$ | **MEDITERRANEAN** | On the waterfront, La Casita (a spin-off of the original in La Romana's downtown) has a contemporary feel; at night dramatic lighting positioned over waterfront tables casts a beautifying glow. Professional waiters guide you through the menu of pastas, risottos, shellfish stew, and paella, which reflects the Spanish owner's heritage. **Known for:** romantic marina front restaurant; fideuà (a variation of paella made with pasta); professional waiters can handle large parties. [$] *Average main: $30* ✉ *Casa de Campo Marina, La Romana* ☎ *809/523–3333* ⏲ *No lunch.*

Peperoni

$$$ | **ECLECTIC** | Although the name may sound as Italian as *amore*, this restaurant's menu is more eclectic than Italian. It has a classy, contemporary white-dominated decor in a dreamy marina setting. **Known for:** beef carpacchio is a staple;

The architecture in the town of Altos de Chavón re-creates a 16th-century Mediterranean village.

international menu; goat cheese salad. *Average main: $21 Casa de Campo Marina, Plaza Portofino 16, La Romana 809/523–2227, 809/523–2228.*

Hotels

★ Casa de Campo

$$$ | RESORT | FAMILY | One of the country's oldest and most famous resorts, which set the benchmark for luxury travel in the Caribbean when it was built in the mid-1970s, is in the top tier of the Dominican Republic's luxury properties. **Pros:** beautiful, modern design; excellent golf and tennis; fine restaurant choices, even for those with meal plans. **Cons:** a bit too sprawling although the golf carts do help; rooms do not have sea views; not the largest beach. *Rooms from: $439 La Romana 809/523–3333, 800/877–3643 www.casadecampo.com.do 300 rooms, 50 villas All-Inclusive.*

Shopping

Altos de Chavón

SHOPPING CENTER | Altos de Chavón is a re-creation of a 16th-century Mediterranean village on the grounds of the Casa de Campo resort, where you can find a church, art galleries, boutiques, restaurants, nightspots, and souvenir shops, and a 5,000-seat amphitheater for concerts grouped around a cobbled square. At the Altos de Chavón Art Studios you can find ceramics, weaving, and screen prints made by local and resident artists. Extra special is the Jenny Polanco Project. A top Dominican fashion designer, she has made an outlet for Dominican, Haitian, and Caribbean craftsmen to sell their wares, from Carnival masks to baskets and carved plates. Tienda Batey sells fine linens handcrafted by women from the sugar plantation *bateys* (poor villages). *Casa de Campo, La Romana www.casadecampo.com.do.*

Casa de Campo Marina
NEIGHBORHOODS | Casa de Campo's top-ranked marina is home to shops and international boutiques, galleries, and jewelers scattered amid restaurants, banks, and other services. The chic shopping scene includes Luxury Shops Carmen Sol and Kiwi St. Tropez for French bathing suits. Polanco-Leon with Dominican designer Jenny Polanco's has resort wear, purses, and jewelry as well as Bibi Leon's tropical-themed home accessories. There's also a marvelous Italian antiques shop, Nuovo Rinascimento, and Club Del Cigarro (Fumo). The *supermercado* Nacional has not only groceries but sundries, postcards, and snacks. ✉ *Casa de Campo Marina, Calle Barlovento, La Romana* 🌐 *www.marinacasadecampo.com.do.*

Bayahibe

11 miles (17 km) east of La Romana via Hwy. 3.

Columbus dropped anchor here in 1494, and Puerto Rican fishermen founded the town in the middle of the 19th century. Now many of the local fishermen either moonlight or have totally given up their poles and nets to skipper the speedboats that bring tourists back from Isla Saona. The small fishing village has flourished in modern times by embracing tourism, and in town Italian immigrants have opened gelato stands and seafood restaurants. Some vestiges remain from earlier times, including the green wooden church on the waterfront, constructed in 1925. It is from this church that a picture of the Virgin Divine Shepherdess, patron saint of Bayahibe, is carried at the front of the annual marine procession. Between the church and the nearby school, an archaeological dig is ongoing, uncovering artifacts from pre-Taíno dwellers, who were potters, as well as an old circular house.

Isla Catalina
ISLAND | This diminutive, picture-postcard Caribbean island lies off the coast of the mainland. Catalina is about a half hour away from Bayahibe by catamaran, and most excursions offer the use of snorkeling equipment as well as a beach barbecue. Some cruise lines also use it as a "private island" experience. ✉ *Isla Catalina* ✣ *30 mins from Bayahibe Bay by boat.*

Isla Saona
ISLAND | Off the east coast of Hispaniola and part of Parque Nacional del Este lies this island, inhabited by sea turtles, pigeons, and other wildlife. Indigenous people once used the caves here. The beaches are beautiful, and legend has it that Columbus once stopped over. However, the island is not nearly as pristine as one might expect for a national park. Getting here, on catamarans and other excursion boats, is half the fun, but it can be a crowded scene once you arrive. Vendors are allowed to sell to visitors, and there are a number of beach shacks serving lunch and drinks. Most boats traveling here leave out of the beach at Bayahibe Village. Most tourists book through their hotel.

⚠ **Please note that there is little to no refrigeration on the island and the sun is strong, so take caution when dining.** ✉ *Bayahibe* ✣ *20 mins from Bayahibe Bay by boat.*

Playa Bayahibe
BEACH | Playa Bayahibe, where several seafood restaurants are situated, is somewhat thin, with hard-packed taupe sand and no lounge chairs. However, as you move away from the village, a 10-minute walk along the shoreline, you'll reach the glorious, half-moon cove. Although you'll be able to get to the cove

and the soft sand, bring a towel (resort security won't let you use the facilities). At night, when no one is on the playa and the silver moon illuminates the phosphorescence, it's the stuff that Caribbean dreams are made of. **Amenities:** food and drink; toilets. **Best for:** partiers; sunset; swimming; walking; windsurfing. ✉ *Near the Dreams resort, Bayahibe* ⊕ *Starts in the center of town.*

Hotels

Iberostar Hacienda Dominicus
$$$ | RESORT | FAMILY | The resort's idyllic beach with its lighthouse bar is that perfect Caribbean postcard; a well-run and-equipped gym and spa help keep it competitive. **Pros:** calm, blue waters and on-site Dressel Divers for water sports; international liquors are available at the lobby lounge; generally a good spirit among the staff. **Cons:** occasional complaints about service, maintenance, and food quality; reservations at à la carte restaurants are difficult to get; room decor is outdated, and restaurants need renovations. *$ Rooms from: $418* ✉ *Playa Dominicus, Bayahibe* ☎ *809/688–3600* 🌐 *www.iberostar.com* *501 rooms* 🍴 *All-Inclusive.*

Viva Wyndham Dominicus Palace
$$ | RESORT | FAMILY | Older Americans looking for an affordable all-inclusive vacation may prefer this classier sister to the nearby Viva Wyndham Dominicus Beach resort, which draws a younger and more family-oriented clientele. **Pros:** professional dive center; lots of stylish European guests; fun resort with a lot of activities. **Cons:** no room service; reservations needed for à la carte restaurants; always heavily occupied, and maintenance cannot keep up. *$ Rooms from: $280* ✉ *Playa Bayahibe, Bayahibe* ☎ *809/686–5658, 800/996–3426* 🌐 *www.vivawyndhamresorts.com* *422 rooms* 🍴 *All-Inclusive.*

Punta Cana

As the sun rises in the Dominican Republic, Punta Cana awakens to the lapping ocean—clear, unspoiled blue brushing up against the pristine stretches of sugar-white sand, with swaying coco palms in the backdrop. A thriving tourism industry fuels the region, and with such plentiful ingredients as sun, sand, and sea, it's no wonder.

The larger area known as Punta Cana encompasses Juanillo (home of the Cap Cana development), Bávaro, and continues all the way around the peninsula to Uvero Alto. Development continues in Galerias Punta-Cana Village, a shopping center that is a draw for visitors from around the area. Five minutes from the village on a gorgeous stretch of beach within the Punta Cana Group's domain is the Westin Punta Cana Resort & Club. Characteristic of this American chain, it is an upscale, non–all inclusive property.

This stretch between Club Med and the Westin Puntacana Resort & Club is one of the most beautiful. Farther up the coast to the Playa El Cortecito section of Bávaro is more how life used to be, with fishermen bringing in their catch, and it is where the wild and crazy restaurant Capitán Cook's is located. Farther north along the coast is a stretch of beach known as Arena Gorda, literally "fat sand," and Playa Bávaro itself. About 20 miles (32 km) from Punta Cana International Airport, it's an area brimming with coconut groves and the location of many resorts. Each has its own strip of sand with rows of chaises longues, and most of these hotels will grant outsiders day passes for a fee. Macao is a pastoral village, but its public beach is no longer a good option, having first been taken over by four-wheeler excursions and now dominated by the huge Hard Rock Hotel & Casino Punta Cana. At the northern end of the peninsula is Uvero Alto.

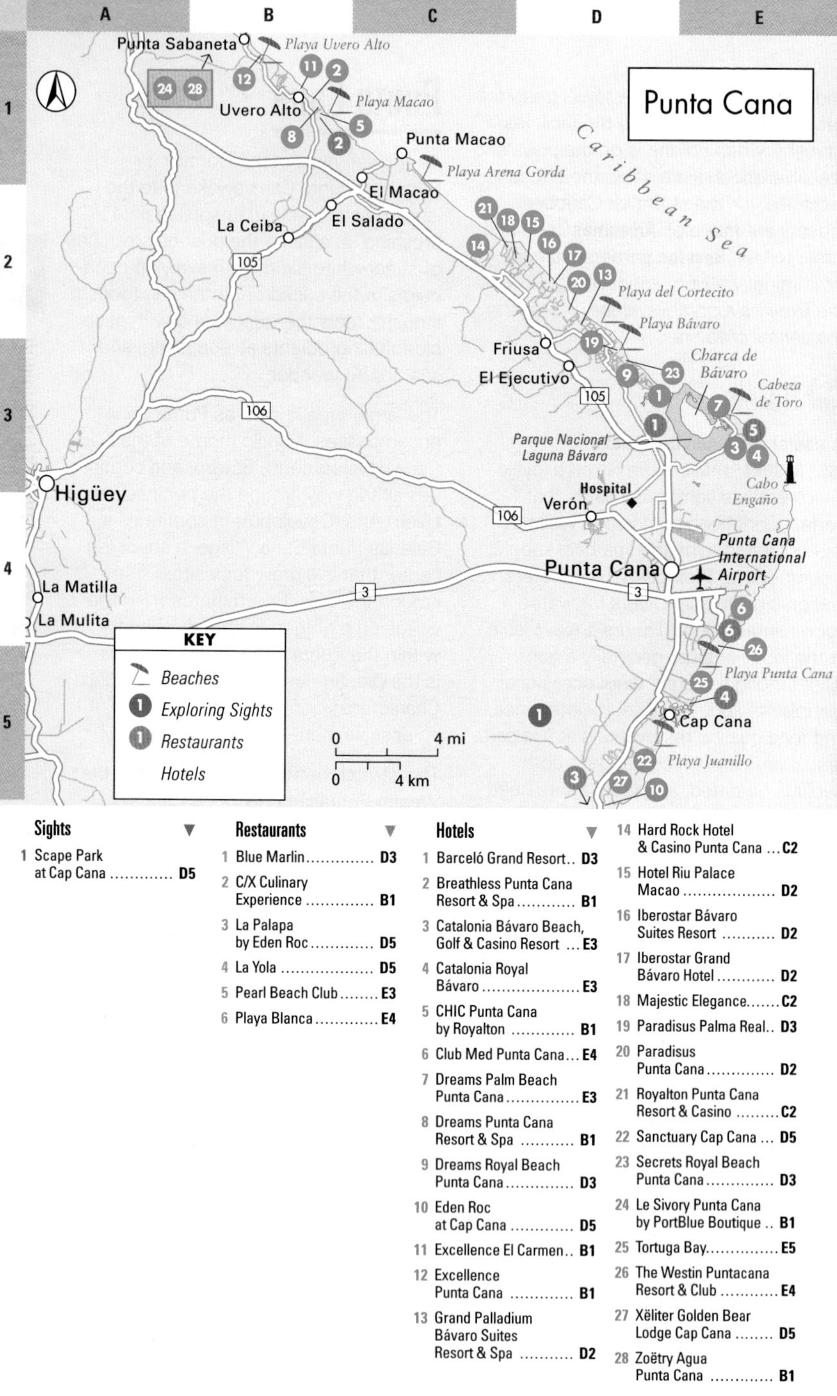

Sights

1 Scape Park at Cap Cana D5

Restaurants

1 Blue Marlin.............. D3
2 C/X Culinary Experience B1
3 La Palapa by Eden Roc D5
4 La Yola D5
5 Pearl Beach Club........ E3
6 Playa Blanca............. E4

Hotels

1 Barceló Grand Resort.. D3
2 Breathless Punta Cana Resort & Spa B1
3 Catalonia Bávaro Beach, Golf & Casino Resort ... E3
4 Catalonia Royal Bávaro E3
5 CHIC Punta Cana by Royalton B1
6 Club Med Punta Cana... E4
7 Dreams Palm Beach Punta Cana................ E3
8 Dreams Punta Cana Resort & Spa B1
9 Dreams Royal Beach Punta Cana.............. D3
10 Eden Roc at Cap Cana D5
11 Excellence El Carmen.. B1
12 Excellence Punta Cana B1
13 Grand Palladium Bávaro Suites Resort & Spa D2
14 Hard Rock Hotel & Casino Punta Cana ... C2
15 Hotel Riu Palace Macao D2
16 Iberostar Bávaro Suites Resort D2
17 Iberostar Grand Bávaro Hotel D2
18 Majestic Elegance....... C2
19 Paradisus Palma Real.. D3
20 Paradisus Punta Cana.............. D2
21 Royalton Punta Cana Resort & Casino C2
22 Sanctuary Cap Cana ... D5
23 Secrets Royal Beach Punta Cana.............. D3
24 Le Sivory Punta Cana by PortBlue Boutique .. B1
25 Tortuga Bay............... E5
26 The Westin Puntacana Resort & Club E4
27 Xëliter Golden Bear Lodge Cap Cana D5
28 Zoëtry Agua Punta Cana B1

Sights

Scape Park at Cap Cana

NATURE SIGHT | FAMILY | This complex in Cap Cana combines beautiful natural scenery with plenty of fun activities for a full day; it can only be visited as part of a daylong tour. The Hoyo Azul combines a tour of the bush with a refreshing swim in a natural cave pool. Another option is the Cenote Indigena Las Ondes, which ends in a swim in a natural sinkhole. The park also has a zipline ecoadventure, a mountain bike ecotrail, Scape Ranch for horseback riding; and the Sunshine Cruise (a booze and snorkeling cruise). Packages can be as short as a half day or as long as a full day, and you have your pick of tours and fun. Lunch, which is a good barbecue meal, can be added but can be a bit busy. Nevertheless, everything is well organized and fun.

TIP→ For the best prices, book through the Park, and you'll be picked up from your Punta Cana, Bávaro, or Uvero Alto resort. ✉ *Cap Cana, Santo Domingo* ☎ *809/469–7484* 🌐 *www.scapepark.com* 🎫 *From $129.*

Beaches

The area encompasses Cabeza de Torres, Playa Bávaro, and continues all the way around the peninsula to Playa de Uvero Alto. Each resort has its own strip of sand with rows of chaises longues; you can call in advance for a day pass, although not all hotels will accommodate outside guests, especially in high season. Playa El Cortecito is more how life used to be, with fishermen bringing in their catch, a few local bars and seafood restaurants, etc. The stretch that includes Club Med and the Puntacana Resort, which encompasses Tortuga Bay and the new Westin, is one of the most beautiful. In theory, it is the only area that should have the designation "Punta Cana," but as tourism and popularity grew, the whole coastal region has been labeled with the name. A new, smooth highway now leads to the more deserted stretches up "north," in Uvero Alto area. Some fine resorts are located here; however, there are few services outside their compounds.

Playa Bávaro

BEACH | Bávaro is the most developed stretch of the 35 miles (56 km) of white-sand beach in the Punta Cana area, which is lined with both midsized and mega-sized all-inclusive resorts. Although it encompasses many smaller towns, the main area, which is past Cabeza de Toro, is thought to begin with the massive Barcelo Bávaro Beach Resort and extend to the funky, fun fishermen's beach, Playa El Cortecito, known for the landmark restaurant Capitán Cook's. The water is characteristically warm and fairly shallow, with seaweed kept in check by hotels. Each resort has its own designated area with its chaise longues lined up in neat rows. Although there are stretches that are idyllically quiet, for the most part it is nonstop action. In several areas there are designated, makeshift markets. **Amenities:** food and drink; toilets; water sports. **Best for:** walking; swimming; windsurfing. ✉ *Playa Bávaro, Bávaro.*

Playa Punta Cana

BEACH | This long stretch of sandy coastline on the Caribbean side of the peninsula is where tourism first began in Punta Cana. This undulating beach with powdery white sand is shaded by lilting coconut palms. Much of it still looks like virgin beach, since there is not the proliferation of all-inclusive hotels you find farther north in Bávaro. The beach extends south to Playa Juanillo, which is similarly incredible and now the site of the Cap Cana development. The waters are generally calm, with more wave action in the winter and during hurricane season. Seaweed has become more of a problem in recent years, and resorts have crews that gather it and rake their stretch of sand. Coral rock can make areas difficult to walk in the water, which is often shallow close to shore; however, the reefs are super for snorkeling and you can walk or swim from shore. The Westin Punta Cana has fresh contemporary food offerings at their beachside restaurant. Playa Blanca is a delightful seafood restaurant adjacent to the Kite-Club and Club Med. **Amenities:** food and drink; toilets; water sports. **Best for:** kitesurfing; snorkeling; swimming; walking; windsurfing. ✉ *Playa Punta Cana, Punta Cana.*

Restaurants

Blue Marlin

$$$$ | **SEAFOOD** | The fresh catch of the day is always the best choice at this restaurant on a palapa-shaded pier overlooking the gentle Caribbean. Dominican specialties are offered, and the plate presentation is relatively simple. **Known for:** Caribbean lobster cakes; South Seas setting (on stilts); fixed price menus. $ *Average main: $70* ✉ *Sanctuary Cap Cana, Blvd. Zona Hotelera, Juanillo* ☎ *809/562–9191* 🌐 *www.sanctuarycapcana.com.*

★ C/X Culinary Experience

$$$$ | **FUSION** | Reservations at this intimate, 20-seat restaurant within the CHIC Resort in Uvero Alto are highly coveted since it welcomes nonresort guests and is not on the resort's all-inclusive plan. The chef's table offers a nightly six-course tasting menu, including wine pairings and choreographed musical accompaniments. **Known for:** open show kitchen; fine dining; food art. $ *Average main: $100* ✉ *CHIC Punta Cana by Royalton, Los Cambrones, Uvero Alto* ☎ *809/468–0404 (ask for the club concierge)* 🌐 *www.chicpuntacana.com* ⏲ *Closed days vary.*

La Palapa by Eden Roc

$$$ | **SEAFOOD** | If you crave waterfront dining, this palapa-roof restaurant is a great option, exuding Caribbean charisma with an Italian accent. The aromas promise exceptional seafood specialties, even hard finds like baby octopus, which is deftly prepared. **Known for:** oceanfront, alfresco dining; delectable gnocchi; an affordable way to experience Eden Roc. $ *Average main: $30* ✉ *Eden Roc Beach Club, Cap Cana, Juanillo* ☎ *809/469–7593, 809/695–5555* 🌐 *www.edenroccapcana.com.*

★ La Yola

$$$ | **MEDITERRANEAN** | Dining on the deck here with the gentle breeze blowing, you feel as if you're actually aboard a *yola* (a small, local fishing boat). The menu, which has always had Mediterranean and Caribbean influences, has been contemporized and given a French flair. **Known for:** strolling musicians; marina front restaurant; professional service. $ *Average main: $29* ✉ *Puntacana Resort & Club Marina, Punta Cana* ☎ *809/959–2262* 🌐 *www.puntacana.com.*

Pearl Beach Club

$$$ | **MEDITERRANEAN** | This trendy, open-air restaurant may be the epitome of beach bars. Mediterranean-Caribbean fusion cuisine as well as upscale burgers and tropical cocktails with fresh ingredients make this a destination worth paying for. **Known for:** daytime parties with DJ; handsome, upscale beach restaurant; infinity pool and sunbeds. $ *Average main: $22* ✉ *Cabeza de Toro, Bávaro* ✣ *Adjacent to the Catalonia Bávaro Beach Casino & Golf Resort* ☎ *809/933–3171, 829/883–5810 WhatsApp* 🌐 *www.pearlbeachclub.com.*

★ Playa Blanca

$$$ | **SEAFOOD** | On a white-sand beach shaded by coco palms, this understatedly cool seafood restaurant is efficient, friendly, and fun. Start with a perfectly executed cocktail—like a lime or mango daiquiri—then dig into the savvy menu, where fresh fish and shrimp done three ways are staples. **Known for:** beachfront bar; chaises are a great place to hang after dining; location between Club Med and the Westin. $ *Average main: $25* ✉ *Puntacana Resort & Club, Playa Blanca, Punta Cana* ☎ *809/959–2262* 🌐 *www.puntacana.com.*

The easternmost coast of the island has 35 miles (56 km) of incredible beach punctuated by coconut palms; add to that a host of all-inclusive resorts, an atmospheric thatch-roof airport that's the busiest in the Dominican Republic (the second busiest in the Caribbean basin), and it's easy to see why this region—despite having more than 50,000 hotel rooms (more than on most other Caribbean islands)—can regularly sell out. Most hotels in the region are clustered around Punta Cana and Bávaro beaches, where more than 90% of the existing properties are all-inclusive. The Westin Puntacana Resort & Club, an upscale American chain hotel, is one of the few that is not all-inclusive. Development continues to press north to the more remote locations of Macao and Uvero Alto, and south to the nearby Juanillo—and several of the newer offerings, such as the Eden Roc Cap Cana, are luxurious and not all-inclusive.

The region commonly referred to as Punta Cana actually encompasses the beaches and villages of Juanillo, Punta Cana, Bávaro, Cabeza de Toro, El Cortecito, Arena Gorda, Macao, and Uvero Alto, which hug an unbroken stretch of the eastern coastline; however, Uvero Alto, the farthest developed resort area to the north, lies some 45 minutes from the Punta Cana International Airport on a significantly improved road.

Barceló Grand Resort

$$$ | **RESORT** | **FAMILY** | Barceló is a glamorous complex of two resorts worthy of gushing praise: the family-friendly Barceló Bávaro Palace is the top of the line, while Barceló Bávaro Beach is adults-only. **Pros:** clean, gorgeous beach; enormous range of entertainment and activity options; no other kids' club is this contemporary. **Cons:** food at buffet is lackluster; club level not a worthwhile upgrade; huge resort draws large conventions and big crowds on both sides. *Rooms from: $435* *Carretera Bávaro, Km 1, Bávaro* *809/686–5797* *www.barcelo.com* *1,991 rooms* *All-Inclusive.*

★ Breathless Punta Cana Resort & Spa

$$$$ | **RESORT** | For adults only, this edgy resort with a sexy yet whimsical vibe is particularly good for singles, filling a void that's been lacking in Punta Cana. **Pros:** the entertainment team works hard to keep the party going; premium liquors are served in the lobby bar Wink and the Xhale club lounge; Xhale level is a worthy upgrade. **Cons:** some staffers lack sufficient English; no reservations needed for à la cartes can mean longish waits; standard rooms are nicely decorated but basic and smallish. *Rooms from: $550* *Playa Uvero Alto, Km 275, Uvero Alto* *809/551–0000* *breathlessresorts.com* *750 rooms* *All-Inclusive.*

Catalonia Bávaro Beach, Golf & Casino Resort

$$ | **RESORT** | **FAMILY** | This sprawling resort, always thought of as a moderately priced playground for families, golfers, and convention attendees, has improved its offering while keeping prices affordably low. **Pros:** no greens fee for guests at Catalonia Caribe Golf Club; extreme value with all of the new upgrades and additions; Pure Chill Out Bar (part of the privileged level). **Cons:** the casino is not inviting; domestic drinks are the norm; can be awfully busy and crowded. *Rooms from: $345* *Cabeza de Toro, Bávaro* *809/412–0000* *cataloniacaribbean.com* *688 rooms* *All-Inclusive.*

★ Catalonia Royal Bávaro

$$ | **RESORT** | This adults-only haven, with meticulously kept grounds and a magical central lake with fountains, is a perfect example of how an all-inclusive resort can offer top-tier hospitality without the herd mentality. **Pros:** less expensive than other deluxe AIs; all rooms have hammocks on terraces; 11 dining options (3 at Royal, 8 at the Bavaro). **Cons:** quality

of food even in Royal restaurants not always spot on; busier than a comparable boutique hotel would be; even the bi-level suites need some maintenance and better lighting. *Rooms from: $375 Playa Bávaro, Bávaro 809/412–0011 www.cataloniahotels.com 377 rooms All-Inclusive.*

★ CHIC Punta Cana by Royalton

$$$ | **ALL-INCLUSIVE** | The adults-only CHIC Punta Cana has been designed with active, younger (twenty- to thirtysomething) partiers in mind, so there is entertainment all day and night, Las Vegas style. **Pros:** food in restaurants generally very good; Wi-Fi and calls to the U.S. and Canada are free; friendly and fun, accommodating staff. **Cons:** service can be slow; house wine is barely potable, so plan on buying better, albeit expensive, bottles; windy beach with lots of wave action. *Rooms from: $450 Carretera Uvero Alta-Punta Cana, Uvero Alto 809/468–0404 royaltonresorts.com 319 rooms All-Inclusive.*

★ Club Med Punta Cana

$$$$ | **RESORT** | **FAMILY** | Whimsy and camaraderie are characteristic of this family-friendly resort—Punta Cana's original all-inclusive—situated on 75 tropical acres, with a coastline of incredibly white sandy shores and a separate luxury reserve for adults only. **Pros:** many theme weeks and events; two-bedroom Tiara suites and Zen Oasis rooms are the best; animated, fun, and interesting global staff. **Cons:** standard rooms are aging and have maintenance issues; peak holiday times, and French school holidays, can be particularly busy; no sea views from the Zen Oasis. *Rooms from: $544 Playa Punta Cana, Punta Cana 809/686–5500, 800/258–2633 www.clubmed.com 631 rooms All-Inclusive.*

Dreams Palm Beach Punta Cana

$$$ | **RESORT** | **FAMILY** | Both family- and American-friendly, the fine Dreams resort is perched on a gorgeous stretch of beach with white-sugar sand and is looking fabulous, offering a wrist-band–free all-inclusive experience. **Pros:** now free Wi-Fi throughout and free calls to U.S. and Canada through concierge; close to the airport; management is especially conscientious. **Cons:** service and maintenance can be inconsistent; time-share sales staff are aggressive; the pool can be very busy, crowded, and loud. *Rooms from: $350 Cabeza de Toro, Bávaro 809/552–6000 www.amrcollection.com 500 rooms All-Inclusive.*

Dreams Punta Cana Resort & Spa

$$$$ | **RESORT** | **FAMILY** | This fun resort in a remote, pastoral setting is super for families, young couples, wedding entourages, honeymooners, ladies getaways—yes, even singles. **Pros:** lovely guest rooms; staff are friendly and personable; nightly entertainment is a cut above. **Cons:** a popular resort that runs at high occupancy; food can leave much to be desired; some rooms still need updating as do some of the older public spaces. *Rooms from: $480 Playa Uvero Alto, Km 269.5, Uvero Alto 809/682–0404, 866/237–3267 in the U.S. www.dreamsresorts.com/punta-cana 620 rooms All-Inclusive.*

Dreams Royal Beach Punta Cana

$$ | **RESORT** | **FAMILY** | This moderately priced branch of the AMResorts family has style as well as a gorgeous beachfront. **Pros:** large housekeeping and entertainment team; within walking distance of shops and off-site cafés; close to the airport. **Cons:** music can be very loud and time-share staff annoying; customer service can be slow; some complaints about maintenance and repairs and uncomfortable beds. *Rooms from: $375 El Cortecito, Av. Alemania s/n, Bávaro 809/221–4646 www.amrcollections.com 639 rooms All-Inclusive.*

★ Eden Roc at Cap Cana
$$$$ | **HOTEL** | Within Cap Cana, the most luxurious resort is unquestionably this all-suite boutique hotel with interior decor straight from the mid-century French Riviera. **Pros:** the charismatic Riva Bar is a great spot for a drink and some piano music; pampering, discreet service; a golf cart is included with rooms. **Cons:** expensive, though promotions are often offered; limited number of one-bedrooms, which are in demand; suites don't have sea views. *Rooms from: $1600* *Cap Cana, Juanillo* *809/469–7469* *www.edenroccapcana.com* *57 units* *Free Breakfast.*

Excellence El Carmen
$$$$ | **ALL-INCLUSIVE** | Slightly more expensive than its neighboring sister property, Excellence Punta Cana, it's equally as beautiful in a more colorful way, particularly the lobby furnishings. **Pros:** everything still feels brand-new; a gorgeous seafront resort; huge variety of good food. **Cons:** rooms are quite a distance to public areas; some might resent the "no shorts" dress code at dinner; exterior facade is gray and institutional. *Rooms from: $576* *Playas de Uvero Alto, Punta Cana* *Five-minute drive before Excellence Punta Cana* *809/285–0000* *www.excellenceresorts.com/resorts/excellence-el-carmen* *492 suites* *All-Inclusive.*

★ Excellence Punta Cana
$$$$ | **RESORT** | This adults-only, all-inclusive is particularly appealing to couples (honeymooners, for sure) and wedding parties, and attracts a younger, fun clientele. **Pros:** no reservations are required at any of the restaurants; super-sized, renovated Excellence Club suites are an expensive but worthy upgrade; free long distance calls to the U.S. and Canada. **Cons:** isolating for singles; waters can be rough off the beach; honeymoon suites and others are far from the restaurants; far from shopping, other restaurants, and nightlife. *Rooms from: $570* *Playa de Uvero Alto, Punta Cana, Uvero Alto* *809/685–9880* *www.excellenceresorts.com* *456 rooms* *All-Inclusive.*

Grand Palladium Bávaro Suites Resort & Spa
$$ | **RESORT** | **FAMILY** | Four sprawling, contiguous resorts (with a shuttle service until 2 am) share these well-kept grounds and feel like a beachside village, and three of these—Grand Palladium Bávaro, Grand Palladium Punta Cana, and Grand Palladium Palace—share one another's facilities, including a top-notch spa and health club. **Pros:** front desk staff is professional and bilingual; excellent offshore snorkeling (though at an extra charge); guest rooms are exceptionally spacious and quiet. **Cons:** Royal Suites area may be too quiet for some; it's a huge resort that can feel busy at times; few rooms have sea views. *Rooms from: $345* *Carretera El Cortecito, El Cortecito, Bávaro* *809/221–8149 Grand Palladium Bávaro, 809/221–0719 Grand Palladium Palace, 800/961–7661 in the U.S.* *www.palladiumhotelgroup.com* *1,823 rooms* *All-Inclusive.*

★ Hard Rock Hotel & Casino Punta Cana
$$$$ | **RESORT** | Hard Rock's first all-inclusive property has its own unique identity, different from any other Dominican resort, and it's a great choice if you want nightlife and a busy, fun atmosphere. **Pros:** music is everywhere; the resort is a lot of fun; very clean. **Cons:** doesn't have a Caribbean feel except at the beach; service can be slow; can be too crowded during the busiest times of the year and Dominican holidays. *Rooms from: $505* *Blvd. Turístico del Este 74, Km 28, Macao* *809/687–0000* *www.hardrockhotels.com* *1,787 rooms* *All-Inclusive.*

★ Hotel Riu Palace Macao
$$$ | **RESORT** | This adults-only resort is the star of the five Riu resorts in Macao. **Pros:** helpful front desk staff, who work well under high-volume pressure; great entertainment staff who try to get guests

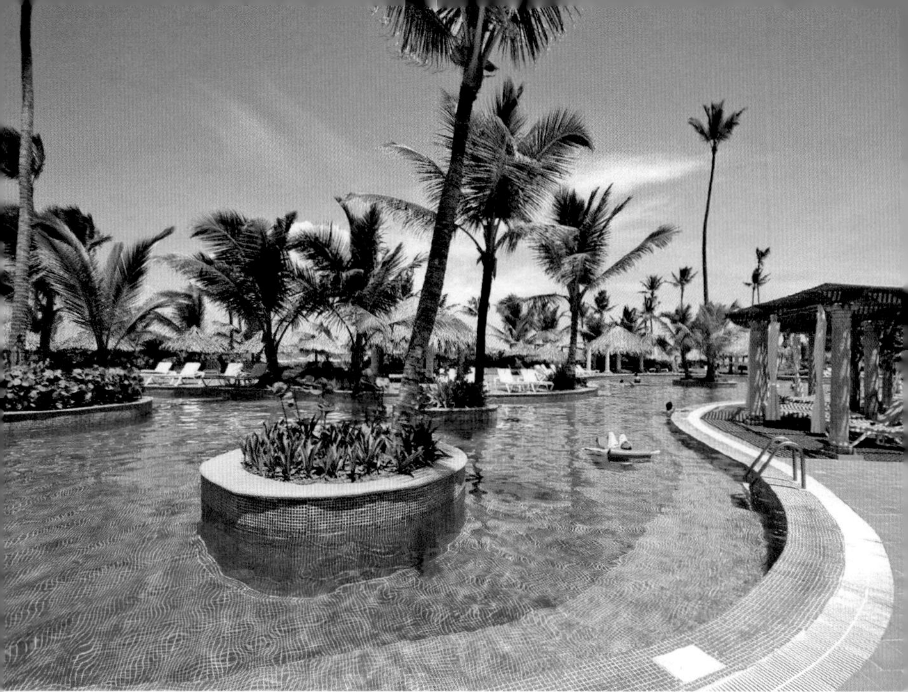

The gorgeous pool at the adults-only Excellence Punta Cana.

to have fun (in a good way); good food. **Cons:** free Wi-Fi is erratic; its new popularity equals high occupancy; excellent value, but still not really luxurious. *Rooms from: $370* ✉ *Playa Arena Gorda, Bávaro* ☎ *809/221–7171* 🌐 *www.riu.com* *424 rooms* *All-Inclusive.*

Iberostar Bávaro Suites Resort

$$$ | **RESORT** | **FAMILY** | Like its two sister resorts, this Spanish entry has panache—evidenced in its lobby, an artistic showpiece, and contemporary guest rooms with plush bedding—making it competitive with Punta Cana's newer properties. **Pros:** extra-special management keeps the staff in fine spirits; great kids' water playground; good specialty restaurants. **Cons:** unrenovated rooms should be avoided; the property is showing its age; buffet not quite as good as it once was. *Rooms from: $379* ✉ *Playa Bávaro, Bávaro* ☎ *809/221–6500, 888/923–2722* 🌐 *www.iberostar.com* *596 rooms* *All-Inclusive.*

★ **Iberostar Grand Bávaro Hotel**

$$$$ | **RESORT** | Iberostar's adults-only resort—an architectural gem—is a knockout from the moment you walk into the glamorous lobby and is one resort where the term "no expense was spared" is actually true. **Pros:** idyllic beach weddings and honeymoons; impressive selection of designer restaurants with contemporary cuisine; excellent lunch buffet at beach. **Cons:** the hotel is pricey for an AI in this area; some inconsistent service in restaurants; although improving, there are still service lapses from lack of English-language skills. *Rooms from: $708* ✉ *Playa Bávaro, Bávaro* ☎ *809/221–6500, 888/923–2722* 🌐 *iberostar.com* *274 rooms* *All-Inclusive.*

Majestic Elegance

$$$ | **RESORT** | The younger of Punta Cana's two Majestic resorts, which is an all-suites property, is the more sophisticated sister—and a busy one. **Pros:** free Wi-Fi in rooms and public areas; fun and welcoming staff is eager to please; premium liquors served at all bars and à la carte restaurants. **Cons:** some rooms are not soundproof; high occupancy makes it feel crowded; guests not in the VIP Club may feel second-class. *Rooms from: $416* *Majestic St., Arena Gorda* *809/221–9898* *www.majestic-resorts.com* *596 rooms* *All-Inclusive.*

★ Paradisus Palma Real

$$$$ | RESORT | FAMILY | This luxury all-inclusive is a visual showstopper. **Pros:** special promos on website offers discounted rates; adjacent to the Palma Real Shopping Center; guests enjoy unlimited golf at Cocotal Golf & Country Club. **Cons:** large resort with little personal service unless you are in one of the special areas; the Reserve does not have sea views, and guests must shuttle to main beach; restaurants and nightlife are far from some rooms. *Rooms from: $486* *Bávaro Beach, Avenida Barceló, Bávaro* *809/688–5000* *www.paradisuspalmareal.com* *554 rooms* *All-Inclusive.*

Royalton Punta Cana Resort & Casino

$$$ | RESORT | FAMILY | Although there are adults-only sections at this resort, including the upper-strata Blue Diamond Club, couples and adults without kids are better served elsewhere; the right demographic for this stunning hotel is young families and groups. **Pros:** just 30 minutes from the airport—important for traveling families; the level of service is quite high, friendly, fun and helpful; free Wi-Fi throughout. **Cons:** butlers at the Blue Diamond Club do not always get high marks; overbooking during high season is a problem; guests have been shunted to less luxurious sister properties; no elevators. *Rooms from: $440* *Playa Arena Gorda, Carretera Macao, Bávaro* *809/468–0404* *www.bluediamondresorts.com* *475 rooms, 10 suites* *Free Breakfast.*

★ Sanctuary Cap Cana

$$$$ | RESORT | The gorgeous stone facade of this adults-only resort—a stellar keystone of Cap Cana—is reminiscent of the 16th-century Alcázar de Colón in Santo Domingo, and the interior public spaces are influenced by Dominican colonial-style mansions. **Pros:** world-class golf is just a swing away at Punta Espada; exceptional breakfast buffet; professional management and many exceptional staffers. **Cons:** food options are not as varied; beach by main pool has coral and shallow, milky water; the standard junior suites are long but narrow. *Rooms from: $500* *Cap Cana, Blvd. Zona Hotelera, Playa Juanillo, Juanillo* *809/562–9191* *www.sanctuarycapcana.com* *298 rooms, 26 villas* *All-Inclusive.*

★ Secrets Royal Beach Punta Cana

$$$ | RESORT | The lobby at this sceney, adults-only all-suites resort is like a modern art gallery, but the Caribbean-accented guest rooms do not quite match these high expectations, though the white-sand beach is glorious. **Pros:** exceptional 17,000-square-foot Spa by Pevonia; nightly entertainment and dancing at the main plaza; fun activities like cooking competitions on the beach. **Cons:** Wi-Fi is slow; all rooms can be loud, but tropical/garden-view rooms especially don't compare; beach vendors and overzealous entertainment crew can be annoying. *Rooms from: $475* *El Cortecito, Av. Alemania s/n, Bávaro* *809/221–4646* *www.amrcollection.com* *641 rooms* *All-Inclusive.*

Le Sivory Punta Cana by PortBlue Boutique

$ | RESORT | The best things really do come in small packages at this romantic boutique hotel, which delivers on its promise of expressly personal service and utter tranquility. **Pros:** near virgin Atlantic beach, albeit not on the calmer Caribbean; prices dropped substantially; free, strong Wi-Fi throughout.

Cons: mosquitoes can be a problem; service can be lacking; no nightlife, and few activities. *Rooms from: $236* ✉ *Playa Sivory, Uvero Alto Rd., Uvero Alto* ☎ *888/774–0040* 🌐 *www.sivorypuntacanaresort.com* *55 rooms* *All-Inclusive.*

★ Tortuga Bay

$$$$ | **RESORT** | Shuttered French windows that open to grand vistas of the sea and a cotton-white private beach are hallmarks of this luxury-villa enclave within the grounds of Puntacana Resort & Club. **Pros:** breakfast poolside with fresh-squeezed OJ; sprawling grounds with virgin beaches; VIP check-in at airport. **Cons:** too isolating for singles; Bamboo restaurant is pricey, as is the resort; little nightlife. *Rooms from: $750* ✉ *Puntacana Resort & Club, Playa Punta Cana, Punta Cana* ☎ *809/959–8229, 888/442–2262* 🌐 *tortugabayhotel.com* *16 units* *Free Breakfast.*

The Westin Puntacana Resort & Club

$$ | **RESORT** | The Punta Cana Group has eschewed the all-inclusive in favor of a beautiful Westin property on a glorious stretch of beach with ocean views from floor-to-ceiling windows and private balconies in every guest room. **Pros:** The Brassa Grill overlooks the sea, illuminated at night; well-trained staff, especially receptionists; the pool segues to the idyllic white-sand beach; bartenders put the happy in the happy hour. **Cons:** not much to do after dinner if there is no entertainment; hotel shuttle has few runs to Punta Cana Village during dinner hours; housekeeping can come too early. *Rooms from: $326* ✉ *Puntacana Resort & Club, Playa Blanca, Punta Cana* ☎ *809/959–2222* 🌐 *www.westinpuntacana.com* *200 rooms* *No Meals.*

Xëliter Golden Bear Lodge Cap Cana

$$$ | **APARTMENT** | A painting of an amber-colored bear—a tribute to golf great Jack Nicklaus—greets guests at this apartment-style property that's possibly the most affordable lodging in the exclusive Cap Cana enclave. **Pros:** spacious guest rooms; safe haven for children; tranquil pool complex. **Cons:** decor somewhat dated; restaurant not wonderful; no activity and may be too quiet for some. *Rooms from: $385* ✉ *Cap Cana* ☎ *809/469–7425* 🌐 *xeliter.com* *91 apartments* *No Meals.*

Zoëtry Agua Punta Cana

$$$ | **RESORT** | At this serene oceanfront resort, rustic, natural beauty and high architectural style blend seamlessly. **Pros:** excellent service; all guests get a complimentary 20-minute spa treatment; top-shelf liquors and fine wines. **Cons:** original rooms need renovations; some low-key entertainment but limited nightlife; open bathrooms mean bugs on ground floor. *Rooms from: $377* ✉ *Playa Uvero Alto, Uvero Alto* ☎ *809/468–0000* 🌐 *www.amrcollection.com* *94 units* *All-Inclusive.*

 Nightlife

With the predominance of all-inclusive hotels, nightlife in Punta Cana tends to center on whatever resort you are staying at. But there's more out there than first meets the eye. Some clubs, casinos, and shows at other resorts have very good reputations and are open to outsiders. Cover charges at the discos vary, ranging from none when it's early on an ordinary night to US$10 or $20 during peak hours, especially when there's live entertainment. Don't forget your ID; when nonguests are allowed into the disco on a resort's grounds, security keeps a close eye on who is coming and going. Some resorts offer nighttime excursions to a local disco, where you can go with a group and return at a scheduled hour.

CocoBongo Club

DANCE CLUBS | This popular Mexican club has opened a branch in Punta Cana. Latin Club music is interspersed with shows (such as celebrity impersonators or samba demos) lasting some 20 minutes, long enough for the dancers to cool off and drink. The atmosphere is loud, hot, and crowded. Paying extra for VIP service may be a good idea if you don't want to compete with the throngs on the main floor, and this includes transportation back to major resorts in the area. ✉ *Downtown Mall, Carretera Barcelo-Vernon, corner El Boulevard, Bávaro* ☎ *809/466–1111* 🌐 *www.cocobongo.com.do.*

★ **Imagine**

DANCE CLUBS | Imagine you were dancing the night away in a natural cave, with earth-rocking acoustics. You can bounce back and forth between the various "cave" rooms with their stalactites and stalagmites, with equally hot dance floors, featuring house/club jams, merengue/salsa/world beats, current Top 40, and more. Theme nights change, like Crazy Thursday might switch to Brazil's Carnaval. Come late and stay early: things start getting steamy well after midnight, when many club crawlers descend via shuttle (round-trip) from the local resorts. The bus is $10 per person round trip. Private options are available. Taxis wait outside for those who can't hang. Tickets are sold online and at the door. The regular open bar for $40 includes international beverages, which differs from other local clubs that only offer national liquors. For just $10 more, premium tickets include an open bar with premium liquors, and the VIP tickets cover entrance for up to six people for $450. ✉ *Carretera Cocoloco–Riu, Coco Loco/Friusa, Bávaro* ☎ *829/838–5353* 🌐 *www.imaginepuntacana.com.*

Shopping

★ **Galerias at Puntacana Village**

SHOPPING CENTER | The Galerias at Puntacana Village lie within a still-blossoming shopping, dining, and residential complex built on the road to the Punta Cana International Airport. Originally the village was built to house employees of the Puntacana Group, but now the shops and restaurants are also a tourist draw. The village is comprised of churches, an international school, and this commercial area with its restaurants, shops, a supermarket, banks (with ATMs), a beauty salon, pharmacy, and doctors' offices. Family-oriented, it has an ice-cream parlor, a playground, and a children's clothing boutique as well as those for adults. The restaurants are less expensive than those at most resorts and very popular. The Sheraton Four Points Puntacana Village is across the street, just a two-minute drive from the airport. ✉ *Blvd. Primero de Noviembre, Punta Cana* 🌐 *www.puntacanavillage.com.*

Plaza Uvero Alto

SHOPPING CENTER | You won't find brand-name shops at Plaza Uvero Alto, but it's a convenient 24-hour shopping center for the hotels in the remote Uvero Alto area of Punta Cana. Especially useful are a bank, outdoor ATM, and a money exchange, followed by a small pharmacy, gift shops, and two minimarkets (one in the front, the other in the back row of booths). ✉ *Carretera Uvero Alto, Uvero Alto.*

North Coast

The Autopista Duarte ultimately leads (via a three- to four-hour drive) from Santo Domingo to the North Coast, sometimes called the Amber Coast because of its large, rich amber deposits. The coastal area around Puerto Plata, notably Playa Dorada, is a region of well-established, all-inclusive resorts and developments; the North Coast has more than 70 miles (110 km) of beaches, with condominiums and villas going up fast.

The farther east you go from Puerto Plata and Sosúa, the prettier and less spoiled the scenery becomes. The autopista runs past Cabarete, a town that's a popular windsurfing haunt, and Playa Grande,

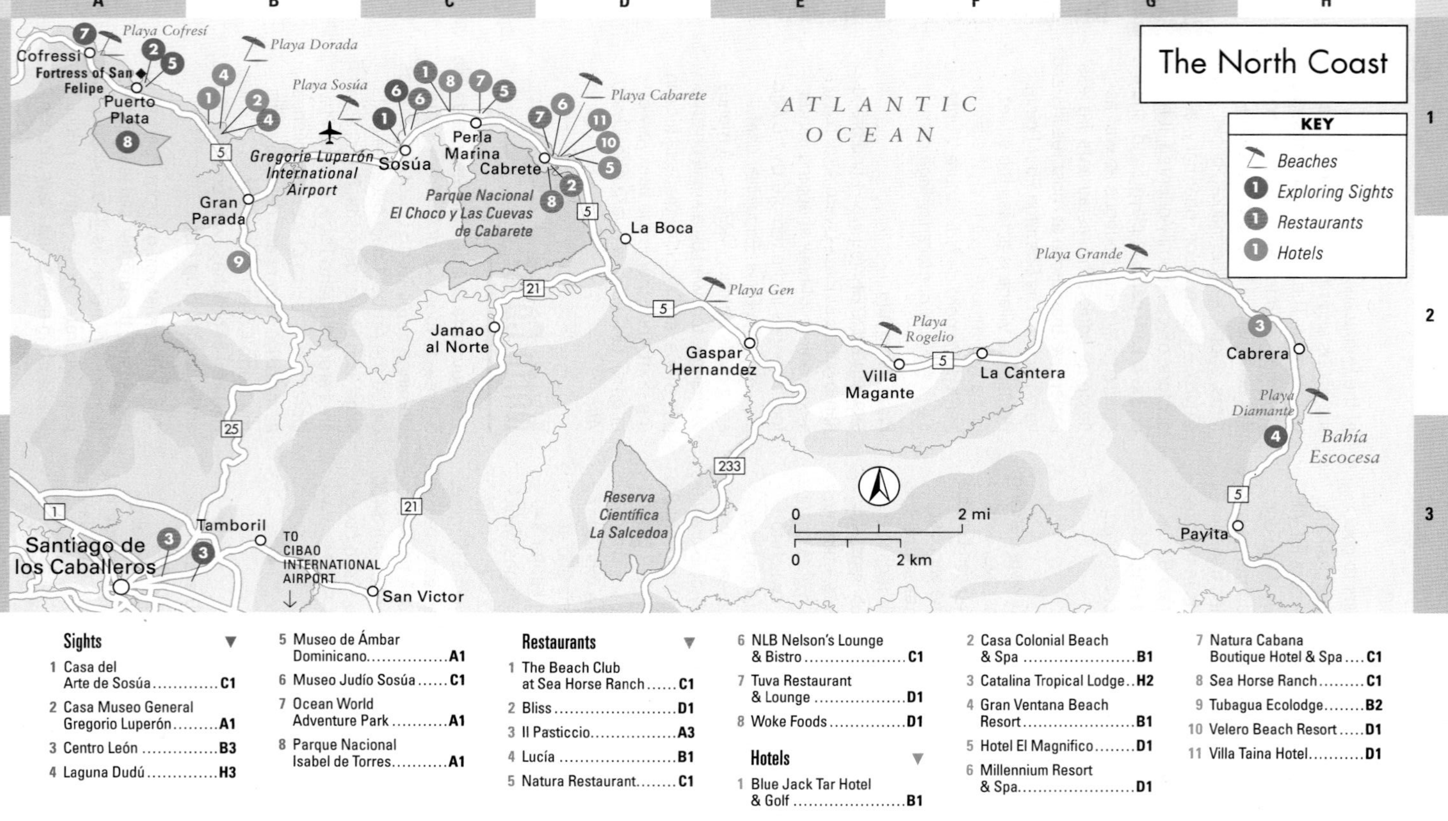

Sights

1 Casa del Arte de Sosúa C1
2 Casa Museo General Gregorio Luperón A1
3 Centro León B3
4 Laguna Dudú H3
5 Museo de Ámbar Dominicano A1
6 Museo Judío Sosúa C1
7 Ocean World Adventure Park A1
8 Parque Nacional Isabel de Torres A1

Restaurants

1 The Beach Club at Sea Horse Ranch C1
2 Bliss D1
3 Il Pasticcio A3
4 Lucía B1
5 Natura Restaurant C1
6 NLB Nelson's Lounge & Bistro C1
7 Tuva Restaurant & Lounge D1
8 Woke Foods D1

Hotels

1 Blue Jack Tar Hotel & Golf B1
2 Casa Colonial Beach & Spa B1
3 Catalina Tropical Lodge H2
4 Gran Ventana Beach Resort B1
5 Hotel El Magnifico D1
6 Millennium Resort & Spa D1
7 Natura Cabana Boutique Hotel & Spa C1
8 Sea Horse Ranch C1
9 Tubagua Ecolodge B2
10 Velero Beach Resort D1
11 Villa Taina Hotel D1

which has an Aman resort and golf club. Surrounded by high cliffs, this incredibly beautiful Playa Grande beach has vendors selling from brightly painted, Victorian-style huts at the end of the beach. There is now a proper parking area, and vehicles can no longer drive on the beach.

Puerto Plata

Although it has been sleeping for decades, this was a dynamic city in its heyday. You can get a feeling for this past in the magnificent Victorian gazebo in the central **Parque Independencia.** Painted a crisp white, the park looks postcard pretty, with gleaming statuary. On the Malecón, the **Fortaleza de San Felipe** protected the city from many a pirate attack and was later used as a political prison. The nearby **lighthouse** has been restored. Much is happening in Puerto Plata and its original hotel zone, Playa Dorada. Nonstop flights are contributing to the area's revival.

The Office of Cultural Patrimony is working with private business owners and investors on a long-term plan to beautify the city, which has hundreds of classic wooden gingerbread buildings. Mansions, including Casa Olivores and the Tapounet family home, are being restored; at the same time new resorts are under development both on and off Playa Dorada's beautiful beachfront.

At Puerto Plata's port, the 30-acre Amber Cove Cruise Center welcomes cruise guests with restaurants, bars, retail shops, and an elaborate pool complex with waterslides.

Sights

Casa Museo General Gregorio Luperón

HISTORIC HOME | A long time in the making, this modest wood-frame house is where Puerto Plata's famous son, General Gregorio Luperón, spent his last years. Known for his courage and patriotic love of his homeland, he led the Dominican revolution against Spain, ending the island's foreign occupation in 1865. The museum's mission is to expose the life and ideals of this national hero to visitors both foreign and domestic. It has been accomplished with quality cultural displays depicting the various stages of Luperón's life, enhanced with signposting in both Spanish and English. The home is a slice of 19th-century life and an emblem of the city's rich history. ✉ *Calle 12 de Julio 54, Puerto Plata* ☎ *809/261–8661* 🎫 *$5* ⏲ *Closed Sun.*

Museo de Ámbar Dominicano

OTHER MUSEUM | In an opulent, galleried mansion, restored to its former Victorian glamour, the museum displays and sells the Dominican Republic's national stone: semiprecious, translucent amber. Amber is essentially prehistoric hardened tree sap, and Dominican amber is considered the best in the world. Many pieces are fascinating for what they have trapped inside, and the small second-floor museum contains a piece with a lizard reported to be 50 million years old, give or take a few millennia. The museum's English text is informative. Shops on the museum's first floor sell authentic, albeit rather expensive, amber, souvenirs, and ceramics. ✉ *Calle Duarte 61, Puerto Plata* ☎ *809/734–2599 museum* 🌐 *www.ambermuseum.com* 🎫 *RD$120* ⏲ *Closed Sun.*

Ocean World Adventure Park

WATER PARK | **FAMILY** | This multimillion-dollar aquatic park in Cofresí has marine and wildlife interactive programs, including dolphin and sea lion shows and encounters, a double-dolphin swim, a tropical reef aquarium, stingrays, shark tanks, an aviary, a rain forest, and a new pirates pool for kids. You must make advance reservations if you want to participate in one of the swims or encounters; children must be at least six years old and accompanied by an adult. The exhilarating (though expensive) double-dolphin swim will produce lifelong memories. If you are brave enough for the (nurse) shark encounter, you will feed them and touch them in the shark cove; the stingray encounter is also included. A photo lab and video service can capture the moment, but there is an extra charge. If you're staying at nearby Lifestyle resorts, or hotels in Puerto Plata, transfers are free. If in Sosúa or Cabarete, transfers are $10 per person; hotels should have the tour schedules.

■ **TIP→ There's a private beach, showers, and a locker room on-site.** ✉ *Calle Principal 3, 3 miles (5 km) west of Puerto Plata, Cofresi* ☎ *809/291–1000* 🌐 *www.ocean-world.net* 🎟 *From $69.*

Parque Nacional Isabel de Torres

MOUNTAIN | Southwest of Puerto Plata, Mount Isabel de Torres soars 2,600 feet above sea level and is notable for its huge statue of Christ. Up there also are botanical gardens that, despite efforts, still are not memorable. If you go independently, you can choose to hire a knowledgeable English-speaking guide. A cable car takes you to the top for a spectacular view. The cars usually wait until filled to capacity before going up—which can make them crowded. You should visit in the morning, preferably by 9 am; by afternoon, the cloud cover rolls in, and you can see practically nothing. That said, some visitors consider this the highlight of a city tour and take dozens of aerial photos from the cable car, which runs continuously until 4:45 pm.

■ **TIP→ The vendors are particularly tenacious here.** ✉ *Av. Manolo Tavárez Justo, off Autopista Duarte (Hwy. 1), follow signs, Puerto Plata* ☎ *809/970–0501* 🌐 *telefericopuertoplata.com* 🎟 *Cable car RD$250.*

Beaches

Playa Cofresí

BEACH | This long stretch of golden sand is good for swimming, and a bit of wave action provides an opportunity for surfing. Locals mainly use the public area, particularly on Sunday. To the immediate north are Ocean World and its marina. To the south, a five-minute walk in the sand, is a semiprivate beach for the Cofresí Palm Beach resort. **Amenities:** food and drink. **Best for:** surfing; swimming; walking. ✉ *Calle Principal, 4½ miles (7 km) west of Puerto Plata town center, just south of Ocean World, Cofresi.*

Restaurants

★ Lucía

$$$ | **CARIBBEAN** | With a setting as artistic as a gallery—befitting its location within Casa Colonial, a refined boutique hotel—and an ambitious Caribbean-fusion menu, Lucía is successful on all fronts. In a room with orchids galore, crisp white linens, and waiters in white guayabera shirts giving impeccable service, guests love the delicious appetizers and signature dessert, the molten chocolate volcano. **Known for:** remarkable main courses are rack of lamb and Caribbean lobster; the ultimate date-night venue; marinated tuna appetizer. 💲 *Average main: $27* ✉ *Casa Colonial, Playa Dorada* ☎ *809/320–3232* 🌐 *www.casacolonialhotel.com* ⊘ *No lunch.*

Hotels

Blue Jack Tar Hotel & Golf

$$$ | **APARTMENT** | **FAMILY** | This condominium complex shares the grounds of the Hotel Blue Jack Tar, providing an upscale option to the generally moderately priced Playa Dorada. **Pros:** beautiful, spacious condos with solid security; condo dwellers can utilize the hotel's facilities; restaurants nearby. **Cons:** first-floor condos do not have views, so you have to go up and pay for that; hotel guests are not as upscale as condo renters; only one restaurant at the hotel. *Rooms from: $300* *Playa Dorada* *809/320–3800* *www.bluejacktar.com* *30 condominiums (7 in the rental pool)* *No Meals.*

★ **Casa Colonial Beach & Spa**

$$$$ | **HOTEL** | Designed by architect Sara Garcia, sophisticated Casa Colonial, a boutique property exuding refinement and relaxation on the quiet end of the long beach, is a surprise among the all-inclusives of Playa Dorada. **Pros:** exceptional gourmet dining in Lucia; architectural gem offering the full luxury, boutique experience; glorious spa. **Cons:** service is attentive but sometimes a bit off; large suites could use a splash of color; can feel empty during the low season. *Rooms from: $520* *Playa Dorada* *809/320–3232, 866/376–7831* *www.casacolonialhotel.com* *50 rooms* *No Meals.*

★ **Gran Ventana Beach Resort**

$ | **RESORT** | **FAMILY** | This longtime all-inclusive has had a rebirth, maintaining its moderate price point but now offering more luxury upgrade options. **Pros:** animated staff are a bit more laid-back than at other resorts; consistently good food and service for this price point; particularly efficient and caring front-desk staff. **Cons:** limited access to à la carte restaurants; charge for safes; a few aspects are still dated. *Rooms from: $250* *Playa Dorada* *809/320–2111* *www.granventanahotel.com* *506 rooms* *All-Inclusive.*

Tubagua Ecolodge

$ | **B&B/INN** | **FAMILY** | The hand-hewn, thatch-roofed wood structures on this mountaintop a short 20 minutes by road from Puerto Plata look over a vast quilt of sugarcane fields to the ocean beyond, offering an authentic Dominican experience in rustic comfort. **Pros:** guests gather over family-style suppers in a spacious social area; free Wi-Fi, small pool, and an artisan shop are on-site; rates including lodging, all meals, and taxes. **Cons:** sounds from the village are sometimes heard at night; remote location has limited transportation and nightlife; too rustic for some. *Rooms from: $60* *Km 19, Ruta Panoramica 25, Tubagua* *809/696–6932* *www.tubagua.com* *8 rooms* *All-Inclusive.*

Playa Dorada

5 miles (8 km) east of Puerto Plata.

One of the Dominican Republic's longest established resort areas, Playa Dorada has benefited both from good reefs, which are right off-shore, and a major beach restoration project. Large condo complexes and resorts line the beach, each with its own private slice of beachfront. The Atlantic waters here are great for kitesurfing, windsurfing, waterskiing, and fishing.

Beaches

Playa Dorada

BEACH | Playa Dorada is one of the island's most established resort areas. Each hotel has its own slice of the beach, which is covered with soft nearly white sand. Reefs for snorkeling are right offshore. Gran Ventana Beach Resort, which is on a point, marks the easternmost end of the beach, followed by Casa Colonial and Blue Bay Villa Doradas. If you're not staying at one of the resorts in the Playa Dorada complex, then it's best to enter the beach before this point. Zealous hotel security guards try to keep you off "their" stretch of beach, but by law they cannot if you walk along the water's edge. They can, however, keep you off the chaise longues and the resort's property. This is a good swimming beach with mild wave action. **Amenities:** none (though resorts on the beach offer full service). **Best for:** fishing; swimming; walking; kitesurfing; windsurfing. *Off Autopista Luperón, at* *the entrance to the Playa Dorada Complex, approximately 10-min drive east of town, Playa Dorada* 🌐 *www.playadorada.com.do.*

Sosúa

15 miles (24 km) east of Puerto Plata.

This small community was settled during World War II by 600 Austrian and German Jews. After the war many of them returned to Europe or went to the United States, and most who remained married Dominicans. Only a few Jewish families reside in the community today, and there's the original one-room wooden synagogue and Museo Judío Sosúa (Jewish Museum). Also, a small park on the waterfront commemorates the Jewish colony.

Sosúa is called Puerto Plata's little sister, and consists of two communities—El Batey, the more modern hotel development, and Los Charamicos, the old quarter—separated by a cove and one of the island's prettiest beaches. The sand is soft and nearly white, the water crystal clear and calm. The walkway above the beach is packed with tents filled with souvenirs, pizzas, and even clothing for sale. In the past, the town had developed a reputation for sex work. Conversely, there are many fine, cultured types here, both Dominican and expats, and the recent opening of a cultural center, Casa del Arte de Sosúa, was a major coup for them.

Sights

Casa del Arte de Sosúa

ARTS CENTER | Sosúa's cultural center is open to the public and free of charge. The ground-floor gallery has rotating exhibitions that primarily feature work by Sosúa and Dominican artists, such as Teddy Tejada. Music and dance lessons, from violin to ballet, are offered to local children on the second floor, as are other culturally minded activities, including photography workshops. ✉ *Pedro Clisante, across from the casino, Sosúa* ☎ *809/571–2442 No phone* 🎟 *Free* ⏲ *Closed Sun.*

Museo Judío Sosúa

HISTORY MUSEUM | While Sosúa is not known for its sights, this museum stands as one of the exceptions, chronicling the immigration and settlement of Jewish refugees in the 1940s. The adjacent small wooden synagogue is the wedding spot for many Jewish couples from abroad. Hours can be irregular, but chances are good that someone will be at the museum to let you in if you get there early in the day.

TIP→ You can try phoning the accommodating Hotel Casa Valeria nearby to confirm if the museum is open. ✉ *Calle Dr. Rosen at David Stern, near Banco Popular, Sosúa* ☎ *809/571–3565 Hotel Casa Valeria* 🌐 *www.sosua-villas.com/jewish-museum* 🎟 *RD$75.*

Beaches

Playa Sosúa

BEACH | This long stretch of beach on Sosúa Bay, renowned for its coral reefs and dive sites, is a 20-minute drive east of Puerto Plata. Here, calm waters gently lap at a shore of soft, golden sand. Swimming is delightful—except after a heavy rain, when litter floats in. But beware of sea urchins in the shallow water—beach shoes are definitely recommended—and bring your own mask and snorkel if possible. You can see mountains in the background, the cliffs that surround the bay, and seemingly miles of coastline. Snorkeling from the beach can be good, but the best spots are offshore, closer to the reefs. The beach is backed by a string of tents where hawkers push souvenirs, snacks, drinks, and water-sports equipment rentals. The weekend scene here is incredible—local families pack the beach, and the roar of Dominican fun fills the air. Don't bring valuables or leave your belongings unattended. There is a small parking area on the beach's north end at the south end of La Puntilla Street. **Amenities:** food and drink; parking (free). **Best for:** snorkeling; swimming; walking. ✉ *Carretera Puerto Plata–Sosúa, El Batey.*

 Restaurants

NLB Nelson's Lounge & Bistro
$ | **CARIBBEAN** | This family-run restaurant is a local favorite among Cabarete and Sosúa expats. The food is good, if unimaginative, and the atmosphere is warm and inviting. **Known for:** dependable food and service; options to please everyone; the small playground for kids. $ *Average main: RD$12* ✉ *Calle Antonio Javier, in front of Super Pola, Sosúa* ☎ *809/571–3253* 🌐 *www.nlbsosua.com/index.php/es/menu.*

 Hotels

Sea Horse Ranch
$$$$ | **HOUSE** | **FAMILY** | This enclave of private homes, each with large front- and backyards and private pool, is an elite bastion set within a vast country club–like setting near Cabarete. **Pros:** one of the country's most organized, well-managed groups of villas; potent security makes your vacation worry-free; all villas have free, unlimited Wi-Fi. **Cons:** guests usually feel the need to rent a car or hire a driver; it's a walk or short drive to reach two petite, communal beaches; complex doesn't have a resort feel. $ *Rooms from: $700* ✉ *Sea Horse Ranch, Route 5, Carretera Principal, Cabarete* ☎ *809/571–3880* 🌐 *www.sea-horse-ranch.com* *14 villas* *No Meals.*

Cabarete

10 miles (15 km) east of Sosúa.

Of the towns within easy reach of the Puerto Plata airport, Cabarete has the best dining, the longest beaches, and the most youthful spirit. A hot destination, especially for the young—and more and more for retired baby boomers as well—one of its main claims to fame is the wind. Nowhere on the island can you find such perfect conditions for kitesurfing. If there's a good breeze, the shoreline flares with bright sails. An annual international competition, Master of the Ocean, takes place the last weekend in February. It's a triathlon of windsurfing, kitesurfing, and surfing.

Those who are afraid to ride the waves or to soar like an eagle propelled by a piece of lightweight fabric can still watch and enjoy these colorful goings-on across the blue horizon. Later, chat up the water adventurers as they barhop and dance the night away. A dozen bars and restaurants have created an imaginative and relaxing setup of tables, Bali beds, and lounges right atop the sand on the main beach in town. It makes for the coast's best beachfront dining and nightlife experience.

 Beaches

Playa Cabarete
BEACH | This is the main business district of Cabarete. If you follow the coastal road east from Playa Dorada, you can't miss it. The beach, which has strong waves after a calm entrance, and ideal, steady wind (from 15 to 20 knots), is an integral part of the international kitesurfing circuit. Segments of this long beach are strips of sand punctuated only by palm trees. The regeneration of Cabarete Beach was a massive engineering project that

made the beach some 115 feet wider, adding an infusion of white sand. In the most commercial area, restaurants and bars are back-to-back, spilling onto the sand. The informal scene is young and fun, with expats and tourists from everywhere. **Amenities:** food and drink; lifeguards; toilets; water sports. **Best for:** partiers; swimming; windsurfing; kitesurfing. ✉ *Sosúa–Cabarete Rd., Cabarete.*

Restaurants

The Beach Club at Sea Horse Ranch
$$$ | **INTERNATIONAL** | Overlooking a craggy shoreline with unobstructed ocean vistas, this renovated restaurant with a global menu is hitting all the high points, offering both delicious food and a fun atmosphere. The menu runs the gamut from pizza to fragrant Tandoori chicken from deliciously light gnocchi to hearty Ethiopian *zilzil* (a dish of braised beef and peppers). **Known for:** safe secure haven with free parking; a gathering place for expats, young bucks, and Sea Horse residents; the view when the ocean is pounding. *Average main: $21* ✉ *Sea Horse Ranch, Carretera Principal Sosua-Cabarete, Cabarete* ☎ *809/571–4995* 🌐 *www.sea-horse-ranch.com* ⏲ *Closed Mon. in low season.*

Bliss
$$$ | **MEDITERRANEAN** | The tables at this tranquil Italian restaurant flank a night-lit pool, offering the kind of intimate, romantic setting tailor-made for a wedding proposal. The young Italian owners have embraced slow food, offering delicious antipastos, carpaccios, and tartares to start and excellent house-made pastas, including feather-light gnocchi and tender half-moons in a sage-and-butter sauce. **Known for:** linguini with lobster fra diavlo; "waterfront" dining in a courtyard overlooking a pool; mahi and salmon carpaccio with rasberry citronette. *Average main: $21* ✉ *Callejón de la Loma 1, Cabarete* ✥ *This home is at the entrance of a residential neighborhood off Sosúa-Cabareta Hwy. 5. The side street is directly across from the Ocean Dreams complex on the other side of the highway* ☎ *809/571–9721* ⏲ *Closed Sun. No lunch.*

Natura Restaurant
$$$ | **SEAFOOD** | If you're staying at this beachfront ecoparadise, you'll likely take most of your meals here; if not, it's worth the trip, not only for the freshest seafood but also for the soothing ambience. The menu changes seasonally but holds tight to some perennial favorites. **Known for:** wines are French, Spanish, and Chilean; oceanfront—listen to the waves; house-made pastas are delectable. *Average main: $23* ✉ *Natura Cabana Boutique Hotel, Paseo del Sol 5, Perla Marina, Cabarete* ☎ *809/571–1507* 🌐 *www.naturacabana.com.*

Tuva Restaurant & Lounge
$$ | **ITALIAN** | The oceanfront vantage point of this Cabarete Beach restaurant is one of its main selling points, but the whimsical kids' corner with its Alice in Wonderland theme doesn't hurt either. The menu features house-made pasta, seafood and grilled meats, all prepared with Mediterranean flair. **Known for:** desserts from panna cotta to tiramisu al limoncello; sophisticated fine dining atmosphere; house-made pastas. *Average main: $20* ✉ *SeaWinds Condominiums, Cabarete* ☎ *809/571–0526* ▭ *No credit cards.*

Woke Foods
$ | **VEGETARIAN** | **FAMILY** | This cute spot tucked away in Cabarete's residential zone is popular among tourists and locals alike. Owner Ysanet Batista Vargas is a U.S.-born Dominican powerhouse known for food justice activism and her catering business operating in New York City; her Cabarete restaurant, a co-op, brings this same level of intensity to an ancestral, plant-based menu that highlights fresh, sometimes raw, organic, and locally sourced food. **Known for:** health conscious and delicious food; plant-based menu; free Wi-Fi. *Average main:*

RD$300 ✉ Callejón de la loma, Cabarete ☎ 849/626–1733 🌐 wokefoods.coop/dominicanrepublic ▭ No credit cards ⏲ No dinner.

Hotels

Hotel El Magnifico

$ | **HOTEL** | You will find a healthy dose of unexpected pleasure at this stellar, boutique hotel made up primarily of one- to three-bedroom condominiums and a few regular hotel rooms tucked in a serene oasis away from the noisy main town. **Pros:** children under 15 stay free; never feels crowded; the interior decor is très chic in many (but not all) units. **Cons:** no in-room phones; no restaurant or bar, though there's a place to get breakfast next door; steep spiral staircases and no elevators. *$ Rooms from: $70 ✉ Calle del Cementerio, Cabarete ☎ 809/571–0868 🌐 www.hotelmagnifico.com 20 apartments No Meals.*

★ Millennium Resort & Spa

$ | **RESORT** | **FAMILY** | If a reasonably priced contemporary and spacious apartment with remarkable ocean vistas is your tropical dream, this small condo resort delivers. **Pros:** two elevators; good, free Wi-Fi throughout the property; comfortable and inviting environment. **Cons:** junior and ocean suites have only a small kitchenette; ocean breezes are often strong here; 15-minute walk along the beach to most bars and restaurants. *$ Rooms from: $150 ✉ Autopista Sosúa/Cabarete Km 1, In front of Ferreteria Linares, Cabarete ☎ 809/571–0407 🌐 www.millenniumcabarete.com 53 apartments No Meals.*

Natura Cabana Boutique Hotel & Spa

$$ | **B&B/INN** | **FAMILY** | If your idea of perfection is thatch-roof cabanas and a quiet, private beach, then this may be your oceanfront nirvana. **Pros:** free Wi-Fi throughout; natural, peaceful beachfront stay; good restaurant. **Cons:** no ocean views from many cabanas; car is an asset, but taxis to town are safer; no TVs, phones, or air-conditioning, but sea breezes. *$ Rooms from: $276 ✉ Playa Perla Marina, Paseo del Sol 5, Cabarete ☎ 809/571–1507 🌐 www.naturacabana.com 12 bungalows Free Breakfast.*

Velero Beach Resort

$ | **HOTEL** | You'll appreciate the location of this well-managed hotel and residential enclave with its own beachfront and gardens, just a few minutes' walk east of the noise of town yet also just minutes from the happening bars and restaurants. **Pros:** high-speed Wi-Fi throughout; blenders, microwaves, and DVD players in the junior suites and above; draped Balinese sun beds at the pool are dreamy. **Cons:** showing some signs of age; standard rooms are not spacious; no elevators—it's a climb up the spiral staircases to the third floor. *$ Rooms from: $140 ✉ Calle la Punta 1, Cabarete ☎ 809/571–9727 🌐 www.velerobeach.com 31 apartments Free Breakfast.*

Villa Taina Hotel

$ | **HOTEL** | Smack amid the action, steps down from the main drag, this simple hotel captures the original spirit of Cabarete, catering to the independent traveler who wants nicer digs than a surf camp. **Pros:** free Wi-Fi; a solid value; efficient and caring owner/staff. **Cons:** standard rooms are small; noise of town can be heard in the building closest to the street; pool is petite, as is the spa. *$ Rooms from: $120 ✉ Calle Principal, Cabarete ✣ behind Friend's restaurant ☎ 809/571–0722 🌐 www.villataina.com 61 rooms, 1 apartment Free Breakfast.*

Nightlife

LAX Ojo Cabarete

BARS | At this perennially popular bar that really comes alive by night, you can sit in the sand in lounge chairs or jump into the action on the outdoor deck, where a DJ will be spinning madly or a live band

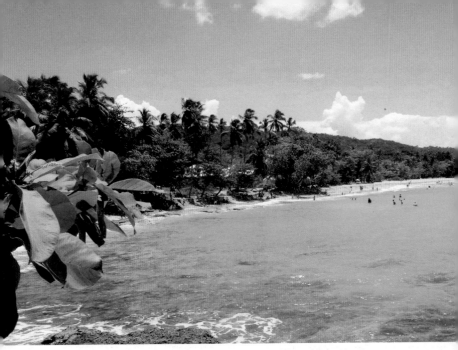

The mile-long Playa Grande is considered by many to be one of the world's best beaches.

might be playing. It's one of the few dance clubs in the area without a cover charge. The inexpensive food is good, and there are special theme nights and drink specials. ✉ *Cabarete Beach, Cabarete* ☎ *829/745–8811*.

Cabrera

60 miles (96 km) east of Cabarete.

Cabrera, Abreu, Río San Juan, and the Playa Grande area are largely unspoiled and pristine coastal areas. There's a raw beauty, with some beaches that are still completely undeveloped, soaring cliffs overlooking pounding ocean waves, and towering inland hills with sweeping vistas not seen elsewhere on the North Coast. In addition, there are some of the most luxurious villa choices in the country, not to mention the island's first Aman resort in Playa Grande. The area's high-end vacation homes, which are far away from the action and the bustle of Sosúa and Cabarete, will appeal primarily to those who wish to avoid noise. The area in general attracts a more moneyed crowd—mostly baby boomers—who want an upscale experience, as well as couples or friends who want to share a house and enjoy the unspoiled beaches.

Cabrera itself is still a sleepy Dominican town centered on its central square. Tourists mingle with locals in the park, and can stop for a drink at one of the adjacent restaurants, such as the thatched-roof Town Square Bar. Decades ago, the area was known for its ranchos, but these days it's the beaches and the famous Playa Grande golf course (now available only to guests of the associated Amanera Resort and members of the club) more than anything else.

Sights

Laguna Dudú
NATURE SIGHT | This memorable natural wonder is a small complex of three natural features a few miles west of Cabrera. It has recently evolved and has been made more like a park. A zipline has been

installed, and you can jump off a cliff into one of the deep swimming holes, where a lifeguard is usually on duty below. The lagoon offers cold, clean water that you can swim in. Nearby is a natural cave you can explore (bring your own flashlight). Then, across the way take stairs down into a spring that flows inside a cave; adventurous types swim into the mouth. A restaurant serves a small menu and cold drinks, and there are toilets and even a shower. ✉ *Carretera Río San Juan, Km 21, La Entrada* 🎫 *RD$100.*

Beaches

★ Playa Grande

BEACH | This dramatic mile-long stretch is widely considered to be one of the top beaches in the world. Many a photo shoot has been staged at this picture-perfect beach with off-white sands and turquoise water. Just east of the famous golf course of the same name, Playa Grande's drama comes from craggy cliffs dropping into the crystalline sea. Shade can be found in the palm trees that thicken into Parque Nacional Cabo Francés Viejo, a jungle preserve south of the beach.

Vendors sell from cutesy, brightly painted Victorian-style huts and have relocated to one end of the beach, where a large parking area was constructed. Security is present, and there are clean restrooms. Surfboards, paddleboards, and boogie boards are for rent—although the surf can swell, it can also be smooth. Two luxury resorts can be found nearby: the Playa Grande Beach Club, just behind the beach and screened by a palm-frond fence, as well as the newer Amanera. **Amenities:** food and drink; toilets. **Best for:** surfing; swimming; walking. ✉ *Carretera Río San Juan–Cabrera, Km 12, Río San Juan* 🌐 *www.playagrande.com* 🎫 *Free.*

Hotels

Catalina Tropical Lodge

$ | **B&B/INN** | This small, family-run hotel offers a lush island getaway from atop a mountain overlooking the Atlantic Ocean. **Pros:** food at restaurant is excellent; stunning views; away from city noise. **Cons:** restaurant is closest option and a long stay adds up; can feel isolating; must have a car to get around. 💲 *Rooms from: $175* ✉ *Calle Vieja 22, Cabrera* ✣ *10 minutes after Cabrera heading toward Puerto Plata* ☎ *809/977–2105* 🌐 *www.catalinatropicallodge.com* 🛏 *12 rooms* 🍽 *No Meals.*

Santiago

The second city of the D.R., where many past presidents were born, sits about 90 miles (145 km) northwest of Santo Domingo and is about an hour's drive from Puerto Plata and 90 minutes from Cabarete via the scenic mountain road. An original route from centuries past, the four-lane highway between Santiago and Puerto Plata is dotted with sugar mills. The Office of Cultural Patrimony is overseeing their restoration. Although an industrial center, Santiago has a surprisingly charming, provincial feel. High on a plateau is an impressive monument honoring the restoration of the republic. Traditional yet progressive, Santiago is still relatively new to the tourist scene but already has several thriving restaurants and hotels. It's definitely worth setting aside some time to explore the city. Colonial-style buildings—with wrought-iron details and tiled porticoes—date from as far back as the 1500s. Others are from the Victorian era, with the requisite gingerbread latticework and fanciful colors, and recent construction is nouveau Victorian. Santiago is the D.R.'s cigar-making center; the Fuente factory is here, though its cigars can be bought on the island only in special designated cigar stores and clubs. (If you see them for sale on the streets, they are counterfeit.)

Sights

★ Centro León

ARTS CENTER | Without question, this is a world-class cultural center for Dominican arts and culture. A postmodern building full of light from a crystal dome, the center includes several attractions, galleries for special exhibits, a sculpture garden, and an aviary. It has a replica of La Aurora's first cigar factory, too. Tobacco money coupled with the Jimenes family's generosity built this wonder. Many visitors are most enthralled with the permanent collection of photography and Dominican art, but temporary art exhibits can also be a draw. There's a first-rate cafeteria and a museum shop, where you can buy high-quality, artsy souvenirs, books, and jewelry.

TIP→ It's best to give advance notice if you want a guided tour in English. ✉ *Av. 27 de Febrero 146, Villa Progreso, Santiago* ☎ *809/582–2315* 🌐 *www.centroleon.org.do* 🎫 *RD$150, guides in English from RD$300; audio guide in English RD$100.*

Restaurants

★ Il Pasticcio

$$ | **ITALIAN** | Everyone from college students to cigar kings, presidents to politicos, photographers to movie stars pack this eccentrically decorated culinary landmark; check out the ornate mirrors and Romanesque plaster sinks in the bathrooms. Chef-owner Paolo's mouthwatering creations are authentic and fresh. **Known for:** owner is larger than life; fun and eccentric decor; menu is written on the ceiling. 💲 *Average main: $15* ✉ *Av. El Lano, corner Calle 3, Gurabo al Medio* ☎ *809/806–1277* 🕒 *Closed Mon.*

Samaná Peninsula

Samaná (pronounced sah-mah-NAH) is a dramatically beautiful peninsula, like an island unto itself, of coconut trees stretching into the sea. This province is full of rural villages and fancy resorts, brand-new highways and muddy dirt roads, verdant mountainsides, tropical forests, street-side fruit vendors, and secluded beaches. Samaná is the name of both the peninsula and its biggest town and the bay to the south. It's worth noting that while the town's official name is Santa Bárbara de Samaná, locals mainly refer to it as simply Samaná. This town makes an excellent departure point for whale-watching or an excursion to Los Haitises Park across the bay. The bay is home to some of the world's best whale-watching from mid-January to late March. It is now the site of Puerto Bahía Marina & Residences and the Bannister Hotel, contemporary, luxurious, yet moderately priced. This complex has given yachts a full-service facility in what has always been a desirable cruising destination. A visit here is about two things: exploring the preserved natural wonders and relaxing at a beachfront hotel. The latter is most readily accomplished in **Las Terrenas,** the peninsula's most touristic area, where you can find beachfront restaurants, accommodations of all types (from small hotels to full-service resorts to luxury condos), and great beaches. In Las Terrenas, you can enjoy peaceful playas, take advantage of the vibrant nightlife, and make all your plans for expeditions on the peninsula. The other pleasures are solitary—quiet beaches, the massive national park Los Haitises, water sports, and hiking. A relatively new toll road connects Santo Domingo to the peninsula; it's now just over a three-hour drive. Small El Catey International Airport is near Las Terrenas and is served by a growing number of airlines.

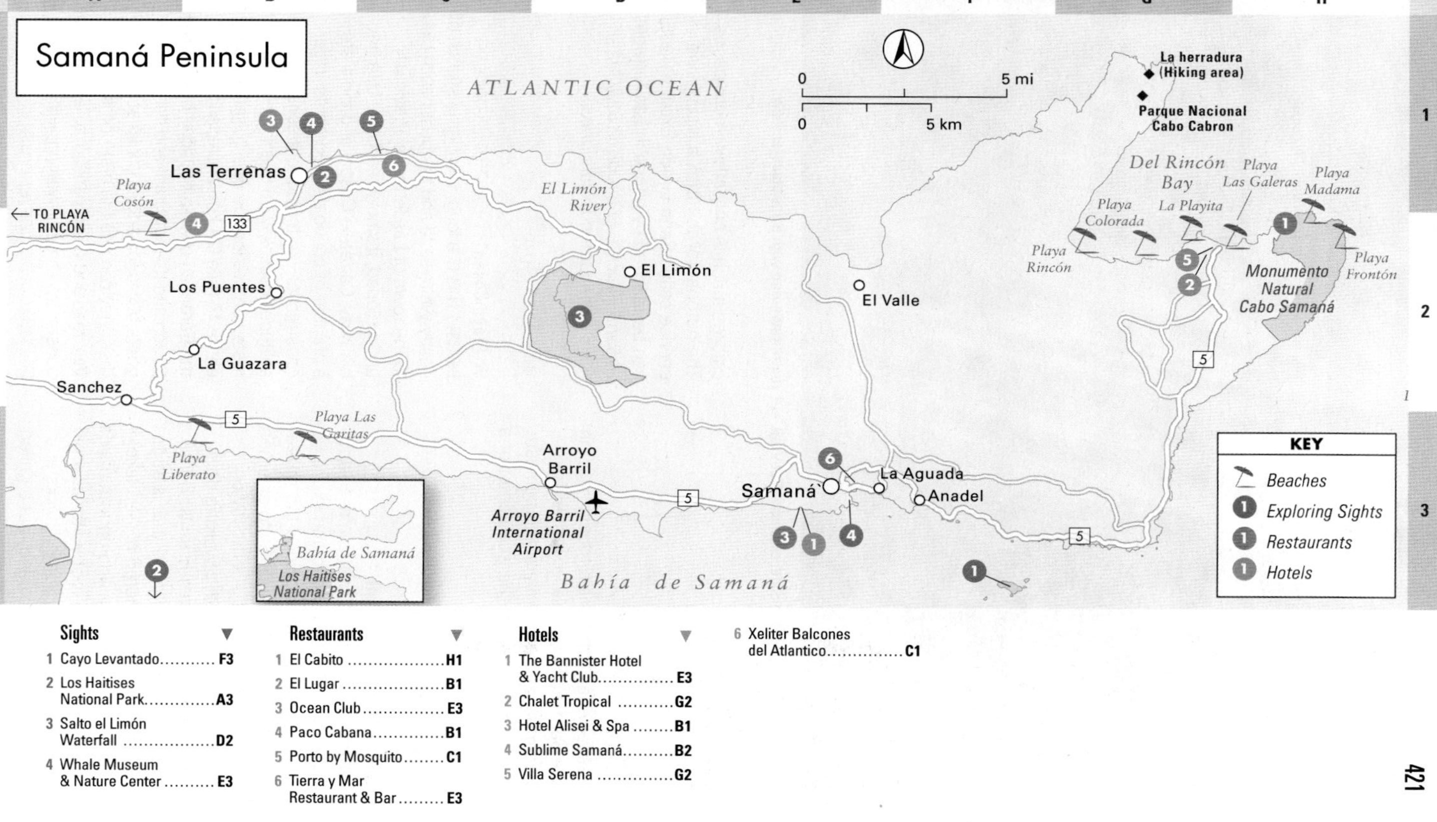

Sights

1 Cayo Levantado.......... F3
2 Los Haitises National Park.............. A3
3 Salto el Limón Waterfall D2
4 Whale Museum & Nature Center E3

Restaurants

1 El Cabito H1
2 El Lugar B1
3 Ocean Club E3
4 Paco Cabana B1
5 Porto by Mosquito C1
6 Tierra y Mar Restaurant & Bar E3

Hotels

1 The Bannister Hotel & Yacht Club.............. E3
2 Chalet Tropical G2
3 Hotel Alisei & Spa B1
4 Sublime Samaná.......... B2
5 Villa Serena G2
6 Xeliter Balcones del Atlantico.............. C1

It's an adventure to get to Salto el Limón Waterfall, but you're rewarded with a spectacular view.

Las Terrenas

22 miles (35 km) northwest of Santa Bárbara de Samaná.

Las Terrenas is the main tourist base on the Samaná Peninsula. It, rather than Santa Bárbara de Samaná, the peninsula's biggest town, is the true center of a visit to the region.

Sights

Salto el Limón Waterfall

WATERFALL | Provided that you're fit and willing to deal with a long and slippery path, an adventurous guided trip (three hours) to the spectacular Salto el Limón Waterfall is a delight. It's mostly on horseback, but includes walking down rocky, sometimes muddy trails. Horse paths are slippery, and the trek is strenuous. The well-mannered horses take you across two rivers and up mountains to El Limón, the 165-foot waterfall amid luxuriant vegetation. Some snacks and drinks are usually included, but a grilled chicken lunch is only a few more pesos. The outpost for the trek, a local guide service called Santi Limón Excursiones, can be reached by phone in Las Terrenas. ✉ *Santi Rancho, El Limón* ☎ *829/342–9976 Santi Limón Excursiones.*

Beaches

★ **Playa Cosón**

BEACH | This is a long, wonderful stretch of nearly white sand and the best beach close to the town of Las Terrenas. Previously undeveloped, it's now reachable by a new highway, Carretera Cosón, and there are a number of condo developments under construction (so the current sense of solitude probably won't last). One excellent restaurant, called The Beach, serves the entire 15-mile (24-km) shore, and there's the European-owned boutique hotel Casa Cosón and its restaurant and bar. If beachgoers buy lunch and/or drinks at either, then they can use the restrooms. **Amenities:** food and drink; parking; toilets. **Best for:** sunset; swimming; walking; kitesurfing. ✉ *Playa Cosón, Las Terrenas.*

Restaurants

El Lugar

$$ | **INTERNATIONAL** | This gastropub is the go-to place for both local expats and tourists with taste. Owner Bruno lends this modest establishment a personality, offering warm welcomes and quality food. **Known for:** dares not to focus on seafood; trendy atmosphere; small and scene-y. *Average main: $17 Calle 27 de Febrero, Las Terrenas 849/248–2580 Closed Tues.*

Paco Cabana

$$ | **FRENCH** | Smack in the middle of Las Terrenas town but on the quiet beach, this social restaurant has French savoir faire, from its contemporary bar with its stainless shine to the cushy couches and Asian beds. Classical French cuisine is coupled with Caribbean flair. **Known for:** feet-in-the sand restaurant; grilled local sardines; lobster-stuffed calamari. *Average main: $17 Calle Libertad 1, Las Terrenas 809/240–5301 Closed Mon.*

Porto by Mosquito

$$ | **SEAFOOD** | This jaw-dropping, beachfront beauty is one of the better players in the ever-evolving, European-accented restaurant scene in Las Terrenas. The nautically themed dining room is by the well-known Dominican designer Patricia Reid. **Known for:** often live entertainment like jazz trios; seafront setting; firepits. *Average main: $18 Playa Las Terrenas, El Limón Directly across the street from Xeliter Balcones del Atlántico 829/877–2844 portobymosquito.com.*

Hotels

Samaná is the name of both the peninsula that curves around the eponymous bay and of the largest town. You can usually arrange flights from Punta Cana and small charters from several D.R. airports. Caribe Tours and other smaller bus companies provide direct routes to Samaná, Las Terrenas, and Las Galeras.

Hotel Alisei & Spa

$ | **HOTEL** | **FAMILY** | An excellent location across from Las Terrenas Beach—within walking distance to town—gives this apart-hotel an edge for those looking for a few resort services to go along with more spacious accommodations. **Pros:** good discounts available in the off-season; windows are double-paned and keep apartments quiet; quiet music is played at the pool. **Cons:** some of the decor and art are dated; not terribly luxurious; mostly international TV. *Rooms from: $156 Calle de la playa, Calle Francisco Alberto Camaño Deñó, Las Terrenas 809/240–5555 www.aliseihotelspa.com 61 units Free Breakfast.*

★ Sublime Samaná

$$ | **HOTEL** | With dramatic, contemporary architecture that allows each suite water views, this resort offers one-bedroom suites and large two- and three-bedroom condo accommodations with designer kitchens and living rooms, two flat-screen TVs, and a balcony that looks down upon the inviting labyrinth of swimming pools lined with draped sun beds. **Pros:** the high-quality mattresses and linens promote sleep; the beach bar offers a great lunch, tropical cocktails, and fresh juices; chic interior furnishings are designed with taste and Caribbean spirit. **Cons:** not a lot of on-site activities; restaurant options are limited, and main dining room has no water views; relatively isolated, so a car is likely necessary. *Rooms from: $225 Bahía de Cosón, Ramal Viva, Las Terrenas 809/240–5050 www.sublimesamana.com 44 units No Meals.*

Xeliter Balcones del Atlantico

$ | **APARTMENT** | **FAMILY** | This condotel on a large tract of virgin land offers beautifully designed, spacious apartments with dreamy bedding and private Jacuzzis on terraces that are basically outdoor rooms. **Pros:** beds are commodious with luxe linens; intelligent and caring concierge staff; ideal for longer stays. **Cons:** phone and maintenance problems continue; isolated location that requires a rental car; not on the beach (it's across the road). $ *Rooms from: $258* ✉ *Carretera Las Terrenas/El Limón Km. 2, across from Porto on Playa Las Terrenas, Las Terrenas* ☎ *809/240–5011* 🌐 *www.xeliter.com* *15 apartments* 🍽 *No Meals.*

Nightlife

Etno Beach Club

LIVE MUSIC | Delivering consistently good meals and good tunes, this club-restaurant breaks the stereotype that you shouldn't eat where you party. The beachside bar regularly hosts local and international DJs with jam sessions covering a wide variety of genres. While the bar provides tried-and-true favorites, the cocktail menu (with non-alcoholic options) is extensive and the drinks are well-made. It's one of the places to be in Las Terrenas. ✉ *Liberty St. 4, Las Terrenas* 🌐 *www.etnobeachclub.com.*

Santa Bárbara de Samaná

22 miles (35 km) southeast of Las Terrenas.

The official name of the city is Santa Bárbara de Samaná; but these days it's just called "Samaná." An authentic port town, it's getting its bearings as a tourist zone, and still is not a magnet like Las Galeras and Las Terrenas. It has a typical *malecón* (seaside promenade) that's ideal for strolling and watching the boats in the harbor. Lookout "towers" have been built; ascend the stairs and see the whales in season or just look out to the horizon. Strong night lighting has been added, too, so you will see Dominicans and tourists alike taking walks after dinner. A small but bustling town, Samaná is filled with friendly residents, skilled local craftsmen selling their wares, and a handful of outdoor, sea-view, and courtyard restaurants.

A big all-inclusive resort, the Bahía Príncipe Cayacoa, is on one end of the bay road up on a hill. Day passes are available (and the resort has the only beach in town). The hotel also operates a block of colorful gift shops and a small casino. This group was the town's first attempt to capture cruise-ship-passenger money. It's the string of buildings called Pueblo Príncipe, which replicates small Victorian buildings painted in Caribbean colors and trimmed in white gingerbread. Along Avenida del Malecón, across from the waterside, is the office of Whale Samaná, ground zero for boat excursions shoving off to see whales from January until late March.

Sights

Cayo Levantado

BEACH | There are no public beaches in Samaná town, but you can hire a boat to take you to Cayo Levantado, which has a wonderful white-sand beach on an island in Samaná Bay. Today the small island has largely been turned into a commercial enterprise to accommodate the 1,500 cruise-ship passengers who anchor here; it has dining facilities, bars, restrooms, and lounge chairs. It can be extremely crowded and boisterous when there's a ship in port. The beach, however, is undeniably beautiful. The Bahía Príncipe Cayo Levantado an upscale, all-inclusive resort with its own launch, sells adults-only day passes. ✉ *Samaná Bay, Samaná* *Public beach free.*

★ Los Haitises National Park

NATIONAL PARK | A highlight of any visit to the Samaná Peninsula is Los Haitises National Park (pronounced *high-TEE-sis*), which is across Samaná Bay. The park is famous for its karst limestone formations, caves, and grottoes filled with pictographs and petroglyphs left by the indigenous Taínos. The park is accessible only by boat, and a professionally guided kayak tour is highly recommended (a licensed guide from a tour company or the government is mandatory for any visitor). You'll paddle around dozens of dramatic rock islands and spectacular cliff faces, while beautiful coastal birds—magnificent frigate birds, brown pelicans, brown booby, egrets, and herons—swirl around overhead. A good tour will also include the caverns, where your flashlight will illuminate Taíno petroglyphs. It's a continual sensory experience, and you'll feel tiny, like a human speck surrounded by geological grandeur. Dominican Shuttles can arrange a park tour and a stay at the adjacent and rustic Paraíso Caño Hondo Ecolodge, which has authentic Creole cuisine and multiple waterfalls. ✉ *Samaná Bay, Samaná* ☎ *809/720–6035 Booking Adventure Tours* 🎫 *$4, not including mandatory use of licensed guide.*

Whale Museum & Nature Center
(*Centro de la Naturaleza*)
SCIENCE MUSEUM | This tiny museum is dedicated to the mighty mammals of the sea. Samaná Bay is part of one of the largest marine mammal sanctuaries in the world and is a center for whale-watching during the winter migration of humpback whales. The Center for Conservation and Ecodevelopment of Samaná Bay and its Environment (CEBSE) manages this facility, which features a 40-foot female humpback skeleton. Information in English is available at the entrance. ✉ *Av. La Marina, Tiro al Blanco, Samaná* ✥ *Turn left from the main section of the Malecón, en route to the hotel Bahía Príncipe Cayacoa, to find the tiny Centro de Naturaleza* ☎ *809/538–2042* 🎫 *RD$150* ⌚ *Closed Sat. and Sun. except for reservations of 8 or more.*

Restaurants

Ocean Club
$$$ | **SEAFOOD** | As the name suggests, seafood is the headliner at this sophisticated marina-side restaurant (formerly Cafe Del Mar), serving Caribbean-influenced Mediterranean cuisine. By day, have lunch outdoors while dipping in and out of the infinity pool. **Known for:** can hear the wind in the riggings; fine dining for lunch and dinner; never overcrowded. [$] *Average main: $23* ✉ *Puerto Bahía Marina, Carretera Sánchez–Samaná, Samaná* ☎ *809/503–6363* 🌐 *www.puertobahiasamana.com.*

Tierra y Mar Restaurant & Bar
$ | **CARIBBEAN** | This locally owned restaurant serves no-frills traditional food done right. Located just off the main strip, the local gem draws both travelers and locals to dine together under its palm roof. **Known for:** lambi or conch in creole sauce; fresh fish in coconut sauce; the best mofongo in town. [$] *Average main: RD$10* ✉ *C. Maria Trinidad Sanchez, Samaná* ☎ *809/538–2436* 💳 *No credit cards.*

Hotels

★ The Bannister Hotel & Yacht Club
$ | **HOTEL** | This stylish marina complex smack on the Bay of Samaná has changed the face of tourism in this area and become the social center for the upscale residents, a safe harbor for visiting yacht owners, and a deluxe, yet reasonably priced option for international visitors. **Pros:** great yacht-watching; wonderful ambience; natural beauty everywhere. **Cons:** service staff is caring but not professional; too far from town to walk; the bedrooms in the one-bedroom accommodations could be more spacious. [$] *Rooms from: $160* ✉ *Puerto Bahía, Carretera Sánchez, Km 5, Samaná*

☎ 809/503–6363 🌐 www.thebannisterhotel.com 🛏 31 units 🍽 Free Breakfast.

Las Galeras

17 miles (28 km) northeast of Santa Bárbara de Samaná.

Las Galeras, a small village between two protected and untouched green mountain capes, used to be a well-kept secret. Tucked away at the very tip of the Samaná Peninsula, this village is home to some of the most stunning beaches on the island (and in the world). Visitors to Las Galeras's beaches can choose their own adventure. Some beaches are home to a few beachfront restaurants. Most of the beaches are within a two-hour hike, some are reachable by car, but the best way to experience them is definitely by boat. Rincón, Frontón, Colorado, La Playita, and Madama are all must-sees. Those interested can most easily hire small fishing boats at Playa Las Galeras, known to locals as Playa Grande. Prices vary depending on the number of beaches and travelers. For Rincón, expect to pay about $35 per person (although prices become much cheaper the larger the group). Because of climbing gas prices, note that some boat captains will not go out with only one or two passengers.

Beaches

★ La Playita

BEACH | La Playita, or Little Beach, is a stunner that's a 15-minute walk from the main Las Galeras beach. Here you'll find a small shack serving fresh fish and a newer, two-story stucco restaurant with a variety of seafood offerings and a full bar. Coconut trees lean far out over the water, and the virgin stretch of Cabo Cabrón extends far along one side, providing incredible views and a sense of privacy and solitude. **Amenities:** food and drink; parking; toilets. **Best for:** partiers; solitude; sunset; swimming; walking. ✉ *Las Galeras* ✥ *1 mile (2 km) by boat, 3 miles (5 km) by road from Las Galeras.*

★ Playa Colorada

BEACH | Only accessible on foot or by boat, this beach is undeveloped save for a hotel at the far end, and it offers solitude on most days. Have your hotel arrange for a small boat to take you there, either privately or with a group. Intrepid travelers who choose to go by foot will enjoy an intermediate, one-hour hike worth every second of the slight climb–especially for the incredible views. To hike here, ask for directions to Casa Dorado and stay on that path until you reach the beach. Bring water and snacks as there are no facilities. In the low season, expect to be among the only visitors. **Amenities:** None. **Best for:** sunbathing; swimming; hiking; solitude. ✉ *Playa Colorada, Las Galeras.*

Playa Las Galeras

BEACH | Playa Las Galeras lies at the end of the highway of this tiny coastal town, a 20-minute drive northeast from Samaná town. The sand is nearly white, the Atlantic waters generally calm. It has been designated a Blue Flag beach, which means that it's clean and unpolluted, though there are several small hotels here. Seaweed is regularly raked up and there is no parking fee, as it is just street parking. That all said, this is really just a departure point for the nearby virgin beaches closer to the cape to the west. **Amenities:** food and drink. **Best for:** partiers; snorkeling; sunset; walking. ✉ *Las Galeras.*

Playa Madama

BEACH | Playa Madama is one of Las Galeras's most well-known beaches and also one of the most charming. Located in a cove a five-minute boat ride away from Playa Las Galeras, on the way to Playa Frontón, this beach is a little slice of undeveloped heaven. The water is fairly low and calm, and the backdrop is a jungle of palms and local trees. Bring your own blankets and drinks, as this beach has no amenities. Adventurous travelers will enjoy the long, solitary trek through the jungle and along several local farms to get here, but boats can also be hired to take you for a fee. Ask your hotel to help you book or head down to Playa Las Galeras, where the bulk of the boats are kept. The larger the group, the cheaper the price. **Amenities:** none. **Best for:** swimming; solitude; snorkeling. ✉ *Playa Madama, Camino a Playa Madama, Las Galeras.*

Playa Rincón

BEACH | Remote Playa Rincón, a stunning white sand beach, is one of the most beautiful beaches in the entire region. Relatively undeveloped, there are no facilities per se, but spread out across the large stretch there are two or three restaurants offering traditional Dominican food. Other vendors may have beach chairs or sell bracelets and kitschy souvenirs or massage and braiding services. The water can be rough, but there are some calmer areas. The beach is cleaned regularly but not often enough. You can reach Rincón by boat, bus, or car from Las Galeras, with a boat the better option. Driving here takes about 30 minutes from town. ⚠ **Theft is a real problem here, so when swimming, watch your belongings, don't bring valuables, and don't stay late. Amenities:** food and drink. **Best for:** partiers; snorkeling; swimming; walking. ✉ *Las Galeras* ✣ *3 miles (5 km) by boat, 9 miles (15 km) by road from Las Galeras.*

Restaurants

El Cabito

$$ | **SEAFOOD** | The simple, off-the-grid palapa seems to exhale with a breezy, unbothered joviality; bring your camera: from this cliffside perch the sea eagle's view of endless ocean makes you feel as if you're at the edge of the world (and in season it's ideal for whale-watching).The menu offers something more creative than the standard fish in coconut sauce: delicious calamari, seafood paella or stew, or stir-fried squid or conch. Vegetarians are well accommodated, too, but you have to call in advance if you want fresh fish, lobster, or paella. **Known for:** one-of-a-kind experience; cliffside setting; creole specialities. *Average main: $17* ✉ *El Cabito, Calle La Caleta, Las Galeras* ✣ *4 miles (6½ km) from the main crossing in Las Galeras, to the right, direction Hotel "Gran Paradise," follow the road. Turn left at the end and then take an immediate right. Signs will help you find the way. Or ask a local* ☎ *829/562–7457* *No credit cards* *Closed Tues.*

Hotels

Chalet Tropical

$ | **APARTMENT** | This family-owned eco-aparthotel offers fully equipped bungalows made of stone and wood and decorated in colors that evoke tropical fruits, flowers, and the sun without being overwhelming. **Pros:** great for longer stays; close to the action but feels away from it all; private pools are refreshing. **Cons:** nature sometimes finds its way into rooms, to be expected during rainy season; hot water sometimes runs out; no on-site food options, but there are plenty of options nearby. *Rooms from: $140* ✉ *Calle Chalet Tropical, Las Galeras* ☎ *809/901–0738, 849/884–2189 Spanish only* *www.chalettropical.com* *11 units* *No Meals.*

Villa Serena

$ | **HOTEL** | Decidedly one of the better hotels in the eastern corner of the peninsula, Villa Serena makes for a wonderful, stress-free Samaná vacation. **Pros:** accommodating, English-speaking front-desk staff and management; small, private beachfront without vendors or loud music; reliable in-room Wi-Fi. **Cons:** no blackout drapes; most rooms have air-conditioning but no TVs; main section is dated. *Rooms from: $117* ✉ *Las Galeras Beach, Las Galeras* ☎ *809/538–0000* *www.villaserena.com* *21 rooms* *Free Breakfast.*

Activities

Although there's hardly a shortage of activities here, the resorts have virtually cornered the market on sports, including every conceivable water sport. In some cases, facilities may be available only to guests of the resorts.

Baseball. Baseball is a national passion, the cultural icon of the D.R., and yes, Sammy Sosa is still a legend in his own time. But he is just one of many celebrated Dominican baseball heroes, including pitcher Odalis Revela. Triple-A Dominican and Puerto Rican players and some American major leaguers hone their skills in the D.R.'s professional Winter League, which plays from October through January. Some games are held in the Tetelo Vargas Stadium, in the town of San Pedro de Macorís, east of Boca Chica.

Biking. Pedaling is easy on pancake-flat beaches, but there are also some steep hills in the D.R. Several resorts rent bikes to guests and nonguests alike.

Boating. Sailing conditions are ideal, with constant trade winds. Favorite excursions include day trips to Catalina and Saona islands—both in the La Romana area—and sunset cruises on the Caribbean. Prices for crewed sailboats of 26 feet and longer, with a capacity of 4 to 12 people, are fixed according to size and duration, from a low of $200 a day to the norm of $700 a day. Charters of powerboats are much more expensive. For example, prices for the fleet at the upscale Cap Cana Marina are as follows: sportfishermen from 47 to 51 feet accommodating up to eight people (crewed with all equipment, snacks, and beverages with sandwiches on all-day trips), $1,800 for four hours, $2,500 for eight hours; a 62-foot custom, luxury power-sail catamaran, $1,650 for two hours (everything included for Cap Cana guests); a 56-foot Sea Ray Sedan Bridge motor yacht, $2,000 for two hours, $2,500 for four hours, $3,500 for eight hours (everything included); and a luxury 90-foot custom motor yacht, ideal for an incentive group, $3,500 for two hours, $5,000 for four hours, $8,500 for eight hours.

Diving. Ancient sunken galleons, undersea gardens, and offshore reefs are among the lures here. Most divers head to the north shore. In the waters off Sosúa alone you can find a dozen dive sites (for all levels of ability) with such catchy names as Three Rocks (a deep, 163-foot dive), Airport Wall (98 feet), and Pyramids (50 feet). Some dive schools are represented on or near Sosúa Beach, in the town of Bayahibe, and in Las Terrenas and Las Galeras on the Samaná Peninsula resorts have dive shops on-site or can arrange trips for you.

Fishing. Big-game fishing is big in Punta Cana, with blue and white marlin, wahoo, sailfish, and dorado among the most common catches in these waters. Several fishing tournaments are held every summer. The Punta Cana Resort & Club hosted the ESPN Xtreme Billfishing Tournament for many years. Blue-marlin tournaments are held at La Mona Channel in Cabeza de Toro. Several tour operators offer organized deep-sea fishing excursions.

Golf. The D.R. has some of the best courses in the Caribbean, designed by top golf architects; among these leading designers are Pete Dye, P. B. Dye, Jack Nicklaus, Robert Trent Jones, Gary Player, Tom Fazio, and Nick Faldo. The country's courses have won awards for customer satisfaction, quality of courses and accommodations, value for money, support from suppliers and tourist boards, and professional conduct. Most courses charge higher rates during the winter high season; some, but not all, reduce their rates between April and October, so be sure to ask. Also, some have cheaper rates in the afternoon (mornings are cooler). And guests of certain hotels get better prices.

Guided Tours. Visitors to the Dominican Republic will have a plethora of excursions to choose from, but many options are not wonderful and are wildly overpriced. Wait until you arrive before booking anything. As for group excursions, "interview" fellow guests to find out if their tour was worth the money and effort, or do research before you arrive. Often the full-day excursions are too long and leave too early. Best are half-day trips—particularly boat excursions. Horseback riding can sound appealing, as the trails usually include some stretches of beach, but horses, equipment, and instruction are often not optimal, and guides often don't speak sufficient English. Clients traveling on a tour-company package tend to book excursions with that company, or through the tour company affiliated with their resort.

NORTH COAST

BIKING AND HIKING

★ Iguana Mama

BIKING | FAMILY | This well-established, safety-oriented company's offerings include mountain bike tours that will take you along the coastal flats or test your mettle on steeper climbs in the national parks. Downhill rides (half- or full-day) include a taxi up to 3,000 feet, as well as breakfast and lunch. Advanced rides on- and off-road are also offered, as are guided day hikes. Other half- and full-day trips include swimming, climbing up and jumping off various waterfalls, rappelling, and natural waterslides, white-water rafting, horseback riding, ecotours, and other adventure sports. The company also organizes longer, multiday excursions that include outdoor activities. ✉ *Calle Principal 74, across from Scotia Bank, Cabarete* ☎ *849/642–8954, 809/571–0908, 809/654–2325* 🌐 *www.iguanamama.com* 🎫 *From $55.*

BOATING

Carib Wind Cabarete

BOATING | A renowned windsurfing center (known for decades as BIC Center) Carib Wind Cabarete has been operating since 1988. Since its founding, it's been transformed into a high-performance Olympic training center for Laser sailors from around the world. Here you can rent Lasers, 17-foot catamarans, bodyboards, ocean kayaks, and paddleboards. ✉ *Cabarete* ☎ *809/571–0640* 🌐 *www.caribwind.com.*

DIVING

Dressel Divers

SCUBA DIVING | One of the best of the area dive centers, Dressel Divers is on the beach in front of the Iberostar Costa Dorada. Spanish-owned, it is part of a global chain and has an international, English-speaking staff and a PADI Five Star rating. Every morning Dressel Divers offers a two-tank dive in the region's best dive spots such as Sosúa Bay, night dives, cavern dives, and Paradise Island dive and snorkeling excursions. Certification from beginner to instructor level is available. Also in the morning, nondivers can rent snorkeling gear. For Iberostar guests, one hour per day of snorkeling equipment, kayak, catamaran, and windsurf is free. The company can arrange a third-party pickup at resorts other than Iberostar. ✉ *Playa Costa Dorada, Carretera Luperón, Km 4, on the beach of Iberostar Costa Dorada, Puerto Plata* ☎ *809/757–1544* 🌐 *www.dresseldivers.com.*

Northern Coast Aquasports

SCUBA DIVING | Located on the main street of Sosúa, this PADI Five Star dive center with a well-stocked retail store offers all levels of PADI courses from Discover Scuba Diving to Instructor, with diving and snorkeling seven days a week. Professionalism is apparent in the initial classroom and pool training. Moreover, the company offers trips to a selection of outstanding sites in the calm, protected waters of Sosúa Bay. This location is not too far from the new Amber Cove cruise ship port in Maímon. All activities are guided by (multilingual) PADI professionals. ✉ *Calle Pedro Clisante 8, Sosúa* ☎ *829/270–8783* 🌐 *www.northerncoast-diving.com.*

GOLF

Playa Dorada Golf Club

GOLF | *Golf Digest* has named Playa Dorada Golf Club one of the top 100 courses outside the United States. It's open to guests of all the hotels in the area. Caddies are mandatory for foursomes (and carry an extra fee); carts are optional. The attractive clubhouse has lockers, a pro shop, a bar, and the Fairways Restaurant. Reservations during high season should be made as far in advance as possible. Guests at certain hotels in the Playa Dorada complex get discounts and can take advantage of packages for multiple plays. ✉ *Playa Dorada Golf Course, Av. Circunvalación Sur, Playa Dorada* ☎ *809/320–4262* 🌐 *www.playadorada-golf.com* 🎫 *$59 for 9 holes, $89 for 18 holes* 🏌 *18 holes, 6730 yards, par 72.*

GUIDED TOURS

Alf's Tours

GUIDED TOURS | In Sosúa, Alf's Tours has been a mainstay for years. Why? It has only multilingual, licensed tour guides, and it's open daily. Plus, it has excursions all over the island for moderate prices, offering complimentary pickup service at any hotel in Sosúa, Puerto Plata, and Cabarete. Vehicles are closer to new than old, and guests are insured whether they are going to the famous waterfall El Limón in Las Terrenas or hopping aboard a Funny Buggy. ✉ *Eugenio Kunhardt 68, El Batey* ☎ *809/571–9904.*

HORSEBACK RIDING

Sea Horse Ranch Equestrian Centre

HORSEBACK RIDING | This equestrian center is a professional, well-staffed operation. The competition ring is built to international regulations, and there is a large schooling ring. Private lessons for experienced riders, including dressage or jumping instruction, are offered by the half-hour; "laissez faire" rides last from 90 minutes to three hours and include drinks and snacks—but make reservations. The most popular ride includes stretches of beach and a bridle path across a neighboring farm's pasture that's full of wildflowers and butterflies. Feel free to tie your horse to a palm tree and jump into the waves. ✉ *Sea Horse Ranch, Sosúa/Cabarete Hwy., Km. 2.5, Cabarete* ✣ *Between Sosúa and Cabarete* ☎ *809/571–3880, 809/571–4462* 🌐 *www.sea-horse-ranch.com* 🎫 *From $35.*

SPAS

Andari Spa

SPAS | This petite spa has quite an adequate menu of services with a particular focus on massages and salon services (especially mani-pedis). Clean and well organized, the spa employs therapists and technicians who are caring, well-trained, and take pride in their work. Before you decide on a treatment, look over the packages, which can be a very good deal. ✉ *Millennium Resort & Spa, Autopista Sosúa/Cabarete Km 1, Ocean Dreams #101, Cabarete* ☎ *809/851–9399* 🌐 *www.cabaretemillennium.com.*

WIND- AND KITESURFING

Cabarete is the wind- and kitesurfing center of the Dominican Republic, if not the entire Caribbean. It's said that if you can learn to kitesurf here, you can do it anywhere. The vast majority of the country's schools are headquartered here. One of the original players was the Carib Wind Cabarete, now also a major sailing center.

GoKite Cabarete

WINDSURFING | **FAMILY** | GoKite is one of the few locally owned kite schools in the country though courses are taught by a mix of local and international instructors. Owner Richard Diaz has been kiting since he was young, and his expertise shows. His school offers individual lessons as well as IKO certification courses for those who'd like to go on to teach themselves. Helmets with radios are available for an extra charge, and proficient riders can rent equipment including boards and kites. ✉ *Kite Beach, 5 km Cabarete, Calle 10, Cabarete* ☎ *829/644–8354 WhatsApp* 🌐 *gokitecabarete.com* 🎫 *Lessons from $75 per hour; rentals $35 per hour.*

SOUTHEAST COAST

BOATING

★ Casa de Campo Marina

BOATING | Casa de Campo Marina has much going on, from sailing to motor yacht charters to socializing at the Casa de Campo Yacht Club. At the sailing school, students learn to conquer the Caribbean Sea from knowledgeable instructors. With everything from a laundry to ship chandlery and shipyard, as well as video surveillance that guarantees security, this is a safe haven for yachtsmen with 350 slips. Those who dock here have access to not only the marina but the amenities of Casa de Campo Resort. ✉ *Casa de Campo, Calle Barlovento 1, La Romana* ☎ *809/523–3333* 🌐 *www.marinacasadecampo.com.do.*

GOLF

★ Casa de Campo Resort

GOLF | The Resort is considered by most to be the premier multiple golf resort in the Caribbean. The famed 18-hole Teeth of the Dog course at Casa de Campo, with seven holes on the sea, is usually ranked as the number-one course in the Caribbean and is among the top courses in the world. Pete Dye regards Teeth of the Dog as one of his best designs and has long enjoyed living at Casa part-time. The Teeth of the Dog requires a caddy for each round (for an additional fee). Pete Dye has designed this and two other globally acclaimed courses here. Dye Fore, now with a total of 27 holes, is close to Altos de Chavón, hugging a cliff that features commanding vistas of the sea, a river, Dominican mountains, and the marina. The Links is a 18-hole inland course. Resort guests must reserve tee times for all courses at least one day in advance; nonguests should make reservations earlier. ✉ *Casa de Campo, La Romana* ☎ *809/523–3333 resort, 855/657–5955* 🌐 *www.casadecampo.com.do* 🎫 *Teeth of the Dog: $395 per round per golfer for nonguests; Dye Fore: $295 for nonguests; The Links: $175 for nonguests* 🏌 *Teeth of the Dog: 18 holes, 6989 yards, par 72; Dye Fore: 18 holes, 7740 yards, par 72; The Links: 18 holes, 6664 yards, par 71.*

GUIDED TOURS

Tour Experts

GUIDED TOURS | **FAMILY** | Formerly known as Tropical Tours, this is the primary and best tour operator on the Southeast Coast, based at Casa de Campo. Prices are even less than some non-pros and cruise-ship excursions. Their vans are new or nearly new and well maintained. Most of their staff speaks English as well as other languages. They can take you on a tour of Santo Domingo, to fascinating caves, and to baseball games in La Romana's baseball stadium. Although most water-based excursions (outback safaris and ziplining, too) now go through the concierges at Casa, Tour Experts does still offer some trips. The company also provides transfers to Las Américas and Punta Cana international airports. ✉ *Casa de Campo, La Romana* ☎ *809/523–2029, 809/523–2028* 🎫 *From $35.*

HORSEBACK RIDING

Equestrian Center at Casa de Campo

HORSEBACK RIDING | The 250-acre Equestrian Center at Casa de Campo has something for both Western and English riders—a dude ranch, a rodeo arena (where Casa's trademark "Donkey Polo" is played), three polo fields, guided trail rides, riding, jumping, and polo lessons. There are early-morning and sunset trail rides, too. Unlimited horseback riding is included in some Casa de Campo packages. Trail rides are offered through the property's private cattle ranch, which houses a herd of water buffalo and lakes populated with ducks as well as the resort's on-site horse-breeding operation. Unlimited horseback riding is included in Casa's all-inclusive experience. Ponies are now available to kids for trail ride. ✉ *Casa de Campo, La Romana* ☎ *809/523–3333* 🌐 *www.casadecampo.com.do* 💴 *From $40.*

SAMANÁ PENINSULA

BOATING

Puerto Bahía Marina

BOATING | This stunning marina on the north end of pristine Samaná Bay is a relatively new entity and is a first-class, full-service facility with slips from 40 to 150 feet. This marina not only has the necessary amenities, including fuel, restrooms with showers, 24-hour security, garbage pickup, Internet access, water taxis, and car rentals, but all the services and facilities of the Bannister Hotel. ✉ *Carretera Sánchez–Samaná, Km 5, Samaná* ☎ *809/503–6363* 🌐 *www.puertobahiasamana.com.*

DIVING

Las Galeras Divers

SCUBA DIVING | This is a professional, safety-conscious operation. Owner Serge is a PADI, OWSI, and nitrox instructor, and every level of PADI course is offered. Diving lessons and trips are offered in English, French, and Spanish, and diving equipment rentals are also available. Discounts are given to groups, families, and divers who want a package deal. ✉ *Calle Principal, Las Galeras* ☎ *809/538–0220, 809/715–4111* 🌐 *www.las-galeras-divers.com* 💴 *From $60.*

SPAS

Mee Spa

SPAS | Walk up the steel spiral staircase to a haven of peace, with New Age music, a professional staff dressed in white, and a chic, sparkling clean environment. Still moderately priced for the quality of the treatments, Mee Spa, formerly known as, NI Spa & Salon, is one of the island's best spa values, with a couples' treatment room, water circuits, and a boutique fitness center. Little English is spoken by the therapists, but they comprehend what you need. There's also a full-service salon. ✉ *The Bannister Hotel, Puerto Bahía Marina, Carretera Sanchez, Km 5, Samaná* ☎ *809/503–6363* 🌐 *www.thebannisterhotel.com.*

SURFING

Surfing, windsurfing, wakeboarding, and kitesurfing are popular in Las Terrenas. Playa Cosón has the best breaks. Playa Bonita is another popular spot, because, as on Cosón, there are no rocks. Two-hour lessons are about $35, and a one-day board rental runs approximately $25; it's usually $15 for a half day.

Carolina Surf School

SURFING | Named for its proprietress, Dominican Republic National Surf Champion Carolina Guiterraz, the school rents surfboards and SUPs in addition to its lessons. Private lessons are $50 for two hours, group $35. She is especially dedicated to teaching children and beginners and has a large local following. ✉ *Hotel Acaya, Playa Bonita, Las Terrenas* ☎ *809/882–5467* 🌐 *carolinasurfschooldr.com* 💴 *Private lesson from $50 for 2 hours.*

WHALE-WATCHING

Humpback whales come to Samaná Bay to mate and give birth each year for a relatively limited period, from approximately January 15 through March 30. Samaná Bay is considered one of the top 10 destinations in the world to watch humpbacks. If you're here during the brief season, this can be the experience of a lifetime. You can listen to the male humpback's solitary courting song and witness incredible displays as the whales flip their tails and breach (humpbacks are the most active species of whales in the Atlantic).

★ Whale Samaná

WILDLIFE-WATCHING | Owned by Kim Beddall, a Canadian who is incredibly knowledgeable about whales and Samaná in general, having lived here for decades, this operation is far and away the region's best, both professional and environmentally sensitive. On board *Pura Mia*, a 55-foot motor vessel, a marine mammal specialist narrates and answers questions in several languages. Kim herself conducts almost all the English-language tours. Normal departure times are 9 for the morning trip and 1:30 for the afternoon trip; she is flexible whenever possible for cruise-ship passengers but does require advance reservations. ✉ *Calle Sra. Morellia Kelly, Samaná* ✣ *Across street from town dock, beside park* ☎ *809/538–2494* 🌐 *www.whalesamana.com* 🎫 *From $59, plus $5 entrance to Marine Mammal Sanctuary.*

SANTO DOMINGO

BASEBALL

Liga de Béisbol Stadiums

BASEBALL & SOFTBALL | Liga de Béisbol Stadiums can be a helpful information source if you're planning an independent trip to a baseball game. The games can get pretty rowdy, so it's best to go with the tour group. ✉ *Santo Domingo* 🌐 *lidom.com.*

GUIDED TOURS

Private tours are a good option in Santo Domingo, but you will have to pay more than $125 a day for a guide—more if the tour guide works with a driver. Your hotel concierge can best arrange these for you, and he or she will know the best English-speaking guides. Be sure you hire a guide who is licensed by the government.

AfrohistoriaRD

WALKING TOURS | **FAMILY** | Most visitors to the country's Colonial Zone are regaled with tales of the exploits of colonizers. Much of the country's African and Indigenous roots are hidden, though if you know where to look they can be found between the lines of the whitewashed retelling of Dominican history. Ruth Pión is looking to change that as a historian and activist. Through walking tours, AfrohistoriaRD tells a different story of the Colonial Zone, one in which enslaved Africans were trafficked into Santo Domingo through back doors and forced to build a city in which they are not depicted. No other tour explores this history, evidenced by the groups of tourists who often pass by the many points of interest Ruth shows during her tour. The stops include sites important to African resistance and are woven together with Ruth's insight as an investigator, a local, and a Black woman. She infuses the subject matter with a quiet passion that makes you want to learn more about the country's true and forgotten history. Bring water, comfortable shoes, and an open mind; the story Ruth tells is brutal and necessary for all to hear. ☎ *849/642-4917 WhatsApp* 🌐 *www.afrohistoriard.com* 🎫 *$65* ⏲ *Closed Sat.* ☞ *Call ahead for meet-up point.*

LA ROMANA

BASEBALL

Estadio Francisco A. Michelli

BASEBALL & SOFTBALL | Estadio Francisco A. Michelli is La Romana's baseball stadium. Know that *la temporada* (the season) is short; your window of opportunity is just October through December, with an occasional game in January.

TIP→ The tours won't take you there if La Romana is on a losing streak. ✉ *Av. Padre Abreu, La Romana* ✣ *Near monument* ☎ *809/556–6188.*

FISHING

Casa de Campo Marina

FISHING | Casa de Campo Marina is the best charter option in the La Romana area. Yachts (22- to 60-footers) are available for deep-sea fishing charters for half or full days. Prices go from $824 for a half day on *Scorpio* to $3,555 for a full day on *Gabriella*. They can come equipped with rods, bait, dinghies, drinks, and experienced guides. Going out for the big billfish that swim the depths of the Caribbean is a major adrenaline rush. The marina hosts the annual Casa de Campo International Blue Marlin Classic Tournament in late March, which is celebrated with a round of parties. Only guests staying on the property can rent. Prices do not include local taxes. ✉ *Casa de Campo, Calle Barlovento 3, La Romana* ☎ *809/523–2247,* 🌐 *www.marinacasadecampo.com.do* 🎟 *Charters from $824.*

PUNTA CANA

FISHING

Marina Cap Cana

FISHING | On the Mona Passage, this is a superb port for sportfishing during the summer season, when the grounds are renowned for an abundance of blue marlin and white marlin. Anglers participating in seasonal fishing tournaments receive favorable dockage rates. For sport fishing, chartered vessels are available for four or eight-hour excursions for marlin, wahoo, tuna, snapper, grouper, etc. (best organized through a Cap Cana hotel). There's also a designated fishing area for snook, tarpon, barracuda, and jack, with guides and equipment for hire. It's a catch-and-release marina. ✉ *Cap Cana, Juanillo* ☎ *809/669–1250* 🌐 *www.marinacapcana.com.*

Puntacana Marina

FISHING | The marine is on the southern end of the resort, where the restaurant La Yola is located. Big-game fishing is what this destination is famous for, and the marina hosts numerous summer tournaments such as ESPN2s Billfishing Xtreme Tournament. All water-sports rentals are handled through the new Punta Cana Aquatic Center, situated between the Westin and Playa Blanca. ✉ *Puntacana Resort & Club, Punta Cana* ☎ *809/959–2262 Punta Cana Aquatic Center* 🌐 *www.puntacana.com.*

GOLF

Barceló Bávaro Golf

GOLF | Integrated within the Barceló Bávaro Beach Golf & Casino Resort complex in the Punta Cana region, this course is open to both resort and nonresort guests. The course traverses a lush inland mangrove forest and features 22 inland lakes and 122 bunkers, and totals 6,655 yards. It was actually the first course in the area and was designed by Juan Manuel Gordillo. ✉ *Barceló Bávaro Beach Golf & Casino Resort, Bávaro* ☎ *809/686–5797* 🌐 *www.barcelobavarogolf.net* 🎟 *$60–$70 for Barceló guests; $90–$100 for nonguests* ⛳ *18 holes, 6655 yards, par 72.*

Corales Golf Club

GOLF | "The Augusta National of the Caribbean" has expansive, finely landscaped grounds. Designed by Tom Fazio, it's a dramatic 18-hole course with six Caribbean seaside holes with a finishing hole that encourages players to cut off as much of the Caribbean off the tee as they dare. Laid out along the natural cliffs and coves of the sea and inland lakes and Coralina quarries, the 700 acres here are part of the extensive Puntacana Resort & Club. The club is open to its members and their guests, guests of Tortuga Bay, and Puntacana Resort guests who purchase the resort's Golf Experience packages, but a limited number of nonguests are allowed to play in both high and low season; inquiries and tee-time requests should be made by email. Caddies are mandatory at Corales. ✉ *Puntacana Resort & Club, Punta Cana* ☎ *809/959–4653* ✉ *golfcorales@puntacana.com* 🌐 *www.puntacana.com* 🎟 *$195–$295 for resort guests; $295–$395 for nonguests (18 holes) with caddies mandatory, $30* ⛳ *18 holes, 7555 yards, par 72.*

Hard Rock Golf Club at Cana Bay

GOLF | This Jack Nicklaus–designed course is just a golf cart ride down from the resort on Macao Beach. It's a challenging and well-maintained course with ocean views and regularly hosts tournaments and other events. The Emerald driving range is close to the golf clubhouse (which rents Calloway clubs). Emblazoned Hard Rock golf carts are included. ✉ *Hard Rock Hotel & Casino Punta Cana, Blvd. Turistico del Este, Km 28, Macao* ☎ *809/687–0000* 🌐 *www.hrhcpuntacana.com* 🎫 *$200 ($130 for "Twilight Play")* 🏌 *18 holes, 7253 yards, par 72.*

★ La Cana Golf Club

GOLF | You will enjoy the ocean views on 14 of the La Cana Golf Club's 27 holes of championship golf designed by P. B. Dye. The three 9s—Tortuga, Hacienda, and Arrecife—make for a very popular offering, particularly the oceanside finish on the La Cana Nine. The latest 9, Hacienda, opened in 2012 not as a full course but rather a set of 9 individual holes; it's punctuated with many lakes amid an unspoiled tropical landscape, a challenging addition to the existing, spectacular courses. All fees include a golf cart, taxes, and use of the expansive practice facility. Caddies are optional. Lessons and golf schools are offered by PGA professional staff. Rental clubs are available and should be reserved two weeks in advance from November through April. Guests of the resort's Westin or Tortuga Bay get discounted rates; nonguests who book with the resort can get transportation included. ✉ *Puntacana Resort & Club, Punta Cana* ☎ *809/959–4653* 🌐 *www.puntacana.com* 🎫 *$140 for resort guests; $175 for nonguests* 🏌 *Tortuga Nine: 9 holes, 3483 yards, par 36; Arrecife Nine: 9 holes, 3676 yards, par 36; Hacienda Nine: 9 holes, 3768 yards, par 36.*

★ Punta Espada Golf Course

GOLF | Jack Nicklaus cast his mark in the Caribbean with the magnificent Punta Espada Golf Course. You will discover a par-72 challenge with striking bluffs, lush foliage, and many gently tumbling fairways with spectacular water vistas. Incidentally, the water often does come into play. Having hosted the PGA Champions Tour, the course is even better in person than it looks on TV, and you won't find smoother putting surfaces! Yes, there's a Caribbean view from all the holes, and eight of them play right along the sea. The course's length can be extended to nearly 7,400 yards, but it's advisable to play a more forward tee. This exceptional golf club has concierge services, a restaurant, the Hole 19 bar, a pro shop, a members' trophy gallery, a library, lockers, an equipment repair shop, and a meeting room. Rates are discounted for guests in any of Cap Cana's accommodations and include golf cart, caddy, tees, water, and practice on the driving range. In high season, reservations are required, and it's best to make them two weeks in advance for tee times. ✉ *Cap Cana, Carretera Juanillo, Juanillo* ☎ *809/469–7767* 🌐 *www.capcana.com* 🎫 *$395 in morning and afternoon; $295 at night* 🏌 *18 holes, 7396 yards, par 72.*

GUIDED TOURS

★ Amstar DMC–Apple Vacations

GUIDED TOURS | Amstar is well managed and reliable, and it is associated with Apple Vacations, a major player that packages all-inclusive vacations in the D.R., particularly in Punta Cana. Once in the area, they can take you on a variety of half- or full-day tours, like to Bávaro Splash, Zipline, and the new Scape Park. They also offer airport transfers, particularly executive and VIP transfers in late-model vehicles with uniformed drivers. ✉ *Car. Beron, Av. Barceló Km 2, Bávaro* ☎ *809/221–6626* 🌐 *www.amstardmc.com.*

★ Go Golf Tours (GGT)

GOLF | Go Golf has services tailored to clients seeking to make golf part of their getaway—whether it's the primary focus or just a one-time outing; the company will help arrange tee times, golf instruction, and transport to courses in Punta Cana or Casa de Campo by private driver at costs that are usually considerably less than those in a private taxi. They can also provide airport transfers. ✉ *Cocotal Golf & Country Club, Bávaro* 🌐 *www.golfreservationcenter.com.*

HORSEBACK RIDING

Adventure Land Punta Cana

HORSEBACK RIDING | Long-established, the former Southfork Ranch (Rancho Pat), which has been the stable of choice in Punta Cana, is now a part of the Barceló resort complex (owners are still the same). Trail rides are along Barceló's "private" beach and on open-country roads. Morning rides start out at 9 and include a mojito break at a typical bar. Another includes an exploratory mission to Taíno caves and culminates in a lobster beach cookout. Then there is the memorable sunset beach ride, which can end with a beach bonfire barbecue. The company also offers other activities, including ATV tours. ✉ *Barceló Resort Complex, Bávaro* ☎ *809/223–8896* 🌐 *adventures-puntacana.com* 🎫 *From $55.*

El Rancho in Punta Cana

HORSEBACK RIDING | El Rancho in Punta Cana is across from the main entrance of the Puntacana Resort & Club. A one-hour trail ride winds along the beach, the golf course, and through tropical forests. The two-hour jungle trail ride has a stopover at a lagoon fed by a natural spring, so wear your swimsuit under your long pants. You can also do a one-hour sunset excursion (weekly) or take riding lessons. The Equestrian Center offers adult riding classes for beginners that include basic horse care. ✉ *Puntacana Resort & Club, Punta Cana* ☎ *829/760–1038, 809/959–9221 resort main number* 🌐 *www.puntacana.com* 🎫 *From $65.*

SPAS

★ Six Senses Spa

SPAS | This spa offers the best treatments in the Dominican Republic. Here you will find master Thai therapists, whose gifted hands will transport you to another zone altogether. Whether you have a special manicure or facial with fresh product, a hot stone massage, or some other sensational therapy, you'll leave satisfied and feeling good. The spa belongs to the Puntacana Resort; everyone is made welcome, as are outside guests. The spa also provides yoga classes and wellness programs.

■ TIP→ An added bonus for resort guests: you can book therapies in your guest rooms or villas. ✉ *Puntacana Resort and Club, Abraham Lincoln No. 960, Punta Cana* ☎ *809/959–7772* 🌐 *www.sixsenses.com/en/spas/punta-cana.*

The Spa at The Sanctuary Cap Cana

SPAS | An overall positive experience, the spa boasts an enjoyable Zen decor and a hydrotherapy section that is better than feel-good-all-over. This may be the only spa located within a "fortress," the castle section of the perennially popular Sanctuary at Cap Cana resort. Bubble in the oversized hot tub, which looks through glass patio doors to the brand-new deck, offering easy access to splendid Juanillo Beach. The spa also offers a full range of salon services, and both the spa and the adjacent fitness center are coed. It's preferred that nonhotel guests make advance appointments so front-gate security can be notified. ✉ *Sanctuary Cap Cana, Blvd. Zona Hotelera, Playa Juanillo, Cap Cana, Juanillo* ⊕ *In the Fortress section* ☎ *809/562–9191* 🌐 *www.sanctuarycapcana.com.*

Chapter 12

GRENADA

Updated by
Akiera Paterson

WELCOME TO GRENADA

TOP REASONS TO GO

★ **Old and New:** Grenada successfully blends a "pure" Caribbean atmosphere with all of the comforts and amenities that you expect.

★ **The Aroma:** The scent of spices fills the air, perfumes the soap, enriches the drinks, and even flavors the ice cream.

★ **Nature Abounds:** Spot monkeys in the mountains, watch birds in the rain forest, join fish in the sea, and build sand castles on the beach.

★ **Local Hospitality:** Grenadians go out of their way to make you feel welcome.

★ **A Great Getaway:** With no megaresorts, you really can get away from it all.

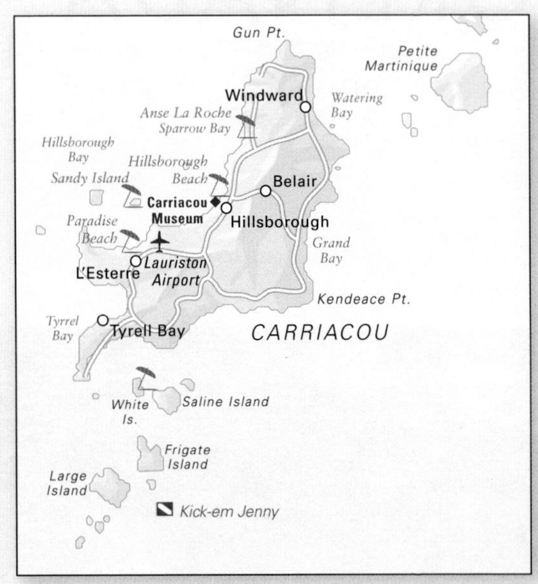

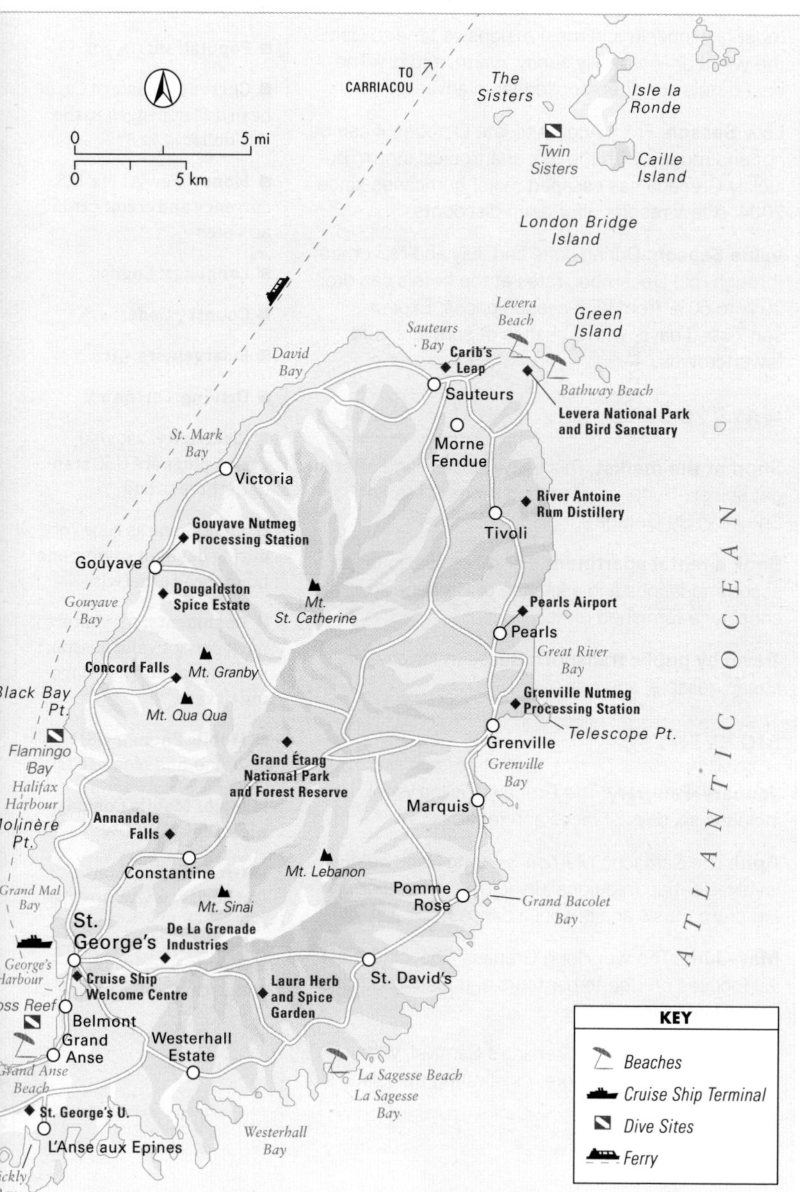
TO CARRIACOU
0
5 mi
0
5 km
The Sisters
Isle la Ronde
Twin Sisters
Caille Island
London Bridge Island
Levera Beach
Green Island
Sauteurs Bay
Carib's Leap
David Bay
Sauteurs
Bathway Beach
Levera National Park and Bird Sanctuary
Morne Fendue
St. Mark Bay
Victoria
River Antoine Rum Distillery
Tivoli
Gouyave Nutmeg Processing Station
Gouyave
Dougaldston Spice Estate
Gouyave Bay
Mt. St. Catherine
Pearls Airport
Pearls
Great River Bay
Concord Falls
Mt. Granby
Black Bay Pt.
Mt. Qua Qua
Grenville Nutmeg Processing Station
Telescope Pt.
Grenville
Flamingo Bay
Halifax Harbour
Grand Étang National Park and Forest Reserve
Grenville Bay
Marquis
Molinère Pt.
Annandale Falls
ATLANTIC OCEAN
Constantine
Mt. Lebanon
Grand Mal Bay
Pomme Rose
Grand Bacolet Bay
Mt. Sinai
St. George's
De La Grenade Industries
St. George's Harbour
Cruise Ship Welcome Centre
St. David's
Laura Herb and Spice Garden
Belmont
Grand Anse
Westerhall Estate
Grand Anse Beach
La Sagesse Beach
La Sagesse Bay
St. George's U.
Westerhall Bay
L'Anse aux Epines
KEY
Beaches
Cruise Ship Terminal
Dive Sites
Ferry

ISLAND SNAPSHOT

WHEN TO GO

High Season: Mid-December through May is the most fashionable and most expensive time to visit; the weather is typically sunny, warm, and dry. The best hotels are often booked far in advance.

Low Season: From August to late October, it can be hot and muggy with the risk of a tropical storm, but luckily Grenada has escaped major hurricanes since 2004. A few resorts offer deep discounts.

Value Season: During June and July and November through mid-December, rates at top hotels can drop 20% to 50% from high-season prices. Expect sun-kissed days, with a chance of showers, and fewer crowds.

WAYS TO SAVE

Shop at the market. This is the spice island after all; get spices, fruits, veggies, and more at Market Square in St. George's.

Book a rental apartment. For more spacious accommodations and a kitchen or kitchenette, consider a furnished rental.

Travel by public transport. Buses (minivans) are cheap, reliable, and fun.

BIG EVENTS

January–February: The Grenada Sailing Week includes six days of races and regattas.

April: The Carriacou Maroon & String Band Festival involves eating traditional dishes, accompanied by big-drum music and quadrille dances.

May–June: The weeklong Grenada Chocolate Festival focuses on tree-to-bar tours and tastings and cacao farm experiences.

August: Spice Mas is Grenada's Carnival, with parades, music, and more, celebrating the island's culture.

AT A GLANCE

- **Capital:** St. George's
- **Population:** 112,579
- **Currency:** Eastern Caribbean dollar; pegged to the U.S. dollar at $2.67
- **Money:** Few ATMs; U.S. currency and credit cards accepted
- **Language:** English
- **Country Code:** 1 473
- **Emergencies:** 911
- **Driving:** On the left
- **Electricity:** 230v/50 cycles; plugs are U.K. standard three-prong
- **Time:** Same as New York during daylight saving; one hour ahead otherwise
- **Documents:** All visitors must carry a valid passport and have a return or ongoing ticket
- **Mobile Phones:** GSM (850, 900, and 1800 bands)
- **Major Mobile Companies:** Digicel, FLOW
- **Grenada Tourism Authority:** www.puregrenada.com
- **Simply Carriacou:** www.simplycarriacou.com

The lush island of Grenada has 45 beaches and countless secluded coves. Crisscrossed by nature trails and laced with spice plantations, its mountainous interior consists mostly of nature preserve and rain forest. Independent since 1974, Grenada has developed a healthy tourism sector and a modern infrastructure, including a variety of hotels and resorts, good roads, up-to-date technology, and reliable utilities.

The nation of Grenada actually consists of three islands: Grenada, the largest, has a population of about 112,579; Carriacou (*car*-ree-a-coo), north of Grenada, has a population of just over 6,000; and Petite Martinique has a population of about 900. Carriacou and Petite Martinique are popular for day trips, fishing adventures, sailing destinations, or diving and snorkeling excursions, but most of the tourist activity is on the island of Grenada itself. People interested in a really quiet, get-away-from-it-all vacation will, however, appreciate the simple pleasures of Carriacou during an extended stay.

St. George's, the capital, is a busy city with buildings and landmarks that date back centuries; its harbor is one of the most picturesque in the Caribbean. Grand Anse, south of the capital, boasts one of the region's finest beaches.

Although Christopher Columbus never set foot on Grenada, he did cruise by in 1498, naming the island Concepción. Spanish sailors following in his wake renamed it Granada, after the city in the hills of their homeland. Adapted to Grenade by French colonists, the transformation of the name to Grenada was completed by the British in the 18th century.

Throughout the 17th century, Grenada was the scene of many bloody battles between the indigenous Carib people and the French. Rather than surrender to the Europeans after losing their last battle in 1651, the Caribs committed mass suicide by leaping off a cliff, now called Caribs' Leap or Leapers Hill, in Grenada's northernmost town of Sauteurs (French for "jumper"). The French were later overwhelmed by the British in 1762, the beginning of a seesaw of power between the two nations. The Treaty of Versailles in 1783 ultimately granted Grenada to the British. Almost immediately, thousands of African slaves were brought in to work the sugar plantations (although slavery in Grenada actually began with the French colonization in 1650). An unsuccessful revolt in 1795, known as

Fédon's Rebellion, attempted to end slavery in Grenada and to allow native French-speaking Grenadians the same dignity and respect enjoyed by British colonists. However, slavery on the island wasn't finally abolished until 1834.

Forts begun by the French to protect St. George's Harbour during their colonization of Grenada were later completed and used by the British during theirs. Today, Ft. George and Ft. Frederick are two of the most visited sights in St. George's. Besides their historical interest, the two locations have magnificent views of the harbor, the capital city itself, and the distant mountains and countryside. Not a single shot was fired from either fort for more than two centuries. In 1983, however, Prime Minister Maurice Bishop and seven others were murdered at Ft. George during a coup d'état. That event triggered the request from Grenada's governor-general and the heads of state of neighboring islands for U.S. troops to intervene, which they did on October 25, 1983. The insurrection came to an immediate halt, perpetrators were imprisoned, and peace was restored.

From that time forward, Grenada's popularity as a vacation destination has increased with each decade, as travelers continue to seek welcoming, interesting, picturesque islands to visit. Most hotels, resorts, and restaurants in Grenada are family-owned and-run (mostly by Grenadians); their guests often become good friends. All Grenadians, in fact, have a well-deserved reputation for their friendliness, hospitality, and entrepreneurial spirit.

Planning

Getting Here and Around

AIR

Nonstop flights to Grenada are available on American Airlines (Miami and Charlotte); JetBlue (New York); Air Canada (Canada); Virgin Atlantic and British Airways (United Kingdom). Regional flights between Grenada and Carriacou and between Grenada and neighboring islands operate several times each day.

Transfers: On Grenada, taxis are always available for transportation between the airport and hotels. Fares to St. George's are $20; to the hotels of Grand Anse and L'Anse aux Épines, $16. On Carriacou, taxis meet every plane; the fare to Hillsborough is $9; to Bogles, $11; to Tyrrel Bay, $15; to Windward, $15.

AIRLINE CONTACTS American Airlines. ☎ *800/744–0006, 473/444–2121 for direct calls to the American Airlines desk* 🌐 *www.aa.com.* **JetBlue Airways.** ☎ *473/444–2583, 855/840–2106* 🌐 *www.jetblue.com.* **LIAT.** ☎ *268/480–5601 for reservations, 268/480–5602* 🌐 *www.liat.com.* **SVG Air Grenada.** ☎ *473/444–3549, 473/444–1475 direct line to SVG desk at MBIA, 473/443–8519 on Carriacou* 🌐 *www.grenada-flights.com.* **Virgin Atlantic.** ✉ *Maurice Bishop's International Airport, Point Salines* ☎ *473/439–0681* 🌐 *www.virginatlantic.com.* **British Airways.** ✉ *Maurice Bishop's International Airport, Point Salines* ☎ *473/439–0681* 🌐 *www.britishairways.com.*

AIRPORT CONTACTS Maurice Bishop International Airport. (*GND*) ✉ *Point Salines* ☎ *473/444–4101, 473/444–4555* 🌐 *www.gaa.gd.*

BUS

Traveling short distances by Grenada's public transit system—privately owned vans—provides an authentic island (often musical) experience. The buses operate throughout the island from 6 am to 9 pm, Monday through Saturday, with frequent service between the main terminal at Market Square in St. George's and Grand Anse. Each bus has a conductor, who collects the fare and will help you find your correct stop. Fares range from about $1 (EC$2.50) to $2.50 (EC$6.50).

CAR

Having a car or jeep is a real convenience if you're staying at a resort in a location other than Grand Anse, which has frequent minibus service. If you don't have a car of your own, round-trip taxi rides can get expensive if you plan to leave the resort frequently for shopping, meals, or visiting other beaches. Driving is also a reasonable option if you want to explore the island on your own. Most of Grenada's 650 miles (1,050 km) of paved roads are kept in fairly good condition—although they are steep, winding, and narrow beyond the Grand Anse area. Driving is on the left, British-style. You'll find gas stations in St. George's, Grand Anse, Grenville, Gouyave, and Sauteurs.

Renting a Car: To rent a car, you need a valid driver's license and a temporary local permit (available at the Central Police Station on the Carenage in the capital city of St. George's and at most car-rental firms), which costs $24 (EC$60). You can also rent a car on Carriacou, even for just a few hours, but it's easier to take taxis.

Most rental agencies impose a minimum age of 25. Rental cars, including four-wheel-drive vehicles, cost $50 to $85 a day or $300 to $550 a week with unlimited mileage—rates are slightly lower in the low season. In high season, there may be a three-day minimum rental. Rental agencies offer free pickup and drop-off at either the airport or your hotel.

CONTACTS ON GRENADA David's Car Rental. ✉ *Maurice Bishop International Airport, Point Salines* ☎ *473/444–3399* 🌐 *www.davidscars.com.* **McIntyre Bros. Ltd..** ✉ *True Blue* ☎ *473/444–3944* 🌐 *www.caribbeanhorizons.com.* **Y&R Car Rentals.** ✉ *Maurice Bishop International Airport, Point Salines* ☎ *473/444–4448* 🌐 *www.carrentalgrenada.com.*

CONTACTS ON CARRIACOU Wayne's Auto Rentals. ✉ *The Esplanade, Main St., Hillsborough* ☎ *473/443–6120.*

FERRY

The best way to travel between Grenada and Carriacou is by air; the high-speed ferry is the next-best choice, as long as you aren't prone to motion sickness. The outbound voyage gets a little rough once you've cleared the island of Grenada; the inbound voyage, by comparison, is a breeze. Reservations for the ferry aren't necessary, but get to the wharf well before the departure time of 9 am and 6 pm in Grenada and 6 am and 3:30 pm in Carriacou to be sure you don't miss the boat.

The high-speed ferry *Osprey Shuttle* makes two round-trip voyages daily from Grenada to Carriacou and on to Petite Martinique. The trip from Grenada to Carriacou takes 2 hours and the fare is $31 each way. For the 30-minute trip from Carriacou to Petite Martinique, the fare is $8 each way. The ferry departs Grenada from The Carenage in St. George's on Monday, Wednesday and Friday at 9 am and 6 pm; the return trips leave from Tyrrel Bay, Carriacou, at 6 am and 3:30 pm.

TAXI

On Grenada, taxis are plentiful, and rates are set. The trip between Grand Anse and St. George's is $20 for up to two people. A fee of $5 is charged for each person added to the ride. Taxis can be hired at an hourly rate of $30, as well.

Water taxis are available along the Esplanade, near the port area. For about $8 (EC$20) a motorboat will transport you on a quick and picturesque cruise between St. George's and the jetty at Grand Anse Beach. Water taxis are privately owned, unregulated, and don't follow any particular schedule—so make arrangements for a pickup time if you need a return trip.

On Carriacou, the taxi fare from the jetty, at Tyrrel Bay, in Harvey Vale to Belair is $18; to Prospect $20, Hillsborough $15, or Windward $22. Carriacou minibus drivers will take up to four people on a 2½–3-hour full-island tour for $92 (EC$250) or a 1½-hour northern or southern tour for $46 (EC$125). A fee of $18 (EC$50) is charged for each person added to the full tour or $9 (EC$25) for each person added to the northern or southern tour.

Beaches

Grenada has some 80 miles (130 km) of coastline, 65 bays, and 45 beaches—many in little coves. The best beaches are just south of St. George's, facing the Caribbean, where many resorts are clustered. Nude or topless bathing that's done in view of others is against the law.

Health and Safety

Grenada is a relatively safe island. Incidents affecting tourists mainly involve petty theft; worse crimes have occurred but are rare. To avoid trouble, stay away from remote beaches and always lock your hotel room or villa and your car. Don't leave your valuables unattended in your room, on the beach, or in your car. Most hotel rooms are equipped with a safe for that purpose. Don't flaunt expensive jewelry or lots of cash either on the beach or in town.

Dengue, chikungunya, and zika have all been reported throughout the Caribbean. We recommend that you protect yourself from these mosquito-borne illnesses by keeping your skin covered and/or wearing mosquito repellent. The mosquitoes that transmit these viruses are as active by day as they are by night and especially emerge after heavy rains. On the beach, tiny sand flies begin to bite after 4 pm, and bugs are often a nuisance when hiking in the rain forest. Apply sun protection whenever you plan to be outdoors for any length of time. You can get sunburned just walking around town—even on cloudy days. Tap water in hotels and restaurants is perfectly safe to drink, and bottled water is always available.

Hotels

Grenada's tourist accommodations are located, for the most part, in the southwestern part of the island—primarily on or near Grand Anse Beach or overlooking small bays along the island's southern coast. Carriacou is a small island, and its hotels and guesthouses are primarily in or around Hillsborough.

Hotels and resorts tend to be small, with friendly and attentive management and staff. All guest rooms are equipped with air-conditioning, an in-room TV, and telephone unless indicated otherwise. Most also offer complimentary Wi-Fi. During the off-season (April 15 to December 15), rates at resorts may be discounted up to 40%; however, rates at some small hotels remain the same year-round.

Hotel reviews have been shortened. For full information, visit Fodors.com.

GUESTHOUSES

Small guesthouses predominate on Carriacou, where no property has more than 25 rooms.

LUXURY RESORTS

Grenada has a handful of luxurious inns and resorts, such as Spice Island Beach Resort and Silversands Resort on Grand Anse Beach, Sandals Grenada and Royalton Grenada in Point Salines, and Laluna in Morne Rouge.

PRIVATE VILLAS AND CONDOS

Grenada was one of the last islands to adopt private villa communities, in which privately owned units are rented to nonowner vacationers through management companies. Only a few such properties are here now or in progress. Silversands on Grand Anse Beach, Laluna Estate in Morne Rouge, and True Blue Bay Resort in True Blue all have associated villa properties. An extensive villa development is underway at Bacolet Bay in St. David, and villas are part of the plan for Port Louis on Lagoon Road in St. George's. Otherwise, villas, apartments, and houses are available for rent for a week or longer on both Grenada and Carriacou. The minimum staff includes a maid and laundress, but a cook, housekeeper, gardener, and others can be arranged.

In Grenada, many rental properties are located in and around L'Anse aux Épines, a beautiful residential peninsula that juts into the sea. In-season rates range from $1,000 a week for a small, two-bedroom house with no pool to $8,000 a week for a five-bedroom house full of amenities, including a pool and beach access. In Carriacou, in-season rates range from $75 a day for a small cottage or in-town apartment suitable for two people to $400 a day for a two-bedroom villa with panoramic views and a swimming pool.

RENTAL CONTACTS Down Island Ltd.—Carriacou. ✉ *Craigston* ☎ *473/443–8182, 473/537–1458* 🌐 *www.islandvillas.com.*

What It Costs in U.S. Dollars

$	$$	$$$	$$$$
RESTAURANTS			
under $12	$12–$20	$21–$30	over $30
HOTELS			
under $275	$275–$375	$376–$475	over $475

Nightlife

Grenada's nightlife consists mainly of live music at resort hotels, a very popular street party, and a handful of nightspots. During the winter season, some resorts present a steel band or other local entertainment several nights a week.

Restaurants

Grenada's crops include all kinds of citrus, along with mangoes, papaya, callaloo (similar to spinach), dasheen (taro, a root vegetable), christophene (a squash, also known as chayote), yams (white, green, yellow, and orange), and breadfruit. All restaurants prepare dishes with local produce and season them with the many spices grown throughout the island. Be sure to try the local flavors of ice cream: soursop, guava, rum raisin, coconut, and nutmeg.

Soups—especially pumpkin and callaloo—are divine and often start a meal. Pepper pot is a savory stew of pork, oxtail, vegetables, and spices. Oildown, the national dish, combines salted meat, breadfruit, onions, carrots, celery, dasheen, and dumplings all boiled in coconut milk until the liquid is absorbed and the savory mixture becomes "oily." A roti—curried chicken, beef, or vegetables wrapped in pastry and baked—is similar to a turnover and more popular in Grenada than a sandwich.

Fresh seafood of all kinds is plentiful, including lobster in season (September–April). Conch, known here as lambi, often appears curried or in a stew. Crab back, though, is not seafood—it's land crab. Most Grenadian restaurants serve seafood and at least some local dishes.

Rum punches are ubiquitous and always topped with grated nutmeg. Clarke's Court, Rivers, and Westerhall are local rums. Carib, the local beer, is refreshing, light, and quite good. If you prefer a nonalcoholic drink, opt for fruit punch—a delicious mixture of freshly blended tropical fruit.

WHAT TO WEAR

Dining in Grenada is casual. At dinner, collared shirts and long pants are appropriate for men (even the fanciest restaurants don't require jacket and tie), and sundresses or dress pants are fine for women. Reserve beachwear and other revealing attire for the beach.

Shopping

Grenada is truly a nation of entrepreneurs—from retail businesses and processing operations, both with employees, to vendors (about one-third of the population) who personally sell their handicrafts in the markets. Note that bargaining isn't customary either in shops or markets.

Stores in Grenada are generally open weekdays from 8 to 4 or 4:30 and Saturday from 8 to 1; some close from noon to 1 during the week. Most are closed Sunday, although tourist shops usually open if a cruise ship is in port; some mall stores, particularly supermarkets, are open for longer hours on weekends.

Unique, locally made goods to look for in gift shops and supermarkets are locally made chocolate bars, nutmeg jam and syrup, spice-scented soaps and body oils, and (no kidding) Nut-Med Pain-Relieving Spray. Grenada's best souvenirs or gifts for friends back home, though, are spice baskets in a variety of shapes and sizes that are filled with cinnamon, nutmeg, mace, bay leaves, cloves, turmeric, and ginger. You can buy them for as little as $5 to $10 in practically every shop, at the open-air produce market at **Market Square** in St. George's, at vendor stalls along the Esplanade near the port, and at the Vendor's Craft & Spice Market on Grand Anse Beach. Vendors also sell handmade fabric dolls, coral jewelry, seashells, spice necklaces, and hats and baskets handwoven from green palm fronds.

Here's some local terminology you should know. If someone asks if you'd like a "sweetie," you're being offered a candy. When you buy spices, you may be offered "saffron" and "vanilla." The "saffron" is really turmeric, a ground yellow root, rather than the (much more expensive) fragile pistils of crocus flowers; the "vanilla" is extracted from locally grown tonka beans rather than from actual (also much more expensive) vanilla beans. No one is trying to pull the wool over your eyes; these are common local terms. That said, the U.S. Food and Drug Administration warns that "vanilla" extracts made from tonka beans can have toxic effects and may pose a significant health risk for individuals taking certain medications.

Sights

Grenada is divided into six parishes, including one named St. George that includes the communities of Grand Anse, Morne Rouge, True Blue, L'Anse aux Épines, and the capital city of St. George's. When exploring this beautiful island, please note that removing bark from trees, taking wildlife from the forest, and taking coral from the sea are all against the law.

Visitor Information

CONTACTS Grenada Hotel & Tourism Association. ✉ *Morne Rouge, Grand Anse* ✣ *Upstairs Ocean House Medical Services* ☎ *473/444–1353* 🌐 *www.ghta.org.* **Grenada Tourism Authority.** ✉ *Burns Point, south end of The Carenage, St. George's* ☎ *473/440–2001, 473/440–2279, 917/929–7892 in U.S.* 🌐 *puregrenada.com.* **Grenada Tourism Authority (Carriacou & Petite Martinique).** ✉ *Main St., Hillsborough* ☎ *473/443–7948* 🌐 *puregrenada.com.*

Weddings

Residency is not required to apply for a marriage license, and securing the license will take two additional workdays; no blood test is necessary. You'll need to present valid passports, birth certificates, proof of single status (e.g., a sworn affidavit), and original or certified copies of divorce decrees or death certificates, if applicable. The marriage license fee is $37 (EC$100) plus a $6 (EC$15) stamp fee. The same-day marriage license fee is $199 (EC$540). The marriage certificate fee is $4 (EC$10) plus a $2 (EC$5) stamp fee. Contact the registrar's office (473/440–2806) for specific information regarding marriage licenses and marriage certificates.

St. George's

Grenada's capital is a bustling West Indian city, much of which remains unchanged from colonial days. Narrow streets lined with shops wind up, down, and across the city. Brick warehouses cling to the waterfront, and pastel-painted homes disappear into steep green hills.

Horseshoe-shape **St. George's Harbour,** a submerged volcanic crater, is arguably the prettiest harbor in the Caribbean. Schooners, ferries, and tour boats tie up along the seawall or at the small dinghy dock. **The Carenage** (pronounced car-a-*nahzh*), which surrounds the harbor, is the capital's center. Warehouses, shops, and restaurants line the waterfront. The *Christ of the Deep* statue sits on the pedestrian plaza at the center of The Carenage; it was presented to Grenada by Costa Cruise Line in remembrance of its ship, *Bianca C,* that burned and sank in the harbor in 1961. *Bianca C* is now a popular dive site.

An engineering feat for its time, the 340-foot-long **Sendall Tunnel** was built in 1895 and named for Walter Sendall, an early governor. The narrow tunnel, used by both pedestrians and vehicles, separates the harbor side of St. George's from The Esplanade on the bay side of town, where you will find the markets (produce, meat, and fish), the Cruise Ship Terminal, the Esplanade Mall, and the public bus station.

TIP→ There are no hotels in St. George's. All of the island's hotels are on or near the beaches south of the city (Grand Anse, Morne Rouge, Lance aux Epines, True Blue, etc.), with a couple more located in the countryside.

Sights

Cathedral of the Immaculate Conception
CHURCH | The Roman Catholic cathedral, high on a hill overlooking the harbor, is the city's most visible landmark. The Gothic tower dates from 1818. ✉ *Church St., St. George's* ☎ *473/440–2999.*

Ft. Frederick
MILITARY SIGHT | Overlooking the city of St. George's and the picturesque harbor, historic Ft. Frederick provides a panoramic view of about one-fourth of Grenada. The French began construction of the fort; the British completed it in 1791. Fort Frederick was the headquarters of the People's Revolutionary Government before and during the 1983 coup. Today, it's simply a peaceful spot with a bird's-eye view of much of Grenada.

TIP→ Visit in the morning for the best photos of the harbor. ✉ *Richmond Hill* ☎ *473/440–2279 Ministry of Tourism Grenada* 🎫 *$2.*

★ **Ft. George**
MILITARY SIGHT | **FAMILY** | Ft. George is perched high on the hill at the entrance to St. George's Harbour. Grenada's oldest fort was built by the French in 1705 to protect the harbor, yet no shots were ever fired here until October 1983, when Prime Minister Maurice Bishop and

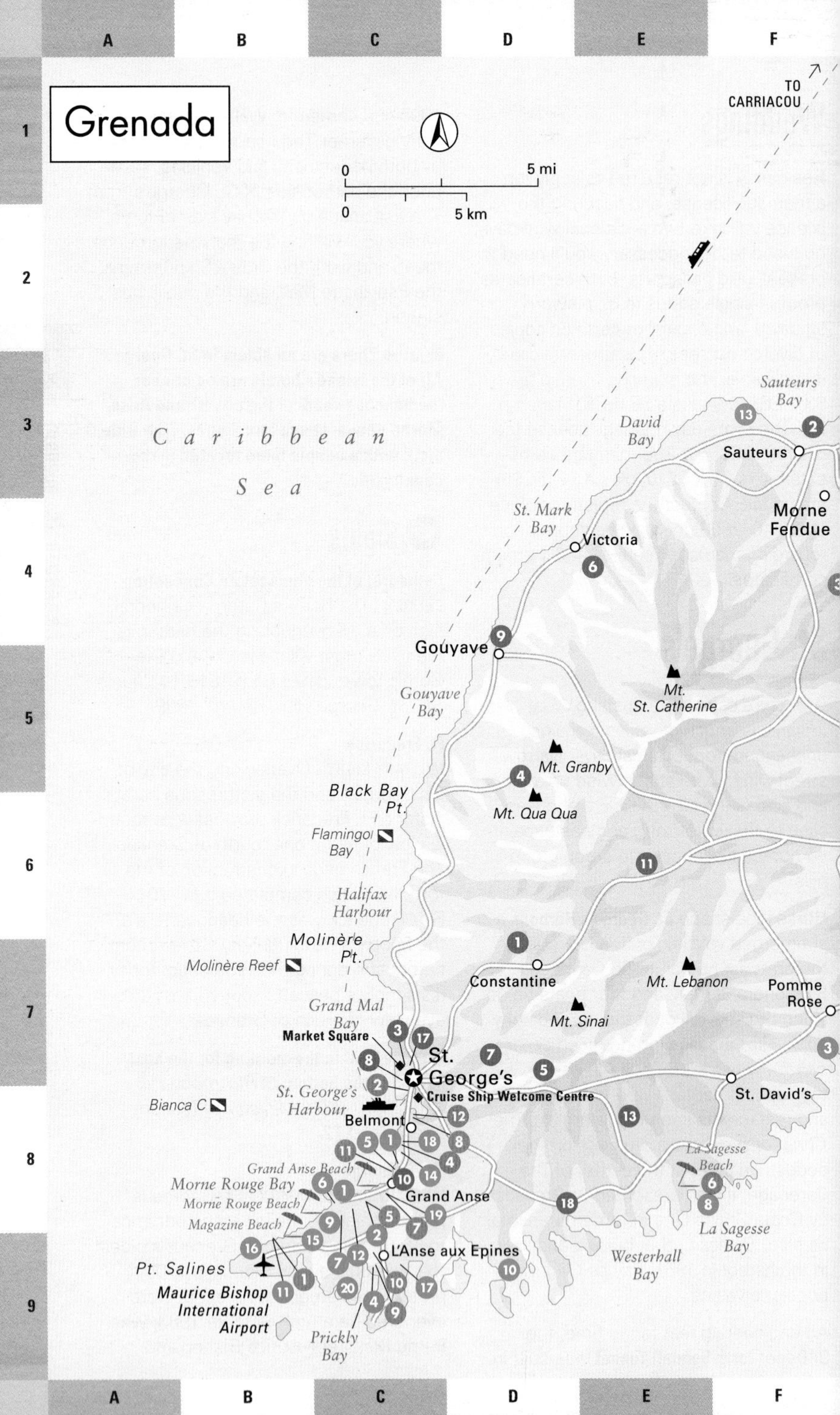

Grenada
0
5 mi
0
5 km
TO CARRIACOU
Caribbean Sea
Sauteurs Bay
David Bay
Sauteurs
Morne Fendue
St. Mark Bay
Victoria
Gouyave
Gouyave Bay
Mt. St. Catherine
Mt. Granby
Mt. Qua Qua
Black Bay Pt.
Flamingo Bay
Halifax Harbour
Molinère Pt.
Molinère Reef
Constantine
Mt. Lebanon
Pomme Rose
Mt. Sinai
Grand Mal Bay
Market Square
St. George's
St. David's
St. George's Harbour
Cruise Ship Welcome Centre
Bianca C
Belmont
La Sagesse Beach
Grand Anse Beach
Morne Rouge Bay
Grand Anse
Morne Rouge Beach
Magazine Beach
La Sagesse Bay
L'Anse aux Epines
Westerhall Bay
Pt. Salines
Maurice Bishop International Airport
Prickly Bay

H I

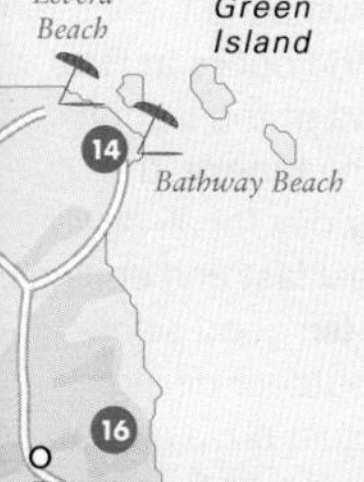

G H I

Sights

1 Annandale Waterfall & Forest Park **D7**
2 Caribs' Leap **F3**
3 Cathedral of the Immaculate Conception **C7**
4 Concord Falls **D5**
5 De La Grenade Industries................ **D7**
6 Diamond Chocolate Factory (Jouvay Chocolate)...... **E4**
7 Ft. Frederick **D7**
8 Ft. George **C7**
9 Gouyave Nutmeg Processing Station **D4**
10 Grand Anse............... **C8**
11 Grand Étang National Park & Forest Reserve **E6**
12 Grenville Nutmeg Processing Station **G6**
13 Laura Herb & Spice Garden **E8**
14 Levera National Park & Bird Sanctuary **G3**
15 Pearls Airport **G5**
16 River Antoine Rum Distillery **G4**
17 St. George's Methodist Church **C7**
18 Westerhall Estate....... **D8**

Restaurants

1 Aquarium Restaurant............... **B9**
2 BB's Crabback Caribbean Restaurant **C7**
3 Belmont Estate........... **F4**
4 Coconut Beach Restaurant................ **C8**
5 La Belle Creole **C8**
6 La Sagesse Restaurant **F8**
7 Oliver's **C8**
8 Patrick's Local Homestyle Restaurant **C8**
9 Rhodes Restaurant...... **C9**
10 Spice Affair by Red Crab.................. **C9**
11 Umbrellas Beach Bar................ **C8**
12 Victory Bar & Restaurant................ **C8**

Hotels

1 Allamanda Beach Resort **C8**
2 Blue Horizons Garden Resort **C8**
3 Cabier Ocean Lodge..... **F7**
4 Calabash Luxury Boutique Hotel **C9**
5 Coyaba Beach Resort... **C8**
6 Gem Holiday Beach Resort **C8**
7 Kalinago Beach Resort..................... **C8**
8 La Sagesse Hotel **E8**
9 Laluna..................... **C8**
10 Le Phare Bleu **D9**
11 Maca Bana.............. **B9**
12 Mount Cinnamon **C8**
13 Petite Anse Hotel **F3**
14 Radisson Grenada Beach Resort **C8**
15 Royalton Grenada Resort & Spa **B9**
16 Sandals Grenada **B9**
17 Secret Harbour Boutique Hotel & Marina........... **C9**
18 Silversands Grenada.... **C8**
19 Spice Island Beach Resort **C8**
20 True Blue Bay Boutique Resort......... **C9**

several of his followers were assassinated in the courtyard. The fort now houses police headquarters but is open to the public daily. The 360-degree view of the capital city, St. George's Harbour, and the open sea is spectacular.

■ TIP→ **Visit in the afternoon for the best photos of the harbor.** ✉ *Grand Étang Rd., St. George's* ☎ *473/440–2279 Ministry of Tourism Grenada* 🎟 *$2.*

St. George's Methodist Church

CHURCH | Built in 1820, the oldest original church building in the city is still in use. It has no spire, unlike the more elaborate churches in St. George's. The building itself was severely damaged by Hurricane Ivan in 2004 but has been completely restored. ✉ *Green St., near Herbert Blaize St., St. George's* ☎ *473/440–2129.*

Restaurants

BB's Crabback Caribbean Restaurant

$$$ | **CARIBBEAN** | **FAMILY** | Overlooking St. George's Harbour, on the north side of The Carenage, BB's Crabback features Grenadian and West Indian dishes prepared by Grenada-born, England-trained, Chef BB (Brian Benjamin). Crabback (local land crab) is a house specialty, but you'll want to try some of his seafood dishes, as well, like prawns in lobster sauce. **Known for:** harborside location; crabback (local land crab), of course; chicken or fish luncheon specials. $ *Average main: $26* ✉ *Progress House, Grand Étang Rd., near Ft. George, St. George's* ☎ *473/435–7058* 🌐 *www.bbscrabback-restaurant.com.*

Patrick's Local Homestyle Restaurant

$$$ | **CARIBBEAN** | The fixed tasting menu of 20 or so local dishes, served family-style, will astound you—it's Grenadian home-style cooking at its casual best. The restaurant, in a tiny cottage on the outskirts of St. George's, is named for the late and very charismatic chef Patrick Levine. **Known for:** truly local atmosphere; usual and unusual local dishes; definitely no rush here. $ *Average main: $23* ✉ *Kirani James Blvd. (Lagoon Rd.), opposite Port Louis Marina, St. George's* ☎ *473/449–7243, 473/440–0364* ⏲ *No lunch weekends.*

Victory Bar & Restaurant

$$$ | **INTERNATIONAL** | Boaters, business-people, vacationers, and anyone else looking for good food in a waterfront atmosphere close to town keep the Victory busy. Overlooking the docks at Port Louis Marina, with views of the lagoon and masts swaying in the breeze, the restaurant is open every day for all-day dining, starting with breakfast and ending with a lively bar. **Known for:** good selection of beer and wine; outdoor dining with a view; best thin-crust pizza on the island. $ *Average main: $22* ✉ *Port Louis Marina, Kirani James Blvd. (Lagoon Rd.), St. George's* ☎ *473/435–7263* ⏲ *victorybargrenada.com.*

Shopping

In St. George's, on the northern side of the harbor, **Young Street** is a main shopping thoroughfare; it rises steeply uphill from The Carenage and then descends just as steeply to **Market Square.** On Melville Street, adjacent to the Cruise Ship Terminal, **Esplanade Mall** has shops that offer duty-free jewelry, electronics, liquor, and gift items, as well as local crafts.

FOOD

House of Chocolate Grenada

CHOCOLATE | **FAMILY** | Part mini-museum, part chocolaterie, part café, part boutique (chocolate boutique, that is)... you can learn how chocolate is processed from cacao beans, enjoy treats made from chocolate (cakes, ice cream, candy, cocoa tea, even chocolate rum), and purchase chocolate bars, cocoa, and other products made in Grenada. ✉ *10 Young St., St. George's* ☎ *473/440–2310* 🌐 *www.houseofchocolategnd.com.*

★ Market Square

CRAFTS | This bustling produce market is open weekday mornings and is the best place to stock up on fresh fruit to enjoy during your stay and to buy packets or baskets of island-grown spices to take home. Saturday morning is busiest. Vendors also sell crafts, leather goods, and decorative objects. ✉ *Foot of Young St., on the north side of town, St. George's.*

Marketing & National Importing Board

FOOD | At this government-run produce market, you'll find fresh fruits and vegetables, spices, hot sauces, and local syrups and jams at lower prices than in most gift shops. ✉ *Young St., St. George's* ☎ *473/440–1791* 🌐 *www.mnib.gd.*

Spice Isle Coffee

OTHER SPECIALTY STORE | The Spice Isle Coffee Company Roasters of Grenada started in 2012 as the dream of the owner Zofia Malisiewicz. Relocating with her husband to Grenada from Poland, she decided to couple her expertise as a chemist with her love for coffee and thus Spice Isle Coffee was born. The company imports the finest quality coffee beans found internationally including from Colombia, Brazil, Ethiopia, Papua New Guinea, Uganda, Guatemala, and Peru, among other countries. Each variety of the coffee beans is roasted to perfection to bring out its best flavor and then blended with love. Each blend is then dubbed with uniquely Grenadian names such as Grenada Forbidden Chocolate, Grand Anse, Forever Nutmeg, Midnight Calypso, Pumpkin Spice, or Sweet Cinnamon. These blends are perfect for making your favorite coffee drink whether your preference is steaming hot or chilled. ✉ *Tanteen, St. George's* ☎ *473/232–3000, 473/458–6309 mobile* 🌐 *www.grenadacoffee.com.*

HANDICRAFTS

Fidel Productions

SOUVENIRS | Fidel Productions is a small cottage industry of local artisans from Carriacou. At this little gift shop at Port Louis Marina, you'll find locally made gifts and souvenirs—hand-printed T-shirts, hand-painted calabashes, Arawak Island soaps and lotions, handmade jewelry, caps, and more. On Carriacou, the shop is inside a bright green shipping container in the Paradise Beach parking lot; a small selection of items is also available at the Carriacou Museum in Hillsborough. ✉ *Port Louis Marina, Kirani James Blvd., St. George's* ☎ *473/435–8866 in Grenada, 473/410–8866 in Carriacou* 🌐 *www.shopfidel.com.*

Elsewhere on Grenada

Sights

Annandale Waterfall & Forest Park

GARDEN | FAMILY | This is a lovely, cool spot for swimming and picnicking. A mountain stream cascades 40 feet into a natural pool surrounded by exotic vines. A paved path leads to the bottom of the falls, and a trail leads to the top. You'll often find local boys diving from the top of the falls—and hoping for a small tip. ✉ *Main interior rd., 15 mins northeast of St. George's, Annandale Estate* ☎ *473/421–4320* 🎟 *$5.*

Caribs' Leap

OTHER ATTRACTION | At Sauteurs (the French word for "jumpers" or "leapers") on the island's northernmost tip, Caribs' Leap (or Leapers Hill) is the 100-foot vertical cliff from which the last of the indigenous Caribs flung themselves into the sea in 1651. After losing several bloody battles with European colonists, they chose suicide over surrender to the French. ✉ *Sauteurs.*

★ Concord Falls

TRAIL | About 8 miles (13 km) north of St. George's, a turnoff from the West Coast Road leads to Concord Falls—actually three separate waterfalls. The first is at the end of the road; when the currents aren't too strong, you can take a dip under the 35-foot cascade. Reaching the two other waterfalls requires a hike into the forest reserve. The hike to the second falls (Au Coin) takes about 30 minutes. The third and most spectacular waterfall (Fontainebleau) thunders 65 feet over huge boulders and creates a small pool. It's smart to hire a guide for that trek, which can take an hour or more. The path is clear, but slippery boulders toward the end can be treacherous without assistance.

TIP→ **It can be dangerous to swim directly under the cascade due to swift currents, an undertow, and falling rocks.** ✉ *Concord Valley, off West Coast Rd., Gouyave* ☎ *473/440–2279 Ministry of Tourism Grenada* 🎫 *Changing room $2.*

De La Grenade Industries

FACTORY | In the suburb of St. Paul's, five minutes east of St. George's, De La Grenade produces syrups, jams, jellies, a nutmeg liqueur, and other homegrown fruits and spices. You're welcome to watch the manufacturing process, visit the shop, and stroll around the adjacent herb and spice gardens. ✉ *St. Paul's, Eastern Main Rd., St. Paul's* ☎ *473/440–3241* 🌐 *www.delagrenade.com* 🎫 *factory tours $4; garden tours $10.*

Diamond Chocolate Factory (Jouvay Chocolate)

FACTORY | Visitors are welcome to this small, farmer-owned chocolate producer in the far northwest of Grenada. A worker will show you the cacao pods growing in the field and explain the bean-to-bar chocolate-making process before giving you a tour of the small factory. You can buy the company's Jouvay-branded dark chocolate bars, cocoa powder, cocoa butter, cocoa nibs, and other products.

TIP→ **Jouvay chocolate is also sold in gift shops throughout Grenada.** ✉ *Diamond St., Victoria* ☎ *473/437–1839* 🌐 *www.jouvaychocolate.com* 🎫 *$5.*

★ Gouyave Nutmeg Processing Station

FACTORY | **FAMILY** | Touring the nutmeg-processing co-op, right in the center of the west-coast fishing village of Gouyave (pronounced *GWAHV*), is a fragrant, fascinating way to spend a half hour. You can learn all about nutmeg and its uses; see the nutmegs laid out in bins; and watch the workers sort them by hand, grade them, and pack them into burlap bags for shipping worldwide. The three-story plant is one of the largest nutmeg processing factories on the island. ✉ *Central Depradine St., Gouyave* ☎ *473/444–8337, 473/440–2117 Grenada Co-operative Nutmeg Association* 🌐 *www.grenadanutmeg.com* 🎫 *$1–$5.*

Grand Anse

BEACH | **FAMILY** | A residential and commercial area about 5 miles (8 km) south of downtown St. George's, Grand Anse is named for the world-renowned beach it surrounds. Grenada's tourist facilities—resorts, restaurants, some shopping, and most nightlife—are concentrated in this general area. **Grand Anse Beach** is a 2-mile (3-km) crescent of sand, shaded by coconut palms and seagrape trees, with gentle turquoise surf. A public entrance is at Camerhogne Park, just a few steps from the main road. Water taxis carry passengers between The Esplanade in St. George's and a jetty on the beach. **St. George's University,** which for years held classes at its enviable beachfront location in Grand Anse, now has its sprawling main campus on a peninsula in True Blue, a nearby residential community. The university's original beachside building in Grand Anse is currently used for student housing. ✉ *Grand Anse.*

★ Grand Étang National Park & Forest Reserve

NATIONAL PARK | FAMILY | A rain forest and wildlife sanctuary deep in the mountainous interior of Grenada, Grand Étang has miles of hiking trails for all levels of ability. There are also lookouts to observe the lush flora and many species of birds and other fauna (including the Mona monkey) and a number of streams for fishing. **Grand Étang Lake** is a 36-acre expanse of cobalt-blue water—1,740 feet above sea level—that fills the crater of an extinct volcano. Although legend has it that the lake is bottomless, maximum soundings have been recorded at just 18 feet. The informative **Grand Étang Forest Center** has displays on the local wildlife and vegetation. A forest ranger is on hand to answer questions; a small snack bar and souvenir stands are nearby. ✉ *Main interior rd. between Grenville and St. George's* ☎ *473/440–6160* 🎫 *$2.*

Grenville Nutmeg Processing Station

FACTORY | FAMILY | Like its counterpart in Gouyave, this nutmeg-processing plant is open to the public for guided tours. You can see and learn about the entire process of receiving, drying, sorting, and packing nutmeg. ✉ *Seaton Browne St., Grenville* ☎ *473/442–7241* 🌐 *www.grenadanutmeg.com* 🎫 *$1–$5.*

Laura Herb & Spice Garden

GARDEN | FAMILY | The 6½ acres of gardens here are part of an old plantation at Laura, near the village of Perdmontemps in St. David Parish and about 6 miles (10 km) east of Grand Anse. On the 20-minute tour, you will learn all about spices and herbs grown in Grenada—including cocoa, clove, nutmeg, pimiento, cinnamon, turmeric, and tonka beans (sometimes used in vanilla substitutes)—and how they're used for flavoring and for medicinal purposes. ✉ *Laura Land, Perdmontemps* ☎ *473/443–2604* 🎫 *$4* ⏲ *Closed weekends.*

Levera National Park & Bird Sanctuary

BEACH | This portion of Grenada's protected parkland encompasses 450 acres at the northeastern tip of the island, where the Caribbean Sea meets the Atlantic Ocean. There's a trail that circles 45-acre Levera Pond. The shallow lagoon by the beach is one of the most important wildlife habitats on the island—thick mangroves provide food and protection for nesting seabirds and seldom-seen parrots—and a natural reef protects swimmers from the rough Atlantic surf at Bathway Beach. The southernmost islets of the Grenadines are visible from the beach. ✉ *At the northeastern tip of the island, 1.9 miles (3 km) east of Sauteurs, Levera* 🎫 *Free.*

Pearls Airport

OTHER ATTRACTION | Pearls, the island's original airport just north of Grenville on the Atlantic coast, was replaced in 1984 by Maurice Bishop International Airport in Point Salines. Here at Pearls, deteriorating Cuban and Soviet planes sit at the end of the old runway. The planes were abandoned after the 1983 intervention, during which Cuban "advisers" helping to construct the airport at Point Salines were summarily removed from the island. Interestingly, three decades later, Cuban workers helped build the new Argyll International Airport in neighboring St. Vincent with no similar international reaction. At Pearls, there's a good view north to the Grenadines and a small beach nearby. ✉ *Pearls.*

★ River Antoine Rum Distillery

DISTILLERY | At this rustic operation, kept open primarily as a museum, a limited quantity of rum is produced by the same methods used since the distillery opened in 1785. River Antoine (pronounced *an-TWYNE*) is the oldest functioning water-propelled distillery in the Caribbean. The process begins with the crushing of sugarcane from adjacent fields; the discarded canes are then used as fuel to fire the boilers. The end result is a potent overproof rum, sold only in Grenada, that will knock your socks off. (A less strong version is also available.) ✉ *River Antoine Estate* ☎ *473/442–7109* 🎫 *Guided tour $2.*

Westerhall Estate

HISTORIC SIGHT | Back in the late 1800s, cocoa, sugarcane, coconuts (the oil was used for soap), and limes (used in perfume) were produced on the 951-acre Westerhall Estate, which was then called Bacaye. More recently, Westerhall has focused on blending and bottling rum. The Westerhall Estate tour includes an explanation of the ruins and sugar-processing machinery on the grounds, along with a small museum comprising the eclectic collection of the Grenadian journalist Dr. Alistair Hughes (1919–2005). Particularly interesting items on display in the museum include old rum bottles and labels, Carib artifacts, a number of vintage sewing machines, a World War I Maxim machine gun, and a 1915 Willys Overland automobile. ✉ *Westerall Heights, Westerhall* ☎ *473/443–5477* 🌐 *www.westerhallrums.com* 🎫 *$3* ⊙ *Closed Sat. and Sun.*

Beaches

Bathway Beach

BEACH | This broad strip of white sand on the northeastern tip of Grenada is part of Levera National Park. A natural coral reef protects swimmers and snorkelers from the rough Atlantic surf; swimming beyond the reef is dangerous. A magnet for local folks on national holidays, the beach is almost deserted at other times. Changing rooms are located at the park headquarters. A vendor or two sometimes sets up shop near the beach, but you're smart to bring your own refreshments. **Amenities:** parking (no fee); toilets. **Best for:** snorkeling; solitude; swimming; walking. ✉ *Levera National Park, Levera.*

★ Grand Anse Beach

BEACH | **FAMILY** | Grenada's loveliest and most popular beach is Grand Anse, a gleaming 2-mile (3-km) semicircle of white sand lapped by gentle surf and punctuated by seagrapes and coconut palms that provide shady escapes from the sun. Brilliant rainbows frequently spill into the sea from the high green mountains that frame St. George's Harbour to the north. Several resorts face the beach, from Mount Cinnamon at the southern end of the beach to Spice Island Beach Resort, Coyaba Beach Resort, Allamanda Beach Resort, Radisson Grenada Beach Resort, and Silversands as you head north. Several of these hotels have dive shops for arranging dive trips or renting snorkeling equipment. A water-taxi dock is at the midpoint of the beach, along with the Grand Anse Craft and Spice Market, where vendors also rent beach chairs and umbrellas. Restrooms and changing facilities are available at Camerhogne Park, which is the public entrance and parking lot. Hotel guests, cruise-ship passengers, and other island visitors love this beach, as do local people who come to swim and play on weekends. There's plenty of room for everyone. **Amenities:** food and drink; parking (no fee); toilets; water sports. **Best for:** sunset; swimming; walking. ✉ *3 miles (5 km) south of St. George's, Grand Anse.*

La Sagesse Beach

BEACH | Surrounding a sheltered bay along the southeastern coast at La Sagesse Nature Centre, this secluded crescent of fine gray sand is a 30-minute drive from Grand Anse. Surrounded by tropical vegetation, the beach provides a lovely, quiet refuge. The water is fairly shallow and always calm along the shoreline. Plan a full day of swimming, sunning, and nature walks, with lunch at La Sagesse Inn's restaurant, which is adjacent to the beach. **Amenities:** food and drink; parking (no fee); toilets. **Best for:** solitude; swimming; walking. ✉ *La Sagesse Nature Center, La Sagesse.*

Magazine Beach

BEACH | Not far from the international airport in Point Salines, Magazine Beach is a magnificent strip of pure white sand that stretches from Aquarium Restaurant and Maca Bana Villas at its southern end to the Royalton Grenada, farther north. Never crowded, it's excellent for swimming and sunbathing; the surf ranges from gentle to spectacular. Cool drinks, snacks, or a full lunch are available at the Aquarium's La Sirena Beach Bar—or stick around for happy hour. You can also rent snorkeling equipment and kayaks there. Access to the beach is next to the restaurant or next to the Royalton. **Amenities:** food and drink; toilets; water sports. **Best for:** snorkeling; sunset; swimming; walking. ✉ *Point Salines.*

Morne Rouge Beach

BEACH | **FAMILY** | One mile (1½ km) south of Grand Anse, a ½-mile-long (¾-km-long) crescent of pure white sand is tucked away on Morne Rouge Bay. The clear turquoise water is excellent for swimming, and the gentle surf makes this beach perfect for families with small children. Light meals and snacks are available at Gem Holiday Resort's beachfront bar and grill or next door at Kalinago Beach Resort. **Amenities:** food and drink; parking (no fee); toilets. **Best for:** sunset; swimming. ✉ *Morne Rouge.*

Restaurants

★ Aquarium Restaurant

$$$ | **SEAFOOD** | **FAMILY** | As the name suggests, fresh seafood is the specialty here and the dinner menu always includes fresh fish and grilled lobster, as well as specialties such as jerk chicken and callaloo cannelloni. Spend the day at adjacent Magazine Beach (you can rent kayaks or snorkeling gear) and then break for a cool drink or satisfying lunch—a salad, sandwich or burger, fresh fish, or pasta—served on the waterfront deck at the restaurant's La Sirena Beach Bar. **Known for:** Sunday beach barbecue; oceanfront dining; congenial bar scene. $ *Average main: $60* ✉ *Magazine Beach, Maurice Bishop Memorial Hwy., Point Salines* ☎ *473/444–1410* 🌐 *www.aquariumgrenada.com* ⏲ *Closed Mon.*

Belmont Estate

$$$ | **CARIBBEAN** | **FAMILY** | If you're visiting the northern reaches of Grenada, plan to stop at Belmont Estate, a 400-year-old working nutmeg and cocoa plantation. A waiter will offer some refreshing local juice and a choice of callaloo or pumpkin soup; then head to the buffet and help yourself to salad, rice, stewed chicken, beef curry, stewed fish, local vegetables, and more. **Known for:** goat dairy, petting farm, and craft market; extensive buffet featuring Grenadian cuisine; scenic, tranquil surroundings. $ *Average main: $27* ✉ *Belmont* ✣ *side road between Hermitage and Tivoli* ☎ *473/442–9524* 🌐 *www.belmontestate.gd* ⏲ *Closed Sat. No dinner.*

★ Coconut Beach Restaurant

$$$ | **CARIBBEAN** | **FAMILY** | Take local seafood, add butter, wine, and Grenadian spices, and you have excellent French-creole cuisine. Throw in a beautiful location at the northern end of Grand Anse Beach, and this West Indian cottage becomes a perfect spot for either an alfresco lunch, snacks at sunset, or dinner by moonlight. **Known for:** vegetarian items, too; lobster prepared in a variety of ways; enjoy lunch at an umbrella table in the sand. $ *Average main: $25* ✉ *Grand Anse Main Rd., northern end of Grand Anse Beach, Grand Anse* ☎ *473/444–4644* 🌐 *www.thecoconutbeachgrenada.com* ⏲ *Closed Tues.*

★ La Belle Creole

$$$$ | **CARIBBEAN** | The marriage of contemporary and West Indian cuisines and a splendid view of the twinkling lights in distant St. George's are the delights of this romantic hillside restaurant. The five-course menu is based on original recipes from the owner's mother, a pioneer in incorporating local fruits, vegetables, and spices into "foreign" dishes. **Known for:** attentive service; upscale local cuisine; lovely view, even at night. *Average main: $35* *Blue Horizons Garden Resort, Morne Rouge Rd., Grand Anse* *473/444–4316* *www.grenadabluehorizons.com.*

★ La Sagesse Restaurant

$$$ | **SEAFOOD** | The perfect spot to soothe a frazzled soul, this open-air seafood restaurant is on a secluded cove in a nature preserve. Combine your lunch or dinner with a nature walk or a day at the beach. **Known for:** all produce and herbs grown organically; stunning view of the bay; alfresco dining in a lovely natural setting. *Average main: $35* *La Sagesse Nature Centre, La Sagesse* *473/444–6458* *www.lasagesse.com.*

★ Oliver's

$$$$ | **CONTEMPORARY** | Enjoy a memorable dining experience at Oliver's, the seaside restaurant at Spice Island Beach Resort. Assistant Head Chef Brenda Joseph, a Grenadian, turns out some of the most delicious, savory, and elegant culinary creations that you'll find on this island. **Known for:** the epitome of fine dining; beautifully crafted, delicious dishes; superb service. *Average main: $85* *Spice Island Beach Resort, Grand Anse* *473/444–4258* *www.spiceislandbeachresort.com.*

★ Rhodes Restaurant

$$$$ | **CONTEMPORARY** | Named for the acclaimed British chef Gary Rhodes, this open-air restaurant is surrounded by palms, flowering plants, and twinkling lights—a wonderful setting for a romantic dinner or special occasion. Local produce and spices have never appeared (or tasted) more elegant. **Known for:** refined, relaxed atmosphere; beautifully prepared, mouthwatering dishes; extensive wine list. *Average main: $50* *Calabash Hotel, L'Anse aux Épines* *473/444–4334* *www.calabashhotel.com* *No lunch.*

Spice Affair by Red Crab

$$$ | **INDIAN** | **FAMILY** | For a real taste treat, head to Spice Affair for Indian cuisine fused with local seafood and Grenadian spices—and an Asian flair. After renovating and modernizing the original Red Crab restaurant, an island institution for many, many years, the chefs here offer a completely different dining experience. **Known for:** vegetarian, vegan, and gluten-free options; dishes are designed for sharing; kids menu, too. *Average main: $21* *L'Anse aux Épines Stretch, L'Anse aux Épines* *473/444–4424* *spiceaffair.gd.*

Umbrellas Beach Bar

$$ | **ECLECTIC** | **FAMILY** | Whether you're spending the day on Grand Anse Beach or just looking for a quick bite, Umbrellas is the place to go. Right on the beach, next to Coyaba Beach Resort, this classic beach bar is open from breakfast until well into the evening. **Known for:** veggie-friendly, too; popular beachside hangout with live music weekends; full menu from burgers to seafood to steak. *Average main: $20* *Grand Anse Beach, next to Coyaba Beach Resort, Grand Anse* *473/439–9149* *www.umbrellas.gd.*

Hotels

Allamanda Beach Resort

$ | **HOTEL** | **FAMILY** | Well-situated facing Grand Anse Beach, many rooms in this small hotel have connecting doors, making Allamanda a good choice for families. **Pros:** easy access to shopping, restaurants, and public transportation; location, location, location; great value. **Cons:** you have to walk down the beach for water sports; no on-site restaurant; don't expect luxury at this price. *Rooms from: $165* *Grand Anse* *473/444–0095* *www.allamandaresort.com* *50 rooms* *No Meals.*

Blue Horizons Garden Resort

$ | **RESORT** | **FAMILY** | Just 300 yards from Grand Anse Beach, "Blue" is especially popular among divers, nature lovers, and family vacationers looking for roomy, self-catering accommodations. **Pros:** pool, playground, family rooms; peaceful, quiet garden environment; walk to shopping and restaurants. **Cons:** few on-site activities; lots of steps up to the hilltop units—which also offer the best view; 5-minute walk to the beach. *Rooms from: $210 Morne Rouge Rd., Grand Anse 473/444–4316, 473/444–4592 www.grenadabluehorizons.com 32 rooms No Meals.*

Cabier Ocean Lodge

$ | **B&B/INN** | **FAMILY** | Definitely off the beaten path and in a truly natural environment, Cabier Ocean Lodge is a combination guesthouse, restaurant/bar, petting zoo, and donkey ranch—all on a remote point of land high above the sea on Grenada's windward (eastern) coast. **Pros:** snorkeling and fishing equipment provided; perfect place to unwind; all rooms have a balcony and sea view. **Cons:** TV only in the lounge; rooms are simply furnished, as guests seem more attracted to the outdoors; a long drive (45 minutes) from the airport or St. George's. *Rooms from: $140 Crochu 473/444–6013 www.cabier.com 15 rooms, 2-unit villa No Meals.*

★ **Calabash Luxury Boutique Hotel**

$$$$ | **HOTEL** | The posh suites here are in 10 two-story cottages distributed in a horseshoe around 8 acres of lawn and gardens that hug the beach on Prickly Bay (L'Anse aux Épines). **Pros:** breakfast served on your verandah; excellent service; love the daily treats and complimentary massage. **Cons:** no kids under 12 from January 15–March 15; rental car suggested to get around the island; small (but lovely) beach, small pool. *Rooms from: $925 L'Anse aux Épines Rd., L'Anse aux Épines 473/444–4334 www.calabashhotel.com Closed Aug. and Sept. 30 suites Free Breakfast.*

Coyaba Beach Resort

$$$ | **RESORT** | Rooms at Coyaba, one of a handful of hotels with direct access to beautiful Grand Anse Beach, are in pavilion-style buildings that surround a 5½-acre beachfront garden of palm trees, hibiscus, frangipani, and bougainvillea. **Pros:** on-site dive center; excellent beachfront location; pool with swim-up bar. **Cons:** restaurant meals mediocre, better to eat elsewhere; "free" water sports have time limits, usually 1 hour per day; rooms are attractive but not extraordinary. *Rooms from: $420 Grand Anse 473/444–4129, 855/626–9222 in U.S. www.coyaba.com 80 rooms No Meals.*

Gem Holiday Beach Resort

$ | **HOTEL** | **FAMILY** | The one- and two-bedroom self-catering apartments are small and simply furnished at this no-frills hotel on pretty Morne Rouge Bay, but the beach it faces is one of Grenada's best. **Pros:** on-site nightclub; best beachfront value; good restaurant and popular beach bar. **Cons:** nightclub attracts a crowd on Wednesday through Saturday nights; no pool; air-conditioning only in bedrooms. *Rooms from: $126 Morne Rouge Rd., Morne Rouge 473/444–4224 www.gembeachresort.com 20 apartments No Meals.*

Kalinago Beach Resort

$ | **HOTEL** | **FAMILY** | This contemporary beachfront hotel on Morne Rouge Bay, next to Gem Holiday Resort and with the same ownership, has stylish suites—all with a patio or deck and a view of the ocean. **Pros:** dive packages; modern rooms; great beach. **Cons:** rooms need better lighting; a rental car is a good idea; walking to Grand Anse—or anywhere—requires negotiating a steep hill. *Rooms from: $200 Morne Rouge Rd., Morne Rouge 473/444–5255 www.kalinagobeachresort.com 29 rooms No Meals.*

La Sagesse Hotel

$ | **B&B/INN** | Secluded on La Sagesse Bay, this country inn boasts its own restaurant and beach bar, along with a salt-pond bird sanctuary, thick mangroves, nature trails, and ½ mile (¾ km) of palm-lined beach—one of the prettiest beaches in the entire Caribbean. **Pros:** excellent restaurant; perfect out-of-the-way escape; great place to commune with nature. **Cons:** not the best choice for families with kids; no air-conditioning (except in one room), no TV, no radios, no phones, no interruptions; far from everything. *Rooms from: $225 ✉ La Sagesse Nature Center, La Sagesse ☎ 473/444–6458 🌐 www.lasagesse.com 12 rooms No Meals.*

★ **Laluna**

$$$$ | **RESORT** | You may think you've landed on an island in the South Pacific when you reach this upscale getaway, hidden away on a pristine beach near Grenada's Quarantine Point. **Pros:** Balinese massage in Laluna Asian Spa; nifty 650 square-foot cottages face a fabulous beach; great restaurant. **Cons:** no kids under 12; most cottages are hillside, requiring a climb up and down; the long, bumpy, access road. *Rooms from: $580 ✉ Morne Rouge ☎ 473/439–0001 🌐 www.laluna.com 16 cottages and 2 villas No Meals.*

Le Phare Bleu

$$ | **APARTMENT** | **FAMILY** | The spacious, self-catering accommodations at the eco-conscious Le Phare Bleu (The Blue Lighthouse) are perfectly situated for those who arrive by boat or who like to be around boats. **Pros:** grocery store nearby; two small beaches and complimentary water sports; poolside restaurant. **Cons:** tiny beaches; rental car advised; somewhat isolated. *Rooms from: $279 ✉ Petite Calivigny Bay, Egmont ☎ 473/444–2400 🌐 www.lepharebleu.com 14 villas No Meals.*

★ **Maca Bana**

$$$$ | **HOUSE** | Clustered on a 2-acre hillside overlooking mile-long Magazine Beach, each of Maca Bana's seven private villas ("banas") has a great view—of the white sand below, out to sea, up the coastline to pretty St. George's Harbour, and beyond toward cloud-capped mountains. **Pros:** free airport shuttle; enormous decks with hot tubs and amazing views; fabulous beach. **Cons:** rental car recommended; tiny pool; steep hill down to the restaurant and beach. *Rooms from: $550 ✉ Maurice Bishop Memorial Hwy., Point Salines ☎ 473/535–1900 cell number, 473/439–5355 🌐 www.macabana.com 7 villas No Meals.*

Mount Cinnamon

$$$$ | **RESORT** | **FAMILY** | On a hillside overlooking Grand Anse Beach, Mount Cinnamon's spacious one-, two-, or three-bedroom villas have full kitchens with a breakfast bar, Bose entertainment systems, cable TV, and convenient extras that include washers and dryers. **Pros:** pool, private beach club on Grand Anse Beach, on-site dive shop; amazing views; great choice for families. **Cons:** mixed reviews on the restaurant meals; 5-minute walk to the beach; villas are on a steep hill, but golf-cart transport to restaurant or beach is available. *Rooms from: $600 ✉ Morne Rouge Rd., Grand Anse ☎ 473/439–9900, 866/720–2616 toll free 🌐 www.mountcinnamongrenada-hotel.com 34 units Free Breakfast.*

Petite Anse Hotel

$$ | **HOTEL** | Experienced travelers love this delightful oceanfront hotel at the northern tip of Grenada; it's surrounded by beautiful gardens on one side and an unobstructed view of the southern Grenadines on the other. **Pros:** surrounded by inviting, woodsy trails; romantic setting; secluded palm-studded beach. **Cons:** long drive from the airport; it's a trek down to the beach; rental car advised. *Rooms from: $297 ✉ Sauteurs ☎ 473/442–5252 🌐 www.petiteanse.com 2 rooms, 13 cottages Free Breakfast.*

Radisson Grenada Beach Resort
$$ | **RESORT** | **FAMILY** | On 20 lovely landscaped acres that stretch along 1,200 feet of Grand Anse Beach, the resort offers comfortable rooms and extensive amenities at a reasonable price. **Pros:** walking distance to Grand Anse shops and restaurants; huge hotel full of amenities, including water sports and a dive shop; beautiful beachfront location. **Cons:** inattentive staff, particularly on the beach; gets crowded when meetings are scheduled; rooms are comfortable but not extraordinary. *Rooms from: $280 Grand Anse Beach, Grand Anse 473/444–4371, 800/333–3333 in U.S. www.radisson.com 229 rooms Free Breakfast.*

Royalton Grenada Resort & Spa
$$$$ | **RESORT** | **FAMILY** | This massive beachfront resort, expanded and upgraded by new owners in 2019, is located on a huge piece of property facing Magazine Beach. **Pros:** minutes from the airport; large play area for kids; two excellent beaches—one quiet, the other for water sports. **Cons:** rather isolated location; wrist bands (not keys) for ID/room entry; quite a hike from room to beach to lobby. *Rooms from: $700 Tamarind Bay, Point Salines 473/444–3333, 809/221–2121 in U.S www.royaltonresorts.com/royalton-grenada 300 rooms All-Inclusive.*

★ **Sandals Grenada**
$$$$ | **RESORT** | Young couples, honeymooners, and second honeymooners love Sandals, and this particular Sandals—a sophisticated, attractive, well-designed enclave on pretty Pink Gin Beach—is one of the company's newer resorts. **Pros:** excellent beachfront location with lots to do; congenial atmosphere; close to the airport. **Cons:** somewhat isolated; rental car suggested to get around the island; expensive for Grenada, though it's all-inclusive and a reliable brand. *Rooms from: $550 Pink Gin Beach, near the airport, Point Salines 473/437–8000, 888/726–3257 in U.S www.sandals.com 257 rooms All-Inclusive.*

Secret Harbour Boutique Hotel & Marina
$$ | **HOTEL** | Completely renovated and reopened in December 2018 after several years of being used for long-term rentals, the self-catering units here are beautifully designed and decorated. **Pros:** quiet and peaceful; bay view from all rooms; eat in or eat out. **Cons:** not recommended for those with physical challenges; rental car advised; small beach. *Rooms from: $300 Mt. Hartman Dr., L'Anse aux Épines 473/444–4449 www.secretharbourgrenada.com 20 units Free Breakfast.*

Silversands Grenada
$$$$ | **RESORT** | The newest luxury resort in Grenada (opened December 2018), Silversands is eyepoppingly exquisite in every respect—the palatial rooms, the furnishings (included treasured artwork), the amazing amenities, the elegant service, the beach, and much, much more. **Pros:** classy rum and cigar lounge; everything here is amazing; beautiful beachfront. **Cons:** ambience is more Miami Beach than Caribbean; definitely adults-oriented, although kids are welcome; extremely expensive. *Rooms from: $1000 Grand Anse Main Rd., Grand Anse 473/533–8888, 833/594–3230 in U.S www.silversandsgrenada.com 43 suites Free Breakfast.*

★ **Spice Island Beach Resort**
$$$$ | **RESORT** | **FAMILY** | Presenting the most luxurious resort experience in Grenada: exquisite rooms fill gleaming white buildings that extend along 1,600 feet of Grand Anse Beach, and the personalized service is impeccable. **Pros:** personalized service and fabulous dining; casually elegant and luxurious; perfect beachfront location. **Cons:** generally older clientele, which is fine if you're older; all the pampering makes it very hard to go home; luxury definitely doesn't come cheap. *Rooms from: $1387 Grand*

Anse ☎ *473/444–4258, 800/501–8603 in U.S.* 🌐 *www.spiceislandbeachresort.com* *64 suites* 🍽 *All-Inclusive.*

True Blue Bay Boutique Resort

$ | RESORT | FAMILY | Families with kids especially appreciate the lawns and gardens at this family-run resort, a former indigo plantation that overlooks True Blue Bay. Colorful villas, rooms, suites, and spacious apartments slope down a seaside cliff. **Pros:** complimentary shuttle to Grand Anse Beach; pleasant environment at reasonable prices; convenient to St. George's University. **Cons:** friendly and fun but not idyllic; rental car recommended; on the water but no beach for swimming. *Rooms from: $202* ✉ *Old Mill Rd., True Blue Bay, True Blue* ☎ *473/443–8783* 🌐 *www.truebluebay.com* *70 rooms* 🍽 *Free Breakfast.*

Nightlife

BARS

Junction Bar & Grill

BARS | An immensely popular meeting place, especially for college students, Junction offers good music, cold beer, and good food Wednesday through Saturday nights. It's the place to be for open mic and karaoke nights on Wednesday, and for party time with DJs and live music on Friday and Saturday. **TIP→ Junction is next door to the West Indies Brewery Co.** ✉ *Lance aux Épines Stretch, L'Anse aux Épines* ☎ *473/457–4227* *Closed Sun. and Mon.*

West Indies Beer Company

BEER GARDENS | Enjoy craft ales, bitter, porter, or cider brewed on-site at the tiny West Indies Beer Company. Awarded Grenada's first new brewery license in 50 years, the brewery itself is in the backroom of the bar and beer garden. Drinks are served from the tap in ice-cold mason jars. A favorite hangout of university students and vacationers alike, the beer garden is open daily from 7 am to 2 am. ✉ *L'Anse aux Épines Stretch, L'Anse aux Épines* ☎ *473/232–2337* 🌐 *www.westindiesbeer.com.*

The Wild Orchid Bar

BARS | Savor the treehouse-type ambience of The Wild Orchid Bar amid prolific vegetation and the 30-foot Annandale Waterfall that is illuminated every evening at 6 pm. Tuesday or "Twosdays" features tacos and margarita specials coupled with shots and games, and "Wine Down Wednesdays" feature live band music and wine specials. "Fridays in the Forest" is the official party night featuring house DJs, cocktail specials, and beer buckets. Immerse yourself in the Saturday night signature event that offers cocktails and a special presentation from the Cuban Circus performers. ✉ *Annandale Waterfall & Forest Park, Annandale Estate* ☎ *473/421–4320.*

DANCE CLUBS

Fantazia 2001

DANCE CLUBS | On Wednesday, Friday, and Saturday nights, you can hear disco, soca, reggae, and international pop music from 10 until the wee hours. There may be a cover charge of EC$10 to EC$30, depending on the entertainment, although admission is often free.

TIP→ You'll mingle here with partygoers who are mostly local, mostly young, and mostly hip. ✉ *Gem Holiday Beach Resort, Morne Rouge Beach, Morne Rouge* ☎ *473/444–4224.*

Shopping

In Grand Anse, a short walk from nearby resorts, **Excel Plaza** has shops and services to interest locals and tourists alike, including a three-screen movie theater. **Grand Anse Shopping Centre** has a supermarket and liquor store, a clothing store, a fast-food restaurant, a pharmacy, an art gallery, several small gift shops, and a doctor's office. **Le Marquis Complex** has restaurants, shops, and tourist services. **Spiceland Mall** has a large, modern supermarket with a liquor section, clothing and shoe boutiques for men and women, housewares stores, a wine shop, gift shops, an art gallery, a food court, a bank, and a video-game arcade.

ART

Susan Mains Gallery

ART GALLERIES | Owned by noted Grenadian artist Susan Mains, this full-service gallery (formerly called Art and Soul Gallery) features original works by local, regional, and international artists—including Mains herself. She also has a second gallery, called Art House 473, located in a renovated pentacostal church in the village of Calliste—at the top of a hill between Grand Anse and the airport. The Spiceland Mall gallery is open daily (except Sunday); Art House 473 is open by appointment. ✉ *Spiceland Mall, Grand Anse* ☎ *473/439–3450* 🌐 *www.arthouse473.com.*

DUTY-FREE GOODS

Duty-free shops at the airport sell liquor at impressive discounts of up to 50%, as well as perfumes, crafts, and Grenadian syrups, jams, and hot sauces. You can shop duty-free at some shops in town, but you must show your passport and outbound ticket to get the duty-free prices.

FOOD

Grenada Chocolate Company

OTHER SPECIALTY STORE | The small Grenada Chocolate Company, founded in 1999, produces its now-famous chocolate bars in a small house-turned-factory in the village of Hermitage. Employees use antique machinery powered by solar energy to roast cocoa beans supplied by a local cooperative of growers representing more than 150 acres of organic cocoa farms. They mix and temper small batches of rich, dark chocolate that are then molded and wrapped by hand into high-quality, organic chocolate bars (cocoa powder and cocoa butter are also available). The company's chocolate bars were awarded silver medals in 2008, 2011, and 2013 by the London Academy of Chocolate. Buy the candy bars in supermarkets or gift shops for about $6 each. ✉ *Hermitage, Belmont* ☎ *473/442–0050* 🌐 *www.grenadachocolate.com* 🕘 *Closed Sat. and Sun.*

Real Value IGA Supermarket

SUPERMARKET | This large, modern supermarket carries a huge variety of familiar products, as well as local produce, meats and seafood, spices, sauces, snacks, sweets, and a broad selection of wines and spirits. ✉ *Spiceland Mall, Grand Anse* ☎ *473/439–2121* 🌐 *www.realvalueiga.com.*

GIFTS

Arawak Islands

SOUVENIRS | This workshop's spice-scented soaps, body oils, perfumes, insect repellents, balms, beeswax candles, and incense are all made by hand from 100% natural products, most of which are grown in Grenada. Visitors are welcome to watch the small group of workers sorting, blending, cutting, shaping, bottling, and labeling the products—and even cutting, sewing, hand-painting, and ironing the little cotton bags used for packaging. Arawak Islands products, including gift baskets, are sold in most gift shops. ✉ *Frequente Industrial Park, Unit 15C, Maurice Bishop Hwy., Point Salines* ☎ *473/444–3577* 🕘 *Closed Sat. and Sun.*

HANDICRAFTS

Grand Anse Craft and Spice Market

CRAFTS | Managed by the Grenada Tourism Authority, this market has 82 booths for vendors who sell art, crafts, spices, music tapes, clothing, produce, and refreshments. It's open daily from 7 to 7. ✉ *Grand Anse Beach, toward the north end, Grand Anse* ☎ *473/440–2001.*

Activities

BOATING AND SAILING

As the "Gateway to the Grenadines," Grenada attracts boatloads of seasoned sailors to its waters. Large marinas are located at Port Louis along the lagoon in St. George's, at Prickly Bay and True Blue on Grenada's southern coast, at Petite

Calivigny Bay and St. David's in southeastern Grenada, and at Tyrrel Bay in Carriacou. You can charter a yacht, with or without crew, for weeklong sailing vacations through the Grenadines. Scenic day sails along Grenada's coast cost about $60 per person for a half-day sail and snorkel and $110 per person for a full-day sail with lunch. Sunset sails cost $40 per person; $65 per person with dinner. A bareboat charter will cost $500 to $1,100 per day, while a crewed charter will cost $1,500 to $2,000 per day, depending on the boat, for up to six people.

Footloose Yacht Charters

BOATING | Operating from The Lagoon in St. George's, Footloose Yacht Charters has a catamaran spacious enough for three couples, as well as a 71-foot ocean ketch and a 47-foot Beneteau sailing yacht. All are available for day trips around Grenada or longer charters to the Grenadines. ✉ *Kirani James Blvd., St. George's* ☎ *473/405–9531* 🌐 *www.sailgrenada.com* 🎫 *$175.*

Horizon Yacht Charters

BOATING | Arrange either bareboat or crewed charters on a fleet of monohulls or catamarans available through Horizon. There's a five-night minimum for bareboat and seven-night minimum for crewed charters. ✉ *Clarke's Court Boat Yard, Grand Anse* ☎ *473/439–1000, 904/638–2373 in U.S.* 🌐 *www.horizonyachtcharters.com* 🕒 *Closed Sat. and Sun.*

DIVING AND SNORKELING

You can see hundreds of varieties of fish and some 40 species of coral at more than a dozen sites off Grenada's southwestern coast—only 15 to 20 minutes away by boat—and another couple of dozen sites around Carriacou's reefs and neighboring islets. Depths vary from 20 to 120 feet, and visibility varies from 30 to 100 feet.

For a spectacular dive, visit the ruins of *Bianca C,* a 600-foot cruise ship that caught fire in 1961, sank to 100 feet, and is now a coral-encrusted habitat for giant turtles, spotted eagle rays, barracuda, and jacks. **Boss Reef** extends 5 miles (8 km) from St. George's Harbour to Point Salines, with a depth ranging from 20 to 90 feet. **Flamingo Bay** has a wall that drops to 90 feet. It teems with fish, sponges, seahorses, sea fans, and coral. **Molinère Reef** slopes from about 20 feet below the surface to a wall that drops to 65 feet. Molinère is also the location of the **Underwater Sculpture Park,** a rather odd artificial reef consisting of more than 55 life-size figures that were sculpted by artist and scuba instructor Jason Taylor and placed on the sea bottom. An underwater bench gives divers a good view of the art gallery. Its most recent addition is a replica of *Christ of the Deep,* the statue that's on the promenade along the Carenage in St. George's. Molinère is a good dive for beginners; advanced divers can continue farther out to view the wreck of the *Buccaneer,* a 42-foot sloop.

Aquanauts Grenada

SCUBA DIVING | Every morning Aquanauts Grenada heads out on two-tank dive trips, each accommodating no more than eight divers, to both the Caribbean and Atlantic sides of Grenada. Also available: guided snorkel trips; beach snorkeling; and special activities, courses, and equipment for children. ✉ *True Blue Bay Resort, True Blue* ☎ *473/444–1126,* 🌐 *www.aquanautsgrenada.com.*

Dive Grenada

SCUBA DIVING | Specializing in wreck diving, particularly the *Bianca C,* and in family snorkeling trips, Dive Grenada heads out twice daily (at 10 am and 2 pm) to local dive sites. ✉ *Mount Cinnamon Hotel, Morne Rouge Rd., Grand Anse Beach, Morne Rouge* ☎ *473/444–1092* 🌐 *www.divegrenada.com.*

EcoDive

SCUBA DIVING | This full-service PADI dive shop offers two trips daily for both drift and wreck dives, as well as weekly trips to dive Isle de Ronde and a full range of diving courses. EcoDive employs two full-time marine biologists who run Grenada's marine-conservation and education center and conduct coral-reef monitoring and restoration efforts. ✉ *Coyaba Beach Resort, Grand Anse Beach, Grand Anse* ☎ *473/444–7777, 877/877–2709 in U.S* 🌐 *www.ecodivegrenada.com.*

ScubaTech Grenada

SCUBA DIVING | With three full-time diving instructors, ScubaTech Grenada offers the complete range of PADI and TDI programs—from "discover scuba," which allows novices to learn the basics and dive for the length of their vacation, to "dive master," the highest level a diver can achieve. Dive trips to local sites leave each morning. ✉ *Calabash Hotel, Prickly Bay Beach, L'Anse aux Épines* ☎ *473/439–4346* 🌐 *www.scubatech-grenada.com.*

FISHING

Deep-sea fishing around Grenada is excellent. The list of likely catches includes marlin, sailfish, yellowfin tuna, and dorado (also known as mahimahi or dolphin). You can arrange sportfishing trips that accommodate up to six people starting at $600 for a half day and $900 for a full day.

True Blue Sportfishing

FISHING | British-born Captain Gary Clifford, who has been fishing since the age of six, has run True Blue Sportfishing since 1998. He offers big-game charters for up to six passengers on the 31-foot *Yes Aye.* The boat has an enclosed cabin, a fighting chair, and professional tackle. Refreshments and transportation to the marina are included. ✉ *Port Louis Marina, Kirani James Blvd., St. George's* ☎ *473/407–4688* 🌐 *www.yesaye.com.*

GOLF

Grenada Golf & Country Club

GOLF | Determined golfers might want to try the 9-hole course at the Grenada Golf & Country Club. Separate tees allow for an 18-hole configuration. Located halfway between St. George's and Grand Anse, the layout features lateral hazards and challenging rough and small, elevated, sloping putting surfaces. Spread over the top of a hill, with strong winds fairly common, the course is more challenging than you might expect. Your hotel can make arrangements for you, and some offer complimentary greens fees. Popular with local businessmen, this course is convenient to most hotels and is the only public course on the island. The club has changing rooms, as well as club rental, a bar, and a restaurant. ✉ *Golf Course Hill, Belmont* ☎ *473/444–4128* *$32; $42 to play the course twice (from separate tees)* *9 holes, 2673 yards, par 34 (18 holes, 5165 yards, par 67, when played twice from different tees).*

GUIDED TOURS

Guided tours offer the historical sights of St. George's, Grand Étang National Park & Forest Reserve, spice plantations and nutmeg-processing stations, rain-forest hikes and treks to waterfalls, snorkeling trips to local islands, and day trips to Carriacou. A full-day sightseeing tour costs $70 to $90 per person, usually including lunch and admissions; a half-day tour, $45 to $60; a guided hike to Concord or Mt. Qua Qua, $60 to $100 per person, depending on the number of hikers. Grenada taxi drivers will conduct island sightseeing tours for $150 per day or $30 per hour for up to four people. Carriacou minibus drivers will take up to four people on a full-island tour for $95 (2½ hours) or a half-island tour for $55 (1½ hours).

Caribbean Horizons

GUIDED TOURS | Personalized half- or full-day tours of historic and natural island sights, market and garden tours, rain-forest hikes, and sailing excursions

Take an exciting safari-style tour of Grenada on an Adventure Jeep Tour.

to Carriacou are all available from this company. ✉ *Maurice Bishop Memorial Hwy., True Blue* ☎ *473/444–1555* 🌐 *www.caribbeanhorizons.com.*

Edwin Frank Taxi & Tours

GUIDED TOURS | **FAMILY** | After 22 years as public relations officer for the Grenada Board of Tourism—and as a radio and TV personality in his own right—Edwin Frank brings to his daily island tours a wealth of information about Grenada's history, geography, politics, culture, flora, fauna, and cuisine, along with a range of contemporary perspectives about life in and on this lovely island. ✉ *Calivigny* ☎ *473/407–5393.*

Henry's Safari Tours

ADVENTURE TOURS | Denis Henry knows Grenada like the back of his hand. He and his team lead adventurous hikes and ATV nature safaris in quad bikes, half- or full-day tours of the island and its attractions—or you can design your own half- or full-day "as you like it" tour. The personalized hiking excursions include trips through rich agricultural land and rain forest to remote waterfalls, the summit of Mt. Qua Qua, and other fascinating spots. ✉ *Woburn* ☎ *473/444–5313, 347/721–9271 in U.S* 🌐 *www.henrysafari.com* ⏲ *Closed Sun.*

Sun Hunters

ADVENTURE TOURS | Sun Hunters is a family-owned business that offers dune buggy and jeep adventure tours along the scenic coast or through mountain road trails that lead to historic and natural sites. Experience a unique land excursion with well-trained, certified tour guides in the latest model Polaris RZR Utility Recreational Vehicles. The tours include the Sunset Adventure Tour, River Lime Tour, Island Tour, Hog Island Tour, or an adventure to Annandale Waterfall and Forest. ✉ *Dr. Grooms Beach Road, Point Salines* ☎ *473/405-4068, 473/423–4868* 🌐 *www.sunhunters-grenada.com* 🎫 *Dune Buggy Tour, $130; Jeep Tour, $169* ⏲ *Sunday.* Guided Tours

Sunsation Tours

GUIDED TOURS | You can visit all the usual sights in Grenada with chartered excursions onboard a 21- or 24-seater bus with Sunsation Tours. The most popular tour experience is the chartered excursions onboard "Woody" a wooden 20-seater bus. Passengers can feel the cool breeze and warmth of the Grenadian sun as they drive by some of the most scenic locations on the island. ✉ *Ocean House, Morne Rouge Rd., Grand Anse* ☎ *473/444–1594.*

HIKING

★ Grand Étang National Park & Forest Reserve

HIKING & WALKING | Mountain trails wind through Grand Étang National Park & Forest Reserve; if you're lucky, you may spot a mona monkey or some exotic birds on your hike. There are trails for all levels—from a self-guided nature trail around Grand Étang Lake to a demanding hike through the bush and across a rocky, mountainous ridge to the peak of Mt. Qua Qua (2,373 feet) or a major all-day trek up Mt. St. Catherine (2,757 feet). Long pants and hiking shoes are recommended. Expect to pay $120 per person for a four-hour guided hike up Mt. Qua Qua; the 7-hour Mt. St. Catherine hike costs $200 per person. (Per-person prices are significantly lower for 2, 3, or more hikers.) ✉ *Grand Étang* ☎ *473/440–6160* *$2 park admission.*

Mandoo Tours

HIKING & WALKING | Mandoo will take you on a short trek to the base of a waterfall, a half-day hike to Mt. Qua Qua, or a full-day adventure to the thundering Seven Sisters Falls. ✉ *Mt. Moritz* ☎ *473/440–1428, 473/407–0024* *www.grenada-tours.com.*

Carriacou

Carriacou, the isle of reefs, is a hilly island with neither lakes nor rivers, so its drinking water comes from rainwater caught in cisterns. It gets quite arid during the dry season (January through May). Nevertheless, pigeon peas, corn, and fruit are grown here, and the climate seems to suit the mahogany trees used for furniture-making and the white cedar that's critical to the island's famed boatbuilding industry.

Hillsborough is Carriacou's main town. Just offshore, Sandy Island is a tiny spit of land with one of the nicest beaches around. Almost anyone with a boat will give you a ride from Paradise Beach or Hillsborough to Sandy Island for a small fee (about $20 round-trip). Rolling hills cut a wide swath through the middle of Carriacou, from Gun Point in the north to Tyrrel Bay in the south.

Despite its tiny size, Carriacou has several distinct cultures. Hillsborough is decidedly English; the southern region, around L'Esterre, reflects French roots; and the northern town of Windward has Scottish ties. African culture, though, is the overarching influence.

The Carriacou Maroon and String Band Music Festival, held annually in April, is an authentic experience of Maroon practices that occur when the seasons shift from harvesting to planting. Maroon is the historical name given to the enslaved Africans that ran away from the plantations to seek refuge in the island's interior. Aspects of the island's Maroon culture are maintained through music, food, singing, and other rituals. The island's unique string band music culture originated from a blend of both African and European cultures.

Sights

Belair

VIEWPOINT | For a great bird's-eye view of Hillsborough and Carriacou's entire west coast, drive to Belair in the north-central part of the island. The vantage point for the magnificent view, 700 feet above sea level, is adjacent to Princess Royal Hospital. On the way to Belair, you'll pass

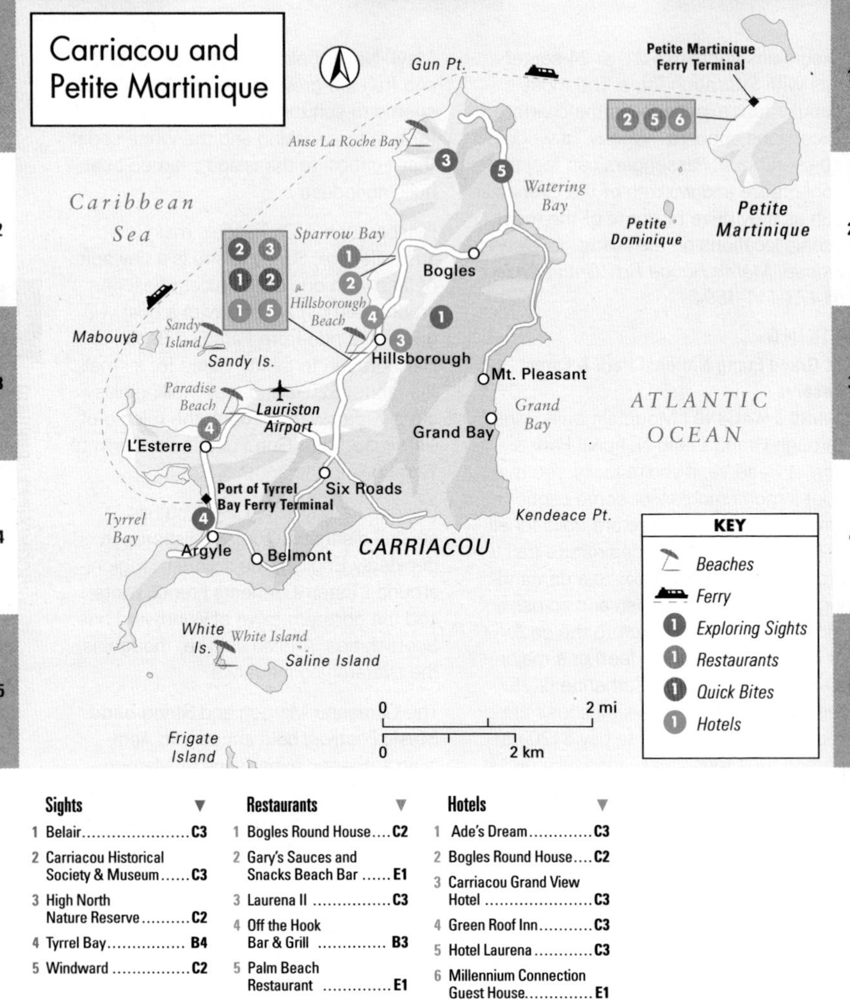

Sights

1 Belair.......................C3

2 Carriacou Historical Society & Museum......C3

3 High North Nature Reserve..........C2

4 Tyrrel Bay................ B4

5 Windward C2

Restaurants

1 Bogles Round House....C2

2 Gary's Sauces and Snacks Beach Bar E1

3 Laurena II C3

4 Off the Hook Bar & Grill B3

5 Palm Beach Restaurant E1

Quick Bites

1 Kayak Kafé & Juice Bar C3

2 Patty's Deli C3

Hotels

1 Ade's Dream.............C3

2 Bogles Round House....C2

3 Carriacou Grand View Hotel C3

4 Green Roof Inn...........C3

5 Hotel Laurena C3

6 Millennium Connection Guest House..............E1

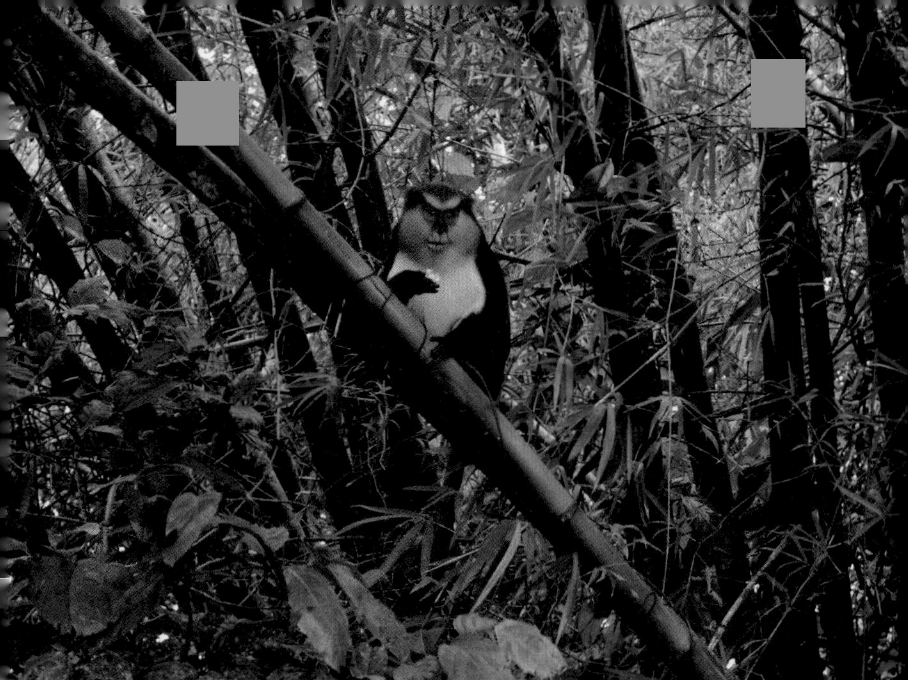
The endangered mona monkey can be found in the Grand Étang National Park & Forest Reserve.

by the photogenic ruins of an old sugar mill. ✉ *Belair.*

Carriacou Historical Society & Museum

OTHER ATTRACTION | Housed in a building that once held a cotton gin (the second-oldest cotton ginnery in the world), and just one block from the waterfront, Carriacou's little museum has exhibitions of Amerindian, European, and African artifacts, a collection of watercolors by native folk artist Canute Caliste, and a small gift shop with local items. Founded in 1976, the museum is supported by the Carriacou Historical Society. Museum manager Clemencia Alexander, one of Caliste's daughters, has worked for the museum for more than 30 years and is happy to give a guided tour. ✉ *Paterson St., Hillsborough* ☎ *473/443–8288* 🌐 *www.carriacoumuseum.com* 🎫 *$5.*

High North Nature Reserve

TRAIL | At 955 feet, the highest peak on Carriacou is in the High North Nature Reserve, a designated national park site that allows breathtaking views as far as Grenada to the south and St. Vincent and all its Grenadines to the north. Visitors can hike the trails, either alone or with a guide, and are likely to encounter iguanas, land tortoises, soldier crabs, and various birds—perhaps even a few macaws—along the way. ✉ *Windward.*

Tyrrel Bay

MARINA/PIER | Tyrrel Bay, a waterfront village in Harvey Vale, surrounds a large protected harbor in southwest Carriacou. Tyrrel Bay is the official port of entry for yachts, the location of a full-service marina, and the terminal for the ferry to Grenada and Petite Martinique. The bay is almost always full of sailboats, powerboats, and working boats—coming, going, or bobbing at their moorings. Restaurants, cafés, and grocery stores face the waterfront. ✉ *Tyrrel Bay.*

Windward

TOWN | The small town of Windward is a boatbuilding community on the northeast coast of Carriacou. At certain times of year, primarily during school vacations, you may encounter a work in progress along the roadside. ✉ *Windward.*

On Carriacou, you'll find some beaches within walking distance of (or a short ride from) Hillsborough—miles of soft, white sand that slopes gently down to the warm (average 83°F), calm sea. Carriacou's best beach experience, though, is a day spent swimming, snorkeling, and picnicking on one of the otherwise uninhabited islands just offshore.

Anse La Roche Bay

BEACH | About a 15-minute hike north from the village of Prospect, on the northwestern tip of Carriacou, this often-deserted beach has white sand, sparkling clear water, and abundant marine life for snorkelers. The beach was named for a huge rock where pelicans gather, so bird-watchers will also be thrilled. And because of its relative inaccessibility, Anse La Roche is never crowded. **Amenities:** none. **Best for:** snorkeling; solitude; swimming; walking. ✉ *Prospect.*

Hillsborough Beach

BEACH | Day-trippers (and others) can take a dip at this strip of sand adjacent to the jetty in the center of town. The beach extends for quite a distance in each direction, so there's plenty of room to swim without interference from any boat traffic. The best parts of the beach are at the northern end, along what's called the Esplanade, and at the southern end in front of Mermaid Beach Hotel and Callaloo Restaurant. Ade's Dream House is across the street from the beach, and snack bars and restaurants are nearby. **Amenities:** food and drink. **Best for:** swimming. ✉ *Hillsborough.*

★ Paradise Beach

BEACH | This long, narrow stretch of beautiful sandy beach in L'Esterre, between Hillsborough and Tyrrel Bay, has calm, clear, inviting water. Popular with local folks on weekends, it's very quiet—often deserted—at other times. The Hardwood Bar, at the southern end of the parking lot, serves local specialties for lunch. **Amenities:** food and drink; parking (no fee); showers; toilets. **Best for:** snorkeling; swimming; walking. ✉ *L'Esterre.*

★ Sandy Island

BEACH | This is a truly deserted sandbar off Paradise Beach—just a few young palm trees on a spit of pure white, powdery soft sand—except for those who come by boat to snorkel and swim in the sparkling clear water. A 5-square-mile (3-square-km) Marine Protected Area surrounds the island. Arrange transportation to the island (about $20 round-trip) with a local boat owner at Paradise Beach, Hillsborough, or Tyrrel Bay; be sure to arrange the pickup time! Wear your bathing suit and bring along snorkeling gear and everything else you'll need (sunscreen, towel, hat, shirt, food and water, etc.), making sure to leave only your footprints when you leave. **Amenities:** none. **Best for:** snorkeling; solitude; swimming. ✉ *L'Esterre Bay, off Paradise Beach.*

White Island

BEACH | On this deserted island off Carriacou's southeastern coast, your choice of beautiful white sandy beaches and calm Caribbean waters awaits you. The island is surrounded by reefs and has beaches on all sides except for the eastern (Atlantic Ocean) side, which has a high cliff. Arrange transportation from Tyrrel Bay for about $30 round-trip, and be sure to bring everything you may need. **Amenities:** none. **Best for:** snorkeling; solitude; swimming; walking. ✉ *Cassada Bay, off the southwestern coast.*

Restaurants

Bogles Round House

$$ | CONTEMPORARY | Surrounded by gardens and a handful of cottages for rent, this small round structure was built with a concrete-filled tree trunk as its central support and a long bench that was once the jawbone of a whale. The food is less peculiar—Chef Roxanne Rock is celebrated for her elegant style of Caribbean cuisine and her three-course menu, which changes according to market availability, may include starters such as fish cakes and cream of callaloo soup and entrées such as rack of lamb au jus and grilled lobster with garlic butter. **Known for:** romantic atmosphere but also kid-friendly; perfectly cooked food; peaceful environment. *Average main: $20 Sparrow Bay, Bogles 473/443–7841 www.boglesroundhouse.com Closed Sun.*

Laurena II

$$ | CARIBBEAN | FAMILY | As you approach this popular restaurant and bar on Main Street, you're greeted by the unmistakable scent of authentic Jamaican jerk chicken and pork. That's the specialty (and personal favorite) of Chef Purgeon Reece, who hails from Jamaica, although his menu also includes other local and regional dishes such as curried goat, baked chicken, or grilled fish with rice and peas. **Known for:** gigantic servings and low prices; takeout options; Jamaican specialties. *Average main: $16 Hotel Laurena, Main St., Hillsborough 473/443–8333, 473/443–8334 hotel-laurena.com Closed Sun.*

Off the Hook Bar & Grill

$$ | CARIBBEAN | FAMILY | Settle into a seat at a colorful picnic table, set right in the sand, and gaze out to sea at the picture-perfect view of Sandy Island. Your mouth will water from the scent of lobster, chicken, fish, and ribs being barbecued on the grill. **Known for:** will arrange water taxi to/from Sandy Island; great beachside barbecue with bonfire; live music Wednesday nights. *Average main: $18 L'Esterre Bay, southern end of Paradise Beach, L'Esterre 473/533–5242.*

Coffee and Quick Bites

Kayak Kafé & Juice Bar

$ | CARIBBEAN | A tiny spot just steps from the jetty, the "dining room" is simply the back porch of a Main Street building with a handful of tables overlooking Hillsborough Bay. Enjoy freshly prepared local food—callaloo soup, lambi (conch) fritters, cracked lambi, fish cakes, fresh fish, fish chowder—or staples such as a good burger, fish-and-chips, delicious sandwiches, tasty wraps, and freshly prepared salads. **Known for:** vegetarian-friendly; diverse menu; fresh local juices. *Average main: $12 Main St., Hillsborough 473/443–6523, 473/406–2151 No credit cards Closed Sun.*

Patty's Deli

$$ | SANDWICHES | At this delicatessen, a short walk from the jetty in "downtown" Hillsborough, you can get takeout sandwiches made to order with freshly sliced meats (ham, smoked turkey, herbed chicken, etc.) and cheeses. Baguettes, croissants, and pastries are baked on-site and fresh daily. **Known for:** perfect picnic lunch provider or provisions for your boat; gourmet food shop and deli; international wine selection. *Average main: $12 Main St., Hillsborough 473/443–6258 www.pattysdeli.com Closed Sun.*

Hotels

Ade's Dream

$ | HOTEL | By the jetty in Hillsborough, Ade's (pronounced add- *ees*) is a convenient—and popular—place to rest your weary head after a day snorkeling at Sandy Island or scuba diving at some of Carriacou's best dive spots. **Pros:** on-site supermarket; right in town, convenient for an overnight on Carriacou; very inexpensive. **Cons:** small rooms, tiny bathrooms; noise may be an issue in street-facing rooms; very basic but very cheap. *Rooms from: $32 Main St., Hillsborough 473/443–7317 www.adesdream.com 23 rooms No Meals.*

Bogles Round House

$ | B&B/INN | Three quaint cottages are in a garden setting five minutes north of Hillsborough and about 60 feet from Sparrow Bay, where guests enjoy swimming, snorkeling, and walks on the beach. **Pros:**

peaceful ambience; the price is right; excellent on-site restaurant. **Cons:** no TV; beach is small and surf can be rough; one step up from camping out. *Rooms from: $60* *Sparrow Bay, Bogles* *473/443–7841* *www.boglesroundhouse.com* *3 cottages* *Free Breakfast.*

Carriacou Grand View Hotel

$ | **HOTEL** | **FAMILY** | Island visitors and local business people alike relish the lovely view, particularly at sunset, from this perch high above Hillsborough Harbour. **Pros:** one child under 12 stays free with parents; truly a grand view, even from the swimming pool; popular restaurant with late-night piano bar. **Cons:** some rooms have no air-conditioning; it's a hot walk uphill from town and the beach; accommodations are basic. *Rooms from: $70* *Belair Rd., Beausejour* *473/443–6348* *www.carriacougrandview.com* *14 rooms* *No Meals.*

Green Roof Inn

$ | **B&B/INN** | You're guaranteed beautiful views of Hillsborough Bay and the offshore cays at this small inn, which is the perfect location for a scuba-diving, snorkeling, or beachcombing vacation. **Pros:** close to town; private jetty for access to boats and water taxis; massage parlor and yoga pavilion. **Cons:** showers only; no air-conditioning, and it can get hot; rooms are small and very basic. *Rooms from: $115* *Hillsborough Bay, Hillsborough* *473/443–6399* *www.greenroofinn.com* *5 rooms, 2 cottages* *Free Breakfast.*

Hotel Laurena

$ | **HOTEL** | **FAMILY** | Within walking distance of downtown Hillsborough, the ferry jetty, shops, and some beaches, Hotel Laurena has large rooms that can accommodate two to four people. **Pros:** some rooms are wheelchair accessible; convenient to town, beach, and restaurants; good dining at associated Laurena II Jerk Center. **Cons:** walk to beach; no pool; not particularly attractive in-town views from rooms. *Rooms from: $55* *Middle St., Hillsborough* *473/443–8334, 877/755–4386 in U.S.* *www.hotellaurena.com* *28 rooms* *No Meals.*

Activities

DIVING AND SNORKELING

There's an active underwater volcano known as **Kick-em Jenny,** with plentiful coral and marine life in the vicinity and, usually, visibility up to 100 feet, though you can't dive down the 500 feet required to reach the actual volcano. **Sandy Island,** in Hillsborough Bay, is especially good for night diving and has fish that feed off its extensive reefs 70 feet below. For experienced divers, **Twin Sisters of Isle de Rhonde** is one of the most spectacular dives in the Grenadines, with walls and drop-offs of up to 185 feet and an underwater cave.

PADI-certified dive operators offer scuba and snorkeling trips to reefs and wrecks, including night dives and special excursions to the *Bianca C.* They also offer resort courses for beginning divers and certification instruction for more experienced divers. It costs about $65 to $85 for a one-tank dive, $110 to $130 for a two-tank dive, and $70 to $85 for night dives. Discounted five- and 10-dive packages are usually offered. Resort courses cost about $150, and open-water certification runs $400 to $550.

Most dive operators will take snorkelers along on dive trips or offer special snorkeling adventures. The best snorkeling in Grenada is at Molinère Point, north of St. George's; in Carriacou, magnificent Sandy Island is just a few hundred yards offshore. Snorkeling trips cost about $30 to accompany a dive trip, or $55 to $80 per person for a full snorkeling excursion to the Underwater Sculpture Park.

Deefer Diving Carriacou

SCUBA DIVING | Deefer Diving has two PADI dive masters and three PADI instructors that provide a full range of diving instruction on their 30-foot, purpose-built catamaran, which accommodates up to 11 divers. The itinerary is flexible, so you can dive when, where, and for as long as you like. There are two guided single-tank dives daily, as well as individually scheduled excursions. ✉ *Main St., Hillsborough* ☎ *473/443–7882* 🌐 *www.deeferdiving.com* 💵 *$120* ⏲ *Closed Sun.*

Dive Carriacou

SCUBA DIVING | Dive Carriacou will take you to some of the area's 30 dive sites and wrecks, on exciting drift dives and lionfish hunts, photo dives, and more. The dive schedule is flexible, with up to five dives per day. PADI courses are available from "Try Diving" to "Advanced." ✉ *Main St., Harvey Vale, Tyrrel Bay* ☎ *473/443–6906* 🌐 *www.divecarriacou.com* 💵 *$110* ⏲ *Sunday.*

GUIDED TOURS

Carriacou minibus drivers will take up to four people on a full-island tour for $95 (2½ hours) or a half-island tour for $50 (1½ hours). A fee of $18 is charged per person to a party of four for the full-island tour and $9 per person added to the half-island tour. Half-island tours include either a northern or southern tour of the island.

Isle of Reefs Tours

GUIDED TOURS | A soft adventure tour operator, Isle of Reefs specializes in guided island tours, hiking treks, turtle-watching (March-August), even a carbon offset tour through the bird sanctuary and mangrove forest (early morning or evening tour). ✉ *Argyle* ☎ *473/404–0415* 🌐 *www.carriacoutours.com.*

Petite Martinique

Ten minutes north of Carriacou by boat or ferry lies the tiny residential island of Petite Martinique. There's a guesthouse or two for tourists interested in peace and quiet, but no major hotels or resorts. Meander along the beachfront and watch boatbuilders at work. If by chance there's a boat launching, sailboat race, traditional wedding, holiday, or festival taking place while you're there, you're in for a treat. The music is infectious, the food bountiful, and the spirit lively.

The island's most popular cultural activity, the Petite Martinique Whitsuntide Regatta Festival, takes place annually from the end of May into June. Rooted in the boat-building culture that is native to Petite Martinique, the festival focuses on sea activities that are fun-filled and action-packed.

Like Carriacou, Saraca is also practiced on the island of Petite Martinique. Saraca is a form of funerary rite indigenous to the Grenadine islands which includes food for the deceased and celebrants, music, special rituals, and folk stories. Saraca food is a unique method of preparing meals for special occasions such as weddings, funerals, boat launching, or a tombstone fete. The dishes include rolled rice, rolled *koo-koo* (made from cornmeal), stewed peas, and a variety of meat.

GETTING HERE AND AROUND

The high-speed ferry Osprey Shuttle makes two round-trip voyages daily from Grenada to Carriacou and on to Petite Martinique. The 30-minute trip from Carriacou to Petite Martinique costs $8 each way.

M.V Charmaine offers daily ferry services between Windward, Carriacou and Petite Martinique. Trips on Monday and Wednesday depart from Petite Martinique at 3 pm and 5 pm while trips on Wednesday and Friday depart at 9 am, 3 pm, and 5 pm. The 15-20-minute trip is $8 one way.

On Petite Martinique, Super Best Taxi offers jeep rentals for $50 (EC $130) per day. Half-day rentals are also offered at a fee of $20 (EC $50). They also offer complimentary pick-up and drop-off to and from the dock in Petite Martinique.

M.V Charmaine. ✉ *Windward Jetty* ☎ *473/406–8537.* **Super Best Taxi.** ✉ *Bellevue* ☎ *473/443–9021, 473/423–7624 mobile.*

Beaches

There are a few beaches on this tiny island including the serene Mang Beach, whose crystal clear waters, white sand, and gentle waves are the perfect setting for long walks, picnicking and sunbathing. A barrier reef protects the shoreline making it ideal for snorkeling and swimming.

Located on the island's scenic southwestern coast, the large stones found at Grand-Ravin Pebble Beach were once used by fishermen and sailors throughout the Grenadines to improve the stability of their boats.

Restaurants

Gary's Sauces and Snacks Beach Bar
$$ | **SEAFOOD** | Just a two-minute walk from the picturesque Mang Beach, this is the go-to spot on the island for quick bites, lunch, and dinner. The owner of the beach bar, Gary Blair, is passionate about cooking and will make dishes that are both on and off the menu for his guests like cracked lambi (conch), grilled lobster, and fish coupled with your choice of sides. **Known for:** burgers and wings; sunset views; grilled lobster. *Average main: $15 Mang Beach 2 minutes' walk from Mang Beach 473/414–3915 No credit cards.*

Palm Beach Restaurant
$$ | **SEAFOOD** | This family-owned business provides a panoramic view of the Grenadine islands from its beach-front property. Menu favorites include the lobster bisque, coconut shrimp, and the cracked conch, but chicken, fish, and pork dishes are also prepared using local herbs and spices. **Known for:** relaxed atmosphere; beachfront location; lobster, conch, and grilled fish. *Average main: $16 Sanchez 473/443–9103 Closed Sun.*

Hotels

Millennium Connection Guest House
$ | **B&B/INN** | Located in Sanchez, this guest house offers visitors a home-away-from-home experience that is complemented by the simplistic, authentic island lifestyle. **Pros:** located on the beach; five minutes' walk from the main jetty; cozy and homely feel. **Cons:** only 4 bedrooms and 1 apartment are available for occupancy. *Rooms from: $50 Sanchez Five minutes' walk from the dock at Petite Martinique 473/443–9243, 473/533–5847 mobile and WhatsApp 4 rooms, 1 apartment No Meals.*

Activities

Bamboo Adventure
GUIDED TOURS | With over ten years of experience in land and sea excursions, this tour company makes unique arrangements for island visitors like guided walking and hiking nature tours. Round-trips from Carriacou are available. Explore the Tobago Cays, Mayreau, Mopion, Saline Island, Chatham Bay, Happy Island and other destinations in a one-of-a-kind sea excursion. *Madam Pierre 473/535–0893 From $30.*

Lose Yourself Tours
GUIDED TOURS | As the name suggests, this company offers immersive experiences as well as land and sea excursions. Saraca In We Pot is a curated culinary experience that has visitors cooking traditional Saraca food. The land and sea tours include guided island tours, nature hikes to the Piton, tours of the Grenadine islands, fishing tours, and the Lose Yourself Retreat for couples. *Sanchez 473/443–9243, 473/533–5847 mobile and WhatsApp From $90.*

Chapter 13

GUADELOUPE

Updated by
Jane Zarem

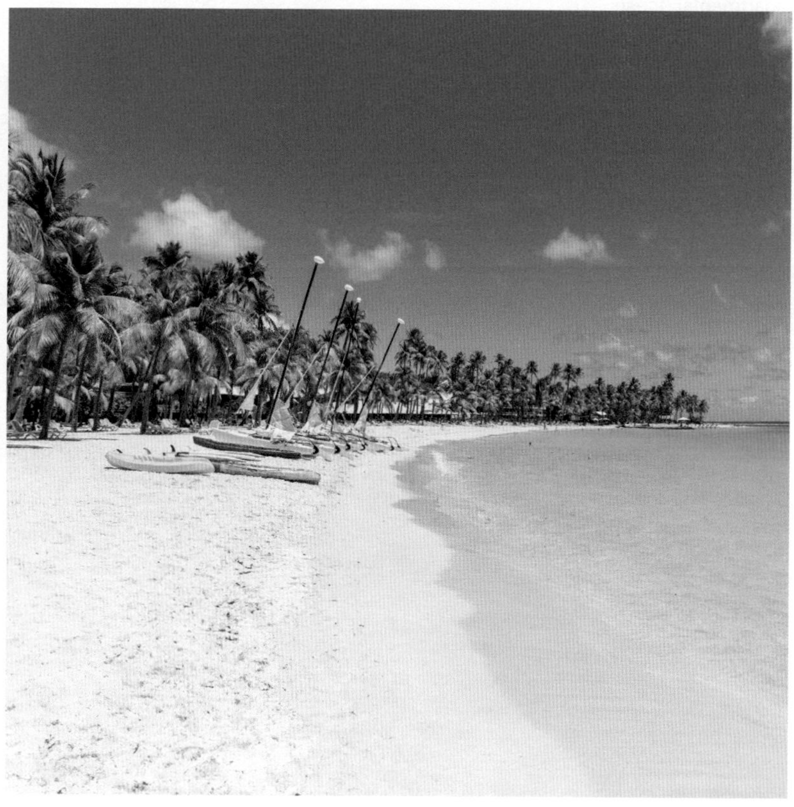

Sights ★★★★☆ Restaurants ★★★☆☆ Hotels ★★☆☆☆ Shopping ★☆☆☆☆ Nightlife ★★☆☆☆

WELCOME TO GUADELOUPE

TOP REASONS TO GO

★ **Creole Flavors:** Guadeloupe's restaurants and hotel dining rooms highlight the island's fine creole cuisine.

★ **Small Inns:** Also called *relais* and *gîtes* (apartments), these intimate accommodations give you a genuine island experience.

★ **Adventure Sports:** Parc National has plenty of activities to keep the adrenaline pumping.

★ **Hiking:** Trek through lush rain forest, past waterfalls and hot springs, and to the peak of a volcano in Basse-Terre.

★ **La Désirade:** Remote and accessible by ferry, "The Forgotten" island provides an escape-from-it-all experience.

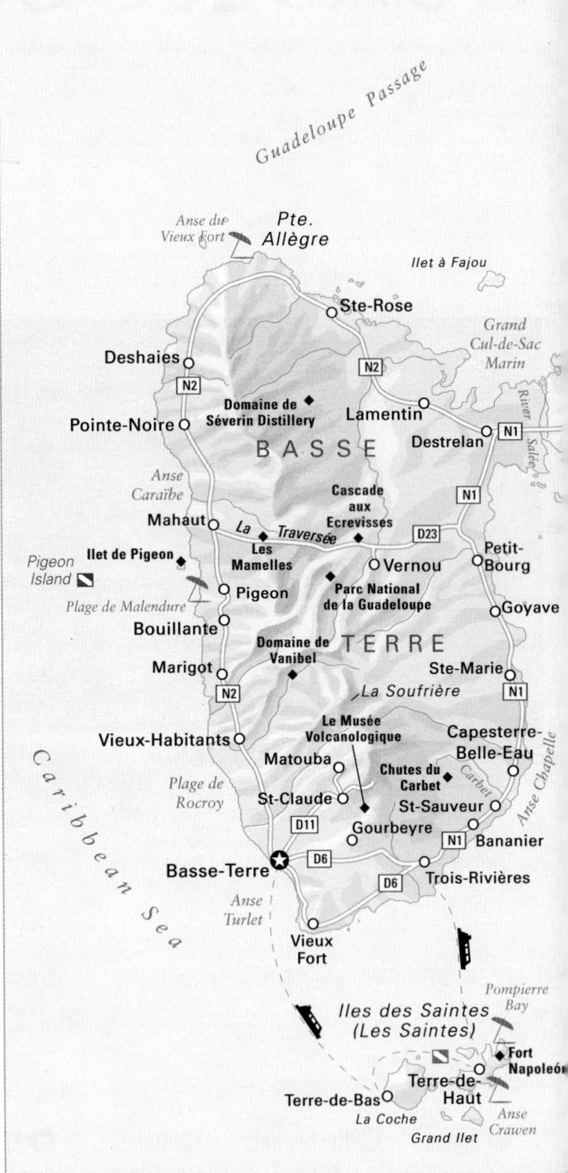

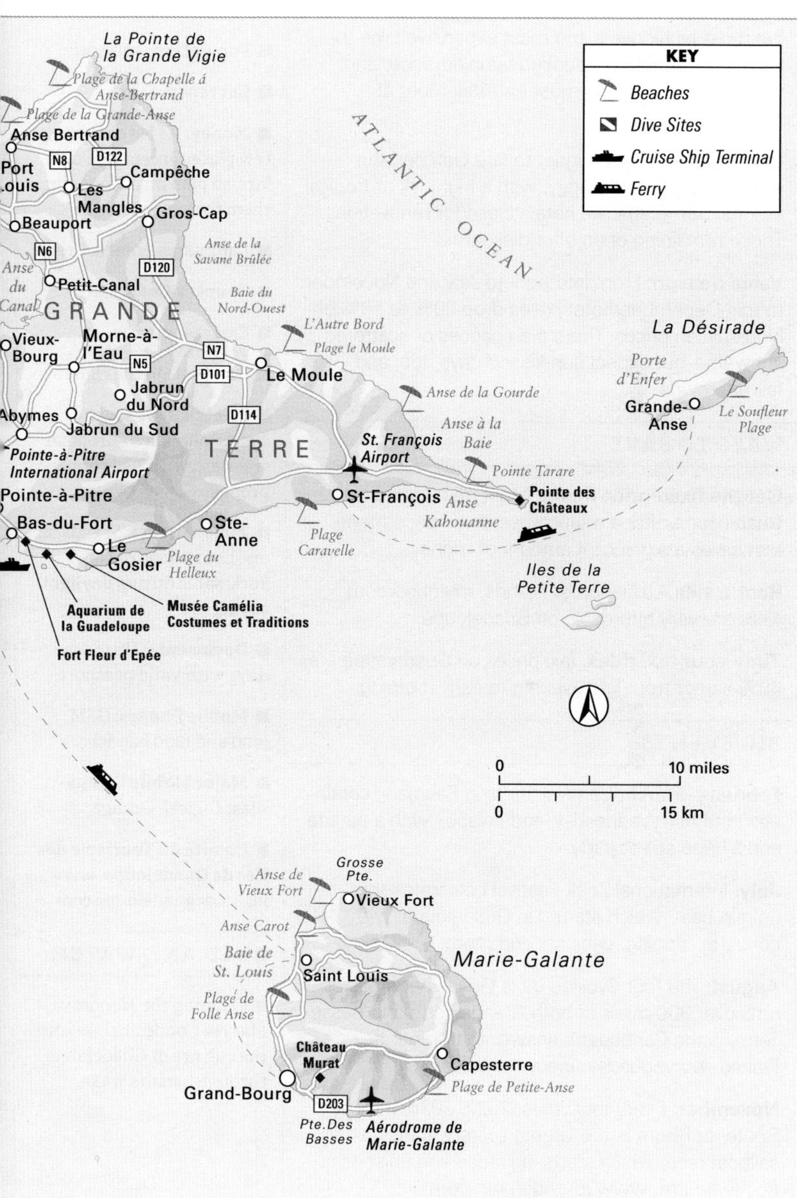
KEY
Beaches
Dive Sites
Cruise Ship Terminal
Ferry
ATLANTIC OCEAN
La Pointe de la Grande Vigie
Plage de la Chapelle á Anse-Bertrand
Plage de la Grande-Anse
Anse Bertrand
Port Louis
N8
D122
Campêche
Les Mangles
Gros-Cap
Beauport
N6
D120
Anse de la Savane Brûlée
Anse du Canal
Petit-Canal
Baie du Nord-Ouest
GRANDE TERRE
L'Autre Bord
Plage le Moule
Vieux-Bourg
Morne-à-l'Eau
N7
N5
D101
Le Moule
Jabrun du Nord
Anse de la Gourde
Abymes
Jabrun du Sud
D114
Anse à la Baie
Pointe-à-Pitre International Airport
St. François Airport
Pointe Tarare
Pointe-à-Pitre
St-François
Anse Kahouanne
Pointe des Châteaux
Bas-du-Fort
Ste-Anne
Le Gosier
Plage du Helleux
Plage Caravelle
Aquarium de la Guadeloupe
Musée Camélia Costumes et Traditions
Fort Fleur d'Epée
La Désirade
Porte d'Enfer
Grande-Anse
Le Soufleur Plage
Iles de la Petite Terre
0
10 miles
0
15 km
Grosse Pte.
Anse de Vieux Fort
Vieux Fort
Anse Carot
Baie de St. Louis
Saint Louis
Marie-Galante
Plage de Folle Anse
Château Murat
Capesterre
Plage de Petite-Anse
Grand-Bourg
D203
Pte.Des Basses
Aérodrome de Marie-Galante

ISLAND SNAPSHOT

WHEN TO GO

High Season: Mid-December through mid-April is the most fashionable and most expensive time to visit. Good hotels are booked far in advance, and you're guaranteed the most entertainment at resorts.

Low Season: From August to late October, the weather is hot and muggy, with a high risk of tropical storms. Some upscale hotels close for renovations. Those remaining open offer discounts.

Value Season: From late April to July and November to mid-December, hotel prices drop 20% to 50% off high-season prices. There are chances of scattered showers—but expect sun-kissed days, too, and fewer crowds.

WAYS TO SAVE

Get the fixed-price menu. Most restaurants on Guadeloupe offer a multicourse, fixed-price menu that saves a significant amount of money.

Rent a villa. Unlike other islands, multibedroom villas are very affordable on Guadeloupe.

Time your taxi rides. Taxi prices on Guadeloupe are 40% higher from late evening to early morning.

BIG EVENTS

February–March: Carnival starts in February, continues until Ash Wednesday, and finishes with a parade and a huge street party.

July: International Zouk Festival celebrates this unique beat, which started in Guadeloupe, with concerts, singing, dancing, and more.

August: The Tour Cycliste de la Guadeloupe, which runs over 800 miles of both Grande-Terre and Basse-Terre, is the Caribbean's answer to the Tour de France. www.guadeloupecyclisme.com

November: Every four years (2022, 2026, etc.) Le Route du Rhum is the largest solitary, transatlantic sailboat race, which starts in France and finishes in Pointe-à-Pitre. www.routedurhum.com

AT A GLANCE

- **Capital:** Basse-Terre
- **Population:** 400,000
- **Currency:** Euro
- **Money:** ATMs common; few places accept U.S. dollars, so plan on exchanging them for euros
- **Language:** French, Creole
- **Country Code:** 590
- **Emergencies:** 17
- **Driving:** On the right
- **Electricity:** 230v/50 cycles; plugs are European standard with two round prongs
- **Time:** Atlantic Standard, one hour ahead of New York; same during daylight saving
- **Documents:** Up to 90 days with valid passport
- **Mobile Phones:** GSM (900 and 1800 bands)
- **Major Mobile Companies:** Digicel, Orange
- **Comité du Tourisme des îles de Guadeloupe:** www.lesilesdeguadeloupe.com

READ AND WATCH

- *Crossing the Mangrove*, Maryse Condé. Insight into the culture of Guadeloupe through a man's wake.

Sail the waters around the Isles of Guadeloupe, and you'll observe nuances in the ocean's color palette as you glide through the gin-clear sea. Things look better from the bow of a sailboat, whether you're viewing the storybook islands of Les Saintes or towns that are less postcard pretty. The Caribbean coastline is dramatic, with white and golden beaches, rocky promontories, and rugged cliffs that span the horizon.

Although Guadeloupe is thought of as one island, it is an archipelago—and each island has its own personality. "The mainland" consists of the nation's two largest islands, Basse-Terre and Grande-Terre, which resemble a butterfly. The outer islands—Îles des Saintes (Les Saintes), Marie-Galante, and La Désirade—are acknowledged as wonderfully unique, unspoiled travel destinations. See which one is your place in the sun. *Vive les vacances!*

It's no wonder that, in 1493, Christopher Columbus welcomed the sight of this emerald paradise, where fresh, sweet water flows in cascades. And it's understandable why France annexed it in 1674 and why the British schemed to wrench it away. In 1749, Guadeloupe mirrored what was happening in the motherland; it, too, was an island divided between royalists and revolutionaries.

The resident British sided with the royalists, so Victor Hugues was sent to banish the Brits. While here, he sent to the guillotine more than 300 planters who were loyal to the royals and freed the slaves, thus all but destroying the plantocracy. An old saying of the French Caribbean refers to *les grands seigneurs de la Martinique et les bonnes gens de la Guadeloupe* (the lords of Martinique and the bourgeoisie of Guadeloupe), and that still rings true. You'll find more aristocratic descendants of the original French planters on Martinique (known as *békés*) and also more "elite" people both living and vacationing there. That historic mass beheading is one of the prime reasons. Napoléon—who ultimately ousted the royals—also ousted Hugues and reestablished slavery. It wasn't until 1848 that an Alsatian, Victor Schoelcher, abolished slavery for good.

Guadeloupe became one of France's *départements d'outremer* in 1946, meaning that it became a dependent of France. The island was designated a region in 1983, making it an actual part of France, albeit a distant part. This brought many benefits to the islanders, from their fine highway system to the French social services and educational system, as well as a high standard of living. Certain tensions still exist, though the anti-colonial resentment harbored by the older generations is dying out. Guadeloupe's young people realize the importance of tourism to the island's future, and you'll find them welcoming, smiling, and practicing the English and tourism skills that they learn in school. Some *Français* is indispensable, though you may receive a bewildering response in Creole.

Guadeloupe reflects quite a bit of France, but the culture of this tropical paradise is decidedly more Afro-influenced. Savor the earthy pleasures here, exemplified by the wonderful potpourri of spices whose heady aromas flood the outdoor markets.

Planning

Getting Here and Around

AIR

Nonstop service is available on JetBlue from New York or Miami and on American Airlines from Miami. Delta codeshares with Air France for flights between Guadeloupe and New York via Miami. Air Antilles and Air Caraïbes offer regional service between Guadeloupe and islands throughout the Caribbean.

Airports and Transfers: Taxi fare to Pointe-à-Pitre is about €35, to Gosier resorts about €40, to Ste-Anne as much as €60, and to St-François nearly €85. Taxis meet all flights at the airport.

AIRLINES Air Antilles Express. ✉ *Les Abymes* ☎ *0590/38–43–22* 🌐 *www.airantilles.com.* **Air Caraïbes.** ☎ *0820/83–58–35* 🌐 *www.aircaraibes.com.* **American Airlines.** ☎ *800/433–7300 in U.S., 0821/98–00–08 in Guadeloupe* 🌐 *www.aa.com.* **Delta.** ☎ *800/221–1212* 🌐 *www.delta.com.* **JetBlue.** ☎ *800/538–2583* 🌐 *www.jetblue.com.*

AIRPORTS Pointe-à-Pitre International Airport (PTP). ✉ *Morne Mamiel, Les Abymes* ☎ *0590/21–14–72* 🌐 *www.guadeloupe.airport.com.*

CAR

If you're based in Gosier or at a large resort, you'll probably need a car only for a day or two of sightseeing. That may be enough, since roundabouts, mountain roads, and fast, aggressive drivers are stressful. Your valid driver's license will suffice for up to 20 days.

Guadeloupeans drive fast and are often impatient—and they tailgate. Driving around Grande-Terre is relatively easy, for there is a well-maintained system of highways. Basse-Terre requires more skill to navigate the hairpin bends on the mountain roads and along the eastern shore; at night, those roads are unlighted and treacherous. Roundabouts (*rond-pointes*) are everywhere. Use your turn signal and proceed cautiously. If you're lost, don't ask people standing on the side of the road; they're usually waiting for a lift and may jump in your car. Instead, look for a gas station. *Je suis perdu!* (I am lost!) is a good phrase to know.

Car Rentals. You can get a rental car from either the airport or your hotel. Count on spending €40 to €65 a day for a small car with standard shift; automatics are more expensive and often must be reserved in advance. Note that some companies, including Europcar, charge a €25 drop-off fee at the airport, even if you pick up the car there. At the end of your stay, plan a full hour to drop off your car at the airport. To avoid getting lost en route, conscientiously follow every sign that has a picture of a plane. You'll leave the car at a car-rental box near the airport, where you catch a shuttle to bring you and your luggage back to the airport. An alternative is to return the car in Gosier and put that €25 drop-off fee that you saved toward a €35 stress-free taxi ride. Also, be sure to return your vehicle with the same amount of gas, or you'll be charged an exorbitant fill-up rate.

CAR RENTALS Avis. ☎ *0590/82-02-71, 800/633–3469 in U.S.* 🌐 *www.avis.com.* **Jumbo Car.** ☎ *0590/91–55–66* 🌐 *www.jumbocar-guadeloupe.com.* **Sixt.** ☎ *0590/91-91-54* 🌐 *www.sixt.com.*

FERRY

Ferry schedules and fares often change, so phone ahead to confirm. You normally travel to the outlying islands in the morning, returning in the afternoon. Comatrile is based in St-François, L'Éxpress des Îles in Point-à-Pitre, and CTM Deher in Trois-Rivières; both Comatrile and L'Éxpress des Isles also operate ferries between Terre-de-Haut and Marie-Galante.

International service is offered by Jeans for Freedom and L'Éxpress des Isles, connecting Pointe-à-Pitre in Guadeloupe with Martinique, Saint Lucia, and Dominica.

CONTACTS Comatrile. ✉ *Gare St-François, St-François* ☎ *0590/91–02–45* 🌐 *comatrile.com.* **Jeans for Freedom.** ✉ *Gare Maritime de Bergevin, Pointe-à-Pitre* ☎ *0590/68–53–09* 🌐 *www.jeansforfreedom.com.* **L'Éxpress des Îles.** ✉ *Gare Maritime de Bergevin, Pointe-à-Pitre* ☎ *0590/91–95–20* 🌐 *www.express-des-iles.fr.*

TAXI

Taxis are metered and fairly pricey. Fares jump by 40% between 7 pm and 7 am and on Sunday and holidays.

CONTACTS CDLG9 Taxi. ✉ *Les Abymes* ☎ *0590/20–74–74.* **Ruddy Taxi.** ✉ *St-François* ☎ *0690/47–47–74.* **Taxi Jean Luc Renault.** ✉ *St-François* ☎ *0590/21–44–99.*

Beaches

Guadeloupe is an archipelago of five magnificent islands surrounded by both the Caribbean and the Atlantic. Its beaches run the spectrum from white to black—long, idyllic stretches of unspoiled beach shaded by coconut palms, with soft, warm sand. Hotel beaches are generally narrow, although well maintained. Some hotels allow nonguests who patronize their restaurants to use their beach facilities. The popular public beaches tend to be cluttered with campers-turned-cafés and cars parked in impromptu lots on the sand. Sunday is the big day, but these same (free) beaches are often quiet during the week.

On the southern coast of Grande-Terre, from Ste-Anne to Pointe des Châteaux, you can find stretches of soft white sand and some sparsely visited areas. The Atlantic waters on the northeast coast are too rough for swimming. Along the western shore of Basse-Terre signposts indicate small beaches. The sand starts turning gray in Malendure and becomes volcanic black farther south. There's only one official nude beach, Pointe Tarare, but topless bathing is common.

Health and Safety

Dengue, chikungunya, and zika have all been reported throughout the Caribbean. We recommend that you protect yourself from these mosquito-borne illnesses by keeping your skin covered and/or wearing mosquito repellent. The mosquitoes that transmit these viruses are as active by day as they are by night.

Hotels and Resorts

Grande-Terre has the big resort hotels that are concentrated primarily in four or five communities on the south coast, whereas wilder Basse-Terre has more locally owned hotels. On the smaller, quieter islands of Îles des Saintes, Marie-Galante, and La Désirade, tourism is only a part of the economy and development is light; any of them will give you a sense of what the Caribbean used to be.

Often, hotel rates include a generous buffet breakfast; ask whether this is included in your quoted rate. (It usually is.) Many smaller properties do not accept American Express. As dictated by French law, all public spaces in hotels are nonsmoking; hotel rooms are considered private, though, and properties can choose to offer smoking rooms.

Relais and Gîtes: These small inns offer a more personal, more authentic Caribbean experience.

Resorts: You can certainly opt for a big, splashy resort with all the amenities. Many of the island's large chain hotels cater to French group tours and are relatively barebones, though an increasing number of them are being renovated to the degree that they will appeal more to Americans, as well.

Villas: Private villas are another option—particularly for families—but the language barrier is often a deterrent for Americans. Best to go through one of the rental agencies recommended here.

Hotel reviews have been shortened. For full information, visit Fodors.com.

What It Costs in Euros

	$	$$	$$$	$$$$
RESTAURANTS	under €12	€12–€20	€21–€30	over €30
HOTELS	under €275	€275–€375	€376–€475	over €475

PRIVATE VILLAS AND RENTALS Prestige Villa Rental. ✉ *Baie-Mahault* ☎ *917/267–7491 in U.S.* 🌐 *www.prestigevillarental.com.*

Nightlife

Guadeloupeans maintain that the beguine began here; and, for sure, the beguine and mazurkas were heavily influenced by the European quadrille and orchestrated melodies. Their merging is the origin of West Indian music, which gave birth to zouk (music with an African-influenced Caribbean rhythm) at the beginning of the 1980s. Still the rage here, zouk has spread not only to France but to other European countries. Many resorts have dinner dancing or offer regularly scheduled entertainment by steel bands and folkloric groups.

Both of the island's casinos are on Grande-Terre and have American-style roulette, blackjack, and stud poker. The legal age for gambling is 21, and French law dictates that everyone show a passport or a local driver's license. Jacket and tie aren't required, but "proper attire" means no shorts, T-shirts, jeans, flip-flops, or sneakers.

Restaurants

Creole cooking is the result of a fusion of influences: African, European, Indian, and Caribbean. It's colorful, spicy, and made up primarily of local seafood and vegetables (including squashlike christophenes), root vegetables, and plantains—and always with a healthy dose of pepper sauce. Favorite appetizers include *accras* (salted codfish fritters), *boudin* (highly seasoned blood sausage), and *crabes farcis* (stuffed land crabs). *Langouste* (lobster), *lambi* (conch), *chatrou* (octopus), and *ouassous* (crayfish) are considered delicacies. *Souchy* (Tahitian-style ceviche), raw fish that is "cooked" when marinated in lime juice or similar marinades, is best at seafront restaurants. *Moules et frites* (mussels in broth served with fries) can be found at cafés, both at the Marina in St-François and Bas du Fort Marina. Many of the best restaurants are

Did You Know?

There are numerous hiking trails that climb La Soufrière volcano, and some of them can be pretty treacherous. Go with a guide, and you can safely take in breathtaking sights—such as the views from Piton Dolomieu.

in Jarry, a commercial area near Pointe-à-Pitre. All restaurants and bars are smoke-free, as decreed by French law.

Diverse culinary options range from pizza and crepes to Indian cuisine. For a quick and inexpensive meal, visit a *boulangerie,* where you can buy luscious French pastries and simple baguette sandwiches. Look for the recommendable chain Baguet. While menu prices may seem high, prices include tax and service—although a small extra tip in cash is expected, just as in France. In most restaurants in Guadeloupe (as throughout the Caribbean), lobster is the most expensive item on the menu.

What to Wear: Dining is casual at lunch, but beach attire is not appropriate except at the most laid-back beachside eateries. Dinner is slightly more formal. Long pants, collared shirts, and skirts or dresses are appreciated, although not required. Guadeloupean ladies like to "dress," particularly on weekends, so don't arrive in flip-flops—they'll be in heels.

Shopping

The island has a lot of desirable French products, from designer fashions and sensual lingerie to French china and liqueurs. As for local handicrafts, you can find attractive wood carvings, madras table linens, island dolls dressed in madras, woven straw baskets and hats, and *salakos*—fishermen's hats made of split bamboo, some covered in madras—which also make great wall decorations. Of course, the favorite Guadeloupean souvenir is rum. Look for *rhum vieux,* the top of the line. Be aware that the only liquor bottles allowed on planes have to be bought in the duty-free shops at the airport. Usually, the shops have to deliver purchases to the aircraft. For foodies, the market ladies sell aromatic fresh spices, crisscrossed with cinnamon sticks, in little baskets lined with madras.

Sights

You'll need to budget at least one day to see each "wing" of the butterfly. They are connected by a bridge, and Grande-Terre has pretty villages along its south coast and the spectacular Pointe des Châteaux. You can see the main sights in Pointe-à-Pitre in a half-day. Touring the rugged, mountainous Basse-Terre, though, is a challenge. If time is a problem, head straight to the west coast; you could easily spend a day traveling its length, stopping for sightseeing, lunch, and a swim. You can also make day trips to the islands, although an overnight or more works best. Leave your heavy luggage in the baggage room of your "mainland" hotel and take a small bag on the ferry.

Visitor Information

CONTACTS Guadeloupe Islands Tourist Board. ✉ *825 3rd Ave., 29th fl., New York* ☎ *212/745–0950* 🌐 *www.guadeloupe-islands.com.* **Office de Tourisme de Désirade.** ✉ *La Capitainerie-Beausejour, waterfront at ferry dock, La Désirade* ☎ *0590/85–00–86.* **Office du Tourisme de Marie-Galante.** ✉ *Rue du Fort, BP 15, Grand-Bourg* ☎ *0590/97–56–51* 🌐 *www.ot-mariegalante.com.*

Weddings

A long residency requirement makes destination weddings prohibitive.

Grande-Terre

Pointe-à-Pitre

The Isles of Guadeloupe have 450,000 inhabitants, most of whom live in the cities. Although Pointe-à-Pitre is not the capital, it is the island's largest city. A commercial and industrial hub in the southwest of Grande-Terre, Pointe-à-Pitre is bustling, noisy, and hot—a place of honking horns and traffic jams and cars on sidewalks for want of a parking place. By day, its pulse is fast; at night, when streets are almost deserted, you may not want to be there.

The city has suffered severe damage over the years from earthquakes, fires, and hurricanes. In recent years, it took heavy hits by hurricanes Frederick (1979), David (1980), Hugo (1989), and Maria (2017). On one side of rue Frébault, you can see the remaining French colonial structures; on the other, the modern city. Some of the downtown area has been rejuvenated. The Centre St-John Perse has transformed old warehouses into a cruise-terminal complex that consists of the spartan Hotel St-John, restaurants, shops, and the port authority headquarters. An impressive terminal serves the ferries that depart for Îles des Saintes, Marie-Galante, Dominica, Martinique, and Saint Lucia.

The heart of the old city is Place de la Victoire; surrounded by wooden buildings with balconies and shutters (including the tourism office) and by sidewalk cafés, the *place* was named in honor of Victor Hugues' 1794 victory over the British. During the French Revolution, Hugues ordered the guillotine set up here so that the public could witness the bloody end of 300 recalcitrant royalists, mainly prosperous plantation owners.

Even more colorful is the bustling marketplace, located between rues St-John Perse, Frébault, Schoelcher, and Peynier. It's a cacophonous place, where shoppers bargain for spices, herbs (and herbal remedies), and a bright assortment of local fruits and vegetables.

Sights

Cathédrale de St-Pierre et St-Paul

CHURCH | If you're fascinated by churches, then stop by the imposing Cathédrale de St-Pierre et St-Paul, built in 1807. Although it has been battered by hurricanes over the years, it has fine stained-glass windows and Creole-style balconies. ✉ *Rue du Général Ruillier, Pointe-à-Pitre* ☎ *0590/82–02–17.*

Musée St-John Perse

HISTORY MUSEUM | Those with a strong interest in French literature and culture will want to visit the Musée St-John Perse, which is dedicated to the poet Alexis Léger, Guadeloupe's most famous son. Better known as Saint-John Perse, Léger was the winner of the Nobel Prize for literature in 1960. Some of his finest poems are inspired by the history and landscape—particularly the sea—of his beloved Guadeloupe. This literary museum, in a restored colonial house, contains a collection of his poetry and some personal belongings. Before you go, look for his birthplace at 54 rue Achille René-Boisneuf. ✉ *9 Rue Louis de Nozières, Pointe-à-Pitre* ☎ *0590/90–01–92* *€2.50* *Closed weekends.*

Restaurants

Caraïbes Café

$$ | **CAFÉ** | This sidewalk café straight out of Paris is an "in" place for lunch and also a spot for a quick breakfast. During the afternoon, order a *pastis* while you people-watch and listen to French crooners. **Known for:** fresh tropical juices; cappuccino; sundaes. *Average main: €18* ✉ *11 rue Bébian, Pointe-à-Pitre* ☎ *0590/82–92–23* *Closed Sun. No dinner.*

Grande-Terre and Basse-Terre

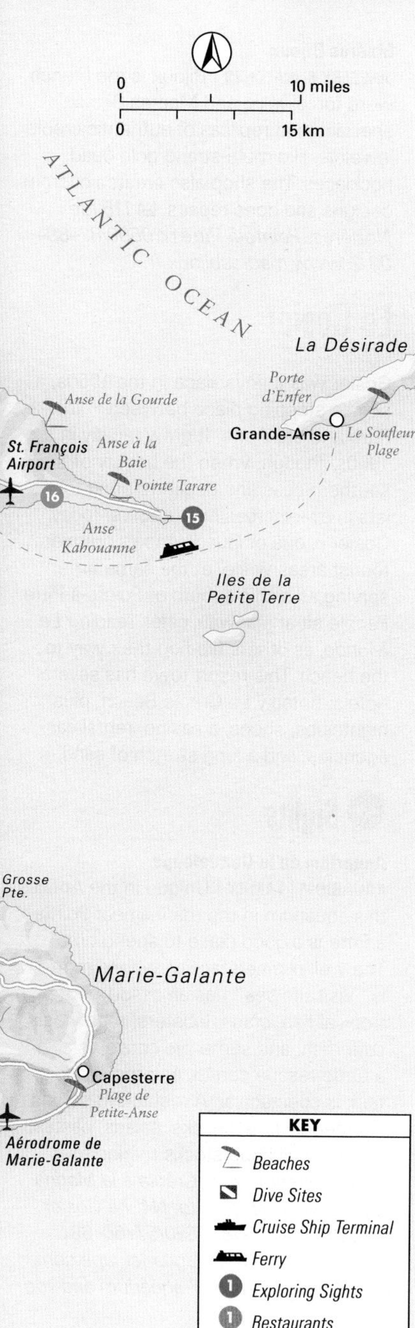

Sights

1 Aquarium de la Guadeloupe **D4**

2 Cascade aux Ecrevisses **B4**

3 Cathédrale de St-Pierre et St-Paul **D4**

4 Domaine de Vanibel.... **B5**

5 Ft. Fleur d'Épée.......... **D4**

6 Îlets Pigeon............. **A5**

7 Jardin Botanique de Deshaies................. **A3**

8 Les Chutes du Carbet ... **C6**

9 Les Mamelles **B4**

10 Morne-à-l'Eau........... **D3**

11 Musée Camélia Costumes et Traditions **E4**

12 Musée du Café/ Café Chaulet............ **A5**

13 Musée St-John Perse.. **D4**

14 Parc National de la Guadeloupe....... **B5**

15 Pointe des Châteaux ... **H4**

16 Port Louis............... **D2**

Restaurants

1 Café Wango **F4**

2 Caraïbes Café........... **D4**

3 La Porte des Indes....... **F3**

4 Le Gran Bleu **E4**

5 Le Mabouya dans la Bouteille **F4**

6 Le Rocher de Malendure **A5**

7 Le Zawag **D4**

8 Restaurant La Savane.. **A3**

9 Restaurant la Vieille Tour.............. **D4**

Hotels

1 Auberge de la Vieille Tour............... **D4**

2 Bwa Chik Hotel & Golf **F4**

3 Caraïb'Bay Hotel........ **A3**

4 Club Med La Caravelle **E4**

5 Habitation Du Comté ... **B3**

6 Habitation Getz.......... **B5**

7 Hôtel Amaudo............ **F4**

8 La Créole Beach Hotel & Spa.............. **D4**

9 Langley Resort Fort Royal................ **A3**

10 La Toubana Hôtel & Spa............... **E4**

11 Le Jardin Malanga Hotel...................... **C7**

12 Le Relais du Moulin **F4**

13 L'Habitation Tabanon.... **C4**

14 Tainos Cottages......... **A3**

15 Tendacayou Ecolodge & Spa.................... **A3**

Shopping

Bustling Point-à-Pitre has obtained the prestigious French label of *Ville d'Art et d'Histoire* (town of art and history). You can browse in the street stalls around the harbor quay and at the two markets (the best is the Marché de Frébault). The town's main shopping streets with lots of French merchandise, from pâté to sexy lingerie, are rue Schoelcher, rue de Nozières, and the busy rue Frébault. At the St-John Perse Cruise Terminal, there's an attractive mall with about two dozen shops.

Destreland

MALL | Destreland, Grande-Terre's largest, most modern shopping mall, has more than 180 boutiques, restaurants, and stores. This commercial center is a few minutes from the airport, which is a shopping destination in its own right. ✉ *Bd. Destrellan, Baie-Mahault, Les Abymes* ☎ *0590/38–53–85* 🌐 *www.destreland.com* 🕓 *Closed Sun. afternoon.*

Dody

MIXED CLOTHING | Across from the market, Dody is the place to go if you want white eyelet lace blouses, skirts, dresses, even bustiers. A single item can cost up to €300. Madras clothing is both traditional and contemporary, and it looks especially cute in children's clothing. A line of colorful, Carnival-inspired, tropical dresses is a knockout. For men, there are Creole suits and cool madras shirts, and there's a line of Bebe Creole. Many styles have reduced prices, and there are special-occasion "costumes"—wedding, communion, and confirmation dresses, all in white eyelet. Those who love designer ensembles based in Guadeloupean tradition can also shop online. ✉ *Spice Market Sq., 40 rue Frébault, Pointe-à-Pitre* ☎ *0590/83–13–73* 🌐 *www.dodyshop.com.*

Madras Bijoux

JEWELRY & WATCHES | Bijoux is the French word for jewelry, and Madras Bijoux specializes in replicas of authentic creole jewelry—like multi-strand gold bead necklaces. The shop also creates custom designs and does repairs. ✉ *115 rue Nozières, Pointe-à-Pitre* ☎ *0590/82–88–03* 🌐 *www.madrasbijoux.fr.*

Le Gosier

Gosier was a tiny village in the 1950s, a simple stopping place between Pointe-à-Pitre and Ste-Anne. It grew rapidly in the 1960s, though, when the beauty of the southern coastline began to bring tourists in ever-increasing numbers. Today, Gosier is one of Guadeloupe's premier tourist areas while, at the same time, serving as a chic suburb of Pointe-à-Pitre. People sit at sidewalk cafés reading *Le Monde*, as others flip-flop their way to the beach. This resort town has several hotels, notably Le Creole Beach, plus nightclubs, shops, a casino, rental-car agencies, and a long stretch of sand.

Sights

Aquarium de la Guadeloupe

AQUARIUM | **FAMILY** | Unique in the Antilles, this aquarium in the marina near Pointe-à-Pitre is a good place to spend time. The well-planned facility, whose motto is "Visit the sea," has an assortment of tropical fish, crabs, lobsters, moray eels, cofferfish, and some live coral. It's also a turtle rescue center, and the shark tank is spectacular. A restaurant serves kid-friendly fare, snacks, salads, pastas, etc. A small shop stocks marine toys and souvenirs. ✉ *Pl. Créole à la Marina de Bas du Fort, off Rte. N4, Le Gosier* ☎ *0590/90–92–38, 0690/57–60–69* 🌐 *www.aquariumdelaguadeloupe.com* 🎟 *€14 aquarium, €27 aquarium and zoo.*

Views of Terre-de-Haut, the largest of the islands in the archipelago known as Îles des Saintes.

Musée Camélia Costumes et Traditions

HISTORY MUSEUM | This museum is a labor of love by its creators. Seeing the dress of black, white, and *métisseé* (mixed-race, or "maroon") societies is a fascinating way to visualize the island's tumultuous history and fascinating heritage. Items that you will remember: madras headdresses, baptism outfits, embroidered maternity dresses, colonial pith helmets, and other various chapeaux, as well as the doll collection. Make sure to go out back and visit the replica of a Guadeloupean *case* circa 1920. A film depicts life of yesteryear. The small museum is privately owned; the founder, Camelia Bausivoir, is a retired English teacher and can act as your guide. The collection was accrued over decades, and Bausivoir sewed many of the costumes. Call for directions before you go and also to make sure that a school group is not there. ✉ *L'Houezel, Le Gosier* ☎ *0690/50–98–16* 🎫 *€10* 🕓 *Closed Mon.*

Restaurants

★ Le Zawag

$$$ | **SEAFOOD** | At this charming hideaway, you'll see the churning sea below and hear waves crashing against the coral rock upon which Le Zawag sits. The interior architecture is all hardwood, with matching furniture and white linen napkins at dinnertime. **Known for:** creole dishes; lobster in cream sauce with pasta; catch of the day. [$] *Average main: €25* ✉ *La Créole Beach Hotel & Spa, Pointe de la Verdure, Le Gosier* ☎ *0590/90–46–46* 🌐 *www.creolebeach.com* 🕓 *No lunch. Closed Sun., Wed., and Sept.*

Restaurant la Vieille Tour

$$$ | **FRENCH** | A historic sugar mill is the backdrop for refined French preparations paired with local produce. The lunch menu is a mix of classic restaurant food and lighter dishes. **Known for:** housemade tropical sorbets; colorful vegetable terrines; choice lamb chops. [$] *Average main: €22* ✉ *Auberge de* *la Vieille Tour, Rte. de Montauban, Le Gosier* ☎ *0590/84–23–23* 🌐 *auberge-vieille-tour.fr.*

Hotels

Auberge de la Vieille Tour

$ | **HOTEL** | At this island classic, built around a historic sugar mill, everyone loves the initial welcome: a cool drink and citrus-scented towels. **Pros:** restaurant is one of the better ones on-island; most rooms have great views; breakfast is a highlight. **Cons:** pool area still needs work, as do some rooms; it's an uphill climb from the beach and pool; exteriors of some sections are an unattractive 1960s style. *Rooms from: €208* ✉ *Rte. de Montauban, Le Gosier* ☎ *0590/84–23–23* 🌐 *www.auberge-vieille-tour.fr* *70 rooms* *Free Breakfast.*

★ **La Créole Beach Hotel & Spa**

$$ | **RESORT** | The magic of this 10-acre complex—with a contemporary, colorful lobby, cosmopolitan bar, and dual pools—lies in the fun atmosphere that the staff is able to create as they unite the disparate, mostly French clientele. **Pros:** piano player in the lobby and a jazz club, too; excellent management and long-term staff; lovely tropical gardens. **Cons:** towels are not plush; beach is nice but small; some rooms far from the lobby. *Rooms from: €275* ✉ *Pointe de la Verdure, Le Gosier* ☎ *0590/90–46–46* 🌐 *www.creolebeach.com* *276 rooms* *Free Breakfast.*

Nightlife

Bar de la Vieille Tour

PIANO BARS | The atmospheric piano bar, with its planters' chairs and whirring fan blades, is as memorable as Rick's Café in *Casablanca.* The terrace tables give you the best views of the Caribbean through multicolored bougainvillea. Accras (saltfish fritters), peanuts, and olives usually arrive with your cocktail, which will be as tasty as it is pretty. A bar menu offers a selection of tapas, and the rum cart is extensive—some available by the flight. The barman makes a perfect piña colada and creates a nightly cocktail du jour. On Wednesday and Friday evenings, there's live piano music; in high season, more live music—like a jazz trio. ✉ *Rte. de Montauban, Le Gosier* ☎ *0590/84–23–23* 🌐 *auberge-vieille-tour.fr.*

La Rhumerie Bar & Lounge

BARS | Something is always happening at La Créole Beach Hotel. Bands often play beguine and zouk or piano with bass, all of which are very danceable and add to the hotel's conviviality. The tom-tom drummers accompanied by a bevy of native dancers are exciting. A steel band also plays, usually on Monday night. On Wednesday, Gwoka (a type of Creole music) plays during Creole Night. The busy bar specializes in quality rums from various Caribbean islands and serves creole tapas, including traditional accras. ✉ *La Créole Beach Hotel & Spa, Pointe de la Verdure, Le Gosier* ☎ *0590/90–46–46* 🌐 *www.creolebeach.com/.*

Le Moule

On the Atlantic coast, and once the capital of Guadeloupe, this port city of 24,000 has had more than its share of troubles: It was bombarded by the British in 1794 and 1809 and by a hurricane in 1928. An important tourist center in past decades, the city is experiencing a comeback. A large East Indian population, which originally came to cut cane, lives here. Canopies of flamboyant trees hang over the narrow streets, where colorful vegetable and fish markets do a brisk business. The town hall, with graceful balustrades, and a small 19th-century neoclassical church are on the main square. Le Moule's beach, protected by a reef, is perfect for windsurfing.

Beaches

L'Autre Bord

BEACH | The waves on this Atlantic beach give the long expanse of sand a wild look. The beach is protected by an extensive coral reef, which makes it safe for children. Farther out, the waves draw surfers and windsurfers. From its location right in the town of Moule, you can stroll along a seaside promenade fringed by flamboyant trees (also known as flame trees). Many shade trees offer protection, the swaying coconut palms are photogenic, and sidewalk cafés provide sustenance. **Amenities:** food and drink; parking (no fee); toilets. **Best for:** surfing; swimming; walking; windsurfing. ✉ *Le Moule.*

Bas du Fort

Sights

Ft. Fleur d'Épée

HISTORIC SIGHT | The main attraction in Bas-du-Fort is this fortress, built between 1759 and 1763, which hunkers down on a hillside behind a deep moat. The fort was the scene of hard-fought battles between the French and the English in 1794. You can explore its well-preserved dungeons and battlements and take in a sweeping view of Îles des Saintes and Marie-Galante. The free guided tour here explores the fort's history and architecture and helps explain the living conditions of the soldiers. Included on the tour is an exploration of its underground galleries, now decorated with graffiti. The fort sometimes has art exhibits. If a bilingual person is on duty, she will explain it all in English. Call ahead to confirm that day's hours. You will only need 30 minutes on your own. Registered as a historic monument since 1979, the fort also provides superb bay views for walkers. ✉ *Rte. du Bas du Fort, Bas du Fort* ☎ *0590/90–94–61* 🎫 *Free.*

Shopping

Bas-du-Fort's two shopping areas are the Cora Shopping Center and the marina, where there are 20 or so shops and some restaurants—many right on the water. This marina has an active social scene.

St-François

This was once a simple little village, primarily involved with fishing and harvesting tomatoes. The fish and tomatoes are still here, as are the old creole houses and the lively market with recommendable food stalls in the *centre ville*; increasingly, though, the St-François marina district is overtaking Gosier as Guadeloupe's most fashionable tourist resort area. Avenue de l'Europe runs between the marina and the fairways and water obstacles of the municipal golf course, which was designed by Robert Trent Jones Sr. On the marina side is a string of shops (including a huge supermarket), hotels, bars, and restaurants. The Bwa Chik Hotel & Golf, an eco-chic study in recyclable materials, is a favorite among golfers. Other attractions include an array of beaches, a lagoon, and the St-François casino. St-François was designated as a Station Balnéaire (nautical resort) by the French government. With its 220-slip marina, this is a sailing mecca and a departure point for catamaran day sails to the out islands—which are in close proximity.

Sights

Pointe des Châteaux

VIEWPOINT | A National Grand Site, the island's easternmost point offers a breathtaking view of the Atlantic crashing against huge rocks, carving them into shapes resembling pyramids. A rocky arm reaching out to the ocean, this spot is a spectacular display of sea versus land. A nine-ton crucifix can be seen for miles out at sea and was erected for the centennial of the Catholic diocese in 1946. There are spectacular views of Guadeloupe's southern and eastern coasts and the island of La Désirade. The beach has few facilities now that most vendors have been relocated to Petit Anse Kahouanne, about a mile up the road; so bring your own food and drink. The Village Artisanal is open every day, and taxis run every hour in high season. ✉ *Rte. de la Pointe des Châteaux, at the end of the road, St-François.*

Need a Break? 

If you don't want to take time for a two-hour French lunch, watch for gas stations such as **Shell Boutique, Total Boutique**, and **Esso Tiger-mart**—which all sell food. The VITO station—on the left going into St-François—has good pizza, as well as tables and chairs. A Total "fillin' station" might have barbecue ribs, chicken, and turkey.

Beaches

Pointe Tarare

BEACH | This secluded strip just before the tip of Pointe des Châteaux is the island's only nude beach. (Technically, nude sunbathing is not allowed by French law.) Small bar-cafés are in the parking area, but it's still best to bring some water, snacks, and beach chairs (there's no place to rent them). What you do have is one of the coast's most dramatic landscapes; rugged cliffs, topped by a huge crucifix, loom over the beach. When approaching St-François Marina, go in the direction of Pointe des Châteaux at the roundabout and drive for about 10 minutes. **Amenities:** food and drink; parking (no fee); toilets. **Best for:** partiers; solitude; sunset; swimming; walking. ✉ *Rte. N4, southeast of St-François on Pointe des Châteaux.*

Restaurants

Café Wango

$$$ | **ECLECTIC** | At this alfresco hot spot, Asian wok dishes, sushi, skewers, fish carpaccios, and tartares dominate the menu—and there are no fewer than five better-than-average salads. The chef, who devotées will know from his previous stint at Iguane Café, is known for his original Asian-, Indian-, Creole-, and African-influenced dishes. **Known for:** French expat crowd; lobster medallions with shrimp, avocado, and citrus chili sauce; ice cream. Ⓢ *Average main: €23* ✉ *Marina St-François, Marines 1, St-François* ☎ *0590/83–50–41* 🌐 *www.facebook.com/cafewango.*

La Porte des Indes

$$$ | **INDIAN** | Dining here is truly a departure: the open-air pergola, the blue gates, the pungent aromas, and the bust of Ganesha. Within the paisley-covered menu, you'll find authentic Indian dishes alongside adaptations for other palates. **Known for:** exotic decor; curried chicken with cashews and raisins; cheese-stuffed naan. Ⓢ *Average main: €28* ✉ *Desvarieux, N5 Dubedou, St-François* ☎ *0590/21–30–87* 🌐 *www.la-porte-des-indes.fr* ⏲ *Closed Mon. and Wed. No lunch Tues., Thurs.-Sat.*

Le Mabouya dans la Bouteille

$$$ | **FRENCH FUSION** | This fine-dining restaurant in St-François offers consistently good, Franco-fusion cuisine. The French couple who owned a Parisian restaurant for eight years before setting up shop here don't always extend the same hospitality to English-speaking tourists as to French patrons; but that (and the impractical, silky, maroon napkins) aside, this open-air venue is cozy and inviting with displays of vintage corkscrews and other knick-knacks. **Known for:** chocolate tart with

cassava ice cream; terrine de foie gras with currants; grilled lobster. *Average main: €27 17 Saline Est, St-François 5-min walk from marina 0590/21–31–14 Closed Thurs. No lunch.*

Hotels

Bwa Chik Hotel & Golf

$ | **HOTEL** | This eco-chic boutique hotel at the marina is the buzz in St-François for its unique decor that combines recycled wood and driftwood with ultra-contemporary Euro furnishings; the lobby has become a gallery for local artists. **Pros:** live jazz nights in season; ideal location, making a car unnecessary; welcoming staff. **Cons:** standard rooms could be larger; no elevators or bellmen; small pool. *Rooms from: €120 Av. d'l Europe, St-François 0590/88–60–60 www.bwachik.com 54 rooms Free Breakfast.*

Hôtel Amaudo

$ | **B&B/INN** | This *hôtel de charme* is now run by an English-speaking manager, who will provide any concierge service you might imagine. **Pros:** well-maintained; a moderate price tag for unobstructed sea views; safe environment, with a mechanized security gate. **Cons:** could be too quiet and peaceful; no activities; car needed because of the remote location. *Rooms from: €185 Anse à la Barque, St-François 0590/88–87–00 www.amaudo.fr 14 rooms No Meals.*

Nightlife

Casino de Saint-François

BARS | The small Casino de St-François has a contemporary élan that makes you want to dress up and come on out. There's a dramatic water installation, leather furniture, and an appealing restaurant, Le Joker, open for both lunch and dinner. The casino has a bar, a piano, and a stage for performers, which also doubles as a disco on Friday and Saturday. The casino is open daily from 10 am.

Need a Break?

There's no wagering at **Hyper Casino**, a *supermarché* on l'avenue de l'Europe at the St-François Marina; but there are esoteric cheeses and baked goods such as pie-size, tropical-fruit tarts. Other supermarkets with good deli or bakery departments are those in the Leader Price and Carrefour chains.

There are 92 slots, as well as English roulette and blackjack. *Lieu-dit-Saint-Marthe, St-François In front of the golf course, opposite the Centre Commercial 0590/88–41–31 www.casinosaint-francois.com.*

Shopping

In St-François, more than a dozen shops surround the marina—some selling French lingerie, swimsuits, and fashions. The supermarket has particularly good prices on French wines and cheeses; pick up a fresh baguette, and you'll have a picnic. (Then get lost at a secluded beach.) Don't forget some island chocolates or individual fruit and custard tarts!

Boutique Le Gall

MIXED CLOTHING | The line of fashionable resort wear for women and children sold here is designed by French painter Jean Claude Le Gall. Pieces have hand-painted figures like turtles and dolphins on high-quality cotton knits. Branches of this French favorite are located at Bas-du-Fort Marina and on Les Saintes. A gift from this store is considered prestigious back in mainland France. *La Marina–La Coursive, Ave. de l'Europe, St-François 0590/88–46–95 Closed daily 12:30–3 pm.*

Ste-Anne

In the 18th century, this town—8 miles (13 km) east of Gosier—was a sugar-exporting center. Today, sand has replaced sugar as the town's most valuable asset. La Caravelle and the other beaches are among the best in Guadeloupe. On the main drag, which parallels the waterfront, you'll find a lively group of inexpensive eateries, shops, and artisan stalls. On a more spiritual note, Ste-Anne has a lovely cemetery with stark-white tombs.

Beaches

Plage Caravelle
BEACH | Just southwest of Ste-Anne, you'll find one of Grande-Terre's longest and prettiest stretches of sand—the occasional dilapidated shack notwithstanding. Protected by reefs, this is also a fine snorkeling spot. Club Med occupies one end of this beach, and nonguests can enjoy its beach and water sports, as well as lunch and drinks, by buying a day pass. You can also have lunch on the terrace of La Toubana Hotel & Spa, then descend the stairs to the beach—or enjoy lunch at La Toubana's beach restaurant, wildly popular on Sunday. **Amenities:** food and drink; parking (no fee); toilets; water sports. **Best for:** partiers; snorkeling; sunset; swimming; walking; windsurfing. ✉ *Rue de la Caravelle, off Rte. N4, southwest of Ste-Anne, Ste-Anne.*

Plage du Helleux
BEACH | Except on Sunday, this long stretch of wild beach—framed by dramatic cliffs—is often completely deserted in the morning or early afternoon. By 4 pm, though, you might find 70 or so young surfers. Many locals take their young children here, but use caution with your own; the current can be strong. The beach has no facilities of its own, but you can get lunch and drinks nearby at the hotel Le Relais du Moulin. To get here, follow the signs to the hotel and pass by, heading right toward the sea to a dirt road down to the beach. **Amenities:** none. **Best for:** partiers; solitude; surfing; swimming; walking. ✉ *Rue de l'Étang Gros Sable, off Rte. N4, 6 km. east of the village of Ste.-Anne, Ste-Anne.*

Restaurants

Le Gran Bleu (*Le Gran Bleu*)
$$$$ | **FRENCH** | Delicious Caribbean-accented French cuisine draws diners to this open-air restaurant, where a specialty is fresh lobster plucked from the petite lagoon that beautifies the deck. The classy, colorful, open-air dining room lounge has deep leather chairs and, on occasion, a piano player and live music. **Known for:** live music; fresh lobster; foie gras. [$] *Average main: €35* ✉ *La Toubana Hotel & Spa, Rte. de l'Hôtel Toubana, off Rte. N4, Ste-Anne* ☎ *0590/88–25–57* 🌐 *toubana.com.*

Hotels

★ **Club Med La Caravelle**
$$$$ | **RESORT** | **FAMILY** | Facing the island's best white-sand beaches, La Caravelle is one of the original clubs in the Caribbean—yet all the facilities, including the seafront restaurant and its deck, have a smashing, contemporary look. **Pros:** exceptional boutique for shoppers; large, fun resort; adults-only area and stunning oceanfront accommodations. **Cons:** speaking French helps; older standard rooms are small; Club Med experience and kid-friendly atmosphere are not for everyone. [$] *Rooms from: €588* ✉ *Quartier Caravelle, Plage de la Caravelle, Ste-Anne* ☎ *0590/85–49–50, 800/258–2633 in US* 🌐 *www.clubmed.us* 🛏 *260 rooms* 🍽 *All-Inclusive.*

Amazing views from Le Grand Bleu at La Toubana Hôtel & Spa

★ La Toubana Hôtel & Spa

$$$$ | **RESORT** | Few hotels on Guadeloupe command such a panoramic view of the sea—spanning four islands, no less—and all the suites offer full sea views, some breathtaking. **Pros:** praise-worthy restaurant; a special boutique experience with sophisticated style; the library/lounge near the pool has remarkable views. **Cons:** beach restaurant can have a long wait for food; bedrooms and TVs are small by American standards; the little beach is down the hill, via a very steep paved path. *Rooms from: €495* ✉ *Rue de l'Hôtel Toubana, off Rte. N4, Ste-Anne* ☎ *0590/88–25–57* *toubana.com* *47 units* *Free Breakfast.*

Le Relais du Moulin

$ | **HOTEL** | With a historic sugar mill as its focal point, the atmosphere here ranges from party-down to relaxing. **Pros:** superior suites have outdoor jacuzzis; most staffers speak English; adults only except December 19-January 6. **Cons:** no beach-front or sea views; very quiet—nothing nearby; need a car. *Rooms from: €235* ✉ *off N4, above Plage du Helleux, Ste-Anne* *between the Village of Ste-Anne and St-Francois* ☎ *0590/88-48-48, 0690/29–19–29* *www.relaisdumoulin.com* *40 rooms* *Free Breakfast.*

Nightlife

Club Med By Night

BARS | Club Med sells night passes that include all cocktails, dinner with wine, and a show in the theater, followed by admission to the disco. Go on Friday for the gala dinner and the most creative show, or on a Tuesday, another special night. A night pass is a good option for single women, who will feel comfortable and safe at the disco, where there are plenty of fun staffers (G.O.s) willing to be dance partners. ✉ *Quartier Caravelle, Plage de la Caravelle, Ste-Anne* ☎ *0590/85–49–50* *www.clubmed.us* *Closed Sept.–early Nov.*

Shopping

Village Artisanal Sainte-Anne

CRAFTS | The village has 15 boutiques offering a wide selection of local crafts, including art composed of shells, wood, and stone. One of the outlets sells authentic Panama hats. It is located under a tent across from the waterfront as you first drive into the village. ✉ *Blvd. Hégesippe Ibéne, Ste-Anne* ☎ *0590/85–43–63.*

Elsewhere on Grande-Terre

Sights

Morne-à-l'Eau

CEMETERY | This agricultural town of about 16,000 people has a cemetery shaped like an amphitheater, with black-and-white-checkerboard tombs, elaborate epitaphs, and multicolor (plastic) flowers. On All Saints' Day (November 1), it's the scene of a moving (and photogenic) candlelight service.

Port Louis

TOWN | This fishing village of about 7,000 people on the northwestern coast of Grand-Terre is best known for Plage du Souffleur. The beach is one of the island's prettiest. Although crowded on weekends, the beach is blissfully quiet during the week. The sand is fringed by flamboyant trees, and there are also spectacular views of Basse-Terre.

Beaches

Plage de la Chapelle à Anse-Bertrand

BEACH | For a delightful day trip to the northern coast of Grande-Terre, aim for this spot—one of the loveliest white-sand beaches, whose gentle mid-afternoon waves are popular with families. The beach is shaded by coconut palms, you can explore the ruins of a chapel, and the sea kayaking is excellent. When the tide rolls in, the beach is equally popular with surfers. Several little terrace restaurants are at the far end of the beach, but you might want to bring your own mat or beach towel; no one rents *chaise longues*. The town has remained relatively undeveloped. **Amenities:** food and drink; showers; toilets. **Best for:** solitude; sunrise; sunset; surfing; swimming; walking; windsurfing. ✉ *Rue de la Coquillages, Anse-Bertrand* ⊕ *4 miles (6½ km) south of La Pointe de la Grand Vigie.*

Basse-Terre

Low on the average tourist's radar, Basse-Terre (which actually translates as "low land") is by far the highest and wildest of the two wings of the Guadeloupe butterfly, with the peak of the Soufrière volcano topping off at nearly 4,811 feet. Basse-Terre, where you can find the island's national park, is also an ecotourist's treasure, with lush, equatorial plant life and adventurous opportunities for hikers and mountain bikers on the old *traces*, routes that porters once took across the mountains. You can still find numerous fishing villages and banana plantations that stretch as far as the eye can see. The northwest coast, between Bouillante and Grande-Anse, is magnificent; the road twists and turns up steep hills smothered in vegetation and then drops down and skirts deep-blue bays and colorful seaside towns. Constantly changing light, towering clouds, and frequent rainbows only add to the beauty. In fact, Basse-Terre is gaining in popularity each year and is especially appreciated by young, sporty couples.

Basse-Terre

Because Pointe-à-Pitre is so much bigger, few people suspect that the little town of Basse-Terre, with 15,000 residents, is the capital and administrative center of Guadeloupe. But if you have any doubts about its relevance, walk up the hill to the state-of-the-art Théâtre Nationale, where some of France's finest theater and opera companies perform.

Vieux-Habitants

As you can tell by its name ("old residents), Vieux-Habitants was the island's first colony, established in 1635. Beaches, a restored coffee plantation, and the oldest church on the island (1666) make this village worth a visit.

Sights

Domaine de Vanibel

FARM/RANCH | Guadeloupean coffee is considered some of the best in the world. Joel Nelson will tell you all about it if you take one of his tours around the grounds of his estate, perched 1,200 feet above sea level. Dress comfortably, as you will be going into the bush to pick vanilla and coffee beans from the trees. Nelson's enthusiasm and passion for what he grows and produces makes what could be a ho-hum walk through the woods a pleasurable learning experience. After some 30 minutes or more, you will be brought back to the stone cottage that is the Habitation Sucrerie for a coffee tasting and fresh tropical fruits. You might want to buy a bag or two of coffee or some of the precious vanilla beans and vanilla powder. Also on the estate, there are simple *gîtes* (cottages) for two to four persons. Tours are in the afternoon, two tours a day from January through April and one tour a day from May through December. ✉ *Cousinière Caféière, Vieux-Habitants* ☎ *0590/98–40–79, 0690/50–63–39* 🌐 *www.vanibel.fr* 🎟 *€7* 🕐 *Closed Sun. and Sept.*

Musée du Café/Café Chaulet

HISTORY MUSEUM | From the riverfront Musée du Café/Café Chaulet, dedicated to the art of coffee making, the tantalizing aroma of freshly ground beans reaches out to the highway. Plaques and photos illustrate the island's coffee history. You will learn that coffee was once Guadeloupe's principal crop and that Chaulets have been planters and exporters since 1900. The shop sells excellent arabica coffee, rum punches, Schrubb (an orange liqueur), hot sauces, sachets of spices, bay-rum lotion, marmalades, and jewelry made from natural materials. Cocoa beans are also grown here. The "resident" chocolate maker, a young Frenchwoman, also crafts bonbons and festive holiday candies with lots of dark chocolate and tropical fruit from the island. You will even see the coffee cars—emblazoned Volkswagen Beetles. The Chaulet family respects traditional procedures while bowing to modernity. Their latest product is coffee capsules. ✉ *Le Bouchu, Vieux-Habitants* ☎ *0590/98–54–96* 🌐 *www.cafe-chaulet.com* 🎟 *Museum €6; shop free* 🕐 *Closed Sun. and Mon.*

Hotels

Habitation Getz

$ | **HOUSE** | **FAMILY** | This former coffee plantation offers unique accommodations in its great house or in unique tree houses—ideal for a family that wants to play Swiss Family Robinson. **Pros:** a good, reasonably priced dinner is offered on Wednesday and Sunday; an impressive labor of love; tree houses are unique in Guadeloupe. **Cons:** towels and linens not changed daily; isolated location means you need a car; tree houses are accessed only by a swinging ladder. $ *Rooms from: €115* ✉ *Rte. de Gery, Vieux-Habitants* ☎ *0690/58–70–20* 🌐 *www.habitation-getz.com/* *5 units* 🍴 *Free Breakfast.*

Ste-Rose

In addition to a sulfur bath, you'll find two good beaches (Amandiers and Clugny) and several interesting small museums in Ste-Rose, a community in northeastern Basse-Terre.

Habitation Du Comté

$ | **B&B/INN** | A decidedly special place, this stalwart, hurricane-proof mansion built in 1948—The County House—was the great house for the owner of a sugar-cane plantation; rooms have artsy decor, luxurious bedding, and quality mattresses—maybe the best in Guadeloupe. **Pros:** 360-degree view of the countryside, mountains, and sea; good blackout shutters; blissfully quiet. **Cons:** no resort-style amenities; isolated location means you need a car; may be too quiet for some travelers. *Rooms from: €140* ✉ *Comté de Lohéac, Ste-Rose* ☎ *0590/21–78–81* 🌐 *www.habitationducomte.com/* *8 units* *Free Breakfast.*

Bouillante

The name means "boiling," and so it's no surprise that hot springs are found here. The biggest attraction, however, is scuba diving on nearby Pigeon Island, which is accessed by boat from Plage de Malendure. There's a small information kiosk on the beach at Plage de Malendure that can help you with diving and snorkeling arrangements.

Îlets Pigeon

ISLAND | Two tiny, rocky islands a few hundred yards off the coast are part of the Jacques Cousteau Underwater Park and Guadeloupe's best scuba and snorkeling site. Although the reefs here are good, they don't rank among the top Caribbean dive spots. Several companies conduct diving trips to the reserve, and it's on the itinerary of some sailing and snorkeling trips. ✉ *off Plage de Malendure, Bouillante.*

Les Mamelles

MOUNTAIN | Two mountain peaks—Mamelle de Petit-Bourg, 2,350 feet, and Mamelle de Pigeon, 2,500 feet—rise in the Parc National de la Guadeloupe. *Mamelle* means "breast"; and when you see the mountains, you'll understand how they got their name. Trails ranging from easy to arduous lace up into the surrounding mountains. There's a glorious view from a lookout point 1,969 feet up Mamelle de Pigeon. If you're a climber, plan to spend several hours exploring this area. If there have been heavy rainfalls, cancel your plans. ✉ *159 Weston Rd., in the National Park, northeast of Bouillante, Bouillante.*

Plage de Malendure

BEACH | Across from Pigeon Island and the Jacques Cousteau Underwater Park, this long, gray, volcanic beach facing the Caribbean's calm waters has restrooms, a few beach shacks offering cold drinks and snacks, and a huge parking lot. Don't come here for solitude, as the beach is a launch point for many dive boats. The snorkeling is good. Le Rocher de Malendure, a seafood restaurant, is perched on a cliff overlooking the bay. Food carts work the parking lot. **Amenities:** food and drink; parking (no fee); toilets. **Best for:** partiers; snorkeling; swimming. ✉ *Rte. N6, Bouillante.*

Restaurants

Le Rocher de Malendure

$$$ | **SEAFOOD** | Guests may at first be attracted to the gorgeous views of dive boats going to Pigeon Island but return again and again for food. After climbing the worn yellow stairs, diners take a seat

on the open, multilevel deck for a delicious meal and the gorgeous panorama. **Known for:** fricassee of octopus; fresh fish; grilled tuna with pesto. 💲 *Average main: €22* ✉ *Bord de Mer, Malendure de Pigeon, Bouillante* ☎ *0590/98–70–84* 🌐 *rocher-malendure.com.*

St-Claude

Sights

Cascade aux Ecrevisses
WATERFALL | Within the Parc National de la Guadeloupe, Crayfish Falls is one of the island's loveliest (and most popular) spots. A marked trail (walk carefully, the rocks can be slippery) leads to this splendid waterfall, which dashes down into the Corossol River—a good place for a dip. Come early, though; otherwise, you definitely won't have it to yourself. ✉ *D23, center island, west of Petit-Bourg, Petit-Bourg.*

Les Chutes du Carbet
WATERFALL | You can reach the first two of the Carbet Falls (the first drops from 65 feet, the second from 360 feet) via a long, steep, marked trail from the village of Habituée. The third and highest waterfall (drops from 410 feet) has been closed since 2008 due to a landslide at the site. On the way up the trail, you pass Grand Étang (Great Pond), a volcanic lake surrounded by interesting plant life. For those who are fans of *The Walking Dead*, there's also the curiously named Étang Zombi, a pond believed to house evil spirits. If there have been heavy rains, don't even think about going here! ✉ *St-Claude.*

Parc National de la Guadeloupe
NATIONAL PARK | This 74,100-acre park has been recognized by UNESCO as a Biosphere Reserve. Before going, pick up a *Guide to the National Park* from the tourist office; the guide rates the hiking trails according to difficulty, and most are quite difficult indeed. Most mountain trails are in the southern half, adjacent to Ste.-Claude. The park is bisected by the route de la Traversée, a 16-mile (26-km) paved road lined with masses of tree ferns, shrubs, flowers, tall trees, and green plantains. It's the ideal point of entry. Wear rubber-soled shoes and take along a swimsuit, a sweater, water, and perhaps food for a picnic. Cruise passengers tend to arrive in the late morning or early afternoon. Check on the weather; if Basse-Terre has had a lot of rain, give it up. In the past, after intense rainfall, rock slides have closed the road for months. ✉ *Habitation Beausoleil-Montéran, via Rte. de la traversée, west from Petit-Bourg, east from Bouillant, Bouillante* ☎ *0590/80–86–00* 🎟 *Free.*

Drainage Ditches

Whether you're driving a car or walking on an unlighted street at night, be aware that there are drainage ditches on the side of the road meant to catch the runoff after a rain. Because parking is at a premium, you will see cars straddling the ditches. Don't do it.

Hotels

L'Habitation Tabanon
$$ | **APARTMENT** | **FAMILY** | This rental complex is in a small market town in the heart of Basse-Terre—the mountainous, wild side of Guadeloupe, where eco-sports and scuba diving are the main draws. **Pros:** well-maintained rooms; a hip place to call home for a week; manager is accommodating and acts as a concierge. **Cons:** no resort services or amenities; three-night minimum stay; you'll need a car. 💲 *Rooms from: €300* ✉ *Moulin de Tabanon, 5 Rte. de Tabanon,*

The inviting Le Jardin Malanga Hotel sits on a former coffee plantation.

Petit-Bourg ☎ 0690069090/41–41–47, 0690/35–06–11 🌐 www.habitation-tabanon.com ⇨ *5 apartments* 🍴 *No Meals.*

Le Jardin Malanga Hotel

$ | B&B/INN | This inviting hillside inn is on a former coffee plantation, where trees laden with fruit are like the temptations of the Garden of Eden. **Pros:** a romantic hideaway with history and character; good food in the restaurant (half- board is a good option); rooms accommodate 3 or 4 people. **Cons:** isolated location far from a beach; no phones in the bungalows to call reception; no TV or Internet in the bungalows. $ *Rooms from: €218* ✉ *60 rte. de l'Hermitage, Trois-Rivières* ☎ *0590/92–67–57* 🌐 *www.jardinmalanga.com* ⇨ *6 rooms* 🍴 *Free Breakfast.*

Deshaies

Sights

Jardin Botanique de Deshaies

GARDEN | FAMILY | This exquisite 10-acre park is filled with parrots and flamingoes. A circuitous walking trail takes you by ponds with floating lily pads, cactus gardens, and every kind of tropical flower and plant— including orchids galore. Amid the exotic ferns and gnarled, ancient trees are little wooden bridges and a gazebo. A panoramic restaurant with a surprisingly sophisticated lunch menu, plus a snack bar, are housed in terraced gingerbread building: one overlooks the park's waterfall, the other, the mountains. The garden has a children's park and nature-oriented playthings in the shop. A local juice and a snack is included with admission. This excursion is delightful and serene, ideal on an overcast day. ✉ *off N2, Deshaies* ☎ *0590/28–43–02* 🌐 *www.jardin-botanique.com* 🎟 *€15.90.*

Beaches

Plage de la Grande-Anse

BEACH | One of Guadeloupe's widest beaches has soft beige sand sheltered by palms. To the west is a round verdant mountain. There's a large parking area and some food stands but no other facilities. The beach can be overrun on Sunday, not to mention littered, due to the food carts. Right past the parking lot, you can see signage for the Creole restaurant Le Karacoli; if you have lunch there (it's not cheap), you can *sieste* on the *chaise longues*. At the far end of the beach, which is more virgin territory, Tainos Cottages has a restaurant. **Amenities:** food and drink; parking (no fee). **Best for:** partiers; solitude; swimming; walking. ✉ *off N2, north of Deshaies, Deshaies.*

Restaurants

Restaurant La Savane

$$$ | **FRENCH** | Even if there's a downpour, the overhanging gingerbread roof over your terrace table will keep you dry as the food and music keep your spirits high. The family-owned restaurant overlooking crystalline Deshaies Bay is a dream fulfilled, and much of its success is directly related to the varied international experiences of the family members. **Known for:** ouassous in coconut milk with red curry; pumpkin and sweet potato soup; chicken with peanut and honey sauce. *Average main: €22* ✉ *238 Blvd. des Poissonniers, Deshaies* ☎ *0590/91–39–58* *Closed Wed. No lunch in low season. No lunch Mon.–Fri. in high season.*

Hotels

Caraïb'Bay Hotel

$ | **B&B/INN** | **FAMILY** | This complex of colorful duplex bungalows may not impress you at first, but its service and customer satisfaction have earned many kudos. **Pros:** innovative bar; homey feel with multilingual library; moderate prices, especially with weekly offers. **Cons:** room decor dated; not luxurious; not directly on the beach. *Rooms from: €160* ✉ *410 Allée du Coeur, Ziotte, Deshaies* ☎ *0590/28–54–43* *www.caraibbayhotel.com* *16 units* *Free Breakfast.*

Langley Resort Fort Royal

$ | **RESORT** | **FAMILY** | This well-priced, friendly, and fun resort offers both simple beachfront bungalows and regular rooms in a mostly all-inclusive environment geared toward less fussy travelers. **Pros:** bedding and mattresses in main building are comfortable; free Wi-Fi; food and service surprisingly good. **Cons:** restaurant gets crowded; bungalows are small and some subject to noise; high-volume, mostly all-inclusive resort that is rare in Guadeloupe. *Rooms from: €180* ✉ *Bas Vent, north of Deshaies, Deshaies* ☎ *0590/68–76–70* *www.fortroyal.eu* *Closed Sept. and Oct.* *215 units* *Free Breakfast.*

Tainos Cottages

$$ | **B&B/INN** | **FAMILY** | The globe-trotting Frenchman who designed these seven Indonesian teak cottages resembling Guadeloupean *cases* from the 1920s that overlook a long unspoiled beach, Plage de Grande-Anse, has passed on; his son and daughter have now taken charge of this small paradise. **Pros:** spacious cottages; a discount for online bookings; family-owned, informal, and English spoken. **Cons:** the mosquito netting's there for a reason—bring repellent; bungalows could use some updating; the rustic experience is not for everyone. *Rooms from: €300* ✉ *Plage de Grande-Anse, Deshaies* ☎ *0590/28–44–42, 0690/53–42–84* *www.tainoscottages.fr/* *Closed late Aug.–late Oct.* *7 bungalows* *Free Breakfast.*

Tendacayou Ecolodge & Spa

$ | **B&B/INN** | The result of a remarkable 10-year saga, this quirky and inventive rain-forest resort consists of both tree houses and ground-level bungalows, as well as a wonderful restaurant—Le

Views of the sea and the town of Capesterre-de-Marie-Galante on the southeast coast of Marie-Galante.

Poisson Rouge—and a moderately priced spa. **Pros:** a boutique jammed with wonderfully exotic treasures from around the world; boardwalks rather than scary ladders access the tree houses; ample homemade breakfast. **Cons:** prices are expensive for what you get; isolated location, with no beach, phones, TVs, or in-room Wi-Fi; no air-conditioning. *Rooms from: €209* *Matouba La Haut, Deshaies* *0590/28–42–72* *www.tendacayou.com* *14 bungalows* *Free Breakfast.*

Marie-Galante

Columbus sighted this 60-square-mile (155-square-km) island on November 3, 1493; named it after his flagship, the *Maria Galanda*; and then sailed on. Marie-Galante is dotted with ruined 19th-century sugar mills, and sugar is still the island's major product. Honey and 59 percent rum are the other important commodities. Make a point to see one of the distilleries. The rolling hills of green cane, still worked by oxen and men with broad-brim straw hats, is like traveling back to the time when all of Guadeloupe was a giant farm. Marie-Galante is a peaceful place for those who want to escape touristic action and simply enjoy the countryside.

Although it's only an hour by high-speed ferry from Pointe-à-Pitre, the country folk here are still, for the most part, sweet and shy; crime is a rarity. That said, driving can be stressful, thanks to young men in dark cars rudely intimidating tourist drivers. You can see swarms of yellow butterflies and maybe a marriage carriage festooned with flowers, pulled by two white oxen. A daughter of the sea, Marie-Galante has some of the archipelago's most gorgeous, uncrowded beaches. Take time to explore the dramatic coast, where you'll find soaring cliffs—such as the Gueule Grand Gouffre (Mouth of the Giant Chasm) and Les Galeries (where the sea has sculpted a natural arcade)—and enormous sun-dappled grottoes, such as Le Trou à Diable, whose underground river can be explored with a guide. Port Louis, the island's "second city," is the new hip spot. The ferry dock is in Port Louis, and it's also on the charts for yachts and regattas. After sunset, the no-see-ums and mosquitoes can be a real irritation, so always be armed with repellent. At different times of year, you might experience a lot of nature trying to enter your hotel.

Château Murat

HISTORIC SIGHT | A mile from town, the Château Murat is a 19th-century sugar plantation and rum distillery housing exhibits on the history of rum making and sugarcane production going back three centuries. This former habitation was once the grandest sugar plantation in Guadeloupe. Various hurricanes left the chateau in ruins, with just remnants of the kitchen still standing. From the rubble rose the eco-museum that celebrates island crafts, and there is a garden for medicinal local plants. ✉ *Murat Estate, Rte. de Capesterre, Grand-Bourg* ☎ *0590/97–48–68* 🎫 *Free.*

★ Habitation Bellevue Distillery

DISTILLERY | If time allows just one distillery here, choose the modern Domaine de Bellevue, whose rum has taken home the gold during official French competitions. Free tastings are just one inviting element. There are award-winning, pure rums (50%–59%) and also excellent tropical liqueurs (punches). Bellevue, in operation since 1821, is the top rum exporter of Guadeloupe/Marie-Galante with the only eco-positive distillery in the world. ✉ *Capesterre-de-Marie-Galante, off Rte. D202, Capesterre-de-Marie-Galante* ☎ *0590/97–29–58, 0690/13–49–00* 🌐 *habitation-bellevue.com* 🎫 *Free.*

Kreol West Indies

HISTORY MUSEUM | This fascinating Creole museum in a renovated bungalow houses information and graphics relating to Guadeloupe's earliest inhabitants, as well as some pirate artifacts. Rooms are furnished with antiques and collectibles that depict island life during various eras through the 1950s. Devoted to Creole culture, the museum also doubles as an art gallery, with attractive contemporary paintings by island artists. This labor of love displays furnishings and descriptives owned by a French "culture lover," Vincent Nicaudie. The gift shop carries quality Marie-Galante logo T-shirts and caps, beachwear, and island food products. Also, this is a Wi-Fi hot spot. ✉ *Plage de Grand Bourg, D 203, toward Capesterre, Grand-Bourg* ✥ *100 meters after exiting the town, continue in the direction of Capesterre and it is on the right-hand side of the road* ☎ *0590/97–21–56* 🌐 *www.kreolwestindies.com* 🎫 *Free* ⏲ *Closed Mon. and Tues.*

Rhum du Père Labat Distillery, Domaine Poisson

DISTILLERY | Located on the 18-century Poisson Estate, the distillery produces Rhum du Père Labat rum (nearly 200,000 liters a year), which is considered among the finest in the Caribbean. The atelier turns out lovely pottery, as well. Tastings are available, but watch out—those samples are quite strong, especially considering that it's open only in the morning. ✉ *Poisson Estate, Rte. N9, Grand-Bourg* ☎ *0590/97–03–79* 🌐 *rhumduperelabat.com* 🎫 *Free.*

Competitions des Boeufs Tirants

The annual ox-pulling competition on Marie-Galante goes on for two weeks in November. Oxen were once used to operate the sugar mills and teams of oxen are still used in local agriculture. Where else will you see this in your lifetime?

Beaches

Anse de Vieux Fort

BEACH | This gorgeous Marie-Galante beach stretches along crystal-clear waters, with a nearby mangrove swamp you can explore on hiking trails. The beaches in this area are wide due to the erosion of the sand dunes. It's also known as a beach for lovers because of the solitude. Bring your own everything. You can pair a visit to Château Murat with your beach day. **Amenities:** none. **Best for:** snorkeling; solitude; sunset; swimming; walking. ✉ *Rte. D205, north of Saint-Louis, St-Louis.*

Plage de Petite Anse

BEACH | This long, golden beach is punctuated by seagrape trees. It's idyllic during the week, but on weekends the crowds of locals and "urban refugees" from the main island arrive. Le Touloulou's great creole seafood restaurant provides the only facilities. The golden sands are ideal for shelling. **Amenities:** food and drink; parking (no fee); toilets. **Best for:** partiers; snorkeling; sunset; swimming; walking. ✉ *Rte. D 203, Capesterre-de-Marie-Galante* ✣ *6½ miles (10 km) east of Grand-Bourg.*

Restaurants

Chez Henri

$$ | CARIBBEAN | This hip place on the water, flanked by the town pier, is named for Henri Vergerolle, the passionate chef-owner—an island character who spent much of his life in France but returned to open this restaurant and cultural center. Everything is fresh here, but the limited menu might have only three main courses available (you can always choose the fish of the day). Just kick back, begin with a rum and fresh-squeezed juice, and listen to African blues. **Known for:** live music; smoked fish; art and sculpture exhibits. [$] *Average main: €17* ✉ *8 Avenue des Caraïbes, St-Louis* ☎ *0590/97–04–57* 🌐 *www.chezhenri.net* ⏲ *Closed Mon.*

★ Manman'dlo the Siren

$$$ | FRENCH FUSION | You may hear that one of the best tables on the island is found at the small *hôtel de charme* La Rose du Brésil—and the rumor is true. Shellfish abounds here, and desserts are inspired by the island's tropical fruits. **Known for:** fresh-squeezed lime daiquiri; sophisticated environment; grilled spiny lobster, shrimp, and scallops. [$] *Average main: €28* ✉ *La Rose du Brésil, Rte. du littoral, D 203, Capesterre-de-Marie-Galante* ☎ *0590/97–47–39, 0690/92–19–95* 🌐 *www.larosedubresil.com/lerestaurantmanmandlo* ⏲ *Closed Wed.*

★ Le Touloulou Le Restaurant

$$ | SEAFOOD | On the curve of Plage de Petite Anse, this casual hotel restaurant is the "happening" place on Marie-Galante. It has tables in the sand, stylish Euro decor, and the freshest, most delicious seafood cooked Franco/Caribbean style. **Known for:** ouassous (jumbo crayfish) in coconut sauce; fricassee of conch or octopus; feet-in-the-sand dining. [$] *Average main: €18* ✉ *Plage de Petite Anse, Capesterre-de-Marie-Galante* ☎ *0590/97–32–63* 🌐 *www.touloulou-mariegalante.com* ⏲ *Closed Thurs. No dinner Sun. and Wed.*

Hotels

Accommodations here are mainly inexpensive, locally owned beachfront bungalows or complexes with international owners. Bwa Chik Hotel in St-François, on the "mainland," offers a package that includes ferry tickets to Marie-Galante.

La Rose du Brésil

$ | B&B/INN | At this tiny boutique hotel, all of the suites have impressive kitchens—though proximity to its good in-hotel restaurant and others nearby may not be an incentive for cooking. **Pros:** quality mattresses are replaced regularly; across from the beach; excellent restaurant plus a tapas bar. **Cons:** tight space; no resort amenities; no sea views

La Désirade

According to legend, this outlying island of Guadeloupe, the "desired land," was so named by the crew of Christopher Columbus, whose tongues were dry for want of fresh water when they spied the island; alas, it was the dry season season. The 8-square-mile (21-square-km) island, 5 miles (8 km) east of St-François, is a chalky plateau with an arid climate, perennial sunshine, cacti, and iguanas.

"Desirable" is the operative word here. This small, safe, somewhat remote island is an absolute find for those who prefer a road less traveled, who want their beaches long and white, and who don't mind that accommodations are simple if the price is right.

Rent a four-wheel drive to climb the zigzag road that leads to the Grande Montagne. Make a photo stop at the diminutive white chapel, which offers a panorama of the sea below. Afraid that you might zig instead of zag down the precipice? Then opt instead for a fun, informative van tour that you join near the tourist office at the harbor near the ferry dock. The ruins of the original settlement—a leper colony—are on the tour.

Only one road runs around the perimeter of the island, and if you're interested in visiting one of the many gorgeous beaches shaded by coconut palms and seagrape trees, you can do that on a scooter. Driving is safer here than most anywhere.

from accommodations. *Rooms from: €78 ✉ Rue du Littoral, D 203, Capesterre-de-Marie-Galante ☎ 0590/97–26–25, 0690/91–19–95, 0590/97–47–39 ⊕ www.larosedubresil.com ⇆ 10 units 🍴 No Meals ☞ Weekly rates.*

Le Soleil Levant Hotel and Resort

$ | **HOTEL** | Low prices, gorgeous hilltop views, and nice dual pools keep this simple, family-owned complex filled. **Pros:** family-friendly; good air-conditioning; free, reliable Wi-Fi in rooms. **Cons:** staff not accustomed to American guests; hotel rooms are not large and get some noise; you'll need a car. *Rooms from: €55 ✉ Section Marie-Louise, 42 rue de la Marine, Les Hauteurs de Capesterre, Capesterre-de-Marie-Galante ☎ 0590/97–31–55 ⊕ lesoleillevant.fr ⇆ 21 units 🍴 No Meals.*

Le Touloulou

$ | **APARTMENT** | Le Touloulou offers four simple stucco one-bedroom bungalows, two of which have kitchenettes, as well as a two-bedroom bungalow, also with a kitchenette; most importantly, you can roll out of your terrace hammock onto the beach. **Pros:** beachfront location at a budget price; adjacent restaurant and fun bar; genial, bilingual chef-owner. **Cons:** simple, no-frills place; lacks the usual resort amenities; can be loud on weekends. *Rooms from: €65 ✉ Plage de Petite-Anse, Capesterre-de-Marie-Galante ☎ 0690/39–13–06 ⊕ www.touloulou-mariegalantecom ⇆ 5 bungalows 🍴 No Meals.*

Le Village de Canada

$ | **APARTMENT** | The decades-old complex offers studios, bungalows, and apartments, some with sea views and a pool but no beach (though one is close by). **Pros:** good central location equidistant between Grand-Bourg and St.-Louis; private terraces; moderate prices, especially on a weekly basis. **Cons:** a car is a must since there is no restaurant; furnishings, TVs, and bedding are dated; not on the beach. *Rooms from: €77 ✉ off D 304,*

Canada Section, St-Louis ☎ 0590/97–86–11 🌐 www.villagedecanada.com ⇆ 10 units 🍽 No Meals.

Shopping

La Suite

OTHER SPECIALTY STORE | This classy boutique is something that you might expect to find in St. Barth or St. Martin, not on the out-island of Marie-Galante. The shop is a mélange of cosmetics, perfumes, beachwear, vintage cards and art, seagrass baskets, and coffee-table books on the island's history and culture. Products are all natural from Guadeloupe and St. Martin—glamorous cosmetics to essential oils, along with bug spray (which you will need on this island). And then there are some accessories like French sunglasses, flip-flop wedgies and utilitarian ones with recycled rubber from Kenya, and beads and original jewelry by island designers like Nathalie Julan. If you're lucky, you may come on a day when an evening soirée is planned—something literary, with a guitarist and flutist performing, or a beauty makeover. *✉ 38 rue du Dr Marcel Etzol, Grand-Bourg ☎ 0590/97–06–90.*

Îles des Saintes

The eight-island archipelago of Îles des Saintes, often referred to as Les Saintes, dots the waters off the southern coast of Guadeloupe. The islands are Terre-de-Haut, Terre-de-Bas, Ilet à Cabrit, Grand Ilet, La Redonde, La Coche, Le Pâté, and Les Augustins. Columbus sighted them on November 4, 1493, and named them Los Santos (Les Saintes in French) in reference to All Saints' Day.

Only Terre-de-Haut and Terre-de-Bas are inhabited, with a combined population of about 3,500. Many of the Saintois are fair-haired, blue-eyed descendants of Breton and Norman sailors. Unless they are in the tourism industry, residents tend to be taciturn and standoffish. Fishing is still their main source of income, and they take pride in their work. The shores are lined with fishing boats and *filets bleus* (blue nets with orange buoys).

Terre-de-Haut

With just five square miles (13 square km) and a population of about 1,500, Terre-de-Haut is the largest and most developed of Les Saintes. Bourg, its "big city," has a single main street lined with bistros, cafés, and shops. Clutching the hillside are trim white houses with bright red or blue doors, balconies, and gingerbread frills.

Terre-de-Haut's ragged coastline is scalloped with lovely coves and beaches, including the semi-nude beach at Anse Crawen. The beautiful bay, complete with a "sugarloaf" mountain, has been called a mini Rio. There are precious few vehicles or taxis on-island, so you'll often find yourself walking despite the hilly terrain. Or you can add to the din and rent a motorbike. Take your time on these rutted roads, as there might be a goat or two or more around any bend. Two traffic lights have brought a small amount of order to the motorbike "traffic." By the way, the scooter agencies neglect to tell you that scootering in town from 9 to noon and from 2 to 4 is prohibited.

This island makes a great day trip, but you can really get a feel for Les Saintes if you stay overnight. With the flavor of St. Barth, Terre-de-Haut is a fraction of the price. Note: Most shops and restaurants close for two hours in the afternoon.

TIP→ The coffee-table book is wonderful introduction to the island, as well as a travel keepsake, and is available in most of the island's shops.

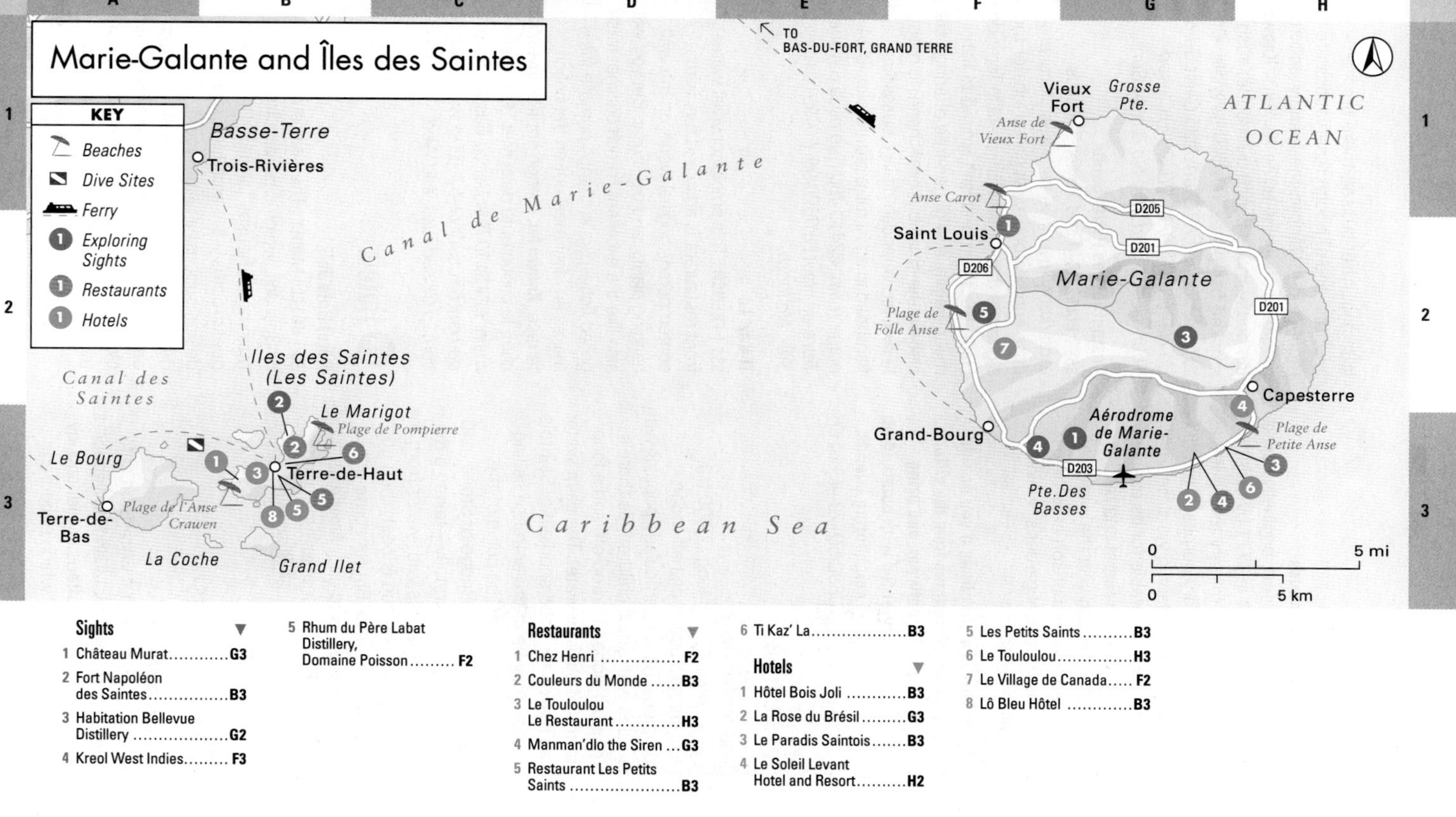

Sights

1 Château Murat............G3
2 Fort Napoléon des Saintes................B3
3 Habitation Bellevue Distillery G2
4 Kreol West Indies......... F3
5 Rhum du Père Labat Distillery, Domaine Poisson......... F2

Restaurants

1 Chez Henri F2
2 Couleurs du Monde B3
3 Le Touloulou Le Restaurant.............H3
4 Manman'dlo the Siren ...G3
5 Restaurant Les Petits Saints B3
6 Ti Kaz' La...................B3

Hotels

1 Hôtel Bois Joli B3
2 La Rose du Brésil G3
3 Le Paradis Saintois.......B3
4 Le Soleil Levant Hotel and Resort..........H2
5 Les Petits Saints B3
6 Le Touloulou...............H3
7 Le Village de Canada..... F2
8 Lô Bleu Hôtel B3

Sights

Fort Napoléon des Saintes

MILITARY SIGHT | This fort, originally called Fort Louis, was built in 1777 by order of King Louis XVI as a military tower. It was never used for military purposes but did serve as a penitentiary in wartime. The museum here is notable for its exhaustive exhibit of the greatest sea battles ever fought. You can visit the well-preserved barracks and prison cells or just admire the botanical gardens, which specialize in cacti.

TIP→ This is a hill climb; if you decide to walk, allow 30 minutes from the village, wear comfortable footwear, and bring water. You'll be rewarded with outstanding views of the bay and neighboring islands. ✉ *Terre-de-Haut* ☎ *0690/50–73–43* 🎫 *€5.*

Beaches

Plage de Pompierre

BEACH | **FAMILY** | This long (2,600 ft.), palm-fringed beach on half-moon Pompierre Bay is particularly popular with families with small children, as there's a gradual slope, no drop-off, and a long stretch of shallow water. The calm water also makes for good snorkeling. Saintois women may be at the entrance selling snacks and drinks. The curve of the beach is called the Bridge of Stone, and you can walk it—carefully—taking a dip in the crater that fills with water from the Atlantic. Morning sun is best; then go to Le Salako Snack Bar for some grilled fresh fish and a cold one. **Amenities:** food and drink. **Best for:** snorkeling; sunrise; swimming; walking. ✉ *Rue de Pont Pierre, Terre-de-Haut.*

Restaurants

Couleurs du Monde

$$ | **CAFÉ** | This colorful waterfront café offers free Wi-Fi, books and newspapers to read, teas and coffees, wine, and icy rum cocktails, all of which encourage lounging. After sunset, there are aperitifs; and although reservations are requested for dinner, the friendly, accommodating staff also takes walk-ins. **Known for:** house-made punch du monde; sushi; smoked fish plates. $ *Average main: €18* ✉ *Le Mouillage, 33 Rue Jean Calot, Terre-de-Haut* ☎ *0590/92–70–98* ⏲ *Closed Thurs., Sept. and Oct. No dinner Sun.*

Restaurant Les Petits Saints

$$$ | **ECLECTIC** | Chef Xavier Simon is remarkably inventive with fresh local produce and seafood, with grilled lobster the signature dish of his restaurant in Terre-de-Haut. But the menu isn't limited to fish; meat, vegan, and gluten-free offerings are also on the small but ever-changing menu. **Known for:** verandah dining; ouassous flambéed in aged rum; profiteroles. $ *Average main: €24* ✉ *480 Rue de la Savane, Terre-de-Haut* ☎ *0590/99–50–99* ⏲ *Closed Sun. No lunch.*

Ti Kaz' La

$$$ | **FRENCH** | This small, convivial waterfront restaurant is artsy and fun, with contemporary, original works on the wall, hanging plants, and hip music. But you will also like the excellent French cuisine: fresh grilled fish—plus authentic *pomme frites*—makes an ideal meal out on the beach terrace. **Known for:** mango soufflé; inventive chef; le choucroute de la mer. $ *Average main: €24* ✉ *10 Rue Benoit Cassin, Terre-de-Haut* ☎ *0590/99–57–63* 🌐 *www.tikazla.com* ⏲ *Closed Tues. and Wed.*

Hotels

Hôtel Bois Joli

$$ | **HOTEL** | **FAMILY** | The seafront section of Bois Joli, which sits apart from the main hotel, houses Terre-de-Haut's best guest rooms—the architecture and design suggest a luxury yacht, including dark wood accents and portholes. **Pros:** organized, clean, and well-serviced; fairly close to nice beaches; an attractive pool traversed by a diminutive bridge. **Cons:** few staff speak English; no bellmen and no elevators in the new section; you'll need an electric car or scooter or take the shuttle. $ *Rooms from: €280* ✉ *Rte. de Bois Joli, Terre-de-Haut* ☎ *0590/99–50–38* 🌐 *www.hotelboisjoli.fr* 🛏 *30 rooms* 🍽 *Free Breakfast.*

Le Paradis Saintois
$ | **APARTMENT** | You'll feel like the king of the hill as you rock yourself to sleep in a hammock on the terrace of your apartment or gaze down on the sea below. **Pros:** discounts for longer stays; lots of fun here; bicycles available for rent. **Cons:** no hotel services; a hike uphill from town; no phones or TVs in some rooms. $ *Rooms from: €58* ✉ *211 Rte. des Prés Cassin, Terre-de-Haut* ☎ *0590/99–56–16* 🌐 *paradis.saintois.pagesperso-orange.fr* 🛏 *8 units* 🍽 *No Meals* ☞ *3-night minimum.*

Les Petits Saints
$ | **B&B/INN** | This charismatic landmark inn, which draws both couples and families, has simple, tile-floor rooms with enviable hillside views overlooking the bay. **Pros:** TV has international channels; free airport and ferry port transfers; village just down the hill. **Cons:** reminiscent of a 1970s island guesthouse; breakfast and check-out are both early; not particularly luxurious. $ *Rooms from: €130* ✉ *480 Rue de la Savane, Terre-de-Haut* ☎ *0590/99–50–99* 🌐 *www.petitssaints.com* ⏲ *Closed Sept.* 🛏 *5 rooms* 🍽 *Free Breakfast.*

Lô Bleu Hôtel
$ | **HOTEL** | **FAMILY** | This small, cheerful beachfront hotel is painted sunset orange with marine-blue trim; dramatic nightlights illuminate the beach area, which is furnished with chaises. **Pros:** right on the bay; large front rooms with sea view and balconies; family-friendly, with baby monitors and some bunk beds. **Cons:** no resort amenities; bar but no restaurant; not all front desk staff speaks English. $ *Rooms from: €126* ✉ *Fond de Curé, Terre-de-Haut* ☎ *0590/92–40–00* 🌐 *www.lobleuhotel.com* 🛏 *10 rooms* 🍽 *No Meals.*

Shopping

Maogany Boutique
MIXED CLOTHING | At this shop, which resembles a yacht, you'll find batik creations and clothing in luminescent seashell and blue shades. Ladies love *pareus* (wraparound fabric for skirts) in the colors of the sea, from pale green to deep turquoise, as well as the jewelry. For both men and ladies, there are authentic Panama hats—tropical fedoras (not inexpensive) in classic white *and* tropical colors. There are also several lines of women's clothing by French designers (like Nathalie Joubert), tunics, crocheted tops, and tiered long skirts. Many items are quite expensive but cool and lightweight. And here, silkscreen is the real deal. ✉ *26 Rue Jean Calot, Terre-de-Haut* ☎ *0590/99–50–12* 🌐 *www.maogany-shop.com.*

Pascal Foy
ART GALLERIES | Artist Pascal Foy produces stunning homages to traditional Creole architecture: paintings of houses that incorporate collage make marvelous wall hangings. As his fame has grown, media attention has expanded and prices have risen. You are more likely to find a family member manning the shop nowadays. ✉ *Rte. de Marigot, Terre-de-Haut* ☎ *0690/43–13–09* ☞ *Call for an appointment.*

Tata Somba
WOMEN'S CLOTHING | This boutique is owned by a Frenchwoman with characteristic good taste. Ladies will find French and Italian fashions here—cool, lightweight skirts and dresses, stylish shade hats for protection from the island's strong sun, jewelry, sandals, accessories, and hip clothes for little girls. ✉ *Rte. de la Fort Napoléon, Terre-de-Haut* ☎ *0590/99–51–65.*

Activities

BOATING AND SAILING

Guadeloupe's craggy coastline and the sea's variegated blues and greens are gorgeous. If you plan to sail these waters, though, you should be aware that the winds and currents tend to be strong. You'll find excellent, well-equipped marinas in Pointe-à-Pitre, Bas-du-Fort, Deshaies, St-François, and Gourbeyre where you can rent a yacht (bareboat or crewed). To make a bareboat charter, companies will evaluate your navigational and seamanship skills. If you do not pass, you must hire a skipper.

Antilles Sail

BOATING | Antilles Sail is a charter operation specializing in catamarans from 40 to 49 feet and a 45-foot trimaran; each accommodates up to eight guests. For those who don't qualify to skipper their own ship or who want to just relax and be pampered, a captain and crew can be hired. Provisioning and meal service can be arranged. The fleet also includes monohulls, from 35 to 55 feet, for cruising from five to 15-days. ✉ *Quai No. 9, Boutique des Moulins Marina, Pointe-à-Pitre* ☎ *0590/90–16–81* 🌐 *www.antilles-sail.com.*

DIVING

The main diving area at the **Cousteau Underwater Park,** just off Basse-Terre near Pigeon Island, offers routine dives to 60 feet. The numerous glass-bottom boats and other craft make the site feel like a marine parking lot; however, the underwater sights are spectacular.

Les Saintes is known for its underwater hills, caves, canyons, and wall dives. Divers can see sponges of varied colors and gorgeous underwater trees that sway. Sec Pate is a famous underwater mountain, off the island's coast, in open seas.

Guides and instructors are certified under the French CMAS (some also have PADI, but none have NAUI). Most operators offer two-hour dives three times per day for about €50 to €55 per dive; three-dive packages are about €120 to €145; six-dive packages, €250. Hotels and dive operators usually rent snorkeling gear.

Les Heures Saines

SCUBA DIVING | **FAMILY** | Les Heures Saines is the premier operator for dives in the Cousteau Underwater Park. Freediving, supervised diving, and instruction from beginner to advanced certification are all available, along with wreck, night, and nitrox diving. The instructors, many of them English speakers, are also excellent with children. ✉ *Rocher de Malendure, Pigeon, Bouillante* ☎ *0590/98–86–63* 🌐 *www.heures-saines.gp.*

Pisquettes Diving Club

SCUBA DIVING | **FAMILY** | Dive master Cedric Phalipon of "Pisquettes Club de Plongée Des Saintes" knows all the best sites. He gives excellent lessons in English, too. Beginners and PADI-certified divers are all welcome. Small tanks are available for kids, who are taken buddy-diving. ✉ *Rue Jean Calot, Terre-de-Haut* ☎ *0590/99–88–80, 0690/49–12–33* 🌐 *www.pisquettes.com.*

PPK (Plaisir Plongée Karokera)

SCUBA DIVING | PPK (Plaisir Plongée Karokera) is well-established and has a good reputation among those who dive off Pigeon Island. One dive boat departs three times a day. A second

En Route

If you're driving from Ste-Anne to the St-François Marina area, follow signs first to St-François, then look for signs to the marina and Pointe des Châteaux—not St-François centre ville, which is the old town and, although a nice detour to see the market, a circuitous route to the marina.

dive boat goes to Les Saintes, with one dive at a wreck, the other at a reef, and lunch included. English-speaking dive masters are PADI-certified. ✉ *Plage de Malendure, Bouillante* ☎ *0590/98–82–43* 🌐 *www.ppk-plongee-guadeloupe.com.*

FISHING

Not far offshore from Pigeon-Bouillante, in Basse-Terre, you'll find a bounty of big-game fish such as bonito, dolphinfish, captain fish, barracuda, kingfish, and tuna. You can also thrill to the challenge of big billfish such as marlin and swordfish. Anglers have been known to come back with as many as three blue marlins in a single day. For Ernest Hemingway wannabes, this is it! To reap this harvest, you'll need to charter one of the high-tech sportfishing boats with flying bridges, competent skippers, and mates. The price ranges from about $430 to $600 a day, with lunch and drinks included. The boats accommodate up to six passengers.

Captain Tony

FISHING | Like father, like son: Tony Burel operates the sportfishing boat that he and his dad, Michel, worked for years. *Veni Vedi Fishi* is outfitted to go into combat with the big-game fish, and he has hauled many a billfish aboard. The boat has the latest generation of electronics and is considered the most commodious sport fisherman on the island. He charges per-person, not for a full boat; nonfishers and kids are welcome at a lower rate and hotel transfers are available for an additional fee. The skipper will be happy to take your picture with your catch of the day. And if you are not into jigging or chumming, check the website for snorkeling adventures and other excursions, like Champagne sunset cruises. ✉ *Plage de Malendure, Bouillante* ☎ *0690/40–15–01.*

GOLF

Golf International de St-François

GOLF | Golf International de St-François is a par-70 course that was designed by Robert Trent Jones in 1978, with later alterations that made it more challenging (though many feel that the putting surfaces could use improvement). The course has an English-speaking pro and electric carts for rent. It's best to reserve tee times a day or two in advance, particularly during high season. There are no caddies. Clubs can be rented for a nominal fee. Guests at Bwa Chik Hotel & Golf get a discount. Le Birdy restaurant serves lunch daily and dinner Wednesday and Friday through Sunday; tapas are offered at the bar. ✉ *Av. d'l Europe, St-François* ☎ *0590/88–41–87* 🌐 *www.golf-saintfrancois.com* 🎟 *€46 for 9 holes, €77 for 18 holes* ⛳ *18 holes, 6550 yards, par 72.*

HIKING

With hundreds of trails and countless rivers and waterfalls, the **Parc National de la Guadeloupe** on Basse-Terre is the main draw for hikers. Some of the trails should be attempted only with an experienced guide. All tend to be muddy, so wear a good pair of boots. Know that even the young and fit can find these outings arduous; the unfit may find them painful. Start off slowly with a shorter hike, then go for the gusto.

Vert Intense

HIKING & WALKING | Vert Intense organizes hikes in the national park and to the volcano. You move from steaming hot springs to an icy waterfall in the same hike. Patient, safety-conscious guides bring you to heights that you never thought you could reach, including the top of La Soufrière. The volcano hike, the least-expensive excursion, must be booked four days in advance. When you are under the fumaroles, you can smell the sulfur (like rotten eggs) and you'll smell like sulfur until you take a shower (as will your clothes until you launder them). A mixed-adventure package spanning three days costs considerably more. The two-day bivouac and other adventures can be extreme; so before you decide to play Indiana Jones, know what to expect—and what's expected. The French-speaking guides, who also know some English and Spanish, can take you to other tropical forests and rivers for canyoning (climbing and scrambling on outcrops, usually along and above the water). If you are just one or two people, the company can team you up with a group. Vert Intense now has a guesthouse, Les Bananes Vertes (The Green Bananas), at the foot of the volcano where you can combine a stay with trekking and other activities. ✉ *Morne Houel, St-Claude* ☎ *0690/55–40–47* 🌐 *www.vert-intense.com.*

HORSEBACK RIDING

Le Haras de Saint-François

HORSEBACK RIDING | A 50-horse stable, the Equestrian Village of Saint-François has English-style instruction and Western-style trail rides for two or three hours. The latter will take you to the beach, where you can ride bareback into the sea. Prices start at €45 for a 90-minute "agricultural" walk and at €65 for a 2½-hour ride to the sea. Riders must be at least 12 years old. (Wear long pants and closed shoes.) ✉ *Chemin de la Princesse, St-François* ☎ *0690/58–99–92.*

KAYAKING

Centre Éconautique

KAYAKING | Centre Éconautique, aka Clear Blue Caraïbes, has mastered the art of underwater exploration without ever getting your hair wet. Rent a glass-bottom kayak, which allows you to see the myriad colors of one of the world's most beautiful bays. Paddleboards and clear-bottom, dinghylike inflatables also enable you to play in the water. The tours, which last either a half or full day, will let you be privy to the marine beauty of the coral reefs and sea life. Trips to the nearby Isle de Cabrito for a picnic and snorkeling are also offered. To find Centre Éconautique, take a left from the main dock, go two blocks, and look for its colorful signage on the right. ✉ *Ruelle Lasserre Lieu dit Mouillage, Terre-de-Haut* ☎ *0690/65–79–81.*

Centre Nautique Bleu Outremer

KAYAKING | Centre Nautique, on Creole Beach, rents sea kayaks (€17/hour), canoes (€25/hour), and stand-up paddleboards (€25/hour)—you must know how to swim! Staff can also arrange other activities—water skiing, towed buoy, diving, and snorkeling. ✉ *Hotel Fleur d'Épée, Bas du Fort, Le Gosier* ☎ *0590/90–85–11* 🌐 *www.plongee-bleu-outremer.com.*

SEA EXCURSIONS

Paradoxe Croisieres

SAILING | In high season, usually on Thursday, the 80-foot sailing catamaran *Paradoxe II* sails from St-François to Marie-Galante, anchoring at St. Louis or, if sea conditions permit, idyllic Anse Canot (€95). The trip usually includes a bus tour around Marie-Galante and a visit to a distillery. Otherwise, the 50-foot motor catamaran *Capresse* departs daily from St-François for Petite-Terre, an uninhabited island that's a nature preserve (€110). Passengers take guided walking tours, always on the lookout for iguanas, and then back to the beach to eat a lunch of grilled fish prepared by the boat's crew. In the afternoon, guests can snorkel in the lagoon. ✉ *St-François Marina, Ave. de l'Europe, St-François* ☎ *0590/88–41–73* 🌐 *paradoxe-croisieres.com.*

Chapter 14

JAMAICA

Updated by
Sheri-kae McLeod

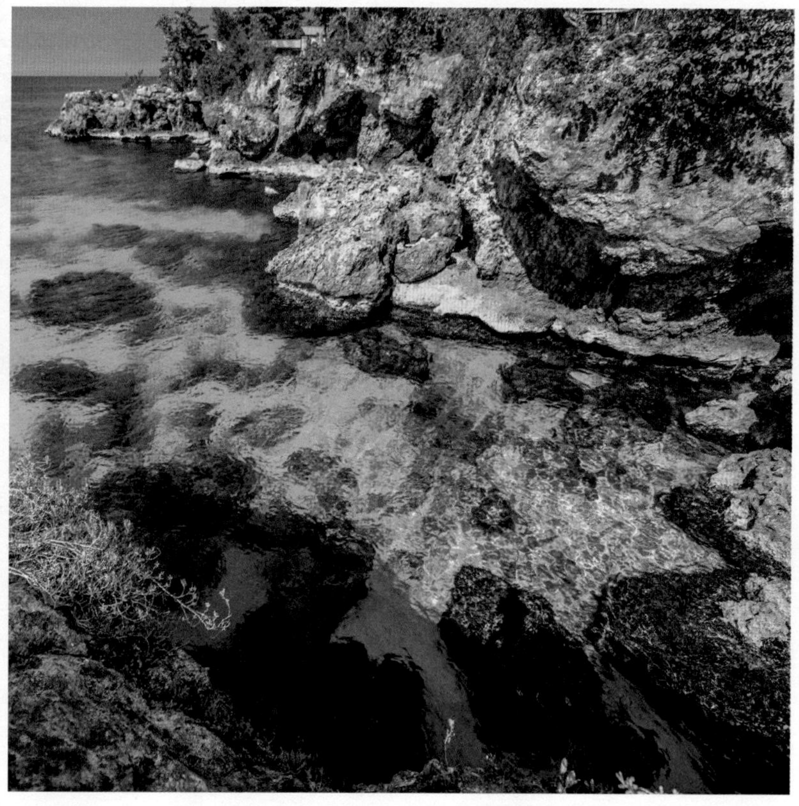

Sights	Restaurants	Hotels	Shopping	Nightlife
★★★★☆	★★★☆☆	★★★★★	★★★☆☆	★★★☆☆

WELCOME TO JAMAICA

TOP REASONS TO GO

★ **All-Inclusive Resorts:** Come to where they were invented.

★ **Delicious Food:** Jamaican cuisine is one of the most beloved in the world.

★ **Fun for the Kids:** Every conceivable activity, great beaches, and many child-friendly resorts appeal to families.

★ **Seven Mile Beach:** It's simply one of the Caribbean's best.

★ **Unique Culture:** Jamaica has rich cultural traditions—particularly local music, art, and cuisine.

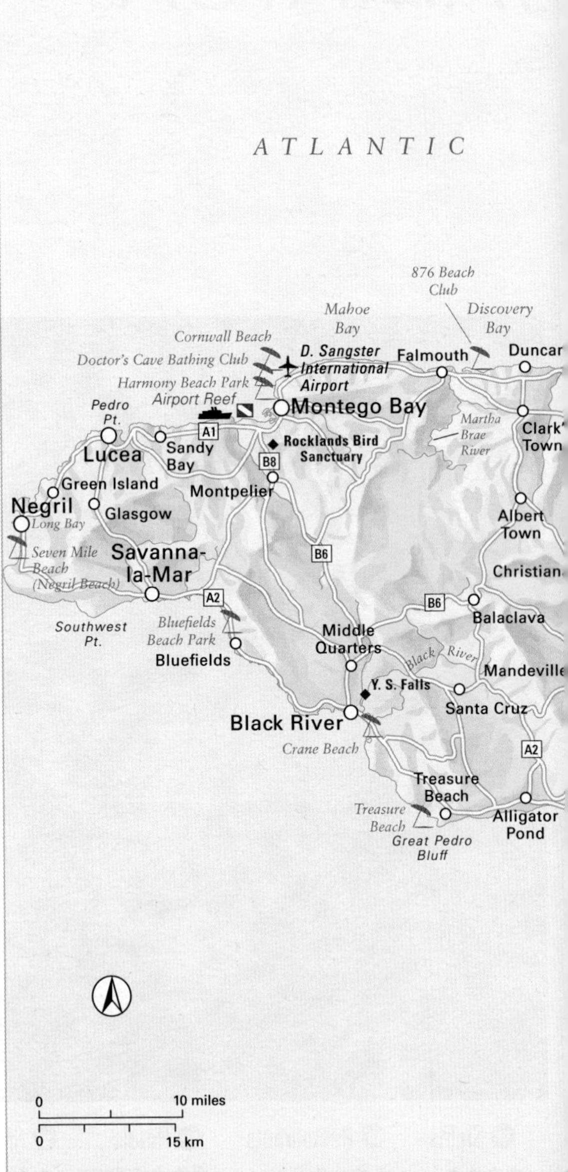

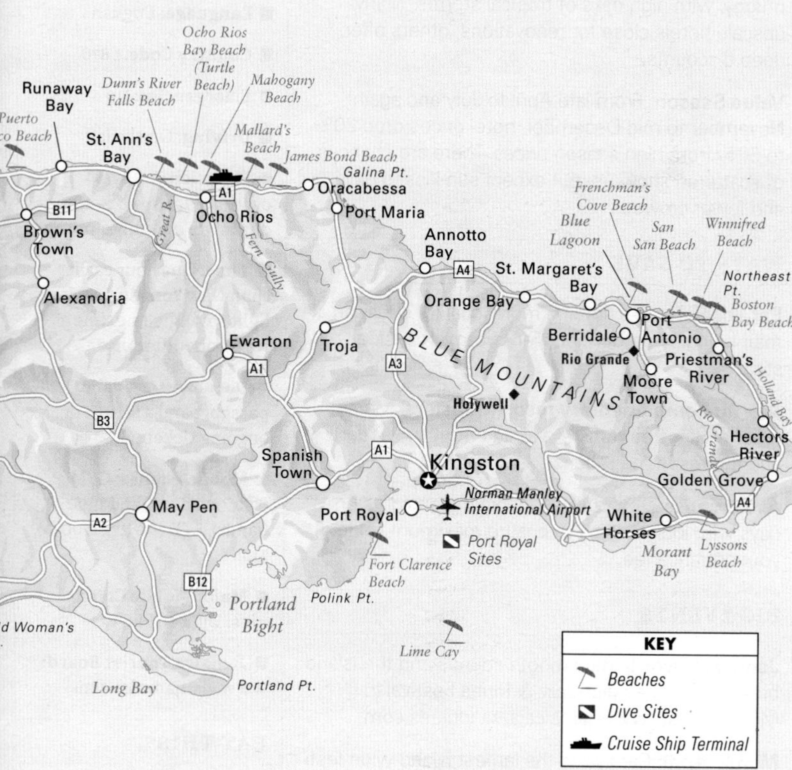
OCEAN
Ocho Rios Bay Beach (Turtle Beach)
Runaway Bay
Dunn's River Falls Beach
Mahogany Beach
Puerto
co Beach
St. Ann's Bay
Mallard's Beach
James Bond Beach
Galina Pt.
Oracabessa
Frenchman's Cove Beach
Brown's Town
Ocho Rios
Port Maria
Blue Lagoon
San San Beach
Winnifred Beach
Great R.
Annotto Bay
Fern Gully
St. Margaret's Bay
Northeast Pt.
Alexandria
Orange Bay
Boston Bay Beach
Port Antonio
Berridale
Ewarton
Troja
BLUE MOUNTAINS
Rio Grande
Priestman's River
Moore Town
Holland Bay
Holywell
Rio Grande
Hectors River
Spanish Town
Kingston
Golden Grove
Norman Manley International Airport
May Pen
Port Royal
White Horses
Port Royal Sites
Lyssons Beach
Morant Bay
Fort Clarence Beach
Portland Bight
Polink Pt.
Lime Cay
Long Bay
Portland Pt.
Caribbean Sea
B11
A1
A4
A3
B3
A2
B12
KEY
Beaches
Dive Sites
Cruise Ship Terminal

ISLAND SNAPSHOT

WHEN TO GO

High Season: Mid-December through mid-April is the most fashionable but most expensive time to visit, when the weather is typically sunny and warm. Good hotels are often booked far in advance, and you're guaranteed the most entertainment at resorts and the most people with whom to enjoy it.

Low Season: From August to late October, temperatures can grow oppressively hot and the weather muggy, with high risks of tropical storms. Many upscale hotels close for renovations; others offer deep discounts.

Value Season: From late April to July and again November to mid-December, hotel prices drop 20% to 50% from high season prices. There are chances of scattered showers, but expect sun-kissed days and fewer crowds.

WAYS TO SAVE

Eat Local. There's nothing more local (or cheaper) than trying some delicious jerk from a roadside stand.

Ask for complimentary resort transfers. Many resorts offer free transfers to and from the airport and the resort, on request.

Avoid cruise ship crowds. Avoid major sights on days with lots of ships to ensure maximum value of your entrance fee.

BIG EVENTS

January: Enjoy some smooth sounds and the island breeze at the Jamaica Jazz & Blues Festival in Montego Bay. www.jamaicajazzandblues.com

March–April: Carnival is the largest island-wide festival; it's held in Kingston, Ocho Rios, and Montego Bay. www.carnivalinjamaica.com

July: Reggae Sumfest is Jamaica's largest reggae concert with two days of musical performances. www.reggaesumfest.com

AT A GLANCE

- **Capital:** Kingston
- **Population:** 2,980,000
- **Currency:** Jamaican dollar; pegged to U.S. dollar
- **Money:** ATMs common; credit cards and U.S. dollars widely accepted
- **Language:** English
- **Country Code:** 1 876
- **Emergencies:** 119
- **Driving:** On the left
- **Electricity:** 110v/50 cycles; plugs are U.S. standard two- and three-prong
- **Time:** One hour earlier than New York during daylight saving; same time as New York otherwise
- **Documents:** A valid passport and a return or ongoing ticket
- **Mobile Phones:** GSM (850, 900, 1800, and 1900 bands), LTE 700 (17), 1700 (4), 2100 (4)
- **Major Mobile Companies:** Digicel, FLOW
- **Jamaica Tourist Board:** www.visitjamaica.com

EAT THIS

- **Jerk chicken:** rubbed with a spicy sauce and cooked over pimento wood.
- **Ackee and saltfish:** cod sautéed with ackee fruit.

Jamaicans define enthusiasm. Whether the topic is track and field or politics, the spirit of this island comes out in every interaction. Although the country is well-known for its tropical beauty, reggae music, and cuisine, you may find that your interactions with local residents are what you truly remember.

The island is rich in beauty, but a quick look around reveals widespread poverty and a disparity between the lives of resort guests and resort employees that is often staggering. Where vacationers opt to stay in Jamaica depends on factors ranging from vacation length to personal interests. With its direct air connections to many U.S. cities, Montego Bay (or MoBay) is favored by Americans taking short trips; many properties are just minutes from the airport. Other parts of Jamaica can be reached from Montego Bay in 60 to 90 minutes, while eastern areas may be more accessible from the other major airport—in the capital, Kingston.

Some of the island's earliest residents were the indigenous Arawak people, who arrived from South America around AD 650 and named the island Xaymaca, or "land of wood and water." Centuries later, the Arawaks welcomed Christopher Columbus on his second voyage to the New World. Later, when the Spanish arrived, the peaceful inhabitants were executed or taken as slaves.

The Spanish maintained control of the island until 1655 when the English arrived. Soon, slavery increased as sugar became a booming industry. In 1834 slavery was abolished, but the sugar, as well as banana industries, continued. Jamaica's plantation owners looked for another source of labor. From 1838 to 1917, more than 30,000 Indians immigrated here, followed by about 5,000 Asians as well as Middle Easterners, primarily from what is now Lebanon. (Today although 95% of the population traces its bloodlines to Africa, Jamaica is a stockpot of cultures, including those of other Caribbean islands, Great Britain, the Middle East, India, China, Germany, Portugal, and South America.)

In the early 1900s, the boats that took the banana crop off the island began returning with travelers. By 1960 the tourism industry was the most important form of income, and in 1962, Jamaica gained independence. Along with tourism, agriculture and mining contribute to the island's considerable self-sufficiency.

Planning

Getting Here and Around

AIR

Most major airlines serve Jamaica, offering direct flights a number of key U.S. and Canadian cities, including Air Canada (Toronto), American (Austin, Charlotte, Chicago, Miami, New York, and Philadelphia), Delta (Atlanta, Detroit, Minneapolis, and New York), Southwest (Baltimore, Chicago, Fort Lauderdale, Houston, and Orlando), and United (Chicago and Newark). Several smaller, often budget-oriented, airlines also fly to Jamaica, including Frontier, JetBlue, Spirit, Virgin Atlantic, and WestJet. Most international flights come into Montego Bay, but some go to Kingston.

DOMESTIC AIRLINE CONTACTS Tim Air. ✉ *Sangster International Airport, Montego Bay* ☎ *876/952–2516* 🌐 *www.timair.net.* **Captain's Aviation.** ✉ *The Towers, 25 Dominica Dr., Kingston* ☎ *876/929–1805* 🌐 *www.captainsaviation.com.*

DOMESTIC AIRPORTS Ian Fleming International Airport. *(OCJ)* ✉ *Oracabessa* ✣ *8 miles (14 km) east of Ocho Rios* ☎ *876/975–3101, 876/975–3734* 🌐 *www.ifia.aero.* **Negril Aerodrome.** ✉ *Norman Manley Blvd., Negril* ☎ *876/957–5016* 🌐 *airportsauthorityjamaica.aero.* **Ken Jones Aerodrome.** ✉ *St. Margarets Bay, Port Antonio* ☎ *876/913–3926* 🌐 *www.airportsauthorityjamaica.aero.*

INTERNATIONAL AIRLINE CONTACTS Caribbean Airlines. ✉ *128 Old Hope Rd., Kingston* ☎ *800/523–5585 for reservations, 876/924–8331* 🌐 *www.caribbean-airlines.com.* **Cayman Airways.** ✉ *91 Owen Roberts Dr.* ☎ *866/759–1372* 🌐 *www.caymanairways.com.*

INTERNATIONAL AIRPORTS Donald Sangster International Airport. *(MBJ)* ✉ *Montego Bay* ☎ *876/952–3124* 🌐 *www.mbjairport.com.* **Norman Manley International Airport.** *(KIN)* ✉ *Kingston* ☎ *876/924–8452* 🌐 *www.nmia.aero.*

BUS

If you have a limited budget and need to get from Montego Bay to Kingston, Ocho Rios, or Negril, book with the **Knutsford Express,** an air-conditioned bus with scheduled service via north and south coasts and shuttle service to both major airports. It's one of the safest and most comfortable ways to travel around the island.

BUS CONTACTS Knutsford Express. ✉ *18 Dominica Dr., Kingston* ✣ *Next to the New Kingston Shopping Center* ☎ *876/971–1822, 876/940–0064* 🌐 *www.knutsfordexpress.com.*

CAR

Driving in Jamaica can be an extremely frustrating endeavor. You must constantly be on guard—for enormous potholes, people and animals darting out into the street, and aggressive drivers. Locals are quick to pass other cars—and sometimes two cars will pass simultaneously. Gas stations are open daily, and most accept credit cards, though you shouldn't count on the card machines always working. Driving in Jamaica is on the left, British-style.

CAR RENTALS

To rent a car, you must be at least 23 years old, have a valid driver's license (from any country), and have a valid credit or debit card. You may be required to post a security deposit before taking possession of your car; ask about it when you make the reservation. Rates can range from $40 to $120 a day after the addition of the compulsory insurance, which you must usually purchase even if your credit card offers it.

CAR RENTAL CONTACTS Avis Jamaica. ✉ *1 Merrick Ave., Kingston 10* ☎ *876/926–8021, 876/952-0762 montego bay airport, 876/924-8293 kingston airport* 🌐 *www.avis.com.jm.* **Budget Car Rental Jamaica.** ✉ *54 South Camp Rd., Kingston*

4, Kingston ☎ 876/759–1793 ⊕ www.budgetjamaica.com. **Fiesta Car Rentals.** ✉ *14 Waterloo Rd., Kingston ☎ 876/926–0133 in Kingston, 800/934–3782 ⊕ www.fiestacarrentals.com.* **Hertz.** ✉ *Norman Manley International Airport, Kingston ☎ 876/952–4250 ⊕ www.hertz.com.* **Island Car Rentals.** ✉ *17 Antiqua Ave., Kingston ☎ 876/929–5875 in Kingston, 866/978–5335 toll-free USA, 876/926–8861 island-wide ⊕ www.islandcarrentals.com.*

TAXI

Some but not all of Jamaica's taxis are metered. If you accept a driver's offer of his services as a tour guide, be sure to agree on a price before the vehicle is put into gear. (Note that a one-day tour should run about US$150 to $200, depending on distance traveled.) All licensed taxis display red Public Passenger Vehicle (PPV) plates. Your hotel concierge can call a taxi for you, or you can flag one down on the street. Rates are per car, not per passenger. In popular tourist areas, 25% is added to the rate between midnight and 5 am. Licensed minivans are also available and bear red PPV plates. JUTA is the largest taxi franchise, with offices in most resort areas.

TAXI CONTACTS JCAL Tours. ✉ *Claude Clarke Ave., Montego Bay ☎ 876/952–7574, 876/952–8277 ⊕ www.jcaltours.com.* **JUTA Tours.** ✉ *80 Claude Clarke Ave., Montego Bay ☎ 876/952–0813, 876/952–0623 ⊕ www.jutatoursltd.com.* **Pat's Car Rental and Taxi.** ✉ *5 Lewis St., Savanna La Mar, Westmoreland ☎ 876/918–0431, 876/919–2297 ⊕ www.patscarrentaljamaica.com.*

Beaches

Although hotel beaches are generally private and restricted to guests above the high-water mark, other beaches are public and open to all kinds of vendors, who can sometimes get aggressive. In resort areas, even if the beach area is considered private, the area below the high-water mark is always public, so vendors will roam longer beaches looking for business. In most cases, a simple "no thanks" will do.

Festivals and Events

There are lots of events and festivals happening in Jamaica, but the largest island-wide festival is Carnival, which is held in Kingston, Ocho Rios, and Montego Bay every March and April. Held in mid-July, Reggae Sumfest is Jamaica's largest reggae concert festival.

Bacchanal Jamaica

FESTIVALS | Kingston is said to be the heartbeat of Jamaica, and at no time does that heart beat louder than during the annual Carnival. This colorful festival begins in March and culminates in a big parade with wonderful costumes the Sunday after Easter. Other events are held around the island. ✉ *Kingston ☎ 876/754–5396, 876/351–2094 ⊕ www.bacchanaljamaica.com.*

Calabash International Literary Festival

FESTIVALS | Three days and nights of both literary and musical talent are featured at this festival, held in May of even-numbered years. Fans come from all over Jamaica and beyond. Past authors have included Rachel Manley, Andrea Levy, and Sonia Sanchez. ✉ *Jakes, Calabash Bay, Treasure Beach ☎ 876/965–3000 ⊕ www.calabashfestival.org.*

Jamaica Food & Drink Festival

FESTIVALS | This nine-day festival takes place every November in Kingston and showcases the best of Jamaica's cuisine, with live entertainment and fun attractions, too. ✉ *Kingston ☎ 876/570–5709 ⊕ www.jafoodanddrink.com.*

★ **Jamaica Jazz & Blues**

FESTIVALS | Held in a stadium 25 minutes east of Montego Bay on the last Thursday–Saturday of January, the music festival attracts followers from around the world. Previous headliners include Mary J. Blige, Michael Bolton, Celine Dion, Kenny Rogers, and Alicia Keys. Tickets usually go on sale online in late November or early December. ✉ *Greenfield Stadium, Trelawny* 🌐 *jamaicajazzandblues.com.*

★ Jamaica Rum Festival

FESTIVALS | Held in Kingston at the end of the winter season around early March, this two-day festival revels in Jamaica's rum culture with seminars, workshops, tastings, and live entertainment. ✉ *Hope Gardens, 231 Old Hope Rd,, Kingston* ☎ *876/999–7867* 🌐 *www.jarumfestival.com.*

Ocho Rios Jazz Festival

FESTIVALS | The biggest event in Ocho Rios, this June jazz festival has been running since 1991, when it was one day. Now eight days, it draws top names in the genre. ✉ *Ocho Rios* ☎ *876/927–3544, 323/857–5358* 🌐 *www.ochoriosjazzja.com.*

★ Rebel Salute

FESTIVALS | Over the years, this has grown to be one of Jamaica's biggest reggae festivals. As a family-oriented, roots-reggae event, no meat or alcohol is served at this two-day celebration held in January. ✉ *Grizzly's Plantation Cove, St. Ann's Bay* ☎ *900/1234–5679* 🌐 *www.rebelsalutejamaica.com.*

Reggae Marathon

FESTIVALS | Runners can test themselves on a 26.2-mile (42.1-km), 13.1-mile (21.1-km), or 6.2-mile (10-km) run along the road by the beach. This event, held the first Saturday of December, draws competitors from around the world and gets bigger every year. ✉ *Long Bay Beach Park, Norman Manley Blvd., Negril* ☎ *876/967–4903* 🌐 *www.reggaemarathon.com.*

★ Reggae Sumfest

FESTIVALS | Those who know and love reggae should visit Montego Bay in mid-July for this weeklong concert, featuring a host of parties that lead up to two days of musical performances that attract big names. Tickets are sold for each night's performances or by multievent passes. ✉ *Montego Bay* ☎ *876/953–2933* 🌐 *www.reggaesumfest.com.*

★ Shaggy and Friends

CONCERTS | This biennial stage show is a charity concert put on by reggae superstar Shaggy in January to benefit Jamaica's Bustamante Hospital for Children. ✉ *Jamaica House, 36 Hope Rd,, Kingston* 🌐 *www.shaggymakeadifferencefoundation.org.*

Health and Safety

Dengue, chikungunya, and zika have all been reported throughout the Caribbean. We recommend that you protect yourself from these mosquito-borne illnesses by keeping your skin covered and/or wearing mosquito repellent, especially during the rainy season (May and September to November). The mosquitoes that transmit these viruses are as active by day as they are by night.

Hotels

Jamaica is the birthplace of the Caribbean all-inclusive resort, which is still the most popular vacation option on the island. Montego Bay has the largest concentration of resorts on the island; Negril, known as the Capital of Casual, is a more relaxed haven on the west coast. Both offer a mix of large and small resorts, plus good nightlife. Runaway Bay and Ocho Rios are more than an hour east of MoBay. Port Antonio, a sleepy, laid-back haven, has a few resorts and a quiet atmosphere and is usually accessed by a short flight or long drive from Kingston. The South Coast has a few small resorts, uncrowded beaches, and only one large resort.

Package prices usually include airport transfers, accommodations, three meals a day, snacks, all bar drinks (often including premium liquors) and soft drinks, a full menu of sports options (including scuba diving and golf at high-end resorts), nightly entertainment, and all gratuities and taxes. At most all-inclusives, the only surcharges are for such luxuries as spa and beauty treatments, phone calls, tours, vow-renewal ceremonies, and weddings (often included at high-end establishments).

The all-inclusive market is especially strong with couples. To maintain a romantic atmosphere (no Marco Polo games in the pool), some resorts have minimum-age requirements between 12 and 18. Other properties court families with supervised kids' programs, family-friendly entertainment, and in-room amenities for young travelers.

Hotel reviews have been shortened. For full information, visit Fodors.com.

What It Costs in U.S. Dollars

	$	$$	$$$	$$$$
RESTAURANTS				
	under $12	$12–$20	$21–$30	over $30
HOTELS				
	under $275	$275–$375	$376–$475	over $475

PRIVATE VILLAS

Ocho Rios is filled with private villas, especially in the Discovery Bay area. In Jamaica, most luxury villas come with a full staff, including a housekeeper, cook, butler, gardener, and often a security guard. Many can arrange for a driver for airport transfers, daily touring, or a prearranged number of days of sightseeing.

Demand for larger, more luxurious properties has increased. Numerous villas have five or more bedrooms in different parts of a building—or in different buildings altogether for extra privacy.

Most villas come with linens, and you can often arrange for the kitchen to be stocked with groceries upon your arrival. Air-conditioning, even in the most luxurious villas, is typically limited to bedrooms.

A four-night minimum is average for many villas, though this can vary by season and property. Gratuities, usually split among the staff, are typically 10%–15%. Several private companies specialize in finding rentals at the right size and price.

RENTAL CONTACTS Jamaica Association of Villas and Apartments. ✉ *Ocho Rios* ☎ *876/208–8905.* **Jamaica Villas by Linda Smith.** ☎ *301/229–4300* 🌐 *www.jamaicavillas.com.* **Luxury Retreats International.** ✉ *Montréal* ☎ *877/993–0100* 🌐 *www.luxuryretreats.com/vacation-rentals/caribbean/jamaica.*

Nightlife

For the most part, the liveliest late-night happenings that tourists take part in are in the major resort hotels and on the beaches in Negril. Some all-inclusives offer a dinner-and-entertainment pass for $50–$100; call ahead and bring a photo ID. *Jamaica Gleaner,* the *Jamaica Observer,* and the *Star* (online and at newsstands) list who's playing when and where. In Negril, cars with loudspeakers sometimes drive the streets in the afternoon announcing that evening's hot spot.

Restaurants

Probably the most famous Jamaican dish is jerk chicken—the ultimate island barbecue. The chicken is covered with a paste of Scotch bonnet peppers, pimento berries (also known as allspice), and other herbs, and cooked slowly over a coal fire. Many aficionados believe the best jerk comes from Boston Beach, near Port Antonio. Jerk pork and fish are also seen on many menus. The ever-so-traditional rice and peas is similar to the *moros y cristianos* of Spanish-speaking islands: white rice cooked with red kidney beans, coconut milk, scallions, and seasonings.

The island's most famous soup—the fiery pepperpot—is a spicy mixture of salt pork, salt beef, ground provisions (yams, sweet potatoes, etc.), okra, and the island green known as callaloo. Patties (spicy meat pies) elevate street food to new heights. Although patties actually originated in Haiti, Jamaicans excel at making them. Curried goat is another island standout: the young goat cooked with spices is more tender and has a gentler flavor than the lamb that immigrants from India used. Salted fish was once the best that islanders could do between catches. Out of necessity, a breakfast staple (and the national dish of Jamaica) was invented. It joins seasonings with saltfish and ackee, a red fruit that grows on trees throughout the island. When cooked in this dish, ackee reminds most people of scrambled eggs.

There are fine restaurants in all the resort areas, many in Kingston and in the resorts themselves. Many restaurants outside the hotels in MoBay and Ocho Rios will provide complimentary transportation.

What to Wear: Dinner dress is usually casual chic (or just plain casual at many local hangouts, especially in Negril). There are a few exceptions in Kingston and at the top resorts; some require semiformal wear (no shorts; collared shirts for men) in the evening during the high season. People tend to dress up for dinner; men might be more comfortable in nice slacks, women in a sundress.

Shopping

Shopping is not really one of Jamaica's high points, though you will certainly find things to buy. Good choices include Jamaican crafts, which range from artwork to batik fabrics to baskets. Wood carvings are a top purchase; the finest are made from the Jamaican national tree, lignum vitae, or tree of life, a dense, blond wood that requires a talented carver to transform it into dolphins, heads, or fish. Bargaining is expected with crafts vendors located on the streets of every resort town. Naturally, Jamaican rum is another top souvenir, as is Tia Maria, the Jamaican-made coffee liqueur. Coffee (both Blue Mountain and the less expensive High Mountain) is sold at nearly every gift shop, but the cheapest prices are often found at local grocery stores, where you can buy coffee beans or ground coffee.

Unless you have an extremely early flight, you'll find plenty of shopping at the Sangster International Airport, which has a large shopping mall. Fine handmade cigars are available there and at the island's many cigar stores. You can buy Cuban cigars almost anywhere, though they can't be taken back legally into the United States. As a rule, only rum distilleries, such as Appleton's and Sangster's, have better deals than the airport stores. Best of all, if you buy your rum at the airport, you don't have to tote all those heavy, breakable bottles. (Note that if you purchase rum—or other liquids, such as duty-free perfumes—outside the airport, you'll need to place them in your checked luggage when returning home. If you purchase liquids inside the secured area of the airport, you may board with them, but, after clearing U.S. Customs on landing, you will need to place them in your checked bag if continuing on another flight.)

Sights

Touring Jamaica can be both thrilling and frustrating. Rugged (albeit beautiful) terrain and winding (often potholed) roads make for slow going. *Always* check conditions before you set off by car, but especially in the rainy season, June through October, when roads can be washed out. Two-lane primary roads that loop around and across the island are not particularly well marked. Numbered addresses are seldom used outside major townships, locals drive aggressively, and people and animals have a knack for appearing out of nowhere. With that said, Jamaica's scenery shouldn't be missed. To be safe and avoid frustration, stick to guided tours and licensed taxis.

If you're staying in Kingston or Port Antonio, set aside at least one day for the capital and another for a guided excursion to the Blue Mountains. There are at least three days of activity along MoBay's boundaries, but also consider a day trip to Negril or Ocho Rios. If you're based in Ocho Rios, be sure to visit Dunn's River Falls; you may also want to stop by Bob Marley's birthplace, Nine Mile, or Firefly, the restored home of Noël Coward. If Negril is your hub, take in the South Coast, including Y. S. Falls and the Appleton Estate.

Tours

Jamaica Get Away Travels

AIR EXCURSIONS | This company offers a range of helicopter sightseeing tours in Kingston, Montego Bay, Ocho Rios, and Port Antonio. They also offer transportation to airports and hotels across the island. ✉ *899 Porto Bello Dr., Montego Bay* ☎ *876/776–0001, 813/556–0903* 🌐 *www.jamaicagetawaytravels.com.*

Captain's Aviation

AIR EXCURSIONS | This outfitter offers transportation from Montego Bay and Kingston airports to hotels across the island. They also provide sightseeing tours to some of Jamaica's most beautiful spots. ✉ *The Towers, 25 Dominica Dr., Kingston* ☎ *876/929–1805* 🌐 *www.captainsaviation.com.*

Visitor Information

CONTACTS Jamaica Tourist Board. ✉ *The Tourism Centre, 64 Knutsford Blvd., Kingston* ☎ *305/665–0557 in Miami, 876/929–9200 in Kingston, 876/952–4425 in Montego Bay* 🌐 *www.visitjamaica.com.*

Weddings

A 24-hour waiting period is required; many resorts offer free wedding packages.

Montego Bay

As the home of the north-shore airport and a busy cruise pier west of town, Jamaica's second-largest city, commonly referred to as "Bay" or "MoBay," is the first taste most visitors have of the island. Travelers from around the world come and go year-round, drawn to the bustling community's all-inclusive resorts and great beaches. Montego Bay's relative proximity to resort towns like Ocho Rios and Negril also make it popular. Adventures and one-of-a-kind experiences, not to mention interesting colonial sights, await in surrounding areas.

The town's main drag is now called Jimmy Cliff Boulevard (formerly Gloucester Avenue), but it's also known as the Hip Strip, as this is where you'll find bars, clubs, and restaurants including Margaritaville, Blue Beat Ultra Lounge, and Pier 1.

Sights

Greenwood Great House

HISTORIC HOME | This historic greathouse may not have a spooky legend to titillate, like Rose Hall, but it's much better at evoking life on a sugar plantation. The Barrett family, from whom the English poet Elizabeth Barrett Browning descended, once owned all the land from Rose Hall to Falmouth; on their vast holdings, they built this and several other greathouses. (The poet's father, Edward Moulton Barrett, "the Tyrant of Wimpole Street," was born at nearby Cinnamon Hill, later the estate of country singer Johnny Cash.) Highlights of Greenwood include oil paintings of the Barretts, china made for the family by Wedgwood, a library filled with rare books from as early as 1697, fine antique furniture, and a collection of exotic musical instruments. There's a pub on-site as well. It's 15 miles (24 km) east of Montego Bay. ✉ *435 Belgrade Ave., Montego Bay* ☎ *876/631-3456* 🌐 *www.greenwoodgreathouse.com* 🎫 *$20.*

Rocklands Bird Sanctuary

OTHER ATTRACTION | A great place to spot birds, this sanctuary is south of Montego Bay. The station was the home of the late Lisa Salmon, one of Jamaica's first amateur ornithologists. Here you can sit quietly and feed a variety of birds—including the doctor bird (also known as the streamer-tail hummingbird), recognizable by its long tail—from your hand. ✉ *Rocklands Rd., Anchovy, Montego Bay* ☎ *876/952–2009* 🌐 *www.rocklandsbirdsanctuary.com* 🎫 *$20.*

★ Rose Hall Great House

HISTORIC SIGHT | In the 1700s, it may well have been one of the greatest greathouses in the West Indies. Today it's popular less for its architecture than for the legend surrounding its second mistress, Annie Palmer. As the story goes, she was born in 1802 in England, but when she was 10, her family moved to Haiti. Soon after, her parents died of yellow fever. Adopted by a Haitian voodoo priestess, Annie became skilled in the practice of witchcraft. She moved to Jamaica, married, and became the mistress of Rose Hall, an enormous plantation spanning 6,600 acres with more than 2,000 slaves.

■ TIP→ A spooky nighttime tour of the property—recommended if you're up for a scare—is offered every evening. After the tour, have a drink at the White Witch pub, in the greathouse's cellar. ✉ *North Coast Hwy., St. James* ✥ *15 miles (24 km) east of Montego Bay* ☎ *876/953–2341* 🌐 *www.rosehall.com* 🎫 *$25.*

CASINOS

Coral Cliff

CASINO | The downstairs of this two-story venue, which is the top entertainment spot on the Hip Strip, is billed "the fun factory" and offers arcade games for the entire family. Upstairs, adults can try their luck at the slot machines and table games. There's also a restaurant and bar, along with a shop serving ice cream, desserts, and snacks. Enjoy live music Wednesday to Saturday and karaoke on Mondays. ✉ *165 Jimmy Cliff Blvd., Montego Bay* ☎ *876/615–3717, 876/952–4131* 🌐 *www.coralcliff.com.*

Mosino Gaming Lounge

CASINO | This lounge has become a favorite for gamers and nongamers alike. It houses a full restaurant and sports bar serving tasty apps and entrées. Visitors can try their luck at any of the 214 machines available here, including an assortment of virtual tables and slot machines. ✉ *Catherine Hall, Montego Bay* ☎ *876/632–2965* 🌐 *www.mosinogaming.com.*

Beaches

Doctor's Cave Bathing Club

BEACH | **FAMILY** | Located along Montego Bay's touristy Hip Strip, this famous beach first gained notoriety for its waters, said to have healing powers. It's a popular beach with a perpetual spring-break feel. The clubhouse has changing rooms, showers, a gift shop, and a restaurant. You can rent beach chairs, pool floats, and umbrellas. Its location within the Montego Bay Marine Park—with protected coral reefs and plenty of marine life—makes it good for snorkeling and glass-bottom boat rides. Chairs, umbrellas, and pool floats are available to rent for $6 per item for the day. **Amenities:** food and drink; lifeguards; parking (fee); showers; toilets; water sports. **Best for:** partiers; snorkeling; sunset; swimming. ✉ *Jimmy Cliff Blvd., Montego Bay* ☎ *876/952–2566* 🌐 *www.doctorscavebathingclub.com* 🎫 *$6.*

★ Harmony Beach Park
BEACH | FAMILY | Renovated and reopened in 2021, this massive park is the top attraction in the center of Montego Bay. In addition to its large beach, it features a multipurpose sports court, a jogging trail, a park, and a kiddies play area. Wi-Fi is available and there are a few shops selling snacks and drinks. You can also rent chairs and an umbrella. **Amenities:** food and drink; lifeguards; parking (fee); showers; toilets. **Best for:** sunset; swimming; walking. ✉ *Jimmy Cliff Blvd., Montego Bay* ☎ *876/656–8031* 🌐 *www.udcja.com/harmony-beach-park* 🎫 *Free; parking JMD $200 per hour.*

Restaurants

★ Margaritaville Montego Bay
$$$ | AMERICAN | FAMILY | Along Montego Bay's Hip Strip, this colorful restaurant is a favorite spot for families thanks to its 110-foot waterslide into the sea, water trampolines and slides, and a sunset deck. When it's time to settle down for lunch, the menu offers some Caribbean-influenced items such as jerk burgers and seafood dishes, along with lots of all-American fare. **Known for:** jerk barbecue cheeseburger; live reggae music; waterslides and water activities. 💲 *Average main: $27* ✉ *Jimmy Cliff Blvd., Montego Bay* ☎ *876/952–4777* 🌐 *www.margaritavillecaribbean.com.*

Marguerite's
$$$$ | SEAFOOD | This romantic seaside restaurant specializes in creative takes on Caribbean seafood, including lobster, shrimp, and fish dishes. The sophisticated style of the menu matches the restaurant's decor, scenery, and overall vibe. **Known for:** stunning views from the terrace; celebrating special occasions; great wine selection. 💲 *Average main: $40* ✉ *Jimmy Cliff Blvd., Montego Bay* ☎ *876/952–4777* 🌐 *www.margueritesjamaica.com* 🕒 *No lunch.*

Pelican Grill
$$ | JAMAICAN | This locals' favorite for more than 50 years on MoBay's Hip Strip offers a wide range of authentic, well-prepared Jamaican dishes, such as escovitch fish, stew peas, and oxtail. Like many restaurants on Jimmy Cliff Boulevard, it's right across from the ocean, but Pelican Grill also boasts a stunning waterfall in the back. **Known for:** escovitch fish; both waterfall and ocean views; delicious local dishes. 💲 *Average main: $18* ✉ *Jimmy Cliff Blvd., Montego Bay* ☎ *876/952–3171.*

★ Pier 1
$$$ | CARIBBEAN | After tropical drinks at the deck bar, you'll be ready to dig into the traditional Jamaican fare and Jamaican-influenced seafood dishes at this open-air restaurant located on Montego Bay's Pier 1 waterfront. Occasional party cruises leave from the marina, and on weekends and holidays the restaurant is mobbed by partying locals. **Known for:** lobster dishes; live music nightly; local rum cocktails. 💲 *Average main: $28* ✉ *off Howard Cooke Blvd., Montego Bay* ☎ *876/952–2452* 🌐 *www.pier1jamaica.com.*

The Pork Pit
$$ | JAMAICAN | A no-frills eatery favored by locals, Pork Pit is an authentic, open-air Jamaican restaurant that serves the best of Jamaican jerk meats and seafood dishes. The restaurant is close to Doctor's Cave Beach and is surrounded by all the attractions of MoBay's Hip Strip. **Known for:** jerk chicken and pork; cheap meals to go; central location. 💲 *Average main: $12* ✉ *27 Jimmy Cliff Blvd., Montego Bay* ☎ *876/940–3008.*

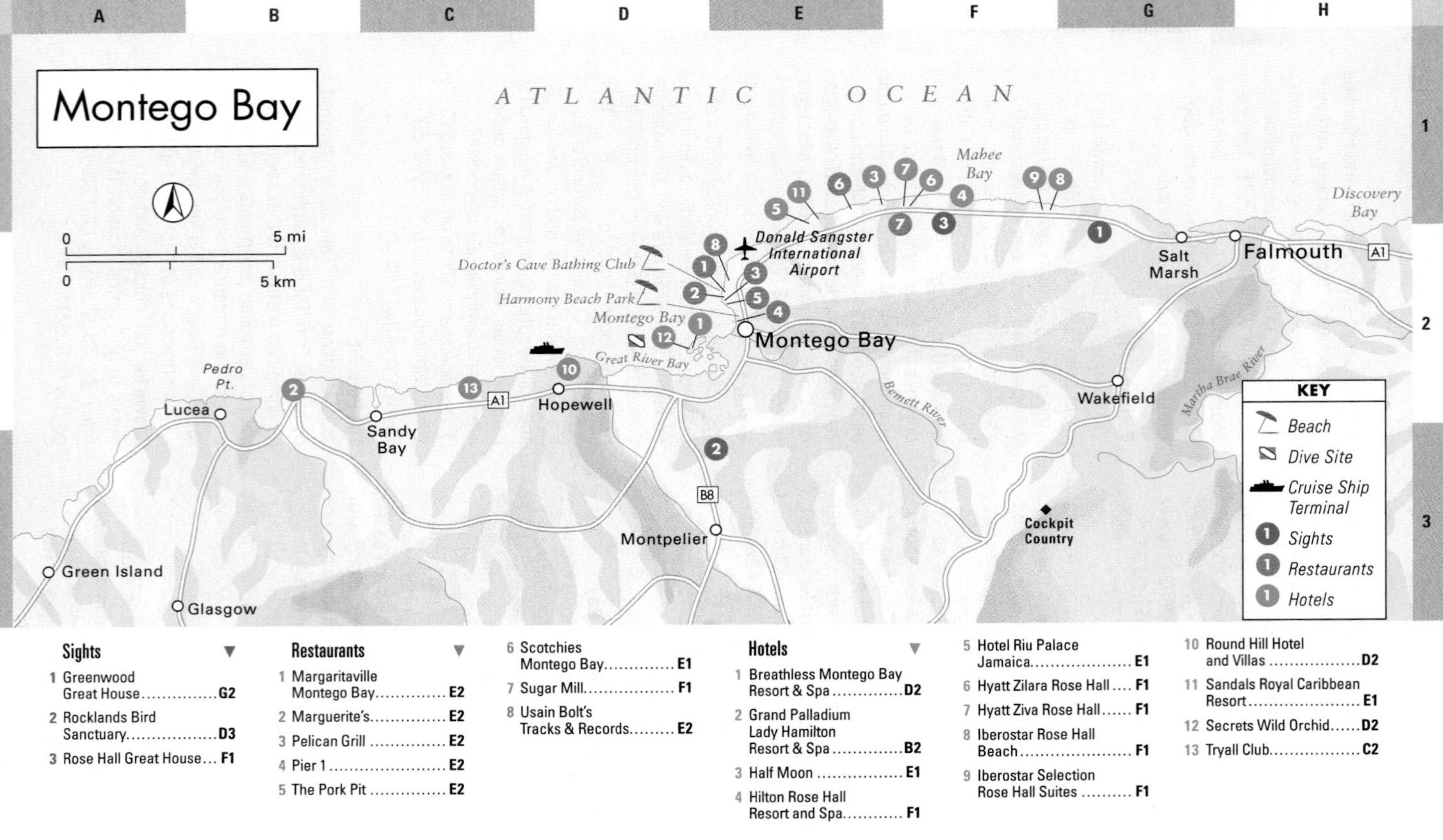

Sights

1 Greenwood Great House.........G2
2 Rocklands Bird Sanctuary.........D3
3 Rose Hall Great House... F1

Restaurants

1 Margaritaville Montego Bay.........E2
2 Marguerite's.........E2
3 Pelican Grill.........E2
4 Pier 1.........E2
5 The Pork Pit.........E2
6 Scotchies Montego Bay.........E1
7 Sugar Mill.........F1
8 Usain Bolt's Tracks & Records.........E2

Hotels

1 Breathless Montego Bay Resort & Spa.........D2
2 Grand Palladium Lady Hamilton Resort & Spa.........B2
3 Half Moon.........E1
4 Hilton Rose Hall Resort and Spa.........F1
5 Hotel Riu Palace Jamaica.........E1
6 Hyatt Zilara Rose Hall.........F1
7 Hyatt Ziva Rose Hall.........F1
8 Iberostar Rose Hall Beach.........F1
9 Iberostar Selection Rose Hall Suites.........F1
10 Round Hill Hotel and Villas.........D2
11 Sandals Royal Caribbean Resort.........E1
12 Secrets Wild Orchid.........D2
13 Tryall Club.........C2

★ Scotchies Montego Bay
$ | **JAMAICAN** | Portland may be the birthplace of jerk cooking, but Scotchies is one of Jamaica's premier jerk eateries. It serves genuine jerk—chicken, pork, fish, sausage, and more—with fiery sauce and delectable side dishes including festival (bread similar to a hush puppy) and rice and peas. **Known for:** local side dishes like festival, bammy (a flatbread made from cassava), and rice and peas; jerk chicken; lively domino games. *Average main: $10 ✉ North Coast Hwy., across from Holiday Inn Montego Bay, Montego Bay ✣ 10 miles (16 km) east of Montego Bay ☎ 876/953–8041.*

Sugar Mill
$$$$ | **ECLECTIC** | The former Running Gut Sugar Estate near the Half Moon Resort Golf Course is the setting for this spot helmed by a top Jamaican chef and serving Caribbean dishes with Asian twists. Dine alfresco on a terrace by a 17th-century watermill, enjoying the signature dishes—seafood, international, or vegetarian—made with island spices; a well-stocked wine cellar complete the experiences. **Known for:** oxtail ravioli; romantic atmosphere; excellent service. *Average main: $50 ✉ Half Moon, North Coast Rd., Montego Bay ✣ 7 miles (11 km) east of Montego Bay ☎ 876/953–2211 ext 43 ⊕ www.halfmoon.com ⊗ No lunch.*

Usain Bolt's Tracks & Records
$$$ | **CARIBBEAN** | This outpost of the Jamaican chain is the most modern in the country, while remaining true to the brand's casual dining and sports-bar ambience. Everything about the restaurant screams "Jamaican pride," from the Usain Bolt statue out front and the gift shop's exclusive Brand Bolt merchandise to the authentic Jamaican food, like jerk seafood, classic red peas soup, jerk chicken and pork, and delicious cocktails. **Known for:** jerk spring rolls; live music; authentic local fare. *Average main: $25 ✉ 7 Jimmy Cliff Blvd., Montego Bay ☎ 876/971–0000 ⊕ www.tracksandrecords.com.*

Hotels

MoBay has miles of hotels, villas, apartments, and duty-free shops. Although without much in the way of must-see culture, at least for the average visitor, it presents a comfortable island backdrop for the many conventions it hosts. And it has the added advantage of being the closest resort town to the Donald Sangster International Airport.

Breathless Montego Bay Resort & Spa
$$ | **RESORT** | Fun and partying take center stage at this luxe contemporary resort set on the peninsula out that juts into the Caribbean sea and offering four restaurants, a stunning rooftop pool, a main pool with a swim-up bar and infinity edge, and a smaller pool that regularly holds foam parties and other events. **Pros:** rooftop restaurant; free access to Secrets resorts' spa and other facilities; lots of pool parties and entertainment. **Cons:** beach is across the street; rooftop pool closes in the evening; gym and spa are located at Secrets Wild Orchid. *Rooms from: $293 ✉ Sunset Dr., Montego Bay ☎ 876/953–6600, 855/652–7328 ⊕ www.amrcollection.com 150 rooms All-Inclusive.*

★ Grand Palladium Lady Hamilton Resort & Spa
$$$ | **RESORT** | **FAMILY** | There's a lot to love about this sprawling, posh resort—about 45 minutes from Montego Bay—with white columns, antique chandeliers, marble floors, and other Roman-inspired design elements and one of the largest pools in the country. **Pros:** a wide variety of restaurants; access to Grand Palladium Resort next door; free water sports. **Cons:** huge property, so there's a long walk to some facilities; rocky beach; nearly an hour's drive from airport. *Rooms from: $422 ✉ Point Lucea, Lucea ☎ 876/619–0000 ⊕ www.palladiumhotelgroup.com 516 rooms All-Inclusive.*

The peaceful Round Hill Hotel and Villas, west of MoBay, is a favorite of celebrities and the wealthy.

Half Moon

$$$$ | **HOTEL** | **FAMILY** | With its many room categories, 28 massive villas (five to seven bedrooms), shopping village, a private beach, water sports, three pools, the luxurious Fern Tree spa, a children's village, golf course, and an equestrian center, this resort feels almost as though it's an entire town. **Pros:** numerous on-site activities; a variety of dining options and meal plans; 10-minute drive from the airport. **Cons:** extra fees for facilities and services; some accommodations are a long walk from public areas; spread out over 400 acres. 💲 *Rooms from: $553* ✉ *Rose Hall, Montego Bay* ☎ *800/626–0592* 🌐 *www.halfmoon.com* 🛏 *210 rooms* 🍽 *Free Breakfast.*

Hilton Rose Hall Resort and Spa

$$ | **RESORT** | **FAMILY** | Popular with couples, conference groups, and families, this self-contained property on a former sugarcane plantation occupies 400 lush acres of well-manicured grounds and has received regular upgrades and enhancements over the years, making it a top choice in Montego Bay. Facilities include a huge water park, complete with lagoons and lazy rafting river, a private beach with deluxe cabanas, and 11 restaurants and bars. **Pros:** huge beach; family-friendly dining and pool; easy access to golf. **Cons:** limited entertainment options; some activities are across the highway; kid-filled pool can be noisy. 💲 *Rooms from: $342* ✉ *Rose Hall Main Rd., St. James* ✣ *15 miles (24 km) east of Montego Bay* ☎ *876/953–2650* 🌐 *www.resortsbyhilton.com* 🛏 *488 rooms* 🍽 *All-Inclusive.*

Hotel Riu Palace Jamaica

$$$$ | **RESORT** | This adults-only beachfront resort with well-appointed rooms is trendy and sophisticated, offering the same all-inclusive service as its neighboring family-friendly sister resort, including a gym, a wellness center, and a spa in addition to freshwater pools and Jacuzzis. **Pros:** double-glass, noise-canceling doors and hydromassage tubs in every room; on the beach and near activities; access to nearby Riu

hotels. **Cons:** property can get noisy at night; small gym; four-night minimum. [$] *Rooms from: $518* ✉ *Blue Mahoe Bay, Ironshore, Montego Bay* ☎ *876/940–8022* 🌐 *www.riupalacejamaica.com* ⇨ *238 rooms* 🍴 *All-Inclusive.*

★ Hyatt Zilara Rose Hall

$$$$ | **RESORT** | As an adults-only resort, the stylish, all-inclusive Hyatt Zilara Rose Hall has all the facilities and services that adults need to enjoy their trip—modern guest rooms (some of which are swim-up rooms and butler suites) with fully furnished private terraces, seven restaurants, a private beach with a beach gazebo and boardwalk, a spacious pool with a swim-up bar and swim-up seating, fitness center, and spa. **Pros:** access to Hyatt Ziva restaurants; short ride from the airport; special add-on packages for couples like candlelit dinners for two or special spa treatments. **Cons:** huge property so a long walk to some amenities; the beach is small; no nightlife options. [$] *Rooms from: $552* ✉ *Rose Hall Rd., Montego Bay* ☎ *876/618–1234* 🌐 *www.hyatt.com* ⇨ *344 rooms* 🍴 *All-Inclusive.*

Hyatt Ziva Rose Hall

$$$ | **RESORT** | **FAMILY** | Unlike its neighboring sister property, Hyatt Ziva caters to families, with a host of activities and entertainment for guests of all ages as well as two pools (one for kids) and 11 restaurants and bars, including a café, coffee bar, and jerk shack. **Pros:** full-service spa; tons of activities for the entire family; access to Hyatt Zilara property. **Cons:** some rooms have dated furniture; not enough variety of restaurants; beach is small. [$] *Rooms from: $405* ✉ *Rose Hall Rd., Montego Bay* ☎ *876/618–1234* 🌐 *www.hyatt.com* ⇨ *387 rooms* 🍴 *All-Inclusive.*

Iberostar Rose Hall Beach

$$ | **RESORT** | **FAMILY** | An extensive array of dining options (including five bars) and activities are offered at this all-inclusive resort just 20 minutes east of the airport and surrounded by beautiful beaches. **Pros:** numerous on-site activities, including lively shows and nightly entertainment; easy access to airport and Montego Bay; complimentary minibar in all rooms. **Cons:** does not have some of the amenities of its sister Iberostar properties; fee for motorized water sports and scuba diving; can be noisy. [$] *Rooms from: $330* ✉ *North Coast Hwy., Montego Bay* ✣ *8 miles (13 km) east of Montego Bay* ☎ *876/680–0000, 888/774–0040* 🌐 *www.iberostarrosehall.com* ⇨ *366 rooms* 🍴 *All-Inclusive.*

Iberostar Selection Rose Hall Suites

$$$ | **RESORT** | **FAMILY** | This all-suites, all-inclusive property is the most stylish and offers more amenities than the other adjacent Iberostar resorts, including a fantastic spa, a beautiful beach, three pools, and a water park for kids. **Pros:** use of facilities at Iberostar Rose Hall Beach; numerous dining options; round-the-clock activities. **Cons:** spotty Wi-Fi connection in suites and outside; bars can be crowded; an outsize, somewhat impersonal feel. [$] *Rooms from: $446* ✉ *North Coast Hwy., Montego Bay* ✣ *8 miles (13 km) east of Montego Bay* ☎ *876/680–0000* 🌐 *www.iberostarrosehallsuite.com* ⇨ *319 suites* 🍴 *All-Inclusive.*

★ Round Hill Hotel and Villas

$$$$ | **HOTEL** | A favorite of celebrities and other wealthy people thanks to its private, elegant villas, this peaceful resort west of MoBay also has stylish hotel rooms in the Pineapple House; the rooms are decorated in a refined Ralph Lauren style done by the designer himself, who has property on the resort's 98 acres. **Pros:** stylish rooms; a number of meal plan options; personal service. **Cons:** some villas do not have pools; no TVs in the rooms; somewhat remote. [$] *Rooms from: $750* ✉ *John Pringle Dr., Montego Bay* ✣ *8 miles (13 km) west of Montego Bay* ☎ *876/956–7050* 🌐 *www.roundhill.com* ⇨ *63 rooms* 🍴 *Free Breakfast.*

Sandals Royal Caribbean Resort

$$$$ | **RESORT** | Four miles (6 km) east of the airport, this elegant resort has Jamaican-style buildings around attractive gardens and a less boisterous atmosphere than Sandals Montego Bay, offering a few more-formal touches, including nightly shows, unlimited fine dining, free nonmotorized water sports, and afternoon tea. **Pros:** complimentary shuttles to airport and other Sandals resorts; lots of room categories; offshore dining. **Cons:** some rooms don't have balconies; smaller beach than Sandals Montego Bay; beachfront cabanas cost extra. *Rooms from: $779 North Coast Hwy., Montego Bay 888/726–3257 www.sandals.com 227 rooms All-Inclusive.*

Secrets Wild Orchid

$$ | **RESORT** | On a peninsula just 20 minutes from the airport, this all-inclusive resort is one of the more luxurious adults-only properties in MoBay—most of its amenities, like the swish spa, beach, casino, shops, and several restaurants and bars, are shared with its sister property, Secrets St. James. **Pros:** chic room decor; a good variety of dining options; lots of activities and nightly entertainment. **Cons:** a long walk to some of the facilities; restaurants can be very noisy; shared amenities with Secrets St. James can make the property feel crowded. *Rooms from: $325 Sunset Dr., Montego Bay 876/953–8436, 866/467–3273 www.amrcollection.com 350 rooms All-Inclusive.*

Tryall Club

$$$$ | **RESORT** | The sumptuous villas—most of which have a private pool—and pampering staff lend a home-away-from-home feel to this golfers' haven west of MoBay; the beautiful seaside golf course is considered one of the toughest in the world and hosts big-money tournaments. **Pros:** complimentary kids' club plus a nanny service; excellent golf; villa experience with convenience of a resort. **Cons:** somewhat formal atmosphere; shared public facilities; rates skyrocket in high season. *Rooms from: $625 North Coast Hwy., Sandy Bay 15 miles (24 km) west of Montego Bay 876/956–5660, 800/238–5290 in U.S. www.tryallclub.com 87 villas No Meals.*

Nightlife

BARS AND CLUBS

Club Ville

DANCE CLUBS | At night, the Margaritaville restaurant turns into a hip and happening nightspot. DJs play reggae, house, and R&B along with occasional live performances. Thursday night is Ladies Night and is especially popular among locals. *Margaritaville, Jimmy Cliff Blvd., Montego Bay 876/952–4777 www.margaritavillecaribbean.com.*

Falmouth

Between two of the most popular tourist locations in Jamaica (MoBay and Ocho Rios) is Falmouth, a laid-back, country town that provides an escape from the bustle of the surrounding cities. The city features many old Georgian-styled buildings, lush greenery, and a quiet and clean atmosphere. There aren't many hotels or tourist attractions in Falmouth and the city center is typically void of crowds of tourists except on the days when cruise ships dock at the port.

Sights

★ Chukka Good Hope Estate

WATER PARK | **FAMILY** | About a 20-minute drive inland from Falmouth, this 2,000-acre estate provides a sense of Jamaica's rich history as a sugar-producing island, incredible views of the Martha Brae River, and loads of fun. An adventure park offers zip-lining, river tubing, a greathouse tour, access to a colonial village, an aviary, a swimming pool, a challenge course for adults, and a kids' play area (with its own challenge course). The Sugar House restaurant serves Jamaican food, and the Caribbean River Bar and a gift shop in the old sugar factory round out the amenities. Park passes get you access to all activities. ✉ *Good Hope Estate, Falmouth, Falmouth* ☎ *876/619–1441, 876/619–1382* 🌐 *www.chukka.com* 🎫 *$69.*

★ **Glistening Waters** (*Luminous Lagoon*)
BODY OF WATER | This is one of Jamaica's most fascinating natural wonders. The lagoon emits a bluish glow caused by microscopic organisms called dinoflagellates, which live in the water and create a natural phenomenon called bioluminescence. There are only five bioluminescent bays in the world, and Jamaica's is said to be the brightest. During one-hour evening tours, guests can touch, take pictures, and even swim in the bioluminescent waters. There's also a marina and a restaurant. ✉ *Hwy. A1, Trelawny* ☎ *876/954–3229* 🌐 *www.glisteningwaters.com* 🎫 *$25.*

Jamaica Swamp Safari Village
NATURE SIGHT | With a large sign declaring that "Trespassers Will Be Eaten," this attraction on the outskirts of Falmouth most fascinates reptile enthusiasts. The village was started as a crocodile farm in the 1970s by American Ross Kananga, who was a stunt man in the James Bond film *Live and Let Die*. Scenes from the film *Papillon,* starring Steve McQueen and Dustin Hoffman, were also shot here. The property is home to a number of Jamaican crocodiles as well as the Jamaican yellow boa snake. There are other exotic animals from South America and colorful tropical birds in the aviary. ✉ *Foreshore Rd., Falmouth* ✣ *Right beside Better Price Hardware Store* ☎ *876/617–2798* 🌐 *www.jamaicaswampsafari.com* 🎫 *$25.*

★ **Martha Brae River**
BODY OF WATER | This gentle waterway takes its name from an Arawak woman who drowned herself because she refused to reveal the whereabouts of a local gold mine. According to legend, she agreed to take her Spanish inquisitors there and, on reaching the river, used magic to change its course, drowning herself and the greedy Spaniards with her. Her *duppy* (ghost) is said to guard the mine's entrance. Rafting on this river is a very popular activity—many operators are on hand to take you for a glide downstream. Admission is for up to two passengers. ✉ *Trelawny* ✣ *4½ miles (7 km) southeast of Falmouth* ☎ *876/952–0889* 🌐 *www.jamaicarafting.com* 🎫 *$77.*

 Beaches

★ **876 Beach Club**
BEACH | Located along Falmouth's scenic coast, this is one of the town's only beaches that isn't attached to a resort. The property does have guestrooms available, but most visitors come for the day to enjoy the clean white-sand beach, which offers a water obstacle course, volleyball, and other beach sports, along with changing rooms, showers, a restaurant and bar (you must call ahead to request permission if bringing your own food and drink). Admission includes beach chairs and cabanas, and Wi-Fi is available. **Amenities:** food and drink; lifeguards; parking (free); showers; toilets; water sports. **Best for:** partiers; sunset; swimming. ✉ *Hwy A1., Falmouth* ☎ *876/475–9090* 🎫 *JMD $1000.*

 Restaurants

Margaritaville Falmouth
$$ | **AMERICAN** | **FAMILY** | Located at Falmouth's port, Margaritaville is a top stop among cruise passengers. In true Margaritaville fashion, this colorful, pirate-style restaurant caters to families, with its hot tub and giant pool featuring a waterfall and swim-up bar. **Known for:** jerk barbecue cheeseburger; lively atmosphere; swim-up bar. Ⓢ *Average main: $20* ✉ *2 King St., Trelawny* ☎ *876/631–1031* 🌐 *www.margaritavillecaribbean.com*

Closed when the cruise port isn't open.

Pepper's Jerk Center

$$$ | **JAMAICAN** | This eatery set in a former slave quarters has a loyal following for authentic Jamaican meals, seafood dishes, and delicious jerk (marked with the restaurant's very own special jerk sauce). The restaurant is in the town's center and is just a short walk away from the Falmouth Port. **Known for:** rum punch; jerk chicken; curry lobster. *Average main: $26 22 Duke St., Trelawny 876/617–3472 www.peppersjerkcenter.com.*

Hotels

Falmouth is a rather quiet town when compared to the resort hubs like Montego Bay and Ocho Rios. There aren't as many resorts here, and the ones that do exist are somewhat secluded, providing the perfect tropical escape for those that want a relaxing stay.

★ Excellence Oyster Bay

$$$$ | **ALL-INCLUSIVE** | This all-inclusive, adult-only resort is Falmouth's most luxurious waterfront property, with a charmed location on a private peninsula with 2 miles of white-sand beach, three pools and four outdoor Jacuzzis, 11 restaurants and bars, a full-service spa, and a health club. **Pros:** variety of dining options and extensive meal plan; secluded location; rooms have private terraces and Jacuzzis. **Cons:** large property so mobility can be an issue, especially for older guests; fewer amenities than other Excellence resorts; limited entertainment options. *Rooms from: $575 Oyster Bay Peninsula, Coopers Pen, Falmouth 876/617–0200 www.excellenceoysterbayresort.com 320 rooms All-Inclusive.*

★ Ocean Coral Spring

$$$$ | **RESORT** | Opened in 2019, the opulent Ocean Coral Spring has given the sleepy town of Falmouth a much-needed tourism boost; everything at this resort is top-notch, from the stunning white-sand beach, lazy river, spa center with a sauna and gym, 9 bars, and 10 restaurants, which include a coffeehouse and ice-cream parlor. **Pros:** a variety of restaurants and bars; rooms are spacious and lavishly appointed; lots of entertainment activities. **Cons:** rocky beach; very expensive gift shop; food at some restaurants isn't great. *Rooms from: $426 Mountain Spring Bay, Falmouth 876/631–4005 www.oceancoralspring.com 513 rooms All-Inclusive.*

Royalton White Sands Resort

$$$ | **RESORT** | **FAMILY** | This stylish, all-inclusive hideaway is perched on a stunning white-sand beach and features two pools (one with a swim-up bar), as well as a luxurious spa with hydrotherapy treatments, a fitness center, multiple dining options, and a tennis court. **Pros:** delicious food at restaurants; lots of family activities; has its own private island. **Cons:** small restaurants; some facilities only accessible to Diamond Club guests; beach areas are small. *Rooms from: $399 Hwy. A1, Trelawny 876/632–7401 www.royaltonwhitesandsresort.com 352 rooms All-Inclusive.*

Runaway Bay

The smallest of Jamaica's resort areas, Runaway Bay is about 50 miles (80 km) east of Montego Bay and about 12 miles (19 km) west of Ocho Rios. It has a handful of modern resorts and an 18-hole golf course.

Nine Miles, the small district where reggae star Bob Marley was born, is a few miles south of Runaway Bay.

Sights

Bob Marley Mausoleum

HISTORIC HOME | The reggae legend was born and is buried at Nine Mile, in the parish of St. Ann, and today his former home is a shrine to his music and values. Tucked behind a tall fence, the site is marked with green and gold flags. Tours are led by Rastafarians, who take visitors through the house and point out the single bed that Marley wrote about in "Is This Love." Visitors also step inside the mausoleum where the singer is interred with his guitar. There is a restaurant, gift shop, and a marijuana farm.

TIP→ If you're driving here yourself, prepare for some bad roads, and the hustlers outside the center are some of Jamaica's most aggressive; it's best to take a guided excursion from one of the resorts. ✉ *Nine Mile, Calderwood Post Office, St. Ann's Bay* ✣ *South of Browns Town* ☎ *876/974–9848* 🎫 *$30.*

Green Grotto Caves

CAVE | A good choice for rainy days, these caves offer 45-minute guided tours that include a look at a subterranean lake. The cave has a long history as a hiding place for everyone from fearsome pirates to runaway slaves to the Spanish governor (he was on the run from the British at the time). It's a good destination if you want to see one of Jamaica's caves without going too far off the beaten path. You'll feel like a spelunker, since you must wear a hard hat throughout the tour. ✉ *North Coast Hwy., Runaway Bay* ✣ *2 miles (3 km) east of Discovery Bay* ☎ *876/973–2841* 🌐 *www.greengrottocavesja.com* 🎫 *$20.*

Beaches

★ Puerto Seco Beach

BEACH | FAMILY | Completely renovated in 2018, this public beach looks out on Discovery Bay, the location where, according to tradition, Christopher Columbus first came ashore on this island. The explorer sailed in search of freshwater but found none, naming the stretch of sand Puerto Seco, or "dry port." Today, the beach is anything but dry. Along with the beach, there's a 150-foot pool, and guests can rent beach chairs, umbrellas, and private cabanas (for larger groups). There's a restaurant and bar, but guests can't bring their own food. There's also a waterpark and a dolphin attraction. **Amenities:** food and drink; lifeguards; parking (no fee); showers; toilets. **Best for:** snorkeling; swimming. ✉ *Discovery Bay, Runaway Bay* ✣ *5 miles (8 km) west of Runaway Bay* ☎ *876/913–5655* 🌐 *www.puertosecojamaica.com* 🎫 *JMD $2000.*

Restaurants

★ L'Escargot

$$$ | FRENCH | This hidden gem of a French restaurant is a rarity on the north coast—a chance to enjoy excellent service and deftly prepared dishes like grilled calamari and salmon fillet. This rarely crowded spot has all-white decor, soft background music, and colorful artwork, and there's an extensive wine list. **Known for:** interesting wines; Sunday brunch; first-rate staff. 💲 *Average main: $30* ✉ *Main St., Runaway Bay* ☎ *876/877–6032, 876/973–5589* 🌐 *www.lescargotja.com* ⏲ *Closed Sun.–Tues.*

Plantation Smokehouse

$$$ | ECLECTIC | Although open only since 2020, this rustic, casual eatery in quiet Richmond has quickly become one of the most popular restaurants on Jamaica's north coast. The menu is divided into Jamaican, American, Asian, and vegetarian sections, and portions are hearty. **Known for:** big portions; live music or DJs; vibrant atmosphere. 💲 *Average main: $25* ✉ *Hwy. A1, Richmond, Priory, Runaway Bay* ☎ *876/488-6404, 876/794–8764* 🌐 *www.plantationsmokehouse.com.*

★ Sharkies Seafood Restaurant

$$$ | SEAFOOD | This hugely popular spot on a stunning stretch of beach in Salem buzzes with guests relaxing over drinks and sea views and listening to DJ tunes on weekend evenings. The menu features best hits of the seafood favorites—lobster, conch, crab, shrimp, and octopus. **Known for:** seating directly on the beach; wide range of seafood dishes; lively atmoshphere. *Average main: $30 ✉ Main St., Hwy. A1, Runaway Bay ☎ 876/973–5472 🌐 www.sharkies-seafood.com.*

Ultimate Jerk Center and Rest Stop
$$ | **JAMAICAN** | A favorite with locals traveling the North Coast Highway, this open-air eatery across from the Green Grotto Caves serves a variety of jerk dishes well as fish and traditional Jamaican side dishes. A separate bar—housed in a colorful rondavel (a round hut with a thatch roof)—serves beverages. **Known for:** lively bar; jerk rabbit; popular Jamaican soups like mannish water (goat soup) and red peas soup. *Average main: $12 ✉ Main St., Runaway Bay ☎ 876/973–2054 🌐 www.ultimatejerkcentre.com.*

Jewel Paradise Cove Beach Resort & Spa
$$ | **RESORT** | Embodying a theme of wellness and rejuvenation, Jewel Paradise Cove comes pretty close to being an actual adults-only tropical paradise with seven dining options and six bars (three of which are swim-up), and the white-glove-service restaurant even has a wine cellar with premium wines. **Pros:** superb spa with many treatment options; excellent dining options; complimentary greens fees at Runaway Bay Golf Club. **Cons:** small beach; over an hour's drive from the airport; spa treatments cost extra. *Rooms from: $340 ✉ Paradise Cove Dr., Runaway Bay ☎ 876/973–4520, 833/325–3935 🌐 www.jewelresorts.com 225 rooms All-Inclusive.*

Ocho Rios

Although Ocho Rios isn't near eight rivers, as its name would seem to indicate, it does have a seemingly endless series of cascades that sparkle from limestone rocks along the coast. (The name Ocho Rios is said to have come about because the English misunderstood the Spanish *las chorreras*—"the waterfalls.") The town itself isn't very attractive and can be traffic-clogged, but the area has several worthwhile attractions, including the very popular Dunn's River Falls. A few steps from the main road in Ocho Rios are some of the Caribbean's most charming inns and oceanfront restaurants. Lying on the sand of what seems to be your own cove or swinging gently in a hammock while sipping a tropical drink, you'll soon forget the traffic that's just a stroll away. The original "defenders" stationed at the Old Fort, built in 1777, spent much of their time sacking and plundering as far afield as St. Augustine, Florida, and sharing their booty with the local plantation owners who financed their missions. In Discovery Bay, 15 miles (24 km) west, where Columbus landed, there's the small, open-air Columbus Park Museum with such artifacts as ships' bells and cannons, and iron pots used for boiling sugarcane. Don't miss a drive through Fern Gully, south of Ocho Rios via the A3 highway.

★ Dolphin Cove
WATER PARK | **FAMILY** | Surrounded by lush rain forest, Dolphin Cove is one of the island's top marine attractions. Packages allow you to touch, dance, or swim with the well-trained and friendly dolphins, who also love to receive a pat or a kiss goodbye. Other water sports and activities, including snorkeling, glass-bottom kayaking, boat rides, swimming with stingrays, and shark shows are offered. In addition to marine life, you can interact with such fauna as iguanas, snakes, and exotic birds on the jungle trail walk. There's also a small ice-cream parlor, restaurant, and gift shop. *✉ Belmont Rd., Ocho Rios ☎ 876/974–5335 🌐 www.dolphincoveja.com From $69 Closed Sun.–Mon. and Thurs.*

★ Dunn's River Falls & Park

WATERFALL | A popular natural attraction that is an eye-catching sight: 600 feet of cold, clear mountain water splashing over a series of stone steps to the Caribbean Sea. The best way to enjoy the falls is to climb the slippery steps in a swimsuit (there are changing rooms at the entrance), as you take the hand of the person ahead of you. The entrance looks like it leads to an amusement park, and it's usually crowded, especially when cruise ships are in port, but it is well organized. It's easy to make arrangements and get trusted guides who will offer bits of local lore while showing you where to step. After the climb, you exit through a crowded market—another reminder that this is one of Jamaica's top tourist attractions. If you can, try to visit on a day when no cruise ships are in port.

■ TIP→ Always climb with a licensed guide at Dunn's River Falls. Freelance guides might be a little cheaper, but the experienced guides can tell you just where to plant each footstep—helping you prevent a fall.

Ask for a guide at the Dunn's River Falls ticket window: Official licensed guides are inside the Dunn's River Falls property, not outside the gate. They should be able to show you credentials if asked. If you arrange the tour through a resort or cruise ship, the guides provided will be licensed. ✉ *Main St., Ocho Rios* ⊕ *Off Hwy. A1, between St. Ann's Bay and Ocho Rios* ☎ *876/974–2857* 🌐 *www.dunnsriverfallsja.com* 🎫 *$25.*

Fern Gully

FOREST | Don't miss this natural canopy of vegetation, which sunlight barely penetrates. (Jamaica has the world's largest number of fern species—more than 570.) The winding road through the gully has been resurfaced, making for a smoother drive, and most tours of the area include a drive through this natural wonder. But to really experience it, stop and take a walk. The 3-mile (5-km) stretch of damp, fern-shaded forest includes many walking paths as well as numerous crafts vendors. ⊕ *Hwy. A3, 2 miles (3 km) south of Ocho Rios.*

Firefly Estate

HISTORIC HOME | Noël Coward's vacation home is now a national monument managed by Chris Blackwell's Island Outpost company. Although the setting is Edenic, the house is surprisingly spartan. Coward decamped uphill from his original home at Blue Harbour to escape the jet-setters who came to visit. He wrote *High Spirits, Quadrille,* and other plays here, and his simple grave is next to a small stage where his works are occasionally performed. Recordings of Coward singing about "mad dogs and Englishmen" echo over the lawns. Tours include a walk through the house and grounds. The view from the house's hilltop perch, which was a lookout for Captain Morgan, is one of the best on the North Coast. Firefly is also a perfect place to host weddings, picnics, photo shoots, stage shows, retreats, full-moon parties, and sunset cocktails. Contact Island Outpost (www.islandoutpost.com) for more information. ✉ *St. Mary* ⊕ *About 20 miles (32 km) east of Ocho Rios* ☎ *876/725–0920* 🌐 *www.firefly-jamaica.com* 🎫 *$20.*

Konoko Falls and Park

GARDEN | Nestled in the hills that overlook Ocho Rios, the beautiful and serene Konoko Falls and Park once served as a settlement site for the Taínos (the original inhabitants of Jamaica). Today, the property has been transformed into a stunning tourist attraction with a waterfall, museum, gift shop, and a small zoo. Visitors can take a guided tour and learn about the history of the island and the Taínos. ✉ *Shaw Park Estate, Shaw Park Rd., Ocho Rios* ☎ *876/622–1712, 876/408–0575* 🌐 *www.konokofalls.com* 🎫 *$20.*

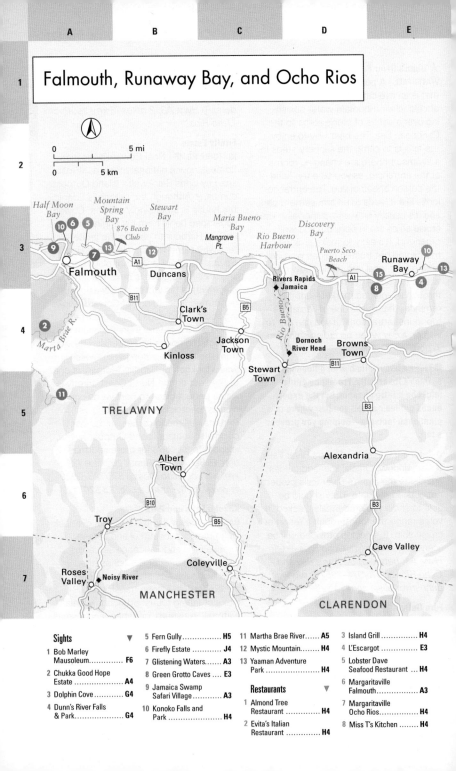

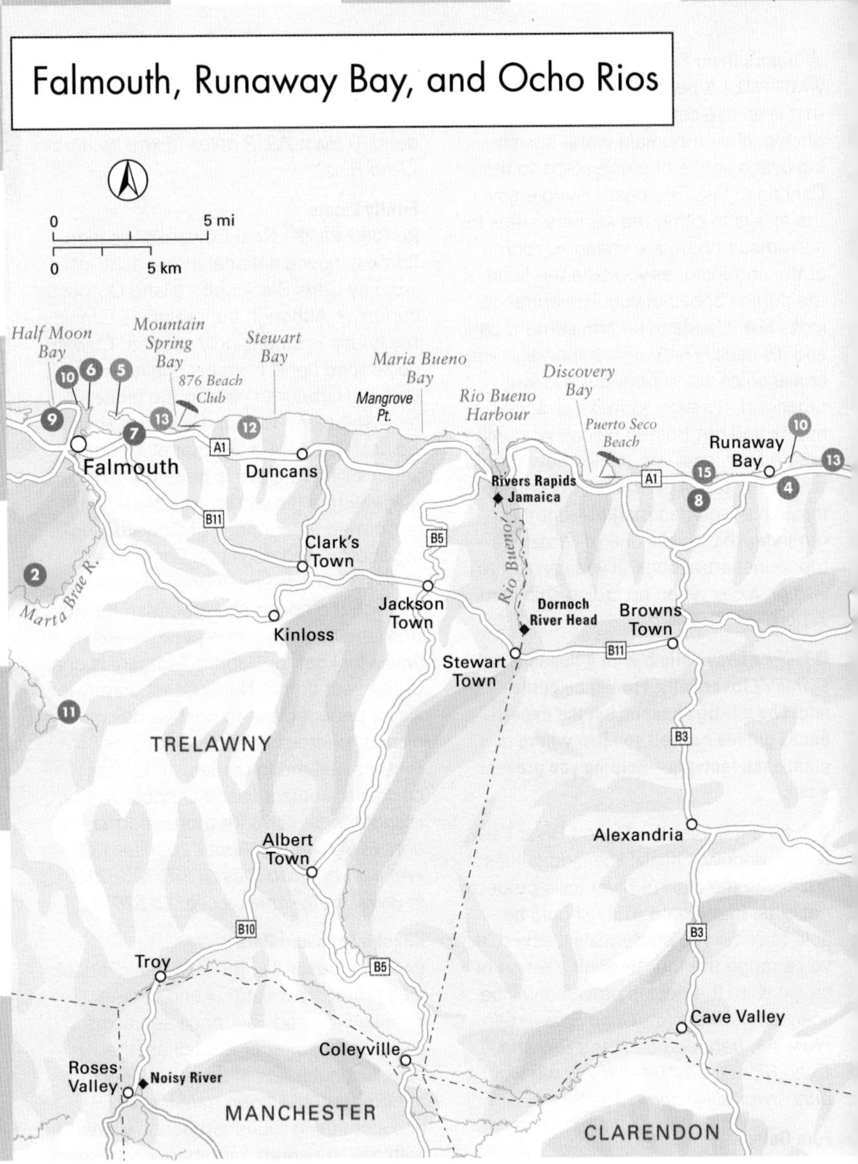

Falmouth, Runaway Bay, and Ocho Rios

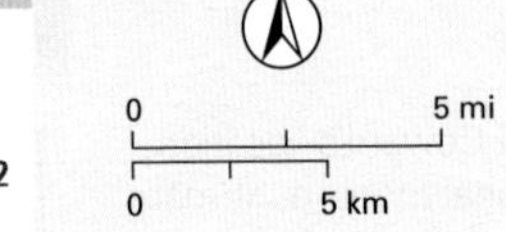

A B C D E
1 2 3 4 5 6 7

Half Moon Bay
Mountain Spring Bay
876 Beach Club
Stewart Bay
Maria Bueno Bay
Mangrove Pt.
Rio Bueno Harbour
Discovery Bay
Puerto Seco Beach
Runaway Bay
Falmouth
Duncans
A1
B11
Rivers Rapids Jamaica
Clark's Town
B5
Rio Bueno
Jackson Town
Dornoch River Head
Browns Town
Kinloss
Marta Brae R.
Stewart Town
TRELAWNY
B3
Alexandria
Albert Town
B10
Troy
Cave Valley
Coleyville
Roses Valley
Noisy River
MANCHESTER
CLARENDON

Sights

1 Bob Marley Mausoleum.............. F6
2 Chukka Good Hope Estate A4
3 Dolphin Cove............ G4
4 Dunn's River Falls & Park..................... G4
5 Fern Gully................ H5
6 Firefly Estate J4
7 Glistening Waters....... A3
8 Green Grotto Caves E3
9 Jamaica Swamp Safari Village............ A3
10 Konoko Falls and Park H4
11 Martha Brae River...... A5
12 Mystic Mountain........ H4
13 Yaaman Adventure Park H4

Restaurants

1 Almond Tree Restaurant H4
2 Evita's Italian Restaurant H4
3 Island Grill H4
4 L'Escargot E3
5 Lobster Dave Seafood Restaurant ... H4
6 Margaritaville Falmouth.................. A3
7 Margaritaville Ocho Rios................ H4
8 Miss T's Kitchen H4

F G H I J

1 2 3 4 5 6 7

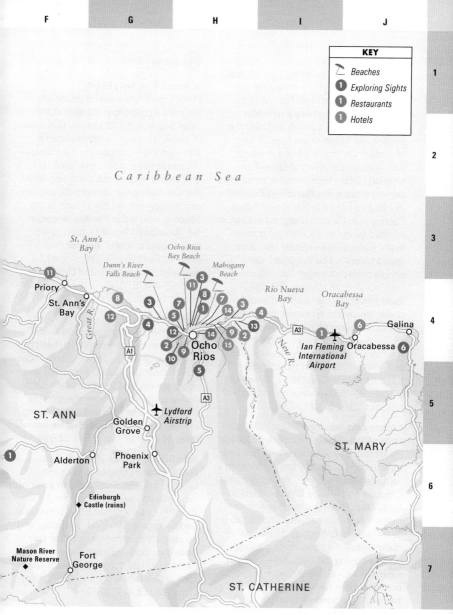

KEY
Beaches
Exploring Sights
Restaurants
Hotels

Caribbean Sea

St. Ann's Bay
Ocho Rios Bay Beach
Dunn's River Falls Beach
Mahogany Beach
Rio Nueva Bay
Oracabessa Bay
Priory
St. Ann's Bay
Great R.
A1
Ocho Rios
A3
New R.
Ian Fleming International Airport
Oracabessa
Galina
Lydford Airstrip
ST. ANN
Golden Grove
Phoenix Park
Alderton
ST. MARY
Edinburgh Castle (ruins)
Mason River Nature Reserve
Fort George
ST. CATHERINE

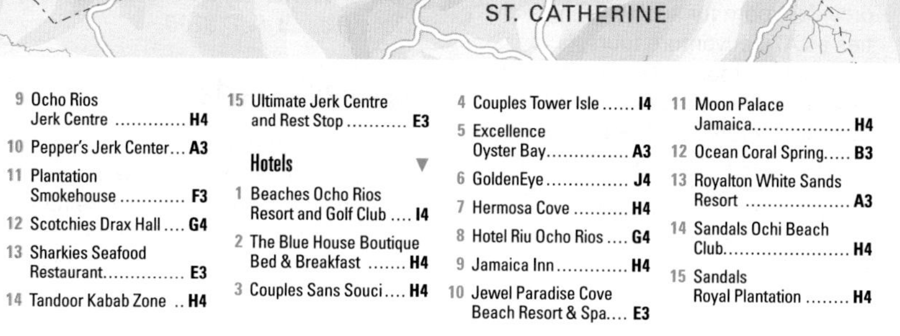

9 Ocho Rios Jerk Centre **H4**

10 Pepper's Jerk Center... **A3**

11 Plantation Smokehouse **F3**

12 Scotchies Drax Hall **G4**

13 Sharkies Seafood Restaurant............... **E3**

14 Tandoor Kabab Zone .. **H4**

15 Ultimate Jerk Centre and Rest Stop **E3**

Hotels ▼

1 Beaches Ocho Rios Resort and Golf Club **I4**

2 The Blue House Boutique Bed & Breakfast **H4**

3 Couples Sans Souci **H4**

4 Couples Tower Isle **I4**

5 Excellence Oyster Bay............... **A3**

6 GoldenEye **J4**

7 Hermosa Cove **H4**

8 Hotel Riu Ocho Rios **G4**

9 Jamaica Inn **H4**

10 Jewel Paradise Cove Beach Resort & Spa.... **E3**

11 Moon Palace Jamaica.................. **H4**

12 Ocean Coral Spring..... **B3**

13 Royalton White Sands Resort **A3**

14 Sandals Ochi Beach Club...................... **H4**

15 Sandals Royal Plantation **H4**

★ Mystic Mountain

AMUSEMENT PARK/CARNIVAL | This attraction covers 100 acres of mountainside rain forest near Dunn's River Falls. Visitors board the Rainforest Sky Explorer, a chairlift that soars through and over the pristine rain forest to the apex of Mystic Mountain. On top, there is a restaurant with spectacular views of Ocho Rios, arts-and-crafts shops, and the attraction's signature tours, the Rainforest Bobsled Jamaica ride and the Rainforest Zipline Canopy ride. Custom-designed bobsleds, inspired by Jamaica's Olympic bobsled team, run downhill on steel rails with speed controlled by the driver, using simple push-pull levers. Couples can run their bobsleds in tandem. The zipline tours streak through lush rain forest under the care of an expert guide who points out items of interest. The entire facility was built using environmentally friendly techniques and materials in order to leave the native rain forest undisturbed. ✉ *North Coast Hwy., Ocho Rios* ☎ *876/618–1553* 🌐 *www.mysticmountain.com* 🎫 *From $49.*

Yaaman Adventure Park

FARM/RANCH | **FAMILY** | Formerly Prospect Plantation, this adventure park has been an attraction since the start of tourism in Jamaica when such visitors as Winston Churchill and Charlie Chaplain planted trees here. There are many activities that are both fun and educational, from camel safaris to Segway tours. Learn about Jamaica's agricultural heritage while enjoying the flora and fauna and excellent views. The 900-acre property provides room for such exciting activities as ATV adventure tours, jitney rides, and cooking tours. ✉ *Hwy. A1, St. Mary* ✣ *4 miles (3 km) east of Ocho Rios* ☎ *876/994–1058, 866/393–5158 toll-free in the U.S.* 🌐 *www.yaamanadventure.com* 🎫 *From $48.*

Beaches

★ Dunn's River Falls Beach

BEACH | You'll find a crowd (especially if there's a cruise ship in town) at the small beach at the foot of the falls, one of Jamaica's most-visited landmarks. Although tiny—considering the crowds—the beach has a great view. Look up for a spectacular vista of the cascading water, the roar from which drowns out the sea as you approach. All-day access to the beach is included in the falls' entrance fee. **Amenities:** lifeguards; parking (no fee); showers; toilets. **Best for:** swimming. ✉ *Ocho Rios* ✣ *Off Hwy. A1, between St. Ann's Bay and Ocho Rios* ☎ *876/974–4767* 🌐 *www.dunnsriverfallsja.com* 🎫 *$20.*

Mahogany Beach

BEACH | This charming but small beach provides an escape from Ocho Rios's bustling town center, and usually doesn't get crowded until a cruise ship docks. There's no admission, and there's a beach bar, a restaurant, and a souvenir stand on the shore. **Amenities:** food and drink; parking (no fee); toilets; showers. **Best for:** swimming. ✉ *Main St., Ocho Rios* 🎫 *Free.*

Ocho Rios Bay Beach (*Turtle Beach*)

BEACH | **FAMILY** | One of the busiest beaches in Ocho Rios caters to a mix of residents and visitors. It looks out over the cruise port and has a bar, but you can also bring your own food. Boat rides and watersport equipment can be rented. **Amenities:** food and drink; lifeguards; parking (no fee); toilets; showers; water sports. **Best for:** swimming. ✉ *Main St., Ocho Rios* 🎫 *JMD $200.*

Restaurants

Almond Tree Restaurant

$$$ | **ECLECTIC** | Named for the massive almond tree growing through the roof, this Ocho Rios restaurant is one of the most romantic restaurants in the resort town. The menu is a mixture of Jamaican and international dishes including seafood, a variety of chicken and beef, and other traditional Jamaican meals. **Known for:** curry goat; large variety of dishes; stunning view. *$ Average main: $25 ✉ Hibiscus Lodge Hotel, 83–85 Main St., Ocho Rios ☎ 876/974–2676 🌐 www.hibiscusjamaica.com.*

★ Evita's Italian Restaurant

$$ | **ECLECTIC** | Set in an 1860s gingerbread house fronted by an old convertible roadster, Evita's—an island institution and the self-proclaimed "Best Little Pasta House in Jamaica"—is a chic, charming restaurant. Its renowned pasta is a spicy mashup of the best of Italian and Jamaican cuisine. **Known for:** One Love Penne; view overlooking the town; lasagna Rastafari. *$ Average main: $20 ✉ Eden Bower Rd., Ocho Rios ☎ 876/974–2333 🌐 www.evitasjamaica.com.*

Island Grill

$ | **JAMAICAN** | With nearly 20 locations across the island, the Ocho Rios branch of this eat-in or take-out restaurant about a block from the main tourist area serves a Jamaican version of fast food. Jerk chicken, sandwiches, soups, and Jamaican dinner combo meals (called *yabbas,* an African-Jamaican term for bowl) are among the specialties. Many meals are served with festival (sweet, fried dumpling) and are spiced for the local palate. **Known for:** yaad-style sandwich (lettuce, tomatoes, grilled chicken, and fried plantains); jerk chicken; local fruit and vegetable juices. *$ Average main: $9 ✉ 59 Main St., Ocho Rios ☎ 876/974–3160 🌐 www.islandgrillja.com.*

★ Lobster Dave Seafood Restaurant

$$$ | **SEAFOOD** | Local celebrities, residents, and tourists frequent this beachside restaurant that serves some of the best seafood in Ocho Rios. The namesake signature dish can be prepared in a variety of ways: curried, jerked, barbecued, cracked, or grilled. **Known for:** lively atmosphere; lobster and other seafood dishes; right by Fisherman's Beach and the port. *$ Average main: $30 ✉ Shop #20, Ocho Rios Shopping Village, Ocho Rios ☎ 876/632–4655, 876/228–8929.*

Margaritaville Ocho Rios

$$ | **ECLECTIC** | If you're looking for a cheeseburger in paradise and blended drinks, come to the familiar Margaritaville. Part of the popular chain (also in Montego Bay, Falmouth, and Negril), the restaurant features Caribbean dishes alongside American favorites, as well as its namesake drink, which comes in tropical flavors like mango, lime, and strawberry. **Known for:** popularity with cruise-ship passengers; swim-up bar; live music. *$ Average main: $20 ✉ Island Village, Turtle Beach Rd., Ocho Rios ☎ 876/675–8800 🌐 www.margaritavillecaribbean.com.*

★ Miss T's Kitchen

$$$ | **JAMAICAN** | The colorful decor, authentic Jamaican food, and rustic, country ambience at Miss T's Kitchen will give you the feel of a true Jamaican culinary experience with a few vegan and vegetarian options thrown in. Anna-Kay Tomlinson, the charming "Miss T," turned her love and passion for Jamaican food into one of the town's most popular Jamaican eateries. **Known for:** special Bob Marley cocktail; Miss T's Famous Oxtail (stew); curry goat (served with white rice or rice and peas). *$ Average main: $25 ✉ 65 Main St., Ocho Rios ☎ 876/795–0099 🌐 www.misstskitchen.com.*

Ocho Rios Jerk Centre

$$ | **JAMAICAN** | This canopied, open-air eatery is a great place for island fare like fiery jerk meals or seafood such as fish and conch, which are perfectly complemented by frosty Red Stripe beers and signature cocktails. Milder barbecued meats—also sold by weight (a quarter- or half-pound makes a good serving)—turn up on the daily chalkboard menu posted on the wall. **Known for:** curry goat served with rice and peas; jerk pork; specialty cocktails. *$ Average main: $12 ✉ 14 DaCosta Dr., Ocho Rios ☎ 876/974–2549.*

Scotchies Drax Hall

$$ | **JAMAICAN** | The Ocho Rios branch of the longtime Montego Bay favorite has been lauded by international chefs for its excellent jerk. The plates of jerk chicken and pork and a variety of other dishes like sausage, fish, and ribs at this open-air restaurant are all accompanied by classic Jamaican side dishes such as festival and bammy. **Known for:** Rum Ribs on Tuesday, Thursday, and Sunday; jerk chicken; fire-breathing hot sauce. *Average main: $12* ✉ *Drax Hall, North Coast Hwy., St. Ann's Bay* ☎ *876/794–9457, 876/564–7993.*

Tandoor Kabab Zone

$$ | **ASIAN FUSION** | As the name suggests, this restaurant is the premier dining destination in Ocho Rios for Asian cuisine, with an emphasis on kebabs. Paired with the signature Asian and Indian dishes and classic Jamaican meals are imported wines, local beers, and cocktails that are served at the wine bar. **Known for:** naan bread; Sikandari Raan (Indian lamb dish); speciality kebabs. *Average main: $16* ✉ *Landmark Plaza, Ocho Rios* ☎ *876/974–8899.*

Hotels

Rivers, waterfalls, fern-shaded roads, and tropical lushness fill this fertile North Coast region, halfway between Port Antonio and MoBay. It's a favorite with honeymooners as well as Jamaicans who like to escape crowded Kingston for the weekend. Resorts, hotels, and villas are all a short drive from the frenetic, traffic-clogged downtown, which has a crafts market, boutiques, duty-free shops, restaurants, and several scenic attractions. Ocho Rios is 67 miles (111 km) east of Montego Bay, just under two hours by car.

Beaches Ocho Rios Resort and Golf Club

$$$$ | **RESORT** | **FAMILY** | The company that specializes in the all-inclusive resort brings its brand of luxury, attention to detail, and attentive staff to this family-oriented property with bright rooms centered on an exquisite beach where you can enjoy water sports and even get scuba certification. **Pros:** access to Sandals Golf & Country Club; excellent children's program; numerous dining options. **Cons:** some rooms and amenities show signs of wear; restaurants not always open; family pools can be crowded. *Rooms from: $708* ✉ *North Coast Hwy., St. Ann's Bay* ☎ *876/975–7777* 🌐 *www.beaches.com* *313 rooms* *All-Inclusive* ☞ *3-night minimum.*

★ **The Blue House Boutique Bed & Breakfast**

$ | **B&B/INN** | This stylish boutique B&B is a nice alternative to North Coast all-inclusives; fabulous feasts (often with Jamaican, Chinese, and international flavors) are available for guests who wish to have dinner as well as breakfast here. **Pros:** homey; great for singles; authentic Jamaican experience. **Cons:** not many rooms, so you need to book early for the busy season; not on the beach; far from amenities. *Rooms from: $160* ✉ *Marcliff, White River Estate, Ocho Rios* ☎ *876/994–1367* 🌐 *www.thebluehousejamaica.com* *5 rooms* *Free Breakfast.*

Couples Sans Souci

$$$$ | **RESORT** | This classy, couples-only, all-inclusive encourages you to check your cares at the entrance and indulge in soul-nurturing pampering. **Pros:** private Au Naturel Beach & Pool; excellent spa; expansive all-inclusive package. **Cons:** few dining options; beaches are not as good as others; some rooms are very isolated and a long walk from public areas. *Rooms from: $512* ✉ *North Coast Hwy., Ocho Rios* ✣ *2 miles (3 km) east of Ocho Rios* ☎ *876/994–1206* 🌐 *www.couples.com* *150 suites* *All-Inclusive* ☞ *3-night minimum.*

Couples Tower Isle

$$$$ | **RESORT** | This all-inclusive has beautiful contemporary designed guest rooms; a handful of villa suites with private

Climbing the 600-foot-tall Dunn's River Falls is a popular sunny day activity in Ocho Rios

plunge pools and private sun terraces; and a private island where you can sunbathe in the buff. **Pros:** multiple dining options; excellent all-inclusive package; great beach facilities. **Cons:** far from town attractions; pools are rather small; far from Montego Bay airport. *Rooms from: $485* *Tower Isle, Rte. A3, St. Mary* *5 miles (8 km) east of Ocho Rios* *876/975–4271* *www.couples.com* *226 rooms* *All-Inclusive* *3-night minimum.*

★ GoldenEye

$$$$ | **HOTEL** | Whether you're a fan of James Bond or luxury getaways in general, this exclusive address 20 minutes east of Ocho Rios holds special appeal as the property was purchased in 1946 by James Bond creator Ian Fleming, who built a villa that is now owned by Island Records founder Chris Blackwell. **Pros:** tree house spa overlooking the lagoon; spacious cottages and villas; plenty of privacy. **Cons:** no all-inclusive packages; limited dining options; remote location. *Rooms from: $620* *North Coast Hwy., Oracabessa* *876/622–9009* *www.goldeneye.com* *48 suites* *No Meals.*

★ Hermosa Cove

$$$ | **RESORT** | Luxury and privacy are hallmarks at Hermosa Cove, where the contemporary one- and two-story villas offer all the conveniences of home in a beautiful tropical setting. **Pros:** yoga, art, and cooking classes available; quiet, stylish, and comfortable suites and villas; safe and secure. **Cons:** isolated location; limited menus at restaurants; small beach. *Rooms from: $450* *Hermosa Lane, Ocho Rios* *876/974–3699* *www.hermosacove.com* *9 rooms* *Free Breakfast.*

Hotel Riu Ocho Rios

$$ | **RESORT** | **FAMILY** | This sprawling resort, built in two U-shape wings each overlooking a pool, is one of the largest in Jamaica. **Pros:** expansive beach; lots of places to eat; large rooms. **Cons:** some rooms show signs of wear; restaurants can get crowded; long walk to beach. *Rooms from: $325* *Mammee Bay*

Nude Beaches

It is perhaps ironic that Jamaica, one of the more conservative, religious islands in the Caribbean, has many opportunities for naturists.

Taking It Off

In most places in Jamaica, letting it all hang out comes at a premium of up to 20% above the regular rates. Clothing-optional beaches are found at Hedonism II, Grand Lido Negril Au Naturel All-Suite-Resort, Couples Negril, Couples Tower Isle, Couples Sans Souci, and Grand Palladium Lady Hamilton.

Keeping It On

If you'd rather enjoy the beach in your swimsuit, remember that most of Jamaica's resorts cater to the traditional beachgoer (and all public beaches require swimsuits by law). "Clothing-optional" means you're free to keep your swimsuit (or as much of it) on as you like. Only beaches deemed "nude" actually have a dress code that requires a birthday suit.

Rd., Mammee Bay ☎ 876/972–2200 🌐 www.riu.com 900 rooms 🍽 All-Inclusive ☞ 2-night minimum.

Jamaica Inn

$$$$ | **HOTEL** | The Jamaica Inn exemplifies the elegance, luxury, and exquisite service of Jamaica's tourism heyday with attention to details such as fresh flower bouquets in the rooms and lovely beach views. **Pros:**; elegant accommodations with old-world charm; various meal plans available; luxurious spa. **Cons:** prices for the all-inclusive options are expensive; no attractions nearby; no in-room TV. *$ Rooms from: $489 ✉ North Coast Hwy., Ocho Rios ✣ 2 miles (3 km) east of Ocho Rios ☎ 876/974–2514 🌐 www.jamaicainn.com 48 suites 🍽 Free Breakfast.*

★ Moon Palace Jamaica

$$$ | **RESORT** | **FAMILY** | With its private beach, 750 minimalist-style rooms, expansive spa, four outdoor pools, and a water park, this sprawling, upscale, all-inclusive resort is as good as it gets (as far as luxury resorts in Jamaica go). **Pros:** rooms are spacious and have private balconies; expansive on-site spa with a pool; lots of water sports and water activities. **Cons:** large property means lots of walking; airport transfers must be arranged at least two weeks in advance; dolphin attractions and scuba diving cost extra. *$ Rooms from: $415 ✉ Main St., Ocho Rios ☎ 800/943–5032 🌐 www.moonpalace.com 750 rooms 🍽 All-Inclusive.*

Sandals Ochi Beach Resort

$$$$ | **RESORT** | This sprawling, couples-only resort began years ago as two separate properties and is now one of the largest resorts in the Sandals group, though it does suffer a bit of a split personality: the Riviera Seaside and Beach Club has babbling brooks, fragrant gardens, and a chic beach club, while across the road (accessible by shuttle or tunnel) is the all-butler-service Riviera Villas and Great House. **Pros:** romantic dining options; lots of privacy; free weddings for guests who stay longer than three nights. **Cons:** over an hour from airport; property can be confusing to navigate; villas a long way from the beach. *$ Rooms from: $600 ✉ 130–131 Main St., Ocho Rios ☎ 888/726–3257 🌐 www.sandals.com 529 rooms 🍽 All-Inclusive ☞ 2-night minimum.*

★ Sandals Royal Plantation

$$$$ | RESORT | During its heyday, guests at what was then called Plantation Inn included British royals, Winston Churchill, and authors Noël Coward and Ian Fleming, but today, it's one of the Caribbean's most popular boutique hotels. **Pros:** free weddings; expansive, stylish accommodations; good dining. **Cons:** not many rooms so bookings should be done far in advance; small pool and beach; guest rooms and beach are on different levels. *Rooms from: $700 ✉ Main St., Ocho Rios ☎ 888/726–3257 🌐 www.sandals.com ⇨ 74 suites 🍽 All-Inclusive.*

Nightlife

BARS AND CLUBS

Club Ville

DANCE CLUBS | After 10, Margaritaville transforms into this club, with a mix of the hottest tunes of the moment, along with occasional live performances from local entertainers. Club Ville also offers free round-trip transportation from most resorts in Ocho Rios. *✉ Margaritaville, Island Village, Ocho Rios ☎ 876/675–8800 🌐 www.margaritavillecaribbean.com.*

8Rivaz Ultra Lounge

DANCE CLUBS | This lounge, with a rooftop dance floor, becomes the hottest club in Ocho Rios each evening. It attracts a younger crowd with themed nights like Campari Mondays, Girlfriends Tuesdays, and Wray (and Nephew) Wednesdays. *✉ Beecham Plaza, 76 Main St., Ocho Rios ☎ 876/826–4967.*

Shopping

Ocho Rios has several malls that draw day-trippers from the cruise ships. The most popular is **Island Village,** a huge shopping mall in Ocho Rios town square with stores (some of which are duty-free) selling clothing, jewelry, souvenirs, and cigars. There's a movie theater, as well as a number of cafés, bars, and restaurants including Margaritaville. Another popular mall on the main street is **Ocean Village.** On the North Coast Highway slightly east of Ocho Rios is **Coconut Grove.**

MARKETS

Ocho Rios Crafts Market

CRAFTS | Ocho Rios's largest market has stalls selling everything from straw hats to wooden figurines to T-shirts. Vendors can be aggressive, and haggling is expected. Your best chance of getting a good price is to come on a day when there's no cruise ship in port. *✉ Main St., Ocho Rios.*

Pineapple Craft Market

CRAFTS | This small, casual market on the outskirts of Ocho Rios has everything from carved figurines to coffee-bean necklaces. *✉ Pineapple St., Ocho Rios.*

Port Antonio

Port Antonio is one of Jamaica's quietest getaways, primarily preferred by long-staying Europeans. Even with the improvement of the North Coast Highway from Ocho Rios and the reopening a decade ago of Trident Hotel, tourism remains slow here.

Port Antonio has also long been a center for some of the Caribbean's finest deep-sea fishing. Dolphin (the delectable fish, not the lovable mammal) is the likely catch here, along with tuna, kingfish, and wahoo. You'll also find some of the best and most authentic jerk chicken and pork here as you will Boston Bay, a small coastal community just 20 minutes away that is the originator of jerk in Jamaica.

Sights

Blue Lagoon

BODY OF WATER | Steeped in lore, Blue Lagoon is one of Port Antonio's best-known attractions. The azure waters of this spring-fed lagoon are a contrast to the warmer waters of the ocean. How deep is it? According to legend, it's bottomless, but it's been measured at 180 feet. There is no fee to access the lagoon, but there are unofficial guides who offer their services and try to make you believe that there is an entry fee. Also, numerous vendors have set up at the entry hawking their wares and creating a noisy juxtaposition to the peaceful natural scenery of the lagoon. ✉ *Port Antonio* ✣ *9 miles (13 km) east of Port Antonio, 1 mile (1½ km) east of San San Beach* 🎫 *Free.*

Folly Lighthouse

LIGHTHOUSE | Since 1888, this red-and-white-stripe masonry lighthouse has stood watch at the tip of Folly Point. Administered by the Jamaica National Heritage Trust, the lighthouse is an often-photographed site near Port Antonio's East Harbour. The lighthouse is down a very rough road that looks abandoned. It is not advisable to go alone. ✉ *Folly Point, Port Antonio* 🌐 *www.jnht.com* 🎫 *Free.*

Folly Ruins

HISTORIC HOME | A favorite photo stop, this structure, little more than ruins, was home to a Tiffany heiress. Built in 1905 and spanning 60 rooms, the house didn't last long because seawater, rather than freshwater, was used in the cement. The ruins have been featured in music videos. In August, the PAN Food Festival is held nearby at the Folly Oval. The property is down a rough road, and it is surrounded by a huge chain-link fence. However, the gate to the fence is wide open. The site is out of the way, and it is probably best not to go there alone. ✉ *Folly Point, Port Antonio* 🎫 *Free.*

★ Reach Falls

WATERFALL | One of Jamaica's most stunning natural waterfalls, Reach Falls was discovered by runaway slaves from nearby plantations who sought refuge in the hills of Portland. One of the waterfall's most fascinating features is the holes in the rocks that have been carved by flowing water—the most fun (and slightly terrifying) is the rabbit hole, which leads to a secret underwater cave that you can swim in! ✉ *off Hwy. A4* ✣ *about 23 miles (37 km) east of Port Antonio* ☎ *876/909–7381, 876/276–8663* 🌐 *www.udcja.com* 🎫 *$10* 🕑 *Closed Mon. and Tues.*

Rio Grande

FOREST | Jamaica's river-rafting operations began here, on an 8-mile-long (13-km-long), swift, green waterway from Berrydale to Rafter's Rest. (Beyond that, the Rio Grande flows into the Caribbean Sea at St. Margaret's Bay.) The trip of about three hours is made on bamboo rafts pushed along by a guide who is likely to be quite a character. You can pack a picnic lunch to enjoy on the raft or on the riverbank; if you lunch onshore, a Red Stripe vendor is likely to appear. A restaurant, a bar, and several souvenir shops can be found at Rafter's Rest. ✉ *Rte. A4, Port Antonio* ✣ *5 miles (8 km) west of Port Antonio* ☎ *876/993–5778* 🎫 *$100 for two-person raft.*

★ Somerset Falls

WATERFALL | On the Daniels River, these falls are in a veritable botanical garden. A concrete walk takes you past the ruins of a Spanish aqueduct and Genesis Falls before reaching Hidden Falls. At Hidden Falls itself you board a boat and travel beneath the tumbling water; more daring travelers can swim in a whirlpool or jump off the falls into a pool of water. There are also waterslides for kids and lifeguards on deck. The bar and restaurant specializes in jerk chicken and local seafood and is a great place to catch your breath. ✉ *Rte. A4, Port Antonio* ✣ *13 miles (21 km) west of Port Antonio* ☎ *876/913–0046* 🎫 *$12.*

Beaches

Boston Bay Beach

BEACH | Considered the birthplace of jerk-style cooking, Boston Bay is the beach that some locals visit just to buy dinner. You can get peppery jerk pork at any of the shacks spewing scented smoke along the small beach, perfect for an after-lunch dip, though these waters are occasionally rough and much more popular for surfing. Boards are available for rent. **Amenities:** food and drink; parking (no fee); toilets; showers. **Best for:** snorkeling; sunrise; surfing; windsurfing. ✉ *Port Antonio* ✣ *11 miles (18 km) east of Port Antonio* 🎫 *JMD $300.*

Frenchman's Cove Beach

BEACH | **FAMILY** | This beautiful, petite, somewhat secluded beach is protected by two outcroppings, creating calm waters good for families. A small stream trickles into the cove. You'll find a bar and restaurant serving fried chicken right on the beach. If this stretch of sand looks familiar, it might be because you've seen it in the movies: *Club Paradise* (1986), *Knight and Day* (2010), and *The Mighty Quinn* (1989). **Amenities:** food and drink; lifeguards; parking (fee); showers; toilets. **Best for:** partiers; sunrise; swimming. ✉ *Frenchman's Cove Resort, Hwy. A4, Port Antonio* ✣ *5 miles (8 km) east of Port Antonio* ☎ *876/993–7270, 876/564–9779* 🌐 *www.frenchmanscove.com* 🎫 *$12 for non Frenchman's Cove Resort guests.*

Winnifred Beach

BEACH | **FAMILY** | This is one of the most popular beaches on Jamaica's east coast, mainly because there is no entry fee. Vendors will, however, ask for a donation to help with upkeep. The beach is clean, with a relaxed atmosphere and a few stalls on the beach selling local food, crafts, and souvenirs. Boat rides and horseback riding are also offered. **Amenities:** food and drink; parking (fee); toilets. **Best for:** swimming. ✉ *Fairy Hill, Port Antonio* ✣ *about 8 miles (12½ km) east of Port Antonio* ☎ *876/290–7150* 🎫 *Free.*

Restaurants

Boston Jerk Centre

$ | **JAMAICAN** | Actually a collection of about half a dozen open-air stands, this is a culinary landmark thanks to its popular jerk pits. Stroll up to the open pits, fired by pimento logs and topped with a piece of corrugated roofing metal, locally known as zinc, and order meat by the quarter-, half-, or full pound. **Known for:** delicious local side dishes like festival and rice and peas; local beers; stands selling jerk meats. 💲 *Average main: $10* ✉ *Boston Bay, Hwy. A4, Port Antonio* ✣ *east of Port Antonio* 💳 *No credit cards.*

★ **Bushbar**

$$$$ | **ECLECTIC** | Located at the luxurious Geejam Hotel, Bushbar stays true to the property's reputation by offering a fine dining experience and stunning views of the surrounding jungle and Caribbean sea. The menu features savory Jamaican seafood and pasta dishes, with an international twist. **Known for:** mango martinis; live bands on weekends; seafood dishes. 💲 *Average main: $44* ✉ *Geejam Hotel, 122 Skippers Blvd., Port Antonio* ☎ *876/993–7000* 🌐 *www.geejamhotel.com.*

★ **The Italian Job**

$$ | **ITALIAN** | A sign on the wall of this friendly pizzeria reads: "You can't buy happiness but you can buy pizza, and that's kind of the same thing." Indeed, here you'll find the best pizza in the area, along with tasty pasta, seafood dishes, and burgers, and a good selection of wines. **Known for:** welcoming staff; delicious pizzas; locally influenced daily specials. 💲 *Average main: $20* ✉ *Shop #18, Shore Bay Plaza, Port Antonio* ☎ *876/573–8603* 🌐 *www.facebook.com/theitalianjobjamaica* 🕒 *Closed Sun.*

★ **Portland Cliff Hanger**

$$$ | **CARIBBEAN** | This restaurant's name perfectly describes its location: directly by the sea cliff, and with spectacular scenery and views. The menu features traditional Jamaican dinner dishes, as well as seafood dishes, soups, and salads. **Known for:** cozy lounge area by the bar; conch salad; lionfish cooked with Jamaican Red Stripe beer and wine. 💲 *Average main: $30* ✉ *Hwy. A4, Ross Craig, Long Bay, Port Antonio* ☎ *876/860–1395* 🌐 *www.seacliff-jamaica.com.*

Woody's Low Bridge Place

$ | **JAMAICAN** | Positive vibes and burgers are featured at this roadside eatery. Charles "Woody" Cousins and wife Cherry serve up simple fare from a whitewashed shack whose walls bear Cherry's handwritten affirmations. **Known for:** veggie burger with plantains; homemade ginger beer; delicious hamburgers. *Average main: $10 ✉ Drapers Main Rd., Port Antonio ☎ 876/993–7888 No credit cards.*

Hotels

For an alternative to the hectic tourist scene in the bustling resort towns of Montego Bay and Ocho Rios, head to this quiet community on Jamaica's east end, 133 miles (220 km) east of Montego Bay. Don't look for mixology classes or limbo dances here. The fun is usually found outdoors, followed by a fine evening meal. The area's must-do activities include rafting Jamaica's own Rio Grande, visiting the beach, taking an ecohike, and having lunch or a drink at a restaurant.

Frenchman's Cove Resort

$ | **RESORT** | This resort has a pristine location and decor that feels like a time capsule, but a far cry from when Queen Elizabeth II stayed in Villa 18. **Pros:** large accommodations; excellent beach; privacy. **Cons:** some rooms don't have TV; long walk to public areas and beach; dated decor. *Rooms from: $145 ✉ Rte. A4, Drapers, Port Antonio ✣ 5 miles (8 km) east of Port Antonio ☎ 876/993–7270, 876/564–9779 ⊕ www.frenchmanscove.com 28 rooms Free Breakfast.*

★ Geejam

$$$ | **HOTEL** | Located 10 minutes east of Port Antonio, this stylish, tech-savvy rockers' getaway (Gwen Stefani recorded an album here, and it's a favorite of Grace Jones) was once a music producer's hideaway. **Pros:** rooms are stylish and clean; complimentary transportation to nearby beaches; personalized service. **Cons:** may be too quiet for some; limited on-site amenities; remote location. *Rooms from: $390 ✉ North Coast Hwy., Port Antonio ☎ 876/993–7000, 888/443–3526 toll-free U.S. and Canada ⊕ www.geejam.com 19 suites Free Breakfast.*

Goblin Hill Villas at San San

$ | **RESORT** | **FAMILY** | Hummingbirds flit about this reasonably priced property, consisting of one- and two-story villas with the conveniences of a hotel, including tennis courts, a pool, and a restaurant and bar that's centered on a 300-year-old ficus tree and looks like a movie set. **Pros:** family-friendly; expansive, lovely grounds; roomy. **Cons:** remote; short walk to the beach; only one restauarant. *Rooms from: $185 ✉ Fairfield Rd., Port Antonio ✣ 3 miles (5 km) east of Port Antonio ☎ 876/993–7443 ⊕ www.goblinhill.com 28 villas No Meals ☞ 2-night minimum.*

Great Huts at Boston Beach

$ | **B&B/INN** | Port Antonio's most unusual accommodation is also its most basic, aimed solely at travelers who don't mind an experience that is, as Jamaicans would say, "rootsy". **Pros:** unfettered, panoramic Caribbean views; fairly good value; unique accommodations. **Cons:** might be too quiet for some; no air-conditioning because of open-air layout; roughing it (even in style) is not for everyone, especially those with mobility issues. *Rooms from: $75 ✉ 8-10 Boston Bay, 15 miles (24 km) east of Port Antonio, Boston Beach ☎ 876/353–3388 ⊕ www.greathuts.com 17 huts Free Breakfast.*

Hotel Mockingbird Hill

$ | **HOTEL** | From the locally sourced bath soaps and stationary to the solar panels and naturally cooled rooms, this ecofriendly boutique hotel is a delight for those who are environmentally conscious and socially aware, while also offering luxury bound to please anyone. **Pros:** numerous ecotourism options; environmentally conscious; carbon offsetting initiatives. **Cons:** not directly on the beach; limited dining options; somewhat remote. $ *Rooms from: $195* ✉ *North Coast Hwy., Point Ann, Port Antonio* ☎ *876/619–1215* 🌐 *www.hotelmockingbirdhill.com* *10 rooms* *Free Breakfast.*

Jamaica Palace Hotel

$ | **HOTEL** | This Port Antonio hotel might be distinctive for its Jamaica-shape swimming pool and surrounding black-and-white pool terrace, but that's just the beginning of its unusual aspects as the all-white building is designed to resemble a 17th-century Italian palace. **Pros:** good on-site dining options; large rooms; large poolside area with plenty of seating. **Cons:** somewhat remote location; basic guest rooms; no beach. $ *Rooms from: $120* ✉ *Rte. A4,, Williamsfield, Port Antonio* ☎ *876/993–7720* 🌐 *www.jamaica-palacehotel.com* *80 rooms* *Free Breakfast.*

Sea Cliff Hotel

$ | **HOTEL** | Perched on a remote cliff in a lush forest and looking out onto the Caribbean sea, this laid-back and rustic resort is a nature lover's paradise—each of the 15 open-air rooms have balconies and hammocks (along with one handy modern feature, free Wi-Fi). **Pros:** very private; great on-site restaurant; spa services available. **Cons:** limited activities; may be too remote for some; most rooms don't have TVs. $ *Rooms from: $177* ✉ *Ross Craig District, Long Bay, Port Antonio* ☎ *876/860–1395, 876/869–5931* 🌐 *www.seacliff-jamaica.com* *15 rooms* *Free Breakfast.*

★ **Trident Hotel**

$$$$ | **HOTEL** | One of Jamaica's most stylish resorts features villas decorated with commissioned artwork and elegant furnishings designed and made especially for the hotel, plus three excellent dining options, including a dinner club with live jazz by the house band or mento music by the famed Jolly Boys. **Pros:**; private beach; movie-screening room; full-service spa. **Cons:** might be too remote for some; not many activities on property; can feel a bit too quiet at times. $ *Rooms from: $864* ✉ *North Coast Hwy., Point Ann, Port Antonio* ☎ *876/633–7100, 800/300–6220* 🌐 *www.thetridenthotel.com* *13 villas* *Free Breakfast.*

Shopping

HANDICRAFTS

Musgrave Market

CRAFTS | This traditional market, unlike those in Ocho Rios and Montego Bay, is primarily aimed at locals. The most popular section of the market is the Port Antonio Craft Market, which offers a wide variety of handmade crafts, clothing, wood carvings, oil paintings, and more. ✉ *West St., Port Antonio.*

Royal Mall Shopping Village

SHOPPING CENTER | In the heart of Port Antonio, this colonial-style mall is home to numerous shops and businesses. From clothing stores to souvenir shops and restaurants; there's even a barber and hairstylist. On the third floor, there's a bar, arcade, and a gym. ✉ *Fort George St., Port Antonio.*

The Village, Port Antonio

CRAFTS | The Village is Port Antonio's most popular shopping center. The stalls are filled with local artists selling fine art and furniture, gift shops with clothes and all kinds of Jamaica memorabilia, and restaurants, including a juice bar. ✉ *3 Allan Ave., Port Antonio* ☎ *876/993–3053.*

Kingston

Few travelers—particularly Americans—take the time to visit Kingston, although guided day trips make the city quite accessible from Ocho Rios and Montego Bay. That's understandable, as Kingston can be a tough city to love. It's big (population 1.25 million) and has a rough reputation, with gang-controlled neighborhoods that can erupt into violence. However, New Kingston is a vibrant and exciting business district with many enjoyable diversions. If you yearn to know more about the heart and soul of Jamaica, Kingston is worth a visit. This government and business center is also a cultural capital, home to numerous dance troupes, theaters, historic sights, and museums. It's also home to the University of the West Indies, one of the Caribbean's largest universities. In many ways, Kingston reflects the true Jamaica—a wonderful cultural mix—more than the sunny havens of the North Coast. As one Jamaican put it, "You don't really know Jamaica until you know Kingston."

The Blue Mountains are a magnificent backdrop for the city, with fabulous homes in the foothills. Views get grander as roads wind up into one of the island's least developed yet most beautiful regions.

GETTING HERE AND AROUND

Kingston is the only city in Jamaica that has "postal zones." Most of the zones are residential areas, but the five most tourists encounter are Kingston CSO (Downtown), Kingston 1 (Port Royal), Kingston 5 (New Kingston), Kingston 6 (Liguanea), and Kingston 10 (Half-Way-Tree).

Sights

Bank of Jamaica Money Museum

BANK | You don't have to be a numismatist to enjoy the exhibits at this museum, which offers a fascinating look at Jamaica's history through its monetary system. It includes everything from glass beads used as currency by the Taíno Indians to Spanish gold pieces to currency of the present day. Ultraviolet lights enable the viewing of detailed features of historic bank notes. There's also a parallel exhibit on the general history of currency through world history. ✉ *Duke St., at Nethersole Pl., Kingston CSO* ☎ *876/922–0750* 🌐 *www.boj.org.jm* 🎫 *Free* 🕙 *Closed weekends.*

★ **Bob Marley Museum**

HISTORIC HOME | At the height of his career, Bob Marley purchased a house on Kingston's Hope Road and added a recording studio—painted Rastafarian red, yellow, and green. It now houses this museum, the capital's best-known tourist sight. The guided tour takes you through rooms wallpapered with magazine and newspaper articles that chronicle his rise to stardom. There's a 20-minute biographical film on Marley's career. You can also see the bullet holes in the walls from a politically motivated assassination attempt in 1976. On the property is a gift shop, record shop, and the One Love Cafe. ✉ *56 Hope Rd., Kingston 6* ☎ *876/630–1588* 🌐 *www.bobmarleymuseum.com* 🎫 *$20 to tour studio; $25 to tour museum and grounds; $40 to tour studio, museum, and grounds.*

Devon House

HISTORIC HOME | Built in 1881 as the mansion of the island's first black millionaire, George Stiebel, who made his fortune from gold mining in South America, this National Heritage Site was bought and restored by the Jamaican government in the 1960s. Visit the two-story mansion, furnished with Venetian-crystal chandeliers and period reproductions, on a guided tour. On the grounds, there are restaurants, crafts shops, a bakery, and a spa. Probably the biggest draw is the Devon House I-Scream shop, where lines of locals form, especially on Sunday, to get a dip of their favorite ice cream, often rum raisin. ✉ *26 Hope Rd., Kingston 10* ☎ *876/929–6602* 🌐 *www.devonhouseja.com* 🎫 *$11 for house; free admission for grounds and shops.*

Emancipation Park

PUBLIC ART | Seven acres of lush greenery make a popular respite from New Kingston's concrete jungle. Locals come to jog, play table tennis, see concerts, and relax. Clowns entertain children, and photographers take romantic pictures of couples by the fountain. At the south entrance, Redemption Song is a pair of monumental statues of slaves, a reminder of the island's colonial past. ✉ *Knutsford Blvd., at Oxford Rd., Kingston* ☎ *876/926–6312* 🌐 *www.emancipationpark.org.jm* 🎫 *Free.*

Hope Royal Botanical Gardens

GARDEN | The Caribbean's largest botanical garden, originally called the Hope Estate, was founded in the 1600s by an English army officer. Today it's often referred to as Hope Gardens, and the 2,000 acres feature areas devoted to orchids, cacti, and palm trees making it the perfect spot for large festivals, picnics, and intimate gatherings. The gardens are also home to the Hope Zoo Kingston. ✉ *231 Old Hope Rd., Kingston 6* ☎ *876/970–3505, 876/977–6047* 🌐 *www.hrbg.org.jm* 🎫 *Free.*

Hope Zoo

ZOO | **FAMILY** | Lucas, a regal male lion, is the zoo's most popular sight, but there are many interesting animals, including iguanas, the Jamaican boa snake, and a colorful array of parrots and other tropical birds. Exhibits also showcase zebras, crocodiles, monkeys, and deer. ✉ *Hope Gardens, Old Hope Rd., Kingston 6* ☎ *876/927–1085* 🌐 *www.hopezookingston.com* 🎫 *JMD $1,500.*

Institute of Jamaica

HISTORY MUSEUM | Dating to 1879, this museum covers early Arawak residents to modern times. Collections span art, literature, and natural history, with exhibits from Jamaican furniture to Marcus Garvey. ✉ *10–16 East St., Kingston CSO* ☎ *876/922–0620* 🌐 *www.instituteofjamaica.org.jm* 🎫 *$10* 🕒 *Closed weekends.*

National Gallery of Jamaica

ART GALLERY | Established in 1974, this gallery is the oldest and largest public art museum in the English-speaking Caribbean. The gallery features early, modern, and contemporary artwork (some of it on permanent view) from Jamaican and Caribbean artists. The gallery offers tours, lectures, exhibitions, and children's programs. There is also a gift shop and a café. ✉ *12 Ocean Blvd., Kingston CSO* ✥ *entrance on Orange St.* ☎ *876/922–1561* 🌐 *www.natgalja.org.jm* 🎫 *JMD $400* 🕒 *Closed Sun. and Mon.*

Peter Tosh Museum

HISTORY MUSEUM | In the heart of New Kingston, this museum is dedicated to one of Jamaica's greatest reggae singers, Peter Tosh (born Winston McIntosh). Tosh, along with two other reggae legends—Bob Marley and Bunny Wailer—formed the Wailers in 1967. After the group split up, Tosh went on to have a successful solo career, spanning a decade, until he was killed during a robbery in 1987. Lots of Tosh's memorabilia, including his custom M16 guitar and unicycle, are on display. ✉ *Pulse Center, 38a Trafalgar Rd., Kingston 10* ☎ *876/960–0049* 🌐 *www.petertosh.com* 🎫 *$20* 🕒 *Closed Sun.*

Trench Town Culture Yard Museum

HISTORY MUSEUM | This restored tenement building where Bob Marley spent much of his youth is now a protected National Heritage Site. Marley wrote frequently about life in the "government yard," and the area is credited with being the birthplace of reggae. It's also where the Wailers band was formed—they recorded *Catch a Fire* here. The project was developed by the Trenchtown Development Association, a group dedicated to breathing new life into what had been one of Kingston's worst slums. There's a museum of Marley and Wailer memorabilia and a souvenir shop.

TIP→ Tours are best arranged by calling in advance, but there is a tour guide on the property, in case you arrive without a reservation. ✉ *6–10 1st St., Kingston CSO* ☎ *876/859–6741* 🌐 *www.ttcultureyard.com* 🎫 *$12 culture yard tour; $18 culture yard and Bob's Mother's house; $30 for the town of Trench Town.*

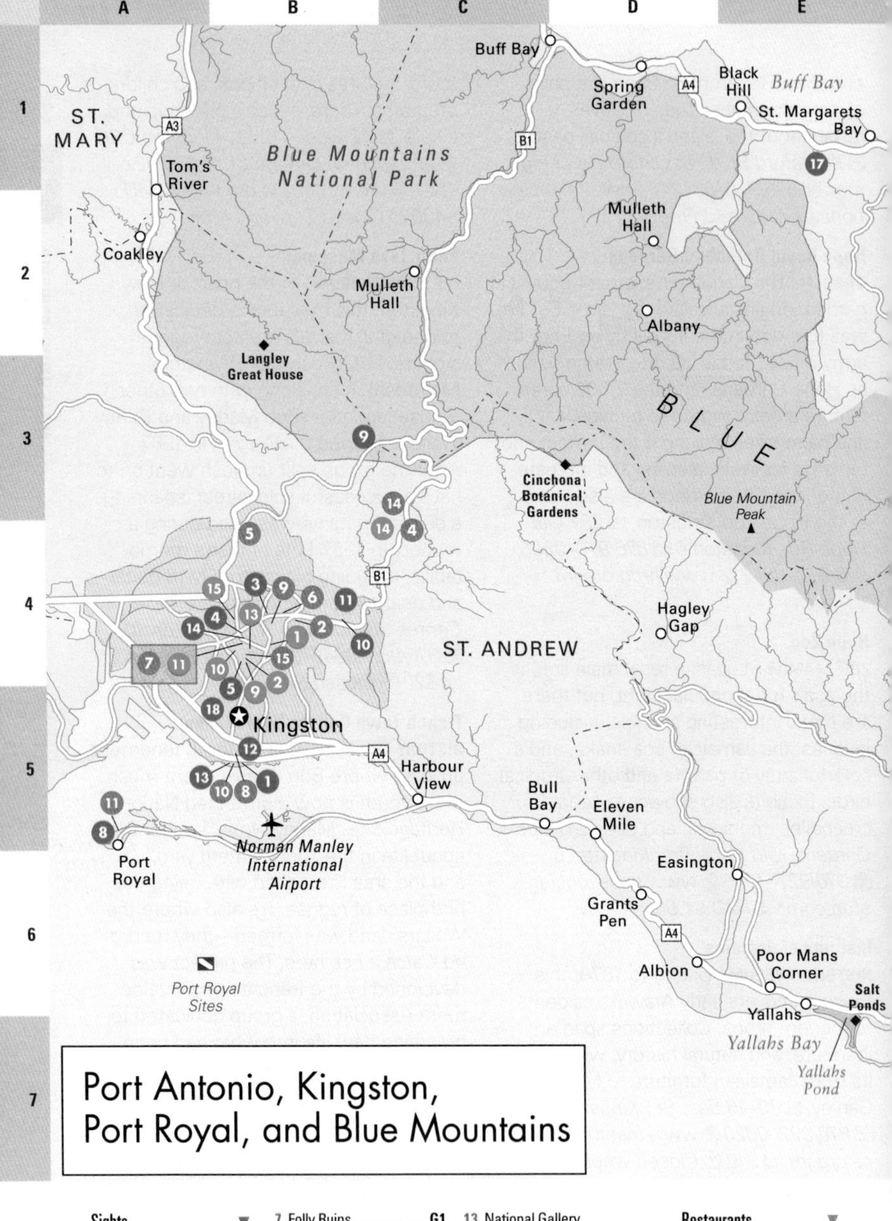

Sights

1 Bank of Jamaica Money Museum B5
2 Blue Lagoon H2
3 Bob Marley Museum... B4
4 Devon House B4
5 Emancipation Park B4
6 Folly Lighthouse G1
7 Folly Ruins G1
8 Fort Charles A5
9 Holywell Park B3
10 Hope Royal Botanical Gardens...... B4
11 Hope Zoo B4
12 Institute of Jamaica B5
13 National Gallery of Jamaica.............. B5
14 Peter Tosh Museum.... B4
15 Reach Falls I4
16 Rio Grande............... F2
17 Somerset Falls E1
18 Trench Town Culture Yard Museum.. B5

Restaurants

1 Boston Jerk Centre H2
2 Broken Plate B4
3 Bushbar G1
4 Cafe Blue C4
5 Cellar 8................... B4
6 Chilitos JaMexican..... B4

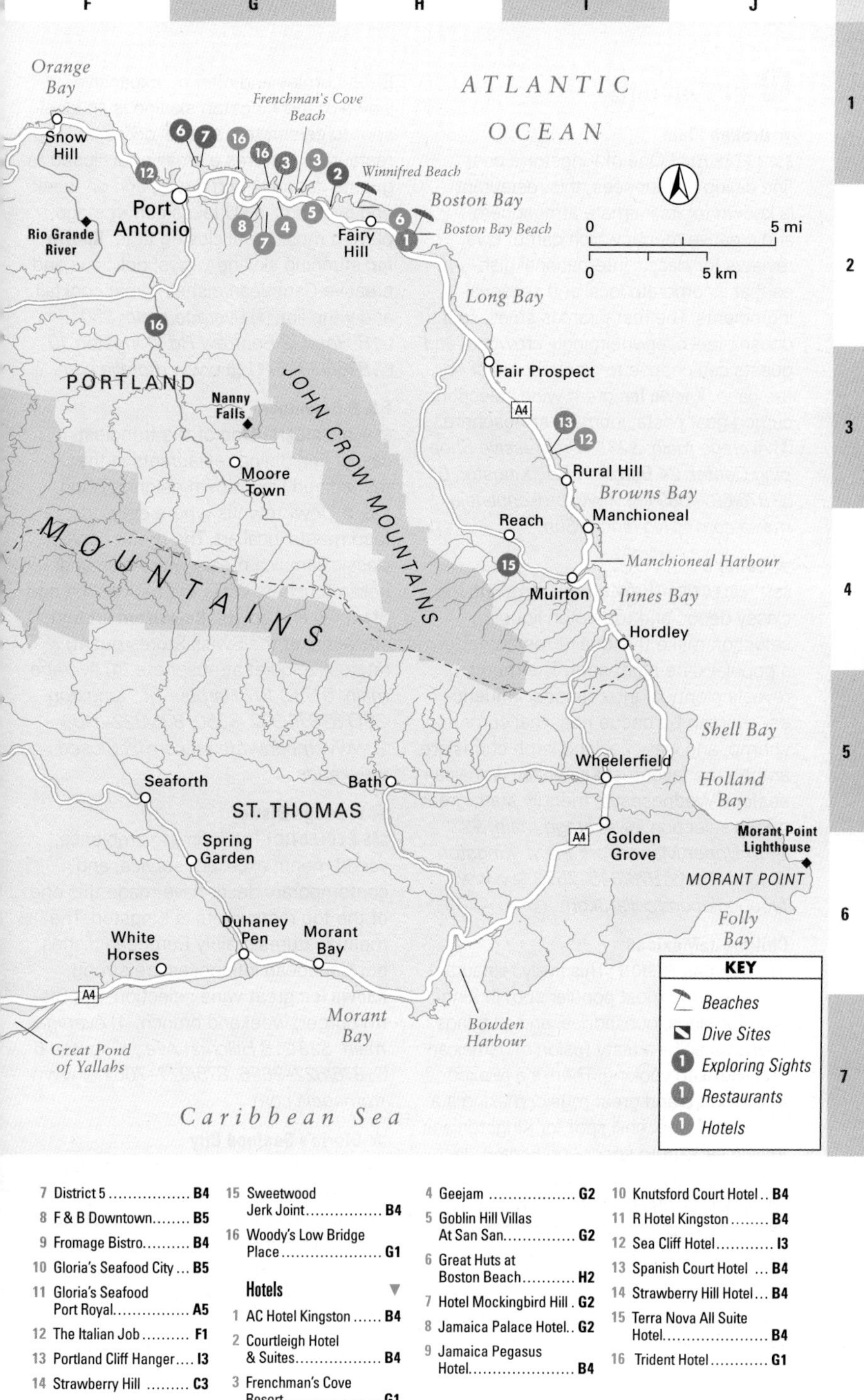

7 District 5 .... **B4**

8 F & B Downtown........ **B5**

9 Fromage Bistro.......... **B4**

10 Gloria's Seafood City ... **B5**

11 Gloria's Seafood Port Royal................ **A5**

12 The Italian Job **F1**

13 Portland Cliff Hanger.... **I3**

14 Strawberry Hill **C3**

15 Sweetwood Jerk Joint................ **B4**

16 Woody's Low Bridge Place **G1**

Hotels

1 AC Hotel Kingston **B4**

2 Courtleigh Hotel & Suites................... **B4**

3 Frenchman's Cove Resort.................... **G1**

4 Geejam **G2**

5 Goblin Hill Villas At San San............... **G2**

6 Great Huts at Boston Beach........... **H2**

7 Hotel Mockingbird Hill . **G2**

8 Jamaica Palace Hotel.. **G2**

9 Jamaica Pegasus Hotel...................... **B4**

10 Knutsford Court Hotel .. **B4**

11 R Hotel Kingston **B4**

12 Sea Cliff Hotel............ **I3**

13 Spanish Court Hotel ... **B4**

14 Strawberry Hill Hotel... **B4**

15 Terra Nova All Suite Hotel...................... **B4**

16 Trident Hotel **G1**

Restaurants

★ Broken Plate

$$$ | **ECLECTIC** | One of Kingston's best fine dining experiences, this restaurant is known for its intimate atmosphere and creative menu, which garner rave reviews for classic international dishes that incorporate local and seasonal ingredients. The restaurant is small, so it doesn't feel overwhelmingly crowded, and guests can choose to dine indoors or on the patio. **Known for:** great wine selection; curried-goat pasta; intimate atmosphere. *Average main: $23 ✉ Progressive Shopping Center, 24 Barbican Rd., Kingston 6 ☎ 876/667–6891 🌐 www.brokenplatejamaica.com ⊙ No dinner Sun.*

★ Cellar 8

$$$ | **ECLECTIC** | The intimate atmosphere, classy decor, and top-notch liquor selection make this quaint restaurant a popular date-night spot. The menu reveals plenty of international influences—Korean barbecue ribs, Thai curried shrimp, and New Zealand lamb chops are among the favorites. **Known for:** Jamaican seafood Wednesdays; friendly staff; great drinks selection. *Average main: $23 ✉ 10 Upper Manor Park Plaza, Kingston 8, Kingston ☎ 876/648–2573 🌐 www.facebook.com/cellar8kgn.*

Chilitos JaMexican

$$ | **MEXICAN FUSION** | This lively restaurant and bar is the most popular spot in Kingston for tacos, quesadillas, and all things "JaMexican"—a tasty fusion of Jamaican and Mexican cooking. There's a relaxed atmosphere and great music, making it a good after-work chill spot for Kingstonians. **Known for:** burrito special on Fridays; taco Tuesdays; margarita Mondays. *Average main: $14 ✉ 88 Hope Rd., Kingston 6 ☎ 876/561–3273, 876/433–3822 🌐 www.chilitosjamexican.com.*

District 5

$$$ | **CARIBBEAN** | Set on the roof of the R Hotel, this Caribbean-fusion restaurant helmed by renowned Jamaican chef Brian Lumley and offering expansive views of the Kingston skyline is an ideal spot to celebrate a special occasion. The restaurant features a small pool closed to guests during dining hours, and on weekend evenings, a DJ takes center stage, playing music until closing time. **Known for:** stunning skyline views; delicious and creative Caribbean dishes; great cocktail and wine list. *Average main: $30 ✉ R Hotel, 2 Renfrew Rd., Kingston 10 ☎ 876/433–6711 🌐 www.rhotelja.com.*

F & B Downtown

$$ | **JAMAICAN** | One of the trendiest casual fine dining restaurants in the reimagined Downtown neighborhood, F & B Downtown is where delicious food meets local art. The menu serves classic Jamaica meals with Asian and Italian touches, while the bar has a range of wines and spirits. **Known for:** art and souvenirs at the Swiss Stores outlet; ratatouille; quiet atmosphere. *Average main: $17 ✉ 107 Harbour St., Kingston CSO ☎ 876/922–8050, 876/922–1109 🌐 www.fnbdowntown.com ⊙ Closed weekends.*

★ Fromage Bistro

$$$ | **ECLECTIC** | The intimate ambience, varied menu, excellent service, and contemporary decor have made this one of the top restaurants in Kingston. The menu features mainly European dishes, but Caribbean influences are strong. **Known for:** great wine selection; the Bistro burger; weekend brunch. *Average main: $23 ✉ 8 Hillcrest Ave., Kingston 6 ☎ 876/622–9856, 876/927–7062 🌐 www.fromageja.com.*

★ Gloria's Seafood City

$$$ | **SEAFOOD** | As part of the restoration of Downtown, Kingston's most beloved seafood restaurant opened a location at the Victoria Pier; the original location is still in Port Royal. The restaurant, designed with windows and glass doors to take in the water views, serves up classic Jamaican seafood dishes with sides like rice and peas, bammy (thick

flatbread made from cassava), and crackers. **Known for:** popular seafood restaurant; harbor views; classic dishes like escovitch fish and brown stew fish. *Average main: $23 ✉ Victoria Pier, Ocean Bvld., Kingston CSO ☎ 876/619–7905 🌐 www.city.gloriasseafoodja.com.*

Sweetwood Jerk Joint

$ | **JAMAICAN** | Located next to Emancipation Park, this jerk joint specializes in spicy jerk meats. It's the perfect spot to relax and dine after a busy day or to take food to go. **Known for:** relaxed atmosphere; jerk lamb and chicken; great post-work spot. *Average main: $7 ✉ 78 Knutsford Blvd., Kingston 6 ☎ 876/906–4854.*

Hotels

Frequented by few vacationers but a popular destination for business travelers and visitors with a deep interest in Jamaican heritage and culture, the sprawling city of Kingston is home to some of the island's finest business hotels. Skirting the city are the Blue Mountains, a completely different world from the urban frenzy of the capital city.

★ **AC Hotel Kingston**

$ | **HOTEL** | Jamaica's first outpost of Marriott's hip, mid-priced AC brand opened in 2019 and appeals greatly to the corporate set but has also become a trendy hotspot with locals, especially the buzzy AC Kitchen and Lounge and the Starbucks in the lobby. **Pros:** stylish and modern design; good dining and lounge options; great business amenities. **Cons:** lounge can get crowded and noisy; expensive food; no meals included. *Rooms from: $184 ✉ 38–42 Lady Musgrave Rd, Kingston 6 ☎ 876/750–3000 🌐 www.marriott.com 219 rooms No Meals.*

Courtleigh Hotel & Suites

$ | **HOTEL** | Aimed at businesspeople, this hotel is in the city's financial district, in the heart of New Kingston and less than a half-hour from Norman Manley International Airport. **Pros:** good business facilities; large rooms; lively nightlife. **Cons:** most rooms lack balconies; noisy location; limited dining options. *Rooms from: $180 ✉ 85 Knutsford Blvd., Kingston 6 ☎ 876/929–9000 🌐 www.courtleigh.com 128 rooms Free Breakfast.*

Jamaica Pegasus Hotel

$ | **HOTEL** | In the heart of the financial district, this 17-story high-rise is popular with corporate travelers due to its central location and ample business amenities. **Pros:** easy access to New Kingston business district; good business travel facilities; nice pool area. **Cons:** area can be unsafe at night; 17 floors can mean a wait for an elevator; limited leisure activities. *Rooms from: $154 ✉ 81 Knutsford Blvd., Kingston 6 ☎ 876/926–3691 🌐 www.jamaicapegasus.com 300 rooms Free Breakfast.*

Knutsford Court Hotel

$ | **HOTEL** | This modest business-district hotel combines business services with a garden-style atmosphere. **Pros:** friendly staff; good value; business amenities. **Cons:** no elevators; small pool area; limited leisure amenities. *Rooms from: $166 ✉ 16 Chelsea Ave., Kingston 6 ☎ 876/929–1000 🌐 www.knutsfordcourt.com 143 rooms Free Breakfast.*

★ **R Hotel Kingston**

$ | **HOTEL** | Although in the midst of the hustle and bustle of central Kingston, this hotel provides comfort and quiet for visitors, its rooms decorated with modern artwork and locally crafted furniture. **Pros:** rooms are stylish and clean; excellent District 5 restaurant; central location. **Cons:** limited breakfast; not many amenities; extremely small pool. *Rooms from: $151 ✉ 2 Renfrew Rd., Kingston 10 ☎ 876/968–6222 🌐 www.rhotelja.com 48 rooms Free Breakfast.*

Spanish Court Hotel

$ | **HOTEL** | A long-time go-to hotel in Kingston, providing service to business travelers, wedding parties, and tourists, this calm oasis in New Kingston features the well-liked and upscale Rojo Restaurant and a roof terrace with a pool and bar. **Pros:** energy-conserving features; 24-hour business center; courteous and helpful staff. **Cons:** limited dining options; street-side rooms can be noisy; not quiet. *$ Rooms from: $169 ✉ 1 St. Lucia Ave., Kingston 6 ☎ 876/926–0000 🌐 www.crissahotels.com 125 rooms 🍽 Free Breakfast.*

★ Terra Nova All Suite Hotel

$ | HOTEL | This graceful former colonial mansion not far from Devon House and several restaurants has refurbished rooms and elegant touches as well as its own eatery offering white-glove-service and sophisticated cuisine. **Pros:** near shops and restaurants; elegant and luxurious; great open-air dining. **Cons:** no spa; so-so fitness center; fills up quickly on weekends. *$ Rooms from: $189 ✉ 17 Waterloo Rd., Kingston 10 ☎ 876/926–2211 🌐 www.terranovajamaica.com 41 suites 🍽 Free Breakfast.*

Nightlife

As a thriving metropolis, Kingston has Jamaica's largest selection of nightlife. Unlike the more tourist-oriented resort communities, nightlife here is aimed at locals and varies from live music to DJs. Some sections of the city are unsafe, so check with your concierge or a knowledgeable local before heading out.

BARS AND CLUBS

Friday nights in Kingston bring on the Friday Night Jam, a street party that begins when office doors close and entrepreneurial chefs roll out oil drums transformed into jerk pits. Street corners sizzle with spicy fare, music blares, and the city launches into weekend mode.

The *Jamaica Gleaner*, the *Jamaica Observer*, and the *Star* have listings of who's playing when and where. Also, look out for roadside posters.

Janga's Soundbar

BARS | One of Kingston's most popular after-work hangouts, this lively bar can get crowded on any given night and is particularly a favorite among the younger crowd. On Friday and Saturday, locals come to dance to DJ sets in the outdoor dining area. *✉ 22 Belmont Rd., Kingston 10 ☎ 876/669–5747.*

★ Regency Bar and Lounge

BARS | At the Terra Nova Hotel, this upscale bar draws well-heeled locals on weekends for delicious cocktails and quick bites. It's less-lively than other bars in town, but a DJ always keeps guests rocking at night. On Friday there's an 'endless cocktails' special. *✉ Terra Nova Hotel, 17 Waterloo Rd., Kingston 10 ☎ 876/926–2211 🌐 www.terranovajamaica.com.*

Usain Bolt's Tracks and Records

BARS | For fans of sprint superstar Usain Bolt, no trip to Kingston would be complete without a visit to the flagship location (there are others in MoBay and Ocho Rios) of his restaurant, a combination casual eatery and sports bar that's designed to look like a stadium. There are (of course) large-screen TVs. Upstairs, on the mezzanine, you can see the running shoes Bolt wore on many of his record-breaking runs as well as signed outfits from medal-winning events. A gift shop sells Bolt gear. On nights when there is live entertainment, the big man himself often shows up at the bar. *✉ The Marketplace, 67 Constant Spring Rd., Kingston 10 ☎ 876/906–3903, 876/926–7875 🌐 www.tracksandrecords.com.*

Shopping

MARKETS

Kingston Crafts Market

MARKET | A large assortment of Jamaican handicrafts, including paintings, sculptures, and inexpensive jewelry, can be found in the market's stalls. Although pickpockets have been a problem in

Jamaica's 2nd International Champ

Reggae legend Bob Marley used to be Jamaica's only international icon. But these days, the fastest man in the world, Usain Bolt, has also reached global icon status and is hero-worshipped on the island. Although retired, Bolt still holds the Olympic record for the 100-meter and 200-meter, successfully defending his own titles, and was part of the Jamaican team to win the 4x100-meter relay. He now holds eight Olympic gold medals for sprinting (he lost his 2008 relay gold medal after a teammate's disqualification) and is an eleven-time world champion. As well as being one of the world's most marketable athletes, he is a goodwill ambassador for Jamaica and undertakes charitable works for children through his Usain Bolt Foundation. Bolt grew up in the parish of Trelawny and now lives in Kingston, where he owns the sports bar Tracks and Records. His winning track shoes and outfits are on display there. Bolt is not the only Jamaican sporting star, as fellow athletes Asafa Powell and Yohan Blake are also champion male runners, while Shelly-Ann Fraser-Pryce won the Olympic 100 meters two consecutive times and three times at the World Championships. Visitors can tour the training ground in Kingston used by these stars and the many other champion Jamaican runners who dominate international sports.

the past, it's much safer now. Some bargaining is tolerated, but don't expect many concessions. ✉ *174 Harbour St., Kingston CSO* ✣ *Between Port Royal St. and Ocean Blvd.*

SHOPPING CENTERS

Shops at Devon House

CRAFTS | This cluster of mostly upscale shops sells clothing, crafts, and other items. The location, at the historic Devon House, makes it a pleasant spot to spend a morning or afternoon. Don't miss the famous Devon House ice cream and popular Devon House patties at the bakery. ✉ *26 Hope Rd., Kingston 10* ☏ *876/929–6602* 🌐 *www.devonhouseja.com.*

Sovereign Centre

MALL | This shopping mall is one of the most popular in eastern Jamaica. There are a large variety of stores and restaurants, a supermarket, and a food court. The movie theater makes it a popular spot among young adults. ✉ *106 Hope Rd., Kingston 6* ☏ *876/978–7416* 🌐 *www.sovereignjamaica.com.*

SPECIALTY ITEMS

Tuff Gong Record Shop

MUSIC | Housed in a studio that's part of the Bob Marley group of companies, this shop carries an impressive collection featuring the legend himself and other reggae greats. Marley and Tuff Gong merchandise is also on sale. The building itself is a tourist attraction, since the studio's international clients include Maxi Priest, Steele Pulse, and Sinéad O'Connor. ✉ *220 Marcus Garvey Dr., Kingston 11, Kingston* ✣ *Entrance on Bell Rd.* ☏ *876/630–1588* 🌐 *www.tuffgong.com.*

Port Royal

Just south of Kingston, Port Royal was called "the wickedest city in the West" until an earthquake tumbled much of it into the sea in 1692. You can no longer down rum in Port Royal's legendary 40 taverns, but a few small bars remain in operation, and the spirits of Henry Morgan and other buccaneers add energy to what remains. The proudest possession of St. Peter's Church, rebuilt in 1726 to replace Christ's Church, is a silver communion set said to have been donated by Morgan himself (who probably obtained it during a raid on Panama). A ferry from the square in downtown Kingston goes to Port Royal at least twice a day, but most visitors arrive by road, continuing past the airport to this small community. If you drive out to Port Royal from Kingston, you pass several other sights, including remains of old forts overgrown with vegetation, an old naval cemetery (which has some intriguing headstones), and a monument commemorating Jamaica's first coconut tree, planted in 1863 (there's no tree there now, just plenty of cacti and scrub brush).

Sights

Fort Charles

MILITARY SIGHT | Built in 1662 and once the city's largest garrison, this is the oldest surviving structure from the British occupation. On the grounds, you can find an old artillery storehouse, called Giddy House, which gained its name after being tilted by the earthquake of 1907. Locals say its slant makes you dizzy. The Fort Charles Maritime Museum is housed in what was once the headquarters for the British Royal Navy. Admiral Horatio Nelson served as a naval lieutenant here in 1779. The museum features a re-creation of Nelson's private quarters, as well as other artifacts from the era, including models of various sailing vessels. Fort Charles is located just past Norman Manley International Airport. ✉ *1 Queen St., Port Royal* ☎ *876/967–8438* 🌐 *www.jnht.com/site_fort_charles.php* 🎫 *$15.*

Restaurants

Gloria's Seafood Port Royal

$$ | **SEAFOOD** | As Port Royal's number-one restaurant, regulars come here for the food and atmosphere. The rustic restaurant is right by the ocean, with a view of the Blue Mountains in the back, and the fishermen's boats docked by the seaside are evidence of the fresh fish, shrimp, lobster, and conch that are caught and prepared here. **Known for:** large portions; fresh seafood; ocean views. [$] *Average main: $17* ✉ *5 Queen St., Port Royal* ☎ *876/967–8066.*

Blue Mountains

Best known as the source of Blue Mountain coffee, these mountains rising out of the lush jungle north of Kingston are a favorite destination with adventure travelers, as well as hikers, birders, and anyone looking to see what lies beyond the beach. You can find guided tours to the mountains from the Ocho Rios and Port Antonio areas, as well as from Kingston.

TIP→ Unless you're traveling with a local, don't try to go on your own; the roads wind and dip without warning and hand-lettered signs blow away, leaving you without a clue as to which way to go. It's best to hire a taxi (look for red PPV license plates to identify a licensed cab) or book a guided tour.

Sights

★ **Holywell Park**

NATURE PRESERVE | In this nature preserve, part of the Blue and John Crow Mountains National Park, nature trails wind through rugged terrain and offer the chance to spot reclusive creatures, including the streamer-tail hummingbird (known as the doctor bird) and the rare swallowtail butterfly. Rustic camping facilities are available, including showers and shelters. It's about 15 miles (25 km) north of Kingston on a very slow and winding road. Bird-watching, guided hikes, and coffee tours are offered. ✉ *Rte. B1, northwest of Newcastle, Kingston* ☎ *876/619–9807, 876/357–9565* 🌐 *www.blueandjohncrowmountains.org* 🎫 *$20 Blue Mountain peak hike; $25 coffee tour.*

Restaurants

Cafe Blue

$$ | **CAFÉ** | Perched on a hillside more than 3,000 feet up in Irish Town, Cafe Blue is one of the most stunning places to enjoy a cup of coffee and a slice of freshly baked cake. The hip hideaway for Kingstonians is also popular with Strawberry Hill Hotel guests because of the variety of beverages made from Blue Mountain coffee. **Known for:** "Blueccino" drinks; terrific local coffee; great breakfast sandwiches. *Average main: $12 ✉ Hwy. B1, Irish Town, Irish Town ☎ 876/944–8918 🌐 www.cafeblue.com ⏲ No dinner.*

★ **Strawberry Hill**

$$$$ | **JAMAICAN** | A favorite with Kingstonians for its elegant Sunday brunch, Strawberry Hill has a stunning location; the open-air terrace has spectacular views of the city and countryside. The restaurant serves an à la carte menu that features dishes with a Jamaican flare and ingredients grown on the Island Outpost Farm. **Known for:** Blackwell Rum Punch; incredible views; romantic ambience. *Average main: $40 ✉ Strawberry Hill, New Castle Rd., Irish Town ☎ 876/944–8403, 876/429–8646 🌐 www.strawberryhillhotel.com.*

Hotels

★ **Strawberry Hill Hotel**

$$$ | **HOTEL** | A 45-minute drive from Kingston—but worlds apart in terms of atmosphere—this exclusive resort was developed by Chris Blackwell, former head of Island Records (the label of Bob Marley, among many others), and features an infinity pool, spa, and pure relaxation in Georgian-style cottages. **Pros:** great for hiking or exploring nearby coffee plantations; stylish accommodations with breathtaking Blue Mountains views; cool retreat from the heat. **Cons:** no fitness center; no surrounding attractions or facilities; remote location a distance from beaches. *Rooms from: $385 ✉ New Castle Rd., Irish Town ☎ 876/944–8400, 800/232–4972 🌐 www.strawberryhillhotel.com 12 cottages Free Breakfast.*

South Coast

Jamaica's South Coast spans four parishes (Westmoreland, St. Elizabeth, Mandeville, and Clarendon), most of which are considered part of rural Jamaica. The South Coast has little commercial activity when compared to tourist towns like Ocho Rios, but this is part of its appeal. Visitors escape here to explore the untouched, natural beauty: secluded beaches, mineral baths, rivers, and waterfalls.

Sights

★ **Appleton Estate**

DISTILLERY | One of the Caribbean's premier rum distillers, Appleton Estate offers guided tours illustrating the history of rum making in the region. The tour begins with a lively discussion of the days when sugarcane was crushed by donkey power, then proceeds to a behind-the-scenes look at the modern facility. Upon being fully educated about rum you can partake of the samples that flow freely. Every visitor receives a complimentary miniature bottle of Appleton. Reservations are not required for the tour are necessary, 24 hours in advance, for lunch. There's also a restaurant, bar, and a gift shop. *✉ Hwy. B6, Siloah ☎ 876/850–0090 🌐 www.appletonestate.com $30 ⏲ Closed Sun.*

Jamaica Standard Products Coffee Factory

FACTORY | Coffee beans grown on nearby plantations—Baronhall Estate Coffee, Island Blue Jamaica Blue Mountain Coffee, and Jamaica High Mountain Coffee—are brought here for processing. Tours aren't offered, but you can stop by the gift shop for a sample taste and purchase their many fine coffee products. *✉ Main Rd., Williamsfield, Mandeville ↔ 5 miles (8 km) east of Mandeville ☎ 876/963–4211 🌐 www.*

jamaicastandardproducts.com 🎫 *Free* ⏲ *Closed weekends.*

Lovers Leap

VIEWPOINT | As legend has it, two slaves in love, Mizzy and Tunkey, chose to jump off this 1,700-foot cliff rather than be captured by their master. At the entrance of the property is a wooden statue dedicated to the tragic pair. This site includes a restaurant with a balcony, a photogenic lighthouse, and stunning sea views. Tours detail Jamaica's history and Mizzy and Tunkey's story. Weddings can be held here. ✉ *Yardley Chase, Southfield, St. Elizabeth* ☎ *876/965–6887* 🌐 *www.jakeshotel.com* 🎫 *JMD $300.*

Mandeville

TOWN | At 2,000 feet above sea level, Mandeville is considerably cooler than the coastal areas about 25 miles (40 km) to the south. Its vegetation is also lusher, thanks to the mists that drift through the mountains. But climate and flora aren't all that separate it from the steamy coast: Mandeville seems a hilly tribute to all that's genteel in the British character. The people here live in tidy cottages with gardens around a village green; there's even a Georgian courthouse and a parish church. The entire scene could be set down in Devonshire, were it not for the occasional poinciana blossom or citrus grove. ✉ *Rte. A2, between Black River and May Pen.*

★ Y. S. Falls

WATERFALL | **FAMILY** | A quiet alternative to Dunn's River Falls in Ocho Rios, these falls are part of a cattle and horse farm and are reached via a tractor and trailer. There is actually a series of seven falls on the property that cascade into natural pools. An exhilarating zipline zooms over them. Other features include a river pool, a garden, a gift shop, and a lounge with food. ✉ *North of A2, just past town of Middle Quarters* ☎ *876/997–6360* 🌐 *www.ysfalls.com* 🎫 *$20 waterfalls; $49 canopy* ⏲ *Closed Mon.*

Although the constant roar of speeding trucks keeps the site from being idyllic, **Bamboo Avenue,** known by locals as Holland Bamboo, the section of Route A1 between Middle Quarters and Lacovia, is an often-photographed stretch of highway that's completely canopied with tall bamboo. Roadside vendors sell chilled coconuts, cracking them with machetes to reveal the jelly inside after you drink the coconut water through a straw.

Beaches

If you're looking for something off the main tourist routes, head for Jamaica's largely undeveloped South Coast. Many of the beaches in these towns feature darker-colored sand. Because the population in this region is sparse, these isolated beaches are some of the island's safest, with hustlers practically nonexistent. You should, however, use common sense; never leave valuables unattended.

Bluefields Beach Park

BEACH | On the South Coast road to Negril, this relatively narrow stretch of sand and rock near the small community of Bluefields is typically crowded only on weekends and holidays. The swimming here is good, although the sea is sometimes rough; and you can get food (mainly jerk chicken and beer) from vendors. **Amenities:** food and drink; lifeguards; parking (fee); showers; toilets. **Best for:** sunset; swimming. ✉ *Hwy. A2, Bluefields* 🎫 *Free.*

Treasure Beach

BEACH | **FAMILY** | The most atmospheric beach in the southwest is in the community of Treasure Beach. Here there are several long stretches of sand and many small coves. With more rocks and darker sand, the beach isn't as pretty as those to the west or north, but it's a bit of the "real" Jamaica. Both locals and visitors use the beach, though you're as likely to find it deserted, beyond a friendly beach dog. Treasure Beach attracts a bohemian crowd, and you won't find as many hustlers as in North Coast resort towns. **Amenities:** food and drink; parking (no fee); lifeguards. **Best for:** solitude; sunset; walking. ✉ *Treasure Beach* 🎫 *Free.*

 Restaurants

★ Floyd's Pelican Bar

$$ | **SEAFOOD** | One of the funkiest places to down a cold Red Stripe, this whimsical structure sits on stilts ½ mile (1 km) offshore between Treasure Beach and Black River, atop a small sandbar, and reachable only by boat. It has become a local legend and a mandatory stop for many visitors to the South Coast. **Known for:** fresh fish (fried or grilled); Jamaican beers; domino games. $ *Average main: $20* ✉ *Parottee Bay, St. Elizabeth* ☎ *876/354–4218, 876/250–3073* 💳 *No credit cards.*

★ Jack Sprat Restaurant

$$ | **ECLECTIC** | It's no surprise that this restaurant shares its home resort's bohemian style (it's the beachside dining spot at Jakes). The menu features jerk dishes, pizzas, and seafood, served with traditional Jamaican sides, and ice cream or pie for dessert. **Known for:** nightly music; jerk crab; lobster dishes (curry lobster, jerk lobster, lobster pizza, and more). $ *Average main: $15* ✉ *Jakes Hotel, Calabash Bay, Treasure Beach* ☎ *876/965–3583* 🌐 *www.jakeshotel.com.*

Little Ochie Seafood Restaurant

$$ | **JAMAICAN** | This casual beachside eatery, a favorite with locals and travelers, is known for genuine Jamaican dishes focused on seafood, most of it supplied by fishermen just yards away. For those staying in Treasure Beach, a popular way to reach Little Ochie is by boat. **Known for:** shrimp dishes (coconut, curry, or garlic); fish soup and jerk chicken; Little Ochie Seafood Fest in July. $ *Average main: $20* ✉ *Alligator Pond* ✥ *about 7 miles (11 km) south of A2* ☎ *876/852–6430.*

★ Murray's Fish and Jerk Hut

$$ | **JAMAICAN** | The location of this casual restaurant makes it popular for those journeying along the south coast—luckily, the food is good, too. As the name suggests, they serve plenty of fish and jerk dishes with a variety of sides at this open-air spot. **Known for:** lively atmosphere; mannish water (Jamaican goat soup); jerk rabbit. $ *Average main: $15* ✉ *Clarendon Park Garden, Toll Gate* ✥ *Between Mandeville and Spanish Town* ☎ *876/867–6572* 🌐 *www.murraysfishandjerkhut.com.*

★ Voilà by Lilee

$ | **ECLECTIC** | This quaint bistro in Mandeville, run by chef Lilee, feels a million miles away from the bustle of the city. Locals favor this spot for breakfast and lunch, where classic burgers, wraps, and delicious pastries highlight the menu. **Known for:** pasta dishes; panini; breakfast sandwiches. $ *Average main: $10* ✉ *Pear Tree Village, 52 Caledonia Rd., Shop #4, Mandeville* ☎ *876/613–0339* 🌐 *www.voilabylilee.com* 🕒 *Closed Sun.*

 Hotels

In the 1970s, Negril was Jamaica's most relaxed place to hang out. Today that distinction is held by the South Coast, a long stretch of coastline ranging from Whitehouse to Treasure Beach. Here local residents wave to cars, and travelers spend their days exploring local communities and their nights in local restaurants. The best way to reach the South Coast is from Montego Bay, driving overland, or via Savanna-la-Mar from Negril. Both methods take around 90 minutes to two hours, depending on your final destination.

★ Jakes Hotel

$ | **HOTEL** | Seaside charm combines with interesting artwork to create a chic place that oozes personality, with each room or cottage designed with unique colors and funky furnishings with signature

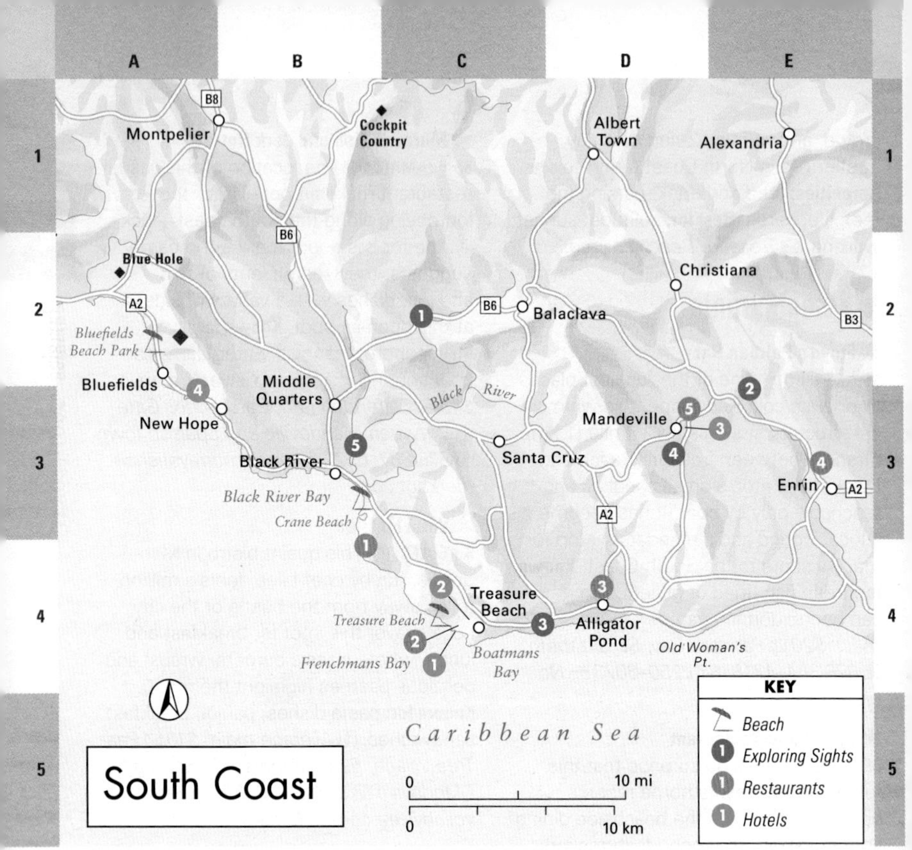

South Coast

KEY
Beach
Exploring Sights
Restaurants
Hotels

Sights

1 Appleton Estate C2
2 Jamaica Standard Products Coffee Factory E3
3 Lovers Leap C4
4 Mandeville................ D3
5 Y. S. Falls................. B3

Restaurants

1 Floyd's Pelican Bar B4
2 Jack Sprat Restaurant................ C4
3 Little Ochie Seafood Restaurant ... D4
4 Murray's Fish and Jerk Hut............. E3
5 Voilà by Lilee D3

Hotels

1 Jakes Hotel............... C4
2 Lashings Boutique Hotel........... C4
3 Mandeville Hotel D3
4 Sandals South Coast .. A3

touches—think mosaic tiles and headboards and concrete walls embedded with colored-glass bottles. **Pros:** personalized service; unique accommodations; South Coast friendliness. **Cons:** food is pricey; long drive from Montego Bay and Kingston airports; can feel cramped when occasional rainy periods keep you inside. *Rooms from: $145 Calabash Bay, Treasure Beach 876/965–3000 www.jakeshotel.com 50 rooms No Meals.*

Lashings Boutique Hotel
$ | **HOTEL** | Bringing an urbane loft aesthetic to the very sleepy seaside village of Treasure Beach, this breezy property with stunning sunset coastal views offers individually appointed rooms with wooden furniture, quirky lighting, and local artwork (you can buy the paintings and sculptures at the hotel's Art Cafe). **Pros:** quiet property; infinity pool with stunning coastal views; a variety of meals of restauarnt. **Cons:** no entertainment activities; guard dogs on the property at night; no TVs in rooms. *Rooms from: $66 Treasure Beach, St. Elizabeth 876/903–6369, 876/512–4476 www.lashings.com 19 rooms No Meals.*

Mandeville Hotel
$ | **HOTEL** | **FAMILY** | Three massive 200-year-old Sandbox trees guard the front of this family-owned hotel that has a friendly aura, tropical gardens wrapping around the main building, and flowers spilling onto the terrace restaurant, where breakfast and lunch are served. **Pros:** quiet property; great views of surrounding hills; staff can set up tours. **Cons:** dated furnishings; no a/c in some rooms; limited nightlife. *Rooms from: $65 4 Hotel St. 876/962–9764 www.mandevillehoteljamaica.com 65 rooms Free Breakfast.*

★ **Sandals South Coast**
$$$$ | **RESORT** | When this resort opened in 2017, it made headlines around the world for its stunning over-the-water bungalows that extend to form the shape of a heart in the ocean; in 2020 Sandals South Coast earned attention by unveiling its first swim-up rondoval suites, all of which feature a private pool, conical ceiling, and a serenity swing. **Pros:** luxurious rooms with ocean views; lots of facilities and activites; stunning beach. **Cons:** long drive from airports; some rooms are far away from restaurants; expensive spa. *Rooms from: $800 Whitehouse, Westmoreland 888/726–3257 www.sandals.com 380 rooms All-Inclusive.*

Negril

In the 18th century, English ships assembled here in convoys for dangerous ocean crossings. The infamous pirate Calico Jack and his crew were captured right here while they guzzled rum. All but two of them were hanged on the spot; Mary Read and Anne Bonny were pregnant at the time, so their executions were delayed.

On the winding coast road 55 miles (89 km) southwest of MoBay, Negril was once Jamaica's best-kept secret, but it has shed some of its bohemian, ramshackle atmosphere for the attractions and activities traditionally associated with MoBay. One thing that hasn't changed about this west-coast center (whose only true claim to fame is a 7-mile [11-km] beach) is a casual approach to life. As you wander from lunch in the sun to shopping in the sun to sports in the sun, you'll find that swimsuits and cover-ups are common attire.

Negril stretches along the coast south from horseshoe-shaped Bloody Bay (named when it was a whale-processing center) along the calm waters of Long Bay to the lighthouse. Nearby, divers spiral downward off 50-foot-high cliffs into the deep green depths as the sun turns into a ball of fire and sets the clouds ablaze with color. Sunset is also the time when Norman Manley Boulevard and West End Road, which intersect, come to life with busy waterside restaurants and reggae stage shows.

Sights

★ Blue Hole Mineral Spring

HOT SPRING | At this mineral spring about 20 minutes from Negril, near the community of Little Bay, you can jump 22 feet off a cliff or climb down a ladder to swim in the hole's icy water. Mud around the water's edge is said to be good for your skin, and the water itself is reputed to have therapeutic properties. For those who cannot jump or climb, water is pumped into a swimming pool at the surface. A bar and grill, a volleyball court, and a motel complete the property. You can also tour a marijuana farm nearby. Take a chartered taxi from Negril, or call to organize a pickup. ✉ *Brighton District, Negril* ✣ *Near Roaring River* ☎ *876/860–8805* 🎟 *$20 for mineral spring; $20 for marijuana farm tour.*

Kool Runnings Adventure Park

WATER PARK | FAMILY | Billing itself as the place where "Jamaica comes to play," this park has 10 waterslides and a ¼-mile (½-km) lazy-river float ride, as well as a go-kart track, kayaking, outdoor laser combat games, and Jamboo rafting (on floating bamboo). There is also a human gyroscope, a "kool kanoe" adventure, a wave pool, and paintball. General admission varies by height and gives guests access to the waterslides, wave pool, and lazy river-ride. Other attractions are an additional fee. ✉ *Norman Manley Blvd., Negril* ☎ *876/957–5418* 🌐 *www.koolrunnings.com* 🎟 *From $40.*

Beaches

★ Seven Mile Beach (*Negril Beach*)

BEACH | Stretching for 7 miles (11 km)—from Bloody Bay in the north along Long Bay to the cliffs on the southern edge of town—this long, white-sand beach is probably Jamaica's finest. Some stretches remain undeveloped, but these are increasingly few. Along the main stretch, the sand is public to the high-water mark, and visitors and vendors parade from end to end. The walk is sprinkled with good beach bars and open-air restaurants, some of which charge a small fee to use their beach facilities. Bloody Bay is lined with large all-inclusive resorts; these sections are mostly private. Jamaica's best-known nude beach, at Hedonism II, is always among the busiest; only resort guests or day-pass holders may sun here. **Amenities:** food and drink; lifeguards; parking (no fee); toilets; showers; water sports. **Best for:** partiers; sunset; swimming; walking. ✉ *Norman Manley Blvd., Negril* 🎟 *Free.*

Restaurants

★ The Caves Restaurant

$$$$ | JAMAICAN | With a reservation, nonguests can savor authentic Jamaican cuisine with a twist at this gorgeous boutique resort on Negril's West End. The price ($150 per person) covers a private, romantic, candlelit five-course dinner in a sea-front cave. **Known for:** great wine and drinks selection; romantic atmosphere; sea views. [$] *Average main: $100* ✉ *The Caves, West End Rd., Negril* ☎ *876/957–0270, 876/618–1081* 🌐 *www.thecaveshotel.com* ⏲ *No lunch.*

★ Chill-Pops Gourmet Paletas

$ | DESSERTS | FAMILY | Opened in 2020, this small dessert shop in the center of the Boardwalk Shopping Village is decorated with bright artistic signs and doles out Mexican paletas, popsicle-like desserts made the traditional (nondairy) way, with real fruit. Ice cream and alcohol-infused pops are also sold. **Known for:** quirky, colorful design; a variety of pops with toppings offered; Blue Mountain coffee fudge pops. [$] *Average main: $4* ✉ *Boardwalk Shopping Village, Norman Manley Blvd, Negril* ☎ *876/957–3278.*

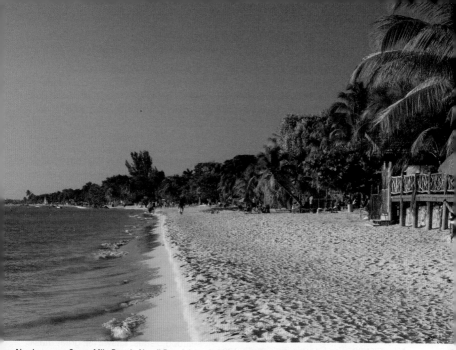

Also known as Seven Mile Beach, Negril Beach is probably one of Jamaica's finest beaches.

★ Fireman's Lobster Pit

$$$ | **SEAFOOD** | This open-air restaurant right on the beach is Negril's go-to for delicious lobster that you select and the staff prepares anyway you like—grilled, curried, or roasted. You can also get delicious king crab here, along with fresh fish and shrimp. **Known for:** ocean views; delicious lobster; king crab. [$] *Average main: $30* ✉ *Ray's Water Sports, Norman Manley Blvd., Negril* ☎ *876/591–1864* 🌐 *www.facebook.com/firelobsterpit.*

★ Ivan's Bar & Restaurant

$$$ | **CARIBBEAN** | Upscale Caribbean cuisine, stunning cliff-side dining, and romance make this one of the best places to eat on Negril's West End. Watch the spectacular sunset while enjoying a cocktail by the simple thatched bar and eatery, decorated with funky art. **Known for:** seafood dishes (coconut lobster, snapper, curry seafood); gorgeous sunset views; pasta dishes. [$] *Average main: $30* ✉ *Catcha Falling Star, West End Rd., Negril* ☎ *876/957–0390, 876/967–0045* 🌐 *www.catchajamaica.com* ⏲ *No lunch.*

Just Natural

$ | **VEGETARIAN** | This low-key eatery with the motto "come and relax" serves made-to-order vegetarian and seafood dishes as well as fresh fruit and vegetable juices, but it's the surroundings—an enchanting garden on Negril's West End—that make it stand out. Mismatched tables and chairs, some of them made from recycled materials, are scattered in the garden, surrounded by orange trees, pretty flowers, and lush vegetation, so that each dining area is private. **Known for:** great breakfasts; beautiful outdoor garden; veggie pasta. [$] *Average main: $10* ✉ *Hylton Ave., Negril* ✣ *½ mile (1 km) after the lighthouse* ☎ *876/957–0235* ▬ *No credit cards.*

★ Kenny's Italian Cafe

$$$ | **ITALIAN** | This popular, open-air spot serves delicious Italian food—pizzas, pasta, and local seafood dishes—in a relaxing atmosphere. The restaurant is beautifully lit with stylish all-white decor in the main dining area, along with private cabanas, an outdoor dining area,

and a bar. **Known for:** jerk chicken; variety of pizza and pasta dishes; club atmosphere with resident DJ. *Average main: $28 Norman Manley Blvd., Negril 876/957–4032 No lunch.*

Kuyaba Restaurant

$$$ | **JAMAICAN** | Open all day and right on the beach, this charming thatch-roof restaurant is one of the top spots for dinner on Negril's 7-mile (11-km) strip of sand. The menu specializes in Jamaican cuisine with an international twist, with meals covering sea, breeze, and land. **Known for:** delicious seafood meals (crab cakes, spicy lobster medley); stunning views; a variety of salads. *Average main: $25 Kuyaba Hotel, Norman Manley Blvd., Negril 876/957–4318 www.kuyaba.com.*

Le Vendome

$$$ | **FRENCH** | The Charela Inn's pretty restaurant is lit up with strings of Christmas lights, with tables set out on the beach (there's also a covered patio area in case it rains). There are Jamaican favorites on the menu along with the likes of escargot, crepes, and soufflés. **Known for:** live music; homemade pizza; delicious desserts. *Average main: $30 Charela Inn, Norman Manley Blvd., Negril 876/379–1505, 876/957–4648 www.charelainn.com.*

★ Margaritaville Negril

$$ | **INTERNATIONAL** | Like its sister properties in Montego Bay and Ocho Rios, Margaritaville Negril is usually packed with young partiers, though this outpost doesn't have waterslides, just a water trampoline to work off those calories. The traditional Margaritaville meals like nachos and cheeseburgers are joined by international fare like fajitas. **Known for:** delicious drinks; beach chairs and umbrellas provided; live music. *Average main: $20 Norman Manley Blvd., Negril 876/957–4467 www.margaritavillecaribbean.com.*

★ Murphy's West End Restaurant

$$$ | **SEAFOOD** | This family-operated restaurant is small and casual, but don't be fooled by its size, as the delicious seafood meals will have you wanting to return again and again. The food is made with fresh, local ingredients and is so beautifully presented, you'd think you were at a much more spendy restaurant. **Known for:** two-for-one lobster specials; a variety of pasta; vegetarian options (stew, burritos). *Average main: $23 West End Rd., Negril About 1 km from Rick's Cafe 876/367–0475.*

Pushcart Restaurant and Rum Bar

$$$ | **JAMAICAN** | Diners can enjoy versions of traditional Jamaican street food in the comfort of a colorful, cliffside restaurant. The menu features traditional house-cooked Jamaican meals and seafood dishes. **Known for:** great music; breathtaking views; braised oxtail (served with callaloo rice) and curry goat (served with steamed rice). *Average main: $25 Rockhouse, West End Rd., Negril 876/957–4373 www.rockhousehotel.com No lunch.*

Rasta Ade Refreshments

$ | **VEGETARIAN** | Rastafarians are masters at vegan food, so don't expect any chicken or pork dishes on the menu of this colorful beachside eatery that's all about organic Jamaican food. Ackee, callaloo, steamed vegetables, and salads are on offer, and most meals are served with traditional Jamaican root staples like yam, potatoes, and boiled dumplings. **Known for:** popular Jamaican porridges; ocean views; vegan options. *Average main: $9 Norman Manley Blvd., Negril 876/957–3898.*

★ Rick's Cafe

$$$ | **CARIBBEAN** | A Negril institution since the hippie days of the 1960s and 1970s, Rick's is one of the resort town's best-known landmarks and attracts busloads of revelers for sunset every evening. Love it or hate it, it's worth experiencing at least once on a trip to Negril. **Known**

for: drink specials using local liquor; live reggae band several times a week; cliff diving. $ *Average main: $28* ✉ *West End Rd., Negril* ☎ *876/957–0380* 🌐 *www.rickscafejamaica.com.*

★ Rockhouse Restaurant

$$$ | **CARIBBEAN** | This restaurant is a must for dinner at least once while visiting Jamaica, as the menu features both traditional Jamaican cooking and Rockhouse's interpretation of "new Jamaican cuisine," inspired by the many cultures that have come to the island. The open-air dining area has huge comfy bamboo sofas where you can relax for an aperitif or after-dinner drink; tables are arranged near the cliff for sensational seaside dining. **Known for:** a variety of seafood dishes; beautiful sunset views; private table dining. $ *Average main: $27* ✉ *Rockhouse, West End Rd., Negril* ☎ *876/957–4373, 876/618–1533* 🌐 *www.rockhouse.com.*

3 Dives Restaurant

$ | **JAMAICAN** | This very casual restaurant housed beneath a big roof (and not much more) is best known for its jerk—it hosts the Negril Jerk Festival every November—but also serves other traditional Jamaican dishes and seafood, like grilled lobsters (in season). Lunch is available, but dinner, thanks to the spectacular sunsets, is always the peak time. **Known for:** large portions; beautiful sunset views; jerk dishes. $ *Average main: $9* ✉ *West End Rd., Negril* ☎ *876/782–9990* ⏲ *No lunch Sun.*

Woodstock Bar and Grill

$$$ | **CARIBBEAN** | This thatched-roof restaurant on Seven Mile Beach draws crowds with its water trampolines, waterbeds, swing chairs, beach chairs, and umbrellas, and there's always some form of entertainment—often it's a live band. But the food is terrific, too, from fresh seafood to traditional Jamaican classics. **Known for:** live entertainment; extensive cocktail selection; water sports and beach activities. $ *Average main: $27* ✉ *Norman Manley Blvd., Negril* ☎ *876/366–5771* 🌐 *www.woodstocknegrilja.com.*

Xtabi Restaurant

$$$$ | **CARIBBEAN** | Along with offering stunning cliffside views, the service here is fast and the staff is extremely friendly and helpful. Breakfast features classic Jamaican dishes, while lunch and dinner are a range of seafood and island favorites. **Known for:** cliff-jumping; curried conch; amazing sunsets. $ *Average main: $36* ✉ *Xtabi Resort, West End Rd., Negril* ☎ *876/957–0121* 🌐 *www.xtabijamaica.com.*

★ Zimbali's Mountain Cooking Studio

$$$$ | **CARIBBEAN** | Zimbali's isn't just a restaurant, it's a culinary experience as guests are taken on a tour of the restaurant's organic farm, before heading back for a delicious farm-to-table meal. The open-air dining space, nestled in the Negril hills, has stadium-style seating with the kitchen in the center, so guests can watch as the chefs prepare seafood and vegetarian meals. **Known for:** variety of cakes for dessert; numerous seafood and vegetarian options; great entertainment. $ *Average main: $70* ✉ *Caanan Mountain, Little London, Negril* ☎ *876/252–3232* 🌐 *www.zimbaliretreats.com* ⏲ *Closed Sun.*

Hotels

Some 50 miles (80 km) west of MoBay, the so-called Capital of Casual was once a hippie hangout, favored for its inexpensive mom-and-pop hotels and laid-back atmosphere. Today there's still a little bohemian flair, but the town is one of the biggest tourist draws on the island, with several large all-inclusives along Bloody Bay, northeast of town. The main strip of Seven Mile Beach and the cliffs are still favored by vacationers who like to get out and explore.

Beaches Negril Resort and Spa
$$ | **RESORT** | **FAMILY** | This family-friendly all-inclusive has something for everyone: a prime Negril Beach location, upscale dining for adults, and multiple attractions for kids and teens—a chief asset is the impressive 18,000-square-foot water park, Pirates Island. **Pros:** great beach; extensive water park; lots of activities for kids of all ages. **Cons:** on major road; children's programs canceled if too few are enrolled; some activities have a surcharge. *Rooms from: $334 Norman Manley Blvd., Negril 888/232–2437 www.beaches.com 215 rooms All-Inclusive.*

Catcha Falling Star
$ | **HOTEL** | Surely one of the prettiest properties on the West End cliffs, this place proclaims "to rekindle the romance," perhaps because the grounds are decorated with pink bougainvillea and other tropical plants, and you can sunbathe or read privately with your loved one in secluded spots throughout the property. **Pros:** every room is individual; rooms for different budgets; romantic atmosphere throughout the property. **Cons:** no kids under the age of 15; no meal plans; no beach. *Rooms from: $175 West End Rd., Negril 876/957–0390 www.catchajamaica.com 17 suites No Meals.*

★ The Caves
$$$$ | **RESORT** | At this boutique resort that's part of former music mogul Chris Blackwell's Island Outpost group, the thatched-roof cottages are individually designed and furnished, most with balconies overlooking the deep water off Negril's West End honeycombed cliffs. **Pros:** unobtrusive but excellent service; intimate spa on cliff top; quiet and friendly. **Cons:** no beach; a couple of rooms have no sea views; limited on-site dining options. *Rooms from: $575 144 One Love Dr., Negril 876/957–0270, 876/618–1081 www.thecaveshotel.com 12 cottages Free Breakfast.*

Charela Inn
$ | **HOTEL** | This quiet, family-run hotel, on one of the nicest parts of Negril Beach, is built hacienda-style around a central courtyard, where there's a round swimming pool and a lush garden. **Pros:** good value for families; various meal plans available; good beach location. **Cons:** not many amenities and activities; facilities are not luxurious; some guest rooms are small. *Rooms from: $163 Norman Manley Blvd., Negril 876/957–4648, 876/957–4277 www.charelainn.com 59 rooms Free Breakfast.*

Couples Negril
$$$$ | **RESORT** | This beachfront, couples-only resort emphasizes romance and relaxation and is a more laid-back alternative to the nearby Sandals Negril. **Pros:** nude beach with hot tub; free weddings with stays of six nights or more; extensive all-inclusive package that includes all land and water activities. **Cons:** a bit of a drive from Negril's attractions; traffic noise can be heard from some rooms; long walk along the beach to action outside the resort. *Rooms from: $532 Norman Manley Blvd., Negril 876/957–5960 www.couples.com 234 rooms All-Inclusive 3-night minimum.*

Couples Swept Away
$$$$ | **RESORT** | For sports-minded couples, this all-suites resort is known for its expansive sports offerings, top-notch facilities (Jamaica's best and among the Caribbean's best), and healthy cuisine. **Pros:** great spa; excellent fitness and sports facilities; complimentary airport shuttle. **Cons:** not many nightlife options; some facilities are across the road; the healthy angle's not for everyone. *Rooms from: $525 Norman Manley Blvd., Negril 876/957–4061 www.couples.com 312 suites All-Inclusive 3-night minimum.*

Hedonism II
$$$ | **RESORT** | At this go-to resort for the uninhibited that promises a perpetual spring break for adults, most

visitors are drawn to the legendary party atmosphere. **Pros:** numerous activities; good beaches; more economical than some adult all-inclusives. **Cons:** basic rooms; nude beach and pool frequently overcrowded; bacchanalian atmosphere not for everyone. *Rooms from: $446 ✉ Norman Manley Blvd., Rutland Point, Negril ☎ 876/957–5200 🌐 www.hedonism.com 280 rooms All-Inclusive.*

Hotel Riu Negril

$ | **RESORT** | **FAMILY** | At the far north end of Negril on Bloody Bay, this massive beachfront resort delivers good bang for the buck, with decent food and extensive activities and facilities. **Pros:** good on-site dining; economical all-inclusive; families find plenty of children. **Cons:** long walk from attractions of Seven Mile Beach; many rooms a long walk from public areas; pools and public areas can be overcrowded with families. *Rooms from: $250 ✉ Bloody Bay Beach, Norman Manley Blvd., Negril ☎ 876/957–5700 🌐 www.riunegrilresort.com 420 rooms All-Inclusive.*

★ **Rockhouse Hotel**

$ | **HOTEL** | A sign reads "Spa Zone—Keep the Vibes Calm," which is not a tall order at this beautiful boutique hotel that attracts discerning travelers, honeymooners, and celebrities who appreciate the cottages and villas placed along a cliff and the rustic but stylish accommodations. **Pros:** great dining options; unique accommodations in a beautiful setting; natural, tropical style that is ecologically aware. **Cons:** no fitness center; may be too quiet for some; no beach. *Rooms from: $195 ✉ West End Rd., Negril ☎ 876/957–4373, 876/618–1533 🌐 www.rockhouse.com 40 rooms No Meals.*

★ **Royalton Negril**

$$$$ | **RESORT** | **FAMILY** | This picturesque, family-friendly retreat on Bloody Bay Beach opened in 2017 and offers tons of water sports and activities for the entire family, along with eight dining options, including a steak house, a teppanyaki restaurant, and a café. **Pros:** spacious and modern rooms; great dining options; free nonmotorized water sports. **Cons:** in-room liquor only for Diamond Club guests; pools can be crowded; spa treatments cost extra. *Rooms from: $490 ✉ Norman Manley Blvd., Negril ☎ 876/632–7401 🌐 www.royaltonresorts.com 407 rooms All-Inclusive.*

Sandals Negril Beach Resort and Spa

$$$$ | **RESORT** | Couples looking for a sports-oriented getaway and a casually elegant atmosphere flock to this resort on one of the best stretches of Negril Beach. **Pros:** good restaurants; complimentary airport shuttle; excellent beach. **Cons:** long drive from the airport; no transportation to sister resorts; on-site nightlife options limited. *Rooms from: $778 ✉ Norman Manley Blvd., Negril ☎ 888/726-3257 🌐 www.sandals.com 226 rooms All-Inclusive.*

Sandy Haven Resort

$$ | **HOTEL** | This small boutique hotel, opened in 2012, is a good value, particularly since it's on a lovely stretch of Negril's famed Seven Mile Beach. **Pros:** good restaurants; good value; lovely beach location. **Cons:** some rooms are outdated; limited on-site lunch options; beach is not private. *Rooms from: $334 ✉ Norman Manley Blvd., Negril ☎ 876/957–3200, 800/583–8365 toll-free in U.S. 🌐 www.sandyhavenresort.com 35 rooms Free Breakfast.*

Skylark Negril Beach Resort

$ | **RESORT** | Located on Negril's Seven Mile Beach, Rockhouse Hotel's sister property is a stylish and modern boutique hotel that has a retro glamorous beach-pad vibe accentuated by bohemian-style decor. **Pros:** rooms are beautfully decorated and clean; complimentary paddle boards and beach games; right on Seven Mile Beach. **Cons:** only two rooms have ocean views; no TV in rooms; hotel lacks a pool and gym. *Rooms from: $195 ✉ Norman Manley Blvd., Negril ☎ 876/957–4364 🌐 www.skylarknegril.com 28 rooms No Meals.*

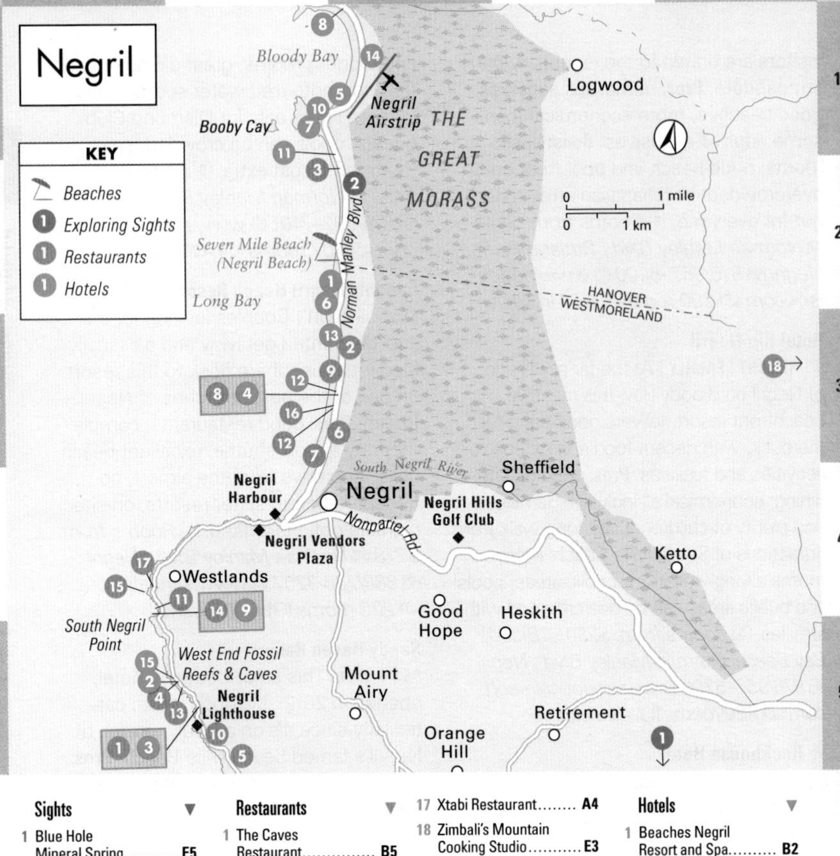

Sights

1 Blue Hole Mineral Spring E5

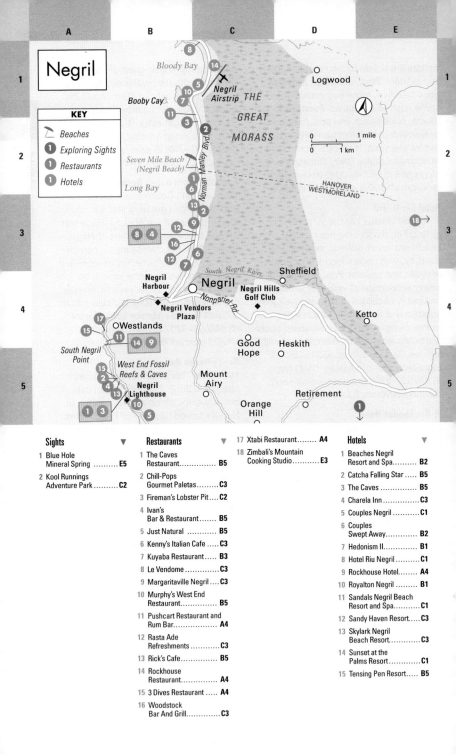

2 Kool Runnings Adventure Park C2

Restaurants

1 The Caves Restaurant............... B5

2 Chill-Pops Gourmet Paletas......... C3

3 Fireman's Lobster Pit.... C2

4 Ivan's Bar & Restaurant....... B5

5 Just Natural B5

6 Kenny's Italian Cafe C3

7 Kuyaba Restaurant..... B3

8 Le Vendome C3

9 Margaritaville Negril C3

10 Murphy's West End Restaurant............... B5

11 Pushcart Restaurant and Rum Bar................. A4

12 Rasta Ade Refreshments C3

13 Rick's Cafe.............. B5

14 Rockhouse Restaurant............... A4

15 3 Dives Restaurant A4

16 Woodstock Bar And Grill.............. C3

17 Xtabi Restaurant........ A4

18 Zimbali's Mountain Cooking Studio........... E3

Hotels

1 Beaches Negril Resort and Spa.......... B2

2 Catcha Falling Star B5

3 The Caves B5

4 Charela Inn C3

5 Couples Negril C1

6 Couples Swept Away............. B2

7 Hedonism II.............. B1

8 Hotel Riu Negril C1

9 Rockhouse Hotel........ A4

10 Royalton Negril B1

11 Sandals Negril Beach Resort and Spa........... C1

12 Sandy Haven Resort..... C3

13 Skylark Negril Beach Resort............ C3

14 Sunset at the Palms Resort............ C1

15 Tensing Pen Resort..... B5

Sunset at the Palms Resort

$$$ | **RESORT** | Surrounded by lush forests and palm trees, this relaxed all-inclusive is a favorite with ecotourists thanks to its emphasis on environmental sustainability. **Pros:** environmentally conscious; beautiful grounds; wedding packages and services available. **Cons:** beach is across street; eco theme not for everyone; not within walking distance of many Negril Beach attractions and restaurants. *Rooms from: $451* ✉ *Norman Manley Blvd., Negril* ☎ *876/854–8160* 🌐 *www.thepalms-jamaica.com* *85 rooms* *All-Inclusive.*

★ **Tensing Pen Resort**

$ | **B&B/INN** | This rustic but elegant resort is hip without being pretentious; it's a top spot for affordable chic and the kind of place that makes you want to check in and just laze in your room, or in a hammock, with a book. **Pros:** spa and yoga services available; unique accommodations; great snorkeling. **Cons:** no fitness center; barking dogs and other noise sometimes interrupts the quiet; perched on the cliffs as it is, you need to work a bit to reach the beach below. *Rooms from: $190* ✉ *West End Rd., Negril* ☎ *876/957–0387* 🌐 *www.tensingpen.com* *22 cottages* *Free Breakfast.*

Nightlife

BARS AND CLUBS

★ **Alfred's Ocean Palace**

LIVE MUSIC | You can find some of Negril's best live music at this bar, which stages reggae band performances right on the beach on Sunday, Tuesday, and Friday nights. ✉ *Norman Manley Blvd., Negril* ✣ *next to Grand Pineapple Beach Resort* ☎ *876/519–1796* 🌐 *www.alfreds.com.*

Bourbon Beach

GATHERING PLACES | This beach bar is popular for its food and daily entertainment. There's live music or a DJ seven days a week, often until the wee hours of the morning, and there's no cover charge. ✉ *Norman Manley Blvd., Negril* ☎ *876/957–4432.*

The Jungle Night Club

DANCE CLUBS | This hot spot has two dance floors, seven bars, and four DJs spinning the latest reggae, dance hall, EDM, and hip-hop tunes. ✉ *Norman Manley Blvd., Negril* ☎ *876/957–4005.*

Margaritaville Negril

DANCE CLUBS | This popular party spot transforms into "Clubville" after hours; it's right on the beach so there's plenty of barefoot fun. Don't miss the sunset beach party every Wednesday. ✉ *Norman Manley Blvd., Negril* ☎ *876/957–4467* 🌐 *www.margaritavillecaribbean.com.*

Rick's Cafe

BARS | One of Jamaica's most popular spots for tourists and locals; sunset brings the crowds for live reggae. ✉ *West End Rd., Negril* ☎ *876/957–0380* 🌐 *www.rickscafejamaica.com.*

Shopping

MARKETS

Negril Craft Market

MARKET | This market on the beach side of the bridge at Negril's town center roundabout sells arts and crafts aplenty. Be sure to bargain with sellers for the best values. ✉ *Norman Manley Blvd., Negril.*

Rutland Point Craft Market

MARKET | With Negril's laid-back atmosphere, it's no surprise that most shopping involves straw hats, woven baskets, and T-shirts, all plentiful at this crafts market on the northern edge of town. The atmosphere is less aggressive here than at similar establishments in Montego Bay and Ocho Rios. ✉ *Norman Manley Blvd., Negril.*

SHOPPING CENTERS

The Boardwalk Village

MALL | Set right on the beach in Negril, this is a nice place to spend half a day perusing souvenir stores, the gaming lounge, and clothing boutiques, and perhaps also having lunch at any of the restaurants. ✉ *Norman Manley Blvd., Negril* ☎ *876/881–2682.*

Time Square Shopping Mall

MALL | The mall is known for its luxury goods and souvenirs, including cigars and jewelry, but there are a few duty free shops and a café as well. ✉ *Norman Manley Blvd., Negril* ☎ *876/957–9263* 🌐 *www.timesquarenegril.com.*

Activities

The tourist board licenses all recreational activity operators and outfitters, which should assure you of fair business practices as long as you deal with companies that display its decals.

BIRD-WATCHING

Jamaica is a major bird-watching destination, thanks to its various natural habitats. The island is home to more than 200 species, some seen only seasonally or in particular parts of the island. Many bird-watchers flock here for the chance to see the vervain hummingbird (the world's second-smallest bird, larger only than Cuba's bee hummingbird) and the Jamaican tody (which nests underground).

PORT ANTONIO

Bespoke Jamaican Birdwatching Tours

BIRD WATCHING | Hotel Mockingbird Hill offers 8-day and 10-day bird-watching tours. Both tours explore a variety of habitats, including mountains and rain forest, quiet rivers and lush valleys. Accommodations and meals are included in the tours. One-day tours can be booked for about $170. ✉ *Hotel Mockingbird Hill, Port Antonio* ☎ *876/619–1215* 🌐 *www.hotelmockingbirdhill.com.*

KINGSTON AND THE BLUE MOUNTAINS

Arrowhead Birding Tours

BIRD WATCHING | This company runs birding tours across the island, including one-day outings ($130 per person for groups of two and $180 for an individual), customized trips, and seven-day trips that include accommodation, meals, and transportation. ✉ *27 Airy Castle Rd., Stony Hill, Kingston* ☎ *876/260–9006* 🌐 *www.arrowheadbirding.com.*

Sun Venture Tours

BIRD WATCHING | This outfit offers 25 different special-interest tours for nature lovers, including bird-watching, across the island. ✉ *32 Russell Heights, Kingston* ☎ *876/924–4515, 876/408–6973.*

DIVING AND SNORKELING

Jamaica isn't a major dive destination, but you can find a few rich underwater regions with a wide array of marine life, especially off the North Coast, which is on the edge of the Cayman Trench. MoBay, known for its wall dives, has **Airport Wall** at its southwestern edge. The site has tropical coral formations and a variety of marine life. The first marine park in Jamaica, the **Montego Bay Marine Park,** was established to protect the natural resources of the bay; it's easy to see the treasures that lie beneath the surface.

Thanks to a marine area protected since 1966, the Ocho Rios region is also a popular diving destination. Through the years, the protected area grew into the **Ocho Rios Marine Park,** stretching from Mammee Bay and Drax Hall in the west to Frankfort Point in the east. Top dive sites in the area include **Jack's Hall,** a 40-foot dive dotted with all types of coral; **Top of the Mountain,** a 60-foot dive near Dunn's River Falls with many coral heads and gorgonians; and the **Wreck of the Katryn**, a 50-foot dive to a deliberately sunk 140-foot former minesweeper.

With its murkier waters, the southern side of the island isn't as popular for diving. However, **Port Royal,** near Kingston's airport, is filled with sunken ships that are home to many varieties of tropical fish; a special permit is required to dive some sites here.

A one-tank dive costs $45–$80. Most large resorts have dive shops, and the all-inclusives sometimes include scuba diving. To dive, you need a certification card, though it's possible to get a taste of scuba and do a shallow dive—usually from shore—after a one-day resort course, which almost every resort with a dive shop offers.

PORT ANTONIO

Wall diving is especially popular in the Port Antonio area. For intermediate and advanced divers, a top spot is **Trident Wall,** lined with stunning black coral. Other favorites include **Alligator Hill,** a moderate to difficult dive known for its tubes and sponges. A beginner site, **Alligator West** is prized for its calm waters.

Lady G'Diver

SCUBA DIVING | The only dive operator in Port Antonio runs trips to interesting sites almost every day. Two-tank dive trips depart the Errol Flynn Marina at 10:30 am. Call two or three days in advance. ✉ *Errol Flynn Marina, Port Antonio* ☎ *876/995–0246* 🌐 *www.ladygdiver.com.*

NEGRIL

Thanks to its protected waters, Negril offers some of the best scuba diving on the island. In addition to the popular **Seven Mile Beach** and **Rockhouse,** there are other sites in the town that are perfect for diving. **Booby Cay** is a small, secluded cay located just off the coast of Negril that's used for snorkeling adventures. Guides also take their visitors to search for fresh seafood to prepare right on the shores. Another popular site is **Negril Reef,** known for its swarms of tiny (and harmless) jellyfish and variety of reef fish.

Negril Adventure Divers

DIVING & SNORKELING | This company offers scuba diving, snorkeling, swimming lessons, life guard preparations, and glass boat rides in dive sites all over Negril. Once you're in town, Negril Adventure will pick you up for free. ✉ *Norman Manley Blvd., Negril* ⊕ *near Merrils Beach Resort II* ☎ *876/412–2502* 🌐 *www.negriladventurediver.com.*

RUNAWAY BAY

Jamaica Scuba Divers

DIVING & SNORKELING | With serious scuba facilities for dedicated divers and beginners, this PADI and NAUI outfit offers nitrox diving and instruction as well as instruction in underwater photography, night diving, and open-water diving. Operations are based at FDR Resort in Runaway Bay. Pickup can be arranged from most hotels and other locations along the North Coast. ✉ *Runaway Bay.*

DOLPHIN SWIM PROGRAMS

Swimming with dolphins is popular in Jamaica; there are three locations on the island.

MONTEGO BAY

Dolphin Cove Montego Bay

WATER SPORTS | FAMILY | This company offers dolphin swims, lower-price dolphin encounters (ages six and up), shark encounters (ages six and over), and admission to the grounds, which includes a short nature walk. Programs cost $99–$189, and reservations are advised. It's open on Monday, Wednesday, and Friday. ✉ *Carretera A1, Montego Bay* ☎ *877/344–3385* 🌐 *www.dolphincoveja.com.*

OCHO RIOS

Dolphin Cove Ocho Rios

WATER SPORTS | This is Jamaica's number one dolphin attraction. Visitors can swim, hold, feed, and interact with dolphins and sharks. There's also a Jungle Trail to see other kinds of animals. Prices range from $69–$199, and it's closed Monday and Thursday. ✉ *Belmont Road, Ocho Rios* ☎ *876/974–5335* 🌐 *www.dolphindiscovery.com.*

Moon Palace Jamaica

WATER SPORTS | As part of the Dolphin Cove attractions, this dolphin program located at Moon Palace Jamaica provides guests with the opportunity to caress, kiss, and even swim with dolphins.

Prices range from \$99–\$199. ✉ *Moon Palace Jamaica, Main St., Ocho Rios* ☎ *888/774–0040, 876/974–5335* 🌐 *www.dolphincoveja.com.*

FISHING

MONTEGO BAY

Lucky Bastard Fishing Charters

FISHING | This company has been providing the best fishing experiences in Montego Bay for over four decades. They offer 4-hour, 6-hour, and 8-hour excursions. Children over five years old are welcome onboard and the charter provides life preservers. Snacks and drinks are included on all trips, with lunch included on the 8-hour trip. There is a maximum of six people per trip and trips start at \$750. ✉ *Sunset Dr., Freeport, Montego Bay* ☎ *876/572–0010* 🌐 *www.fishinginjamaica.com.*

FALMOUTH

Glistening Waters Marina

FISHING | Offering deep-sea fishing and other charter trips from Glistening Waters (20 minutes east of Montego Bay), this marina also runs night tours of the lagoon, which is iridescent due to microscopic dinoflagellates that glow when they move. ✉ *North Coast Hwy., Falmouth* ☎ *876/954–3229* 🌐 *www.glisteningwaters.com.*

FOUR-WHEELING

OCHO RIOS

Chukka Caribbean Adventures

FOUR-WHEELING | Chukka offers ATV adventure combo packages that can include horse-back riding, cliff jumping, tubing, and ziplining, or the all-inclusive 4-play package. Prices range from \$99 to \$179. ✉ *Island Village, Turtle River Rd., Ocho Rios* ☎ *876/619–1441, 876/619–1382, 877/424–8552 in U.S.* 🌐 *chukka.com.*

Wilderness ATV Tours

FOUR-WHEELING | Wilderness ATV Tours offers two different tours. One takes you to Murphy Hill, the highest point in Ocho Rios, and the other heads to Dunn's River Falls. ATV tour is \$80 per person. All tours, offered daily, start at Reynolds Pier, so they're popular with cruise passengers. Transportation is included if you're staying in nearby hotels. ✉ *Reynolds Pier, Main St., Ocho Rios* ☎ *876/382–4029* 🌐 *www.wildernessatvtours.com* ⏲ *Closed Sun.*

NEGRIL

Jamwest Motorsports & Adventure Park

FOUR-WHEELING | This massive adventure park in Little London has its own dirt trail. ATV Tours last one hour, \$115 per person. They also offer ziplining, horseback riding, and bobsledding. A safari and a circuit track are also on the property. Pickups can be arranged from hotels in Negril. ✉ *Old Hope, Little London, Negril* ☎ *876/957–4474, 876/475–7588* 🌐 *www.jamwest.com.*

GOLF

MONTEGO BAY

Cinnamon Hill Gold Course

GOLF | On 400 lush acres on the Rose Hall estate, this course, designed by Robert von Hagge and Rick Baril, takes you to the water's edge and up into the hilly jungles. Rates include greens fees, cart, caddy, and tax, and Nike clubs are available for rent. ✉ *Rose Hall, North Coast Hwy., St. James* ☎ *876/953–2984, 876/953–2341* 🌐 *www.rosehall.com/cinnamon-hill* 🎫 *\$179 in winter, \$139 in summer, \$49 replay* 🏌 *18 holes, 6828 yards, par 72.*

Half Moon Golf Course

GOLF | Swaying palms, abundant bunkering, and large greens greet you on this flat Robert Trent Jones Sr.–designed course, home of the Jamaica Open. The course has been redesigned by Jones's protégé Roger Rulewich to better position the hazards for today's longer hitters. The Half Moon Golf Academy offers one-day sessions, multiday retreats, and hour-long private sessions. ✉ *Half Moon, North Coast Hwy., Montego Bay* ✥ *7 miles (11 km) east of Montego Bay* ☎ *876/953–2560* 🌐 *www.halfmoon.com/golf* 🎫 *Nonguests:*

$275 for 18 holes, $150 for 9 holes ⛳ *18 holes, 7141 yards, par 72.*

★ Tryall Club Golf Course

GOLF | At an exclusive country club 15 miles (24 km) west of Montego Bay, this championship course on the site of a 19th-century sugar plantation blends first-class golf with traces of history. The ambience is peaceful; no one is hurried and playing with a caddy is the norm. The layout takes in the Caribbean coast—the 4th-hole green hugs the sea—before heading up into the hills for expansive vistas. Designed by Ralph Plummer, the course has hosted events such as the Johnnie Walker World Championship. ✉ *Tryall Club, North Coast Hwy., Sandy Bay* ☎ *876/956–5660* 🌐 *www.tryallclub.com* 🎫 *$150 for 18 holes ($115 guests), $115 for 9 holes ($85 guests)* ⛳ *18 holes, 6836 yards, par 71.*

White Witch Golf Course

GOLF | One of the nicest courses in Montego Bay, if not Jamaica, is the White Witch course, named for Annie Palmer, the wicked 19th-century plantation mistress, whose greathouse looms above the course. The course was designed by Robert von Hagge and Rick Baril. Annie's Revenge is one of five tournaments hosted at the course that occupies mountainous terrain high above the sea and features bold, attractive bunkering and panoramic views. Legend has it that Annie still haunts the area, but not your golf game. Rental clubs are available for $55. Prebooking is recommended. ✉ *Rose Hall Main Rd., Rose Hall, St. James* ☎ *876/953–2341* 🌐 *www.rosehall.com* 🎫 *$179 in winter, $139 in summer, $49 replay* ⛳ *18 holes, 6758 yards, par 71.*

KINGSTON

Caymanas Golf and Country Club

GOLF | About 8 miles (12 km) west of the city center, Jamaica's first major championship 18-hole course opened in 1957. On the property is a clubhouse, restaurant, bar, and pro shop. ✉ *Hwy 2000, between Kingston and Spanish Town* ☎ *876/665–9993, 876/746–9000* 🌐 *www.caymanasgolf.com* 🎫 *$70 for 18 holes, $38 for 9 holes* ⛳ *18 holes, 6844 yards, par 72.*

Constant Spring Golf Club

GOLF | Designed by Stanley Thompson, a mentor of Robert Trent Jones Sr., in 1920, this short course is in one of Kingston's nicest neighborhoods. There's a clubhouse, restaurant, bar, and pro shop. ✉ *152 Constant Spring Rd., Kingston 8, Kingston* ✥ *Next to Immaculate Conception convent and high school* ☎ *876/924–1610* 🎫 *$45 weekdays, $50 weekends and public holidays* ⛳ *18 holes, 6094 yards, par 70.*

NEGRIL

Negril Hills Golf Club

GOLF | Inland from Jamaica's longest stretch of private beach, this course is 1½ hours west of Montego Bay. High points are the lush tropical foliage, picturesque water hazards, elevated tees, gently rolling fairways, tropical mountain vistas, and hard-sloping greens. The 6,333-yard course is walkable but plays longer due to elevated putting surfaces. ✉ *Negril* ☎ *876/957–4638* 🌐 *www.negrilhillsgolfclub.com* 🎫 *$80 for 18 holes, $50 for 9 holes* ⛳ *18 holes, 6333 yards, par 72.*

GUIDED TOURS

Because most vacationers avoid renting cars for safety and cost reasons, guided tours with hotel pickup are popular options for exploring. Jamaica's size and slow interior roads mean that you can't expect to see the entire island on one trip; even full-day tours concentrate on one part of the island. Most tours are similar in both content and price. From Montego Bay, tours often include one of the area's plantation houses. Several Negril-based companies offer tours to Y. S. Falls on the South Coast. Tours from Ocho Rios might include top attractions such as Dunn's River Falls or Kingston. In almost all cases, you arrange the tour through your resort.

MONTEGO BAY

Glamour Destination Management

GUIDED TOURS | One of the island's large tour operators, this company offers a wide selection of guided visits to tourist attractions in and around Montego Bay. They also offer fully customized tour options. ✉ *Shop #26, Blue Diamond Plaza, Montego Bay* ☎ *876/539–7689* 🌐 *www.glamourdmc.com.*

★ Island Routes Caribbean Adventures

PRIVATE GUIDES | Run by Sandals, this company provides a host of luxury group and private guided tours (with certified partners) to guests and nonguests. Guests can book via the website or at an Island Routes tour desk at participating resorts. ✉ *Queens Dr., Montego Bay* ☎ *877/959–0220 in U.S., 800/744–1150 in the Caribbean* 🌐 *www.islandroutes.com.*

JUTA Tours

ADVENTURE TOURS | The island's largest tour operator offers a greathouse tour and a rafting tour, as well as tours to other parts of the island like Black River, Negril, and Ocho Rios. ✉ *80 Claude Clarke Ave., Montego Bay* ☎ *876/979–0778, 876/952–0813, 876/952–0623* 🌐 *www.jutatoursja.com.*

Uton Tours

GUIDED TOURS | Uton Tours is licensed by the Jamaica Tourist Board and offers tours from Montego Bay, Negril, Ocho Rios, and Falmouth. They specialize in a variety of customized Jamaica tour and excursion packages at great prices. ✉ *Fairfield Cres, Montego Bay* ☎ *876/456–6323, 876/815–7666* 🌐 *www.utontours.com.*

FALMOUTH

Liberty Tours Jamaica

GUIDED TOURS | Tours are available from Falmouth cruise ships to some of the town's most popular attractions including the Irie Blue Hole, Luminous Lagoon, Martha Brae River, and Nine Mile. Personalized tour packages are also available, as are tours in Ocho Rios and Montego Bay. ✉ *Trelawny* ☎ *876/448–0473* 🌐 *www.libertytoursjamaica.com.*

OCHO RIOS

Jamaica Tours Limited

GUIDED TOURS | This operator offers several tours with stops that include gardens and Dunn's River Falls. ✉ *Ocho Rios* ☎ *876/953–8100* 🌐 *www.jamaicatoursltd.com.*

PORT ANTONIO

Blissful Jamaica Tours

GUIDED TOURS | Blissful Jamaica Tours offers a special Portland Paradise Tour that showcases the best of Portland. Entry fees, boat rides, and transportation are included. ✉ *West Palm Ave., Port Antonio* ☎ *876/366–4030* 🌐 *www.facebook.com/blissfuljamaicatours* 💵 *JMD $6500.*

KINGSTON

Numerous operators offer tours of the Kingston area, as well as excursions into the Blue Mountains. Professional tour operators provide a valuable service, as neither destination is particularly suited to exploration without a guide. In Kingston, certain areas can be dangerous; an organized tour provides a measure of security. Think twice before roaming in the Blue Mountains, as roads are narrow or in poor condition and signs are few and far between.

Typical city tours include a city overview with stops at Devon House, the Bob Marley Museum, and Port Royal. Niche operators such as Olde Jamaica Tours provide theme tours, including a tour of churches and museums and one that visits the athletic grounds where Usain Bolt and other sprinters have trained.

Olde Jamaica Tours

CULTURAL TOURS | This company runs heritage and cultural tours—churches, greathouses, and the like—as well as visits to a cricket field and the training ground where Usain Bolt and others have developed their sporting prowess. Though island-wide trips are offered, the

The championship course at Tryall Club is built on the site of a former sugar plantation.

focus is on Kingston. ✉ *The Trade Center, Shop #3A, 30-32 Red Hills Rd., Kingston 10* ☎ *876/362–9319* 🌐 *www.oldejamaicatours.com.*

Sun Venture Tours

GUIDED TOURS | A tour company offering many packages covering the island to meet different interests. ✉ *Kingston* ☎ *876/924–4515.*

SOUTH COAST

Countrystyle Community Experiences Tours

CULTURAL TOURS | Combining your choice of accommodation—whether homestay or hotel—with your interests, these tour packages match you with residents to showcase rural community lifestyles, helping you enjoy Jamaican culture, heritage, cuisine, and music. Tours cost $85 and include transportation, a community tour, lunch, and a gift. ✉ *Mandeville* ☎ *876/507–6326* 🌐 *www.accesscommunitytourism.com.*

Jakes Biking Tour

BIKING | Jakes offers bike tours around the area. In one three-hour tour, a guide leads the way through the Little Park farming district, then to Great Bay. Since Treasure Beach is flat, almost all fitness levels can participate. You can also chart your own course—one-day bike rentals are $25. ✉ *Jakes Hotel, Treasure Beach* ☎ *876/564–3000* 🌐 *www.jakeshotel.com.*

NEGRIL

In addition to tours from Montego Bay that give day-trippers a chance to experience Negril, there are several tours available to those who are staying here, including trips to the waterfalls.

The North Coast is known for Dunn's River Falls, and the South Coast for Y. S. Falls (both accessible from Negril on a day tour), but the Negril area is home to some impressive waterfalls of its own. A top activity for travelers tired of the beach, Mayfield Falls is tucked into the Dolphin Head Mountains near Glenbrook. These falls have been the stuff of legend since the 1700s, when locals swore a mermaid lived in these mineral-rich pools. Today the "mermaids" are tourists from Negril and Montego

Bay who come to enjoy the waterfalls and underwater caves. Fifty-two varieties of fern are found here, as well as many types of tropical flowers. A visit here includes a guided hike up the river with a stop at a bar and grill along the way. Several operators offer tours, usually with transportation from nearby hotels and lunch included.

Jamaica Onestop

GUIDED TOURS | In collaboration with Malcolm Brothers Transfer and Tours, Jamaica Onestop has offered car rentals and private tours to all of Negril's best attractions. Tour rates include private transfers, entrance fees, and lunch. ✉ *Negril* ☎ *876/532–6363, 876/879–8457* 🌐 *www.jamaicaonestop.com.*

Rhodes Hall Eco Tours

ECOTOURISM | Just 15 minutes from Negril, this former sugar plantation offers ecotours in a nature reserve with a crocodile lake and bird sanctuary. Other adventures include horseback riding, glass-bottom boating, and bathing in Rhodes Hall's Magic Blue Mud Mineral Spring Bath. Help to arrange transportation from Negril area hotels is provided. ✉ *Green Island* ☎ *876/957–6883, 876/957–6334* 🌐 *www.rhodeshallplantation.net* 🎫 *$70.*

Tropical Tours

ADVENTURE TOURS | A variety of tours are available including adventure, beach and sun, historic sights, nature, and more. Pickups are arranged from your hotel. ✉ *Norman Manley Blvd., Negril* ☎ *876/952–1126* 🌐 *www.tropicaltoursja.com.*

HIKING

PORT ANTONIO

El Sol Vida Fun Tours

GUIDED TOURS | This company specializes in private day tours to attractions in Port Antonio, including a Blue Mountain Hike and Coffee tour for six hours ($150 per person). There's a minimum of two adults per tour. ✉ *Port Antonio* ☎ *876/630–0664, 877/839–3924 in U.S.* 🌐 *www.fun.tours* ⏲ *Closed Sun.*

HORSEBACK RIDING

MONTEGO BAY

Braco Stables

HORSEBACK RIDING | These stables are in the Braco area near Duncans in Trelawny, between Montego Bay and Ocho Rios. Two daily estate rides ($70) include transportation ($20 commission if transportation is not needed) and complimentary refreshments served poolside at the Braco greathouse. Experienced riders, or those who want private rides, can also opt for a mountain ride ($100) for a more rugged two-hour tour. ✉ *Braco, Duncans* ☎ *876/954–0185.*

Chukka Caribbean Adventures

HORSEBACK RIDING | From its location west of Montego Bay at Sandy Bay, this outfit offers tours for riders of all levels. You travel through rain forest and open countryside before heading to the sea for an exhilarating ride through the surf. The two-hour excursion is available for riders 6 and older. A horseback ride-and-swim is $99. ✉ *Sandy Bay, Sandy Bay* ☎ *876/619–1441, 876/619–1382, 877/424–8552 in U.S.* 🌐 *chukka.com* 🎫 *From $99.*

OCHO RIOS

With its combination of hills and beaches, Ocho Rios is a natural for horseback excursions. Most are guided tours taken at a slow pace and perfect for those with no previous equestrian experience. Many travelers opt to wear long pants for horseback rides, especially those away from the beach.

★ **Chukka Caribbean Adventures**

HORSEBACK RIDING | The two-hour ride-and-swim tour ($99) travels along Papillon Cove (where the 1973 movie *Papillon* was filmed) as well as to locations used in *Return to Treasure Island* (1985) and *Passion and Paradise* (1988). The trail continues along the coastline to Chukka Beach and a bareback ride in the sea. Chukka has a location west of Montego

Bay and handles other activities and tours, too. ✉ *Chukka Cove, Llandovery, Ocho Rios* ☎ *876/619–1441, 876/619–1382, 877/424–8552 in U.S.* 🌐 *chukka.com* 🎫 *$99.*

KAYAKING

OCHO RIOS

Chukka Caribbean Adventures

KAYAKING | Chukka offers kayak trips, for persons 6 years old and over, down the White River Valley. Kayaking trips are approximately two hours. ✉ *Chukka White River Valley, Ocho Rios* ☎ *876/619–1441, 876/619–1382, 877/424–8552 in U.S.* 🌐 *chukka.com* 🎫 *$99.*

MOUNTAIN BIKING

OCHO RIOS

Blue Mountain Bicycle Tours

BIKING | This company leads guided rides in the spectacular Blue Mountains. The all-day excursion, for all levels of riders, starts high and glides downhill, ending with a dip in a waterfall. Transportation from Ocho Rios, Montego Bay, Runaway Bay, Trelawny, or Kingston; lunch; and equipment are included. ✉ *121 Main St., Ocho Rios* ☎ *876/974–7075, 876/369–8997* 🌐 *www.bmtoursja.com* 🎫 *From $100.*

RIVER BOATING AND RAFTING

Jamaica's many rivers mean a multitude of freshwater experiences, from mild to wild. The island's first tourist activity off the beaches was relaxing rafting trips aboard bamboo rafts poled by local boatmen, which originated on the **Rio Grande.** Jamaicans had long used rafts to transport bananas downriver. Decades ago actor and local resident Errol Flynn saw the rafts and thought they'd make a good tourist attraction. Today the slow rides are a favorite with romantic travelers and anyone looking to get off the beach for a few hours. The popularity of the Rio Grande's trips spawned similar trips down the **Martha Brae River,** about 25 miles (38 km) from MoBay. Near Ocho Rios, the **Great River** has lazy river rafting as well as energetic kayaking.

MONTEGO BAY

Jamaica Tours Limited

WHITE-WATER RAFTING | This big tour company offers various tour packages that include raft trips down the Martha Brae and Great Rivers. Price depends on number of people and pickup location. Hotel tour desks can book it. ✉ *Providence Dr., Montego Bay* ☎ *876/953–8100* 🌐 *www.jamaicatoursltd.com.*

Rio Grande Tours

WHITE-WATER RAFTING | Guided raft trips down the Rio Grande depart around 9 am and take about two hours, unless you stop to swim and have lunch. ✉ *St. Margaret's Bay* ☎ *876/993–5778* 🎫 *$80.*

River Raft Ltd.

WHITE-WATER RAFTING | This company leads 1½-hour trips down the Martha Brae River, about 25 miles (38 km) from most MoBay hotels. ✉ *Martha Brae Rafting Village* ☎ *876/940–7018, 876/952–0889, 876/940–6398* 🌐 *www.jamaicarafting.com* 🎫 *$77.*

OCHO RIOS

Chukka Caribbean Adventures

WHITE-WATER RAFTING | The big activity outfitter offers the Chukka River Tubing Safari on the White River, an easy trip that doesn't require previous tubing experience. The three-hour tour lets you travel in your very own tube through gentle rapids. ✉ *Chukka White River Valley, Ocho Rios* ☎ *876/619–1441, 876/619–1382, 877/424–8552 in U.S.* 🌐 *chukka.com* 🎫 *$99.*

SAILING

MONTEGO BAY

★ Dreamer Catamaran Cruises

SAILING | Five catamarans, from 53 to 65 feet, take cruises that include a snorkel stop and visit to Margaritaville. Foot massages for women are followed by dance instruction for all. Children are allowed on only the morning and sunset cruises. They also offer a Montego bay to Negril cruise. ✉ *2 Kent Ave., Montego Bay* ☎ *876/979–0101* 🌐 *www.dreamercatamarans.com* 🎫 *From $95.*

OCHO RIOS

Cool Runnings Catamaran Cruises

SAILING | Several sailing and partying options are available through this company's catamaran cruises: romantic dinner sails (only available on Friday), the Wet and Wild Cruise (adults only), and the daily trip to Dunn's River Falls. ✉ *1 Marvin's Park St., White River, Ocho Rios* ☎ *876/974–0164, 876/618–2052* 🌐 *www.coolrunningscatamarans.com.*

PORT ANTONIO

Errol Flynn Marina

BOATING | This official national port of entry has 24-hour customs and immigration services. The 32-berth marina, reached via a deepwater channel, includes 24-hour security, an Internet center, swimming pool, laundry, and 100-ton boat lift—the only area facility that can handle vessels of 600 feet. Scuba diving and other water-sports attractions are also here. ✉ *Ken Wright Dr., Port Antonio* ☎ *876/715–6044* 🌐 *www.errolflynnmarina.com.*

NEGRIL

SOCCER

National Stadium of Jamaica

SPORTS VENUE | Constructed in 1962, this 35,000-seat arena (nicknamed "the Office") hosts national and international soccer matches. It's the home of Jamaica's national team, dubbed the Reggae Boyz, which made strong showings in world competitions several years ago. One of the statues in front of the main entrance honors not a soccer star, but music legend Bob Marley, paying homage to an iconic moment in Jamaican history. During the 1970s, Jamaica was torn by political unrest when the ruling Jamaican Labor Party met a strong challenge by the People's National Party. Armed gangs representing the parties battled in the streets. On April 22, 1978, while Bob Marley and the Wailers were performing the song "Jammin'" at the packed stadium, he called for the leaders of both parties to join him on stage and made a spirited plea for peace and unity. For the night, at least, civility and harmony prevailed. ✉ *Independence Park, Arthur Wint Dr., Kingston* ☎ *876/926–1514.*

Chapter 15

MARTINIQUE

Updated by
Tracy Laville

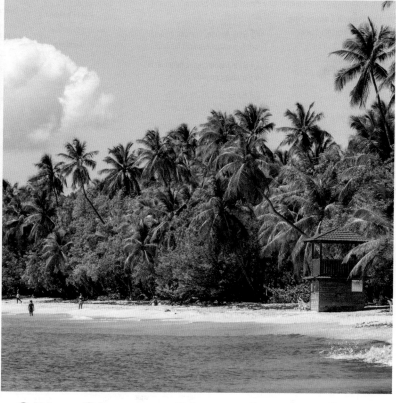

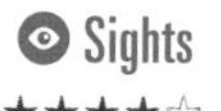

★★★★☆

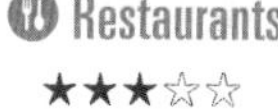

★★★☆☆

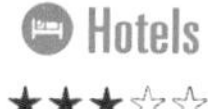

★★★☆☆

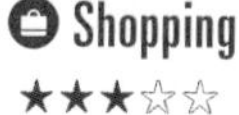

★★★☆☆

★★☆☆☆

WELCOME TO MARTINIQUE

TOP REASONS TO GO

★ **The Romance:** A magical atmosphere infuses everything; ample peace and quiet make it easy to kick back and enjoy.

★ **Beautiful Beaches:** A full roster of beautiful beaches will let you enjoy sun and sand.

★ **The French Connection:** Excellent French food, not to mention French music and fashion, make the island a paradise for those in search of the finer things.

★ **Hiking:** With plenty of nature reserves and lush trails, this is prime hiking territory, especially around the island's volcano, Mont Pelée.

★ **Inviting Waters:** The sea, Caribbean; the ocean, Atlantic—experience the water in a kayak or on a sailboat. Journey to Les Fonds Blancs where Joséphine Bonaparte once swam.

★ **Distilleries:** Sample rum at one of the many excellent distilleries on Martinique, such as Depaz and Distillerie JM.

1 **Fort-de-France.** Martinique's capital.

2 **Le François.** Noted for snorkeling.

3 **Les Trois-Îlets.** Charming village leading to beaches.

4 **Le Diamant.** Diving with views of Diamond Rock.

5 **Le Marin.** Yachting capital that hosts carnival.

6 **Ste-Anne.** Lively town with a white-sand beach.

7 **Ste-Luce.** Beaches with a young crowd.

8 **Balata.** Quiet town with beautiful gardens.

9 **St-Pierre.** Learn about the eruption of Mont Pelée in this town.

10 **Le Morne Rouge.** Resort spot with access to Mont Pelée.

11 **Macouba.** The wild side of Martinique has scenic drive.

12 **Ste-Marie.** Rum distillery and natural beauty.

13 **Tartane.** Rugged beach popular with surfers.

14 **Le Carbet.** Great restaurant and Paul Gauguin museum.

15 **Le Prêcheur.** Village surrounded by hot springs.

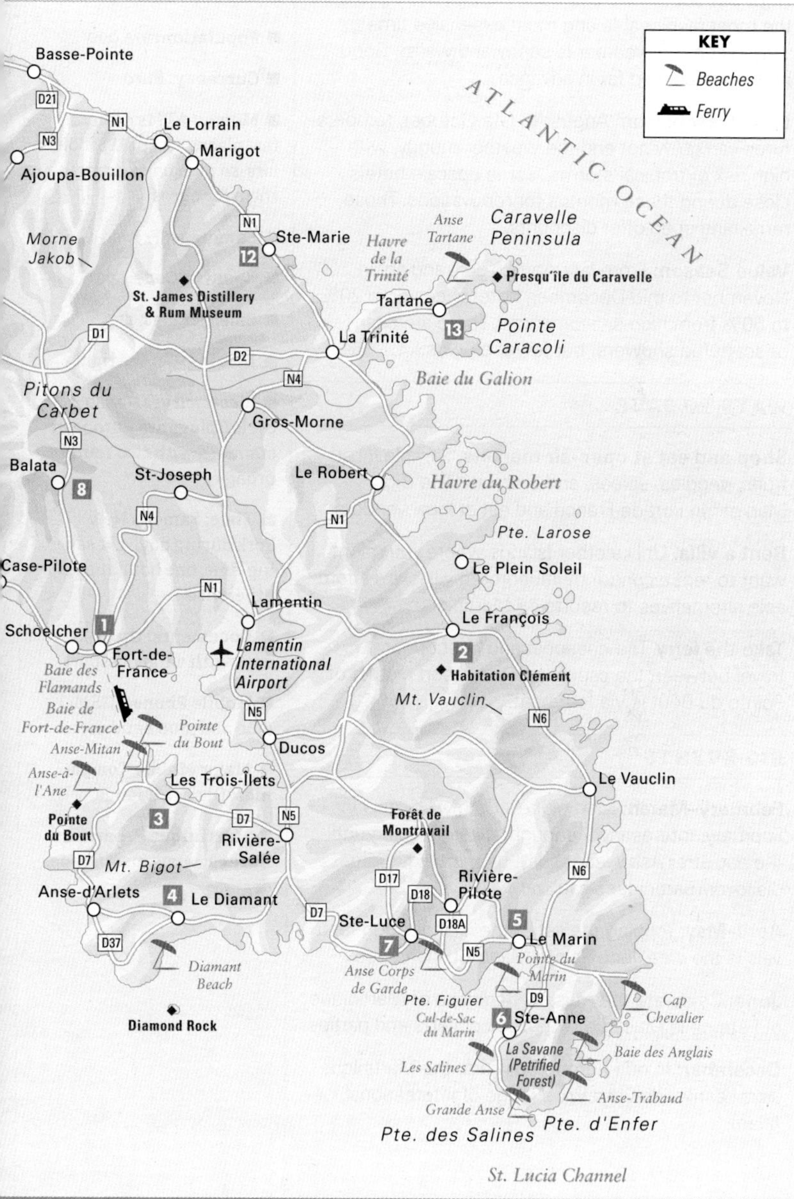
KEY
Beaches
Ferry
ATLANTIC OCEAN
Basse-Pointe
Le Lorrain
Marigot
Ajoupa-Bouillon
Morne Jakob
Ste-Marie
St. James Distillery & Rum Museum
Havre de la Trinité
Anse Tartane
Caravelle Peninsula
Presqu'île du Caravelle
Tartane
Pointe Caracoli
La Trinité
Baie du Galion
Pitons du Carbet
Gros-Morne
Balata
St-Joseph
Le Robert
Havre du Robert
Pte. Larose
Le Plein Soleil
Case-Pilote
Lamentin
Schoelcher
Fort-de-France
Le François
Lamentin International Airport
Habitation Clément
Baie des Flamands
Baie de Fort-de-France
Mt. Vauclin
Pointe du Bout
Anse-Mitan
Ducos
Anse-à-l'Ane
Les Trois-Îlets
Le Vauclin
Pointe du Bout
Forêt de Montravail
Rivière-Salée
Mt. Bigot
Rivière-Pilote
Anse-d'Arlets
Le Diamant
Ste-Luce
Le Marin
Anse Corps de Garde
Pointe du Marin
Diamant Beach
Pte. Figuier
Cap Chevalier
Diamond Rock
Cul-de-Sac du Marin
Ste-Anne
La Savane (Petrified Forest)
Baie des Anglais
Les Salines
Anse-Trabaud
Grande Anse
Pte. d'Enfer
Pte. des Salines
St. Lucia Channel

ISLAND SNAPSHOT

WHEN TO GO

High Season: Mid-December through mid-April is the most fashionable and most expensive time to visit, when the weather is sunny and warm. Good hotels are booked far in advance.

Low Season: From August to late October, temperatures can grow hot and the weather muggy, with high risk of tropical storms. Some upscale hotels close during these months for renovations. Those remaining open offer discounts.

Value Season: From late April to July and again November to mid-December, hotel prices drop 20% to 50% from high-season prices. There are chances of scattered showers, but fewer crowds.

WAYS TO SAVE

Shop and eat at open-air markets. Sample local fruits, veggies, spices, and more at "The Big Market" in Fort-de-France and eat at local vendors.

Rent a villa. Unlike other islands where you might want to rent a condo, multibedroom villas are affordable alternatives to resorts on Martinique.

Take the ferry. The cheapest and best option to travel between the capital and the resort district of Pointe du Bout is via ferryboat.

BIG EVENTS

February–March: Martinique's Carnival begins in February. Interestingly enough, it keeps going until the day after Ash Wednesday. us.martinique.org/discover/martiniques-carnival

April–May: Topping the list of the island's food festivals is the weeklong Sainte-Marie Culinary Week.

June: Celebrate the musical traditions of Martinique at Fête de la Musique with free concerts and parties.

December: In odd-numbered years, the Martinique Jazz Festival draws a wide range of international talent.

AT A GLANCE

- **Capital:** Fort-de-France
- **Population:** 375,000
- **Currency:** Euro
- **Money:** ATMs common; few places accept U.S. dollars, so plan on exchanging them for euros
- **Language:** French, Creole
- **Country Code:** 596
- **Emergencies:** 17
- **Driving:** On the right
- **Electricity:** 220v/50 cycles; plugs are European standard with two round prongs
- **Time:** Same as New York during daylight saving time; one hour ahead otherwise
- **Documents:** Up to 90 days with valid passport
- **Mobile Phones:** GSM (900 and 1800 bands)
- **Major Mobile Companies:** Digicel, Orange
- **Martinique Promotion Bureau:** www.martinique.org

Numerous scattered ruins and other historical monuments reflect the richness of Martinique's sugarcane plantation past, *rhum*, and the legacy of slavery. Called the Rum Capital of the World, it is widely considered the best gourmet island in the Caribbean. It stirs the passions with its distinctive brand of culinary offerings. If you believe in magic, Martinique has it, along with plenty of romance and opportunities for rest and relaxation. It has become known as the island of *revenants*, those who always return. *Et pourquoi pas?*

Martinique is simply one of the most enchanting destinations in the western hemisphere. Francophiles adore this island for its food, rum, *musique*, and élan, and the availability of the finest French products, from Chanel fashions to Limoges china. It is endowed with lots of tropical beauty, including white-sand beaches and rain forests. The volcano Mont Pelée looms over the harbor town of St-Pierre, known as the Pompeii of the Caribbean. Its largest city, Fort-de-France, comes with lots of charm as well as some great restaurants and clubs.

Christopher Columbus first sighted this gorgeous island in 1502, when it was inhabited by the Caraïbes, who had pushed out the peace-loving Arawaks. The Arawaks called their home Madinina (the Isle of Flowers), and for good reason. Wild orchids, frangipani, anthurium, jade vines, flamingo flowers, and hundreds of vivid varieties of hibiscus still thrive here.

The island reflects its rich cultural history. In colonial days Martinique was the administrative, social, and cultural center of the French Antilles; this rich, aristocratic island was quite famous. The island even gave birth to an empress, Napoléon's Joséphine. It saw the full flowering of a society ruled by planters who often flaunted their wealth.

Martinique's economy still depends on *les bananes* (bananas), *l'ananas* (pineapples), cane sugar, rum, and fishing. It's also the largest remaining stronghold of the *békés*—the descendants of the original French planters—and they are still the privileged class on any of the French-Caribbean islands. Numbering around 4,000, many control Martinique's most profitable businesses, from banana plantations and rum distilleries to car dealerships. The elite dress in designer outfits straight off the Paris runways. In general, the islanders have style. In the airport waiting room you can almost always tell the Martiniquaises by their fashionable clothes.

Of the island's 375,000 inhabitants, 100,000 live in Fort-de-France and its environs. It has 34 separate municipalities. Though the actual number of French residents from the Metropole (France) does not exceed 15% of the total population, Martinique is a part of France, an overseas *département* to be exact; and French is the official language, though the vast majority of the residents also speak Creole.

Thousands are employed in government jobs offering more paid holidays than most Americans can imagine. Martinicans work hard and enjoy their time off, celebrating everything from *le fin de la semaine* (the weekend) to feast days, sailboat races, and Carnival. Their *joie de vivre* is infectious. Once you experience it, you'll be back.

Planning

Getting Here and Around

AIR

There are nonstop flights from the United States on American Airlines, flying out of Miami. Most travelers are able to connect in San Juan or in Miami and to Air France, as well, which departs Miami with a stop in a neighboring island.

CONTACTS Air Antilles Express. ☎ *0890/64–86–48, 0596/42–18–07* 🌐 *www.airantilles.com.* **Air Canada.** ☎ *888/247–2262* 🌐 *www.aircanada.com.* **Air Caraïbes.** ☎ *0820/83–58–35, 0590/82–47–47 in Guadeloupe, reservations* 🌐 *www.aircaraibes.com.* **Air France.** ☎ *0970/01-98-01, 0596/55–34–72, 800/237–2747 in U.S., 0596/82–61–61* 🌐 *www.airfrance.com.* **American Airlines.** ☎ *800/433–7300* 🌐 *www.aa.com.*

AIRPORT

CONTACTS Martinique Aimé Césaire Airport (FDF). ✉ *Le Lamentin* ☎ *0596/42-19-95* 🌐 *www.martinique.aeroport.fr.*

BUS

Many locals take *bus collectifs* (white vans holding up to 10 passengers) that cost just a few euros and depart from Pointe Simon, on the waterfront in Fort-de-France, to all parts of the island. Don't be shy; the difference can be €3 versus, say, €60 for a taxi to reach the same destination. Drivers don't usually speak English, and there's no air-conditioning.

Bus Mozaik

The air-conditioned buses of this private company stop within the city; they service Lamentin, Fort-de-France suburbs such as Schoelcher, and as far into the interior of the island as St. Joseph. Buses leave from Pointe Simon, on the waterfront, where the public buses and shared-taxis (white vans) congregate. Fares start at €1.25 one-way; €2.30 for round-trip, if tickets are purchased at a Moziak Kiosk. If bought on the bus, those same rates would be €1.80 and €2.50. For schedules, visit the website. 🌐 *www.aquelleheure.fr/bus.htm.*

CAR

The main highways, about 175 miles (280 km) of well-paved and well-marked roads, are excellent, but only in a few areas are they lighted at night. Many hotels are on roads that are barely passable, so get wherever you're going by nightfall or you could lose your way. Then tell a stranger, *"Je suis perdu!"* ("I am lost!"). If they say, *"Suivez-moi!"*—that's "Follow me!"—stay glued to their bumper. Finally, drive defensively; drivers can be aggressive.

Martinique, especially Fort-de-France and environs, is plagued with heavy traffic; if you must drive into Fort-de-France, do it on a weekend. Absolutely avoid the Lamentin Airport area and Fort-de-France during weekday rush hours, roughly 7 to 10 am and 4 to 7:30 pm, and on Sunday night going in the direction of Fort-de-France. That's when everyone comes off the beaches and heads back to the city. Even smaller towns such as La Trinité have rush hours. Watch, too, for *dos d'ânes* (literally, donkey backs), speed bumps that are hard to spot—particularly at night. Gas is costly, at about triple U.S. prices. Diesel is somewhat cheaper, but if you rent an economy car for a full week, you should budget a sufficient amount for fuel.

Be aware that the French gendarmes set up roadblocks, often on Sunday, to stop speeders and drunk drivers, and just to check papers. Now they even have video cameras on the highways. Visitors are not absolved from speeding tickets, because you can be tracked down through the rental car's license plate.

Renting a Car: It's worth the hassle to rent a car—if only for a day or two—so that you can explore more of this beautiful island. Just be prepared for a manual shift, steep mountainous roads, and heavy traffic. Prices are expensive, "in season" about €80 per day or €450 per week (unlimited mileage) for a manual shift, perhaps more for an automatic, which must be ordered in advance (and not all agencies have them). You may save money by waiting to book your car rental on the island for a reduced weekly rate from a local agency. Some of the latter, though, make up their own rules, and they will not be in your favor. There's an extra charge (about $20) if you drop the car off at the airport after having rented it somewhere else on the island. A valid U.S. driver's license or International Driver's Permit is needed to rent a car for up to 20 days.

TIP→ Often, the airline you fly in with will have a discount coupon for a rental car, right on the ticket, or in their in-flight magazine. Also, local publications have ads with discounts that can be as much as 40% off (in low season). You can find these at the Tourism Information counter in the airport.

CONTACTS Avis. ☎ *0596/42–11–00* 🌐 *www.avis-antilles.fr.* **Budget.** ✉ *Martinique Aimé Césaire Airport, Le Lamentin* ☎ *0596/42–04–04* 🌐 *www.budget-martinique.com.* **Europcar.** ☎ *0596/42–42–42* 🌐 *www.en.europcar-martinique.com.* **Hertz.** ✉ *Martinique Aime Cesare Airport, Le Lamentin* ☎ *0596/51–01–01, 0810/32–31–13* 🌐 *www.hertzantilles.com.* **JumboCar.** ✉ *Martinique Aimé Césaire Aéroport, Le Lamentin* ☎ *0596/42–17–01, 0820/22–02–30* 🌐 *en.jumbocar-martinique.com.* **Sixt.** ✉ *Martinique Aimé Césaire Airport, Le Lamentin* ☎ *0596/60–14–16* 🌐 *www.sixt.fr.*

FERRY

Weather permitting, *vedettes* (ferries) operate daily between Quai d'Esnambuc in Fort-de-France and the marinas in Pointe du Bout, Anse-Mitan, and Anse-à-l'Ane and are the best way to go into the capital. Any of these trips takes about 20 minutes. Ferries depart every 30 minutes on weekdays; less often in the low season and weekends. Round-trip tickets cost €6.50.

CONTACTS Compagnie Maritime West Indies. ☎ *0696/21–77–76, 0596/74–93–38 in Martinique, 0758/452–8757 in Saint Lucia* 🌐 *www.accueil-martinique.fr.* **Jeans for Freedom.** ✉ *Pl. du Marche, rue Victor Hugo, St-Pierre* ☎ *0825/01–01–25, 0596/78–11–50* 🌐 *www.jeansforfreedom.com.* **L'Express des Îles.** ✉ *Terminal Inter Isles Quai Ouest, Fort-de-France* ☎ *0590/91–98–53 in Guadeloupe* 🌐 *www.express-des-iles.com.*

TAXI

Taxis, which are metered, are expensive, though you can try bargaining by offering to pay a flat rate to your destination or offering them an hourly rate—try for €40, but you may have to compromise at €50. Taxis generally charge substantially more at night and on Sunday.

CONTACTS J. Peloponese Taxis. ☎ *0696/25–61–02.* **M. Martial Mercedes Taxis.** ☎ *0696/45–69–07 mobile.* **Taxi de Place.** ✉ *rue Victoire Sévre, Fort-de-France* ☎ *0596/63–63–62 Martinique Taxis, 0596/70–40–10 Madinina Taxis.*

Sights

The northern part of the island will appeal to nature lovers, hikers, and mountain climbers. The drive from Fort-de-France to St-Pierre is particularly impressive, as is the one across the island, via Morne Rouge, from the Caribbean to the Atlantic. This is Martinique's wild side—a place of waterfalls, rain forest, and mountains. The highlight is Mont Pelée. The south is the more developed half of the island, where the resorts and restaurants are located, as well as the beaches.

Beaches

Take to the beach in Martinique and experience the white sandbars known as Les Fonds Blancs aka Josephine's Baths, where Napoléon's wife Joséphine would bathe. All of Martinique's beaches are open to the public, but hotels charge a fee for nonguests to use chaise longues, changing rooms, and other facilities. There are no official nudist beaches, but topless bathing is prevalent, as is the case on most French islands. Unless you're an expert swimmer, steer clear of the Atlantic waters, except in the area of Cap Chevalier (Cape Knight) and the Presqu'île de Caravelle (Caravelle Peninsula). The white-sand beaches are south of Fort-de-France; to the north, the sand turns darker, and there are even beaches with silvery-black volcanic sand. Some of the most pleasant strips of sand are around Ste-Anne, Ste-Luce, and Havre du Robert. Some 15 minutes from Le François harbor, the white sandbars that form Josephine's Baths stand in the middle of the sea.

Restaurants

Martinique cuisine, a fusion of African and French, is international and sophisticated. The influx of young chefs, who favor a contemporary and lighter approach, has brought exciting innovations to the table. This haute-nouvelle creole cuisine emphasizes local products, predominantly starchy tubers such as plantains, white yams, yuca, and island sweet potatoes, as well as vegetables such as breadfruit, christophene (also known as chayote), and taro leaves. Many creole dishes have been Frenchified, transformed into mousselines, terrines, and gratins topped with creamy sauces. And then there's the bountiful harvest of the sea—*lambi* (conch), *langouste* (clawless local lobsters), and dozens of species of fish predominate, but you can also find *écrevisses* (freshwater crayfish, which are as luscious as jumbo prawns).

Some local creole specialties are *accras* (cod or vegetable fritters), which are the signature appetizer of Martinique, *crabes farcis* (stuffed land crab), and *feroce* (avocado stuffed with saltfish and farina). You can perk up fish and any other dish with a hit of hot *chien* (dog) sauce. Not to worry—it's made from onions, shallots, hot peppers, oil, and vinegar. To cool your jets, have a 'ti punch—four parts white rum and one part sugarcane syrup.

Supermarkets often have snack bars that serve sandwiches, as do the bakeries and larger gas stations such as Esso and Total. Supermarkets, such as Carrefour, have good deli sections and sell French wines for significantly less than at home. Another French chain, Le Baguet Shop, has locations in most tourist areas. Travelers on a budget will find creperies and pizzerias, even an African pizza place in Le François. And there may be times when you just want to drive in to Mickey Ds—however, brace yourself for the price hike.

In Fort-de-France's city market, ladies serve up well-priced creole prix-fixe meals that can include accras, fricassee of octopus and conch, chicken in coconut milk, or grilled whole fish.

As for euro sticker shock, the consolation is that although menu prices may seem steep, they include tax and service. Prix-fixe menus, sometimes with wine, can help keep costs in line.

What to Wear. For dinner, casual resort wear is appropriate; collared shirts and sundresses are typical. At dinnertime, beach attire is too casual for most restaurants. Both the French (expats) and the Martiniquais often "dress." They have an admirable French style, and almost always wear high heels.

Health and Safety

In Fort-de-France, an increased police presence and video cameras have helped lower the crime rate. However, you should exercise the same safety precautions you would in any city. It's best to go downtown at night only as part of a group. Never leave jewelry, money, or designer sunglasses unattended on the beach or in your car. Keep your laptop under wraps and put valuables in hotel safes.

Dengue, chikungunya, and zika have all been reported throughout the Caribbean. We recommend that you protect yourself from these mosquito-borne illnesses by keeping your skin covered and/or wearing mosquito repellent. The mosquitoes that transmit these viruses are as active by day as they are by night.

Hotels and Resorts

On Martinique, you can stay in tiny inns called *relais créoles,* boutique hotels, and private villas as well as splashy tourist resorts. Several hotels are clustered in Pointe du Bout on Les Trois-Ilets Peninsula, which is connected to Fort-de-France by ferry. Other clusters are in Ste-Luce, and Le François has become known for its boutique properties. Hotels and relais can be found all over the island. Because Martinique is the largest of the Windward Islands, this can mean a substantial drive to your hotel after a long flight or ferry trip. You may want to stay closer to the airport on your first night—for instance, at the Hotel Galleria, a no-nonsense hotel within a shopping mall just 10 minutes from the airport, or at a hotel in Fort-de-France. If you need to make a last-minute hotel reservation, head for the Tourism Information counter in the airport arrival hall (0596/42–18–05); it is open between 8 am and 9 pm every day except Sunday, when it's open from 2 pm to 9 pm.

Large Resorts: There are only a few deluxe properties on the island. Those that lack megastar ratings offer an equally appealing mixture of charisma, hospitality, and French style. Larger hotels often have the busy, slightly frenetic feel that the French seem to like.

Relais Créoles: Small, individually owned inns are still available on Martinique, though they may be far removed from the resorts.

Villas: Groups and large families can save money by renting a villa, but the language barrier can be problematic if you only know English, and often you will need a car.

Hotel reviews have been shortened. For full information, visit Fodors.com.

What It Costs in Euros

	$	$$	$$$	$$$$
RESTAURANTS				
	under €12	€12–€20	€21–€30	over €30
HOTELS				
	under €275	€275–€375	€376–€475	over €475

PRIVATE VILLAS AND CONDOS

If you're staying a week or longer, you can often save money by renting a villa or apartment with a kitchen for preparing your own meals. The more upscale rentals come with French-speaking maids and cooks. Don't forget to add the cost of a car rental to your vacation budget.

RENTAL CONTACTS **French Caribbean International.** ✉ *Santa Barbara* ☎ *805/967–9850 U.S. office* 🌐 *www.frenchcaribbean.com.* **Prestige Villa Rental.** ✉ *3617 Bd. Marquis at Mahaut de Houelbourg* ☎ *917/267–7491 in U.S., 336/85-18-53–01* 🌐 *www.prestigevillarental.com.*

Nightlife and Performing Arts

There are lively discos and nightclubs in Martinique. For art openings and other cultural events, check with the Fondation Clément (🌐 www.fondation-clement.org), which runs the Habitation Clément, to see what's coming up. In addition to its art exhibits, the foundation throws some of the best parties on the island, which are a chance to toast and clink rum glasses with some of Martinique's movers and shakers.

Your hotel or the tourist office can put you in touch with the current popular places. It's also wise to check on opening and closing times and cover charges. Several free tourist publications that can be found at hotels tell of the latest happenings at the clubs. For the most part, the discos draw a mixed crowd of Martinicans and travelers, and although a younger crowd is the norm, people of all ages go dancing here.

Jazz musicians, like their music, tend to be informal and independent. Zouk mixes Caribbean rhythm with Creole lyrics. Jacob Devarieux is the leading exponent of this style, and he occasionally performs on the island. Otherwise, you're likely to hear one of his followers.

To enter a casino, French law requires everyone to show a passport; the legal gambling age is 18.

Most leading hotels offer nightly entertainment in season, including the marvelous **Grands Ballets de Martinique,** one of the finest folkloric dance troupes in the Caribbean. Consisting of a bevy of musicians and dancers dressed in traditional outfits, the ballet revives the Martinique of yesteryear through dance rhythms such as the beguine and the mazurka.

Shopping

French fragrances; designer clothes, scarves, and sunglasses; fine china and crystal; leather goods; wine (inexpensive at supermarkets); and liquor are all good buys in duty-free Fort-de-France. Purchases are further sweetened by the 20% discount on luxury items when paid for with certain credit cards. Among the items produced on the island, look for *bijoux creole* (local jewelry, such as hoop earrings and heavy bead necklaces); white, dark, and aged rum; and handcrafted straw goods, pottery, and tapestries.

The striking 215,000-square-foot Cour Perrinon Mall in Fort-de-France, bordered by rue Perrinon, houses a Carrefour supermarket, a bookstore, perfume shops, designer boutiques, a French bakery, and a café–brasserie. The area around the cathedral in Fort-de-France has a number of small shops that carry luxury goods. Of particular note are the shops on rue Victor Hugo, rue Moreau de Jones, rue Antoine Siger, and rue Lamartine. Ongoing efforts to be more inviting to the North American market—with particular emphasis on offering English-language classes to staff—have dozens of shops participating. The **Galleries Lafayette** department store on rue Schoelcher in downtown Fort-de-France sells everything from perfume to pâté. On the outskirts of Fort-de-France, the **Centre Commercial de Cluny, Centre Commercial de Dillon, Centre Commercial de Bellevue,** and **Centre Commercial la Rond Point** are among the major shopping malls.

You can find more than 100 thriving businesses—from shops and department stores to restaurants, pizzerias, fast-food outlets, a superb supermarket, and the simple Galleria Hotel (the closest hotel to the airport)—at **La Galleria** in Lamentin. In Pointe du Bout there are a number of appealing tourist shops and boutiques, both in and around **Village Créole,** which alone has more than 20, plus some 10 restaurants–bars, an ice-cream shop, free Wi-Fi, and the Residence Village Creole, with small and family-size furnished apartments, available by the night, the week, or longer, for moderate prices. Village Creole often has live entertainment at night in the courtyard.

Visitor Information

CONTACTS Comité Martiniquais du Tourisme. ✉ *Immeuble Beaupre, Pointe de Jaham, Schoelcher* ☎ *0596/61–61–77* 🌐 *www.martinique.org.* **Martinique Promotion Bureau.** ✉ *825 3rd Ave., 29th fl., New York* ☎ *212/838–6887 in New York* 🌐 *www.martinique.org.* **Martinique Central Tourist Office.** ✉ *29 rue Victor Hugo, Fort-de-France* ☎ *0596/80–00–70.*

Weddings

Martinique has a long residency requirement, so it's not really feasible to plan a wedding on the island. It is, however, a very romantic place for honeymoons.

Fort-de-France

Martinique's capital is entering its latest renaissance. With its historic fort and superb location beneath the towering Pitons du Carbet on the Baie des Flamands, Fort-de-France—home to about one-quarter of the island's 375,000 inhabitants—is coming up fast. The bay has received the designation one of the "Most Beautiful Bays in the World."

Already done are the renovation of the park, La Savane, and the construction of a spectacular waterfront promenade. The bayfront Pointe Simon Business and Tourist Center, which includes the sophisticated, 94-room Simon Hotel and a luxury apartment building has opened. The white complex dazzles in the sunlight as it looks over the boat traffic in one of the world's most beautiful bays. The hotel/residence, Fort Savane, opened on rue Liberté, right across from its namesake. Near the mall is the former Hôtel de Ville (mayor's office), in a gorgeous and ornate Italianate building. Aimé Césaire, the statesman, playwright, and civil rights leader, for whom the airport was renamed, maintained an office there for more than 50 years. One of the best-preserved examples of neoclassical architecture in the Caribbean, its construction spanned from 1884 to 1901. It now houses a museum dedicated to art exhibits and cultural performances held in the courtyard and theater.

There is a small Office of Tourism de Fort-de-France at 29 rue Victor Hugo. It has some brochures in English and helpful, English-speaking staffers. They can organize English-language tours with advance notice. Another Point d'Information Touristique is near the cathedral, at the junction of rues Antoine Siger and Victor Schoelcher, and a third is at Kiosk number 1 in La Savane; you can now arrange a tour to Fort Louis at that kiosk for about €8.

The Stewards Urbains, easily recognized by their red caps and uniforms, are able to answer most visitors' questions about the city and give directions. These young gals and *garçons* are multilingual and knowledgeable. When a large cruise ship is in port, they are out in force, positioned in heavily trafficked tourist zones and at the front entrance of Lafayette's department store.

The most pleasant districts of Fort-de-France—Didier, Bellevue, and Schoelcher—are up on the hillside, and you need a car (or a taxi) to reach them. But if you try to drive here, you may find yourself trapped in gridlock in the narrow streets downtown. Parking is difficult, and it's best to try one of the garages or—as a second choice—outdoor public parking areas. Come armed with some euro coins for this purpose. A taxi, TCSP bus, or ferry from Pointe du Bout may be a better alternative. Even if your hotel isn't there, you can drive to the marina and park nearby.

There are some fine shops with Parisian wares (at Parisian prices), including French lingerie, St. Laurent clothes, Cacharel perfume, and stiletto heels. Near the harbor is a lively indoor marketplace (*grand marché*), where produce and spices are sold.

A playground on the Malecón, which has a half-mile wooden boardwalk, has swings, trampolines, benches, and grounds for playing *pétanque.* The urban beach between the Malecón and the fort, La Française, is covered with white sand that was brought in.

An inviting oasis of nature and serenity amid the hustle and bustle of Fort-de-France, La Savane is a prime spot for walks, picnics, and meeting up with friends. Freshly squeezed juices, cocktails, sandwiches, pizzas, panini, pasta, cassava cakes, deliciously flavored homemade ice creams, creole, Indonesian, and vegetarian food, sushi, crepes, and locally made candies are all available from vendors here; street merchants sell everything from jewelry to human hairpieces. The tourism kiosk on the historic Place de La Savane is open from 9 to 4:30 Tuesday through Saturday, 9 to 4 on Sunday (0596/80–00–70).

The Martinique cruise sector is also booming. Widespread improvements in the island's overall product, including capital improvements at the cruise ports in Fort-de-France, new and renovated attractions, and the redoubled efforts of the Martinique Tourism Authority are among the factors of this success.

As more U.S. cruise lines have committed to Martinique, many local merchants have started accepting U.S. dollars. (This is indicated by a sign on the door.) Also, more than 200 staffers from local stores enrolled in English classes. The island is rolling out the proverbial red carpet for American cruise passengers.

Just across from the Savane, the downtown landmark Hotel L'Impératrice, a product of the 1950s, is a good option to overnight downtown (its boutique guest rooms have a colonial look with Creole furnishings like four-poster, mahogany beds). It's within walking distance to the interisland ferries and closer to the airport than the resort properties. Le Josephine, the in-house restaurant, offers superb views of the Savane to go with its own elegant and eye-catching decor—dark-wood furniture, crisp white linens, and some refined creole cuisine. Its outdoor café, which serves only drinks, spills out to the sidewalk.

Fort-de-France is patrolled by about 20 civilians called Mediation Officers, one team on foot and bikes, easily recognized by their blue-and-orange uniforms, and a second team on motorbikes and in cars.They complement the presence of the police. Alas, the heat and exhaust fumes still exist, so by day, dress to stay cool, and rehydrate often. There are some piano bars, hot jazz venues, new late-night restaurants, and younger-crowd bars.

If you plan to go into the city at night, it's still best to go with a group. Hiring an English-speaking driver to take you on a club-crawl is wise.

Sights

Bibliothèque Schoelcher
LIBRARY | This wildly elaborate Romanesque public library was named after Victor Schoelcher, who led the fight to free the slaves in the French West Indies in the 19th century. The eye-popping, historic structure was built for the 1889 Paris Exposition, after which it was dismantled, shipped to Martinique, and reassembled piece by piece. ✉ *1 rue de la liberté, along the west side of La Savane, Fort-de-France* ☎ *0596/55–68–30* 🎫 *Free* 🕑 *Closed Mon. morning, Sat., Sun., and holidays.*

Fort St-Louis
HISTORIC SIGHT | Fort St-Louis (pronounced *lou-EE*) is an imposing stone fortress that has guarded the island's principal port city since the 17th century. Originally carved out from a rocky promontory jutting out into the Bay of Fort-de-France, Fort St-Louis towers nearly 200 feet over the city at its highest point, affording visitors panoramic views of the surrounding seaside urban landscape. A view-experience and photo op, with a spyglass, one could see any threatening warships coming for miles in advance. Guided tours are available in English, French, Spanish, and Italian. Walking shoes are recommended. Visitors must first check-in at the Office of Tourism, on 29 rue Victor Hugo. ✉ *Bd. Chevalier, Sainte-Marthe, Fort-de-France* ☎ *0596/80–00–70* 🌐 *www.tourisme-centre.fr* 🎫 *€8* 🕑 *Fort closed for tours Sun.–Mon.*

La Savane
CITY PARK | The heart of Fort-de-France, La Savane is a 12½-acre oceanside park filled with trees, fountains, and benches. A massive revitalization made it the focal point of the city again, with entertainment, shopping, and a pedestrian mall. Attractive wooden stands have been constructed along the edge of the park that house public restrooms, arts-and-crafts vendors, a crepe stand, an ice-cream stand, and numerous other eateries.

The Hotel L'Imperatrice, directly across from the park, has become a real gathering place—particularly for its café, which opens to the sidewalk. The hotel also has one of the best kiosks in the Savane for lunch and snacks. The newer Fort Savane, a residence (apartments) for the business and leisure market, is also right across from its namesake park. The Simon Hotel is a short stroll away. Diagonally across from La Savane, you can catch the ferries for the 20-minute run across the bay to Pointe du Bout and the beaches at Anse Mitan and Anse à l'Ane. It's relatively cheap as well as stress-free—much safer, more pleasant, and faster than by car.

The most imposing historic site in Fort-de-France is Fort St-Louis, which runs along the east side of La Savane. Now a military installation, it's again open to the public. However, you have to arrange a guided tour in advance at the tourist information kiosk in La Savane. They will sell you a ticket for under a euro and rent you an audio guide. ✉ *Fort-de-France.*

Musée d'Archéologie Précolombienne et de Préhistoire
HISTORY MUSEUM | A hidden treasure with an unassuming entrance just down the street from the Hotel L'Impératrice, this multistory archaeological museum

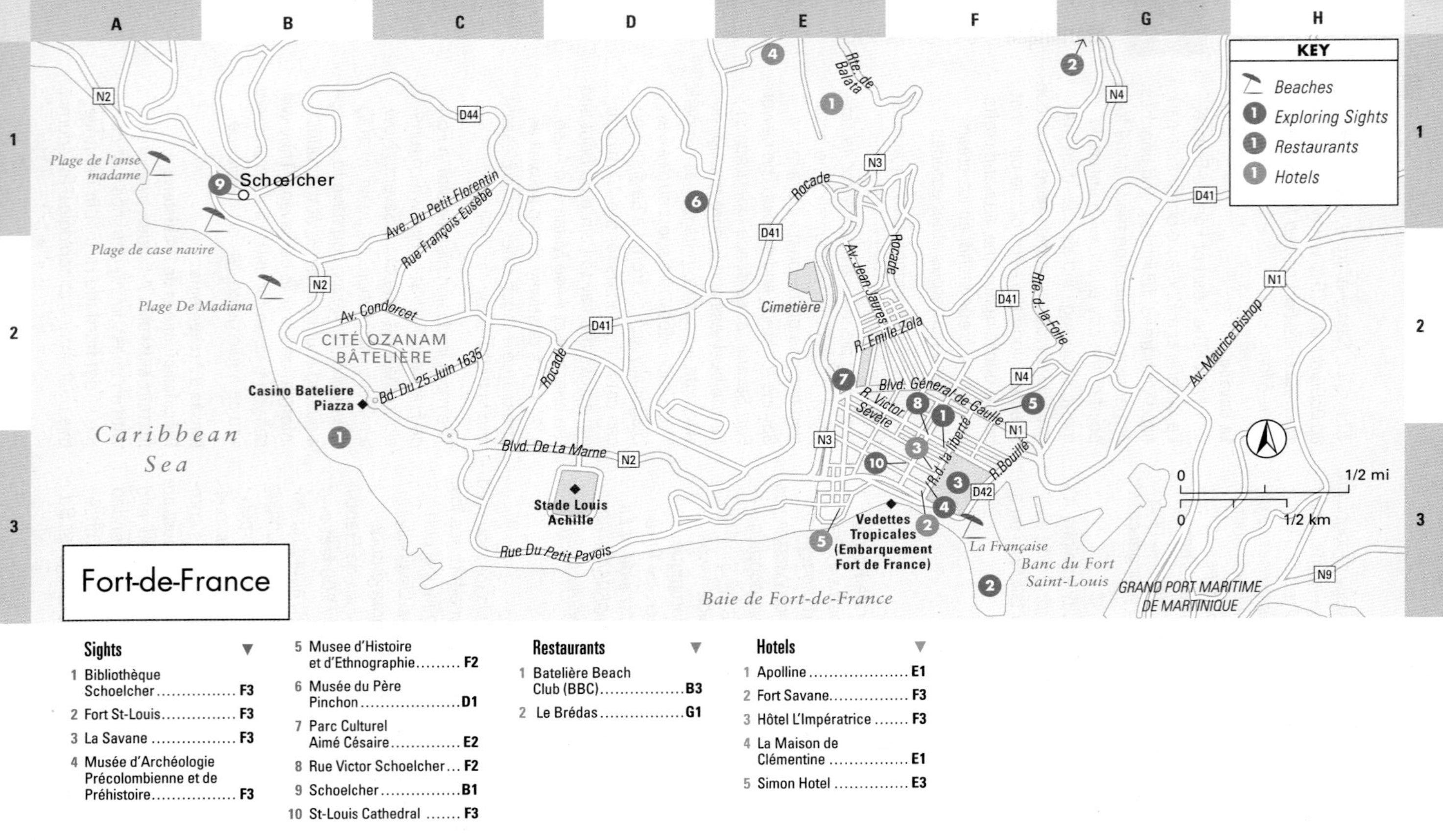

Fort-de-France
KEY
Beaches
Exploring Sights
Restaurants
Hotels
A
B
C
D
E
F
G
H
1
2
3
Caribbean Sea
Plage de l'anse madame
Plage de case navire
Plage De Madiana
Schœlcher
Ave. Du Petit Florentin
Rue François Eusèbe
Av. Condorcet
CITÉ OZANAM BÂTELIÈRE
Bd. Du 25 Juin 1635
Casino Bateliere Piazza
Rocade
Blvd. De La Marne
Stade Louis Achille
Rue Du Petit Pavois
Rte. de Balata
Cimetière
Av. Jean Jaures
R. Emile Zola
Blvd. Géneral de Gaulle
R. Victor Sévère
R.d. la liberté
R.Bouillé
Rte. d. la Folie
Av. Maurice Bishop
Vedettes Tropicales (Embarquement Fort de France)
La Française
Banc du Fort Saint-Louis
Baie de Fort-de-France
GRAND PORT MARITIME DE MARTINIQUE
N1
N2
N3
N4
N9
D41
D42
D44
0
1/2 mi
1/2 km
Sights
1 Bibliothèque Schoelcher ... F3
2 Fort St-Louis ... F3
3 La Savane ... F3
4 Musée d'Archéologie Précolombienne et de Préhistoire ... F3
5 Musee d'Histoire et d'Ethnographie ... F2
6 Musée du Père Pinchon ... D1
7 Parc Culturel Aimé Césaire ... E2
8 Rue Victor Schoelcher ... F2
9 Schoelcher ... B1
10 St-Louis Cathedral ... F3
Restaurants
1 Batelière Beach Club (BBC) ... B3
2 Le Brédas ... G1
Hotels
1 Apolline ... E1
2 Fort Savane ... F3
3 Hôtel L'Impératrice ... F3
4 La Maison de Clémentine ... E1
5 Simon Hotel ... E3

houses some 2,000 Indigenous artifacts. English-speaking guides are sometimes available. Kids take to this museum, "digging" the early peashooters, poison darts, hammocks that took a year to make, and the shaman's headdress. Also fascinating is the jewelry fashioned from natural materials, boar tusks, and bird feathers. A good time to sample this dose of prehistory is on a typically hot city day, for the air-conditioning is frigid. ✉ *9 rue de Liberté, Fort-de-France* ☎ *0596/71–57–05* 🎟 *€4.*

Musée d'Histoire et d'Ethnographie

HISTORY MUSEUM | This museum is best undertaken at the beginning of your vacation, so you can better understand the history, background, and people of the island. Housed in an elaborate former military residence (circa 1888) with balconies and fretwork, the museum displays gold jewelry as well as the sorts of rooms that a middle-class Martinican would have lived in. Oil paintings, engravings, and old historical documents also help sketch out the island's culture. ✉ *10 bd. Général de Gaulle, Fort-de-France* ☎ *0596/72–81–87* 🎟 *€3* ⏲ *Closed Tues. morning and Sat. afternoon.*

Musée du Père Pinchon

SCIENCE MUSEUM | This museum explores Martinique's diverse fauna and flora. Ten thousand species can be discovered, from the different types of mangroves to reptiles. Père Pinchon was a natural science professor and a priest who moved to Martinique in 1945 and dedicated his life to researching and listing all the existing species on the island. ✉ *33 rue Professeur Raymond Garcin, Fort-de-France* ☎ *0596/42–12–30* 🌐 *collectivitedemartinique.mq* 🎟 *Free* ⏲ *Closed on Tues. morning, Sat. afternoon, and Sun.*

Parc Culturel Aimé Césaire

CITY PARK | On the site of an ancient hospital, the Parc Floral Aimé Césaire is in the northeastern corner of the city center. After restorations parts of the park have reopened, as has the Grand Carbet theater. The park contains the island's official cultural center, where there are events that include beauty pageants and free evening concerts, especially during the International Festival or on memorial days. The live music is often jazz, classical music, and opera. ✉ *Pl. José-Marti, Sermac, Bd. du Marechal de Lattre, Fort-de-France* ☎ *0596/60–59–00* 🎟 *Free.*

Rue Victor Schoelcher

STREET | Stores sell Paris fashions and French perfume, china, crystal, and liqueurs, as well as local handicrafts along this street running through the center of the capital's primary shopping district, a six-block area bounded by rue de la République, rue de la Liberté, rue Victor Sévère, and rue Victor Hugo. ✉ *Fort-de-France.*

Schoelcher

TOWN | Pronounced shell- *share,* this upscale suburb of Fort-de-France is home to the University of the French West Indies and Guyana, as well as Martinique's largest convention center, Palais de Congres de Madiana. Schoelcher was named after abolitionist Victor Schoelcher, who is credited with ending slavery on the island. ✉ *Schoelcher.*

St-Louis Cathedral

CHURCH | This Romanesque cathedral with lovely stained-glass windows was built in 1878, the sixth church on this site (the others were destroyed by fires, hurricanes, and earthquakes). Classified as a historical monument, it has a marble altar, an impressive organ, and carved wooden pulpits. ✉ *Rue Victor Schoelcher, Schoelcher* ☎ *0596/60–59–00.*

Restaurants

Batelière Beach Club (BBC)

$$$ | **CARIBBEAN** | At this thatch-roof beach bar, on any given day DJs might be spinning local and international sounds. The bar puts out strong (and pricey) tropical cocktails, though the food is less expensive than at the hotel's restaurant. Just plan not to be in a hurry, especially on the weekends. **Known for:** amazing view over the Batelière Beach; trendy party atmosphere; live music or DJ. $ *Average main: €25 ✉ L'Hôtel La Batelière, Schoelcher ☎ 0596/10–64–26.*

Le Brédas

$$$$ | **CARIBBEAN** | This culinary experience necessitates a trip into the island's interior, down winding roads where the dense foliage is junglelike. It's best navigated, at least the first time, by day, so come for Sunday lunch. **Known for:** tender, marinated beef tenderloin; contemporary, authentic Martinican cuisine; perfectly executed foie gras appetizer. $ *Average main: €34 ✉ Entrée Presqu'île, St-Joseph ☎ 0596/57–65–52 ⏲ Closed Mon.–Wed. No lunch Sat. No dinner Sun.*

Hotels

★ Apolline

$ | **HOTEL** | A home away from home in the heights of Fort-de-France, Apolline is a modernist-style mansion with spacious rooms tucked away in a lush garden setting. **Pros:** authentic Creole cuisine; heated infinity pool overlooking Fort-de-France; friendly and helpful English-speaking staff. **Cons:** only the suite has bay views; staff is not at the hotel 24/7; garden needs a little maintenance. $ *Rooms from: €180 ✉ 61 rue Marie Therese Lung Fu, Fort-de-France ☎ 0596/10–82–62 🌐 apollinematinique.com 5 rooms 🍽 Free Breakfast.*

Fort Savane

$ | **APARTMENT** | Not to be confused with the military installation (Fort St-Louis) up the hill, this accommodation bills itself as a residence for both business travelers and tourists, though it doesn't have the full range of hotel amenities. **Pros:** excellent location across from the Savane; personalized concierge service can even obtain a bottle of Champagne after midnight; cordial, English-speaking receptionists. **Cons:** reception desk is not manned after 8 pm or on weekends (guests must enter with a code); no restaurant or bar on-site; cheapest rooms are small. $ *Rooms from: €144 ✉ 5 rue de la Liberté, Fort-de-France ☎ 0596/80–75–75 🌐 www.fortsavane.fr 14 units 🍽 No Meals.*

Hôtel L'Impératrice

$ | **HOTEL** | Right across from La Savane stands this hotel, which has been owned by the same caring, Martinican family since the 1950s; like the park, it's another landmark that's been revived in recent years. **Pros:** central location; personalized service; some rooms have terraces that overlook the park. **Cons:** some maintenance worries, mainly broken air-conditioning units; narrow hallways; the small standard rooms in back are quiet but otherwise not desirable. $ *Rooms from: €124 ✉ 15 rue de la Liberté, Fort-de-France ☎ 0596/63–06–82 🌐 www.limperatricehotel.fr 22 rooms 🍽 Free Breakfast.*

La Maison de Clémentine

$ | **B&B/INN** | This small B&B in a suburban house (about 10 minutes from Fort-de-France) has deluxe suites with contemporary decor, as well as Wi-Fi and other attractive amenities and high-end touches. **Pros:** rooms are attractive, particularly rooms 2 and 5; nearby restaurants; unique on the island. **Cons:** not all the benefits of a hotel; really need a car here; charming manager does not speak English—owners do. $ *Rooms from: €160 ✉ 22 rte. de l'Union Didier, Fort-de-France ☎ 0596/64–96–00 🌐 www.lamaisondeclementine.com 5 rooms 🍽 Free Breakfast.*

Simon Hotel

$ | **HOTEL** | Long awaited, the futuristic Simon Hotel is one of the best innovations in the capital, with eye-stopping, contemporary interior design, commodious beds, and memorable bay views. **Pros:** two great restaurants; it's all new; downtown, bayfront location. **Cons:**

in-room Wi-Fi is not totally dependable; some employees need more training; rooms are not totally soundproof. *Rooms from: €220* ✉ *1 rue Loulou Bois Laville, Fort-de-France* ☎ *596/50–22–22* 🌐 *www.hotel-simon.com* *94 rooms* *No Meals.*

Nightlife

Casino Batelière Plazza

THEMED ENTERTAINMENT | On the outskirts of Fort-de-France, the Casino Batelière Plaza was built in a striking nouveau-plantation-house style, all cranberry and white. Slots open at 10 am, but table games (American roulette, blackjack, and stud poker) don't start until after 8 pm and close at 3:00 am. There's always a bar open, and you can often catch live entertainment on weekends after 8. It's open Sunday night, when most places are shut tight. Restaurant Le Club Seven, which serves Franco-creole food, offers themed parties on weekends. A new concert hall is impressive as well. ✉ *Rue des Alizés, Schoelcher* ☎ *0596/61–73–23* 🌐 *www.casinobateliereplazza.com.*

Le Bolibar

COCKTAIL LOUNGES | Located within the modern four-star hotel Le Simon, Le Bolibar lounge and restaurant offers a breathtaking view on la Baie des Flamands. Open from 5 pm to 10 pm; you can enjoy your cocktail and tapas on the terrace at sunset. The service can take time. ✉ *1 Avenue Loulou, Boislaville, Fort-de-France* ☎ *0596/50–22–22* 🌐 *hotel-simon.com* ☞ *Free parking for Le Bolibar's clients.*

Shopping

Bois Nature

CRAFTS | This place is all about mood and mystique and ecosensitivity. Gift items at Bois Nature begin with scented soap, massage oil, aromatherapy sprays, and perfumes. Then there are wind chimes, mosquito netting, shell mobiles, and sun hats made of coconut fiber. The interior decor accessories are unique and worth carrying home on the plane, but they can also ship things home for you. The big stuff includes natural wood-frame mirrors and furniture à la Louis XV. ✉ *Parking Centre, Commercial place d'armes, Le Lamentin* ☎ *0596/65–77–65* 🌐 *www.boisnature.fr.*

La Chamade

MIXED CLOTHING | So you wanna look French? *Femmes,* this urban boutique is a good start, although the chic doesn't come cheap here. You will recognize some well-known brands like Paul Smith, Mellow Yellow, and Calarena, and the French shoes are nearly irresistible. The shop does have some good *soldes* (sales), though—and make sure you check the second level. ✉ *25 rue Schoelcher, Fort-de-France* ☎ *0596/73–28–78.*

Lynx Optique

OTHER SPECIALTY STORE | Lynx Optique has the latest designer sunglasses from such major brands as Chanel, Gucci, Dior, Cartier, and Versace. (French designer brands are less expensive here.) And if you need a pair of prescription lenses or a repair, they can take care of that, too. The staff are professional, polite, and English is spoken. There are several locations throughout the island, this being the most centrally located. ✉ *51 rue Victor Hugo, Fort-de-France* ☎ *0596/71–38–48* 🌐 *www.lynx-optique.com.*

Pascal de Rogatis Jewelry

JEWELRY & WATCHES | Authentic Creole-style jewelry, popularized after the abolition of slavery and seen in many museums, is for sale here at the number-one jewelry store in Martinique. Most creations are in 18-karat gold, but 9-karat is an option. ✉ *47 rue Isambert, Fort-de-France* ☎ *0596/71–36–78.*

Tendance Bikini

SWIMWEAR | Tendance Bikini is a beachwear paradise where you can find a wide variety of bathing suits, beach clothes, and "sandales" (slippers). The salespeople are friendly, and they can help you put an outfit together. You will notice Martinicans love a unique piece that stands out, especially in August for the famous sailing race: "le tour des yoles." ✉ *57 rue Victor Schoelcher, Fort-de-France* ☎ *0596/72–05–39.*

Le François

With some 16,000 inhabitants, this is the main city on the Atlantic coast (and the area's largest). Many of the old wooden buildings remain and are juxtaposed with concrete structures. The classic West Indian cemetery, with its black-and-white tiles, is still here, and a marina is at the end of town. One of Martinique's best hotels is in this area (Hotel Plein Soleil), as well as some of the island's most upscale residences and most visited distillery estates, Habitation Clément and Habitation Simon A1710. Le François is also noted for its snorkeling at les fonds blancs.

Sights

★ Habitation Clément

HISTORIC SIGHT | Get a glimpse into Martinique's colonial past at this estate and rum distillery, the site of a former sugar cane plantation. Visitors are given a multilingual audio headset, which explains tour highlights. Signage further describes the rum-making process and other aspects of plantation life. The Palm Grove, with an avenue of palms and park benches, is a delightful place to reflect; the contemporary sculpture is fascinating. It was all built with the wealth generated by its rum distillery, and its 18th-century splendor has been lovingly preserved. The plantation's Creole house illustrates the adaption to life in the tropics up through the 20th century. An early French typewriter, a crank-up telephone, and decades-old photos of the Cléments and Hayots (béké families), are juxtaposed with modern Afro-Caribbean art. The newest building houses an art gallery that showcases contemporary, Caribbean art, and sculpture. Enjoy the free tastings at the bar of the retail shop. Consider the Canne Bleu, Grappe Blanche, or one of the aged rums, some bottled as early as 1952.

TIP→ Children get a discount. Also, allow 1½–2 hours to see everything. The ticket office closes at 5. ✉ *Domaine de l'Acajou, Le François* ☎ *0596/54–62–07* 🌐 *www.habitation-clement.fr* 🎫 *€12.*

Habitation Simon A1710

DISTILLERY | Gustatory and olfactory delights await at this bio rum distillery, one of few where the sugarcane is still cut by hand. La "belle Aline," the shiny copper alembic, steals the show. To discover more in-depth, you can even participate in the rum production (available upon reservation). ✉ *Le François* ☎ *0596/50–58–42* 🌐 *rhum-a1710.com* 🎫 *15€* ⏲ *Closed Sat. afternoon and Sun.* ✍ *Reservations required for guided tour.*

★ Les Fonds Blancs (*Joséphine's Baths*)

NATURE SIGHT | Offshore from Le François, les fonds blancs baths draw snorkelers to the privately owned Ilets de l'Impératrice. The islands received that name because, according to legend, this is where Empress Joséphine Bonaparte came to bathe in the shallow basins, known as les fonds blancs because of their white-sand bottoms. Group boat tours leave from the harbor and include lunch and drinks and one can even buy a package that includes an overnight stay on the remote and romantic Îlet Oscar. Prices vary. You can also haggle with a fisherman to take you out for a while on his boat. There's a fine bay 6 miles (10 km) farther along the coast where you can swim and go kayaking. The town itself is rather lackluster but authentic, and you'll find a number of different shops, a gas station, and supermarkets. ✉ *Ilets de l'Impératrice, Le François.*

Restaurants

★ Le Plein Soleil Restaurant

$$$$ | **FRENCH FUSION** | Perennially popular with the chic set, Le Plein Soleil's restaurant has a smashing contemporary, Creole look, but it's the inventive, beautifully executed menu that cements its well-deserved reputation. It continues to draw applause for the use of the latest techniques from France coupled with remarkable twists on local products. **Known for:** fine dining; sophisticated, trendy ambience; sea views from the terrace. *Average main: €50* *Hôtel Le Plein Soleil, Pointe Thalèmont, Le François* *0596/38–07–77* *hotelpleins-oleil.fr* *No lunch Mon.–Thurs.*

Coffee and Quick Bites

Le Grand Trianon Boulangerie

$ | **BAKERY** | If you need a fast French lunch break in Le François, try this bakery in town, near the Carrefour Supermarket. Crisp baguettes and luscious pastries and ice cream are sold, as are prix-fixe lunches with sandwiches or salads. **Known for:** salads and sandwiches; quick lunch; French-style baked goods. *Average main: €5* *Centre Cial Ancienne Usine, Le François* *0596/56–89–81.*

Hotels

★ Hotel Plein Soleil

$ | **HOTEL** | Long one of our favorites, this heavenly hideaway is now a modern, Martinique landmark, with accommodations in Creole *cases* (cottages)—painted red, purple, and subtle earth tones—with contemporary bathrooms, and terraces that maximize the glorious sea views. **Pros:** deluxe breakfast; owner is on-site and accessible; sophisticated and artistic ambience is unique in Martinique. **Cons:** Wi-Fi is free but seldom works within guest accommodations; smallest rooms have small bathrooms; rough road (particularly in rainy season) to somewhat remote, hilltop location. *Rooms from: €215* *Pointe Thalèmont, Le François* *0596/38–07–77* *www.hotelpleins-oleil.fr* *Closed Sept.–mid-Oct.* *16 rooms* *Free Breakfast.*

Les Trois-Îlets

Named after the three rocky islands nearby, this charming little village (population 3,000) has brilliant beaches and unusual brick-and-wood buildings roofed with antique tiles. It's known for its pottery, straw, and woodwork, but above all as the birthplace of Napoléon's empress, Joséphine. In the square, where there's also a market and a fine *mairie* (town hall), you can visit the simple church where she was baptized Marie-Joseph Tascher de la Pagerie. The Martinicans have always been enormously proud of Joséphine, even though her husband reintroduced slavery on the island and most historians consider her to have been rather shallow. After a quick look around, head out to the touristic Pointe du Bout.

Sights

Musée de la Pagerie

HISTORY MUSEUM | A stone building that held the kitchen of the estate where Joséphine grew up houses the Musée de la Pagerie. It contains an assortment of memorabilia pertaining to her life and rather unfortunate loves, including a marriage certificate and a love letter written straight from the heart by Napoléon in 1796. The main house blew down in the hurricane of 1766, when she was three, and the family lived for years above the sugarcane factory—a hot, smelly, and fly-ridden existence. At 16 she was wed (an arranged marriage because her father was a gambling man in need of money) to Alexandre de Beauharnais. After he was assassinated during the Revolution, she married Napoléon and substantially

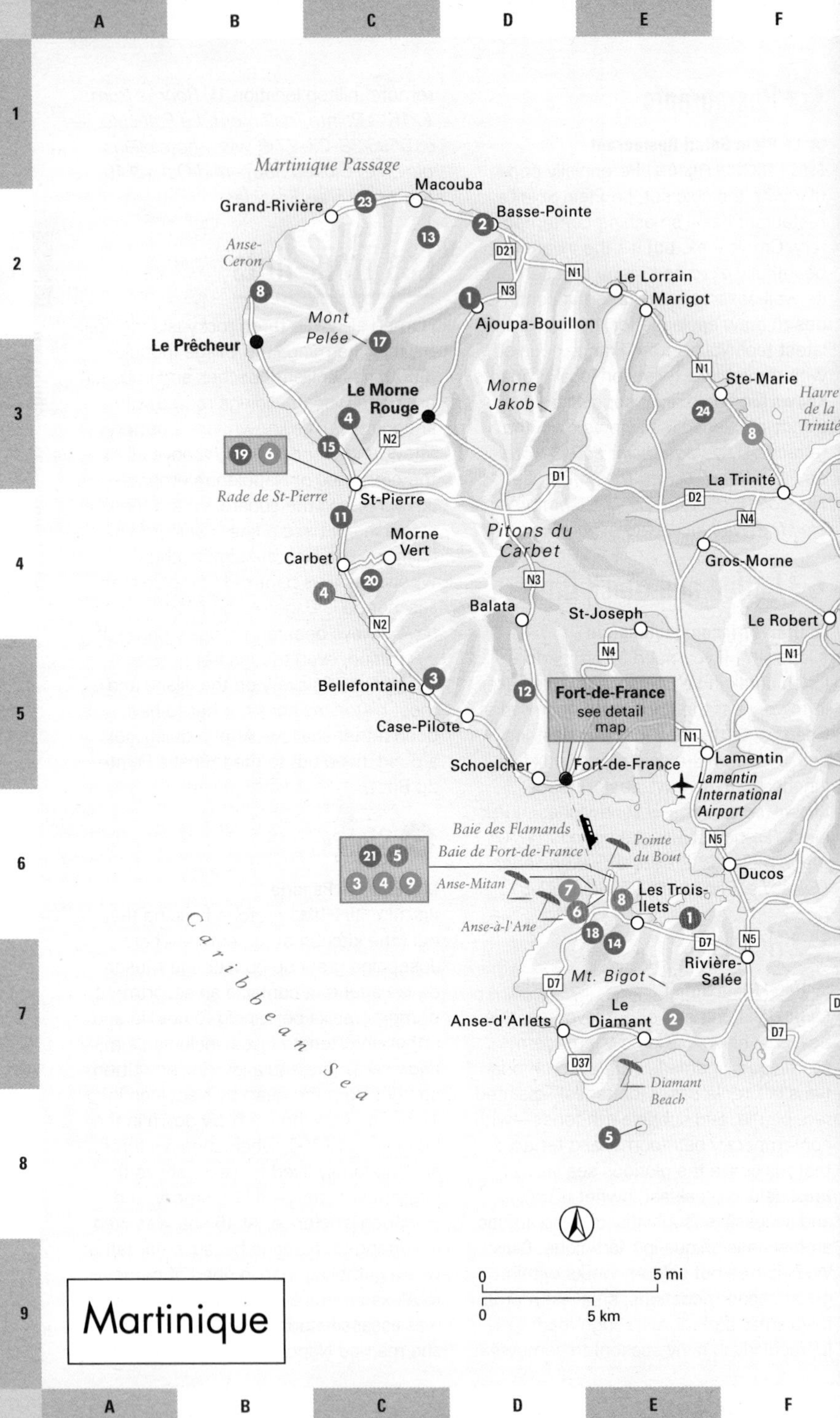

Martinique
Martinique Passage
Macouba
Grand-Rivière
Basse-Pointe
Anse-Ceron
Le Lorrain
Marigot
Ajoupa-Bouillon
Mont Pelée
Le Prêcheur
Ste-Marie
Havre de la Trinité
Le Morne Rouge
Morne Jakob
Rade de St-Pierre
St-Pierre
La Trinité
Pitons du Carbet
Morne Vert
Carbet
Gros-Morne
Balata
St-Joseph
Le Robert
Bellefontaine
Fort-de-France
see detail map
Case-Pilote
Schoelcher
Lamentin
Lamentin International Airport
Baie des Flamands
Baie de Fort-de-France
Pointe du Bout
Anse-Mitan
Les Trois-Ilets
Ducos
Anse-à-l'Ane
Rivière-Salée
Mt. Bigot
Le Diamant
Anse-d'Arlets
Diamant Beach
Caribbean Sea
0
5 mi
5 km

Sights

1 Ajoupa-Bouillon......... **D2**
2 Basse-Pointe............ **D2**
3 Bellefontaine............ **C5**
4 Depaz Distillery **C3**
5 Diamond Rock........... **E8**
6 Dubuc Castle........... **G3**
7 Forêt de Montravail **G7**
8 Habitation Céron........ **B2**
9 Habitation Clément..... **G5**
10 Habitation Simon A1710.................... **G6**
11 Interpretation Center Paul Gauguin............ **C4**
12 Jardin de Balata **D5**
13 La Distillerie J. M........ **C2**
14 La Savane des Esclaves **E7**
15 Le Centre de Découverte des Sciences de la Terre **C3**
16 Les Fonds Blancs....... **H6**
17 Mont Pelée.............. **C3**
18 Musée de la Pagerie **E6**
19 Musée Volcanologique Franck Perret............ **C3**
20 Neisson Distillery **C4**
21 Pointe du Bout **E6**
22 Presqu'île du Caravelle................. **G3**
23 Route to Grand' Rivière............ **C2**
24 St. James Distillery & Rum Museum.......... **E3**

Restaurants

1 La Baraqu' Obama...... **G7**
2 Le Dubuc Restaurant... **G3**
3 Le Plein Soleil Restaurant.............. **G5**
4 Le Petibonum............ **C4**
5 Le Pitaya.................. **E6**
6 Le Zandoli............... **D6**
7 Liv'Bar.................... **G7**
8 Restaurant Le Golf....... **E6**
9 Zanzibar.................. **G7**

Quick Bites

1 Coup d'Coeur............. **E6**
2 Le Grand Trianon Boulangerie **G5**

Hotels

1 Club Med Buccaneer's Creek..... **G8**
2 Domaine de la Palmeraie................. **E7**
3 Hôtel Bakoua............. **E6**
4 Hôtel La Pagerie **E6**
5 Hotel Plein Soleil........ **G5**
6 Hotel Villa Saint Pierre................ **C3**
7 La Suite Villa............. **E6**
8 Le Domaine Saint Aubin............... **F3**
9 Résidence Le Village Créole..................... **E6**
10 Résidence Oceane **G3**

improved her station in life. This museum is not a must-do in Martinique, but if you have some time and are in Trois-Îlets it offers an interesting bit of island history about a girl who made good.

■ TIP→ Museum hours sometimes change, so be sure to call in advance. ✉ *D38, Les Trois-Îlets, Les Trois-Îlets* ☎ *0596/80-71-00* 🎫 *€5* ⏲ *Closed Mon.*

Pointe du Bout
NEIGHBORHOOD | This beachy tourist area has a marina and several resort hotels, among them the deluxe Hotel Bakoua and the Hôtel La Pagerie. The ferry to Fort-de-France leaves from here. The Village Creole complex with its "residences" for tourists, its cluster of boutiques, ice-cream parlors, and rental-car agencies, forms the hub from which various restaurants and hotels radiate. It's a pretty quiet place in the low season. The beach at Anse-Mitan, which is a little west of Pointe du Bout proper, is one of the best on the island. There are also several small restaurants and inexpensive guesthouses there. ✉ *Les Trois-Îlets.*

La Savane des Esclaves (*The Savannah of the Slaves*)
MUSEUM VILLAGE | Down a dirt road, in the countryside outside the tourist zone, stands La Savane des Esclaves, a re-created "free" village of former enslaved people (circa 1800). This labor of love was created by Gilbert Larose, who has a fascination with his ancestors who were "Nèg'Marrons," enslaved people who fled the plantations to live free, off the land. The Antan Lontan Village, the name Larose gave his settlement, reveals much about this major element in Martinique's history and culture, with food tastings and artisan demonstrations. His gardens of fruits, vegetables, and medicinal herbs are cultivated in the traditional manner. Shows utilizing the various groups of Martinican folkloric dancers are held several times a year, both by day and by night. On Saturday from 9 to noon, there are often more elaborate tastings, demonstrations, and traditional dance lessons. Allow an hour and 15 minutes for the guided tour in French. There is some signage in English. ✉ *Quartier La Ferme, Les Trois-Îlets* ☎ *0596/68–33–91* 🌐 *www.lasavanedesesclaves.fr* 🎫 *€12* ⏲ *Closed Sun. afternoon.*

Beaches

Anse-Mitan
BEACH | There are often yachts moored offshore in these calm waters. This long stretch of beach can be particularly fun on Sunday. Small, family-owned seaside restaurants are half-hidden among palm trees and are footsteps from the lapping waves. Nearly all offer grilled lobster and some form of music on weekends, perhaps a zouk band. Inexpensive waterfront hotels line the clean, golden beach, which has excellent snorkeling just offshore. Chaise longues are available for rent from hotels, and there are also usually vendors on weekends. When you get to Pointe du Bout, take a left at the yellow office of Budget Rent a Car, then the next left up a hill, and park near the little white church. **Amenities:** food and drink. **Best for:** partiers; snorkeling; swimming; walking. ✉ *Pointe du Bout, Les Trois-Îlets.*

Pointe du Bout
BEACH | **FAMILY** | The beaches here are small, man-made, and lined with resorts. Each little strip is associated with its resident hotel, and security guards and closed gates make access difficult. However, if you take a left across from the main pedestrian entrance to the marina, after the taxi stand, then go left again, you will reach the beach for Hotel Bakoua, which has especially nice facilities and several options for lunch and drinks. If things are quiet (particularly during the week) one of the beach attendants may rent you a chaise; otherwise, just plop your beach towel down, face forward, and enjoy the delightful view of the Fort-de-France skyline. The water is dead calm

and quite shallow, but it eventually drops off if you swim out a bit. **Amenities:** food and drink; showers. **Best for:** snorkeling; sunset; swimming. ✉ *Pointe du Bout, Les Trois-Îlets.*

 Restaurants

Le Pitaya

$$$ | **FRENCH FUSION** | This award-winning hotel restaurant is not only good but affordable. The menu changes nightly, but many items do find their way back regularly. **Known for:** open-air dining; menu du jour; lobster. $ *Average main: €25* ✉ *Hotel La Pagerie, rue Chacha, Pointe du Bout, Les Trois-Îlets* ☎ *0596/66–05–30* 🌐 *www.hotel-lapagerie.com.*

★ Le Zandoli

$$$$ | **FRENCH FUSION** | Although "le zandoli" is the Creole term for the lowly gecko, there's nothing humble about the culinary presentation or the wildly colorful dining room here, which are as slick as anything you might encounter in Paris. Both the lunch and dinner chefs have worked in Michelin-starred restaurants in France. **Known for:** a cream puff of the day; daily fish tartare; sweetbreads of veal. $ *Average main: €45* ✉ *La Suite Villa, rte. du Fort d'Alet, Anse Mitan, Les Trois-Îlets* ☎ *0596/59–88–00,* 🌐 *www.la-suite-villa.com* ⏲ *No lunch Mon.–Wed.*

Restaurant Le Golf

$$$ | **MODERN FRENCH** | You may not expect a golf course to house a great restaurant, but once you're at this terraced, alfresco location, you will find yourself wowed as you look out on acres of rolling greens and the turquoise blue of the Caribbean beyond. The real accomplishment, however, is on the plates. **Known for:** traditional desserts like crème brûlée; the view; red snapper fillet elevated to fine art. $ *Average main: €25* ✉ *Golf de Trois-Îlets, Quartier la Pagerie, Les Trois-Îlets* ☎ *0596/48–20–84* ⏲ *No dinner Sun. and Mon.*

 Coffee and Quick Bites

Coup d'Coeur

$ | **BAKERY** | If perusing the Poterie Village, look no farther for a lunch spot or a tea break. This *patisserie–salon de thé* is on the right, as you first enter the village. **Known for:** quiche, pizza, sandwiches; fresh baked goods; daytime go-to. $ *Average main: €10* ✉ *Village de la Poterie, Les Trois-Îlets* ☎ *0596/69–70–32* ⏲ *No dinner.*

 Hotels

Hôtel Bakoua

$ | **RESORT** | Wrought-iron gates open to this lovely beachfront hotel, a throwback to gracious estate living, where you can cocoon yourself in colonial-era style. **Pros:** infinity pool with sea and mountain view; vintage Caribbean charisma; you don't necessarily need a car. **Cons:** can be busy and loud on weekends; facades are not all pretty; some rooms are outdated. $ *Rooms from: €230* ✉ *Pointe du Bout, Les Trois-Îlets* ☎ *0596/66–02–02* 🌐 *www.hotel-bakoua.fr/en* 🛏 *132 rooms* 🍴 *No Meals.*

Hôtel La Pagerie

$ | **HOTEL** | Ideally located in Pointe du Bout, this affordable hotel with a palm-lined swimming pool and lots of local art is one of the area's best. **Pros:** poolside restaurant and lively bar on site; spacious guest rooms; helpful, warm staff. **Cons:** in-room furnishings are not high-end; no sea vistas (but pool views); service, while friendly, not always up to four-star standards. $ *Rooms from: €180* ✉ *rue Chacha, Pointe de Bout, Les Trois-Îlets* ☎ *0596/66–05–30* 🌐 *hotel-lapagerie.com* 🛏 *98 rooms* 🍴 *No Meals.*

★ La Suite Villa

$$$ | **HOTEL** | This hilltop boutique hotel gives Les Trois-Îlets some art-infused glamour and manages to maximize the Caribbean views from every room—even the bathrooms. **Pros:** inimitable,

whimsical style with a profusion of Caribbean colors; spa, infinity pool, restaurant, and bar on site; upbeat social scene. **Cons:** no beach (nearest one is a half-mile away); pool is petite with few chaises; no elevator in three-story greathouse. $ *Rooms from: €405* ✉ *Rte. du Fort d'Alet, Anse Mitan, Les Trois-Îlets* ☎ *0596/59–88–00* 🌐 *www.la-suite-villa.com* *15 units* *No Meals.*

Résidence Le Village Créole

$ | **APARTMENT** | **FAMILY** | The "village" is comprised of very reasonably priced apartments surrounding a courtyard that houses some 20 shops and 10 restaurants/bars. **Pros:** a lot of square footage for the euro; caring, English-speaking management; ample amenities. **Cons:** apartments are sparsely furnished; check-out during high season is early, at 10 am; reception office not always staffed. $ *Rooms from: €126* ✉ *Village Créole, Pointe du Bout, Les Trois-Îlets* ☎ *0596/66–03–19* 🌐 *www.villagecreole.com* *23 apartments* *No Meals.*

Nightlife

Casino Trois-Îlets

THEMED ENTERTAINMENT | The interior of this small casino was designed in a French Quarter style and houses slot machines, blackjack, U.S. roulette, stud poker, and craps (Friday and Saturday). The casino is open daily from 10 am to 3 am, but the gaming tables don't start cranking until 9. On weekends in high season, a DJ spins Caribbean, Creole, and international beats, and there's a dance floor. The restaurant serves up a marriage of refined creole and international fare, with fresh local produce; however, the tables are right in the middle of the floor, which is not conducive to fine dining.

TIP→ There is often a cover charge when there is an event. ✉ *Rte. de Pointe du Bout, near rte. de Trois-Îlets, Les Trois-Îlets* ☎ *596/66–00–30.*

Hôtel Bakoua

LIVE MUSIC | The quality entertainment here ranges from piano concerts to singers to jazz combos on up to full swimsuit fashion shows or splashy variety shows. You can also go to the hotel's waterfront Le Coco Bar or the tropical Le Gommier bar and order a cocktail. There's a litany of island rums, from white to amber and rhum vieux. It's usually best to call the hotel first to learn what's on the schedule, since events taper off during the low season. ✉ *Les Trois-Îlets* ☎ *0596/66–02–02.*

Infinity

LIVE MUSIC | This two-story bar and gourmet food boutique has live entertainment on weekends and a sophisticated bar with tables, some on a small terrace. The cuisine is contemporary Italian, the presentation is artistic, and the service is praiseworthy. It serves late into the night, closing at midnight, and it opens at 11 am for lunch. ✉ *Village Creole, Pointe du Bout, Les Trois-Îlets* ☎ *0596/38–71–68.*

Le Kano Bar Lounge Restaurant

BARS | At this trendy, beachfront bar and lounge/restaurant, creole-influenced tapas and brochettes as well as creative Caribbean cocktails are happily consumed while relaxing Caribbean music plays in the background; a full menu is available, too. Spacious with several open rooms leading to the beach, it is wheelchair accessible, and the contemporary Euro furniture is inviting. Guests enjoy some of the best Martinican dark (aged) rum. Happy hours are fun, and in season, a DJ cranks until 3 am on Friday and Saturday nights. The beach party on Sunday afternoons rocks. Kano is across the street from the Casino des Trois-Îlets, and the ample parking there makes it easy to visit both. ✉ *31 rue des Bougainvilliers, facing the casino, Les Trois-Îlets* ☎ *0569/78–40–33.*

La Marine

PUBS | La Marine is a busy bar and restaurant with live entertainment, mainly a local band on Saturday nights. Open daily, expats and boaters hang here for the reasonably priced, good pizza and old-world Italian and French classics. As one expat puts it, "It will probably be here for life!" There's nothing contemporary about this place—on quiet nights you can hear the wind in the riggings and check out the boat action on the docks. ✉ *Marina Pointe du Bout, Les Trois-Îlets* ☎ *0596/66–02–32.*

 Shopping

Artisanat & Poterie des Trois-Îlets

SHOPPING CENTER | At this group of shops, a major tourist attraction in the area, you can watch the creation of Arawak- and Carib-style pots, vases, and jars; plus, there are shops with interesting gifts, jewelry, and clothing, especially pareos (wraparound skirts). Several appealing restaurants (particularly the bakery) also make it a good stopover for lunch. There's also a go-kart track and kayaking. ✉ *Rte. des Trois-Îlets, Les Trois-Îlets* ☎ *0596/68–03–44.*

L'Atelier du Parfum Tropical

PERFUME | The trained staff here can formulate your very own eau du parfum from more than 50 available fragrances. The ingredients are natural and from the island. The store also sells soaps and body oils that include a natural bronzer with oil of roucou and a coconut oil base. One purse-size spray that everyone should carry is an anti-mosquito oil with eucalyptus and citronella. Many of the spray atomizers (non aerosol) are less than 3 ounces and can be carried aboard your homebound plane. ✉ *Village Creole, Pointe du Bout, Les Trois-Îlets* ☎ *0696/80–80–04, 0596/62–22–90* 🌐 *www.parfums-des-iles.com.*

Caz' Art

CRAFTS | This is one of those artsy souvenir shops that is so chockablock full that you are fascinated, amazed at every turn. There are many small items that would fit in luggage, such as colorful, metallic sculptures. Some of the most fanciful items are home accessories. Luc Ferrari, a designer (and importer) of art deco, showcases his wares here. ✉ *Village de la Poterie, Les Trois-Îlets* ✥ *When you first drive in the village, pass the bakery (patissiere) and then this shop is next, also on the right* ☎ *0596/48–17–38.*

Coté Plage Sarl

MIXED CLOTHING | Stop in here for French sailor jerseys in creative colors, youthful straw purses in bold hues, fun jewelry, and bathing suits. ✉ *Village Créole, Pointe du Bout, Les Trois-Îlets* ☎ *0596/66–13–00.*

Galerie de Sophen

ART GALLERIES | Across from the Village Créole, this gallery combines Sophie and Henry, both in name and content. On sale are the originals and limited prints of a French couple who live aboard their sailboat and paint the beauty of the sea and the island, from exotic birds to banana trucks. ✉ *Pointe du Bout, Les Trois-Îlets* ☎ *0596/66–13–64.*

La Petite Boutique

CHILDREN'S CLOTHING | La Petite Boutique offers a unique children's collection, including jewelry, and madras dollies. There are also contemporary mini-styles from upscale kid companies. ✉ *Village Créole, Pointe du Bout, Les Trois-Îlets* ☎ *0596/38–00–65, 0696/83–27–67.*

Diamond Rock is one of the island's top dive sites.

Le Diamant

While most tourists don't find their way to Le Diamant, it's a good, off-the-beaten-path stop for those who like outdoor pursuits, including diving and hiking.

Sights

Diamond Rock

VIEWPOINT | This volcanic mound, 1 mile (1½ km) offshore from the small, friendly village of Le Diamant, is one of the island's best diving spots. In 1804, during the squabbles over possession of the island between the French and the English, the latter commandeered the rock, armed it with cannons, and proceeded to use it as a strategic battery. The British held the rock for nearly a year and a half, attacking any French ships that came along. The French got wind that the British were getting cabin fever on their isolated island and arranged for barrels of rum to float up on the rock. The French easily overpowered the inebriated sailors, ending one of the most curious engagements in naval history. ✉ *Le Diamant.*

Forêt de Montravail

FOREST | A few miles north of Ste-Luce, this tropical rain forest is ideal for a short hike. Look for the interesting group of Carib rock drawings. ✉ *Le Diamant.*

Beaches

Diamant Beach

BEACH | The island's longest beach has a splendid view of Diamond Rock, but the Atlantic waters are rough, with lots of wave action—it's not known as a surfers' beach, though. Diamant is often deserted, especially midweek, which is more reason to be careful if you do go swimming. The sand is black here, and it is an experience to snorkel above it. Happily, it's a great place for picnicking and beachcombing; there are shade trees aplenty, and parking is abundant and free. The hospitable, family-run Diamant Les Bains hotel is a good lunch spot; if you eat lunch there, the management may let you wash off in the pool overlooking the beach. From Les Trois-Îlets, go in the direction of Rivière Salée, taking the secondary road to the east, toward Le Diamant. A coastal route, it leads to the beach. **Amenities:** food and drink; parking. **Best for:** solitude; snorkeling; walking. ✉ *Le Diamant.*

 Hotels

Domaine de la Palmeraie

$$ | **B&B/INN** | Unique in Martinique, this contemporary Caribbean villa complex is secluded amid acres of Zen-like gardens yet a short drive to Diamant's beach and town, making it more of a slice of real island life than a tourist destination. **Pros:** strong Wi-Fi; private enclave; good for families. **Cons:** no air-conditioning in second-floor bedrooms except in the spacious Villa Papaye; a rental car is almost a necessity; some might prefer to be closer to Trois-Îlets or other tourist areas. $ *Rooms from: €325* ✉ *Quartier Thoraille, Allée de la Palmeraie Quartier Thoraille, Le Diamant* ☎ *0696/50–24–40* 🌐 *www.domainedelapalmeraie.com* *6 villas* *Free Breakfast.*

Le Marin

The yachting capital of Martinique, Le Marin is also known for its colorful August carnival and its Jesuit church, circa 1766. It's also one of the few scene-y towns on the island. From Le Marin a narrow road leads to picturesque Cap Chevalier, about 1 mile (1½ km) from town. Most of the buildings are white and very European. The marina, a hub for charter boats, is often buzzing with charter sailboats departing and celebrities on impressive yachts pulling in. There are waterfront restaurants and clubs that are a magnet for the younger crowd as well as for sailors and tourists at large. For dinner try Mango Bay overlooking the water, or Liv Bar; beside it is a crepe restaurant, Sucre Sale. The upscale restaurant Zanzibar is on boulevard Allegre and on that same street is Le Country and Le Marin Mouillage.

 Restaurants

Liv'Bar

$ | **CARIBBEAN** | Facing the beach, this lively restaurant bar has great views and solid Caribbean food and cocktails. Fresh grilled seafood plates with a side of rice and local vegetables are prominent on the menu. **Known for:** sea views; grilled seafood plates; inventive cocktails. $ *Average main: €20* ✉ *19 blvd. Allegre, Le Marin* ☎ *696/37–76–53* 🌐 *livbar-bar.business.site* ⏲ *Closed Mon. No dinner Tues.*

★ **Zanzibar**

$$ | **CREOLE** | One of the best restaurants in Le Marin, this upscale open-air restaurant uses local ingredients from the nearby market and fisheries to create tantalizing Creole dishes. Dine on the terrace with a glass of wine in hand for a memorable view of sailboats floating on the sea. **Known for:** freshest local fish; romantic setting; sea views. $ *Average main: €25* ✉ *Plage du Bourg, 11 blvd. Allègre, Le Marin* ☎ *596/74–08–46* 🌐 *en.restaurantzanzibar.com/restaurant* ⏲ *Closed Mon.*

Ste-Anne

A long, nearly white-sand beach and a Catholic church are the highlights of this town on the island's southern tip. A bevy of small, inexpensive cafés offer seafood and creole dishes, pizza parlors, produce markets, and barbecue joints—it's a fun and lively place. To the south of Ste-Anne is Pointe des Salines, the southernmost tip of the island and site of one of Martinique's best beaches.

Les Salines

BEACH | **FAMILY** | A short drive south of Ste-Anne brings you to a mile-long (1½-km-long) cove lined with soft white sand and coconut palms. The beach is awash with families and children during holidays and on weekends, but quiet during the week. The far end—away from the makeshift souvenir shops—is most appealing. The calm waters are safe for swimming, even for the kids. You can snorkel, but it's not that memorable. Food vendors roam the sand, and there are also pizza stands and simple seafood restaurants. From Le Marin, take the coastal road toward Ste-Anne. You will see signs for Les Salines. If you see the sign for Pointe du Marin, you have gone too far. **Amenities:** food and drink; parking; showers; toilets. **Best for:** partiers; swimming; walking. ✉ *Ste-Anne.*

Pointe du Marin

BEACH | Stretching north from Ste-Anne, this is a good windsurfing and waterskiing spot. It's also a popular family beach, with restaurants, campsites, and clean facilities available for a small fee. Club Med is on the northern edge, and you can purchase a day pass. From Le Marin, take the coastal road to Ste-Anne. Make a right before town, toward Domaine de Belfond. You can see signs for Pointe du Marin. **Amenities:** food and drink; toilets. **Best for:** swimming; walking; windsurfing. ✉ *Ste-Anne.*

★ Club Med Buccaneer's Creek

$$$ | **RESORT** | One of the French chain's most upscale, sophisticated all-inclusive resorts offers a lot of fun, good food, and a huge, seaside pool to an international mix of singles, couples, and families (though there is no kids' club). **Pros:** enjoyable, professional entertainment in lounge before dinner; on one of the island's best beaches; in-room Wi-Fi and even waterskiing is included. **Cons:** some rooms feel dated; Ste. Anne village is not that close; no small catamarans or windsurfing. $ *Rooms from: €385* ✉ *Pointe Marin, Ste-Anne* ☎ *0596/76–72–72* 🌐 *www.clubmed.us* *292 rooms* 🍽 *All-Inclusive.*

Club Med Buccaneer's Creek

LIVE MUSIC | At Club Med Buccaneer's Creek, you can buy a night pass that will give you all the food, drinks, and entertainment you can handle from 7 pm until the disco closes at 1 am. While it comes at a hefty price, it includes an extensive buffet dinner with wine, a show in the theater, and drinks and dancing afterward. Friday is the best night to come since both the food and shows are most elaborate. Entertainment changes based on a two-week cycle. Following the show, it's on to dancing at the disco if you can hang. ✉ *Pointe du Marin, Ste-Anne* ☎ *0596/76–83–36.*

Ste-Luce

One of the most delightful towns in the south, this quaint fishing village has a sleepy main street with tourist shops and markets. Many young people live in this town; you can see some cool types taking a Pernod. From the sidewalk cafés there are panoramic sea views of Saint Lucia, and nearby are excellent beaches and several resorts. To the east is Pointe Figuier, an excellent spot for scuba diving. On the way, the Trois-Rivières Distillery is just off the highway, and Club Med is nearby, on its own peninsula.

Anse Corps de Garde

BEACH | On the southern Caribbean coast, this is one of the island's best long stretches of white sand. The public

Traditional madras costumes in Martinique

beach has picnic tables, restrooms, seagrape trees (which offer some shade), and crowds on weekends, when you'll also usually find plenty of food vendors. During the week, the beach is much less busy. The water is calm, with just enough wave action to remind you that it's the sea. There are no beach-chair rentals. From Fort-de-France, exit to the right before you get to the town of Ste-Luce. You first see signs for the Karibea Hotels and then one for Corps de Garde, which is on the right. At the stop sign take a left. **Amenities:** food and drink; toilets. **Best for:** partiers; swimming; walking. ✉ *Ste-Luce.*

Restaurants

La Baraqu' Obama
$$$ | **SEAFOOD** | If you're looking for a seafront restaurant that specializes in conch and lobster, Obama's is recommended. During lunchtime the alfresco terrace fills up mainly with French tourists supping on grilled lobster with either saltfish or black pudding or veggies, and a dessert. **Known for:** 4-foot poster of Obama; lobster and conch; grilled fresh catch of the day. $ *Average main: €24* ✉ *Bord de Mer, bd. Kennedy, Ste-Luce* ☎ *0696/80–78–75.*

Balata

Not much happens here, but the quiet little town has a few sights worth visiting. Built in 1923 to commemorate those Martinicans who fought and died in World War I, **Balata Church** is a replica of Paris's Sacré-Coeur Basilica. The gardens, **Jardin de Balata,** are lovely.

Sights

Jardin de Balata (*Balata Gardens*)
GARDEN | The Jardin de Balata has thousands of varieties of tropical flowers and plants, showing why Martinique is called "the Island of Flowers;" its owner is a dedicated horticulturist. There are shaded benches from which to take in the mountain views and a plantation-style house furnished with period furniture.

Le Morne Rouge is a good base where you can start the climb up the 4,600-foot Mont Pelée.

An aerial path gives visitors an astounding, bird's-eye view of the gardens and surrounding hills, from wooden walkways suspended 50 feet in the air. There is no restaurant, though beverages are for sale. It's 15 minutes from Fort-de-France, in the direction of St-Pierre. You can order anthuriums and other tropical flowers to be delivered to the airport from the mesmerizing flower boutique here.

TIP→ The gardens close at 6, but the ticket office will not admit anyone after 4:30. Children get a discount. ✉ *Km. 10, rte. de Balata, Balata* ☎ *0596/64–48–73* 🌐 *www.jardindebalata.fr* 🎫 *€14.*

St-Pierre

The rise and fall of St-Pierre is one of the most remarkable stories in the Caribbean and one of its worst disasters. Martinique's modern history began here in 1635. By the turn of the 20th century St-Pierre was a flourishing city of 30,000, known as the Paris of the West Indies. As many as 30 ships at a time stood at anchor. By 1902 it was the most modern town in the Caribbean, with electricity, phones, and a tram. On May 8, 1902, two thunderous explosions rent the air. As the nearby volcano erupted, Mont Pelée split in half, belching forth a cloud of burning ash, poisonous gas, and lava that raced down the mountain at 250 mph. At 3,600°F, it instantly vaporized everything in its path; 30,000 people were killed in two minutes.

The **Cyparis Express,** a small tourist train, will take you around to the main sights with running narrative (in French) for an hour Monday through Saturday, starting at 11 am, with reservations (0596/55–50–92, 0696/81–88–70) for €15.

An Office du Tourisme is on the *moderne* seafront promenade. Stroll the main streets and check the blackboards at the sidewalk cafés before deciding where to lunch. At night some places have live music. Like stage sets for a dramatic opera, there are the ruins of the island's first church (built in 1640), the imposing theater, and the toppled statues. This city, situated on its naturally beautiful harbor and with its narrow, winding streets, has the feel of a European seaside hill town. With every footstep, you touch a page of history. Although many of the historic buildings need work, stark modernism has not invaded this burg.

Sights

Ajoupa-Bouillon

TOWN | A good day trip from nearby St-Pierre, this 17th-century village surrounded by pineapple fields and filled with flowers is the jumping-off point for several sights. The **Saut Babin**, a 40-foot waterfall, is a half-hour walk from Ajoupa-Bouillon. The **Gorges de la Falaise** is a river gorge where you can swim. ✉ *Ajoupa-Bouillon.*

★ Depaz Distillery

DISTILLERY | An excursion to Depaz Distillery is one of the best things to do on the island. Established in 1651, it sits at the foot of the volcano. After a devastating eruption in 1902, the fields of blue cane were replanted, and in time, the rum-making began all over again. A self-guided tour includes the workers' gingerbread cottages. The tasting room sells Depaz rum, including its golden and aged rums, as well as liqueurs made from orange, ginger, and basil (among other flavors) that can enhance your cooking. Unfortunately, the plantation's greathouse, or château, is unlikely to be open. Allow time and make a reservation for Depaz's restaurant, **Le Moulin a Canne** (☎ *0596/69–80–44*). Open only for lunch (even on Sunday when the distillery is closed), it has the views, the service, and flavorful creole specialties as well as some French classics on the menu, plus—you guessed it—Depaz rum to wash it down. It's "on the house."

TIP→ Shutters are drawn at the tasting room and the staff leave at exactly 5 pm (4 on Saturday), so plan to be there at least an hour before. ✉ *Mount Pelée Plantation, St-Pierre* ☎ *0596/78–13–14* 🌐 *www.depaz.fr/en* 🎫 *Distillery free* ⏲ *Closed Sun.*

Did You Know?

One man survived the eruption of Mont Pelée. His name was Cyparis, and he was a prisoner in an underground cell in the town's jail, locked up for public drunkenness. Later, he went on the road with the Barnum & Bailey Circus as a sideshow attraction. Le Petit Train, that gives tours of the town, is named after him, "Cyparis Express."

Le Centre de Découverte des Sciences de la Terre

SCIENCE MUSEUM | If you want to know more about volcanoes, earthquakes, and hurricanes, check out Le Centre de Découverte des Sciences de la Terre. Housed in a sleek building that looks like a dramatic white box, this earth-science museum has high-tech exhibits and interesting films. Watch the documentary on the volcanoes in the Antilles, highlighting the eruption of the nearby Mount Pelée. Le Centre has fascinating Wednesday summer programs on dance, food, and ecotourism.

TIP→ The Depaz Distillery is nearby, and it's easy to visit both on the same day. ✉ *Habitation Perinelle, Quartier la Galere, St-Pierre* ☎ *0596/52–82–42* 🌐 *cdst.e-monsite.com* 🎫 *€5.*

Musée Volcanologique Franck Perret

HISTORY MUSEUM | **FAMILY** | For those interested in Mount Pelée's eruption of 1902, the Musée Vulcanologique Franck Perret is a must. It was established in 1933 by Franck Perret, a noted American volcanologist. Small but fascinating and insightful, the museum houses photographs of the old town before and after the eruption, documents, and a number of relics—some gruesome—excavated from the ashy ruins, including molten glass, melted iron, the church bell, and contorted clocks stopped at 8 am. The 30-minute film is a good way to begin. An English-speaking guide is often available and may tell you that the next lava flow is expected within 50 years. (No wonder the price of real estate in St-Pierre is among the lowest on the island.) ✉ *Rue Victor Hugo (D10) at rue du Theatre, St-Pierre* ☎ *0596/78–15–16* 🎫 *€5.*

Hotels

Hotel Villa Saint Pierre

$ | **HOTEL** | Simple, modern decor typifies this modest bayfront property that is somewhere between a boutique hotel and a French business hotel. **Pros:** only real hotel in St. Pierre; caring managers; downtown location. **Cons:** price is somewhat high for the relatively small rooms; not on a good beach; little English spoken. $ *Rooms from: €147* ✉ *108 rue Bouillé, St-Pierre* ☎ *0596/78–68–45* 🌐 *www.hotel-villastpierre.fr* *8 rooms* 🍴 *Free Breakfast.*

Le Morne Rouge

This town sits on the southern slopes of the volcano that destroyed it in 1902. Today it's a popular resort spot and offers hikers some fantastic mountain scenery. From Le Morne Rouge you can start the climb up the 4,600-foot Mont Pelée.

Sights

Mont Pelée

VOLCANO | This active 4,600-ft volcano is the site of an eruption in 1902 that killed 30,000 people (its last eruption was in 1932). There is a long and quite difficult hike you can do here that leaves from Le Morne Rouge, but don't try scaling this volcano without a guide unless you want to get buried alive under pumice stones. Instead, drive up to L'Auberge de la Montagne Pelée. (Ask for a room with a view.) From the parking lot it's 1 mile (1½ km) up a well-marked trail to the summit. Bring a hooded sweatshirt because there's often a mist that makes the air damp and chilly. From the summit follow the route de la Trace (Route N3), which winds south of Le Morne Rouge to St-Pierre. It's steep and winding, but that didn't stop the *porteuses* (female porters) of old: balancing a tray, these women would carry up to 100 pounds of provisions on their heads for the 15-hour trek to the Atlantic coast. ✉ *Le Morne-Rouge.*

Macouba

Sights

Named after the Carib word for "fish," this village was a prosperous tobacco town in the 17th century. Today its cliff-top location affords magnificent views of the sea, the mountains, and—on clear days—the neighboring island of Dominica. (Do not confuse it with Cap Macabou, which is near Le Vauclin.)

Basse-Pointe

TOWN | On the route to this village on the Atlantic coast at the island's northern end—the wild side of Martinique—you pass many banana and pineapple plantations. Just south of Basse-Pointe is a Hindu temple, which was built by descendants of the East Indians who settled in this area in the 19th century. The view of Mont Pelée from the temple is memorable. Basse-Pointe is a short drive from Macouba and is best experienced as a day excursion. ✉ *Basse-Pointe.*

★ **La Distillerie J. M.**

DISTILLERY | J. M. offers the most innovative and contemporary exhibits in addition to tastings. Long considered to be among the top echelon of Martinique rums, it does not have the same name recognition as some of the other popular

The town of St-Pierre is beneath the 4,600-foot Mont Pelée.

labels, like Clément, for example. That is partly because J. M.'s best *rhum vieux* is considerably more expensive than your average bottle. The 10-year-old vintages (44.8 proof) truly rival France's fine cognacs, and a tasting is among the complimentary offerings that are available. Displays allow you to inhale the various aromas of the products, from vanilla and orange to almonds and exotic fruits. Some of the visuals are very high-tech. It is said that J. M. rum is made special by the pure mountain water of Macouba, where the outstanding rain forest is among the only sightseeing options.

TIP→ Plan to couple a visit to this destination distillery with one to Carbet and St. Pierre, then the Depaz Distillery, in time to take lunch at their fine restaurant. Then proceed to J. M. It is best to either have a designated driver, or hire an English-speaking driver for a half or full day. ✉ *Macouba* ☎ *0596/78–92–55* 🌐 *rhum-jm-la-distillerie.com* 🎫 *Free.*

Route to Grand' Rivière

SCENIC DRIVE | Macouba is the starting point for a spectacular drive, the 6-mile (10-km) Route to Grand' Rivière on the northernmost point. This is Martinique at its greenest: groves of giant bamboo, cliffs hung with curtains of vines, and human-size tree ferns that seem to grow as you watch them. Literally at the end of the road is Grand' Rivière, a colorful, sprawling fishing village at the foot of high cliffs. The Syndicat d'Initiative Riverain, the local tourism office in Macouba, can arrange hiking and boating excursions. ✉ *Macouba* ☎ *0596/55–72–74.*

Ste-Marie

The winding, hilly route to this town of some 20,000 offers breathtaking views of the rugged Atlantic coastline. Ste-Marie is the commercial capital of the island's north. Look for a picturesque mid-19th-century church here. Most come to the area to visit the St. James Distillery and its Musée du Rhum, but the north is also filled with immense natural beauty.

Sights

St. James Distillery & Rum Museum

DISTILLERY | The Musée du Rhum, operated by the St. James Rum Distillery, is housed in a graceful, galleried Creole house. Interestingly, the distillery was founded in 1765 in Ste-Pierre by a priest who was also an alchemist. It was relocated to Ste-Marie after the 1902 eruption of Mont Pelée. Guided tours can take in the plantation and the displays of the tools of the trade, the art gallery, and include a visit and tasting at the distillery. You can opt to take a little red train tour for €5 that traverses the cane fields and runs between here and the nearby banana museum, while a guide narrates; it runs on many Tuesday and Thursday mornings and Saturday afternoons. Just be aware the detailed commentary is in French.

TIP→ The museum and distillery are closed during the cane harvest, and weekend hours sometimes change; tours may not happen during December. It's a good idea to call ahead. ✉ *Plan d l'union, St. James Distillery, Ste-Marie* ☎ *0596/69–30–02* *Free.*

Hotels

Le Domaine Saint Aubin

$ | **APARTMENT** | Apartments at this private estate—perched on a verdant hilltop offering breathtaking views overlooking the Atlantic—are divided between a 19th-century Creole plantation house and newer, freestanding cottages. **Pros:** wheelchair-accessible rooms (and the pool has a chair lift); daydream yourself into the past; sea views. **Cons:** meals limited to breakfast and dinner, which cost extra; original rooms have character but are not stylin'; somewhat remote location requires a car. $ *Rooms from: €159* ✉ *Petite Rivière Salée, off Rte. 1, La Trinité* ☎ *0596/69–34–77, 0696/40–99–59* 🌐 *www.domaine-saint-aubin.com* *30 rooms* *No Meals.*

Tartane

One of the few sights to see in Tartane is its castle, but it's also a surfer's haunt.

Sights

Dubuc Castle

CASTLE/PALACE | At the eastern tip of the Presqu'île de Caravelle are the ruins of this castle, once the home of the Dubuc de Rivery family, who owned the peninsula in the 18th century. Constructed in the middle of a sugar plantation in the 1700s, the Dubuc castle had an exceptional location and ocean view. It was the castle that slavery built, as its solitary position enabled the Dubuc family to devote its efforts to an intense traffic of enslaved people with the English Antilles. You can park your car right after the turnoff for Résidence Oceane and walk the dirt road to the ruins. The castle still has a skeleton of stone walls, but it is mostly rubble. Hikers go for the dramatic ocean views, raw nature, and birdlife, but for others, it might not be worth the price of admission. It now has a map and interactive self-guide and sometimes an in-person guide, but mainly it is all in French so English visitors are not as satisfied. Also, you can buy a light picnic and ice cream and there are tables. ✉ *Tartane* *€4.*

Presqu'île de Caravelle

NATURE PRESERVE | Much of the Caravelle Peninsula, which juts 8 miles (13 km) into the Atlantic Ocean, is under the protection of the Regional Nature Reserve and offers places for trekking, swimming, and sailing. This is also the site of Anse-Spoutourne, an open-air sports and leisure center operated by the reserve. The town of Tartane has a popular surfing beach with brisk Atlantic breezes. ✉ *Tartane.*

Beaches

Anse Tartane

BEACH | This patch of sand is on the wild side of the Presqu'île du Caravelle. Ungroomed and in a fairly natural state, it's what the French call a *sauvage* beach. The only people you are likely to see are brave surfers who ride the high waves or some local families. Bliss, the surf school here, has re-opened and has taught many kids. Résidence Oceane, mainly for surfers, looks down on all of this action; it doesn't have a restaurant, but you can get a drink. **Amenities:** parking; toilets (at surf school); water sports. **Best for:** partiers; surfing; walking. ✉ *Tartane, La Trinité* ✢ *Turn right before you get to La Trinité, and follow the rte. de Château past the Caravelle hotel. Instead of following the signs to Résidence Oceane, veer left and go downhill when you see the ocean. The road runs right beside the beach. There are several bays and pointes here, but if you keep heading to the right, you can reach the surf school.*

Restaurants

Le Dubuc Restaurant

$$ | **CREOLE** | Come to Le Dubuc for a relaxed atmosphere and tasty Creole cuisine with a view of Tartane Beach. Note that the waiters are friendly, but they generally do not speak English. **Known for:** fresh fruit juices and colorful cocktails; great location near the beach; Creole style chatrou (octopus). $ *Average main: €20* ✉ *La Trinité, Tartane* ☎ *0596/74-27-16.*

Hotels

Résidence Oceane

$ | **HOTEL** | Garden and water views are abundant at this lovely secluded hotel in La Trinité, close to the beach and to the Caravelle nature preserve. **Pros:** close to Bliss surf school; sea views; pool. **Cons:** no restaurant or bar on-site; caters mostly to French-speaking guests; basic rooms but they have kitchenettes. $ *Rooms from: €85* ✉ *28 rue du Surf, La Trinité* ☎ *596/58-73-73* 🌐 *www.residenceoceane.com* *25 studios* *No Meals.*

Nightlife

Le Jardin des Lucioles

LIVE MUSIC | If you want European specialties, this restaurant-bar is the place to be. The duck breast burger is a must-try. On weekends, there is a live band or DJ. ✉ *Blvd. Francois Mitterand, La Trinité, Tartane* ☎ *0596/58-07-25.*

Le Carbet

There are two reasons to go to Carbet: the destination restaurant Le Petibonum and the museum for painter Paul Gauguin.

Sights

Bellefontaine

TOWN | A 20-minute drive from Le Carbet, Bellefontaine is a colorful fishing village with pastel houses on the hillsides and beautifully painted *gommiers* (fishing boats) bobbing in the water. Look for the restaurant built in the shape of a boat. ✉ *Bellefontaine.*

Interpretation Center Paul Gauguin

ART MUSEUM | Martinique was a brief stop in Paul Gauguin's wanderings, but a decisive moment in the evolution of his art. He arrived from Panama in 1887 with friend and fellow painter Charles Laval and, having pawned his watch at the docks, rented a wooden shack on a hill above Carbet. Dazzled by the tropical colors and vegetation, Gauguin developed a style, his Martinique period, that directly anticipated his Tahitian paintings. Also remembered here is the writer Lafcadio Hearn. In his endearing book *Two Years in the West Indies* he provides the

Dining in Martinique

Dining in Martinique is a delightful culinary experience, but as with driving here, it is best to get some directions before you head out. First of all, as in France, *entrées* are appetizers; the main courses will usually be labeled as follows: *poissons* (fish); *viandes* (meat); or *principal plats* (main dishes). The appetizers are almost as expensive as the mains—and if the appetizer is foie gras, you'll pay just as much as for a main course.

Entrecôte is a sirloin steak, usually cut thin. A filet mignon is a rarity, but you will see *filet mignon du porc*, which is pork tenderloin. *Ecrivesses* (known also as *ouassous* or *z'habitants*) are incredible freshwater crayfish, usually served with their heads on. Similarly, if a fish dish does not specify fillet, it will be served whole—bones, stones, and eyeballs.

Every respectable restaurant has an admirable wine *carte*, and the offerings will be almost completely French, with few half bottles. Wines by the glass are often swill and best avoided.

Finally, don't ever embarrass yourself by asking for a doggie bag, unless you're willing to risk being considered gauche.

most extensive description of the island before St-Pierre was buried in ash and lava. A major renovation created unique white cottages that house an interactive multimedia exhibit. The front gallery features some of Gauguin's original works. Throughout are exhibits detailing his life on Martinique. Space has also been set aside for temporary exhibitions for Martinican and Caribbean artists like a recent one for Carnival masks. In addition there are painting classes. The entryway displays a large, wooden sculpture by the island's well-known artist, Hector Charpentier. ✉ *Anse-Turin, Carbet* ☎ *0696/80–80–96* 🎫 *€8.50.*

Neisson Distillery

DISTILLERY | The producers of one of the best rums on the island, Neisson is a small, family-run operation. Its rum is distilled from pure sugarcane juice rather than molasses. The distillery is open for tours and tastings, and the shop sells *rhum extra-vieux* (vintage rum) that truly rivals cognac. Neisson is one of the distilleries that consistently brings home the gold (and the silver) from rum competitions in France. A passion for history and tradition characterizes the distillery, as does the design of its bottles. Proud of its independence, at a time when most distilleries are absorbed by large groups, the distillery is now run by the daughter and grandson of Hildevert Pamphille Neisson, who founded the distillery in 1931. ✉ *Domaine Thieubeurt-Bourg, Carbet* ☎ *0596/78–03–70* 🎫 *Free.*

Restaurants

★ Le Petibonum

$$ | **SEAFOOD** | This marriage of French island funkiness and South Beach gloss is one-of-a-kind in Martinique. So is charismatic owner Guy Ferdinand, who has made this a destination restaurant in the north coast's tiny town of Carbet. **Known for:** social scene; chef/owner is a local celebrity; signature jumbo crayfish in a vanilla sauce. $ *Average main: €18* ✉ *Le Coin, Le Bord de Mer, Carbet* ☎ *0596/78–04–34* 🌐 *www.petibonum.com.*

Le Prêcheur

This quaint village, the last on the northern Caribbean coast, is surrounded by volcanic hot springs. It was the childhood home of Françoise d'Aubigné, who later became the Marquise de Maintenon and the second wife of Louis XIV. At her request, the Sun King donated the handsome bronze bell that still hangs outside the church. The Tomb of the Carib Indians commemorates a sadder event: It's a formation of limestone cliffs, from which the last of the Caraïbes are said to have flung themselves to avoid capture by the marquise's forebears.

Sights

Habitation Céron

GARDEN | Once a cacao, sugarcane, and cassava plantation dating back to 1665, today Habitation Céron is a luxuriant garden where you can wander among tropical flowers and a prestigious 350-year-old Zamana tree. The giant tree was once integral to cocoa production; it protected the cocoa from the sun and filtered raindrops through its leaves. Be sure to visit the restaurant and gift shop with locally made dark chocolate. ✉ *Anse Céron, Le Prêcheur* ☎ *0596/48–27–53* 🎫 *€8.*

Activities

BOATING AND SAILING

You can rent Hobie Cats, Sunfish, and Sailfish by the hour from most hotel beach shacks. As for larger craft, bareboat charters (that is, ones with no crew) can be had for $1,900 to $7,000 a week, depending on the season and the size of the craft. The Windward Islands are a joy for experienced sailors, but the channels between islands are often windy and have high waves. You must have a sailing license or be able to prove your nautical prowess, though you can always hire a skipper and crew. Before setting out, you can get itinerary suggestions; the safe ports in Martinique are many. If you charter for a week, you can go south to Saint Lucia or Grenada or north to Dominica, Guadeloupe, and Les Saintes. One-way sailing to St. Martin or Antigua is a popular choice.

TIP→ Don't even consider striking out on the rough Atlantic side of the island unless you're an experienced sailor. The Caribbean side is much calmer—more like a vast lagoon.

Punch Croisières

BOATING | A local, French-owned charter company, Punch Croisières has a fleet of 18 sailboats, 15 of which are catamarans from 38 to 49 feet; three monohulls are 40 to 48 feet. They go out bareboat or crewed, and you can take a boat to a neighboring island. They are comfortably equipped to go down to the Grenadines or just over to Guadeloupe, Saint Lucia, or Dominica. This company has been here since 1995 while other charter operations, from the Moorings to Windward Islands Cruising, have pulled out. The staff is really accommodating and English is spoken. Rentals from a weekend to one week to 11 months are available. ✉ *Marina, Bd. Allègre, Port de Plaisance, Le Marin* ☎ *0596/74–89–18* 🌐 *www.punch-croisieres.com.*

CANOPY TOURS

Mangofil

ZIP LINING | This professionally run zipline park is overseen by the proprietors of a similar park in France. All of the platforms, ladders, and stations were installed by members of a special union in France that specializes in such work. Safety is key here, but there's also a lot of fun; there are upgraded food offerings and a picnic area. **TIP→ It's just a small add-on if a "Big Mango" (adult) comes with a little Parcabout (kid).** ✉ *Forêt Rateau, rte. de Trois-Îlets, near Le Potterie, Les Trois-Îlets* ☎ *0596/68–08–08* 🌐 *www.mangofil.com* 🎫 *From €5 to €40* 🕐 *Closed Mon. and Tues.*

CANYONING

Bureau de la Randonnée et du Canyoning

HIKING & WALKING | Since 1995, the professionals at this company have been leading hikes that take in the island's gorges, canyons, and volcanic landscape. The tours also include some canyoning, which involves climbing up, down, in, and around rocky areas, which are usually near falls or along a stream. For this adrenaline rush, you must be fit and able to hike in the forest for hours. If you are not sure about that, book just the half-day trip, not the full day. These tropical adventures can take you to the Presqu'île du Caravelle, through canals, to Mont Pelée, even to the borders of the craters. Price depends on the destination and the duration. ✉ *Jolimont, Morne Vert* ☎ *0596/55–04–79 canyoning, 0696/24–32–25 hiking* 🌐 *www.bureau-rando-martinique.com.*

DAY SAILS

Kata Mambo

SAILING | The catamaran *Kata Mambo* offers two full-day excursions now. You can sail north to historic St-Pierre and snorkel in clear, Atlantic waters, or you can have a sail coupled with a 4x4 adventure through sugarcane and banana plantations in the south of the island. The full-day trips include rum drinks and a good, multicourse creole lunch. The boat pulls into its slip at the marina at 5 pm. This is a fun day, and you're likely to meet some dolphins. Also, someone in the crew will speak English. This operation has been in the biz since the early 1990s; that longevity attests to its professionalism. ✉ *Pointe du Bout Marina, Les Trois-Îlets* ☎ *0696/25–23–16, 0596/66–11–83* 🌐 *www.kata-mambo.com* 🎟 *From €95.*

La Belle Kréole

BOATING | One of the most popular excursion boats takes you to *les fonds blancs,* also known as Empress Joséphine's baths. (These are natural, shallow pools with white-sand bottoms.) You can experience the unique Martinican custom of "baptism by rum" (tilt your head back while standing in waist-deep water, and one of the crew pours rum into your mouth). The cost of the day trip depends in part on what you choose to have for lunch, which is taken on the remote Îlet Thierry. There's planter's punch and dancing to Martinican music. Yes, it is touristy—you're basically on a booze cruise that lasts from 9 to 5, with lots of loud music—but it's equally popular with locals and families. A two-hour excursion directly to the baths is also available on a smaller boat with capacity for nine guests. ✉ *Baie du Simon, Slip 36, Le François* ☎ *0596/54–95–57, 0595/54–96–46* 🌐 *www.baignoiredejosephine.com* 🎟 *From €65.*

★ **Les Ballades du Delphis**

SAILING | This full-day tour uses one of three commodious catamarans, with two departure points: François Bay and Anse Spoutourne (Tartane). The sail from François takes in the famous fonds blancs and then the Baie du Robert and îlet Chancel to see sea iguanas and ruins. The Tartane route heads to Treasure Bay, one of the most appealing nature preserves on the island. You'll be served planter's punch, accras (fritters), and a creole-style lunch with fish or chicken. A new offering is a day cruise with an overnight at the guesthouse on islet Oscar, a magical setting, with meals included. All of these cruises can be idyllic travel memories, especially when you are sailing from islet to islet, between coral reefs and swimming in shallow pools with white-sand bottoms. The boats are available for private party charters or a romantic couple sail. These comfortable catamarans have a capacity for 23 guests and are even wheelchair accessible. ✉ *Port de Pêche, François, Baie du Simon, Le François* ☎ *0696/90–90–36, 0596/62–20–19* 🌐 *catamaran-martinique.com* 🎟 *From €95.*

Kayaking is a popular activity on Martinique.

DIVING AND SNORKELING

Martinique's underwater world is decorated with multicolor coral, crustaceans, turtles, and seahorses. Expect to pay €50 to €55 for a single dive; a package of three dives is around €120.

GOLF

Golf de l'Impératrice Josephine (*Martinique Golf and Country Club*)

GOLF | Although it's named in honor of Empress Joséphine Bonaparte, this Robert Trent Jones Sr. course is completely American in design, with an English-speaking pro, a pro shop, a bar, and an especially good restaurant. The best hole on the course may just be the par-5 15th. Sandwiched between two good par-3s, the 15th plays to an island fairway and then to a green situated by the shore. Try not to be mesmerized by the turquoise waters. (You can finish your visit here with foie gras torchon or a full meal at Restaurant Le Golf.) The club offers special greens fees to cruise-ship passengers. Club trolleys (called "chariots") are €6 for 18 holes, €4 for 9. There are no caddies. ✉ *Quartier la Pagerie, Les Trois-Îlets* ☎ *0596/52–04–13* 💳 *€15 for 9 holes, €22,50 for 18; carts €25 for 9 holes, €40 for 18* 🏌 *18 holes, 6640 yards, par 71.*

GUIDED TOURS

Your hotel front desk can help arrange a personalized island tour with an English-speaking driver. It's also possible to hire a taxi for the day or half day; there are set rates for certain itineraries, and if you share the ride with others, the per-person price will be whittled down. The Office du Tourisme de Fort-de-France (29 Victor Hugo) also arranges tours, from walking tours of the city (on demand for €15) to bus excursions, and can find you English-speaking guides, too.

HIKING

Parc Naturel Régional de la Martinique

HIKING & WALKING | Two-thirds of Martinique is designated as protected land, and trails—all 31 of them—are well marked and maintained. At the beginning of each, a notice is posted advising on the level of difficulty, the duration of a hike, and any interesting facts. The Parc Naturel Régional de la Martinique organizes inexpensive guided excursions year-round. If there have been heavy rains, though, give it up. The tangle of ferns, bamboo trees, and vines is dramatic, but during the rainy season, the wet, muddy trails will temper your enthusiasm. ✉ *9 bd. Général de Gaulle, Fort-de-France* ☎ *0596/64–45–64.*

HORSEBACK RIDING

Ranch Jack

HORSEBACK RIDING | **FAMILY** | Equipped with a large stable of some 30 horses, Ranch Jack's (English-style) trail rides cross some beautiful country for 90 minutes to two hours. Half-day excursions (inquire about transfers from nearby hotels) go through the fields and forests to the beach. Short rides ranging from an hour are also available. The company has a wonderful program to introduce kids ages three to seven to horses. Online comments reflect riders' satisfaction with the professionalism of the stable and the beautiful acreage they traverse. Their mounts are Creole horses, descended from Spanish horses that have adapted to the tropical climate. ✉ *Morne habitué, Les Trois-Îlets* ☎ *0596/68–37–69, 0696/92–26–58* ✉ *ranch.jack@wanadoo.fr* 🎫 *From €60.*

KAYAKING

It can be great fun to skim the shallow bay while paddling to bird and iguana reserves. Rent colorful fiberglass kayaks to explore the crystalline Havre du Robert, with its clear, shallow pools (called *fonds blancs*), petite beaches, and islets, such as Iguana Island.

Les Kayaks du Robert

KAYAKING | You'll receive one of the island's warmest welcomes at Les Kayaks du Robert. After a memorable paddle through shallow lagoons and mangrove swamps chasing colorful fish, you can enjoy a complimentary glass of juice or planter's punch. An English-speaking guide is available with advance reservation, and reservations are necessary if you are taking a lunch package. If you're going without a guide, ask how to get to various small islets, especially Iguana Island. A waterproof box for your belongings is complimentary; masks and fins are available, and it's a joy to snorkel in the fonds blancs. ✉ *Pointe Savane, Le Robert* ☎ *0696/27–08–68* 🎫 *From €20.*

WINDSURFING

Bliss, École de Surf de Martinique

SURFING | In addition to surfing lessons for adults, adolescents, and kids, this school also rents equipment and offers instruction for bodyboards and stand-up paddling. The multilingual and certified team operates a surf camp and can arrange accommodations in clean, spartan digs for a night or a week or more and can provide airport transfers. Both group and private lessons are available. Online promotions are also offered regularly. ✉ *Anse Bonneville, 28 Rue du Surf, near Résidence Oceane, Tartane* ☎ *0596/58–00–96* 🎫 *From €35.*

Chapter 16

PUERTO RICO

Updated by
Paulina Salach

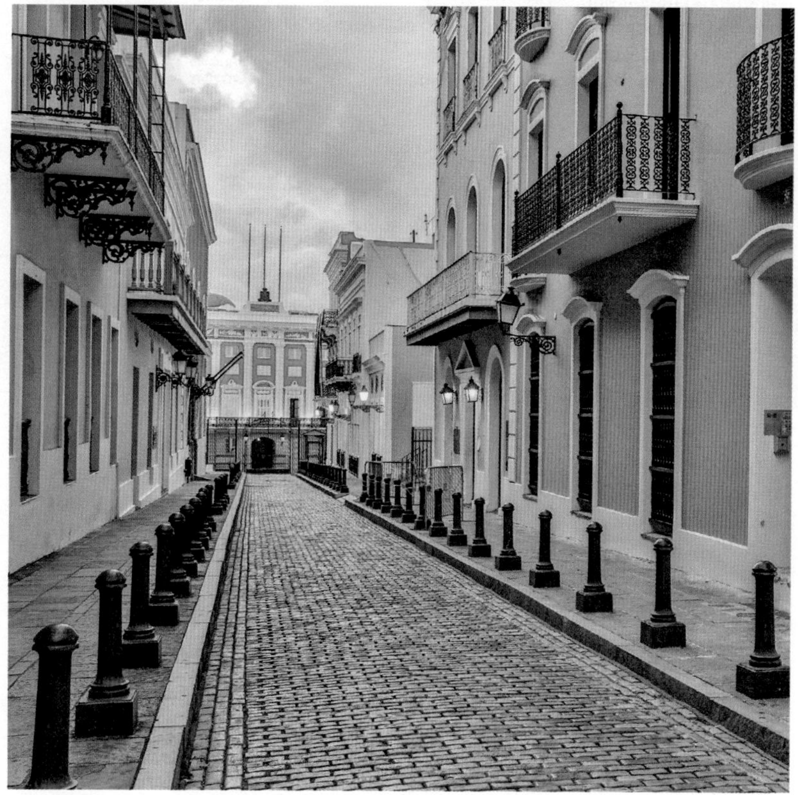

Sights	Restaurants	Hotels	Shopping	Nightlife
★★★★★	★★★★☆	★★★★☆	★★☆☆☆	★★★☆☆

WELCOME TO PUERTO RICO

TOP REASONS TO GO

★ **The Nightlife:** Happening clubs, discos, and cocktail bars make San Juan one of the Caribbean's nightlife capitals, rivaling even Miami.

★ **The Food:** Great restaurants run the gamut from elegant places in San Juan to casual spots serving delicious *comida criolla* (creole food).

★ **The Beaches:** Both developed and wild, beaches here suit the needs of surfers, sunbathers, and families.

★ **The Nature:** Nature abounds, from the underground Río Camuy to El Yunque, the only Caribbean national forest.

★ **The Unexpected:** Puerto Mosquito—kayak after dark on the astounding bioluminescent bay on Vieques Island.

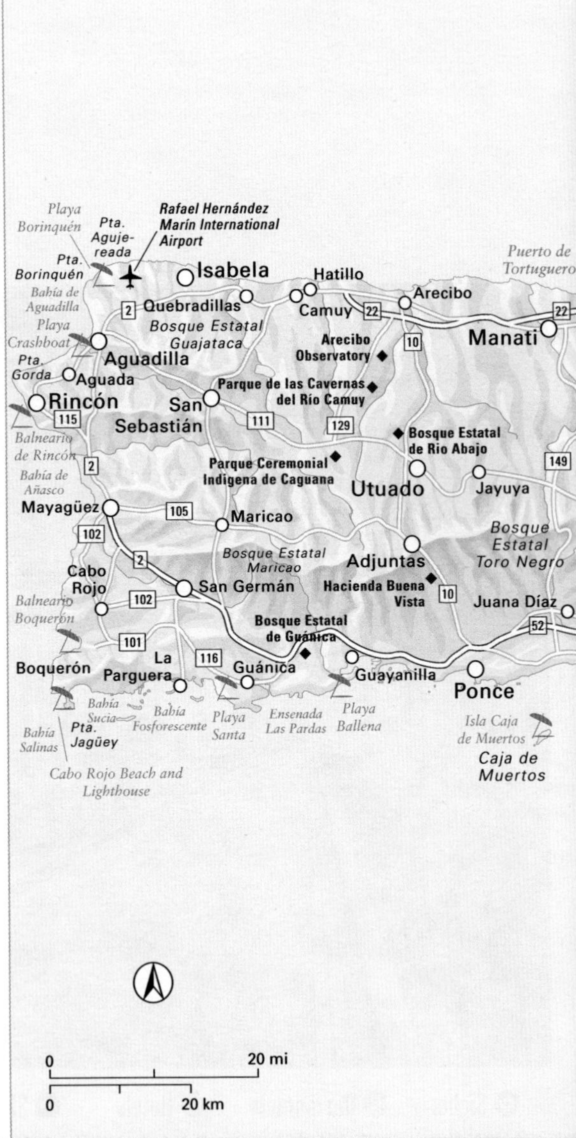

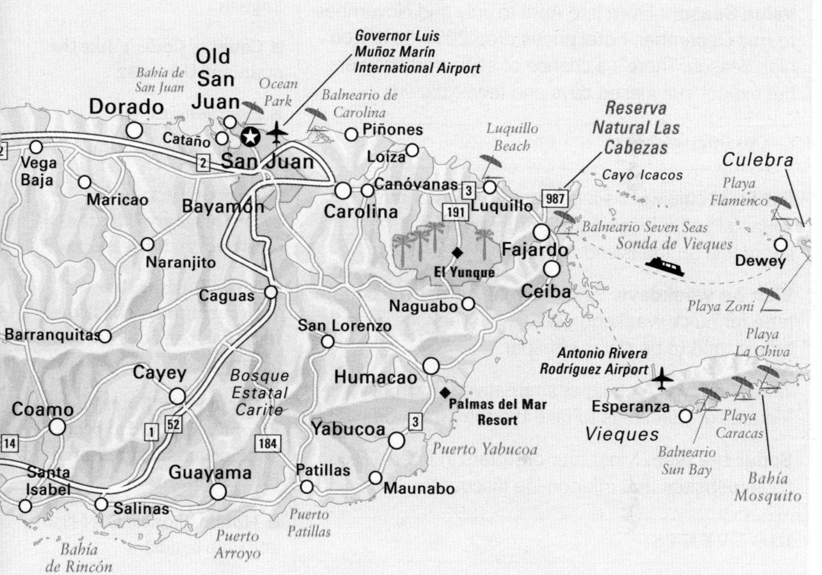
ATLANTIC OCEAN
Governor Luis Muñoz Marín International Airport
Old San Juan
Bahía de San Juan
Ocean Park
Balneario de Carolina
Dorado
Cataño
San Juan
Piñones
Loíza
Vega Baja
Maricao
Bayamón
Canóvanas
Carolina
Luquillo Beach
Luquillo
Reserva Natural Las Cabezas
Cayo Icacos
Culebra
Playa Flamenco
Balneario Seven Seas
Sonda de Vieques
Fajardo
Dewey
El Yunque
Naranjito
Ceiba
Caguas
Naguabo
Playa Zoni
Barranquitas
San Lorenzo
Playa La Chiva
Antonio Rivera Rodríguez Airport
Cayey
Bosque Estatal Carite
Humacao
Palmas del Mar Resort
Esperanza
Vieques
Coamo
Yabucoa
Playa Caracas
Puerto Yabucoa
Balneario Sun Bay
Bahía Mosquito
Santa Isabel
Guayama
Patillas
Maunabo
Salinas
Puerto Patillas
Puerto Arroyo
Bahía de Rincón
Caribbean Sea
2
3
191
987
1
52
14
184

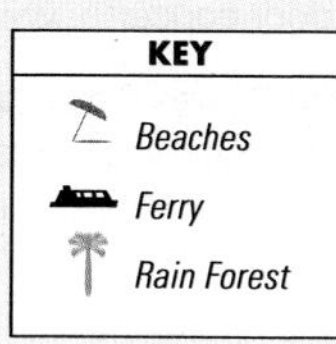
KEY
Beaches
Ferry
Rain Forest

ISLAND SNAPSHOT

WHEN TO GO

High Season: From mid-December through mid-April, the weather is typically sunny and warm. Good hotels are often booked far in advance, everything is open, and prices are highest.

Low Season: From August to late October, temperatures can climb to oppressive heights and the weather grows muggy, with a high risk of tropical storms. Many upscale hotels offer deep discounts.

Value Season: From late April to July and November to mid-December, hotel prices drop 20%–50% from high season. There's a chance of scattered showers, but expect sun-kissed days and fewer crowds.

WAYS TO SAVE

Eat local cuisine. As a general rule, restaurants serving Puerto Rican cuisine tend to be the most affordable on the island.

Visit on weekdays. Since so many Americans come here for quick weekend getaways, weekday prices at hotels tend to be much cheaper.

Take the ferry. A cheaper alternative to flying to Vieques or Culebra is to take the ferry from Ceiba.

Scour the web. Most tour outfitters in Puerto Rico have websites that offer online discounts.

BIG EVENTS

January: The annual Fiestas de la Calle San Sebastián feature four nights of live music as well as food festivals and *cabezudos* parades. www.discoverpuertorico.com

March: The annual Heineken JazzFest attracts some 15,000 aficionados to San Juan for four days of outdoor concerts. www.prheinekenjazz.com

April: Puerto Rico's largest culinary event, Saborea Puerto Rico, is a three-day extravaganza held at Vivo Beach Club in San Juan. www.saboreapuertorico.com

AT A GLANCE

- **Capital:** San Juan
- **Population:** 3,679,086
- **Currency:** U.S. dollar
- **Money:** ATMs common; credit cards widely accepted
- **Language:** Spanish, English
- **Country Code:** "1" like the mainland U.S. + 787
- **Emergencies:** 911
- **Driving:** On the right
- **Electricity:** 120v/60 cycles; plugs are U.S. standard two- and three-prong
- **Time:** Same as New York during daylight savings time; one hour ahead otherwise
- **Documents:** Enter Puerto Rico as you would another state; no passport required for U.S. citizens
- **Mobile Phones:** GSM (850 and 1900 bands)
- **Major Mobile Companies:** AT&T, Claro, Open Mobile, Sprint, T-Mobile US

Sunrise and sunset are both worth waiting for when you're in Puerto Rico. The pinks and yellows that hang in the early-morning sky are just as compelling as the sinewy reds and purples that blend into the twilight. It's easy to compare them, as Puerto Rico is small enough to have breakfast in Fajardo, looking eastward over the boats headed to Vieques and Culebra, and lobster dinner in Rincón as the sun is sinking into the inky-blue water.

Known as the Island of Enchantment, Puerto Rico conjures a powerful spell. Here traffic actually leads you to a "Road to Paradise," whether you're looking for a pleasurable, sunny escape from the confines of urbanity or a rich supply of stimulation to quench your cultural and entertainment thirst. On the island you have the best of both worlds, natural and urban thrills alike, and although city life is frenetic enough to make you forget you're surrounded by azure waters and warm sand, traveling a few miles inland or down the coast can easily make you forget you're surrounded by development.

Puerto Rico was populated primarily by the Taíno people when Columbus landed in 1493. In 1508 Ponce de León established a settlement and became the first governor; in 1521 he founded what is known as Old San Juan. For centuries, while Africans worked in the coastal sugarcane fields, the French, Dutch, and English tried unsuccessfully to wrest the island from Spain. In 1898, as a result of the Spanish-American War, Spain ceded the island to the United States. In 1917 Puerto Ricans became U.S. citizens, and in 1952 Puerto Rico became a semiautonomous commonwealth.

Since the 1950s, Puerto Rico has developed exponentially, as witnessed in the urban sprawl, burgeoning traffic, and growing population (estimated at nearly 4 million); yet *en la isla* (on the island) a strong Latin sense of community and family prevails. Puertorriqueños are fiercely proud of their unique blend of heritages.

Music is another source of Puerto Rican pride. Like wildflowers, *velloneras* (jukeboxes) pop up almost everywhere, and when one is playing, somebody will be either singing or dancing along—or both. Cars often vibrate with *reggaetón,* an aggressive beat with lyrics that express social malaise. Salsa, a fusion of West African percussion, jazz, and other Latin beats, is the trademark dance. You may choose to try it out by doing some clubbing *a la vida loca* made famous by pop star Ricky Martin. Nightlife options are on par with any cosmopolitan city—and then some.

By day you can drink in the culture of the Old World; one of the richest visual experiences in Puerto Rico is Old San Juan. Originally built as a fortress by the Spaniards in the early 1500s, the Old City has myriad attractions that include restored 16th-century buildings and 200-year-old houses on cobblestone streets. Spanish traditions are also apparent in the countryside festivals celebrated in honor of small-town patron saints. For quiet relaxation or experiences off the beaten track, visit coffee plantations, colonial towns, or outlying islets where nightlife is virtually nonexistent.

And you don't come to a Caribbean island without taking in some of the glorious sunshine and natural wonders. In the coastal areas the sun shines, and you're immediately healed by soft waves and cool breezes. In the misty mountains, you can wonder at the flickering night flies and the star-studded sky while the *coquís* (tiny local frogs) chirp their legendary sweet lullaby. On a moonless night, watch the warm ocean turn into luminescent aqua-blue speckles on your skin. Then there are the island's many acres of golf courses, numerous tennis courts, rain forests, and dozens of beaches that offer every imaginable water sport.

Planning

Getting Here and Around

AIR

San Juan's busy Aeropuerto Internacional Luis Muñoz Marín (SJU) receives flights from all major American carriers, and there are dozens of daily flights to Puerto Rico from the United States. Nonstop options fly from cities including Chicago, Dallas, Miami, New York–JFK, Atlanta, Boston, Fort Lauderdale, Hartford, Newark, Orlando, and Tampa, Houston, Philadelphia, Washington, D.C.–Dulles, Charlotte, and more.

SJU is a major regional hub; many travelers make connections here to other islands in the Caribbean. Sometimes known as Isla Grande, San Juan's other airport, the Aeropuerto Fernando L. Ribas Dominicci (SIG), is in Miramar near the Convention Center. It handles mainly short hops to Vieques and other nearby islands, though both airports offer flights to Culebra, Vieques, and other destinations on Puerto Rico and throughout the Caribbean. Air Flamenco and Vieques Air Link offer daily flights from SJU and SIG to Vieques and Culebra. Cape Air flies from SJU to Vieques and Culebra.

AIRPORTS Aeropuerto Internacional Luis Muñoz Marín. *(SJU)* ✉ *Carolina* ☎ *787/253–2329* 🌐 *www.aeropuertosju.com.* **Aeropuerto Fernando L. Ribas Dominicci.** *(SIG)* ✉ *Calle Lindbergh, San Juan* ☎ *787/729–8715.*

CAR

In San Juan it's often more trouble than it's worth to rent a car. Elsewhere a car is probably a necessity. A valid driver's license from your country of origin can be used in Puerto Rico for three months. Rates start as low as $25 a day. Several well-marked multilane highways link population centers. Driving distances are posted in kilometers, but speed limits are posted in miles per hour. Road signs are in Spanish.

LOCAL AGENCIES Charlie Car Rental. ✉ *6050 Isla Verde Ave., Carolina* ☎ *787/728–2418* 🌐 *www.charliecars.com.* **Vias.** ✉ *Hotel Villa del Sol, 4 Rosa St., Isla Verde* ☎ *787/791–4120* 🌐 *www.viascarrental.com.*

FERRY

Ferries all depart from Ceiba, about 90 minutes by car west of San Juan. Some of these ferries carry cars, but rental agencies won't let you take their vehicles between the mainland and islands. A municipal parking lot next to the ferry costs $5–$7 per day. Fares are cheap: $2 per person from Fajardo to Vieques, $2.25 to Cuelbra; there are discounts for children and seniors, and passengers over 75 are free. They are also faster than they used to be, with travel to Vieques taking only 30 minutes, Culebra 45 minutes on the fast ferries. No ferries link Vieques and Culebra at present. There's limited seating, so arrive at least an hour ahead of the departure time (more on busy weekends, particularly for the early morning departures and mid-afternoon returns). You cannot reserve or pay for the ferries online; everything must be done in person.

CONTACTS Ceiba Ferry Terminal. ✉ *Roosevelt Roads, 69HJ+XM4, Marina Dr., Ceiba* ☎ *787/497–7740* 🌐 *www.puertoricoferry.com.*

TAXI

Taxis turísticos—painted white, with the garita (sentry box) logo—run from the airport and cruise-ship piers to Isla Verde, Condado, Ocean Park, and Old San Juan. They charge set rates based on zones (usually $10–$20); make sure to agree on a price before you get inside. City tours start at $36 per hour.

Although you can hail cabs on the street, virtually every San Juan hotel has taxis waiting outside to transport guests; if none are available, have one called. (Once called, taxis may charge an extra $1 for the pickup.)

Uber, the popular ride-sharing company, has entered the Puerto Rico market and operates in the San Juan metro area. Fares are generally lower than those of traditional taxis, and cars are readily available. Uber is not allowed to pick up at the airport, but it can drop you off.

CONTACTS Go Puerto Rico Shuttle. ✉ *Calle Sirio, Urb Los Angeles #80, Isla Verde* ☎ *787/400–2100* 🌐 *www.puertoricoshuttle.com.* **Metro Taxi.** ✉ *959 Calle Suau, Miramar* ☎ *787/945-5555.*

Beaches

In Puerto Rico the Foundation for Environmental Education, a nonprofit agency, designates Blue Flag beaches. They have to meet 27 criteria, focusing on water quality, the presence of trained staff, and the availability of facilities such as water fountains and restrooms. Surprisingly, two such beaches are in San Juan: Balneario El Escambrón, in Puerta de Tierra, and Balneario de Carolina, in Isla Verde. The government maintains 13 (public beaches), which are gated and equipped with dressing rooms, lifeguards, parking, and, in some cases, picnic tables, playgrounds, and camping facilities.

Dining

In cosmopolitan San Juan, European, Asian, Middle Eastern, and chic fusion eateries vie for attention with family-owned restaurants specializing in seafood or (creole cooking). Many of the most innovative chefs here have restaurants in the city's large hotels, but don't be shy about venturing into stand-alone establishments—traditionally concentrated in Condado and Old San Juan. The historic center is also home to new restaurants and cafés offering artisanal cuisine—crop-to-cup coffee, rustic homemade pizzas, and creative vegetarian food—at affordable prices. But as the San Juan metro area develops, great restaurants are popping up in other parts of the city, including Santurce, Miramar, and Ocean Park. Throughout the island, there's a radiant pride in what the local land can provide, and enthusiastic restaurateurs are redefining what Puerto Rican food is, bite by tasty bite.

What to Wear: Dress codes vary greatly, though a restaurant's prices are a fairly good indicator of its formality. For less expensive places, anything but beachwear is fine. When in doubt, do as the Puerto Ricans often do and dress up.

Health and Safety

Dengue, chikungunya, and zika have all been reported in the Caribbean. We recommend that you protect yourself from these mosquito-borne illnesses by keeping your skin covered and/or wearing mosquito repellent. The mosquitoes that transmit these viruses are as active by day as they are by night.

Lodging

If you want easy access to shopping, dining, and nightlife, then you should stay in San Juan, which also has decent—though by no means the island's best—beaches. Most other large, deluxe resorts are along the northeast coast, but there are a few along the southern coast. Rincón, in the west, has a concentration of resorts and great surfing. Other small inns and hotels are in the interior, including a few around El Yunque. Look to Vieques and Culebra if you want to find excellent beaches and little development. Many larger resorts in Puerto Rico charge resort fees, which are uncommon elsewhere in the Caribbean.

In San Juan, the best beaches are in Isla Verde, though Condado is more centrally located. Old San Juan offers easy access to dining and nightlife. Outside San Juan, particularly on the east coast, you can find self-contained luxury resorts that cover hundreds of acres. Around the island, government-sponsored paradores are rural inns, others offer no-frills apartments, and some are large hotels close to either an attraction or beach.

Big Hotels: San Juan's beaches are lined with large-scale hotels that include happening restaurants and splashy casinos. Most are spread out along Condado and Isla Verde beaches.

Paradores: Small inns (many offering homestyle cooking) are spread around the island, though they are rarely on the beach.

Upscale Beach Resorts: All over the island—but particularly along the north coast—large tourist resorts offer all the amenities along with a hefty dose of isolation. Just be prepared for expensive food and few off-resort restaurants nearby.

Restaurant and hotel reviews have been shortened. For full information, visit Fodors.com.

What It Costs in U.S. Dollars

	$	$$	$$$	$$$$
RESTAURANTS				
	under $12	$12–$20	$21–$30	over $30
HOTELS				
	under $275	$275–$375	$376–$475	over $475

Nightlife

Wherever you go, dress to impress. Puerto Ricans have flair, and both men and women love getting dressed up to go out. Bars are usually casual, but if you have on jeans, sneakers, and a T-shirt, you may be refused entry at swankier nightclubs and discos.

In Old San Juan, Calle San Sebastián is lined with bars and restaurants. Evenings begin with dinner and stretch into the wee hours (often until 3 or 4) at bars at the more upscale SoFo (south of Fortaleza) end. An eclectic crowd heads to the Plaza del Mercado in Santurce after work to hang out in the plaza or enjoy drinks and food in one of the small establishments skirting the farmers' market. Condado and Ocean Park have their share of nightlife, too. Most are restaurant-and-bar environments.

Just east of San Juan along Route 187, funky Piñones has a collection of open-air seaside eateries that are popular with locals. On weekend evenings many places have merengue combos, Brazilian jazz trios, or reggae bands. In Ponce, people embrace the Spanish tradition of the paseo, an evening stroll around the Plaza de las Delicias, and the boardwalk at La Guancha is also a lively scene. Live bands often play on weekends. Elsewhere *en la isla,* nighttime activities center on the hotels and resorts. *Qué Pasa,* the official visitor's guide, has listings of events in San Juan and out on the island. The local blog puertoricodaytrips.com is another great source for event listings.

Shopping

San Juan has the island's best range of stores (many closed on Sunday), but it isn't a free port, so you won't find bargains on electronics and perfumes. You can, however, find excellent prices on china, crystal, clothing, and jewelry. When shopping for local crafts, you'll find tacky along with treasures; in many cases you can watch the artisans at work. Popular items include (small carved figures of saints or religious scenes), hand-rolled cigars, handmade lace from Moca, (colorful masks used during Carnival and local festivals) from Loíza and Ponce, and fancy men's shirts called guayaberas.

Old San Juan—especially Calles Fortaleza and Cristo—has T-shirt emporiums, crafts stores, bookshops, art galleries, jewelry boutiques, and even shops that specialize in made-to-order Panama hats. Calle Cristo has factory outlets, including Coach and Dooney & Bourke.

With many stores selling luxury items and designer fashions, the shopping spirit in the San Juan neighborhood of Condado is reminiscent of Miami. Avenida Ashford, the heart of San Juan's fashion district, has plenty of high-end clothing stores.

Visitor Information

Puerto Rico Tourism Company. ☎ *787/721–2400, 800/866–7827* 🌐 *www.discoverpuertorico.com.*

San Juan

Old San Juan

Old San Juan, the original city founded in 1521, contains carefully preserved examples of 16th- and 17th-century Spanish colonial architecture. More than 400 buildings have been beautifully restored. Graceful wrought-iron and wooden balconies with lush hanging plants extend over narrow streets paved with *adoquines* (blue-gray stones originally used as ballast on Spanish ships). The Old City is partially enclosed by walls that date from 1633 and once completely surrounded it. Designated a U.S. National Historic Zone in 1950, Old San Juan is chockablock with shops, open-air cafés, colorful homes, tree-shaded squares, monuments, and people. You can get an overview on a morning's stroll, which includes some steep climbs. However, if you plan to immerse yourself in history or to shop, you'll need a couple of days.

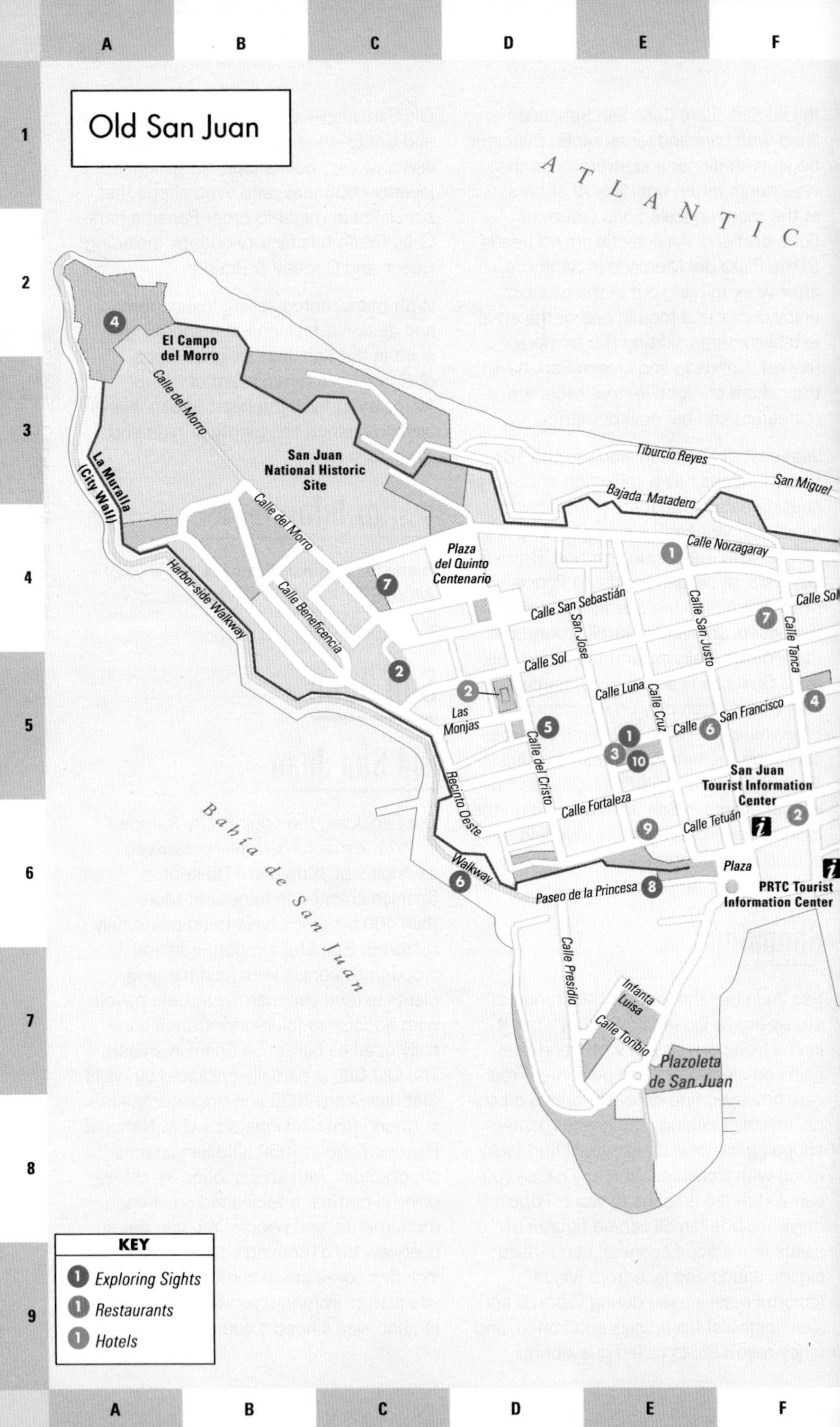

A
B
C
D
E
F
1
2
3
4
5
6
7
8
9
Old San Juan
ATLANTIC
El Campo del Morro
Calle del Morro
La Muralla (City Wall)
San Juan National Historic Site
Tiburcio Reyes
San Miguel
Bajada Matadero
Calle Norzagaray
Calle del Morro
Harbor-side Walkway
Plaza del Quinto Centenario
Calle Beneficencia
Calle San Sebastián
San Jose
Calle San Justo
Calle Sol
Calle Tanca
Calle Sol
Calle Luna
Calle Cruz
Las Monjas
Calle San Francisco
Calle del Cristo
San Juan Tourist Information Center
Recinto Oeste
Calle Fortaleza
Calle Tetuán
Bahía de San Juan
Walkway
Paseo de la Princesa
Plaza
PRTC Tourist Information Center
Calle Presidio
Infanta Luisa
Calle Toribio
Plazoleta de San Juan
KEY
Exploring Sights
Restaurants
Hotels

Sights

1 Casa Alcaldía de San Juan E5
2 Casa Blanca C5
3 Castillo San Cristóbal I4
4 Castillo San Felipe del Morro A2
5 Catedral de San Juan Bautista D5
6 La Fortaleza D6
7 Museo de las Américas C4
8 Paseo de la Princesa E6
9 Plaza Colón G5
10 Plaza de Armas E5

Restaurants

1 Café Berlin G4
2 Café Cuatro Sombras ... F6
3 Café 4 Estaciones E5
4 Cafeteria Mallorca F5
5 Caficultura G4
6 Casa Cortés ChocoBar E5
7 El Jibarito F4
8 Marmalade G5
9 Señor Paleta E6

Hotels

1 The Gallery Inn E4
2 Hotel El Convento D5

Casa Alcaldía de San Juan

(*San Juan City Hall*)

GOVERNMENT BUILDING | San Juan's city hall was built between 1602 and 1789. In 1841, extensive alterations made it resemble Madrid's city hall, with arcades, towers, balconies, and an inner courtyard. Renovations have refreshed the facade and some interior rooms, but the architecture remains true to its colonial style. Only the patios are open to public viewings. A municipal tourist information center and an art gallery with rotating exhibits are in the lobby. Call ahead to schedule a free tour. ✉ *153 Calle San Francisco, Plaza de Armas, Old San Juan* ☎ *787/480–2910* 🌐 *www.sanjuanciudadpatria.com* 🎫 *Free* ⏲ *Closed weekends.*

Casa Blanca

HISTORIC HOME | The original structure here was a wooden house built in 1521 as a home for Ponce de León; he died in Cuba without ever living here. His descendants occupied the house's sturdier replacement, a lovely colonial mansion with tile floors and beamed ceilings, for more than 250 years. It was the home of the U.S. Army commander in Puerto Rico from the end of the Spanish-American War in 1898 to 1966. Several rooms decorated with colonial-era furnishings are open to the public. The lush garden, complete with watchtower, is a quiet place to unwind. ✉ *1 Calle San Sebastián, Old San Juan* ☎ *787/725–1454* 🎫 *$3* ⏲ *Closed Mon. and Tues.*

★ Castillo San Cristóbal

MILITARY SIGHT | **FAMILY** | This huge stone fortress, built between 1634 and 1783, guarded the city from land attacks from the east. The largest Spanish fortification in the New World, San Cristóbal was known in the 17th and 18th centuries as "the Gibraltar of the West Indies." Five freestanding structures divided by dry moats are connected by tunnels. You're free to explore the gun turrets (with cannon in situ), officers' quarters, re-created 18th-century barracks, and gloomy passageways. Along with El Morro, San Cristóbal is a National Historic Site administered by the U.S. National Park Service; it's a UNESCO World Heritage Site as well. Rangers conduct tours in Spanish and English. ✉ *Calle Norzagaray at Av. Muñoz Rivera, Old San Juan* ☎ *787/729–6777* 🌐 *www.nps.gov/saju* 🎫 *$10, includes Castillo San Felipe del Morro.*

★ Castillo San Felipe del Morro (*El Morro*)

MILITARY SIGHT | **FAMILY** | At the northwestern tip of Old San Juan, El Morro (the promontory) was built by the Spaniards between 1539 and 1790. Rising 140 feet above the sea, the massive six-level fortress was built to protect the port and has a commanding view of the harbor. It is a labyrinth of cannon batteries, ramps, barracks, turrets, towers, and tunnels, through which you're free to wander. The cannon emplacement walls and the dank secret passageways are a wonder of engineering. A small but enlightening museum displays ancient Spanish guns and other armaments, military uniforms, and blueprints for Spanish forts in the Americas, although Castillo San Cristóbal has more extensive and impressive exhibits. There's also a gift shop. The fort is a National Historic Site administered by the U.S. National Park Service, and a UNESCO World Heritage Site as well. Various tours and a video are available in English. ✉ *Calle del Morro, Old San Juan* ☎ *787/729–6960* 🌐 *www.nps.gov/saju* 🎫 *$10, includes Castillo San Cristóbal.*

Catedral de San Juan Bautista

CHURCH | The Catholic shrine of Puerto Rico had humble beginnings in the early 1520s as a thatch-roofed wooden structure. After a hurricane destroyed the church, it was rebuilt in 1540, when it was given a graceful circular staircase and vaulted Gothic ceilings. Most of the work on the present cathedral, however, was done in the 19th century. The remains of Ponce de León are behind a marble tomb in the wall near the transept, on the north side. The trompe-l'oeil work on the inside of the dome is breathtaking. Unfortunately, many of the other frescoes have suffered water damage. ✉ *151 Calle Cristo, Old San Juan* ☎ *787/722–0861* 🎫 *$1 suggested donation.*

La Fortaleza

GOVERNMENT BUILDING | Sitting atop the fortified city walls overlooking the harbor, La Fortaleza was built between 1533 and 1540 as a fortress, but it proved insufficient, mainly because it was built inside the bay. It was attacked numerous times and occupied twice, by the British in 1598 and the Dutch in 1625. When the city's other fortifications were finished, this became the governor's palace. Changes made over the past four centuries have resulted in the current eclectic yet eye-pleasing collection of marble and mahogany, medieval towers, and stained-glass galleries. It is still the official residence of the island's governor, making it the western hemisphere's oldest executive mansion in continuous use. Guided tours of the gardens and exterior are conducted several times a day in English and Spanish; call ahead, as the schedule changes daily. Proper attire is required: no sleeveless shirts or very short shorts. Tours begin near the main gate in a yellow building called the Real Audiencia, housing the Oficina Estatal de Conservación Histórica (State Historic Preservation Office). ✉ *West end of Calle Fortaleza, Old San Juan* ☎ *787/721–7000* 🌐 *www.fortaleza.pr.gov* 🎫 *Free* 🕑 *Closed weekends.*

Museo de las Américas

ART MUSEUM | On the second floor of the imposing former military barracks, Cuartel de Ballajá, this museum houses four permanent exhibits covering folk art, African and Native American heritage, and colonization. You'll also find temporary exhibitions of works by regional and international artists. A wide range of handicrafts is available in the gift shop. Before visting, it's best to check the website for current hours. ✉ *Calle Norzagaray and Calle del Morro, Old San Juan* ☎ *787/724–5052* 🌐 *www.museolasamericas.org* 🎫 *$6* 🕑 *Closed Mon.–Tues.*

Paseo de la Princesa

PROMENADE | Built in the mid-19th century to honor the Spanish princess of Asturias, this street has a broad pedestrian walkway and is spruced up with flowers, trees, benches, and streetlamps. Unfurling westward from Plaza del Inmigrante along the base of the fortified city walls, it leads to the Fuente Raíces, a striking fountain depicting the various ethnic groups of Puerto Rico. Take a seat, and watch boats zip across the water. Beyond the fountain is the beginning of Paseo del Morro, a well-paved shoreline path that hugs Old San Juan's walls, leading past the city gate at Calle San Juan and continuing to the tip of the headland, beneath El Morro. ✉ *Paseo de la Princesa, Old San Juan.*

Plaza Colón

PLAZA/SQUARE | A statue of Christopher Columbus stands atop a soaring column and fountain in this bustling Old San Juan square, catercorner to Castillo San Cristóbal. Once called St. James Square, it was renamed in 1893 to honor the 400th anniversary of Columbus's arrival in Puerto Rico; bronze plaques on the statue's base relate episodes in his life. Local artisans often line the plaza, so it's a good place to hunt for souvenirs. Cool off with a fresh fruit frappé or smoothie at the kiosk. ✉ *Old San Juan.*

Plaza de Armas

PLAZA/SQUARE | The Old City's original main square was once used as military drilling grounds. Bordered by Calles San Francisco, Rafael Cordero, San José, and Cruz, it has a fountain with 19th-century statues representing the four seasons as well as a bandstand, a small café, and a kiosk selling snacks and fruit frappés. The

Hear your footsteps echo throughout Castillo San Felipe's vast network of tunnels, designed to amplify the sounds of approaching enemies.

Alcaldía commands the north side. This is a popular, bustling meeting place, often filled with artists sketching caricatures, pedestrians in line at the food stands, and hundreds of pigeons waiting for handouts. ✉ *Calle San José, Old San Juan.*

Restaurants

Café Berlin

$$ | **INTERNATIONAL** | **FAMILY** | A handful of tables spill onto a sidewalk deck adorned with tiny lights at this romantic, bohemian restaurant overlooking Plaza Colón. There's something on the international menu for everyone, including a good selection of vegan and vegetarian dishes. **Known for:** street-side dining; breakfast; variety of vegan and vegetarian choices. *$ Average main: $19 ✉ 407 Calle San Francisco, Old San Juan ☎ 787/722–5205 🌐 www.cafeberlinpr.com.*

★ Café Cuatro Sombras

$ | **CAFÉ** | **FAMILY** | If you want to try local, single-origin, shade-grown coffee, this micro-roastery and café is the place to do it. Owners Pablo Muñoz and Mariana Suárez grow their beans in the mountains of Yauco on a hacienda that has been in the Muñoz family since 1846. **Known for:** coffee tastings; locally grown coffee; pastries and sandwiches. *$ Average main: $7 ✉ 259 Calle Recinto Sur, Old San Juan ☎ 787/724–9955 🌐 www.cuatrosombras.com ⏲ No dinner.*

Café 4 Estaciones

$ | **CAFÉ** | At this tiny kiosk, the tables and chairs under a canvas canopy that's surrounded by potted plants invite you to put down your shopping bags and rest your tired feet. Grab a *café con leche* (coffee with hot milk), an espresso, or cold drink, and watch the children chase the pigeons. **Known for:** quesitos; café con leche; mallorcas. *$ Average main: $2 ✉ Plaza de Armas, Old San Juan 💳 No credit cards.*

Cafetería Mallorca

$ | **CAFÉ** | **FAMILY** | The specialty at this old-fashioned, 1950s-style diner is the *mallorca*, a sweet pastry that's buttered, grilled, and then sprinkled with powdered sugar. Wash one down with a cup of café con leche. **Known for:** café con leche; old-school diner feel; mallorcas. *Average main: $10 ✉ 300 Calle San Francisco, Old San Juan ☎ 787/724–4607 ⌚ No dinner.*

Caficultura

$$ | **CAFÉ** | Caficultura prides itself on its full coffee-bar, its mimosas made with fresh juice, and its all-day breakfast and brunch menu (try the coconut-milk French toast with pineapple jam and coconut shavings). Numerous vegetarian options are available, especially at lunch, when you'll also find many delicious gourmet sandwiches and heartier dishes. **Known for:** outside seating; all-day breakfast; beautifully presented lattes. *Average main: $15 ✉ 401 Calle San Francisco, Old San Juan ☎ 787/723–7731 ⌚ No dinner.*

★ **Casa Cortés ChocoBar**

$$ | **CONTEMPORARY** | The Cortés family has been making bean-to-bar chocolate for more than 90 years, and, in 2013, they opened Puerto Rico's first "chocobar" to share their passion. The walls in this vivid, modern space are decorated with ads from the 1950s, original chocolate-bar molds, a timeline of chocolate, and two flat screens showing the chocolate-making process. **Known for:** locally made chocolates; chocolate incorporated into many dishes; breakfast specialties and pastries. *Average main: $12 ✉ 210 Calle San Francisco, Old San Juan ☎ 787/722–0499 🌐 www.casacortespr.com ⌚ No dinner weekdays.*

El Jibarito

$$ | **PUERTO RICAN** | **FAMILY** | The menus are handwritten, and the tables wobble, but locals in the know have favored this no-frills, family-run restaurant—tucked away on a quiet cobblestone street—for years. The *bistec encebollado,* goat fricassee, and shredded beef stew stand out on the comida criolla menu. **Known for:** gentle prices; traditional Puerto Rican comfort food; casual atmosphere. *Average main: $14 ✉ 280 Calle Sol, Old San Juan ☎ 787/725–8375.*

★ **Marmalade**

$$$$ | **ECLECTIC** | Peter Schintler, the U.S.-born owner-chef of Old San Juan's hippest—and finest—restaurant, apprenticed with Raymond Blanc and Gordon Ramsay. His dishes incorporate local and organic ingredients, and his cuisine is influenced by both California and French styles of cooking, resulting in complex flavors and strong aromas. **Known for:** excellent wine list; varying prix-fixe menus; exceptional service. *Average main: $32 ✉ 317 Calle Fortaleza, Old San Juan ☎ 787/724–3969 🌐 www.marmaladepr.com ⌚ Closed Sun.*

★ **Señor Paleta**

$ | **CAFÉ** | **FAMILY** | There's nothing more refreshing on a hot day than an ice pop from Señor Paleta. All the ingredients used to make these artisanal *paletas* are fresh, and many use local fruits. **Known for:** fruity ice pops on a stick; long waits on weekends; ice cream. *Average main: $4 ✉ 153 Calle Tetuan, Old San Juan ☎ 787/724–2337.*

Hotels

The Gallery Inn

$ | **B&B/INN** | No two rooms in this 200-year-old mansion are alike, but all have four-poster beds, handwoven tapestries, and quirky antiques; indeed, every nook and cranny here is adorned with owner Jan D'Esopo's paintings, bronze sculptures, ceramic busts, and plaques. **Pros:** wonderful classical music concerts; one-of-a-kind lodging; ocean views. **Cons:** sometimes-raucous pet macaws and cockatoos; an uphill walk from the rest of Old San Juan; several narrow, winding staircases. *Rooms from: $150 ✉ 204–206 Calle Norzagaray, Old San Juan ☎ 787/722–1808 🌐 www.thegallery-inn.com 25 rooms Free Breakfast.*

Hotel El Convento is a 350-year-old former convent in Old San Juan.

★ Hotel El Convento

$ | HOTEL | There's no longer anything austere about this 350-year-old former convent: all the guest rooms are lavish and inviting, with wrought-iron and hand-hewn wood furniture, shuttered windows, and mahogany-beamed ceilings joining high-tech amenities like Wi-Fi and flat-screen TVs. **Pros:** plenty of nearby dining options; lovely historic building; atmosphere to spare. **Cons:** small bathrooms; small pool; near some noisy bars. *Rooms from: $200* ✉ *100 Calle Cristo, Old San Juan* ☎ *787/723–9020* 🌐 *www.elconvento.com* *58 rooms* *No Meals.*

Nightlife

BARS AND CLUBS

El Batey

BARS | This legendary dive bar won't win any prizes for decor, but it has an irresistibly artsy and welcoming vibe. Add your own message to the graffiti-covered walls—they have a "B.Y.O.S." policy (Bring Your Own Sharpie)—or hang your business card alongside the hundreds that cover the light fixtures. The jukebox has the best selection of oldies in town, and locals crowd the back room for billiards. ✉ *101 Calle Cristo, Old San Juan* ☎ *No phone* 🌐 *www.elbateytavernpr.com.*

★ La Factoría

BARS | La Factoría, the former Hijos de Borinquen, is hands-down the best cocktail bar in San Juan. Here, artisanal drinks are crafted with the highest-quality ingredients. Many bitters are homemade, as is the ginger beer, which is used in the popular Lavender Mule. Whether it's sweet, spicy, bitter, or something completely out of the box, these drinks will blow your mind. Behind the bar, there is a secret wooden door that leads to Vino Wine Bar, which has a great speakeasy feel. Tasty tapas are available and can be enjoyed in the adjacent room. These bars stay open till sunup, and a DJ spins in the back room on weekends. Salsa is played on Sunday and Monday. There's no sign on the door, so just look for the terra-cotta building at the corner of San Sebastián and San José. ✉ *148 Calle San Sebastián, Old San Juan* ☎ *787/594–5698.*

La Taberna Lúpulo

BARS | If you love beer, don't leave Puerto Rico without visiting Lúpulo. At the island's largest craft beer bar you'll find over 25 varieties on tap and more than 100 bottles of the finest European and American brews. This casual hipster bar is open late and a great option for night bites. ✉ *151 Calle San Sebastián, Old San Juan* ☎ *787/721–3772.*

The Mezzanine

BARS | Set in the former headquarters of the Nationalist Party, this contemporary take on a 1920s speakeasy is a chic space that's conducive to sipping a creative cocktail. Tapas are served all day, making this an even more refreshing stop after walking the hills of Old San Juan. Although the Mezzanine is typically closed on Monday, from Tuesday to Friday it hosts one of the best happy hours in town, with half-price select tapas and cocktails. You can't beat that in San Juan! Weekend brunch is also very popular. ✉ *St. Germain Bistro & Café, 156 Calle Sol, 2nd fl., Old San Juan* ☎ *787/724–4657* ⏲ *Closed Mon.*

Shopping

ART GALLERIES

Galería Botello

ART GALLERIES | This influential gallery displays art by the late Angel Botello, who was hailed as the Caribbean Gauguin as far back as 1943. (His works also hang in the Museo de Arte de Puerto Rico.) His paintings often feature the bright colors of the tropics and usually depict island scenes. Also on display here are works by other prominent local artists, Puerto Rican santos, and sculptures by Botello. ✉ *208 Calle Cristo, Old San Juan* ☎ *787/723–9987* 🌐 *www.botello.com* ⏲ *Closed Sun.*

CIGARS

Cigar House

TOBACCO | The Cigar House has an eclectic selection of local and imported cigars from Nicaragua, Honduras, and the Dominican Republic. At the lounge and bar, you can enjoy your purchase with a glass of your favorite spirit. ✉ *257 Calle Fortaleza, Old San Juan* ☎ *787/723–5223* 🌐 *www.facebook.com/thecigarhouse.*

CLOTHING

Cappalli

WOMEN'S CLOTHING | Noted local designer Lisa Cappalli sells her feminine, sensuous designs in this elegant boutique, which specializes in ready-to-wear and custom fashions including a small collection of whimsical, lacy wedding gowns. ✉ *206 Calle O'Donnell, Old San Juan* ☎ *787/289–6565* 🌐 *www.lisacappalli.com.*

GIFTS

Eclectika

SOUVENIRS | Here the inventory, most of it Indonesian, ranges from bedspreads and furnishings to beaded jewelry and hand fans. ✉ *204 Calle O'Donnell, Plaza Colón, Old San Juan* ☎ *787/721–7236.*

Haitian Gallery

CRAFTS | This shop carries Haitian masks, statues, paintings, and wooden works of art. The second floor houses a large selection of paintings from the Caribbean. ✉ *367 Calle Fortaleza, Old San Juan* ☎ *787/725–0986.*

Spicy Caribbee

SOUVENIRS | Kitchen items, cookbooks, jams, spices, and sauces from around the Caribbean are on offer. ✉ *154 Calle Cristo, Old San Juan* ☎ *888/725–7259* 🌐 *www.spicycaribbee.com.*

JEWELRY

Catalá Joyeros

JEWELRY & WATCHES | Family-run since the 1930s, this store is known for its large selection of pearls and precious stones, as well as for its jewelry design. ✉ *Plaza de Armas, 152 Calle Rafael Cordero,*

Old San Juan ☎ *787/722–3231* 🌐 *www.catalajoyeros.com.*

SOUVENIRS

Mi Pequeño San Juan

CRAFTS | You might find a reproduction of your hotel at this shop, which specializes in tiny ceramic versions of San Juan doorways. The works are created by hand in the shop, which also carries fine art prints. ✉ *152 Calle Fortaleza, Old San Juan* ☎ *787/721–5040.*

Puerto de Tierra

Just east of the Old City, Puerta de Tierra is home to a few notable hotels, a nice public beach, several parks, and some high-end furniture stores.

Sights

El Capitolio

GOVERNMENT BUILDING | The white-marble Capitol, a fine example of Italian Renaissance style, dates from 1929. The grand rotunda, which can be seen from all over San Juan, was completed in the late 1990s. Fronted by eight Corinthian columns, it's a dignified home for the Commonwealth's constitution. Although the Senate and House of Representatives have offices in the more modern buildings on either side, the Capitol is where the legislators meet. Guided tours, which last about an hour and include the rotunda, are by appointment only. ✉ *Av. Constitución, Puerta de Tierra* ☎ *787/724–2030, 787/721–5200 for guided tours* 🎟 *Free* ⏲ *Closed weekends.*

Activities

BIKING

Only some areas lend themselves to bike travel. Avoid main thoroughfares, as the traffic is heavy and bike lanes are scarce. The Paseo Piñones is an 11-mile (18-km) bike path that skirts the ocean east of San Juan. The entire southwest coast of Cabo Rojo also makes for good biking, particularly the broad beach at Boquerón. Parts of Route 466, in Isabela, that are still free from development, make for gorgeous rides with breathtaking views of the ocean.

Rent the Bicycle

BIKING | For about $40 per day, this friendly operation offers bicycle rental with free delivery to all major San Juan hotels. They also offer guided tours of Old San Juan and greater San Juan beaches and parks. The bilingual guides are authorized by the National Park Service to give tours of the forts. ✉ *Capitolio Plaza, 100 Calle del Muelle, Suite 205, Old San Juan* ☎ *787/661–2728* 🌐 *www.rentthebicycle.com.*

Condado

For multiple dining options within walking distance of one another, look to Condado. Home to many of the city's moneyed elite, it's the most vibrant pedestrian neighborhood outside of Old San Juan. Here you'll find old Spanish-style homes next to sleek, modern apartment buildings and beachfront hotels (although the beach isn't as big or alluring as those in Isla Verde). The main street, Avenida Ashford, is fun to stroll, but quieter residential areas are also very attractive.

Sights

CASINOS

Stellaris Casino

CASINO | The crowd is casual and the decor tropical and bubbly at this spacious gaming room. Right outside, there's a huge bar where Latin musicians perform on weekends, and an adjacent café. ✉ *San Juan Marriott Resort, 1309 Av. Ashford, Condado* ☎ *787/722–7000.*

Beaches

Condado Beach

BEACH | **FAMILY** | East of Old San Juan and west of Ocean Park, this long, wide beach is overshadowed by an unbroken string of hotels and apartment buildings. Beach bars, water-sports outfitters, and chair-rental places abound. You can access the beach from several roads off Avenida Ashford, including Calles Cervantes, Vendig, Condado, and Candina. The protected water at the small stretch of beach west of the Condado Plaza Hilton hotel is particularly calm and popular with families; surf elsewhere in Condado can be a bit strong. The stretch of sand near Calle Vendig (behind the Atlantic Beach Hotel) is especially popular with the gay community. If you're driving, street parking is your only option. **Amenities:** none. **Best for:** partiers; people-watching. ✉ *Av. Ashford, Condado.*

Restaurants

★ 1919 Restaurant

$$$$ | **ECLECTIC** | Michelin-starred, Puerto Rico–born chef Juan José Cuevas operates this successful fine-dining restaurant in San Juan's most striking hotel, built in 1919 by the Vanderbilt family. The international dishes—served prix fixe or à la carte—change seasonally and emphasize local ingredients. **Known for:** elegant setting; focus on organic, locally grown ingredients; prix-fixe and tasting menus. *Average main: $36* ✉ *Condado Vanderbilt Hotel, 1055 Av. Ashford, Condado* ☎ *787/724–1919* 🌐 *www.1919restaurant.com* *Closed Sun. and Mon. No lunch.*

Hotels

Coral Princess Hotel

$ | **HOTEL** | This affordable boutique hotel is a good choice for a quiet, romantic getaway: the hotel is only a block from the neighborhood's main drag, and the beach is a three-minute walk away. **Pros:** friendly staff; comfortable common areas; Wi-Fi in rooms. **Cons:** limited parking; small pool; not directly on the beach. *Rooms from: $175* ✉ *1159 Av. Magdalena, Condado* ☎ *787/977–7700* 🌐 *www.coralpr.com* *25 rooms* *No Meals.*

★ La Concha—A Renaissance Resort

$$ | **RESORT** | Not only does this property epitomize the chic Caribbean resort, but it's also an icon of tropical modernist architecture—from the undulating ceiling in the sprawling lobby to Perla, the shell-shape event space. **Pros:** beachfront location; numerous on-site social activities; beautiful guest rooms. **Cons:** pricey bar; beach can be narrow at high tide; noisy bar/lobby, particularly when there's live music. *Rooms from: $350* ✉ *1077 Av. Ashford, Condado* ☎ *787/721–7500* 🌐 *www.laconcharesort.com* *483 rooms* *No Meals.*

★ O:live Boutique Hotel

$$ | **HOTEL** | Tucked away on a quiet street overlooking the lagoon, this luxurious, all-suites boutique hotel recalls the south of France, with artwork from Italy, Spain, Morocco, and France. **Pros:** rooftop terrace; beautiful decor; close to shops and restaurants. **Cons:** no parking lot; see-through bathrooms not for everyone; small pool. *Rooms from: $350* ✉ *55 Calle Aguadilla, Condado* ☎ *787/705–9994* 🌐 *www.oliveboutiquehotel.com* *15 suites* *Free Breakfast.*

San Juan Marriott Resort & Stellaris Casino

$$$ | **RESORT** | **FAMILY** | The shape and color of a cardboard box, this lively, popular hotel doesn't add much to the skyline of Condado, but step inside the impressive lobby—with its stunning coral sculpture carved from wood, chic spots for lounging, and welcoming bar—and you'll feel you've arrived in the Caribbean. **Pros:** lots of amenities; on one of the area's best beaches; near dozens of dining options. **Cons:** noise from lobby; lots of conventions; uninspired architecture. *Rooms from: $400* ✉ *1309 Av. Ashford, Condado* ☎ *787/722–7000, 787/631–0595* 🌐 *www.marriottsanjuan.com* *527 rooms* *No Meals.*

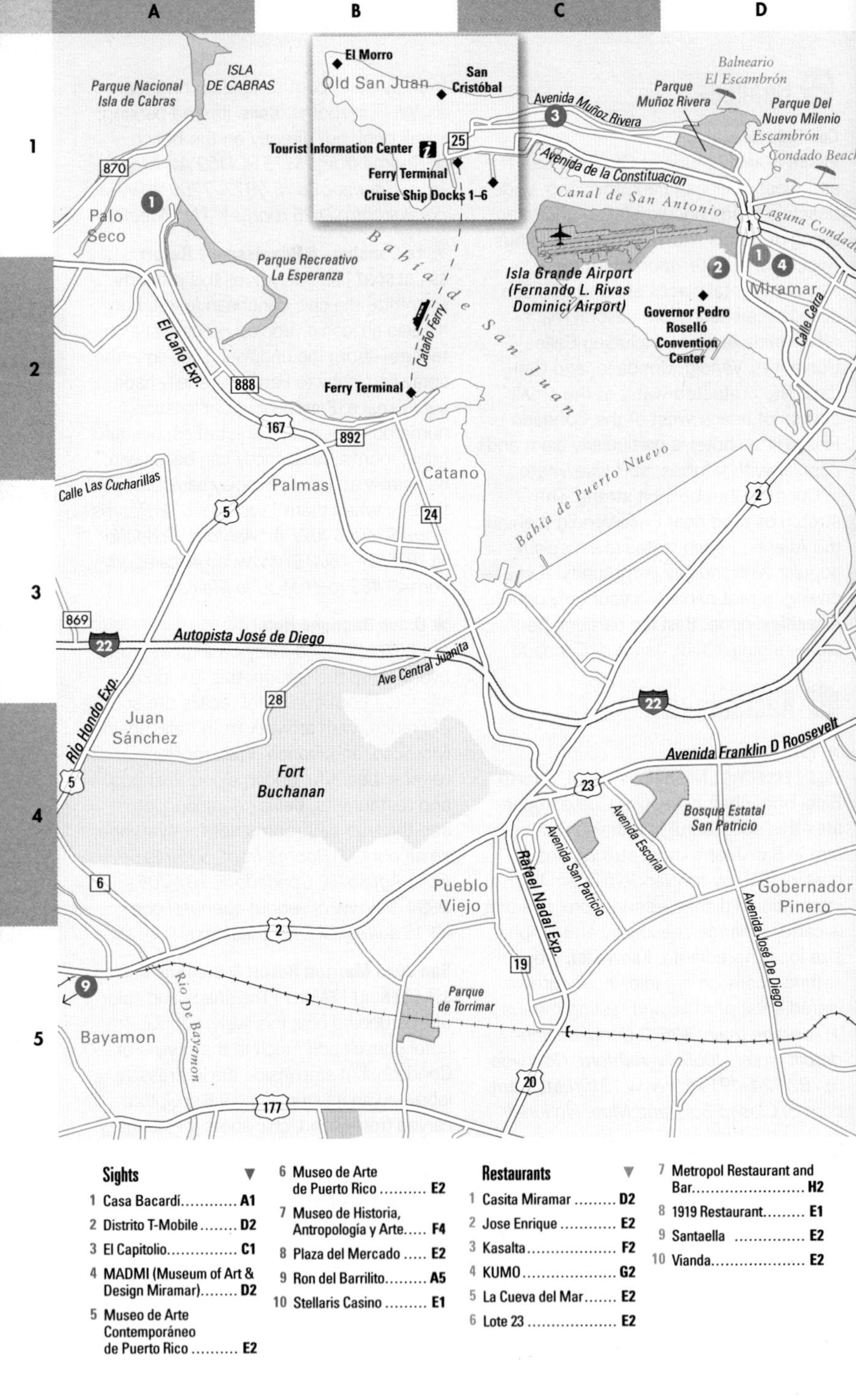
A
B
C
D
1
2
3
4
5
El Morro
Old San Juan
San Cristóbal
Tourist Information Center
Ferry Terminal
Cruise Ship Docks 1–6
ISLA DE CABRAS
Parque Nacional Isla de Cabras
Palo Seco
Parque Recreativo La Esperanza
El Caño Exp.
Bahía de San Juan
Cataño Ferry
Ferry Terminal
Avenida Muñoz Rivera
Avenida de la Constituacion
Canal de San Antonio
Parque Muñoz Rivera
Balneario El Escambrón
Parque Del Nuevo Milenio
Escambrón
Condado Beach
Laguna Condado
Isla Grande Airport (Fernando L. Rivas Dominici Airport)
Governor Pedro Roselló Convention Center
Miramar
Calle Cerra
Calle Las Cucharillas
Palmas
Catano
Bahía de Puerto Nuevo
Autopista José de Diego
Ave Central Juanita
Río Hondo Exp.
Juan Sánchez
Fort Buchanan
Avenida Franklin D Roosevelt
Bosque Estatal San Patricio
Avenida San Patricio
Avenida Escorial
Rafael Nadal Exp.
Pueblo Viejo
Gobernador Pinero
Avenida José De Diego
Parque de Torrimar
Rio De Bayamon
Bayamon
870
888
167
892
5
24
869
22
28
25
1
2
23
6
19
20
177
Sights
1 Casa Bacardí A1
2 Distrito T-Mobile D2
3 El Capitolio C1
4 MADMI (Museum of Art & Design Miramar) D2
5 Museo de Arte Contemporáneo de Puerto Rico E2
6 Museo de Arte de Puerto Rico E2
7 Museo de Historia, Antropología y Arte F4
8 Plaza del Mercado E2
9 Ron del Barrilito A5
10 Stellaris Casino E1
Restaurants
1 Casita Miramar D2
2 Jose Enrique E2
3 Kasalta F2
4 KUMO G2
5 La Cueva del Mar E2
6 Lote 23 E2
7 Metropol Restaurant and Bar H2
8 1919 Restaurant E1
9 Santaella E2
10 Vianda E2

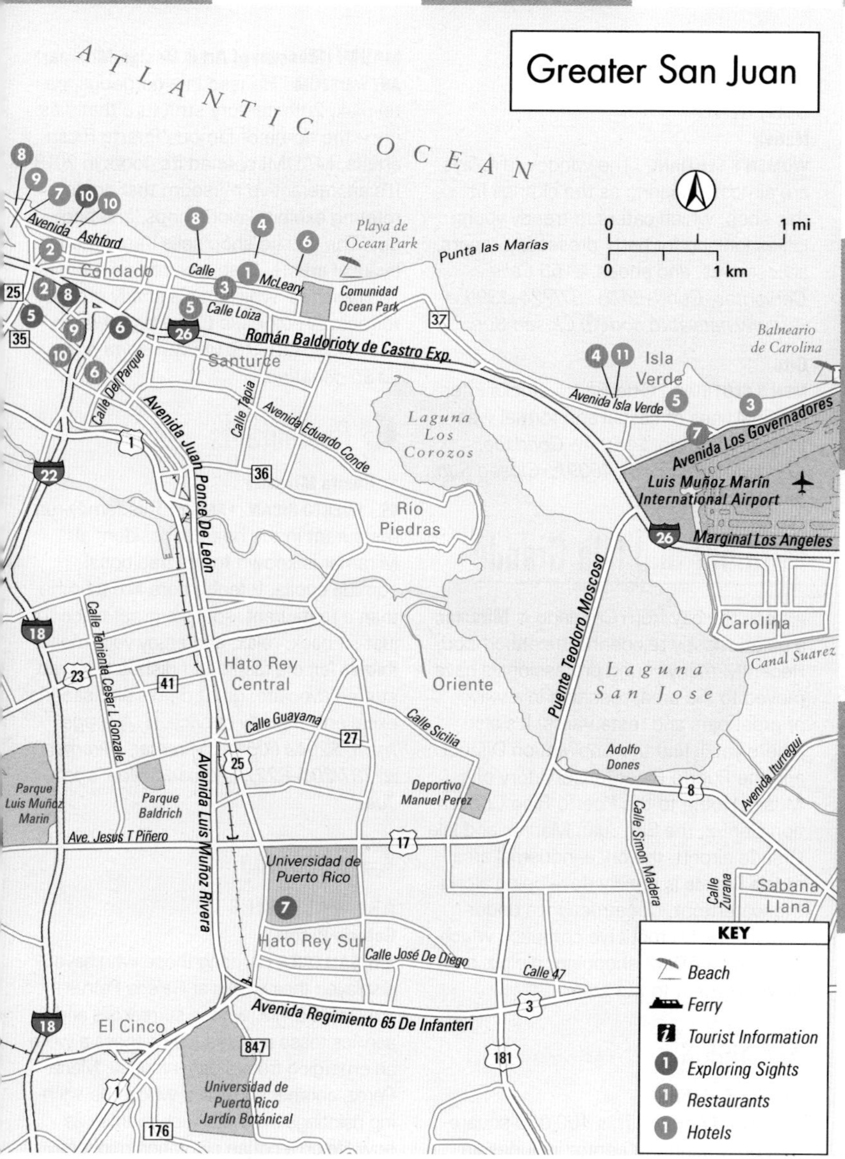

Greater San Juan

Hotels ▼

1 Andalucia Guest House............. **F2**

2 Coral Princess Hotel ... **E2**

3 Courtyard by Marriott Isla Verde Beach Resort........... **H2**

4 The Dreamcatcher **F2**

5 Fairmont El San Juan Hotel...................... **H2**

6 Hostería del Mar........ **F2**

7 La Concha— A Renaissance Resort **E1**

8 Numero Uno Beach House............ **E2**

9 O:live Boutique Hotel... **E1**

10 San Juan Marriott Resort & Stellaris Casino.................... **E1**

11 San Juan Water Beach Club Hotel....... **G2**

Shopping

CLOTHING

Nativa

WOMEN'S CLOTHING | The window displays are almost as daring as the clothes at this shop, which caters to trendy young ladies looking for party dresses, jumpers, accessories, and shoes. *55 Calle Cervantes, Condado* *787/724–1396* *www.nativabtq.com* *Closed Sun.*

Otto

MEN'S CLOTHING | Otto Bauzá stocks international lines of casual and formal wear for younger men. *69 Av. Condado, Condado* *787/722–4609* *Closed Sun. and Mon.*

Miramar and Isla Grande

Across the bay from Condado is **Miramar,** a quiet, mostly residential neighborhood. Recently, many young professionals have moved to the area, resulting in a wave of great bars and restaurants. It's also where you'll find the Convention District and the Puerto Rico Conservatory of Music. Home to the Puerto Rico Convention Center, the San Juan Marina, and Isla Grande airport, the once-industrial area of **Isla Grande** is rapidly developing along the waterfront. Construction is underway for the District Live complex, which will bring a mix of shopping, dining, and entertainment to the area.

Sights

Distrito T-Mobile

OTHER ATTRACTION | This 400,000-square-foot entertainment center includes an arcade, several restaurants, shops, a music venue, and a movie theater. There's even a zipline. *Convention Center, 250 Convention Blvd., Isla Grande* *distritot-mobile.com.*

MADMI (Museum of Art & Design Miramar)

ART MUSEUM | Housed in a gorgeous, pastel-pink, 20th-century structure that was once the home of famous Puerto Rican artists, MADMI opened its doors in 2018. It's an interactive museum that hosts rotating exhibits, workshops, and pop-ups. The on-site shop sells items made by local artists. Grab a coffee next door at La Hacienda, which has a shady outdoor terrace. *607 Calle Cuevillas, Miramar* *787/995–7063* *www.madmi.org* *$5 donation.*

Restaurants

★ **Casita Miramar**

$$ | **PUERTO RICAN** | **FAMILY** | This family-run restaurant in the heart of residential Miramar is known for its traditional comida criolla. It feels more like a home than a restaurant, so it's a great place to just sit back, relax, and enjoy your meal. **Known for:** old-fashioned dishes like crab-stuffed avocado; great drinks and sangria; excellent, friendly service. *Average main: $20* *605 Av. Miramar, Miramar* *787/200–8227* *Closed Mon. and Tues.*

Shopping

ART GALLERIES

Galería Petrus

ART GALLERIES | Among those who have displayed their works at Galería Petrus are Dafne Elvira, whose surreal oils and acrylics tease and seduce (witness a woman emerging from a banana peel); Marta Pérez, another surrealist, whose bewitching paintings examine such themes as how life on a coffee plantation might have been; and Elizam Escobar, a former political prisoner whose oils depict typically dark subjects. Exhibitions change frequently and focus on local artists like Bobby Cruz and Carlos Dávila. *Galeria Petrus, 726 Calle Hoare, Miramar* *787/289–0505* *www.petrusgallery.com.*

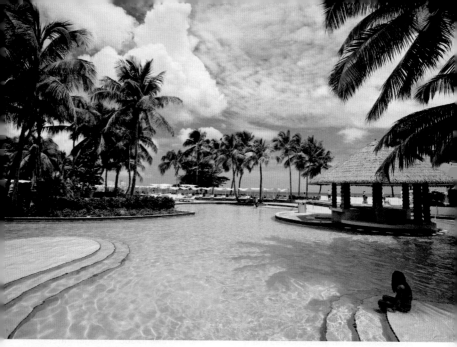

The beautiful pool at the El San Juan Hotel.

Santurce and Hato Rey

Venture into **Santurce** to explore a mostly commercial district with a growing artistic community, thanks to the Museo de Arte de Puerto Rico and the Museo de Arte Contemporáneo. You'll also find a thriving nightlife scene on weekends. Nearby, **Hato Rey** is a busy financial district that's home to the large Plaza Las Américas Mall.

Sights

Museo de Arte Contemporáneo de Puerto Rico

ART MUSEUM | This Georgian-style structure, once a public school, displays a dynamic range of works by established and up-and-coming Latin American artists. Many works have strong political messages, including pointed commentaries on Puerto Rico's status as a commonwealth. Only part of the permanent collection's more than 900 works is on display at a time, but it might be anything from ceramics to videos. ✉ *1220 Av. Ponce de León, at Av. R. H. Todd, Santurce* ☎ *787/977–4030* 🌐 *www.mac-pr.org* *$5* *Closed Sun. and Mon.*

★ Museo de Arte de Puerto Rico

ART MUSEUM | One of the Caribbean's biggest museums, this beautiful neoclassical building was once the San Juan Municipal Hospital. The collection of Puerto Rican art starts with the colonial era, when most art was commissioned for churches. Works by José Campeche, the island's first great painter, include his masterpiece, *Immaculate Conception,* finished in 1794. Also well represented is Francisco Oller, who was the first to move beyond religious subjects to paint local scenes; another room has the works of artists who were inspired by him. The original building, built in the 1920s, proved too small to house the collection. A newer east wing is dominated by a five-story, stained-glass window by local artist Eric Tabales. The museum also has a beautiful garden with native flora and a 400-seat theater with a remarkable hand-crocheted lace curtain. ✉ *299 Av. José de Diego, Santurce* ☎ *787/977–6277* 🌐 *www.mapr.org* 🎫 *$6* ⏲ *Closed Mon. and Tues.*

Plaza del Mercado (*La Placita*)
MARKET | Though often overlooked by tourists, charming La Placita (as it's known by locals) is one of San Juan's liveliest spots. At its center is a market hall (circa 1910) where you—perhaps alongside chefs from the city's top restaurants—can shop for fruits and vegetables, including exotic options like *guanábana* and *caimito*. The many restaurants and bars facing the central square are quiet during the day but busy in the evening, especially on weekends. Nearby are Santaella, a stellar restaurant by renowned chef Jose Santaella, and Jungle Bar, known for its craft and tiki cocktails. The area also has many *botánicas*—small shops that sell herbs, candles, and religious items. The square is between the Museo de Arte de Puerto Rico and the Museo de Arte Contemporáneo de Puerto Rico, making it a good place to stop for dinner and drinks after a day of museum-hopping. ✉ *Calle Dos Hermanos, at Calle Capital, Santurce.*

Restaurants

Jose Enrique
$$$ | PUERTO RICAN | Although it recently moved from Santurce to Condado, the restaurant of chef Jose Enrique—who's been nominated for the prestigious James Beard Award multiple times—remains popular with locals and visitors for its elevated Puerto Rican cuisine. The setting is casual, and the menu is ever-changing, though it always includes *carne guisada* (a local beef stew), fritters, and a catch of the day. **Known for:** celebrity chef; focus on locally grown produce and other ingredients; ever-changing menu. 💲 *Average main: $30* ✉ *1021 Av. Ashford, Condado* ☎ *787/705–8130* ⏲ *Closed Sun. and Mon.*

Lote 23
$$ | ECLECTIC | FAMILY | Over a dozen kiosks here showcase the gastronomic offerings of the city's chefs and entrepreneurs. You'll find roast-pork sandwiches, poké bowls, thin-crust pizzas cooked in a stone oven, artisanal ice-cream pops, fried chicken, mofongo, and more. **Known for:** live music some nights; family-friendly; al fresco dining. 💲 *Average main: $13* ✉ *1552 Av. Ponce de León, Santurce* ☎ 🌐 *lote23.com* ⏲ *Closed Mon.*

★ **Santaella**
$$$ | PUERTO RICAN | A career working with top chefs and a successful catering business prefaced chef José Santaella's namesake restaurant in La Placita marketplace. The menu is dominated by tapas, and favorites include the ahi tuna skewers, goat-cheese quesadilla, and *morcilla* (blood sausage) fritters. **Known for:** great cocktails; small plates of nouveau Puerto Rican specialties; trendy ambience. 💲 *Average main: $29* ✉ *La Placita de Santurce, 219 Calle Canals, Santurce* ☎ *787/725–1611* 🌐 *www.santaellapr.com* ⏲ *Closed Sun. and Mon. No lunch Sat.*

Vianda
$$$ | ECLECTIC | Driven by local ingredients and seasonality, chef Francis Guzman's dishes are culinary delights (think: California cuisine with Puerto Rican and Caribbean influences). The service is fantastic, and the wine list and cocktail menu are strong—anything with mezcal is a particularly good choice. **Known for:** farm-to-table-focused menu; fantastic crudos; excellent service. 💲 *Average main: $24* ✉ *1413 Av. Ponce de León, Santurce* ☎ *939/475–1578* 🌐 *www.viandapr.com* ⏲ *Closed Mon. and Tues., No lunch.*

Ocean Park

Ocean Park is a partially gated residential community with a laid-back feel. If you dream of staying in a quiet guesthouse on a more secluded beach—away from the crowds—this might be the spot for you.

Beaches

Playa de Ocean Park

BEACH | The residential neighborhood east of Condado and west of Isla Verde is home to this 1½-km-long (1-mile-long) stretch of golden sand. The waters are often choppy but still swimmable—take care, however, as there are no lifeguards on duty. Windsurfers say the conditions here are nearly perfect. The tranquil beach is popular with young people as well as gay men—particularly on weekends. Parking is a bit difficult, as many of the streets are gated and restricted to residents. **Amenities:** none. **Best for:** partiers; windsurfing. ✉ *Calle Santa Ana, Ocean Park.*

Restaurants

Kasalta

$$ | CAFÉ | FAMILY | This local bakery is always buzzing with locals and tourists. Display cases are full of luscious pastries, including the *quesito* (cream cheese–filled puff pastry), and sandwiches include the *medianoche,* made famous when President Obama ordered one while campaigning. **Known for:** sometimes curt service; great baked goods, including cream cheese–filled quesitos; medianoche sandwiches. *Ⓢ Average main: $16* ✉ *1966 Calle McLeary, Ocean Park* ☎ *787/727–7340* 🌐 *www.kasalta.com.*

La Cueva del Mar

$$ | SEAFOOD | FAMILY | Families with kids, beachgoers in flip-flops, and businesspeople all flock to this casual, marine-themed restaurant, renowned for its seafood dishes. Grouper tacos, lightly fried and topped with a spicy slaw, are a best-seller—don't leave without trying at least one. **Known for:** fish tacos; conch in season; house-made hot sauce. *Ⓢ Average main: $15* ✉ *1857 Calle Loíza, Ocean Park* ☎ *787/726–8700* 🌐 *www.lacuevatogo.com.*

Hotels

Andalucía Guest House

$ | B&B/INN | In a Spanish-style house, this friendly little inn evokes its namesake region with such details as hand-painted tiles and ceramic pots filled with greenery. **Pros:** gorgeous courtyard; terrific value; helpful hosts. **Cons:** could use an update; some rooms smaller than others; not right on the beach. *Ⓢ Rooms from: $174* ✉ *2011 Calle McLeary, Ocean Park* ☎ *787/309–3373* 🌐 *www.andalucia-puertorico.com* *11 rooms* *No Meals.*

★ The Dreamcatcher

$ | B&B/INN | Each room of this guesthouse—a relaxing oasis in the heart of Ocean Park and just steps from the beach—is uniquely decorated with vintage furniture and works of art that the owner has collected over the years. **Pros:** two blocks from beach; house chef on-site; yoga offered daily. **Cons:** no in-room TVs; some rooms share bathrooms; no pool. *Ⓢ Rooms from: $180* ✉ *2009 Calle España, Ocean Park* ☎ *787/455–8259* 🌐 *www.dreamerspuertorico.com* *18 rooms* *No Meals.*

Hostería del Mar

$ | **B&B/INN** | Second-floor rooms have ocean views at this small, secluded inn with an unbeatable location right on the beach in a gated community. **Pros:** beach-side dining; plasma TVs; right on the beach. **Cons:** hot water can be inconsistent; needs a face-lift; long walk to other restaurants. *Rooms from: $148 ✉ 1 Calle Tapia, Ocean Park ☎ 787/727–3302 🌐 www.lahosteriadelmar.com 25 rooms No Meals.*

Numero Uno Beach House

$$ | **HOTEL** | This relaxing inn is so close to the beach that you can hear the crashing waves. **Pros:** on the beach; friendly atmosphere; on-site, beachfront dining. **Cons:** rooms are fairly basic; small pool; in a residential neighborhood far from other tourist areas. *Rooms from: $340 ✉ 1 Calle Santa Ana, Ocean Park ☎ 787/726–5010, 866/726–5010 🌐 www.numerounobeachhouse.com 11 rooms No Meals.*

Isla Verde and Carolina

If you came to work on your tan—and you came to do it on a big, beautiful Caribbean beach—then Isla Verde, home to the nicest beach in the metropolitan area, is your place. The main commercial strip is not especially attractive: it's filled with fast-food restaurants and other businesses. You'll also need a car or taxi to get anywhere. That said, the resort-style hotels (many of them beachfront) offer so many amenities and so many restaurants on-site, you may not want—or need—to leave very often.

Beaches

Balneario de Carolina

BEACH | **FAMILY** | When people talk about a "beautiful Isla Verde beach," this Blue Flag beach is the one—even though it's so close to the airport that leaves rustle when planes take off. Thanks to an offshore reef, the surf here is not as strong as at other nearby beaches, so it's good for families. There's plenty of room to spread out underneath the palm and almond trees, and there are picnic tables and grills. Although there's a charge for parking, there's not always someone to take the money. On weekends, the beach is crowded; get here early to nab parking. The Vivo Beach Club offers lounge chairs and beautiful facilities for food and drink, including a brewery. **Amenities:** food and drink; lifeguards; parking (fee); showers; toilets. **Best for:** swimming; walking. *✉ Av. Los Gobernadores, Carolina Parking $4.*

Restaurants

KUMO

$$ | **JAPANESE** | On the roof of Aire de O:live, this sexy, bohemian spot offers some of Isla Verde's best ocean views. The Japanese-inspired menu offers creative sushi rolls, charcoal-grilled skewers, *sakanas* (Japanese snacks served with sake), and a selection of excellent cocktails. **Known for:** creative Asian cuisine; trendy rooftop; incredible ocean views. *Average main: $20 ✉ San Juan Water Beach Club Hotel, 2 Calle Tartak, Isla Verde ☎ 787/725–4664 🌐 www.waterbeachhotel.com.*

Metropol Restaurant and Bar

$$ | **CARIBBEAN** | **FAMILY** | Across the street from a string of major hotels, this casual restaurant doesn't look like much from the outside, but inside it's decorated in warm, tropical colors. The kitchen turns out delicious versions of Cuban and Puerto Rican favorites at reasonable prices. **Known for:** family-friendly atmosphere; local vibe; large portions of typical dishes like churrasco and ropa vieja. *Average main: $15 ✉ Av. Isla Verde, Anexo Club Gallistico, Isla Verde ☎ 787/791–5585 🌐 www.metropolrestaurant.com.*

Hotels

Courtyard by Marriott Isla Verde Beach Resort

$$ | **RESORT** | **FAMILY** | This 12-story resort tries to be all things to all people—and succeeds to a great degree. **Pros:** good value; on a great beach; family-friendly environment. **Cons:** far from Condado and Old San Juan; lobby is busy and noisy; you can hear airport noise from some rooms. *Rooms from: $339* *7012 Av. Boca de Cangrejos, Isla Verde* *787/791–0404, 787/999–6300* *www.sjcourtyard.com* *281 rooms* *No Meals.*

★ **Fairmont El San Juan Hotel**

$$$ | **RESORT** | **FAMILY** | Post-hurricane renovations gave the rooms a more modern look (with shades of blue, white, and cream), but elsewhere, this hotel's classic appeal remains, including in the lobby, which has intricately carved mahogany walls. **Pros:** large guest rooms; beautiful pool; fantastic beach. **Cons:** small bathrooms; parking lot a long walk from hotel entrance; noise in lobby from bars. *Rooms from: $395* *6063 Av. Isla Verde, Isla Verde* *787/791–1000* *www.elsanjuanhotel.com* *388 rooms* *No Meals.*

San Juan Water Beach Club Hotel

$ | **HOTEL** | Water is everywhere—from droplets in the reception area to cataracts running down the elevators' glass walls—at this ultramodern hotel, where most guest rooms have ocean views and all have feather beds and minimalist white color schemes with splashes of turquoise. **Pros:** rooftop pool and bar; fun atmosphere; interesting design. **Cons:** beach is across the street; small pool; dark hallways. *Rooms from: $252* *2 Calle Tartak, Isla Verde* *787/728–3666, 888/265–6699* *www.waterbeachhotel.com* *80 rooms* *No Meals.*

Río Piedras

The mostly residential Río Piedras area is home to the University of Puerto Rico, on whose campus you'll find the Botanical Garden and an interesting museum.

Sights

Museo de Historia, Antropología y Arte

ART MUSEUM | The Universidad de Puerto Rico's small Museum of History, Anthropology and Art offers rotating exhibitions in three areas. Its archaeological and historical collection covers the Native American influence on the island and the Caribbean, the colonial era, and the history of slavery. There's also a small collection of Egyptian antiquities. Art holdings include a range of Puerto Rican popular, graphic, folk, and fine art; the museum's prize exhibit is the painting *El Velorio* (*The Wake*), by the 19th-century artist Francisco Oller. If you're looking to see something in particular, call before you go, as only a small portion of the collection is on display at a time. Guided tours in English are available; call for reservations. *Universidad de Puerto Rico, Av. Ponce de León, Río Piedras* *787/763–3939* *museo.uprrp.edu* *Free* *Closed Sat. and Sun.*

Cataño and Bayamón

Cataño, bordered by the Bahía de San Juan in the north, is an industrial suburb, perhaps most noted for its distillery belonging to Bacardí. Bayamón can be reached in 15–30 minutes from central San Juan; if you come by car, stop by the attractive central park, bordered by historic buildings and take a walk along the waterfront promenade—the views of Old San Juan are stunning.

Sights

Casa Bacardí

DISTILLERY | The Bacardí family built a small rum distillery in the 1950s after they were exiled from Cuba. It's now the world's largest distillery, able to produce 100,000 gallons of spirits a day, which translates to 21 million cases a year. Book a mixology class or rum tasting tour, both include a welcome cocktail at the pavilion and a trolley ride through the property. A ferry is available from Pier 2 ($0.50) but then you'll have to Uber, or you can drive. ✉ *Bay View Industrial Park, Rte. 165, Km 2.6, at Rte. 888, Cataño* ☎ *787/788–8400* 🌐 *www.visitcasabacardi.com* 🎟 *$75 (mixology class or rum tasting).*

★ Ron del Barrilito

DISTILLERY | Although Ron del Barrilito's handcrafted Puerto Rican rum isn't often seen outside the island, it's a local favorite that has been around since 1880. A visit to its distillery, which only produces about 14,000 cases a year, offers a more authentic experience than a trip to larger operations. It's also a great way to ensure you take home a truly special island souvenir. The rum's four varieties are differentiated by how long they're aged. Most places only carry the 2- and 3-star bottles; the rarer 4-star version is aged up to 20 years, and the extremely limited 5-star variety spends 35 years in oak casks. Although you can sample rum at the visitor center, for a more in-depth look at things, book a Heritage Tour, Rum Tasting Tour, or Mixology Class. ✉ *Hacienda Santa Ana, Carretera 5, Km. 5.5, Bayamón* ☎ *787/415–8601* 🌐 *rondelbarrilito.com* 🎟 *$30–$60, depending on tour* ⏲ *Closed Sun.*

Río Grande

35 km (21 miles) southeast of San Juan.

This urban cluster of about 54,000 residents proudly calls itself "The City of El Yunque," as it's the closest community to the rain forest and most of the reserve falls within its municipal borders. Two images of the rare green parrot, which makes its home in El Yunque, are found on the city's coat of arms; another parrot peeks out at you from the town's flag.

Río Espíritu Santo, which runs through Río Grande, begins in El Yunque's highest elevations. It was once used to transport lumber, sugar, and coffee from plantations, and immigrants flocked to the region to take advantage of the employment opportunities.

Restaurants

Richie's Café

$$$ | **SEAFOOD** | Perched on a mountaintop, this restaurant—a convenient option for Wyndham Grand Río Mar guests who don't want to dine on-site but are willing to pay resort prices—has a pair of open-air dining rooms with views to Vieques on a clear day. The atmosphere is festive; there's often a game playing on one of the big screens or a local band jamming on the weekend. **Known for:** ocean views; fresh seafood, especially whole red snapper; fried plantains stuffed with seafood. $ *Average main: $25* ✉ *Rte. 968, Km 2.0* ☎ *787/887–1435* 🌐 *www.richiesrestaurantpr.com.*

Hotels

Hyatt Regency Grand Reserve Puerto Rico

$$$$ | **RESORT** | **FAMILY** | This massive resort on a stretch of pristine coastline does a decent job of being all things to all people, with oversized suites, many of which have plunge pools or patio Jacuzzis, spread among two-story bungalows and even larger suites that have features like an adults-only pool and private check-in. **Pros:** short walk to beach; beautiful setting; lovely pool area. **Cons:** iguanas near pool bother some guests; blank and uninviting facade; scarce parking. $ *Rooms from: $500* ✉ *200 Coco Beach*

Spanning 28,000 acres, El Yunque is the only tropical rainforest in the U.S. National Forest System.

Blvd. ☎ *787/809–1770* 🌐 *www.hyatt.com* *579 suites* 🍽 *No Meals.*

★ **St. Regis Bahia Beach Resort, Puerto Rico**

$$$$ | **RESORT** | Between El Yunque National Forest and the Río Espíritu Santo, this luxurious, environmentally aware property, with 3 km (2 miles) of pristine private beach, is an oasis of calm that hums with local wildlife. **Pros:** luxurious amenities; privacy; impeccable service. **Cons:** very, very expensive; slim off-property restaurant selection; isolated location. $ *Rooms from: $1300* ✉ *Rte. 187, Km 4.2* ☎ *787/809–8000* 🌐 *www.stregisbahiabeach.com* *174 rooms* 🍽 *No Meals.*

Wyndham Río Mar Golf & Beach Resort

$$$ | **RESORT** | **FAMILY** | This sprawling resort offers a host of outdoor activities, including championship golf and tennis as well as hiking in the nearby rain forest. **Pros:** casino; expansive beachfront; good restaurants. **Cons:** far from off-site restaurants; occasionally long lines at check-in; expensive resort fee. $ *Rooms from: $450* ✉ *6000 Río Mar Blvd.* ☎ *787/888–6000* 🌐 *www.wyndhamriomar.com* *400 rooms* 🍽 *No Meals.*

El Yunque

The more than 100 billion gallons of precipitation that El Yunque receives annually spawns rushing streams and cascades, outsize impatiens and ferns, and 240 tree species. In the evening millions of inch-long coquís (tree frogs) begin their calls. El Yunque is also home to the *cotorra,* Puerto Rico's endangered green parrot, as well as 67 other types of birds.

El Yunque is the only tropical rain forest in the U.S. National Forest System, spanning 28,000 acres, reaching an elevation of more than 3,500 feet, and receiving an estimated 200–240 inches of rain each year. The forest's 13 hiking trails are well maintained; many are easy to navigate and less than 1 mile (1½ km) long. The trails on the north side of El Yunque, the park's main tourist hub, tend toward folks

Puerto Rico

A B C D

1 2 3 4 5

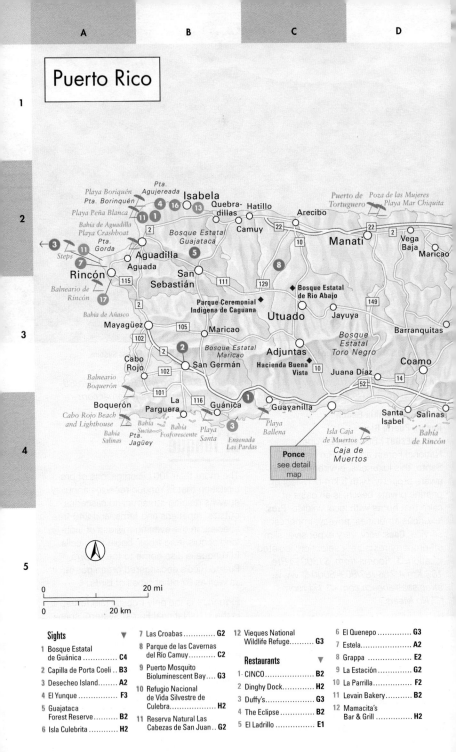

Pta. Agujereada
Playa Boriquén
Pta. Borinquén
Playa Peña Blanca
Bahía de Aguadilla
Playa Crashboat
Pta. Gorda
Steps
Isabela
Quebradillas
Hatillo
Camuy
Arecibo
Puerto de Tortuguero
Poza de las Mujeres
Playa Mar Chiquita
Manati
Vega Baja
Maricao
Bosque Estatal Guajataca
Aguadilla
Aguada
Rincón
Balneario de Rincón
San Sebastián
Bosque Estatal de Rio Abajo
Parque Ceremonial Indigena de Caguana
Utuado
Jayuya
Barranquitas
Bahía de Añasco
Mayagüez
Maricao
Bosque Estatal Toro Negro
Bosque Estatal Maricao
Adjuntas
Cabo Rojo
San Germán
Hacienda Buena Vista
Juana Díaz
Coamo
Balneario Boquerón
Boquerón
La Parguera
Guánica
Guayanilla
Santa Isabel
Salinas
Cabo Rojo Beach and Lighthouse
Bahía Sucia
Bahía Fosforescente
Playa Santa
Ensenada Las Pardas
Playa Ballena
Isla Caja de Muertos
Caja de Muertos
Bahía de Rincón
Bahía Salinas
Pta. Jagüey

Ponce see detail map

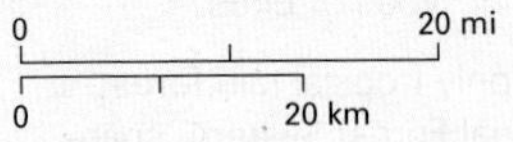

Sights

1 Bosque Estatal de Guánica C4
2 Capilla de Porta Coeli .. B3
3 Desecheo Island........ A2
4 El Yunque F3
5 Guajataca Forest Reserve.......... B2
6 Isla Culebrita H2
7 Las Croabas G2
8 Parque de las Cavernas del Río Camuy........... C2
9 Puerto Mosquito Bioluminescent Bay.... G3
10 Refugio Nacional de Vida Silvestre de Culebra.................. H2
11 Reserva Natural Las Cabezas de San Juan.. G2
12 Vieques National Wildlife Refuge.......... G3

Restaurants

1 CINCO.................... B2
2 Dinghy Dock............ H2
3 Duffy's.................... G3
4 The Eclipse B2
5 El Ladrillo E1
6 El Quenepo G3
7 Estela...................... A2
8 Grappa E2
9 La Estación.............. G2
10 La Parrilla................ F2
11 Levain Bakery........... B2
12 Mamacita's Bar & Grill H2

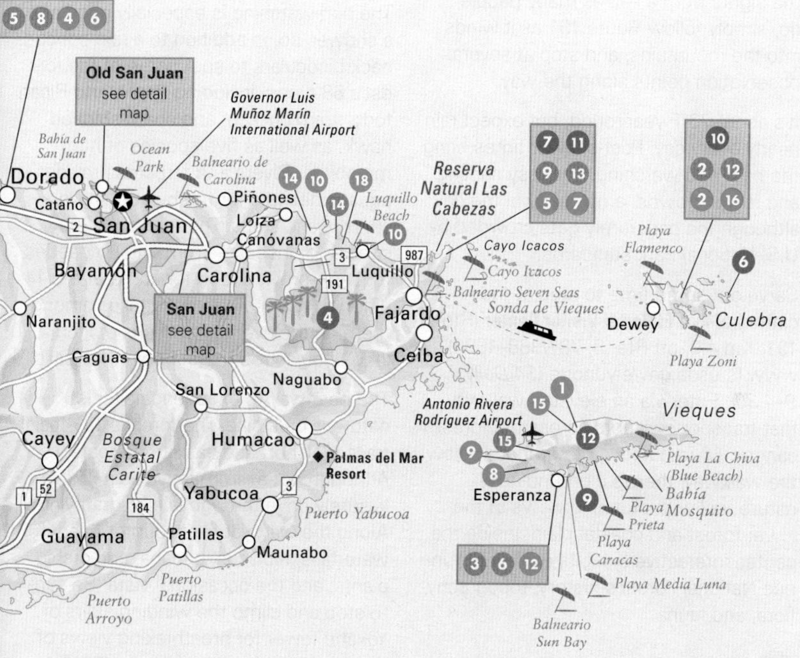

13 Pasión por el Fogón G2
14 Richie's Café............ F2
15 Tin Box.................. G3
16 Uma's Playa Jobos B2

Hotels ▼

1 Bravo Beach Hotel G3
2 Club Seabourne......... H2
3 Copamarina Beach Resort and Spa B4
4 Dorado Beach, a Ritz-Carlton Reserve......... E2
5 El Conquistador Resort...................... G2
6 Embassy Suites by Hilton Dorado del Mar Beach Resort........... E2
7 Fajardo Inn G2
8 Hacienda Tamarindo ... G3
9 Hix Island House........ G3
10 Hyatt Regency Grand Reserve Puerto Rico ... F2
11 Lazy Parrot Inn.......... A2
12 Malecón House.......... G3
13 Royal Isabela............ B2
14 St. Regis Bahia Beach Resort, Puerto Rico............. F2
15 Sea Gate Hotel.......... G3
16 Tamarindo Estates...... H2
17 Tres Sirenas............. A3
18 Wyndham Río Mar Golf & Beach Resort......... F2

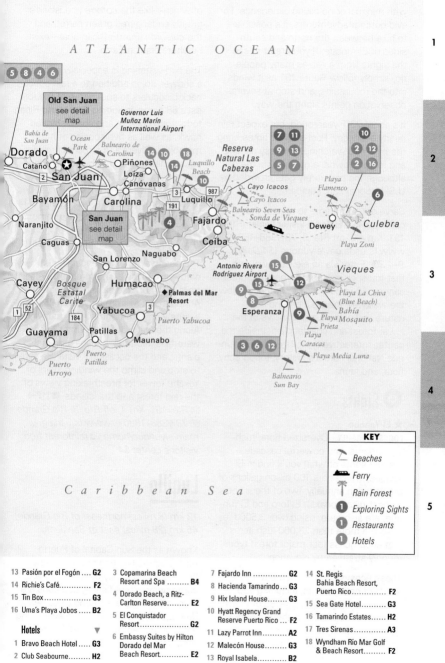

with minimal or no hiking experience. For avid outdoor adventurers, it's possible to hike between the north and south sides of El Yunque. If you prefer to see the sights from a car, as many people do, simply follow Route 191 as it winds into the mountains, and stop at several observation points along the way.

It's about 73°F year-round, but expect rain nearly every day. Post-shower times bring the best bird-watching. For easy parking and fewer crowds, arrive early in the day, although the park rarely gets crowded by U.S. National Park standards.

Carve out some time to stop at the cathedral-like **El Portal Visitor Center** (Rte. 191, Km 4.3, off Rte. 3, 787/888–1880) www.fs.usda.gov/elyunque (*$4 Daily 9–4:30*). Enter via an elevated walkway that transports visitors across the forest canopy, 60 feet above the ground. Below the walkway, there's a ground-level nature trail with stunning views of the lower forest and coastal plain. Inside the center, interactive exhibits explain El Yunque National Forest's history, topography, flora, and fauna.

Sights

★ El Yunque

FOREST | FAMILY | Oversized flora, rushing streams, and powerful cascades are just some of what you'll find in El Yunque, which gets 100 billion gallons of precipitation annually. Two of the island's highest *picos* (peaks), El Toro and El Yunque, are also here, rising over 3,500 feet amid the more than 28,000 lush acres that encompass four major forest types, roughly stratified by elevation.

These ecosystems are home to thousands of native plants, including 150 fern and 240 tree species—88 of them rare and endemic, 23 of them found here exclusively. There are no monkeys or large cats (and no poisonous snakes, either). Rather, El Yunque is populated with small creatures, some of which—like the *cotorra* (the island's greatly endangered green parrot) and the *culebrón* (Puerto Rican boa)—exist nowhere else on Earth.

The bird-watching is especially good after a shower, so, in addition to a rain poncho, pack binoculars to spot some of the forest's 68 types, including the Puerto Rican tody, lizard cuckoo, and sharp-shinned hawk, as well as five species of hummingbirds. Rivers and streams provide aquatic habitats for freshwater snails, shrimp, and crabs. The forest's 1,200 species of insects—from ants to beetles to flies—provide food for some of the 14 different types of lizards, geckos among them. In the evening, millions of inch-long *coquís* (tree frogs) begin their calls.

The best way to experience all this nature is on a hike. The forest's 13 official trails are short and easy to navigate. Although not as immersive as a hike, a leisurely drive-through is also gratifying. Along the way, you'll encounter beautiful waterfalls; hibiscus, banana, and orchid plants; and the occasional vista. Be sure to stop and climb the winding stairs of Yokahu Tower for breathtaking views of the rain forest and the islands. **TIP→** ✉ *Rte. 191, Km 4, off Rte. 3, Río Grande* ☎ *787/888–1880* 🌐 *www.fs.usda.gov/main/elyunque/home* 🎫 *rainforest free; visitor's center $4.*

Luqillo

13 km (8 miles) northeast of Río Grande; 45 km (28 miles) east of San Juan.

Known as the Sun Capital of Puerto Rico, Luquillo has one of the island's best-equipped family beaches. It's also a community where fishing traditions are respected. On the east end of Balneario de Luquillo, past the guarded swimming area, fishermen launch small boats and drop nets in open stretches between coral reefs.

Like many other Puerto Rican towns, Luquillo has its own signature festival—in this case, the Festival de Platos Típicos (Festival of Typical Dishes), a late-November or early-December culinary event that revolves around one ingredient: coconut. During the festivities, many of the community's 20,000 residents gather in the Plaza de Recreo to sample treats rich with coconut or coconut milk. There's also plenty of free entertainment, including folk shows, troubadour contests, and salsa bands.

Beaches

Luquillo Beach (*Balneario La Monserrate*)
BEACH | FAMILY | Signs refer to this gentle beach off Route 3 as "Balneario La Monserrate," but everyone simply calls it Luquillo Beach. Lined with lifeguard stations and shaded by soaring palm trees, it's a magnet for families and has picnic areas and more than 60 kiosks serving fritters and drinks—making it a local hangout. Lounge chairs and umbrellas are available to rent, as are kayaks and Jet Skis. One very distinctive feature here is the *Mar Sin Barreras* (Sea Without Barriers), a gradual ramp into the water that allows wheelchair users to take a dip. On busy days, the beach can be crowded and characterized by a party atmosphere. **■TIP→ There is a nominal fee for using the shower facilities, so bring small bills for this purpose. Amenities:** food and drink; lifeguards; parking (fee); showers; toilets; water sports. **Best for:** partiers; swimming; walking. ✉ *Off Rte. 3, Luquillo* ☎ *787/889–5871* *$4 plus tax, per car (cash only).*

Restaurants

La Parrilla
$$$ | SEAFOOD | FAMILY | There are dozens of *kioskos,* or food stands, along Route 3 on the way to Luquillo Beach, most offering humble local fare, much of it fried. This full-service restaurant raises the bar for its culinary counterparts. **Known for:** steaks for the non-fish eaters; good grilled seafood; alfresco dining. $ *Average main: $28* ✉ *Luquillo Beach, Rte. 3, Kiosk 2, Luquillo.*

Activities

HORSEBACK RIDING

Horseback riding is a well-established family pastime in Puerto Rico, with *cabalgatas* (group day rides) frequently organized on weekends through mountain towns.

Carabalí Rainforest Park
HORSEBACK RIDING | FAMILY | A family-run operation, this hacienda is a good place to jump in the saddle and ride one of Puerto Rico's Paso Fino horses. Hour-long rides take you around the 600-acre ranch, while two-hour treks take you to a river where you and your horse can take a dip. If you prefer something more high-tech, rent a four-wheeler for an excursion through the foothills of El Yunque. ✉ *Rte. 3, Km 31.6, Luquillo* ☎ *787/889–4954* 🌐 *www.carabalirainforestpark.com.*

Fajardo

11 km (7 miles) southeast of Luquillo; 55 km (34 miles) southeast of San Juan.

Fajardo, founded in 1772, was once notorious as a piratical pit stop. It later developed into a fishing community and an area where sugarcane flourished. Today it's a hub for yachts that use its marinas, divers who head to its good offshore sites, and day-trippers who travel by catamaran, ferry, or plane to the islands of Culebra and Vieques from nearby Ceiba. With the most significant docking facilities on the island's eastern side, Fajardo is a bustling city of 37,000—so bustling, in fact, that its unremarkable and somewhat battered downtown is often congested and difficult to navigate. Much of the tourist activity in Fajardo centers on the northern reaches of Las Croabas, near the gigantic Conquistador Resort.

Sights

Las Croabas

NATURE SIGHT | FAMILY | A few miles north of Fajardo is this fishing area, where seafood is sold in open-air restaurants along the ocean. A small park in the middle of town has a lovely waterfront walk, and it's easy to find outfitters for any kind of ocean adventure, from kayak excursions to sailing trips. ✉ *Rte. 3, Km 51.2, Fajardo.*

★ Reserva Natural Las Cabezas de San Juan

NATURE PRESERVE | The 316-acre reserve on a headland north of Fajardo is owned by the nonprofit Conservation Trust of Puerto Rico. You ride in open-air trolleys and wander down boardwalks through seven ecosystems, including lagoons, mangrove swamps, and dry-forest areas. Green iguanas skitter across paths, and guides identify other endangered species. A half-hour hike down a wooden walkway brings you to the mangrove-lined **Laguna Grande,** where bioluminescent microorganisms glow at night. The restored **Fajardo Lighthouse** is the final stop on the tour. Its Spanish-colonial tower has been in operation since 1882, making it Puerto Rico's second-oldest lighthouse. The first floor houses ecological displays, and a winding staircase leads to an observation deck. The only way to see the reserve is on a guided tour; reservations are required and can be made through the trust's website. ✉ *Rte. 987, Km 6, Fajardo* ☎ *787/722–5882* 🌐 *www.paralanaturaleza.org* 🎟 *$12.*

Beaches

Balneario Seven Seas

BEACH | FAMILY | One of Puerto Rico's prized Blue Flag beaches, this long stretch of powdery sand near the Reserva Natural Las Cabezas de San Juan has calm, clear waters that are perfect for swimming. There are plenty of picnic tables, as well as restaurants just outside the gates. **Amenities:** food and drink; parking (fee); showers (fee); toilets. **Best for:** swimming. ✉ *Rte. 195, Km 4.8, Las Croabas* ☎ *787/863–8180* 🎟 *Parking $5.*

★ Cayo Icacos

BEACH | Cayo Icacos is one of about 10 small islands that make up the Cordillera Nature Reserve just off the coast of Puerto Rico. It's a beautiful beach with good snorkeling offshore. Icacos can only be reached by a 15- to 20-minute boat ride, so pack whatever you might need for the day. Several tour operators in Fajardo offer day-trips here, or you can hire a boat in Las Croabas. **Amenities:** none. **Best for:** snorkeling, solitude, swimming, walking. ✉ *La Cordillera Nature Reserve, Las Croabas* ✣ *Off the coast 15 to 20 minutes by boat from Las Croabas.*

Restaurants

★ La Estación

$$$ | PUERTO RICAN | This laid-back spot has elevated Puerto Rican street food to an art form, thanks to two New Yorkers (one Puerto Rican) with restaurant pedigrees who decided to leave the big city and open a new spot dedicated to barbecue in an old gas station outside the Conquistador Resort. Highlighting products obtained from local fishermen and farmers, and smoking their own meats in an outdoor kitchen, Idalia García and Kevin Roth's awesome joint is one of Puerto Rico's don't-miss culinary treats. **Known for:** friendly service; locally sourced produce and meats; delicious barbecue. 💲 *Average main: $28* ✉ *Rte. 987, Km 4, Las Croabas* ☎ *787/863–4481* 🌐 *www.laestacionpr.com* 🕐 *Closed Tues. and Wed.*

Pasión por el Fogón

$$$ | CARIBBEAN | FAMILY | At this beloved Fajardo restaurant, Chef Myrta Pérez Toledo transforms traditional dishes into something special. Succulent cuts of meat and fish are presented in unexpected ways. **Known for:** great desserts; contemporary Caribbean cuisine; fresh seafood. *$ Average main: $28 ✉ Rte. 987, Km 2.3, Fajardo ☎ 787/863–3502 🌐 www.pasionporelfogon.net ⏲ Closed Mon. and Tues.*

Hotels

El Conquistador Resort

$$$$ | RESORT | FAMILY | Despite extensive, post–Hurricane Maria renovations, this sprawling complex remains one of the island's most popular resorts—a place where pastel-painted "villages" of ultra-modern accommodations are arranged on an oceanside bluff and a shuttle whisks guests to a beach on Palomino Island. **Pros:** good dining options; bright, spacious rooms; unbeatable views of nearby islands. **Cons:** hidden fees including parking and kids club (and you need a car); long waits at funicular running between levels; large-scale, post-hurricane renovation in progress. *$ Rooms from: $400 ✉ 1000 Av. El Conquistador, Fajardo ☎ 787/863–1000, 888/543–1282 🌐 www.conquistadorresort.com 299 rooms Free Breakfast.*

Fajardo Inn

$ | HOTEL | FAMILY | The buildings that make up this hilltop hotel offer lovely views of islands poking out of the Atlantic Ocean. **Pros:** good value; pretty grounds; family-friendly environment. **Cons:** lacks amenities; motel-like rooms; not on the beach. *$ Rooms from: $130 ✉ 52 Parcelas Beltrán, Rte. 195, Beltrán Sector, Fajardo ☎ 787/860–6000, 888/860–6006 🌐 www.fajardoinn.com 125 rooms No Meals.*

Activities

BOATING AND SAILING

East Island Excursions

SAILING | This outfit operates 45- to 65-foot catamarans, three of which are powered to cut down on travel time to outlying islands. Trips may include offshore snorkeling, stops at isolated beaches, and a lunch buffet. Trips are offered to Cayo Icacos and Isla Palomino, within La Cordillera Nature Reserve. An evening excursion to Vieques to see the bioluminescent bay includes dinner at a local restaurant. All of the plush craft are outfitted with swimming decks, freshwater showers, and full-service bars. *✉ Marina Puerto del Rey, Rte. 3, Km 51.4, Fajardo ☎ 787/860–3434, 877/937–4386 🌐 www.eastislandpr.com.*

DIVING AND SNORKELING

The diving is excellent off Puerto Rico's south, east, and west coasts, as well as its nearby islands. Particularly striking are dramatic walls created by a continental shelf off the south coast near La Parguera and Guánica. There's also some fantastic diving near Fajardo and around Vieques and Culebra, two small islands off the east coast. It's best to choose specific locations with the help of a guide or outfitter. Escorted half-day dives range from $65 to $120 for one or two tanks, including all equipment; in general, double those prices for night dives. Packages that include lunch and other extras are more. Snorkeling excursions, which include transportation, equipment rental, and sometimes lunch, start at $50. Equipment rents for about $5 to $10.

Sea Ventures Pro Dive Center

SCUBA DIVING | Here you can get diving certification, arrange dive trips to Culebra, and organize boating and sailing excursions. *✉ Marina Puerto del Rey, Rte. 3, Km 51.2, Fajardo ☎ 787/863–3483, 800/739–3483 🌐 www.divepuertorico.com.*

GOLF

Arthur Hills Golf Course at El Conquistador

GOLF | Named for its designer, this 18-hole course is famous for mountainous terrain with elevation changes of more than 200 feet—a rarity in the Caribbean. From the highest spot, on the 15th hole, you have great views of the surrounding mountains and rain forest.

Views of an islet off of the picturesque Blue Beach on Vieques.

Trade winds challenge every shot—as if the gorgeous views, strategic bunkering, and many water hazards aren't distracting enough. You are also likely to spot the harmless and generally timid iguana that populate the area. ✉ *El Conquistador Resort, 1000 Av. El Conquistador, Fajardo* ☎ *787/863–6784* 🌐 *www.conquistador-resort.com* 🎫 *From $60 for non–hotel guests* 🏌 *18 holes, 6746 yards, par 72.*

KAYAKING

Kayaking Puerto Rico

WATER SPORTS | FAMILY | This adventure outfitter has an excursion for all types of water- (and kayak-) lovers. They offer a host of day and night trips—such as kayaking the glowing waters of Fajardo's bioluminescent lagoon, paddling along Culebra's reefs, snorkeling with local turtles, and piloting an eco-friendly, inflatable speedboat across crystal clear waters. Group rates and specials can be found online. ✉ *PR-987, Km. 5, Las Croabas, Fajardo* ☎ *787/435–1665, 787/245–4545* 🌐 *www.kayakingpuertorico.com* 🎫 *From $52.*

Vieques

13 km (8 miles) southeast of Fajardo.

Looking for a place to play Robinson Crusoe? Look no further than Vieques, where you can wander along almost any stretch of sand and rarely see another soul. You can while away the hours underneath coconut palms, wade in the warm water, or get a mask and snorkel and explore coral reefs that ring the island.

For many years the island was known mostly for the conflict between angry islanders and aloof federal officials. Over the course of six decades the U.S. Navy used two-thirds of Vieques, mostly on the island's eastern end, as a bombing range, and the western tip as an ammunition dump. After an April 1999 bombing accident took the life of one resident, waves of protests brought the maneuvers to a standstill, and political pressure from the island's governor helped force the military to leave on May 1, 2003.

Ironically, the military presence helped keep the island pristine by keeping resort developers away. Today the military's former holdings have been turned into the Vieques National Wildlife Refuge. The woodsy western end of the island is laced by trails that offer fabulous cycling around the base of Monte Pirata, the island's highest peak. More and more of the eastern part of the island is being opened every year, granting access to stupendous beaches shelving into calm turquoise waters. The park also protects Puerto Mosquito, a flask-shape bay populated by microscopic organisms that glow when disturbed at night—a thrilling experience for kayakers.

Just because Vieques is sleepy doesn't mean there's nothing to do besides hit the beach. There are two communities—Isabel Segunda and Esperanza—where you can dine at a variety of excellent restaurants, stock up on supplies, or book a trip to the astonishing Puerto Mosquito, perhaps the world's most luminous bioluminescent bay.

Sights

★ Puerto Mosquito Bioluminescent Bay

NATURE SIGHT | East of Esperanza, Puerto Mosquito is one of the world's best spots for a glow-in-the-dark experience with undersea dinoflagellates—microorganisms that light up when the water around them is agitated. Local operators offer kayak trips or excursions on nonpolluting boats to see the bay's light show. Look behind your boat at the twinkling wake. Even the fish that swim through and jump from the water bear an eerie glow. The high concentration of dinoflagellates sets the bay apart from other spots (including in Puerto Rico) that are home to these microorganisms. The experience is best when there's little or no moonlight; rainy nights are beautiful, too, because drops hitting the water produce ricochets that shimmer like diamonds. Note that licensed operators are prohibited from leading tours on the day before, during, and after a full moon. ✉ *Unpaved roads off Rte. 997.*

Vieques National Wildlife Refuge

WILDLIFE REFUGE | A portion of the west and the entire eastern end of the island is administered by the U.S. Fish and Wildlife Service as the Vieques National Wildlife Refuge. With almost 18,000 acres, it's Puerto Rico's biggest protected natural reserve; in 2015, it was voted the fourth best refuge in the entire Fish and Wildlife system. Many of the beaches on the northern and southern coasts—where an asphalt road leads to six of them—are open to the public. Hiking, biking, and horseback riding are allowed on designated trails. Fishing (both shore and from kayak), swimming, snorkeling, and diving are also permitted in designated zones. Much, though not all, of the eastern region is pristine, astonishingly beautiful, and well forested, with a hilly center region overlooking powder-white sandy beaches and a coral-ringed coastline. Some of the refuge—including 900 acres that once served as a naval bombing range—remains off-limits to visitors, though, as authorities continue to search for unexploded munitions and contaminants, the byproducts of the area's 60 years as a military base. ✉ *Rte. 997, Km 3.2* ☎ *787/741–2138* 🌐 *www.fws.gov/refuge/vieques.*

Beaches

Balneario Sun Bay

BEACH | FAMILY | Just east of Esperanza, this mile-long stretch of sand skirts a perfect crescent-shape bay. Dotted with picnic tables, this beach gets packed on holidays and weekends. On weekdays, when crowds are thin, you might see wild horses grazing among the palm trees. There is a small fee for parking, but often there is no one at the gate to take your money. **Amenities:** food and drink; parking (fee); showers; toilets. **Best for:** snorkeling; swimming; walking. ✉ *Rte. 997, Esperanza* ☎ *787/741–8198* 🎫 *Parking $2.*

★ Pata Prieta (*Secret Beach*)
BEACH | The not-so-secret Secret Beach is a heavenly cove for those seeking privacy. This tiny yet beautiful horseshoe-shape stretch of sand, reached via a rambling dirt road, is calm and secluded. You can find yourself completely alone or in the company of just a few couples embracing in the crystal clear water. **Amenities:** none. **Best for:** solitude; snorkeling; swimming. ✉ *Off Rte. 997, east of Playa Caracas.*

Playa Caracas (*Red Beach*)
BEACH | One of the first stretches of sand east of Esperanza, this well-maintained beach boasts covered cabañas for lounging. Less rustic than other nearby beaches, it is sheltered from waves. **Amenities:** parking (no fee); toilets. **Best for:** snorkeling; swimming; walking. ✉ *Off Rte. 997.*

Playa Media Luna
BEACH | Ideal for families because the water is calm and shallow, this is also a good spot to try snorkeling. There are no facilities. **Amenities:** none. **Best for:** families; snorkeling; swimming. ✉ *Off Rte. 997* ✣ *East of Balneario Sun Bay.*

Restaurants

Duffy's
$$ | CARIBBEAN | At some point during your time in Vieques, you should end up at Duffy's, the island's most popular hangout, where customers tend to sit elbow-to-elbow around the bar (the owner is a real character, and locals love to to chew the fat with him). Don't dismiss the food, though: in addition to burgers, fries, and other standards, there are chalkboard specials like conch fritters, scallop ceviche, grilled rib eye, or pan-seared pork loin—all a cut above the usual beach fare. **Known for:** cheap drinks; good bar food; lively atmosphere and waterfront location. $ *Average main: $12* ✉ *140 Calle Flamboyán, Esperanza* ☎ *787/435–6585* 🌐 *www.duffysesperanza.com* ⏲ *Closed Sun. and Mon.*

★ El Quenepo
$$$ | ECLECTIC | This elegant yet unpretentious spot (the owners, Scott and Kate Cole, don't mind if you show up in anything from a dripping wet bikini with a cover-up to a ball gown) brings fine dining and a touch of class to the Esperanza waterfront. Local herbs and fruits, such as quenepas and breadfruit, appear in artfully prepared dishes that the Coles call "fun, funky island food." Scott is the chef, known for seafood specials highlighting the daily catch, as well as dishes you're unlikely to find elsewhere in Puerto Rico, such as braised goat masala. **Known for:** good choice of wine and cocktails; fresh fish and seafood; excellent service. $ *Average main: $30* ✉ *148 Calle Flamboyán, Esperanza* ☎ *787/741–1215* 🌐 *www.elquenepovieques.com* ⏲ *Closed Sun. No lunch.*

★ Tin Box
$$ | BARBECUE | FAMILY | Tin Box is, quite literally, a tin box serving barbecue platters and po'boys piled high with smoked chicken, pork, fried shrimp, or ribs, served with classic sides like coleslaw, baked beans, and cornbread. A sushi bar rounds out the offerings—you can't go wrong with one of the rolls made with local spiny lobster. **Known for:** best sushi and barbecue on the island; watermelon margaritas and martinis; house-cured bacon. $ *Average main: $18* ✉ *Rte. 996 at Rte. 201* ☎ *787/435–6064* 🌐 *www.facebook.com/tinboxvqs* ⏲ *Closed Mon. and Tues.*

Bravo Beach Hotel
$ | HOTEL | FAMILY | Several blocks north of the ferry dock in Isabel Segunda, this simple but attractive hotel makes a good home base for island exploration. **Pros:** friendly management; gorgeous building; beautiful pools. **Cons:** no on-site

restaurant; can't swim on property's beach; out-of-the-way location in residential neighborhood. *Rooms from: $210* *1 North Shore Rd., Isabel Segunda* *787/741–1128* *www.bravobeachhotel.com* *11 rooms* *No Meals.*

★ Hacienda Tamarindo

$ | **HOTEL** | Taking its name from a centuries-old tamarind tree rising more than three stories through the center of its main building, this plantation-style property—with a barrel-tile roof and wood-shuttered windows—was once a dance hall but is now one of the island's prettiest hotels. **Pros:** excellent breakfast included; beautiful views; nicely designed rooms. **Cons:** no elevator; no full-service restaurant; must drive to beaches. *Rooms from: $265* *Rte. 997, Km 4.5, Esperanza* *787/741–8525* *www.haciendatamarindo.com* *17 rooms* *Free Breakfast.*

Hix Island House

$$ | **HOTEL** | Constructed entirely of concrete and set in a tropical forest, the four buildings of this luxurious hotel echo the granite boulders strewn around Vieques, blending with the surroundings. **Pros:** friendly staff; acclaimed eco-friendly architecture; very secluded setting. **Cons:** no Wi-Fi in rooms (although it's free in public areas); no air-conditioning, TVs, or phones; the lack of window screens means bugs get in. *Rooms from: $300* *Rte. 995, Km 1.5* *787/435–4590* *www.hixislandhouse.com* *19 rooms* *Free Breakfast.*

Malecón House

$ | **B&B/INN** | Raising the bar for Vieques lodging are posh boutique hotels like this immaculate seaside escape, where rooms are decorated with rich wood furniture, luxurious stone flooring, and high-end linens. **Pros:** welcoming hosts; affordable waterfront property; tasty breakfast. **Cons:** surrounding area can be noisy; rather small pool; in-town location not for those seeking seclusion. *Rooms from: $200* *105 Calle Flamboyán, Esperanza* *939/239–7113* *www.maleconhouse.com* *13 rooms* *Free Breakfast.*

Sea Gate Hotel

$ | **HOTEL** | This hilltop hotel—the oldest on Vieques—overlooks the island's picturesque, historic fort and is about 10 minutes by foot (downhill) from Isabel Segunda. **Pros:** continental breakfast included; friendly and helpful owner-manager; complimentary pickup at ferry or airport. **Cons:** presence of farm animals and dogs might be problematic for some; no restaurant; small rooms. *Rooms from: $125* *Barrio Fuerte, Isabel Segunda* *201/450–8238* *www.seagatehotel.com* *15 rooms* *Free Breakfast.*

Activities

BOATING AND KAYAKING

Various outfitters offer trips to Puerto Mosquito, the island's celebrated bioluminescent bay. Most trips are made in single-person kayaks, which can be a challenge if you lack experience or endurance. A better option for most people is electric-powered boat—gas-powered engines harm the environment.

Abe's Snorkeling and Bio-Bay Tours

KAYAKING | Abe is one of Vieques's most animated characters, so it's no surprise that his kayaking tours to Puerto Mosquito are the most popular. Over the course of two hours, guests kayak into the glowing bay for a once-in-a-lifetime experience. For an entire day on the water, Abe's All-in-One Tour involves kayaking through mangrove lagóons, snorkeling coral reefs, watching the sunset on a secluded beach, and visiting the bio-bay after dark. Lunch is provided. *278 Calle Flamboyan, Esperanza* *787/435–1362* *www.abessnorkeling.com* *Night tours from $60, five-hour tours from $150.*

Culebra

28 km (17 miles) east of Fajardo by ferry.

"Open some days, closed others," reads the sign on a food kiosk near the canal that cuts through a part of this island. It's a pretty good motto for most of Culebra, which—if you can imagine it—is even more laid-back than Vieques. Visitors don't come here for highbrow entertainment. They come for one thing: beaches. Culebra is known around the world for its curvaceous coastline. Playa Flamenco, the island's most famous stretch of sand, is considered one of the top 10 best beaches in the world. If Playa Flamenco gets too crowded, as it often does around Easter or Christmas, many other neighboring beaches will still be nearly deserted. And if it's complete privacy you're after, hire a motorboat to take you to one of the nearby islets, such as Isla Culebrita or Cayo Luis Peña. It won't be difficult to find a little cove that you can have all to yourself.

Archaeological evidence shows that Taíno and Carib people lived on Culebra long before the arrival of the Spanish in the late 15th century. The Spanish didn't bother laying claim to it until 1886; a lack of freshwater made it an unattractive location for a settlement. The U.S. Navy and Marine Corps, however, thought it was a very valuable piece of real estate. Although President Theodore Roosevelt created a wildlife refuge here in 1909, the military later used this island, as well as nearby Vieques, for target practice and amphibious assault training, beginning in WWII. Despite having a smaller population than Vieques, the residents of Culebra staged a number of sit-ins and succeeded in ousting the military in 1975.

Sights

★ Isla Culebrita

ISLAND | Part of the Refugio Nacional de Vida Silvestre de Culebra, uninhabited Isla Culebrita is clearly visible from the northeast corner of Culebra. An essential day-trip excursion, this islet is a favorite destination for sunbathers, snorkelers, and boating enthusiasts. Isolation amid a palette of crystalline, turquoise waters, and dewy, lush greens makes for a one-of-a-kind natural experience. On weekends and holidays however, the island can get crowded. On the northern shore there are several tidal pools; snuggling into one of them is like taking a warm bath. Snorkelers and divers love that they can reach the reef from the shore and carouse with sea turtles, rays, and schools of colorful fish. Bring your sneakers: in about 20–30 minutes you can hike to the islet's peak, where the spectacular ruins of an old lighthouse await. Views of the surrounding Caribbean are sublime from the top of the structure, but you may not be able to climb its 54 steps; the lighthouse is currently being restored. Several tour operators offer excursions to the island. 🌐 *www.paralanaturaleza.org.*

★ Refugio Nacional de Vida Silvestre de Culebra

WILDLIFE REFUGE | Commissioned by President Theodore Roosevelt in 1909, the Culebra National Wildlife Refuge is one of the nation's oldest. The total protected area comprises some 1,500 acres of the island. It's a lure for hikers and bird-watchers: Culebra teems with seabirds, from laughing gulls and roseate terns to red-billed tropic birds and sooty terns. Maps of trails in the refuge are hard to come by, but you can stop by the U.S. Fish and Wildlife Service office east of the airport to find out about trail conditions and determine whether you're headed to an area that requires a permit. The office also can tell you whether the leatherback turtles are nesting. From mid-April to mid-July, volunteers help monitor and tag these creatures, which nest on nearby beaches, especially Playa Resaca and Playa Brava. ✉ *Rte. 250, north of Dewey* ☎ *787/742–0115* 🌐 *www.fws.gov/refuge/culebra.*

Beaches

★ Playa Flamenco
BEACH | FAMILY | Consistently ranked one of the most beautiful beaches in the world, this stretch has snow-white sands, turquoise waters, and lush hills rising on all sides. During the week, it's pleasantly uncrowded; on weekends it fills up with day-trippers from the mainland. With kiosks selling simple dishes and vendors for lounge-chair and umbrella rentals, it's easy to make a day of it. There's great snorkeling past the old dock. Tanks on the northern end of the beach are a reminder that the area was once a military base. **Amenities:** food and drink; parking (no fee); showers; toilets. **Best for:** snorkeling; swimming; walking. ✉ *Rte. 251, west of the airport* ☎ *787/742–0700.*

Restaurants

Dinghy Dock
$$ | SEAFOOD | This restaurant takes its name from the nearby site of Culebra's heaviest traffic—the arrival and departure of the water taxi. The menu leans toward grilled meats, from hamburgers and wraps to sirloin steaks. **Known for:** laid-back atmosphere; creole-style seafood; burgers and other bar food. $ *Average main: $20* ✉ *Calle Fulladoza, Dewey* ☎ *787/742–0233.*

Mamacita's Bar & Grill
$$ | CARIBBEAN | Pull your dinghy up to the dock, and watch the resident iguanas plod past this simple, open-air, tin-roof restaurant on a rough-plank deck beside the Dewey canal. Tarpon cruise past, and the to-and-fro of boaters completes the show at Culebra's favorite watering hole and gringo hangout. **Known for:** casual setting; grilled seafood; lunchtime burgers. $ *Average main: $18* ✉ *66 Calle Castelar, Dewey* ☎ *787/742–0090.*

Hotels

★ Club Seabourne
$ | HOTEL | The most sophisticated place in Culebra is an assemblage of lovely plantation-style cottages on a picturesque hilltop overlooking Fulladoza Bay. Though just a five-minute drive south of Dewey, it feels completely isolated—in a good way. **Pros:** airport or ferry transfers included; lush gardens; nice pool. **Cons:** spotty Internet and mobile phone reception; no full-service on-site restaurant; some steps to negotiate. $ *Rooms from: $249* ✉ *Rte. 252, northwest of town* ☎ *787/742–3169* 🌐 *www.clubseabourne.com* *13 rooms* 🍽 *Free Breakfast.*

Tamarindo Estates
$ | APARTMENT | A few of the one- and two-bedroom cottages at this 60-acre estate, hidden away on Culebra's western coast, sit directly on a long, sandy beach; most cottages, however, are a bit farther inland, though they have great coastal views from covered verandas. **Pros:** all apartments have full kitchens; peaceful location; pretty pool area. **Cons:** no housekeeping service; isolated, far from dining options; short walk to the beach. $ *Rooms from: $169* ✉ *Off Rte. 251* ☎ *787/742–3343* 🌐 *www.tamarindoestates.com* *12 cottages* 🍽 *No Meals.*

Activities

DIVING AND SNORKELING

Aquatic Adventures
BOATING | Captain Taz Hamrick takes guests out on snorkeling and PADI-certified scuba trips, as well as charters to the surrounding keys. Two-tank dive trips start at $110. ✉ *372 Sector Fulladoza, Dewey* ☎ *515/290–2310* 🌐 *www.diveculebra.com.*

Culebra Divers
SCUBA DIVING | The island's premier dive shop caters to scuba newbies and old hands alike. The company's 25-foot cabin

cruisers travel to more than 50 local sites to see spotted eagle rays, octopus, moray eels, and turtles. You can also rent a mask and snorkel to explore on your own. Two-tank dive trips start at $125. ✉ *4 Calle Pedro Márquez, Dewey* ☎ *787/742–0803* 🌐 *www.culebradivers.com.*

Dorado

27 km (17 miles) west of San Juan.

This small and tidy town is one of the oldest vacation spots on the island, having gotten a boost in 1955, when Laurance Rockefeller bought the pineapple, coconut, and grapefruit plantation of Dr. Alfred Livingston and his daughter Clara and built a resort on the property. Sadly, the Hyatt Dorado Beach Resort & Country Club closed in 2005. Its excellent golf courses—among the best-known in Puerto Rico—are still open, however, and the property has been redeveloped as a private residential resort. Those looking for upscale accommodations evoking the erstwhile golden age still have an option here, thanks to the Dorado Beach, a Ritz-Carlton Reserve. The town of Dorado itself is fun to visit; its winding road leads across a bridge to a main square, with small bars, restaurants, and shops nearby. Most visitors, however, don't stray too far from the beach.

GETTING HERE AND AROUND

As is the case throughout most of Puerto Rico, the best means of getting to and around Dorado and the surrounding towns is by car. Public transportation is virtually nonexistent outside San Juan, and when it is available, it's rarely reliable. A map and a sense of adventure will be your greatest assets.

Beaches

★ Playa Mar Chiquita

BEACH | The beaches along Puerto Rico's northern coast are unique in that many of them are formed from natural pools surrounded by limestone walls that protect these swimming holes from the rough waters of the Atlantic Ocean. This half-moon shaped, natural pool is one of the Island's most visited and the crashing waves are a spectacular sight. Food trucks selling all of PR's fave fried goodies are always set up here, and arts vendors come out on the weekends when the beach is busier. The water gets rough in the winter months, and swimming may not always be a good idea. **Amenities:** food and drink; parking (no fee). **Best for:** snorkeling; swimming; walking ✉ *Playa Mar Chiquita, Manatí* ✢ *end of Route 684; 21 miles west of Dorado.*

★ Poza de las Mujeres

BEACH | Poza de las Mujeres is another natural North Coast swimming hole protected by rock formations, which split the beach almost in two. On the left-hand side, the water is shallow, calm, and protected from the rougher waters outside the natural barricade. On the right-hand side, however, the rocks do not form a protective barrier and the water is much rougher year-round. **Amenities:** parking (no fee). **Best for:** snorkeling; swimming; walking. ✉ *Tierras Nuevas Poniente, Manatí* ✢ *22 miles west of Dorado.*

Restaurants

El Ladrillo

$$$ | **STEAKHOUSE** | Original paintings cover brick walls (*ladrillo* means "brick") from floor to ceiling at this restaurant, popular among locals for more than 40 years. It's known primarily for steaks—and offers an excellent filet mignon—but given its coastal location, there's also a wide selection of fresh seafood. **Known for:** filet mignon; ample wine cellar; zarzuela. $ *Average main: $28* ✉ *334 Calle*

Mendéz Vigo, Dorado ☏ 787/796–2120 ⊕ www.elladrillorest.com ⊙ Closed Mon. and Tues.

★ **Grappa**

$$$ | ITALIAN | Dorado's most charming restaurant—and perhaps the most appealing one on the North Coast—Grappa is spectacular, both in design and on the plate. Specializing in Italian fare, the kitchen staff makes pasta by hand, and it's served with fruits of the sea or delicious, tender beef. **Known for:** house-made pastas; romantic setting; fresh seafood. *$ Average main: $27 ✉ 247 Calle Mendéz Vigo, Dorado ☏ 787/796–2674 ⊕ www.grappapr.com ⊙ Closed Sun.–Tues.*

Hotels

★ **Dorado Beach, a Ritz-Carlton Reserve**

$$$$ | RESORT | Luxurious accommodations, spectacular golf courses, and 5 km (3 miles) of exquisite coast are among the many draws at this resort, set on 1,400 acres that were once part of Laurance Rockefeller's estate. **Pros:** excellent spa and gourmet dining; all rooms are beachfront; activities galore. **Cons:** occasional service lapses; exceedingly expensive; $150 daily resort fee. *$ Rooms from: $3000 ✉ 100 Dorado Beach Dr., Dorado ☏ 787/626–1100 ⊕ www.ritzcarlton.com 114 rooms No Meals.*

Embassy Suites by Hilton Dorado del Mar Beach Resort

$ | HOTEL | FAMILY | This resort, directly on the beach, is much like an Embassy Suites anywhere else in the world, offering a consistent, quality experience but little local flavor. **Pros:** suites have kitchenettes; on a gorgeous beach; breakfast and happy hour included. **Cons:** limited on-site food options; noisy common areas; $35 resort fee. *$ Rooms from: $240 ✉ 201 Dorado del Mar Blvd., Dorado ☏ 787/796–6125 ⊕ embassysuites3.hilton.com 209 suites Free Breakfast.*

Activities

GOLF

TPC Dorado Beach

GOLF | Two, 18-hole, regulation courses blend Caribbean luxury and great golf at this iconic property with a storied tradition. Designed by Robert Trent Jones Sr. and renovated by his son in 2011, the famous **East** course is secluded along 3 km (2 miles) of northeasterly shore within the former Rockefeller estate. A plantation course—the challenging **Sugarcane**—completes the offerings. Both were purchased by the Tournament Players Club (TPC) in 2015. *✉ 5000 Plantation Dr., Dorado ☏ 787/262–1010 ⊕ www.tpc.com East Course $282, Sugarcane Course $170 East Course: 18 holes, 7200 yards, par 72; Sugarcane: 18 holes, 7119 yards, par 72.*

Arecibo

60 km (38 miles) west of Dorado.

The town of Arecibo was founded in 1515 and is known as the Villa of Capitán Correa because of a battle fought here by Captain Antonio Correa and a handful of Spanish soldiers to repel a British sea invasion in 1702. Today it's a busy manufacturing center, and serves as a link to the Parque de las Cavernas del Río Camuy and deeper exploration of the central mountain region. For one of the best ocean drives on the island, get off the main road at Barceloneta and take Route 681 through Arecibo's waterfront district.

GETTING HERE AND AROUND

To get to Arecibo from San Juan, take Route 22 west toward Arecibo and get off exit 77b. Then Route 129 south to Km 20. Signs will guide you to the caves once you get off the main highway.

Sights

Parque de las Cavernas del Río Camuy

CAVE | The 268-acre Parque de las Cavernas del Río Camuy contains one of the world's largest cave networks. A tram takes you down a trail shaded by bamboo and banana trees to Cueva Clara, where stalactites and stalagmites turn the entrance into a toothy grin. Hour-long guided tours in English and Spanish lead you on foot through the 180-foot-high cave, which is teeming with wildlife. You're likely to see blue-eyed river crabs and long-legged tarantulas. More elusive are the more than 100,000 bats that make their home in the cave; they don't come out until dark, but you can feel the heat they generate at the cave's entrance (not to mention smell their presence). The visit ends with a tram ride to Tres Pueblos sinkhole, where you can see the third-longest underground river in the world pass from one cave to another. Tours are first-come, first-served; plan to arrive early on weekends, when local families join the crowds. Tours are sometimes canceled if it's raining, as the steep walkways can get slippery. There's a picnic area, cafeteria, and gift shop. ✉ *Rte. 129, Km 18.9, Camuy* ☎ *787/898–3100* 🎫 *$18* ⏲ *Closed Mon. and Tues.*

Rincón

93 miles (150 km) southwest of San Juan.

Jutting out into the ocean along the rugged western coast, Rincón ("corner" in Spanish) may have gotten its name because it's tucked into a bend of the coastline. Some, however, trace the town's name to Gonzalo Rincón, a 16th-century landowner who let poor families live on his land. Whatever the history, the name suits the town, which is like a little world unto itself.

The most famous hotel in the region is the Horned Dorset Primavera. Although a couple of other larger hotels, including the Rincón of the Seas and Rincón Beach Resort, have been built, Rincón remains a laid-back place. The town is a mecca for wave-seekers—particularly surfers from the East Coast of the United States, who often prefer the relatively quick New York–Aguadilla flight to the long Pacific haul. The town caters to all sorts of travelers, however.

The pace picks up October–April, when the waves are at their best, but tourists can be found here year-round, and many American mainlanders have settled here. Budget travelers will most likely find discount accommodations in August and September, when tourism is slow. Hurricane season runs June–November, bringing occasional swells for the surf crowd.

GETTING HERE AND AROUND

Rincón itself is a spread-out labyrinth of unmarked streets without any apparent logic to its layout. The city is built on a hillside, so most streets are narrow and steep, weaving erratically through the intermingled residential-business zones. There are three main highways to keep in mind; Route 115 cuts through the middle of "downtown" (the administrative center) and runs north to the Aguadilla airport and south to the Mayagüez airport. Route 413 snakes along the hillsides, past villas and local restaurants. The smaller Route 4413 follows the water, past Punta Higuero Lighthouse, and ends at the Bonus Thermonuclear Energy Plant.

AIR

San Juan's international airport is the most commonly used on the island and is approximately two hours from Rincón. The closest airports, however, are in Mayagüez and Aguadilla—only 20 minutes' drive in either direction. A taxi from either airport into town costs around $20, but the best option is to rent a car at the

The boutique inn, Tres Sirenas, in the town of Rincon

airport, since you'll need it for transportation during your trip.

CAR

To reach Rincón from San Juan, take Route 22, which merges Route 2 after Arecibo. Follow it past the northwestern tip of the island, just beyond Aguadilla. Then take Route 115 southwest past Aguada until you reach Rincón's Route 413, "the Road to Happiness."

Sights

Desecheo Island

ISLAND | Protected by the U.S. Fish and Wildlife Service, this uninhabited island—about 20 km (13 miles) off the coast of Rincón—is home to lizards, rats, and rhesus monkeys, first introduced in 1967 from Cayo Santiago. Among divers, it's known for abundant reef and fish life. The main draw here is "Candyland," a rocky bottom that rims the island and slopes to 120 feet. Long tunnels and caverns covered with purple hydrocoral distinguish one formation known as Yellow Reef. With visibility of 150 feet, this is also a popular snorkeling spot. Other sites have plentiful fish and coral in shallower water just off Rincón's shores. ✉ *Rincón.*

Beaches

Balneario de Rincón

BEACH | **FAMILY** | Families enjoy the tranquil waters, playground, and shelters for seaside picnics. The beach is within walking distance to the center of town. **Amenities:** parking (no fee); showers; toilets. **Best for:** sunset; swimming. ✉ *Calle Cambija, Rincón.*

Steps (*Tres Palmas*)

BEACH | This beach, which takes its name from the mysterious concrete steps at the water's edge, is home to the Tres Palmas Marine Reserve. It's a good place to find sea glass; on calm days, it's also an excellent snorkeling spot. At other times, the waves can be huge. Indeed, on a handful of days each year, the waters deliver epic rides that draw surfers from around the globe. A small food truck serves coconut water, fish tacos, empanadas, and other treats. The beach is hard to find—look for the turnoff at a whale-shape sign reading "Playa Escalera." **Amenities:** none. **Best for:** snorkeling; sunsets. ✉ *Rte. 413, north of turnoff for Black Eagle Marina, Rincón.*

Restaurants

★ Estela

$$$ | **CARIBBEAN** | On weekends, patrons come from as far as San Juan to dine at this cozy restaurant. Operated by husband-and-wife team Juan and Nerylu, it's found a niche in Rincón offering dishes made using locally sourced ingredients—you may even see a fisherman pull up with a giant yellowfin tuna. **Known for:** good wine list; fresh seafood; farm-to-table dining. *Average main: $25* ✉ *Rte. 115, Km 14, Rincón* ☎ *787/823–1795* *Closed Sun. and Mon. No lunch.*

Hotels

Lazy Parrot Inn

$ | **HOTEL** | **FAMILY** | Though its guest rooms are more subdued, this mountainside hotel—painted in eye-popping tropical hues and with an open lobby featuring colorful murals of its namesake bird—makes a statement without taking itself too seriously. **Pros:** great pizza at on-site restaurant; in-room microwaves; beautiful pool. **Cons:** some may consider the whimsical style tacky; stairs to climb; not on the beach. *Rooms from: $200* ✉ *Rte. 413, Km 4.1, Rincón* ☎ *787/823–5654, 800/294–1752* *www.lazyparrot.com* *22 rooms* *No Meals.*

★ Tres Sirenas

$ | **B&B/INN** | Waves gently lap against the shore at the "Three Mermaids" (a nod to the owners' daughters), a boutique inn set in a luxurious two-story villa on one of Rincón's calmer beaches. **Pros:** tastefully decorated; beachfront; spotless. **Cons:** long walk to restaurants; pricey in high season; often fully booked far in advance. *Rooms from: $230* ✉ *26 Seabeach Dr., Rincón* ☎ *787/823–0558* *www.tressirenas.com* *5 rooms* *Free Breakfast.*

Activities

SURFING

After hosting the World Surfing Championship in 1968, Rincón became a popular surfing destination. Today, locals and tourists flock to this small, laid-back town every winter to catch the season's best waves. But you don't need to be a pro to vacation in Rincón. There are several surfing schools that offer lessons for beginners, and the town's chill vibe is the perfect place to unwind, relax, and soak up the sun.

Mar Azul

SURFING | One of the best surf shops on the entire island has Rincon's finest selection of performance surfboards and stand-up paddleboards to buy or rent. Rent a board for $25 a day or $150 for an entire week. ✉ *Rte. 413, Km 4.4, Rincón* ☎ *787/823–5692* *www.puertoricosurfinginfo.com.*

Puntas Surf School

SURFING | With more than a decade of surf-coaching experience, Puntas is a great surf school for beginners and kids. ✉ *Rincón* ☎ *787/366–1689* *www.puntassurfschool.com.*

Rincón Surf School

SURFING | This popular surf school offers private and group lessons. ✉ *Rte. 413, Km 4.4, Rincón* ☎ *787/823–0610* *www.rinconsurfschool.com.*

Surf Lessons Puerto Rico

SURFING | Ex–pro surfer Ramse Morales has been conducting high-quality surfing classes since 2000. ✉ *Maria's Beach, Maria's Beach, Rincón* ☎ *787/617–4731* *www.surflessonspuertorico.com* *From $75 for private 2-hr lessons.*

Boquerón

5 km (3 miles) south of Joyuda.

Once a quiet fishing village, Boquerón still has its share of seaside shanties. Its narrow streets are quiet during the week but come alive on the weekend, when vendors appear with carts full of clams and oysters you can slurp down on the spot, and when bars and restaurants throw open their doors—if they have any, that is. Many of the establishments here are open to the breeze, making this a Puerto Rican party spot where the music (and the people) can be heard until 2 in the morning. Boquerón is also a water-sports center; many companies operate from or near the docks of the imposing Club Nautico de Boquerón, which is easy to find at the end of Route 100.

GETTING HERE AND AROUND

To reach Boquerón from Mayagüez, take Route 2 south to Route 100. After you pass Cabo Rojo heading south, take Route 101 and follow the signs south-west to Boquerón. The small town can easily be explored on foot.

Beaches

Balneario Boquerón
BEACH | FAMILY | The long stretch of sand at this beach off Route 101 is a favorite with islanders, especially on weekends. This is a Blue Flag beach, meaning it is recognized for its adherence to high environmental standards. **Amenities:** lifeguards; parking (no fee); picnic tables; playground; showers; toilets. **Best for:** relaxing; swimming. ✉ *Off Rte. 101, Boquerón.*

Aguadilla

18 km (12 miles) north of Rincón.

Resembling a fishing village, downtown Aguadilla has narrow streets lined with small wooden homes. Weathered but lovely, the faded facades recall the city's long and turbulent past. Officially incorporated as a town in 1775, Aguadilla subsequently suffered a series of catastrophes, including a devastating earthquake in 1918 and strong hurricanes in 1928 and 1932. Determined to survive, the town rebuilt after each disaster, and by World War II it had become known for the sprawling Ramey Air Force Base. The base was an important link in the U.S. defense system throughout the Cold War. Ramey was decommissioned in 1973; today this area comprises some small businesses, a golf course, a university, and the region's most important airport. As a result of tourism, the north end of town is budding with international restaurants, surf shops, and even an outdoor mall.

Perhaps the town's greatest draw is its surfing at local spots like Playa Wilderness, Playa Crashboat, and Playa Gas Chamber. Famous for their right-hand barrels, these beaches have hosted a variety of amateur and professional surfing events, including the 1968 and 1988 International Surfing Association (ISA) World Championships and the 2010 Association of Surfing Professionals (ASP) World Tour.

Beaches

★ Playa Borínquen
BEACH | This big, beautiful stretch of white sand leads to large rocks and a cliff that juts into the sea. The water can be too rough and choppy for swimming in the winter, but the summer months are great for swimming and snorkeling. During low tide, you'll find a small cave at the far end. **Amenities:** parking (free). **Best for:** snorkeling; swimming; walking. ✉ *Av. Borínquen, Aguadilla.*

Playa Crashboat
BEACH | Named for the rescue boats used when nearby Ramey Air Force Base was in operation, this beach has soft, sugary sand, water as smooth as glass, and the

sort of colorful fishing boats pictured on postcards. A food stand serves the catch of the day with cold beer. **Amenities:** food and drink; parking (free); showers; toilets. **Best for:** partiers; snorkeling; swimming. *End of Rte. 458, off Rte. 107, Aguadilla.*

★ Playa Peña Blanca

BEACH | Swimming in the crystal clear waters of Peña Blanca is best in the summer months during low tide. In the winter months, the waters reach the rocks around the beach, eliminating the already fairly small shoreline. Regardless, the views here are stunning. **Amenities:** parking (free in winter, fee in summer when it's busy). **Best for:** snorkeling; walking. *Calle Wishin Wells, Aguadilla.*

Restaurants

CINCO

$$ | **PUERTO RICAN** | **FAMILY** | Although the menu at this family-friendly restaurant includes pizza and pasta dishes, it's a good place to dine on hearty Caribbean fare, including Puerto Rican specialties like mofongo, churrasco, and bistec encebollado. The wine list is short but well-curated, and the cocktails are creative and affordable. **Known for:** friendly staff; mofongo; churrasco. *Average main: $18 Rte. 110, Km 32, Aguadilla 787/658–6078.*

Levain Bakery

$ | **BAKERY** | **FAMILY** | This small bakery across the street from the airport makes some of the best breads and croissants on the island. They also serve lattes and breakfast items such as cinnamon buns, as well as sandwiches and quiche for lunch. **Known for:** weekend brunch; great coffee; excellent fresh breads and croissants. *Average main: $9 333 Wing Rd., Aguadilla 787/658–6220 www.levainpr.com No dinner; Closed Mon. and Tues.*

Isabela

20 km (13 miles) east of Aguadilla.

Founded in 1819 and named for Spain's Queen Isabella, this small town on the northwestern tip of the island skirts tall cliffs that overlook the rocky shoreline. Locals have long known of the area's natural beauty, and lately more offshore tourists have begun coming to this niche, which offers secluded hotels, sprawling golf courses, fantastic beaches, excellent surf, and hiking through one of the island's forest reserves.

Sights

Guajataca Forest Reserve

NATURE PRESERVE | Explore karst topography and subtropical vegetation at the 2,357-acre Guajataca State Forest, between the towns of Quebradillas and Isabela. On more than 46 walking trails you can see 186 species of trees, like royal palm and ironwood, and 45 species of birds—watch for red-tailed hawks and Puerto Rican woodpeckers. Bring a flashlight and descend into the **Cueva del Viento** (Cave of the Wind) to find stalagmites, stalactites, and other strange formations. At the forest entrance there's a small ranger station where you can pick up a decent hiking map (get here early, as the rangers don't always stay until closing time). *Rte. 446, Km 10, Isabela 787/872–1045 Free Ranger station closed weekends.*

Restaurants

The Eclipse

$$$ | **ECLECTIC** | Beautiful beachfront dining, farm-to-table ingredients, and fantastic service are worth the drive from San Juan. The setting is rustic yet elegant, and the view is unbeatable. **Known for:** unbeatable beachfront location; great pizza; weekend brunch. *Average main: $28 Villa Montaña, Rte. 4466, Km 1.9,*

Isabela ☎ *787/872–9554* 🌐 *www.villamontana.com.*

Uma's Playa Jobos

$$ | EUROPEAN | This family-run restaurant, a Rockaway Beach (New York City) outpost on Playa Jobos, serves Euro-Asian cuisine with a tropical twist. You can sip a creative cocktail on the wooden deck and chow down on unique dishes like Korean carrot and green papaya salad, pumpkin manti, or Hawaiian poke bowl with local yellowfin tuna. **Known for:** live reggae on Saturday; great Caribbean-inspired, Euro-Asian fare; perfect beachfront location. $ *Average main: $13* ✉ *Playa Jobos, Rte. 4466, Km 7.2, Isabela* ☎ *917/865–6261.*

 Hotels

★ Royal Isabela

$$$$ | RESORT | The area's most luxurious property, this 2,200-acre paradise is a must for anyone remotely interested in golf—it has one of the best courses in Puerto Rico. **Pros:** access to a private beach; great views; luxurious accommodations. **Cons:** long walk to the beach; 15-minute drive from other dining options; luxury isn't cheap. $ *Rooms from: $500* ✉ *396 Av. Noel Estrada, Isabela* ☎ *787/609–5888* 🌐 *www.royalisabela.com* *20 casitas* *No Meals.*

 Activities

GOLF

★ Golf Links at Royal Isabela

GOLF | Mixing luxurious service, ecological sensitivity, and an incomparable setting, this 18-hole course is considered one of the Caribbean's best. Designed and developed by Stanley and Charlie Pasarell with assistance from course architect David Pfaff, it can play to as much as 7,667 yards and a par of 72 or 73, depending upon how you play the fork-in-the-road 6th. The course has many signature moments—from the 6th to the island green at No. 9 to the carry over the sea at No. 12. Carts are available, although walking is encouraged and caddies are mandatory. Note too that the course is open to guests staying at the Royal Isabela. ✉ *396 Av. Noel Estrada, Isabela* ☎ *787/609–5888* 🌐 *www.royalisabela.com* *$250 (guests $125); caddie $90 for 2 players* *18 holes, 7667 yards, par 73.*

HORSEBACK RIDING

Tropical Trail Rides

HORSEBACK RIDING | FAMILY | Group rides depart Playa Shacks, one of the region's prettiest beaches. The two-hour tours cost approximatly $100 per person and take you along the beach and through a forest of almond trees. At the end you have a chance to take a dip in the ocean. The company also offers hiking trips to the limestone caves at Survival Beach. ✉ *400 Bo Bajuras, Rte. 4466, Km 1.9, Isabela* ☎ *787/872–9256* 🌐 *www.tropicaltrailrides.com.*

Ponce

34 km (21 miles) southwest of Coamo.

"Ponce is Ponce and the rest is parking" is the adage used by residents of Puerto Rico's second-largest city (population 166,000) to express their pride in being *ponceños.* The rivalry with the island's capital began in the 19th century, when European immigrants from England, France, and Spain settled here. Because the city limits extend from the Caribbean to the foothills of the Cordillera Central, it's a lot hotter in climate than San Juan. Another contrast is the neoclassical architecture of the elegant homes and public buildings that surround the main square.

Many of the 19th-century buildings in Ponce Centro, the downtown area, have been renovated, and the Museo de Arte de Ponce—endowed by its late native son and former governor of Puerto Rico,

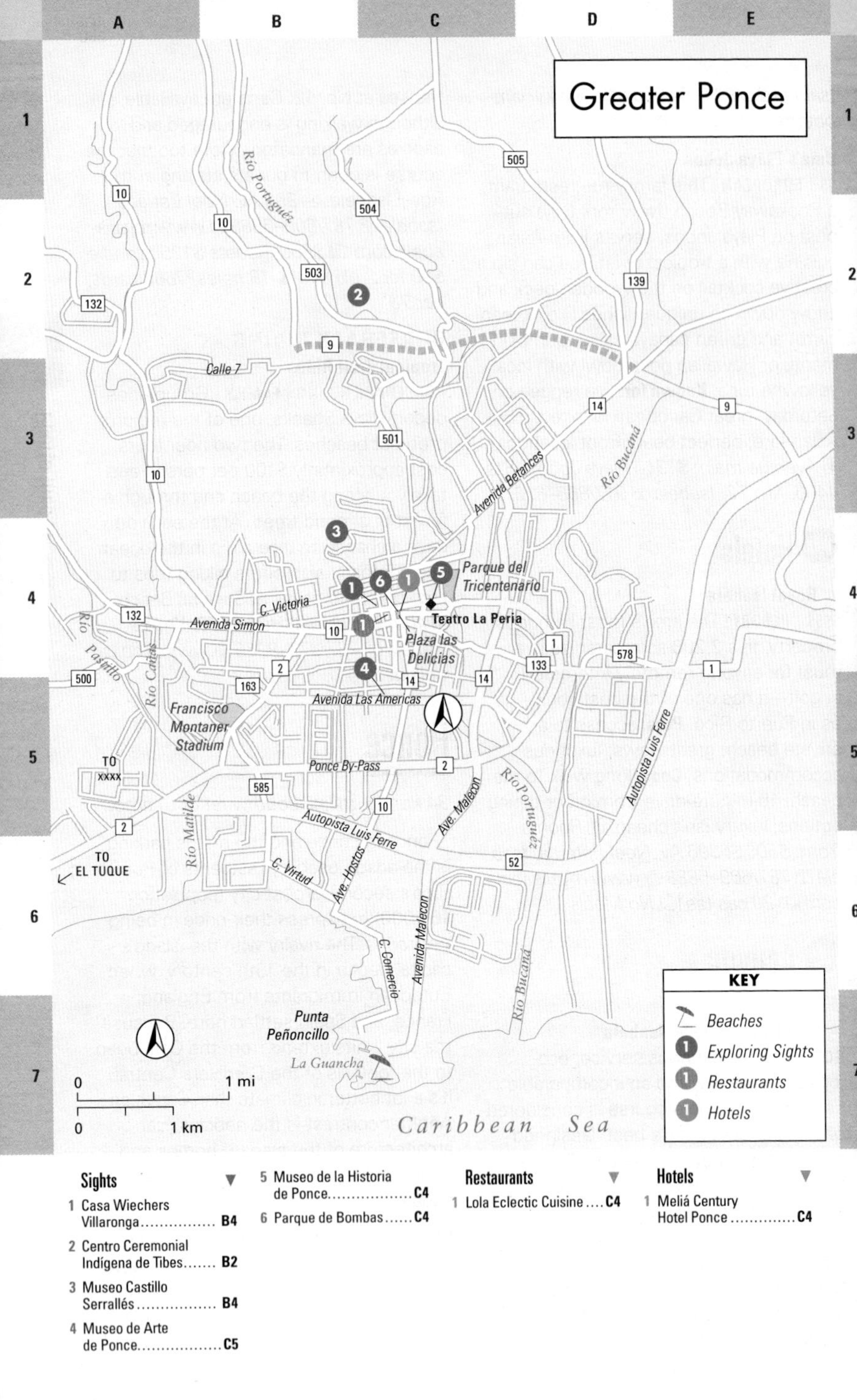

A
B
C
D
E
1
2
3
4
5
6
7
Greater Ponce
Río Portuguéz
505
504
10
503
139
132
9
Calle 7
14
501
Avenida Betances
Río Bucaná
Parque del Tricentenario
C. Victoria
Teatro La Perla
Avenida Simon
Plaza las Delicias
Río
Pastillo
Río Cañas
500
163
Avenida Las Americas
133
578
1
2
Francisco Montaner Stadium
TO XXXX
Ponce By-Pass
585
Autopista Luis Ferre
Ave. Malecon
Río Matilde
TO EL TUQUE
C. Virtud
Ave. Hostos
52
C. Comercio
Avenida Malecon
Río Bucaná
Punta Peñoncillo
La Guancha
0
1 mi
1 km
Caribbean Sea
KEY
Beaches
Exploring Sights
Restaurants
Hotels
Sights
1 Casa Wiechers Villaronga B4
2 Centro Ceremonial Indígena de Tibes B2
3 Museo Castillo Serrallés B4
4 Museo de Arte de Ponce C5
5 Museo de la Historia de Ponce C4
6 Parque de Bombas C4
Restaurants
1 Lola Eclectic Cuisine C4
Hotels
1 Meliá Century Hotel Ponce C4

Luis A. Ferré—is considered one of the Caribbean's finest art museums. Just as famous is Ponce's pre-Lenten carnival. The colorful costumes and *vejigante* (mischief-maker) masks worn during the festivities are famous throughout the world. The best dining in Ponce is just west of town. Seafood restaurants line the highway in an area known as Las Cucharas, named for the spoon-shape bay you'll overlook as you dine.

Sights

★ Casa Wiechers Villaronga

HISTORIC HOME | In a city filled with neoclassical confections, this is one of the most elaborate. Alfredo B. Wiechers, who returned to his native Ponce after studying architecture in Paris, designed the house. Though small in scale compared with some of its neighbors, it makes a big impression with details like huge arched windows and a massive rooftop gazebo. No wonder that soon after it was completed in 1911 the Villaronga-Mercado family decided to make it their own. Check out the stained-glass windows and other fanciful touches. The house, restored by the Institute of Puerto Rican Culture, now operates as the Museum of Puerto Rican Architecture, so, in addition to original furnishings, you'll find exhibits on Wiechers and other Ponce architects of his era. ✉ *106 Calle Reina, at Calle Méndez Vigo, Ponce* ☎ *848-7016* 🎟 *Free* ⏲ *Closed Mon. and Tues.*

Centro Ceremonial Indígena de Tibes

(*Tibes Indigenous Ceremonial Center*)
RUINS | This archaeological site, discovered after flooding from a tropical storm in 1975, is the island's most important. Dating from AD 300–700, it includes nine playing fields used for a ritual ball game that some think was similar to soccer. The fields are bordered by smooth stones, some of which are engraved with petroglyphs that might have ceremonial or astronomical significance. In the eye-catching Plaza de Estrella (Plaza of the Star), stones are arranged in a pattern resembling a rising sun, perhaps used to chart the seasons. A village with thatched huts has been reconstructed. Visit the small museum before taking a walking tour of the site. Last entry varies from day to day, so call ahead to confirm. ✉ *Rte. 503, Km 2.5, Barrio Tibes* ☎ *787/840–2255, 787/840–2255* 🌐 *www.nps.gov/nr/travel/prvi/pr15.htm* 🎟 *$3* ⏲ *Closed Mon.*

★ Museo Castillo Serrallés

HISTORIC HOME | This lovely Spanish-style villa—so massive that townspeople dubbed it a castle—was built in the 1930s for Ponce's wealthiest family, the makers of Don Q rum. Guided tours provide a glimpse into the lifestyle of a sugar baron, and a permanent exhibit explains the area's sugarcane and rum industries. Highlights include the dining room, with original hand-carved furnishings, and the extensive garden, with sculptured bushes and a shimmering reflection pool. A large cross looming over the house is an observatory; from the top, you can see the Caribbean. ✉ *17 El Vigía, El Vigía* ☎ *787/259–1774* 🌐 *www.museocastilloserralles.com* 🎟 *From $15* ⏲ *Closed Tues. and Wed.*

★ Museo de Arte de Ponce

ART MUSEUM | Designed by Edward Durell Stone, who also designed the original Museum of Modern Art in New York City and the Kennedy Center in Washington, D.C., Ponce's art museum is easily identified by the hexagonal galleries on its second story. It has one of the best art collections in Puerto Rico, which is why residents of San Juan frequently make the trip. The 4,500-piece collection includes works by famous Puerto Rican artists such as Francisco Oller, represented by a lovely landscape called *Hacienda Aurora*. European works include paintings by Peter Paul Rubens and Thomas Gainsborough, as well as pre-Raphaelite paintings, particularly the mesmerizing *Flaming June*, by Frederic Leighton, which has become the museum's unofficial

Today it's a museum, but for more than 100 years Parque de Bombas served as Ponce's main firehouse.

symbol. The museum also offers special exhibits, three sculpture gardens, and a café. ✉ *Museo de Ponce, 2325 Bul. Luis A. Ferré Aguayo (Hwy. 163), Sector Santa María* ☎ *787/840–1510* 🌐 *www.museoarteponce.org* 🎫 *$6* ⏲ *Closed Tues.*

Museo de la Historia de Ponce

HISTORIC HOME | Housed in two adjoining neoclassical mansions, this museum includes 10 rooms with exhibits covering the city's residents, from the indigenous Taíno people to Spanish settlers to the mix of the present. Guided tours in English and Spanish give an overview of the city's history. Although descriptions are mostly in Spanish, displays of clothing from different eras are interesting. ✉ *53 Calle Isabel, at Calle Mayor, Ponce* ☎ *787/844–7071* 🎫 *Free* ⏲ *Closed Sun. and Mon.*

★ **Parque de Bombas**

NOTABLE BUILDING | **FAMILY** | After El Morro in Old San Juan, this distinctive red-and-black-striped building may be the second-most-photographed structure in Puerto Rico. Built in 1882 as a pavilion for an agricultural and industrial fair, it was converted the following year into a firehouse. In 1990, it took on new life as a small museum tracing the history—and glorious feats—of Ponce's fire brigade. Kids love the antique fire truck on the lower level. Short tours in English and Spanish are given on the hour starting at 10; if the trolley is running, you can sign up for free tours of the historic downtown here, too. Helpful tourism officials staff a small information desk inside. ✉ *Plaza de las Delicias, Ponce* ☎ *787/284–3338* 🌐 *www.visitponce.com* 🎫 *Free.*

Beaches

Isla Caja de Muertos (*Coffin Island*)

BEACH | **FAMILY** | Named for its shape, this island, which stretches for 3 km (2 miles) and is 8 km (5 miles) off the coast, has the best beaches near Ponce and some of the best snorkeling in southern Puerto Rico. Due to hawksbill turtle nesting (May–December), the island is protected by the Reserva Natural Caja de Muertos, but you can still swim, snorkel, and dive here. A 30-minute hike across the island leads to a small lighthouse dating from 1887. Scheduled boats leave La Guancha Friday–Sunday at 9:30 am, daily in high season. Island Venture is one outfitter that leaves from La Guancha for Caja de Muertos. Alternatively, you can ask one of the many boatmen at La Guancha to take you out for about $30 round-trip. You must pack in what you need (food and drink) and pack out your garbage. **Amenities:** toilets. **Best for:** snorkeling; swimming; walking. ✉ *La Guancha, end of Rte. 14, Ponce.*

Restaurants

Lola Eclectic Cuisine
$$$ | **ECLECTIC** | This trendy bistro in the heart of downtown has an eclectic menu to match the decor. Grab a seat in a red-velvet booth, and start with the sampler of mahimahi nuggets, bruschetta, fried plantains, and egg rolls. **Known for:** blackened ahi tuna served with seaweed; Lolita Martini (grapefruit, cranberry, champagne, lime, and rum); showcase for local artists. *Average main: $27* ✉ *Ponce Plaza Hotel & Casino, Calle Reina, at Calle Union, Ponce* ☎ *787/813–5033,* *www.lolacuisine.com* *Closed Mon. and Tues. No lunch.*

Meliá Century Hotel Ponce
$ | **HOTEL** | In the heart of the city, this family-owned hotel has been a local landmark for more than 125 years; in fact, it claims to be the island's oldest hotel. **Pros:** budget-friendly; great location on the main square; good dining options nearby. **Cons:** Internet service is often spotty; front rooms can be noisy; somewhat dated decor. *Rooms from: $150* ✉ *75 Calle Cristina, Ponce* ☎ *787/842–0260* *www.meliacenturyhotel.com* *84 rooms* *No Meals.*

Guánica

24 miles (38 km) west of Ponce.

Juan Ponce de León first explored this area in 1508, when he was searching for the elusive Fountain of Youth. Nearly 400 years later U.S. troops landed first at Guánica during the Spanish-American War in 1898. The event is commemorated with an engraved marker on the city's *malecón,* or jetty. Sugarcane dominated the landscape through much of the 1900s, and the ruins of the old Guánica Central sugar mill, closed in 1980, loom over the town's western area, known as Ensenada. Today Guánica's biggest draws are its beaches and forests.

Bosque Estatal de Guánica
(*Guánica State Forest*)
FOREST | This 9,900-acre United Nations Biosphere Reserve is a great place for hiking. An outstanding example of a subtropical dry forest, it has some 700 species of plants, from the prickly-pear cactus to the gumbo limbo tree, and offers superb bird-watching; its more than 100 species include the pearly-eyed thrasher, lizard cuckoo, and nightjar.

The popular **Ballena Trail,** which begins at the ranger station on Route 334, is an easy 2-km (1¼-mile) walk that follows a partially paved road past a mahogany plantation to a dry plain covered with stunted cactus. A sign reading "Guayacán centenario" leads you to an extraordinary guayacán tree with a 6-foot-wide trunk. The moderately difficult, 5½-km (3½-mile) **Fuerte Trail** leads to an old fort built by the Spanish Armada. It was destroyed in the Spanish-American War in 1898, but you can see ruins of the old observatory tower.

In addition to using the main entrance on Route 334, you can enter on Route 333, which skirts the forest's southwestern quadrant. You may also wish to explore the less-trafficked area west of the town of Guánica, off Route 325. ✉ *Rte. 334, Guánica* ☎ *787/821–5706* 🎫 *Free.*

Hotels

★ Copamarina Beach Resort and Spa

$ | **RESORT** | The most beautiful resort on the southern coast is set on 16 palm-shaded acres facing the Caribbean. **Pros:** good-size guest rooms; plenty of activities; great dining options. **Cons:** beach just OK; expensive 20% resort fee; somewhat distant from other attractions. [$] *Rooms from: $230* ✉ *Copamarina Beach Resort and Spa, Rte. 333, Km 6.5, Rte. 333, Km 6.5, Guánica* ☎ *787/821–0505, 800/468–4553* 🌐 *www.copamarina.com* *104 rooms* *Free Breakfast.*

San Germán

10 km (6 miles) north of La Parguera, 166 km (104 miles) southwest of San Juan.

During its early years, San Germán was a city on the move. Although the first settlement's exact founding date and location remains at issue, the town is believed to have been established in 1510 near Guánica. Plagued by mosquitoes, settlers moved north along the west coast, where they encountered French pirates and smugglers. In the 1570s they fled inland to the current location, but they endured further harrassment. Determined and creative, they dug tunnels and moved beneath the city (the tunnels are now part of the water system). Today San Germán has a population of 35,000, and its intellectual and political activity is anything but underground. This is very much a college town, and students and professors from the Inter-American University often fill the bars and cafés.

Around San Germán's two main squares—Plazuela Santo Domingo and Plaza Francisco Mariano Quiñones (named for an abolitionist)—are buildings in every conceivable style of architecture found on the island, including mission, Victorian, criollo, and Spanish colonial. The city's tourist office offers a free guided trolley tour. Most of the buildings are private homes; two of them—the Capilla de Porta Coeli and the Museo de Arte y Casa de Estudio—are museums. Strip malls surround the historic center.

Sights

Capilla de Porta Coeli

(*Heaven's Gate Chapel*)

CHURCH | One of the oldest religious buildings in the Americas, this mission-style chapel overlooks the long, rectangular Plazuela de Santo Domingo. It's not a grand building, but its position at the top of a stone stairway gives it a noble air. Queen Isabel Segunda decreed that the Dominicans should build a church and monastery in San Germán, so a rudimentary building was erected in 1609, replaced in 1692 by the structure seen today. (Sadly, most of the monastery was demolished in 1866, leaving only a vestige of its facade.) The chapel functions as a museum of religious art, displaying painted wooden statuary by Latin American and Spanish artists. ✉ *East end of Plazuela Santo Domingo, San Germán* ☎ *787/892–5845* 🎫 *$3.*

Chapter 17

ST. BARTHÉLEMY

Updated by
Sheryl Nance-Nash

Sights	Restaurants	Hotels	Shopping	Nightlife
★★★★☆	★★★★★	★★★★★	★★★★★	★★★☆☆

WELCOME TO ST. BARTHÉLEMY

TOP REASONS TO GO

★ **The Scene:** The island is active, hedonistic, and hip, and the party is always on by the sparkling-blue sea.

★ **Super Style:** Growing ever more chic, St. Barth combines French style with Caribbean flair.

★ **Great Dining:** New restaurants tempt gourmets and gourmands.

★ **Shopping Galore:** If you're a shopper, you'll find bliss stalking the latest in French clothes and accessories with prices up to 30% less than in the States.

★ **Getting Out on the Water:** Windsurfing, kitesurfing, and other water sports make going to the beach more than just a lounging experience.

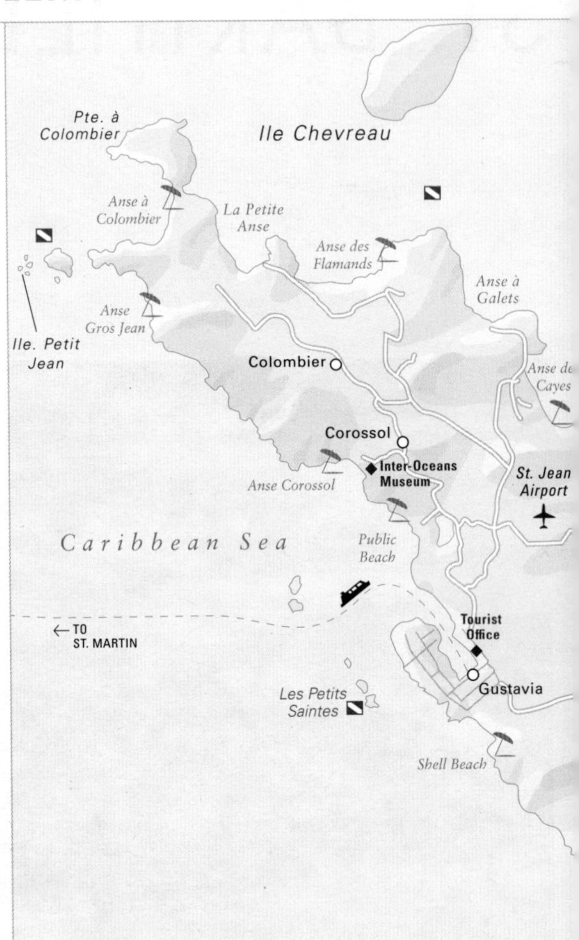

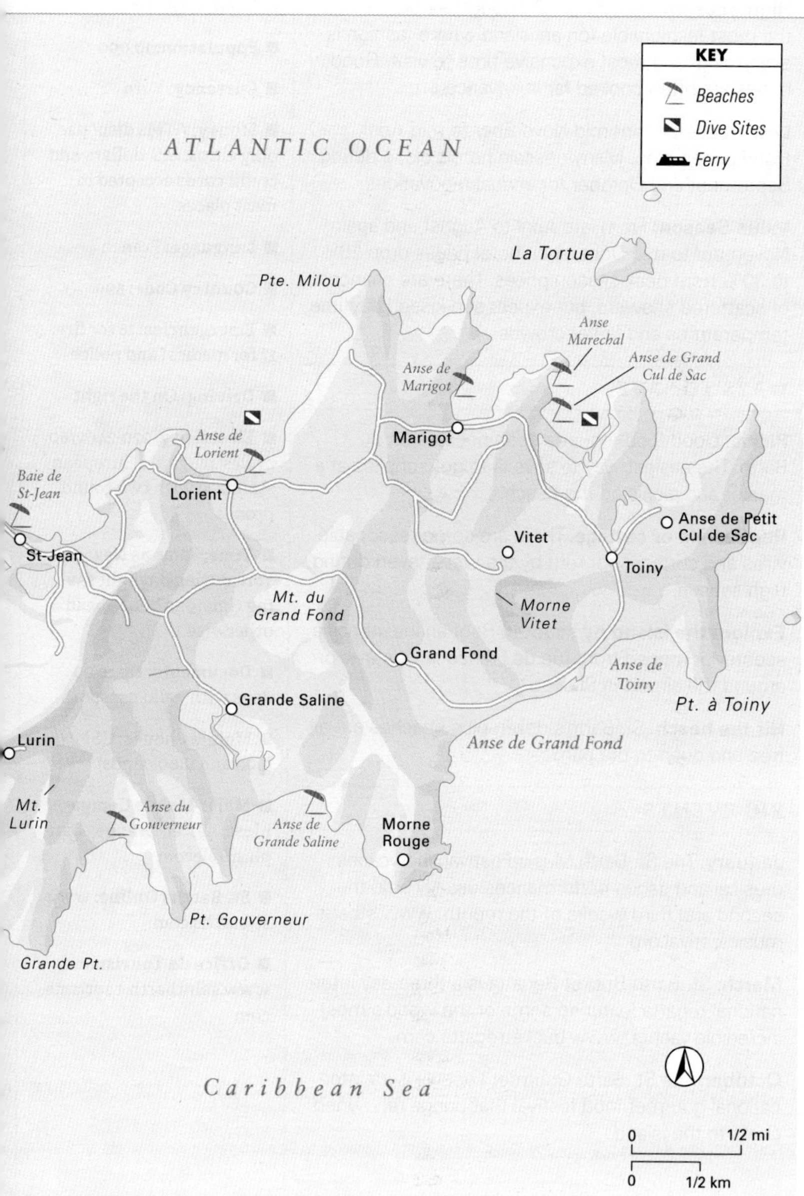
KEY
Beaches
Dive Sites
Ferry
ATLANTIC OCEAN
La Tortue
Pte. Milou
Anse Marechal
Anse de Grand Cul de Sac
Anse de Marigot
Marigot
Anse de Lorient
Lorient
Baie de St-Jean
St-Jean
Vitet
Anse de Petit Cul de Sac
Toiny
Mt. du Grand Fond
Morne Vitet
Grand Fond
Anse de Toiny
Pt. à Toiny
Grande Saline
Anse de Grand Fond
Lurin
Mt. Lurin
Anse du Gouverneur
Anse de Grande Saline
Morne Rouge
Pt. Gouverneur
Grande Pt.
Caribbean Sea
0
1/2 mi
0
1/2 km

ISLAND SNAPSHOT

WHEN TO GO

High Season: December 26 through January 2 is the most fashionable (on an island where fashion is everything) and most expensive time to visit. Good hotels are often booked far in advance.

Low Season: From mid-November to mid-April. Hotel prices drop. Many upscale hotels close during September and October for annual renovations.

Value Season: From late April to August and again November to mid-December, hotel prices drop 20% to 30% from peak-season prices. There are chances of scattered showers, but expect sun-kissed daytime temperatures and fewer crowds.

WAYS TO SAVE

Picnic. Good food requires deep pockets on St. Barth. The easiest way to save is to get supplies at a market and picnic on the beach.

Rent a villa or cottage. There are some reasonable villas and cottages for rent by the week, even during high season.

Explore the island by scooter. Rent an inexpensive scooter or moped from rue de France in Gustavia or around the airport in St-Jean.

Hit the beach. St. Barth's dozen-plus beaches are all free and open to the public.

BIG EVENTS

January: The St. Barth Music Festival showcases musical and dance performances usually held the second and third weeks of the month. www.stbarts-musicfestival.org

March: St. Barth Bucket Regatta is a three-day international regatta featuring some of the world's most incredible yachts. www.bucketregatta.com.

October: The St. Barth Gourmet Festival is an international gourmet food festival that brings renowned chefs to the island.

AT A GLANCE

- **Capital:** Gustavia
- **Population:** 10,000
- **Currency:** Euro
- **Money:** ATMs dispense only euros; U.S. dollars and credit cards accepted in most places.
- **Language:** French
- **Country Code:** 590
- **Emergencies:** 18 for fire; 17 for medical and police
- **Driving:** On the right
- **Electricity:** 220-240v/60 cycles; plugs are European standard with two round prongs
- **Time:** Same as New York during daylight saving time; one hour ahead otherwise
- **Documents:** Up to 90 days with valid passport
- **Mobile Phones:** GSM (900 and 1800 bands)
- **Major Mobile Companies:** Digicel, Orange, Dauphin Telecom
- **St. Barths Online:** www.st-barths.com
- **Office du Tourisme:** www.saintbarth-tourisme.com

St. Barthélemy blends the respective essences of the Caribbean, France, and *Architectural Digest* in perfect proportions. A sophisticated but unstudied approach to relaxation and respite prevails: you can spend the day on a beach, try on the latest French fashions, catch a gallery exhibition, and watch the sunset while nibbling tapas over Gustavia Harbor, then choose from 80 excellent restaurants for an elegant or easy evening meal. You can putter around the island, scuba dive, windsurf on a quiet cove, or just admire the lovely views.

A mere 8 square miles (21 square km), St. Barth is a hilly island, with many sheltered inlets and picturesque, quiet beaches. The town of Gustavia wraps itself around a modern harbor lined with everything from size-matters megayachts to rustic fishing boats to sailboats of all descriptions. Red-roof villas dot the hillsides, and glass-front shops line the streets. Beach surf runs the gamut from kiddie-pool calm to serious-surfer dangerous, beaches from deserted to packed. The cuisine is tops in the Caribbean, and almost everything is tidy, stylish, and up-to-date. French *savoir vivre* prevails.

Christopher Columbus came to the island—called "Ouanalao" by its native Caribs—in 1493; he named it for his brother Bartolomé. The first French colonists arrived in 1648, drawn by its location on the West Indian Trade Route, but they were wiped out by the Caribs, who dominated the area. Another small group from Normandy and Brittany arrived in 1694. This time the settlers prospered—with the help of French buccaneers, who took advantage of the island's strategic location and protected harbor. In 1784 the French traded the island to King Gustav III of Sweden in exchange for port rights in Göteborg. The king dubbed the capital Gustavia, laid out and paved streets, built three forts, and turned the community into a prosperous free port. The island thrived as a shipping and commercial center until the 19th century, when earthquakes, fires, and hurricanes brought financial ruin. Many residents fled to newer lands of opportunity, and Oscar II of Sweden returned the island to France. After briefly considering selling it to America, the French took possession of St. Barthélemy again on August 10, 1877.

Today the island is a free port, and in 2007 it became a Collectivité, a French-administered overseas territory. Arid, hilly, and rocky, St. Barth was unsuited to sugar production and thus never developed an extensive slave base. Some of the residents are descendants of the tough Norman and Breton settlers of three centuries ago, but you are more likely to encounter attractive French twenty- and thirtysomethings from Normandy and Provence, who are friendly, English-speaking, and here for the sunny lifestyle.

Planning

Getting Here and Around

AIR

Because of its tiny, hillside runway, there are no direct major-airline flights to St. Barth. Most North Americans fly first into St. Maarten's Princess Juliana International SXM Airport, from which the island is a quick 15 minutes by air. Winair has frequent flights from St. Maarten every day. Through Winair's affiliation with major airlines, you can check your luggage from your home airport through to St. Barth under certain circumstances. Tradewind Aviation has regularly scheduled service from San Juan and also does VIP charters. Anguilla Air Services and St. Barth Commuter have scheduled flights and also do charters. *Leave ample time between your scheduled flight and your connection in St. Maarten: 90 minutes is the minimum recommended* (and be aware that luggage frequently doesn't make the trip; your hotel or villa-rental company may be able to send someone to retrieve it). It's a good idea to pack a change of clothes, required medicines, and a bathing suit in your carry-on—or better yet, pack very light and don't check baggage at all.

AIRPORTS Jean Remi de Haenen (SBH). ✉ *St. Jean Rd., St-Jean* ☎ *0590/27–75–81.*

AIRLINES St. Barth Commuter. ☎ *0590/27–54–54* 🌐 *www.stbarthcommuter.com.* **Tradewind Aviation.** ☎ *203/267–3305* 🌐 *www.flytradewind.com.* **Trans Anguilla Airways.** ☎ *264/498–5922* 🌐 *www.transanguilla.com.* **Winair.** ☎ *0590/27–61–01, 866/545-4237* 🌐 *www.fly-winair.com.*

BOAT AND FERRY

St. Barth can be reached via ferry service from St. Maarten/St. Martin to Quai de la République in Gustavia. Voyager offers at least twice daily round-trips for about $100, economy class per person from Marigot. Great Bay Express has multiple round-trips daily from the Dutch side of Sint Maarten for roughly €110 if reserved in advance, €115 for same-day tickets, and €70 each way for a same-day round-trip. Private boat charters are also available, but they are very expensive; MasterSki Pilou offers transfers from St. Maarten.

CONTACTS Great Bay Express. ✉ *Quai Gustavia, Gustavia* ☎ *721/520–5015* 🌐 *www.greatbayexpress.com.* **Master Ski Pilou.** ☎ *0590/27–91–79* 🌐 *www.master-ski-pilou.com.* **Voyager.** ☎ *0590/87–10–68* 🌐 *www.voy12.com.*

CAR

Roads are sometimes unmarked, so get a map and look for signs, nailed to posts at all crossroads, pointing to a destination. Roads are narrow and sometimes very steep, but have been improved; even so, check the brakes and low gears before driving away from the rental office. Maximum speed is 30 mph (50 kph). Driving is on the right, as in the

United States and Europe. Parking is an additional challenge. There are two gas stations on the island, one near the airport and one in Lorient. They aren't open after 5 pm or on Sunday, and pumps at the station near the airport now accept chip-and-pin credit cards. Considering the short distances, a full tank should last most of a week.

TIP→ Ask your car rental company about Blue Parking Tags, which give you 1½ hours of parking for free.

Car Rentals: You must have a valid driver's license and be 25 or older to rent, and in high season there may be a three-day minimum. During peak periods, such as Christmas week and February, arrange for your car rental ahead of time. Rental agencies operate out of Jean Remi de Haenen airport; some will bring your car to your hotel. Alternately, when you make your hotel reservation, ask if the hotel has its own cars available to rent; some hotels provide 24-hour emergency road service—something most rental companies don't. Expect to pay at least $55 per day, and note the company will usually hold about $500 until the car is returned.

TIP→ For a green alternative, consider renting an electric car. They're available for about $85 per day.

MOPED, SCOOTER, AND BIKE

Several companies rent motorbikes, scooters, mopeds, ATVs, and mountain bikes. Motorbikes go for about $30 per day and require a $100 deposit. ATV rental starts at $40 per day. Helmets are required. Scooter and motorbike rental places are mostly along rue de France in Gustavia and around the airport in St-Jean. If you have not driven an ATV or "quad" before, St. Barth may not be the best place to try it out. The roads, though not jammed with traffic, are quite narrow, and navigating the hilly terrain can be quite a challenge.

CONTACTS Barthloc Rental. ✉ *Rue de France, Gustavia* ☎ *0590/27–52–81* 🌐 *www.barthloc.com.* **Chez Béranger.** ✉ *21 rue du général de Gaulle, Gustavia* ☎ *0590/27–89–00* 🌐 *www.beranger-rental.com.*

TAXI

Taxis are expensive and not particularly easy to arrange, especially in the evening. There's a taxi station at the airport and another at the ferry dock in Gustavia; from elsewhere you must contact a dispatcher in Gustavia or St-Jean. Fares are regulated by the Collectivity, and drivers accept both dollars and euros. If you go out to dinner by taxi, let the restaurant know if you will need a taxi at the end of the meal, and they will call one for you.

CONTACTS Taxis. ☎ *0590/52–40–40, 0590/27–75–81.* **Taxi Prestige.** ☎ *0590/27–70–57.*

Beaches

There is a beach in St. Barth to suit every taste. Wild surf, complete privacy in nature, a dreamy white-sand strand, and a spot at a chic beach club close to shopping and restaurants—they're all within a 20-minute drive.

There are many *anses* (coves) and nearly 20 *plages* (beaches) scattered around the island, each with a distinct personality; all are open to the public, even if they front a tony resort. Because of the number of beaches, even in high season you can find a nearly empty one, despite St. Barth's tiny size. That's not to say that all beaches are equally good or even equally suitable for swimming, but each has something to offer. Unless you are having lunch at a beachfront restaurant with lounging areas set aside for patrons, you should bring an umbrella, beach mat, and drinking water (all of which are easily obtainable all over the island). Topless sunbathing is common, but nudism is

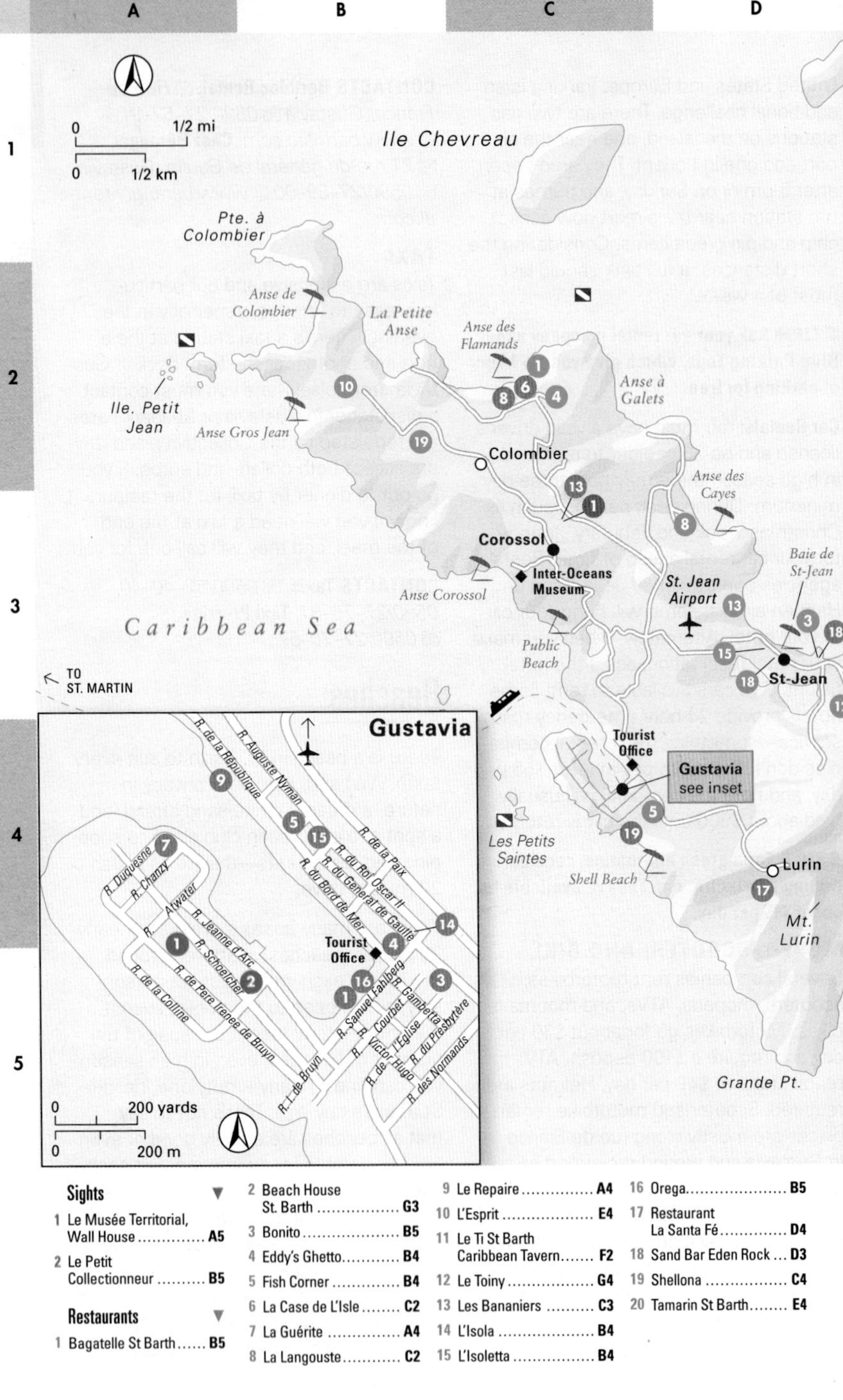
A
B
C
D
1
2
3
4
5
0 1/2 mi
0 1/2 km
Ile Chevreau
Pte. à Colombier
Anse de Colombier
La Petite Anse
Anse des Flamands
Anse à Galets
Ile. Petit Jean
Anse Gros Jean
Colombier
Anse des Cayes
Corossol
Inter-Oceans Museum
Anse Corossol
Baie de St-Jean
St. Jean Airport
Public Beach
St-Jean
Caribbean Sea
TO ST. MARTIN
Gustavia
Tourist Office
Gustavia see inset
Les Petits Saintes
Shell Beach
Lurin
Mt. Lurin
Grande Pt.
R. de la République
R. Auguste Nyman
R. de la Paix
R. du Roi Oscar II
R. du Général de Gaulle
R. du Bord de Mer
R. Duquesne
R. Chanzy
Atwater
R. Jeanne d'Arc
R. Schoelcher
R. de Pere Irenee de Bruyn
R. de la Colline
R. Samuel Fahlberg
R. Gambetta
R. Courbet
R. Victor Hugo
R. de l'Eglise
R. du Presbytère
R. des Normands
R. I. de Bruyn
0 200 yards
0 200 m
Sights
1 Le Musée Territorial, Wall House A5
2 Le Petit Collectionneur B5
Restaurants
1 Bagatelle St Barth B5
2 Beach House St. Barth G3
3 Bonito B5
4 Eddy's Ghetto B4
5 Fish Corner B4
6 La Case de L'Isle C2
7 La Guérite A4
8 La Langouste C2
9 Le Repaire A4
10 L'Esprit E4
11 Le Ti St Barth Caribbean Tavern....... F2
12 Le Toiny G4
13 Les Bananiers C3
14 L'Isola B4
15 L'Isoletta B4
16 Orega...................... B5
17 Restaurant La Santa Fé............. D4
18 Sand Bar Eden Rock ... D3
19 Shellona C4
20 Tamarin St Barth........ E4

St. Barthélemy

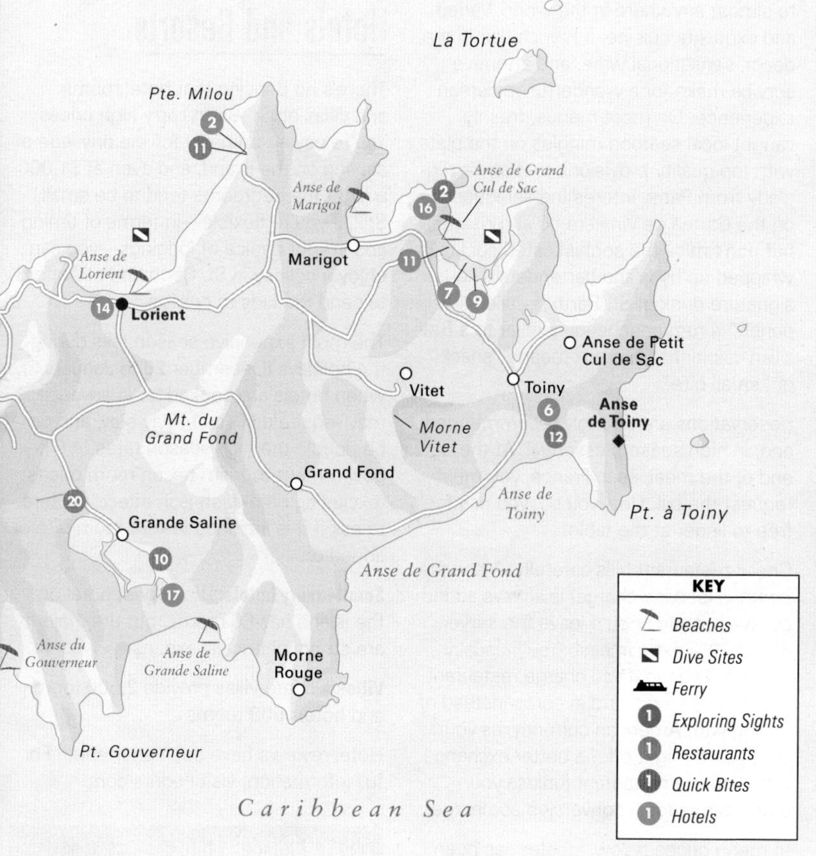

Quick Bites ▼

1 La Petite Colombe **C3**

Hotels ▼

1 Cheval Blanc St-Barth Isle de France........... **C2**

2 Christopher............. **F2**

3 Eden Rock St Barths ... **D3**

4 Hôtel Baie des Anges.................... **C2**

5 Hôtel Barrière Le Carl Gustaf........... **C4**

6 Hotel Le Toiny........... **G3**

7 Hotel Les Ondines Sur La Plage............. **G3**

8 Hotel Manapany........ **D3**

9 Le Barthélemy Hotel & Spa............. **G3**

10 Le P'tit Morne **B2**

11 Le Sereno................ **G3**

12 Le Village St. Barth Hotel **D3**

13 Les Îlets de la Plage.... **D3**

14 Les Mouettes............ **E3**

15 Pearl Beach Saint Barth **D3**

16 Rosewood Le Guanahani St. Barth **G3**

17 Salines Garden Cottages **E4**

18 Villa Les Lataniers **D3**

19 Villa Marie Saint-Barth.............. **B2**

supposedly forbidden—although both Grande Saline and Gouverneur are de facto nude beaches, albeit less than in the past. Shade is scarce.

Restaurants

Dining on St. Barth compares favorably to almost anywhere in the world. Varied and exquisite cuisine, a French flair in the decor, sensational wine, and attentive service make for a wonderful epicurean experience. On most menus, freshly caught local seafood mingles on the plate with top-quality provisions that arrive regularly from Paris. Interesting selections on the Cartes de Vins are no surprise, but don't miss the sophisticated cocktails whipped up by island bartenders. The signature drink of St. Barth is called "'ti punch," a rum concoction similar to a Brazilian caipirinha. *Ti creux* means "snack" or "small bite."

Reservations are strongly recommended and, in high season, essential. At the end of the meal, as in France, you must request the bill. Until you do, you can feel free to linger at the table.

Check restaurant bills carefully. A *service compris* (service charge) is always added by law, but you should leave the server 5% to 10% extra in cash. You'll usually come out ahead if you charge restaurant meals on a credit card in euros instead of paying with American currency, as your credit card might offer a better exchange rate than the restaurant (unless your credit card adds a conversion surcharge).

In menu prices below, lobster has been left out of the range.

What to Wear: A bathing suit and gauzy top or shift is acceptable at beachside lunch spots, but not really in Gustavia. St. Barth is for fashionistas. You can't go wrong in a tank dress or a nice top with white jeans, high sandals, and flashy accessories. The sky is the limit for high fashion at nightclubs and lounges in high season, when you might (correctly) think everyone in sight is a model. Jackets are never required and are rarely worn, but most people do dress fashionably for dinner. Leave some space in your suitcase; you can buy the perfect outfit here on the island. Pack a light sweater or shawl for the occasional breezy night.

Hotels and Resorts

There's no denying that hotel rooms and villas on St. Barth carry high prices. You're paying primarily for the privilege of staying on the island, and even at $1,000 a night the bedrooms tend to be small. Still, if you're flexible—in terms of timing and in your choice of lodgings—you can enjoy a holiday in St. Barth and still afford to send the kids to college.

The most expensive season falls during the holidays (December 26 to January 2), when hotels are booked far in advance, may require a 10- or 14-day stay, and can be double the high-season rates. A 5% government tourism tax on room prices (excluding breakfast) is in effect; be sure to ask if it is included in your room rate or added on.

Small luxury hotels: The largest hotel on the island has 66 rooms, but the majority are stratospherically expensive.

Villas: Private villas provide 2,500 rooms and hotels 500 rooms.

Hotel reviews have been shortened. For full information, visit Fodors.com.

What It Costs in Euros

$	$$	$$$	$$$$
RESTAURANTS			
under €12	€12–€20	€21–€30	over €30
HOTELS			
under €275	€275–€375	€376–€475	over €475

PRIVATE VILLAS AND CONDOS

On St. Barth the term *villa* describes anything from a small cottage to a luxurious, modern estate. Today more than half of St. Barth's accommodations are in villas, a great option, especially if traveling with friends or family. Even more advantageous to Americans, villa rates are usually quoted in dollars, thus bypassing unfavorable euro fluctuations. Most villas have a small private swimming pool and maid service daily except Sunday. They are well furnished with linens, kitchen utensils, and such electronic necessities as smart-phone docks, TV, and Internet. Weekly low-season rates range from $3,000 + to "oh-my-gosh." Some villa-rental companies also have offices in the United States and have extensive websites that enable you to see pictures or panoramic videos of the place you're considering; their local offices oversee maintenance and housekeeping and provide concierge services. Just be aware that there are few beachfront villas, so if you have your heart set on "toes in the sand" and a cute waiter delivering your Kir Royale, stick with the hotels or villas operated by hotel properties.

Nightlife

Most of the nightlife in St. Barth is centered in Gustavia, though there are a few places to go outside of town. "In" clubs change from season to season, so you might ask around for the hot spot of the moment, but none really get going until about midnight. Theme parties are the current trend. Check the daily *St. Barth News* or *Le Journal de Saint-Barth* for details. A late (10 pm or later) reservation at one of the club–restaurants will eventually become a front-row seat at a party.

Shopping

St. Barth is a duty-free port, and its sophisticated visitors find shopping in its 200-plus boutiques a delight, especially for beachwear, accessories, jewelry, and casual wear. It's no overstatement to say that shopping for fashionable clothing, jewels, and designer accessories is better in St. Barth than anywhere else in the Caribbean. New shops open all the time, so there's always something to discover. Some stores close from noon to 3, but they are open until 8 pm. Many are closed on Sunday. A popular afternoon pastime is strolling the two major shopping areas in Gustavia and St-Jean. While high fashion is as pricey here as everywhere, French brands sell for up to 30% less than in the U.S.

Health and Safety

There's relatively little crime on St. Barth. Visitors can travel anywhere on the island with confidence. Most hotel rooms have safes for your valuables. As anywhere, don't tempt loss by leaving cameras, laptops, or jewelry out in plain sight in your hotel room or villa or in your car or car trunk. Also, don't walk barefoot at night: there are venomous centipedes that can inflict a remarkably painful sting. If you ask residents, they will tell you that they drink only bottled water, although most cook or make coffee with tap water.

Dengue, chikungunya, and zika have all been reported throughout the Caribbean. We recommend that you protect yourself from these mosquito-borne illnesses by keeping your skin covered and/or wearing mosquito repellent. The mosquitoes that transmit these viruses are as active by day as they are by night. Small hand-held mosquito zappers are available in some supermarkets.

Visitor Information

CONTACT Office du Tourisme. ✉ *10 rue de France, Gustavia* ☎ *0590/27–87–27* 🌐 *www.saintbarth-tourisme.com.*

Gustavia

You can easily explore all of Gustavia during a two-hour stroll. Some shops close from noon to 3 or 4, so plan lunch accordingly, but stores stay open past 7 in the evening. Parking in Gustavia is a challenge, especially during vacation times. A good spot to park is rue de la République, alongside the catamarans, yachts, and sailboats.

Sights

★ Le Musée Territorial, Wall House

HISTORY MUSEUM | **FAMILY** | On the far side of the harbor known as La Pointe, the charming Municipal Museum on the first floor of the restored Wall House has watercolors, portraits, photographs, traditional costumes, and historic documents detailing the island's history over many hundreds of years, as well as displays of the island's flowers, plants, and marine life. There are also changing contemporary art exhibitions. It's a must-stop on your St. Barth visit, and it's free. ✉ *La Pointe, Gustavia* ☎ *0590/29–71–55* 🌐 *visitersaintbarthelemy.com/musee-territorial-de-gustavia* 🎫 *Free.*

Le Petit Collectionneur

OTHER MUSEUM | Encouraged by family and friends, André Berry opened this private museum in his home to showcase his lifelong passion for collecting fascinating objects such as 18th-century English pipes and the first phonograph to come to the island. Today there are more than 1,000 pieces here, ranging from cannon balls to coins that are hundreds of years old. Berry will happily show you his treasures. ✉ *La Pointe, Gustavia* ☎ *0590/27-67-77* 🎫 *€2.*

Backup Ferry

Even if you are flying to St. Barth, it's a good idea to keep the numbers and schedules for the ferry companies handy, in case your flight is delayed. If you are planning to spend time in St. Maarten before traveling on to St. Barth, the ferry may be lower in cost, and you can leave from Marigot or Philipsburg.

Beaches

Shell Beach

BEACH | Because of its rather sheltered southward-facing location on the coast south of downtown Gustavia, this small beach sees high numbers of shells washing ashore. Despite that, the unspoken rule here is "Take nothing but pictures, leave nothing but footprints." A taxi will be happy to take you here, but for most people it's a relatively easy walk. Have lunch at Shellona for music and relaxed island vibes. **Best for:** walking. **Amenities:** food and drink; restrooms. ✉ *Gustavia.*

Restaurants

★ Bagatelle St Barth

$$$$ | **MODERN FRENCH** | Watch the yachts on Gustavia harbor from the terrace of this sophisticated St-Tropez–inspired restaurant while enjoying cocktails and French and Mediterranean cuisine. Fans of sister establishments in Dubai, London, and elsewhere will recognize the friendly service, lively atmosphere, and great music provided by resident DJs. **Known for:** chic crowd; haute cuisine in an elegant harborside location; late-night partying. 💲 *Average main: €45* ✉ *24 Rue Samuel Fahlberg, Gustavia*

Did You Know?

The largest hotel on St. Barth has only about 70 rooms, which means you get a great deal of personal service and attention wherever you stay.

☎ *0590/27–51–51* 🌐 *www.bistrotbagatelle.com* ⊙ *Closed Sun. No lunch.*

★ Bonito

$$$$ | LATIN AMERICAN | Combining cuisines from France, Peru, and all over the Americas, Bonito delivers a spectrum of artistically assembled flavors, textures, and aromas that you'd find challenging to locate elsewhere. Located on a hill overlooking Gustavia harbor, the restaurant indulges you with big white canvas couches for lounging, tables around the sides, an open kitchen, and three bar areas. **Known for:** caring owners; artistically presented dishes; elegance. 💲 *Average main: €60* ✉ *Rue Lubin Brin, Gustavia* ☎ *0590/27–96–96* 🌐 *www.ilovebonito.com* ⊙ *Closed late Aug.–Nov. 1, no lunch.*

Eddy's Ghetto

$$$ | FRENCH | By local standards, dinner in the pretty, open-air, tropical garden here is reasonably priced. The cooking is French and Creole, and everything is fresh and delicious. **Known for:** authentic French and local dishes; beautiful tropical gardens; attentive service regardless of how busy they are. 💲 *Average main: €28* ✉ *12 rue Samuel Fahlberg, Gustavia* ☎ *0590/27–54–17* ⊙ *Closed Sun. and Sept. through late Oct. No lunch.*

Fish Corner

$$$$ | MEDITERRANEAN | This comfy, intimate spot, noted for its lobster tank, serves mostly local fish with Caribbean flair. You'll have a hard time deciding between the fish tacos, tuna burgers on sesame brioche bun, lobster risotto, or Chilean sea bass with white bean velouté truffle oil. **Known for:** fresh veggies; relaxed vibe; adjacent fish market. 💲 *Average main: €32* ✉ *41 rue de la Republic, Gustavia* ☎ *0590/51–36–33* 🌐 *www.instagram.com/fishcornerstbarth* ⊙ *Closed Sun., no dinner except Thurs.–Sat.*

La Guérite

$$$$ | MEDITERRANEAN | A sister of a well-beloved Cannes hot spot, this stylish Greek-influenced restaurant is at the far side of Gustavia Harbor. The room is beautiful, overlooking the yachts; the service helpful and friendly; and the food is fresh, tasty, healthy, and well prepared, featuring many locally caught types of seafood. **Known for:** Black Angus rib eye; fish or veal Milanaise; wahoo, sea bass, mahimahi, and tuna entrées. 💲 *Average main: €45* ✉ *La Pointe, Gustavia* ☎ *0590/27-71-83* 🌐 *www.saintbarth.restaurantlaguerite.com.*

Picking the Right Beach

For long stretches of powder-soft pale sand choose La Saline, Gouverneur, or Flamands. For seclusion in nature, pick the tawny grains of Corossol. But the most remarkable beach on the island, Shell Beach, is right in Gustavia and hardly has sand at all! Millions of tiny pink shells wash ashore in drifts, thanks to an unusual confluence of ocean currents, sea-life beds, and hurricane action.

Le Repaire

$$$ | BRASSERIE | FAMILY | Overlooking the harbor, this friendly classic French brasserie is busy from its 7 am opening to its late-night closing. The flexible hours are great if you arrive on the island midafternoon and need a substantial snack. **Known for:** well-prepared, simple food; St. Barth's only early breakfast restaurant; reliable any time of day. 💲 *Average main: €30* ✉ *Rue de la République, Gustavia* ☎ *0590/27–72–48.*

★ L'Isola

$$$$ | ITALIAN | The chic sister of Santa Monica, California's Via Veneto packs in happy guests for classic Italian dishes, dozens of house-made pasta dishes, prime meats, and a huge, well-chosen wine list. Restaurateur Fabrizio Bianconi

Gustavia Harbor welcomes ships to St. Barth.

wants it to feel like a big Italian party, and with all the celebrating in this pretty and romantic room, he has certainly succeeded. **Known for:** the daily catch; house-made pasta; festive atmosphere. *Average main: €45 rue du Roi Oscar II, Gustavia 0590/51–00–05 www.lisolastbarth.com Closed Sept. and Oct. No lunch.*

L'Isoletta

$$$$ | **PIZZA** | This casual Roman-style pizzeria run by the popular L'Isola restaurant is a lively, chic lounge-style gastropub serving delicious thin-crust pizzas by the slice or the meter. There are even dessert pizzas, and excellent tiramisu. **Known for:** wait times at peak hours; meter-long pizzas; lively atmosphere. *Average main: €38 Rue du Roi Oscar II, Gustavia 0590/52–02–02 www.lisolettastbarth.com.*

★ Orega

$$$$ | **JAPANESE FUSION** | One of St. Barth's very best, this Franco-Japanese fusion restaurant draws legions of admirers for its top-notch sushi and fish, imported directly from sushi markets in Tokyo, New York, and Paris. The pretty room in which it's served is decorated in natural woods, neutral linen, and attractive art. **Known for:** Franco-Japanese fusions like Pomme Shiso; extraordinary sushi and fish; outstanding service. *Average main: €54 13 rue Samuel Fahlberg, Gustavia 0590/52–45–31 www.oregastbarth.com Closed Sun.*

★ Shellona

$$$$ | **GREEK** | The sounds of Ibiza and Mykonos, in the form of live bands and DJs, fill the air at Shellona as patrons chill with a cocktail on comfortable couches and sunbeds. Lunch here is all about Greek sharing dishes with a side of Caribbean Sea views. **Known for:** grilled meats with herbs; music on the beach; cocktails. *Average main: €47 Shell Beach, Gustavia 0590/29–06–66 shellonabeach.com No dinner.*

Hotels

★ Hôtel Barrière Le Carl Gustaf

$$$$ | HOTEL | The only hotel on the island with panoramic views of the port of Gustavia, this sophisticated hillside hotel is the last word in luxury and French-style charm. **Pros:** close to Shell Beach, the port, shopping, and attractions; excellent restaurant; beautiful spa. **Cons:** not on the beach; not budget-friendly; on a hill. *Rooms from: €1100 ✉ rue des Normands, Gustavia ☎ 0590/29–79–00 🌐 www.hotelsbarriere.com ⏲ Closed late Aug. – late Oct. 21 rooms 🍽 Free Breakfast.*

Nightlife

Bar de l'Oubli

BARS | Locals and visitors mingle over drinks at this landmark bar, which is a good breakfast option, too. The service can be slow, though, so it's best if you're not in a hurry. *✉ 3 Rue de la France, Gustavia ☎ 0590/27–70–06 🌐 www.bardeloubli.com ☞ No credit cards.*

Le Repaire

BARS | This restaurant lures a crowd for cocktail hour and its pool table. It's great for dinner and people-watching. *✉ Rue de la République, Gustavia ☎ 0590/27–72–48.*

★ Le Sélect

GATHERING PLACES | Quite possibly the inspiration for Jimmy Buffett's "Cheeseburger in Paradise," St. Barth's original hangout has been around since 1949. In the boisterous garden, the barefoot boating set gathers for a cold Carib beer at lower-than-usual prices while listening to a local band or DJ. And yes, you can grab a legendary "Cheeseburger in Paradise" here and not get indigestion when you see the surprisingly modest bill. *✉ Rue de la France, Gustavia ☎ 0590/27–86–87.*

Shopping

In Gustavia, boutiques pack the three major shopping streets. Quai de la République, which is right on the harbor, rivals New York's Madison Avenue or Paris's avenue Montaigne for high-end designer retail, including shops for **Louis Vuitton, Bulgari, Cartier, Chopard, Erès,** and **Hermès.** These shops often carry items that are not available in the United States. The elegant Carré d'Or plaza and the adjacent **Coeur Ven dôme** are great fun to explore. Shops are also clustered in **La Savane Commercial Center** (across from the airport), **La Villa Créole** (in St-Jean), and **Espace Neptune** (on the road to Lorient). It's worth working your way from one end to the other at these shopping complexes—just to see or, perhaps, be seen. Boutiques in all three areas carry the latest in French and Italian sportswear, charming children's togs, and some haute couture. Bargains may be tough to come by, but you might be able to snag that Birkin that has a long waiting list stateside, and in any case, you'll have a lot of fun hunting around.

BOOKS

Clic

BOOKS | Devoted to books on photography and monthly exhibits of fine modern photography, as well as arty things to wear, this concept gallery–bookstore is an outpost of those in SoHo (New York) and the Hamptons. It's the brainchild of Calypso founder Christiane Celle. *✉ Rue de la République, Gustavia ☎ 0590/29–70–17 🌐 www.clic.com ⏲ Closed Sun.*

La Case Aux Livres

BOOKS | This full-service bookstore and newsstand has hundreds of English titles for adults and kids. Its blog lists author appearances, which may well be worth a stop if you're around. *✉ 9 rue de la République, Gustavia ☎ 0590/27–15–88 🌐 www.lacaseauxlivres.com.*

Shoppers flock to Gustavia's Rue de France for high-end boutiques.

CLOTHING

Boutique Lacoste

MIXED CLOTHING | This store has a huge selection of the once-again-chic alligator-logo wear for adults and kids. ✉ *Rue du Bord de Mer, Gustavia* ☎ *0590/27–66–90.*

Hermès

MIXED CLOTHING | This independently owned franchise (closed September and October) has prices slightly below those in the States, a welcome notion among the sky-high prices here. ✉ *Le Carré d'Or, Gustavia* ☎ *0590/27–66–15* ⏲ *Closed Sun.*

Kokon

MIXED CLOTHING | This boutique offers a nicely edited mix of designs for on-island or off from of-the-moment fashion lines, and cute shoes to go with them. ✉ *Rue Samuel Fahlberg, Gustavia* ☎ *0590/29–74–48.*

Laurent Effel

MIXED CLOTHING | This St. Barth institution operates three attractive shops next to each other, offering comfy and colorful driving mocs for adults, well-tailored linen shirts and shorts in a rainbow of candy colors, and accessories. ✉ *Rue du Générale de Gaulle, Gustavia* ☎ *0590/27–54–02.*

PaSha St Barth

MIXED CLOTHING | PaSha St. Barth's concept store stocks cheeky slogan T-shirts, swimsuits, edgy hats, gifts, and accessories for adults. ✉ *14 Rue Oscar II, Gustavia* ☎ *0590/39–01–99.*

Linen

MEN'S CLOTHING | This shop offers tailored linen shirts for men in a rainbow of soft colors and soft slip-on driving mocs in classic styles. ✉ *Rue du Générale de Gaulle, Gustavia* ☎ *0590/27–54–26* 🌐 *www.facebook.com/Linensbh.*

L.Joy Boutique

MIXED CLOTHING | Look for lovely high-end silk tunics, evening wear, and elegant accessories. Brides-to-be and the glitter/sparkle-obsessed should not miss the collection of beaded and rhinestone-set headbands and sparkly sandals. ✉ *Rue* *du Bord de Mer* ☎ *0590/27–14–89* 🌐 *www.facebook.com/ljoyboutique.*

Lolita Jaca

MIXED CLOTHING | This store has trendy, tailored sportswear and floaty silk charmeuse and cotton gauze tunics perfect for the beach. ✉ *Le Carré d'Or, Gustavia* ☎ *0590/27–59–98* 🌐 *www.lolitajaca.com.*

Mademoiselle Hortense

MIXED CLOTHING | Charming tops and dresses in pretty prints are made on the island. Great crafty bracelets and necklaces to accent your new styles are also here. ✉ *Rue de la République, Gustavia* ☎ *0590/27–13–29.*

Pati de St Barth

MIXED CLOTHING | This is the largest of the three shops that stock the chic, locally made T-shirts, totes, and beach wraps that have become the de facto logo of St. Barth. The newest styles have hand-done graffiti-style lettering. The shop also has some handicrafts and other giftable items. ✉ *Rue du Bord de Mer, Gustavia* ☎ *0590/27–78–04* 🌐 *www.patidestbarth.com.*

Poupette St. Barth

MIXED CLOTHING | All the brilliant color-crinkle silk, chiffon batik, and embroidered peasant skirts and tops are designed by the owner. There also are great belts and beaded bracelets. ✉ *Rue de la République, Gustavia* ☎ *0590/27–94-49* 🌐 *www.poupettestbarth.com.*

Saint-Barth Stock Exchange

MIXED CLOTHING | On the far side of Gustavia Harbor, the island's consignment and discount shop is a blast to explore. ✉ *Rue Schoelcher, La Pointe, Gustavia* ☎ *0590/27–68–12.*

Vanita Rosa

MIXED CLOTHING | This store showcases beautiful lace and linen sundresses and peasant tops, plus poncho/kaftans, accessories galore, and very cool designer vintage. ✉ *Rue Oscar II, Gustavia* ☎ *0590/87-46-91* 🌐 *www.vanitarosa.com* 🕑 *Closed Sun.*

Voila St Barth

MIXED CLOTHING | Find beautifully made linen and cotton resort sportswear mostly in a classic blue-and-white palette at this polished shop. The classic styles are wearable by all ages. There is a sister shop in St-Jean. ✉ *4 rue de la Suède, Gustavia* ☎ *0590/27–99–53* 🌐 *www.voilastbarth-shop.com/en/.*

Volver St Barth

MIXED CLOTHING | The attractive shop stocks a fashion-forward selection by SeeByChloé, Alexander Wang, ba&sh, forte_forte, Lisa Marie Fernandez, Thurley, and remarkable folkloric, one-of-a-kind garments. ✉ *Rue de France, Gustavia* ☎ *0590/27–55–90* 🌐 *www.volverstbarth.com.*

FOODSTUFFS

AMC

FOOD | This supermarket is a bit older than Marché U in St-Jean but can supply nearly anything you might need. ✉ *Quai de la République, Gustavia* ☎ *0590/27–52–00* 🕑 *Closed Sun.* ☞ *Additional locations in Lorient and St.-Jean.*

JEWELRY

Cartier

JEWELRY & WATCHES | For fine jewelry, visit this branch of the famous jeweler. ✉ *Quai de la République, Gustavia* ☎ *0590/27–66–69* 🌐 *stores.cartier.com/france/st-barthelemy/quai-de-la-republique-gustavia* 🕑 *Closed Sun.*

Diamond Genesis

JEWELRY & WATCHES | A good selection of watches, including Patek Philippe and Chanel, can be found at this store. Pendants and charms in the shape of the island, available in gold, are popular purchases, as are high-end jewels by Graff and Pomellato. ✉ *Rue de la République, Gustavia* ☎ *0590/27–66–94* 🌐 *www.diamondgenesis.com.*

Fabienne Miot

JEWELRY & WATCHES | Unusual and artistic jewelry features rare stones and cultured pearls, watches, and jewelry. ✉ *Rue de la République, Gustavia* ☎ *0590/27–73–13* 🌐 *www.fabiennemiot.com.*

Kalinas Perles

JEWELRY & WATCHES | Beautiful freshwater pearls are knotted onto the classic St. Barth–style leather thongs by artist Jérémy Albaledejo, who also showcases other artisans' works. Tahitian black pearls are featured. ✉ *23 rue du Général de Gaulle, Gustavia* ☎ *0690/65–93–00* 🌐 *www.kalinasperles.com.*

Time

JEWELRY & WATCHES | This store specializes in exclusive watches by Breitling, Bell and Ross, Giuliano Mazzuoli, BRM, Boucheron, and more. ✉ *Rue de la République, Gustavia* ☎ *0590/27–99–10* 🌐 *www.access.sb/en/st-barts/shopping/watchmakers/time.*

LEATHER GOODS AND ACCESSORIES

Human Steps

SHOES | This popular boutique stocks a well-edited selection of chic shoes and leather accessories from names like YSL, Givenchy, Balenciaga, Miu Miu, and Jimmy Choo. ✉ *39 rue de la République, Gustavia* ☎ *0590/27–93–79* 🌐 *www.human-steps.fr.*

LIQUOR AND TOBACCO

Couleurs des Iles 120% Lino

TOBACCO | This shop has many rare varieties of smokables, including Cuban cigars, plus the original Panama hats, and good souvenir T-shirts, too. Head to the back for the stash of rare Puro Vintage. ✉ *Rue du Général de Gaulle, Gustavia* ☎ *0590/27–79–20.*

La Cave du Port Franc

WINE/SPIRITS | This store has a huge selection of wine, especially from France. ✉ *Rue de la République, Gustavia* ☎ *0590/27–65–27* 🌐 *www.lacaveduportfranc.com.*

M'Bolo

WINE/SPIRITS | Sample infused rums, including lemongrass, ginger, and the island favorite, vanilla, and bring some home in beautiful handblown bottles. Laguiole knives and local spices are sold, too, plus artisan products like homemade jam. ✉ *Rue du Général de Gaulle, Gustavia* ☎ *0590/27–90–54* 🌐 *mbolo-rum.com/en.*

Anse de Toiny

Over the hills beyond Grand Cul de Sac is this much-photographed coastline. Stone fences crisscross the steep slopes of Morne du Vitet, one of many small mountains on St. Barth, along a rocky shore that resembles the rugged coast of Normandy. Nicknamed the "washing machine" because of its turbulent surf, it is not recommended even to expert swimmers because of the strong undertow.

TIP→ There is a tough but scenic hike around the point. Take the road past Le Toiny hotel to the top to the start of the trail.

Restaurants

Le Toiny

$$$$ | **MODERN FRENCH** | Hôtel Le Toiny's dramatic cliffside dining porch showcases nature and gastronomy in equal parts. The food is notable for its innovation and extraordinary presentation, and the warm but consummately professional service sets a high standard. **Known for:** relaxing setting; exquisite views; attention to detail. $ *Average main: €50* ✉ *Hôtel Le Toiny, Anse de Toiny* ☎ *0590/27–88–88* 🌐 *www.letoiny.com* ⏲ *Closed Sept.–mid-Oct.*

Hotels

★ **Hôtel Le Toiny**

$$$$ | **HOTEL** | The privacy, serenity, and personalized service at this remote, beachy chic hotel will make you never want to leave. **Pros:** environmental

awareness; suites have private pool and outdoor shower; lovely alfresco restaurant. **Cons:** must take a hotel shuttle to reach the beach (though they're readily available); pricey, as are most St. Barth properties; isolated (at least half an hour's drive from town). *Rooms from: €1980 Anse de Toiny 0590/27–88–88 www.letoiny.com Closed Sept.–late Oct. 22 suites Free Breakfast.*

Colombier

Beaches

Anse de Colombier

BEACH | The beach here is the island's least accessible, thus the most private; to reach it you must take either a rocky footpath from Petite Anse or brave the 30-minute climb down (and back up) a steep, cactus-bordered trail from the top of the mountain behind the beach. Appropriate footgear is a must, and on the beach, the only shade is a rock cave. But this is a good place to snorkel. Boaters favor this cove for its calm anchorage. **Amenities:** none. **Best for:** snorkeling; swimming. *Colombier.*

Restaurants

Les Bananiers

$$$ | **FRENCH** | **FAMILY** | Ask the locals where to eat, and they will surely recommend this casual spot in Colombier, adjacent to a wonderful bakery. The food is classic French (though they're also well known for pizza), the service is warm, the prices are gentle (a rarity here), and you can eat in or take out. **Known for:** a can't-miss bakery next door; thin-crust pizza; reasonable prices. *Average main: €26 Rte. de Colombier, Colombier 0590/27–93–48.*

Coffee and Quick Bites

La Petite Colombe

$ | **BAKERY** | If you're in Colombier (or Lorient, where there's a second location) pop into La Petite for pastries, bread, and baguettes that are the stuff of dreams. You can grab and go or sit for a spell here. **Known for:** picnic fixings; coffee and baked goodies; sandwiches and salads. *Average main: €10 D209, Colombier 0590/27–95–27 Colombier, 0590/29–74–30 Lorient www.facebook.com/petitecolombestbarth No dinner.*

Hotels

Le P'tit Morne

$ | **B&B/INN** | Each of the modestly furnished but clean and freshly decorated, painted mountainside studios has a private balcony with panoramic views of the coastline. **Pros:** helpful management; reasonable rates; great area for hiking. **Cons:** not on the beach; remote location; rooms are basic. *Rooms from: €231 Colombier 0590/52–95–50 www.timorne.com 14 rooms Free Breakfast.*

Villa Marie Saint-Barth

$$$$ | **HOTEL** | Airy bungalows with views of the Bay of Flanders, some with private pools, paint a picture of understated luxury at this boutique hotel in Colombier. **Pros:** great service; good restaurant and spa; peaceful getaway. **Cons:** farther from the action; pricey, as with all St. Barth properties; not on the beach. *Rooms from: €700 Colombier 0590/77–52–52 en.saint-barth.villamarie.fr 23 rooms Free Breakfast.*

Corossol

Traces of the island's French provincial origins are evident in this two-street fishing village with a little rocky beach. Stop for the scenery on the way up to Anse de Colombier; it's a 10-minute drive from Gustavia.

Dinner at Le Toiny is private and romantic.

Flamands

Beaches

Anse des Flamands

BEACH | This is the most beautiful of the hotel beaches—a roomy strip of silken sand. Come here for lunch and then spend the afternoon sunning, enjoying long beach walks, and swimming in the turquoise water. From the beach, you can take a brisk hike along a paved sidewalk to the top of the now-extinct volcano believed to have given birth to St. Barth. **Amenities:** food and drink; toilets. **Best for:** snorkeling; swimming; walking. ✉ *Anse des Flamands.*

Restaurants

★ La Case de L'Isle

$$$$ | MODERN FRENCH | You can't top the view or the service at this waterfront restaurant at the renowned Cheval Blanc St-Barth Isle de France, and at night there is no more romantic spot on the island. Lighter versions of traditional French fare are served. **Known for:** romantic ambience; creative preparations; toes-in-the-sand dining. $ *Average main: €52* ✉ *Cheval Blanc St-Barth Isle de France, Flamands Beach, Anse des Flamands* ☎ *0590/27–61–81* 🌐 *www.chevalblanc.com/en.*

La Langouste

$$$ | FRENCH FUSION | This small but friendly beachside restaurant in the pool courtyard of Hôtel Baie des Anges lives up to its name by serving fresh-grilled local lobster—and lobster thermidor—at prices that are somewhat gentler than at most other island venues. Try starters like crab and guacamole tiramisu, grilled scallops, or one of soups, including classic Caribbean fish soup and lobster bisque. **Known for:** classic French desserts; pick-your-own lobster from the tank; lobster thermidor. $ *Average main: €28* ✉ *Hôtel Baie des Anges, Anse des Flamands* ☎ *0590/27–63–61* 🌐 *www.hotel-baie-des-anges.com* ⏲ *Closed Tues. and late Aug.–mid-Oct.*

Hotels

★ Cheval Blanc St-Barth Isle de France
$$$$ | **RESORT** | Nestled along a pristine white-sand beach, in tropical gardens, or on a hillside, the spacious suites and villas of this intimate, casual resort are private and luxurious. **Pros:** great spa; prime beach location; excellent restaurant. **Cons:** pricey, like everything on the island; you may not want to leave; car needed to get around. *Rooms from: €1625 ✉ Baie des Flamands, Anse des Flamands ☎ 0590/27–61–81 🌐 www.chevalblanc.com ⏲ Closed late Aug.–late Oct. 61 rooms 🍽 Free Breakfast.*

Hôtel Baie des Anges
$$ | **HOTEL** | **FAMILY** | Everyone is treated like family at this casual retreat with 10 clean, spacious units, two of which are modern two-bedroom oceanfront suites, one with a Jacuzzi. **Pros:** excellent value; on St. Barth's longest beach; family-friendly. **Cons:** the boutique is good but not likely to cover all your shopping needs; not super fancy; a bit remote from town, so you'll need a car. *Rooms from: €300 ✉ Anse des Flamands ☎ 0590/27–63–61 🌐 www.hotel-baie-des-anges.com ⏲ Closed Sept. 10 rooms 🍽 No Meals.*

Gouverneur

Beaches

Anse du Gouverneur
BEACH | **FAMILY** | Because it's so secluded, this beach continues to be a popular place for nude sunbathing. Truly beautiful, it has blissful swimming and views of St. Kitts, Saba, and St. Eustatius. Venture here at the end of the day and watch the sun set behind the hills. The road here from Gustavia also offers spectacular vistas. Legend has it that pirates' treasure is buried in the vicinity. There are no restaurants, toilets, or other services here, so plan accordingly. **Amenities:** parking (no fee). **Best for:** nudists; sunset; swimming; walking. ✉ *Le Gouverneur.*

Grand Cul de Sac

Beaches

Anse de Grand Cul de Sac
BEACH | **FAMILY** | The shallow, reef-protected beach is nice for small children, fly-fishermen, kayakers, and windsurfers—and for the amusing frigate birds that dive-bomb the water fishing for their lunch. You needn't do your own fishing; you can have a wonderful lunch at one of the excellent restaurants nearby and use their lounge chairs for the afternoon. You may see some turtles in the shallow water. After storms the water may be a bit murky. **Amenities:** food and drink; parking (no fee); toilets; water sports. **Best for:** swimming; walking. ✉ *Grand Cul de Sac.*

Restaurants

Beach House St. Barth
$$$ | **MEDITERRANEAN** | Rosewood Le Guanahani's open-air restaurant serves fresh Mediterranean-Caribbean fare, family-style. After lunch, sunbathe on the lounge deck with a cocktail. **Known for:** Mediterranean bites; waterfront dining; casual luxury. *Average main: €30 ✉ Rosewood Le Guanahani, Grand Cul de Sac ☎ 0590/52–90–01 🌐 www.rosewood-hotels.com.*

Hotels

Hotel Les Ondines Sur La Plage
$$$$ | **APARTMENT** | **FAMILY** | Right on the beach, this reasonably priced, intimate gem comprises modern, comfortable apartments with room to spread out. **Pros:** airport transfers included; close to restaurants and water sports; nice pool. **Cons:** you'll need a car; narrow beach; not a resort. *Rooms from: €680 ✉ Grand Cul de Sac ☎ 0590/27–69–64 🌐 www.*

st-barths.com/les-ondines ⏲ Closed Sept.–mid-Oct. 6 units | Free Breakfast.

★ Le Barthélemy Hotel & Spa

$$$$ | **HOTEL** | **FAMILY** | Perched on a crescent bay, this beachfront hotel exudes Parisian chic with Caribbean flair. **Pros:** ultimate luxury; restaurants, rooftop bar, and spa on-site; spacious villas with kitchens and private pools. **Cons:** not budget-friendly; high levels of service may spoil you; service can be relaxed. *Rooms from: €1450 ✉ Baie de Grand Cul de Sac, Grand Cul de Sac ☎ 0590/77–48–48 🌐 www.lebarthelemyhotel.com/en* *44 rooms* | *Free Breakfast.*

★ Le Sereno

$$$$ | **RESORT** | Those seeking a restorative, sensuous escape discover nirvana at the quietly elegant, aptly named Le Sereno, set on a beachy cove of turquoise sea, between the island's highest mountain and the foamy waves. **Pros:** spa and restaurant on-site; beach location; super-chic comfort. **Cons:** air-conditioning could be better in bathrooms; pricey, as with most St. Barth properties; you won't want to go home. *Rooms from: €1300 ✉ B.P. 19 Grand-Cul-de-Sac, Grand Cul de Sac ☎ 0590/29–83–00 🌐 www.lesereno.com ⏲ Closed late Aug.–mid-Oct.* *42 units* | *Free Breakfast.*

★ Rosewood Le Guanahani St. Barth

$$$$ | **RESORT** | **FAMILY** | The island's largest resort has luxurious suites, most with ocean views and 20 with private swimming pools, plus impeccable service. **Pros:** has one of the island's few children's programs; fantastic spa; beachside sports. **Cons:** steep walk to beach; pricey; lots of walking around property. *Rooms from: €1850 ✉ Grand Cul de Sac ☎ 0590/52–90–00 🌐 www.rosewoodhotels.com ⏲ Closed late Aug.–Oct.* *66 rooms* | *Free Breakfast ☞ Day passes available.*

Shopping

ART

Chez Pompi

ART GALLERIES | This is little more than a cottage whose first room is a gallery for the naive paintings of Pompi (Louis Ledée). You must call to make a reservation to visit. *✉ Rte. de Toiny, Petit Cul de Sac ☎ 0590/29–76–90.*

Grande Saline

Beaches

★ Anse de Grande Saline

BEACH | With its peaceful seclusion and sandy ocean bottom, this is just about everyone's favorite beach and is great for swimming, too. Without any major development, it's an ideal Caribbean strand, though there can be a bit of wind at times. In spite of the prohibition, young and old alike go nude. The beach is a 10-minute walk up a rocky dune trail, so wear sneakers or water shoes, and bring a blanket, umbrella, and beach towels. There are several good lunch restaurants near the parking area, but the beach itself is just sand, sea, and sky. The big salt ponds here are no longer in use, and the place looks a little desolate on approach, but don't despair. **Amenities:** parking (no fee). **Best for:** nudists; swimming; walking. *✉ Grande Saline.*

Restaurants

★ L' Esprit

$$$$ | **MODERN FRENCH** | **FAMILY** | Renowned chef Jean-Claude Dufour (formerly of Eden Rock) brings innovative dishes to a romantic terrace close to Saline Beach. The menu has lots of variety, from light French dishes with a Provençal twist to interesting salads that have included soba noodles with shrimp and lime to dishes such as roasted pigeon with foie gras, steak, and vegetarian options.

Known for: excellent wine list; creative menu items; outstanding service. *Average main: €41 ✉ Anse de Grande Saline, Grande Saline ☎ 0590/52–46–10 ⊙ Closed Sun. and Mon. No lunch.*

Restaurant La Santa Fé
$$$$ | FRENCH | FAMILY | Perched at the top of the Lurin hills on the way to Gouverneur Beach, this relaxed and scenic restaurant serves panoramic views with both lunch and dinner. The chef comes from Provence and trained at some of its best restaurants before moving to the Caribbean. **Known for:** generous portions; incredible views of neighboring islands; beautiful presentation. *Average main: €42 ✉ Rte. de Lurin, Lurin ☎ 0590/27–61–04 ⊙ Closed Tues., Wed., and late June-Sept.*

★ Tamarin St Barth
$$$$ | INTERNATIONAL | With a beautiful tropical garden that shades the lounge chairs surrounding the palapa of the restaurant, Tamarin is tops for dinner near Grande Saline Beach. The service is attentive and friendly, and the wine list is excellent. **Known for:** great service; superb outdoor dining; variety of entrées. *Average main: €45 ✉ Grande Saline, Grande Saline ☎ 0590/29–27–74 ⊕ www.tamarinstbarth.com ⊙ Closed Mon.*

Salines Garden Cottages
$ | HOUSE | FAMILY | Budget-conscious beach lovers who don't require a lot of coddling need look no further than these petite garden cottages, a short stroll from St. Barth's best beach. **Pros:** good restaurants nearby; only property walkable to Grande Saline Beach; quiet. **Cons:** strict cancellation policy; not very private; far from town. *Rooms from: €250 ✉ Grande Saline ☎ 0590/41–94–29 ⊕ www.salinesgarden.com ⇆ 5 cottages ⟟ Free Breakfast.*

Lorient

Anse de Lorient
BEACH | FAMILY | This beach is popular with families and surfers, who like its waves and central location. Be aware of the level of the tide, which can come in very quickly. Hikers and avid surfers like the walk over the hill to Pointe Milou in the late afternoon, when the waves roll in. **Amenities:** parking (no fee). **Best for:** snorkeling; surfing; swimming. ✉ *Lorient.*

Les Mouettes
$ | HOUSE | FAMILY | This guesthouse offers clean, simply furnished, and economical bungalows with kitchenettes that open directly onto the beach but are also very close to the road. **Pros:** less expensive than many St. Barth options; on the beach; family-friendly. **Cons:** no pool, but you're on the beach; strict prepayment and cancellation policies; basic rooms without TVs. *Rooms from: €270 ✉ Lorient ☎ 0590/27–77–91 ⊕ www.lesmouetteshotel.com ⇆ 7 bungalows ⟟ No Meals.*

Shopping

COSMETICS

Ligne St. Barth
OTHER HEALTH & BEAUTY | Superb skin-care products are made on-site from local tropical plants. ✉ *Rte. de Saline, Lorient ☎ 0590/27–82–63 ⊕ www.lignestbarth.com.*

FOODSTUFFS

Bacchus
WINE/SPIRITS | Fine wines and gourmet delicacies, teas, and Nespresso coffee can be found here, an outpost of the St. Martin distributor. ✉ *Place des Marais, Lorient ☎ 0590/29–19–22 ⊕ www.bacchussxm.com.*

St. Barth's Spas

Visitors to St. Barth can enjoy more than the comforts of home by taking advantage of the myriad wellness, spa, and beauty treatments available on the island. Major hotels—the Cheval Blanc St-Barth Isle de France and Christopher among them—have beautiful, comprehensive, on-site spas. Others, including Le Village St. Barth Hotel, Le Sereno, (with its waterfront treatment pavillion) and Hôtel Le Toiny, have added spa cottages, where treatments and services can be arranged on-site. Depending on availability, all island visitors can book services at these locations. There's a new wellness retreat here, with metabolic and detox programs available. In addition, scores of independent therapists will come to your hotel room or villa and provide any therapeutic discipline you can think of, including yoga, Thai massage, shiatsu, reflexology, and even manicures, pedicures, and hairdressing. You can get recommendations at the tourist office in Gustavia.

JoJo Supermarché

SUPERMARKET | This well-stocked counterpart to Gustavia's supermarket gets daily deliveries of bread and produce. JoJoBurger, next door, is the local surfers' spot for a (very good) quick burger. ✉ *Lorient* ☎ *0590/27–63–53.*

Pointe Milou

Restaurants

★ **Le Ti St Barth Caribbean Tavern**

$$$$ | **ECLECTIC** | Owner Carole Gruson captures the island's wild spirit in her popular hilltop spot. Come to dance to great music with the attractive bar crowd, lounge at a pillow-strewn banquette, or chat on the torch-lighted terrace. **Known for:** legendary barbecue; fun nights from beginning to end; lively crowd. $ *Average main: €66* ✉ *Pointe Milou* ☎ *0590/27–97–71* 🌐 *www.tist-barth.com.*

Hotels

★ **Christopher**

$$$$ | **RESORT** | **FAMILY** | This longtime favorite of European families delivers a high standard of professionalism and courteous service. **Pros:** good value; comfortable elegance; family-friendly. **Cons:** there's a bit of walking to get around the complex; three-night minimum; on the water but not on a beach. $ *Rooms from: €1850* ✉ *Pointe Milou* ☎ *0590/27–63–63* 🌐 *www.hotelchristopher.com* ⏲ *Closed mid-Aug.–mid-Oct.* *45 units* *Free Breakfast* ☞ *3-night minimum.*

St-Jean

There is a monument at the crest of the hill that divides St-Jean from Gustavia. Called *The Arawak,* it symbolizes the soul of St. Barth. A warrior, one of the earliest inhabitants of the area (AD 800–1,800) holds a lance in his right hand and stands on a rock shaped like the island; in his left hand he holds a conch shell, which sounds the cry of nature; perched beside him are a pelican (which symbolizes the air and survival by fishing) and an

The secluded beach at Eden Rock is a sunbather's dream.

iguana (which represents the earth). The half-mile-long crescent of sand at St-Jean is the island's favorite beach. A popular activity is watching and photographing the hair-raising airplane landings (but it is *extremely* dangerous to stand at the beach end of the runway). Some of the best shopping on the island is here as are several restaurants.

 Beaches

Baie de St-Jean

BEACH | FAMILY | Like a mini Côte d'Azur—beachside bistros, terrific shopping, bungalow hotels, bronzed sunbathers, windsurfing, and day-trippers who tend to arrive on *big* yachts—the reef-protected strip is divided by the Eden Rock promontory. Except when the hotels are filled, you can rent chaises and umbrellas at the Pearl Beach restaurant or Eden Rock, where you can lounge for hours over lunch. **Amenities:** food and drink; toilets. **Best for:** partiers; walking. ✉ *St-Jean.*

 Restaurants

★ Sand Bar Eden Rock

$$$$ | ECLECTIC | Eden Rock hotel is legendary; this laid-back beach restaurant is just one more reason to love it. Lunch time is lively but relaxed with a DJ pumping tunes by the sparkling sea, and there are many tempting gourmet pizzas on offer. **Known for:** music; black truffle fontina cheese pizza; fresh herbs from the hotel's garden. [$] *Average main: €52* ✉ *Eden Rock, Baie de St-Jean, St-Jean* ☎ *0590/29–81–86* 🌐 *www.oetkercollection.com.*

 Hotels

★ Eden Rock St Barths

$$$$ | RESORT | FAMILY | Even on an island known for gourmet cuisine and luxury hotels, this iconic luxury hotel stands out thanks to top-tier Jean-Georges Vongerichten eateries, spacious rooms, stunning bay views, and cosseting service. **Pros:** beach setting; chic clientele; stylish facilities. **Cons:** car needed to tour the entire island; some construction or site work may continue for a bit; some suites near street are noisy. *Rooms from: €900 ✉ Baie de St-Jean, St-Jean ☎ 0590/29–79–99, 877/992–0070 in U.S. 🌐 www.oetkercollection.com ⏲ Closed late Aug.–Nov. 1 37 units 🍴 Free Breakfast.*

★ Hotel Manapany

$$$$ | **RESORT** | On a private beach of Anse des Cayes, this breezy yet luxurious B Signature resort (the first outside of mainland France) is an eco-friendly paradise, with solar panels and electric cars on property. **Pros:** open-air restaurant; five minutes to the airport with complimentary transfers; spa faces the sea. **Cons:** you may be spoiled by high levels of service; pricey, like everything here; not in the action of Baie St-Jean. *Rooms from: €1030 ✉ Anse de Cayes, St-Jean ☎ 0590/27-66-55 🌐 hotelmanapany-st-barth.com 43 units 🍴 Free Breakfast.*

★ Le Village St. Barth Hotel

$$ | **HOTEL** | **FAMILY** | For two generations the Charneau family has offered friendly hotel service, villa advantages, and reasonable rates, making guests feel like a part of the family. **Pros:** on-site spa and gym; convenient location near beach and town; wonderful management. **Cons:** rooms close to street can be noisy; not in the center of the action; steep walk to hotel, many steps. *Rooms from: €295 ✉ Colline de St-Jean, St-Jean ☎ 0590/27–61–39, 800/651–8366 in U.S. 🌐 www.levillagestbarth.com 25 units 🍴 Free Breakfast.*

Les Îlets de la Plage

$$$$ | **B&B/INN** | **FAMILY** | On the far side of the airport and the far corner of Baie de St-Jean, these well-priced, island-style one-, two-, and three-bedroom bungalows are nestled either on the beach itself or among lush tropical gardens on the hillside, with stunning views of the Bay. The units have small kitchens, open-air sitting areas, and comfortable bathrooms. **Pros:** front porches; beach location; apartment conveniences. **Cons:** near airport, so you will hear some small planes taking off; limited air-conditioning; only small pets allowed. *Rooms from: €550 ✉ Plage de St-Jean, St-Jean ☎ 0590/27–88–57 🌐 www.lesilets.com ⏲ Closed Sept. 1- Oct. 15 12 units 🍴 Free Breakfast.*

Pearl Beach Saint Barth

$$$$ | **HOTEL** | This chic but casual boutique property on busy St-Jean beach is fun for social types; the nonstop house party may well spill onto the terraces and last into the wee hours. **Pros:** many places of interest are walking distance away; party central at beach, restaurant, and pool; in town. **Cons:** you'll need a car to get to other beaches; some noise from the airport; trendy social scene is not for everybody, especially light sleepers. *Rooms from: €635 ✉ Plage de St-Jean, St-Jean ☎ 0590/52–81–20 🌐 pearlbeachstbarth.com 14 rooms 🍴 Free Breakfast.*

Villa Les Lataniers

$$$$ | **B&B/INN** | With breathtaking views of the ocean and St. Barth's famous red tile roofs plus personalized service, this hillside villa is the ultimate private getaway. **Pros:** private, comfortable luxury; 24/7 concierge service; infinity pool with sweeping views. **Cons:** since this is a private villa, you lose the convenience of resort life (like restaurant and spa on-site); pricey; need a car if you want to venture beyond St. Jean. *Rooms from: €6000 ✉ Wimco Villas, St-Jean ☎ 800/932–3222 🌐 wimco.com 1 private villa 🍴 Free Breakfast ☞ price is per week.*

Nightlife

Le Nikki Beach

BARS | This place rocks on weekends at lunch—especially Sunday—when the scantily clad young and beautiful lounge on the white canvas banquettes. *✉ St-Jean ☎ 0590/27–64–64 🌐 www.nikkibeach.com.*

CLOTHING

Bamboo St Barth

MIXED CLOTHING | Beach fashions like cotton tunics, cocktails-on-the-yacht dresses, and sexy Australian swimsuits by Nicole Olivier and Seafolly can be paired with sassy sandals and costume jewelry. ✉ *Pelican Beach, St-Jean* ☎ *0590/52–08–82* 🌐 *www.facebook.com/bamboo.stbarth.*

Black Swan

MIXED CLOTHING | This shop has an unparalleled selection of bathing suits, and it also offers beach dresses, hats, caps, and sunglasses. ✉ *La Villa Créole, St-Jean* ☎ *0590/87–44–60* 🌐 *facebook.com/blackswanstbarth.*

Cabane Saint-Barth

MIXED CLOTHING | Stocked with stenciled cotton, gauzy beach tops, great straw fedoras, caftans (for all ages), plus beachy shoes and accessories, this shop is open nonstop every day. ✉ *Pélican, St-Jean* ☎ *0590/51–21–02* 🌐 *facebook.com/cabanesaintbarth.*

Filles des Iles

MIXED CLOTHING | In addition to high-quality, flattering French attire and sophisticated swimwear for all ages, this shop stocks delicious artisanal fragrances and chic accessories, like beautiful sandals. ✉ *8 Villa Créole, St-Jean* ☎ *0590/29–04–08.*

Iléna St Barth

MIXED CLOTHING | Incredible beachwear and lingerie by Papueen , Sarda, and others includes Swarovski crystal–encrusted bikinis for the trendy set. ✉ *La Villa Créole, St-Jean* ☎ *0590/29–84–05* 🌐 *www.facebook.com/Ilena.StBarth.*

KiWi Saint-Tropez

MIXED CLOTHING | This popular boutique for adults and kids has beach and resort wear for everyone, as well as a variety of beach bags and towels. ✉ *3 Villa Créole, St-Jean* ☎ *0590/27–57–08* 🌐 *www.kiwi.fr.*

Lili Belle

MIXED CLOTHING | Their great selection includes chic, French designer beachwear and resort clothing. ✉ *Pelican Plage, St-Jean* ☎ *0590/87–46–14.*

Morgan

MIXED CLOTHING | There's a great selection of trendy feminine clothing, accessories, shoes, hats, bags, and more at Morgan. ✉ *La Villa Créole, St-Jean* ☎ *0590/27–57–22.*

SUD SUD St Barth

HANDBAGS | This store stocks bags, beachy shell jewelry, as well as gauzy cover-ups. ✉ *La Villa Creole, St-Jean* ☎ *0590/27-98-75* 🌐 *https://www.facebook.com/Sud-Sud-St-Barth-1519235571710326/.*

FOODSTUFFS

Eden to Go

FOOD | This is the place to go for prepared picnics, meals, salads, and more. The emphasis is on freshness, so menu items change according to season and availability. This is not your average "boxed lunch" place; you could well get shrimp rolls on homemade bread, custom picnic baskets, or pork burgers. ✉ *Les Galeries du Commerce, St-Jean* ☎ *0590/29–83–70* 🌐 *edentogo.com.*

Super U

FOOD | This modern, fully stocked supermarket across from the airport has a wide selection of French cheeses, pâtés, cured meats, produce, fresh bread, wine, and liquor. There is also a good selection of prepared foods and organic items. ✉ *Face à l'aéroport, St-Jean* ☎ *0590/27–68–16* ⏲ *Closed Sun.*

HANDICRAFTS

Couleurs Provence

HOUSEWARES | This store stocks beautiful, handcrafted, French-made items like jacquard table linens in brilliant colors; decorative tableware, including trays in which dried flowers and herbs are suspended; and the island home fragrance line by L'Occitane. ✉ *Rte. de Saline, St-Jean* ☎ *0590/52–48–51* 🌐 *www.facebook.com/CouleursProvence.*

HOME FURNISHINGS

French Indies Design

HOUSEWARES | This beautiful shop is the brainchild of Karine Bruneel, a St. Barth–based architect and interior designer. There are lovely items to accent your home (or yacht) including furniture, textiles, glassware, and unusual decorative baskets, candles, and pottery. ✉ *Centre Les Amandiers, St-Jean* ☎ *0590/29–66–38* 🌐 *www.frenchindiesdesign.fr.*

Activities

BOATING AND SAILING

St. Barth is a popular yachting and sailing center, thanks to its location midway between Antigua and St. Thomas.

Gustavia's harbor, 13 to 16 feet deep, has mooring and docking facilities for 40 yachts. There are also good anchorages at Public, Corossol, and Colombier. You can charter sailing and motorboats in Gustavia Harbor for as little as a half day, staffed or bareboat. Ask at the Gustavia tourist office or your hotel for a list of recommended charter companies.

Carib Waterplay

WINDSURFING | On St. Jean beach for over 35 years, this outfit lets you try windsurfing, kayaking, surfing, and stand-up paddling; rents waterbikes; and offers lessons for all ages. ✉ *St-Jean* ☎ *0665/95–43–52* 🌐 *www.caribwaterplay.com.*

Jicky Marine Service

BOATING | This company offers private full-day outings on motorboats, Zodiacs, and 47-foot catamarans to the uninhabited Île Fourchue for swimming, snorkeling, cocktails, or lunch, as well as scheduled cruises including weekly half- and full-day group cruises and twice-weekly group sunset catamaran cruises. Private fishing charters are also offered, as is private transport from St. Martin. Skippered motorboat rentals run about €1,400 per day. A one-hour group Jet Ski tour of the island is also offered, as are private tours. ✉ *33 rue Jeanne D'Arc, Gustavia* ☎ *0590/27–70–34* 🌐 *www.jickymarine.com.*

St Barth Sailing

SAILING | Captain Eric offers his 47′ sailing catamaran *Okeanos* for day trips for up to 16 people and charters for up to six. Half-day, full-day, and sunset-champagne cruises are available with all the amenities you could ask for either standard or available, or you can charter the boat and sail to the British Virgin Islands, Antigua and Barbuda, or St. Martin and Anguila, all available as seven-day, six-night sailing adventures. ☎ *690/19–00–15* 🌐 *www.saintbarthsailing.com.*

St Barth Sailor

SAILING | Want to rent a bareboat or crewed catamaran and take off for your own tour of several islands? Captain Miguel Danet enables you to do exactly that, for a full-day, half-day, or sunset cruise. Extras are available, from special dining choices aboard to massage to scuba to underwater scooters. ☎ *690/18–60–66* 🌐 *www.stbarthsailor.com.*

Top Loc Boat Rental

BOATING | Charter a catamaran for a day of fun on the water. Rental for a half-day on the catamaran including an open bar is €750. Other rates/itineraries available. ✉ *Airport Office, St-Jean* ☎ *0590/29–02–02* 🌐 *www.top-loc.com.*

DIVING AND SNORKELING

Several dive shops arrange scuba excursions. Depending on weather conditions, you may dive at **Pain de Sucre, Coco Island,** or toward nearby **Saba.** There's also an underwater shipwreck, plus sharks, rays, sea tortoises, coral, and the usual varieties of colorful fish. The waters on the island's leeward side are the calmest.

For the uncertified, there's a shallow reef right off the beach at Anse des Cayes, which you can explore with mask and fins, and a hike down to the beach at Corossol brings you to a very popular snorkeling spot.

Ouanalao Dive

DIVING & SNORKELING | This well-regarded company offers PADI and CMAS, night dives, private dives and snorkeling, rental of fins, mask and snorkel, and more. Organized dives, a good dive shop, and instruction are offered at the Grand Cul-de Sac beach location. A two-tank dive is €170. A two-hour snorkeling trip to a nearby island starts at €70 per person. ✉ *Grand Cul de Sac* ☎ *0690/63–74–34* 🌐 *www.ouanalaodive.com*.

Plongée Caraïbes

DIVING & SNORKELING | **FAMILY** | Recommended for its up-to-the-minute equipment, dive boat, and scuba discovery program, this company offers nitrox diving and certification. They also run two-hour group snorkeling trips on the *Blue Cat Catamaran* (€75 per person), or you can enjoy a private charter from €590. ✉ *Quai de la République, Gustavia* ☎ *0590/27–55–94* 🌐 *www.sbhonline.com/activities/scuba/plongee-caraibes/*.

Réserve Naturelle de Saint-Barthélemy

SCUBA DIVING | Most of the waters surrounding St. Barth are protected in the island's nature reserve, which provides information from its Gustavia office. The diving here isn't nearly as rich as in more dive-centered destinations like Saba and St. Eustatius (Statia), but the options aren't bad either. ✉ *Gustavia* ☎ *0590/27–88–18* 🌐 *www.reserves-naturelles.org/saint-barthelemy*.

Splash

SCUBA DIVING | This company offers PADI and CMAS (Confédération Mondiale des Activités Subaquatiques—World Underwater Federation) diver training at all levels. Instructors speak French and English. The boat leaves several times during the day and in the evening for a night dive; times are adjusted to suit preferences. Seabob scuba scooters are available at reasonable rates. ✉ *Gustavia* ☎ *0590/56–90–24*.

FISHING

Most fishing is done in the waters north of Lorient, Flamands, and Corossol. Popular catches are tuna, marlin, wahoo, and barracuda. The annual St. Barth Open Fishing Tournament, organized by Océan Must, is in mid-July.

GUIDED TOURS

You can arrange island tours by minibus or car at hotel desks or through taxi operators in Gustavia or at the airport. The tourist office runs a variety of tours for about €50 for a half day for up to eight people. You can also download up-to-the-minute walking and driving tour itineraries from the office's website.

Hélène Bernier

GUIDED TOURS | St. Barth native Hélène gives complete island tours. Her family has lived on the island since the 17th century; she is also president of Barth Essential, a non-profit organization she started to focus on preservation and environmental protection. ☎ *0690/63–46–09*.

JC Taxi

DRIVING TOURS | Since 1986, native-born Jean-Claude has been providing safe and comfortable transportation in a 9-passenger van with executive seats. Island tours and night driving are available. ✉ *Gustavia* ☎ *0690/31–59–00 (WhatsApp)*.

St. Barth Mobilité

SPECIAL-INTEREST TOURS | This company offers transportation, tours, and guided help for those with limited mobility. ☎ *0690/77–66–73* 🌐 *www.stbarthmobilite.com*.

Chapter 18

ST. KITTS AND NEVIS

Updated by
Amber Love Bond

Sights ★★★☆☆ Restaurants ★★★★☆ Hotels ★★★★☆ Shopping ★★★☆☆ Nightlife ★★★☆☆

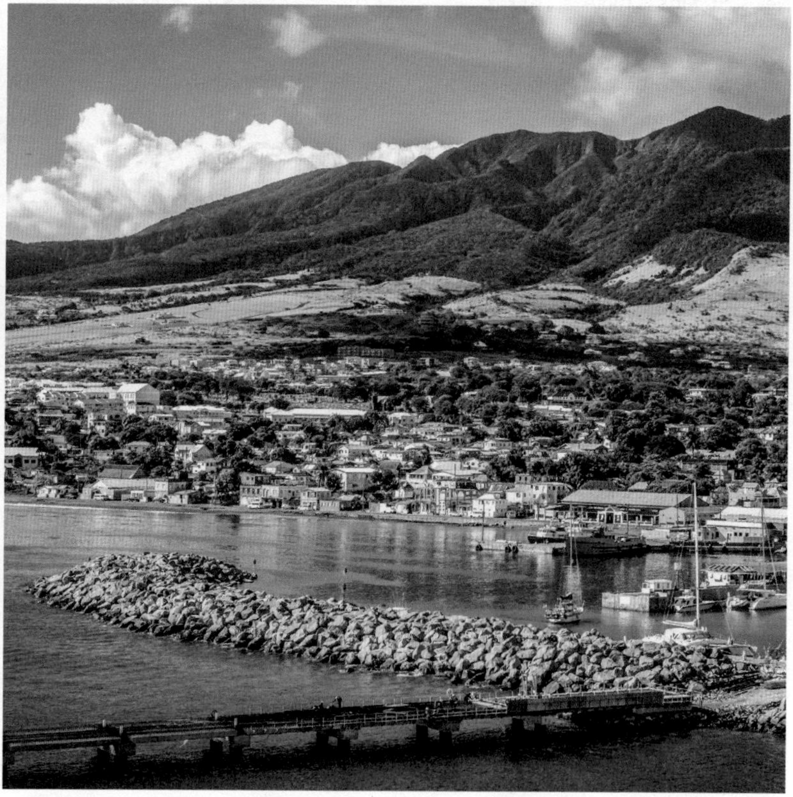

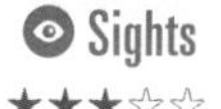

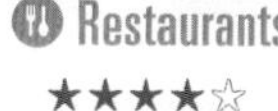

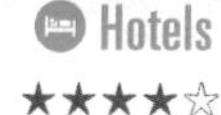

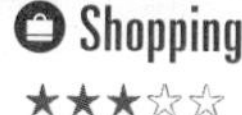

WELCOME TO ST. KITTS AND NEVIS

TOP REASONS TO GO

★ **History:** Both St. Kitts and Nevis are steeped in history; Brimstone Hill Fortress is a UNESCO World Heritage Site.

★ **Luxury:** Luxurious, restored plantation inns can still be found on Nevis; St. Kitts is more focused on upscale developments, such as the Park Hyatt.

★ **Landscape:** Both islands have extinct volcanoes and luxuriant rain forests ideal for hikes, as well as fine diving and snorkeling sites.

★ **Unspoiled:** You'll find less development—particularly on Nevis—and more cordial and courteous islanders than on more touristy islands.

★ **Water Activities:** Both islands feature aquatic activities aplenty, with fine sailing, deep-sea fishing, diving (especially off St. Kitts), and windsurfing (especially around Nevis).

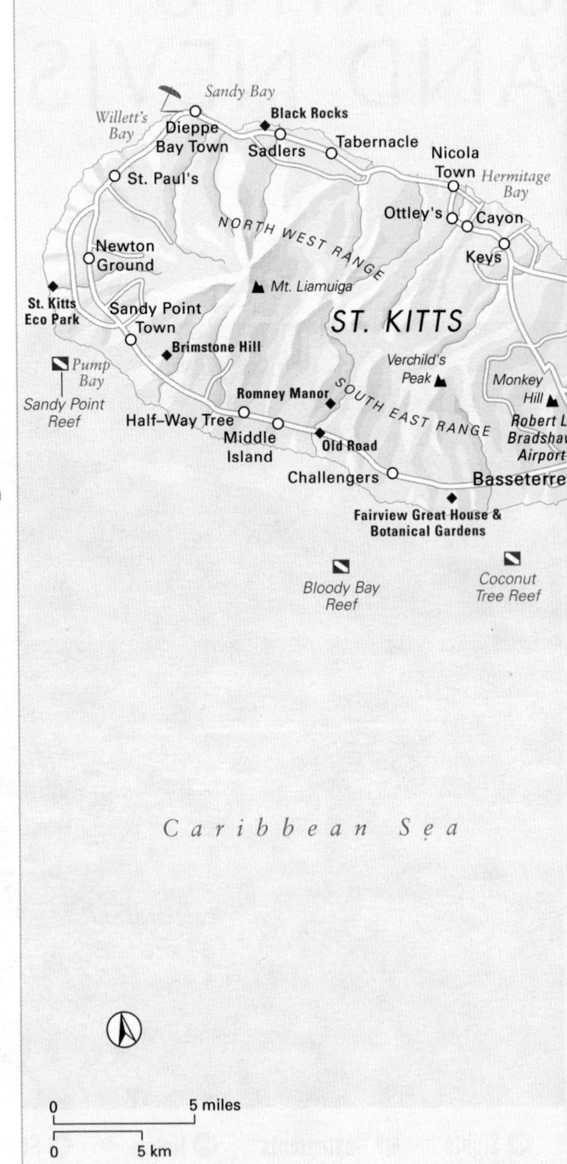

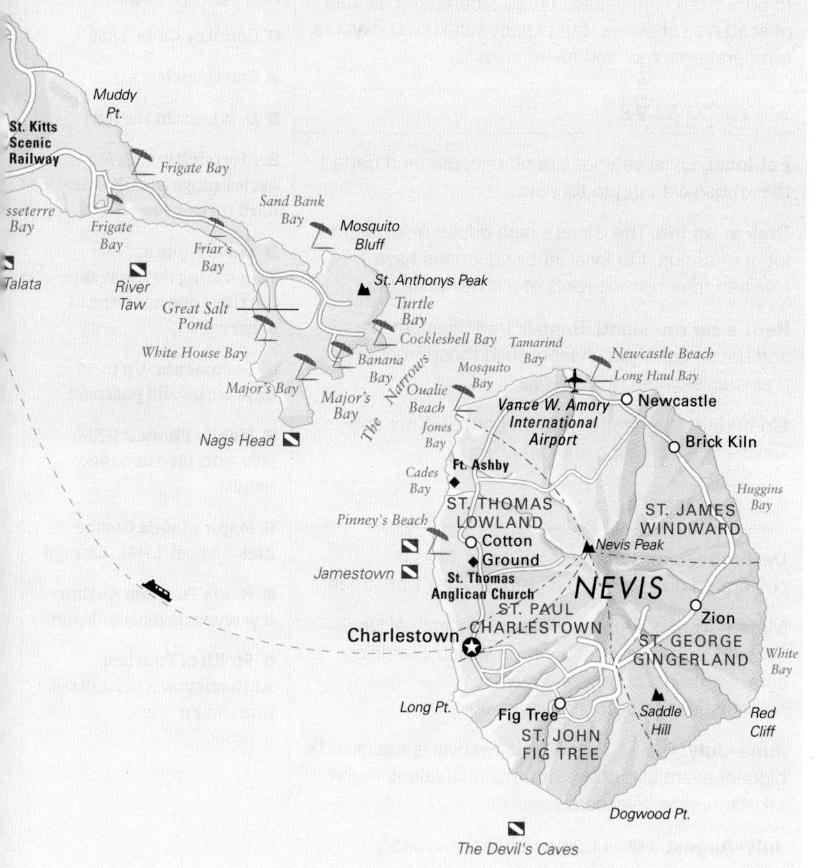
ATLANTIC OCEAN
Muddy Pt.
St. Kitts Scenic Railway
Frigate Bay
Basseterre Bay
Frigate Bay
Sand Bank Bay
Mosquito Bluff
Friar's Bay
Talata
River Taw
St. Anthonys Peak
Great Salt Pond
Turtle Bay
Cockleshell Bay
White House Bay
Banana Bay
Major's Bay
Major's Bay
The Narrows
Nags Head
Tamarind Bay
Mosquito Bay
Newcastle Beach
Long Haul Bay
Oualie Beach
Vance W. Amory International Airport
Newcastle
Jones Bay
Brick Kiln
Cades Bay
Ft. Ashby
Huggins Bay
ST. THOMAS LOWLAND
ST. JAMES WINDWARD
Pinney's Beach
Cotton Ground
Nevis Peak
Jamestown
St. Thomas Anglican Church
NEVIS
ST. PAUL CHARLESTOWN
Zion
Charlestown
ST. GEORGE GINGERLAND
White Bay
Long Pt.
Fig Tree
Saddle Hill
Red Cliff
ST. JOHN FIG TREE
Dogwood Pt.
The Devil's Caves

ISLAND SNAPSHOT

WHEN TO GO

High Season: Mid-December through mid-April is the most popular time to visit as it has the best weather and the most options. Lodging options usually book up fast though, so plan ahead.

Low Season: From August to late October, the weather is hot and muggy, with high risks of tropical storms. Some hotels close for annual renovations, while others offer deep discounts.

Value Season: From late April to July and again November to mid-December, hotel prices drop 20% to 50% from high-season prices. There are chances of scattered showers, but expect sun-kissed daytime temperatures, too, and fewer crowds.

WAYS TO SAVE

Eat local. Local eateries are far cheaper (and better) than those catering to tourists.

Stay at an inn. The island's high-priced resorts get a lot of attention, but local inns and lodges have retained their historic roots at a lower price tag.

Rent a car on-island. Rentals from local retailers and hotels are often cheaper than those from larger agencies secured on the Web.

Go hiking. The nature trails on both St. Kitts and Nevis are exhilarating and dirt cheap.

BIG EVENTS

December–January: Carnival on St. Kitts is celebrated during the 10 days right after Christmas.

March–April: Spectators flock to the annual Nevis–St. Kitts Cross Channel Swim to watch championship swimmers compete. www.nevistostkittscrosschannelswim.com

June–July: The St. Kitts Music Festival is the island's biggest event and draws international talent. www.stkittsmusicfestival.com

July–August: Nevis Culturama is the island's summer carnival. www.culturamanevis.com

AT A GLANCE

- **Capital:** Basseterre
- **Population:** 53,192
- **Currency:** Eastern Caribbean dollar; pegged to the U.S. dollar
- **Money:** Few ATMs; credit cards accepted at resorts, cash elsewhere. U.S. dollars commonly accepted
- **Language:** English
- **Country Code:** 1 869
- **Emergencies:** 911
- **Driving:** On the left
- **Electricity:** 230v/60 cycles; plugs are UK standard three-prong
- **Time:** Same as New York during daylight saving time; one hour ahead otherwise
- **Documents:** Up to 90 days with valid passport
- **Mobile Phones:** GSM (850, 900, 1800 and 1900 bands)
- **Major Mobile Companies:** Digicel, LIME, Orange
- **Nevis Tourism Authority:** www.nevisisland.com
- **St. Kitts Tourism Authority:** www.stkitts-tourism.kn

These idyllic sister islands, 2 miles (3 km) apart at their closest point, offer visitors a relatively authentic island experience. Both have luxuriant mountain rain forests; uncrowded beaches; historic ruins; towering, long-dormant volcanoes; charming if slightly dilapidated Georgian capitals in Basseterre (St. Kitts) and Charlestown (Nevis); intact cultural heritage; friendly, if shy, people; and restored 18th-century sugar plantation inns run by elegant, if sometimes eccentric, expatriate owners.

The islands' history follows the usual Caribbean route: Amerindian settlements, Columbus's voyages, fierce colonial battles between the British and French, a boom in sugar production second only to that of Barbados. St. Kitts became known as the mother colony of the West Indies: English settlers sailed from here to Antigua, Barbuda, Tortola, and Montserrat, and the French dispatched colonists to Martinique, Guadeloupe, St. Martin, and St. Barth.

St. Kitts and Nevis, in addition to Anguilla, achieved self-government as an associated state of Great Britain in 1967. Anguillians soon made their displeasure known, separating immediately, whereas St. Kitts and Nevis waited until 1983 to become an independent nation. The two islands, despite their superficial similarities, have taken increasingly different routes regarding tourism. Nevis received an economic boost from the Four Seasons, which helped establish it as an upscale destination. St. Kitts, however, had yet to define its identity at a point when most islands had found their tourism niche but is now making up for lost time and notoriety with several high-profile high-end projects, including Kittitian Hill and Christophe Harbour, with a Park Hyatt. A fierce sibling rivalry has ensued.

Though its comparative lack of development is a lure, the Kittitian government is casting its economic net in several directions. Golf, ecotourism, and scuba diving are being aggressively promoted. The island offers a surprisingly diverse vacation experience while retaining its essential Caribbean flavor. Divers have yet to discover all its underwater attractions, and nature lovers are pleasantly surprised by the hiking. There's now every kind of accommodation, as well as gourmet dining, golf, and gaming.

Meanwhile, Nevis seems determined to stay even more unspoiled (there are still no traffic lights). Its natural attractions and activities certainly rival those of St. Kitts, from mountain biking and ecohiking to windsurfing and deep-sea fishing, though lying in a hammock and dining on romantic candlelit patios remain cherished pursuits. Pinney's Beach, despite occasional hurricane erosion, remains a classic Caribbean strand. Its historic heritage, from the Caribbean's first hotel to Alexander Hamilton's childhood home, is just as pronounced, including equally sybaritic plantation inns that seem torn from the pages of a romance novel.

Perhaps it's a warning sign that many guests call the catamaran trip to Nevis the high point of their stay on St. Kitts—and many Kittitians build retirement and second homes on Nevis. The sister islands' relationship remains outwardly cordial if slightly contentious. Nevis papers sometimes run blistering editorials advocating independence, though one plebiscite has already failed. St. Kitts and Nevis may separate someday, but for now their battles are confined to ad campaigns and political debates. Fortunately, well-heeled and barefoot travelers alike can still happily enjoy the many energetic and easygoing enticements of both blissful retreats.

Planning

Getting Here and Around

AIR

St. Kitts' **Robert L. Bradshaw International Airport** (SKB) is 2½ miles (4 km) northeast of downtown Basseterre, a 10-minute drive in light traffic. The airport's KayanJet Lounge (aka YU Lounge) is available not just to private jet passengers but also to commercial travelers willing to pay for a restful, hassle-free, executive retreat that eliminates the need to go through Customs and Immigration (it offers its own approved security screening). Nevis's **Vance W. Amory International Airport** (NEV) is in New Castle at the northern tip of the island.

There are no nonstop flights to Nevis from the United States. Many travelers connect in Tortola, St. Thomas, Anguilla, or San Juan. To Nevis, it's almost always cheaper to fly into St. Kitts and then take a regularly scheduled ferry, but check the schedules or book a transfer from your resort (if available) in advance. **American** has nonstop flights from Miami into St. Kitts (once daily) and weekly flights from Charlotte, New York's JFK, and (late May–mid-August) Dallas. **Delta** also offers nonstop flights to St. Kitts from Atlanta (twice weekly in high season, with a third flight during the Christmas holidays). **United** offers twice-weekly nonstop flights from Newark to St. Kitts during peak season.

Several major domestic airlines (including Delta once-weekly from Atlanta) fly from their eastern hubs either into Antigua, St. Maarten, San Juan, or St. Thomas, where connections to St. Kitts (and, less frequently, to Nevis) can be made on **LIAT**. **Seaborne** offers service from San Juan to both St. Kitts and Nevis. Passengers can take advantage of its code-share agreements with American, Delta, and JetBlue. **Winair** flies to both Nevis and St. Kitts from St. Maarten.

AIRLINE CONTACTS LIAT. ☎ *268/480–5601, 268/480–5602* 🌐 *www.liat.com.* **Seaborne.** ☎ *801/401–9100* 🌐 *www.seaborneairlines.com.* **Winair.** ☎ *712/545–4237* 🌐 *www.fly-winair.sx.*

AIRPORT CONTACTS Robert L. Bradshaw International Airport. *(SKB)* ✉ *Golden Rock* ☎ *869/465–8472.* **Vance W. Amory International Airport.** *(NEV)* ✉ *Newcastle* ☎ *869/469–9040.*

CAR

One well-kept main road circumnavigates St. Kitts and is usually clearly marked, making it difficult to get lost, though the northeast can get a bit bumpy, and the access roads to the plantation inns are notoriously rough.

The roads on Nevis are generally smooth, at least on the most traveled north, west, and south sides of the island. The east coast has some potholes, and pigs, goats, and sheep still insist on the right-of-way all around the island. Drivers on both islands tend to travel at a fast clip and pass on curves, so drive defensively. Driving is on the left, British-style, though you will probably be given an American-style car.

Renting a Car: You can get by without a car if you are staying in the Frigate Bay–Basseterre area, but elsewhere you'll need to rent one. On Nevis it's often easier to just take taxis and guided tours. On St. Kitts, present your valid driver's license and $25 (for three months, or $47 for a year) at the police station traffic department on Cayon Street in Basseterre or fire station in Frigate Bay to get a temporary driving permit (on Nevis the car-rental agency will help you obtain the $25 local license at the police station). The license is valid on both islands. On either island, car rentals start at about $40 per day for a compact; expect to pay a few extra bucks for air-conditioning. Most agencies offer substantial multiday discounts.

CONTACTS IN ST. KITTS Avis. ✉ *Bay Rd, Basseterre* ☎ *869/465–6507, 954/284–5331 for U.S. reservations* 🌐 *www.avis-stkitts.com.* **Hertz.** ✉ *C. A. P. Southwell Industrial Park, Basseterre* ☎ *869/465–7822* 🌐 *www.hertz.com.* **TDC/Thrifty Rentals.** ✉ *West Independence Sq., Central St., Basseterre* ☎ *869/465–23160,* 🌐 *tdcgrouplimited.com/vehicle-rentals.*

CONTACTS IN NEVIS Funky Monkey Tours and Rentals. ✉ *Cades Bay* ☎ *869/665–6045, 869/665–6245* 🌐 *www.funkymonkeytours.com.* **Nevis Car Rentals.** ✉ *Shaws Rd., Newcastle* ☎ *869/469–9837* 🌐 *www.neviscarrentals.com.* **Noel's Courtesy Garage.** ✉ *Farm Estate* ☎ *869/469–5199.* **Striker's Car Rental.** ✉ *Hermitage Rd., Gingerland* ☎ *869/469–2654* 🌐 *www.strikerscarrentals.com.* **TDC/Thrifty Rentals.** ✉ *Bay Rd., Charlestown* ☎ *869/465–3160* 🌐 *www.tdcgrouplimited.com/vehicle-rentals.*

FERRY

There are several ferry services between St. Kitts and Nevis, all with schedules that are subject to abrupt change. Most companies make two or three trips daily. All the ferries take about 30 to 45 minutes and cost $8–$10. An additional EC$1 tax for port security is paid separately on departure.

CONTACT Ferry Schedule. 🌐 *www.scaspa-sea.com.*

TAXI

Taxi rates are government regulated and posted at the airport, the dock, and in the free tourist guide. Be sure to clarify whether the fare is in EC or U.S. dollars. There are fixed rates to and from all the hotels and to and from major points of interest.

Airport Transfers: On St. Kitts the fares from the airport range from EC$32 to Frigate Bay to EC$80 for the farthest point. From the airport on Nevis it's EC$27 to Nisbet Plantation, EC$54 to the Four Seasons, and EC$67 to Montpelier. There is a 50% surcharge between 10 pm and 6 am.

CONTACTS Nevis Taxi Service. ☎ *869/469–5631, 869/469–9790 for the airport, 869/469–5515 after dark.* **St. Kitts Taxi Association.com.** ☎ *869/465–8487, 869/465–4253, 869/465–7818 after hrs.*

Hotels and Restaurants

St. Kitts has a wide variety of places to stay: full-service affordable hotels, simple beachfront cottages, comfortable condos, and all-inclusive resorts. One large resort—the Marriott—is more midrange than upscale and attracts large groups and package tourists. Choose St. Kitts if you want a wider choice of activities and accommodations (you can always do Nevis as a day trip). Nevis is a small island with no large resorts, and most accommodations are upscale—primarily plantation inns and the luxurious Four Seasons. It's much quieter than St. Kitts, so choose it if you want to get away from the hectic island scene and simply relax in low-key comfort and surprisingly high style.

Luxury Resorts: Really in a class by itself, the Four Seasons Resort Nevis was the only sizable, lavish, high-end property on either island until the 126-room Park Hyatt St. Kitts opened on Banana Bay in 2017 as part of the massive upscale Christophe Harbour development. Both resorts certainly rank among the Caribbean's finest (with prices to match); recent renovations improved on near-perfection at the Four Seasons.

Plantation Inns: St. Kitts and Nevis feature renovated, historic plantation houses that have been turned into upscale inns, though the fate of the last such lodging, Ottley's, on St. Kitts is undetermined after being sold to Chinese developers. On Nevis, the inns are the most distinctive form of lodging. They are usually managed by hands-on owner-operators and offer fine cuisine and convivial hospitality; though not usually on a beach, most of these inns have beach clubs with free private shuttle service.

Hotel reviews have been shortened. For full information, visit Fodors.com.

What It Costs in U.S. Dollars

	$	$$	$$$	$$$$
RESTAURANTS				
	under $12	$12–$20	$21–$30	over $30
HOTELS				
	under $275	$275–$375	$376–$475	over $475

Health and Safety

Dengue, chikungunya, and zika have all been reported throughout the Caribbean. We recommend that you protect yourself from these mosquito-borne illnesses by keeping your skin covered and/or wearing mosquito repellent. The mosquitoes that transmit these viruses are as active by day as they are by night.

Visitor Information

CONTACTS Nevis Tourism Authority. ✉ *A. L. Evenlyn Bldg., Main St., Charlestown* ☎ *869/469–7550* 🌐 *www.nevisisland.com.* **St. Kitts Tourism Authority.** ✉ *Pelican Mall, Basseterre* ☎ *869/465–4040* 🌐 *www.stkittstourism.kn.* **St. Kitts and Nevis Hotel and Tourism Association.** ✉ *Sands Complex, Unit C9, Basseterre* ☎ *869/465–5304* 🌐 *www.stkittsnevishta.org.*

Weddings

Two-business-day residency requirement. License and application are EC$200. Valid passport or birth certificate required; if divorced, a divorce decree; if widowed, a death certificate of the deceased spouse.

St. Kitts

Mountainous St. Kitts, the first English settlement in the Leeward Islands, offers a surprisingly diverse vacation experience. Divers have yet to discover all its underwater attractions, history buffs will marvel at Brimstone Hill—known in the 18th century as the Gibraltar of the West Indies—and nature lovers will be pleasantly surprised by the hiking, whether in a rain forest replete with waterfalls or a central mountain range home to a long-dormant crater. There's also now every kind of accommodation, as well as gourmet dining, golf, and gaming, plus white-sand beaches concentrated around Frigate Bay and the Southeast Peninsula with views onto quiet Nevis.

Major developments including the Kittitian Hill and Christophe Harbour have added to the landscape of the island. Kittitian Hill is a sustainable resort development that's home to four luxury farm-style villa properties, a destination spa in a mango forest, and Irie Fields—an 18-hole Championship Golf Course.

GETTING HERE AND AROUND

You can explore Basseterre, the capital city, in a half hour or so, and should allow four hours for an island tour. Main Road traces the northwestern perimeter of the island through seas of sugarcane and past breadfruit trees and stone walls. Villages with tiny pastel-color houses of stone and weathered wood are scattered across the island, and the drive back to Basseterre around the island's other side passes through several of them. The most spectacular stretch of scenery is on Dr. Kennedy Simmonds Highway, which goes to the tip of the Southeast Peninsula. This modern road twists and turns through the mostly undeveloped grassy hills that rise between the calm Caribbean and the windswept Atlantic, passing the shimmering pink Great Salt Pond, a volcanic crater, and seductive beaches.

Sights

On the south coast, St. Kitts's walkable capital, Basseterre, is graced with tall palms and flagstone sidewalks; although many of the buildings appear run-down, there are interesting shops, excellent art galleries, and some beautifully maintained houses. Duty-free shops and boutiques line the streets and courtyards radiating from the octagonal **Circus,** built in the original style of London's famous Piccadilly Circus.

Black Rocks

NATURE SIGHT | This series of lava deposits was spat into the sea ages ago when the island's volcano erupted. It has since been molded into fanciful shapes by centuries of pounding surf, and it's a magical place to see where the Atlantic Ocean meets the Caribbean. The government has added much-needed railings and viewing platforms as well as a collection of colorful, faux chattel houses that double as crafts and food stalls. ✉ *Atlantic coast, outside town of Sadlers, Sandy Bay, Sand Bank Bay.*

Brimstone Hill

HISTORIC SIGHT | This 38-acre fortress, a UNESCO World Heritage Site, is part of a national park dedicated by Queen Elizabeth in 1985. After routing the French in 1690, the English erected a battery here; by 1736 the fortress held 49 guns, earning it the moniker "Gibraltar of the West Indies." In 1782, 8,000 French troops laid siege to the stronghold, which was defended by 350 militia and 600 regular troops of the Royal Scots and East Yorkshires. When the English finally surrendered, they were allowed to march from the fort in full formation out of respect for their bravery (the English afforded the French the same honor when they surrendered the fort a mere year later). A hurricane severely damaged the fortress in 1834, and in 1852 it was evacuated and dismantled. The beautiful stones were carted away to build houses.

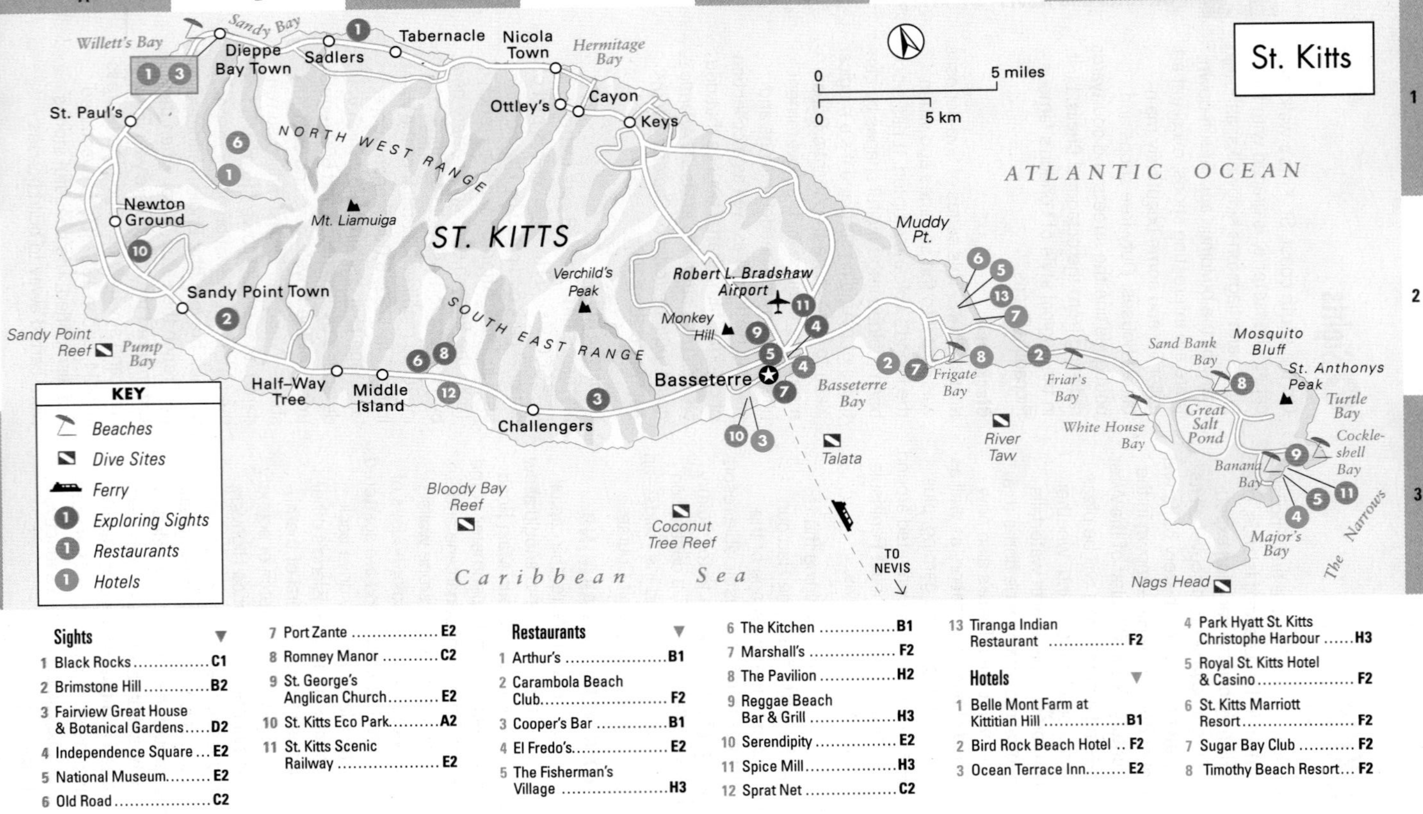

St. Kitts
A
B
C
D
E
F
G
H
1
2
3
0
5 miles
0
5 km
ATLANTIC OCEAN
Caribbean Sea
ST. KITTS
NORTH WEST RANGE
SOUTH EAST RANGE
Mt. Liamuiga
Verchild's Peak
Monkey Hill
Robert L. Bradshaw Airport
Basseterre
Willett's Bay
Sandy Bay
Dieppe Bay Town
Sadlers
Tabernacle
Nicola Town
Hermitage Bay
Ottley's
Cayon
Keys
St. Paul's
Newton Ground
Sandy Point Town
Sandy Point Reef
Pump Bay
Half–Way Tree
Middle Island
Challengers
Bloody Bay Reef
Coconut Tree Reef
Talata
TO NEVIS
Muddy Pt.
Basseterre Bay
Frigate Bay
Friar's Bay
River Taw
White House Bay
Sand Bank Bay
Mosquito Bluff
St. Anthonys Peak
Great Salt Pond
Turtle Bay
Cockle-shell Bay
Banana Bay
Major's Bay
Nags Head
The Narrows
KEY
Beaches
Dive Sites
Ferry
Exploring Sights
Restaurants
Hotels
Sights
1 Black Rocks C1
2 Brimstone Hill B2
3 Fairview Great House & Botanical Gardens D2
4 Independence Square ... E2
5 National Museum......... E2
6 Old Road C2
7 Port Zante E2
8 Romney Manor C2
9 St. George's Anglican Church.......... E2
10 St. Kitts Eco Park.......... A2
11 St. Kitts Scenic Railway E2
Restaurants
1 Arthur's B1
2 Carambola Beach Club......................... F2
3 Cooper's Bar B1
4 El Fredo's................... E2
5 The Fisherman's Village H3
6 The Kitchen B1
7 Marshall's F2
8 The Pavilion H2
9 Reggae Beach Bar & Grill H3
10 Serendipity E2
11 Spice Mill................... H3
12 Sprat Net C2
13 Tiranga Indian Restaurant F2
Hotels
1 Belle Mont Farm at Kittitian Hill B1
2 Bird Rock Beach Hotel .. F2
3 Ocean Terrace Inn......... E2
4 Park Hyatt St. Kitts Christophe Harbour H3
5 Royal St. Kitts Hotel & Casino F2
6 St. Kitts Marriott Resort....................... F2
7 Sugar Bay Club F2
8 Timothy Beach Resort... F2

Cannons at Brimstone Hill, a UNESCO World Heritage Site on St. Kitts

The citadel has been partially reconstructed and its guns remounted. It's a steep walk up the hill from the parking lot. A seven-minute orientation film recounts the fort's history and restoration. You can see remains of the officers' quarters, redoubts, barracks, ordnance store, and cemetery. Its museum collections were depleted by hurricanes, but it still has some weaponry, uniforms, photographs, old newspapers, pre-Columbian artifacts, and objects pertaining to the African heritage of the island's slaves (such as masks and ceremonial tools). The spectacular view includes Montserrat and Nevis to the southeast; Saba and St. Eustatius to the northwest; and St. Barth and St. Maarten to the north. Nature trails snake through the tangle of surrounding hardwood forest and savanna (a fine spot to catch the green vervet monkeys—inexplicably brought by the French and now outnumbering the residents—skittering about). ✉ *Main Rd., Brimstone Hill* ☎ *869/465–2609* 🌐 *www.brimstonehillfortress.org* 🎫 *$15.*

Fairview Great House & Botanical Gardens

HISTORIC HOME | Parts of this French colonial greathouse set on more than 2 lush tropical acres date back to 1701, with an impeccably restored interior in period fashion. Each room is painted in different colors from pomegranate to lemon. Furnishings include a 16-seat mahogany dinner table set with china and silver; docents relate fascinating factoids (chaises were broadened to accommodate petticoats—or "can-can skirts," in local parlance). Cross the cobblestone courtyard to the original kitchen, replete with volcanic stone and brick oven, and bathing room (heated rocks warmed spring water in the tub). The fieldstone cellar now contains the gift shop, offering local pottery, art, and honey harvested on-site at the apiary. You can wander meticulously maintained gardens with interpretive signage, filled with chattering birds and monkeys. They hold occasional rum tastings, cooking classes, or other special events—often by the pool. ✉ *Artist's Level Hill, Boyd's* ☎ *869/465–3141* 🌐 *www.kantours.com* 🎫 *$27.*

Independence Square

PLAZA/SQUARE | There are lovely gardens and a fountain on this site of a former slave market at Independence Square. The square is surrounded on three sides by 18th-century Georgian buildings. ✉ *Off Bank St., Basseterre.*

National Museum

HISTORY MUSEUM | In the restored former treasury building, the National Museum presents an eclectic collection of artifacts reflecting the history and culture of the island. ✉ *Bay Rd., Basseterre* ☎ *869/465–5584* 🎫 *$7.*

Old Road

TOWN | This site marks the first permanent English settlement in the West Indies, founded in 1624 by Thomas Warner. Take the side road toward the interior to find some Carib petroglyphs, testimony of even earlier habitation. The largest depicts a female figure on black volcanic rock, presumably a fertility goddess. Less than a mile east of Old Road along Main Road is **Bloody Point,** where French and British soldiers joined forces in 1629 to repel a mass Carib attack; reputedly so many Caribs were massacred that the stream ran red for three days. ✥ *Main Rd. west of Challengers.*

Port Zante

MARINA/PIER | Port Zante is an ambitious, ever-growing 27-acre cruise-ship pier and marina in an area that has been reclaimed from the sea. The domed welcome center is an imposing neoclassical hodgepodge, with columns and stone arches, shops, walkways, fountains, and West Indian–style buildings housing both cheap souvenir and luxury shops, galleries, restaurants, and a small casino. The crafts and T-shirt booths of the Amina Marketplace sit at the entrance beyond the Pelican Mall. A second pier, 1,434 feet long, has a draft that accommodates even leviathan cruise ships. The selection of shops and restaurants (Twist serves global fusion cuisine and rocks with DJs several nights of the week) continues to expand. ✉ *Waterfront, behind Circus, Basseterre* 🌐 *www.portzante.com; www.portzantemarina.com.*

★ **Romney Manor**

HISTORIC HOME | A somewhat restored house (once the property of Thomas Jefferson's great-great-great-grandfather Samuel) and surrounding replicas of chattel-house cottages are set in 8 acres of glorious tiered gardens, with exotic flowers, an old bell tower, and an enormous, gnarled 400-year-old saman tree (sometimes called a rain tree). Inside, at Caribelle Batik, you can watch artisans hand-printing fabrics by the 2,500-year-old Indonesian wax-and-dye process known as batik. You can also stroll to the 17th-century ruins (including sugar equipment, a still, and cistern) of Wingfield Manor, site of the first land grant in the British West Indies and home to a ziplining outfit. A bar serves luscious homemade rum cake and affords splendid panoramas of the rain forest. Look for signs indicating a turnoff for Romney Manor near Old Road. ✉ *Old Road Town* ☎ *869/465–6253* 🌐 *www.caribellebatikstkitts.com* 🎫 *$3* ⊗ *Closed Sun. year-round and Sat. Apr.–Oct.*

St. George's Anglican Church

CHURCH | This handsome stone building (and largest church in Basseterre) has a crenellated tower originally built by the French in 1670 that is called Nôtre-Dame. The British burned it down in 1706 and rebuilt it four years later, naming it after the patron saint of England. Since then it has suffered a fire, an earthquake, and hurricanes, and was once again rebuilt in 1869. ✉ *Cayon St., Basseterre.*

St. Kitts Eco Park

GARDEN | **FAMILY** | Created in collaboration with the Taiwanese government (and now under sole Kittitian ownership), St. Kitts Eco Park essentially functions as an agritourism demonstration farm, with soaring, light-filled glass and fiber-reinforced concrete structures that are powered by state-of-the-art solar trackers.

Antique cannons and old-fashioned gas lamps lead to the handsome Victorian plantation-style visitors center, divided into Kittitian and Taiwanese sections, each selling local foodstuffs and specialty items (ceramics for St. Kitts, tea and technology for Taiwan). You can stroll through the greenhouse, viewing orchids in the working nursery, then scale the watchtower for scintillating views of the farm and the Caribbean, with Saba and Statia in the distance. Kids will love challenging the map mazes (plantings shaped like the partner nations), while parents can wander the orchards and desert garden or savor bush tea in the herb gazebo. The property provides environmental edutainment while delivering on its so-called 4G promise: greenhouse, green beauty, green energy, green landscape. ✉ *Sir Gillies Estate, Sandy Point* ☎ *869/465–8755* 🌐 *www.ecopark.kn; www.stkittstourism.kn/activities/excursions/st-kitts-eco-park* 🎫 *$8.*

St. Kitts Scenic Railway

TRAIN/TRAIN STATION | FAMILY | The old narrow-gauge train that had transported sugarcane to the central sugar factory since 1912 is all that remains of the island's once-thriving sugar industry. Two-story cars bedecked in bright Kittitian colors circle much of the island (the final segment is aboard a bus) in just under three hours (a Rail and Sail option takes guests going or returning via catamaran). Each passenger gets a comfortable, downstairs air-conditioned seat fronting vaulted picture windows and an upstairs open-air observation spot. The conductor's running narration encompasses not only the history of sugar cultivation but also the railway's construction, local folklore, island geography, even other agricultural mainstays from papayas to pigs. You can drink in complimentary tropical beverages (including luscious guava daiquiris) along with the sweeping rain-forest and ocean vistas, accompanied by an a cappella choir's renditions of hymns, spirituals, and predictable standards like "I've Been Workin' on the Railroad." ✉ *Needsmust Estate* ☎ *869/465–7263* 🌐 *www.stkittsscenicrailway.com* 🎫 *$128.*

Beaches

Beaches on St. Kitts are free and open to the public (even those occupied by hotels). The best beaches, with powdery white sand, are in the Frigate Bay area or on the lower peninsula. The Atlantic waters are rougher, and many black-sand beaches northwest of Frigate Bay double as garbage dumps.

Banana/Cockleshell Bays

BEACH | These twin connected eyebrows of glittering Champagne-color sand—stretching nearly 2 miles (3 km) total at the southeastern tip of the island—feature majestic views of Nevis and are backed by lush vegetation and coconut palms. The first-rate restaurant-bar Spice Mill (next to Rasta-hued Lion Rock Beach Bar—order the knockout Lion Punch) and Reggae Beach Bar & Grill bracket either end of Cockleshell, and the posh Park Hyatt is here as well. The water is generally placid, ideal for swimming. The downside is irregular maintenance, with seaweed (particularly after rough weather) and occasional litter. Follow Simmonds Highway to the end and bear right, ignoring the turnoff for Turtle Beach. **Amenities:** food and drink; parking. **Best for:** partiers; snorkeling; swimming; walking. ✉ *Banana Bay.*

Friar's Bay

BEACH | Locals consider Friar's Bay, on the Caribbean (southern) side, the island's finest beach. It's a long, tawny scimitar, where the water always seems warmer and clearer. The upscale Carambola Beach Club, which has co-opted roughly one third of the strand, is popular with cruise ship passengers at lunch. Still, several happening bars—including Godfather Beach Bar, ShipWreck, and Discovery Beach—serve terrific, inexpensive local food and cheap, frosty drinks. Chair rentals cost around $10 for two, though if you order lunch, you can typically negotiate a freebie. Friar's is the first major beach along Southeast Peninsula Drive (aka Simmonds Highway), approximately a mile (1½ km) southeast of Frigate Bay. **Amenities:** food and drink. **Best for:** snorkeling; swimming; walking. ✉ *South Friar's Bay.*

Frigate Bay

BEACH | The Caribbean side offers talcum-powder-fine beige sand framed by coconut palms and seagrapes, and the Atlantic side (a 15-minute stroll)—sometimes called North Frigate Bay—is a favorite with horseback riders. South Frigate Bay is bookended by the Timothy Beach Club's Sunset Café and the popular, pulsating Buddies Beach Hut. In between are several other lively beach spots, including Cathy's (fabulous jerk ribs), Chinchilla's, Vibes, and Mr. X Shiggidy Shack. Most charge $3 to $5 to rent a chair, though they'll often waive the fee if you ask politely and buy lunch. Locals barhop late into Friday and Saturday nights. Waters are generally calm for swimming; the rockier eastern end offers fine snorkeling. The incomparably scenic Atlantic side is—regrettably—dominated by the Marriott (plentiful dining options), attracting occasional pesky vendors. The surf is choppier and the undertow stronger here. On cruise-ship days, groups stampede both sides. **Amenities:** food and drink; water sports. **Best for:** partiers; snorkeling; swimming; walking. ✉ *Frigate Bay* ✣ *Less than 3 miles (5 km) from downtown Basseterre.*

Sand Bank Bay

BEACH | A dirt road, nearly impassable after heavy rains, leads to a long mocha crescent on the Atlantic. The shallow coves are protected here, making it ideal for families, and it's usually deserted. Brisk breezes lure the occasional windsurfer, but avoid the rocky far left area because of fierce sudden swells and currents. This exceptionally pretty beach lacks shade; Christophe Harbour has constructed several villas and a beach club (whose upscale Pavilion restaurant is open to the public only for dinner). As you drive southeast along Simmonds Highway, approximately 10 miles (16 km) from Basseterre, look for an unmarked dirt turnoff to the left of the Great Salt Pond. **Amenities:** none. **Best for:** solitude; swimming; windsurfing. ✉ *Sand Bank Bay.*

White House Bay

BEACH | The beach is rocky, but the snorkeling, taking in several reefs surrounding a sunken tugboat, as well as a recently discovered 18th-century British troop ship, is superb. It's usually deserted, though the calm water (and stunning scenery) makes it a favorite anchorage of yachties. There is little shade, but also little seaweed. Christophe Harbour's sexy beach bar (open from late afternoon), Salt Plage, anchors one end. A dirt road skirts a hill to the right off Simmonds Highway approximately 2 miles (3 km) after Friar's. **Amenities:** food and drink. **Best for:** snorkeling; solitude. ✉ *White House Bay.*

Restaurants

St. Kitts restaurants range from funky beachfront bistros to elegant plantation-style dining rooms; most fare is tinged with the flavors of the Caribbean. Many restaurants offer West Indian specialties such as curried mutton, pepper pot (a stew of vegetables, tubers, and meats), and Arawak chicken (seasoned and served with rice and almonds on breadfruit leaf).

What to Wear. Throughout the island, dress is casual at lunch (but no bathing suits). Dinner, although not necessarily formal, definitely calls for long pants and sundresses.

Arthur's

$$$ | **CARIBBEAN** | Named for the beloved late owner of the Golden Lemon Inn, this breezy, beachfront, semi-alfresco eatery on the black sand of Dieppe

Bay makes a perfect spot to watch the colorful fishing boats ply the waters. The marine decor—dried sea fans and ship's lanterns—suggest what's best on the sea-to-fork menu, though landlubbers can happily dig into burgers or pulled pork sandwiches. **Known for:** fab lobster pot pie, coconut seafood chowder, and other fish dishes; delightful seaside setting; charming staff. *Average main: US$22 Dieppe Bay 869/465–1004 www.bellemontfarm.com/food-arthurs Closed Mon. and Tues.*

Carambola Beach Club

$$$$ | ECLECTIC | At this ultra-stylish restaurant, which unfurls sensuously down South Friar's Bay, more casual lunches take full advantage of the beachfront setting, with white tents and hedonistic beach beds (often overflowing with cruise ship passengers). But nighttime is truly spectacular, as outdoor fiber-optic fountains enhance the visual flair of the vast, sleek-but-not-slick interior, replete with eat-in wine cellar and tile-and-layered-wood sushi bar. **Known for:** sophisticated decor; superb seafood, including sushi; glorious beachfront. *Average main: US$31 South Friar's Bay 869/465–9090 www.carambolabeachclub.com.*

Cooper's Bar

$ | CARIBBEAN | Barely more than a royal blue shack, dressed with vivid murals of cavorting monkeys and replete with a chicken coop, Cooper's (aka Glenda's Place after the owner) is the quintessential local dining experience—as good a place as any to try Caribbean staples like stewed mutton or macaroni pie. There are only two picnic tables, so most locals order their food to go; if you stay, ask for takeout containers anyway (the lids come in handy to repel flies in between bites). **Known for:** luscious house-cooked fare; enormous servings; cheap prices. *Average main: US$8 Main St., Gibbons Hill, Dieppe Bay 869/664–7162 No credit cards Closed Sun. No dinner some nights.*

El Fredo's

$$ | CARIBBEAN | The decor is basic at this humble wooden shack across from the waterfront, but locals swear that the bounteous dishes, some of the best local fare on St. Kitts, will cure—or at least absorb—any hangover. It's also a terrific place to eavesdrop on local gossip, with politicians and expats grabbing a quick lunch alongside local workers, who shyly banter with the servers. **Known for:** authentic island ambience; traditional fare (swordfish creole, curry goat, garlic conch, dumplings); heaping helpings. *Average main: US$14 Newtown Bay Rd. at Sanddown Rd., Basseterre 869/466–8871 No credit cards Closed Sun.–Mon. No dinner.*

The Fisherman's Village

$$$$ | SEAFOOD | This casual eatery at the Park Hyatt has a splendid dockside setting looking out toward Nevis. Fittingly, the seafood is so fresh that you half expect it to jump onto your patio table (you can see it being prepared in the open kitchen), and the handsome space cannily incorporates traditional ceramic pots, lobster traps, and other fishing implements. **Known for:** happy hours, theme nights, and buffet evenings take the sting out of otherwise exorbitant prices; glorious patio seating; stellar seafood. *Average main: US$31 Park Hyatt St. Kitts Christophe Harbour, Banana Bay 869/468–1234 Closed Mon. and Tues.*

The Kitchen

$$$ | CARIBBEAN | This stunner in the so-called greathouse—the soaring stone-steel-and-wood space of Belle Mont Farm at Kittitian Hill—serves sustainable seasonal treats, sourced from the farm itself and other local suppliers who practice ethical farming, fishing, and animal husbandry. Begin your evening with ultra-fresh, handcrafted cocktails in the handsome Mill Bar, and then repair to the main dining room or Caribbean-view terrace for an array of delightful dinner options. **Known for:** Sunday champagne brunch attracts island movers and shakers; stunning split-level space; warm service. *Average main: US$25 ✉ Belle Mont Farm at Kittitian Hill, Frigate Bay ☎ 869/465–7388 🌐 www.bellemontfarm.com.*

Marshall's

$$$ | **ECLECTIC** | The pool area of Horizons Villa Resort is transformed into a stylish eatery thanks to smashing ocean views, potted plants, serenading tree frogs, and elegant candlelit tables. Jamaican chef Verral Marshall fuses ultra-fresh local ingredients with global influences. Artfully plated, most dishes are more along the lines of what you'd find at a steakhouse (grilled ribeye), but the Caribbean portion of the menu is where dishes shine, like the curry chicken with pineapple and coconut. **Known for:** delicious desserts, including homemade sorbets; superlative seafood; refined ambience. *Average main: US$30 ✉ Horizons Villa Resort, Frigate Bay ☎ 869/466–8245 🌐 www.marshallsdining.com ⏲ Closed Mon.-Tues. No lunch.*

★ The Pavilion

$$$$ | **ECLECTIC** | Imagine a semi-alfresco cathedral of raw limestone coral overlooking a sandy, palm-fringed crescent: that's this ritzy Christophe Harbour beach club (open to nonmembers for dinner only), whose soaring interior contrasts a curved exhibition kitchen, streamlined bar stools, and abstract pendant lamps with sea fans and driftwood, antique settees, and 19th-century black-and-white photos of island scenes. The kitchen similarly combines tradition with innovation, juxtaposing textures, flavors, and colors so that even "traditional" fare like conch fritters is goosed with pickled ginger, passion-fruit coulis, and swirls of jerk mayo. **Known for:** thoughtful wine and aged-rum offerings; gorgeous setting; impeccable presentation and service. *Average main: US$38 ✉ Christophe Harbour, Sand Bank Bay ☎ 869/465–8304 🌐 www.christopheharbour.com ⏲ No dinner Sun. and Mon. No lunch for nonmembers.*

Reggae Beach Bar & Grill

$$ | **ECLECTIC** | Treats at this popular daytime watering hole include honey-mustard ribs, coconut shrimp, grilled lobster, banana bread pudding with rum sauce, and lots of tempting tropical libations. Business cards and pennants plaster the bar, and the open-air space is decorated with fishnets, turtle shells, and other nautical accoutrements. **Known for:** host of aquatic activities on tap; chill vibe with free beach chairs and Wi-Fi; live music on Sunday and bonfire-dinner on Friday. *Average main: US$21 ✉ S.E. Peninsula Rd., Cockleshell Beach ☎ 869/762–5050 🌐 www.reggaebeachbar.com ⏲ No dinner Sun. and Mon.*

★ Serendipity

$$$$ | **ECLECTIC** | This stylish restaurant occupies an old Creole home whose charming enclosed patio offers lovely views of Basseterre and the bay. The interior lounge is even more conducive to romantic dining—with cushy sofas, patterned hardwood floors, porcelain lamps, and African carvings—and the ambitious menu reflects co-owner-chef Alexander James's peripatetic postings: crispy fried Brie, spring rolls with plum dipping sauce, mahimahi with a cheese-and-basil crust, teriyaki-glazed tiger shrimp. **Known for:** well-considered wine list; affordable lunches with gargantuan tapas-style selections; creative vegetarian options. *Average main: US$34 ✉ 3 Wigley Ave., Basseterre ☎ 869/465–9999 🌐 www.serendipitystkitts.net ⏲ No lunch Sun.*

★ Spice Mill

$$$$ | **ECLECTIC** | The cuisine at this beachfront beauty references the Caribbean's melting pot of African, French, English, Iberian, Asian, and Dutch influences. But the kitchen and barefoot-chic bar, which is open daily and serves light snacks, also adopt a locavore philosophy, sourcing as much as possible from Kittitian farmers and fishermen (who might troop through the restaurant with 30 just-caught snapper). **Known for:** fresh fish dishes (try

Pavilion at the ritzy Christophe Harbour beach club is only open to nonmembers for dinner.

the Panko-crusted crab cakes or seafood risotto); lively clientele; lovely beachfront setting. *Average main: US$35 ✉ Cockleshell Beach ☎ 869/765–6706, 869/762–2160 🌐 www.spicemillrestaurant.com.*

Sprat Net

$$ | SEAFOOD | This simple cluster of picnic tables—an island hot spot sheltered by a brilliant-turquoise corrugated-tin roof and decorated with driftwood, life preservers, photos of coastal scenes, and fishnets—sits on a sliver of sand. There's nothing fancy on the menu: just grilled fish, lobster, ribs, and chicken served with mountains of coleslaw and peas and rice. **Known for:** homemade pizza and fab fresh seafood; great bands weekends; old-style Caribbean flavor in both senses. *Average main: US$15 ✉ Main Rd., Old Road Town ☎ 869/466–7535 No credit cards ⏲ Closed Mon., Tues., and Sept. No lunch.*

Tiranga Indian Restaurant

$$ | INDIAN | FAMILY | This colorful spot offers an authentic Indian dinner experience. from the food down to the dark, but welcoming decor. A favorite for locals, but well-liked by tourists, this spot focuses heavily on bringing Indian culture to life, with its plethora of traditional dishes from paneer to fish vindaloo to lamb biriyani. **Known for:** an impressive array of naan; vegetarian friendly; super-helpful staff. *Average main: US$14 ✉ Royal St. Kitts Hotel, Frigate Bay ☎ 869/662–5846 🌐 www.tirangarestaurantsk.com ⏲ No lunch.*

Hotels

St. Kitts has an appealing variety of places to stay—full-service, affordable hotels, simple beachfront cottages, and all-inclusive resorts. There are also several guesthouses and self-serve condos. Increasing development has been touted (or threatened) for years. The ritzy 126-unit Park Hyatt debuted its first Caribbean property on Banana Bay, in partnership with the grand Christophe Harbour development, which sprawls across the Southeast Peninsula, offering spectacular villas, beach clubs, celebrity restaurants, a mega-yacht marina replete with retail village, a Tom Fazio–designed golf course, and other boutique hotels. Several upscale villa compounds have been developed, such as the culture-oriented, ecocentric Kittitian Hill (architect Bill Bensley designed some of Thailand's most remarkable resorts), which includes an "edible" golf course (greens will intersect with farmland), spa, cosmopolitan retail village, farm-to-table restaurants, and a variety of sustainable lodgings in vernacular style, most with fabulous views. Several other luxury hotels are slated to be built within St. Kitts in the coming years.

★ Belle Mont Farm at Kittitian Hill

$$$ | **RESORT** | Atop a hill with majestic valley and Caribbean views, this grouping of luxurious "standard" guesthouses, farmhouses, and villas comprise the Kittitian Hill development, built with sustainably sourced materials (from Canadian cedar-shake roofs to andasite stone quarried on-site) and featuring a 400-acre organic farm that provides ingredients for offerings in the restaurants and the spa, and Irie Fields—a 9-hole "edible" golf course that's one of only three such developments in the world. **Pros:** technologically state-of-the-art; ecofriendly; luxurious. **Cons:** beach club a bumpy ride away; still-water design features attract mosquitoes; pricey. *Rooms from: US$500 ✉ St. Paul's ☎ 855/846–3951 reservations, 869/465–7388 🌐 www.bellemontfarm.com 41 units 🍽 No Meals.*

Bird Rock Beach Hotel

$ | **RESORT** | Two-story buildings in carnival colors wind through small gardens at this basic scuba-set resort, which crowns a bluff above Basseterre and delivers amazing views of the town, sea, and mountains. **Pros:** excellent value, including free Frigate Bay shuttle; exuberant international clientele; great diving as well as bike and kayak rentals. **Cons:** dilapidated decor and spotty Wi-Fi; insufficient parking; small man-made beach. *Rooms from: US$95 ✉ 2 miles (3 km) east of Basseterre, Basseterre ☎ 869/465–8914, 800/403–5966 🌐 www.birdrockbeachhotel.com 46 units 🍽 Free Breakfast.*

★ Ocean Terrace Inn

$ | **HOTEL** | "OTI," as locals call it, is a rarity: a smart, intimate, "boutique-y" business hotel that also appeals to vacationers. **Pros:** walking distance to Basseterre; excellent service; fine facilities (including great restaurants) for a small hotel. **Cons:** hard for those with physical disabilities to navigate; sprawling layout; must drive to beaches. *Rooms from: US$110 ✉ Wigley Ave., Basseterre ☎ 869/465–2754, 800/524–0512 🌐 www.oceanterraceinn.com 34 rooms 🍽 Free Breakfast.*

Park Hyatt St. Kitts Christophe Harbour

$$$$ | **RESORT** | The upscale Christophe Harbour development unfurls elegantly along Banana Bay, everything designed to bring an "if luxe could kill" experience to St. Kitts. **Pros:** ultra-comfortable digs; attentive cordial service; stunning views from most rooms. **Cons:** very spread out, meaning long walks to amenities; extremely expensive; grounds terribly lit at night. *Rooms from: US$775 ✉ Banana Bay ☎ 869/468–1234 🌐 www.hyatt.com 126 rooms 🍽 No Meals.*

Royal St. Kitts Hotel & Casino

$ | **HOTEL** | This attractive property, which now affects a budget boutique look, has seen many changes over the years—like the addition of two adjacent mini-malls with restaurants, retail outlets (including a supermarket), and a spa/salon. **Pros:** on-site laundry facility and free Wi-Fi; terrific value, including regular package deals; friendly staff. **Cons:** limited facilities (and casino is closed indefinitely); eyesore cinder-block buildings; can be loud when booked with tour groups. *Rooms from: US$179 ✉ Zenway Blvd., Frigate Bay ☎ 869/465–8651, 866/607–6242 🌐 www.royalstkittshotel.com 282 rooms 🍽 No Meals.*

St. Kitts Marriott Resort

$$$ | **RESORT** | From families to conventioneers and golfers to gamblers, this big, bustling beachfront resort has something for everyone, scoring points for its sizable rooms (albeit many without direct beach access or true sea views), soothing Emerald Mist Spa, sexy Bohemia beach bar, fine golf course, and decent casino with the trendy Sky Lounge. **Pros:** many packages offer good value, especially off-season; enormous main pool and great range of activities; good bars and plentiful duty-free shopping. **Cons:** mostly mediocre food; surprise extra resort charges; occasional time-share pitches. *Rooms from: US$376* ✉ *858 Frigate Bay Rd., Frigate Bay* ☎ *869/466–1200, 800/845–5249* 🌐 *www.stkittsmarriott.com* *393 rooms* *No Meals.*

Sugar Bay Club

$ | **HOTEL** | This sprawling property borders Frigate Bay's wild Atlantic side, offering varied accommodations in an architectural mishmash ranging from Creole-style cottages to cinder-block eyesores. **Pros:** great value; family-friendly; on-site mini-mart and restaurants. **Cons:** inadequate facilities compared with comparably sized hotels; unmaintained beach with seaweed and rough surf; several units used for student housing. *Rooms from: US$125* ✉ *Frigate Bay* ☎ *869/465-8037* 🌐 *www.sugarbayclub.com* *89 rooms* *No Meals.*

Timothy Beach Resort

$ | **RESORT** | The only affordable St. Kitts resort directly on a Caribbean beach is a great find thanks not only to reasonable pricing and an incomparable location, but also to a restful atmosphere, smiling service, and simple but sizable apartments. **Pros:** plentiful deals; close to the beach action; lovely pool deck overlooking the sea. **Cons:** no view from most bedrooms; can hear boisterous beach bar music weekend nights; occasionally worn decor. *Rooms from: US$175* ✉ *1 South Frigate Bay Beach, Frigate Bay* ☎ *869/465–8597, 845/201–0047, 888/229–2747* 🌐 *www.timothybeach.com* *60 apartments* *No Meals.*

Nightlife

Most nightlife revolves around the hotels, which host folkloric shows and calypso and steel bands of the usual limbo-rum-and-reggae variety. The growing Frigate Bay "strip" of beach bars—including Mr. X Shiggidy Shack, Patsy's, Cathy's, Monkey Bar, Inon's, Buddies Beach Hut, Chinchilla, and Vibes—is the place to party hearty on weekend nights.

Look for hard-driving local exponents of soca music (such as Nu-Vybes, Grand Masters, Small Axe, and Royalton 5) as well as the "heavy dance-hall" reggae group House of Judah. The Marriott's large, glitzy casino has table games and slots.

Great Room Lobby Bar at the Marriott

BARS | Sushi, tapas, and 'tinis with 'tude are all on tap at this low-key, surprisingly classy hangout. ✉ *St. Kitts Marriott Resort, Frigate Bay* ☎ *869/466–1200.*

Lemongrass

BARS | This Thai spot, a favorite happy-hour watering hole, is a second-floor eatery whose verandah offers views of the harbor and the activity on the Circus. ✉ *Bay Rd., Basseterre* ☎ *869/465–0143.*

Mr. X's Shiggidy Shack

LIVE MUSIC | Mr. X's Shiggidy Shack is known for its sizzling Thursday-night bonfire parties (replete with fire-eaters) and its raucous karaoke Saturdays. For locals it's also a must-stop on the Friday-night liming circuit of Frigate Bay bars. ✉ *Frigate Bay* ☎ *869/663–4578* 🌐 *www.shiggidyshack,com.*

★ **Salt Plage**

BARS | This happening beachfront nightspot merges with the handsomely recycled, rusting ruins of a former salt-storage chattel house (the lavatories are particularly creative, incorporating old depth meters and a reclaimed engine room). Turquoise tables and white chairs dot the multitiered, bleached-wood deck, all optimally placed for sunset viewing. DJs and live bands are on tap most nights; boaters often anchor at the dock, joining in the fun. The menu and drinks list conjure a Cannes in the Caribbean feel. Savory light bites (priced between $10 and $20) include fish tacos, ceviches, and lobster kebabs. Bottle service (but of course!) and a small but savvy wine list help to further lessen inhibitions. ✉ *White House Bay* ☎ *869/466–7221* 🌐 *www.christopheharbour.com.*

Shopping

All Kind of Tings

MARKET | All Kind of Tings, a peppermint-pink edifice on Liverpool Row at College Street Ghaut, functions as a de facto vendors' market, where several booths sell local crafts and cheap T-shirts. Its courtyard frequently hosts folkloric dances, fashion shows, poetry readings, and steel-pan concerts. ✉ *Liverpool Row, Basseterre.*

Caribelle Batik

CRAFTS | Caribelle Batik sells gloriously colored batik wraps, kimonos, caftans, T-shirts, dresses, wall hangings, and the like; you can watch the process in back. ✉ *Romney Manor, Old Road Town* ☎ *869/465–6253* 🌐 *www.caribellebatik-stkitts.com.*

Crafthouse

CRAFTS | The Crafthouse is one of the best sources for local dolls, wood carvings, and straw work. ✉ *Southwell Industrial Site, Bay Rd., Basseterre* ☎ *869/465–7754.*

★ Kate Design

CRAFTS | As artist Kate Spencer summers in Sicily, you must call ahead for an appointment to visit her studio outside Rawlins Plantation (note that she typically closes from May through October). It's very much worth doing so, though, to shop for her truly unique and brilliantly colored original paintings, serigraphs, note cards, scarves, and other lovely pieces. ✉ *Mount Pleasant House, St. Paul's* ☎ *869/465–7740* 🌐 *www.katespencerfineart.com.*

Palms Court Gardens

OTHER SPECIALTY STORE | Talk about multitasking: this little oasis offers a restaurant, an infinity pool and hot tub with bay views, miniature botanical gardens, and the ShellWorks atelier and gift shop, where artisans fashion graceful napkin holders, candlesticks, stemware, wall hangings, and jewelry from coral, sea fans, mother-of-pearl, and other marine materials. The $2 admission is refunded with a purchase. ✉ *Corner of Wilkin and Wigley Sts., Basseterre* ☎ *869/465–6060* 🌐 *www.palmscourtgardens.com.*

Pelican Mall

SHOPPING CENTER | This shopping arcade, designed to look like a traditional Caribbean street, has more than 20 stores (purveying mostly resort wear, souvenirs, and liquor), a restaurant, tourism offices, and a bandstand near the cruise-ship pier. ✉ *Bay Rd., Basseterre.*

Port Zante Mall

SHOPPING CENTER | Directly behind Pelican Mall, on the waterfront, is Port Zante, the deepwater cruise-ship pier where a much-delayed upscale shopping–dining complex has become a 50-shop area (including the large, ubiquitous jewelry concerns like Abbott's, Diamonds International, and Kay). If you're looking for inexpensive, local T-shirts, souvenirs, and crafts, check out Amina Market, a series of vendors' huts behind Pelican Mall to the right of Port Zante as you face the sea. ✉ *Cruise Ship Pier, Basseterre* 🌐 *www.portzante.com.*

Shoreline Plaza

SHOPPING CENTER | Shoreline Plaza is next to the Treasury Building, right on Basseterre's waterfront. The shops mainly sell T-shirts and locally made handicrafts and souvenirs. ✉ *Basseterre.*

Spencer Cameron Art Gallery

ART GALLERIES | In addition to a wide selection of exceptional work by regional and local artists and artisans, this gallery sells Caribbean island charts and other historical reproductions, as well as owner Rosey Cameron Smith's popular Carnevale clown prints. It also showcases Glass Island's seductively colored, sinuously shaped, art-glass frames, plates, and other items. In addition, one section is devoted to the Potter's House, the atelier of Carla Astaphan, who celebrates her Afro-Caribbean heritage with beautifully glazed ceramics and masks. Another section houses the NOMAD Chic clothing boutique. Rosey's daughter Leah runs a courtyard café that sells scrumptious baked goods. With so much on offer, it's good to know that the gallery ships worldwide. ✉ *10 N. Independence Sq., Basseterre* ☎ *869/465–1617, 869/664–4157* 🌐 *www.roseycameronsmith.com.*

TDC Mall

SHOPPING CENTER | TDC Mall is just off the Circus in downtown, with a few boutiques, selling mostly island wear. ✉ *Bank St., Basseterre.*

Activities

BOATING AND FISHING

Most operators are on the Caribbean side of Frigate Bay, known for its gentle currents. Turtle Bay offers stronger winds and stunning views of Nevis. Though not noted for big-game fishing, several steep offshore drop-offs do lure wahoo, barracuda, shark, tuna, yellowtail snapper, and mackerel. Rates are occasionally negotiable; figure approximately $450 for a four-hour excursion with refreshments.

Leeward Island Charters

BOATING | The knowledgeable Todd Leypoldt of Leeward Island Charters takes you out on his charter boats, *Spirit of St. Kitts*, *Caona*, and *Eagle*. He's also available for snorkeling charters, beach picnics, and sunset-moonlight cruises. ✉ *Basseterre* ☎ *869/465–7474* 🌐 *www.leewardislandschartersstkitts.com.*

Mr. X's Watersports

BOATING | Found within Mr. X's Shiggidy Shack this shop rents small craft, including motorboats (waterskiing and Jet Skiing are available). Paddleboats and sailboats can be rented by the hour. Deep-sea fishing charters, snorkeling tours, water taxis, sunset cruises, and private charters with captain and crew are available. Mr. X and his cohorts are usually hanging out at the adjacent open-air Monkey Bar. ✉ *Frigate Bay* ☎ *869/465–0673* 🌐 *www.shigiddyshack.com.*

Reggae Beach Bar & Grill

BOATING | This establishment rents kayaks and snorkeling equipment from the restaurant, offers sailing lessons, and can also arrange fishing trips, as well as water taxis to Nevis via St. Kitts Water Sports. ✉ *S. E. Peninsula Rd., Cockleshell Beach* ☎ *869/762–5050* 🌐 *www.reggaebeachbar.com.*

St. Kitts Water Safaris

BOATING | This all-purpose outfit operating out of Vibes Beach Bar on Frigate Bay rents banana boats ($15 an hour) and Jet Skis ($75 for 30 minutes, $150 for an hour). It also offers historical Jet Ski tours ($150) and sunset cruises. ✉ *Vibes Beach Bar, Frigate Bay* ☎ *869/669–5046* 🌐 *www.saintkittswatersafaris.com.*

DIVING AND SNORKELING

Though unheralded as a dive destination, St. Kitts has more than a dozen excellent sites, protected by several marine parks. The surrounding waters feature shoals, hot vents, shallows, canyons, steep walls, and caverns at depths from 40 to nearly 200 feet. The St. Kitts Maritime Archaeological Project, which surveys, records, researches, and preserves the island's underwater treasures, has charted several hundred wrecks of galleons, frigates, and freighters dating back to the 17th century. **Bloody Bay Reef** is noted for its network of underwater grottoes daubed with purple anemones, sienna bristle worms, and canary-yellow sea fans that seem to wave you in. **Coconut Tree Reef,** one of the largest in the area, includes sea fans, sponges, and anemones, as well as the Rocks, three enormous boulders with impressive multilevel diving. The only drift-dive site, **Nags Head,** has strong currents, but experienced divers might spot gliding rays, lobsters, turtles, and reef sharks. Since it sank in 50 feet of water in the early 1980s, the *River Taw* makes a splendid site for less experienced divers. **Sandy Point Reef** has been designated a National Marine Park and includes Paradise Reef, with swim-through 90-foot sloping canyons, and Anchors Away, where anchors have been encrusted with coral formations. The 1985 wreck of the *Talata* lies in 70 feet of water; barracudas, rays, groupers, and grunts dart through its hull.

Dive St. Kitts

SCUBA DIVING | This PADI–NAUI facility offers competitive rates (including a price-matching guarantee), computers to maximize time below, a wide range of courses from refresher to rescue, and friendly, laid-back dive masters. The Bird Rock location features superb shore diving (unlimited when you book packages): common sightings 20 to 30 feet out include octopuses, nurse sharks, manta and spotted eagle rays, seahorses, even barracudas George and Georgianna. It also offers kayak and snorkeling tours. ✉ *2 miles (3 km) east of Basseterre, Frigate Bay* ☎ *869/465–8914* 🌐 *www.divestkitts.com.*

Kenneth's Dive Center

SCUBA DIVING | Kenneth Samuel, the owner of this PADI company, takes small groups of divers with C cards to nearby reefs on his two custom-built catamarans. Rates average $80 for single-tank dives, $110 for double-tank dives; add $10 for equipment. Night dives, including lights, are $80–$100. After over 40 years' experience, former fisherman Samuel is considered an old pro (Jean-Michel Cousteau requested his guidance upon his first visit in the 1990s) and strives to keep groups small and prices reasonable. ✉ *Bay Rd., Basseterre* ☎ *869/465–2670* 🌐 *www.kennethdivecentre.net.*

Pro-Divers

SCUBA DIVING | Owned by Auston Macleod, a PADI-certified dive master–instructor, this outfitter offers resort and certification courses running $160–$700, including specialty options from deep diving to digital underwater photography. Dive computers are included gratis. He also takes groups to snorkeling sites accessible only by boat via his custom-built 38-foot catamaran, *Kuriala.* ✉ *Fisherman's Wharf, Ocean Terrace Inn, Basseterre* ☎ *869/660–3483* 🌐 *www.prodiversstkitts.com.*

GOLF

Royal St. Kitts Golf Club

GOLF | This 18-hole links-style championship course underwent a complete redesign by Thomas McBroom to maximize Caribbean and Atlantic views and increase the challenge (there are 12 lakes and 83 bunkers). Holes 15 through 17 (the latter patterned after Pebble Beach No. 18) skirt the Atlantic in their entirety, lending new meaning to the term sand trap. The sudden gusts, wide but twisting fairways, and extremely hilly terrain demand pinpoint accuracy and finesse, yet holes such as 18 require pure power. The development includes practice bunkers, a putting green, a short-game chipping area, and the fairly high-tech Royal Golf Academy. Twilight and super-twilight discounts are offered. ✉ *St. Kitts Marriott Resort, 858 Zenway Blvd., Frigate Bay* ☎ *869/466–2700, 866/785–4653* 🌐 *www.royalstkittsgolfclub.com* 🎫 *$150 for Marriott guests in high season, $165 for nonguests* 🏌 *18 holes, 6900 yards, par 71.*

GUIDED TOURS

The taxi driver who picks you up will probably offer to act as your guide to the island. Each driver is knowledgeable and does a three-hour tour of Nevis for $75 or a four-hour tour of St. Kitts for $80. He can also make a lunch reservation at one of the plantation restaurants, and you can incorporate this into your tour.

Kantours

GUIDED TOURS | On St. Kitts, Kantours offers comprehensive general island tours on both St. Kitts and Nevis, as well as a variety of specialty excursions, including ATV expeditions and SNUBA adventures. ✉ *Liverpool Row, Basseterre* ☎ *869/465–2631, 869/465–3054, 869/469–0136 in Nevis* 🌐 *www.kantours.com.*

Tropical Tours

GUIDED TOURS | The friendly guides at Tropical Tours can run you around St. Kitts (from $36 per person); arrange kayaking, snorkeling, and deep-sea fishing trips (from $137 per person); and take you on volcano or rain-forest hiking or horseback-riding adventures ($87 per person and up). ✉ *22 Cayon St., Basseterre* ☎ *869/465–4167, 869/465–4039* 🌐 *www.tropicaltoursstkitts-nevis.com.*

HIKING

Trails in the central mountains vary from easy to don't-try-it-by-yourself. Monkey Hill and Verchild's Peak aren't difficult, although the Verchild's climb will take the better part of a day. Don't attempt Mt. Liamuiga without a guide. You'll start at Belmont Estate—at the west end of the island—on horseback, and then proceed on foot to the lip of the crater, at 2,600 feet. You can go down into the crater—1,000 feet deep and 1 mile (1½ km) wide, with a small freshwater lake—clinging to vines and roots and scaling rocks, even trees. Expect to get muddy. There are several fine operators (each hotel recommends its favorite); tour rates generally range from $50 for a rain-forest walk to $95 for a volcano expedition and usually include round-trip transportation from your hotel and picnic lunch.

Greg's Safaris

HIKING & WALKING | Greg Pereira, whose family has lived on St. Kitts since the early 19th century, takes groups on half-day trips ($75 and up) into the rain forest and on full-day hikes up the volcano and through the grounds of a private 18th-century greathouse. The rain forest trips include visits to sacred Carib sites, abandoned sugar mills, and an excursion down a 100-foot coastal canyon containing a wealth of Amerindian petroglyphs. The Off the Beaten Track 4X4 Plantation Tour provides a thorough explanation of the role sugar and rum played in the Caribbean economy and colonial wars. He and his staff relate fascinating historical, folkloric, and botanical information. ☎ *869/465–4121* 🌐 *www.gregsafaris.com.*

HORSEBACK RIDING

Wild North Frigate Bay and desolate Conaree Beach are great for riding, as is the rain forest.

Trinity Stables

HORSEBACK RIDING | Guides from Trinity Stables offer beach rides and trips into the rain forest, both including hotel pickup. The latter is intriguing, as guides discuss plants' medicinal properties along the way (such as sugarcane to stanch bleeding) and pick oranges right off a tree to squeeze fresh juice. The staffers are cordial but shy; this isn't a place for beginners' instruction. ✉ *Palmetto Point* ☎ *869/465–3226, 869/726–3098* *www.facebook.com/trinitystableskn.*

SEA EXCURSIONS

In addition to the usual snorkeling, sunset, and party cruises (ranging in price from $50 to $110), most companies offer whale-watching excursions during the winter migrating season, January through April. And on land, turtle-watches during nesting season are becoming popular.

Blue Water Safaris

SAILING | Blue Water Safaris offers half-day snorkeling trips or beach barbecues on deserted cays, as well as sunset and moonlight cruises on its 65-foot catamarans *Irie Lime* and *Swaliga,* and the smaller *Falcon.* Prices include refreshments and/or meals. It also runs kayaking tours. Boats depart from Port Zante, rates start at $69 per person. ✉ *Princess St., Basseterre* ☎ *869/466–4933* 🌐 *www.bluewatersafaris.com.*

Leeward Island Charters

SAILING | This reliable outfit offers day and overnight charters on two catamarans—the 67-foot *Eagle* and 78-foot *Spirit of St. Kitts,* as well as the 47-foot *Caona.* Day sails are from 9:30 to 4:30 and include a barbecue, an open bar, and use of snorkeling equipment. The Nevis trip stops at Pinney's Beach for a barbecue and at Shooting Bay, a tiny cove in the bullying shadow of a sheer cliff, where petrels and frigate birds inspect your snorkeling skills. The crews are mellow, affable, and knowledgeable about island life. ✉ *586 Fort St., Basseterre* ☎ *869/465–7474* 🌐 *www.leewardislandscharters.com.*

ZIP LINING

Sky Safari Tours

ZIP LINING | **FAMILY** | On these popular tours, would-be Tarzans and Janes whisk through the "Valley of the Giants" (so dubbed for the towering trees) at speeds up to 50 mph (80 kph) along five cable lines; the longest (nicknamed "The Boss") stretches 1,350 feet through towering turpentine and mahogany trees draped thickly with bromeliads, suspended 250 feet above the ground. Following the Canadian-based company's mantra of "faster, higher, safer," it uses a specially designed trolley with secure harnesses attached. Many of the routes afford unobstructed views of Brimstone Hill and the sea beyond. The outfit emphasizes environmental and historic aspects. Guides provide nature interpretation and commentary, and the office incorporates Wingfield Estate's old sugar plantation, distillery, and church ruins, which visitors can explore. Rates run from $45 to $296, depending on the tour. ✉ *Wingfield Estate, Wingfield Estate* ☎ *869/466–4259, 869/465–4347* 🌐 *www.skysafaristkitts.com.*

Nevis

Nevis's charm is its rusticity: there are no traffic lights, goats still amble through the streets of Charlestown, and local grocers announce whatever's in stock on a blackboard (anything from pig snouts to beer).

Few islands remain as unspoiled as Nevis, the quiet sister island of St. Kitts. While its natural attractions and activities certainly captivate—there's great ecohiking, windsurfing, and deep-sea fishing to be had—lying in a hammock, strolling on Pinney's Beach, and dining on romantic candlelit patios remain cherished pursuits. Nevis's historic heritage, from the Caribbean's first hotel to Alexander Hamilton's childhood home, is just as pronounced, and visitors can look forward to sybaritic plantation inns that seem torn from the pages of a romance novel and scenes of overgrown sugar mills almost everywhere you look.

GETTING HERE AND AROUND

Nevis's Main Road makes a 21-mile (32-km) circuit through the five parishes; various offshoots of the road wind into the mountains. You can tour Charlestown, the capital, in a half hour or so, but you'll need three to four hours to explore the entire island.

Sights

About 1,500 of Nevis's nearly 12,000 inhabitants live in the capital. If you arrive by ferry, as most people do, you'll walk smack onto Main Street from the pier. It's easy to imagine how tiny Charlestown, founded in 1660, must have looked

Mt. Nevis rising behind the Botanical Gardens of Nevis.

in its heyday. The weathered buildings still have fanciful galleries, elaborate gingerbread fretwork, wooden shutters, and hanging plants. The stone building with the clock tower (1825, but mostly rebuilt after a devastating 1873 fire) houses the courthouse and second-floor library (a cool respite on sultry days). The little park next to the library is Memorial Square, dedicated to the fallen of World Wars I and II. Down the street from the square, archaeologists have discovered the remains of a Jewish cemetery and synagogue (Nevis reputedly had the Caribbean's second-oldest congregation), but there's little to see.

Alexander Hamilton Birthplace

HISTORY MUSEUM | The Alexander Hamilton Birthplace, which contains the Hamilton Museum, sits on the waterfront. This bougainvillea-draped Georgian-style house is a reconstruction of what is believed to have been the American patriot's original home, built in 1680 and likely destroyed during a mid-19th-century earthquake. Born here in 1755, Hamilton moved to St. Croix when he was about 12. He moved to the American colonies to continue his education at 17; he became George Washington's Secretary of the Treasury and died in a duel with political rival Aaron Burr in 1804. The Nevis House of Assembly occupies the second floor; the museum contains Hamilton memorabilia, documents pertaining to the island's history, and displays on island geology, politics, architecture, culture, and cuisine. The gift shop is a wonderful source for historic maps, crafts, and books on Nevis. ✉ *Low St., Charlestown* ☎ *869/469–5786* 🌐 *www.nevisheritage.org* 🎫 *$5; combination ticket $7, includes Museum of Nevis History.*

★ **Botanical Gardens of Nevis**

GARDEN | In addition to terraced gardens and arbors, this remarkable 7.8-acre site in the glowering shadow of Mt. Nevis has natural lagoons, streams, and waterfalls, superlative bronze mermaids, Buddhas, egrets and herons, and extravagant fountains. You can find a proper rose garden, sections devoted to orchids and bromeliads, cacti, and flowering trees and shrubs—even a bamboo garden. The entrance to the Rain Forest Conservatory, which attempts to include every conceivable Caribbean ecosystem and then some, duplicates an imposing Mayan temple. A splendid re-creation of a plantation-style greathouse contains the appealing Oasis Thai restaurant with sweeping sea views (and wonderfully inventive variations on classic cocktails utilizing local ingredients), and the Galleria Gift Shop selling art, textiles, glass items, and jewelry. ✉ *Montpelier Estate* ☎ *869/469–3509* 🌐 *www.botanicalgardennevis.com* 🎟 *$13.*

Eden Brown Estate

HISTORIC HOME | This government-owned mansion, built around 1740, is known as Nevis's haunted house, or haunted ruins. In 1822 a Miss Julia Huggins was to marry a fellow named Maynard. However, come wedding day, the groom and his best man killed each other in a duel. The bride-to-be became a recluse, and the mansion was closed down. Locals claim they can feel the presence of "someone" whenever they go near the eerie old house with its shroud of weeds and wildflowers. Though memorable more for the story than the hike or ruins, it's always open, and it's free. ✉ *East Coast Rd., between Lime Kiln and Mannings, Eden Brown Bay.*

Ft. Ashby

MILITARY SIGHT | Overgrown with tropical vegetation, this site overlooks the place where the settlement of Jamestown fell into the sea after a tidal wave hit the coast in 1680. Needless to say, this is a favorite scuba-diving site. ✉ *Main Rd., Asbby Fort* ✣ *1½ miles (2½ km) southwest of Hurricane Hill.*

Fothergills Nevisian Heritage Village

MUSEUM VILLAGE | On the grounds of a former sugar plantation–cotton ginnery, this ambitious, ever-expanding project traces the evolution of Nevisian social history, from the Caribs to the present, through vernacular dwellings that re-create living conditions over the centuries. The Carib chief's thatched hut includes actual relics such as weapons, calabash bowls, clay pots, and cassava squeezers. Wattle-and-daub structures reproduce slave quarters; implements on display include coal pots and sea fans (used as sieves). A post-emancipation gingerbread chattel house holds patchwork quilts and flour-bag dresses. There's a typical sharecropper's garden explaining herbal medicinal folklore and blacksmith's shop. Docents are quite earnest and go on at great (mostly fascinating) length. If you're lucky, one of the ladies might have brought in home-baked bread or goat water. ✉ *Fothergills Estate, Gingerland* ☎ *869/469–5521, 869/469–2033* 🎟 *$4* ⏲ *Closed Sun.; Sat. by appointment only.*

★ Malcolm Guishard Recreational Park

CITY PARK | **FAMILY** | A collaboration between Nevis and Taiwan, this 11-acre sustainable park is dedicated in memory of the former minister of tourism of Nevis. It features an open-air amphitheater, playgrounds, a basketball court, LED-lit splash-pad fountains, a jogging path, and a boardwalk. Those looking to cool off can pop inside the on-site game arcade, and families are encouraged to stop by on the weekends for movies in the park. ✉ *Charlestown.*

Museum of Nevis History

HISTORY MUSEUM | Purportedly this is the Western Hemisphere's largest collection of Lord Horatio Nelson memorabilia, including letters, documents, paintings, and even furniture from his flagship. Nelson was based in Antigua but came on military patrol to Nevis, where he met and eventually married Frances Nisbet, who lived on a 64-acre plantation here. Half the space is devoted to often-provocative displays on island life, from leading families to vernacular architecture to the adaptation of traditional African customs, from cuisine to Carnival. The shop is an excellent source for gifts, from homemade soaps to historical guides. ✉ *Bath Rd., Charlestown* ☎ *869/469–0408* 🌐 *www.nevisheritage.org* 🎫 *$5; combination ticket $7, includes Alexander Hamilton Birthplace* ⏲ *Closed Sun., and Sat. June–November.*

Nevis Hot Springs

HOT SPRING | The Caribbean's first lodging, the Bath Hotel (built by businessman John Huggins in 1778), was so popular in the 19th century that visitors, who included Samuel Taylor Coleridge, traveled months by ship to "take the waters" in the property's hot springs. It suffered extensive hurricane and earthquake damage over the years and long languished in disrepair. Local volunteers have cleaned up the spring and built stone pools and steps to enter the waters, though signs still caution that you bathe at your own risk, especially if you have heart problems. The development houses the Nevis Island Administration offices; there's still talk of adding massage huts, changing rooms, a restaurant, and a culture and history center on the original hotel property. ✉ *Charlestown* ✣ *Follow Main St. south from Charlestown.*

St. John's Figtree Church

RELIGIOUS BUILDING | Among the records of this church built in 1680 is a tattered, prominently displayed marriage certificate that reads "Horatio Nelson, Esquire, to Frances Nisbet, Widow, on March 11, 1787." ✉ *Church Ground* ✣ *Located about 10 mins south of Charlestown on the main road.*

St. Thomas Anglican Church

RELIGIOUS BUILDING | The island's oldest church was built in 1643 and has been altered many times over the years. The gravestones in the old churchyard have stories to tell, and the church itself contains poignant embedded crypts and memorials to Nevis's early settlers. The prospects over the sea are so lovely that this site has become an unexpected if somewhat macabre picnic spot. ✉ *Main Rd., Jessup* ✣ *Just south of Cotton Ground.*

Beaches

All beaches on Nevis are free to the public (the plantation inns cordon off "private" areas on Pinney's Beach for guests), but there are no changing facilities, so wear a swimsuit under your clothes.

Newcastle Beach

BEACH | This broad swath of soft ecru sand shaded by coconut palms and patrolled by pelicans is near Nisbet Plantation, on the channel between St. Kitts and Nevis. It's popular with snorkelers, but beware stony sections and occasional strong currents that kick up seaweed and roil the sandy bottom. **Amenities:** food and drink. **Best for:** snorkeling. ✉ *Newcastle.*

Oualie Beach

BEACH | South of Mosquito Bay and north of Cades and Jones Bays, this beige-sand beach lined with palms and seagrapes is where the folks at Oualie Beach Hotel can mix you a drink and fix you up with water-sports equipment. There's excellent snorkeling amid calm water and fantastic sunset views with St. Kitts silhouetted in the background. Several beach chairs and hammocks (free with lunch, $3 rental without) line the sand and the grassy "lawn" behind it. Oualie is at the island's northwest tip, approximately 3 miles (5 km) west of the airport. **Amenities:** food and drink; water sports. **Best for:** snorkeling; sunset. ✉ *Oualie Beach.*

Pinney's Beach

BEACH | The island's showpiece has soft golden sand on the calm Caribbean, lined with a magnificent grove of palm trees. The Four Seasons Resort is here, as are the plantation inns' beach clubs and casual beach bars such as Sunshine's and Lime—their off-shoot, the Cabanas at Lime, has a relaxed atmosphere with light bites and drinks, highlighted by a famed Lobster Fest on Thursdays). Beach chairs are gratis when you purchase a drink or lunch. Regrettably, the waters can be murky and filled with kelp if the weather has been inclement anywhere within a hundred miles, depending on the currents. **Amenities:** food and drink; water sports. **Best for:** swimming; walking. ✉ *Pinney's Beach.*

Restaurants

★ Bananas

$$$ | **ECLECTIC** | The wildly diverse experiences of peripatetic English owner Gillian Smith inform every aspect of this restaurant, which is set in a classic plantation greathouse she herself painstakingly built and decorated with an array of items: colonial pith helmets, carved pineapple chairs, calabash chandeliers, dressmaker dummies, Turkish kilims, and Moroccan lamps. From bourbon-glazed guava ribs to lobster linguine in saffron cream, the dishes are equally eclectic, and the selection of aged rum—from Appleton to Zacapa—is sterling. **Known for:** luscious local dishes with international flair; delightfully whimsical yet elegant decor; warm staff. $ *Average main: US$30* ✉ *Upper Hamilton Estate* ☎ *869/469–1891* 🌐 *www.bananasnevis.com* ⏲ *No lunch Sun.*

Drift

$$$ | **CARIBBEAN** | A farm-to-sea-to-table purveyor inside a quaint beach house right along the water serving up a creative menu that changes with the season. Sure there's quintessential coconut shrimp and jerk chicken, but guests will also find dishes like a fresh catch of the day smothered in whatever sauce the chef comes up with on the spot. **Known for:** curry of the day; great shareable appetizer platters; Nevis lobster salad. $ *Average main: US$30* ✉ *Newcastle* ☎ *869/469–2777* 🌐 *www.driftnevis.com.*

EsQuilina

$$$ | **MEDITERRANEAN** | Come sundown, the Four Seasons breakfast space morphs into a stylish trattoria offering a tapestry of tapas-style tastes—from a silken pear-hazelnut burrata with black truffle and local greens to a pumpkin ravioli that brilliantly counterpoints smoky bacon, crunchy sunflower seeds, and crisped sage with a sweet, satiny filling. Although the interior is a handsome symphony of gold and ecru art deco–inspired accents, the prime seating is on the patio. **Known for:** warm, winning service; Mediterranean cuisine artfully adapted to the tropics; exceptional raw bar. $ *Average main: US$30* ✉ *Pinney's Beach* ☎ *869/469–8111* 🌐 *www.fourseasons.com* ⏲ *No lunch.*

The Gin Trap

$$$ | **ECLECTIC** | This split-level space lives up to its "Let the Evening Be Gin" mantra, but succulent seafood and myriad house-made items (from pastas to infused oils to baked goods) ensure that gin isn't the sole reason to visit. The inlaid-wood bar—where free popcorn is served in whimsical oversize glasses—and adjacent patio make smart settings for the mixologist's wizardry; cushy leather seating with Union Jack and American flag throw pillows, huge model boats doubling as drink carts, and steamer trunks serving as coffee tables complete the fun, funky look. **Known for:** affordable bar bites; stunning sunsets from patio; extraordinary selection of gin with tasting flights. $ *Average main: US$30* ✉ *Main Rd., Jones Bay* ☎ *869/469–8230* 🌐 *www.thegintrapnevis.com.*

★ Hermitage Plantation Inn

$$$ | **ECLECTIC** | After cocktails in the antiques-filled parlor, head to the verandah for a dinner featuring dishes often made with ingredients from the inn's herb garden, fruit trees, and livestock collection. The scrumptious cured meats, baked goods, preserves, and ice creams are homemade, and the traditional wood-burning oven yields incredible thin-crust pizza. **Known for:** phenomenal roast pig and pizza nights; delightful hosts and clientele; legendary knockout rum punches and intriguing wines. $ *Average main:*

US$30 ✉ Gingerland ☎ 869/469–3477 🌐 www.hermitagenevis.com.

Indian Summer

$ | **INDIAN** | Serving authentic Indian cuisine in a dimly lit casual atmosphere, this relaxing spot serves heaping portions of tikka masala, mutton vindaloo, and fluffy basmati rice. The menu is separated into appetizers, vegetarian, seafood, and lamb specialties. **Known for:** plenty of vegan and vegetarian options; pickup and delivery available; delicious fresh naan. *$ Average main: US$11 ✉ Cades Bay ☎ 869/662–5410 🌐 www.indiansummernevis.com ⏲ No lunch Mon.*

★ Luna Restaurant & Tapas Bar

$$$$ | **CARIBBEAN** | Focusing on Caribbean flavors with heavy influences from Africa, the Middle East, and a bit of Italy, this spot is situated in a courtyard surrounded by a lush tropical garden. Begin with tapas-style dishes like the seafood au gratin and wild mushroom tartelette shine, before moving on to exciting entrées like the fire-grilled local lobster seasoned with star anise and cinnamon, served with saffron rice and lobster butter sauce. **Known for:** daily-changing smoked wahoo dish; perfectly plated dishes; well-spiced and-flavored options. *$ Average main: US$35 ✉ Newcastle ☎ 869/469–8111 🌐 www.lunanevis.com ⏲ Closed Mon. No lunch.*

★ Mango

$$$$ | **CARIBBEAN** | This sophisticated beach bar at the Four Seasons is a perennial hot spot thanks, in part, to an outdoor deck overlooking the illuminated water and a farm- and sea-to-table menu (half of which is gluten free) showcasing local ingredients—many grown by the staff. Dishes might include cornmeal-dusted soft shell crab over curried black beans and shishito peppers in coriander-lime sour cream, slow-roasted goat tamale, lobster fritters with lime aioli, or mango-Myer's rum baby back ribs. **Known for:** hip decor and sizzling music; artful, inventive takes on Caribbean classics; fab drinks and more than 100 rum selections. *$ Average main: US$39 ✉ Four Seasons Resort, Pinney's Beach ☎ 869/469–1111, 869/469–6238 🌐 www.fourseasons.com ⏲ No lunch Mon.–Sat.*

★ On The Dune

$$$ | **CARIBBEAN** | **FAMILY** | The newest restaurant at the Four Seasons, On The Dune is an upscale poolside spot with stunning views of the ocean and the entire property. Guests can nosh on local queen snapper tiradito, conch fritters, and seafood paella at lunch and dinner. **Known for:** plenty of gluten-free options; loaded lobster fries; great service. *$ Average main: US$25 ✉ Four Seasons Nevis, Pinney's Beach 🌐 www.fourseasons.com.*

The Rocks at Golden Rock

$$$$ | **ECLECTIC** | This glam eatery's tiered garden is a masterpiece: glass panels and ceilings display the night sky while reflecting patio lights; silvery waterfalls, pools, and fountains filigree the grounds; strategically placed boulders resemble hulking Henry Moore sculptures; and flowers as well as fire-engine-red directors' chairs and a tarp add pops of color. Contemporary and colonial artworks from Mali and Afghanistan grace the interior, where the kitchen doesn't always match the setting's creativity; still the jerk pork, pan-roasted snapper, or justly celebrated conch chowder (perfectly chunky with a touch of heat offsetting the creamy base) are solid choices. **Known for:** fabulous lobster rolls at lunch; striking design; expert re-inventions of Caribbean classics. *$ Average main: US$32 ✉ Golden Rock Inn, Gingerland ☎ 869/469–3346 🌐 www.goldenrocknevis.com.*

Sip on the Square

$ | **MODERN AMERICAN** | **FAMILY** | A charming little café and brunch spot for those craving Nutella-covered French toast or a BLT. Perched on the second floor of a cute home in the middle of downtown Charlestown, this is a spot beloved by locals, and often missed

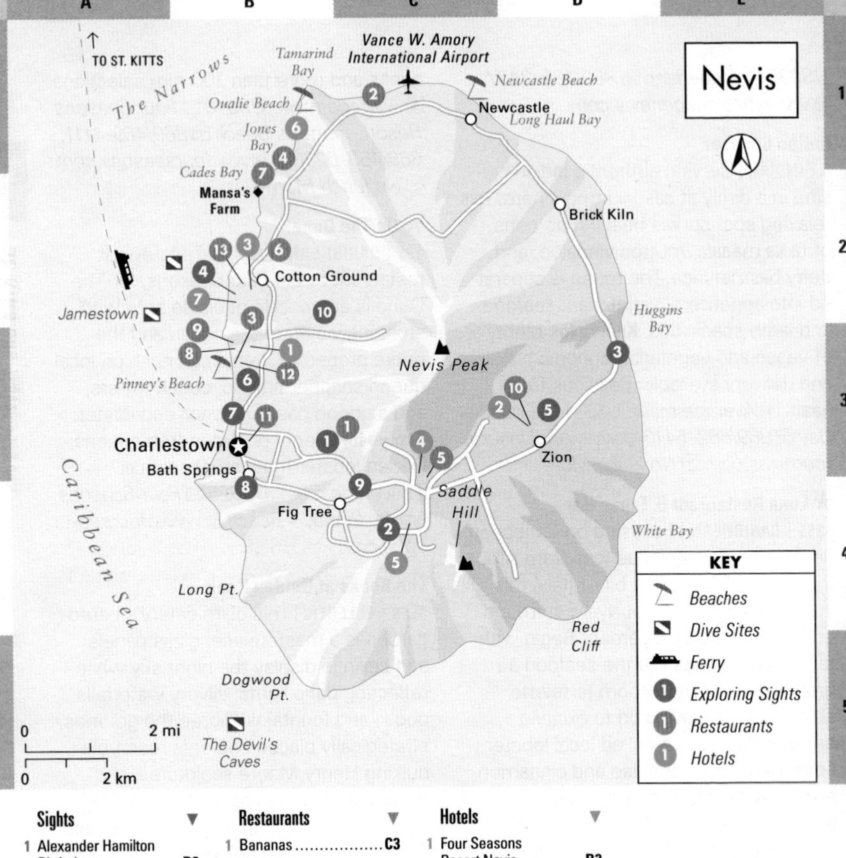

Sights

1 Alexander Hamilton Birthplace B3
2 Botanical Gardens of Nevis C4
3 Eden Brown Estate D3
4 Ft. Ashby B2
5 Fothergills Nevisian Heritage Village D3
6 Malcolm Guishard Recreational Park B3
7 Museum of Nevis History B3
8 Nevis Hot Springs B4
9 St John's Figtree Church C4
10 St. Thomas Anglican Church B2

Restaurants

1 Bananas C3
2 Drift........................ C1
3 EsQuilina................. B3
4 The Gin Trap............. B1
5 Hermitage Plantation Inn C3
6 Indian Summer B2
7 Luna Restaurant & Tapas Bar................ B2
8 Mango B3
9 On The Dune B3
10 The Rocks at Golden Rock.......... D3
11 Sip on the Square....... B3
12 Sunshine's............... B3
13 Yachtsman Grill B2

Hotels

1 Four Seasons Resort Nevis............ B3
2 Golden Rock Inn D3
3 The Hamilton Beach Villas & Spa B2
4 The Hermitage C3
5 Montpelier Plantation & Beach C4
6 Oualie Beach Resort ... B1
7 Paradise Beach Nevis B2

by visitors. **Known for:** quaint environment; friendly staff; hearty sandwiches. *Average main: US$10* ✉ *Charlestown* ☎ *869/469-6488* 🌐 *www.facebook.com/siponthesquarenevis.*

★ Sunshine's

$$ | **CARIBBEAN** | Everything about this beach shack is larger than life, from the Rasta man Llewellyn "Sunshine" Caines himself to the walls plastered with flags and license plates that reflect a very international clientele, to the picnic tables and palm trees splashed with bright sunrise-to-sunset color. With the restaurant's addition of VIP cabanas, locals say "it gone upscaled," but fishermen still cruise up with their catch, keeping things real and ensuring that the lobster rolls and snapper creole are truly fresh. **Known for:** occasional celebrity sightings; Killer Bee rum punch ("One and you're stung; two, you're stunned; three, it's a knockout"); boisterous crowd. *Average main: US$19* ✉ *Pinney's Beach* ☎ *869/469–5817* 🌐 *www.sunshinesnevis.com.*

Yachtsman Grill

$$$$ | **ECLECTIC** | This beachfront eatery features nautical decor (sailboat models, keels, fishing rods, outboard motors) and seafood to match (pick your own lobster from the tank). Steaks, barbecue ribs, and lamb chops are also on offer, and there's a wood-fired pizza oven. **Known for:** house-baked goods and pizzas; enviable beach setting; excellent, fairly reasonable wine list. *Average main: US$32* ✉ *Hamilton Beach Villas, Nelson Spring* ☎ *869/469–1382* 🌐 *www.yachtsmangrill.com* *No credit cards.*

Hotels

Many Nevis lodgings are in restored manor or plantation houses scattered throughout the island's five parishes (counties). The owners often live at these inns, and it's easy to feel as if you've been personally invited down for a visit. Before dinner you may find yourself in the drawing room having a cocktail and conversing with the family, other guests, or visitors who have come for a meal. Most inns offer free shuttles to their "private" stretches of beach as well as meal plans that include breakfast and dinner (plus afternoon tea). If you require TVs and air-conditioning, you're better off staying at hotels and simply dining with the engaging inn owners.

★ Four Seasons Resort Nevis

$$$$ | **RESORT** | **FAMILY** | This beachfront beauty impeccably combines world-class elegance—ever dazzling and sleek, never overwhelming or overdone—with West Indian hospitality while scrupulously maintaining, upgrading, and refreshing its facilities. **Pros:** marvelous food; superlative luxury and service without attitude; stunning golf course and spa. **Cons:** berms (storm-surge defenses) impede some beachfront room views; sometimes overrun by conventions and incentive groups (off-season mainly); pricey. *Rooms from: US$925* ✉ *Pinney's Beach* ☎ *869/469–1111, 869/469–6238, 800/332–3442 in U.S., 800/268–6282 in Canada* 🌐 *www.fourseasons.com/nevis* *250 units* *No Meals.*

Golden Rock Inn

$$ | **HOTEL** | Acclaimed artists Brice Marden and wife Helen Harrington have imparted a chic, modernist sensibility to this 18th-century estate property while respecting its storied past: the old cistern is now the spring-fed swimming pool; the sugar mill has become a honeymoon retreat; and the vividly hued gingerbread cottages (each holding two rooms) contrast pristine white floors, curtains, and bedspreads with hardwood or bamboo furnishings, pineapple friezes, and colorful Berber throw rugs. **Pros:** free Wi-Fi and laundry; ecofriendly property with glorious grounds; artsy crowd. **Cons:** foliage blocks some of the water views; lack of air-conditioning can be uncomfortable on still days; no actual beach though there's a beach club. *Rooms from:*

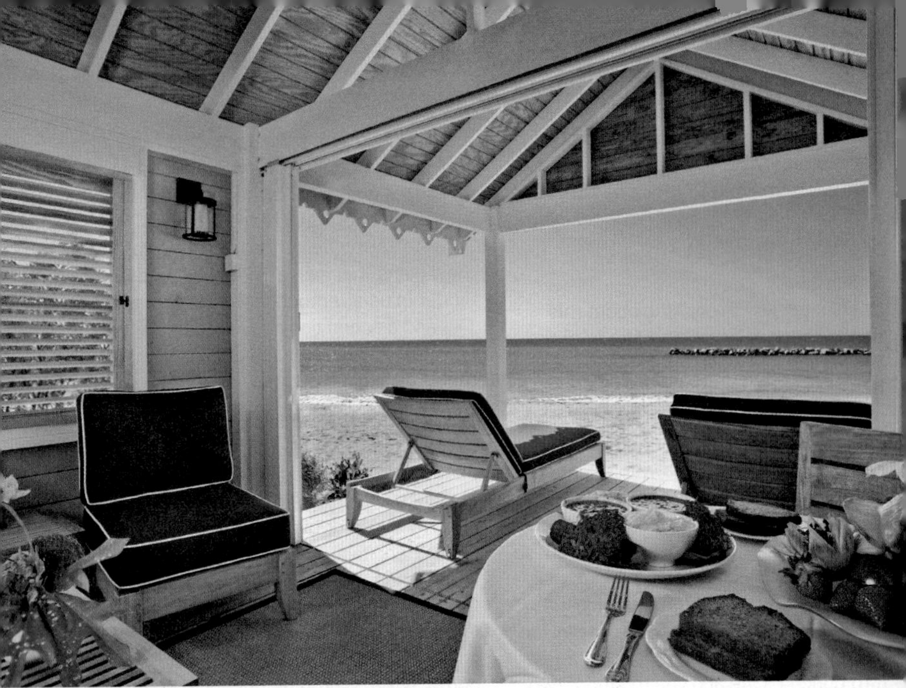

The beach-front Four Seasons Resort Nevis is ultimate luxury.

US$325 ⊠ Gingerland ☎ 869/469–3346 🌐 goldenrocknevis.com ⊙ Closed mid-Aug.–mid-Oct. ⇆ 17 rooms 🍽 Free Breakfast.

The Hamilton Beach Villas & Spa
$$$ | **APARTMENT** | **FAMILY** | Located right along popular Pinneys Beach, and one of the island's newest properties with views of not only the Caribbean, but also lush gardens and Nevis Peak. **Pros:** one of the newer options on the island; washer and dryer in unit; pre-stock fridge if requested. **Cons:** only one on-site dining option; few decor highlights in rooms; no "beach activities". [$] *Rooms from: US$380 ⊠ Charlestown ☎ 869/469-5320 🌐 www.hamiltonnevis.com ⇆ 79 rooms 🍽 No Meals.*

★ The Hermitage
$$ | **HOTEL** | A snug 1670 greathouse (reputedly the Caribbean's oldest surviving wooden building) forms the heart of this hillside hideaway, run by two (going on three) generations of charmingly "loopy" Lupinaccis, who keep things lively, down to earth, and family friendly—rare for such a refined, smart-set retreat. **Pros:** lovely breezes eliminate the need for air-conditioning; wonderful sense of history; delightful owners and clientele. **Cons:** some rooms too warm on still days; hard for people with disabilities to negotiate the hillside setting; long drive to beach. [$] *Rooms from: US$300 ⊠ Hermitage Rd., Gingerland ☎ 869/469–3477, 800/682–4025 🌐 www.hermitage-nevis.com ⇆ 17 units 🍽 Free Breakfast.*

★ Montpelier Plantation & Beach
$$$ | **RESORT** | This Nevisian beauty, a Rélais & Châteaux property, epitomizes understated elegance and graciously updated plantation living: a fieldstone greathouse replicates the 18th-century original, a sugar mill houses an intimate restaurant, and hillside cottages—each with a private sea-view verandah—dot 30 acres of ravishing gardens. **Pros:** exquisite gardens; impeccable service and attention to detail; lovely cuisine. **Cons:** no TVs for those who care; no beach on-site; some may find it a little stuffy. [$] *Rooms from: US$500 ⊠ Montpelier*

Estate ☎ *869/469–3462, 800/735–2478* 🌐 *www.montpeliernevis.com* ⏲ *Closed mid-Aug.–early Oct.* *19 units* 🍽 *Free Breakfast.*

Oualie Beach Resort

$ | **RESORT** | These Creole-style, cotton-candy-color, gingerbread cottages sit steps from a beach facing St. Kitts and are staggered to ensure sea views from all the rooms, some of which have mahogany canopy four-poster beds and granite vanities. **Pros:** appealing beach; fantastic water-sports operations; affordable (especially with recreational packages). **Cons:** food is average; not ideal for less active types; showing some wear. $ *Rooms from: US$100* ✉ *Oualie Beach* ☎ *869/469–9735* 🌐 *www.oualiebeach.com* *32 rooms* 🍽 *Free Breakfast.*

Paradise Beach Nevis

$$$$ | **B&B/INN** | This exclusive South Sea–inspired enclave cascades down a lush hill to Pinney's Beach, providing posh, pampering, Bali "high" stays in thatched-roof villas that have 30-foot ceilings with hand-carved beams and private, vine-swaddled, split-level, sea-view patios with plunge pools. **Pros:** private and quiet; ultra-luxurious; well-equipped. **Cons:** not the nicest stretch of Pinney's Beach; few on-site facilities; pricey and requires a three-night minimum stay. $ *Rooms from: US$1,800* ✉ *Pinney's Beach* ☎ *869/469–7900* 🌐 *www.paradisebeachnevis.com* *12 units* 🍽 *No Meals.*

Nightlife

In season it's usually easy to find a local calypso singer or a steel or string band performing at one of the hotels, notably the Four Seasons and Oualie Beach (which also features string musicians on homemade instruments Tuesday evening), as well as at the Pinneys' bars. Scan the posters plastered on doorways announcing informal jump-ups. Though Nevis lacks high-tech discos, many restaurants and bars have live bands or DJs on weekends.

★ Chrishi Beach Club

GATHERING PLACES | **FAMILY** | Though more of a daytime hangout—especially Sunday when local families descend on the lovely beach—this spot keeps hopping into the night, thanks to vivacious Norwegian expats Hedda and Christian "Chrishi" Wienpahl. Sprawl on beach waterbeds in the shady Love Shack + Bar or on comfy chaises in the "stripper" lounge, replete with a pole for shimmying. Enjoy the righteous lounge mix (and mixology), the wildly popular movie nights, and the DJs on Sexy Saturday Nights. Browse Hedda's fun, funky HWD line of jewelry, which incorporates leather, coins, and found objects. Dine on salads, pizzas, sandwiches, and sushi as well as more substantial dishes like butterflied prawns in garlic-parsley sauce. Kids even have their own club with fresh-fruit smoothies. The adjacent Zenith Beach villa development has some spectacular units. ✉ *Next to Sea Bridge and Mansa's, Cades Bay* ☎ *869/469–5959, 869/662–3959* 🌐 *www.chrishibeachclub.net.*

Crowned Monkey Rum Bar

COCKTAIL LOUNGES | A trendy and sophisticated bar located inside the Four Seasons, this is the spot for a relaxed, but upscale happy hour, quick pre-dinner drink, or nightcap. As the name implies there's an extensive list of rums (and rum tastings available), including the bespoke signature Crowned Monkey Rum—14 year-aged in single bourbon barrels—that's only available at Four Seasons Nevis. It's also a prime spot to perch yourself to enjoy the live music that often happens at the hotel. ✉ *Four Seasons Nevis, Pinney's Beach* 🌐 *www.fourseasons.com.*

★ Water Department Barbecue

GATHERING PLACES | The Water Department Barbecue is the informal name for a lively Friday-night jump-up that's run by two fellows (nicknamed the Pump Boys) from the local water department. Friday afternoons the tents go up, and the grills are fired. Cars line the streets, and the guys dish up fabulous barbecue ribs and chicken—as certain customers lobby to get their water pressure adjusted. It's a classic Caribbean scene. ✉ *Pump Rd., Charlestown.*

Shopping

CraftHouse

CRAFTS | This marvelous source for local specialties, from vetiver mats to leather moccasins, also has a smaller branch in the Cotton Ginnery. ✉ *Pinney's Rd., Charlestown* ☎ *869/469–5505.*

Eva Wilkin Gallery

ART GALLERIES | Nevis has produced one artist of some international repute, the late Dame Eva Wilkin, who for more than 50 years painted island people, flowers, and landscapes in an evocative art naïf style. Her originals are now quite valuable, but prints are available in some local shops. The Eva Wilkin Gallery occupies her former atelier (hours are extremely irregular; you must call ahead for appointments). If the paintings, drawings, and prints are out of your price range, consider buying the lovely note cards based on her designs; the owners are also promoting promising regional artists and craftspeople. ✉ *Clay Ghaut Estate, Gingerland* ☎ *869/469–2673.*

★ Indigo Blue

SOUVENIRS | Annie Lupinacci's bright, cheery shop carries delightful local and imported gift items, including her line of painted boats, as well as chic household goods, beachwear, and art. There's also a branch at The Hermitage. ✉ *Riviere House, Upper Government Rd., Charlestown* ☎ *869/661–3544* ⊙ *Closed Sun.*

Island Fever

MIXED CLOTHING | The island's classiest clothing shop carries an excellent selection of everything from bathing suits and dresses to straw bags and jewelry. ✉ *Main St., Charlestown* ☎ *869/762–8799.*

★ L & L Rum Shop

WINE/SPIRITS | Owner Mark Theron's passion for rum (he leads tastings at top hotels) led him to create the Clifton Estate brand of artisanal spiced rum as well as the affordable line of silver and gold Moko Jumbie rums. Both are on sale at this gleaming shop, which stocks an astonishing array of rum from around the world—putting the (sugar) cane in arcane—in addition to other spirits. While you're browsing, you can sip homemade limoncello or orange rum liqueur. If you call ahead, Mark may be able to organize a tasting of his products. ✉ *Upper Prince William St., Charlestown* ☎ *869/661–0627* 🌐 *www.cliftonestaterums.com.*

Newcastle Pottery

CRAFTS | This cooperative has continued the age-old tradition of hand-built red-clay pottery fired over burning coconut husks. It's possible to watch the potters and purchase wares at their small Newcastle factory. ✉ *Main Rd., Newcastle* ☎ *869/469–9746.*

Activities

BIKING

Windsurfing Nevis/Wheel World

BIKING | This shop offers mountain-bike rentals, apparel, and specially tailored tours on Gary Fisher, Trek, Hybrid, and MTB bikes. The tours ($65–$85), led by Winston Crooke, a master windsurfer and competitive bike racer, encompass lush rain forest, majestic ruins, and spectacular views. Costs vary according to itinerary and ability level but are aimed generally at experienced riders. Winston and his team delight in sharing local knowledge, from history to culture. For those just renting (rates from $25 daily, $150 weekly), Winston determines your performance level and suggests appropriate routes. ✉ *Oualie Beach* ☎ *869/469–9682* 🌐 *www.bikenevis.com.*

★ Nevis Adventure Tours

BIKING | Offering both biking and hiking tours for every skill level, these tours give adventurers a two- or three-hour island experience with stops at historic sites all over the island. ✉ *Charlestown* ☎ *869/664–0992, 869/765–4158* 🌐 *www.nevisadventuretours.com.*

DIVING AND SNORKELING

The **Devil's Caves** make up a series of grottoes where divers can navigate tunnels, canyons, and underwater hot springs while viewing lobsters, sea fans, sponges, squirrelfish, and more. The village of **Jamestown,** which washed into the sea around Ft. Ashby, just south of Cades Bay, makes for superior snorkeling and diving. Reef-protected Pinney's Beach offers especially good snorkeling. Single-tank dives are usually $100, two-tank dives $120; packages provide deep discounts.

Scuba Safaris

SCUBA DIVING | **FAMILY** | This PADI Five Star facility and NASDS Examining Station is staffed by experienced dive masters who offer everything from a resort course to full certification to nitrox. Their equipment is always state-of-the-art, including underwater scooters. It also provides a snorkeling learning experience that enables you not only to see but to listen to sea life, including whales and dolphins, as well as an exhilarating underwater scooter safari, night dives, and kids' bubble-makers. ✉ *Oualie Beach* ☎ *869/665–1516* 🌐 *www.divenevis.com.*

FISHING

Black Fin Charters

FISHING | With 32-foot boats, there's plenty of deck space for fishing, relaxing, and enjoying the day on the water. Options include deep sea (up to 20-miles out) or reef fishing for full and half days. ☎ *869/663–3301* 🌐 *www.blackfincharters.net.*

Fishing here focuses on kingfish, wahoo, grouper, tuna, and yellowtail snapper, with marlin occasionally spotted. The best areas are Monkey Shoals and around Redonda. Charters cost approximately $450–$500 per half day, $850–$1,000 per full day, and usually include an open bar.

GOLF

★ Four Seasons Golf Course

GOLF | The Robert Trent Jones Jr.–designed Four Seasons Golf Course is beautiful and impeccably maintained. The front 9 holes are fairly flat until hole 8, which climbs uphill after your tee shot. Most of the truly stunning views are along the back 9. The signature hole is the 15th, a 660-yard monster that encompasses a deep ravine; other holes include bridges, steep drops, rolling pitches, extremely tight and unforgiving fairways, sugar-mill ruins, and fierce doglegs. Attentive attendants canvass the course in beverage buggies, handing out chilled, peppermint-scented towels and preordered Cubanos to help test the wind. There are kids', twilight, and off-season discounts. ✉ *Four Seasons Resort Nevis, Pinney's Beach* ☎ *869/469–1111* 🌐 *www.fourseasons.com* 🎫 *$270; rental clubs $85* 🏌 *18 holes, 6766 yards, par 72.*

GUIDED TOURS

★ Nevis Sun Tours

GUIDED TOURS | FAMILY | Led by the former CEO of the Nevis Tourism Authority, they offer a handful of tour offerings, from an early-morning walk through the quiet villages or a food-themed tour highlighting authentic cuisines of the island, these guided tours range from $40 to $100 and last up to 2-hours. This outfit is also a one-stop shop that handles everything from villa booking to airport transfers and dining options (5 or 7-day options available) within both Nevis and St. Kitts. ✉ *Charlestown* ☎ *869/469–1299, 321/710–9765* 🌐 *www.nevissuntours.com.*

Queen City ATV Adventures

ADVENTURE TOURS | FAMILY | Go off-roading and see the island from a different view point while cruising on your own ATV. These lively tours are guided and full of adventure. Most hotels are happy to help guests set up this experience. ✉ *Charlestown* ☎ *869/667–7610* 🌐 *www.facebook.com/qcaanevis.*

HIKING

The center of the island is Nevis Peak—also known as Mt. Nevis—which soars 3,232 feet and is flanked by Hurricane Hill on the north and Saddle Hill on the south. If you plan to scale Nevis Peak, a daylong affair, it's highly recommended that you go with a guide. Your hotel can arrange it (and a picnic lunch) for you. The 9-mile (15-km) **Upper Round Road Trail** was constructed in the late 1600s and cleared and restored by the Nevis Historical and Conservation Society. It connects the Golden Rock Plantation Inn, on the east side of the island, with Nisbet Plantation Beach Club, on the northern tip. The trail encompasses numerous vegetation zones, including pristine rain forest, and impressive plantation ruins. The original cobblestones, walls, and ruins are still evident in many places.

Sunrise Tours

HIKING & WALKING | Run by Lynell and Earla Liburd (and their son Kervin), Sunrise Tours offers a range of hiking trips, but their most popular is Devil's Copper, a rock configuration full of ghostly legends. Local people gave it its name because at one time the water was hot—a volcanic thermal stream. The area features pristine waterfalls and splendid bird-watching. They also do a Nevis village walk, a Hamilton Estate Walk, a Charlestown tour, an Amerindian walk along the wild southeast Atlantic coast, and trips to the rain forest and Nevis Peak. They love highlighting Nevisian heritage, explaining time-honored cooking techniques, the many uses of dried grasses, and medicinal plants. Hikes range from $25 to $40 per person, and you receive a certificate of achievement. ☎ *869/469–2758* 🌐 *www.nevisnaturetours.com.*

HORSEBACK RIDING

Nevis Equestrian Centre

HORSEBACK RIDING | The Nevis Equestrian Centre offers leisurely beach rides as well as more demanding canters through the lush hills, starting at $85. Lessons are sometimes available ($30 group, $40 private). ✉ *Clifton Estate, Nevis Main Rd., Clifton Estate, Cotton Ground* ☎ *869/662–9118* 🌐 *www.nevishorseback.com.*

Chapter 19

SAINT LUCIA

Updated by
Diane Bair

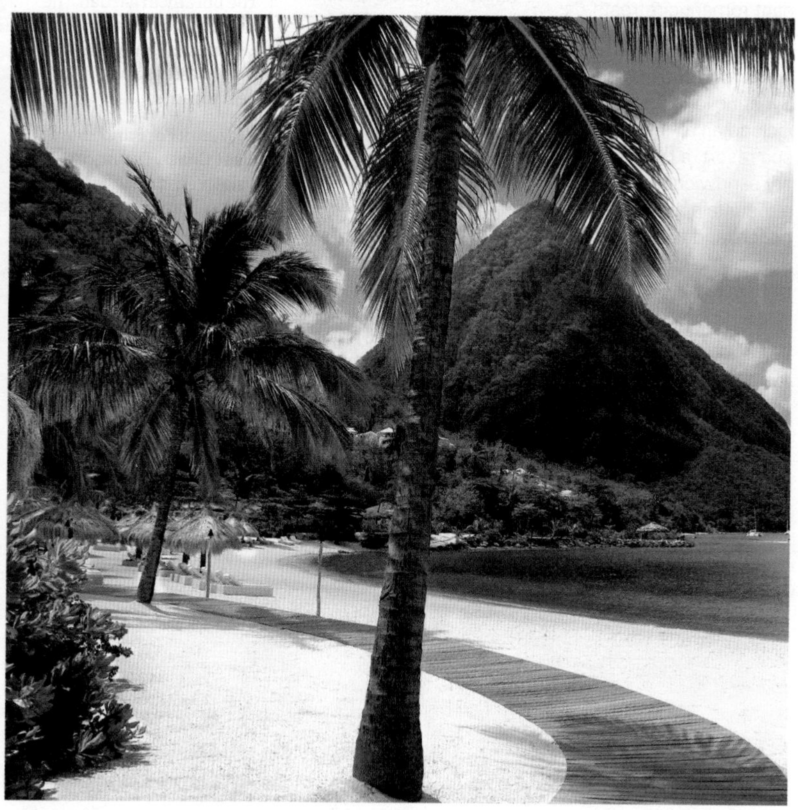

Sights	Restaurants	Hotels	Shopping	Nightlife
★★★★★	★★★★★	★★★★★	★★★☆☆	★★★☆☆

WELCOME TO SAINT LUCIA

TOP REASONS TO GO

★ **The Natural Beauty:** Magnificent, lush scenery makes Saint Lucia one of the most beautiful Caribbean islands.

★ **The Romance:** A popular honeymoon spot, Saint Lucia has abundant romantic retreats.

★ **Indulgent Accommodations:** Sybaritic lodging options include an all-inclusive spa resort, a posh sanctuary sandwiched between a mountain and the beach, and two resorts with prime locations between the Pitons.

★ **The Music:** Performers and fans from around the world come for the annual Saint Lucia Jazz and Arts Festival.

★ **The Welcome:** The friendly Saint Lucians love sharing their island and their cultural heritage with visitors.

Saint Lucia, 27 miles (43½ km) by 14 miles (22½ km), is a volcanic island covered to a large extent by lush rain forest, much of which is protected as a national park. The most notable geological features are the Pitons, half-mile-high twin peaks designated a UNESCO World Heritage Site in 2004.

1 Rodney Bay and the North. The lovely harbor has a marina, great restaurants, and a few places to stay. Some of the most luxurious resorts and a popular public golf course are at Cap Estate, in the far north.

2 Castries. The lively capital city has an active market and small hotels; lovely resorts are tucked into the coastline.

3 Marigot Bay. Between Castries and Soufrière, the "village" surrounding the man-made lagoon has an active marina, large resorts and small hotels, lots of restaurants, and shopping.

4 Soufrière and the Southwest Coast. The island's oldest town is also the location of the Pitons, the botanical garden, the drive-in volcano, and waterfalls. There are also great resorts and restaurants.

5 Vieux Fort and the East Coast. In and around relatively quiet Vieux Fort—home to the airport and a pair of resorts—you can explore some of the island's unique ecosystems.

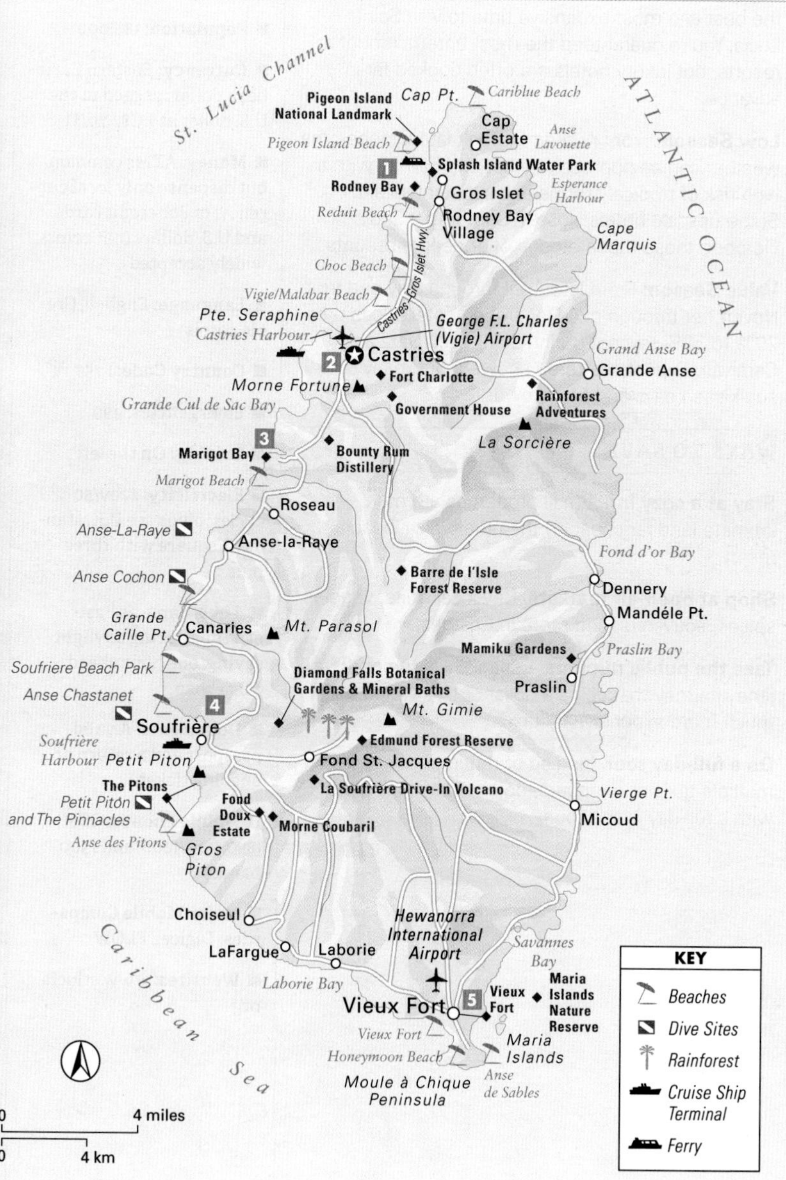
St. Lucia Channel
ATLANTIC OCEAN
Caribbean Sea
Pigeon Island National Landmark
Cap Pt.
Cariblue Beach
Cap Estate
Anse Lavouette
Pigeon Island Beach
Splash Island Water Park
Rodney Bay
Gros Islet
Esperance Harbour
Reduit Beach
Rodney Bay Village
Cape Marquis
Choc Beach
Castries–Gros Islet Hwy.
Vigie/Malabar Beach
Pte. Seraphine
George F.L. Charles (Vigie) Airport
Castries Harbour
Castries
Grand Anse Bay
Grande Anse
Morne Fortune
Fort Charlotte
Grande Cul de Sac Bay
Government House
Rainforest Adventures
La Sorcière
Marigot Bay
Bounty Rum Distillery
Marigot Beach
Roseau
Anse-La-Raye
Anse-la-Raye
Fond d'or Bay
Anse Cochon
Barre de l'Isle Forest Reserve
Dennery
Mandéle Pt.
Grande Caille Pt.
Canaries
Mt. Parasol
Mamiku Gardens
Praslin Bay
Soufriere Beach Park
Diamond Falls Botanical Gardens & Mineral Baths
Praslin
Anse Chastanet
Mt. Gimie
Soufrière
Soufrière Harbour
Edmund Forest Reserve
Petit Piton
Fond St. Jacques
The Pitons
Petit Pitón and The Pinnacles
Fond Doux Estate
La Soufrière Drive-In Volcano
Vierge Pt.
Morne Coubaril
Micoud
Anse des Pitons
Gros Piton
Choiseul
Hewanorra International Airport
Savannes Bay
LaFargue
Laborie
Laborie Bay
Vieux Fort
Maria Islands Nature Reserve
Vieux Fort
Vieux Fort
Maria Islands
Honeymoon Beach
Anse de Sables
Moule à Chique Peninsula
0
4 miles
0
4 km
1
2
3
4
5
KEY
Beaches
Dive Sites
Rainforest
Cruise Ship Terminal
Ferry

ISLAND SNAPSHOT

WHEN TO GO

High Season: Mid-December through mid-April is the best and most expensive time to visit Saint Lucia. You're guaranteed the most entertainment at resorts, but luxury hotels are often booked far in advance.

Low Season: From August through late October, the weather can be oppressively hot and humid, with a high risk of tropical storms and substantial rain. Some upscale hotels close in September and October; those that are open offer deep discounts.

Value Season: From late April through July and from November through mid-December, hotel prices drop 20% to 50% (except during Saint Lucia Jazz and Carnival). Expect scattered showers but many sun-kissed days and few crowds.

WAYS TO SAVE

Stay at a cozy inn. Small properties are more intimate (and far cheaper) than the typical beach resort.

Shop at open-air markets. Buy local fruits, veggies, spices, souvenirs, and more in Castries.

Take the public minibus. Especially in the north, a jitney journey that costs a dollar or two would be much more expensive by taxi.

Do a full-day tour. Instead of renting a car or taking multiple taxis or minitours, do an attractions blitz with a full-day island tour.

AT A GLANCE

- **Capital:** Castries
- **Population:** 184,000
- **Currency:** Eastern Caribbean dollar; pegged to the U.S. dollar at EC$2.70/$1
- **Money:** ATMs common but dispense only local currency; major credit cards and U.S. dollars (not coins) widely accepted
- **Language:** English, Creole patois
- **Country Code:** 1 758
- **Emergencies:** 999
- **Driving:** On the left
- **Electricity:** 220v/50 cycles; plugs are U.K. standard, square with three pins
- **Time:** Same as Eastern time during daylight saving; one hour ahead otherwise
- **Documents:** A valid passport and a return or ongoing ticket
- **Mobile Phones:** GSM (850, 900, 1800, and 1900 bands)
- **Major Mobile Companies:** Digicel, FLOW
- **Websites:** www.stlucia.org

A verdant, mountainous island located halfway between Martinique and St. Vincent, Saint Lucia has evolved into one of the Caribbean's most popular vacation destinations—particularly for honeymooners and other romantics enticed by the island's striking natural beauty, many splendid resorts and appealing inns, and welcoming atmosphere.

The capital city of Castries and nearby villages in the northwest are home to 40% of the 184,000 Saint Lucians. This area, Cap Estate and Rodney Bay Village (farther north), Marigot Bay (just south of the capital), and Soufrière (southwestern coast) are the destinations of most vacationers. In central and southwestern areas, dense rain forest, jungle-covered mountains, and vast banana plantations dominate the landscape. A tortuous road follows most of the coastline, bisecting small villages, cutting through mountains, and passing fertile valleys. Petit Piton and Gros Piton, unusual twin peaks that anchor the southwestern coast and rise up to 2,600 feet, are familiar landmarks for sailors and aviators, as well as a UNESCO World Heritage Site. Divers are attracted to the reefs in the National Marine Reserve between the Pitons and extending north past Soufrière, the capital during French colonial times. Most of the natural tourist attractions are in this area, along with several fine resorts and inns.

The pirate François Le Clerc, nicknamed Jambe de Bois (Wooden Leg) for obvious reasons, was the first European "settler." In the late 16th century Le Clerc holed up on Pigeon Island, just off Saint Lucia's northernmost point, using it as a staging ground for attacking passing ships. Now, Pigeon Island National Landmark is a public park connected by a causeway to the mainland; Sandals Grande Saint Lucian Spa & Beach Resort, one of the largest resorts in Saint Lucia, and the Landings, a luxury villa community, sprawl along that causeway.

Like most of its Caribbean neighbors, Saint Lucia was first inhabited by Arawaks and then the Carib people. British settlers attempted to colonize the island twice in the early 1600s, but it wasn't until 1651, after the French West India Company suppressed the local Caribs, that Europeans gained a foothold. For 150 years, battles between the French and the British over the island were frequent, with a dizzying 14 changes in power before the British finally took possession in 1814. The Europeans established sugar plantations, using slaves from West Africa to work the fields. By 1838, when the slaves were emancipated, more than 90% of the population was of African descent—roughly the same proportion as today.

On February 22, 1979, Saint Lucia became an independent state within the British Commonwealth of Nations, with a resident governor-general appointed by the Queen. Still, the island appears to have retained more relics of French influence—notably the island's patois, cuisine, village names, and surnames—than of the British. Most likely, that's because the British contribution primarily involved the English language, the educational and legal systems, and the political structure, whereas the French culture historically had more influence on the arts—culinary, dance, and music. Speaking of music, Saint Lucians love jazz—and, interestingly, country music—while the beat of Caribbean music also resonates throughout the island.

MAJOR REGIONS

Except for a small area in the extreme northeast, one main highway circles all of Saint Lucia. The road snakes along the coast, cuts across mountains, makes hairpin turns and sheer drops, and reaches dizzying heights. It takes at least four hours to drive the whole loop. Even at a leisurely pace with frequent sightseeing stops, and whether you're driving or being driven, the curvy roads make it a tiring drive in a single outing.

Between Castries and Cap Estate, in the far north, the road is mainly flat. The area is built up with businesses, resorts, and residences, so the two-lane road is often clogged with traffic—especially just north of **Castries** and around **Rodney Bay Village** but less as you approach Pigeon Island and Cap Estate. Frequent bus service is available on this route.

The West Coast Road between Castries and **Soufrière** (a 1½-hour journey) has steep hills and sharp turns, but it's well marked and incredibly scenic. South of Castries, the road tunnels through Morne Fortune, skirts the island's largest banana plantation (more than 127 varieties of bananas, called "figs" in this part of the Caribbean, grow on the island) and the road to **Marigot Bay,** and then passes through tiny fishing villages. Just north of Soufrière, the road negotiates the island's fruit basket, where most of the mangoes, breadfruit, tomatoes, limes, and oranges are grown. In the mountainous region that forms a backdrop for Soufrière, you will notice 3,118-foot Mt. Gimie (pronounced Jimmy), Saint Lucia's highest peak. Approaching Soufrière, you'll have spectacular views of the Pitons; the plume of smoke wafting out of the thickly forested mountainside just east of Soufrière emanates from the so-called drive-in volcano.

The landscape changes dramatically between the Pitons and **Vieux Fort** on the island's southeastern tip. Along the South Coast Road traveling southeasterly from Soufrière, the terrain starts as steep mountainside with dense vegetation, progresses to undulating hills, and finally becomes rather flat and comparatively arid. Anyone arriving at Hewanorra International Airport, which is in Vieux Fort, and staying at a resort near Soufrière will travel along this route, a journey of about 45 minutes each way.

From Vieux Fort north to Castries, a 1½-hour drive, the East Coast Road twists through Micoud, Dennery, and other coastal villages. It then winds up, down, and around mountains, crosses Barre de l'Isle Ridge, and slices through the rain forest. Much of the scenery is breathtaking. The Atlantic Ocean pounds against rocky cliffs, and acres and acres of bananas and coconut palms blanket the hillsides. If you arrive at Hewanorra and stay at a resort in Marigot Bay, Castries, Rodney Bay, or Cap Estate, you'll travel along the East Coast Road.

Planning

Getting Here and Around

AIR

American Airlines flies nonstop from Charlotte, Chicago, Philadelphia, and Miami to Hewanorra (UVF) in Vieux Fort, with connecting service from New York and other major cities. Delta flies nonstop from Atlanta to UVF. JetBlue flies nonstop to UVF from Boston and New York (JFK). United flies nonstop to UVF from Newark and Chicago. LIAT flies to George F. L. Charles Airport (SLU) in Castries from several neighboring islands. Air Canada and Westjet both offer direct flights from Toronto. British Airways flies directly from London Gatwick.

Airports and Transfers. Saint Lucia has two airports. Hewanorra International Airport (UVF), which accommodates large jet aircraft, is at the southeastern tip of the island in Vieux Fort. George F. L. Charles Airport (SLU), also referred to as Vigie Airport, is at Vigie Point in Castries in the northwestern part of the island and accommodates only small prop aircraft due to its location and runway limitations.

Some large resorts—particularly the all-inclusive ones—and package tour operators provide round-trip airport transfers. That's a significant amenity if you're landing at Hewanorra, as the one-way taxi fare is expensive: about $80 to $100 for four passengers for the 90-minute ride to Castries and the north; about $75–$80 for the 45-minute ride to Soufrière. Taxis are always available at the airports.

If you land at George F. L. Charles Airport, it's a short drive to resorts in the north and about 20 minutes to Marigot Bay but more than an hour on a winding road to Soufrière.

Some people opt for a helicopter transfer between Hewanorra and Castries, a quick 12-minute ride with a beautiful view at a one-way cost of $165 per passenger. Helicopters operate in daylight hours only and carry up to six passengers; luggage usually follows by ground transportation.

AIRPORTS George F. L. Charles Airport. *(SLU) ✉ Vigie ☎ 758/457–6149 🌐 www.georgeflcharlesairport.com.* **Hewanorra International Airport.** *(UVF) ✉ Vieux Fort ☎ 758/457–6160 🌐 www.hewanorrainternationalairport.com.*

AIR TRANSFERS St. Lucia Helicopters. *✉ Sunny Acres, George F. L. Charles Airport, Vigie ☎ 758/453–6950 🌐 www.stluciahelicopters.com.*

BOAT AND FERRY

Visitors combining a visit to Saint Lucia with a visit to Martinique, Dominica, or Guadeloupe may opt for the L'Express des Iles fast ferry, a modern, high-speed catamaran that calls in Castries four days a week. The trip between Saint Lucia and Fort de France, Martinique, takes 1½ hours; Roseau, Dominica, 3½ hours; and Point à Pitre, Guadeloupe, 5½ hours.

Water taxis are available to shuttle passengers between Soufrière and Marigot Bay or Castries. When cruise ships are in port in Castries, a water taxi shuttles back and forth between Pointe Seraphine on the north side of the harbor and La Place Carenage on the south side of the harbor for $2 per person each way.

CONTACTS Feel Good Water Taxi & Tours. *✉ 14 Victoria St., Soufrière ☎ 758/721–2174 🌐 www.feelgoodwatertaxiandtours.com.* **Israel King Water Taxi & Tours.** *✉ Rodney Bay Marina, Rodney Bay ☎ 758/717–3301 🌐 www.israelkingwatertaxi.com.* **L'Express des Iles.** *✉ Castries Ferry Terminal, Castries ☎ 758/456–5000 🌐 coxcoltd.com/lexpress-des-iles/.* **Solomon Water Taxi & Tours.** *✉ Boulevard St., Soufrière ☎ 758/384-4087 🌐 www.solomon-saintlucia.com.*

BUS

Privately owned and operated minivans constitute Saint Lucia's bus system, an inexpensive and efficient means of transportation used primarily by local people. Buses have green number plates beginning with the letter *M.* They are a good way to travel between Castries and the Rodney Bay area; the fare is EC$2.50 (ideally paid in local currency). You can also travel from Castries to Soufrière or Vieux Fort (two-plus hours, EC$10), but those are definitely arduous rides. Wait at a marked stop and hail the passing minivan. Let the conductor or driver know where you need to go, and he'll stop at the appropriate place.

CAR

Roads in Saint Lucia are winding and mountainous, except north of Castries, making driving a challenge for timid or apprehensive drivers and exhausting for everyone else. Between Castries and Rodney Bay, traffic jams are not uncommon, particularly during rush hours. You drive on the left, British-style. Seat belts are required, and speed limits (32 mph/51 kmh in urban areas) are enforced, especially in and around Castries.

Car Rentals. To rent a car you must be at least 25 years old and provide a valid driver's license and a credit card. If you don't have an international driver's license, you must buy a temporary Saint Lucia driving permit at the car-rental office for $20 (EC$54), which is valid for three months. Car-rental rates are usually quoted in U.S. dollars and start at $50 per day or $300 per week.

CONTACTS Avis. ✉ *Hewanorra International Airport, Vieux Fort* ☎ *758/454–6325, 758/452–2046 George F. L. Charles Airport* 🌐 *www.avis.com.* **Cool Breeze Jeep/Car Rental.** ✉ *Soufrière* ☎ *758/459–7729* 🌐 *www.coolbreezecarrental.com.* **Cost Less Rent-a-Car.** ✉ *Harmony Suites, Rodney Bay* ☎ *758/285-2183, 908/818–8506 in U.S.* 🌐 *www.costless-rentacar.com.* **Courtesy Car Rentals.** ✉ *Rodney Bay* ☎ *758/452–8140, 315/519–7684 in U.S.* 🌐 *www.courtesycarrentals.com.* **Hertz.** ✉ *Hewanorra International Airport, Vieux Fort* ☎ *758/454–9636* 🌐 *www.hertz.com.*

TAXI

Fully licensed taxis have number plates beginning with *TX.* They are unmetered, although fares are fairly standard. Sample fares for up to two passengers are: Castries to Rodney Bay, $20; Rodney Bay to Cap Estate, $25; Castries to Cap Estate, $20; Castries to Marigot Bay, $30; Castries to Anse La Raye, $60; Castries to Soufrière, $80; and Castries to Vieux Fort, $75; and Soufriere to Vieux Fort, $65. Charge per extra passenger ranges from $5 to $10. Always ask the driver to quote the price before you get in, and be sure that you both understand whether it's quoted in EC or U.S. dollars. Drivers are generally careful, knowledgeable, and courteous. Drivers can also be hired for an hourly rate of about $40 per hour for up to three people.

Beaches

The sand on Saint Lucia's beaches ranges from warm gold to silvery black, and the island has some of the best off-the-beach snorkeling in the Caribbean—especially along the western coast just north of Soufrière.

Saint Lucia's longest, broadest, and most popular beaches are in the north, which is also the flattest part of this mountainous island and the location of most resorts, restaurants, and nightlife. Many of the island's biggest resorts front the beaches from Choc Bay to Rodney Bay and north to Cap Estate. Elsewhere, tiny coves with inviting crescents of sand offer great swimming and snorkeling opportunities. Beaches are all public, but hotels flank many along the northwestern coast. A few secluded stretches of beach on the southwestern coast, south of Marigot Bay and accessible primarily by boat, are popular swimming and snorkeling stops on catamaran day sails or powerboat sightseeing trips. Don't swim along the windward (eastern) coast, as the Atlantic Ocean is too rough—but the views are spectacular. Coconut Bay Beach Resort and Serenity by Coconut Bay, both in Vieux Fort, share a beautiful beach facing the Atlantic at the southernmost tip of the island. The water is rough—but an artificial reef makes it safe for swimming and water sports, especially kitesurfing.

Festivals and Events

Anse la Raye Seafood Friday. For a taste of Saint Lucian village life, head for this street festival, held every Friday night beginning at 6:30. The main street in this tiny fishing village—about halfway between Castries and Soufrière—is closed to vehicles, and residents prepare what they know best: fish cakes, grilled or stewed fish, hot bakes (biscuits), roasted corn, boiled crayfish, and lobster (grilled before your eyes). Prices range from a few cents for a fish cake or bake to $15 or $20 for a whole lobster. Walk around, eat, chat with locals, and listen to live music until the wee hours. 🌐 www.facebook.com/AnseLaRayeSeafoodFriday

Gros Islet Jump-Up. The island's largest street party is a Friday-night ritual. Huge speakers set up on the street blast Caribbean music all night long. Sometimes there are live bands. When you take a break from dancing, you can buy barbecue fish or chicken, rotis (turnovers filled with meat and/or vegetables), beer, and soda from villagers who set up grills along the roadside. It's the ultimate carnival fête. 🌐 www.facebook.com/fridaystreetparty

Health and Safety

Dengue, chikungunya, and zika have all been reported throughout the Caribbean. We recommend that you protect yourself from these mosquito-borne illnesses by keeping your skin covered and/or wearing mosquito repellent. The mosquitoes that transmit these viruses are as active by day as they are by night. Beyond that, use sunblock to protect yourself from sunburn, as the sun is more intense than you think. The water in Saint Lucia is safe to drink, although bottled water is always available.

Hotels and Resorts

Nearly all Saint Lucia's resorts and small inns face or are near unspoiled beaches or are hidden away on secluded coves or tucked into forested hillsides in three locations along the calm Caribbean (western) coast. They're in the greater Castries area between Marigot Bay, a few miles south of the city, and Labrelotte Bay in the north; in and around Rodney Bay Village and north to Cap Estate; and in and around Soufrière on the southwest coast near the Pitons. There are two sister resorts in Vieux Fort, near Hewanorra. The advantage of being in the north is that you have access to a wider range of restaurants and nightlife; in the south, you are close to most of Saint Lucia's natural wonders.

Beach Resorts: Most people—particularly honeymooners—choose to stay in one of Saint Lucia's many beach resorts, the majority of which are upscale and fairly pricey. Several are all-inclusive, including three Sandals resorts, two Sunswept resorts (The Body Holiday and Rendezvous), St. James's Club Morgan Bay, and East Winds Inn, Coconut Bay Beach Resort, and Serenity at Coconut Bay. Others may offer an all-inclusive option.

Small Inns: If you're looking for something more intimate and perhaps less expensive, a locally owned inn or small hotel is a good option; it may or may not be directly on the beach.

Villas and Condos: Luxury villa and condo communities are an important part of the accommodations mix on Saint Lucia, as they can be an economical option for families, other groups, or couples vacationing together. Several communities have opened in recent years, and more are on the way. The villa units themselves are privately owned, but nonowners can rent individual units directly from the property managers for a vacation or short-term stay, much like reserving hotel accommodations. Units with fully equipped kitchens, up to three bedrooms, and as many baths run $200 to $2,500 per night, depending on the size and the season.

Local real-estate agencies will arrange vacation rentals of privately owned villas and condos that are fully equipped. Most private villas are in the hills of Cap Estate in the very north of the island, at Rodney Bay or Bois d'Orange, or in Soufrière among Saint Lucia's natural treasures. Some are within walking distance of a beach.

All rental villas are staffed with a cook who specializes in local cuisine and a housekeeper; in some cases, a caretaker lives on the property, and a gardener and night watchman are on staff. All properties have telephones, and most will have Internet access. Telephones may be barred against outgoing overseas calls; plan to use a phone card or calling card. Most villas also have TVs and other entertainment options and/or connectivity. All private villas have a swimming pool; condos share a community pool. Vehicles are generally not included in the rates, but rental cars can be arranged for and delivered to the villa upon request. Linens and basic supplies (such as bath soap, toilet paper, and dish detergent) are included. Pre-arrival grocery stocking can be arranged.

CONTACTS Airbnb. ☎ *415/800–5959 in U.S.* 🌐 *www.airbnb.com.* **Discover Villas of Saint Lucia.** ✉ *Cap Dr., Cap Estate* ☎ *758/484–3066, 758/450–0002* 🌐 *discovervillasstlucia.com.* **Blue Sky Luxury.** ✉ *Cap Estate* ☎ *758/450–8240* 🌐 *www.blueskyluxurystlucia.com.*

Hotel reviews have been shortened. For full information, visit Fodors.com.

What It Costs in U.S. Dollars

$	$$	$$$	$$$$
RESTAURANTS			
under $12	$12–$20	$21–$30	over $30
HOTELS			
under $275	$275–$375	$376–$475	over $475

Nightlife

Most resort hotels have entertainment—island music, calypso singers, or steel bands, as well as disco, karaoke, or staff/guest talent shows—every night in high season and a night or two each week in the off-season. Otherwise, Rodney Bay Village is the best bet for nightlife. The many restaurants and bars there attract a crowd nearly every night.

Restaurants

Bananas, mangoes, passion fruit, plantains, breadfruit, okra, avocados, limes, pumpkins, cucumbers, papaya, yams, christophenes (also called chayote), and coconuts are among the fresh fruits and vegetables that grace Saint Lucian menus. The French influence is strong, and most chefs cook with a creole flair. Resort buffets and restaurant fare include standards like steaks, chops, pasta, and pizza—and every menu lists fresh fish along with the ever-popular lobster, which is available in season—August through March.

Soups and stews are traditionally prepared in a coal pot—unique to Saint Lucia—a rustic clay casserole on a matching clay stand that holds the hot coals. Chicken and pork dishes and barbecues are also popular here. As they do throughout the Caribbean, local vendors set up barbecues along the roadside, at street fairs, and at Friday-night "jump-ups" and do a bang-up business selling grilled fish or chicken legs, bakes (fried biscuits), and beverages. Piton is the local brew; Bounty, the local rum. You can get a full meal for less than $10.

Guests at Saint Lucia's all-inclusive resorts take meals at hotel restaurants—which are generally quite good and in some cases exceptional—but it's fun when vacationing to try some of the local restaurants, as well, for lunch when sightseeing or for a special night out.

What to Wear: Dress on Saint Lucia is casual but conservative. Shorts are usually fine during the day, but bathing suits and immodest clothing are frowned upon anywhere but at the beach. Nude or topless sunbathing is prohibited. In the evening, the mood is casually elegant, but even the fanciest places generally expect only a collared shirt and long pants for men and a sundress or slacks for women.

Shopping

The island's best-known products are artwork and wood carvings, straw mats, clay pottery, and clothing and household articles made from batik and silk-screened fabrics that are designed and produced in island workshops. You can also take home straw hats and baskets and locally grown cocoa, coffee, spices, sauces, and flavorings.

Duty-free shopping areas are at **Pointe Seraphine,** an attractive Spanish-motif complex on Castries Harbour with a dozen shops that are open mainly when a cruise ship is in port, and **La Place Carenage,** an inviting three-story complex on the opposite side of the harbor a short walk from the market. You can also find duty-free items at stores in Baywalk Mall and J.Q.'s Rodney Bay Mall, in a few small shops at the arcade at the Mystique Royal Saint Lucia hotel—all in Rodney Bay Village—and, of course, in the departure lounge at Hewanorra International Airport. You must present your passport and airline ticket to purchase items at the duty-free price.

Vieux Fort Plaza, near Hewanorra International Airport in Vieux Fort, is the main shopping center in the southern part of Saint Lucia. It has a bank, supermarket, bookstore, toy shop, and clothing stores. Pointe Seraphine is a duty-free shopping complex on the north side of the bay, about a 20-minute walk or 2-minute cab ride from the city center; a launch ferries passengers across the harbor when cruise ships are in port.

Visitor Information

CONTACTS Saint Lucia Tourism Authority. ☎ *800/210-0921, 800/456–3984 in U.S., 758/458–7101* 🌐 *www.stlucia.org.*

Weddings

Marriage licenses cost $125 with a required three-day waiting period or $200 with no waiting period, plus $60 for the associated registrar and certificate fees. There is no residency requirement, but you will need to produce valid passports and original or certified copies of birth certificates and, if applicable, divorce decrees or death certificates. Some resorts offer free weddings when combined with a honeymoon stay.

Rodney Bay and the North

Hotels, popular restaurants, a huge mall, and dance clubs surround a natural bay and an 80-acre man-made lagoon named for Admiral George Rodney, who sailed the British navy out of Gros Islet in 1780 to attack and ultimately destroy the French fleet. With 253 slips and a 4½-acre boatyard, Rodney Bay Marina is one of the Caribbean's premier yachting centers; each December, it's the destination of the Atlantic Rally for Cruisers, a transatlantic sailing competition for racing yachts. Yacht charters and sightseeing day trips can be arranged at the marina. Rodney Bay Village is about 15 minutes north of Castries.

Sights

Pigeon Island National Landmark

BEACH | FAMILY | Jutting out from the northwest coast, Pigeon Island connects to the mainland via a causeway. Tales are told of the pirate Jambe de Bois (Wooden Leg), who once hid out on this 44-acre hilltop islet—a strategic point during the French and British struggles for control of Saint Lucia. Now Pigeon Island is a national park and a venue for concerts, festivals, and family gatherings. There are two small beaches with calm waters for swimming and snorkeling, a restaurant, and picnic areas. Scattered around the grounds are ruins of barracks, batteries, and garrisons that date from 18th-century French and English battles. In the Museum and Interpretative Centre, housed in the restored British officers' mess, a multimedia display explains the island's ecological and historical significance. The site is administered by the Saint Lucia National Trust. ✉ *Pigeon Island* ☎ *758/452–5005* 🌐 *www.slunatrust.org/sites/pigeon-island-national-landmark* 🎫 *$10.*

★ **Splash Island Water Park**

WATER PARK | FAMILY | The Eastern Caribbean's first open-water-sports park, installed just off Reduit Beach a dozen or so yards from the sand in front of Bay Gardens Beach Resort, thrills kids and adults alike—but mostly kids. They spend hours on the colorful, inflatable, modular features, which include a trampoline, climbing wall, swing, slide, hurdles, and water volleyball net. Children must be at least six, and everyone must wear a life vest. A team of lifeguards is on duty when the park is open. ✉ *Reduit Beach, Reduit Beach Rd., Rodney Bay* ✢ *Facing Bay Gardens Beach Resort* ☎ *758/457–8532* 🌐 *www.saintluciawaterpark.com* 🎫 *From $13 per hr.*

Beaches

Pigeon Island Beach

BEACH | FAMILY | This small beach within the national landmark, on the northwestern tip of Saint Lucia, has golden sand, a calm sea, and a view that extends from Rodney Bay to Martinique. It's a perfect spot for picnicking, and you can take a break from the sun by visiting the nearby Pigeon Island Museum and Interpretive Centre. **Amenities:** food and drink; toilets. **Best for:** snorkeling; solitude; swimming. ✉ *Pigeon Island National Landmark, Pigeon Island Causeway, Pigeon Island* 🎫 *$10 park admission.*

★ **Reduit Beach**

BEACH | FAMILY | Many feel that Reduit (pronounced *red-WEE*) is the island's finest beach. The long stretch of golden sand that frames Rodney Bay is within walking distance of many hotels and restaurants in Rodney Bay Village. Bay Gardens Beach Resort and Mystique St. Lucia by Royalton face the beachfront; Harmony Suites is across the road. At Mystique's water-sports center, you can rent sports equipment and beach chairs and take windsurfing or waterskiing lessons. Kids (and adults alike) love Splash Island Water Park, an open-water inflatable playground near Bay Gardens Beach Resort with a trampoline, climbing wall, swing, slide, and more. **Amenities:** food and drink; toilets; water sports. **Best for:** snorkeling; sunset; swimming; walking; windsurfing. ✉ *Rodney Bay.*

Restaurants

Buzz Seafood & Grill

$$$ | **SEAFOOD** | Opposite the Mystique Royal St. Lucia hotel and Reduit Beach, this dining spot is part of Rodney Bay's "restaurant central." After cool drinks and warm appetizers at the bar, diners make their way to the dining room or garden for some serious seafood or a good steak, West Indian pepperpot stew, spicy Moroccan-style lamb shanks, or simple chicken and chips. The seared yellowfin tuna, potato-crusted red snapper, and seafood Creole are big hits, too. **Known for:** flashy tropical cocktails; indoor and outdoor seating; happy hour every evening. [$] *Average main: US$30* ✉ *Reduit Beach Rd., Rodney Bay* ☎ *758/458–0450* 🌐 *www.facebook.com/buzzrestaurant.*

★ The Cliff at Cap

$$$$ | **ECLECTIC** | High on top of a cliff at the northern tip of Saint Lucia, the open-air dining room at Cap Maison welcomes diners to what executive chef Craig Jones calls "nouveau" French–West Indian cuisine. True, he incorporates local vegetables, fruits, herbs, and spices with the best meats and fresh-caught seafood you'll find on the island; but the technique and presentation—and the service—lean more toward the French. **Known for:** daily (pricey) tastings in the wine cellar; superb dining; panoramic view. [$] *Average main: US$36* ✉ *Cap Maison, Smuggler's Cove Dr., Cap Estate* ☎ *758/457–8681* 🌐 *www.thecliffatcap.com.*

★ Jacques Waterfront Dining

$$$$ | **FRENCH** | Chef-owner Jacky Rioux creates magical dishes in his waterfront restaurant set within the gardens of Harmony Suites Hotel in Rodney Bay. The cooking is decidedly French, as is Rioux, but fresh produce and local spices create a memorable fusion cuisine. **Known for:** jazz brunch on Sunday; long-standing reputation for quality cuisine; waterfront location. [$] *Average main: US$34* ✉ *Harmony Suites Hotel, Reduit Beach Ave., Rodney Bay* ☎ *758/458–1900* 🌐 *www.jacquesrestaurant.com* 🕓 *No dinner Sun. No lunch Mon.*

The Naked Fisherman

$$$$ | **SEAFOOD** | The rather sophisticated beachside seafood restaurant at Cap Maison is tucked into a cliff surrounding a crescent of sand at the northern tip of Saint Lucia. During the day, stare across the sea as far as Martinique; in the evening, candlit lanterns grace the alfresco dining deck as the surf gently laps the sand. **Known for:** 92 steps down to the beach (and back up); sophisticated cuisine on the beach; excellent wine list. [$] *Average main: US$35* ✉ *Cap Maison, Smugglers Cove Dr., Cap Estate* ☎ *758/457–8694* 🌐 *nakedfishermanstlucia.com.*

★ Tao

$$$$ | **ASIAN FUSION** | For a special evening, head for this Cap Estate restaurant on the premises of BodyHoliday Saint Lucia resort. On a second-floor balcony at the edge of Cariblue Beach, you'll enjoy a pleasant breeze and a starry sky while you dine on fusion cuisine—mouthwatering Asian tastes with a Caribbean touch. **Known for:** romantic atmosphere; sophisticated cuisine; top-drawer service. [$] *Average main: US$35* ✉ *BodyHoliday Saint Lucia, Cariblue Beach, Cap Estate* ☎ *758/450–8551, 758/457–7800 hotel front desk* 🌐 *www.thebodyholiday.com* 🕓 *No lunch.*

Ti Bananne

$$$ | **CARIBBEAN** | **FAMILY** | Poolside at the Coco Palm hotel, this alfresco bistro and bar attracts mostly hotel guests for breakfast but a wider clientele for lunch and dinner—and happy hour—especially when there's live entertainment. The dinner menu focuses on Caribbean favorites such as jerk baby back ribs with guava barbecue sauce, perfectly grilled fish or steak with coconut curry sauce and local vegetables, a huge lamb shank, and always a pasta dish or two. **Known for:** poolside snacks; easy, breezy dining; friendly bar. *Average main: US$27 Coco Palm Resort, Off Reduit Beach Ave., Rodney Bay 758/456–2800 www.coco-resorts.com.*

Hotels

Bay Gardens Beach Resort & Spa

$$$ | **RESORT** | **FAMILY** | One of four Bay Gardens properties in Rodney Bay Village, this family-friendly resort has a prime location on beautiful Reduit Beach and its six three-story buildings wrap around a large, lagoon-style pool. **Pros:** perfect beach location; kitchenettes are great for families and those who like to self-cater; complimentary passes to Splash Island Water Park just offshore. **Cons:** some rooms a bit tired; plan to eat elsewhere; cruise passengers with day passes crowd the beach (and beach chairs). *Rooms from: US$383 Reduit Beach Ave., Rodney Bay 758/457–8514, 877/620–3200 in U.S. www.baygardensresorts.com 78 rooms No Meals.*

Bay Gardens Hotel

$ | **HOTEL** | Modern, colorful, and surrounded by pretty flower gardens, the hotel is a short walk to beautiful Reduit Beach (shuttle service also available), several popular restaurants, and shopping malls. **Pros:** complimentary passes to Splash Island Water Park; close to nightspots and shopping; unlimited use of Bay Gardens Beach Club loungers and nonmotorized water sports. **Cons:** on the main road, so noise may be an issue for some rooms; heavy focus on business travelers; not beachfront, although there's a beach shuttle. *Rooms from: US$206 Castries–Gros Islet Hwy., Rodney Bay 758/457–8010, 877/620–3200 in U.S. www.baygardensresorts.com 87 rooms Free Breakfast.*

★ BodyHoliday Saint Lucia

$$$$ | **RESORT** | At this adults-only wellness resort on picturesque Cariblue Beach—where daily treatments are included in the rates—you can customize your own "body holiday" online even before you leave home. **Pros:** interesting activities, such as archery, include free instruction; special rates for solo travelers; all rooms have at least a partial ocean view. **Cons:** no room service; lots of steps to the spa, though you can take an elevator; expensive (but includes a lot of amenities). *Rooms from: US$838 Cariblue Beach, Cap Estate 758/457–7800, 800/544–2883 www.thebodyholiday.com 155 rooms All-Inclusive.*

★ Calabash Cove Resort & Spa

$$$ | **RESORT** | The luxurious suites and Balinese-inspired cottages at this inviting boutique resort spill gently down a tropical hillside to a secluded beach on Bonaire Bay, just south of Rodney Bay. The private cottages, constructed of mahogany, stone, and other natural materials, all face the sea to take advantage of the sunset. **Pros:** wedding parties can reserve the entire resort; stylish, sophisticated, and friendly atmosphere; great food served in lovely alfresco setting. **Cons:** few on-site activities; steps to the cottages and beach may be difficult for those with mobility issues; the long, bone-crunching dirt road to the entrance. *Rooms from: US$430 Bonaire Estate, Marisule Estate Off Castries–Gros Islet Hwy., south of Rodney Bay 758/456–3500, 800/917–2683 in U.S. www.calabashcove.com 26 rooms Free Breakfast.*

★ Cap Maison

$$$$ | **RESORT** | **FAMILY** | Prepare to be spoiled by the doting staffers at this intimate villa resort—the luxurious service includes unpacking (if you wish) and a personal butler for any little needs that arise. **Pros:**; private and elegant with outstanding service; cocktails with a view at Cliff Bar or surf side at Rock Maison; rooftop plunge pools in most suites. **Cons:** meals are expensive (but delicious) with few nearby options; 92 steps to the beach; books up quickly in high season. *Rooms from: US$580 Smuggler's Cove Dr., Cap Estate 758/457–8670, 800/331-2713 in U.S. www.capmaison.com 49 rooms Free Breakfast.*

Coco Palm

$ | **HOTEL** | **FAMILY** | This popular hotel in Rodney Bay Village overlooks an inviting pool and a separate cozy guesthouse, Kreole Village, at the edge of the property. **Pros:** walk to restaurants, bars, and shopping in Rodney Bay Village; swim-up rooms; poolside entertainment. **Cons:** nightly music can be loud (until 10); skip the all-inclusive package, as good restaurants are nearby; not directly on the beach. *Rooms from: US$130 Off Reduit Beach Ave., Rodney Bay 758/456–2800 www.coco-resorts.com 103 rooms Free Breakfast.*

East Winds Saint Lucia

$$$$ | **RESORT** | Guests keep returning to this small, all-inclusive resort on a secluded beach halfway between Castries and Rodney Bay, where 12 acres of botanical gardens surround 30 gingerbread-style cottages, ocean-view rooms, and a beach house. **Pros:** peaceful and quiet; lovely beach; excellent dining. **Cons:** three-night minimum; very expensive; not the best choice for kids, though they're welcome. *Rooms from: US$650 La Brelotte Bay, Gros Islet 758/452–8212 www.eastwinds.com 30 suites All-Inclusive.*

Harmony Marina Suites

$ | **HOTEL** | Guests at this inexpensive, adults-only hotel are generally scuba divers, boaters, or others who don't need luxury but appreciate comfort and want to be on the waterfront. **Pros:** easy access to Reduit Beach; marina location with waterfront suites; walk to restaurants, nightspots, and shopping. **Cons:** waterfront rooms can be a little noisy; bathrooms need renovating; most rooms are fairly basic. *Rooms from: US$130 Flamboyant Dr., Rodney Bay Off Reduit Beach Ave. 758/452–8756, 888/790–5264 in U.S. www.harmonymarinasuites.net 30 rooms No Meals.*

★ The Landings Resort & Spa

$$$$ | **RESORT** | **FAMILY** | On 19 acres along the Pigeon Point Causeway at the northern edge of Rodney Bay, this villa resort surrounds a private, 34-slip marina where guests can dock their own yachts, literally, at their doorstep. **Pros:** kids' club and playground; spacious, beautifully appointed units; perfect for yachties, couples, families, even business travelers. **Cons:** all-inclusive option carries surcharges for some menu items and premium drinks; it's a hike to beach from some rooms; town-house atmosphere. *Rooms from: US$517 Pigeon Island Causeway, Gros Islet 758/458–7300, 866/252–0689 in U.S. www.landingsstlucia.com 80 suites Free Breakfast.*

Mystique by Royalton

$$ | **RESORT** | **FAMILY** | This beautifully situated all-suites resort on Saint Lucia's best beach caters to every whim—for the whole family. **Pros:** great location on Reduit Beach; two suites equipped for guests with disabilities; convenient to Rodney Bay restaurants, clubs, and shops. **Cons:** rooms ready for a little TLC; food and extras are pricey; get your snacks at the nearby supermarket. *Rooms from: US$295 Reduit Beach Ave., Rodney Bay 758/457–3131 www.mystiqueresorts.com 95 rooms No Meals.*

★ Sandals Grande St. Lucian

$$$$ | **RESORT** | Perched on the narrow Pigeon Island Causeway at Saint Lucia's northern tip, Sandals Grande offers panoramic views of Rodney Bay on one side and the Atlantic Ocean on the other. **Pros:** free scuba for certified divers; grand accommodations, especially the over-the-water bungalow suites; 12 restaurants and countless activities. **Cons:** while romantic, it's not peaceful or quiet; beach can be crowded; really long ride (at least 90 minutes) from/ to Hewanorra, but transfers are complimentary. *Rooms from: US$650* ✉ *Pigeon Island Causeway, Pigeon Island* ☎ *758/455–2000, 888/726-3257* 🌐 *www.sandals.com/grande-st-lucian* *311 rooms* *All-Inclusive.*

Nightlife

DANCE CLUBS

Most dance clubs with live bands have a cover charge of around $7 (EC$20), and the music usually starts at 11 pm.

Ultra Lounge

DANCE CLUBS | It's open all afternoon, but nights are when partygoers come to hang out, sip drinks, munch tapas, and dance in an ultra-contemporary atmosphere. ✉ *Reduit Beach Ave., Rodney Bay* ☎ *758/458–5872* 🌐 *www.facebook.com/ultraloungeslu/.*

Verve

DANCE CLUBS | At what is considered the hottest party spot in Rodney Bay Village, you can dance to the DJ's awesome vibes (and sometimes live bands) every night until 2 am (or later). ✉ *Reduit Beach Ave., Rodney Bay* ☎ *758/728-3666* 🌐 *www.facebook.com/Vervestlucia.*

Shopping

CLOTHING AND TEXTILES

Sea Island Cotton Shop

SOUVENIRS | High-quality T-shirts, clothing and resort wear, and colorful souvenirs are sold at reasonable prices and duty free. ✉ *Baywalk Mall, Reduit Beach Ave., Rodney Bay* ✥ *Off Castries–Gros Islet Hwy.* ☎ *758/452-3674* 🌐 *www.seaisland-saintlucia.com.*

SHOPPING MALLS

Baywalk Mall

SHOPPING CENTER | **FAMILY** | With more than 45 stores and a half-dozen restaurants, this two-level complex boasts boutiques, banks, a beauty salon, jewelry and souvenir stores, a large supermarket (great for snacks, picnic items, or a bottle of wine), a playground for kids, and the island's only (so far) casino. ✉ *Rodney Bay Ave., Rodney Bay* ☎ *758/452–6666* 🌐 *www.baywalkslu.com.*

J. Q.'s Shopping Mall

SHOPPING CENTER | Along with boutiques, restaurants, and other businesses that sell services and supplies, a large supermarket is the focal point here. ✉ *Corner Gros Islet Hwy. and Rodney Bay Village Strip* ☎ *758/458–0700* 🌐 *www.shop-jqmall.com.*

Castries

Castries, a busy commercial city that wraps around sheltered Castries Harbour, is Saint Lucia's capital; Castries Quarter, which stretches over 30 square miles, is home to some 70,000 residents. Morne Fortune rises sharply to the south of the city, creating a dramatic green backdrop. The charm of Castries lies almost entirely in its current liveliness rather than its history, because four fires between 1796 and 1948 destroyed most of the colonial buildings. Freighters (exporting bananas, coconut, cocoa, mace, nutmeg, and citrus fruits) and cruise ships come and go frequently, making Castries Harbour one of the Caribbean's busiest ports.

Sights

Antillia Brewing Company

BREWERY | Antillia brews handcrafted wheat beers, stout, and specialty ales in its brewery at Emerald Farm in Soufriere. Their niche is beer aged and brewed with citrus, passionfruit, cocoa nibs and other add-ins. You can take a tour of the brewery, but it's easier (and more fun) to enjoy a pint or two—or a flight—at the company's Antillia Beer Garden, adjacent to the cruise terminal at Pointe Seraphine in Castries, or at the TapShack on the beach at Anse Chastenet. ✉ *Odsan Industrial Park, Pointe Seraphine* ☎ *758/459–0844* 🌐 *www.facebook.com/antilliabrewing/.*

★ Castries Central Market

MARKET | FAMILY | Under a brilliant orange roof, this bustling market is at its liveliest on Saturday morning, when farmers bring their produce and spices to town, as they have for more than a century. (It's closed Sunday.) Next door to the produce market is the **Craft Market,** where you can buy pottery, wood carvings, handwoven straw articles, and innumerable souvenirs, trinkets, and gewgaws. At the **Vendors' Arcade,** across Peynier Street from the Craft Market, you'll find still more handicrafts and souvenirs. ✉ *55 John Compton Hwy., Castries.*

Cathedral of the Immaculate Conception

CHURCH | Directly across Laborie Street from Derek Walcott Square is the Roman Catholic Cathedral of the Immaculate Conception, which was built in 1897. Though it's rather somber on the outside, colorful murals by St. Lucian artist Dunstan St. Omer decorate the interior walls. The murals were reworked prior to the visit of Pope John Paul II in 1985. The church has an active parish and is open daily for both public viewing and religious services. ✉ *Cor. Micoud & Laborie Sts., Castries* ☎ *758/452–2272.*

Derek Walcott Square

PLAZA/SQUARE | This green oasis, bordered by Brazil, Laborie, Micoud, and Bourbon streets, honors the hometown poet who won the 1992 Nobel Prize in Literature—one of two Nobel laureates from Saint Lucia. The late Sir W. Arthur Lewis won the 1979 Nobel in economics. (Interestingly, both Nobel laureates shared the same birthday, January 23.) Some of the few 19th-century buildings that survived fire, wind, and rain can be seen on Brazil Street, the square's southern border. On the Laborie Street side, there's a huge, 400-year-old *saman* (monkeypod) tree with leafy branches that shade a good portion of the square. ✉ *Laborie St., Castries.*

Fort Charlotte

CEMETERY | Begun in 1764 by the French as the Citadelle du Morne Fortune, Fort Charlotte was completed after 20 years of battling and changing hands. Its old barracks and batteries are now government buildings and local educational facilities, but you can drive around and look at the remains of redoubts, a guardroom, stables, and cells. You can also walk up to the Inniskilling Monument, a tribute to the 1796 battle in which the 27th (Inniskilling) Regiment of Foot wrested the Morne from the French. At the military cemetery, first used in 1782, faint inscriptions on the tombstones tell the tales of French and English soldiers who died in Saint Lucia. Six former governors of the island are also buried here. From this point atop Morne Fortune, you have a beautiful view of Castries Harbour, Martinique farther north, and the Pitons to the south. ✉ *Morne Fortune.*

Government House

HISTORIC HOME | The official residence of the governor-general—and one of the island's few remaining examples of Victorian architecture—is perched high above Castries, halfway up Morne

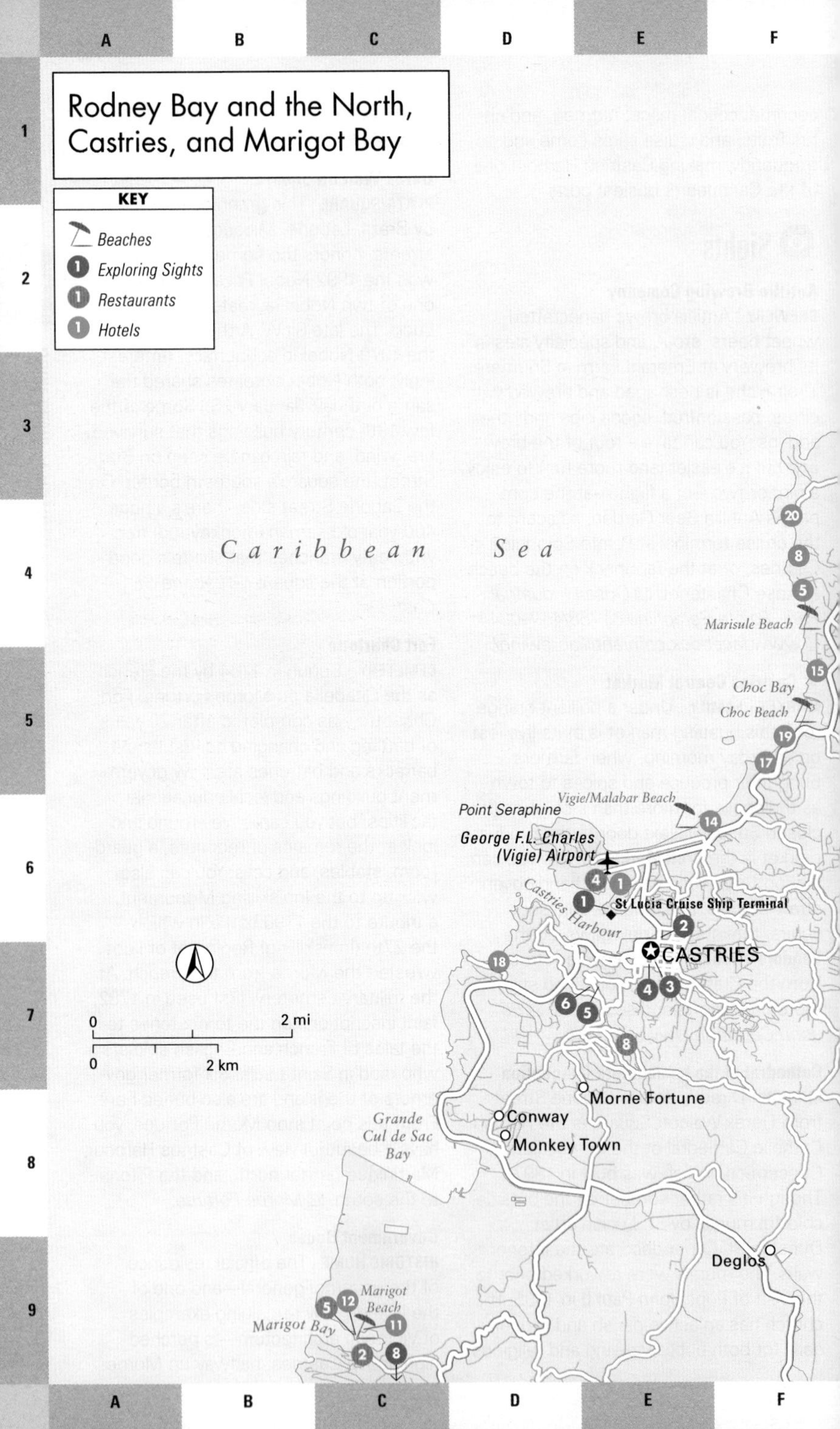

Rodney Bay and the North, Castries, and Marigot Bay
KEY
Beaches
Exploring Sights
Restaurants
Hotels
Caribbean Sea
Marisule Beach
Choc Bay
Choc Beach
Vigie/Malabar Beach
Point Seraphine
George F.L. Charles (Vigie) Airport
Castries Harbour
St Lucia Cruise Ship Terminal
CASTRIES
Morne Fortune
Conway
Monkey Town
Grande Cul de Sac Bay
Deglos
Marigot Beach
Marigot Bay
0
2 mi
0
2 km
A
B
C
D
E
F
1
2
3
4
5
6
7
8
9

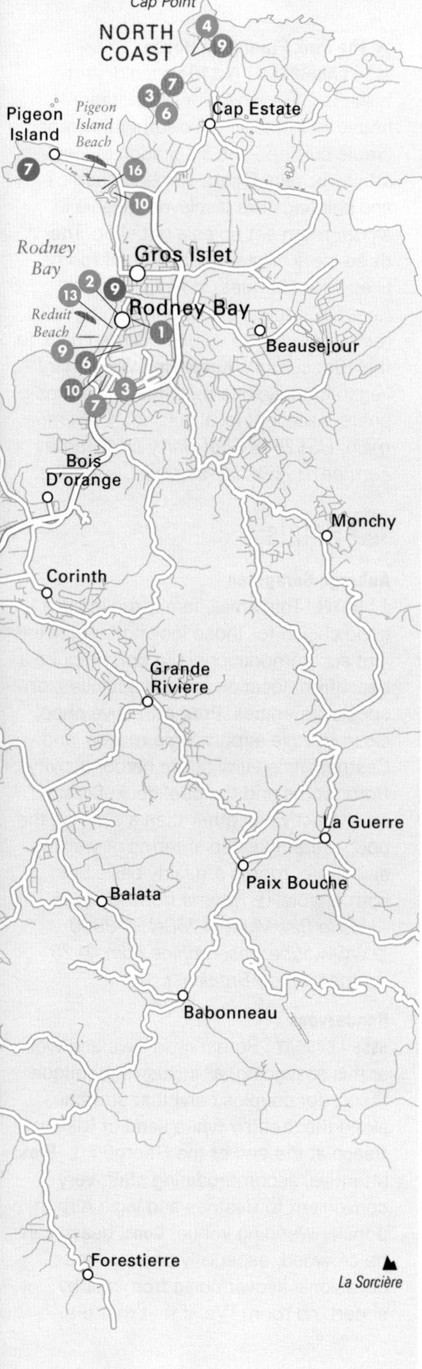

Sights ▼

1 Antillia Brewing Company E6
2 Castries Central Market E6
3 Cathedral of the Immaculate Conception E7
4 Derek Walcott Square E7
5 Fort Charlotte E7
6 Government House E7
7 Pigeon Island National Landmark G2
8 St. Lucia Distillers Group of Companies C9
9 Splash Island Water Park G2

Restaurants ▼

1 Buzz Seafood & Grill G3
2 Chateau Mygo House of Seafood C9
3 The Cliff at Cap H1
4 The Coal Pot Restaurant E6
5 DOOlittle's Restaurant + Bar C9
6 Jacques Waterfront Dining G3
7 The Naked Fisherman H1
8 The Pink Plantation House E7
9 Tao H1
10 Ti Bananne G3

Hotels ▼

1 Auberge Seraphine E6
2 Bay Gardens Beach Resort & Spa G3
3 Bay Gardens Hotel G3
4 BodyHoliday Saint Lucia H1
5 Calabash Cove Resort & Spa F4
6 Cap Maison H1
7 Coco Palm G3
8 East Winds Saint Lucia F4
9 Harmony Marina Suites G3
10 The Landings Resort & Spa G2
11 Mango Beach Inn C9
12 Marigot Beach Club & Dive Resort C9
13 Mystique by Royalton G3
14 Rendezvous E6
15 St. James's Club Morgan Bay F5
16 Sandals Grande St. Lucian G2
17 Sandals Halcyon Beach Resort & Spa F5
18 Sandals Regency La Toc D7
19 Villa Beach Cottages F5
20 Windjammer Landing Villa Beach Resort F4

Fortune (Hill of Good Fortune), which forms a backdrop for the capital city. Morne Fortune has also seen more than its share of *bad* luck, including devastating hurricanes and four fires that leveled Castries. Within Government House is Le Pavillon Royal Museum, which houses important historical photographs and documents, artifacts, crockery, silverware, medals, and awards; original architectural drawings of the house are displayed on the walls. Open Tuesday and Thursday from 10 am to 4 pm. ✉ *Morne Fortune* ☎ *758/452–2481* 🌐 *www.governorgeneral.govt.lc.* 🎟 *Free.*

Beaches

Vigie/Malabar Beach

BEACH | FAMILY | This 2-mile (3-km) stretch of lovely white sand runs parallel to the George F. L. Charles Airport runway in Castries and continues on past the Rendezvous resort, where it becomes Malabar Beach. In the area opposite the airport departure lounge, a few vendors sell refreshments. **Amenities:** food and drink. **Best for:** swimming. ✉ *Castries* ✣ *Adjacent to George F. L. Charles Airport runway.*

Restaurants

★ The Coal Pot Restaurant

$$$$ | FRENCH | Popular since it opened in 1968, this tiny waterfront restaurant overlooks pretty Vigie Cove. Come for a light lunch—perhaps a bowl of creamy pumpkin soup, Greek salad with chicken or shrimp, or broiled fresh fish—or enjoy an exquisite French-inspired dinner under the stars. **Known for:** repeat customers who love the place; outstanding cuisine and service; picturesque harbor views. $ *Average main: US$32* ✉ *Seraphine Rd., Vigie* ☎ *758/452–5566* ⏲ *Closed Sun. No lunch Sat.*

★ The Pink Plantation House

$$$ | CARIBBEAN | A 140-year-old, pretty-in-pink, French Colonial plantation house is the setting for authentic French creole cuisine—the inspiration of local artist Michelle Elliott, whose ceramics and paintings are displayed for sale in a cozy room set up as a gift shop. The three-story house, a labyrinth of rooms filled with antiques, is wrapped in a forest of tropical plants and trees; you'll really feel like you've been carried back to the 19th century. **Known for:** vegetarian/vegan-friendly; charming historic atmosphere; excellent local cuisine. $ *Average main: US$25* ✉ *Chef Harry Dr., Morne Fortune* ☎ *758/452–5422* ⏲ *Closed Sat.*

Hotels

Auberge Seraphine

$ | HOTEL | This small, family-run inn is a good choice for those looking for convenient accommodations, but don't require a beachfront location, on-site activities, or special amenities. **Pros:** attractive price; close to Vigie airport, Vigie marina, and Castries; nice view of the harbor activity from rooms and the pool deck. **Cons:** no on-site activities other than a swim in the pool; rather isolated in terms of walking anywhere; rooms are fairly basic but comfortable. $ *Rooms from: US$125* ✉ *Vielle Bay, Vigie* ☎ *758/456–3000* 🌐 *www.aubergeseraphine.com* *28 rooms* *Free Breakfast.*

Rendezvous

$$$$ | RESORT | Romance is alive and well at this easygoing, all-inclusive, boutique resort (for couples only) that stretches along the dreamy white sand of Malabar Beach at the end of the George F. L. **Pros:** attentive, accommodating staff; very convenient to Castries and Vigie Airport; popular wedding venue. **Cons:** beach can be crowded, especially on weekends; occasional flyover noise from nearby airport; no room TVs, if that matters.

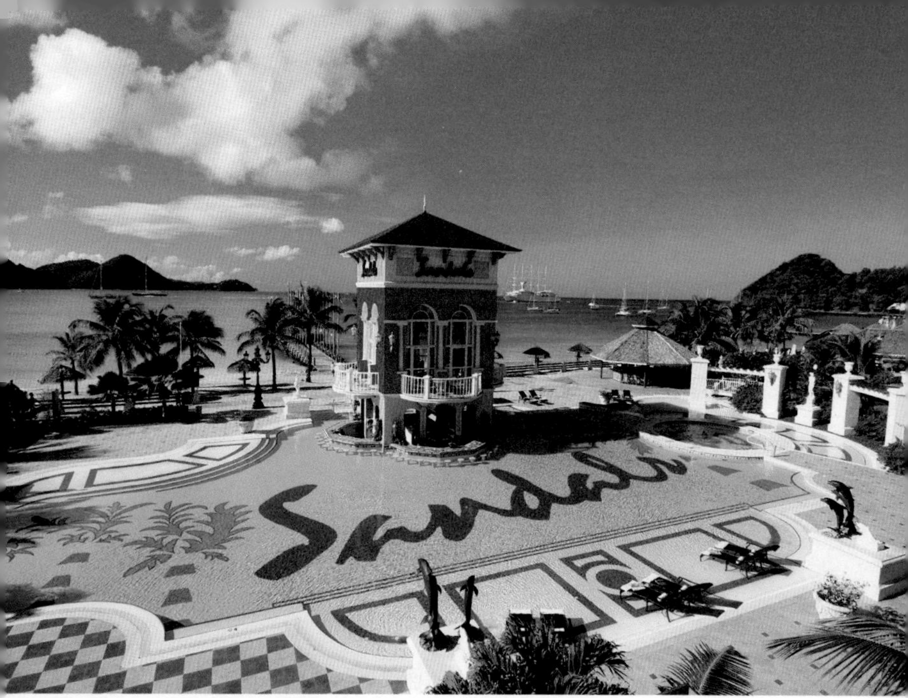
The beautiful pool at the Sandals Grande St. Lucian is just steps from the ocean.

[$] *Rooms from: US$875* ✉ *Malabar Beach, Vigie* ☎ *758/457–7900, 800/544–2883 in U.S.* 🌐 *www.theromanticholiday.com* 🛏 *100 rooms* 🍽 *All-Inclusive.*

St. James's Club Morgan Bay

$$$$ | **RESORT** | **FAMILY** | Singles, couples, and families enjoy tons of sports and activities at this all-inclusive resort on 22 secluded acres surrounding a stretch of white-sand beach. **Pros:** free waterskiing, sailing, and tennis; six restaurants, six bars, four pools, four tennis courts, and more; children's club. **Cons:** Wi-Fi only in some rooms and for a fee; they charge a nightly resort fee; huge resort can be very busy, especially when full. [$] *Rooms from: US$790* ✉ *Choc Bay, Choc* ☎ *758/457–3700, 866/830–1617* 🌐 *www.stjamesclubmorganbay.com* 🛏 *335 rooms* 🍽 *All-Inclusive.*

★ Sandals Halcyon Beach Resort & Spa

$$$$ | **RESORT** | This is the most intimate and low-key of the three Sandals resorts on Saint Lucia; like the others, it's beachfront, all-inclusive, for couples only, and loaded with amenities and activities—including personalized butler service in some suites. **Pros:** exchange privileges (including golf) at other Sandals properties; all the Sandals amenities in a more intimate setting; lots of dining and activity choices. **Cons:** rooms at back of property, nearest the main road, can be noisy at night; small and popular, so book well in advance; it's Sandals, so it's a theme property that's not for everyone. [$] *Rooms from: US$576* ✉ *Choc Bay, Choc* ☎ *758/453–0222, 888/726–3257* 🌐 *www.sandals.com/halcyon-beach* 🛏 *169 rooms* 🍽 *All-Inclusive.*

Sandals Regency La Toc

$$$ | **RESORT** | The second-largest of the three Sandals on Saint Lucia, this resort distinguishes itself with a 9-hole executive-style golf course (for Sandals guests only); like the others, though, this Sandals is all-inclusive and for couples only. **Pros:** on-site 9-hole golf course; lots to do—never a dull moment; complimentary airport shuttle. **Cons:** lots of hills and steps; expert golfers will prefer Sandals Saint Lucia Golf & Country

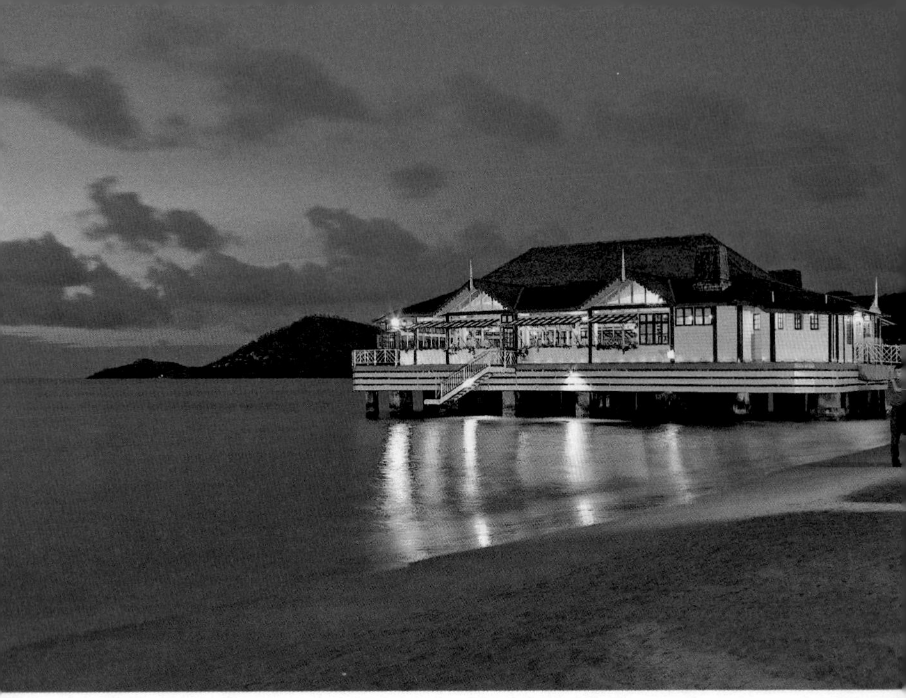

Kelly's Dockside is one of the dining options at Sandals Halcyon Beach.

Club; somewhat isolated location on a bluff west of Castries. [$] *Rooms from: US$470* ✉ *La Toc Rd., Castries* ☎ *758/452–3081, 888/726–3257* 🌐 *www.sandals.com/regency-la-toc* *323 rooms* 🍽 *All-Inclusive.*

Villa Beach Cottages
$$ | **HOTEL** | Tidy housekeeping cottages with gingerbread-laced facades are steps from the beach at this family-run establishment 3 miles (5 km) north of the airport in Castries. **Pros:** peaceful and quiet environment; just feet from the water; beautiful sunsets from your balcony. **Cons:** beach is quite narrow and pools are small; rent a car, as you'll go out for meals (or groceries); close quarters. [$] *Rooms from: US$290* ✉ *John Compton (Castries-Gros Islet) Hwy., Choc* ☎ *758/450–2884, 866/542–1991 in U.S.* 🌐 *www.villabeachcottages.com* *20 rooms* 🍽 *No Meals.*

Windjammer Landing Villa Beach Resort
$$ | **RESORT** | **FAMILY** | Mediterranean-style villas—which are as appropriate for a family or group vacation as for a romantic getaway—climb the hillside on one of Saint Lucia's prettiest bays. **Pros:** five restaurants, four bars, in-villa dining, room service ... you choose; lovely, spacious units with seating areas and kitchenettes; amazing sunset views from every villa. **Cons:** some villa sitting rooms are open-air, meaning no air-conditioning and occasional insects; meal and bar costs add up fast unless you choose the all-inclusive option; far from main road, so you'll need a car if you plan to leave the property often. [$] *Rooms from: US$294* ✉ *Trouya Point Rd., La Brellotte Bay, Bois d'Orange* ☎ *758/456–9000, 877/522–0722 in U.S.* 🌐 *www.windjammer-landing.com* *330 rooms* 🍽 *Free Breakfast.*

Shopping

Along the harbor in Castries, rambling structures with bright-orange roofs cover several open-air markets that are open from 6 am to 5 pm Monday through Saturday. Saturday morning is the busiest and most colorful time to shop.

Embracing Kwéyòl

English is Saint Lucia's official language, but most Saint Lucians speak Kwéyòl—a French-based Creole language—and often use it for informal conversations among themselves. Primarily a spoken language, Kwéyòl in its written version doesn't look at all like French; pronounce the words phonetically, though—*entenasyonnal* (international), for example, or the word *Kwéyòl* (Creole) itself—and you indeed sound as if you're speaking French.

Pretty much the same version of the Creole language, or patois, is spoken in the nearby island of Dominica. Otherwise, the Saint Lucian Kwéyòl is quite different from that spoken in other Caribbean islands that have a French and African heritage, such as Haiti, Guadeloupe, and Martinique—or elsewhere, such as Mauritius, Madagascar, and the state of Louisiana. The Kwéyòl spoken in Saint Lucia and Dominica is mostly unintelligible to people from those other locations—and vice versa.

Saint Lucia embraces its Creole heritage by devoting the month of October each year to celebrations that preserve and promote Creole culture, language, and traditions. Events and performances highlight Creole music, food, dance, theater, native costumes, church services, traditional games, folklore, native medicine—a little bit of everything, or *tout bagay*, as you say in Kwéyòl.

Creole Heritage Month culminates at the end of October with all-day events and activities on Jounen Kwéyòl Entenasyonnal, or International Creole Day, which is recognized by all countries that speak a version of Creole.

For more than a century, farmers' wives have gathered at the **Castries Market** to sell produce—which you can enjoy on the island but, alas, can't bring to the United States. You can, however, take spices (such as cocoa sticks or balls, turmeric, cloves, bay leaves, ginger, peppercorns, cinnamon sticks, vanilla beans, nutmeg, and mace), as well as locally bottled hot-pepper sauces—all of which cost a fraction of what you'd pay back home. The adjacent **Craft Market** has aisles and aisles of baskets and other handmade straw work, rustic brooms made from palm fronds, wood carvings, leather work, clay pottery, and souvenirs—all at affordable prices. The **Vendors' Arcade,** across the street from the Craft Market, is a maze of stalls and booths where you can find handicrafts among the T-shirts and costume jewelry.

Duty-free shopping areas are at **Pointe Seraphine,** an attractive Spanish-motif complex on Castries Harbour with a dozen shops, and **La Place Carenage,** an inviting three-story complex on the opposite side of the harbor.

CLOTHING AND TEXTILES

Howelton Estate

SOUVENIRS | This arts-and-crafts shop and studio (formerly Caribelle Batik), high atop Morne Fortune, is named for the old Victorian mansion in which the enterprise is housed. Craftspeople demonstrate the art of batik and silk-screen printing, which you can buy in the shop—along with chocolate products, coconut oil products, and gift items, all made in Saint Lucia. There's a terrace where you can have a cool drink and a garden full of tropical orchids and lilies. You can also take a tour of the estate. ✉ *Howelton*

House, Old Victoria Rd., Morne Fortune ☎ *758/452–3785* 🌐 *www.howelton-estate.com.*

HANDICRAFTS

Eudovic's Art Studio

ART GALLERIES | This workshop, studio, and art gallery has wall plaques, masks, and abstract figures hand-carved by sculptor Vincent Joseph Eudovic from local mahogany, red cedar, and eucalyptus wood. ✉ *West Coast Rd., Goodlands, Morne Fortune* ☎ *758/452–2747* 🌐 *www.eudovicart.com.*

AREAS AND MALLS

Gablewoods Mall

MALL | **FAMILY** | This mall has about 35 shops that sell groceries, wines and spirits, jewelry, clothing, crafts, books and overseas newspapers, music, souvenirs, household goods, and snacks. ✉ *Sunny Acres, Gros Islet Hwy., Choc Bay, Castries* ✣ *A couple miles north of downtown Castries* ☎ *758/453–7752* 🌐 *www.facebook.com/Shops-at-Gablewoods-Mall-1816458811898957/.*

Marigot Bay

This is one of the prettiest natural harbors in the Caribbean. In 1778, British admiral Samuel Barrington sailed into this secluded bay-within-a-bay and, the story goes, covered his ships with palm fronds to hide them from the French. Today this small community, just 4 miles (7 km) south of Castries, is a favorite anchorage for boaters and a peaceful destination for landlubbers, with a luxury resort, several small inns and restaurants, and a marina village with a snack shop, grocery store, and boutiques. A 24-hour ferry (EC$5 round-trip) connects the bay's two shores—a voyage that takes a minute or so each way.

Sights

St. Lucia Distillers Group of Companies

DISTILLERY | St. Lucia Distillers, which produces the island's own Bounty and Chairman's Reserve rums, offers 90-minute Rhythm of Rum tours that cover the history of sugar, the background of rum, a detailed description of the distillation process, colorful displays of local architecture, a glimpse at a typical rum shop, Caribbean music, and a chance to sample the company's rums and liqueurs. The distillery is at the Roseau Sugar Factory in the Roseau Valley, on the island's largest banana plantation a few miles south of Castries and not far from Marigot. Reservations for the tour are essential. ✉ *Roseau Sugar Factory, West Coast Rd., Roseau Valley, Marigot Bay* ☎ *758/456–3192* 🌐 *www.saintluciarums.com* 🎫 *$12* 🕓 *Closed weekends* ✍ *Reservations required.*

Beaches

Marigot Beach (*La Bas Beach*)

BEACH | **FAMILY** | Calm waters rippled only by passing yachts lap a sliver of sand on the north side of Marigot Bay adjacent to the Marigot Beach Club & Dive Resort, across the bay from Marigot Bay Resort & Marina, and a short walk from Mango Beach Inn. Studded with palm trees, the tiny beach on extremely picturesque Marigot Bay is accessible by a ferry (EC$5 round-trip) that operates continually from one side of the bay to the other, with pickup at the Marina Village dock. You can find refreshments at adjacent or nearby restaurants. **Amenities:** food and drink; toilets; water sports. **Best for:** swimming; sunset. ✉ *Marigot Bay.*

Restaurants

★ **Chateau Mygo House of Seafood**

$$$ | **SEAFOOD** | **FAMILY** | Walk down a garden path to Chateau Mygo (a colloquial corruption of "Marigot") or sail up on your boat, pick out a table on the deck of this popular dockside restaurant, and soak up the waterfront atmosphere of what may be the Caribbean's prettiest bay. The tableau is mesmerizing—and that's at lunch, when you can order a sandwich, burger, roti, fish- or chicken-and-chips, salads, grilled fish or savory coconut chicken with peas and rice and vegetables, and ice cream. **Known for:** live local music and dancing (weekly); casual waterside dining on Marigot Bay; Happy Hour daily from 5 to 6 pm. *$ Average main: US$25 ✉ Marigot Bay ☎ 758/458–3947 🌐 www.chateaumygo.com.*

DOOlittle's Restaurant + Bar

$$$ | **SEAFOOD** | **FAMILY** | Named for the protagonist in the original (1967) *Dr. Doolittle* movie, part of which was filmed in Marigot Bay, this indoor-outdoor restaurant at Marigot Beach Club & Dive Resort is on the north side of the bay. **Known for:** evening entertainment; casual atmosphere; close to the beach. *$ Average main: US$28 ✉ Marigot Beach Club & Dive Resort, Marigot Bay ✣ North side of bay ☎ 758/451–4974 🌐 www.marigotbeachclub.com.*

Hotels

Mango Beach Inn

$ | **B&B/INN** | When the Marigot Bay ferry delivers you to the dock across the bay, a small gate opens to a stone staircase that leads through a jungle of trees and flowers to this delightful, tidy little B&B. **Pros:** lovely hosts and personalized service; spectacular views of Marigot Bay; beach, restaurants, and activities nearby. **Cons:** steps to the inn may be difficult for anyone with mobility issues; only showers in the bathrooms; tiny garden rooms. *$ Rooms from: US$240 ✉ North side of bay, Marigot Bay ☎ 758/485–1621 🌐 www.mangobeachmarigot.com 6 rooms Free Breakfast.*

Marigot Beach Club & Dive Resort

$ | **RESORT** | **FAMILY** | Divers love this place, and everyone loves the location facing the little palm-studded beach at Marigot Bay. Some accommodations are right on the beachfront; others are on the hillside with a sweeping view of the bay. **Pros:** deeply discounted rates off-season; beautiful views of Marigot Bay from every room; good casual dining with live entertainment on Saturday night. **Cons:** adjacent beach is tiny; hillside rooms require a trek; rooms and public areas are fairly basic and could use updating. *$ Rooms from: US$213 ✉ Marigot Bay ☎ 758/451–4974 🌐 www.marigotbeachclub.com 38 rooms No Meals.*

Soufrière and the Southwest Coast

The oldest town in Saint Lucia and the island's colonial capital, Soufrière was founded by the French in 1746 and named for its proximity to the volcano of the same name. The wharf is the center of activity in this sleepy town (population, 9,000), particularly when a cruise ship anchors in pretty Soufrière Bay. French colonial influences are evident in the second-story verandahs, gingerbread trim, and other appointments of the wooden buildings that surround the market square. The market building itself is decorated with colorful murals.

The site of much of Saint Lucia's renowned natural wonders, Soufrière is the destination of most sightseeing trips. Here you can get up close to the iconic Pitons and visit Saint Lucia's "drive-in" volcano, magnificent botanical gardens, working plantations, waterfalls, and countless other examples of the natural beauty for which the island is deservedly famous.

Sights

★ Diamond Falls Botanical Gardens and Mineral Baths

GARDEN | These splendid gardens are part of Soufrière Estate, a 2,000-acre land grant presented by King Louis XIV in 1713 to three Devaux brothers from Normandy in recognition of their services to France. The estate is still owned by their descendants; Joan Du Boulay Devaux maintains the gardens. Bushes and shrubs bursting with brilliant flowers grow beneath towering trees and line pathways that lead to a natural gorge. Water bubbling to the surface from underground sulfur springs streams downhill in rivulets to become Diamond Waterfall, deep within the botanical gardens. Through the centuries, the rocks over which the cascade spills have become encrusted with minerals tinted yellow, green, and purple. Near the falls, mineral baths are fed by the underground springs. King Louis XVI of France provided funds in 1784 for the construction of a building with a dozen large stone baths to fortify his troops against the Saint Lucian climate. It's claimed that the future Joséphine Bonaparte bathed here as a young girl while visiting her father's plantation nearby. During the Brigand's War, just after the French Revolution, the bathhouse was destroyed. In 1930 André Du Boulay had the site excavated, and two of the original stone baths were restored for his use. Outside baths were added later. For a small fee, you can slip into your swimsuit and soak for 30 minutes in one of the outside pools; a private bath costs slightly more. ✉ *Soufrière Estate, Diamond Rd., Soufrière* ☎ *758/459–7155* 🌐 *www.diamondstlucia.com* 🎟 *$7, public bath $6, private bath $7.*

Edmund Forest Reserve

FOREST | **FAMILY** | Dense tropical rain forest that stretches from one side of Saint Lucia to the other, sprawling over 19,000 acres of mountains and valleys, is home to a multitude of exotic flowers, trees, plants, and rare birds—including the brightly feathered Jacquot parrot. The Edmund Forest Reserve, on the island's western side, is most easily accessed from the road to Fond St. Jacques, which is just east of Soufrière. A trek through the verdant landscape, with spectacular views of mountains, valleys, and the sea beyond, can take three or more hours. The ranger station at the reserve entrance is a 30-minute drive from Soufrière and 90 minutes or more from the northern end of Saint Lucia. You'll need a four-wheel-drive vehicle to drive inland to the trailhead, which can take another hour. The trek itself is a strenuous hike, requiring stamina and sturdy hiking shoes. Your hotel can help you obtain permission from the Saint Lucia Forestry Department to access reserve trails and to arrange for a naturalist or forest officer guide—necessary because the vegetation is so dense. ✉ *Soufrière* ☎ *758/468–5649 Forestry Dept.* 🎟 *Nature trails $10, guide $25.*

★ Fond Doux Estate

FARM/RANCH | **FAMILY** | One of the earliest French estates established by land grants (1745 and 1764), this plantation still produces cocoa, citrus, bananas, coconuts, and vegetables on 135 hilly acres within the UNESCO World Heritage Site of Soufrière. The restored 1864 plantation house is still in use, as well. A 90-minute guided walking tour begins at the cocoa *fermentary*, and takes you through the chocolate-making process. You then follow a lushly-planted nature trail, where a guide points out various fruit- or spice-bearing trees, tropical flowers, and indigenous birds (and their unique songs). Additional trails lead to old military ruins, a religious shrine, and a vantage point for viewing the spectacular Pitons. Cool drinks and an optional Creole buffet lunch are served after the tour. Souvenirs, including freshly-made chocolate sticks, are sold at the boutique. ✉ *Vieux Fort Rd., Château Belair* ☎ *758/459–7545* 🌐 *www.fonddouxresort.com* 🎟 *$25, $40 with lunch.*

Did You Know?

The Devaux family has owned Soufrière Estate, the location of Diamond Falls Botanical Gardens, since 1713; mineral-rich water cascading over Diamond Falls for centuries causes the rocks underneath to sparkle in different colors.

★ Morne Coubaril Historical Adventure Park

FARM/RANCH | FAMILY | On the site of an 18th-century estate, a 250-acre land grant in 1713 by Louis XIV of France, the original plantation house has been rebuilt and a farmworkers' village has been re-created. Both do a good job of showing what life was like for both the owners (a single family owned the land until 1960) and those who did all the hard labor over the centuries producing cotton, coffee, sugarcane, and cocoa. Cocoa, coffee, coconuts, and tropical fruits are still grown on the estate using traditional agricultural methods. On the 30-minute Historical Estate Tour, guides show how coconuts are de-husked and dried for use in a variety of products. On the cocoa side, a guide will cut open a cocoa pod, offering samples of cocoa beans, and demonstrate how cocoa is fermented, dried, polished (by dancing on the beans), and transformed into chocolate sticks. They also offer a 40-minute Rum & Chocolate Tour. The grounds are lovely for walking or hiking, with spellbinding views of mountains and Soufrière Bay. More adventurous visitors will enjoy ziplining beneath Petit Piton and through the adjacent rain forest. ✉ *West Coast Rd., Soufrière* ✣ *2 miles (3 km) south of Soufrière Harbour* ☎ *758/712–5808* 🌐 *www.mornecoubarilestate.com* 🎫 *$11 estate tour, $75 zipline, $35 rum & chocolate tour.*

★ The Pitons

MOUNTAIN | Rising precipitously from the cobalt-blue Caribbean just south of Soufrière Bay, these two unusual mountains—named a UNESCO World Heritage Site in 2004—have become the iconic symbol of Saint Lucia. Covered with thick tropical vegetation, the massive outcroppings were formed by a volcanic eruption 30 to 40 million years ago. They are not identical twins, since 2,619-foot Gros Piton is taller and 2,461-foot Petit Piton is broader. It's possible to climb the Pitons, but it's a strenuous trek. Gros Piton is the easier climb and takes about four hours round-trip. Either climb requires permission and a guide; register at the base of Gros Piton. ✉ *Soufrière.*

★ Sulphur Springs Park

HOT SPRING | FAMILY | As you approach Sulphur Springs Park and the crater of the "drive-in volcano," your nose will pick up a strong scent emanating from more than 20 belching pools of murky water, crusty sulfur deposits, and other multicolor minerals baking and steaming on the surface. You don't actually drive all the way in. Rather, you drive within a few hundred feet of the gurgling, steaming mass and then walk behind your guide (whose service is included in the admission price) around a fault in the substratum rock. (Don't worry... the volcano hasn't erupted since the 1700s, probably because it continues to let off steam.) Following the fascinating, educational half-hour tour, you're welcome to take a quick dip in the nearby hot, mineral-rich bathing pools—they can also be pretty stinky on a hot day, but your skin (and joints) will thank you!

TIP→ You can rinse off under the waterfall. ✉ *Malgretoute, Soufrière* ✣ *Off West Coast Rd., south of town* ☎ *758/714–8900* 🌐 *sulphurspringstlucia.com* 🎫 *$10 tour, $5 bath, $13 combo; from $120 for half- or full-day tours with hotel transportation.*

Beaches

★ Anse Chastanet

BEACH | FAMILY | In front of the resort of the same name and Jade Mountain, this palm-studded, dark-sand beach just north of Soufrière Bay has a backdrop of green mountains, brightly painted fishing skiffs bobbing at anchor, calm waters for swimming, and some of the island's best reefs for snorkeling and diving right from shore. Anse Chastanet Resort's gazebos are among the palms; its dive shop, restaurant, and bar are on the beach and open to the public. The mile-long dirt road from Soufrière, though, is a challenge even for taxi drivers, given its (by design) state of disrepair. **Amenities:** food and drink; parking (no fee); toilets; water sports. **Best for:** snorkeling; sunset; swimming. ✉ *Anse Chastanet Rd., Soufrière* ⊕ *1 mile (1½ km) north of Soufrière.*

★ Anse Cochon

BEACH | FAMILY | This dark-sand beach in front of Ti Kaye Resort & Spa is accessible by boat or by jeep via Ti Kaye's mile-long, tire-crunching access road—and then 166 steps down to the beach. The calm water and adjacent reefs, part of the National Marine Reserve, are superb for swimming, diving, and snorkeling. Most catamaran cruises to Soufrière stop here on the northbound leg so that day-trippers can take a quick swim. Moorings are free, and boaters and swimmers can enjoy refreshments at Ti Kaye's beach bar. Snorkeling equipment is available at the dive shop on the beach. **Amenities:** food and drink; toilets; water sports. **Best for:** snorkeling; swimming. ✉ *Off West Coast Rd.* ⊕ *3 miles (5 km) south of Anse la Raye.*

★ Anse des Pitons (*Sugar Beach, Jalousie Beach*)

BEACH | The white sand on this crescent beach, snuggled between the Pitons, was imported years ago and spread over the natural black sand. Accessible through the Viceroy resort, or by boat, Anse des Pitons (aka Sugar Beach, Jalousie Beach) offers crystal-clear water for swimming, excellent snorkeling and diving, and breathtaking scenery—you're swimming right between the Pitons, after all. The underwater area here is protected as part of the National Marine Reserve. Neighboring resorts provide shuttle service to the beach for their guests, but if you're not staying nearby, prepare to pay a hefty fee. **Amenities:** food and drink; toilets; water sports. **Best for:** snorkeling; sunset; swimming. ✉ *Val des Pitons, Soufrière* ⊕ *3 miles (5 km) south of Soufrière.*

Soufrière Beach Park

BEACH | FAMILY | This stretch of beachfront on Soufrière Bay was designated Soufrière Beach Park in spring 2019. Formerly called Hummingbird Beach, the park stretches in front of Hummingbird Beach Resort. The park offers beachgoers a restaurant, spa, smoothie bar, beach bar, pizzeria, souvenir shop, outdoor showers, and a tourism information center. You can also rent nonmotorized water sports equipment. **Amenities:** food and drink; parking (no fee); showers; toilets; water sports. **Best for:** snorkeling; sunset; swimming. ✉ *Bridge Rd., Soufrière.*

Restaurants

Apsara

$$$ | INDIAN | India has had an important influence on the Caribbean islands, from the heritage of their people to the colorful madras plaids and the curry flavors that are a staple of Caribbean cuisine. At night, Anse Chastanet's Trou au Diable restaurant transforms into Apsara, an extraordinarily romantic, candlelit, beachfront dining experience with modern Indian cuisine. **Known for:** exotic cuisine in an island setting; accessible by land or water; chef visits with diners at table to discuss cuisine. $ *Average main: US$26* ✉ *Anse Chastanet, 1 Anse Chastanet Rd., Soufrière* ☎ *758/459–7000* 🌐 *www.apsarastlucia.com* ⏲ *Closed Tues. No lunch.*

Bamboo and The Creole Pot at Fond Doux Eco Resort

$$$ | CARIBBEAN | FAMILY | The small, rustic pair of restaurants are two of the most popular spots to enjoy a Creole lunch when touring the natural sights in and around Soufrière. Bamboo offers à la carte options at both lunch and dinner while the Creole Pot has a buffet lunch of stewed chicken, grilled fish, rice and beans, macaroni and cheese, caramelized plantains, figs (green bananas), breadfruit balls, purple yams, salad, and more. **Known for:** farm tours before or after your

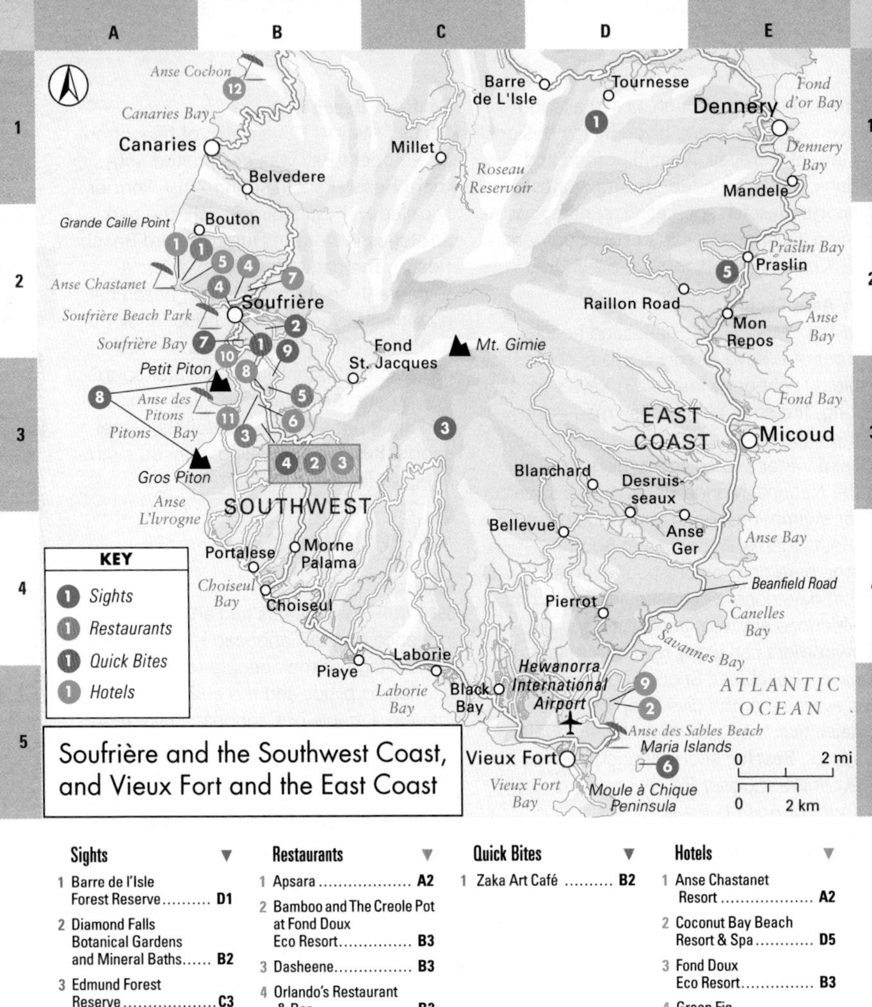

Soufrière and the Southwest Coast, and Vieux Fort and the East Coast

Sights

1. Barre de l'Isle Forest Reserve **D1**
2. Diamond Falls Botanical Gardens and Mineral Baths...... **B2**
3. Edmund Forest Reserve **C3**
4. Fond Doux Estate **B3**
5. Mamiku Gardens **E2**
6. Maria Islands Nature Reserve **D5**
7. Morne Coubaril Historical Adventure Park **B2**
8. The Pitons **B3**
9. Sulphur Springs Park... **B3**

Restaurants

1. Apsara **A2**
2. Bamboo and The Creole Pot at Fond Doux Eco Resort............... **B3**
3. Dasheene................ **B3**
4. Orlando's Restaurant & Bar **B2**
5. Rabot Restaurant **B3**

Quick Bites

1. Zaka Art Café **B2**

Hotels

1. Anse Chastanet Resort **A2**
2. Coconut Bay Beach Resort & Spa **D5**
3. Fond Doux Eco Resort.............. **B3**
4. Green Fig Resort & Spa **B2**
5. Jade Mountain.......... **B2**
6. Ladera Resort........... **B3**
7. La Haut Resort **B2**
8. Rabot Hotel.............. **B3**
9. Serenity at Coconut Bay............. **D5**
10. Stonefield Villa Resort **B2**
11. Sugar Beach, A Viceroy Resort........ **B3**
12. Ti Kaye Resort & Spa..................... **B1**

Amazing views of the Pitons from Dasheene at Ladera.

meal; farm-to-table Creole cuisine; natural environment. *Average main: US$25* *Fond Doux Eco Resort, West Coast Rd., Château Belair* *758/459–7545* *fonddouxresort.com/dining.*

★ Dasheene

$$$$ | CARIBBEAN | The terrace restaurant at Ladera Resort has breathtaking, close-up views of the Pitons and the sea between them, especially beautiful at sunset. The atmosphere is casual by day and magical at night. **Known for:** live local music most evenings; fresh, stylish island cuisine; Pitons views. *Average main: US$35* *Ladera Resort, West Coast Rd., Soufrière* *3 miles (5 km) south of Soufrière* *758/459–6623* *www.ladera.com/dining.*

Orlando's Restaurant & Bar

$$$$ | CARIBBEAN | A man on a mission, chef Orlando Sachell opened his original restaurant in downtown Soufrière to present his "Share the Love" (or STL) style of Caribbean cooking. Breakfast and lunch are served here, and dinner is served at his second Orlando's Restaurant, which opened in Rodney Bay in 2020. **Known for:** casual courtyard dining; star chef yet always accommodating; exquisite small plates and excellent wine. *Average main: US$38* *Bridge St., Soufrière* *758/459–5955* *www.facebook.com/Orlandos.Restaurant.Soufriere.St.Lucia/* *Closed Tues. No dinner.*

★ Rabot Restaurant

$$$$ | CARIBBEAN | Located on the Rabot Estate, a working cocoa farm, chocolate is infused into nearly every dish. Starters include an organic citrus salad with cashew nuts and white chocolate-coconut dressing, and sea scallops marinated with cacao, seared and basted in a cacao citrus sauce. **Known for:** sunset at the bar with a cacao Bellini; "pioneering" cacao cuisine; open-air dining room with Pitons views. *Average main: US$38* *Rabot Hotel, Rabot Estate, West Coast Rd., Soufrière* *3 miles (5 km) south of Soufrière* *758/459–7966* *hotelchocolat.com/restaurant.*

Jade Mountain is one of Saint Lucia's best adults-only resorts.

Coffee and Quick Bites

★ Zaka Art Café

$ | **CAFÉ** | **FAMILY** | Stop in for a chat and a cup of coffee—and, of course, Zaka's rather brilliant artwork. In his studio, artist and craftsman Simon "Zaka" Gajhadhar (and his team of local artists and wood carvers) fashion totems and masks from driftwood, branches, and other environmentally friendly wood sources—taking advantage of the natural nibs and knots that distinguish each piece. **Known for:** hand-carved wood art; coffee. *Average main: US$5* *1 Sulphur Springs Rd., Soufrière* *758/384-2925* *zaka-art.com* *No credit cards.*

Hotels

Anse Chastanet Resort

$$$$ | **RESORT** | Spectacular, individually designed rooms—some with fourth walls wide open to the stunning Pitons view—peek out of the thick rain forest that cascades down a steep hillside to the beach. **Pros:** great location for divers; the open-wall Pitons views; attractive room furnishings and artwork. **Cons:** no pool; air-conditioning only in beachfront rooms; steep hillside not conducive to strolling or to guests with mobility or cardiac issues. *Rooms from: US$665* *1000 Anse Chastanet Rd., Soufrière* *758/459-7000, 800/223-1108 in U.S.* *www.ansechastanet.com* *49 rooms* *No Meals.*

★ Fond Doux Eco Resort

$$$ | **RESORT** | **FAMILY** | At this laid-back "eco resort" on one of Soufrière's most active agricultural farms, nine historic homes salvaged from all around the island have been rebuilt on the 135-acre estate and refurbished as guest accommodations with luxury bathrooms and period furniture, and surrounded by dense tropical foliage and marked trails that meander through the property. **Pros:** free beach shuttle; an exotic, eco-friendly experience; striking location on an 18th-century plantation. **Cons:** a car is advised, as local sights are a few miles away; no air-conditioning in some

cottages; no room TVs. $ *Rooms from: US$395* ✉ *Fond Doux Estate, Soufrière* ✥ *4 miles (7 km) south of Soufrière* ☎ *758/459–7545* 🌐 *www.fonddouxresort.com* 🛏 *17 rooms* 🍽 *Free Breakfast.*

Green Fig Resort & Spa

$ | **RESORT** | Opened in 2021, this small hillside resort overlooking Soufrière Bay gets rave reviews from guests, who don't mind walking stairs—100-plus, in some cases—to get to their digs (those with the fewest stairs are rooms 101, 103, and 104), which reward the effort with beautiful views of the Pitons. **Pros:** staff is friendly and accommodating; good value for the area; amazing views of the Pitons. **Cons:** sounds of dogs and roosters during the night in open-air rooms; Wi-Fi is not always reliable; many stairs and no wheelchair access. $ *Rooms from: US$175* ✉ *Upper Palmiste Rd.* ☎ *758/518–6106* 🌐 *www.greenfigresort.com* 🛏 *25 rooms.*

★ Jade Mountain

$$$$ | **RESORT** | This premium-class, premium-priced, adults-only hotel is an architectural wonder perched on a picturesque mountainside overlooking the Pitons and the Caribbean. **Pros:** open fourth wall with Pitons views in every "sanctuary"; access to Anse Chastanet beach, water sports, restaurants, and spa; huge in-room pools. **Cons:** not recommended for anyone with physical disabilities; no air-conditioning (except in one "sky suite"); sky-high rates. $ *Rooms from: US$1285* ✉ *Anse Chastanet, Anse Chastanet Rd., Soufrière* ☎ *758/459–4000, 800/223–1108 in U.S.* 🌐 *www.jademountain.com* 🛏 *29 rooms* 🍽 *No Meals.*

★ Ladera Resort

$$$$ | **RESORT** | The elegantly rustic Ladera Resort, perched 1,000 feet above the sea directly between the two Pitons, is one of the most sophisticated small inns in the Caribbean but, at the same time, takes a local, eco-friendly approach to furnishings, food, and service. **Pros:** open fourth walls and private plunge pools provide breathtaking views; excellent cuisine at Dasheene; hand-hewn furniture makes each room unique. **Cons:** no air-conditioning (but breezy, so no real need); steep drops make this the wrong choice for people with physical disabilities; communal infinity pool is small. $ *Rooms from: US$840* ✉ *Rabot Estate, Soufrière–Vieux Fort Hwy., Soufrière* ✥ *3 miles (5 km) south of town* ☎ *758/459–6600, 844/785–8242 in U.S.* 🌐 *www.ladera.com* 🛏 *37 suites* 🍽 *Free Breakfast.*

La Haut Resort

$ | **B&B/INN** | **FAMILY** | "La Haut" is French for "the height," so it's all about the view—the Pitons, of course—plus the appeal of staying in an intimate and affordable family-run inn. **Pros:** complimentary fresh fruit daily; lovely for weddings and honeymoons but also for families; stunning Pitons views. **Cons:** vehicle recommended; spotty Wi-Fi access; no air-conditioning in some rooms. $ *Rooms from: US$200* ✉ *West Coast Rd., Colombette, Soufrière* ✥ *Just north of Soufrière* ☎ *758/459–7008, 866/773–4321 in U.S.* 🌐 *www.lahaut.com* 🛏 *16 rooms* 🍽 *No Meals.*

★ Rabot Hotel

$$$$ | **HOTEL** | Anyone who loves chocolate will love this themed, adults-only boutique hotel just south of Soufrière and within shouting distance of the Pitons. **Pros:** self-guided trail walks and cocoa tours throughout the estate; pool with a view and daily beach shuttle service; chocolate lover's dream. **Cons:** no children 18 or under; no TV, but a preloaded iPod and free Wi-Fi; no air-conditioning, but naturally breezy. $ *Rooms from: US$876* ✉ *Rabot Estate, West Coast Rd., Soufrière* ✥ *2 miles (3 km) south of Soufrière* ☎ *758/459–7966* 🌐 *www.thehotelchocolat.com/uk/rabothotel.html* 🛏 *25 rooms* 🍽 *Free Breakfast.*

Stonefield Villa Resort

$$ | **RESORT** | The 18th-century plantation house and cottage-style villas that dot this 26-acre family-owned estate, a former lime and cocoa plantation that spills down a tropical hillside, afford eye-popping views of Petit Piton. **Pros:** great sunset views from villa decks; quiet, natural, very private setting; beautiful pool. **Cons:** no room TVs; fitness facility could use air-conditioning; car recommended to go off-site. *Rooms from: US$345 ✉ West Coast Rd., Soufrière ✥ 1 mile (1½ km) south of Soufrière ☎ 758/459–7037, 800/420–5731 in U.S. 🌐 www.stonefieldresort.com 17 villas Free Breakfast.*

★ **Sugar Beach, A Viceroy Resort**

$$$$ | **RESORT** | **FAMILY** | Located in Val des Pitons, the steep valley between the Pitons and the most dramatic 100 acres in Saint Lucia, magnificent private villas are tucked into the dense tropical foliage that covers the hillside and reaches down to the sea. **Pros:** complimentary Wi-Fi and use of iPad during stay; exquisite accommodations, scenery, service, and amenities; huge infinity pool. **Cons:** rental car advised; fairly isolated, so a meal plan makes sense; very expensive. *Rooms from: US$768 ✉ Val des Pitons, Soufrière ✥ 2 miles (3 km) south of town ☎ 800/235–4300 in U.S., 758/456–8000 🌐 www.viceroyhotelsandresorts.com/sugarbeach 128 rooms No Meals.*

★ **Ti Kaye Resort & Spa**

$$$ | **RESORT** | Rustic elegance is not an oxymoron at this upscale, adults-only cottage community that spills down a hillside above fabulous Anse Cochon beach. **Pros:** great for a wedding, honeymoon, or getaway (adults only); excellent dining at Kai Manje; on-site dive shop. **Cons:** those 166 steps down to (and up from) the beach; room TV costs extra; location is far from anywhere—rent a car to get around. *Rooms from: US$441 ✉ Anse Cochon, off West Coast Rd., Anse La Raye ✥ Halfway between Anse la Raye and Canaries ☎ 758/456–8101, 888/300–7026 in U.S. 🌐 www.tikaye.com 33 cottages Free Breakfast.*

Shopping

Choiseul Art Gallery

CRAFTS | Leo and Hattie Barnard, who came to Saint Lucia from England, offer paintings and handmade greeting cards that capture the beauty of the island, along with souvenirs, palm crafts, and wood carvings made locally by Leo and others. *✉ River Doree ☎ 758/715–5740 🌐 choiseulartgallery.com ⏲ Closed Sun., Mon., Aug., and Sept.*

Cacoa Sainte Lucie

CHOCOLATE | As locally made souvenirs go, they don't get much sweeter than a box of gorgeous truffles from this artisan chocolate maker in rural Canaries. Led by owner-pastry chef Maria Jackson, the team creates small-batch chocolates on-site using cocoa from local farms. Get a glimpse of the process through the viewing windows, alongside display cases filled with their signature pink sea salt caramels, mango-basil bonbons, and other tempting confections. They also offer chocolate "sensory" tastings (US$20 per person); truffle-making classes (US$50 per person), and farm excursions. *✉ Belvedere, Anse La Raye ✥ Canaries ☎ 758/459-4401 🌐 www.cacoasaintelucie.com ⏲ Closed Saturday.*

Vieux Fort and the East Coast

Saint Lucia's second largest town is also the location of Hewanorra International Airport. From the Moule à Chique peninsula, the island's southernmost tip, you can see much of Saint Lucia to the north and the island of St. Vincent 21 miles (34 km) to the south. This is where the clear waters of the Caribbean Sea blend with the deeper blue Atlantic Ocean. Although less developed for tourism than the island's north and west, the area around Vieux Fort and points north along the eastern coast (en route to Castries) are home to some of Saint Lucia's unique ecosystems and interesting natural attractions.

Sights

Barre de l'Isle Forest Reserve

FOREST | **FAMILY** | Saint Lucia is divided into eastern and western halves by Barre de l'Isle ridge. A mile-long (1½-km-long) trail cuts through the reserve, and four lookout points provide panoramic views. Visible in the distance are Mt. Gimie (pronounced *Jimmy*), immense green valleys, both the Caribbean Sea and the Atlantic Ocean, and coastal communities. The trailhead is a half-hour drive from Castries. It takes about an hour to walk the trail—an easy hike—and another hour to climb Mt. LaCombe Ridge. Permission from the Saint Lucia Forestry Department is required to access the trail in Barre de l'Isle; a naturalist or forest officer guide will accompany you. ✉ *Micoud Hwy., Ravine Poisson* ✥ *Midway between Castries and Dennery* ☎ *758/468–5649 Forestry Dept.* 🎫 *$20, $10 for the guide* ☞ *Call weekdays 8:30–4:30.*

Mamiku Gardens

GARDEN | One of Saint Lucia's loveliest botanical gardens surrounds the hilltop ruins of the Micoud Estate. Baron Micoud, an 18th-century colonel in the French army and governor-general of Saint Lucia, deeded the land to his wife, Madame de Micoud, to avoid confiscation by the British during one of the many times when Saint Lucia changed hands. Locals abbreviated her name to "Ma Micoud," which, over time, became Mamiku. (The estate did become a British military outpost in 1796, but shortly thereafter was burned to the ground by slaves during the Brigand's War.) The estate is now primarily a banana plantation, but the gardens themselves—including several secluded or "secret" gardens—are filled with tropical flowers and plants, delicate orchids, and fragrant herbs. The bird watching is excellent here; three species of hummingbirds have been spotted on the grounds. ✉ *Micoud Rd., Praslin* ✥ *Off Micoud Hwy., south of Praslin* ☎ *758/714-4824* 🌐 *www.mamikugardens.com* 🎫 *$8, guided tour $12* ☞ *Guided tours must be booked at least 3 days in advance.*

Maria Islands Nature Reserve

ISLAND | **FAMILY** | Two tiny islands in the Atlantic Ocean off Saint Lucia's southeastern coast make up the reserve, which has its own interpretive center. The 25-acre Maria Major and the 4-acre Maria Minor are inhabited by two rare species of reptiles: the colorful Zandoli Terre ground lizard and the harmless Kouwes grass snake. They share their home with frigate birds, terns, doves, and other wildlife. There's a small beach for swimming and snorkeling, as well as an undisturbed forest, a vertical cliff covered with cacti, and a coral reef for snorkeling or diving. The St. Lucia National Trust offers tours, including a local fishing boat trip to the islands, by appointment only; bring your own picnic lunch, as there are no facilities. ✉ *Vieux Fort* ☎ *758/454–5014 for tour reservations* 🌐 *slunatrust.org/sites/maria-island-nature-reserve* 🎫 *$50.*

Hotels

Coconut Bay Beach Resort & Spa

$$$ | **RESORT** | **FAMILY** | Coconut Bay is a sprawling (85 acres), family-friendly, seaside retreat minutes from Hewanorra International Airport. **Pros:** five minutes from the airport; separate section for families with kids; excellent kitesurfing. **Cons:** nothing else nearby; rough surf beyond the reef; bathrooms have showers only. 💲 *Rooms from: US$378* ✉ *Off Micoud Hwy., Vieux Fort* ☎ *758/459–6000, 833/300–0146 in U.S.* 🌐 *www.cbayresort.com* 🛏 *250 rooms* 🍽 *All-Inclusive.*

★ Serenity at Coconut Bay

$$$$ | ALL-INCLUSIVE | An upscale yet casual, private yet social, adults-only (age 21 and over) enclave tucked into a corner of the expansive oceanfront gardens surrounding sister property, Coconut Bay Beach Resort, Serenity certainly lives up to its name. **Pros:** full access to all of Coconut Bay Resort's restaurants/activities; perfect choice for a romantic interlude, honeymoon, or anniversary; five minutes from Hewanorra International Airport. **Cons:** very expensive, even with special offers; long walk or shuttle to the resort's beach; remote location vis-à-vis island sights/outside activities. *Rooms from: US$981 ✉ Eau Piquant, Vieux Fort ✥ Adjacent to Coconut Bay Beach Resort & Spa ☎ 758/459–6064, 877/252-0304 🌐 serenityatcoconutbay.com 36 rooms All-Inclusive.*

Activities

BIKING

Bike St. Lucia

BIKING | Small groups of mountain bikers are accompanied on jungle biking tours (from $45 per person) along 8 miles (13 km) of groomed trails—with naturally occurring challenges (such as rocks and roots) and a few mud holes to challenge purists—that meander through the remnants of the 18th-century Anse Mamin Plantation, part of the 600-acre Anse Chastanet Estate in Soufrière. Stops are made to explore the French colonial ruins, study the beautiful tropical plants and fruit trees, have a picnic lunch, and take a dip in a river swimming hole or at the beach. There's an orientation loop for learning or brushing up on off-road riding skills, and there are beginner, intermediate, and advanced tracks. If you're staying in the north, you can arrange a tour that includes transportation to the Soufrière area and lunch at Anse Chastanet Resort. If you want to repeat the tour a second day, the charge drops to $25 per person. *✉ Anse Mamin Plantation, Anse Chastanet Adventure Center, Soufrière ☎ 758/459–7755 🌐 www.bikestlucia.com.*

BOATING AND SAILING

Rodney Bay and Marigot Bay are centers for bareboat or crewed yacht charters. Their marinas offer safe anchorage, shower facilities, restaurants, groceries, and maintenance for yachts sailing the waters of the eastern Caribbean. Charter prices range from $1,900 to $10,000 or more per week, depending on the season and the type and size of vessel, plus about $400 more per day if you want a skipper and cook. Some boat charter companies do not operate in August and September—the height of the hurricane season.

Bateau Mygo

BOATING | FAMILY | Choose a monohull or catamaran sailboat or a luxury power yacht for your half-, full-, or two-day cruise along the west coast, or charter by the week and explore neighboring islands. *✉ Chateau Mygo, Marigot Bay ✥ Adjacent to Marina Village ☎ 758/721–7007 🌐 www.sailsaintlucia.com.*

Destination St. Lucia Ltd. (*DSL*)

BOATING | FAMILY | For its bareboat yacht charters, DSL's vessels include two catamarans (42 and 44 feet) and several monohulls ranging in length from 32 to 46 feet. *✉ Rodney Bay Marina, Rodney Bay ☎ 758/452–8531 🌐 www.dsl-yachting.com.*

The Moorings St. Lucia

BOATING | FAMILY | Bareboat and crewed catamarans and monohulls are available for charter. You can also plan a one-way sail through the Grenadines, either picking up or dropping off at the company's facility in Grenada. *✉ Rodney Bay Marina, Rodney Bay ☎ 758/451–4357, 888/350–3575 in U.S. 🌐 www.moorings.com.*

DIVING AND SNORKELING

You'll find on-site dive shops at several resorts, including BodyHoliday St. Lucia, Sandals Grande, Royal St. Lucia, and Rendezvous in the north; Marigot Bay

Resort and Ti Kaye farther south; and Anse Chastanet and Sugar Beach, A Viceroy Resort, in Soufrière. Nearly all dive operators, regardless of their own location, provide transportation from Rodney Bay, Castries, Marigot Bay, or Soufrière. Depending on the season, the particular trip, and whether you rent or have your own gear, prices range from about $40 for a one-tank shore dive and $90 for a two-tank boat dive to $225 to $320 for a six-dive package over three days and $350 to $500 for a 10-dive package over five days—plus a Marine Reserve permit fee of $5 to $15, depending on the number of days. Dive shops provide instruction for all levels (beginner, intermediate, and advanced). For beginners, a resort course (pool training), followed by one open-water dive, runs from about $20 to $160, depending on the number of days and dives included. Snorkelers are generally welcome on dive trips and usually pay $60 to $75. All prices usually include taxi/boat transfers, refreshments, and equipment.

Anse Chastanet, near the Pitons on the southwest coast, is the best beach-entry dive site. The underwater reef drops from 20 feet to nearly 140 feet in a stunning coral wall.

A 165-foot freighter, *Lesleen M,* was deliberately sunk in 60 feet of water near **Anse Cochon** to create an artificial reef; divers can explore the ship in its entirety and view huge gorgonians, black coral trees, gigantic barrel sponges, lace corals, schooling fish, angelfish, sea horses, spotted eels, stingrays, nurse sharks, and sea turtles.

Anse La Raye, midway up the west coast, is one of Saint Lucia's finest wall and drift dives and a great place for snorkeling.

At the **Pinnacles,** four coral-encrusted stone piers rise to within 10 feet of the surface.

Superman's Flight is a dramatic drift dive along the steep walls beneath the Pitons. At the base of **Petit Piton** a spectacular wall drops to 200 feet, where you can view an impressive collection of huge barrel sponges and black coral trees; strong currents ensure good visibility.

DIVE OPERATORS

Dive Fair Helen

SCUBA DIVING | **FAMILY** | In operation since 1992 and owned by a Saint Lucian environmentalist, this PADI dive center offers half- and full-day excursions on two custom-built dive boats to wreck, wall, and marine reserve areas, as well as night dives and instruction. ✉ *Marina Village, Marigot Bay* ☎ *758/451–7716* 🌐 *www.divefairhelen.com.*

★ Dive Saint Lucia

DIVING & SNORKELING | Operating out of a LEED platinum-certified building at Rodney Bay Marina, Saint Lucia's state-of-the-art dive center has a purpose-built training pool, fully equipped classrooms for adult and junior instruction, fully equipped compressors, a PADI 5-star Instructor Development Center (IDC), equipment rental and storage, guided dives, and two specialized dive boats (46-foot Newton)—each with a 30-diver capacity. Facilities are handicap-accessible and include a motorized lift chair. Dive trips include lunch, drinks, and hotel transfers (north of Castries). ✉ *Rodney Bay Marina, Castries-Gros Islet Hwy., Rodney Bay* ☎ *758/451–3483* 🌐 *www.divesaintlucia.com.*

Island Divers

DIVING & SNORKELING | **FAMILY** | At the edge of the National Marine Park, with two reefs and an offshore wreck accessible from shore, this dive shop at Ti Kaye Resort & Spa offers guided shore dives ($40), boat dives, PADI certification, equipment rental, and an extensive list of specialty courses. Hotel transfers available. ✉ *Ti Kaye Resort & Spa, Off West Coast Rd., Anse La Raye* ✣ *Between Anse la Raye and Canaries* ☎ *758/456–8110* 🌐 *www.tikaye.com/diving.*

Did You Know?

Anse Chastanet, near the Pitons, is the best beach-entry site for divers. The underwater reef drops to nearly 140 feet in a stunning coral wall.

Scuba St. Lucia

SCUBA DIVING | FAMILY | Daily (and nightly) beach and boat dives and resort and certification courses are available from this PADI 5-Star facility located on Anse Chastanet. They also offer underwater photography and snorkeling equipment. ✉ *Anse Chastanet Resort, Anse Chastanet Rd., Soufrière* ☎ *758/459–7755, 800/223–1108 in U.S.* 🌐 *www.scubastlucia.com.*

FISHING

Among the deep-sea creatures you can find in Saint Lucia's waters are dolphin (the fish, not the mammal, also called dorado or mahimahi), barracuda, mackerel, wahoo, kingfish, sailfish, and white and blue marlin. Sportfishing is generally done on a catch-and-release basis, but the captain may permit you to take a fish back to your hotel to be prepared for your dinner. Neither spearfishing nor collecting live fish in coastal waters is permitted. Half- and full-day deep-sea fishing excursions can be arranged at Vigie Marina. A half day of fishing on a scheduled trip runs about $120 per person; a private charter costs $660 to $1,700 for up to six or eight people, depending on the size of the boat and the length of time. Beginners are welcome.

Captain Mike's

FISHING | FAMILY | Named for Captain Mike Hackshaw and run by his sons, Bruce and Andrew, this operation has a fleet of powerboats that accommodate up to eight anglers for half- or full-day sportfishing charters (tackle and cold drinks are supplied). Customized sightseeing or whale/dolphin-watching trips (from $60 per person) can also be arranged for four to six people. ✉ *Vigie Marina, Vigie* ☎ *758/452–7044* 🌐 *www.captmikes.com.*

Hackshaw's Boat Charters

FISHING | FAMILY | In business since 1953, this company runs group and private deep-sea sports fishing charters on *Blue Boy,* a 31-foot Bertram; *Limited Edition,* a 47-foot custom-built Buddy Davis; and *Lady Anne,* a 50-foot luxury power catamaran used for custom fishing, snorkeling, whale-watching, and sunset cruises. ✉ *Vigie Marina, Seraphine Rd., Vigie* ☎ *758/453–0553* 🌐 *www.hackshaws.com.*

GOLF

Sandals St. Lucia Golf & Country Club at Cap Estate

GOLF | FAMILY | Situated at the island's northern tip, this championship 18-hole course features broad views of both the Atlantic and the Caribbean, as well as many spots adorned with orchids and bromeliads. Wind and the demanding layout present challenges. The Sports Bar is a convivial meeting place all day long. You can arrange lessons at the pro shop and perfect your swing at the 350-yard driving range. Carts are mandatory; club and shoe rentals are available. Reservations are essential. ✉ *Cap Estate* ☎ *758/450–8523* 🌐 *www.sandals.com/golf/st-lucia* 🎫 *$175 for 18 holes, $135 for 9 holes* 🏌 *18 holes, 6744 yards, par 71.*

GUIDED TOURS

Taxi drivers are well informed and can give you a full tour and often an excellent one, thanks to government-sponsored training programs. Full-day island tours cost about $140 for up to four people, depending on the route and whether entrance fees and lunch are included; half-day tours, $100. If you plan your own day, expect to pay the driver $40 per hour plus tip.

Island Routes

ADVENTURE TOURS | This Sandals partner offers dozens of adventure and sightseeing tours, including a six-hour tour that features a rum factory, Anse La Raye, a waterfall swim, the Tet Paul Nature Trail, and lunch ($236). A catamaran cruise down the west coast from Rodney Bay to Soufrière (with stops at the Sulphur Springs and Marigot Bay) is a more leisurely experience (seven hours, $114). Other tours include hiking, biking, horseback riding, ziplining, and many, many more. ✉ *Castries* ☎ *877/768–8370 in U.S., 758/455–2000* 🌐 *www.islandroutes.com.*

Jungle Tours

GUIDED TOURS | This company specializes in rain-forest hiking tours in small groups and for all ability levels. You're required only to bring hiking shoes or sneakers and have a willingness to get wet and have fun. The cost is around $120 per person, depending on the hike and the number of people in your party, and includes lunch, fees, and transportation via an open Land Rover truck. ✉ *Cas en Bas* ☎ *758/715–3438* 🌐 *www.jungle-toursstlucia.com.*

Rainforest Adventures

GUIDED TOURS | **FAMILY** | Ever wish you could get a bird's-eye view of the rain forest? Or at least experience it without hiking up and down miles of mountain trails? Here's your chance. Depending on your athleticism and spirit of adventure, choose a two-hour aerial tram ride, a zipline experience, or both. Either activity guarantees a magnificent view as you peacefully ride above or actively zip through the canopy of the 3,442-acre Castries Waterworks Rain Forest in Babonneau, 30 minutes east of Rodney Bay. On the tram ride, eight-passenger gondolas glide slowly among the giant trees, twisting vines, and dense thickets of vegetation accented by colorful flowers, as a tour guide explains and shares anecdotes about the various trees, plants, birds, and other wonders of nature found in the area. You might even spot a Jacquot parrot! The zipline, on the other hand, is a thrilling experience in which you're rigged with a harness, helmet, and clamps that attach to cables strategically strung through the forest. Short trails connect 18 platforms, so riders come down to earth briefly and hike to the next station before speeding through the forest canopy to the next stop. There's even a nighttime zipline tour. By the way, you can take a guided trail hike, too.

TIP→ Bring binoculars and a camera. ✉ *Chassin, Babonneau* ☎ *758/461–5151* 🌐 *www.rainforestadventure.com* 🎫 *$75 tram, $65 zipline, $85 tram and zipline, $45 trail hike.*

St. Lucia Helicopters

AIR EXCURSIONS | How about a bird's-eye view of the island? A 10-minute North Island tour ($127 per person) leaves from the hangar in Castries, continues up the west coast to Pigeon Island, then flies along the rugged Atlantic coastline before returning inland over Castries. The 20-minute South Island tour ($204 per person) starts at Pointe Seraphine and follows the western coastline, circling beautiful Marigot Bay, Soufrière, and the majestic Pitons before returning inland over the volcanic hot springs and tropical rain forest. A complete island tour combines the two and lasts 30 minutes ($248 per person). All tours require a minimum of four passengers; the copter holds six. ✉ *George F. L. Charles Airport, Island Flyers Hangar, Vigie* ☎ *758/453–6950* 🌐 *stluciahelicopters.com.*

★ **Saint Lucia National Trust**

ECOTOURISM | Among the trust's fascinating Eco-South Tours (located in and around the southeast of Saint Lucia) are a hike through a mangrove forest, a boat trip and trek to Maria Islands Nature Reserve, a native fishing tour on a traditional pirogue, handicraft production, horseback riding, or sea moss harvesting. ✉ *Pigeon Island National Landmark, Pigeon Island* ☎ *758/452–5005 Maria Islands Interpretation Centre, Vieux Fort, 758/454–5014* 🌐 *slunatrust.org/tours/toureco-south-tours.*

HIKING

Saint Lucia Forestry Department

HIKING & WALKING | **FAMILY** | Trails under this department's jurisdiction include the Barre de L'Isle Trail (just off the highway, halfway between Castries and Dennery but currently closed for construction), the Forestiere Trail (20 minutes east of Castries), the Des Cartiers Rain Forest Trail (west of Micoud), the Edmund Rain Forest Trail and Enbas Saut Waterfalls (east of Soufrière), the Millet Bird Sanctuary

Trail (east of Marigot Bay), and the Union Nature Trail (north of Castries). Most are two-hour hikes on 2-mile (3-km) loop trails; the bird-watching tour lasts four hours. The Forestry Department charges $25 for access to the hiking trails ($10 for nature trails), and provides guides ($20 to $30, depending on the hike) who explain the plants and trees that you'll encounter and keep you on the right track. Seasoned hikers climb the Pitons, the two volcanic cones rising 2,461 feet and 2,619 feet from the ocean floor, just south of Soufrière. Casual hiking is recommended only on Gros Piton, which offers a steep but safe trail to the top. The first half of the hike is moderately difficult; reaching the summit is challenging and should be attempted only by those who are physically fit. The view from the top is spectacular. Tourists are also permitted to hike Petit Piton, but the second half of the hike requires a good deal of rock climbing, and you'll need to provide your own safety equipment. Hiking either Piton requires permission from the Forestry Department and a knowledgeable guide. ✉ *Union Forestry Complex, Union, Castries* ☎ *758/468–5649, 758/489–0136 for Pitons permission* 🌐 *www.forestryeeunit.blogpost.com.*

Tet Paul Nature Trail

HIKING & WALKING | Climb the natural "stairway" for a stunning 360-degree view of Saint Lucia including the entire southern coast (and neighboring St. Vincent in the distance), Mt. Gimie in the island's center, the Pitons on the nearby west coast, and as far north as Martinique on a clear day. This Saint Lucia Heritage Site, just 10 minutes from downtown Soufrière, is an easy-to-moderate, 45-minute hike, with stops along the way to observe the scenery and a picnic area. ✉ *West Coast Rd., Soufrière* ✣ *3 miles (5 km) south of town behind Fond Doux Plantation* ☎ *758/723–2930* 🌐 *www.tetpaulnaturetrail.com* ☞ *$10 entry fee includes guide.*

HORSEBACK RIDING

Creole horses, a breed native to South America and popular on Saint Lucia, are fairly small, fast, sturdy, and even-tempered animals suitable for beginners. Established stables can accommodate all skill levels. They offer countryside trail rides, beach rides with picnic lunches, farm tours, carriage rides, and lengthy treks. Prices run about $40–$75 for a guided ride and $65–$120 for a beach ride with swimming (with your horse), depending on the distance and how long you're in the saddle. Local people sometimes appear on beaches with their steeds and offer 30-minute rides for $15 to $20; ride at your own risk.

Atlantic Shores Riding Stables

HORSEBACK RIDING | FAMILY | One- and two-hour trail rides roam along the beach, three-hour rides traverse the countryside, and private rides can be arranged. Beginners and children are welcome. Prices range from $65 to $95 per person. ✉ *Micoud Hwy., Savannes Bay, Vieux Fort* ☎ *758/454–8660* 🌐 *www.atlanticridingstables.com.*

Trim's National Riding Stable

HORSEBACK RIDING | FAMILY | At the island's oldest riding stable, they offer four riding sessions per day, including beach tours and trail rides, plus riding lessons, party rides, pony rides, and horse-and-carriage tours to Pigeon Island. Prices range from $50 for a one-hour ride to $95 for a three-hour ride with a barbecue lunch. Transportation is provided from nearby hotels if necessary. ✉ *Cas en Bas* ☎ *758/484-9799* 🌐 *www.facebook.com/trimsnationalridingstables/.*

KITESURFING

Kitesurfers congregate at Anse de Sables (Sandy) Beach in Vieux Fort, at the southeastern tip of Saint Lucia, to take advantage of the blue-water and high-wind conditions that the Atlantic Ocean provides.

Aquaholics

LOCAL SPORTS | FAMILY | Want to learn to kitesurf, or boost your skills in a glorious environment? You can't go wrong with Aquaholics. Their classroom is a beautiful, crescent-shape bay at the northeastern tip of Saint Lucia, where the Atlantic Ocean meets the Caribbean Sea and the trade winds are consistent from November to June. All lessons are private; prices range from $60 for an introductory course (one hour) to $450 for a three-day, six hour course. ✉ *Cas-En-Bas Beach, Cotton Bay, Cap Estate* ☎ *758/726–0600* 🌐 *www.aquaholicsstlucia.com.*

The Reef Kite + Surf

WINDSURFING | FAMILY | This water-sports center offers equipment rental and lessons from certified instructors. Kitesurfing equipment rents for $60 half day, $80 full day. The three-hour starter costs $200, including equipment and safety gear; the one-hour "taster" lesson, $90. Kitesurfing is particularly strenuous, so participants must be excellent swimmers and in good health. ✉ *The Reef Beach Café, Sandy Beach, Micoud Hwy., Vieux Fort* ☎ *758/454–3418* 🌐 *www.stluciakitesurfing.com.*

SEA EXCURSIONS

A day sail or sea cruise from Rodney Bay or Vigie Cove to Soufrière and the Pitons is a wonderful way to see Saint Lucia and get to its distinctive natural sites. Prices for a full-day sailing excursion to Soufrière run about $110 per person and include a land tour to the Diamond Falls Botanical Gardens, the "drive-in" volcano, lunch, a stop for swimming and snorkeling, and a swing through pretty Marigot Bay. You might even add ziplining! Half-day cruises to the Pitons, three-hour whale-watching tours, and two-hour sunset cruises along the northwest coast cost about $50 per person.

Captain Mike's

RAFTING | FAMILY | With 20 species of whales and dolphins living in Caribbean waters, your chances of sighting some are very good—90 percent of the time, they say—on these 3½-hour whale- and dolphin-watching trips ($60 per person) aboard Captain Mike's *Free Willie.* ✉ *Vigie Marina, Ganthers Bay, Castries* ☎ *758/452–7044* 🌐 *www.captmikes.com.*

★ **Carnival Sailing**

BOATING | FAMILY | Carnival Sailing has a fleet of eight catamarans that accommodate from 30 to 170 passengers and they run a variety of trips along the coast to Soufrière—tours, entrance fees, lunch, and drinks included. Prices vary for the menu of day tours, adventure tours, sunset cruises, and private charters. ✉ *Reduit Beach Ave., Rodney Bay* ☎ *758/452–5586* 🌐 *carnivalsailing.com.*

Mystic Man Ocean Adventures

BOATING | FAMILY | The glass-bottom boat, sailing, catamaran, deep-sea fishing, snorkeling, and/or whale- and dolphin-watching tours are all great family excursions; there's also a sunset cruise. Most trips depart from Soufrière. ✉ *Bay St., Soufrière* ✣ *On bay front* ☎ *758/459–7783, 800/401–9804* 🌐 *www.mysticmantours.com.*

Sea Spray Cruises

BOATING | FAMILY | Sail down the west coast from Rodney Bay to Soufrière on *Mango Tango* (a 52-foot catamaran), *Jus Tango* (a 65-foot catamaran), Go Tango (an 80-foot double-deck catamaran), *Calypso Cat* (a 42-foot double-deck power catamaran), or *Tango* (a 78-foot power catamaran). The all-day Tout Bagay (a little bit of everything tour; adults, $125; children, $60) includes a visit to the sulfur springs, drive-in volcano, and Morne Coubaril Estate. The view of the Pitons from the water is majestic. You'll have lunch and drinks onboard, plenty of music, and an opportunity to swim at a remote beach. ✉ *Rodney Bay Marina, Rodney Bay* ☎ *758/458–0123* 🌐 *www.seaspraycruises.com.*

Chapter 20

ST. MAARTEN AND ST. MARTIN

Updated by
Riselle Celestina

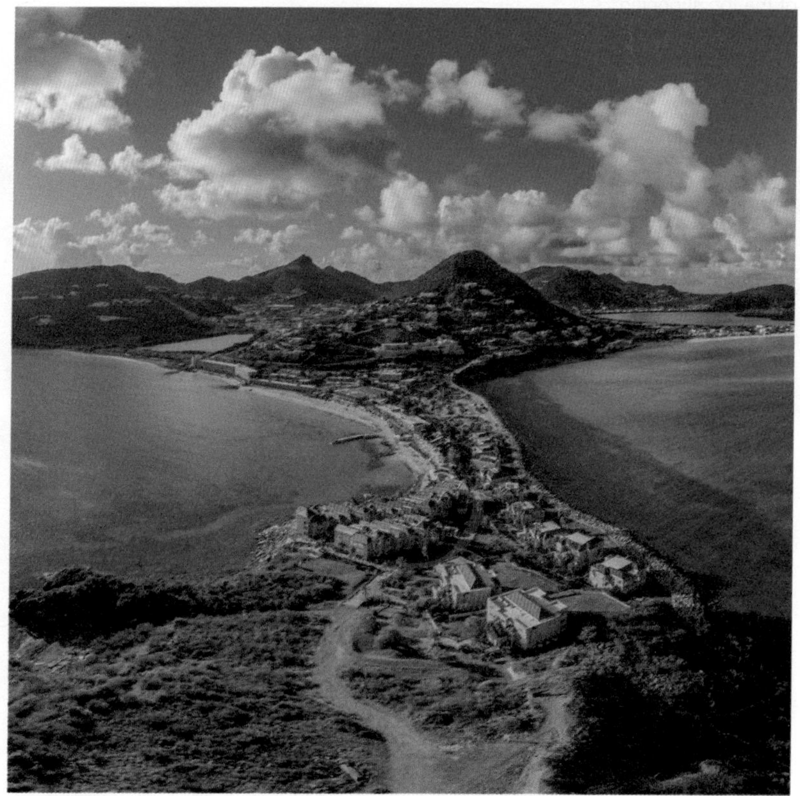

Sights ★★★★★ | Restaurants ★★★★★ | Hotels ★★★★☆ | Shopping ★★★★★ | Nightlife ★★★★☆

WELCOME TO ST. MAARTEN AND ST. MARTIN

TOP REASONS TO GO

★ **Great Food:** The island has so many good places to dine that you could eat out for a month (or six) and never repeat a restaurant visit.

★ **Lots of Shops:** Philipsburg is one of the top shopping spots in the Caribbean and the galleries and boutiques of Marigot and Grand Case bring a touch of France.

★ **Beaches Large and Small:** Thirty-seven picture-perfect beaches are spread out across the island; some are clothing-optional.

★ **Sports Galore:** The wide range of land and water sports adventures will satisfy almost any need and give you the perfect excuse to try everything from ATVs to ziplines.

★ **Variety of Nightlife:** After-dark entertainment options include shows, lounges, discos, beach bars, and casinos.

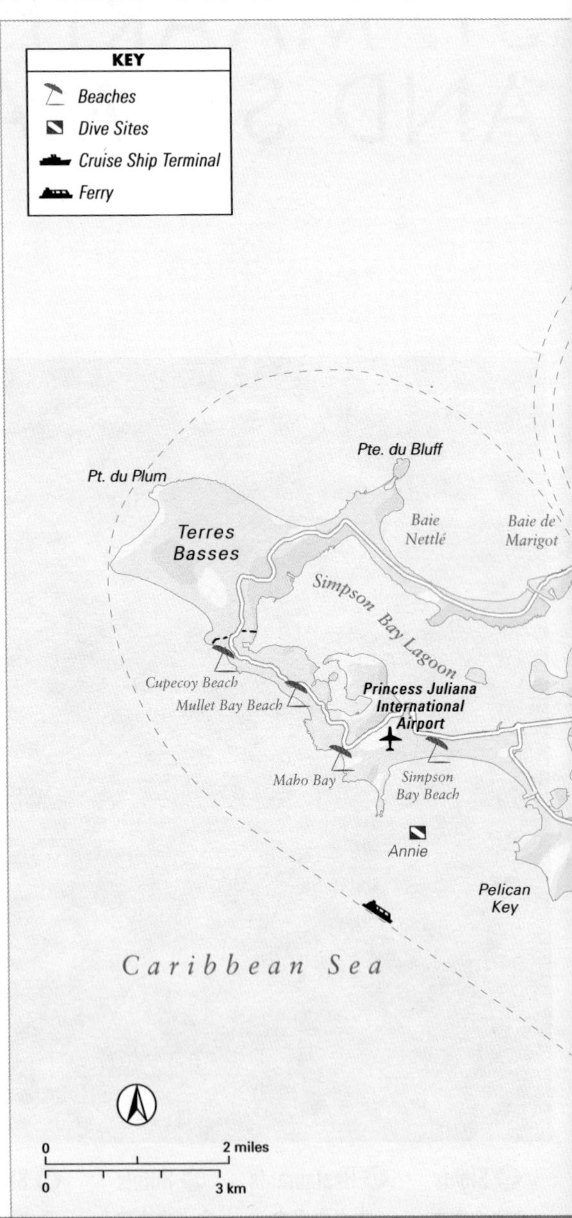

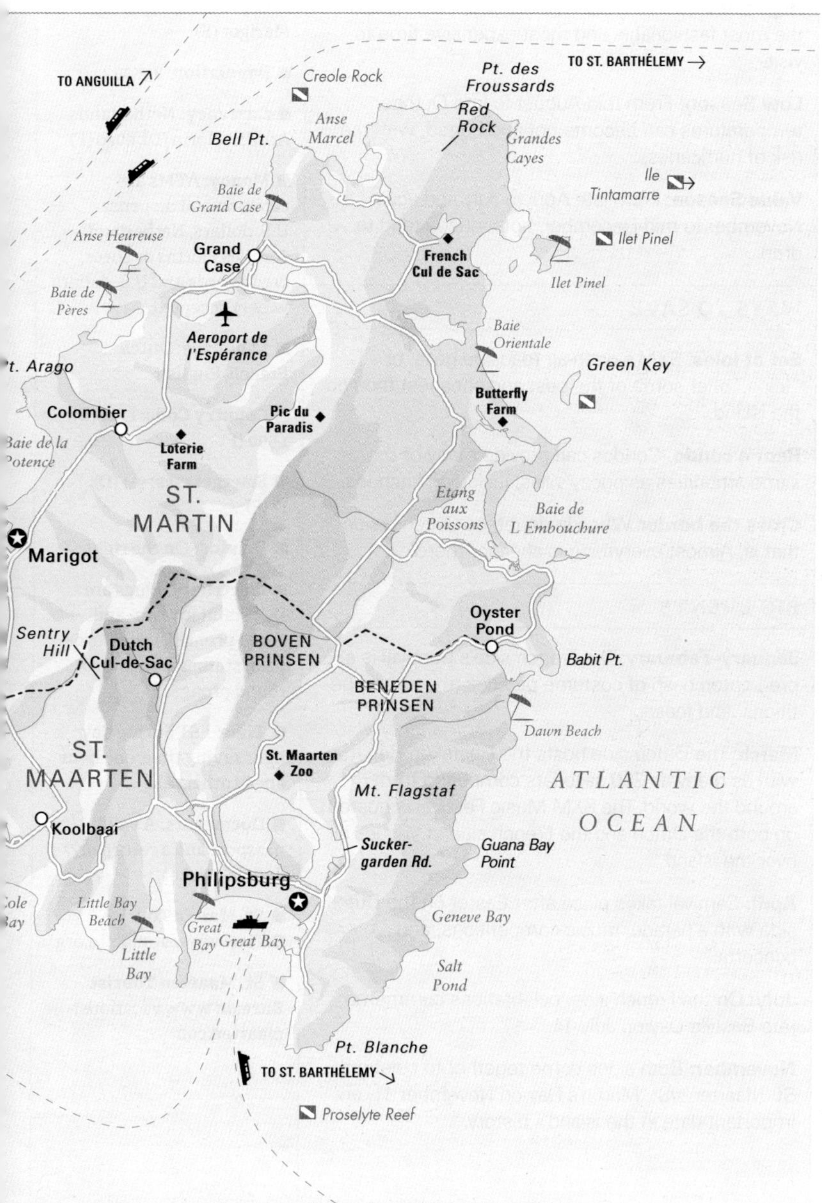

TO ANGUILLA
Creole Rock
Pt. des Froussards
TO ST. BARTHÉLEMY
Anse Marcel
Bell Pt.
Red Rock
Grandes Cayes
Ile Tintamarre
Baie de Grand Case
Anse Heureuse
Grand Case
French Cul de Sac
Ilet Pinel
Ilet Pinel
Baie de Pères
Aeroport de l'Espérance
Baie Orientale
Green Key
Pt. Arago
Butterfly Farm
Colombier
Pic du Paradis
Baie de la Potence
Loterie Farm
ST. MARTIN
Etang aux Poissons
Baie de L Embouchure
Marigot
Oyster Pond
Sentry Hill
Dutch Cul-de-Sac
BOVEN PRINSEN
Babit Pt.
BENEDEN PRINSEN
Dawn Beach
ST. MAARTEN
St. Maarten Zoo
ATLANTIC OCEAN
Mt. Flagstaf
Koolbaai
Suckergarden Rd.
Guana Bay Point
Philipsburg
Little Bay Beach
Great Bay
Great Bay
Geneve Bay
Little Bay
Salt Pond
Pt. Blanche
TO ST. BARTHÉLEMY
Proselyte Reef

ISLAND SNAPSHOT

WHEN TO GO

High Season: Mid-December through mid-April is the most fashionable and most expensive time to visit.

Low Season: From mid-August to late October, temperatures can become hot and humid, with the risk of hurricanes.

Value Season: From late April to July and again November to mid-December, hotel prices tend to drop.

WAYS TO SAVE

Eat at lolos. SXM's open-air roadside grills, or "lolos," offer some of the best and cheapest food on the island.

Rent a condo. Condos can provide many of the same amenities as pricey villas, including kitchens.

Cross the border. When in doubt, go Dutch... side that is. Almost everything is cheaper there.

BIG EVENTS

January–February: The French side's Carnival is a pre-Lenten bash of costume parades, music competitions, and feasts.

March: The Dutch side hosts the Heineken Regatta, with as many as 200 sailboats competing from around the world. The SXM Music Festival is hosted on both the Dutch and the French side at venues all over the island.

April: Carnival takes place after Easter on the Dutch side with a parade, music competitions, and concerts.

July: On the French side, celebrations commemorate Bastille Day on July 14.

November: Both sides come together to celebrate St. Maarten's/St. Martin's Day on November 11, an important date in the island's history.

AT A GLANCE

- **Capital:** Phillipsburg (D); Marigot (F)
- **Population:** 81,535
- **Currency:** Netherlands Antilles florin (D); euro (F)
- **Money:** ATMs are common and dispense U.S. dollars, Netherlands Antilles Florins or euros; credit cards and U.S. dollars widely accepted.
- **Language:** Dutch, French, English
- **Country Code:** 1 721 (D); 1 590 (F)
- **Emergencies:** 911 (D); 17 (F)
- **Driving:** On the right
- **Electricity:** Plugs are U.S. standard two- and three-prong (D) and European standard with two round prongs (F)
- **Time:** EST during daylight saving time; one hour ahead otherwise
- **Documents:** A valid passport and a return or ongoing ticket
- **St. Martin Tourist Office:** www.st-martin.org
- **St. Maarten Tourist Bureau:** www.vacationst-maarten.com

St. Maarten/St. Martin is unique among Caribbean destinations. The 37-square-mile (96-square-km) island is a seamless place (there are no border gates), but it is governed by two nations—the Netherlands and France—and has residents from more than 100 countries. A call from the Dutch side to the French is an international call, currencies are different, electric current differs, and even the vibe is different. Only the island of Hispaniola, which encompasses Haiti and the Dominican Republic, is in a similar position in the Caribbean.

Happily for Americans, who make up the majority of visitors to St. Maarten/ St. Martin, English works in both nations. Dutch St. Maarten might feel particularly comfortable for Americans: the prices are a bit lower (not to mention in U.S. dollars), the big hotels have casinos, and there is more nightlife. Huge cruise ships disgorge masses of shoppers into the Philipsburg shopping area at midmorning, when roads may become congested. But once you pass the meandering, unmarked border to the French side, you find a hint of the south of France: quiet countryside, fine cuisine, and in Marigot, a walkable harbor area with outdoor cafés, a great outdoor market, and some shops to explore.

Almost 4,000 years ago, it was salt and not tourism that drove this little island's economy. The Arawak people, the island's first known inhabitants, prospered until the warring Caribs invaded, adding the peaceful Arawaks to their list of conquests. Columbus spotted the isle on November 11, 1493, and named it after St. Martin (whose feast day is November 11), but it wasn't populated by Europeans until the 17th century, when it was claimed by the Dutch, French, and Spanish. The Dutch and French finally joined forces to claim the island in 1644, and the Treaty of Concordia partitioned the territory in 1648. According to legend the border was drawn along the line where a French man and a Dutch man, walking from opposite coasts, met.

Both sides of the island offer a touch of European culture along with a lot of laid-back Caribbean ambience. Water sports both serene and extreme abound—diving, snorkeling, sailing, windsurfing, kitesurfing, ziplining, and even hover-boarding. With soft trade winds cooling the subtropical climate, it's easy to while away the day relaxing on one of the 37 beaches, strolling Philipsburg's boardwalk, shopping along Philipsburg's Front Street or the harbors of Marigot. Although luck is an important commodity at St. Maarten's dozen or so casinos, chance plays no part in finding a good meal at the hundreds of excellent restaurants or after-dark fun in the subtle to sizzling nightlife.

When cruise ships are in port on the Dutch side (there can be as many as nine at once), shopping areas are crowded and traffic moves at a snail's pace. Instead spend those days at your resort or one of the full-service beach clubs, or out on the water, and plan shopping excursions for the early morning or at cocktail hour, after "rush hour" traffic calms down. Still, these are minor inconveniences compared with the feel of the sand between your toes or the breeze through your hair, gourmet food sating your appetite, and being able to crisscross freely between two nations on one island.

Planning

Getting Here and Around

AIR

More than 20 carriers fly to the island. There are nonstop flights from Atlanta (Delta, seasonal), Boston (JetBlue, seasonal), Charlotte (American), Miami/Ft. Lauderdale (American and JetBlue), New York–JFK (American, Delta, JetBlue), Newark, Chicago, and Dulles (United, seasonal), Ft. Lauderdale (JetBlue, Spirit), Orlando (Frontier), and Philadelphia (American). Nonstop flights also arrive from both Paris (Air France) and Amsterdam (KLM) as well as Panama (Copa, which has many connections from and to the U.S.). There are also direct flights from Montreal and Toronto and some nonstop charter flights (including some from Boston). You can also connect in San Juan on Seabourne and Winair, the St. Maarten–based local carrier. Many smaller Caribbean-based airlines, including Air Caraïbes, Air Antilles, Anguilla Air Services, Caribbean Airlines, Air Sunshine, St. Barth Commuter, and Winair (Windward Islands Airways), offer service from other islands in the Caribbean.

AIRPORTS Aéroport de L'Espérance. *(SFG) ✉ Rte. de l'Espérance, Grand Case ☎ 0590/27–11–00 🌐 www.saintmartin-airport.com.* **Princess Juliana International Airport.** *(SXM) ☎ 721/546–7542 🌐 www.sxmairport.com.*

BOAT AND FERRY

You can take ferries to St. Barth (45–60 minutes, €55–€90 from the French side, though you can pay in dollars or $85–$115 from the Dutch side); to Anguilla (25 minutes, €25 from the French side); and to Saba (one to two hours, $90–$100 from the Dutch side).

CONTACTS Aqua Mania Adventures. *✉ Simpson Bay Resort Marina Plaza, Simpson Bay ☎ 721/544–2640 🌐 www.stmaarten-activities.com.* **Great Bay Express.** *✉ Bobby's Marina Village, Philipsburg ☎ 721/542–0032 Dutch side 🌐 www.greatbayexpress.com.* **Link Ferries.** *✉ Marigot ☎ 264/772–4901 🌐 www.linkferry.com.* **Voyager.** *✉ Marigot ☎ 0590/87–10–68 🌐 www.voy12.com.* **Makana Ferry Service.** *☎ 721/543-8915 🌐 www.makanaferryservice.com.* **Calypso Charters.** *✉ Blowing Point Ferry Terminal, Blowing Point, for ferry service between St. Barth, Anguilla, and St. Maarten/Martin ☎ 264/462-8504.*

CAR

It's easy to get around the island by car. Virtually all roads are paved and in generally good condition. However, they can be crowded, especially during high season; you might experience traffic jams, particularly around Marigot around noon and Simpson Bay from 3 pm. Be alert for occasional potholes and unpainted speed bumps (small signs warn you), as well as the island tradition of stopping in the middle of the road to chat with a friend or yield to someone entering traffic. Be aware that there is no stopping in a roundabout to allow someone to enter the roundabout. Few roads are identified by name or number, but most have signs indicating the destination. Driving is on the right. There are gas stations all over the island, but gas tends to be cheaper on the French side.

Car Rentals: You can book a car at Princess Juliana International SXM Airport, where all major rental companies have booths, but it is often *much* cheaper to reserve a car in advance from home. That's also an especially wise move in high season when some companies may run out of cars. A shuttle to the rental-car companies' lots is provided. Rates are among the best in the Caribbean, as little as $25–$40 per day in low season, but at least $240/week, and up, in high season. You can also rent a car on the French side, but this rarely makes sense for Americans because of the exchange rates.

CAR-RENTAL CONTACTS Avis. ✉ *Airport Rd., Simpson Bay* ☎ *888/777–2847, 721/545-2847* 🌐 *www.avis.com.* **Budget.** ☎ *800/472–3325, 721/587–2847* 🌐 *www.sxmbudget.com.* **Dollar/Thrifty Car Rental.** ✉ *102 Airport Rd.* ☎ *721/545–2393* 🌐 *www.dollarthriftysxm.com.* **Empress Rent-a-Car.** ☎ *721/545–2062* 🌐 *www.empressrentacar.com.*

TAXI

There is a government-sponsored taxi dispatcher at the airport and the harbor. Posted fares are for one or two people. Add $5 for each additional person, half price for kids. The first bag is free; after that it's $1 per bag. It costs about $18 from the airport to Philipsburg or Marigot, and about $30 to Dawn Beach. After 10 pm fares go up 25%, and after midnight 50%. Licensed drivers can be identified by the "taxi" or new "T" license plate on the Dutch side and the TXI license plate on the French side. Avoid any uninsured illegal cabs that may appear; they have no such plates, and police have been cracking down on them across the island. Fixed fares apply from Juliana International Airport and the Marigot ferry to hotels around the island.

TAXI CONTACTS Dutch St. Maarten Taxi Association. ☎ *721/543–7815, 721/524–4978* 🌐 *www.taxistmaarten.com.* **Juliana Airport Taxi Dispatch.** ☎ *721/542–1681* 🌐 *www.sxmairporttaxis.com.* **Marigot Taxi Dispatch.** ☎ *0590/87–56–54.*

Sights

The best way to explore St. Maarten/St. Martin is by car. Though sometimes congested, especially around Philipsburg and Marigot, the roads are fairly good, though narrow and winding, with some speed bumps, potholes, roundabouts, and an occasional wandering goat herd or stray oxen. Few roads are marked with their names, but destination signs are somewhat common. Besides, the island is so small that it's hard to get really lost.

If you're spending a few days, get to know the area with a scenic loop around the island. Be sure to pack a towel and some water shoes, a hat, sunglasses, and sunblock. Head up the east shoreline from Philipsburg, and follow the signs to Dawn Beach and Oyster Pond. The road winds past soaring hills, turquoise waters, quaint West Indian houses, and wonderful views of St. Barth. As you cross over to the French side, keep following the road toward Orient Bay, the St-Tropez of the Caribbean. Continue to Anse Marcel, Grand Case, and Marigot. From Marigot, the flat neighboring island of Anguilla is visible. Completing the loop through Sandy Ground and the French lowlands brings you past Cupecoy Beach, through Maho and Simpson Bay, where Saba looms on the southern horizon, and back over the mountain road into Philipsburg. A few have called it "the Great Circle Route," for good reason.

Beaches

For such a small island, St. Maarten/St. Martin has a wide array of beaches, from the long expanse of Baie Orientale on the French side to powdery-soft Mullet Bay on the Dutch side.

Several of the best Dutch-side beaches are developed and have large-scale resorts. But others, including Simpson Bay and Cupecoy, have comparatively little development. You'll sometimes find vendors or beach bars to rent chairs and umbrellas (but not always).

Almost all of the French-side beaches, whether busy Baie Orientale or less busy Baie des Pères (Friar's Bay), have beach clubs and restaurants. For about $20–$25 a couple you get two chaises (*transats*) and an umbrella (*parasol*) for the day, not to mention chair-side service for drinks and food. Only some beaches have bathrooms and showers, so if that is your preference, inquire.

Warm surf and a gentle breeze can be found at the island's 37 beaches, though breezes are generally a bit stronger on the windward Eastern shore. Every beach is open to the public. Try several. Each is unique: some bustling and some bare, some refined and some rocky, some good for snorkeling and some for sunning. Whatever your fancy, it's here, including a clothing-optional beach at the south end of beautiful Baie Orientale (Orient Beach). And several of the island's gems don't have big hotels lining their shores. Many beaches have chair rental concessions and beach bars, too.

TIP→ Petty theft from cars in beach parking lots occasionally happens. Leave nothing in your parked car, not even in the glove compartment or especially the trunk.

Restaurants

Although most people come to St. Maarten/St. Martin for sun and fun, they leave praising the incredible cuisine available on both sides of the island. On an isle that covers only 37 square miles (96 square km), there are literally hundreds of restaurants.

Some of the best restaurants are in Grand Case (on the French side), but many other fine dining restaurants now are in Simpson Bay and Porto Cupecoy, both on the Dutch side. Don't limit your culinary adventures to one area. Try the hopping upscale restaurants of Cupecoy, the tourist-friendly low-key eateries of Simpson Bay, and the many *lolos* (roadside barbecue stands) throughout. Loyalists on both "sides" will cheerfully try to steer you to their favorites. Do remember that some French-side restaurants may still offer a one-to-one exchange rate if you use cash.

During high season, it's essential to make reservations. Sometimes you can make them the same day. Dutch-side restaurants may include a 15% service charge, so check your bill before tipping. On the French side, service is usually included (worth checking, here, too), but it is customary to leave 5%–10% extra. Don't leave tips on your credit card—it's customary to tip in cash. A taxi is probably the easiest solution to the parking problems in Grand Case, Marigot, and Philipsburg. Grand Case has two pay lots—each costs several dollars—at each end of the main boulevard, and there's one well-lit free lot toward the northern end of town, which usually fills up by 8 pm. Restaurants will be happy to call you a cab to return at the end of the meal.

What to Wear: Although appropriate dining attire ranges from swimsuits to sport jackets, casual dress is usually just fine. A nice shirt and pants or a skirt will take you almost anywhere. Jeans are fine in less formal eateries.

Hotels and Resorts

The island, though small, is well developed—some say overdeveloped—and offers a wide range of lodging. The larger resorts and time shares are on the Dutch side; the French side has more intimate properties. Just keep in mind that the popular restaurants around Grand Case, on the French side, are a long drive from most Dutch-side hotels—but there are now lots of great restaurants in Simpson Bay and at Porto Cupecoy. French-side hotels charge in euros. Be wary of very low–price alternatives, short-term housing for temporary workers, or properties used by very low-end tour companies. Some locations very close to the airport can be a bit noisy.

Resorts and Time-Shares: Virtually every SXM time-share and resort has been rebuilt better and stronger in the past few years due to hurricanes. There are several resorts with all-inclusive options, but before you lock yourself into a meal plan, keep in mind that restaurants at all price points are easily accessible (and that opting for an all-inclusive resort could deprive you of some seriously memorable dining experiences).

Small Inns: Small guesthouses and inns can be found on both sides of the island. It's worth considering these, especially if you are not the big-resort type. Several are quite modern and attractive, and located beachfront.

Villas and Condos: Both sides of the island have hundreds of villas and condos for every conceivable budget. Some of the resorts offer villa alternatives, which make for a good compromise, and perhaps better security. In addition, many high-end condo developments offer unsold units as rentals—and some are brand-new and terrific bargains.

Hotel reviews have been shortened. For full information, visit Fodors.com.

What It Costs in U.S. Dollars			
$	$$	$$$	$$$$
RESTAURANTS			
under $12	$12–$20	$21–$30	over $30
HOTELS			
under $275	$275–$375	$376–$475	over $475

St. Maarten/St. Martin accommodations range from modern megaresorts to condos, villas, and stylish intimate guesthouses. On the Dutch side some hotels cater to groups, and although that's also true to some extent on the French side, you can find a larger collection of intimate accommodations there.

TIP→ Off-season rates (April through the beginning of December) can be as little as half the high-season rates.

TIME-SHARE RENTALS

Time-share properties are concentrated on the Dutch side. There's no need to buy a share, as these condos are rented out by the resorts or by time-share owners themselves whenever the owners are not in residence. If you stay in one, try to avoid a sales pitch—they can last up to two hours. Some rent by the night, but there are substantial savings if you secure a weekly rate. Not all offer daily maid service.

PRIVATE VILLAS

Villas are a great lodging option, especially for families who don't need to keep the kids occupied, or for groups of friends who like hanging out together. Since these are for the most part freestanding houses, their greatest advantage is privacy. Properties are scattered throughout the island, often in gated communities or on secluded roads. Although a few have bare-bones furnishings, most are quite luxurious, sometimes with gyms, theaters, game rooms, and several different pools. There are private chefs, gardeners, maids, and other staffers to care for both the villa and its occupants.

Villas are secured through rental companies. They offer weekly prices that range from reasonable to more than many people make in a year. Check around, as prices for the same property vary from agent to agent. Rental companies usually provide airport transfers and concierge service, and for an extra fee will even stock your refrigerator.

HomeAway
This listing service is the world's leading vacation rentals marketplace. To rent a condo, you contact the owner directly. ⊕ *www.homeaway.com.*

Island Properties
This company's properties are scattered around the island. ✉ *62 Welfare Rd., Simpson Bay* ☎ *721/544–4580, 866/978–0470 in U.S.* ⊕ *www.remaxislandproperties.com.*

Island Real Estate Team / IRE Vacations
Island Real Estate Team and its IRE Vacations division offer both sales and rentals of villas, condominiums, businesses, property, and more on both the French and Dutch sides of SXM. ✉ *91-b Welfare Rd., Simpson Bay* ☎ *721/544–4240* ⊕ *www.ireteam.com.*

Jennifer's Vacation Villas
Jennifer's specializes in vacation villas across the island, handling both short- and long-term rentals as well as villa purchases. ✉ *Plaza del Lago, Welfare Rd., Simpson Bay* ☎ *721/544–3107, 631/546–7345* ✎ *www.jennifersvacationvillas.com.*

St. Maarten Sotheby's International Realty
St. Maarten Sotheby's International Realty sells and rents luxury villas, many in gated communities. ✉ *One Cupecoy, 1 Niger Rd., Cupecoy* ☎ *721/545–3626, 213/805–0840* ⊕ *www.stmartinsir.com.*

Villas of Distinction
This company rents villas worldwide. ☎ *800/289–0900 in U.S.* ⊕ *www.villasofdistinction.com.*

WIMCO
This outfit has more hotel, villa, apartment, and condo listings in the Caribbean than many, and it has over 30 years of experience. ☎ *401/239–0319 in U.S., 888888/997–3970 toll-free* ⊕ *www.wimco.com.*

Nightlife

St. Maarten has lots of evening and late-night action. To find out what's going on, pick up *St. Maarten Nights,* distributed free in the tourist office and hotels, or the Thursday edition of *The Daily Herald,* the Dutch-side newspaper. The glossy *Discover St. Martin/St. Maarten* magazine, also free, has articles on island history and on the newest shops, discos, and restaurants.

The island's many casinos are only on the Dutch side. All have craps, blackjack, roulette, and slot machines. You must be 18 or older to gamble. Dress is casual (but not bathing suits or skimpy beachwear). Most casinos are in hotels, but there are also some that are free-standing; all are open to the public.

Shopping

Shopaholics are drawn to the array of stores—and jewelry, watches, and high-end handbags in particular are big business on both sides of the island, with the greatest concentration of jewelers on Front Street in Philipsburg. Start at the center of town near the historic Court House on Front Street. Many of the best stores are closest to the Court House. In addition, duty-free shops can offer substantial savings—about 15% to 30% below U.S. and Canadian prices—on cameras, liquor, cigars, and designer clothing, but prices are not always better, so make sure you know U.S. prices beforehand—and bargain hard. Stick with the big vendors that advertise in the tourist press to get the best quality. Be alert for idlers: they've been known on rare occassions to snatch unwatched purses.

Prices are in dollars on the Dutch side, and in euros on the French side. More bargains are to be had on the Dutch side; prices on the French side may be higher than back home, and prices in euros don't help. Merchandise may not be from the newest collections, especially with regard to clothing, but there are items available on the French side that are not available on the Dutch side.

Visitor Information

CONTACTS Dutch-side Tourist Information Bureau. ☎ *721/542–2337* 🌐 *www.vacationstmaarten.com.* **French-side Office de Tourisme.** ✉ *Rte. de Sandy Ground, Marigot* ☎ *0590/87–57–21* 🌐 *www.st-martin.org.*

Weddings

There's a three-day waiting period on the Dutch side—but wait, it's worse: paperwork may take several weeks to process, so be sure your venue or wedding planner has a couple of months (preferably) to get everything done for you. Yes, you can do a memorable tropical wedding on a beach, but no, you can't possibly do it tomorrow. Getting married on the French side is not a viable option because of long residency requirements.

St. Maarten (Dutch Side)

Philipsburg

The capital of Dutch St. Maarten stretches about a mile (1½ km) along an isthmus between Great Bay and the Salt Pond and has five parallel streets. Most of the village's dozens of shops and restaurants are on Front Street, narrow and cobblestone, closest to Great Bay. It can be congested when cruise ships are in port because of its many duty-free shops and several casinos, but on the busiest days, it's closed off to vehicular traffic so Front Street becomes a pleasant pedestrian mall. Little lanes called *steegjes* connect Front Street with Back Street, where locals shop for clothes and sundries. Along the beach is a ½-mile-long (1-km-long) boardwalk with restaurants, souvenir shops, and beach concessions where you can rent chairs and umbrellas for about $20, sometimes with cold drinks included. There are many Wi-Fi hot spots. The boardwalk—technically called the "Great Bay Beach Promenade"—is being further extended at its eastern end all the way to the Cruise & Cargo Facilities, which will make for a much more scenic and enjoyable walk from the port to downtown Philipsburg.

Sights

Rainforest Adventures St. Maarten
AMUSEMENT PARK/CARNIVAL | FAMILY | This eco-adventure park, designed so it would minimally impact the island's nature, offers 360-degree views of the island and

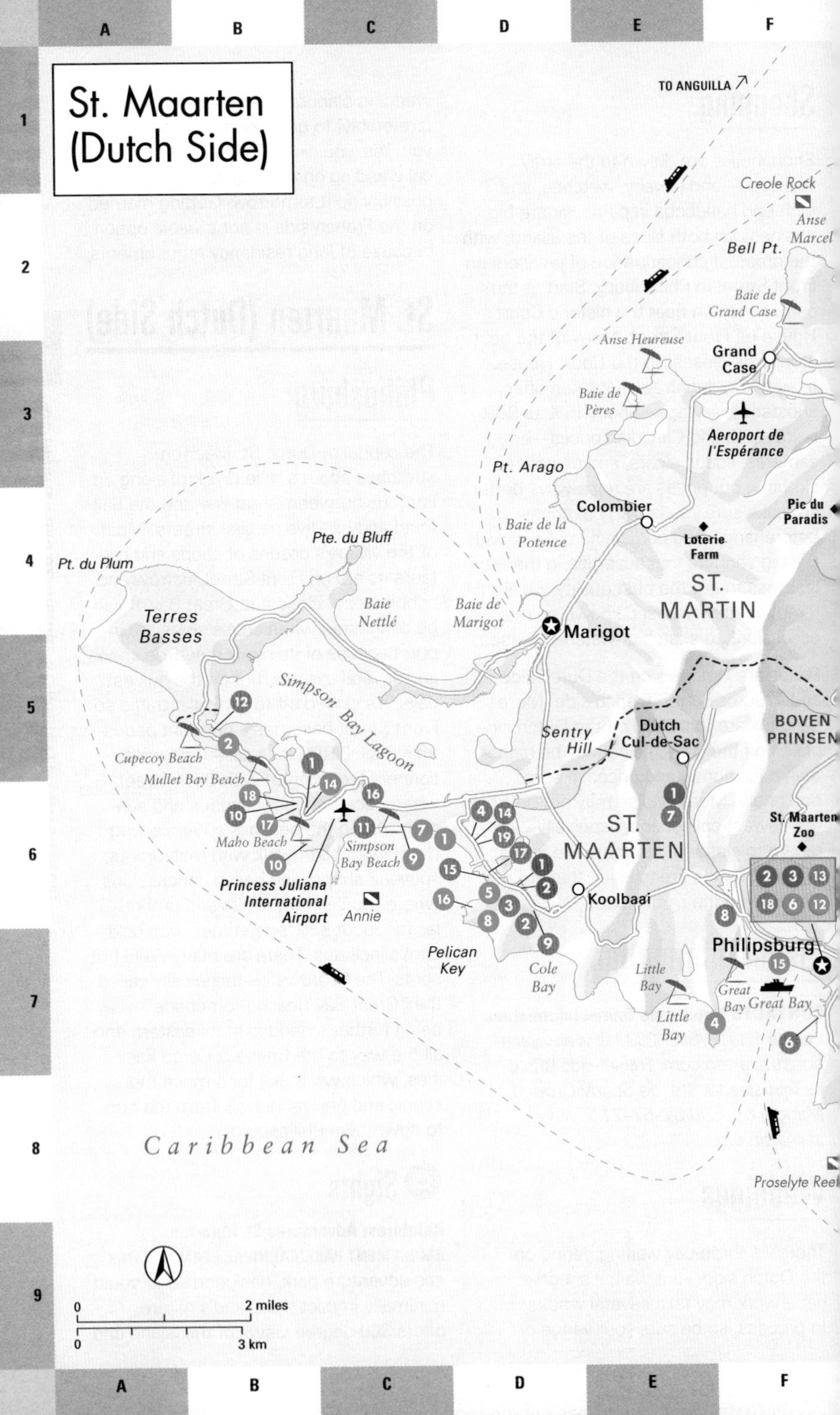

St. Maarten (Dutch Side)
A
B
C
D
E
F
1
2
3
4
5
6
7
8
9
TO ANGUILLA
Creole Rock
Anse Marcel
Bell Pt.
Baie de Grand Case
Anse Heureuse
Grand Case
Baie de Pères
Aeroport de l'Espérance
Pt. Arago
Colombier
Pic du Paradis
Baie de la Potence
Loterie Farm
Pte. du Bluff
Pt. du Plum
ST. MARTIN
Terres Basses
Baie Nettlé
Baie de Marigot
Marigot
Simpson Bay Lagoon
Sentry Hill
Dutch Cul-de-Sac
BOVEN PRINSEN
Cupecoy Beach
Mullet Bay Beach
ST. MAARTEN
St. Maarten Zoo
Maho Beach
Simpson Bay Beach
Koolbaai
Princess Juliana International Airport
Annie
Pelican Key
Cole Bay
Philipsburg
Little Bay
Great Bay
Caribbean Sea
Proselyte Reef
0
2 miles
3 km

Sights

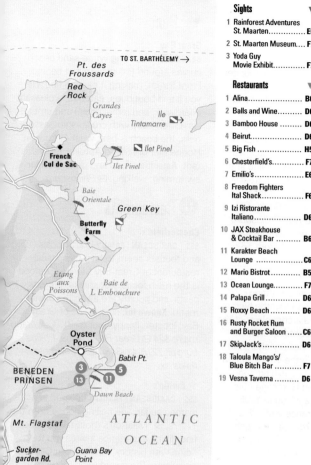

1 Rainforest Adventures St. Maarten E6
2 St. Maarten Museum F7
3 Yoda Guy Movie Exhibit F7

Restaurants

1 Alina B6
2 Balls and Wine D6
3 Bamboo House D6
4 Beirut D6
5 Big Fish H5
6 Chesterfield's F7
7 Emilio's E6
8 Freedom Fighters Ital Shack F6
9 Izi Ristorante Italiano D6
10 JAX Steakhouse & Cocktail Bar B6
11 Karakter Beach Lounge C6
12 Mario Bistrot B5
13 Ocean Lounge F7
14 Palapa Grill D6
15 Roxxy Beach D6
16 Rusty Rocket Rum and Burger Saloon C6
17 SkipJack's D6
18 Taloula Mango's/ Blue Bitch Bar F7
19 Vesna Taverna D6

Quick Bites

1 Top Carrot D6
2 Zee Best D6

Hotels

1 Azure Hotel & Art Studio C6
2 The Cliff at Cupecoy Beach B5
3 Coral Beach Club H5
4 Divi Little Bay Beach Resort F7
5 Festiva Atrium Beach Resort and Spa D6
6 Holland House Beach Hotel F7
7 The Horny Toad C6
8 La Vista Resort D6
9 Mary's Boon Beach Resort & Spa C6
10 The Morgan Resort & Spa B6
11 Oyster Bay Beach Resort H5
12 Pasanggrahan Royal Inn F7
13 Princess Heights H5
14 Royal Islander Club La Terrasse B6
15 Sea Palace Resort F7
16 Simpson Bay Resort and Marina D6
17 Sonesta Maho Beach Resort & Casino B6
18 Sonesta Ocean Point ... B6

adrenaline pumping rides. Nose around the Emilio Wilson museum and learn about the island's history before you take the chair lift all the way to the top of Sentry Hill to the sky explorer, a wooden deck from which you can enjoy the most incredible views of the island. Get a cold beverage at the Sky Bar and work up the nerve to go down the hill with either the Sentry Hill zipline, the schooner ride or–if you dare–the famous Flying Dutchman, also known as the steepest zipline in the world. After all the excitement, treat yourself to a nice lunch at Emilio's restaurant located on the property. ✉ *Rockland Estates, 59 L.B. Scott Rd., Philipsburg* ☎ *721/543–1135* 🌐 *www.rainforestadventure.com/st-maarten* 🎟 *From $52* ⏲ *Closed Fri.*

St. Maarten Museum

HISTORY MUSEUM | Hosting rotating cultural exhibits that address the history, industry, geology, and archaeology of the island, the museum contains artifacts ranging from Arawak pottery shards to objects salvaged from the wreck of HMS *Proselyte.* An interesting exhibit about hurricanes focuses on Hurricane Luis, which devastated the island in 1995. There is a good reference and video library as well. ✉ *7 Front St., Philipsburg* ☎ *721/542–4917* 🌐 *www.sintmaartenmuseum.org* 🎟 *Free, but donations are welcome.*

★ Yoda Guy Movie Exhibit

OTHER MUSEUM | **FAMILY** | This odd-sounding exhibit is actually a nonprofit museum run by Nick Maley, a movie-industry artist who was involved in the creation of Yoda and other icons. You can learn how the artist worked while enjoying the models and memorabilia on display—a must-see for *Star Wars* fans but of interest to most movie buffs. Maley is often on-hand and is happy to answer questions as time allows, and to autograph souvenirs for sale. ✉ *19a Front St., Philipsburg* ☎ *721/542–4009.*

Beaches

Great Bay

BEACH | This bustling white-sand beach curves around Philipsburg just behind Front Street, making it easy to find. Here you'll find boutiques, eateries, a pleasant boardwalk, and rental chairs and umbrellas. Often busy with cruise-ship passengers, the beach is best west of Captain Hodge Pier or around Antoine Restaurant. **Amenities:** food and drink. **Best for:** swimming; walking. ✉ *Philipsburg.*

Restaurants

Chesterfield's

$$$ | **CARIBBEAN** | **FAMILY** | Both locals and tourists seem to love this casual restaurant at Great Bay Marina. Seafood is the main focus, but steaks, burgers, pasta, and poultry are all on the dinner menu. **Known for:** nice views of Great Bay; lobster; happy hour (5–7). $ *Average main: $24* ✉ *Great Bay Marina, Philipsburg* ☎ *721/542–3484* 🌐 *www.chesterfields.sx.*

★ Emilio's

$$$ | **CARIBBEAN** | **FAMILY** | Located in a historic sugarcane boiling house from the 1700's, St. Maarten's most talked-about fine dining experience invites you to "dine with history" on nouveau Caribbean cuisine. The award-winning restaurant is named after Emilio Wilson, who bought the plantation on which his grandparents worked and died as enslaved people and which today is the location of the restaurant and Rainforest Adventure park. **Known for:** historic atmosphere in a chic setting; impressive wine selection; exceptional menu, cocktails, and Sunday brunch. $ *Average main: $28* ✉ *59 L.B. Scott Rd., Philipsburg* ☎ *721/522–1848* 🌐 *www.emilios-sxm.com* ⏲ *Closed on Mon. Closed for dinner on Sun.*

Freedom Fighters Ital Shack

$ | **CARIBBEAN** | **FAMILY** | Made famous by the late Anthony Bourdain after he stopped here in 2000, this local, vibrant spot on the edge of town is well known for its colorful exterior and animated owner. Serving ital food (vegan and organic) made of strictly local ingredients from either their own land out back or from local farmers, the Ital Shack has a very loyal following. **Known for:** colorful decor inspired by the Rastafarian belief; organic, vegan meals; fresh juice made from local fruits and veggies. *Average main: $10* *7 Bush Rd., Philipsburg* *721/542–0055* *www.sxmfreedom-fighters.com* *No credit cards* *No breakfast and lunch Sat. Closed on Sun.* *Cash only.*

Ocean Lounge

$$$$ | **ECLECTIC** | **FAMILY** | An airy modern verandah perched on the Philipsburg boardwalk gives a distinct South Beach vibe. You'll want to linger over fresh fish and steaks as you watch tourists pass by on romantic strolls by night or determined cruise-ship passengers surveying the surrounding shops by day. **Known for:** easy place to relax and people-watch; gathering place for Philipsburg movers and shakers; beachfront lounge. *Average main: $35* *Holland House Beach Hotel, 45 Front St., Philipsburg* *721/542–2572* *www.hhbh.com.*

Taloula Mango's/Blue Bitch Bar

$$ | **ECLECTIC** | **FAMILY** | Ribs and burgers are the specialty at this casual beachfront restaurant, but Gouda cheese sticks and quesadillas, not to mention the flatbread pizza options, are not to be ignored. Opt to have lunch on the beach; beach chairs and umbrellas are complimentary with lunch and beach service is available. **Known for:** beach views and people watching; location on the Philipsburg boardwalk; delicious tapas. *Average main: $19* *Sint Rose Arcade, Philipsburg* *Off Front St. on the boardwalk* *721/542–1645* *www.bluebitchbar.com.*

Hotels

Holland House Beach Hotel

$ | **HOTEL** | This hotel is in an ideal location for shoppers and sun worshippers; it faces Front Street and to the rear are the boardwalk and a long stretch of Great Bay Beach. **Pros:** in the heart of Philipsburg; easy access to beach and shops; all rooms have balconies. **Cons:** getting there by car is challenging when many cruise ships visit; no pool; busy downtown location can be noisy. *Rooms from: $255* *45 Front St., Philipsburg* *721/542–2572* *www.hhbh.com* *55 rooms* *Free Breakfast.*

Pasanggrahan Royal Inn

$ | **B&B/INN** | One of the few remaining authentic West Indian properties on St. Maarten is steeped in history; in fact, the island's oldest hotel once served as the governor's mansion. **Pros:** inexpensive; in the heart of Philipsburg; historic. **Cons:** street side can be noisy; beach can be crowded; on the main drag, which can be loaded with people. *Rooms from: $154* *15 Front St., Philipsburg* *721/542–3588* *www.pasanhotel.net* *19 rooms* *No Meals.*

Sea Palace Resort

$ | **TIMESHARE** | **FAMILY** | This hotel and time-share, which is right on the beach in Philipsburg, is painted an eye-popping shade of coral that is hard to miss. **Pros:** on Great Bay beach and the Promenade (boardwalk); walking distance to shopping; fully equipped kitchens. **Cons:** can be a bit noisy during the day due to traffic; not much for kids to do; area is crowded when cruise ships dock. *Rooms from: $229* *147 Front St., Philipsburg* *721/542–2700, 866/998–5333* *www.seapalaceresort.com* *32 units* *No Meals.*

Nightlife

Axum Art Café and Gallery

CAFÉS | This 1960s-style gallery and jazz café offers local cultural activities as well as live music and poetry readings. It's open Thursday, Friday, and Saturday 10–5. ✉ *7L Front St., Philipsburg* ✣ *Near the Guavaberry Emporium toward the east end of Front St.* ☎ *590/88–96–63 French side phone number* 🌐 *www.axumartcafe.com.*

★ **Ocean Lounge**

BARS | Sip a guavaberry colada and sample tapas with your chair pointed toward the boardwalk at this popular, genuinely Caribbean venue. There's free parking for patrons until midnight; enter on Back Street, and look for the Holland House banner. ✉ *Holland House Beach Hotel, 43 Front St., Philipsburg* ☎ *721/542–2572* 🌐 *www.hhbh.com.*

Shopping

Philipsburg's **Front Street** reinvented itself several years ago and continues to evolve. Now it's mall-like, with a redbrick walk and streets, some palm trees lining the sleek boutiques, jewelry stores, souvenir shops, and outdoor restaurants. Here and there a school or a church appears to remind visitors there's much more to this island than shopping. On Back Street, the **Philipsburg Market Place** is a daily open-air market where you can haggle over handicrafts, souvenirs, and beachwear. **Old Street,** off Front Street, has little stores, boutiques, and island mementos.

Ballerina Jewelers

JEWELRY & WATCHES | One of the most popular jewelry stores on the island, Ballerina has jewelry by Tacori and Pandora, and watches by Bell & Ross, Franck Muller, and other luxury brands. ✉ *56 Front St., Philipsburg* ☎ *721/542–4399* 🌐 *www.ballerina-jewelers.com.*

★ **Caribbean Gems**

JEWELRY & WATCHES | One of St. Maarten's oldest and most popular jewelers, Caribbean Gems has two Philipsburg locations, at both 22 and 40 Front Street, an easy walk especially for cruise ship passengers. The store features one-of-a-kind jewelry and watches in all price ranges, including many sold exclusively there. Known for impeccable customer service, Caribbean Gems has a wide selection and competitive pricing. ✉ *22 Front St. and 40 Front St.* ☎ *721/542–2176, 646/472–7996* 🌐 *www.caribbeangems.com.*

Guavaberry Emporium

WINE/SPIRITS | Visitors come for free samples at the small factory where the Sint Maarten Guavaberry Company sells its famous liqueur. The many versions include one made with jalapeño peppers. Check out the hand-painted bottles. The store also sells a gourmet barbecue and hot sauce collection and souvenir hats. ✉ *8–10 Front St., Philipsburg* ☎ *721/542–2965* 🌐 *www.guavaberry.com.*

Little Europe

JEWELRY & WATCHES | Come here to buy fine jewelry, crystal, and china; they carry many top brands. They have two stores in Philipsburg on 2 Front St. and 80 Front St., and one in Marigot on Rue de General de Gaulle. ✉ *80 Front St., Philipsburg* ☎ *721/542–4371* 🌐 *www.littleeurope.com.*

Oro Diamante

JEWELRY & WATCHES | Specializing in diamonds, this store carries loose diamonds, jewelry, and watches. ✉ *62-B Front St., Philipsburg* ☎ *599/543–0342, 800/764–0884 in U.S.* 🌐 *www.oro-diamante.com.*

Shipwreck Shop

CRAFTS | With multiple SXM outlets, this chain stocks a little of everything: colorful hammocks, handmade jewelry, and local Guavaberry liqueur. But the main store has the largest selection. ✉ *42 Front St.,*

Philipsburg ☎ *721/542–2962* 🌐 *www.shipwreckshops.com.*

★ Zhaveri Jewelers & Luxury
JEWELRY & WATCHES | A fixture on Front Street for more than 30 years, Zhaveri has a huge selection of loose diamonds, jewelry, watches, and gifts, plus designer handbags from Hugo Boss, Georgio Armani, Emporio Armani, Kartell, Furla, and Carmen Sol, as well as jewelry pieces sold nowhere else on SXM. They pay no fees to cruise lines, which makes their pricing highly competitive. ✉ *68 Front St.* ☎ *721/543–1075* 🌐 *www.zhaveri.com.*

Cupecoy

Beaches

★ Cupecoy Beach
BEACH | Near the Dutch-French border, this highly picturesque area of sandstone cliffs, white sand, and shoreline caves is actually a string of small beaches that come and go according to the whims of the sea. The surf can be rough, and it's a steep walk down to parts of the beach. Despite some "no nudity" signs at the neighboring Shore Pointe condos, this beach has been "clothing optional" for decades—but wait until you're on the beach itself before disrobing. Friendly "Dany's Beach Bar," located at the top of the stairs to the beach, serves all kinds of drinks and snacks, and sometimes fresh Caribbean spiny lobster. It's also a superb place for meeting people who gather here from around the world. **Amenities:** food, drink; chair and umbrella rentals. **Best for:** relaxation; sunsets. ✉ *Between Baie Longue and Mullet Bay, Cupecoy.*

★ Mullet Bay Beach
BEACH | **FAMILY** | Many believe that this mile-long, powdery white-sand beach behind the Mullet Bay Golf Course is the island's best. You can rent umbrellas and chairs here. Swimmers like it because the water is usually calm. Be cautious here; undertow can be challenging. Always swim with others nearby, since there are no lifeguards.The comparatively calm cove at the south end is good for kids. Listen for the "whispering pebbles" as the waves wash up. Beach bars serve lunch and cold drinks. **Amenities:** food and drink. **Best for:** families; snorkeling; swimming. ✉ *South of Cupecoy and Northwest of the Maho area, Mullet Bay.*

Restaurants

★ Mario Bistrot
$$$$ | **ECLECTIC** | **FAMILY** | With stunning views of the ocean, Mario Bistrot's new location at The Cliff offers incredible sunsets, a memorable atmosphere, and culinary excellence that ensures its ongoing popularity. Though the menu is in English and French, the cooking is an eclectic mix of Continental and Caribbean with a little Asian flare. **Known for:** extraordinary desserts; culinary creativity; generous portions (they happily provide take-home boxes). 💲 *Average main: $35* ✉ *The Cliff, Rhine Rd., Cupecoy* ☎ *721/523–2760* 🌐 *www.mariobistrot.com.*

Hotels

The Cliff at Cupecoy Beach
$$$ | **APARTMENT** | These luxurious, high-rise condos are rented out when the owners are not in residence; depending on the owner's personal style, they can be downright fabulous. **Pros:** great views; good for families; close to SXM airport and Maho and Porto Cupecoy restaurants. **Cons:** traffic and some nearby construction; getting to Orient Beach or Philipsburg is a chore from here; limited services. 💲 *Rooms from: $425* ✉ *Rhine Rd., Cupecoy* ☎ *721/546–6600, 721/520–6655* 🌐 *www.cliffsxm.com* *72 units* *No Meals.*

Maho

Beaches

Maho Beach

BEACH | People flock to the island's most famous beach to see dramatically low plane landings to Princess Juliana; they seem to pass just above your head. Be careful; the planes are loud and cause strong wind. Standing under the jet blast directly behind the plane can be dangerous and is not advised. Alternatively, you can watch from a more comfortable distance at one of two bars on either side of the beach or at the nearby Sonesta Ocean Point or Sunset Bar and Grill. **Amenities:** food and drink **Best for:** walking; windsurfing *Maho Reef.*

Restaurants

★ Alina

$$$ | JAPANESE FUSION | Located above Casino Royale in the the heart of the Maho entertainment area, Alina is the island's latest Japanese restaurant from the inspiring mind of expert Chef Ken. The restaurant is popular not only for the delectable Japanese dishes infused with local flavors, but also for the views from its open design. **Known for:** trendy atmosphere; creative sushi rolls like the curry lobster roll; multi-course omakase. *Average main: $30* *Above Casino Royale, 1 Rhine Rd., Maho Reef* *721/587–8858* *www.alinarestaurant.com* *Closed Sun.*

JAX Steakhouse & Cocktail Bar

$$$$ | STEAKHOUSE | Diners have been flocking to JAX for Certified Angus beef steaks since the restaurant opened in 2019. The attractive ambience and great service are a tribute to the owner's years of experience as a restaurateur on the island. **Known for:** central location in Maho; superior cocktails and quality steaks; great ambience and service to match. *Average main: $39* *Sonesta Maho Resort, 1 Rhine Rd., Maho Reef* *721/588–8884* *No lunch.*

Hotels

★ The Morgan Resort & Spa

$$$ | RESORT | This boutique resort next to popular Maho Beach opened its doors in 2021 to rave reviews; the majority of its 124 rooms overlook the exceptional beach-style infinity pool below. **Pros:** complimentary airport shuttle; pool with swim-up bar and cabanas; great location near bars and restaurants. **Cons:** rooms are rather simple for the price you pay; noise from planes at adjacent airport can be heard throughout the hotel; no beach. *Rooms from: $449* *2 Beacon Hill Rd., Simpson Bay* *721/545–4000, 833/966–7426 in U.S.* *www.themorganresort.com* *124 rooms* *No Meals.*

Royal Islander Club La Terrasse

$$ | TIMESHARE | FAMILY | This smaller and somewhat nicer sister time-share resort to the Royal Islander Club La Plage is right across the street and shares many of the same amenities, including the larger resort's beach. **Pros:** convenient underground parking; in a hip area, near restaurants and bars; suites have nice views. **Cons:** proximity to airport means it's sometimes noisy here; because this is a time-share, rooms can be hard to book during peak periods; not on the beach. *Rooms from: $309* *1 Rhine Rd., Maho Reef* *721/545–2388* *www.royalislander.com* *76 units* *No Meals.*

Sonesta Maho Beach Resort & Casino

$$$ | RESORT | FAMILY | The island's largest hotel, which is on Maho Beach and typically caters to big groups, isn't luxurious or fancy, but it's a vibrant, attractive property. **Pros:** nonstop activities; family-friendly; views of landing planes at nearby airport. **Cons:** resort does not have a beach but is just steps aways from one; not for a quiet getaway; large resort, not remotely intimate. $ *Rooms from: $468* ✉ *1 Rhine Rd., Maho Reef* ☎ *721/545–2115* 🌐 *www.sonesta.com/mahobeach* *420 rooms* *All-Inclusive.*

★ Sonesta Ocean Point

$$$$ | RESORT | The roomy suites in this sophisticated, luxurious enclave are some of the very best accommodations on the island. **Pros:** private dining; brand-new comfortable rooms; great design. **Cons:** fairly long walk to all the Maho-area restaurants and bars (golf carts available); proximity to airport gives you a lot of chances to watch the dramatic plane landings, but it can be noisy during take-offs; access is through the Sonesta Maho complex. $ *Rooms from: $880* ✉ *14 A Rhine Rd., Maho Reef* ☎ *721/545–3100* 🌐 *www.sonesta.com/oceanpoint* *130 rooms* *All-Inclusive.*

 Nightlife

Casino Royale

THEMED ENTERTAINMENT | Casino Royale boasts more than 21,000 square feet of gaming and is home to the biggest theater on the island. With an amplitude of tables and slot machines, a free tiered Players Club membership, a private high-roller area, a new Sportsbook with self-service kiosks, free Vegas-style production shows weekly, a VIP Lounge, and more, it is St. Maarten's top-rated casino. ✉ *Sonesta Maho Beach Resort & Casino, 1 Rhine Rd., Maho Reef* ☎ *721/545–2590* 🌐 *www.playmaho.com.*

Mimosa Skylounge

BARS | After dinner at Alina, take the stairs to the top floor to Mimosa Skylounge. This rooftop cocktail lounge offers 180-degree views of the Maho area, artful concoctions by expert mixologists, and music by renowned local and international DJs. ✉ *Above Casino Royale, 1 Rhine Rd., Maho Reef* ☎ *721/588–9988* 🌐 *www.mimosa-skylounge.com* ⏲ *Closed Sun.*

Sunset Bar and Grill

BARS | This popular plane spotting bar and restaurant near the ocean edge of the Princess Juliana International Airport runway has a relaxed, anything-goes atmosphere. Watch big planes fly very low over your head a few seconds before landing, while you enjoy a BBC (Bailey's banana colada), or a bucket of beers. Bring your camera for stunning photos, but expect a high noise level. Note: drinks here can be quite pricey, and it is very busy when cruise ships are in port. There's live music on Sunday and occasionally on week nights. ✉ *Maho Beach, Beacon Hill # 2, Maho Reef* ☎ *721/545–2084* 🌐 *www.facebook.com/SunsetBeachBarSXM.*

Oyster Pond

Dawn Beach

BEACH | True to its name, this is a great place to be at sunrise with your camera. Located on the Atlantic side of Oyster Pond, just south of the French border, it's a first-class beach for sunning and snorkeling, but the winds and rough water mean only strong swimmers should attempt to take a dip (there are no lifeguards). It's not usually crowded, and there are some good restaurants in the area. Locals often fish here in early mornings or evenings—as do brown pelicans. To find the beach, follow the signs to Oyster Bay Beach Resort, Big Fish Restaurant, or Coral Beach Club. **Amenities:** food and drink. **Best for:** snorkeling (particularly at the northern end); sunrise. ✉ *South of Oyster Pond, Dawn Beach.*

Restaurants

★ Big Fish

$$$ | ECLECTIC | Big portions of fresh-caught fish, sushi, and steaks are served in a modern, Miami Beach atmosphere. The service is friendly and attentive. **Known for:** creative cocktails; South Beach vibes; spicy Hurricane shrimp. *Average main: $28* ⊠ *14 Emerald Merit Rd., Oyster Pond* ☎ *721/543–6288.*

Hotels

★ Coral Beach Club

$$$$ | **RESORT** | The luxurious private villas in this condo-style complex are right on the ocean or overlooking Oyster Pond. **Pros:** private plunge pool; attention to detail; private parking and use of Oyster Bay Resort amenities. **Cons:** expensive; isolated location; car needed if you want to see more of the island. *Rooms from: $950* ⊠ *3 Emerald Merit Rd., Oyster Pond* ☎ *721/543–6303, 866/978–7278 toll free* ⊕ *www.coralbeach-club.com* *24 villas* *No Meals.*

Oyster Bay Beach Resort

$$ | **RESORT** | **FAMILY** | Jutting out into the Atlantic and Oyster Pond, this condo/time-share resort sits overlooking Dawn Beach and is convenient to groceries and restaurants; it appeals to those who want a relaxing atmosphere without being too far from everything else. **Pros:** infinity pool; lots of activities; nightly entertainment. **Cons:** older units are smaller than new units; need a car to get around; isolated location. *Rooms from: $315* ⊠ *10 Emerald Merit Rd., Oyster Pond* ☎ *721/543–6040, 888/784–6685 Toll free* ⊕ *www.OBBR.com* *182 units* *No Meals.*

Princess Heights

$ | **HOTEL** | Perched on a hill hundreds of feet above the Atlantic, spacious suites offer privacy, luxury, and white-balustrade balconies with a smashing view of St. Barth. **Pros:** gorgeous vistas; away from the crowds; friendly staff. **Cons:** not easy to find; numerous steps to climb in the older building; not on the beach and need a car to get around. *Rooms from: $225* ⊠ *156 Oyster Pond Rd., Oyster Pond* ☎ *800/881–1744, 721/543–6906* ⊕ *www.princessheights.com* *51 suites* *No Meals.*

Pelican Key

Hotels

Festiva Atrium Beach Resort and Spa

$ | **RESORT** | **FAMILY** | Lush tropical foliage in the glassed-in lobby—hence the name—makes a great first impression at this good base for island explorations. **Pros:** free shuttle to Philipsburg; family-friendly environment; short walk to restaurants and close to the beach. **Cons:** taxes and service charges add a whopping 25% to basic rates; neighborhood is crowded; some rooms lack private balconies. *Rooms from: $227* ⊠ *6 Billy Folly Rd., Pelican Key* ☎ *721/544-2126, 888/992–8748* ⊕ *www.festiva-atrium.com* *87 rooms* *No Meals.*

La Vista Resort

$ | **TIMESHARE** | **FAMILY** | Hibiscus and bougainvillea line brick walkways that connect the bungalows and beachfront suites of this intimate and friendly, family-owned time-share resort perched at the foot of Pelican Key. The accommodations, which have completed renovations, are beautifully furnished and have small bathrooms, but the balconies have awesome views. **Pros:** centrally located; close to restaurants and bars; nearest good beach is at Simpson Bay Resort, very walkable. **Cons:** nothing fancy; beach is a bit rocky; no-frills furnishings. *Rooms from: $205* ⊠ *53 Billy Folly Rd., Pelican Key* ☎ *721/544–3005* ⊕ *www.lavistaresort.com* *50 units* *No Meals.*

★ Simpson Bay Resort and Marina

$ | **RESORT** | **FAMILY** | Tucked away on Pelican Key, Simpson Bay Resort borders both the bay and the ocean, giving you a front-row seat for island sunsets from your terrace. **Pros:** close to SXM airport; family-friendly resort on the beach; close to restaurants and nightlife options. **Cons:** capitals are each at least 20 minutes away in perfect conditions; busy area; housekeeping service only weekly. *Rooms from: $208* ⊠ *7 Billy Folly Rd.,*

Pelican Key ☎ *888/721–4407, 954/736–5807* 🌐 *www.simpsonbayresort.com* *355 units* *No Meals.*

 Nightlife

Buccaneer Beach Bar

BARS | **FAMILY** | Conveniently located on Kim Sha Beach, between the Atrium Beach Resort and the Simpson Bay Beach Resort, this bar can provide you delicious frozen drinks, a slice of pizza, burgers and fish from the grill, a beautiful sunset, and a beach bonfire on Sunday. Live music on Wednesday and Sunday and a daily happy hour from 5 to 7 makes this spot popular with both travelers and locals. Their small parking lot fills quickly; there is some on-street parking near the entrance, but parking can be a huge challenge here. ✉ *10 Billy Folly Rd., behind Festiva Atrium Beach Resort, Pelican Key* ☎ *721/523–0401* 🌐 *www.buccaneerbeachbar.com.*

Hollywood Casino

THEMED ENTERTAINMENT | Centrally located to the Simpson Bay area, the Hollywood Casino is part of Pelican Key, and is right across from Simpson Bay Resort. This casino, mostly slot machines and dice, enjoys the Hollywood Star Theme. Isola Restaurant, a very busy authentic Italian dining spot, is part of the complex. It has many traditional upscale offerings and excellent brick-oven pizzas. ✉ *37 Billy Folly Rd., Pelican Key* ☎ *721/544–4463* 🌐 *www.hollywoodcasino.info.*

Princess Casino

THEMED ENTERTAINMENT | One of the island's largest gaming halls has a wide array of restaurants and entertainment options. It's just a quick trip across the Simpson Bay Lagoon Causeway from the Simpson Bay area. ✉ *Port de Plaisance, 155 Union Rd., Cole Bay* ☎ *721/544–5222.*

Simpson Bay

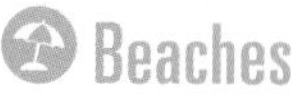

★ Simpson Bay Beach

BEACH | This half-moon stretch of white sand on the island's Caribbean side is a hidden gem. It's mostly surrounded by private residences, with no big resorts, few Jet Skiers, and no crowds. It's just you, the sand, and the water (along with one funky beach bar, Karakter, at the beach's northern end, to provide some chairs and nourishment). The beach is sometimes a bit noisy when planes depart nearby. To find the beach, follow the signs southeast of the airport to Mary's Boon and the Horny Toad guesthouses. **Amenities:** food and drink; showers; toilets. **Best for:** solitude; swimming; walking. ✉ *Simpson Bay.*

 Restaurants

★ Balls and Wine

$$ | **ECLECTIC** | **FAMILY** | This quaint restaurant with a quirky name, located in the corner of the Paradise Mall, is a hidden gem. Owners Eduar and wife Alejandra serve appetizing tapas, delicious wine, and craft cocktails that have garnered the restaurant quite a following. **Known for:** friendly owners; Taco Tuesday and Wine Wednesday; intimate yet convivial atmosphere. *Average main: $18* ✉ *Paradise Mall, Welfare Rd., Simpson Bay* ☎ *721/527–6146* 🌐 *www.ballsandwine.com* *No credit cards* *Closed Sun.* ☞ *Cash only.*

★ Bamboo House

$$$ | **ASIAN FUSION** | Located in hilltop villa overlooking Simpson Bay, Bamboo House blends stunning views with a lively atmosphere and top-notch sushi. Chefs from spots like Nobu and Morimoto to blend contemporary Asian flavors and Mediterranean traditions with complexity and innovation. **Known for:** views at sunset; sushi and sashimi; dynamic, upbeat ambience. [$] *Average main: $27* ✉ *150 Union Rd., Simpson Bay* ☎ *721/523-1508* 🌐 *www.bamboohouse-sxm.com* ⏲ *Closed Mon.*

Beirut

$$ | **LEBANESE** | **FAMILY** | Beirut serves delicious, fresh Middle Eastern specialties such as falafel, kebabs, and salads, as well as meze such as baba ghanoush. The friendly owners make everyone feel right at home, and there's a hookah bar in the back in the evening. **Known for:** reasonable prices; casual, welcoming atmosphere; friendly staff. [$] *Average main: $18* ✉ *29 Airport Rd., Simpson Bay* ☎ *721/545–3612* 🌐 *www.beirutsxm.com.*

★ Izi Ristorante Italiano

$$$ | **ITALIAN** | **FAMILY** | The award-winning former chef and owner of La Gondola serves up sharable portions of more than 400 dishes in this popular, cheerful, centrally located space. For something fun, diners are invited to create their own menu: pick a pasta and sauce, then add your choice of meat, fish, and veggies. **Known for:** homemade desserts that are worth saving room for; creative, hands-on chef; unequaled tasting menu. [$] *Average main: $29* ✉ *Paradise Mall, 67 Welfare Rd., Simpson Bay* ☎ *721/544–3079* 🌐 *www.izirestaurant.com* ⏲ *Closed Mon.*

Karakter Beach Lounge

$$$ | **ECLECTIC** | **FAMILY** | This charming modern beach bar, right behind the airport, serves up fun, great music, relaxation, and a lot of style. Open from 9 am until 10 pm, with nightly live music in the evening, the restaurant makes fruit smoothies, tropical cocktails, pastas, seafood, and tapas. **Known for:** on the beach; funky surroundings (an old school bus); good food. [$] *Average main: $24* ✉ *121 Simpson Bay Rd., Simpson Bay* ☎ *721/523–9983* 🌐 *www.karakterstmaarten.com.*

Palapa Grill

$$$ | **FRENCH FUSION** | French-Caribbean fusion dishes that change with the seasons keep the menu fresh at this lively restaurant in the middle of the popular Simpson Bay strip. Like the menu, each section of the restaurant is thoughtful; its varying decor creates different vibes, but still offers the intimacy of a hidden oasis. **Known for:** lively lounge with DJ and creative cocktails; trendy decor; delicious tapas. [$] *Average main: $28* ✉ *28 Airport Rd., Simpson Bay* ☎ *721/559–1901* 🌐 *www.palapagrillsxm.com* ⏲ *Closed Sun.*

Roxxy Beach

$$$ | **ASIAN FUSION** | Located in the entertainment mecca of the island, Simpson Bay, this beach bar and restaurant combines the alluring vibes of St-Tropez and Miami Beach with the flavors of Asia and the Mediterranean. Live music by well known local and international DJs make this a popular stop for many. **Known for:** sushi and tapas; beach party atmosphere; great happy hour with sunset views. [$] *Average main: $28* ✉ *127 Welfare Rd., Simpson Bay* ☎ *721/520–2001* 🌐 *www.roxxybeach.com* ⏲ *Closed Mon.*

Rusty Rocket Rum and Burger Saloon

$$ | **BURGER** | **FAMILY** | This lively and fun spot next to the airport is famous for serving the island's best burgers. Built mostly from wooden palettes and wine boxes, the bar exudes Caribbean charm. Jimmy, the owner, has an amusing imagination, and the menu is testament to that. **Known for:** creative and tasty burgers; fun atmosphere, especially on the weekend; guest names written all over the bar. [$] *Average main: $15* ✉ *Across from the Winair office, 130 Airport Rd., Simpson Bay* ☎ *721/556–3300* 🌐 *www.facebook.com/RustyRocket* ⏲ *Closed Tues. and Wed.*

SkipJack's

$$$ | **SEAFOOD** | **FAMILY** | Arguably the island's top seafood restaurant, SkipJack's is located right on Simpson Bay lagoon. It is popular for crowd-pleasers such as its fried calamari, shrimp cocktail, sandwiches, and a good variety of fresh seafood. **Known for:** seasoned, friendly, knowledgeable staff; lobster from Saba; one of the biggest and busiest SXM restaurants. *$ Average main: $21 ✉ Welfare Rd., Simpson Bay ☎ 721/544–2313 🌐 www.skipjacks-sxm.com.*

Vesna Taverna

$$$ | **ECLECTIC** | **FAMILY** | Centrally located just north of the Simpson Bay drawbridge, this casual restaurant is open all day long, with French and Mediterranean specials nightly and incredible house-made desserts. In the morning, you can order American breakfasts (including their famous Bagel Tower, plus omelets, pancakes, and more), and at lunch they offer tasty but healthy options like smoothies, sandwiches, salads, and burgers. **Known for:** delicious house-made desserts; Greek specialties; house-made bagels. *$ Average main: $25 ✉ 9 La Palapa Marina, Simpson Bay ↔ In front of Soggy Dollar Bar on Simpson Bay lagoon ☎ 721/524–5283 🌐 www.vesnataverna.com ⏲ No dinner Sun. Closed Mon.*

Coffee and Quick Bites

★ Top Carrot

$$ | **VEGETARIAN** | **FAMILY** | Open from 8 am to 5 pm, this friendly café and juice bar is a popular healthy breakfast and lunch stop. It features fresh and tasty vegetarian entrées, sandwiches, salads, and homemade pastries. **Known for:** great gift shop; crowd-pleasing menu; casual, cozy little dining room. *$ Average main: $15 ✉ Airport Rd., near Simpson Bay Yacht Club, Simpson Bay ☎ 721/544–3381 ⏲ Closed Sun. and Mon. No dinner.*

★ Zee Best

$ | **CAFÉ** | This friendly bistro serves one of the most popular breakfasts on the island. There's a huge selection of fresh-baked pastries—try the almond croissants—plus sweet and savory crepes, omelets, quiches, and other treats from the oven. **Known for:** St. Martin omelet and the zee bagel; pastry basket; breakfast served until 2. *$ Average main: $8 ✉ Plaza del Lago, Simpson Bay ☎ 721/544–2477 🌐 www.zeebestrestaurant.com No credit cards ⏲ No dinner.*

Hotels

Azure Hotel & Art Studio

$ | **HOTEL** | **FAMILY** | Azure is a funky, wonderful boutique hotel located on a serene stretch of Simpson Bay Beach. **Pros:** on the beach; central location; inexpensive. **Cons:** a car is needed to get to Philipsburg or the French side; no on-site restaurant (but there are kitchenettes); no pool. *$ Rooms from: $90 ✉ 6 Roberts Dr., Simpson Bay ☎ 721/581–3858 🌐 www.azurehotelsxm.com 8 rooms No Meals.*

★ The Horny Toad

$ | **B&B/INN** | Because of its stupendous view of Simpson Bay and the simple but comfortable rooms with creative decor, this lovely guesthouse is widely considered one of the best on this side of the island. **Pros:** beautiful beach that's usually deserted; tidy rooms; friendly vibe and fantastic owners. **Cons:** no pool (but you're on the beach); no kids under seven; need a car to get around. *$ Rooms from: $130 ✉ 2 Vlaun's Dr., Simpson Bay ☎ 721/545–4323 🌐 www.thtgh.com 8 rooms No Meals.*

Mary's Boon Beach Resort & Spa

$ | **HOTEL** | **FAMILY** | A shaded courtyard welcomes guests at this quirky, informal guesthouse on a 3-mile-long (5-km-long) stretch of Simpson Bay Beach, which has the funky feel of the Florida Keys. **Pros:** owners are usually on-site; small and intimate; interesting history. **Cons:** basic bathrooms; because of airport proximity, it can be noisy during takeoffs; very small pool. *Rooms from: $135* *117 Simpson Bay Rd., Simpson Bay* *721/545–7000* *www.visitmarysboon.com* *34 rooms* *No Meals.*

Nightlife

Nowhere Special Rum Bar & Grill

BARS | This cozy, colorful roadside bar close to the draw bridge in Simpson Bay has become quite the hot spot since opening in 2018. Tamarind sours, sour sop martinis, and other island cocktails are mixed behind the bar as locals and visitors come together in a blend of happy faces and swaying hips. Nightly live music by local bands guarantee the audience a great time. Of course, it wouldn't be an island hot spot without food. Caribbean-style tapas like the oxtail bowl, mahi ceviche, goat meat triangle, and conch fritters keep people coming back. *88 Welfare Rd., Simpson Bay* *721/544–2440* *www.nowheresxm.com* *Closed Mon.*

Pineapple Pete

BARS | **FAMILY** | You can groove to nightly live music or hit the game room for a couple of rounds of pool or video games. *Airport Rd., Simpson Bay* *721/544–6030* *www.pineapplepete.com* *Closed Tues.*

The Red Piano

PIANO BARS | The Red Piano is one of the island's most popular entertainment venues, welcoming piano players from around the world. Famous for its "Church on Monday" event featuring a live local band, the bar has live music nightly, tasty cocktails, and a pool table. Smoking is permitted. *Across from Simpson Bay Resort, 35 Billy Folly Rd., Pelican Key* *721/527–4266.*

Little Bay

Beaches

★ Little Bay

BEACH | Despite its occasional use by snorkelers, divers, kayakers, and boating enthusiasts, Little Bay isn't usually crowded. It does boast panoramic views of neighboring islands St. Eustatius (Statia) and Saba, and arriving and departing cruise ships. The beach is on the same peninsula as Fort Amsterdam and accessible via the Divi Little Bay Beach Resort, and most beachgoers are hotel guests. **Amenities:** food and drink at the resort; parking; toilets. **Best for:** snorkeling; swimming; walking. *Little Bay Rd., Little Bay.*

Hotels

★ Divi Little Bay Beach Resort

$$ | **RESORT** | **FAMILY** | Bordering gorgeous Little Bay, this centrally located property is awash with water sports, restaurants, and an awesome multilevel pool with breathtaking views of neighboring islands. **Pros:** completely renovated; good location; lovely beach with nearby restaurants. **Cons:** car necessary to venture off-site; inconvenient entrance from the main road; some construction in the area. *Rooms from: $275* *Little Bay Rd., Little Bay* *721/542–2333* *www.diviresorts.com/divi-little-bay-beach-resort* *309 rooms.*

St. Martin (French Side)

Marigot

It is great fun to spend a few hours exploring the harbor, shopping stalls, open-air cafés, and boutiques of French St. Martin's capital, especially on Wednesday and Saturday, when the daily open-air crafts markets expand to include fresh fruits and vegetables, spices, and all manner of seafood. The market might remind you of Provence, especially when aromas of delicious cooking waft by. Be sure to climb up to the Fort St. Louis for the panoramic view, stopping at the museum for an overview of the island. Marina Port La Royale is the shopping–lunch spot central to the port, but rue de la République and rue de la Liberté, which border the bay, have some duty-free shops and boutiques. The West Indies Mall offers a deluxe (and air-conditioned) shopping experience. There's less bustle here than in Philipsburg, but the open-air cafés are still tempting places to sit and people-watch. From the harborfront you can catch ferries to Anguilla and St. Barth. Parking can be a real challenge during the business day, and even at night during high season.

Fort Louis

RUINS | Though not much remains of the structure itself, Fort Louis, completed by the French in 1789, is great fun if you want to climb the 92 steps to the top for the wonderful views of the island and neighboring Anguilla. On Wednesday and Saturday there is a market in the square at the bottom. ✉ *Marigot.*

Baie des Pères (*Friar's Bay*)

BEACH | **FAMILY** | This quiet, occasionally rocky cove close to Marigot has beach grills and bars, with chaises and umbrellas, usually calm waters, and a lovely view of Anguilla. 978 Beach Lounge, open daily for lunch and (weather permitting) dinner, has a cool jazzy vibe. It's the best place to be on the full moon, with music, dancing, and a bonfire, but you can get lunch, beach chairs, and umbrellas anytime. Friar's Bay Beach Café is a French bistro on the sand, open from breakfast to sunset. To get to the beach, take National Road 7 from Marigot, go toward Grand Case to the Morne Valois hill, and turn left on the dead-end road at the sign. Note the last 200 yards of road to the beach is dirt and quite bumpy. **Amenities:** food and drink; toilets. **Best for:** partiers; swimming; walking. ✉ *Anse des Pères.*

Happy Bay Beach (*Anse Heureuse*)

BEACH | Not many people know about this romantic, hidden gem. Happy Bay has powdery sand and stunning views of Anguilla. The snorkeling is also good. To get here, turn onto the rather rutted dead-end road to Baie des Péres (Friar's Bay). The beach itself, which is clothing-optional, is a 10- to 15-minute easy hike from the northernmost beach bar on Friar's Bay. **Amenities:** food and drink; toilets (only at adjacent Friar's Bay). **Best for:** snorkeling; solitude; swimming; walking. ✉ *Happy Bay.*

Restaurants

Bistro Nu

$$ | **FRENCH** | It's hard to top the authentic French comfort food and reasonable prices you can find at this intimate restaurant tucked in a Marigot alley. Traditional French dishes like steak au poivre, sweetbreads with mushroom sauce, and sole meunière are served in a friendly, intimate dining room, which is now air-conditioned. **Known for:** wine list; French comfort food; good value prix-fixe menu. *Average main: €20* ✉ *Allée de l'Ancienne Geôle, Marigot* ☎ *0690/28–16–32* ⏲ *Closed Sat. and Sun.*

★ **Friar's Bay Beach Café**

$$ | **BISTRO** | **FAMILY** | There is a sophisticated vibe at this quiet, rather elegant beach club that may make you feel as if you're on a private beach. You can rent lounge chairs and umbrellas (half price with lunch) and spend the whole day relaxing, drinking, and dining. **Known for:** good specials; beachside dining; informal atmosphere. *Average main:*

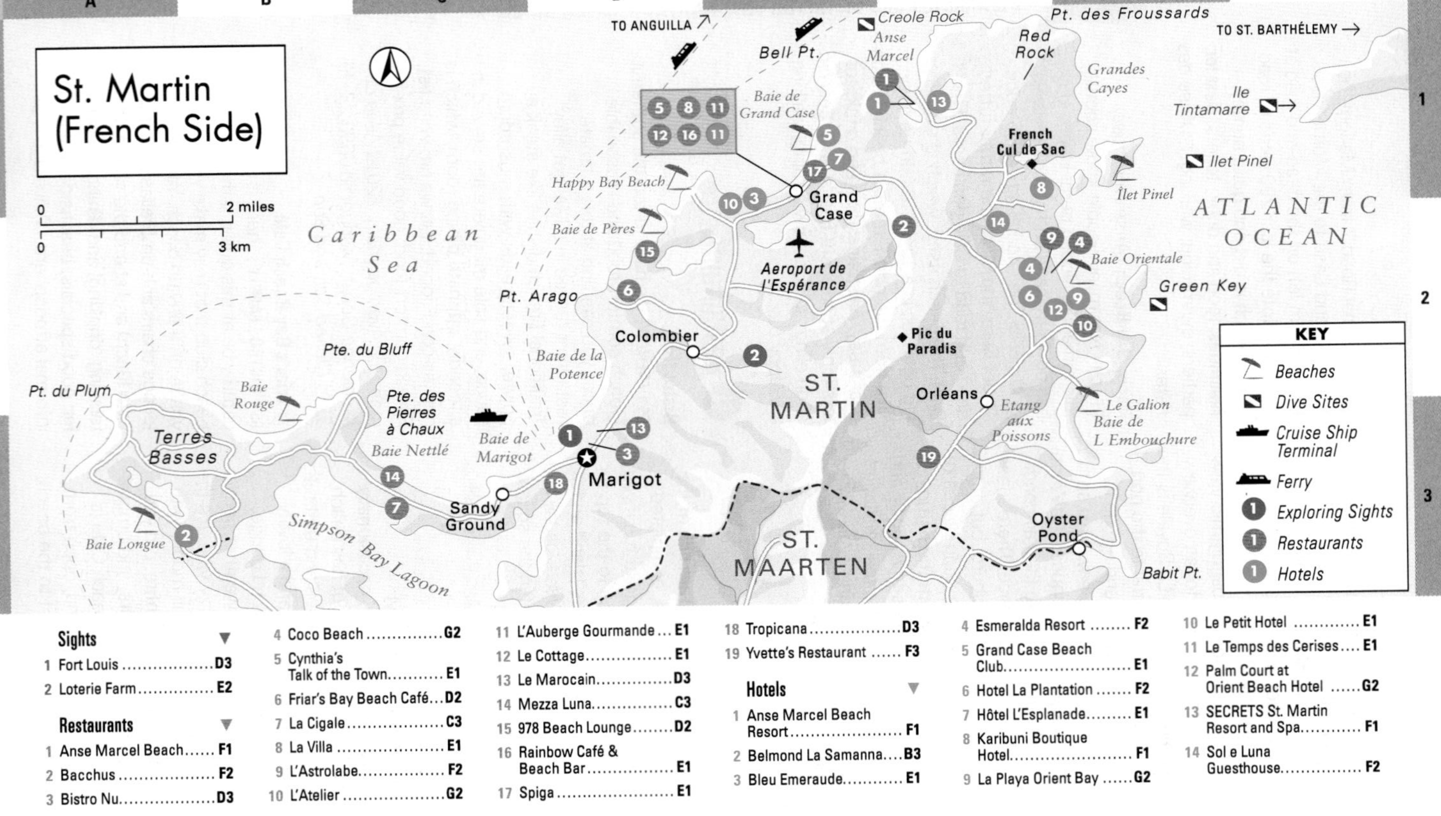

Sights

1 Fort Louis D3
2 Loterie Farm E2

Restaurants

1 Anse Marcel Beach...... F1
2 Bacchus F2
3 Bistro Nu..................D3
4 Coco Beach G2
5 Cynthia's Talk of the Town........... E1
6 Friar's Bay Beach Café...D2
7 La Cigale C3
8 La Villa E1
9 L'Astrolabe.................F2
10 L'Atelier G2
11 L'Auberge Gourmande ... E1
12 Le Cottage.................E1
13 Le Marocain...............D3
14 Mezza Luna................C3
15 978 Beach Lounge........D2
16 Rainbow Café & Beach Bar E1
17 Spiga E1
18 Tropicana D3
19 Yvette's Restaurant F3

Hotels

1 Anse Marcel Beach Resort.....................F1
2 Belmond La Samanna....B3
3 Bleu Emeraude............E1
4 Esmeralda Resort F2
5 Grand Case Beach Club.......................E1
6 Hotel La Plantation F2
7 Hôtel L'Esplanade.........E1
8 Karibuni Boutique Hotel.......................F1
9 La Playa Orient Bay G2
10 Le Petit Hotel E1
11 Le Temps des Cerises....E1
12 Palm Court at Orient Beach Hotel G2
13 SECRETS St. Martin Resort and Spa............F1
14 Sol e Luna Guesthouse................F2

Get the best sunset view over Marigot from Fort Louis.

€18 ✉ Friar's Bay Rd., Anse des Pères ☎ 0690/49–16–87 ▭ No credit cards ⏲ No dinner. Closed Tues.

★ Le Marocain

$$ | MOROCCAN | Years after being destroyed by Hurricane Irma, the old Marrakech is back with the same ownership but a new name, Le Marocain. The decor transports you straight to Morocco as you dine on fragrant, authentic Moroccan classics in a romantic space with an open garden and a new rooftop. **Known for:** affable staff; tagine and couscous; rooftop lounge. *[$] Average main: €20 ✉ 169 rue de Hollande, Marigot ☎ 0590/27–54–48 🌐 www.le-marocain.com ⏲ Closed Sun. No lunch.*

978 Beach Lounge

$$ | CREOLE | FAMILY | Feel the St. Martin culture at this beach bar and restaurant (previously Kali's, but now under new ownership). Flavorful local Creole dishes and island inspired cocktails are served on the beach. **Known for:** live music on weekends; all-white full moon beach party; Creole and Cajun delicacies. *[$] Average main: €20 ✉ Friar's Bay, 61 rue de Friar's Bay, Anse des Pères ☎ 0590/690–828–000 🌐 www.978sxm.com ⏲ Closed Mon. and Tues.*

Tropicana

$$$ | FRENCH | This bustling and popular bistro at the Marina Port La Royale stays busy thanks to a varied menu, (relatively) reasonable prices, and friendly staff. Salads are superb lunch options, especially the salade Niçoise with medallions of crusted goat cheese. **Known for:** crème brûlée; inside and outside dining; steak and seafood. *[$] Average main: €22 ✉ Marina Port La Royale, Marigot ☎ 0590/87–79–07.*

Shopping

Max Mara

MIXED CLOTHING | These beautifully made, tailored clothes have an elegant attitude. *✉ 33 rue du Kennedy, Marigot ☎ 0590/52–99–75 ⏲ Closed Sun.*

A Tale of Two Islands

The smallest island in the world to be shared between two different countries, St. Maarten/St. Martin has existed peacefully in its divided state for more than 370 years. The Treaty of Concordia, which subdivided the island, was signed in 1648 and was really inspired by the two resident colonies of French and Dutch settlers (not to mention their respective governments) joining forces to repel a common enemy, the Spanish, in 1644. Although the French were promised the side of the island facing Anguilla and the Dutch the south side of the island, the boundary itself wasn't firmly established until 1817 and only then after several disputes (16 of them, to be exact).

Visitors to the island will likely not be able to tell that they have passed from the Dutch to the French side unless they notice the border monuments at the side of the roads—and that roads on the French side feel a little smoother. In 2003 the population of St. Martin (and St. Barthélemy) voted to secede from Guadeloupe, the administrative capital of the French West Indies. That detachment became official in 2007, and St. Martin is now officially known as the Collectivité de Saint-Martin.

Minguet Art Gallery

ART GALLERIES | On Rambaud Hill between Marigot and Grand Case, this gallery is managed by the daughter of the late artist Alexandre Minguet. It carries original paintings, lithographs, posters, and postcards depicting island flora and landscapes by Minguet and is a popular tourist attraction on the island. Call before visiting to be sure they're open. ✉ *Rambaud Hill, Rambaud* ☎ 🌐 *www.minguet.com.*

French Cul de Sac

North of Orient Bay Beach, the French colonial mansion of St. Martin's mayor is nestled in the hills. Little red-roof houses look like open umbrellas tumbling down the green hillside. The area is peaceful and good for hiking. From the beach here, shuttle boats make the five-minute trip to Îlet Pinel, an uninhabited island that's fine for picnicking, snorkeling, sunning, and swimming. There are full-service restaurants and beach clubs there, so just pack the sunscreen and head over.

Beaches

★ Îlet Pinel

BEACH | FAMILY | A protected nature reserve, this kid-friendly island is a five-minute ferry ride from French Cul de Sac (about €12 per person round-trip). The ferry runs every half hour from midmorning until 4 pm. The water is clear and shallow, and the shore is sheltered. Snorkelers can swim a trail between both coasts of this pencil-shape speck in the ocean. You can rent equipment on the island. There are two restaurants, Karibuni and Yellow Beach; both offer great service, with cocktail tables in the water. Chairs and umbrellas can be rented for about €25 for two. It can get busy on Sunday. **Amenities:** food and drink; parking. **Best for:** snorkeling; sunning; swimming. ✉ *Ilet Pinel.*

Hotels

Karibuni Boutique Hotel

$$ | HOTEL | Tucked away in a tropical oasis overlooking turquoise water and distant islets like Îlet Pinel and Tintamarre, this family-owned and-operated boutique hotel offers well-designed rooms in an idyllic setting. **Pros:** private, intimate, and peaceful; personalized service; complimentary kayaks, transportation to Pinel island, and beach chairs. **Cons:** location is far from main areas so you'll need a car to get around; not on the beach (but you have a plunge pool); no kids under 13. *Rooms from: €350 Cul de Sac Bay, Cul de Sac 0590/690–64–38–58 www.lekaribuni.com Closed Sept. to mid Oct. Free Breakfast.*

Anse Marcel

Restaurants

★ Anse Marcel Beach

$$$ | MODERN FRENCH | Beachside calm with a side order of chic is on the menu at this lovely and private cove restaurant/beach club that was designed with the environment in mind. It's good for a beach day, a sunset cocktail, and great swimming. **Known for:** beachfront dining; seafood, especially the local catch; modern, pleasant atmosphere. *Average main: €24 Anse Marcel Beach, Anse Marcel 0690/26–38–50 www.ansemarcelbeach.com.*

Hotels

Anse Marcel Beach Resort

$ | RESORT | FAMILY | This classic property on 148 acres of lush gardens borders the exceptionally beautiful and secluded beach in Anse Marcel. **Pros:** beachfront setting; all-inclusive option; lovely gardens. **Cons:** beach is shared; need a car to get around; some rooms have round bathtubs in middle of room. *Rooms from: $147 26 rue de Lonvillier, Anse Marcel 0590/26–38–50 Closed Sept.–Oct. 129 rooms No Meals.*

Secrets St. Martin Resort and Spa

$ | RESORT | Reopened in 2021, this all-inclusive hotel has 300 rooms from partial ocean view to swim-out suites, plus multiple dining options, including Asian, Italian, French restaurants, a café, and a poolside grill. **Pros:** great beach and huge pool; secluded and intimate; activities galore. **Cons:** a car is necessary to explore outside of resort; beach may be busy; remote. *Rooms from: €269 BP 581, Anse Marcel 0590/87–67–00 www.secretsresorts.com 300 rooms All-Inclusive.*

Sol e Luna Guesthouse

$$ | B&B/INN | Independent couples who don't want a big resort love the six comfortable suites in this hillside guesthouse overlooking a pretty pool, a salt pond, and on to Orient Bay. Beautifully decorated in a modern Italian style with tropical details, the attractive and spacious suites have Italian marble baths, compact kitchenettes, and dining patios. **Pros:** excellent on-site restaurant; spacious suites; good location for exploring. **Cons:** quite a few steps to climb around the property; need a car; not a full-service hotel. *Rooms from: €280 61 Mont Vernon, Baie Orientale 0590/29–08–56 Closed Sept. 6 suites Free Breakfast.*

Baie Nettlé

Beaches

Baie Rouge

BEACH | Here you can bask with millionaires renting big-ticket villas in the "neighborhood" of Terres Basses—the French lowlands. The gorgeous beach and its salt ponds make up a nature preserve, site of the oldest habitation in the Caribbean. This area is widely thought to have the best snorkeling on the island. You can swim the crystal waters along the point and explore a swim-through cave, but beware: the water can be rough. There is a sign and a right turn after you leave Baie Nettlé. **Amenities:** none. **Best for:** snorkeling; swimming; walking. *Baie Rouge.*

Anse Marcel Beach is a great spot for swimming, dining, and lounging.

Restaurants

★ La Cigale

$$$$ | **FRENCH** | On the edge of Baie Nettlé, this restaurant has wonderful views of the lagoon from its dining room and open-air patio, but the charm comes from the devoted attention of adorable owner Olivier, helped by his mother and brother and various cousins. The delicious food is edible sculpture: lobster bisque under a pastry dome, fresh sea bass with a leek fondue, and their signature "Le Cigale," a foie gras emulsion soup. **Known for:** convenient location near Marigot; artistic presentation; excellent service. *$ Average main: €32 ✉ 101 Laguna Beach, Baie Nettlé ☎ 0590/87–90–23 🌐 www.lacigalerestaurantsxm.com ⏲ Closed Sun. and Sept. and Oct. No lunch.*

Mezza Luna

$$$ | **ITALIAN** | **FAMILY** | Sit with your feet in the sand and enjoy the views at this restaurant, popular for its pizzas and beach terrace. Their chalkboard describes all the varieties, which are many, and the pricing is very reasonable. **Known for:** reasonable prices; variety of pizza; house-made pasta. *$ Average main: €22 ✉ 501 Nettlé Bay Beach Club, Baie Nettlé ☎ 0590/690–73–19–18 🌐 www.facebook.com/mezzalunasxm ⏲ Closed Sun.*

Grand Case

"The Culinary Capital of the Caribbean" is back. Years after rebuilding from big damages sustained during Hurricane Irma, Grand Case's popular eateries on its renowned "Restaurant Row" are once again serving exquisite dishes. It's an easy 10-minute drive from either Orient Bay or Marigot, stretching along a narrow beach overlooking Anguilla. At lunchtime, or with kids, head to the casual *lolos* (open-air grills) and feet-in-the-sand beach bars. At night, stroll the strip and preview the sophisticated offerings on the menus posted outside before you settle in for a long and sumptuous meal (reservations are required for some of the top restaurants, and they're essential in winter, high season).

 Beaches

Baie de Grand Case

BEACH | FAMILY | Along this skinny stripe of a beach bordering the culinary village of Grand Case, the old-style gingerbread architecture sometimes peeps out between the bustling restaurants and boutiques. The sea is usually quite calm, and there are tons of fun lunch options from bistros to beachside grills (called *lolos*). Several of the restaurants rent chairs and umbrellas; some include their use for lunch patrons. The main street, nicknamed "Restaurant Row" is where some of the best restaurants on the island can be found. In between there is a bit of shopping—for beach necessities but also for handicrafts and beach couture. **Amenities:** food and drink; toilets. **Best for:** swimming; walking. ✉ *Grand Case.*

 Restaurants

★ Bacchus

$$$ | FRENCH | The best wine importer in the Caribbean, Benjamin Laurent, and his wife Magali have built a lively, immaculate, deliciously air-conditioned wine cellar that also happens to serve outstanding starters, salads, and main courses made from top ingredients brought in from France. The place is well worth the effort it may take to find it, in the Hope Estate commercial area south of the main road (Deviation de Grand Case). **Known for:** strong coffee; great wine; chic bistro setting. $ *Average main: €28* ✉ *18–19 Hope Estate, Grand Case Rd., Grand Case* ☎ *0590/87–15–70* 🌐 *www.bacchussxm.com* ⏲ *Closed Sun. No dinner.*

★ Cynthia's Talk of the Town

$$ | CARIBBEAN | FAMILY | One of the five lolos in the middle of the village on the water side, Cynthia's (better known simply as "Talk of the Town") is a fun, relatively cheap, and iconic St. Martin meal. With plastic utensils and paper plates, it couldn't be more informal, and the menu includes everything from succulent grilled ribs to stewed conch, fresh snapper, and grilled lobster. **Known for:** low pricing and big portions; lobster; succulent ribs. $ *Average main: €14* ✉ *Bd. de Grand Case, Grand Case* 💳 *No credit cards.*

L'Auberge Gourmande

$$$ | FRENCH | With a formal, French-provincial dining room framed by elegant arches, L'Auberge Gourmande is in one of the island's oldest Creole houses. On the walls are small etchings that look like they're 100 years old, but they're actually contemporary works by renowned island impressionist Sir Roland Richardson. **Known for:** creative desserts; high-end traditional dining; Dover sole in almond butter. $ *Average main: €27* ✉ *89 bd. de Grand Case, Grand Case* ☎ *0590/87–73–37* 🌐 *www.laubergegourmande.com* ⏲ *Closed Sept. No lunch.*

La Villa

$$$ | FRENCH | FAMILY | Diners flock here for the friendly management, the spectrum of well-prepared French cuisine, and the easy-to-find location in the middle of Grand Case. You can choose what you like from their €52 three-course menu (additional charges for foie gras and lobster), or go à la carte. **Known for:** three-course fixed-price menu; classic seafood preparations; friendly service. $ *Average main: €28* ✉ *93 bd. de Grand Case, Grand Case* ☎ *0590/690–501–204* 🌐 *www.lavillasxm.com* ⏲ *No lunch. Closed Wed.*

Le Cottage

$$$ | FRENCH | French cuisine with Caribbean flavors is prepared with a light touch and presented with flair at Le Cottage, where a lively community gathers on the street-front porch. With an amazing wine cellar and a sommelier from the Burgundy region, the restaurant offers a great wine-pairing menu at €89. **Known for:** coveted porch seating that should be reserved in advance; loyal following; wine pairing menu. *Average main: €30* *97 bd. de Grand Case, Grand Case* *0590/690–622–686* *www.lecottagesxm.com* *No lunch.*

★ Rainbow Café & Beach Bar

$$$ | **MODERN FRENCH** | With a highly Instagrammable Bohemian look, this restaurant brings style, wit, and a bit of panache to the beach bar genre. Rainbow delivers a memorable breakfast, lunch, sunset drinks, sushi and tapas on the beach, their beachfront deck, or on the covered rooftop. **Known for:** people-watching; SXM's most upscale beach bar; beach parties. *Average main: €30* *176 bd. de Grand Case, Grand Case* *590/690–888–444* *www.rainbowcafesxm.com* *Closed Sept.*

Spiga

$$$ | **ITALIAN** | In a beautifully restored Creole house, exceptional cuisine fuses Italian and occasionally some Caribbean ingredients and cooking techniques. Follow one of the ample appetizers with an excellent pasta, fresh fish, or meat dish, such as the braised Angus beef short rib with porcini mushroom risotto. **Known for:** outstanding desserts; creative Italian cuisine; porch dining. *Average main: €26* *4 rte. de L'Espérance, Grand Case* *0590/52–47–83* *www.spiga-sxm.com* *Closed mid-Sept.–late Oct. and Tues. No lunch.*

Hotels

Bleu Emeraude

$$$ | **APARTMENT** | **FAMILY** | Be lulled to sleep by the sounds of the ocean below at one of the 11 spacious apartments in this tidy complex that sits right on a sliver of Grand Case Beach. **Pros:** attractive decor; modern and updated; walk to restaurants. **Cons:** can be an hour or more from the airport on busy days; far from Philipsburg, the island's shopping capital; neighborhood can be noisy. *Rooms from: €390* *240 bd. de Grand Case, Grand Case* *0590/690–37–07–00, 0590/690-71–12–16* *www.bleuemeraude.com* *11 units* *Free Breakfast.*

Grand Case Beach Club

$$ | **RESORT** | **FAMILY** | Easily the finest beach resort in Grand Case, "GCBC" has a friendly staff and incredible sunset views. **Pros:** walking distance to fine-dining restaurants; reasonably priced for what you get; access to two beaches; Grand Case beach and La Petite Plage. **Cons:** need a car to explore; some ongoing minor renovations; narrow road to hotel gets congested on Sunday. *Rooms from: €326* *21 rue de la Petite Plage, at East / North end of bd. de Grand Case, Grand Case* *0590/87–51–87, 800/344–3016 in U.S.* *www.grandcasebeachclub.com* *72 apartments* *No Meals.*

★ Hôtel L'Esplanade

$$$ | **HOTEL** | **FAMILY** | Fans return year after year to the classy, loft-style suites in this immaculate family-owned and-operated boutique hotel, located on a hill overlooking Grand Case village and its harbor. **Pros:** highly attentive management; clean and beautiful; family-friendly. **Cons:** lots of stairs; not on the beach; the pool, spa, and yoga area are a bit of a walk from the rooms. *Rooms from: €415* *Grand Case* *0590/87–06–55, 866/596–8365 in U.S.* *www.lesplanade.com* *24 units* *Free Breakfast.*

★ Le Petit Hotel

$$ | **HOTEL** | With some of the best restaurants in the Caribbean just steps away, this attractive beachfront boutique hotel exudes charm and has the same caring, attentive management as Hotel L'Esplanade. **Pros:** clean, bright, updated rooms; walking distance to everything in Grand Case; friendly staff. **Cons:** on-site parking is tight; no pool; some stairs to climb. *Rooms from: €275* *248 bd. de Grand Case, Grand Case* *0590/29–09–65* *www.lepetithotel.com* *10 rooms* *Free Breakfast.*

★ Le Temps des Cerises

$$ | **B&B/INN** | Named for the classic 19th-century French chanson, Le Temps des Cerises is the first hotel representing the fashion house of the same name based in Marseille; right on the sands of Grand Case beach, the boutique inn is the picture of current French chic. **Pros:** right on the beach; chic decor; comfortable rooms. **Cons:** a car is necessary to see the sights; across the island from Princess Juliana airport; can be a bit noisy. *Rooms from: €290 ✉ 158 bd. de Grand Case, Grand Case ☎ 590/51–36–27 🌐 www.letempsdescerises.com/en/saint-martin-beach-hotel ⏲ Closed Sept. 8 rooms 🍽 No Meals.*

Shopping

Tropismes Gallery

ART GALLERIES | Contemporary Caribbean artists showcased here include Paul Elliot Thuleau, who is a master of capturing the sunshine of the islands, and Nathalie Lepine, whose portraits show a Modigliani influence. This is a serious gallery with some very good artists. It's open 10–1 and 5–9 daily. *✉ 107 bd. de Grand Case, Grand Case ☎ 690/54–62–69 🌐 www.tropismesgallery.com ⏲ Closed Sun.*

Voila!!!

MIXED CLOTHING | The trendy beach attire, artsy accessories, and souvenirs are fun to try on and buy here. They're open until 9 pm, which means you can shop here before dinner. *✉ 101 bd. de Grand Case, Grand Case ☎ 0590/690–37–72–41 ⏲ Closed Sun. morning.*

Orléans

North of Oyster Pond and the Étang aux Poissons (Fish Lake) is the island's oldest settlement, also known as the French Quarter. You can still see a few vibrantly painted West Indian–style homes with the original gingerbread fretwork. There are also large areas of the nature and marine preserve working to save the island's fragile ecosystem.

Beaches

Le Galion

BEACH | **FAMILY** | A coral reef borders this quiet, naturally well-protected beach, part of the French side's nature reserve. The water is calm, clear, and quite shallow, so it's a paradise for young kids. Kiteboarders and windsurfers like the trade winds at the far end of the beach and will find the beach satisfactory if they don't need those "services." On Sunday there still may be some groups picnicking and partying, but during the week Le Galion is a rather desolate place better avoided. **Amenities:** parking. **Best for:** small children; swimming; windsurfing. *✉ Quartier d'Orléans.*

Restaurants

Yvette's Restaurant

$$ | **CARIBBEAN** | **FAMILY** | Follow the locals to Yvette's Kitchen, in a private house, for the island's best creole-Cajun cooking. All the St. Martin favorites are dished up in big portions at a reasonable price. **Known for:** curry goat; pickled conch; hot johnnycakes. *Average main: €19 ✉ Quartier d'Orléans ✣ Off the main road of Quartier d'Orleans, across the road from the pharmacy ☎ 721/524–6946 ▭ No credit cards ⏲ Closed Wed.*

Pic Paradis

Between Marigot and Grand Case, Paradise Peak (Pic Paradis), at 1,492 feet, is the island's highest point. There are two observation areas. From them, the tropical forest unfolds below, and the vistas are breathtaking. The road is quite isolated and steep, best suited to a four-wheel-drive vehicle. There continue to be some problems with crime in this area,

St. Maarten vs. St. Martin

If this is your first trip to St. Maarten/St. Martin, you're probably wondering which side will better suit your needs. That's hard to say, because in some ways the difference between the two can seem as subtle as the open boundary dividing them. But there are some major distinctions.

St. Maarten, the Dutch side, has the casinos, more nightlife, smaller price tags (thanks in part to the French side's euro), and bigger hotels. Cruise ships dock here. St. Martin, the French side, has no casinos, less nightlife, and hotels that are smaller and more intimate. Many have kitchenettes, and most include breakfast. If you're looking for fine dining, that used to be concentrated in Grand Case on the French side, but now there's extraordinary dining from one end of the island to the other; look especially now at both Porto Cupecoy and Simpson Bay on the Dutch side.

so it might be best to go hiking with an experienced local guide, if at all; better to visit Loterie Farm, which is off the main road headed to Pic Paradis.

Sights

★ Loterie Farm

NATURE PRESERVE | FAMILY | Almost halfway up the road to Pic Paradis is a peaceful 150-acre private nature preserve, opened to the public in 1999 by American expat B. J. Welch. There are trail maps, so you can hike on your own or hire a guide. Marked trails traverse native forest with tamarind, gum, mango, and mahogany trees—the same as it was hundreds of years ago. You might well see some wild vervet monkeys, now rather common here. The Jungle Pool is a lovely tropical garden with a large pool and Jacuzzi area plus lounge chairs, great music, roaming iguanas, and chic tented cabanas with a St. Barth–meets–Wet 'n' Wild atmosphere. A delicious, healthy lunch or dinner can be had poolside, and if you are brave—and over 4 feet 5 inches tall—you can try soaring over trees on one of the longest ziplines in the western hemisphere. (There is a milder version, but people love the more extreme one.) On Sundays you can enjoy music, played by a dj in the tree booth. Called "TreeJ" this wild party by the pool is from 1pm to 5pm on Sundays, and is has more of an adults vibe. If the festive pool area is not your thing, head to the Jungle Room for a tasty lunch, great ambience, tapas, and strong cocktails. ✉ *103 rte. de Pic du Paradis, Rambaud* ☎ *0590/87–86–16* 🌐 *www.loteriefarm.com* 🎫 *Hiking €10, zipline €40–€60, cabanas from €85, and day beds at €25* ✍ *cabana reservation recommended.*

Baie Orientale

Beaches

★ Baie Orientale (*Orient Bay*)

BEACH | FAMILY | The beach is as vibrant as ever (wider even, with more sand to enjoy now than in years past). Many consider this the island's most beautiful beach, with 2 miles (3 km) of champagne sand, underwater marine reserve, a variety of water sports, and trendy beach clubs. At its southern end, "naturists" enjoy the Club Orient area's clothing-optional policy, limited by regulation to that portion of the beach only. (Topless sunbathing is allowed on the entire beach.) Naturally, cameras are forbidden and may be confiscated. Plan to spend the day at

Belmond La Samanna is known for its great beach and spa.

one of the clubs; each bar has different color umbrellas, and most boast excellent restaurants and lively entertainment. To get here from Marigot, take the main road north past Grand Case, past the French side Aéroport de L'Espérance, and watch for the left turn. **Amenities:** food and drink; parking; toilets; water sports. **Best for:** nudists; partiers; swimming; walking; windsurfing. ✉ *Baie Orientale.*

Restaurants

Coco Beach

$$$ | FRENCH FUSION | This trendy beach restaurant captivates guests with its chic decor and relaxing vibes. Enjoy beach service or hang by the bar for flavorful cocktails. **Known for:** tartare, lobster, and oysters; beachfront relaxation; Sunday entertainment. *Average main: €30* ✉ *Orient Bay Beach, Baie Orientale* ☎ *0590/690–64–14–94* *www.cocobeach.restaurant* *No dinner, closed Sept.*

★ L'Astrolabe

$$$ | FRENCH | L'Astrolabe gets raves for its modern interpretations of classic French cuisine served around the pool at this cozy, relaxed restaurant in the Esmeralda Resort. Menu highlights include lobster and cognac bisque, fresh sea scallops and smoked pork belly, foie gras over brioche, Angus beef filet mignon, and fresh vanilla crème brûlée. **Known for:** live music on Monday and Friday; classic French dining, by the pool; fixed-price lobster menu on Friday. *Average main: €28* ✉ *Esmeralda Resort, Baie Orientale* ☎ *0590/87–11–20* *www.astrolabe-sxm.com* *No lunch. No dinner Wed.*

L'Atelier

$$$$ | FRENCH FUSION | Located on the square in Orient Bay village, this popular French restaurant enthralls with flavors for every palate. Owner Alexandre's food is inspired by his grandmother; tasteful dishes made with simple, fresh ingredients have become a staple. **Known for:** exciting menu presented on a blackboard; steaks and bone marrow appetizers; cocktails by expert mixologists. *Average main: €35 Orient Bay village square, Baie Orientale 0590/690–22–10–22 Closed Sun. and Aug.*

Hotels

Esmeralda Resort

$ | **RESORT** | **FAMILY** | Esmeralda has traditional Caribbean-style, kitchen-equipped villas that can be configured to meet guests' needs, have their own pool, and offer the fun of Orient Beach a short walk away. **Pros:** plenty of activities; beachfront location; private pools. **Cons:** main airport and capital is a distance away, especially with traffic; iffy Wi-Fi service; need a car to get around. *Rooms from: €262 Baie Orientale, 44 Main St., Baie Orientale 0590/87–36–36 www.esmeralda-resort.com Closed Sept. 65 rooms Free Breakfast.*

★ **Hotel La Plantation**

$$ | **HOTEL** | **FAMILY** | This quaint, colonial-style hotel is a charmer; French doors open to a wraparound verandah with an expansive view of the bay. **Pros:** lots of area restaurants; relaxing atmosphere; seating privileges at nearby restaurants. **Cons:** car or taxi needed to get to other major tourist areas; beach is a 10-minute walk away; small pool. *Rooms from: €283 C5 Parc de La Baie Orientale, Baie Orientale 0590/29–58–00, 800/480-8555 toll free www.laplantationhotel.com Normally closed Sept.–mid-Oct. 51 rooms Free Breakfast.*

★ **La Playa Orient Bay**

$$ | **RESORT** | You can't miss the multi-story white villas right on beautiful Orient Beach, beautifully renovated after Hurricane Irma; guests flock here for reasonable though not cheap prices, huge rooms, and the friendly, relaxed atmosphere. **Pros:** attractive beach location; spacious rooms; friendly atmosphere. **Cons:** getting to the airport can take up to an hour on weekdays (traffic); car needed to visit other tourist areas; minimum length stay may be required in high season. *Rooms from: $296 116 Parc de la Baie Orientale, Baie Orientale 0590/87–42–08 www.laplayaorientbay.com 56 rooms Free Breakfast.*

★ **Palm Court at Orient Beach Hotel**

$ | **HOTEL** | **FAMILY** | The romantic beachfront units of this *hôtel de charme* are steps from the fun of Orient Beach yet private, quiet, and stylish. **Pros:** nice garden; big rooms; romantic decor. **Cons:** daily except Sunday, driving in traffic to the airport can take an hour; car required to get to distant key tourist areas; across from, but not on, the beach. *Rooms from: €231 Parc de la Baie Orientale, Baie Orientale 800/480–8555, 0590/87–41–94 www.sxm-palm-court.com Closed Oct. 21 rooms Free Breakfast.*

Shopping

Antoine Chapon

ART GALLERIES | Reflecting the peaceful atmosphere of St. Martin and the sea surrounding it, the watercolor paintings of Antoine Chapon can be seen at the artist's studio in Cul de Sac. Call for an appointment. *Terrasses de Cul de Sac, Cul de Sac 0590/87–40–87 www.chaponartgallery.com.*

Baie Longue

Beaches

Baie Longue (*Long Bay*)

BEACH | Though it extends over the French Lowlands, from the cliff at La Samanna to La Pointe des Canniers, the island's longest beach has no facilities or vendors. It's a great place for a romantic walk, but be aware that getting here isn't as easy as it once was since you must now pass through Lowlands security. Note that the beach faces westward and can get very hot; there's no shade from trees, either. This beach is on the leeward, less breezy side of the island. To get here, take National Road 7 south of Marigot. Baie Longue Road is the first entrance to the beach. It's worth a splurge for lunch or a sunset cocktail at the elegant La Samanna. **Amenities:** none. **Best for:** solitude; walking. Note: beach faces westward and can get very hot; there's no shade from trees, either. This beach is on the leeward, less breezy side of the island. ✉ *Baie Longue.*

Hotels

★ Belmond La Samanna

$$$$ | RESORT | FAMILY | A complete redesign of the rooms, villas, and restaurants in 2019 has helped keep La Samanna, bordered by a pristine, white-sand beach, the island's top luxury resort. **Pros:** beach cabanas, convenient location; chic decor; great beach and spa. **Cons:** car required to get to off-site restaurants and shopping; some rooms are small for the price; expensive. *$ Rooms from: €1071* ✉ *Baie Longue* ☎ *0590/87–64–00, 800/854–2252 in U.S.* 🌐 *www.belmond.com/lasamanna* *Usually closed Sept. and Oct.* *91 rooms* *No Meals.*

Activities

BIKING AND SCOOTERS

Biking is a great way to explore the island. Beginner and intermediate cyclists can ride the coastal roads from Cay Bay to Fort Amsterdam or Mullet Beach. More serious bikers can cruise from Bellevue Trail and Port de Plaisance to Marigot. Bring your bathing suit—along the way you can stop at Baie Rouge or Baie des Prunes for a dip. Biking to Fort Louis offer fabulous views. The most challenging ride is up Pic Paradis. You should only tackle this route with a guide, because of crime here; ask at one of the bike shops. Several locally known guides can help you make this trip. There are no bike lanes and many roads are narrow, so pedal with caution and be aware of nearby traffic.

TriSport

BIKING | FAMILY | Rental bikes here come with helmets, water bottles, locks, and repair kits. Rates are $20 per day, $25 overnight, and $110 per week. A variety of guided bicycle tours focusing on hard terrain, or historical insight are offered for $49–$75. TriSport also rents kayaks and stand-up paddle boards, and arranges hikes, outings, and even triathlons. **TIP→ If you are on the French side, there is a location in Marigot.** ✉ *14B Airport Rd., Simpson Bay* ☎ *721/545–4384* 🌐 *www.trisportsxm.com.*

BOATING AND SAILING

The water and winds are perfect for skimming the surf. It'll cost you anywhere between $700 and $3,000 per day to rent a powerboat, considerably less if you join one of the many sailing tours available. Drinks and lunch are usually included on crewed day charters, and some tours are eco-oriented.

★ Pyratz Gourmet Sailing

SAILING | FAMILY | This company offers the ultimate sailing experience on their power catamaran, complete with a gourmet four-course lunch, wine, cocktails, and activities such as a floating mat, kayaking, paddle boarding, and snorkeling. Everything from the water toys to the reef-safe sunscreen is provided, making it easy to relax and enjoy a full day on the water. Or, you can watch the sun go down on their sunset cruise in a group of eight on the *Bali 4.5* or on the *Lagoon 450 S* power catamaran. Rent both vessels for larger groups. The company prides itself on its sustainability efforts and environmentally friendly practices. ✉ *50 Airport Rd., Simpson Bay* ☎ *0590/690–88–81–11* 🌐 *www.pyratzsxm.com* ☞ *Shared charters on Tues.*

Random Wind

BOATING | FAMILY | This company offers full-day sailing and snorkeling trips on a catamaran, also called *Random Wind*. Charter prices depend on the size of the group and whether lunch is served. The regularly scheduled Paradise Daysail (10–3, $119 per person for adults, $95 kids 5–12) includes food and drink, snorkeling equipment, and stand-up paddleboard. Departures, weekdays at 9:45, are from near the cruise ship terminal in Philipsburg or from Simpson Bay, by prearrangement. Everyone loves "flying" from the Tarzan swing.

TIP→ You can get the best rates from the website rather than hotels or cruise lines. ✉ *Simpson Bay* ☎ *721/587–5742, 757/660–5624* 🌐 *www.randomwind.com.*

Rhino Safari

BOATING | FAMILY | Take a 2½-hour guided water tour around the island on a 10-foot inflatable watercraft. The boats are stable, easy to pilot, and riding the waves is a blast. The tour includes 45 minutes of snorkeling (equipment provided) at Creole Rock, the best snorkeling spot on the island. Choose from several departures and routes every day. There is a $6 marina park fee to be paid at check in. ✉ *58 Welfare Rd., Simpson Bay* ☎ *721/544–3150* 🌐 *www.rhinotours.com* 🎫 *From $75 per person.*

St. Maarten 12-Metre Challenge

BOATING | Sailing experience is not necessary as participants compete on 68-foot racing yachts, including Dennis Connor's *Stars and Stripes* (the actual boat that won the America's Cup in Freemantle, Australia, in 1987), *Canada II*, and *True North I*. Everyone is allocated a crew position, either grinding winches, trimming sails, punching the stopwatch, or bartending. The thrill is priceless, but book well in advance; this is one of the most popular shore excursions in the Caribbean. It is offered up to four times daily and lasts 2½–3 hours. Children over 12 (9 with sailing experience) may participate. ✉ *Bobby's Marina, Philipsburg* ☎ *721/542–0045* 🌐 *www.12metre.com.*

DIVING

Diving in St. Maarten/St. Martin has become a major attraction, with reef expeditions and sunken boats easily accessible offshore. The seawater temperature here is rarely below 78°F and visibility is often 60 to 100 feet. The island has more than 30 dive sites, from wrecks to rocky labyrinths. Right outside Philipsburg, 55 feet under the water, is the HMS *Proselyte,* once explored by Jacques Cousteau. Although it sank in 1801, the boat's cannons and coral-encrusted anchors are still visible.

Off the northwest coast, in the protected and mostly current-free Grand Case Bay, is **Creole Rock.** The water here ranges in depth from 10 feet to 25 feet. Other sites off the northern coast include **Î let Pinel,** with shallow diving; **Green Key,** with its vibrant barrier reef; and **Tintamarre,** with its sheltered coves and geologic faults. On average, one-tank dives start at $65; two-tank dives are about $115. Certification courses start at about $450.

The Dutch side offers several full-service outfitters and SSI (Scuba Schools International) and/or PADI certification. There are no hyperbaric chambers on the island.

Dive Safaris

SCUBA DIVING | Certified divers who have dived within the last two years can watch professional feeders give reef sharks a little nosh in a half-hour shark-awareness dive. The company also offers a full PADI training program and can tailor dive excursions and sophisticated, sensitive instruction to any level. ✉ *16 Airport Rd., Simpson Bay* ☎ *721/520–3618* 🌐 *www.divesafarisstmaarten.com.*

Ocean Explorers Dive Center

SCUBA DIVING | St. Maarten's oldest dive shop offers different types of certification courses. Serious divers like the eight-person-maximum policy on trips, but this means you must reserve in advance. Have a small group? You can easily reserve the entire boat, given sufficient notice. Learn to dive with their on-site PADI courses or get started from home with their PADI e-Learning. ✉ *113 Welfare Rd., Simpson Bay* ☎ *721/544–5252* 🌐 *www.stmaartendiving.com.*

FISHING

You can angle for yellowtail snapper, grouper, marlin, tuna, and wahoo on deep-sea excursions. Costs range from $150 per person for a half day to $250 and up for a full day. Prices usually include bait and tackle, instruction for novices, and refreshments. Ask about licensing and insurance. Most boats give you some fillets but otherwise keep the fish, so if you want to keep yours, arrange it in advance.

Rudy's Deep Sea Fishing

FISHING | One of the more experienced sport-angling outfits runs private charter trips. Half-day excursions for up to four people start at $625. Rudy is reasonable; you can have the fillets you need and he keeps the rest.

TIP→ Check the website for great tips on fishing around St. Maarten. ✉ *14 Airport Rd., Simpson Bay* ☎ *721/545–2177, 721/522–7120* 🌐 *www.rudysdeepseafishing.com.*

KAYAKING

Kayaking continues to be very popular and is frequently offered at the many water-sports operations on both the Dutch and the French sides. Rental starts at roughly $15–$20 per hour for a single and up to about $25 for a double.

★ TriSports

KAYAKING | **FAMILY** | This company has a full slate of reasonably priced kayaking activities, but they also offer bike tours. TriSports organizes leisurely 2½-hour combination kayaking and snorkeling excursions in addition to its biking and hiking tours. Prices vary but a fee of roughly $49 includes all equipment. ✉ *Airport Rd., 14B, Simpson Bay* ☎ *721/545–4384* 🌐 *www.trisportsxm.com.*

SEA EXCURSIONS

★ Aqua Mania Adventures

BOATING | **FAMILY** | You can take day cruises to Prickly Pear Cay, off Anguilla, aboard the *Lambada,* or sunset and dinner cruises on the 65-foot sail catamaran *Tango. The Edge* goes to Saba and St. Barth. There are tours on inflatable boats, scuba and snorkel trips, and motor cruises around the island. ✉ *Simpson Bay Beach Resort and Marina, Pelican Key* ☎ *721/544–2640, 721/544–2631* 🌐 *www.stmaarten-activities.com.*

★ Celine Charters

BOATING | **FAMILY** | Perhaps SXM's most well-known, well-respected, and experienced captain is Neil Roebert, whose new sailing catamaran *Enigma* is docked behind Nowhere Special in Simpson Bay. Neil has a number of scheduled trips in addition to the boat's availability for charter. Whether you choose a private charter, a Fun in the Sun tour of SXM's beaches, or the Anguilla fantasy trip, you'll return relaxed and filled with great memories and quite possibly several new friends. Although Celine Charters is the name of the business (named for Neil's daughter), his current boat is named *Enigma*. Especially fun are full-day sails aboard *Enigma* which feature snorkel equipment, lunch, and top shelf drinks, all included. ✉ *Boat is moored behind Nowhere Special in Simpson Bay, Wellfare Rd., Simpson Bay* ☎ *721/526–1170 Neil's cell phone is usually answered quickly.* 🌐 *www.sailstmaarten.com.*

Golden Eagle III

BOATING | **FAMILY** | Three sleek catamarans, *Golden Eagle I, II* and *III*, take day-sailors on eco-friendly excursions to outlying islets and reefs for snorkeling and partying. They can pick you up from your hotel or condo. The same company offers other boat and land tours, including the double-deck *Explorer* for cruises in

Simpson Bay Lagoon. ✉ *Bobby's Marina, Jurancho Yrausquin Bd., Philipsburg* ☎ *721/543–0068* 🌐 *www.toursxm.com.*

Sail Arawak

BOATING | FAMILY | The 52-foot, competition-savvy sailing catamaran accommodates a maximum of just 12 people, enabling an intimate, enjoyable sailing experience. Arawak provides regular full- and half-day trips in St. Maarten/St. Martin, and day trips to neighboring Anguilla. Swimming, snorkeling, and a leisurely sail are just some what you can expect on any of the sail tours. No specific sailing experience is required since a captain and crew are onboard, but passengers can assist them and experience racing in a safe and secure way. An open bar, lunch, and snacks are offered onboard. *Arawak* is built for speed! Private charters are also available. ✉ *Billy Folly Rd. 10, Pelican Key* ☎ *721/554-1973* 🌐 *www.sailarawaksxm.com.*

SNORKELING

Some of the best snorkeling on the Dutch side can be found around the rocks below Fort Amsterdam off Little Bay Beach; in the southern end of Maho Bay, near Beacon Hill; off Pelican Key; and around the reefs off the northern end of Dawn Beach, near Oyster Bay Beach Resort. On the French side, the area around Baie Orientale—including Caye Verte (Green Key) and Tintamarre—is especially beautiful and is officially classified and protected as a regional underwater nature reserve. Sea creatures also congregate around Creole Rock at the point of Baie de Grand Case, though the shallows in that area are said to offer superior snorkeling activity. The average cost of an afternoon snorkeling trip is $55–$75 per person.

Blue Bubbles

SNORKELING | FAMILY | This company offers both boat and shore snorkel excursions, ATV and Jeep tours, as well as Jet Skiing, and SNUBA for beginner divers. Snorkel excursions are $55 for two hours and $75 for four hours. ✉ *153 Front St., Philipsburg* ☎ *721/556–8484* 🌐 *www.bluebubblessxm.com.*

SPAS

Spas have added a pampering dimension to some properties on both the French and Dutch sides of the island. Be sure to book in advance, however, as walk-ins are hardly ever accommodated. There are massage cabanas on some beaches, more on the French side than the Dutch, and some of the beach clubs on Baie Orientale have a blackboard where you can sign up. Hotels that don't have spas can usually arrange in-room treatments.

★ La Samanna Spa

SPAS | You don't have to be a guest at the hotel to enjoy a treatment or a day package at this heavenly retreat, easily one of the top spas on the island. In a lovely tropical garden setting, immaculate treatment rooms feature walled gardens with private outdoor showers. There are dozens of therapies for body, face, hair, and spirit on the spa menu; any can be customized to your desires or sensitivities. ✉ *Belmond La Samanna, Baie Longue* ☎ *0590/87–65–69* 🌐 *www.belmond.com/lasamanna* ⏲ *Closed Sun.*

TENNIS

SXM Padel Club

RAQUET SPORTS | Join the local padel and pétanque communities at this club, the first of its kind on the island. Open to adults and kids, the club welcomes non-members and offers classes on one of its two padel courts. Two well-lit pétanque lanes can be found in the back of the bar. Rent or buy equipment at the on-site retail store and, after sweating it on the court, get a refreshing cold drink at the bar. Make reservations via the free SXM Padel app. ✉ *24 Kangaroo Rd., Philipsburg* 🌐 *www.sxmpadelgroup.com* *By reservation only* ⏲ *Closed Sun.*

Chapter 21

TURKS AND CAICOS ISLANDS

Updated by
Sheri-kae McLeod

Sights
★★★★★

Restaurants
★★★★☆

Hotels
★★★★★

Shopping
★★★☆☆

Nightlife
★★★☆☆

WELCOME TO TURKS AND CAICOS ISLANDS

TOP REASONS TO GO

★ **Beautiful Beaches:** Even on Provo, there are miles of deserted beaches without any beach umbrellas in sight.

★ **Excellent Diving:** The world's third-largest coral reef system is one of the globe's top dive sites.

★ **Easy Island-Hopping:** Island-hopping beyond the beaten path gives a feel for the country as a whole.

★ **The Jet Set:** Destination spas, penthouse suites, and exclusive villas and resorts make celebrity spotting a possibility; keep your eyes open!

★ **Exploring on the Sea:** You'll find excellent fishing and boating among the uninhabited coves and cays.

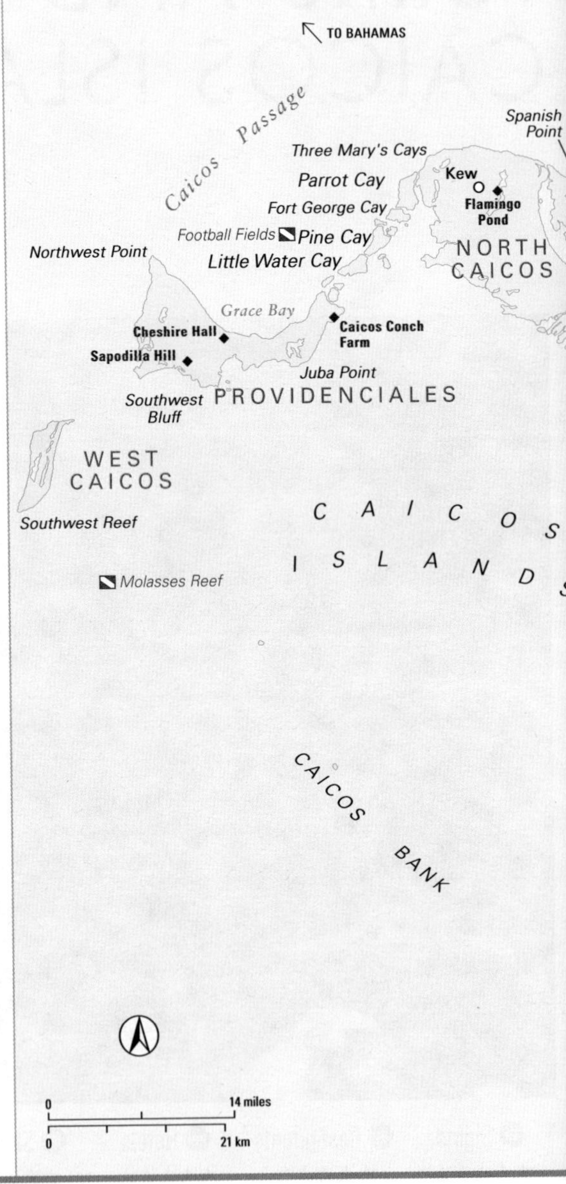

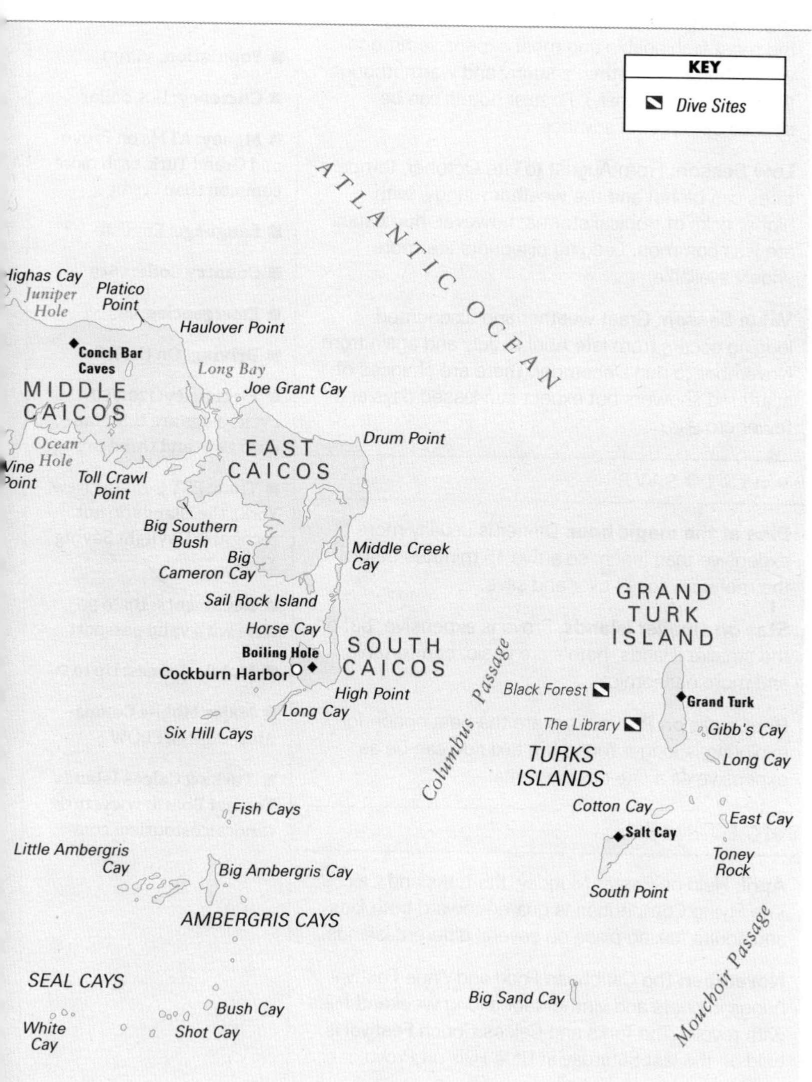
KEY
Dive Sites
ATLANTIC OCEAN
Highas Cay
Juniper Hole
Platico Point
Haulover Point
Conch Bar Caves
Long Bay
Joe Grant Cay
MIDDLE CAICOS
Ocean Hole
Vine Point
Toll Crawl Point
EAST CAICOS
Drum Point
Big Southern Bush
Big Cameron Cay
Middle Creek Cay
Sail Rock Island
Horse Cay
Boiling Hole
Cockburn Harbor
SOUTH CAICOS
High Point
Long Cay
Six Hill Cays
Columbus Passage
GRAND TURK ISLAND
Black Forest
Grand Turk
The Library
Gibb's Cay
Long Cay
TURKS ISLANDS
Fish Cays
Cotton Cay
East Cay
Salt Cay
Toney Rock
Little Ambergris Cay
Big Ambergris Cay
South Point
AMBERGRIS CAYS
Mouchoir Passage
SEAL CAYS
Big Sand Cay
Bush Cay
White Cay
Shot Cay

ISLAND SNAPSHOT

WHEN TO GO

High Season: Mid-December through mid-April is the most fashionable and most expensive time to visit, when the weather is sunny and warm (though the water can be chilly). Popular hotels can be booked up a year in advance.

Low Season: From August to late October, temperatures can be hot and the weather muggy, with higher risks of tropical storms; however, hurricanes are less common. Lodging discounts are more widely available.

Value Season: Great weather and discounted lodging occurs from late April to July and again from November to mid-December. There are chances of scattered showers but expect sun-kissed days and fewer crowds.

WAYS TO SAVE

Dine at the magic hour. Dinner is usually more expensive than lunch, so arrive 15 minutes before the menu switches over and save.

Stay on smaller islands. Provo is expensive, but on the smaller islands, hotels are basic, comfortable, and more economical.

Rent a car on Provo. Cars are the best option for exploring; a longer round-trip taxi ride can be as expensive as a one-day car rental.

BIG EVENTS

April: Held on Easter Monday, the Turks and Caicos Kite Flying Competition is geared toward both kids and adults, taking place on several different islands.

November: The Caribbean Food and Wine Festival brings in chefs and vintners for a long weekend filled with revelry. The Turks and Caicos Conch Festival is held on the last Saturday in Blue Hills on Provo.

December: The Junkanoo New Year's Eve street party with live bands, parades, and fireworks erupts in Grace Bay.

AT A GLANCE

- **Capital:** Cockburn Town
- **Population:** 38,700
- **Currency:** U.S. dollar
- **Money:** ATMs on Provo and Grand Turk; cash more common than credit.
- **Language:** English
- **Country Code:** 1 649
- **Emergencies:** 999
- **Driving:** On the left
- **Electricity:** 120v/60 cycle; plugs are U.S. standard two- and three-prong
- **Time:** EST (same as New York); the islands do not recognize Daylight Saving Time
- **Documents:** Up to 90 days with valid passport
- **Mobile Phones:** Up to 5G
- **Major Mobile Companies:** Digicel, FLOW
- **Turks & Caicos Islands Tourist Board:** www.turksandcaicostourism.com

In this paradise with crystal-clear turquoise waters, you may find it difficult to stray far from the beach. You may find no need for museums, and no desire to see ruins or even to read books. You may simply find yourself hypnotized by the myriad ocean blues. And because the beaches are among the most incredible you will ever see, don't be surprised if you wake up on your last morning to realize that you didn't find a lot of time for anything else.

Although ivory-white, soft, sandy beaches and breathtaking turquoise waters are shared among all the islands, the landscapes are a series of contrasts, from the dry, arid bush and scrub on the flat, coral islands of Salt Cay, Grand Turk, South Caicos, Pine Cay, and Providenciales, to the greener, foliage-rich undulating landscapes of Middle Caicos, North Caicos, and Parrot Cay.

A much-disputed legend has it that Columbus first discovered these islands in 1492. Despite being on the map for longer than most other island groups, the Turks and Caicos (pronounced *kay*-kos) Islands still remain part of the less discovered Caribbean. More than 40 islands—only 8 inhabited—make up this self-governing overseas territory of the United Kingdom that lies just 575 miles (925 km) southeast of Miami on the third-largest coral reef system in the world.

The political and historical capital of the country is the island of Grand Turk; however, Providenciales is the tourist hub, thanks to the beauty of Grace Bay and its incredible crescent of powder-soft sand. Once home to a population of around 500 people plus a few donkey carts, Provo is now the center of activity, where you enjoy resorts, spas, restaurants, and water sports. Condo-style hotels or one of the many self-contained villa residences house most visitors who come to the Turks and Caicos.

The country's colonial past is evident in the wood-and-stone, Bermudian-style clapboard houses—often wrapped in deep-red bougainvillea—that line the streets on the quiet islands of Grand Turk, Salt Cay, and South Caicos. Donkeys roam freely in and around the salt ponds, which are a legacy from a time when residents of these island communities worked hard as both slaves and then laborers to rake salt (then known as "white gold") bound for the United States and Canada. In Salt Cay, the remains of wooden windmills are now home to large osprey nests. In Grand Turk and South Caicos, the crystal-edged tidal ponds are regularly visited by flocks of rose-pink flamingos hungry for the brine shrimp and blue-green algae found in the shallow waters.

Sea Island cotton, considered to be of the highest quality, was produced on the Loyalist plantations in the Caicos Islands from the late 1700s. The cotton plants can still be seen dotted among the stone remains of former plantation houses in the more fertile soils of Middle Caicos and North Caicos. The elders, still residing in their tiny, traditional settlements scattered around the islands, have retained age-old skills using the locally grown fanner grasses, silver palms, and sisal to create exceptional straw baskets, bags, mats, and hats.

In all, just under 40,000 people live in the Turks and Caicos Islands; fewer than half are "Turks Islanders," the native population that is mainly descended from Loyalist and Bermudian slaves who settled here beginning in the 1600s. Most residents work in tourism, fishing, and offshore finance. Indeed, for residents and visitors alike, life in "TCI" is anything but taxing. But even though most visitors come to do nothing—a specialty in the islands—it doesn't mean there's nothing to do.

Planning

Getting Here and Around

AIR

You can fly nonstop from several cities in the U.S.: Atlanta (Delta), Boston (JetBlue), Dallas (American), Charlotte (American), Fort Lauderdale (JetBlue), Miami (American), New York (Delta, JetBlue, United), and Philadelphia (American).

Although carriers and schedules vary seasonally, there are many nonstop and connecting flights to Providenciales from several U.S. cities on American, Delta, JetBlue, and United Airways. There are also flights connecting with other parts of the Caribbean: Antigua (British Airways); Cap Haitien, Haiti (Caicos Express, InterCaribbean); Kingston, Jamaica (InterCaribbean); Nassau, Bahamas (Bahamasair); Port au Prince, Haiti (InterCaribbean); Puerto Plata, Dominican Republic (InterCaribbean); Santiago, Dominican Republic (InterCaribbean). Airlines connecting with the Canadian cities of Toronto and Montréal are WestJet and Air Canada. European cities are accessed through London on British Airways.

Airports: The main gateway into the Turks and Caicos Islands is the Providenciales International Airport (PLS). For private planes, Provo Air Center is a full-service FBO (Fixed Base Operator) offering refueling, maintenance, and short-term storage, as well as on-site customs and immigration clearance, a lounge, and concierge services. There are smaller airports on Grand Turk (GDT), North Caicos (NCS), South Caicos (XSC), and Salt Cay (SLX). Other than on Grand Turk, if you're going on to other islands in the chain, you'll stop first in Provo to clear custom and then continue from there.

AIRPORT CONTACTS Turks & Caicos Islands Airport Authority. ✉ *Providenciales International Airport (PLS), Airport Rd., Airport* ☎ *649/946–4420 general inquiries* 🌐 *www.tciairports.com.*

BOAT AND FERRY

Despite the islands' relative proximity, ferry service is limited in Turks and Caicos. You can take a ferry from Provo to North Caicos and to South Caicos. There's also a ferry from Grand Turk to Salt Cay; however, the service is often inconsistent due to weather. Air service or private boat charter is your best bet for Salt Cay.

CONTACTS Caribbean Cruisin'. ✉ *Walkin' Marina, Heaving Down Rock, Leeward Hwy. E, Leeward* ☎ *649/946–5406, 649/231–4191* 🌐 *tciferry.tciferry.com.* **Salt Cay Community Ferry.** ✉ *Balfour Town* ✥ *Departs from Deane's Dock* ☎ *649/241–1009.*

CAR

Driving here is on the left side of the road, British-style; when pulling out into traffic, remember to look to your right. Give way to anyone entering a roundabout; stop even if you're on what appears to be the primary road. The maximum speed is 40 mph (64 kph), 20 mph (30 kph) through settlements; speed limits, as well as the use of seat belts, are enforced.

If you are staying on Provo, you may find it useful to have a car; it's nice to enjoy a few days of exploring or to get away from your hotel for dinner. On Grand Turk, you can rent a car, but you probably won't need to. Car- and jeep-rental rates average $39 to $100+ per day on Provo, plus a $15 surcharge per rental as a government tax. Be sure to check if your rental company includes insurance with your rental. Many do not include liability. Reserve well ahead of time during peak season. Most agencies offer unlimited mileage and airport-pickup service. Major agencies with offices on Providenciales include Alamo, Budget, Payless, and Sixt. You might also try local Provo agencies such as Grace Bay Car Rentals, Rent a Buggy, Tropical Auto Rentals, and Caicos Wheels. There are a number of local operators on Grand Turk as well as on North Caicos, where they meet the ferries when they arrive at Sandy Point.

CONTACTS Alamo. ✉ *Providenciales International Airport, Airport* ☎ *649/941–3659* 🌐 *www.alamo.com.* **Budget.** ✉ *Butterfield Square, Downtown* ✥ *Downtown on your left just before Airport Rd.* ☎ *649/946–4079* 🌐 *www.budget.com.* **Caicos Wheels.** ✉ *Ports of Call Plaza, Grace Bay Rd., Grace Bay* ☎ *954/363–1119 US Vonage, 649/946–8302 local number* 🌐 *www.caicoswheels.com.* **Grace Bay Car Rentals.** ✉ *Grace Bay Plaza, Grace Bay Rd., Grace Bay* ✥ *Next to Island Scoop* ☎ *649/941–8500 main hotline, 649/946–4404* 🌐 *www.gracebaycarrentals.com.* **Rent a Buggy.** ✉ *1081 Leeward Hwy., next door to Mac Motors and Central Plaza, Downtown* ☎ *649/946–4158* 🌐 *www.rentabuggy.tc.* **Scooter Bob's.** ✉ *Turtle Creek Dr., Turtle Cove* ✥ *just after the Marina entrance, next to Turtle Cove Inn* ☎ *649/946–4684* 🌐 *www.scooterbobstci.com.* **Tony's Car Rental.** ✉ *Outside cruise-terminal gates, Grand Turk Cruise Terminal* ☎ *649/231–1806* 🌐 *www.tonyscarrental.com.* **Tropical Auto Rentals.** ✉ *Tropicana Plaza, Leeward Hwy., Grace Bay* ✥ *At Leeward Hwy. and Sand Castle Dr.* ☎ *649/946–5300* 🌐 *www.tropicalautorental.com.* **Sixt Car Rental.** ✉ *Blue Heron Rd., Airport* ✥ *Across from the airport* ☎ *649/941–3966* 🌐 *www.sixt.com.* **Payless Car Rental.** ✉ *Kew Town Settlement, Airport* ☎ *649/946–8592* 🌐 *www.payless.tc.* **TCI Car Rental.** ✉ *Suzy Turn, Leeward* ☎ *649/941–8824* 🌐 *www.tcicarrental.com.*

TAXI

Taxis are available at the airports on both Provo and Grand Turk. Many resorts will arrange guest transfers; ask for assistance if this service isn't included. When booking accommodations, ask upfront about the arrangements. A trip via taxi between Provo's airport and most major hotels runs between $15 and $23 per person. Taxis (actually large vans) in Providenciales are regulated by the government at a per-person rate, based on travel zones. On Grand Turk, a trip from the airport to Cockburn Town is about $8. You can also get from the ferry dock on North Caicos by taxi. On the family islands, taxis are not metered, so it's best to discuss the cost of your trip in advance.

Health and Safety

Dengue, chikungunya, and zika have all been reported throughout the Caribbean. We recommend that you protect yourself from these mosquito-borne illnesses by keeping your skin covered and using mosquito repellent. The mosquitoes that transmit these viruses are as active by day as they are by night.

Hotel and Resorts

The Turks and Caicos can be expensive. Most hotels in Providenciales are pricey, but there are some moderate options; most accommodations are condo-style, and not all resorts are family-friendly. You'll find a sprinkling of upscale properties on the outer islands—including the famous Parrot Cay—but the majority of places are smaller inns and private self-contained villas. What you give up in luxury, however, you gain back tenfold in island charm. Though the smaller islands are relatively isolated, their quiet ambience and "beauty by nature" is what makes them so attractive.

Resorts: Most of the resorts in Provo are upscale; most are condo-style and feature kitchens, allowing the option of preparing some meals in or having a private chef prepare something extra special for you. There are limited all-inclusive resorts on Provo. A few resorts close for a short period during the fall for maintenance. Double-check if your heart is set on a particular property.

Small Inns: Most of the more modest inns with fewer amenities are on the outlying islands, with a few such options on Provo. Some are devoted to diving.

Villas and Condos: Villas and condos are plentiful, particularly on Provo, and usually represent good value for families. However, there are also larger villas with full staffs that offer the ultimate in pampering. Many of the more popular properties book up to two years in advance, so you need to plan ahead to get what suits you best.

Hotel reviews have been shortened. For full information, visit Fodors.com.

What It Costs in U.S. Dollars

	$	$$	$$$	$$$$
RESTAURANTS	under $12	$12–$20	$21–$30	over $30
HOTELS	under $275	$275–$375	$376–$475	over $475

Tours

★ **Big Blue Collective**
ECOTOURISM | FAMILY | This exceptional and experienced outfitter's educational ecotours include three-hour kayak trips and other guided journeys throughout the cays northeast of the island, as well as on North, Middle, and South Caicos. The Coastal Ecology and Wildlife tour is a kayak adventure through red mangroves to bird habitats, rock iguana hideaways, and natural fish nurseries. The Heart of the Islands Eco Tour gets you on a bike to explore North and Middle Caicos; it includes plantation ruins, inland lakes, and a flamingo pond with a stop for lunch. Costs range from $125 to $295 per person. ✉ *Leeward Marina, Marina Rd., Leeward* ✣ *Next to Blue Haven Resort* ☎ *649/946–5034 main office, 649/231–6455 mobile* 🌐 *www.bigbluecollective.com.*

Visitor Information

The tourist offices on Grand Turk and Providenciales are open weekdays.

CONTACTS Turks & Caicos Islands Tourist Board, Grand Turk. ✉ *Front St., Cockburn Town* ☎ *649/946–2321* 🌐 *www.*

turksandcaicostourism.com. **Turks & Caicos Islands Tourist Board, Providenciales.** ✉ *Ventura Dr., Grace Bay* ☎ *649/946–4970* 🌐 *www.turksandcaicostourism.com.* **Turks & Caicos Reservations.** ✉ *1 Caribbean Pl., 1254 Leeward Hwy., Leeward* ☎ *877/774–5486 U.S., 649/432–1708 local* 🌐 *www.turksandcaicosreservations.com.*

Weddings

The residency requirement for both parties is 48 hours, after which you can apply for a marriage license to the registrar in Grand Turk with the exception of those arriving by cruise ship, for whom special permission can be granted for same-day arrival. Both parties must present a valid passport, original birth certificate, proof of current marital status, and a copy of immigration entry. All documents must be notarized and sealed. Both individuals must be 21 or older; all others require written parental consent. No blood tests are required. The license fee is $250.

Providenciales

The sight of the shallow, crystal-clear turquoise waters of Chalk Sound National Park never fails to dazzle visitors as they approach the island by plane. With an increasing number of visitors arriving each year, Provo—as the island is commonly called—is a top Caribbean destination. But don't worry. There are plenty of gorgeous beaches and world-class services to go around. Although you may start to believe that every road leads to a large, luxurious resort, there are plenty of sections of beach where you can escape the din. Most of the modern resorts, exquisite spas, water-sports operators, shops, restaurants, and the island's only golf course are scattered along the north shore, fringed by the exquisite stretch of Grace Bay Beach. And even though almost all of the country's grand condo resorts are found on Provo, it's still possible to find deserted stretches of ivory-white shoreline, particularly on the more secluded southern shores and the western tip of the island.

Although you may be quite content enjoying the beachscape and top-notch amenities on Provo, it's also a great jumping-off point for island-hopping tours by sea or by air, as well as both fishing and diving trips. The well-maintained road network enables you to get around easily and make the most of the main sightseeing spots. Remember: driving is on the left-hand side.

All the beaches of Turks and Caicos have bright white sand that's soft like baby powder. An added bonus is that no matter how hot the sun gets, your feet never burn. The soft sand extends to the ocean, so there's little fear of stepping on rocks or coral. Even the beach areas with coral for snorkeling have clear, clean sand for water entry.

Whichever Provo restaurant you choose, you can expect fresh seafood specials, artistic presentations, and a full range of Caribbean spices. You'll also find a range of international restaurants representing many regions around the globe. Very few restaurants close during the slow season; however, there are a few that do, so check ahead.

Pick up a free copy of *Where When How's Dining Guide,* an island-wide guide with menus, websites, and photos of most well-established restaurants.

Most of the resorts on Providenciales are on Grace Bay, but a few are off the beaten track. You'll find choices dotted along smaller bays around the island or even off the beach.

Although Provo isn't known for nightlife, there are some live bands and bars worth checking out. Popular singers such as Brentford Handfield, Justice, Correy

Forbes, and Quinton Dean perform at numerous restaurants and barbecue bonfires. Danny Buoy's, where you can always watch the latest game on big video screens, gets going late at night. Be sure to see if any ripsaw—aka rake-and-scrape—bands are playing; this is one of the quintessential local music genres (it's popular at restaurants in Blue Hills). You can also find karaoke around the island.

Late-night action can be found at Casablanca Casino, where many end the night. And every Sunday, Seven Stars features a beach bonfire and barbecue with live music while you dine. Reservations are required.

There are several main shopping areas in Provo: Grace Bay has the newer **Saltmills** complex and **Graceway Plaza, Regent Village,** and the original **Ports of Call** shopping village.

Except for Parrot Cay, Provo is the best Turks and Caicos destination for a spa vacation. The spas offer treatments with all the bells and whistles. All of Provo's high-end resorts have spas, but if you're staying at a villa, Spa Tropique or Teona Spa can bring their services to you.

Private Villa Rentals

On Provo, you can rent a self-catering apartment or a private house. For the best villa selection, make your reservations six months to a year in advance. Most villas are listed on multiple vacation rental sites, which act as booking agents, and most have property managers or owners to assist you. Vacation Rentals By Owners (VRBO) offers an excellent overview of what's available.

RENTAL CONTACTS

Coldwell Banker TCI
Several agents at Coldwell Banker will assist you in selecting a property islandwide. ✉ *Caicos Cafe Plaza, Grace Bay Rd.* ☎ *649/946–4969* 🌐 *www.coldwellbankertci.com.*

Engel & Volkers
Engel & Volkers offers modest to magnificent condos and villas throughout Providenciales. ✉ *229 Grace Bay Rd., Grace Bay* ☎ *649/231–2220* 🌐 *www.evrealestate-turks-and-caicos.com.*

T.C. Safari
Based in Florida, T.C. Safari offers reservation services for numerous properties around Provo. ☎ *649/941–5043 local number with answering service, 904/491–1415 in U.S.* 🌐 *www.tcsafari.com.*

The Bight

 Beaches

★ The Bight Beach
BEACH | The Bight Beach blends right into Grace Bay Beach as the western extension of Provo's Princess Alexandra National Park; visitors generally think of the two beaches are one and the same. Unlike its world-famous counterpart, Bight Beach has off-the-beach snorkeling where the fringing reef comes in to touch the shore. The Provo Sailing Academy gives lessons to residents some Sundays. The beach also holds the Annual Fools Regatta in June, which everyone can enjoy. Both are held at the far western end in the Children's Park. **Amenities:** food and drink; parking (free). **Best for:** snorkeling; swimming; walking. ✉ *Lower Bight Rd., The Bight* ✣ *Children's Park is at Pratt's Rd. and Lower Bight Rd.*

Restaurants

★ Indigo
$$$$ | **INTERNATIONAL** | Helmed by Australian chef and passionate fisherman Andrew Mirosch, this stylish spot at Wymara Resort serves internationally inflected dishes using sustainably sourced ingredients. Consider Australian rack of lamb, Jamaican jerk shrimp, and

any of the interesting vegetarian options, like compressed-watermelon carpaccio or grilled cauliflower steak. **Known for:** local sustainable seafood; wellness menu with healthy options; sushi and raw bar specialties. *Average main: $44 Wymara Resort, Lower Bight Rd, The Bight 649/941–7555 wymararesortandvillas.com.*

★ Mr. Grouper's

$$$ | CARIBBEAN | The name gives it away—Mr. Grouper's is where you'll find some of the best grouper dishes in Provo. **Known for:** live music on Tuesday nights and weekends; blackened or coconut-crusted grouper; relaxed atmosphere. *Average main: $29 73 Princess Dr., The Bight Settlement, The Bight 649/242–6780 www.mrgrouper.com.*

★ Somewhere Café and Lounge

$$ | MEXICAN | Right on Grace Bay Beach overlooking tranquil waters, this is a perfect spot to enjoy midday, as bathing attire is perfectly acceptable, with the incredible Coral Gardens snorkeling only a few steps away. Much of the Mexican and Tex-Mex fare—including desserts—is made from scratch. **Known for:** live music; adult-only upper-deck bar with amazing views; great salsas and guacamole. *Average main: $22 Coral Gardens Resort, Lower Bight Rd., The Bight 649/941–8260 www.somewherecafeandlounge.com.*

Hotels

Coral Gardens Resort

$$$ | RESORT | FAMILY | From the wicker-filled rooms at this small and peaceful hideaway, you're just steps away from Bight Reef, one of the most stunning in the Caribbean and an incredible spot for snorkeling. **Pros:** access to Provo's best snorkeling; suites have fully equipped kitchens; terrific restaurant with live music. **Cons:** pools are small; not many on-site activities; somes rooms have outdated decor. *Rooms from: $399 Penn's Rd., The Bight 800/532–8536 www.coralgardens.com Closed mid-Sept–mid-Oct 32 rooms No Meals.*

West Bay Club

$$$$ | RESORT | A prime location on a pristine stretch of Grace Bay Beach just steps away from the best off-the-beach snorkeling makes this elegant, contemporary resort with two restaurants and a landscaped pool a top pick. **Pros:** suites have beach views; amazing luxury for the price; on the widest section of Grace Bay Beach. **Cons:** somewhat limited dining options; only in-room spa treatments available; secluded location away from shopping. *Rooms from: $630 242 Lower Bight Rd., The Bight 649/946–8550, 855/749–5750 www.thewestbayclub.com 46 suites Free Breakfast.*

★ Windsong Resort

$$ | RESORT | FAMILY | On a gorgeous beach lined with spectacular ocean views, Windsong makes you feel right at home with its friendly and efficient reception and huge rooms outfitted with oversize bathrooms, stainless-steel appliances, marble floors, and dark woods and whites contrasted with warm golden tones. **Pros:** amazing setting for romance or weddings; unusual pool with waterfalls; huge, gorgeous bathrooms. **Cons:** not many restaurants within walking distance; breakfast is nothing spectacular; studios have only a refrigerator and microwave. *Rooms from: $350 Stubbs Rd., The Bight Between Coral Gardens and Beaches Resort 649/946–3766, 800/946–3766 www.windsongresort.com 50 rooms Free Breakfast.*

★ Wymara Resort & Villas

$$$$ | RESORT | South Beach Miami meets island time at this gorgeous resort with modern, chic furnishings, a minimalistic vibe, and bathrooms like no others on the island, complete with waterfalls cascading into tubs from the ceiling and huge rain showers. **Pros:** hip yet unpretentious;

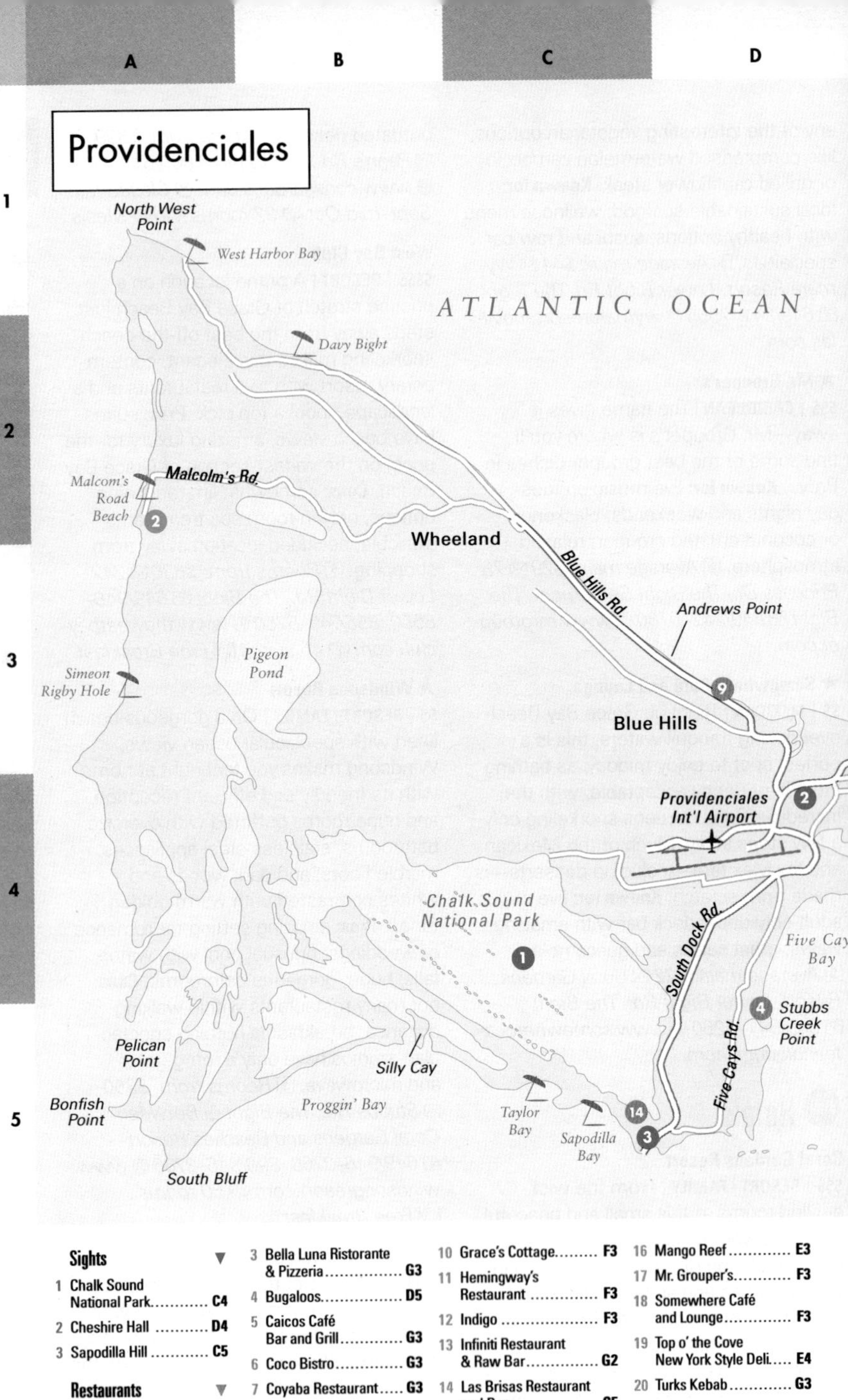

Sights ▼

1 Chalk Sound National Park............ C4
2 Cheshire Hall D4
3 Sapodilla Hill C5

Restaurants ▼

1 Baci Ristorante E3
2 Bay Bistro F3
3 Bella Luna Ristorante & Pizzeria................ G3
4 Bugaloos.................. D5
5 Caicos Café Bar and Grill............. G3
6 Coco Bistro............... G3
7 Coyaba Restaurant..... G3
8 Crackpot Kitchen G3
9 Da Conch Shack........ D3
10 Grace's Cottage......... F3
11 Hemingway's Restaurant F3
12 Indigo F3
13 Infiniti Restaurant & Raw Bar............. G2
14 Las Brisas Restaurant and Bar C5
15 Magnolia Wine Bar and Restaurant E3
16 Mango Reef E3
17 Mr. Grouper's............ F3
18 Somewhere Café and Lounge............... F3
19 Top o' the Cove New York Style Deli..... E4
20 Turks Kebab G3

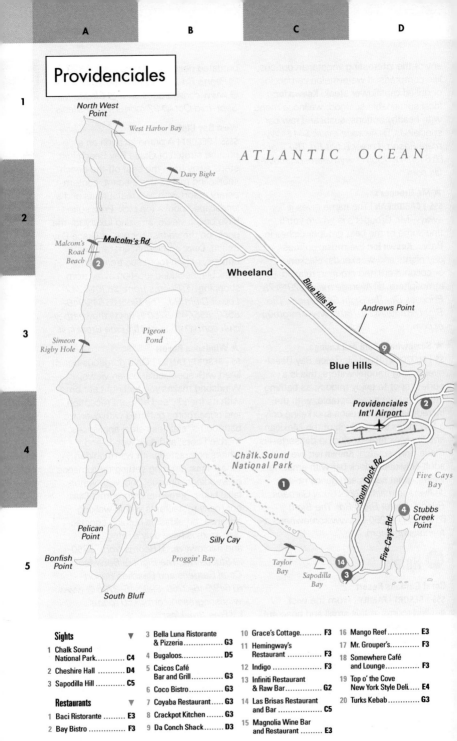

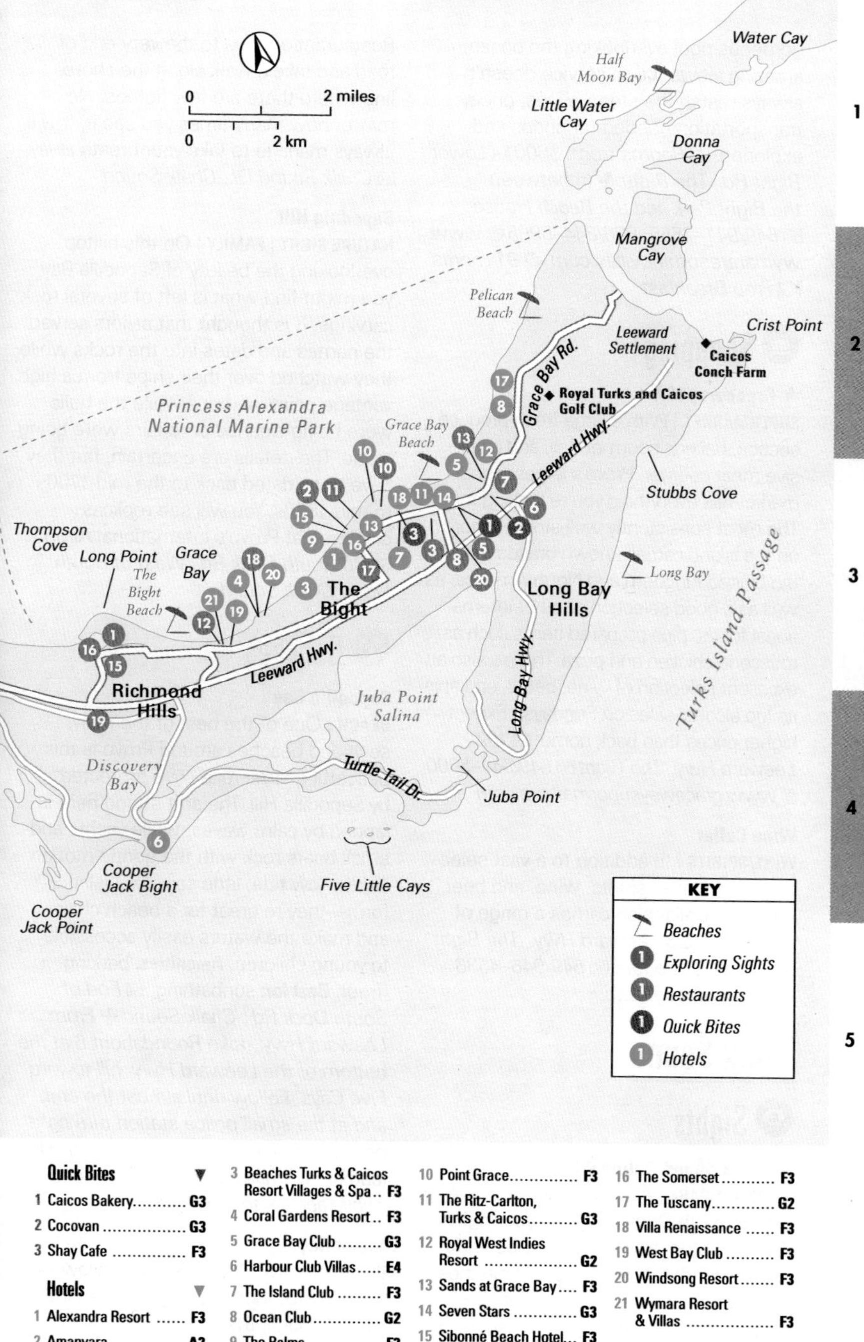

Quick Bites ▼

1 Caicos Bakery........... **G3**
2 Cocovan **G3**
3 Shay Cafe **F3**

Hotels ▼

1 Alexandra Resort **F3**
2 Amanyara................ **A2**
3 Beaches Turks & Caicos Resort Villages & Spa.. **F3**
4 Coral Gardens Resort.. **F3**
5 Grace Bay Club **G3**
6 Harbour Club Villas..... **E4**
7 The Island Club **F3**
8 Ocean Club.............. **G2**
9 The Palms **F3**
10 Point Grace............. **F3**
11 The Ritz-Carlton, Turks & Caicos.......... **G3**
12 Royal West Indies Resort **G2**
13 Sands at Grace Bay.... **F3**
14 Seven Stars **G3**
15 Sibonné Beach Hotel... **F3**
16 The Somerset **F3**
17 The Tuscany............. **G2**
18 Villa Renaissance **F3**
19 West Bay Club **F3**
20 Windsong Resort....... **F3**
21 Wymara Resort & Villas **F3**

gorgeous pool overlooking the ocean; amazing views. **Cons:** service doesn't always match the steep prices; pricey; transportation needed for shops and exploring. *$ Rooms from: $600 ⊠ Lower Bight Rd., The Bight ✣ In between the Bight Park and the Beach House ☎ 649/941–7555, 888/844–5986 🌐 www.wymararesortandvillas.com 91 rooms 🍽 Free Breakfast.*

Shopping

★ Graceway IGA
SUPERMARKET | With a large fresh-produce section, bakery, gourmet deli, and extensive meat counter, Provo's largest supermarket has everything you're looking for. The most consistently well-stocked store on the island carries known brands from the United Kingdom and North America, as well as a good selection of other international foods, plus prepared items such as rotisserie chicken and pizza. There's also an excellent selection of wine, beers, and spirits (no alcohol sales on Sundays). Expect higher prices than back home. *⊠ 102 Leeward Hwy., The Bight ☎ 649/941–5000 🌐 www.gracewaysupermarkets.com.*

Wine Cellar
WINE/SPIRITS | In addition to a vast selection of duty-free spirits, wine, and beer, the Wine Cellar also carries a range of cigars. *⊠ 1025 Leeward Hwy., The Bight ✣ East of Suzie Turn ☎ 649/946–4536 🌐 www.winecellar.tc.*

Chalk Sound

Sights

★ Chalk Sound National Park
NATIONAL PARK | As you drive out to the end of South Dock Road, on your right you will catch glimpses of the beautiful Chalk Sound; the water here is luminescent. The best places to stop for pictures are on Chalk Sound Drive. You can enjoy lunch overlooking the park at Las Brisas Restaurant or drive to the very end of the road and take a walk along the shoreline where there are few homes. No matter how many times you see it, it will always manage to take your breath away. *⊠ Chalk Sound Dr., Chalk Sound.*

Sapodilla Hill
NATURE SIGHT | **FAMILY** | On this hilltop overlooking the beauty of Sapodilla Bay, you might find what is left of several rock carvings. It is thought that sailors carved the names and dates into the rocks while they watched over their ships from a high vantage point, perhaps while the hulls were being cleaned or repairs were being made. The details are uncertain, but they have been dated back to the mid-1700s to mid-1800s. You will see replicas displayed at Provo's International Airport. *⊠ Off South Dock Rd., West of South Dock, Chalk Sound.*

Beaches

Sapodilla Bay
BEACH | One of the best of the many secluded beaches around Provo is this peaceful quarter-mile cove protected by Sapodilla Hill. The soft strand here is lapped by calm waves, while yachts and small boats rock with the gentle motion. During low tide, little sandbar "islands" form—they're great for a beach chair and make the waters easily accessible to young children. **Amenities:** parking (free). **Best for:** sunbathing. *⊠ End of South Dock Rd., Chalk Sound ✣ From Leeward Hwy., take Roundabout 6 at the bottom of the Leeward Hwy. hill toward Five Cays. Follow until almost the end, and at the small police station turn right onto Chalk Sound Dr. The road on the left leads to a small parking area that offers public access to the beach.*

Taylor Bay
BEACH | **FAMILY** | Taylor Bay is shallow for hundreds of feet, making it the perfect place for kids; they become giddy at the fact that they can run free through

shallow waters without their parents worrying about them. The beach also offers gorgeous views of the villas that hang over the shoreline on one side of the bay with natural coastline on the other. As it has had many amazing reviews over the years, don't expect to have this one all to yourself. There is even the odd tour that pulls up. **Amenities:** none. **Best for:** sunbathing; wading. ✉ *Sunset Dr., Chalk Sound* ✣ *From Leeward Hwy., take the roundabout exit toward Five Cays at the bottom of the Leeward Hwy. hill. Follow the road until almost the end, and at the small police station, take a right onto Chalk Sound Dr. Take a left at Ocean Point Dr., and park next to the tennis courts where there are big boulders blocking a sand path. Follow this path to the beach.*

West Harbour Bay
BEACH | This is about as isolated as it gets on Provo. West Bay has long stretches of beaches to walk and possibly not see another person for hours. You might see large red starfish in the water here, or if you walk out to Bonefish Point you may spot small reef sharks and the odd ray hunting in the shallows. Don't leave valuables in your car, as there have been break-ins reported in the past. **Amenities:** none. **Best for:** exploring; solitude; swimming; walking. ✉ *Northwest Point* ✣ *Traveling west on Millennium Hwy. past Blue Hills, take the last left before Provo's landfill site. Continue for 5 miles (8 km) along a relatively rough road until you come to the ocean's edge. Walk along the shoreline to get to the caves. Walk right to Bonefish Point.*

Restaurants

★ Las Brisas Restaurant and Bar
$$$$ | **INTERNATIONAL** | **FAMILY** | With exquisite views of Chalk Sound, the restaurant terrace and elevated gazebo offer picture-postcard views of the intensely blue waters. This is the only restaurant on Provo that offers an authentic paella (if you order this, give it time—the flavors have to simmer), and everything here is made to order; you pick out your fish or meat, decide how you want it prepared, and choose a sauce for it. **Known for:** extensive tapas selection; spectacular views; seafood paella. [$] *Average main: $36* ✉ *Neptune Villas, #533 Chalk Sound Dr., Chalk Sound* ✣ *Off South Dock Rd.* ☎ *649/946–5306* 🌐 *www.neptunevillastci.com.*

Grace Bay

The "hub" of the island is the stunning Grace Bay Beach, a graceful curve of soft sand along Provo's north shore. Between it and the Lower Bight Road, which runs parallel to the beach, you'll find most of the island's shops, restaurants, and resorts. There are sidewalks and streetlights, cafés and coffeehouses, restaurants, spas, tour operators, and specialty stores. This is the area where most tourists stay, especially if it's their first visit.

Beaches

★ Grace Bay Beach
BEACH | The world-famous sweeping stretch of ivory-white, powder-soft sand on Provo's north shore is simply breathtaking. Protected within the Princess Alexandra National Park, it's home to migrating starfish, as well as many schools of tiny fishes. The majority of Provo's beachfront resorts are along this shore, and it's the primary reason Turks and Caicos is a world-class destination. **Amenities:** food and drink; parking (free); water sports. **Best for:** sunset; swimming; walking. ✉ *Grace Bay Rd., along the north shore, Grace Bay.*

Restaurants

★ Bay Bistro

$$$$ | **ECLECTIC** | **FAMILY** | You simply can't eat any closer to the beach than at this breezy bistro on Grace Bay Beach, where you can dine on a covered deck, on an open-air patio, or with your feet in the sand, surrounded by palm trees with the sound of lapping waves. The coffee-rubbed tuna appetizer—with a hint of wasabi—is the best, but also consider the fish-and-chips, beef tenderloin, and seasonal lobster, which is brought to the back door daily by local fishermen. Around the full moon, call for the date of their memorable beach barbecue: grilled lobster, jerk lamb, side fixings—all enjoyed around a wonderful beach bonfire. **Known for:** homemade ice cream; dining right on the beach; weekend brunch with mimosas. *Average main: $33 ✉ Sibonné Beach Hotel, Princess Dr., Grace Bay ☎ 649/946–5396 🌐 www.baybistrorestaurant.com.*

★ Bella Luna Ristorante & Pizzeria

$$$ | **ITALIAN** | In the heart of Grace Bay, you'll find the soul of Italy at this hip pizzeria and elegant trattoria with charmingly rustic decor, lush green vines, an herb garden, and softly lighted outdoor seating surrounded by trees. The native Italian owner has created a superb menu of authentic red and white pizzas plus calzones in the casual parlor. **Known for:** banana with caramel sauce for dessert; impressive wine list; friendly staff. *Average main: $30 ✉ 6 Grace Bay Rd., Grace Bay ☎ 649/946–5214 restaurant, 649/941–5128 Pizzeria 🌐 www.bellaluna.tc ⏲ Closed Sun. No lunch.*

★ Caicos Café Bar and Grill

$$$$ | **ECLECTIC** | Here the fresh and carefully prepared island dishes come with an Italian twist, from bread baked fresh daily at the bakery next door to handcrafted gourmet pastas. On windy nights, the inland setting offers protection from the breezes, and the large flamboyant tree is quite spectacular, especially when it is in full bloom. (Bug spray at night may be necessary.) **Known for:** Mediterranean-style seafood casserole; plenty of vegetarian options; oven-warm fresh baked bread. *Average main: $36 ✉ Caicos Café Plaza, Governor's Rd., Grace Bay ☎ 649/946–5278 🌐 www.caicoscaferestaurant.com ⏲ Closed Sun. No lunch.*

★ Coco Bistro

$$$$ | **INTERNATIONAL** | With tables set dramatically within a mature palm grove, this hugely popular restaurant serves continental-style dishes with Caribbean flair, with local seafood leading the way. Be sure to try the Caicos lobster bisque: it's served flambé with cognac and a hint of spicy cream. **Known for:** famous coconut pie; dining under the palms; fresh-from-the-sea lobster. *Average main: $44 ✉ Governor's Rd., Grace Bay ✣ Just down from Sunshine Nursery ☎ 649/946–5369 🌐 www.cocobistro.tc ⏲ Closed Mon. No lunch.*

Coyaba Restaurant

$$$$ | **ECLECTIC** | Directly behind Grace Bay Club at Caribbean Paradise Inn, this posh little restaurant with a palm-fringed setting serves nostalgic favorites with tempting, tropical twists. Don't skip the excellent chocolate fondant for dessert. **Known for:** deconstructed beef Wellington; innovate modern cuisine; delectable desserts. *Average main: $48 ✉ Bonaventure Crescent, Grace Bay ✣ Just off Grace Bay Rd., west of Club Med ☎ 649/946–5186 🌐 www.coyabarestaurant.com ⏲ Closed Tues. No lunch.*

★ Crackpot Kitchen

$$$ | **CARIBBEAN** | This casual local hot spot is one of the only restaurants in Grace Bay that serves authentic and traditional Turks and Caicos cuisine (beyond the standard cracked conch or conch salad). From braised oxtail with butter beans to curried goat, you'll find items on this menu that you won't find elsewhere, all infused with life and love from Chef Nik. **Known for:** warm and welcoming service;

traditional island food in a tourist-friendly setting; Friday-night happy hour. *Average main: $30 Port of Call Plaza, Grace Bay Rd., Grace Bay 649/941–3330 www.crackpotkitchen.com Closed Thurs. No lunch Sun.*

Grace's Cottage

$$$$ | **CARIBBEAN** | This is one of the prettiest settings on Provo, and the name says it all: Imagine dining under the stars in an English-style garden or at one of the tables placed artfully upon the graceful covered verandah skirting the gingerbread cottage. Tangy and exciting entrées include Caicos bouillabaisse, duck confit cassoulet, and a succulent tomahawk steak for sharing. **Known for:** chocolate soufflé that's worth the wait; dining under the stars; Caribbean flavors with creative twists. *Average main: $44 Point Grace, Off Grace Bay Rd., Grace Bay 649/946–5096 www.pointgrace.com No lunch.*

Hemingway's Restaurant

$$$$ | **ECLECTIC** | **FAMILY** | The casual yet gorgeous setting, with a patio and deck offering unobstructed views of Grace Bay, makes this one of the most popular dining venues on the island. At lunch, you can't miss the conch, served however you prefer, but the mango shrimp salad is also excellent. **Known for:** great kids' menu at lunch; lobster, with your choice of preparations; views of Grace Bay. *Average main: $38 The Sands at Grace Bay, Grace Bay Rd., Grace Bay 649/941–8408 www.hemingwaystci.com.*

★ **Infiniti Restaurant & Raw Bar**

$$$$ | **ECLECTIC** | This chic palapa-style, waterfront restaurant has the most romantic setting along Grace Bay—some would say the most romantic in all of the Turks and Caicos Islands. Despite the elite clientele and higher prices, the restaurant offers a memorable dining experience minus any formality or attitude—oil lamps create an evening glow, and the murmur of trade winds adds to the Edenic ambience. **Known for:** farm- and sea-to-table ingredients; raw bar; romantic, mesmerizing ocean views. *Average main: $45 Grace Bay Club, Grace Bay Circle Rd., Grace Bay 649/946–5050 www.gracebayresorts.com No lunch.*

★ **Turks Kebab**

$$ | **MEDITERRANEAN** | Operating by the roadside on Allegro Road, this restaurant is one of the hidden food gems in Grace Bay, and the only place serving eastern Mediterranean food, including kebabs, gyros, Turkish-style pizzas, and souvlaki. The kitchen keeps things simple but traditional, using locally sourced ingredients, and there's a wide selection of spirits, wines, and cocktails. **Known for:** best gyro in Provo; lamb and beef kebabs; delicious baklava for dessert. *Average main: $20 Allegro Rd., Grace Bay A block from Graceway IGA 649/431–9964 www.turkskebab.com Closed Sun.*

Coffee and Quick Bites

★ **Caicos Bakery**

$ | **BAKERY** | At this little takeout-only bakery you will find the perfect coffee, freshly baked croissants or doughnuts, an assortment of fresh bread, French desserts, traditional cakes, and more. Be sure to get there early though, as there's often a line waiting for them to open! **Known for:** fresh-baked savory breads; coconut rum eclairs; pastries worth jumping early out of bed for. *Average main: $6 Caicos Plaza, Grace Bay 649/232–1003 www.facebook.com/frederictatiana No credit cards Closed Sun. No dinner.*

★ **Cocovan**

$$ | **ECLECTIC** | With so many incredible restaurants in Provo, you might wonder how a food truck made it to the top of the pack. Every bite that comes out the kitchen, housed in an authentic 1974 Airstream van, is absolutely delicious, and seating is at airy picnic tables. **Known for:**

shrimp mac and cheese balls; delicious food truck fare; fun outdoor dining. *Average main: $19 ✉ 10 Oak Ave., Grace Bay ☎ 649/231–8226 🌐 www.cocovan.tc ⏲ No lunch.*

Shay Cafe

$ | **CAFÉ** | This cozy spot provides some of the best breakfast and brunch options in Grace Bay, plus a variety of coffee and organic teas, along with tasty wraps, crepes, and other breakfast sandwiches. Mimosas are served all day on weekends. **Known for:** homemade gelato; weekend brunch; creative sandwiches. *Average main: $11 ✉ Le Vele Plaza, Grace Bay Rd., Grace Bay ☎ 649/941–4959 🌐 shaycafelounge.restaurantsnapshot.com ⏲ No dinner.*

Hotels

Alexandra Resort

$$$$ | **ALL-INCLUSIVE** | **FAMILY** | This all-inclusive beachfront resort, on a fine stretch of Grace Bay Beach, offers spacious accommodations with large decks or balconies and kitchens or kitchenettes, plus amenities that include a lagoon-style pool, tennis courts, water-sports equipment, and other perks that appeal to families as well as couples. **Pros:** large pool; kids 12 and under stay and eat free; spectacular stretch of beach just steps away. **Cons:** it's a 15-minute shuttle ride to sister property; service is often on island time; some rooms lack king beds. *Rooms from: $700 ✉ Princess Dr., Grace Bay ✣ next to the Palms Resort ☎ 649/946–5807, 800/284–0699 🌐 www.alexandraresort.com 90 rooms All-Inclusive.*

★ **Beaches Turks & Caicos Resort Villages & Spa**

$$$$ | **RESORT** | **FAMILY** | Designed for families to spend some time together and reconnect and recharge, Beaches is the largest resort in the Turks and Caicos Islands, and it offers much to see and do, including more than 20 dining options, a full-service spa, and myriad water sports and activities. **Pros:** a diverse range of dining options; tons of cool family diversions; gorgeous pools. **Cons:** per-person rates; excursions such as the catamaran trip can get crowded; the extensive all-inclusive plan means you may miss out on the dining at the island's other great restaurants. *Rooms from: $1200 ✉ Lower Bight Rd., Grace Bay ☎ 649/946–8000, 888/232–2437 🌐 www.beaches.com 758 rooms All-Inclusive.*

Grace Bay Club

$$$$ | **RESORT** | **FAMILY** | The stylish Grace Bay Club has always been a number-one choice on Providenciales, constantly meeting the demands of the discerning visitor and staying consistently ahead of all expectations, and the helpful, attentive staff and unpretentious elegance have helped it to retain a loyal following. **Pros:** lots of activities to entertain kids of all ages; gorgeous pools and restaurants; adult-only sections. **Cons:** have to travel into town to purchase basic amenities; expensive; must stay in Estates section to use its beautiful pool. *Rooms from: $962 ✉ Bonaventure Crescent, Grace Bay ✣ Off Governor's Rd. ☎ 649/946–5050, 800/946–5757 🌐 www.gracebayresorts.com 82 suites No Meals.*

The Island Club

$$ | **RESORT** | This small, reasonably priced condo complex right next door to Saltmills Plaza and within walking distance of many restaurants and Graceway IGA, is in the heart of it all—and within only a few minutes' walk of the beach. **Pros:** laundry facilities on-site; you can't get a better deal on Provo; centrally located so you can walk everywhere. **Cons:** three-night minimum stay; a block from the beach; only a few condos in the complex are in the short-term rental pool, so availability is limited. *Rooms from: $275 ✉ 375 Grace Bay Rd., Grace Bay ☎ 649/344–8558, 844/428–8757 🌐 www.islandclubturks.com 24 units No Meals.*

What Is a Potcake?

Feral dogs in the Bahamas and Turks and Caicos Islands are called potcakes. Traditionally, they would be fed from the leftover scraps of food that formed at the bottom of the pot; this is how they got their name. Much is being done these days to control the stray dog population. The TCSPCA and Potcake Place are two agencies working to adopt out the puppies. You can "travel with a cause" by adopting one of these gorgeous pups; they come with all their shots and all the papers required to bring them back home to the United States or Canada. Even if you don't adopt, you can help by volunteering as a carrier—bringing one back to its adoptive family. Customs in the U.S. is actually easier when you are bringing back a potcake! You can also choose to borrow a pup for a couple of hours to take it for a walk, an activity that has become increasingly popular with those who are sad to have had to leave their canines back at home. For more information on how you can help, check out the website for Potcake Place (www.potcakeplace.com).

Ocean Club

$$ | RESORT | FAMILY | Enormous, locally painted pictures of hibiscus make a striking first impression as you enter the reception area at one of the island's most well-established condominium resorts, which enjoys a quiet location away from busier developments. **Pros:** fully equipped kitchens and gas grills; family-friendly resort with shuttles between the two shared properties; screened balconies and porches. **Cons:** rooms are starting to show their age; the sister properties are a shuttle ride or 20-minute beach walk apart; if you don't have a rental car, you have to take the shuttle to get closer to the "hub." *Rooms from: $375 118 Grace Bay Rd., Grace Bay Next to The Tuscany 649/946–5880, 800/457–8787 www.oceanclubresorts.com Closed Sept. 174 suites No Meals.*

★ The Palms

$$$$ | RESORT | FAMILY | Consistently ranked among the world's top luxury beach resorts, this swanky spread on the Grace Bay waterfront boasts a supremely inviting 25,000-square-foot spa with a central reflection pool, several shops, two restaurants, and stylishly appointed rooms with an enchanting old-world-meets-modern-Caribbean feel. **Pros:** wide range of amenities; lively; one of the best spas in the Caribbean. **Cons:** island-time service doesn't always match the high rates; expensive; in the summer, the sunken pool bar area can get hot when the trade winds die. *Rooms from: $850 Princess Dr., Grace Bay Between the Alexandra and the Somerset 649/946–8666, 866/630–5890 www.thepalmstc.com 72 suites Free Breakfast.*

Point Grace

$$$$ | RESORT | Keeping history in mind, this resort was built with a turn-of-the-20th-century British colonial feel; dark mahogany, granite, marble, and teak create a sense of warmth and comfort within each of the 28 luxurious one- to four-bedroom suites and penthouses. **Pros:** relaxing environment; beautiful pool; attentive service. **Cons:** can be extremely quiet (signs around the pool remind you); decor is dated; service can be inconsistent. *Rooms from: $660 Grace Bay Rd., Grace Bay Next door to the Sands 649/946–5097, 888/209–5582 toll-free reservations www.pointgrace.com Closed Sept.–mid-Oct. 28 rooms No Meals.*

★ **The Ritz-Carlton, Turks & Caicos**

$$$$ | **RESORT** | With Grace Bay's reputation for unparalleled refinement, it's no surprise that the vaunted Ritz-Carlton brand opened its first Turks and Caicos property here; indeed, the resort's opulence stands out from the moment you're greeted with a glass of champagne and continues as you enjoy the shimmering amenities, including a casino, oceanside spa, and one of Provo's top beaches. **Pros:** tons of water sports and activities; close to Grace Bay shopping and dining; amazing water views from rooms. **Cons:** junior rooms are smaller than at comparable hotels; spotty service; dining options are pricey and nothing spectacular. *Rooms from: $1300 Grace Bay Rd., Grace Bay 649/339–2222 www.ritzcarlton.com 147 rooms No Meals.*

Royal West Indies Resort

$$$ | **RESORT** | With a contemporary take on colonial architecture and the outdoor feel of a botanical garden, this unpretentious resort on Grace Bay Beach has plenty of garden-view and beachfront studios and suites for moderate self-catering budgets. **Pros:** daily happy hour; great bang for your buck; on one of the longest stretches of Grace Bay Beach. **Cons:** most activities cost extra; units at the back of the resort are far from the beach; Club Med next door can be noisy. *Rooms from: $405 Bonaventure Crescent, Grace Bay Between Club Med and The Oasis 649/946–5004, 800/332–4203 www.royalwestindies.com 115 suites No Meals.*

Sands at Grace Bay

$$$ | **RESORT** | **FAMILY** | Spacious gardens and winding pools set the tone for one of Provo's most family-friendly resorts, a 6-acre beachfront spread with helpful service and excellent amenities that include a spa, a good-size fitness room, water sports, tennis, and basketball, as well as on-site dining. **Pros:** screened-in balconies and porches; ideal for families; central to shops and restaurants. **Cons:** lots of kids can make poolside rooms less than relaxing; restaurant is busy; courtyard rooms aren't worth the price. *Rooms from: $440 Grace Bay Rd., Grace Bay 649/941–5199, 877/777–2637 www.thesandstc.com 114 suites No Meals.*

★ **Seven Stars**

$$$$ | **RESORT** | **FAMILY** | Fronting gorgeous Grace Bay Beach, the tallest property on the island also sets a high mark for luxury within its three buildings, a magnificent heated saltwater pool, full-service spa, tennis courts, and large in-room bathrooms. **Pros:** lots to keep the kids entertained; Moët Champagne shack next to the beach; walking distance to everything in Grace Bay. **Cons:** restaurants are pricey; can feel crowded; some find the resort too big. *Rooms from: $740 Grace Bay Rd., Grace Bay 649/941–7777, 866/570–7777 www.sevenstarsgracebay.com 123 suites Free Breakfast.*

Sibonné Beach Hotel

$ | **HOTEL** | Dwarfed by most nearby resorts, the smallest hotel on Grace Bay Beach has snug (by Provo's spacious standards) but pleasant rooms with Bermudan-style balconies and a tiny circular pool that's hardly used because the property is right on the beach. **Pros:** small and unimposing; closest property to the beach; the island's best bargain. **Cons:** lacks amenities; some rooms have a double bed; pool is small and dated. *Rooms from: $185 Princess Dr., Grace Bay next to Somerset 649/946–5547, 888/570–2861 www.sibonne.com 30 rooms No Meals.*

★ **The Somerset**

$$$$ | **RESORT** | This luxury resort plenty of wow factor, starting with the architecture and ending in your luxuriously appointed suite, but what sets the Somerset apart is that it's more focused on your comfort and enjoyment than on attracting a celebrity clientele. **Pros:** lots of added amenities, including a sunscreen bar; Provo's

most beautiful architecture; you can walk to snorkel and to shops. **Cons:** breakfast is nothing special; in-room Wi-Fi can be spotty; the cheapest rooms can get noisy. *Rooms from: $700 Princess Dr., Grace Bay Between the Palms and Sibonné 649/339–5900, 888/386–8770 www.thesomerset.com 53 suites Free Breakfast.*

The Tuscany

$$$$ | HOTEL | FAMILY | Located at the far eastern end of Grace Bay, this quiet, upscale self-catering resort is the place for mature, independent travelers to unwind without the need for resort amenities, thanks in part to its immaculate gardens and prime setting on a long and secluded beach shared mostly just with its sister property, the Venetian. **Pros:** beautiful pool; luxurious; all condos have ocean views. **Cons:** can feel like no one else is on the property; very expensive for a self-catering resort; no restaurant or reception, and it's at the far end of the hub. *Rooms from: $775 Governor's Rd., Grace Bay Across from the golf course 649/941–4667, 866/359–6466 www.thetuscanyresort.com 30 units No Meals.*

Villa Renaissance

$$$$ | HOTEL | Guests love the quiet, residential feel of this posh short-term-rentals property modeled after a Tuscan villa and comprising one-, two-, and three-bedroom suites in either the four-story oceanfront building or housed in the pool/garden-view suites. **Pros:** peaceful and quiet; luxury for less; one of the prettiest courtyards in Provo. **Cons:** too quiet for some; limited food and beverage options; not a full-service resort. *Rooms from: $514 Ventura Dr., Grace Bay Between Regent Grand and the Mansions 649/941–5300, 800/234–0346 www.villarenaissanceturksandcaicos.com 32 units No Meals.*

Nightlife

Danny Buoy's

BARS | This popular Irish pub has lots of slot machines, as well as big-screen TVs airing major sporting events. Tuesday and Thursday are karaoke, Friday is country night with line dancing, and Saturday night has a DJ. It's open until the wee hours except Sunday when they call it a night at midnight. It's also a great spot for a late-night bite. *Grace Bay Rd., Grace Bay Across from Regent Village 649/946–5921.*

Shopping

★ Anna's Art Gallery

ART GALLERIES | This trove of fabulous original artworks, silk-screen paintings, sculptures, and handmade sea-glass jewelry, most made by local artists and artisans, is almost impossible to visit without picking up a little something to take home with you. Anna's Too, just a couple of doors down, is filled with fantastic women's wear—all cotton, comfortable, and colorful. Tucked alongside are books and pillows as well as other home decor items. *Saltmills Plaza, Grace Bay Rd., Grace Bay 649/941–8841 www.anna.tc.*

ArtProvo

ART GALLERIES | This gallery features a wide selection of designer wall art, but native crafts, jewelry, handblown glass, candles, and other gift items are also available, including locally made bath products. Mary, the gallery's owner, has lived in TCI for more than 40 years and has developed relationships with many local artists and artisans. She features creations by the island's own Jill Segal, Alexis, and Dwight Outten. Sandra Knuyt's cigar-smoking female characters are a favorite. *Regent Village, Regent St., Grace Bay Turn off Grace Bay Rd. at Caicos Adventures 649/941–4545 www.artprovo.tc Closed Sun.*

Best Spas in Provo and Beyond

A Turks Island Salt Glow, in which the island's sea salt is mixed with gentle oils to exfoliate, smooth, and moisturize the skin, is just one of the treatments you can enjoy at a Provo spa. Being pampered spa-style has become as much a part of a Turks and Caicos vacation as sunning on the beach. Marine-based ingredients fit well with the Grace Bay backdrop at the Thalasso Spa at **Point Grace**, where massages take place in two simple, bleached-white cottages standing on the dune line, which means you have a spectacular view of the sea-blue hues—if you manage to keep your eyes open. The Spa at **The Palms** offers individual treatments, with a water feature by day, champagne, and chocolates under the stars by night. The signature body scrub uses hand-crushed local conch shells to smooth the skin. The widest choice of Asian-inspired treatments (and the most unforgettable scenery) can be found at the 6,000-square-foot Como Shambhala Spa at the **Parrot Cay Resort**, which has outdoor whirlpools and a central beech-wood lounge overlooking the shallow turquoise waters and mangroves. Another more than luxurious experience is the spa at Amanyara, situated in total seclusion along the northwest shoreline.

Provo also has a noteworthy day spa that's not in one of the Grace Bay resorts. **Spa Tropique** blends Swedish, therapeutic, and reflexology massage techniques using oils made from natural plants and products produced locally and within the Caribbean region. The mango and passion fruit scrub is one of the most popular treatments.

Making Waves Art Studio

ART GALLERIES | Alex, the owner and resident artist, paints turquoise scenes, often on wood that doesn't require framing. She's happy to discuss the possibility of transforming your thoughts and emotions about one special spot onto canvas as the perfect souvenir. You'll find artists working on-site—come and meet them in their natural habitats. They don't mind being fed! And bring wine! ✉ *Ocean Club West Plaza, 337 Grace Bay, Unit 1, Grace Bay* ☎ *649/242–9588* 🌐 *www.makingwavesart.com.*

Turtle Cove

Restaurants

★ Baci Ristorante

$$$ | **ITALIAN** | Aromas redolent of Mediterranean cuisine waft from the open kitchen as you enter this local favorite directly on Turtle Cove. Outdoor seating is on a lovely canal-front patio, or enjoy your meal from a table in the open-air, covered restaurant. **Known for:** a nice break from the standard American or island fare; delicious pizzas; authentic, made-from-scratch Italian desserts. $ *Average main: $30* ✉ *Harbour Towne, Turtle Cove* ☎ *649/941–3044* 🌐 *www.baci-ristorante.com* ⏲ *Closed Sun. No lunch Sat.*

Magnolia Wine Bar and Restaurant
$$$$ | ECLECTIC | The hands-on owners ensure a terrific experience at this hilltop spot with great views of Turtle Cove Marina and the north shore. Expect well-prepared, uncomplicated dishes, such as cognac–garlic butter escargot and sesame-encrusted, rare-seared tuna. **Known for:** well-curated wine list; banoffee and lemon-lime-curd pies; European fare with Caribbean flair. *Average main: $42 Miramar Hotel, 76 Sunburst Rd., Turtle Cove Just off Lower Bight Rd. 649/941–5108 www.magnoliaprovo.com Closed Mon. No lunch.*

★ Mango Reef
$$$ | ECLECTIC | FAMILY | Dine alfresco while watching yachts sail in and out of the Turtle Cove Marina at this restaurant located well west of the hustle and bustle of Grace Bay. Casual and popular with families, Mango Reef serves standard island and American fare for lunch and dinner, including lots of conch, quesadillas, burgers, and salads. **Known for:** casual island fare; outdoor dining; Dominican seafood paella when in season. *Average main: $25 Turtle Cove Marina, Turtle Cove 649/946–8200 www.mangoreef.com.*

Top o' the Cove New York Style Deli
$ | SANDWICHES | Order a coffee, tea, bagel, deli sandwich, salad, or dessert at this island institution (opened in 1992) on Leeward Highway, just south of Turtle Cove. There's also great pizza, which you can order by the slice or by the pie, and the deli case and market shelves offer all the foods—plus some beer and wine—you need for a fancy picnic. **Known for:** shaded outdoor patio; bagels; hearty breakfasts. *Average main: $10 Turtle Creek Drive, Turtle Cove 649/946–4694 www.topothecove.com No dinner.*

Hotels

Harbour Club Villas
$$ | B&B/INN | FAMILY | Although not on the beach, this small complex of of six one-bedroom cottages along a ridge overlooking the Caicos Banks and inland Flamingo Lake is right by the marina, making it a good base for scuba diving, bonefishing, or a quieter vacation. **Pros:** great base for divers; just a five-minute drive from Grace Bay; great value. **Cons:** not much in the way of amenities; have to drive to a beach; need a car to get around the island. *Rooms from: $325 36 Turtle Tail Dr., Turtle Cove Next to South Side Marina 888/240–0447 www.harbourclubvillas.com 6 villas No Meals.*

Elsewhere on Providenciales

Sights

Cheshire Hall
RUINS | Just east of downtown Provo are the eerie remains of an 18th-century cotton plantation owned by the Loyalist Thomas Stubbs. A trail weaves through the ruins, where guided interpretive tours tell the story of the island's doomed cotton industry and about the plantation itself. A variety of local plants are also identified. Contact the Turks & Caicos National Trust to visit; the $10 fee helps preserve the nation's heritage. If this piques your interest, a visit to the North Caicos Wades Green plantation or the Turks and Caicos National Museum in Grand Turk provides more of the story. *Leeward Hwy., next to the entrance into the National Hospital (Providenciales), Downtown 649/941–5710 www.tcnationaltrust.org $10 Closed Sun.*

Half Moon Bay's white sand and turquoise water are minutes from Provo by boat.

Beaches

★ Half Moon Bay

BEACH | Only minutes from Provo's eastern tip, Half Moon Bay is one of the most gorgeous beaches in the country. This natural ribbon of sand linking two uninhabited cays is only inches above the sparkling turquoise waters. There are small limestone cliffs to explore on either end where rock iguanas sun themselves, as well as small, sandy coves. Most of the island's tour companies run excursions here or simply offer a beach drop-off. As an alternative, rent a kayak from Big Blue Collective and venture over independently. **Amenities:** none. **Best for:** solitude; swimming; walking. ✉ *Between Big Water Cay and Little Water Cay* 🌐 *www.bigbluecollective.com.*

Malcolm's Road Beach

BEACH | This is one of the most stunning beaches you'll ever see, but you'll need to tread carefully; the road is a little rough in spots, and there have been reports of break-ins at the parking area. Don't bring any valuables with you, and never go alone. Also pack your own food and drinks because there are no facilities for miles around. **Amenities:** parking (free). **Best for:** solitude; swimming; walking. ✉ *Malcolm's Beach Rd., Northwest Point* ✥ *Off hard-packed sand section of Millennium Hwy.; follow the somewhat rough road until it ends.*

Pelican Beach

BEACH | Pelican Beach is a gorgeous stretch of beach that blends right into Grace Bay Beach at its eastern extension, within Princess Alexandra National Park. There is little distinction between where one beach ends and the other begins—some people refer to a small stretch in between as Leeward Beach. Because of a cut in the reef, you may find wonderful shells here—but remember that you are within the national park, so they must be left behind for others to see long after you have gone home. This end of the bay is slightly quieter than the rest, as there is much less development here. Enjoy. **Amenities:** parking (free).

Best for: solitude; swimming; walking. ✉ *Nightjar, Leeward* ⊕ *Off Grace Bay Rd. via Sandpiper La.*

Restaurants

★ Bugaloos

$$ | **CARIBBEAN** | Dinner and lunch is served island-style at this fabulous spot overlooking the Caicos Banks on the southern shores of Providenciales. Fine local cuisine and a wide selection of drinks are served, and there's live music—you grab the mike most nights to belt out a favorite tune, and dancing to the island beat is encouraged. **Known for:** live music and dancing; near the ocean; the best cracked conch. [$] *Average main: $20* ✉ *Five Cay's Rd., Five Cay's* ⊕ *Next door to Sunny's Fish Plant* ☎ *649/941–3863, 649/333–7321 reservations* 🌐 *www.bugaloostci.com.*

★ Da Conch Shack

$$ | **CARIBBEAN** | **FAMILY** | An institution on Provo for years, this brightly colored beach shack with live music is justly famous for its seafood and the island's freshest conch, which is fished fresh out of the shallows and broiled, spiced, cracked, or fried to absolute perfection. They also have Johnny fries, a local tradition of french fries with a black-bean-and-local-pepper sauce. **Known for:** toes-in-the-sand dining; fresh-as-it-gets conch; day and night parties. [$] *Average main: $18* ✉ *Blue Hills Rd., Blue Hills* ⊕ *Next to Kalooki's* ☎ *649/946–8877, 649/332–8501* 🌐 *www.daconchshack.com.*

Hotels

★ Amanyara

$$$$ | **RESORT** | With the ultimate zenlike atmosphere, this breathtaking luxury resort with 38 timber-shingled guest pavilions and 20 villas harmoniously blends with the indigenous vegetation and is *the* place for peace and quiet in a remote waterfront setting. **Pros:** best full-service secluded beach on Provo; fabulous restaurants; incredible spa with pool and yoga pavilion. **Cons:** expensive; far from restaurants, outside excursion companies, and other beaches; isolated. [$] *Rooms from: $2000* ✉ *Northwest Point* ⊕ *Off Millennium Hwy.* ☎ *649/941–8133* 🌐 *www.aman.com* *58 rooms* *No Meals.*

Nightlife

Blue Haven Resort, The Pool Bar

BARS | Servers at the Pool Bar are more than happy to keep the drinks flowing by delivering them to your quiet spot on the water's edge, with Mangrove Cay and the mega-yachts of the marina as a dramatic backdrop. Three gas fireplace seating areas are absolutely wonderful spots from which to enjoy a breezy evening. ✉ *Blue Haven Resort, Leeward Marina, Leeward* ⊕ *Far eastern tip of the island* ☎ *649/946–9900 hotel, front desk* 🌐 *www.bluehaventci.com.*

Shopping

After 5 Island Concierge

OTHER SPECIALTY STORE | Sometimes you just need help before or during your trip. After 5 Island Concierge can do anything to ease your vacation worries, from grocery delivery and meal reservations to organizing private wine tastings and sorting out bulk wine delivery for that special party or event. They'll also help you arrange for a personal chef or catering services. ☎ *649/244–9720* 🌐 *www.islandconciergetc.com.*

Smart

SUPERMARKET | IGA's downtown location is another North American–style supermarket but offers more to locals at lower prices (the logo is $mart). You can cut your travel budget considerably by purchasing Essential Everyday brand items, and there are alcoholic beverages. ✉ *Town Centre Mall, Downtown* ☎ *649/946–5525* 🌐 *www.gracewaysupermarkets.com.*

BICYCLING

Most hotels have bicycles available for guests, or you can rent one from an independent company. Stick to the sidewalks on Grace Bay Road; drivers don't pay much attention to bikes. But the island thanks you for cycling, as you're creating less dust within this arid environment.

★ Caicos Cyclery

BIKING | Comfortable beach cruisers are available from Caicos Cyclery from $25 a day, as well as the wider-tired Choppers, mountain bikes, and hybrids. Delivery to a private villa is possible. There's a tandem bike available for rent as well. You can also look forward to a 50% discount with a two-week rental. They offer guided cycling tours of Provo and North & Middle Caicos. ✉ *Saltmills Plaza, Grace Bay Rd., Grace Bay* ✥ *Adjoining Big Al's Island Grill* ☎ *649/941–7544, 649/431–6890 mobile* 🌐 *www.caicoscyclery.com.*

BOATING AND SAILING

Provo's calm, reef-protected seas combine with constant easterly trade winds for excellent sailing conditions. Several multihulled vessels offer charters with snorkeling stops, food and beverage service, and sunset vistas. Prices range from $90 per person for group trips (subject to passenger minimums) to upwards of $600 or more for private charters.

★ Caicos Dream Tours

BOATING | Caicos Dream Tours offers several boating options, including one that has you diving for conch before lunch off a gorgeous beach. You may choose from two different excursions shared with others, starting at $112/person, or charter a private boat for as many as 12 people, beginning at $1,200 for a half day. With 10 boats in their fleet, Dream Tours is able to accommodate a few hundred guests at the same time, so wedding parties and conference groups have the option of enjoying a day out together. Maximum capacity on one boat is 90 including crew. They also offer a bottom-fishing charter for up to 12 people for those die-hard fisherpeople traveling together. Note that Caicos Dream Tours is the only island excursion operator that offers a combo of bottom-fishing and snorkeling on the same charter; this one makes the whole family happy! ✉ *Alexandra Resort, 1 Princess Dr., Grace Bay* ☎ *649/231–7274* 🌐 *www.caicosdreamtours.com.*

★ Island Vibes

BOATING | **FAMILY** | Turks and Caicos–born and raised, the owner-operators of Island Vibes make their excursions stand out. If conditions are right, they'll take you to snorkel out over the wall, where the reef drops an amazing 3,000 feet. With a 12-foot curve slide off the roof, a diving board, and spacious bathroom onboard with freshwater showers, these fun excursion boats can add a little more excitement to your day. Join a group for the half-day snorkel at $125 per person, or throw yourself into the full-day barbecue adventure ($250 per person), which combines an amazing lunch set up under the shade of tall island pines with exploring small cays, snorkeling, conch diving, and beach strolling. There's also a sunset tour in the evenings for $80 per person and private cruises nightly. ✉ *One Season Plaza,, Grace Bay Rd., Turtle Cove* ☎ *649/231–8423* 🌐 *www.islandvibestours.com* 🎫 *From $80 per person.*

Silver Deep

BOATING | Silver Deep excursions include several half-day and full-day trip options. Choose from all types of fishing, a dedicated snorkeling adventure, exploration of North and Middle Caicos, and the most popular: a Native Beach Barbecue. Their most unique opportunity is the night-fishing private charter, just in case your days are too busy with naps and enjoying the beach. Other private charters may be arranged starting at $1,200; your itinerary may be personalized to include a multitude of activities, keeping all members in your group happy. ✉ *Ocean Club West Plaza, Grace Bay Rd., Grace Bay* ✣ *Right across from Caicos Café Plaza* ☎ *649/946–5612* 🌐 *www.silverdeep.com* 🎫 *From $99 per person.*

★ Sun Charters

BOATING | FAMILY | The *Atabeyra*, operated by Sun Charters, is a 70-foot schooner with a big wide belly. It's a local favorite for special events, as it's by far the most family-friendly adventure. Kids can run around without too many worries about going overboard, and the boom overhead is strong enough for them to sit and survey the seascape—just as a pirate would have done. Although primarily known as a private charter service, Sun also offers an amazing sunset rum punch party and glowworm excursions as their specialty, with a weekly Sail & Snorkel for individuals to join. During Night with da Stars trips, the *Atabeyra* sails at sunset and then throws anchor in a secluded spot; a night sky app and laser discussion will introduce you to a light-pollution-free night sky. The boat accommodates up to 50 people. ✉ *Blue Haven Resort, Marina Rd., Leeward* ✣ *Operates from the resort's VIP dock in front of Fire and Ice Restaurant* ☎ *649/231–0624* 🌐 *www.suncharters.tc.*

Undersea Explorer

BOATING | FAMILY | For sightseeing below the waves, try the *Undersea Explorer*, a semi-submarine operated by Caicos Tours out of Turtle Cove Marina. It's an ocean adventure that takes you into the underwater world without getting wet. Your one-hour tour of the reef is led by a knowledgeable captain and viewed through large windows below the surface on either side, all in air-conditioned comfort. It's the perfect trip for young and old alike. Your choice: the Mermaid Adventure, which is a theatrical voyage with a "surprise" spotting of Mermaid Bella along the way and a pirate captain making a guest appearance, or the Turtle Reef Adventure, which sticks strictly to the business of exploring the reef as an informative voyage. ✉ *Turtle Cove Marina, Lower Bight Rd., Turtle Cove* ☎ *649/432–0006* 🌐 *www.caicostours.com* 🎫 *$80* ⏲ *Closed Sun.*

DIVING AND SNORKELING

The island's many shallow reefs offer excellent and exciting snorkeling relatively close to shore. Try **Smith's Reef** over Bridge Road east of Turtle Cove, or the Bight Reef in front of Coral Gardens, to explore the reef where it touches the shoreline. A third option is the patch of coral just off Babalua Beach, between the north shore's Turtle Cove and Thompson Cove; you will need a car to get there.

Scuba diving in the crystalline waters surrounding the islands ranks among the best in the Caribbean. The reef and wall drop-offs thrive with bright, unbroken coral formations and lavish numbers of fish and marine life. Mimicking the idyllic climate, waters are warm all year, averaging 76°F to 78°F in winter and 82°F to 84°F in summer. With minimal rainfall and soil runoff, visibility is usually very good and frequently superb, ranging from 60 feet to more than 150 feet. An extensive system of marine national parks and boat moorings, combined with an ecoconscious mindset among dive operators, contributes to an uncommonly pristine underwater environment.

Dive operators in Provo regularly visit sites at **Grace Bay** and **Pine Cay** for spur-and-groove coral formations and bustling reef diving. They make the longer journey to the dramatic walls at **North West Point** and **West Caicos** depending on weather conditions. Instruction from the major diving agencies is available for all levels and certifications, including technical diving. An average one-tank dive costs $75; a two-tank dive is $145; they go upwards from there depending on the number of divers, where the dive sites are, and what services are included. There are also two live-aboard dive boats available for charter working out of Provo.

Diving with stingrays is a popular activity on Turks and Caicos.

Aqua TCI

DIVING & SNORKELING | Founded by experienced divers Bill and Stephanie Wallwork, Aqua TCI offers daily excursions to dive sites off Northwest Point, Sandbore Channel, West Caicos, and French Cay. Up to eight passengers are allowed on the boat. If you're not certified, they also offer private charter snorkeling adventures. The cost is $1,500 for four people; lunch and snacks included. And if you're looking to get certified as a diver, you can check their various PADI courses. ✉ *Venetian Rd.* ☎ *649/432–2782* 🌐 *www.aquatci.com.*

★ **Big Blue Collective**

DIVING & SNORKELING | **FAMILY** | This ecotour operator got its start offering dive excursions in 1997, but has since widened its scope considerably. Big Blue offers several educational kayak ecotours, as well as very popular stand-up paddleboard (SUP) safari tours, though these don't cover quite as much territory as kayak tours. Big Blue also has outposts on Middle, North, and South Caicos, with an extensive network of guides, bikes, kayaks, and boats. They're an interactive and ecofriendly way to learn more about what Turks and Caicos has to offer. Private charters up to 12 passengers can incorporate a snorkeling adventure to the reef off the outer islands or on the Caicos Banks near French Cay and West Caicos. They are also the only operator offering excursions to the pristine coral reefs surrounding South Caicos. And they're recognized for outstanding kiteboarding and kitesurfing instruction, downwinders, and kite safaris. The Cabrinha Kite and Board gear is used for both instruction and rentals. ✉ *Leeward Marina, Marina Rd., Leeward* ☎ *649/946–5034* 🌐 *www.bigbluecollective.com.*

Caicos Adventures

SCUBA DIVING | **FAMILY** | Run by the well-known and friendly Frenchman Fifi Kunz, Caicos Adventures offers daily excursions out of their private marina on the south side of Provo to sites off West Caicos, French Cay, and Southwest Reef. The company runs two dive boats, with groups up to 20 able to dive together. If you are not yet certified, you may enjoy one of their snorkel adventures as an alternative. They also have the *Lady K*, a luxury motorboat, available for private charters operating out of Blue Haven Marina on the eastern tip of the island. It's best to book over the phone. ✉ *Regent Village, Grace Bay Rd., Grace Bay* ✣ *Private marina is off Venetian Rd.* ☎ *649/941–3346* 🌐 *www.caicosadventures.com.*

★ Dive Provo

SCUBA DIVING | Dive Provo is a PADI Five Star operation that runs daily one- and two-tank dives to popular Grace Bay sites, as well as to West Caicos. In addition, they offer the exciting night dive, as well as their unique three-tank Scuba Safari, where they head out to dive sites farther afield, such as Molasses Reef, Sandbore Channel, and Southwest Reef. This excursion includes one tank of nitrox to make it easier on the diver to spend as much time as possible under the water. Note that this is not offered to junior divers. Dive Provo has a full array of dive courses: Discover Scuba, Open Water Certification, Advanced Open Water, and Nitrox Certification. They also offer snorkeling excursions. Check out their packages including accommodation; it's a great way to save money on your next dive holiday. ✉ *Saltmills Plaza, Grace Bay Rd., Grace Bay* ☎ *649/946–5040, 800/234–7768* 🌐 *www.diveprovo.com.*

★ Flamingo Divers

DIVING & SNORKELING | Flamingo Divers is a PADI Five Star Gold Palm Facility offering high-end service in small groups of up to a maximum of eight divers. Operating out of their south-side location, Mickey and Jayne will take you through amazing sites off Northwest Point and West Caicos, as well as French Cay when the seas permit. With more than 20 years of experience diving the waters around Provo, they know the territory. ✉ *Venetian Rd.* ☎ *649/333–3483* 🌐 *www.flamingodivers.com.*

FISHING

The islands' fertile waters are great for angling—anything from bottom and reef-fishing (most likely to produce plenty of bites and a large catch) to bonefishing (among the finest in the Caribbean) and deep-sea fishing. Every July, the Caicos Classic IGFA Billfish Release Tournament attracts anglers from across the islands, as well as internationally, who compete to catch the biggest Atlantic blue marlin, Atlantic sailfish, and white marlin—all indigenous to the waters surrounding TCI. For any fishing activity, you are required to purchase a visitor's fishing license ($10 per day or $30 for a month); operators generally furnish all equipment, drinks, and snacks. While die-hard anglers have a wide range of fishing to choose from, families may look forward to a combination excursion incorporating family-friendly fishing along with a beach barbecue featuring the catch of the day. Prices range from $700 upward, depending on the length of trip and size of the boat.

Grand Slam Fishing Charters

FISHING | For deep-sea fishing trips in search of marlin, sailfish, wahoo, and tuna, look up this company. Grand Slam operates three boats: a 45-foot Hatteras, a 42-foot Pursuit, and a 252 Mako Center Console. ✉ *Turtle Cove Marina, Turtle Cove* ☎ *649/231–4420* 🌐 *www.gsfishing.com.*

Silver Deep

FISHING | FAMILY | Silver Deep has been operating out of Provo for more than 30 years. In the fishing department, they offer the full range: deep-sea, bone, fly, night, and bottom fishing. Families can choose to participate in a private excursion where fishing, beach time, and snorkeling can all be included to keep every member content. With a large fleet of boats, there is the perfect fit for all occasions—no matter the charter request or the water conditions on any given day. ✉ *Ocean Club West Plaza, Grace Bay Rd., Grace Bay* ✣ *Opposite Caicos Café Plaza* ☎ *649/232–5612* 🌐 *www.silverdeep.com.*

Diving the Turks and Caicos Islands

Scuba diving was the original water sport that lured visitors to the Turks and Caicos Islands in the 1970s. Aficionados are still drawn by the abundant marine life, including humpback whales in winter, the pristine waters of TCI's warm and calm seas, and the intrigue of its wall diving, with continuous vertical faces of hundreds of feet. And the magnificent fringing coral reef that runs the full length of the country's north shore is the third-largest in the world! Diving the Turks and Caicos—especially off Grand Turk, South Caicos, and Salt Cay—remains among the finest in the world.

Off Providenciales, many dive sites are found along the north shore, with boat times of anywhere from 10 to 45 minutes. Dive sites feature spur-and-groove coral formations atop a coral-covered slope. Popular stops such as **Aquarium**, **Pinnacles**, and **Grouper Hole** have large schools of fish, turtles, nurse sharks, and gray reef sharks. From the south side, dive boats go to **French Cay**, **West Caicos**, **South West Reef**, and **Northwest Point**, with longer boat access times. Known for typically calm conditions and excellent visibility, the West Caicos Marine National Park is a favorite stop. The area has dramatic walls and marine life, including sharks, eagle rays, and octopus, with large stands of pillar coral and huge barrel sponges.

Off Grand Turk, the 7,000-foot coral wall is actually within swimming distance of the beach. Buoyed sites along the wall have swim-through tunnels, cascading sand chutes, imposing coral pinnacles, dizzying vertical drops, and undercuts where the wall goes beyond the vertical and fades beneath the reef.

GOLF

★ Provo Golf Club

GOLF | Among the Caribbean's top courses, the 18 holes here (par 72) are a combination of lush greens and fairways, rugged limestone outcroppings, and freshwater lakes. Rack rates are $210 for 18 holes, but you can save through twilight specials, a multi-round pass, or a biweekly or monthly pass. The club also offers two hard-court, floodlit tennis courts, which are among the island's best. Nonmembers can play until 5 pm for $20/hour, with racket rentals available. Inquire at the pro shop about tennis lessons. ✉ *Grace Bay Rd., Grace Bay* ☎ *649/946–5991 pro shop, 877/218–9124* 🌐 *www.provogolfclub.com* 🎟 *$210 for 18 holes, $125 for 9 holes with shared cart* ⛳ *18 holes, 6705 yards, par 72.*

HORSEBACK RIDING

Provo's Long Bay Beach and secluded laneways are ideal for horseback riding.

Provo Ponies

HORSEBACK RIDING | **FAMILY** | Provo Ponies offers morning and afternoon rides along quiet dirt roads, through short brush trails, and then out onto the beauty of Long Bay Beach, where you and your horse may take a dip in the shallow waters of the Caicos Banks before heading back to the stable. Horses are matched according to your riding ability, with no rider under seven and no double riding allowed. Reservations are required, and there is a 240-pound weight limit and only seven horses that can carry riders who weigh more than 150 pounds. Pick-up at your Grace Bay hotel or villa can be arranged for an additional $10 per person, which is great for those who've decided

Provo Golf Club is one of the Caribbean's top 18-hole courses.

not to hire a rental car. It's closed on Sundays to give the horses their well-deserved rest and Saturday afternoon rides are available by special request only. ✉ *32 Dolphin La., Long Bay* ✣ *Take Leeward Hwy. east to Long Bay Hills Rd. Turn left onto Lignumvitae and left again onto Dolphin La.* ☎ *649/241–6350* 🌐 *www.provoponies.com* 🎫 *$143 for 60-min ride, $169 for 90-min ride; additional fee for a private ride* 🕓 *Closed Sun.*

SPAS

Anani Spa at Grace Bay Club

SPAS | Anani Spa at Grace Bay Club is on the villas side of the complex. There are eight treatment rooms in total, but treatments can also be performed on your terrace if you're staying at the resort, or in the spa tent on the oceanfront. Spa packages are available so that you can enjoy a combination of treatments designed to work together. One of their signature treatments is the Exotic Lime and Ginger Scrub; you will emerge refreshed and polished! ✉ *Villas at Grace Bay Club, Bonaventure Crescent, Grace Bay* ☎ *649/946–5050* 🌐 *www.gracebayresorts.com.*

The Palms Resort and Spa

SPAS | Widely considered one of the best spas in the Caribbean, the Palms Spa is an oasis of relaxation. In the main facility you will find a pedicure/manicure space, gym, boutique, and yoga and Pilates pavilion, as well as men's and women's steam rooms and saunas. Outdoors, white tented cabanas grace the edge of a beautiful reflection pool, its waters catching images of towering palms and flowering bougainvillea. However, you don't even have to leave your room; massages may be arranged so that you can enjoy the wonderful sea views right from your very own balcony. Guests are encouraged to indulge in one of the locally inspired signature treatments: a mother-of-pearl body exfoliation incorporating the queen conch shell, or the 90-minute Zareeba herbal cleansing and detox. Rest a while and sip herbal tea or replenish with citrus-infused water before or after your treatment. ✉ *The Palms, Princess*

Dr., Grace Bay ☎ *649/946–8667* 🌐 *www.thepalmstc.com.*

Spa Tropique

SPAS | You pick the place, and this spa comes to your hotel room or even your isolated villa. Or, you can go to one of their five locations scattered throughout the Grace Bay area. They offer all the standard treatments as well as a Thai massage that, when combined with the relaxed vibe of the island, will relieve you of any tension you brought with you on vacation. ✉ *Ports of Call, Grace Bay Rd., Grace Bay* ☎ *649/331–2400* 🌐 *www.spatropique.com.*

Teona Spa

SPAS | The spa for Bianca Sands, the Villa Renaissance, and the Somerset, Teona also provides a mobile service offering most of their treatments in the comfort of your hotel or villa. Their spaces exude a peace-filled ambience, with every detail carefully thought out. Hush as you enter, and relax while you're there. It is the spa choice for many island residents. Take a peek at the spa specials; there is always a combination package put together for special times of the year. Or try one of the spa parties. What better way to spend time with a young one than a Mommy and Me day? The team also offers wedding packages that include makeup and hair. ✉ *Bianca Sands Resort, Ventura Dr., Grace Bay* ✣ *Turn off Grace Bay Rd. at the Goldsmiths into Regent Village* ☎ *649/941–5051 main spa, 649/339–5900 Somerset location* 🌐 *www.teonaspa.com.*

Thalasso Spa at Point Grace

SPAS | Thalasso Spa at Point Grace offers their services from within three white-washed open-air cabanas set upon the dunes overlooking Grace Bay. They share the European philosophy of the famous Thalgo Spas of France and combine it with the perfect Caribbean ambience for your enjoyment. Treatments combine elements of the ocean, including sea mud, seaweed, and sea salt, with the properties of seawater to pamper you from head to toe. The setting alone, with the salt air and sea breezes, is worth the visit. This is another favorite with residents. ✉ *Point Grace Resort, Grace Bay Rd., Grace Bay* ☎ *649/946–5096* 🌐 *www.pointgrace.com.*

Parrot Cay

Once said to be a hideout for Calico Jack Rackham and his fellow pirates Mary Read and Anne Bonny, this 1,000-acre cay between Fort George Cay and North Caicos is now the site of a luxury resort.

The only way to reach Parrot Cay is by private boat or the resort's private ferry from its dock in Leeward.

GETTING THERE

The only way to reach Parrot Cay is by private boat or the resort's private ferry from its own dock in Leeward. If you are staying on Provo and would like to go to Parrot Cay for lunch or spa treatments, you must make a reservation with the resort and pay for a day pass, which includes the transfer over. The private ferry to Parrot Cay runs only for guests; with a reservation, your name will be added to the passenger list.

 Hotels

★ **Parrot Cay Resort**

$$$$ | **RESORT** | This private paradise, on its own island, pairs tranquility with stellar service and features exquisite oceanfront villas along the beach, with an Asian-inspired look that contrasts with the simple hillside terra-cotta and stucco building that houses the rooms and spacious suites. **Pros:** one of the world's most acclaimed spas; impeccable service; gorgeous, secluded beach. **Cons:** very remote; excursions are expensive; only two restaurants to choose from island-wide. 💲 *Rooms from: $1020* ✣ *Northeastern tip of Parrot Cay* ☎ *649/946–7788, 866/388–0036*

Parrot Cay Resort is on its own private island.

www.parrotcay.com 113 rooms
Free Breakfast.

Pine Cay

15 to 20 minutes by boat from Provo.

Pine Cay's 2½-mile-long (4-km-long) beach is among the most beautiful in the archipelago. The 800-acre private island, which is in the string of small cays between Provo and North Caicos, is home to a secluded resort and almost 40 private residences. The beach alone is a reason to stay here: the sand seems a little whiter, the water a little brighter than beaches on the other cays. Nonguests of the Meridian Club can make reservations for lunch. Expect to pay $85 plus taxes for the day, plus a fee for the boat transfer; there are themed buffets on Sunday.

GETTING THERE

There are three ways to reach Pine Cay: by private boat, on the Meridian Club's private shuttle, or by small private plane. There is no schedule for the shuttle: it operates as needed.

Hotels

★ **The Meridian Club, Turks & Caicos**
$$$$ | RESORT | On one of the most beautiful beaches in Turks and Caicos, the Meridian Club is the place to de-stress—guest rooms lack phones and TVs (even cell-phone use is frowned upon), and the simple beachfront rooms and cottages, most of the staff, and what is perhaps the world's smallest airport (in truth, a gazebo with thatched roof) have all stayed pretty much the same over the years. Choose from the 12 oceanfront rooms, two cottages, or one of the private homes around the island. **Pros:** perfect place to completely unwind; one of the finest beaches in the Caribbean; rates include exceptional food. **Cons:** the simplicity comes at a cost; expensive to get back to Provo; no TVs or phones—you're truly unplugged here. *Rooms from: $1095 North Shore 649/946–7758, 888/286–7993 www.pinecay.*

Local Souvenirs

What should you bring home after a fabulous vacation in the Turks and Caicos Islands? Here are a few suggestions, some of which are free.

You can bring home up to three conch shells (shells only). If you do not call the U.S. or Canada home, check your country's import regulations for conch. For some, you will need a formal letter from TCI's DEMA (Department of Environment and Marine Affairs).

The Middle Caicos Co-op shop features a local artisan from 11 to 3 daily, while their local handicrafts along with others from around the islands may also be found at Paradise Arts in Saltmills Plaza, Art Provo in Regent Village, Turks & Caicos National Trust in Town Center Mall, as well as Mama's in Ports of Call—all located right on Provo.

The Conch Farm sells beautiful, affordable jewelry made from conch shells and freshwater pearls.

One of the best souvenirs is the hardcover coffee-table cookbook from the Red Cross. Not only is it gorgeous, featuring recipes from all the great chefs of the Turks and Caicos, but the proceeds help the Red Cross.

If you're a dog lover, then maybe the best free souvenir would be to adopt a potcake puppy. Dogs come with a carrier, papers, and all their shots—and one will remind you year after year of your terrific vacation.

com ⏲ *Closed Aug.–Oct.* 🛏 *28 rooms* 🍽 *Free Breakfast.*

North Caicos

This 41-square-mile (106-square-km) island is the lushest in the Turks and Caicos chain. With an estimated population of only 1,400, the expansive island allows you to get away from it all. Bird lovers can observe the large resident flock of flamingos here, anglers will take delight in the ease of access to shallow creeks and banks plentiful in bonefish, while history buffs can visit the ruins of a Loyalist plantation. Although there's little traffic, almost all the roads are paved, so bicycling is an excellent way to sightsee. Even though it's a quiet place, you can find some small eateries around the settlements and in Whitby, giving you a chance to try local and seafood specialties, sometimes served with home-grown okra or corn. The beaches are in a natural state here, so are often scattered with seaweed and pine needles, as no major resorts rake them daily. Nevertheless, these secluded, less manicured strands of soft sand are breathtaking and offer beachcombing—while those on Provo do not.

North Caicos may be described as rustic, especially in comparison with the much more polished Provo. Accommodations are clean but fairly basic. Locals are consistently friendly, and life always seems to move slowly here.

Sights

★ Flamingo Pond

NATURE SIGHT | The pond is home to approximately 2,000 resident flamingos. These spectacular pink birds come and go during the day, so if you miss them on your drive down the island, be sure to double-check at the end of the day. Bring binoculars to get a better look; they feed quite a ways out, and you're not allowed to hike closer. ✉ *Whitby Hwy., Whitby* ✢ *South of Whitby, east of Kew.*

Kew

TOWN | This settlement includes a small school and a number of churches, as well as tropical fruit trees that produce limes, papayas, and the more exotic custard apples. Nearby are the well-preserved ruins—old cauldrons, main house structure, and other outbuildings—of Wade's Green Plantation. The fully intact ruins of a historic Baptist church sits roadside just past the modern Church of God of Prophecy as you enter the village. Kew's heartbeat is still present, and visiting will give you a better understanding of the daily life of the islanders before development; it's wonderful to see the more traditional lifestyle coexisting with the present day. Contact the National Trust to make special arrangements to view the plantation. It is usually open weekdays 10:30 to 3:30 pm. ✉ *Kew* ☎ *649/232–6284 National Trust* 🌐 *tcnationaltrust.org* 🎫 *$10, which includes a 30-minute tour* ⏲ *Closed Sun.*

Three Mary Cays

ISLAND | Three small rocky cays within swimming distance of Whitby Beach give you some of the best secluded snorkeling in all of the Turks and Caicos. You will often find ospreys nesting there, too. This is a wildlife protection area, so don't feed the fish, touch any of the corals, or disturb the birds. ✢ *Off Whitby Beach.*

★ Wades Green

HISTORIC SIGHT | FAMILY | You wander down the shaded laneway, bordered by walls made from the rocks once found in the fields of this cotton plantation established by Loyalist Wade Stubbs in 1789. The walls of the great house still stand, albeit with foliage now growing on the inside. Giant iron cauldrons, once used to prepare meals for enslaved people, rest in the yard. There are also partial remains of the kitchen, the overseer's house, slave quarters, and several storage buildings. A lookout tower provides views for miles. TCI National Trust offers visits and 30-minute tours from Monday to Saturday, 10:30–3:30. ✉ *Kew* ☎ *649/232–6284 TCI National Trust* 🌐 *tcnationaltrust.org* 🎫 *$10* ⏲ *Closed Sun.*

Restaurants

Barracuda Beach Bar

$$$ | CARIBBEAN | It's doesn't get more Caribbean than this shack right on the beach. The menu here is casual, with tacos, hamburgers, and fries plus local favorites like cracked conch, snapper, and lobster salad (when in season). **Known for:** delicious cocktails; stunning ocean view; very welcoming staff. 💲 *Average main: $25* ✉ *Pelican Beach Hotel, Whitby* ☎ *649/243–4794, 649/245–9449* 🌐 *www.pelicanbeachhotel.com.*

My Dee's Restaurant

$$ | CARIBBEAN | Nearly everyone in North Caicos dines at this restaurant, a laid-back spot that serves three meals a day. The menu showcases delicious local favorites: grilled shrimp and snapper, crab and rice, along with delicious lobster. **Known for:** Jamaican dishes; Friday night barbecue; cracked lobster. 💲 *Average main: $20* ✉ *Airport Rd., Bottle Creek* ☎ *649/946–7059, 649/245–1239.*

Hotels

★ Hollywood Beach Suites

$$ | B&B/INN | With 7 miles (11 km) of secluded beach and few others to share it with, this property with four upscale and tastefully furnished three-bedroom units is utterly simple and relaxing—each has a master bedroom with king-size bed; an open-concept kitchen, living room, and dining room; and a large screened-in sunroom with dining and lounging possibilities. **Pros:** daily light housekeeping; secluded and tranquil; updated furnishings. **Cons:** you have to be happy doing nothing much; four-night minimum; might feel a little too secluded. 💲 *Rooms from: $375* ✉ *Hollywood Beach Dr., Whitby* ☎ *649/231–1020,*

800/551–2256 🌐 www.hollywood-beachsuites.com 🛏 4 suites 🍴 No Meals.

Pelican Beach Hotel

$ | **HOTEL** | North Caicos islanders Susan and Clifford Gardiner built this small, palmetto-fringed hotel in the 1980s on this quiet and almost deserted beach in Whitby, and the couple's friendliness and insights into island life help create a full island ambience. **Pros:** perfect spot to get away from it all; the beach is right outside your room; the owners make you instantly feel at home. **Cons:** not much entertainment; location may be too remote and sleepy for some; property is tired. *$ Rooms from: $225 ✉ Whitby ☎ 649/245-9449 🌐 pelicanbeachhotel.com ⏲ Closed Sept.–Oct. 🛏 6 rooms 🍴 Free Breakfast ☞ Stay may include breakfast plan.*

Middle Caicos

At 48 square miles (124 square km) and with fewer than 300 residents, this is the largest and least developed of the inhabited islands within the Turks and Caicos chain. A limestone ridge runs to about 125 feet above sea level, creating dramatic cliffs on the north shore and a cave system farther inland. Middle Caicos has rambling trails along the coast; the **Crossing Place Trail,** maintained by the National Trust, follows the path used by the early settlers to go between the islands. Inland are quiet settlements with friendly residents. This is the real thing.

GETTING THERE

The only way to reach Middle Caicos is by car over a causeway that connects it to North Caicos. It's therefore possible to take a ferry from Provo to North Caicos, rent a car, and explore both North Caicos and Middle Caicos.

Sights

★ Conch Bar Caves

CAVE | **FAMILY** | These limestone caves make up one of the largest cave systems in the Caribbean, with good examples of stalactites and stalagmites, as well as small—and slightly eerie—underground bodies of water. Archaeologists have discovered Lucayan artifacts in the caves and the surrounding area; these natives to the island would have used the caves to weather the storm season. Currently, the caves are inhabited by five species of bats—some of which are endangered and bring scientists here annually to study them—but they don't bother visitors. Half-hour tours are available through TCI's National Trust. Guides provide flashlights and a sense of humor. It's best to wear sturdy shoes, as the ground is rocky and damp in places. If you don't have much time, Indian Cave is a smaller version that's worth exploring. Watch for the sign on your left after leaving the causeway. It's only a few steps off the road, parallel with Dragon Cay Resort. *✉ Conch Bar ✣ Main cave system is just outside Conch Bar; Indian Cave is near Dragon Cay Resort on main highway. ☎ 649/941–5710 🌐 www.tcnationaltrust.org 🎟 $20 ⏲ Closed Sun.*

Restaurants

★ Mudjin Bar and Grill

$$ | **SEAFOOD** | The restaurant at Dragon Cay Resort is a fabulous spot to enjoy lunch or dinner, or as an afternoon respite over a refreshing cocktail. The view overlooking the beautiful Mudjin Harbour and miles of north shore beach just may be the best in Turks and Caicos. **Known for:** the only vegetarian options around; best views for early evening cocktails; tasty seafood. *$ Average main: $25 ✉ Dragon Cay Resort, Mudjin Harbour ✣ Just after the causeway on your left ☎ 649/246–4472 🌐 www.dragoncayresort.com ⏲ Closed Sept.*

Hotels

★ Dragon Cay Resort

$$ | HOTEL | At this property, dramatic cliffs skirt one of the most beautiful beaches in the Turks and Caicos, while turquoise-roofed cottages dot the hillside, all with outstanding views of the coastline and reef beyond. **Pros:** hiking, kayaking, and beaching for adventure enthusiasts; breathtaking views of Mudjin Harbour from the rooms; lack of development makes you feel like you're away from it all. **Cons:** three-night minimum; may be too isolated for some; need a car to explore. *Rooms from: $280* ✉ *Mudjin Harbour* ✣ *Just after crossing the causeway on your left* ☎ *649/232–4102, 888/354–7290* 🌐 *www.dragoncayresort.com* *7 rooms* *No Meals.*

Activities

★ Cardinal Arthur

BIRD WATCHING | Although exploring Middle Caicos on your own can be fun, a guided tour with Cardinal can illuminate the island's secret spots, from caves to where flamingos flock. He has lived on Middle Caicos all his life, so his stories go way back, and his local knowledge of the flora and fauna satiates the appetite of budding naturalists. He can tell you the history of every nook and cranny of both Middle and North, as well as drop you off on hidden beaches—some accessible only by skiff. He can arrange almost anything and also runs a taxi service—the only one on the island. ✉ *Conch Bar* ☎ *649/241–0730.*

South Caicos

This 8½-square-mile (21-square-km) island was once an important salt producer; today it's the heart of the fishing industry. Nature prevails, with long, white beaches, jagged bluffs, quiet backwater bays, and salt flats. Diving and snorkeling on the pristine wall and reefs are a treat enjoyed by only a few.

In 2017, hurricanes Irma and Maria dealt South Caicos a devastating blow. Although the island continues to recover, the few independent dive operators that were here have disappeared. The only way to dive (other than independently) is through the shop at East Bay Resort.

The biggest draw to South Caicos is its excellent diving and snorkeling on the wall and reefs (with an average visibility of 100 feet). It's practically the only thing to do on South Caicos other than lie on the lovely beaches, enjoy a mountain bike ride, or go kayaking. Making up the third-largest reef in the world, the coral walls surrounding South Caicos are dramatic, dropping from 50 feet to 6,000 feet in the blink of an eye. Several local fishermen harvest spiny lobsters for consumption in the Turks and Caicos, as well as for export.

GETTING THERE

The only way to reach South Caicos is by air on interCaribbean Airways, private charter, or by the ferry operated by Caribbean Cruisin' out of Provo. Some of the resorts book complimentary flights for guests who book directly with them.

Sights

At the northern end of the island are fine white-sand beaches. The south coast is great for scuba diving along the drop-off, and there's excellent snorkeling off the windward (east) coast, where stands of elkhorn and staghorn coral shelter a wide variety of marine life. Spiny lobster and queen conch are found on the shallow Caicos Bank to the west and are harvested for export by local processing plants. The bonefishing here is some of the best in the West Indies.

Boiling Hole

NATURE SIGHT | Abandoned *salinas* (natural salt pans) make up the center of this island, the largest receiving its water directly from an underground cave system that is connected directly to the ocean through this "boiling" hole. Don't expect anything too dramatic, other than a sense of what the industry once was. Multiple hurricanes have clogged the connection to the ocean.

Cockburn Harbour

TOWN | The best natural harbor in the Caicos chain hosts the Big South Regatta each May. It began as a sailing regatta where all the families with traditional Caicos sloops would come over from Middle and North to race, but sloops are now being replaced with conch boats hosting 85-hp motors for a rip-roaring race. *Cockburn Harbour.*

Restaurants

Restaurant choices on South Caicos are limited and no one consistently takes credit cards, so you definitely should bring cash. The Dolphin Grill at Ocean and Beach Resort is the only restaurant that operates with regular hours. Here you can find a wide range on the menu including fresh catch and a fully stocked bar. **Sunset Cafe** (also known as Darryl's, on Stubbs Road) is a more casual restaurant, along with the Triple J Grill; expect to pay $10 to $20 for what they have available. Ask around to find out when (or if) these local favorites will be open; if you're staying over, your accommodations can assist you in making "reservations." There are a couple of other dining spots operated directly out of a private residence.

Sunset Cafe

$$ | CARIBBEAN | Consider this South Caicos staple your go-to for some delicious lobster tail. The menu has local favorites—shrimp, blackened snapper, and cracked conch are signature offerings—or to sample a bit of everything, try the seafood platter. **Known for:** the seafood platter; deck with harbor views; welcoming proprietors. *Average main: $20 Stubb's Street, Cockburn Harbour 649/242–7109, 649/342–0160 Closed Sun.*

Hotels

★ East Bay Resort

$$$ | RESORT | Fans of the ocean and watersports appreciate this calm, polished resort by the beach and surrounded by the shores of Shark Bay—it's the only resort in South Caicos dedicated to divers and beach-goers, and it offers snorkeling, diving, paddleboarding, and kayaking. **Pros:** quiet and laid-back; lots of watersports; delicious breakfasts included. **Cons:** limited restaurant offerings; limited equipment at the gym; Wi-Fi is slow and spotty. *Rooms from: $429 1 4th St., Cockburn Harbour 639/946–3612, 649/232–6444 mobile www.eastbayresort.com 86 suites Free Breakfast.*

★ Sailrock Resort

$$$$ | RESORT | This completely secluded high-end resort with a secluded setting overlooks both the Caribbean Sea and the Atlantic Ocean and is one of the most luxurious on South Caicos, offering two restaurants, a fitness center, a bar, a pool, and an array of water sports and spa treatments. **Pros:** very friendly staff; secluded location; rooms are modern and well-kept. **Cons:** menus at the restaurants lack variety; limited spa services; property is very remote and less than ideal for kids. *Rooms from: $527 Front St. 649/946–3777, 800/929–7197 www.sailrockresort.com 35 rooms Free Breakfast.*

Grand Turk

Just 7 miles (11 km) long and a little more than 1 mile (1½ km) wide, this island, the capital and seat of the Turks and Caicos government, has been a longtime favorite destination for divers eager to explore the 7,000-foot coral-encrusted wall that drops down within yards of the shoreline. This tiny, quiet island is home to white-sand beaches, the National Museum, and a small population of wild horses and donkeys, which leisurely meander past the white-walled courtyards, pretty churches, and bougainvillea-covered colonial inns on their daily commute into town. But things aren't entirely sleepy: a cruise-ship complex at the southern end of the island brings about 1 million visitors per year. That said, the dock is self-contained and is about 3 miles (5 km) from the tranquil, small hotels of Cockburn Town, Pillory Beach, and the Ridge and far from most of the western-shore dive sites.

Pristine beaches with vistas of turquoise waters, small local settlements, historic ruins, and native flora and fauna are among the sights on Grand Turk. Just under 5,000 people live on this 7½-square-mile (19-square-km) island, and it's easy to find your way around, as there aren't many roads.

The buildings in the country's capital and seat of government reflect a 19th-century Bermudian style. Narrow streets are lined with low stone walls and old street lamps. The once-vital *salinas* (natural salt pans, where the sea leaves a film of salt) have been restored, and covered benches along the sluiceways offer shady spots for observing the many wading birds, including flamingos, that frequent the shallows. Be sure to pick up a copy of the TCI Tourist Board's *Heritage Walk* guide to discover Grand Turk's rich architecture.

Conch in every shape and form, fresh grouper, and lobster when it's in season are favorite dishes at the laid-back restaurants found along the historic waterfront. Away from these more touristy areas, smaller and less expensive eateries serve chicken and ribs, curried goat, peas and rice, and other native island specialties. If you are driving around, don't hesitate to stop and try what's offered at roadside stands; the food is most often incredibly tasty. Be prepared for higher prices than in the United States, as almost everything that goes with the catch of the day must be imported.

Accommodations include original Bermudian-style inns, more modern but small beachfront hotels, as well as self-catering options. Almost all hotels offer dive packages, which are usually excellent value.

Cockburn Town

Sights

Her Majesty's Prison

JAIL/PRISON | This prison was built out of stone in the 1830s to incarcerate men and women who had committed mostly petty crimes. As time passed, the prison expanded, housing even modern-day drug runners until it closed in the 1990s. Tours are self-guided, and there's not much to see from outside the tall limestone walls—but check it out if you happen to pass through the area. ✉ *Pond St., Cockburn Town* 🌐 *www.visittci.com* 🎫 *$7.*

★ Turks and Caicos National Museum

HISTORY MUSEUM | **FAMILY** | In one of the island's oldest stone buildings, the National Museum houses several interactive exhibits, as well as a super little gift shop with books and local handicrafts. The complete collection of preserved artifacts raised from the noteworthy Molasses Reef Wreck is here. Dating back to the early 1500s, it's the earliest European shipwreck yet excavated in the New World. There is also a natural-history exhibit including artifacts left by the Taíno (or Lucayans), the earliest migrants to settle in the Turks and Caicos Islands. The museum also has a 3-D coral reef exhibit that complements its presentation on the history of diving. Another gallery is dedicated to Grand Turk's involvement

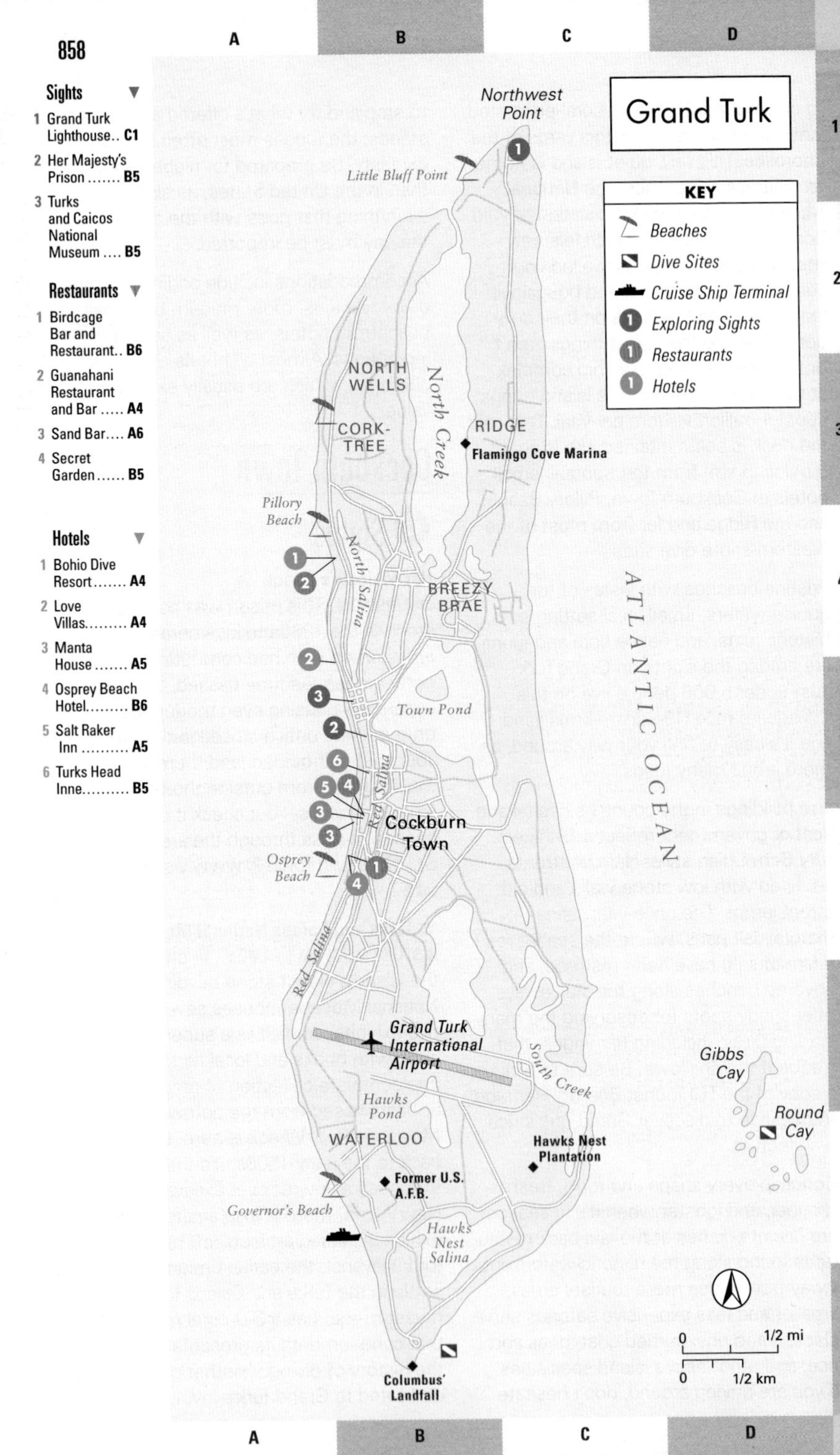
Sights
1 Grand Turk Lighthouse.. C1
2 Her Majesty's Prison B5
3 Turks and Caicos National Museum B5
Restaurants
1 Birdcage Bar and Restaurant.. B6
2 Guanahani Restaurant and Bar A4
3 Sand Bar.... A6
4 Secret Garden...... B5
Hotels
1 Bohio Dive Resort....... A4
2 Love Villas......... A4
3 Manta House A5
4 Osprey Beach Hotel......... B6
5 Salt Raker Inn A5
6 Turks Head Inne.......... B5
A
B
C
D
1
2
3
4
5
6
7
8
9
Grand Turk
KEY
Beaches
Dive Sites
Cruise Ship Terminal
Exploring Sights
Restaurants
Hotels
Northwest Point
Little Bluff Point
NORTH WELLS
North Creek
CORK-TREE
RIDGE
Flamingo Cove Marina
Pillory Beach
North Salina
BREEZY BRAE
ATLANTIC OCEAN
Town Pond
Red Salina
Cockburn Town
Osprey Beach
Red Salina
Grand Turk International Airport
South Creek
Gibbs Cay
Round Cay
Hawks Pond
WATERLOO
Hawks Nest Plantation
Former U.S. A.F.B.
Governor's Beach
Hawks Nest Salina
0
1/2 mi
0
1/2 km
Columbus' Landfall

in the Space Race. John Glenn made landfall here after being the first American to orbit Earth. Locals are quite put out that the movie *Hidden Figures* inaccurately portrayed the landing as having taken place in the Bahamas just north of Turks and Caicos. A fascinating display is a collection of "messages in a bottle" that have washed ashore from all over the world. This is the perfect spot to start your walking tour of the historic waterfront. ✉ *Guinep House, Front St., Cockburn Town* ☎ *649/946–2160, 649/247–2160* 🌐 *www.tcmuseum.org* 🎫 *$7* ⏲ *Hours based on when ships are in port.*

Restaurants

Birdcage Bar and Restaurant

$$$ | **CARIBBEAN** | This restaurant is a little more upscale than most of the other dining spots on the island, with a lovely view of the ocean and tablecloths in the evening. It's become the place to be on Saturday nights, when a sizzling menu of barbecue ribs, chicken, and lobster (in season) combines with live music. **Known for:** best spot for live island music; fall-off-the-bone barbecue ribs; sunset views. $ *Average main: $30* ✉ *Osprey Beach Hotel, 1 Duke St., Cockburn Town* ☎ *649/946–2666* 🌐 *www.ospreybeachhotel.com.*

★ Sand Bar

$$ | **CARIBBEAN** | Run by two Canadian sisters, this popular beachside bar is very good value and the perfect spot to enjoy island time—no shoes or shirt required. The menu includes fresh-caught fish, lobster, and conch, as well as typical North American fare—burgers, quesadillas, and chicken and ribs—served island-style with peas and rice. **Known for:** beachside dining; sunsets that will take your breath away; downhome island cooking. $ *Average main: $20* ✉ *Duke St., Cockburn Town* ☎ *649/243–2666* 🌐 *www.grandturk-mantahouse.com* 💳 *No credit cards* ⏲ *Closed Sat.*

Secret Garden

$$ | **ECLECTIC** | This locally beloved open-air spot is tucked away amid tall tamarind and neem trees in a courtyard garden behind the historical Salt Raker Inn. The Secret Garden serves simply prepared, local dishes such as grilled grouper and snapper, conch, and lobster, and there's live music many evenings. **Known for:** best place on island for breakfast; homemade desserts; great spot to mix with locals. $ *Average main: $18* ✉ *Salt Raker Inn, Duke St., Cockburn Town* ☎ *649/946–2260, 649/243–5522* 🌐 *www.saltrakerinn.com.*

Hotels

★ Love Villas

$$ | **APARTMENT** | These three spacious condo-style villas offer upscale amenities that are unmatched on the island, including a communal barbecue, floats and paddleboards to enjoy the beach out front, and fat-tire bikes for easy off-road exploration. **Pros:** each units comes with its own electric car; contemporary; right on the beach. **Cons:** books up early; ground floor patio is communal; no restaurant on property. $ *Rooms from: $375* ✉ *West Rd., Cockburn Town* ☎ *804/366–3150* 🌐 *www.lovegrandturk.com* *3 units* 🍽 *No Meals.*

★ Manta House

$ | **HOTEL** | Owned by the Canadian sisters who run the Sand Bar across the street, this funky, laid-back island hotel has three units immediately opposite the beach, and although there aren't many amenities and activities, it's clean and comfortable and the owners make you feel at home the minute you arrive. **Pros:** you can run a tab at the Sand Bar across the street; across the street from a relaxing beach; fully outfitted kitchens. **Cons:** books up fast; Sand Bar crowd can get loud; no amenities. $ *Rooms from: $200* ✉ *Duke St., Cockburn Town* ☎ *649/243–2666* 🌐 *www.grandturk-mantahouse.com* *3 rooms* 🍽 *No Meals.*

Osprey Beach Hotel

$ | **HOTEL** | You can't get any closer to the water's edge than this two-story oceanfront hotel and the adjacent guesthouse-style Atrium overlooking a tropical courtyard. **Pros:** you'll likely have the beach all to yourself; within walking distance of several waterfront restaurants and dive operators; affordable and charming, if basic. **Cons:** courtyard suites lack atmosphere; very thin walls; rocky beachfront. *Rooms from: $165* ✉ *1 Duke St., Cockburn Town* ☎ *649/946–2666* 🌐 *www.ospreybeachhotel.com* *34 rooms* *No Meals.*

Salt Raker Inn

$ | **B&B/INN** | An unpretentious inn filled with island character and charm, this 19th-century house was built by shipwright Jonathan Glass in the 1850s, complete with its quirky nautical features. **Pros:** perfect spot to completely unwind; ambience and character; an easy walk to everything on the historical waterfront. **Cons:** no views from ground-floor rooms; dated furnishings and fittings; spotty Wi-Fi. *Rooms from: $125* ✉ *Duke St., Cockburn Town* ☎ *649/946–2260* 🌐 *www.saltrakerinn.com* *13 rooms* *No Meals.*

★ Turks Head Inne

$ | **B&B/INN** | Set in an enclosed courtyard that was built circa 1830, this inn by the beach strikes a balance between a historic inn that has maintained its colonial charm and a charming modern accommodation with snorkeling equipment, paddleboards, and boogie boards provided free of cost. **Pros:** beachfront location; free breakfast; historic property. **Cons:** no TVs in rooms; some rooms have no windows; spotty Wi-Fi. *Rooms from: $150* ✉ *Duke St., Cockburn Town* ☎ *649/431–1830, 649/247–6574* 🌐 *www.turksheadinne.com* *7 rooms* *Free Breakfast.*

Beyond Cockburn Town

Sights

Grand Turk Lighthouse

LIGHTHOUSE | More than 150 years ago, the main structure of the lighthouse was prefabricated in the United Kingdom and then transported to the island; once erected, it helped prevent ships from wrecking on the northern reefs for more than 100 years. It was originally designed to burn whale oil as its light source. You can use this landmark as a starting point for a breezy cliff-top walk by following the donkey trails to the deserted eastern beach. The cruise-ship world has made its mark here, so you'll find the location's solitude can be interrupted and the view has been marred by a zipline. If you are stretched for time, you might want to take a pass. ✉ *Lighthouse Rd., North Ridge* 🌐 *visittci.com* *$3.*

Beaches

Governor's Beach

BEACH | Directly in front of the official British governor's residence, known as Waterloo, is a long stretch of beach framed by tall casuarina trees that provide plenty of natural shade. The beach can be a bit crowded on days when cruise ships are in port. There are a couple of picnic tables where you can enjoy a picnic lunch, and there is a decent snorkeling spot just offshore. **Amenities:** none. **Best for:** swimming; walking. *20–30-min walk north of the Cruise Center.*

★ Pillory Beach

BEACH | It's said that Columbus made his New World landfall here, just north of Cockburn Town on the protected west shore. And why not? This is the prettiest beach on Grand Turk; it also has great off-the-beach snorkeling. As you enjoy the powdery white sand, you may be visited by one of the many donkeys that pass by. The Bohio Dive Resort is on Pillory

Beach, so you can enjoy a wonderful lunch or a cold drink while there. **Amenities:** food and drink; parking (free); toilets. **Best for:** snorkeling; swimming; walking. ✉ *Pillory Beach.*

Restaurants

★ Guanahani Restaurant and Bar

$$$ | **INTERNATIONAL** | Off the town's main drag, this restaurant sits on a stunning but quiet stretch of beach just north of Cockburn Town and serves exceptional food that goes beyond the usual Grand Turk fare. There's an international theme-night buffet on Tuesdays, each week featuring the cuisine of a different country. **Known for:** Sunday brunch by the beach; English high tea, island-style; Saturday night rake-and-scrape music and barbecue. *$ Average main: $38 ✉ Bohio Dive Resort, Pillory Beach ☎ 649/231–3572 🌐 www.bohioresort.com.*

Hotels

★ Bohio Dive Resort

$ | **RESORT** | **FAMILY** | Divers are drawn to this basic yet comfortable hotel, whose on-site dive shop means there's no wait for some of the world's best diving (dive packages are offered). **Pros:** steps away from awesome snorkeling (plus winter whale-watching); great restaurant; on a gorgeous beach. **Cons:** you'll need a bike or car to get around; beach can get crowded when cruise ships are in port; drinks and dinner not included in all-inclusive packages. *$ Rooms from: $240 ✉ Pillory Beach ☎ 649/231–3572, 800/494–4310 🌐 www.bohioresort.com 16 rooms All-Inclusive.*

Nightlife

Grand Turk is a quiet place where most people come to relax and unwind, perhaps do a bit of diving. Most of the nightlife consists of little more than happy hour at sunset. Most restaurants turn into gathering places where you can talk with new friends you've made that day, or enjoy live music such as traditional rake-and-scrape. The Bohio encourages dancing! Once you get yourself settled, ask around to find out the where and when.

Shopping

Shopping in Grand Turk is hard to come by—choices are slim. Let's just say that no true shopaholic would choose to vacation here. You can get the usual T-shirts and dive trinkets at all the dive shops, and souvenirs from the National Museum's gift shop. When a ship is in port, the shops at the pier are open, increasing your options dramatically.

Activities

BICYCLING

Out of all the islands in Turks and Caicos, Grand Turk is the perfect island for biking: it's small enough that it is possible to tour it all that way. The island's mostly flat terrain isn't very taxing, and most roads have hard surfaces. Take water with you: there are few places to stop for refreshments. Most hotels have bicycles available, but you can also rent them for $20 a day from Grand Turk Diving across from the Osprey Hotel with a $200 deposit.

DIVING AND SNORKELING

With the wall just yards offshore, diving doesn't get any better than in Grand Turk. Divers may explore undersea cathedrals, coral gardens, and countless tunnels, or watch an octopus dance down a sandy slope. But take note: you must present your valid certification before you're allowed to dive. As its name suggests, the **Black Forest** offers staggering black-coral formations as well as the occasional black-tip shark. In the **Library,** you can study fish galore, including large numbers of yellowtail snapper. The Columbus Passage separates South Caicos from Grand Turk, each side of

Cockburn Town, Grand Turk is a good place to relax by stunning blue water.

the 22-mile-wide (35-km-wide) channel dropping 7,000 feet. From January through March, humpback whales pass through en route to their winter breeding grounds. **Gibb's Cay,** a small cay a couple of miles off Grand Turk, is where you can swim with stingrays.

★ Blue Water Divers

SCUBA DIVING | In operation on Grand Turk since 1983, Blue Water Divers is the only PADI Green Star Award-recipient dive center on the island, priding themselves on their personalized service and small group diving. There won't be more than eight of you headed out for a dive. In addition, Blue Water Divers offers Gibbs Cay snorkel and Salt Cay trips. ✉ *Osprey Beach Hotel, The Atrium, 1 Duke St., Cockburn Town* ☎ *649/946–2432* 🌐 *www.grandturkscuba.com.*

Crystal Seas Adventures

BOATING | Proprietor Tim Dunn, who is an actual descendent of the original owners of Salt Cay's historic White House, knows the waters around Grand Turk and Salt Cay as well as anybody. His company offers a variety of excursions: swimming with stingrays at Gibbs Cay, excursions to secluded cays, snorkel trips, plus whale-watching from mid-January through mid-April. Crystal Seas Adventures will cater to Salt Cay visitors as well. ✉ *Grand Turk Cruise Terminal* ✣ *Next to the Cruise Terminal* ☎ *649/243–3291, 510/926–3904 in the U.S.* 🌐 *www.crystalseasadventures.com.*

Grand Turk Diving

BIKING | This company offers full-service dives, as well as trips to nearby Gibbs Cay and Salt Cay. They also offer whale-watching tours January through March when humpback whales migrate from Iceland to the Silver Banks and Turks Bank. In addition, they offer bicycles for hire at $20 for a 24-hour period as well as sunset cruises and the popular champagne tour. ✉ *Duke St., Cockburn Town* ✣ *Across from the Osprey Beach Hotel* ☎ *649/946–1559* 🌐 *www.gtdiving.com.*

Oasis Divers

FISHING | Oasis Divers provides excellent personalized service, with full gear handling and dive site briefing included. In addition, Oasis Divers offers a variety of other tours, including their land-based one on Segways, glass-bottom kayak tours, and whale-watching when the animals migrate past. It's a good spot to rent a kayak or paddleboard for some solo exploration, and if it's fishing you want to do, they offer deep-sea and reef fishing starting at $650 for a half-day charter. ✉ *Duke St., Cockburn Town* ☎ *649/946–1128* 🌐 *www.oasisdivers.com.*

KAYAKING

Oasis Divers (see "Diving and Snorkeling" above) offers glass-bottom kayak and ecosafari tours. Check out their website (www.oasisdivers.com) for options.

Salt Cay

Just a little over 100 people live on this 2½-square-mile (6-square-km) dot of land, their unassuming lifestyle set against a backdrop of whitewashed cottages, stone ruins, and weathered wooden windmills standing sentry in the abandoned salinas. Bordered by beaches where weathered green and blue sea glass and pretty shells often wash ashore, Salt Cay lives up to its reference as "the island that time forgot." Beneath the waves, 10 dive sites are minutes from the shore, while humpback whales pass by on their way south to their breeding grounds from January through March.

Sights

Salt sheds and salinas are silent reminders of the days when the island was a leading producer of salt, for a period of time the largest harvester of salt in the world. Now the ponds attract abundant birdlife, both migratory and resident.

What little development there is on Salt Cay is found in its main community, Balfour Town. It's home to the majority of accommodations, a few small shops, and some restaurants. As a visitor, you can cover the entire island on foot if you're inclined, though some visitors zip around by motorized golf cart. Renting a sea kayak to explore the coastline is a great way to see the island from a different view.

White House

HISTORIC HOME | This grand stone and plaster house, which once belonged to a wealthy salt merchant, is testimony to Salt Cay's heyday. Still owned by the descendants of the original family, it's sometimes open for tours when Tim Dunn, one of the successors, is on island. He's pleased to share the house, where you will see some of the original furnishings, books, and a medicine cabinet that dates back to around 1835. ✉ *Victoria St., Balfour Town* 🎫 *Free.*

Beaches

★ North Beach

BEACH | This beach is the best reason to visit Salt Cay; it might be the finest beach in the Turks and Caicos. Part of the beauty lies not just in the soft, powdery sand and beautiful blue waters, but also in its isolation; it's very likely that you will have this lovely beach all to yourself. **Amenities:** none. **Best for:** snorkeling; solitude; swimming; walking. ✥ *North shore near Castaways.*

Restaurants

★ Oceanaire Bistro

$$$ | **CARIBBEAN** | Fondly thought of as *the* gathering spot, this bistro with a full bar and occasional live music is a block from the dock and overlooking the salina. It offers simple but good breakfast, lunch, and dinner fare that changes depending on what's available. **Known for:** locally sourced food; tacos and ribs theme nights; salsa nights. *Average main: $26 ✉ Chapel Street, Balfour Town ☎ 649/341–3363 🌐 www.facebook.com/oceanairebistro.*

Hotels

Tradewinds Guest House

$ | **B&B/INN** | This guest house may be simple in its design and furnishings, but the ocean view is spectacular, and it's a short walk or pedal (you can borrow a free bike) to the Oceanaire Bistro. **Pros:** owner is friendly and accommodating; property is right on the beach; close to one of Salt Cay's only restaurants. **Cons:** may be too remote for some; few amenities; property is a bit dated. *Rooms from: $133 ✉ Victoria St, Balfour Town ☎ 649/241–1009, 649/946–6906 🌐 www.tradewinds.tc 5 rooms No Meals.*

Activities

DIVING AND SNORKELING

There are 10 excellent dive sites offshore from Salt Cay, or as an alternative, scuba divers can explore the wreck of the *Endymion,* a British 44-gun warship that went down in 1790. Coral-encrusted cannons and anchors can still be seen, a 45-minute boat ride away.

★ Salt Cay Divers

DIVING & SNORKELING | Salt Cay Divers conducts daily dive trips and rents out all necessary equipment, with night diving upon request. Snorkeling trips to some amazing sites are also available. The exclusive Cotton Cay private island offers some of the best snorkeling in the entire Turks and Caicos, and SC Divers has the exclusive rights to take guests there for a unique snorkeling and econature tour. In season, SC Divers also offers whale-watching excursions. *✉ Balfour Town ☎ 649/341–5027 Dive Shop, 540/336–8600 (U.S. number) 🌐 saltcaydivers.com.*

KAYAKING

If you fancy exploring the coastline of Salt Cay, renting sea kayaks from Salt Cay Divers (www.saltcaydivers.com) is another option for visitors to this tiny island.

WHALE-WATCHING

During the winter months (January–April), Salt Cay is a center for whale-watching, when some 2,500 humpback whales migrate past close to shore. Whale-watching trips can most easily be organized through your inn or guesthouse; out of Salt Cay you can choose from Salt Cay Divers or Crystal Seas Adventures, who will come over from Grand Turk for the excursion.

Chapter 22

UNITED STATES VIRGIN ISLANDS

Updated by
Carol Bareuther

Sights	Restaurants	Hotels	Shopping	Nightlife
★★★☆☆	★★★★☆	★★★★☆	★★★☆☆	★★★☆☆

WELCOME TO UNITED STATES VIRGIN ISLANDS

TOP REASONS TO GO

★ **Incomparable Sailing:** St. Thomas is one of the Caribbean's major sailing centers.

★ **Great Hiking:** Two-thirds of St. John is a national park that's crisscrossed by excellent hiking trails.

★ **Beaches:** Though Magens Bay on St. Thomas and Trunk Bay on St. John are two of the most perfect beaches you'll ever find, St. Croix's West End beaches are fetching in their own way.

★ **Shopping:** Shopping on both St. Thomas and St. Croix is stellar.

★ **Deep-Sea Fishing:** St. Thomas is one of the best places to catch Atlantic blue marlin between the months of June and October.

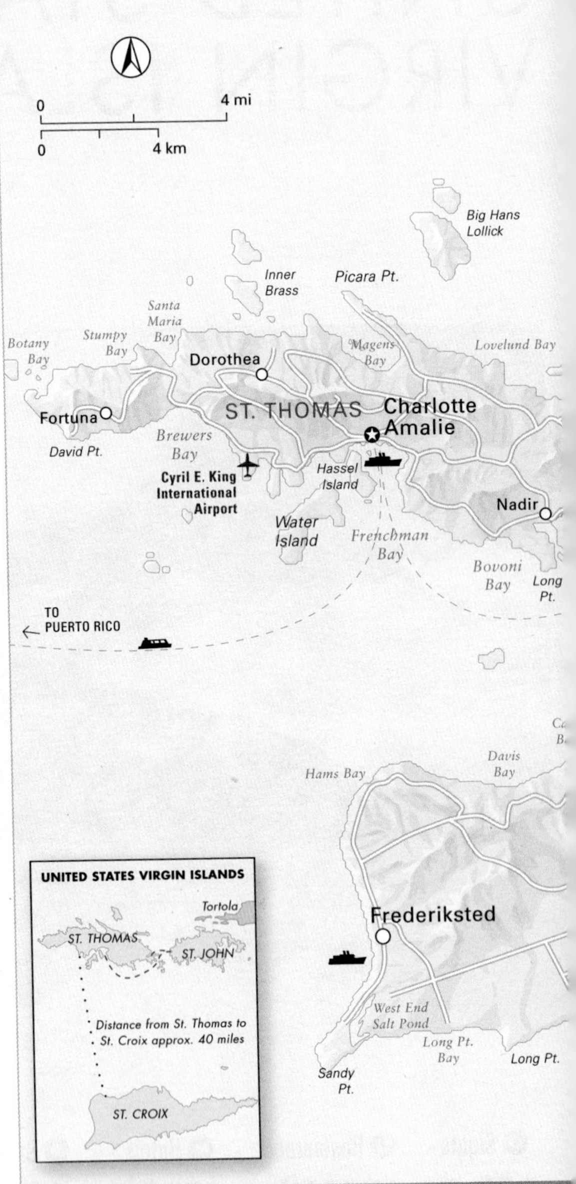

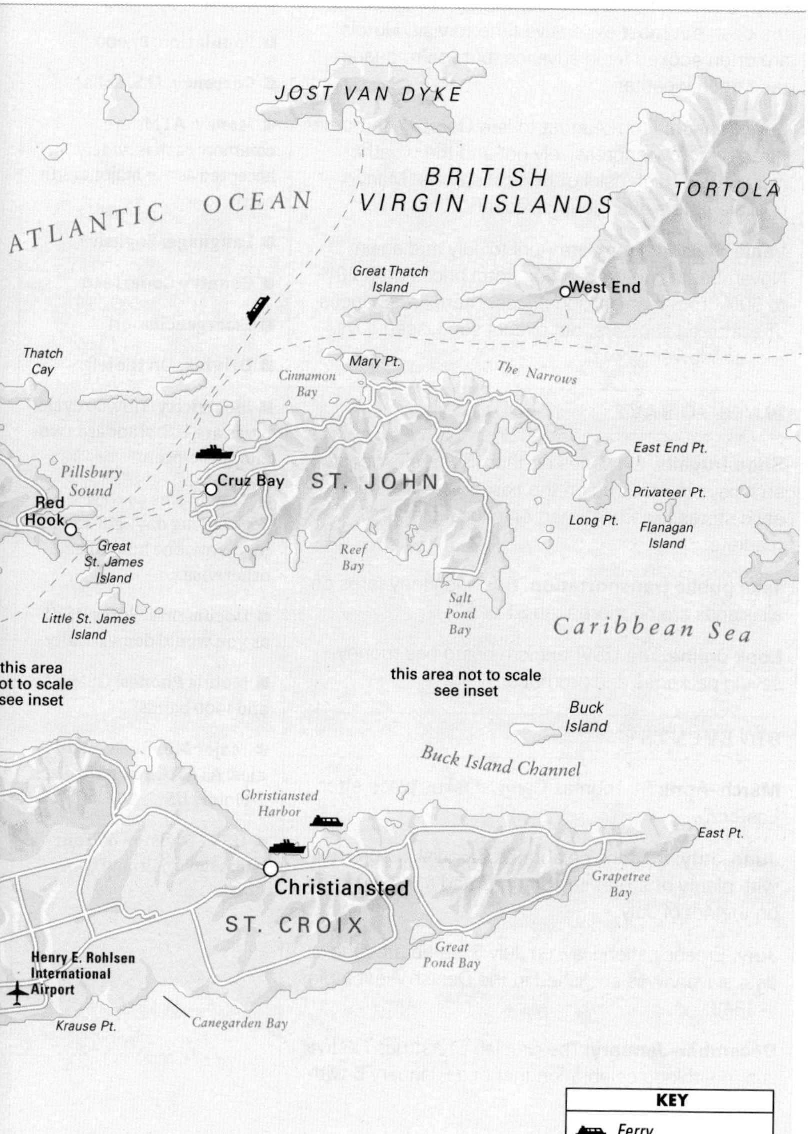
JOST VAN DYKE
BRITISH
VIRGIN ISLANDS
TORTOLA
ATLANTIC OCEAN
Great Thatch
Island
West End
Thatch
Cay
Mary Pt.
Cinnamon
Bay
The Narrows
East End Pt.
Pillsbury
Sound
Red
Hook
Cruz Bay
ST. JOHN
Privateer Pt.
Long Pt.
Flanagan
Island
Great
St. James
Island
Reef
Bay
Little St. James
Island
Salt
Pond
Bay
Caribbean Sea
this area
ot to scale
see inset
this area not to scale
see inset
Buck
Island
Buck Island Channel
Christiansted
Harbor
East Pt.
Christiansted
Grapetree
Bay
ST. CROIX
Great
Pond Bay
Henry E. Rohlsen
International
Airport
Krause Pt.
Canegarden Bay
KEY
Ferry
Cruise Ship Terminal

ISLAND SNAPSHOT

WHEN TO GO

High Season: Mid-December through mid-April is the best, but most expensive time to visit. Hotels are often booked far in advance, but you're guaranteed good weather.

Low Season: From August to late October, temperatures can grow oppressively hot and the weather muggy, with high risks of tropical storms. Many upscale hotels offer deep discounts.

Value Season: From late April to July and again November to mid-December, hotel prices drop 20% to 50% from high-season prices. There are chances of scattered showers, but expect sun-kissed days, too, and fewer crowds.

WAYS TO SAVE

Shop frugally. Groceries on the USVI are expensive, so it pays to stock up on the basics at warehouse-style stores like PriceSmart or in local farmers' markets.

Take public transportation. Bus and jitney fares on all islands are no more than $1 or $2.

Look online. The USVI tourism board has money-saving packages and promotions.

BIG EVENTS

March–April: St. Thomas Carnival takes place after Easter.

June–July: St. John celebrates Carnival in summer with plenty of street celebrations and a huge parade on the 4th of July.

July: Emancipation Day, on July 3, celebrates the date slavery was abolished in the Danish West Indies in 1848.

December–January: The Crucian Christmas Festival is a monthlong celebration that ends January 6 with a huge parade.

AT A GLANCE

- **Capital:** Charlotte Amalie
- **Population:** 87,000
- **Currency:** U.S. dollar
- **Money:** ATMs are common; cash is widely accepted as are major credit cards
- **Language:** English
- **Country Code:** 1 340
- **Emergencies:** 911
- **Driving:** On the left
- **Electricity:** 110v/60 cycle; plugs are U.S. standard two- and three-prong
- **Time:** Same as New York during daylight savings time; one hour ahead otherwise
- **Documents:** Enter USVI as you would domestically
- **Mobile Phones:** GSM (850 and 1900 bands)
- **Major Mobile Companies:** AT&T, Choice Wireless, T-Mobile US
- **USVI Division of Tourism:** www.visitusvi.com

The U.S. Virgin Islands—St. Thomas, St. John, and St. Croix—may fly the American flag, but "America's Paradise" is in reality a mix of the foreign and familiar that offers something for everyone to enjoy. The history, beautiful beaches, myriad activities, good food, and no-passport-required status make the Virgin Islands an inviting beach destination for many Americans.

With three islands to choose from, you're likely to find your piece of paradise. Check into a beachfront condo on the East End of St. Thomas; then eat burgers and watch football at a waterfront bar and grill. Or stay at an 18th-century plantation greathouse on St. Croix, go horseback riding at sunrise, and then dine that night on local seafood classics. Rent a villa in the pristine national park on St. John; then take a hike, kayak off the coast, read a book, or just listen to the sounds of the forest. Or dive deep into "island time" and learn the art of limin' (hanging out, Caribbean-style) on all three islands.

History books give credit to Christopher Columbus for discovering the New World. In reality, the Virgin Islands, like the rest of the isles in the Caribbean chain, were populated as long ago as 2000 BC by nomadic waves of seagoing settlers as they migrated north from South America and eastward from Central America and the Yucatán Peninsula.

Columbus met the descendants of these original inhabitants during his second voyage to the New World, in 1493. He anchored in Salt River, a natural bay west of what is now Christiansted, St. Croix, and sent his men ashore in search of fresh water. Hostile arrows rather than welcoming embraces made for a quick retreat, but Columbus did have time to name the island Santa Cruz (Holy Cross) before sailing north. He eventually claimed St. John, St. Thomas, and what are now the British Virgin Islands for Spain and at the same time named this shapely silhouette of 60-some islands Las Once Mil Virgenes, for the 11,000 legendary virgin followers of St. Ursula. Columbus believed the islands barren of the costly spices he sought, so he sailed off, leaving more than a century's gap in time before the next Europeans arrived.

Pioneers, planters, and pirates from throughout Europe ushered in the era of colonization. Great Britain and the Netherlands both claimed St. Croix in 1625. This peaceful coexistence ended abruptly when the Dutch governor killed his English counterpart, thus launching years of battles for possession that would see seven flags fly over this southernmost

Virgin isle. Meanwhile, St. Thomas's sheltered harbor proved a magnet for pirates such as Blackbeard and Bluebeard. The Danes first colonized the island in 1666, naming their main settlement Taphus for its many beer halls. In 1691 the town received the more respectable name of Charlotte Amalie in honor of Danish king Christian V's wife. It wasn't until 1718 that a small group of Dutch planters raised their country's flag on St. John. As on the other Virgin Islands, a plantation economy soon developed.

Plantations depended on slave labor, and the Virgin Islands played a key role in the triangular route that connected the Caribbean, Africa, and Europe in the trade of sugar, rum, and human cargo. By the early 1800s a sharp decline in cane prices because of competing beet sugar and an increasing number of slave revolts motivated Governor-General Peter von Scholten to abolish slavery in the Danish colonies on July 3, 1848. This holiday is now celebrated as Emancipation Day.

After emancipation, the island's economy slumped. Islanders owed their existence to subsistence farming and fishing. Meanwhile, during the American Civil War the Union began negotiations with Denmark for the purchase of the Virgin Islands in order to establish a naval base. However, the sale didn't happen until World War I, when President Woodrow Wilson paid the Danes $25 million for the three largest islands; an elaborate Transfer Day ceremony was held on the grounds of St. Thomas's Legislature building on March 31, 1917 to commemorate the occasion. A decade later, Virgin Islanders were granted U.S. citizenship. Today the U.S. Virgin Islands is an unincorporated territory, meaning that citizens govern themselves and vote for their own governors and congressional representative, but cannot vote for the U.S. president.

Nowadays, Virgin Islanders hail from more than 60 nations. The Danish influence is still strong in architecture and street names. Americana is everywhere, too, most notably in recognizable fast-food chains, familiar TV shows, and name-brand hotels. Between this diversity and the wealth that tourism brings, Virgin Islanders struggle to preserve their culture. Their rich, spicy West Indian–African heritage comes to full bloom at Carnival time, when celebrating and playing *mas* (with abandon) take precedence over everything else.

There's evidence, too, of growing pains. Traffic jams are common, a clandestine drug trade fuels crime, and there are few beaches left that aren't fronted by a high-rise hotel. Despite fairly heavy development, wildlife has found refuge here. The brown pelican is on the endangered list worldwide but is a common sight here. The endangered native boa tree is protected, as is the hawksbill turtle, whose females lumber onto the beaches to lay eggs.

Planning

Getting Here and Around

AIR

Fly nonstop to St. Thomas on American (Charlotte, Chicago, Dallas, Miami, New York–JFK, Philadelphia), Delta (Atlanta, Boston, New York–JFK), Frontier (Miami, Orlando, San Juan), JetBlue (Boston, Newark, New York–JFK, San Juan), Spirit (Fort Lauderdale, Miami, Orlando), and United (Chicago, Houston, New York–JFK, Washington–Dulles). Fly nonstop to St. Croix on American (Charlotte, Miami), Delta (Atlanta), and Spirit (Fort Lauderdale). The above flights range from daily to weekly depending on the route, and some increase in frequency or are offered only in winter.

Additionally, you can fly to St. Thomas and St. Croix from San Juan on Cape Air and Seaborne Airlines, and to St. Thomas from Antigua on LIAT. You can also book a seaplane (on demand) through Sea Flight to fly among the USVI. The only other option for St. John is a ferry from either Red Hook or Charlotte Amalie in St. Thomas. The Westin St. John has a private ferry.

AIRLINE CONTACTS Cape Air. ☎ *800/227–3247* 🌐 *www.capeair.com.* **Seaborne Airlines.** ☎ *787/946–7800, 866/359–8784* 🌐 *www.seaborneairlines.com.* **LIAT.** ☎ *268/480–5602* 🌐 *www.liat.com.*

AIRPORTS Cyril E. King Airport. *(STT)* ✉ *Rte. 30, Lindbergh Bay* ☎ *340/774–5100.* **Henry Rohlsen Airport.** *(STX)* ✉ *Airport Rd., off Rte. 66, Christiansted* ☎ *340/778–1012.*

BOAT AND FERRY

There's frequent service among the three main USVI and their neighbors, the BVI. Check with the ferry companies for the current schedules, which are also printed in the free *St. Thomas + St. John This Week* magazine and online at vinow.com.

There's frequent daily service from both Red Hook and Charlotte Amalie to Cruz Bay, St. John. About every hour there's a car ferry, which locals call the barge. You should arrive at least 15 minutes before departure.

FERRY CONTACTS Inter-Island Boat Service. ☎ *340/776–6597 in St. John.* **Native Son.** ☎ *340/774–8685 in St. Thomas* 🌐 *www.nativesonferry.com.* **Smith's Ferry.** ☎ *340/775–7292 in St. Thomas* 🌐 *www.bviferryservices.com.* **Speedy's.** ☎ *284/495–5240 in Tortola* 🌐 *www.bviferries.com.*

CAR

Driving is on the left, British-style. The law requires that *everyone* wear a seat belt. Traffic can be bad during rush hour on all three islands.

Car Rentals in St. Thomas: Avis, Budget, and Hertz all have counters at Cyril E. King Airport, but there are some other offices as well; in addition, there are local companies.

Car Rentals in St. John: All the car-rental companies in St. John are locally owned. Most companies are just a short walk from the ferry dock. Those a bit farther away will pick you up.

Car Rentals in St. Croix: There are both local and national companies on St. Croix; if your company doesn't have an airport location, you'll be picked up or a car will be delivered to you.

ST. THOMAS CAR RENTAL CONTACTS Avis. ✉ *Cyril E. King Airport, 70 Lindbergh Bay, Lindbergh Bay* ✣ *4 miles (6½ km) west of Charlotte Amalie* ☎ *340/774–1468* 🌐 *www.avis.com.* **Budget.** ✉ *Cyril E. King Airport, 70 Lindbergh Bay, Lindbergh Bay* ✣ *4 miles (6½ km) west of Charlotte Amalie* ☎ *340/776–5774* 🌐 *www.budgetstt.com.* **Discount Car Rental.** ✉ *Cyril E. King Airport, 70 Lindbergh Bay* ✣ *4 miles (6½ km) west of Charlotte Amalie; car rental is located adjacent to the entrance road of the airport, 1 min from the terminal* ☎ *340/643–4222, 877/478–2833* 🌐 *www.discountcar.vi.* **Hertz.** ✉ *Cyril E. King Airport, 70 Lindbergh Bay, Lindbergh Bay* ✣ *4 miles (6½ km) west of Charlotte Amalie* ☎ *340/774–1879* 🌐 *www.hertz.com.*

ST. JOHN CAR RENTAL CONTACTS Best. ✉ *Near library, Cruz Bay* ☎ *340/693–8177.* **Cool Breeze.** ✉ *1 block east of the passenger ferry dock, Cruz Bay* ☎ *340/776–6588* 🌐 *www.coolbreezecarrental.com.* **Courtesy.** ✉ *Near St. Ursula's Church, Cruz Bay* ☎ *340/776–6650* 🌐 *www.courtesycarrental.com.* **Denzil Clyne.** ✉ *North Shore Rd., across from creek, Cruz Bay* ☎ *340/776–6715.* **O'Connor Car Rental.** ✉ *Rte. 104, near the roundabout, Cruz Bay* ☎ *340/776–6343* 🌐 *www.oconnorcarrental.com.* **St. John Car Rental.** ✉ *Bay St., near Wharfside Village, Cruz Bay* ☎ *340/776–6103* 🌐 *www.stjohncarrental.com.*

ST. CROIX CAR RENTAL CONTACTS
Avis. ✉ *Henry E. Rohlsen Airport* ☎ *340/778–9636, 800/352–7900* 🌐 *www.avis.com.* **Budget.** ✉ *Henry E. Rohlsen Airport* ☎ *340/778–4663, 888/264–8894, 340/778–7201* 🌐 *budgetstcroix.com.* **Hertz.** ✉ *Henry E. Rohlsen Airport* ☎ *340/778–1402, 888/248–4261, 340/778–9744* 🌐 *www.rentacarstcroix.com.* **Judi of Croix.** ☎ *340/773–2123, 877/903–2123* 🌐 *www.judiofcroix.com.* **Olympic.** ✉ *Rte. 70, Christiansted* ☎ *340/718–3000* 🌐 *www.olympicstcroix.com.*

TAXI

USVI taxis don't have meters; fares are per person, set by a schedule, and drivers usually take multiple fares, especially from the airport, ferry docks, and cruise-ship terminals. Many taxis are open safari vans, but some are air-conditioned vans.

ST. THOMAS East End Taxi. ✉ *Urman Victor Fredericks Marine Terminal, 6117 Red Hook Quarters, off Rte. 38, Red Hook* ☎ *340/775–6974.* **Islander Taxi Services.** ✉ *Fortress Storage, Bldg. K, Suite 2025, at the intersection of Rtes. 313 and 38, Charlotte Amalie* ☎ *340/774–4077* 🌐 *www.islandertaxiservice.com.* **Virgin Islands Taxi Association.** ✉ *68A Estate Contant, Charlotte Amalie* ☎ *340/774–4550, 340/774–7457* 🌐 *vitaxiassociation.com.*

ST. JOHN Paradise Taxi. ✉ *Waterfront, Cruz Bay* ☎ *340/714–7913.*

ST. CROIX St. Croix Taxi Association. ✉ *Henry E. Rohlsen Airport* ☎ *340/778–1088.*

Health and Safety

Dengue, chikungunya, and zika have all been reported in the Caribbean. We recommend that you protect yourself from these mosquito-borne illnesses by keeping your skin covered and/or wearing mosquito repellent. The mosquitoes that transmit these viruses are as active by day as they are at night.

Hotels and Resorts

St. Thomas is the most developed of the Virgin Islands; choose it if you want extensive shopping opportunities and a multitude of activities and restaurants. St. John, the least developed of the three, has a distinct following; it's the best choice if you want a small-island feel and easy access to great hiking. However, most villas there aren't directly on the beach. St. Croix is a sleeper. The diversity of the accommodations means that you can stay in everything from a simple inn to a luxury resort, but none of the beaches is as breathtaking as those on St. Thomas and St. John.

Resorts: Whether you are looking for a luxury retreat or a moderately priced vacation spot, there's going to be something for you in the USVI. St. Thomas has the most options. St. John has only one large upscale resort. St. Croix's resorts are more midsize.

Small Inns: Particularly on St. Croix, you'll find a wide range of attractive and accommodating small inns; if you can live without being directly on the beach, these friendly, homey places are a good option. St. Thomas also has a few small inns in the historic district of Charlotte Amalie.

Villas: Villas are plentiful on all three islands, but they are especially popular on St. John, where they represent the majority of the available lodging. They're always a good bet for families who can do without a busy resort environment.

Hotel reviews have been shortened. For full information, visit Fodors.com.

What It Costs in U.S. Dollars

	$	$$	$$$	$$$$
RESTAURANTS				
	under $12	$12–$20	$21–$30	over $30
HOTELS				
	under $275	$275–$375	$376–$475	over $475

Visitor Information

CONTACTS USVI Department of Tourism. ☎ *340/774–8784, 800/372–8784* 🌐 *www.visitusvi.com.*

Weddings

Apply for a marriage license at the Superior Court. There's a $100 application fee and $100 license fee. You have to wait eight days after the clerk receives the application to get married, and licenses must be picked up in person weekdays or on weekends for an additional $150, though you can apply by mail. A marriage ceremony at the Superior Court costs $400 in St. John and $200 in St. Thomas.

CONTACTS St. Croix Superior Court. ☎ *340/778–9750.* **St. Thomas Superior Court.** ☎ *340/774–6680.*

St. Thomas

If you fly to the 32-square-mile (83-square-km) island of St. Thomas, you land at its western end; if you arrive by cruise ship, you come into one of the world's most beautiful harbors. Either way, one of your first sights is the town of Charlotte Amalie. From the harbor you see an idyllic-looking village that spreads into the lower hills. If you were expecting a quiet hamlet with its inhabitants hanging out under palm trees, you've missed that era by about 300 years. Although other islands in the USVI developed plantation economies, St. Thomas cultivated its harbor, and it became a thriving seaport soon after it was settled by the Danish in the 1600s.

The success of the naturally perfect harbor was enhanced by the fact that the Danes—who ruled St. Thomas with only a couple of short interruptions from 1666 to 1917—avoided involvement in some 100 years' worth of European wars. Denmark was the only European country with colonies in the Caribbean to stay neutral during the War of the Spanish Succession in the early 1700s. Thus, products of the Dutch, English, and French islands—sugar, cotton, and indigo—were traded through Charlotte Amalie, along with the regular shipments of slaves. When the Spanish wars ended, trade fell off, but by the end of the 1700s Europe was at war again, Denmark again remained neutral, and St. Thomas continued to prosper. Even into the 1800s, while the economies of St. Croix and St. John foundered with the market for sugarcane, St. Thomas's economy remained vigorous. This prosperity led to the development of shipyards, a well-organized banking system, and a large merchant class. In 1845 Charlotte Amalie had 101 large importing houses owned by the English, French, Germans, Haitians, Spaniards, Americans, Sephardim, and Danes.

Charlotte Amalie is still one of the world's most active cruise-ship ports. On almost any day at least one and sometimes as many as eight cruise ships are tied to the docks or anchored outside the harbor. Gently rocking in the shadows of these giant floating hotels are just about every other kind of vessel imaginable: sleek sailing catamarans that will take you on a sunset cruise complete with rum punch and a Jimmy Buffett sound track, private megayachts for billionaires, and barnacle-bottom sloops—with laundry draped over the lifelines—that are home to world-cruising gypsies. Huge container ships pull up in Sub Base, west of the harbor, bringing in everything from breakfast cereals to tires. Anchored right along the waterfront are down-island barges that ply the waters between the Greater Antilles and the Leeward Islands, transporting goods such as refrigerators, cellphones, and disposable diapers.

The waterfront road through Charlotte Amalie was once part of the harbor. Before it was filled in to build the highway, the beach came right up to the back door of the warehouses that now line the thoroughfare. Two hundred years ago those warehouses were filled with indigo, tobacco, and cotton. Today the stone buildings house silk, crystal, and diamonds. Exotic fragrances are still traded, but by island beauty queens in air-conditioned perfume palaces instead of through open market stalls. The pirates of old used St. Thomas as a base from which to raid merchant ships of every nation, though they were particularly fond of the gold- and silver-laden treasure ships heading to Spain. Pirates are still around, but today's versions use St. Thomas as a drop-off for their contraband: illegal immigrants and drugs.

Hop on the Bus 

On St. Thomas the island's large buses make public transportation a very comfortable—though slow—way to get from east and west to Charlotte Amalie and back (service to the north is limited). Buses run about every 30 minutes from stops that are clearly marked with "Vitran" signs. Fares are $1 between outlying areas and town and 75¢ in town. There are also safari taxis (open-air seats with a roof built on the back of a pickup truck) or "dollar buses" that run the same routes for $1 a ride.

GETTING HERE AND AROUND

To explore outside Charlotte Amalie, rent a car or hire a taxi. Your rental car should come with a good map, and you can also rent a GPS device (or use the GPS app on your cell phone) to better navigate the island. Cell service is available everywhere, though, it's prudent to save maps on your phone or pick up the pocket-size "St. Thomas–St. John Road Map" at a tourist information center. Roads are marked with route numbers, but they're confusing and seem to switch numbers suddenly. Roads are also identified by signs bearing the St. Thomas–St. John Hotel and Tourism Association's mascot, Tommy the Starfish. More than 100 of these color-coded signs line the island's main routes. Orange signs trace the route from the airport to Red Hook, green signs identify the road from town to Magens Bay, Tommy's face on a yellow background points from Mafolie to Crown Bay through the north side, red signs lead from Smith Bay to Four Corners via Skyline Drive, and blue signs mark the route from the cruise-ship dock at Havensight to Red Hook. Allow yourself at least a day to explore, especially if you want to stop to take pictures or to enjoy a light bite or refreshing swim. Most gas stations are on the island's more populated eastern end, so fill up before heading north or west. And remember that driving is on the left!

TAXIS Dolphin Water Taxi. ✉ *American Yacht Harbor, Red Hook, Hwy. 32, Red Hook* ☎ *340/774–2628* 🌐 *www.dolphin-shuttle.com.*

RENTAL CARS Paradise Rental Car. ✉ *Cyril E. King Airport, 70 Lindbergh Bay, Contant* ☎ *340/643–2692* 🌐 *www.pdiseinc.com.*

BEACHES

All 44 St. Thomas beaches are open to the public, although you can reach some of them only by walking through a resort. Hotel guests frequently have access to lounge chairs and floats that are off-limits to nonguests; for this reason, you may feel more comfortable at one of the beaches not associated with a resort, such as Magens Bay or Lindquist Beach (which both charge an entrance fee to cover beach maintenance) or Coki Beach, the latter abutting Coral World Ocean Park and offering the island's best off-the-beach snorkeling. Remember to remove all your valuables from the car and keep them out of sight when you go swimming. Break-ins are possible on all three of the U.S. Virgin Islands; most locals recommend leaving your windows down and leaving absolutely nothing in your car.

RESTAURANTS

The beauty of St. Thomas and its sister islands has attracted a cadre of professionally trained chefs who know their way around fresh fish and local fruits. You can dine on terrific cheap local dishes such as goat water (a spicy stew) and fungi (a cornmeal side dish that's similar to polenta) as well as imports that include sushi and strawberries in crème fraîche.

Restaurants are spread all over, although fewer are found on the west and northwest parts of the island. Most restaurants out of town are easily accessible by taxi and have ample parking. If you dine in Charlotte Amalie, take a taxi. Parking close to restaurants can be difficult to find, and walking around after dark isn't always safe.

If your accommodations have a kitchen and you plan to cook, there's good variety in St. Thomas's mainland-style supermarkets. Just be prepared for grocery prices that are about 20% to 30% higher than those in the United States. As for drinking, a beer in a bar that's not part of a hotel will cost between $6 and $7 and a piña colada $10 or more.

What to Wear: Dining on St. Thomas is informal. Virtually no restaurants require a jacket and tie. Still, at dinner in the snazzier places, shorts and T-shirts are inappropriate; men would do well to wear slacks and a collared shirt. Dress codes on St. Thomas rarely require women to wear skirts, but you can never go wrong with something flowing.

HOTELS

Of the USVI, St. Thomas has the most rooms and the greatest number and variety of resorts. You can let yourself be pampered at a luxurious resort—albeit at a price of $400 to more than $600 per night, not including meals. For much less, there are fine hotels (often with rooms that have a kitchen and a living area) in lovely settings throughout the island. There are also guesthouses and inns with great views and great service at about half the cost of what you'll pay at the beachfront pleasure palaces. Many of these are east and north of Charlotte Amalie or overlooking hills—ideal if you plan to get out and mingle with the locals. There are also inexpensive lodgings (most right in town) that are perfect if you just want a clean room to return to after a day of exploring or beach bumming.

East End condominium complexes are popular with families. Although condos are pricey (winter rates average $450 per night for a two-bedroom unit, which usually sleeps six), they have full kitchens, and you can definitely save money by cooking for yourself—especially if you bring some of your own nonperishable foodstuffs. (Virtually everything on St. Thomas is imported, and restaurants and shops pass shipping costs on to you.) Though you may spend some time laboring in the kitchen, many condos ease your burden with daily maid service and on-site restaurants; a few also have resort amenities, including pools and tennis courts. The East End is convenient to St. John, and it's a hub for the boating crowd, with some good restaurants.

The prices below reflect rates in high season, which runs from December 15 to April 15. Rates are 25% to 50% lower the rest of the year.

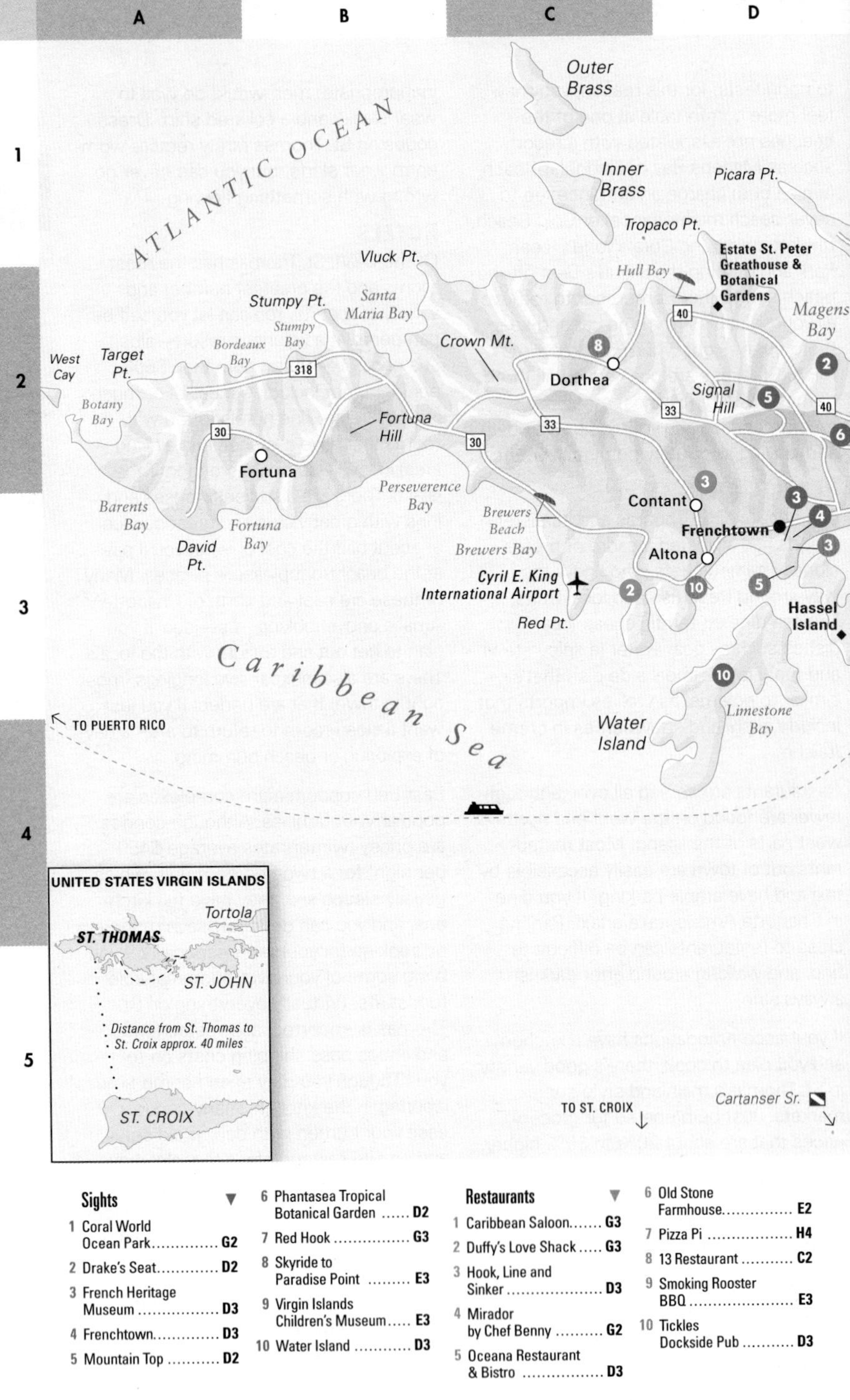

A
B
C
D
1
2
3
4
5
ATLANTIC OCEAN
Outer Brass
Inner Brass
Picara Pt.
Tropaco Pt.
Vluck Pt.
Hull Bay
Estate St. Peter Greathouse & Botanical Gardens
Magens Bay
Santa Maria Bay
Stumpy Pt.
Stumpy Bay
Bordeaux Bay
West Cay
Target Pt.
318
Crown Mt.
Dorthea
40
Signal Hill
33
Botany Bay
30
Fortuna Hill
Fortuna
Perseverence Bay
Contant
Barents Bay
Fortuna Bay
Brewers Beach
Brewers Bay
Frenchtown
David Pt.
Altona
Cyril E. King International Airport
Red Pt.
Hassel Island
Caribbean Sea
Limestone Bay
Water Island
TO PUERTO RICO
UNITED STATES VIRGIN ISLANDS
Tortola
ST. THOMAS
ST. JOHN
Distance from St. Thomas to St. Croix approx. 40 miles
ST. CROIX
TO ST. CROIX
Cartanser Sr.
Sights
1 Coral World Ocean Park G2
2 Drake's Seat............. D2
3 French Heritage Museum D3
4 Frenchtown.............. D3
5 Mountain Top D2
6 Phantasea Tropical Botanical Garden D2
7 Red Hook G3
8 Skyride to Paradise Point E3
9 Virgin Islands Children's Museum..... E3
10 Water Island D3
Restaurants
1 Caribbean Saloon....... G3
2 Duffy's Love Shack..... G3
3 Hook, Line and Sinker D3
4 Mirador by Chef Benny G2
5 Oceana Restaurant & Bistro D3
6 Old Stone Farmhouse............... E2
7 Pizza Pi H4
8 13 Restaurant C2
9 Smoking Rooster BBQ E3
10 Tickles Dockside Pub D3

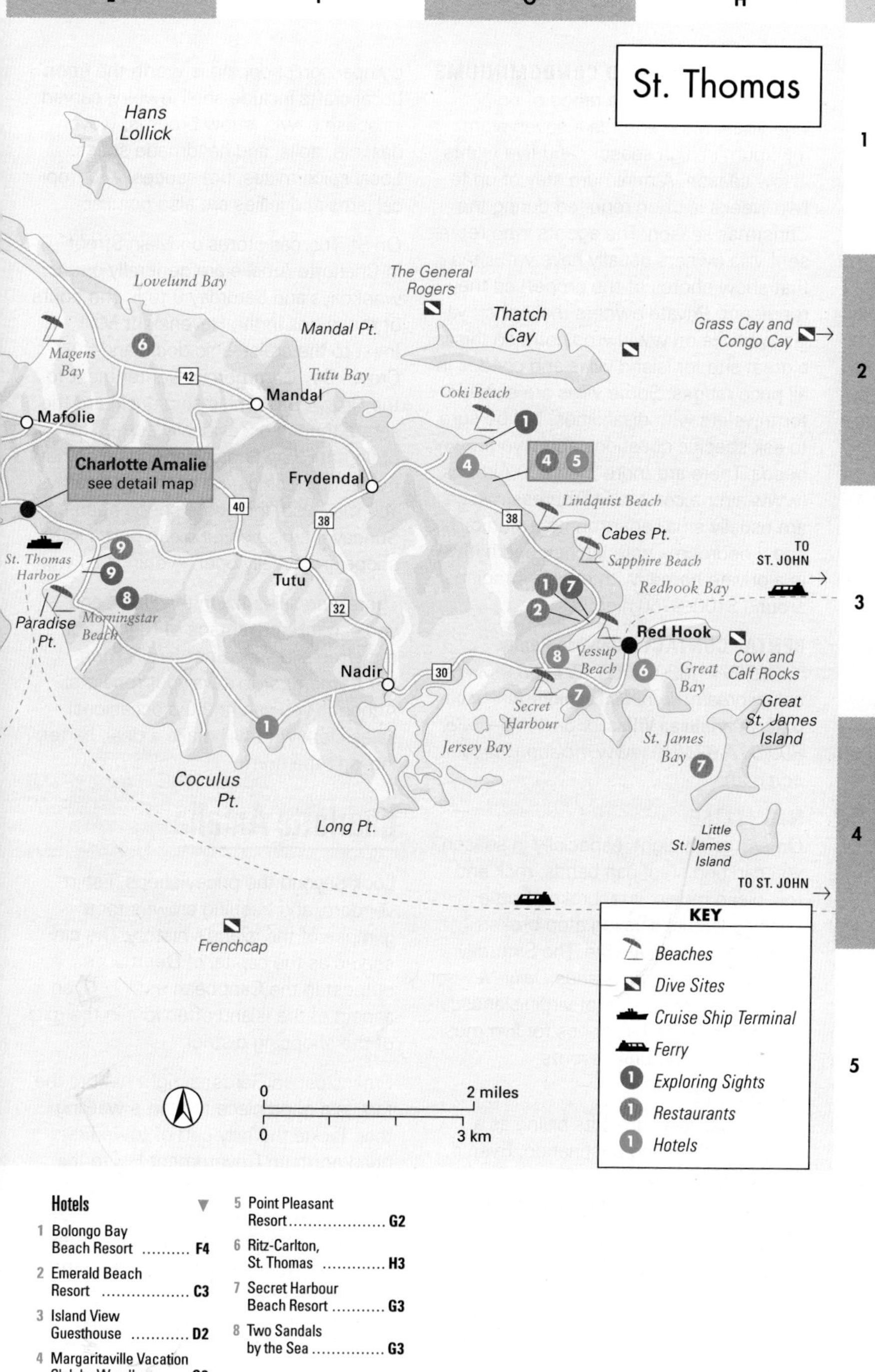

Hotels

1 Bolongo Bay Beach Resort F4
2 Emerald Beach Resort C3
3 Island View Guesthouse D2
4 Margaritaville Vacation Club by Wyndham G2
5 Point Pleasant Resort G2
6 Ritz-Carlton, St. Thomas H3
7 Secret Harbour Beach Resort G3
8 Two Sandals by the Sea G3

PRIVATE VILLAS AND CONDOMINIUMS

St. Thomas has a wide range of private villas. Most enforce a seven-night minimum in high season, and five nights in low season. A minimum stay of up to two weeks is often required during the Christmas season. The agents who represent villa owners usually have websites that show photos of the properties they represent. Private owners make their villas available on www.vrbo.com, so this is a great site for island villas and condos in all price ranges. Some villas are suitable for travelers with disabilities, but be sure to ask specific questions about your own needs. There are more than 800 Airbnbs (www.airbnb.com) in St. Thomas, which are usually small apartments—studio, 1-, and 2-bedrooms with kitchen and bath—in a private home, with rates averaging around $100–$150 nightly.

RENTAL CONTACTS Calypso Realty. ☎ *340/774–1620, 800/747–4858* 🌐 *www.calypsorealty.com.* **McLaughlin-Anderson Luxury Caribbean Villas.** ☎ *340/776–0635, 800/537–6246* 🌐 *www.mclaughlinanderson.com.*

NIGHTLIFE

On any given night, especially in season, you can find steel-pan bands, rock and roll, piano music, jazz, broken-bottle dancing (actual dancing atop broken glass), pop, and karaoke. The Saturday edition of the *Virgin Islands Daily News* or the Island Life section of virginislandsdailynews.com carries listings for live music and other community events.

SHOPPING

St. Thomas lives up to its billing as a duty-free shopping destination. Even if shopping isn't your idea of how to spend a vacation, you still may want to slip in on a quiet day (check the cruise-ship listings—Monday and Sunday are usually the least crowded) to browse. Among the best buys are liquor, linens, china, crystal (most stores will ship), and jewelry. The amount of jewelry available makes this one of the few items for which comparison shopping is worth the effort. Local crafts include shell jewelry, carved calabash bowls, straw brooms, woven baskets, dolls, and handmade soaps. Local spice mixes, hot sauces, and tropical jams and jellies are also popular.

On St. Thomas stores on Main Street in Charlotte Amalie are generally open weekdays and Saturday 9 to 5. The hours of the shops in the Havensight Mall (next to the cruise-ship dock) and the Crown Bay Commercial Center (next to the Crown Bay cruise ship dock) are the same, though occasionally some stay open until 9 on Friday, depending on how many cruise ships are anchored nearby. You may also find some shops open on Sunday if cruise ships are in port. Hotel shops are usually open evenings as well.

There's no sales tax in the USVI, and you can take advantage of the $1,200 duty-free allowance per family member (remember to save your receipts). Although you can find the occasional sales clerk who will make a deal, bartering isn't the norm.

Charlotte Amalie

Look beyond the pricey shops, T-shirt vendors, and bustling crowds for a glimpse of the island's history. The city served as the capital of Denmark's outpost in the Caribbean until 1917, an aspect of the island often lost in the glitz of the shopping district.

Emancipation Gardens, right next to the fort, is a good place to start a walking tour. Tackle the hilly part of town first: head north up Government Hill to the historic buildings that house government offices and have incredible views. Several regal churches line the route that runs west back to the town proper and the old-time market. Virtually all the alleyways that intersect Main Street lead to eateries serving frosty drinks, sandwiches, and West Indian fare. There are public

Fort Christian (1672–80) is the oldest surviving structure in St. Thomas.

restrooms in this area, too. Allow an hour for a quick view of the sights.

A note about the street names: In deference to the island's heritage, the streets downtown are labeled by their Danish names. Locals will use both the Danish name and the English name (such as Dronningens Gade and Norre Gade for Main Street), but most people refer to things by their location ("a block toward the waterfront off Main Street" or "next to the Little Switzerland Shop"). You may find it more useful if you ask for directions by shop names or landmarks.

TOURS

Downtown Walking Tours

WALKING TOURS | Join a member of the St. Thomas Historical Trust for a guided two- to three-hour walking tour through Charlotte Amalie's 400-year history. Highlights include Fort Christian, the 99 Steps, and the Camille Pissarro building. Tours start at 9 and leave from the Trust's office and museum on Raadets Gade. ✉ *5332 Raadets Gade, Charlotte Amalie* ✣ *across from Emancipation Gardens* ☎ *340/774–5541* 🌐 *www.stthomashistoricaltrust.org* *Suggested donation: $30 per person per tour.* ☞ *Reservations requested 24 hours in advance.*

Sights

All Saints Episcopal Church

RELIGIOUS BUILDING | Built in 1848 from stone quarried on the island, the church has thick, arched window frames lined with the yellow brick that came to the islands as ballast aboard ships. Merchants left the brick on the waterfront when they filled their boats with molasses, sugar, mahogany, and rum for the return voyage. The church was built in celebration of the end of slavery in the USVI. ✉ *13 Commandant Gade, near the Emancipation Garden U.S. Post Office, Charlotte Amalie* ☎ *340/774–0217.*

Educators Park

MONUMENT | A peaceful place amid the town's hustle and bustle, the park has memorials for three famous Virgin Islanders: educator Edith Williams, J.

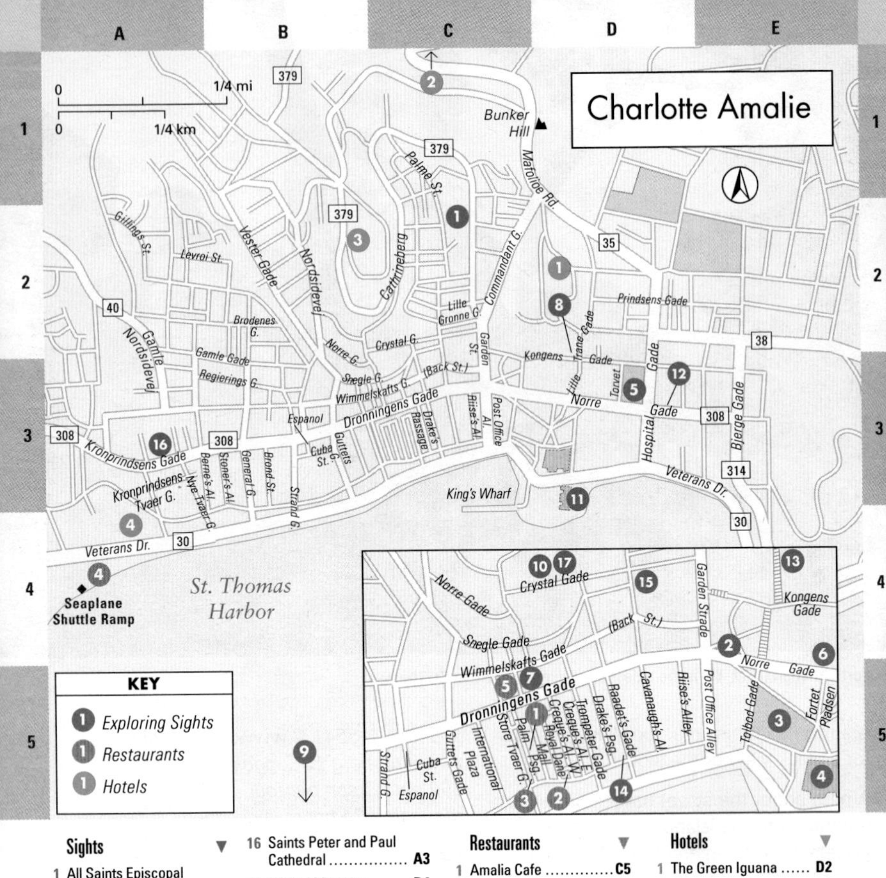

Sights

1 All Saints Episcopal Church **C2**

2 Educators Park........... **E4**

3 Emancipation Garden... **E5**

4 Fort Christian............. **E5**

5 Franklin D. Roosevelt Memorial Park **D3**

6 Frederick Evangelical Lutheran Church......... **E4**

7 Gallery Camille Pissarro................... **C5**

8 Government House..... **D3**

9 Hassel Island **B5**

10 Hebrew Congregation of St. Thomas............ **C4**

11 Legislature Building **D3**

12 Memorial Moravian Church **D3**

13 99 Steps................... **E4**

14 St. Thomas Historical Trust Museum........... **D5**

15 St. Thomas Reformed Church.................... **D4**

16 Saints Peter and Paul Cathedral **A3**

17 Weibel Museum **D4**

Restaurants

1 Amalia Cafe **C5**

2 Gladys' Cafe............. **D5**

3 Greenhouse Bar and Restaurant...... **C5**

4 Petite Pump Room...... **A4**

5 Virgilio's.................. **C5**

Hotels

1 The Green Iguana **D2**

2 Mafolie Hotel............. **C1**

3 Villa Santana **B2**

4 Windward Passage Hotel...................... **A4**

Antonio Jarvis (a founder of *The Virgin Islands Daily News*), and educator and author Rothschild Francis. The last gave many speeches here. ✉ *Main St., across from Emancipation Garden post office, Charlotte Amalie.*

Emancipation Garden

MONUMENT | A bronze bust of a freed slave blowing a conch shell commemorates slavery's end in 1848—the garden was built to mark emancipation's 150th anniversary in 1998. The gazebo here is used for official ceremonies. One other monument shows a scaled-down model of the U.S. Liberty Bell, with a plaque remembering the Virginia-bound English settlers who stopped here in 1607, a month before they established Jamestown. ✉ *Between Tolbod Gade and Fort Christian, next to Vendor's Plaza, Charlotte Amalie.*

Fort Christian

MILITARY SIGHT | **FAMILY** | St. Thomas's oldest extant structure, this remarkable building was built between 1672 and 1680 and is now U.S. National Historic Landmark. Over the years, it was used as a jail, governor's residence, town hall, courthouse, and church. In 2005, a multimillion-dollar renovation project started to stabilize the structure and halt centuries of deterioration. This project was completed in 2017 in time to commemorate the centennial of the U.S. purchase of the territory from Denmark in 1917. You can tour the museum inside on your own or take a guide tour at 10 or 1:45. Outside, look for historic features, like the four renovated faces of the famous 19th-century clock tower. ✉ *Forte Strande and Waterfront Hwy., Adjacent to Emancipation Garden, Charlotte Amalie* ☎ *340/714–3678* 🎟 *$10* ⏲ *Closed weekends.*

Franklin D. Roosevelt Memorial Park

CITY PARK | **FAMILY** | The former Coconut Park was renamed in honor of Franklin D. Roosevelt in 1945. It's a great place to put your feet up and people-watch. Five granite pedestals represent the five branches of the military, bronze urns commemorate special events and can be lighted, and inscribed bronze plaques pay tribute to the territory's veterans who died defending the United States. There's also a children's playground. ✉ *Intersection of Norre Gade and Rte. 35, adjacent to the Memorial Moravian Church, Charlotte Amalie.*

Frederick Evangelical Lutheran Church

RELIGIOUS BUILDING | This historic church has a massive mahogany altar, and its pews—each with its own door—were once rented to families of the congregation. Lutheranism is the state religion of Denmark, and when the territory was without a minister, the governor—who had his own elevated pew—filled in. ✉ *7 Norre Gade, across from Emancipation Garden, Charlotte Amalie* ☎ *340/776–1315* 🌐 *www.felcvi.org.*

Gallery Camille Pissarro

NOTABLE BUILDING | Housing an antiques shop and an art gallery, this was the birthplace and childhood home of the acclaimed 19th-century impressionist painter Camille Pissarro, who lived for most of his adult life in France. The art gallery on the second floor contains three original pages from Pissarro's sketchbook and two pastels by Pissarro's grandson, Claude. ✉ *14 Dronningens Gade (Main St.), between Raadets Gade and Trompeter Gade, Charlotte Amalie.*

Government House

GOVERNMENT BUILDING | Built in 1867, this neoclassical, white, brick-and-wood structure houses the offices of the governor of the Virgin Islands. Outside, the bright red Danish-style guard house is a perfect place for a photo. The view of the harbor is picture-postcard pretty from the First Lady's garden directly across the street.

■ TIP→ The inside of the building is currently closed to visitors. ✉ *Government Hill, 21–22 Kongens Gade, Charlotte Amalie* ✥ *On the hill above the Frederick Lutheran Church* ☎ *340/774–0001.*

Hassel Island

ISLAND | East of Water Island in Charlotte Amalie harbor, Hassel Island is part of the Virgin Islands National Park. On it are the ruins of a British military garrison (built during a brief British occupation of the USVI during the 1800s) and the remains of a marine railway (where ships were hoisted into dry dock for repairs). The St. Thomas Historical Trust leads 2- to 2½-hour walking tours, with boat transportation to and from St. Thomas, by advance request. ✉ *Charlotte Amalie harbor, Charlotte Amalie* ☎ *340/774–5541 St. Thomas Historical Trust* 🌐 *www.stthomashistoricaltrust.org* ✍ *Tours are given only on request, and cost varies by size of group.*

Hebrew Congregation of St. Thomas

RELIGIOUS BUILDING | The synagogue's Hebrew name, *Beracha Veshalom Vegmiluth Hasidim,* translates as the Congregation of Blessing, Peace, and Loving Deeds. The small building's white pillars contrast with rough stone walls, as does the rich mahogany of the pews and altar. The sand on the floor symbolizes the exodus from Egypt. Since the synagogue first opened its doors in 1833, it has held a weekly service, making it the oldest synagogue building in continuous use under the American flag and the second-oldest (after the one on Curaçao) in the western hemisphere. Guided tours can be arranged. Brochures detailing the key structures and history are also available. Next door the Weibel Museum showcases Jewish history on St. Thomas. ✉ *Synagogue Hill, 15 Crystal Gade, Charlotte Amalie* ☎ *340/774–4312* 🌐 *www.synagogue.vi.*

Legislature Building

GOVERNMENT BUILDING | Its light yellow colonial-style exterior is the face of the vociferous political wrangling of the Virgin Islands Senate. Constructed originally by the Danish as a police barracks, the building was later used to billet U.S. Marines, and much later it housed a public school. You're welcome to sit in on sessions in the upstairs chambers. ✉ *Waterfront Hwy. (aka Rte. 30), across from Fort Christian, Charlotte Amalie* ☎ *340/774–0880* 🌐 *www.legvi.org.*

Memorial Moravian Church

RELIGIOUS BUILDING | Built in 1884, this church was named to commemorate the 150th anniversary of the Moravian Church in the Virgin Islands. ✉ *17 Norre Gade, next to Roosevelt Park, Charlotte Amalie* ☎ *340/776–0066* 🌐 *www.memorialmoravianvi.org.*

99 Steps

STREET | This staircase "street," built by the Danes in the 1700s, leads to the residential area above Charlotte Amalie. Although historic Blackbeard's Castle, at the top, has been closed due to hurricane damage since 2017, the splendid views are worth the trek. If you count the stairs as you go up, you'll discover, as thousands have before you, that there are more than the name implies. ✉ *Charlotte Amalie* ✣ *Look for steps heading north from Government Hill.*

Saints Peter and Paul Cathedral

RELIGIOUS BUILDING | This building was consecrated as a parish church in 1848, and serves as the seat of the territory's Roman Catholic diocese. The ceiling and walls are covered with 11 murals depicting biblical scenes; they were painted in 1899 by two Belgian artists, Father Leo Servais and Brother Ildephonsus. The marble altar and walls were added in the 1960s. Over a dozen statues of handcrafted saints represent the many nationalities of the congregants who worship here. Guided tours available. ✉ *22-AB Kronprindsens Gade, 1 block west of Market Sq., Charlotte Amalie* ☎ *340/774–0201* 🌐 *www.cathedralvi.com.*

St. Thomas Historical Trust Museum

HISTORY MUSEUM | Tours of the museum, which are by appointment only, take 30 minutes and include a wealth of pirate artifacts, as well as West Indian antique furniture and art (some of which dates to the 1600s), old-time postcards, and historic books. The Trust office, also at the museum, is where you can book 2- to 2½ hour historic Charlotte Amalie walking tours and three-hour Hassel Island tours. ✉ *5332 Raadets Gade, Charlotte Amalie* ☎ *340/774–5541* 🌐 *www.stthomashistoricaltrust.org* *Free, but donations appreciated* ⏲ *Open by appointment only.*

St. Thomas Reformed Church
RELIGIOUS BUILDING | This church has an austere loveliness that's amazing considering all it's been through. Founded in 1744, it's been rebuilt twice after fires and hurricanes. The unembellished cream-color hall is quite peaceful. The only other color is the forest green of the shutters and the carpet. Call ahead if you wish to visit at a particular time, as the doors are sometimes locked. Services are held at 9 am each Sunday. ✉ *5 Crystal Gade at Nye Gade, Charlotte Amalie* ✥ *1½ blocks north of Main St.* ☎ *340/776–8255* 🌐 *www.strchurch.org.*

Weibel Museum
HISTORY MUSEUM | This museum next to the Synagogue of Beracha Veshalom showcases 300 years of Jewish history on St. Thomas. The small gift shop sells a commemorative silver coin celebrating the anniversary of the Hebrew congregation's establishment on the island in 1796. There are also tropically inspired items, such as menorahs painted to resemble palm trees. ✉ *Synagogue Hill, 15 Crystal Gade, Charlotte Amalie* ✥ *From Main St., walk up Raadets Gade (H. Stern is on the corner) to the top of the hill; turn left and it's the 2nd bldg. on the right* ☎ *340/774–4312* 🌐 *www.synagogue.vi* *Free* ⏲ *Closed weekends.*

Restaurants

★ Amalia Cafe
$$$$ | **SPANISH** | The menu and surroundings speak Old World European elegance, from the signature paella to the beautiful stone walls that line the 18th-century Palm Passage venue where the restaurant sits open-air and alleyside. Owners Antiguan-born Randolf Maynard and German-born wife, Helga, offer small plate tapas, Spanish-style entrées such as the Costa Brava-style Seafood Casserole, rich, thick and delicious with snapper, clams, and shrimp. **Known for:** historic setting; delicious paella; power lunch spot for business workers. $ *Average main: $32* ✉ *5143 Palm Passage, Charlotte Amalie* ☎ *340/714–7373* 🌐 *www.amaliacafe.com.*

★ Gladys' Cafe
$$ | **CARIBBEAN** | This cozy alleyway restaurant is rich in atmosphere, with its mahogany bar and native stone walls, making dining a double delight. Try the local specialties like conch in butter sauce, jerk pork, or panfried yellowtail snapper. **Known for:** local West Indian cuisine; service with a smile; homemade hot sauce. $ *Average main: $16* ✉ *5600 Royal Dane Mall, Suite 9, Charlotte Amalie* ☎ *340/774–6604* 🌐 *www.gladyscafe.com* ⏲ *No dinner.*

Greenhouse Bar and Restaurant
$$ | **AMERICAN** | **FAMILY** | Fun-lovers come to this waterfront restaurant to eat, listen to music, and play games, including video lottery terminals. Even the most finicky eater should find something to please on the eight-page menu that offers burgers, salads, and pizza all day long, along with peel-and-eat shrimp, Caribbean lobster tail, Alaskan king crab, and Black Angus filet mignon for dinner. **Known for:** eight-page menu with huge selection of American-style fare; family-friendly vibe; live music. $ *Average main: $18* ✉ *Waterfront Hwy. at Store*

Tvaer Gade, Charlotte Amalie ☎ 340/774–7998 🌐 www.thegreenhouserestaurant.com.

★ **Petite Pump Room**

$$ | **CARIBBEAN** | While sitting and watching the boats in Charlotte Amalie harbor come and go, sample Virgin Islands specials like conch in butter sauce, stewed oxtail, and callaloo soup, along with American-style burgers, sandwiches, salads, and steaks. Michael and Judy Watson are hospitable second-generation owners who can tell you everything from the ingredients they use in their flavorful dishes to what to see and do around the island. **Known for:** watching boats and ferries; lobster- and conch-filled omelets at breakfast; local Virgin Islands fare. *Average main: $15 ✉ Edward Wilmoth Blyden Building, Veterans Dr., 2nd floor, Charlotte Amalie ☎ 340/776–2976 🌐 www.petitepumproom.com ⏲ No dinner.*

Virgilio's

$$$$ | **ITALIAN** | For the island's best northern Italian cuisine, don't miss this intimate, elegant hideaway that's on a quiet side street. Come here for more than 40 homemade pastas topped with superb sauces, like capellini with fresh tomatoes and garlic or peasant-style spaghetti in a rich tomato sauce with mushrooms and prosciutto. **Known for:** eclectic art and decor; tender osso buco; rich creamy tiramisu. *Average main: $32 ✉ 18 Dronningens Gade, Charlotte Amalie ☎ 340/776–4920 🌐 www.virgilios-vi.com ⏲ Closed Sun.*

Hotels

Accommodations in and near town mean that you're close to the airport, shopping, and a number of restaurants. The downside is that this is the most crowded and noisy area of the island. Crime can also be a problem. Don't go for a stroll at night in the heart of town. Use common sense and take the same precautions you would in any major city. Properties along the hillsides are less likely to have crime problems, and they also get a steady breeze from the cool trade winds. This is especially important if you're visiting in summer and early fall.

The Green Iguana

$ | **HOTEL** | Atop Blackbeard's Hill, this value-priced small hotel offers the perfect mix of gorgeous harbor views, proximity to shopping (five-minute walk), and secluded privacy provided by the surrounding showy trees and bushy hibiscus. **Pros:** personalized service; near the center of town; laundry on premises. **Cons:** need a car to get around; not too many frills; noise from town, especially during events. *Rooms from: $155 ✉ 1002 Blackbeard's Hill, Charlotte Amalie ☎ 340/776–7654, 855/473–4733 🌐 www.thegreeniguana.com 9 rooms No Meals.*

★ **Mafolie Hotel**

$$ | **B&B/INN** | The view and the value are the selling points of this simply furnished family-run hotel perched 800 feet above Charlotte Amalie's harbor. **Pros:** friendly staff; fantastic views; nice restaurant and bar. **Cons:** need a car to get around; on a busy street; tiny pool. *Rooms from: $280 ✉ 7091 Estate Mafolie, off Rte. 35, Charlotte Amalie ☎ 340/774–2790, 800/225–7035 🌐 www.mafolie.com 22 rooms Free Breakfast.*

Villa Santana

$ | **HOTEL** | Built by exiled General Antonio López Santa Anna of Mexico, this 1857 landmark provides a panoramic view of the harbor and plenty of West Indian charm, which will make you feel as if you're living in a slice of Virgin Islands history. **Pros:** modern amenities like good Wi-Fi; historic charm; plenty of privacy. **Cons:** need a car to get around; no restaurant; not on a beach. *Rooms from: $250 ✉ 2602 Bjerge Gade, 2D Denmark Hill, Charlotte Amalie ☎ 340/776–1311 🌐 www.villasantana.com 6 rooms No Meals.*

Windward Passage Hotel

$ | **HOTEL** | Business travelers, tourists on their way to the British Virgin Islands, and laid-back vacationers who want the convenience of being able to walk to duty-free shopping, sights, and restaurants favor this harbor-front hotel. **Pros:** across from BVI ferry terminal; walking distance to Charlotte Amalie; nice harbor views. **Cons:** no water sports, but dive shop is on property; on a busy street; basic rooms. *Rooms from: $180* ✉ *Veterans Dr., Charlotte Amalie* ☎ *340/774–5200, 718/624–2211, 800/524–7389* 🌐 *www.windwardpassage.com* *180 rooms* *No Meals.*

Charlotte Amalie used to be the center of St. Thomas's nightlife scene, but as tourism has grown elsewhere on the island, the nightlife scene has mostly migrated.

Greenhouse Bar and Restaurant

BARS | Once this popular eatery puts away the salt-and-pepper shakers after 10 pm on the weekends, it becomes a rock-and-roll club with a DJ or live reggae bands bringing the weary to their feet. ✉ *Waterfront Hwy., at Storetvaer Gade, Charlotte Amalie* ☎ *340/774–7998* 🌐 *www.thegreenhouserestaurant.com.*

The prime shopping area in **Charlotte Amalie** is between the Emancipation Gardens Post Office and Market Square; it consists of two parallel streets that run east–west (Waterfront Highway and Main Street) and the alleyways that connect them. Particularly attractive are the historic **A. H. Riise Alley, Drake's Passage, Royal Dane Mall,** and **Palm Passage.**

Vendors Plaza, on the waterfront side of Emancipation Gardens in Charlotte Amalie, is a central location for vendors selling handmade earrings, necklaces, and bracelets; straw baskets and handbags; T-shirts; fabrics; African artifacts; and local fruits. Look for the many brightly colored umbrellas.

ART

Camille Pissarro Art Gallery

ART GALLERIES | This second-floor gallery, at the birthplace of St. Thomas's famous artist, offers a fine collection of original paintings and prints by local and regional artists. ✉ *14 Main St., Charlotte Amalie* ☎ *340/774–4621.*

CAMERAS AND ELECTRONICS

Boolchand's

ELECTRONICS | This store sells brand-name cameras, audio and video equipment, and binoculars. ✉ *Havensight Mall, Bldg. II, Suite C, Rte. 30, Havensight* ☎ *340/776–0302* 🌐 *www.boolchand.com.*

Royal Caribbean

ELECTRONICS | Find a wide selection of cameras, camcorders, stereos, watches, and clocks at this store. There are also branches at the Crown Bay Center. ✉ *33 Main St., Charlotte Amalie* ☎ *340/776–4110* 🌐 *www.royalcaribbeanvi.com.*

CHINA AND CRYSTAL

Little Switzerland

GLASSWARE | This popular Caribbean chain carries crystal from Baccarat, Waterford, and Orrefors; and china from Kosta Boda, Rosenthal, and Wedgwood. There's also an assortment of Swarovski cut-crystal animals, gemstone globes, and many other affordable collectibles. The Main Street location features separate boutiques showcasing timepieces from Omega, TAG Heuer, Patek Philippe, David Yurman, and Breitling. A branch at the Crown Bay Center is open when ships are in port, and locations are in Havensight Mall and at the Ritz Carlton. ✉ *5182 Dronningens Gade, Charlotte Amalie* ☎ *248/809–5560 ext. 10110* 🌐 *www.littleswitzerland.com.*

CLOTHING

Local Color

WOMEN'S CLOTHING | FAMILY | This St. Thomas chain has clothes for men, women, and children among its brand names, which include Jams World, Fresh Produce, and Urban Safari. You can also find St. John artist Sloop Jones's colorful, hand-painted island designs on cool dresses, T-shirts, and sweaters. The tropically oriented accessories include big-brimmed straw hats, bold-color bags, and casual jewelry. There's another location at the Havensight Mall. ✉ *5332–5333 Raadets Gade, Charlotte Amalie* ☎ *340/774–2280* 🌐 *www.localcolorvi.com.*

FOOD AND DRINK

A. H. Riise Liquors and Tobacco

TOBACCO | This giant duty-free liquor outlet carries a large selection of tobacco (including imported cigars), as well as cordials, wines, and rare vintage Armagnacs, cognacs, ports, and Madeiras. It also stocks fruits in brandy and barware from England. Enjoy rum samples at the tasting bar. ✉ *37 Main St., at Riise's Alley, Charlotte Amalie* ☎ *340/777–2222* 🌐 *www.ahriise.com.*

★ The Belgian Chocolate Factory

CHOCOLATE | Whet your appetite while watching these handcrafted chocolates being made behind the glass in the store's kitchen. Milk, dark, and white chocolate come in over 50 varieties with fillings like pralines, marshmallow, fruits, and caramel. Gift boxes make these sweets an easy souvenir or present for friends back home. ✉ *5093 Dronningens Gade, Ste. 3, Charlotte Amalie* ✣ *Located in the A. H. Riise Mall in Hibiscus Alley* ☎ *340/777–5247.*

HANDICRAFTS

Made in the U.S. Virgin Islands

CRAFTS | This pop-up shop is open from Thanksgiving until early January each year and is located in a historic building across from Fort Christian. Inside, you'll find a treasure trove for bona fide made-in-the-Virgin Islands arts, crafts, and local food products that make the perfect gifts. There are soaps, hot sauces, hand-tied palm brooms, native dolls, books by local authors, T-shirts, jewelry, and much more. Signs next to displays tell you about the respective artists. ✉ *23 Dronningens Gade, across from Fort Christian, Charlotte Amalie* ☎ *340/714–1700.*

JEWELRY

★ Cardow Jewelers

JEWELRY & WATCHES | You can get gold in several lengths, widths, sizes, and styles, along with jewelry made of diamonds, emeralds, and other precious gems from this small chain's main store. You're guaranteed 40% to 60% savings off U.S. retail prices, or your money will be refunded within 30 days of purchase. There's also a line of classy commemorative Virgin Islands watches made on-site. Branches located at the Cyril E. King Airport; Ritz-Carlton, St. Thomas; and Crown Bay Center. ✉ *5195 Dronningens Gate, across from Emancipation Garden, Charlotte Amalie* ☎ *340/776–1140* 🌐 *www.cardow.com.*

Diamonds International

JEWELRY & WATCHES | At this large chain with several outlets on St. Thomas, just choose a diamond, emerald, or tanzanite gem and a mounting, and you can have your dream ring set in an hour. Famous for having the largest inventory of diamonds on the island, this shop welcomes trade-ins, has a U.S. service center, and includes diamond earrings with every purchase. Branches located at Crown Bay Center and Havensight Mall. ✉ *31 Main St., Charlotte Amalie* ☎ *340/774–3707* 🌐 *www.diamondsinternational.com.*

Rolex Watches at A. H. Riise

JEWELRY & WATCHES | A.H. Riise is the official Rolex retailer of the Virgin Islands, and this shop offers one of the largest new and pre-owned selections these fine timepieces in the Caribbean. An After Sales Service Center helps you keep your Rolex ticking for a lifetime. ✉ *37 Main*

St., at Riise's Alley, Charlotte Amalie ☎ *340/777–6789* 🌐 *www.ahriise.com.*

LEATHER GOODS

A.H. Riise Mall

HANDBAGS | Find designer leather bags from Kipling, Vince Camuto, Milano and more in hand- to suitcase-sizes. ✉ *5189 Dronningens Gade, Charlotte Amalie* ☎ *340/777–2222* ✉ *info@ahriise.com* 🌐 *www.ahriise.com.*

★ Zora's

LEATHER GOODS | This store specializes in fine, made-to-order leather sandals. There's also a selection of locally made backpacks, purses, and briefcases in durable, brightly colored canvas. ✉ *34 Norre Gade, across from Roosevelt Park, Charlotte Amalie* ☎ *340/774–2559.*

LINENS

Fabric & Fashion Playroom

FABRICS | Silks and fancy fabrics share space with colorful batiks, African Kente, and Caribbean madras prints, ribbons, and accessories in this small shop off the beaten path. ✉ *5412 Store Gade, Charlotte Amalie* ✥ *1/2 block north of the Greenhouse Restaurant* ☎ *340/714–4410.*

Mr. Tablecloth

FABRICS | This store has prices to please, and the friendly staff here will help you choose from the floor-to-ceiling selection of linens, which include Tuscan lace tablecloths and Irish linen pillowcases. ✉ *6 Main St., Charlotte Amalie* ☎ *340/774–4343* 🌐 *www.mrtablecloth-vi.com.*

East End

Although the eastern end has many major resorts and spectacular beaches, don't be surprised if a cow or a herd of goats crosses your path as you drive through the relatively flat, dry terrain. Proximity to St. John and BVI ferry service makes this side of the island, especially Red Hook, a hub for watersports, from fishing to sailing.

Sights

★ Coral World Ocean Park

AQUARIUM | **FAMILY** | This interactive aquarium and water-sports center lets you experience a variety of sea life and other animals. In the 2-acre dolphin habitat, you can swim with these graceful creatures. There are also several outdoor pools where you can pet baby sharks, feed stingrays, touch starfish, and view endangered sea turtles. During the Sea Trek Helmet Dive, you walk along an underwater trail wearing a helmet that provides a continuous supply of air. You can also try Snuba, a cross between snorkeling and scuba diving. Swim with a sea lion for the chance to play ball or get a big, wet, whiskered kiss. The park also has an offshore underwater observatory, an 80,000-gallon coral reef exhibit (one of the largest in the world), and a nature trail with native ducks and tortoises. Daily feedings take place at most exhibits. ✉ *6450 Estate Smith Bay, Estate Smith Bay* ✥ *Coki Point Rd. north of Rte. 38* ☎ *340/775–1555* 🌐 *www.coralworldvi.com* 🎟 *$23.50.*

Red Hook

MARINA/PIER | The IGY American Yacht Harbor marina here has fishing and sailing charter boats, a dive shop, and powerboat-rental agencies. There are also several bars and restaurants, including the Caribbean Saloon, The Tap & Still, Island Time Pub, Raw Sushi & Sake Bar, and Duffy's Love Shack. Other services include mail service, drug and grocery stores, and medical services. Ferries depart from here en route to St. John and BVI. ✉ *Red Hook, Rtes. 38 and 32, Red Hook.*

Beaches

Coki Beach

BEACH | **FAMILY** | Funky beach huts selling local foods such as pates (fried turnovers with a spicy ground-beef filling), quaint vendor kiosks, and a brigade of hair

Coral World Ocean Park offers interactive sea-life encounters.

braiders and taxi men make this beach overlooking picturesque Thatch Cay feel like a carnival. But this is the best place on the island to snorkel and scuba dive. Fish—including grunts, snappers, and wrasses—are like an effervescent cloud you can wave your hand through. **Amenities:** food and drink; lifeguards; parking; showers; toilets; water sports. **Best for:** partiers; snorkeling. ✉ *End of Rte. 388, off Rte. 38, Estate Smith Bay* ✣ *Next to Coral World Ocean Park.*

Lindquist Beach

BEACH | FAMILY | The newest of the Virgin Islands' public beaches has a serene sense of wilderness that isn't found on the more crowded beaches. A lifeguard is on duty between 8 am and 5 pm. Picnic tables are available. Try snorkeling over the offshore reef. **Amenities:** lifeguards; parking; showers; toilets. **Best for:** snorkeling; solitude. ✉ *Rte. 38, at end of a bumpy road past the paved parking lot* *$4 per person; $2 per vehicle to park.*

Sapphire Beach

BEACH | FAMILY | A steady breeze makes this beach a windsurfer's paradise. The swimming is great, as is the snorkeling, especially at the reef near Pettyklip Point. Beach volleyball is big on the weekends as is a Sunday live music beach jam. There's a small restaurant serving breakfast and lunch. **Amenities:** parking; toilets. **Best for:** snorkeling; swimming; windsurfing. ✉ *Rte. 38, Sapphire Bay* ✣ *½ mile (1 km) north of Red Hook.*

Secret Harbour

BEACH | Placid waters make it easy to stroke your way out to a swim platform offshore from the Secret Harbour Beach Resort & Villas. Nearby reefs give snorkelers a natural show. There's a bar and restaurant as well as a dive shop where you can rent beach lounge chairs. **Amenities:** food and drink; parking; toilets; water sports. **Best for:** snorkeling; sunset; swimming. ✉ *Rte. 322, Nazareth* ✣ *Take 1st right off Rte. 322.*

Vessup Beach

BEACH | This wild, undeveloped beach is lined with seagrape trees and century plants. It's close to Red Hook harbor, so you can watch the ferries depart. The calm waters are excellent for swimming. It's popular with locals on weekends. **Amenities:** parking; water sports. **Best for:** swimming. ✉ *Off Rte. 322, Nazareth.*

Restaurants

Caribbean Saloon

$$$ | **AMERICAN** | Sports on wide-screen TVs and live music on weekends are two added attractions at this hip sports bar that's in the center of the action in Red Hook. The menu ranges from finger-licking barbecue ribs to more sophisticated fare, such as the signature filet mignon wrapped in bacon and smothered in melted Gorgonzola cheese. **Known for:** live music on the weekends; fresh catch of the day; late-night menu. $ *Average main: $28* ✉ *American Yacht Harbor, Bldg. B, Rte. 32, Red Hook* ☎ *340/775–7060* 🌐 *www.caribbeansaloon.com.*

Duffy's Love Shack

$$ | **ECLECTIC** | If the floating bubbles don't attract you to this zany eatery billed as the "ultimate tropical drink shack," the lime-green shutters, loud rock music, and fun-loving waitstaff just might. The menu has a selection of burgers, tacos, burritos, and salads, and bartenders shake up such exotic concoctions as the Love Shack Volcano—a 50-ounce flaming extravaganza. **Known for:** tropical cocktails; grilled fish tacos; the Caribbean Pu-Pu platter sampler. $ *Average main: $19* ✉ *Red Hook Shopping Center, Rte. 32 and 6500 Red Hook Plaza, Red Hook* ✣ *In the parking lot* ☎ *340/779–2080* 🌐 *www.duffysloveshack.com.*

Mirador by Chef Benny

$$$ | **INTERNATIONAL** | Arrive before sunset for the magnificent view and handcrafted cocktails at the Pineapple Bar, but stay for the Latin meets American mix of dinner selections. Chef Benny is from Puerto Rico and he cooks the food he grew up with—garlic tostones, chicken breast with garlic and truffle *mofonguitos,* and braised pork *masitas*—which is showcased during his Thursday special, a Puerto Rican–style buffet; save room for the Coquito Rum Cake. **Known for:** romantic setting; Puerto Rican–style buffets on Thursday; fantastic views across the ocean. $ *Average main: $28* ✉ *Point Pleasant Resort, 6600 Estate Smith Bay, Estate Smith Bay* ☎ *340/775–7200 Ext. 3* 🌐 *miradorbychefbenny.com* ⏲ *No lunch.*

★ Old Stone Farmhouse

$$$$ | **ECLECTIC** | At this beautifully restored plantation house, guests can dine on sophisticated small plates such as warm olives and basil focaccia or simple entrées such as New Zealand lamb chop or a lobster-based seafood medley. Personalized attention makes dining here a delight, as does the incredible decor—think 18th-century stone walls meets modern-day elegance, with fine silver and china set on white-tablecloth-topped hardwood tables. **Known for:** well-prepared dishes; excellent service; elegant setting. $ *Average main: $45* ✉ *Rte. 42, Lovenlund* ✣ *1 mile (1½ km) west of entrance to Mahogany Run Golf Course* ☎ *340/777–6277* 🌐 *www.oldstonefarmhouse.net* ⏲ *Closed Mon. and Tues.*

★ Pizza Pi

$$ | **PIZZA** | **FAMILY** | Sail up in a boat, paddle by in a kayak, or drive out in a dinghy to pick up freshly made New York–style pizza from this "floating" food truck. This 37-foot motor sailor is an authentic brick-oven pizzeria, serving pizzas topped with locally grown basil and fresh lobster. **Known for:** inventive toppings; one-of-a-kind location; delicious pizza. $ *Average main: $16* ✉ *Christmas Cove, Great St. James Island* ✣ *Across from Cowpet Bay, on the east end of St. Thomas* ☎ *340/643–4674* 🌐 *www.pizza-pi.com.*

You can find most of the large, luxurious beachfront resorts on St. Thomas's East End. The downside is that these properties are about a 30-minute drive from Charlotte Amalie and a 45-minute drive from the airport (substantially longer during peak hours). On the upside, they tend to be self-contained, plus there are a number of good restaurants, shops, and water-sports operators in the area. Once you've settled in, you don't need a car to get around.

★ Margaritaville Vacation Club by Wyndham
$$$$ | **RESORT** | The laid-back, flip-flop vibe is alive and well here at this Jimmy Buffett–themed beachfront resort, along with all the comforts and conveniences you'd expect from upscale tropical accommodations. **Pros:** beachfront property; restaurant on-site; quiet setting. **Cons:** need a car to get around; might not be a great fit among non–Parrot Heads; small beach. *Rooms from: $625 ✉ 6080 Estate Smith Bay, Estate Smith Bay ✣ Next to Coki Beach and Coral World Ocean Park ☎ 340/775–8300 🌐 www.margaritavillevacationclub.com ⇨ 80 rooms 🍽 No Meals.*

Point Pleasant Resort
$$$ | **RESORT** | Hilltop suites give you an eagle's-eye view of the East End and beyond, and those in a building adjacent to the reception area offer incredible sea views, but the sea-level junior suites, where the sounds of lapping waves lull you to sleep, are smaller. **Pros:** pleasant pools; there's a resort shuttle; convenient kitchens. **Cons:** some rooms need refurbishing; need a car to get around; steep climb from beach. *Rooms from: $475 ✉ 6600 Estate Smith Bay, off Rte. 38, Estate Smith Bay ☎ 340/775–7200, 888/619–4010 🌐 www.pointpleasantresort.com ⇨ 128 suites 🍽 No Meals.*

Ritz-Carlton, St. Thomas
$$$$ | **RESORT** | **FAMILY** | Everything sparkles at the island's most luxurious resort, from the in-room furnishings and amenities to the infinity pool, white-sand, eco-friendly Blue Flag–designated beach, and turquoise sea beyond. **Pros:** airport shuttle; gorgeous views; great water-sports facilities; beautiful beach. **Cons:** half-hour or more drive to town and airport; food and drink can lack flair and are expensive ($19 hamburger, $12 piña colada); steep resort fee. *Rooms from: $1425 ✉ 6900 Estate Great Bay, off Rte. 317, Estate Great Bay ☎ 340/775–3333, 800/241–3333 🌐 www.ritzcarlton.com ⇨ 180 rooms 🍽 No Meals.*

Secret Harbour Beach Resort
$$$ | **APARTMENT** | There's not a bad view from these low-rise studios and one- and two-bedroom condos, which are either beachfront or perched on a hill overlooking an inviting cove. **Pros:** secluded location; beautiful beach and great snorkeling; good restaurant. **Cons:** condo owners can be territorial about beach chairs; small pool; car needed to get around. *Rooms from: $460 ✉ Rte. 317, Nazareth ☎ 340/775–6550, 800/524–2250 🌐 www.secretharbourvi.com ⇨ 69 suites 🍽 No Meals.*

Two Sandals by the Sea
$$ | **B&B/INN** | This cozy bed-and-breakfast feels like a home away from home because of its casual ambience, picturesque setting overlooking Red Hook Harbor, and the friendliness of the owners. **Pros:** breakfast included in price; quaint and clean; close to beaches. **Cons:** no pool; need a car to get around; a little too intimate for some. *Rooms from: $320 ✉ On Ridge Rd., 6264 Estate Nazareth, Nazareth ☎ 340/998–2395 🌐 www.twosandals.com ⇨ 6 rooms 🍽 Free Breakfast.*

Charlotte Amalie's historic center and shopping district are great places to explore.

Nightlife

Several bars and restaurants make Red Hook a great spot for food, drink, and live music on the weekends.

Duffy's Love Shack

BARS | At this island favorite, funky cocktails, a loud sound system, and dancing under the stars are the big draws for locals and visitors alike. ✉ *Red Hook Plaza, Rte. 32, Red Hook* ☎ *340/775-4122* 🌐 *www.duffysloveshack.com.*

Shopping

Red Hook has **American Yacht Harbor,** a waterfront shopping area with a dive shop, a tackle store, clothing and jewelry boutiques, a bar, and a few restaurants.

FOOD AND DRINK

Food Center

FOOD | This supermarket sells fresh produce, meats, and seafood. There's also an on-site bakery and deli with hot and cold prepared foods, which are the big draw here, especially for those renting villas, condos, or charter boats in the East End area. ✉ *Rte. 32, 1 mile (2 km) west of Red Hook, Estate Frydenhoj* ☎ *340/777–8806* 🌐 *www.foodcentervi.com.*

Moe's Fresh Market

FOOD | This gourmet market near the ferry to St. John has the best deli cheeses, prepared-to-order subs, and selection of organic foods, coffees, and wines on the island. Two other locations are at Yacht Haven Grande near the cruise ship dock in Havensight and at the corner of Waterfront Drive and Espanole Strade in Charlotte Amalie. ✉ *6502 Smith Bay Rd., Rte. 32, Red Hook* ☎ *340/693–0254* 🌐 *www.moesvi.com.*

JEWELRY

Little Switzerland

JEWELRY & WATCHES | Designer jewelry available in this major chain includes David Yurman, Bulgari, Chopard, and Penny Preville. The selection of watches is also extensive. ✉ *Ritz-Carlton, St. Thomas, Rte. 322, Nazareth* ☎ *248/809–5560 ext. 10050* 🌐 *www.littleswitzerland.com.*

Southeast Shore

The southeast shore of St. Thomas connects Charlotte Amalie to the East End of the island via a beautiful road that rambles along the hillside with frequent peeks between the hills for a view of the ocean and, on a clear day, of St. Croix some 40 miles (64 km) to the south. The resorts here are on their own beaches and offer several opportunities for water sports, as well as land-based activities, upscale dining, and evening entertainment.

Sights

Skyride to Paradise Point
VIEWPOINT | FAMILY | Fly skyward in a seven-minute gondola ride to Paradise Point, an overlook with breathtaking views of Charlotte Amalie, the harbor, and the neighboring islands of St. Croix to the south and Vieques and Culebra, Puerto Rico, to the west. You'll find several shops, a bar (the specialty here is the Bushwacker, a creamy frozen cocktail), and a restaurant. Alternatively, you could skip the $25 gondola ride and take a taxi to the top for $7 per person from the Havensight Dock. ✉ *Rte. 30, across from Havensight Mall, Havensight* ☎ *340/774–9809* 🌐 *www.paradisepointvi.com* 🎟 *$25.*

★ Virgin Islands Children's Museum
CHILDREN'S MUSEUM | FAMILY | Giant bubble makers, a rainbow-colored gear table, and a larger-than-life abacus are just a few of the interactive exhibits at this indoor, family-friendly, play-and-learn museum. Science was never so fun! ✉ *Buccaneer Mall, Rte. 30, Havensight* ✥ *Across from the cruise ship dock* ☎ *340/643–0366* 🌐 *www.vichildrensmuseum.org* 🎟 *$10* ⏲ *Closed Mon.*

★ Water Island
ISLAND | FAMILY | This island, the fourth largest of the U.S. Virgin Islands, sits about a ¼ mile (½ km) out in Charlotte Amalie harbor. A ferry between Crown Bay Marina and the island ($15 round-trip) operates several times daily, Monday through Saturday from 7 to 6 and Sunday and holidays 8 to 6. From the ferry dock, it's a hike of less than half a mile to Honeymoon Beach (though you have to go up a big hill), where Brad Pitt and Cate Blanchett filmed a scene of the movie *The Curious Case of Benjamin Button*. Get lunch from a food truck or Dinghy's Beach Bar & Grill on the far south side of the beach. Monday night is Movie Night at Honeymoon Beach, a fun activity for the whole family after a day on the beach. ✉ *Charlotte Amalie harbor, Water Island* ☎ *340/690–4159 for ferry info* 🌐 *www.waterislandferry.com* 🎟 *$15 round-trip.*

Restaurants

Smoking Rooster BBQ
$$ | BARBECUE | House-smoked, hand-rubbed meats with a side of rum are the specialty here. Order the sampler platter for a taste of everything: choice of two meats like pulled pork and beef brisket, two sides such as potato mac salad (a mishmash of two favorites with a flavor all its own) and brisket beans, plus pickled veggies and Texas toast. **Known for:** house-pickled veggie sides; barbecue with house-made dry rubs; artisan craft beer and huge rum selection. 💲 *Average main: $19* ✉ *Havensight Mall, Rte. 30, Charlotte Amalie* ☎ *340/715–2625* 🌐 *www.thesmokingrooster.com.*

Hotels

Bolongo Bay Beach Resort

$$$ | RESORT | FAMILY | All the rooms at this family-run resort tucked along a palm-lined beach have balconies with ocean views; down the beach are nine condos with full kitchens. **Pros:** water sports abound; family-run property; on the beach. **Cons:** need a car to get around; on a busy road; a bit run-down. *Rooms from: $435 ✉ Rte. 30, Bolongo ☎ 340/775–1800, 800/524–4746 ⊕ www.bolongobay.com 74 rooms No Meals.*

Nightlife

Iggies Oasis

LIVE MUSIC | Bolongo Bay's poolside bar and restaurant offers live music on the weekends. *✉ Bolongo Bay Beach Resort, Rte. 30, Bolongo ☎ 340/775–1800 ⊕ www.iggiesbeachbar.com.*

Shopping

Havensight Mall, next to the cruise-ship dock, may not be as charming as downtown Charlotte Amalie, but it does have more than 60 shops, including a bank, a pharmacy, and smaller branches of many downtown stores. The shops at **Port of $ale,** adjoining Havensight Mall (its buildings are pink instead of brown), include a bakery, a bar and restaurant, a shoe store, and a tobacco shop. Next door to Port of $ale is the **Yacht Haven Grande** complex, a stunning megayacht marina with beautiful, safe walkways and some shops.

East of Charlotte Amalie on Route 38, **Tillett Gardens** is an oasis of artistic endeavor. The late Jim and Rhoda Tillett converted this Danish farm into an artists' retreat in 1959. Today you can take art classes, watch artisans produce candles, and shop.

Tutu Park Shopping Mall, across from Tillett Gardens, is the island's only enclosed mall. More than 50 stores and a food court are anchored by Kmart and the Plaza Extra grocery store. Archaeologists have discovered evidence that Arawak Indians once lived near the grounds.

ART

Mango Tango

ART GALLERIES | This gallery sells and displays works by popular local artists—originals, prints, and note cards. There's a one-person or multiple-person show at least one weekend a month. *✉ 4003 Raphune Hill, off Rte. 38, Raphune Hill, above the Paint Depot, ½ mile (1 km) east of Charlotte Amalie, Raphune ☎ 340/777–3060 ⊕ www.mangotangoart.com.*

CAMERAS AND ELECTRONICS

Boolchand's

ELECTRONICS | This store sells brand-name cameras, audio and video equipment, and binoculars. *✉ Havensight Mall, Rte. 30, Bldg. II, Suite C, Havensight ☎ 340/725–1614 ⊕ www.boolchand.com.*

CHINA AND CRYSTAL

Caribbean Gems

CERAMICS | Find the best of Scandinavia here, including Royal Copenhagen, Georg Jensen, Kosta Boda, and Orrefors. There's also a large selection of jewels like white diamonds, rainbow sapphires, and Caribbean topaz. *✉ Havensight Mall, Bldg. III, Rte. 30, Havensight ✣ The last store closest to cruise ship dock ☎ 340/714–2162.*

FOOD AND DRINK

★ **Fruit Bowl**

FOOD | This grocery store is the best place on the island to go for fresh fruits and vegetables. There are many ethnic, vegetarian, and health-food items as well as a fresh meat area, seafood department, and extensive salad and hot food bar. *✉ Wheatley Center, Intersection of Rtes. 38 and 313, Charlotte Amalie ☎ 340/774–8565 ⊕ www.thefruitbowlvi.com.*

JEWELRY

Omni Jewelers

JEWELRY & WATCHES | Diamonds are the star of the show. Find a variety of carat sizes in bracelets and bangles, rings and earrings, and pendants and necklaces. Settings come in gold or silver. There's also a location in the Crown Bay Center. ✉ *Havensight Mall, 9002, Rte. 30, Havensight* ☎ *340/715–2692* 🌐 *www.omnijewelers.com.*

LIQUOR AND TOBACCO

Tobacco Discounters

TOBACCO | This duty-free outlet carries a full line of discounted brand-name cigarettes, cigars, and tobacco accessories. ✉ *9100 Port of $ale Mall, Rte. 30, next to Havensight Mall, Havensight* ☎ *340/774–2256.*

West End

A few properties are in the hills overlooking Charlotte Amalie to the northwest or near Frenchtown, which is otherwise primarily residential. Views are often spectacular due to the higher elevations.

Sights

Drake's Seat

VIEWPOINT | Sir Francis Drake was supposed to have kept watch over his fleet from this vantage point, looking for enemy ships. The panorama is especially breathtaking (and romantic) at dusk, and if you plan to arrive late in the day, you'll miss the hordes of day-trippers on taxi tours who stop here to take pictures. ✉ *Rte. 40, Mafolie* ✣ *Located ¼ mile (½ km) west of the intersection of Rtes. 40 and 35.*

French Heritage Museum

HISTORY MUSEUM | The museum houses fishing nets, accordions, tambourines, mahogany furniture, photographs, and other artifacts illustrating the lives of the island's French descendants during the 18th through 20th centuries. Admission is free, but donations are accepted. ✉ *Rue de St. Anne and rue de St. Barthélemy, next to Joseph Aubain Ballpark, Frenchtown* ☎ *340/714–2583* 🌐 *www.frenchheritagemuseum.com* 🎟 *Free, donations accepted.*

Frenchtown

BUSINESS DISTRICT | Popular for its bars and restaurants, Frenchtown is also the home of descendants of immigrants from St. Barthélemy (St. Barth). You can watch them pull up their brightly painted boats and display their equally colorful catch of the day along the waterfront. If you chat with them, you can hear speech patterns slightly different from those of other St. Thomians. Get a feel for the residential district of Frenchtown by walking west to some of the town's winding streets, where tiny wooden houses have been passed down from generation to generation. ✉ *Turn south off Waterfront Hwy. (Rte. 30) at post office, Frenchtown.*

Mountain Top

VIEWPOINT | **FAMILY** | Head out to the observation deck—more than 1,500 feet above sea level—to get a bird's-eye view that stretches from Puerto Rico's out-island of Culebra in the west all the way to the British Virgin Islands to the north. There's also a restaurant, restrooms, and duty-free shops that sell everything from Caribbean art to nautical antiques, ship models, and touristy T-shirts. ✉ *Estate St. Peter* ✣ *Head north off Rte. 33, look for signs* ☎ *340/774–2400* 🌐 *www.mountaintopvi.com* 🎟 *Free.*

Phantasea Tropical Botanical Garden

GARDEN | Orchids, palms, cactus, and bromeliads are a few of the stunning plants that bloom along the self-guided hiking trails. These gardens are the essence of peace and quiet; they are located high on the island's lush north side. There are critters here too: peacocks, hummingbirds, and hermit crabs, to name a few. ✉ *Bishop Dr. (intersection of Rtes. 334 and 33)* ✣ *On the road to Mountain Top* ☎ *340/774–2916* 🌐 *www.stthomasbotanicalgarden.com* 🎟 *$10* ⏲ *Mondays.*

Beaches

Brewers Beach

BEACH | Watch jets land at the Cyril E. King Airport as you dip into the usually calm seas. Rocks at either end of the shoreline, patches of grass poking randomly through the sand, and shady tamarind trees 30 feet from the water give this beach a wild, natural feel. Civilization has arrived, in the form of one or two mobile food vans parked on the nearby road. Buy a fried-chicken leg and johnnycake or burgers and chips to munch on at the picnic tables. **Amenities:** food and drink; lifeguards; parking; toilets. **Best for:** sunset; swimming. ✉ *Rte. 30, west of University of the Virgin Islands.*

★ **Magens Bay**

BEACH | FAMILY | Deeded to the island as a public park, this heart-shaped stretch of white sand is considered one of the most beautiful in the world. The bottom of the bay is flat and sandy, so this is a place for sunning and swimming rather than snorkeling. On weekends and holidays, the sounds of music from groups partying under the sheds fill the air. There's a bar, snack shack, and beachwear boutique; bathhouses with restrooms, changing rooms, and saltwater showers are close by. Kayaks and paddleboards are available for rent at the water-sports kiosk. **Amenities:** food and drink; lifeguards; parking (fee); showers; toilets; water sports. **Best for:** partiers; swimming; walking. ✉ *Magens Bay, Rte. 35, at end of road on north side of island* ☎ *340/777–6300* 🌐 *www.magensbayauthority.com* 🎫 *Adults $5, parking $2.*

Restaurants

Hook, Line and Sinker

$$$ | SEAFOOD | FAMILY | Anchored on the breezy Frenchtown waterfront and close to the pastel-painted boats of the local fishing fleet, this harbor-view eatery serves high-quality seafood dishes, as well as steaks, burgers, and salads. This is one of the few independent restaurants serving Sunday brunch. **Known for:** just a few feet from the water; creative seafood dishes; Sunday brunch. 💲 *Average main: $24* ✉ *Frenchtown Mall, 62 Honduras St., Frenchtown* ✣ *at Frenchtown Marina docks* ☎ *340/776–9708* 🌐 *www.hlsvi.com.*

★ **Oceana Restaurant & Bistro**

$$$$ | ECLECTIC | In the old Russian consulate house at the tip of the Frenchtown peninsula, this restaurant offers superb views along with an eclectic array of dishes expertly prepared by longtime Virgin Islands chef Patricia LaCorte and her staff. Choose from the more casual bistro-style menu, which features taste-and-share charcuterie and artisanal cheese plates and entrées like flatbreads and burgers, or splurge on the more formal dinner selections like butter-poached local lobster and filet mignon. **Known for:** near Frenchtown nightlife; seaside view; indulgent dishes. 💲 *Average main: $42* ✉ *Villa Olga, 8A Honduras, Frenchtown* ☎ *340/774–4262* 🌐 *www.oceanavi.com* ⏲ *No dinner Sun.*

13 Restaurant

$$$ | SOUTHERN | Off the beaten path and unassuming on the outside, this mountainside eatery is a find. Inside, the decor is light and bright, the view of the Atlantic Ocean and the British Virgin Islands beyond is awesome, and the Southern-inspired cooking is terrific—consider the fried-green tomato appetizer, seafood gumbo, and crispy cornmeal-breaded fried catfish. **Known for:** cinnamon croissant French toast at Sunday brunch; fabulous views; decadent Southern and Cajun fare. 💲 *Average main: $29* ✉ *13a Estate Dorothea Northside* ☎ *340/774–6800* 🌐 *www.13restaurant.com* ⏲ *Closed Mon. and Tues. No lunch.*

Tickles Dockside Pub

$$ | AMERICAN | FAMILY | Nautical types and locals come here for casual fare with homey appeal: chicken-fried steak, meat loaf with mashed potatoes, and baby

back ribs. Hearty breakfasts feature eggs and pancakes, and lunch is an array of burgers, salads, sandwiches, and soups. **Known for:** Sunday brunch; marina views; hearty food. *Average main: $18 8168 Crown Bay Marina, Suite 308, Contant off Rte. 304 340/777–8792 www.ticklesdocksidepub.com.*

Hotels

Emerald Beach Resort

$ | **HOTEL** | You get beachfront ambience at this reasonably priced mini-resort tucked beneath the palm trees, but the trade-off is that it's directly across from a noisy airport runway. **Pros:** great Sunday brunch; beachfront location; good value. **Cons:** limited water sports; on a busy road; airport noise until 10 pm. *Rooms from: $240 8070 Lindbergh Bay, Lindbergh Bay 340/777–8800 www.emeraldbeach.com 90 rooms Free Breakfast.*

Island View Guesthouse

$ | **B&B/INN** | Perched 545 feet up the face of Crown Mountain, this small, homey inn has hands-on owners who can book tours or offer tips about the best sightseeing spots. **Pros:** good value; spectacular views; friendly atmosphere. **Cons:** need a car to get around; no air-conditioning in some rooms; small pool. *Rooms from: $180 Scott Free Rd., 11-1 C, Contant Immediately east of the intersection of Rte. 33 and Rte. 332 340/774–4270 www.islandviewstthomas.com 12 rooms No Meals.*

Activities

AIR TOURS

Caribbean Buzz Helicopters

AIR EXCURSIONS | Near to the UVI field, Caribbean Buzz Helicopters offers a minimum 30-minute tour that includes St. Thomas, St. John, the west end of Tortola, Jost Van Dyke, and all the cays in between. It's a nice ride if you can afford the splurge (tours are from $190 per person for up to three people), but in truth, you can see most of the aerial sights from Paradise Point or Mountain Top, and there's no place you can't reach easily by car or boat. *Jet Port, 8202 Lindbergh Bay, Charlotte Amalie 340/775–7335 www.caribbean-buzz.com.*

BOATING AND SAILING

Calm seas, crystal waters, and nearby islands (perfect for picnicking, snorkeling, and exploring) make St. Thomas a favorite jumping-off spot for day- or weeklong sails or powerboat adventures. With over 100 vessels from which to choose, St. Thomas is the charter-boat center of the U.S. Virgin Islands. You can go through a broker to book a sailing vessel with a crew or contact a charter company directly. Crewed charters start at approximately $3,800 per person per week, and bareboat charters can start at $2,700 per person for a 45- to 50-foot sailboat (not including provisioning), which can comfortably accommodate up to six people. If you want to rent your own boat, hire a captain. Most local captains are excellent tour guides.

Single-day charters are also a possibility. You can hire smaller boats for the day, including the services of a captain if you wish to have someone take you on a guided snorkeling trip around the islands.

Island Yachts

BOATING | The sailboats from Island Yachts are available for charter with or without crews. *6100 Red Hook Quarter, 18B, Red Hook 340/344–2143 www.iyc.vi.*

★ **Magic Moments**

BOATING | *Luxury* is the word at Magic Moments, where crews aboard the 45-foot Sea Rays offer pampered island-hopping snorkeling cruises for between $1,900 and $2,700 for up to six people. Nice touches include a chilled prawns-and-Champagne lunch and icy-cold eucalyptus-infused washcloths for freshening up. *American Yacht Harbor, 6501 Red Hook Plaza, Suite 201, Docks*

B and C, Red Hook ☎ *340/775–5066* 🌐 *www.yachtmagicmoments.com.*

The Moorings

BOATING | Three- and four-cabin sailing and power catamarans are available for bareboat or crewed charter from this U.S.-headquartered company with bases around the world. ✉ *Marina at Yacht Haven Grande St. Thomas, 5304 Yacht Haven Grande, Charlotte Amalie* ☎ *800/416–0814* 🌐 *www.moorings.com.*

St. Thomas Boat Rental

BOATING | Rental selections range from a 20-foot Caribe inflatable dinghy for $495 per day—it's perfect for exploring nearby islands—to a 60-foot luxury motor yacht complete with gourmet tapas and open bar at $2,800, plus gas, for up to eight. ✉ *Sapphire Beach Marina, off Rte 38, Estate Smith Bay* ☎ *813/465–2665* 🌐 *www.stthomasboatrental.com.*

Stewart Yacht Charters

BOATING | Run by longtime sailor Ellen Stewart, this company is skilled at matching clients with yachts and crews for weeklong charter holidays. ✉ *6501 Red Hook Plaza, Suite 20, Red Hook* ☎ *340/775–1358, 800/432–6118.*

DIVING AND SNORKELING

Popular dive sites include such wrecks as the *Cartanser Sr.*, a beautifully encrusted World War II cargo ship sitting in 35 feet of water, and the *General Rogers*, a Coast Guard cutter resting at 65 feet. Here you can find a gigantic resident barracuda. Reef dives offer hidden caves and archways at **Cow and Calf Rocks,** coral-covered pinnacles at **Frenchcap,** and tunnels where you can explore undersea from the Caribbean to the Atlantic at **Thatch Cay, Grass Cay,** and **Congo Cay.** Many resorts and charter yachts offer dive packages. A one-tank dive starts at $110; two-tank dives are $140 and up. Call the USVI Department of Tourism to obtain a free guide to Virgin Islands dive sites. There are plenty of snorkeling possibilities, too.

Admiralty Dive Center

SCUBA DIVING | Boat dives, rental equipment, and a retail store are available from this dive center. You can also get multiple-tank packages if you want to dive over several days. ✉ *Frenchtown Marina, 59 Honduras St., Charlotte Amalie* ☎ *340/777–9802* 🌐 *www.admiralty-dive.com.*

B.O.S.S. Underwater Adventure

SCUBA DIVING | As an alternative to traditional diving, try an underwater motor scooter called B.O.S.S., or Breathing Observation Submersible Scooter. A 3½-hour tour, including snorkel equipment, rum punch, and towels, is $135 per person. ✉ *Crown Bay Marina, Rte. 304, Charlotte Amalie* ☎ *340/201–9352* 🌐 *www.bossusvi.com.*

Coki Dive Center

SCUBA DIVING | FAMILY | Snorkeling and dive tours in the fish-filled reefs off Coki Beach are available from this PADI Five Star outfit, as are classes, including one on underwater photography. It's run by the avid diver Peter Jackson. ✉ *Rte. 388 at Coki Point, Estate Smith Bay* ☎ *340/775–4220* 🌐 *www.cokidive.com.*

St. Thomas Dive Center

SCUBA DIVING | FAMILY | This PADI Five Star center offers boat dives to the reefs around Buck Island and nearby offshore wrecks, as well as multiday dive packages. ✉ *Bolongo Bay Beach Resort, Rte. 30, Bolongo* ☎ *340/776–2381* 🌐 *www.stthomasdivingclub.com.*

Snuba of St. Thomas

SCUBA DIVING | FAMILY | In Snuba, a snorkeling and scuba-diving hybrid, a 20-foot air hose connects you to the surface. The cost is $85. Children must be age eight or older to participate. This company also operates at Trunk Bay on St. John. ✉ *Rte. 388 at Coki Point, Estate Smith Bay* ☎ *340/693–8063* 🌐 *www.visnuba.com.*

FISHING

Fishing here is synonymous with blue marlin angling—especially from June through October. Four 1,000-pound-plus blues, including three world records, have been caught on the famous North Drop, about 20 miles (32 km) north of St. Thomas. A day charter for marlin with up to six anglers costs $1,600 for the day. If you're not into marlin fishing, try hooking sailfish in winter, dolphinfish (the fish that's also known as mahimahi, not the mammal) in spring, and wahoo in fall. Inshore trips for four hours start at $700. To find the trip that will best suit you, walk down the docks at either American Yacht Harbor or Sapphire Beach Marina in the late afternoon and chat with the captains and crews.

Abigail III

FISHING | Captain Red Bailey's *Abigail III* specializes in marlin fishing. ✉ *Sapphire Beach Marina, Rte. 38, ¼ mile (½ km) northwest of Red Hook, Sapphire Bay* ☎ *340/775–6024* 🌐 *www.visportfish.com.*

★ Double Header Sportfishing

FISHING | **FAMILY** | This company offers trips out to the North Drop on its 40-foot sportfisher and half-day reef and bay trips aboard its two speedy 37-foot center consoles. ✉ *Oasis Cove Marina, Rte. 32, Estate Frydenhoj* ☎ *340/777–7317* 🌐 *www.doubleheadersportfishing.net.*

Offshore Adventures

FISHING | **FAMILY** | Get hooked on delicious game fish like mahimahi, tuna, and big blue marlin with Captain Rob Richards. Rates range from $650 for a half-day inshore trip to $1,400 for a full-day marlin trip. Bait, beverages, and fishing gear are provided. Although based on St. John, Offshore Adventures offers pickup from any resort or public dock on St. Thomas. ✉ *Estate Chocolate Hole and Great Cruz Bay* ☎ *340/513–0389* 🌐 *www.sportfishingstjohn.com.*

GUIDED TOURS

VI Taxi Association Tropical Paradise St. Thomas Island Tour

GUIDED TOURS | Aimed at cruise-ship passengers, this two-hour tour for two people is done in an open-air safari bus or enclosed van. Most vehicles can accommodate wheelchairs. The $29 tour includes stops at Drake's Seat and Mountain Top. Other tours include a three-hour trip to Coki Beach with a shopping stop in downtown Charlotte Amalie for $35 per person, a three-hour trip to the Coral World Ocean Park for $45 per person, and a five-hour beach tour to St. John for $75 per person. For $35 to $40 for two, you can hire a taxi for a customized three-hour drive around the island. Make sure to see Mountain Top, as the view is wonderful. ☎ *340/774–4550* 🌐 *vitaxiassociation.com/tours.html.*

SEA EXCURSIONS

Landlubbers and seafarers alike can experience the wind in their hair and salt spray in the air while exploring the waters surrounding St. Thomas. Several businesses can book you on a snorkel-and-sail to a deserted cay for a half-day that starts at $85 per person or a full day (at least $120 per person). An excursion over to the British Virgin Islands starts at $155 per person, not including $65 per person customs fees. A luxury daylong motor-yacht cruise complete with lunch is $475 or more per person, plus fuel.

St. Thomas Water Sports

BOATING | **FAMILY** | For a soup-to-nuts choice of sea tours including a stand-up paddleboard safari, full- and half-day sails, sunset cruises, fishing trips, powerboat rentals, and kayak tours, contact this reliable outfitter. ✉ *Marriott's Frenchman's Cove, Rte. 315, Estate Bakkero* ☎ *340/473–5708, 340/998–6789* 🌐 *www.watersportsvi.com.*

SEA KAYAKING

The best way to experience the mangroves of any island is on the water, ideally by kayak. These boats are very stable sit-on-top types and come in both single and double sizes. You don't need any experience, just a little stamina to paddle and guide your boat, making for a slow-paced and relaxing soft-adventure voyage.

★ Virgin Islands Ecotours

KAYAKING | FAMILY | Fish dart, birds sing, and iguanas lounge in trees as your paddle on three- or five-hour guided kayak trips in the Mangrove Lagoon, as well as excursions to Henley, Cas, and Patricia cays. There's also a three-hour stand-up paddleboard and snorkel tour of the lagoon. Three-hour trips include snacks; five-hour trips include lunch. ✉ *Mangrove Lagoon, Rte. 32, 2 miles (3 km) east of Rte. 30, Nadir* ☎ *340/779–2155* 🌐 *www.viecotours.com.*

WINDSURFING

Expect some spills, anticipate the thrills, and try your luck clipping through the seas. Most beachfront resorts rent Windsurfers and offer one-hour lessons for about $140.

West Indies Windsurfing

WINDSURFING | Owner John Phillips makes this sport accessible with $140 per hour lessons and rigs for rent. There are stand-up paddleboards and kayaks available, too, ideal for this usually calm yet consistently breezy bay. ✉ *9-B Estate Nazareth, Vessup Bay, Red Hook* ☎ *340/775–6530, 340/998–4658.*

ZIP LINING

Tree Limin' Extreme

ZIP LINING | FAMILY | Ride through rain forest and then break into clearings with views that stretch to the British Virgin Islands. Six ziplines mean wait times are low, even on busy cruise-ship days. Two sky bridges and a really cool "yo-yo" zip (yes, it makes you feel like the old-time kids toy) sets this apart from standard zipline tours. ✉ *7406 St. Peter, Estate St. Peter* ☎ *340/777–9477* 🌐 *www.ziplinest-thomas.com.*

St. John

St. John's heart is the Virgin Islands National Park, a treasure that takes up a full two-thirds of the island's 20 square miles (53 square km). The park helps keep the island's interior in its pristine and undisturbed state, but if you go at midday, you'll probably have to share your stretch of beach with others, particularly at Trunk Bay.

The island has just 4,000 full-time residents, but they're joined by more than 800,000 visitors each year. It can get crowded at ever-popular Trunk Bay Beach during the busy winter season, and parking woes plague the island's main town of Cruz Bay, but you won't find traffic jams or pollution. It's easy to escape from the fray, however: just head off on a hike or go early or late to the beach. The sun won't be as strong, and you may have that perfect crescent of white sand all to yourself.

St. John doesn't have a major agrarian past like her sister island, St. Croix, but if you're hiking in the dry season, you may stumble upon the stone ruins of old plantations. The less adventuresome can visit the restored ruins at the park's Annaberg Plantation, Cinnamon Bay, and Catherineberg Estate.

In 1675 Jorgen Iverson claimed the unsettled island for Denmark. By 1733 there were more than 1,000 slaves working more than 100 plantations. In that year the island was hit by a drought, hurricanes, and a plague of insects that destroyed the summer crops. With famine a real threat and the planters keeping them under tight rein, the slaves revolted on November 23, 1733. They captured the fort at Coral Bay, took control of the island, and held it for six months. During this period, about 20% of the island's black and white residents were killed. The rebellion was eventually put down with the help of French troops from Martinique. Slavery continued until 1848, when slaves in St. Croix marched on Frederiksted to demand their freedom from the Danish government. This time it was granted. After emancipation, St. John fell into decline, with its inhabitants eking out a living on small farms. Life continued in much the same way until the national park opened in 1956 and tourism became a viable industry.

Of the three U.S. Virgin Islands, St. John has the strongest sense of community, which is primarily rooted in a desire to protect the island's natural beauty. Despite the growth, there are still many pockets of tranquility. Here you can truly escape the pressures of modern life for a day, a week—perhaps forever.

GETTING HERE AND AROUND

St. John is an easy place to explore. One road runs along the northern shore, another across the center of the mountains. There are a few roads that branch off here and there, but it's hard to get lost. Pick up a map at the Virgin Islands National Park's visitor center in Cruz Bay before you start out. Few residents refer to the official route numbers, so have your map in hand if you stop to ask for directions. Bring along a swimsuit for stops at some of the most beautiful beaches in the world. You can spend all day or just a couple of hours exploring, but be advised that the roads are narrow and wind up and down steep hills, so take your time. For lunch, there are food trucks at Trunk Bay and Maho Bay and restaurants in Coral Bay, or you can do what the locals do—find a secluded spot for a picnic. The grocery stores in Cruz Bay sell coolers just for this purpose.

If you plan to do a lot of touring, renting a car will be cheaper and give you much more freedom than relying on taxis; on St. John taxis are shared safari vans, and drivers are reluctant to go anywhere until they have a full load of passengers. Although you may be tempted to rent an open-air Suzuki or jeep, a conventional SUV will let you lock up your valuables. You can get just about everywhere on the paved roads without four-wheel drive unless it rains—then four-wheel drive will help you get up the wet, hilly roads. You may be able to share a van or open-air vehicle (called a safari bus) with other passengers on a tour of scenic mountain trails, secret coves, and eerie bush-covered ruins.

BEACHES

St. John is blessed with many beaches, and all of them fall into the good, great, and don't-tell-anyone-else-about-this-place categories. Some are more developed than others—and many are crowded on weekends, holidays, and in high season—but by and large they're still pristine. Beaches along the southern and eastern shores are quiet and isolated. Break-ins occur on all the U.S. Virgin Islands; most locals recommend leaving your windows down and leaving absolutely nothing in your car, rather than locking it up and risking a broken window.

RESTAURANTS

The cuisine on St. John seems to get better every year, with chefs vying to see who can come up with the most imaginative dishes, whether you're at one of the white-tablecloth establishments in Cruz Bay or the casual joints in Coral Bay. For quick lunches, try the West Indian food stands and trucks in Cruz Bay and along Centerline Road (Route 10) en route to Coral Bay. The cooks prepare fried chicken legs, pâtés (meat- and saltfish-filled pastries), and callaloo.

Some restaurants close for vacation in September and even October. If you have your heart set on a special place, call ahead to make sure it's open.

HOTELS

St. John doesn't have many beachfront hotels, but that's a small price to pay for all the pristine sand. However, the island's largest resort, the Westin St. John Resort and Villas, *is* on the beach. Most villas are in the residential south-shore area, a 15-minute drive from the north-shore beaches. If you head east, you come to the laid-back community of Coral Bay, where there are growing numbers of villas and cottages. A stay outside Coral Bay will be peaceful and quiet.

If you're looking for West Indian village charm, there are a few inns in Cruz Bay. Keep in mind that when bands play at any of the town's bars (some of which stay open until the wee hours), the noise can be a problem. Your choice of accommodations also includes condominiums near town; and luxurious villas, often with a pool or a hot tub (sometimes both) and a stunning view.

If you're a camper—or glamper—there's everything from bare sites to pitch a tent to eco-tents and cottages at the Cinnamon Bay Beach & Campground. The tented units at Concordia Eco-Resort past Coral Bay are for glampers, while the small, basic dome tents at Camp St. John in Susanaberg are geared for campers.

If your lodging comes with a fully equipped kitchen, you'll be happy to know that St. John's handful of grocery stores sell everything you're likely to need—though the prices will take your breath away. If you're on a budget, consider bringing some staples (pasta, canned goods, paper products) from home, or stock up at big box stores in St. Thomas like Cost-U-Less or PriceSmart (the latter requires a $35 membership fee) before ferrying across to St. John. Hotel rates throughout the island are fairly expensive, but they do include endless privacy and access to most water sports.

Many of the island's condos are just minutes from the hustle and bustle of Cruz Bay, but you can find more scattered around the island.

PRIVATE CONDOS AND VILLAS

Here and there between Cruz Bay and Coral Bay are about 500 private villas and condos (prices range from $ to $$$$). With pools or hot tubs, full kitchens, and living areas, these lodgings provide a fully functional home away from home. They're perfect for couples and extended groups of family or friends. You need a car, since most lodgings are in the hills and very few are at the beach. Villa managers usually pick you up at the dock, arrange for your rental car, and answer questions on arrival as well as during your stay. Prices drop in the summer season, which is generally after May 15. Some companies begin off-season pricing a week or two later, so be sure to ask.

If you want to be close to Cruz Bay's restaurants and boutiques, a villa in the Chocolate Hole and Great Cruz Bay areas will put you a few minutes away. The Coral Bay area has a growing number of villas, but you'll be about 20 minutes from Cruz Bay. Beaches lie out along the North Shore, so you won't be more than 15 minutes from the water no matter where you stay.

RENTAL CONTACTS Carefree Getaways. ✉ *Cruz Bay* ☎ *340/779–4070, 888/643–6002* 🌐 *www.carefreegetaways.com.* **Caribbean Villas of St. John, USVI.** ✉ *Cruz Bay* ☎ *340/776–6152, 800/338–0987* 🌐 *www.caribbeanvilla.com.* **Catered to Vacation Homes.** ✉ *Cruz Bay* ☎ *340/776–6641, 800/424–6641* 🌐 *www.cateredto.com.* **Island Getaways.** ✉ *Cruz Bay* ☎ *340/693–7676, 888/693–7676* 🌐 *www.islandgetawaysinc.com.* **Seaview Homes.** ✉ *Cruz Bay* ☎ *340/776–6805* 🌐 *www.seaviewhomes.com.* **Star Villas.** ✉ *Cruz Bay* ☎ *340/626–5118* 🌐 *www.starvillas.com.* **St. John Properties.** ✉ *PO Box 710, Cruz Bay* ☎ *800/283–1746, 340/693–8485* 🌐 *www.stjohnproperties.com.* **St. John**

Ultimate Villas. ✉ *Cruz Bay* ☎ *340/513–3864, 888/851–7588* 🌐 *www.stjohnultimatevillas.com.* **Vacation Vistas.** ✉ *Cruz Bay* ☎ *340/776–6462, 340/244–9465, 888/334–5222* 🌐 *www.vacationvistas.com.* **Windspree Vacation Homes.** ✉ *7924 Emmaus, Coral Bay* ☎ *340/201–3002, 340/693–5423* 🌐 *www.windspree.com.*

NIGHTLIFE

St. John isn't the place to go for glitter and all-night partying. Still, after-hours Cruz Bay can be a lively little town in which to dine, drink, dance, chat, or flirt. Notices posted on the bulletin board outside the Connections business center—up the street from the ferry dock in Cruz Bay—or listings in the online *St. John Source* (www.stjohnsource.com) will keep you apprised of special events, comedy nights, movies, and the like.

Cruz Bay

St. John's main town may be compact (it consists of only several blocks), but it's definitely a hub: the ferries from St. Thomas and the British Virgin Islands pull in here, and it's where you can get a taxi or rent a car to travel around the island. There are plenty of shops, a number of watering holes and restaurants, and a grassy square with benches where you can sit back and take everything in. Look for the current edition of the handy, amusing "St. John Activity Road Map."

Sights

★ Virgin Islands National Park

NATIONAL PARK | Covering more than two-thirds of St. John, Virgin Islands National Park preserves the island's natural environments and is a must if you're interested in bird-watching, snorkeling, camping, history, or just strolling in beautiful environs. At Francis Bay there's a boardwalk through the mangroves, where birds may be plentiful; Trunk Bay boasts an underwater snorkel trail while Salt Pond Bay offers pleasant snorkeling too; Cinnamon Bay's campground offers bare sites, eco tents. and cottages; and you can explore plantation history at Annaberg Sugar Mill and Catherineberg Estate ruins.

There are more than 20 trails on the north and south shores, with guided hikes along the most popular routes. A full-day trip to Reef Bay is a highlight; it's an easy hike through lush and dry forest, past the ruins of an old plantation, and to a sugar factory adjacent to the beach. It can be a bit arduous for young kids, however. The nonprofit Friends of the Virgin Islands National Park runs a $60 per person ranger-guided tour to Reef Bay that includes a safari bus ride to the trailhead and a boat ride back to the visitor center. The schedule changes from season to season; call for times and to make reservations, which are essential. To pick up a useful guide to St. John's hiking trails, see various large maps of the island, and find out about current Park Service programs—including guided walks and cultural demonstrations—stop by the park visitor center at the western tip of the park in Cruz Bay on North Shore Road. ✉ *North Shore Rd., near creek, Cruz Bay* ☎ *340/776–6201* 🌐 *www.nps.gov/viis.*

Free Parking

Cruz Bay's parking problem is maddening. Your best bet is to rent a car from a company that allows you to park in its lot. Make sure you ask before you sign on the dotted line if you plan to spend time in Cruz Bay.

Restaurants

Café Roma

$$$ | ITALIAN | FAMILY | This second-floor restaurant in the heart of Cruz Bay is *the* place for traditional Italian cuisine, so don't let the underwhelming ambience turn you away. The lasagna, spaghetti and meatballs, and seafood manicotti are all delicious, as are the small pizza—they're available at your table, but larger ones are for takeout or at the bar. **Known for:** Raju Cajun (chicken and penne tossed in a Cajun sherry cream sauce); authentic Italian cuisine; lively atmosphere. *Average main: $28 1-C King St., Cruz Bay 340/776–6524 www.caferomastjohn.com No lunch.*

★ Lime Inn

$$$$ | ECLECTIC | The vacationers and mainland transplants who call St. John home like to flock to this alfresco spot for the congenial hospitality and good food. Fresh lobster is the specialty, and the menu also includes shrimp-and-steak dishes and rotating chicken and pasta specials. **Known for:** local crowd; Lime Out, a floating taco bar off the east end of the island; fresh lobster. *Average main: $32 Lemon Tree Mall, King St., Cruz Bay 340/776–6425 thelimeinn.com Closed Sun. No lunch.*

Morgan's Mango

$$$$ | INTERNATIONAL | A melting pot of cuisines is what you'll find at this open-air, family-run restaurant. The tasty food runs the gamut from Peruvian fusion ceviche to Jamaican-style rib eye steak to Argentinian-style osso buco. **Known for:** Tuesday and Saturday lobster nights; Caribbean-fusion cuisine; friendly staff. *Average main: $34 18-1 Enighed, Northshore Road, Rte. 20, Cruz Bay Across from the VINP visitor center 340/693–8141 www.morgansmango.com.*

North Shore Deli

$ | ECLECTIC | At this air-conditioned (but no-frills) sandwich shop you place your order at the counter and wait for it to be delivered to your table or for takeout. The classic Reuben is a favorite, but other sandwiches, like the turkey pesto and vegan Greek flatbread pita with hummus and veggies, also get rave reviews. **Known for:** grab-and-go menu makes great picnic fixings; hearty sandwiches; tropical fruit smoothies. *Average main: $10 Mongoose Junction Shopping Center, North Shore Rd., Cruz Bay 340/777–3061 www.northshoredelistjohn.com No dinner.*

Sam and Jack's Deli

$$ | SANDWICHES | The sandwiches are scrumptious, but this deli also dishes up wonderful meals to-go that just need heating. There are a few seats inside, but most folks opt to eat at the tables in front of the deli. **Known for:** villa and yacht provisioning available; picnic-ready meals; The Wolf (crispy fried rock shrimp with Cajun remoulade). *Average main: $14 Marketplace Shopping Center, Rte. 104, 3rd fl., Cruz Bay 340/714–3354 www.samandjacksdeli.com.*

Hotels

Coconut Coast Villas

$$$ | HOTEL | This small condominium complex with studio, two-, and three-bedroom apartments is a 10-minute walk from Cruz Bay, but it's insulated from the town's noise in a sleepy suburban neighborhood. **Pros:** walk to Cruz Bay; good snorkeling; full kitchens. **Cons:** nearby utility plant can be noisy; some uphill walks; small beach. *Rooms from: $389 268 Estate Enighed, Near pond, Turner Bay, Cruz Bay 340/693–9100, 800/858–7989 www.coconutcoast.com 9 units No Meals.*

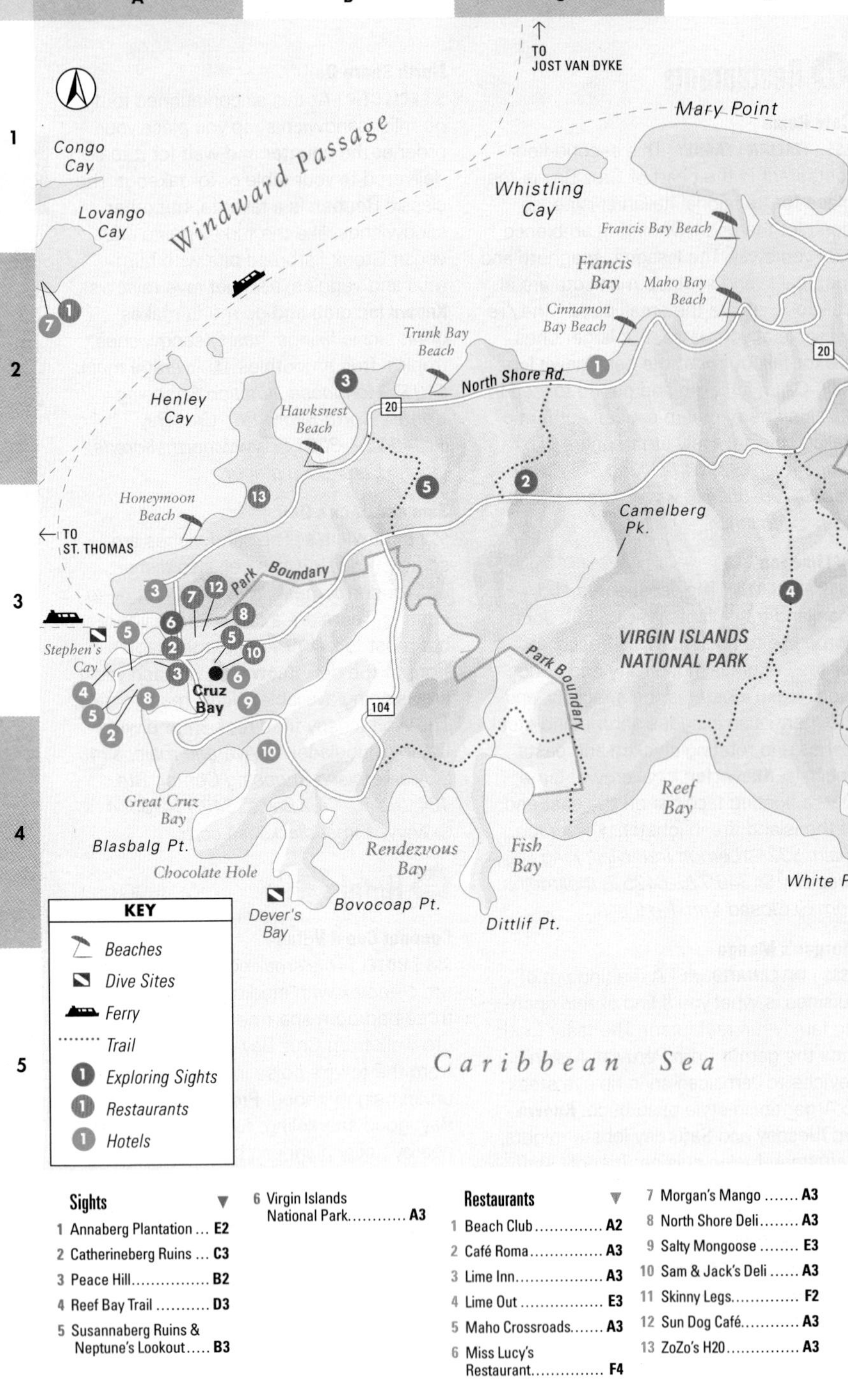

Sights

1 Annaberg Plantation ... **E2**
2 Catherineberg Ruins ... **C3**
3 Peace Hill................ **B2**
4 Reef Bay Trail **D3**
5 Susannaberg Ruins & Neptune's Lookout..... **B3**
6 Virgin Islands National Park............ **A3**

Restaurants

1 Beach Club.............. **A2**
2 Café Roma............... **A3**
3 Lime Inn.................. **A3**
4 Lime Out **E3**
5 Maho Crossroads....... **A3**
6 Miss Lucy's Restaurant............... **F4**
7 Morgan's Mango **A3**
8 North Shore Deli........ **A3**
9 Salty Mongoose **E3**
10 Sam & Jack's Deli **A3**
11 Skinny Legs............. **F2**
12 Sun Dog Café............ **A3**
13 ZoZo's H20............... **A3**

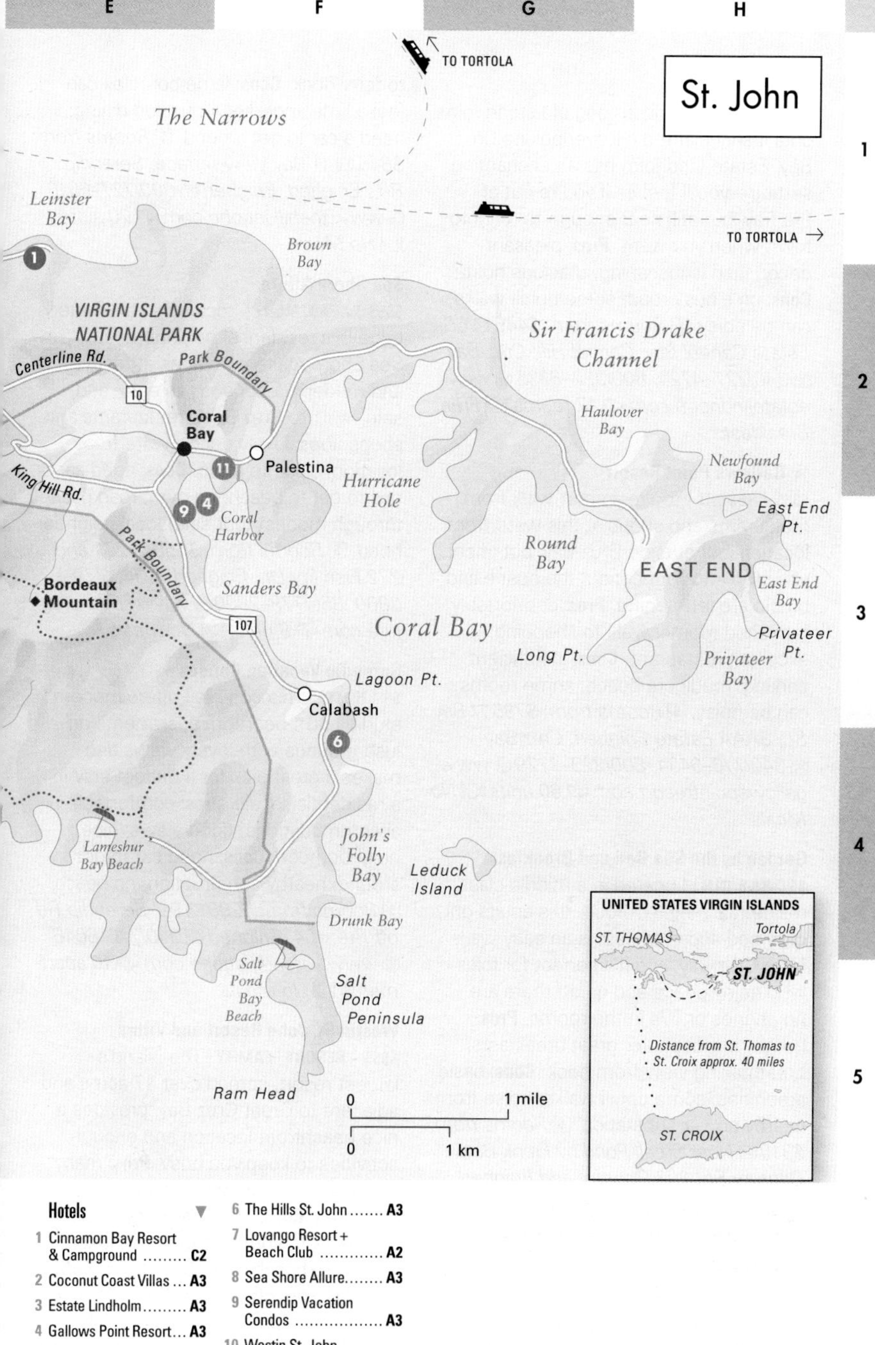

Hotels ▼

1 Cinnamon Bay Resort & Campground **C2**
2 Coconut Coast Villas ... **A3**
3 Estate Lindholm......... **A3**
4 Gallows Point Resort... **A3**
5 Garden by the Sea Bed and Breakfast **A3**
6 The Hills St. John **A3**
7 Lovango Resort + Beach Club **A2**
8 Sea Shore Allure........ **A3**
9 Serendip Vacation Condos **A3**
10 Westin St. John Resort and Villas **B4**

Estate Lindholm

$$$ | **B&B/INN** | Built among old stone ruins on a lushly planted hill overlooking Cruz Bay, Estate Lindholm has an enchanting setting—you'll feel as if you're out of the fray, but still near enough to run into town when you want. **Pros:** pleasant decor; lush landscaping; gracious host. **Cons:** on a busy road; some uphill walks; can be noisy. *Rooms from: $445 ✉ 6B Estate Caneel Bay, Caneel Hill, Cruz Bay ☎ 340/227–4724, 800/322–6335 🌐 www.estatelindholm.com 17 rooms Free Breakfast.*

★ **Gallows Point Resort**

$$$$ | **RESORT** | You're a short walk from restaurants and shops at this waterfront location just outside Cruz Bay, but once you step into your condo, the hustle and bustle are left behind. **Pros:** comfortably furnished rooms; walk to shopping; excellent restaurant. **Cons:** insufficient parking; mediocre beach; some rooms can be noisy. *Rooms from: $795 ✉ Bay St., 3AAA Estate Enighed, Cruz Bay ☎ 340/776–6434, 800/323–7229 🌐 www.gallowspointresort.com 60 units No Meals.*

Garden by the Sea Bed and Breakfast

$$ | **B&B/INN** | Located in a middle-class residential neighborhood, this adults-only, cozy bed-and-breakfast is an easy walk from Cruz Bay, and it's perfect for folks who enjoy peace and quiet: there are no phones or TVs in the rooms. **Pros:**; homey atmosphere; great breakfasts; breathtaking view from deck. **Cons:** basic amenities; some uphill walks; noise from nearby power substation. *Rooms from: $310 ✉ Near Small Pond by Frank Bay, Century St., 203 Contant and Enighed, Enighed ☎ 340/779–4731 🌐 gardenbythesea.com 3 rooms Free Breakfast.*

The Hills St. John

$$$$ | **RESORT** | This Mediterranean-style villa resort perched on a hill overlooking Cruz Bay offers panoramic views of the island, seas, and St. Thomas beyond. **Pros:** luxurious; incredible views; close to ferry dock. **Cons:** large complex can feel a little impersonal; limited dining; need a car to get around. *Rooms from: $645 ✉ 11 Bay View Terrace, Serendip Rd., Enighed, Enighed ☎ 800/727–6610 🌐 www.thehillsstjohn.com 20 suites No Meals.*

Sea Shore Allure

$$$$ | **APARTMENT** | Located at the water's edge in a residential neighborhood, Sea Shore Allure combines attractive and modern decor with an easy, and safe, walk to Cruz Bay's restaurants and shops. **Pros:** lovely decor; waterfront location; close to town. **Cons:** need car or taxi to get to beach; no gym; road passes through modest (but safe) local neighborhood. *Rooms from: $550 ✉ 271 and 272 Fish Fry Dr., Enighed ☎ 340/779–2800, 855/779–2800 🌐 www.seashoreallure.com 8 units No Meals.*

Serendip Vacation Condos

$$ | **HOTEL** | This complex offers modern studio and 1-bedroom apartments on lush grounds with lovely views and makes a great pick for a budget stay in a residential locale. **Pros:** comfortable accommodations; good views; nice neighborhood. **Cons:** need car to get around; nearby construction; no beach. *Rooms from: $299 ✉ 9-7 Serendip Rd., off Rte. 104, Enighed ☎ 340/776–6646 🌐 www.serendipstjohn.com 10 apartments No Meals.*

Westin St. John Resort and Villas

$$$$ | **RESORT** | **FAMILY** | The island's largest resort, spread over 47 acres and adjacent to Great Cruz Bay, provides a nice beachfront location and enough activities to keep you busy. **Pros:** many activities; restaurants on property; pretty pool area. **Cons:** need car to get around; long walk to some parts of the resort; mediocre beach. *Rooms from: $657 ✉ 300B Chocolate Hole, Rte. 104, Estate Chocolate Hole and Great Cruz Bay ☎ 340/693–8000, 800/845-5279 🌐 www.westinresortstjohn.com 296 units No Meals.*

Cruz Bay, St. John's main town, is filled with restaurants, bars, shopping opportunities, and dive centers.

Nightlife

Cruz Bay Landing

LIVE MUSIC | At this lively spot, you can count on live music by local artists 6 to 9 every night in season, and weekends off-season. The tunes are eclectic, but most often it's a mix of R&B, soft rock, and island tunes. Order a craft cocktail, like the signature rum-based Jumbie Juice or baby-back ribs, lobster, and fish tacos for dinner. Or, if you're not hungry or thirsty, you can sit on the benches outside in the Franklin A. Powell Sr. Park and tap your toes to the tunes. ✉ *Franklin A. Powell Sr. Park, Prince and Strand Sts., 6D Cruz Bay, Cruz Bay* ☎ *340/776–6908* 🌐 *cruzbaylanding.com.*

Woody's Seafood Saloon

BARS | Folks like to gather here, a short walk from the ferry dock, where the sidewalk tables provide a close-up view of Cruz Bay action. There's live entertainment on weekends. American country music star Kenny Chesney often stops here when on island and sings a song or two. ✉ *Prince and King Sts., Cruz Bay* ✣ *2 blocks east of the ferry dock* ☎ *340/779–4625* 🌐 *www.woodysseafood.com.*

Shopping

Luxury goods and handicrafts are widely available on St. John. Most shops carry a little of this and a bit of that, so it pays to poke around. The Cruz Bay shopping district runs from **Wharfside Village,** just around the corner from the ferry dock, to **Mongoose Junction,** an inviting shopping center on North Shore Road. (The name of this upscale shopping mall, by the way, is a holdover from a time when those furry island creatures gathered at a nearby garbage bin.) Out on Route 104, stop in at the **Marketplace** to explore its shops and art gallery. On St. John, store hours run from 9 or 10 to 5 or 6. Wharfside Village and Mongoose Junction shops in Cruz Bay are often open into the evening.

ART

★ Bajo el Sol Gallery, Art Bar & Rum Room

ART GALLERIES | This gallery sells pieces from a roster of the island's best artists. You can shop for oils, pastels, watercolors, and turned-wood pieces as well as ceramic and metal works. Find potable art in the form of a full bar in the back. There's espresso, craft cocktails. and a good selection of aged rums, the latter of which you can sample in curated tasting flights. ✉ *Mongoose Junction Shopping Center, North Shore Rd., Hwy. 20, Cruz Bay* ☎ *340/693–7070* 🌐 *www.bajo-el-sol-gallery.business.site.*

Coconut Coast Studios

ART GALLERIES | This waterside shop, a five-minute walk from the center of Cruz Bay, showcases the work of Elaine Estern. She specializes in undersea scenes. ✉ *Frank Bay, Tobacco Rd., Cruz Bay* ☎ *340/776–6944* 🌐 *www.coconut-coaststudios.com.*

Kimberly Boulon Fine Art Gallery

ART GALLERIES | Landscapes and seascapes come to life in oils and pastels by this California native and 40-year-plus St. John resident, whose love of nature is shared by her husband, a long-time employee at the Virgin Islands National Park. Find other island artists' works here, too. There are carved bowls made out of Caribbean hardwood lignum vitae and blue-hued ceramics painted with 18th-century scenes. ✉ *The Marketplace, 2nd fl., Hwy. 104, Cruz Bay* ☎ *340/690–3332* 🌐 *www.kimberlyboulon.com.* Art

BOOKS

★ Friends of the Park Store

BOOKS | Find books, maps, and beachwear—like tee's printed with turtle and petroglyph designs—at this store run by the nonprofit group that raises money for Virgin Islands National Park. It's a great spot to buy educational materials for kids and books about the island. ✉ *Mongoose Junction Shopping Center, North Shore Rd., Hwy 20., Cruz Bay* ☎ *340/779–4940* 🌐 *www.friendsvinp.org.*

National Park Headquarters Bookstore

BOOKS | **FAMILY** | The bookshop at Virgin Islands National Park Headquarters sells several good histories of St. John, including *St. John Backtime: Eyewitness Accounts From 1718 to 1956*, by Ruth Hull Low and Rafael Lito Valls, and, for intrepid explorers, longtime resident Pam Gaffin's *St. John Feet, Fins and Four-Wheel Drive*, a "complete guide to all of the island's beaches, trails, and roads." ✉ *1300 Cruz Bay Creek, Hwy. 20, Cruz Bay* ☎ *340/776–6201* 🌐 *www.nps.gov/viis.*

CLOTHING

Big Planet Adventure Outfitters

MIXED CLOTHING | You knew when you arrived that someplace on St. John would cater to the outdoors enthusiasts who hike up and down the island's trails. This store sells flip-flops and Reef footwear, along with colorful and durable cotton clothing and accessories by Billabong. The store also sells children's clothes. ✉ *Mongoose Junction Shopping Center, North Shore Rd., Hwy. 20, Cruz Bay* ☎ *340/776–6638* 🌐 *www.big-planet.com.*

FOOD

If you're renting a villa or condo, or camping, and doing your own cooking, there are several good places to shop for food; just be aware that prices are higher than those at home.

Starfish Market

FOOD | The island's largest store usually has the best selection of meat, fish, and produce. ✉ *The Marketplace, Rte. 104, Cruz Bay* ☎ *340/779–4949* 🌐 *www.starfishmarket.com.*

GIFTS

Bamboula

SOUVENIRS | This multicultural boutique carries unusual housewares, rugs, bedspreads, accessories, and men's and women's clothes and shoes that owner Jo Sterling has found on her world travels. ✉ *Mongoose Junction Shopping*

Center, North Shore Rd., Cruz Bay ☎ *340/693–8699* 🌐 *www.bamboulast-john.com.*

Donald Schnell Studio

SOUVENIRS | You'll find distinctive clay pieces, unusual handblown glass, wind chimes, kaleidoscopes, fanciful fountains, and pottery bowls here. Your purchases can be shipped worldwide. ✉ *Amore Center, 27 Southside Rd., near roundabout, Enighed* ☎ *340/776–6420, 800/253–7107* 🌐 *donaldschnell.com/the-studio.*

Gallows Point Resort Gift & Gourmet

SOUVENIRS | The gift shop at Gallows Point Resort has a bit of this and a bit of that. Shop for Caribbean books, picture frames decorated with shells, and T-shirts with tropical motifs. Residents and visitors also drop by for a cup of coffee or espresso. ✉ *Gallows Point Resort, Bay St., Cruz Bay* ☎ *340/693–7730, 800/323–7229 ext. 608* 🌐 *www.gallowspointconcierge.com.*

Pink Papaya

SOUVENIRS | Head to this shop and art gallery for the work of longtime Virgin Islands resident Lisa Etre. There's also a huge collection of one-of-a-kind gifts, including bright tableware, trays, and tropical jewelry. ✉ *Lemon Tree Mall, King St., Cruz Bay* ☎ *340/693–8535* 🌐 *www.pinkpapaya.com.*

St. John Spice

SOUVENIRS | Spices, hot sauces, and rubs are the trademark of this island-style country store. Find other Caribbean favorites, such as locally made soaps, bath products, cookbooks, St. John engraved mugs, and scenic island matted prints. ✉ *Adjacent to the ferry dock, Prince St., Cruz Bay* ☎ *340/693–7046* 🌐 *www.stjohnspice.com.*

JEWELRY

Freebird Creations

JEWELRY & WATCHES | This is your on-island destination for special handcrafted jewelry—earrings, bracelets, pendants, chains—as well as a good selection of water-resistant watches. ✉ *Dockside Mall, next to ferry dock, Cruz Bay* ☎ *340/693–8625* 🌐 *www.freebirdcreations.com.*

Little Switzerland

JEWELRY & WATCHES | A branch of the St. Thomas store, Little Switzerland carries diamonds and other jewels in attractive yellow- and white-gold settings, as well as strings of creamy pearls, watches, and other designer jewelry. ✉ *Mongoose Junction Shopping Center, North Shore Rd., Cruz Bay* ☎ *248/809–5560, ext. 10040* 🌐 *www.littleswitzerland.com.*

★ **R&I PATTON goldsmithing**

JEWELRY & WATCHES | This store is owned by Rudy and Irene Patton, who design most of the lovely silver and gold jewelry on display. The rest comes from various designer friends. Sea fans (those large, lacy plants that sway with the ocean's currents) in filigreed silver, starfish and hibiscus pendants in silver or gold, and gold sand-dollar-shape charms and earrings are choice selections. ✉ *Mongoose Junction Shopping Center, North Shore Rd., Cruz Bay* ☎ *340/776–6548, 800/626–3445* 🌐 *www.pattongold.com.*

North Shore

Perhaps one of the most spectacular drives on the island, the North Shore is home to the best-known Virgin Islands National Park beaches. Accommodations include rental villas and the campground at Cinnamon Bay.

Sights

★ **Annaberg Plantation**

RUINS | In the 18th century, sugar plantations dotted the steep hills of this island. Enslaved people and free Danes and Dutchmen toiled to harvest the cane that was used to create sugar, molasses, and rum for export. Built in the 1780s, the partially restored plantation at Leinster Bay was once an important sugar mill. Although there are no official visiting hours, the National Park Service hosts tours, and some well-informed taxi drivers can show you around. Occasionally, you may see a living-history demonstration—someone making johnnycakes or weaving baskets. For information on tours and cultural events, contact the National Park visitor center. ✉ *Leinster Bay Rd., Annaberg* ☎ *340/776–6201* 🌐 *www.nps.gov/viis.*

Peace Hill
VIEWPOINT | It's worth stopping here, just past the Hawksnest Bay overlook, for great views of St. John, St. Thomas, and the BVI. On the flat promontory is an old sugar mill. ✉ *Off Hwy. 20, Estate Denis Bay.*

Beaches

Facilities at most of the North Shore's beaches include parking, picnic tables, grills, food trucks, and restrooms.

Cinnamon Bay Beach
BEACH | FAMILY | This long, sandy beach faces beautiful cays and abuts the National Park campground. There's excellent snorkeling off the point to the right; look for the big angelfish and large schools of purple triggerfish. Afternoons on Cinnamon Bay can be windy—a boon for windsurfers but an annoyance for sunbathers—so arrive early to beat the gusts. The Cinnamon Bay hiking trail begins across the road from the beach parking lot; ruins mark the trailhead. There are actually two paths here: a level nature trail (with signs to identify flora) that loops through the woods and passes an old Danish cemetery and a steep trail that starts where the road bends past the ruins and heads straight up to Route 10. **Amenities:** parking; toilets. **Best for:** snorkeling; swimming; walking; windsurfing. ✉ *North Shore Rd., Hwy. 20, Cinnamon Bay* ✣ *About 4 miles (6 km) east of Cruz Bay* 🌐 *www.nps.gov/viis.*

Francis Bay Beach
BEACH | Because there's little shade, this beach gets toasty in the afternoon, when the sun comes around to the west, but the rest of the day it's a delightful stretch of white sand. The only facilities are a few picnic tables tucked among the trees and a portable restroom, but folks come here to watch the birds that live in the swampy area behind the beach. There's also a boardwalk here for bird-watching. In addition, the park offers weekly bird-watching hikes; sign up at the visitor center in Cruz Bay. To get here, turn left at the Annaberg intersection. **Amenities:** parking; toilets. **Best for:** snorkeling; swimming; walking. ✉ *North Shore Rd., Hwy. 20, Francis Bay* ✣ *¼ mile (½ km) from Annaberg intersection* 🌐 *www.nps.gov/viis.*

Hawksnest Beach
BEACH | Seagrapes and waving palm trees line this narrow beach, and there are portable toilets, cooking grills, and a covered shed for picnicking. It's the closest drivable beach to Cruz Bay, so it's often crowded with locals and visitors. A patchy reef just offshore means snorkeling is an easy swim away, but the best underwater views are reserved for ambitious snorkelers who head farther to the east along the bay's fringes. Watch out for boat traffic: although a channel of buoys marks where dinghies or other small vessels can come up onto the sand to drop off or pick up passengers, the occasional boater strays into the swim area. **Amenities:** parking; toilets. **Best for:** snorkeling; swimming. ✉ *North Shore Rd., Hwy 20, Estate Hawksnest* ✣ *About 2 miles (3 km) east of Cruz Bay* 🌐 *www.nps.gov/viis.*

Honeymoon Beach
BEACH | FAMILY | Hike in to this off-the-beaten-path seagrape-lined strip of white sand via the Lind Point Trail, which starts at the Virgin Islands National Park visitors center in Cruz Bay. A popular draw here is Bikinis on the Beach, a combo restaurant,

Sugar mill ruins at Annaberg Plantation.

gift shop, and water sports and cabana rental shop that makes this a great getaway beach for the day—day passes, which include water sports gear and beach chairs, cost $49 per person. **Amenities:** food and drink. **Best for:** snorkeling, walking. ✉ *North Shore Rd., Hwy. 20, 1 mile east of Cruz Bay, Estate Caneel Bay* ☎ 🌐 *www.viecotours.com.* Beaches

Maho Bay Beach

BEACH | This gorgeous strip of sand sits right along the North Shore Road. It's a popular place, particularly on weekends, when locals come out in droves to party at the picnic tables on the south end of the beach. The snorkeling along the rocky edges is good, but the center is mostly sea grass. If you're lucky, you'll cross paths with turtles. There are portable toilets at the end of the beach. Across the beach is Maho Crossroads, with food trucks, a bar, and a couple of shops. **Amenities:** food and drink; parking; toilets. **Best for:** snorkeling; swimming. ✉ *North Shore Rd., Hwy. 20, Estate Maho Bay* 🌐 *www.nps.gov/viis.*

★ Trunk Bay Beach

BEACH | St. John's most photographed beach is also the preferred spot for beginning snorkelers because of its underwater trail. (Cruise-ship passengers interested in snorkeling for a day flock here, so if you're looking for seclusion, arrive early or later in the day.) Crowded or not, this stunning beach is one of the island's most beautiful. There are changing rooms with showers, bathrooms, a food concession, picnic tables, a gift shop, phones, lockers, and snorkeling-equipment rentals. The parking lot often overflows, but you can park along the road as long as the tires are off the pavement. **Amenities:** food and drink; lifeguards; parking; showers; toilets; water sports. **Best for:** snorkeling; swimming; windsurfing. ✉ *North Shore Rd., Hwy. 20, Estate Trunk Bay* ✣ *About 2½ miles (4 km) east of Cruz Bay* 🌐 *www.nps.gov/viis* 🎫 *$5.*

Restaurants

Maho Crossroads

$ | **AMERICAN** | There's a back-to-the '60s hippie vibe at this eco-friendly pop-up village across from Maho Bay Beach—the food truck is an old VW bus. Hot dogs and hamburgers, plus tacos, mahimahi sandwiches, and veggie burgers are among the standards. *Average main: $11 ✉ Maho Bay, Northshore Rd., Hwy. 20, 5½ miles east of Cruz Bay, Estate Maho Bay ⊕ www.mahocrossroads.com ⊙ No dinner.*

★ Sun Dog Café

$$ | **ECLECTIC** | There's an unusual assortment of dishes at this charming alfresco restaurant, which you'll find tucked into a courtyard in the upper reaches of the Mongoose Junction shopping center. The Jamaican jerk chicken salad and the black-bean quesadilla are good choices. **Known for:** live music on weekends; eclectic menu; white pizza with artichoke hearts. *Average main: $18 ✉ Mongoose Junction Shopping Center, North Shore Rd., Hwy. 20, Cruz Bay ☎ 340/693–8340 ⊕ www.sundogcafe.com.*

★ Zozo's H20

$$$$ | **ECLECTIC** | Creative takes on true classics coupled with artfully presented plates draw crowds to this Mediterranean-inspired restaurant at Caneel Bay. Start with appetizers like scallop ceviche with mango, avocado, and heirloom tomatoes, then move on to the filet mignon with lobster demi-glace, cauliflower puree, and broccolini. **Known for:** mango-and-coconut pannacotta; breathtaking seaside views; romantic ambience. *Average main: $130 ✉ Caneel Bay, Northshore Rd., Hwy. 20, 1½ miles east of Cruz Bay, Estate Caneel Bay ☎ 860/450–6649 ⊕ www.zozosatcaneelbay.com ⊙ No dinner weekends.*

Hotels

Cinnamon Bay Resort & Campground

$ | **RESORT** | **FAMILY** | Sleep near the beach in one of 55 eco-tents or 31 bare sites at this Virgin Islands National Park Campground—tents come with a queen-size bed, cooking equipment, locked storage box, electric lights, and an electrical outlet, while bare sites have a wooden-platform base and shaded awning. **Pros:** restaurant and food truck on-site; steps from Cinnamon Bay Beach; nature immersive experience. **Cons:** fans in eco-tents, but no air-conditioning; communal bathrooms; no-see-um bugs can be bad at sunset. *Rooms from: $150 ✉ Cinnamon Bay, North Shore Rd., Hwy. 20, 4¼ miles east of Cruz Bay, Cinnamon Bay ☎ 340/714–7144 ⊕ www.cinnamonbayvi.com 86 units No Meals.*

Lovango Cay

A 10-minute ferry ride from Cruz Bay, St. John, or a 20-minute ride from Red Hook, St. Thomas, about a third of this 118-acre island is occupied by the snazzy Lovango Resort + Beach Club, which opened in 2020. Apart from a scattering of private homes, the island offers a wonderfully off-the-beaten-track vibe with hiking trails and deserted beaches.

Restaurants

Beach Club

$$$$ | **ECLECTIC** | At Lovango Resort's stylish eatery, enjoy lunch in the open-air dining room or in a cabana by the pool, or dinner on the deck. Start with the Caribbean lobster guacamole, before graduating to oyster, ahi tuna, caviar, and other selections from the raw bar, and then braised black Angus short ribs. **Known for:** elegant atmosphere; extensive raw bar; s'mores torte for dessert. *Average main: $32 ✉ Lovango Resort ☎ 340/625–0400 ⊕ www.lovangovi.com.*

Lovango Resort + Beach Club
$$$$ | **RESORT** | **FAMILY** | At this posh secluded-island resort, choose from an eco-friendly villa on the south shore facing St. John—complete with its own pool—or a luxury treehouse or glamping tent overlooking uninhabited Congo Cay and the Atlantic Ocean beyond. **Pros:** eco-friendly; stunning natural surroundings; quiet solitude. **Cons:** only two restaurants; remote location; long walks from accommodations to facilities. *Rooms from: $1100 ✉ Lovango Cay ☎ 340/625–0400, 833/568–2646 🌐 www.lovangovi.com 9 units Free Breakfast ☞ 3- to 7-night minimum stays.*

Mid Island

The least habited area of the island, it's all about nature and nurture in the Mid-Island including hiking trails and secluded camping and rental villas.

Catherineberg Ruins
RUINS | At this fine example of an 18th-century sugar and rum factory, there's a storage vault beneath the windmill. Across the road, look for the round mill, which was later used to hold water. In the 1733 slave revolt Catherineberg served as headquarters for the Amina warriors, a tribe of Africans that had been captured into slavery. ✉ *Catherineberg Rd., off Rte. 10, St. John.*

★ **Reef Bay Trail**
TRAIL | This is one of the most interesting hikes on St. John, but it's only for the physically fit as the 2-mile return climb, rising 900 feet from sea level back to the trailhead, is a real workout. Along the way, one short side trail to the west takes you to a small pool where indigenous inhabitants carved petroglyphs into the rock. Another short side trail to the east leads to the plantation's greathouse, a gutted but mostly intact structure with vestiges of its former beauty. Down at sea level, walk around the sugar factory ruins. The beach here makes a great place to cool off before hiking back up. *Difficult.* ✉ *Rte. 10, Reef Bay* ☎ *340/776–6201* 🌐 *www.nps.gov/viis, www.friendsvinp.org.*

Susannaberg Ruins & Neptune's Lookout
RUINS | Bird's-eye views of St. John's north-shore beaches, offshore cays, and the British Virgin Islands beyond are breathtaking from this 1700s-era ruins of a windmill and plantation house that was once Estate Susannaberg. Grab a cold drink at the Windmill Bar, where you can often catch live music on weekends. Or, stay the night next door at Camp St. John, which rents two-person dome tents. ✉ *Hwy. 10, Estate Susannaberg, Susannaberg* ☎ *340/514–4798, 340/244–6002* 🌐 *www.neptuneslookout.com.*

Coral Bay and Environs

This laid-back community at the island's dry eastern end is named for its shape rather than for its underwater life—the word *coral* comes from *krawl*, Dutch for "corral." Coral Bay is growing fast, but it's still a small, neighborly place. You'll probably need a four-wheel-drive vehicle if you plan to stay at this end of the island, as some of the rental houses are up unpaved roads that wind around the mountain. If you come just for lunch, a regular car will be fine.

Lameshur Bay Beach
BEACH | This seagrape-fringed beach is toward the end of a partially paved, rut-strewn road (don't attempt it without a four-wheel-drive vehicle) on the southeast coast. The reward for your bumpy drive is good snorkeling and a chance to spy on some pelicans. The beach has a

St. John Archaeology

Archaeologists have unraveled some of St. John's past through excavations at Trunk Bay and Cinnamon Bay, both prime tourist destinations within Virgin Islands National Park.

Work began back in the early 1990s, when the park wanted to build new bathhouses at the popular Trunk Bay. In preparation for that project, the archaeologists began to dig, turning up artifacts and the remains of structures that date to AD 900. The site was once a village occupied by the Taíno, a group that lived in the area until AD 1500. A similar but slightly more recent village was discovered at Cinnamon Bay.

By the time the Taíno got to Cinnamon Bay, roughly a century later, their society had developed to include chiefs, commoners, workers, and slaves. The location of the national park's hurricane-damaged Cinnamon Bay campground was once a Taíno temple that belonged to a king or chief. When archaeologists began digging in 1998, they uncovered several dozen *zemis*, which are small clay gods used in ceremonial activities, as well as beads, pots, and many other artifacts.

Near the end of the Cinnamon Bay dig archaeologists turned up another less ancient but still surprising discovery. A burned layer indicated that a plantation slave village had also stood near Cinnamon Bay campground; it was torched during the 1733 revolt because its slave inhabitants had been loyal to the planters. Since the 1970s, bones from slaves buried in the area have been uncovered at the water's edge by beach erosion.

couple of picnic tables, rusting barbecue grills, and a portable restroom. The ruins of the old plantation are a five-minute walk down the road past the beach. The area has good hiking trails, including a trek (nearly 2 miles [3 km]) up Bordeaux Mountain before an easy walk to Yawzi Point. **Amenities:** parking; toilets. **Best for:** snorkeling; swimming; walking. ✉ *Off Rte. 107, Lameshur Bay* ✣ *About 1½ miles (2½ km) from Salt Pond* ☎ *340/776–6201* 🌐 *www.nps.gov/viis.*

Salt Pond Bay Beach

BEACH | If you're adventurous, this rocky beach on the scenic southeastern coast—next to rugged Drunk Bay—is worth exploring. It's a short hike down a hill from the parking lot, and the only facilities are a portable toilet and a few picnic tables scattered about. Tide pools are filled with all sorts of marine creatures, and the snorkeling is good, particularly along the bay's edges. A short walk takes you to a pond where salt crystals collect around the edges. Hike farther uphill past cactus gardens to Ram Head for see-forever views. Leave nothing valuable in your car, as thefts are common. **Amenities:** parking; toilets. **Best for:** snorkeling; swimming; walking. ✉ *Rte. 107, about 3 miles (5 km) south of Coral Bay, Concordia* ☎ *340/776–6201* 🌐 *www.nps.gov/viis.*

Restaurants

★ Lime Out

$$ | **MEXICAN** | Jump on a boat, rent a dinghy, or paddle by SUP or kayak to this floating taco boat anchored in Coral Harbor. This cottage on pontoons, built by three men who grew up in Coral Bay, serves tacos—try the rum rib, ceviche, fresh tuna, or surf-and-turf versions—and cocktails. **Known for:** creative cocktails;

fun, floating setting; tasty tacos. $ *Average main: $14 ✉ West Fortsberg Bay, east side of Coral Harbor, Coral Bay ☎ 340/643–5333 🌐 www.limeoutvi.com ⏲ Closed Sept.*

Miss Lucy's Restaurant

$$$ | **CARIBBEAN** | Sitting seaside at remote Friis Bay, Miss Lucy's dishes up Caribbean food with a contemporary flair, like tender conch fritters, spicy callaloo stew, fried local fish, and a generous paella with seafood, sausage, and chicken. Sunday brunches are legendary, and if you're around at the time, stop by for the monthly full-moon parties. **Known for:** outdoor dining; Sunday brunch; full-moon parties. $ *Average main: $28 ✉ Rte. 107, Friis Bay ☎ 340/693–5244 ⏲ Closed Mon. No dinner Sun.*

Salty Mongoose

$$ | **AMERICAN** | Build your own pizza or salad at this bay-side open-air restaurant with eclectic ingredients, including prosciutto, bacon, and locally grown greens. Beer on tap, frozen and rum-based cocktails, and even a small selection of wines are also on offer. **Known for:** key lime pie; good selection of beer and cocktails; live music on Fridays and Saturdays. $ *Average main: $15 ✉ Isola Shops Building, Rte. 107, Coral Bay ☎ 340/643–8486 🌐 www.saltymongoose.com.*

★ Skinny Legs

$$ | **AMERICAN** | Sailors who live aboard boats anchored offshore and an eclectic coterie of residents and visitors gather for lunch and dinner at this funky spot in the middle of a boatyard and shopping complex. It's a great place for burgers (they're served with potato chips, not fries—there's no deep fryer), fish sandwiches, and whatever sports are on the satellite TV. **Known for:** local flavor; people-watching; pub food. $ *Average main: $13 ✉ Rte. 10, Coral Bay ☎ 340/779–4982 🌐 www.skinnylegsvi.com ⏲ Closed Mon.*

Nightlife

Skinny Legs

BARS | Landlubbers and old salts listen to music and swap stories at this popular casual restaurant and bar on the far side of the island. ✉ *Rte. 10, Coral Bay ☎ 340/779–4982 🌐 www.skinnylegsvi.com.*

Shopping

CLOTHING

★ Sloop Jones

MIXED CLOTHING | This store's worth the trip all the way out to the island's East End to shop for made-on-the-premises clothing and pillows, in fabrics splashed with tropical colors. The clothes are made from cotton, gauze, and modal, and are supremely comfortable. Sloop also holds painting workshops. ✉ *Off Rte. 10, East End ☎ 340/779–4001 🌐 www.sloopjones.com.*

FOOD

Dolphin Market

FOOD | Find fresh produce, meats, dairy, deli, snacks, dry goods. and a fair-size liquor selection at this largest grocery on the island's east side. This chain has two other locations in Cruz Bay. ✉ *Cocoloba Mall, Rte. 107, Coral Bay ☎ 340/776–5327 🌐 www.dolphinmarkets.com.* Food

GIFTS

Mumbo Jumbo

SOUVENIRS | With what may be the best prices in St. John, Mumbo Jumbo carries tropical clothing, stuffed sea creatures, local hot sauces, and other gifty items in a cozy little shop. ✉ *Skinny Legs Shopping Complex, Rte. 10, Coral Bay ☎ 340/779–4277.*

Activities

BOATING AND SAILING

If you're staying at a hotel or campground, your activities desk will usually be able to help you arrange a sailing excursion aboard a nearby boat. Most day sails leaving Cruz Bay head out along St. John's north coast. Those that depart from Coral Bay might drop anchor at some remote cay off the island's East End or even in the nearby British Virgin Islands. Your trip usually includes lunch, beverages, and at least one snorkeling stop. Keep in mind that inclement weather could interfere with your plans, though most boats will still go out if rain isn't too heavy.

Ocean Runner

BOATING | For a speedier trip to the cays and remote beaches off St. John, you can rent a powerboat with a captain from Ocean Runner. The company has everything from a 60-foot Sunseeker luxury yacht for up to 12 people for $4,500 to 15-foot runabouts for up to 4 people for $395 per day. Gas and oil will run you $100 to $300 a day extra, depending on how far you're going. ✉ *Adjacent to Wharfside Village, Bay St., Waterfront, Cruz Bay* ☎ *340/693–8809* 🌐 *www.oceanrunnerusvi.com.*

St. John Concierge Service

BOATING | The capable staff can find a charter sail or powerboat that fits your style and budget. The company also books fishing and scuba trips. ✉ *Henry Samuel St., booth across from post office, Cruz Bay* ☎ *340/514–5262* 🌐 *www.stjohnconciergeservice.com.*

DIVING AND SNORKELING

Although just about every beach has nice snorkeling—Trunk Bay, Cinnamon Bay, and Waterlemon Cay at Leinster Bay get the most praise—you need a boat to head out to the more remote snorkeling locations and the best scuba spots. Sign on with any of the island's water-sports operators to get to spots farther from St. John. Their boats will take you to hot spots between St. John and St. Thomas, including the tunnels at **Thatch Cay,** the ledges at **Congo Cay,** and the wreck of the *General Rogers*. Dive off St. John at **Stephens Cay,** a short boat ride out of Cruz Bay, where fish swim around the reefs as you float downward. At **Devers Bay,** on St. John's south shore, fish dart about in colorful schools. **Carval Rock,** shaped like an old-time ship, has gorgeous rock formations, coral gardens, and lots of fish. It can be too rough here in winter, though. Count on paying $110 for a one-tank dive and $155 for a two-tank dive. Rates include equipment and a tour. If you've never dived before, try an introductory course, called a resort course. Or if certification is in your vacation plans, the island's dive shops can help you get your card.

Cruz Bay Watersports

SCUBA DIVING | Regular reef, wreck, and night dives, as well as USVI and BVI snorkel tours, are among this operator's offerings. There's a second location at the Ritz Carlton on St. Thomas. ✉ *The Westin St. John, 300 Chocolate Hole, Cruz Bay* ☎ *888/492–9923, 340/776–6234* 🌐 *www.cruzbaywatersports.com.*

Low Key Watersports

SCUBA DIVING | This PADI Five Star training facility offers two-tank dives, night dives, and specialty courses. ✉ *1 Bay St., Cruz Bay* ☎ *340/693–8999* 🌐 *www.divelowkey.com.*

FISHING

Well-kept charter boats—approved by the U.S. Coast Guard—head out to the north and south drops or troll along the inshore reefs, depending on the season and what's biting. The captains usually provide bait, drinks, and lunch, but you need to bring your own hat and sunscreen. Fishing charters run about $1,200 for the full-day trip.

Offshore Adventures

FISHING | FAMILY | An excellent choice for fishing charters, Captain Rob Richards is patient with beginners—especially kids—but also enjoys going out with more experienced anglers. He runs the 32-foot and 40-foot center consoles, *Mixed Bag II and III*. ✉ *The Westin St. John, 300A Chocolate Hole Rd., Estate Chocolate Hole and Great Cruz Bay* ☎ *340/513–0389* 🌐 *www.sportfishingstjohn.com.*

GUIDED TOURS

In St. John, taxi drivers provide tours of the island, making stops at various sites, including Trunk Bay and Annaberg Plantation. Prices run $8 to around $15 a person one-way. The taxi drivers congregate near the ferry in Cruz Bay. The dispatcher will find you a driver for your tour. A two- to three-hour tour ranges from $25 to $35 per person for two or more passengers and includes the north-shore beaches out to Annaberg and back.

★ **Friends of the Virgin Islands National Park**

HIKING & WALKING | Held November–June, the Fridays with Friends Seminar Series offers guided hikes, walks, and turtle talks. Learn about cultural plants, hike from Salt Pond to Ram Head, and discover how turtles hatch and find their way back to the sea. Seminars run about two to three hours. The cost to nonmembers is $30; it's free for members, and an annual membership costs just $30, making it well worth the cost. ✉ *Mongoose Junction Shopping Center, Northshore Rd., Hwy. 20, Cruz Bay* ☎ *340/779–4940* 🌐 *www.friendsvinp.org.*

V.I. National Park Visitors Center

HIKING & WALKING | Along with providing trail maps and brochures about Virgin Islands National Park, the park service gives guided tours, both on- and offshore. Some are offered only during particular times of the year, and some require reservations. ✉ *Cruz Bay* ☎ *340/776–6201* 🌐 *www.nps.gov/viis.*

HIKING

Virgin Islands National Park has more than 20 trails from which to choose. Guided trips with the park service are a popular way to explore and are highly recommended, but you can also set out on your own. To find a hike that suits your ability, stop by the park's visitor center in Cruz Bay and pick up the free trail guide; it details points of interest, trail lengths, and estimated hiking times, as well as any dangers you might encounter. Although the park staff recommends long pants to protect against thorns and insects, most people hike in shorts because it can get very hot. Wear sturdy shoes or hiking boots even if you're hiking to the beach. Don't forget to bring water and insect repellent.

HORSEBACK RIDING

Carolina Corral

HORSEBACK RIDING | FAMILY | Clip-clop along the island's byways for a slower-paced tour of St. John. Carolina Corral offers horseback trips and donkey wagon rides down scenic roads with owner Dana Bartlett. She has a way with animals and calms even novice riders. It's $85 for a two-hour ride. ✉ *Off Rte. 10, Coral Bay* ☎ *340/693–5778* 🌐 *www.horsesstjohn.com.*

SEA KAYAKING

Poke around the clear bays here and explore undersea life from an easy-to-paddle sit-on-top kayak. Rental rates run about $65 for a full day in a double kayak. Tours start at $110 for a half-day.

Arawak Expeditions

KAYAKING | This company uses traditional and sit-on-top kayaks for exploring the waters around St. John. They also rent stand-up paddleboards (SUP). Multiday kayak and SUP paddle and beach camping tours to neighboring deserted islands are also offered. ✉ *Mongoose Junction Shopping Center, North Shore Rd., Cruz Bay* ☎ *340/693–8312, 800/238–8687* 🌐 *www.arawakexp.com.*

Cinnamon Bay Watersports
KAYAKING | You can also rent kayaks, stand-up paddleboards, bodyboards, small sailboats, and surfboards at this outfitter. ✉ *Rte. 20, Cinnamon Bay* ☎ *340/693–5902, 340/626–4769.*

Crabby's Watersports
BOATING | Explore Coral Bay Harbor and Hurricane Hole on the eastern end of the island in a sea kayak or on a stand-up paddleboard from Crabby's, which also rents snorkel gear, beach chairs, umbrellas, coolers, and floats. ✉ *Rte. 107, next to Cocoloba shopping center, Coral Bay* ☎ *340/626–1570* 🌐 *www.crabbyswatersports.com.*

Virgin Islands Ecotours
KAYAKING | Coral reefs, lush seagrass beds filled with marine life, and even sea turtles are among the interesting sights you can encounter when renting kayaks, SUPs, and snorkel gear from this outfitter at Honeymoon Beach, along the northwest coast of St. John. ✉ *Honeymoon Beach, Rte. 20, Estate Caneel Bay* ☎ *340/779–2155, 877/684–2441* 🌐 *www.viecotours.com.*

St. Croix

History is a big draw in St. Croix: among the island's visitors are Danes who come to explore the island's colonial past as well as spending some time sunning at the island's powdery beaches, getting pampered at the hotels, and dining at interesting restaurants.

Until 1917, Denmark owned St. Croix and her sister Virgin Islands, a fact reflected in street names in the main towns of Christiansted and Frederiksted as well as the surnames of many island residents. In the 18th and 19th centuries, some of those early Danish settlers, as well as other Europeans, owned plantations, worked by African slaves and white indentured servants lured to St. Croix to pay off their debts. Some of the plantation ruins—such as the Christiansted National Historic Site, the ruins at St. George Village Botanical Garden, and those at Estate Mount Washington—are open for easy exploration. Others are on private land, but a drive around the island reveals the ruins of plantations here and there on St. Croix's 84 square miles (218 square km). Their windmills, greathouses, and factories are all that's left of the hundreds of plantations that once grew sugarcane, tobacco, and other crops. Many local place names still bear the "Estate" monikers established by the Dutch centuries ago.

An economic downturn began in 1801, when the British briefly occupied the island. The end of the slave trade in 1803, an additional British occupation (from 1807 to 1815), droughts, the development of the sugar-beet industry in Europe, political upheaval, and an economic depression all sent the island into a downward economic spiral.

An 1848 slave revolt led to all remaining slaves on St. Croix being freed, but subsequent harsh labor laws saw the former slaves working in conditions little changed from their days of being treated as property. In 1878, a bloody, women-led labor revolt known as the Fireburn resulted in marginally improved conditions; put down brutally, the Fireburn is nonetheless remembered with pride on the island. In a move overwhelmingly supported by Crucians, Denmark sold St. Croix, St. John, and St. Thomas to the United States in 1916, and island residents were made U.S. citizens in 1927. Prohibition, however, crippled the island's rum industry, and President Herbert Hoover called the territory an "effective poorhouse" during a 1931 visit. The rise of tourism in the late 1950s and 1960s brought some economic improvements coupled with an influx of residents from other Caribbean islands (notably from Puerto Rico) and the mainland. The Limetree Bay oil refinery was an economic stimulus until it shuttered its doors in 2012; the facility reopened in 2021. The economy is mostly recovered from the aftereffects of the two hurricanes—Irma and Maria—that hit St. Croix in 2017; most businesses that closed due to storm damage have reopened, but some remain temporarily or permanently shuttered.

Today suburban subdivisions fill the fields where sugarcane once waved in the tropical breeze. Condominium complexes line the beaches along the north coast outside Christiansted. Large houses dot the rolling hillsides. Modern strip malls and shopping centers sit along major roads, and it's as easy to find a McDonald's as it is Caribbean fare. Yet it only takes only a little effort to get away from 21st-century civilization and step back into the island's past.

GETTING HERE AND AROUND

Visitors to St. Croix generally fly into Henry Rohlsen International Airport in Christiansted (which has direct flights from many U.S. cities), debark from a cruise ship, or take a ferry from St. Thomas. Although there are plenty of things to see and do in St. Croix's "twin cities," Christiansted and Frederiksted (both named after Danish kings), there are also lots of interesting spots in between and to the east of Christiansted. Just be sure you have a map in hand or downloaded to your cell phone: many secondary roads are unmarked. If you get confused, ask for help—locals are happy to point you in the right direction.

BEACHES

St. Croix's beaches aren't as spectacular as those on St. John or St. Thomas. But that's not to say you won't find some good places to spread out for a day on the water. The best beach is on nearby Buck Island, a national monument where a marked snorkeling trail leads you through an extensive coral reef while a soft, sandy beach beckons a few yards away. Other great options are the West End beaches both south and north of Frederiksted. You can park yourself at any of the handful of restaurants north of Frederiksted. Some rent loungers, and you can get food and drink right on the beach. Remember: Never leave valuables in the car or unattended on the beach.

RESTAURANTS

Seven flags have flown over St. Croix, and each has left its legacy in the island's cuisine. Fresh local seafood is plentiful and always good; wahoo, mahimahi, and conch are most popular. Island chefs often add Caribbean twists to familiar dishes. For a true island experience, stop at a local restaurant for goat stew, curried chicken, or roti. In most places you eat, your meal will be an informal affair. As is the case everywhere in the Caribbean, prices are higher than you'd pay on the mainland. Some restaurants may close for a week or two in September or October, so if you're traveling during these months, it's best to call ahead.

HOTELS

If you stay in either the Christiansted or Frederiksted areas, you'll be closest to shopping, restaurants, and nightlife. Most of the island's other hotels will put you just steps from the beach. St. Croix has several smaller properties that offer personalized service. If you like all the comforts of home, you may prefer a condominium or villa. Rates on St. Croix are competitive with those on other islands, and if you travel off-season, you can find steep discounts. Many properties offer money-saving honeymoon and dive packages, too. Whether you stay in a hotel, a condominium, or a villa, you'll enjoy up-to-date amenities, including Wi-Fi. Most properties have room TVs, but at some bed-and-breakfasts there might be only one in the common room.

Although a stay right in historic Christiansted may mean putting up with a little urban noise, you probably won't have trouble sleeping. Christiansted rolls up the sidewalks fairly early, and humming

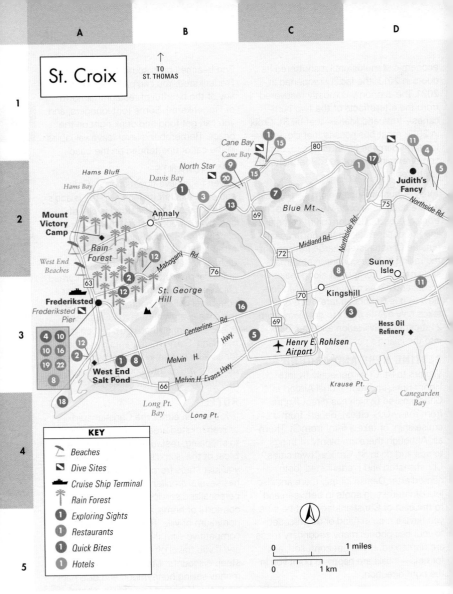

TO ST. THOMAS

1
2
3
4
5

Cane Bay
Cane Bay
North Star
Hams Bluff
Davis Bay
Hams Bay
Mount Victory Camp
Annaly
Blue Mt.
Judith's Fancy
Northside Rd.
Midland Rd.
Northside Rd.
Mahogany Rd.
Rain Forest
West End Beaches
Sunny Isle
Kingshill
St. George Hill
Frederiksted
Frederiksted Pier
Centerline Rd.
Hess Oil Refinery
Henry E. Rohlsen Airport
Melvin H. Hwy.
Melvin H. Evans Hwy.
West End Salt Pond
Krause Pt.
Canegarden Bay
Long Pt. Bay
Long Pt.
80
75
69
72
76
63
70
69
66

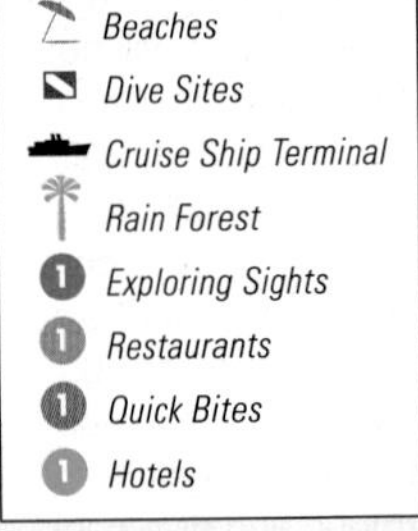

0 1 miles
0 1 km

Sights

1 Annaly Bay Tide Pools . **B2**
2 Buck Island Reef National Monument.... **G1**
3 Captain Morgan Distillery **C3**
4 Caribbean Museum Center for The Arts..... **A3**
5 Cruzan Rum Distillery .. **C3**
6 D. Hamilton Jackson Park **E2**
7 Estate Mount Washington Plantation................ **C2**
8 Estate Whim Museum .. **B3**
9 Fort Christiansvaern.... **E2**
10 Fort Frederick **A3**
11 Government House ... **E2**
12 Little La Grange Farm and Lawaetz Museum....... **A3**
13 Mt. Eagle................ **B2**
14 Old Danish Customs House **E2**
15 Point Udall............... **H2**
16 St. George Village Botanical Garden....... **B3**
17 Salt River Bay National Historical Park and Ecological Preserve.... **D2**
18 Sandy Point National Wildlife Refuge.......... **A4**
19 Scale House............. **E2**
20 Steeple Building **E2**

Restaurants

1 AMA at Cane Bay....... **C1**
2 Beach Side Café........ **A3**
3 Café Christine **E2**
4 Duggan's Reef **G2**
5 40 Eats and Drinks...... **E2**
6 The Galleon............. **F2**
7 Goat Soup and Whiskey **G2**
8 La Reine Chicken Shack **C2**
9 The Landing Beach Bar........................ **B2**

E F G H

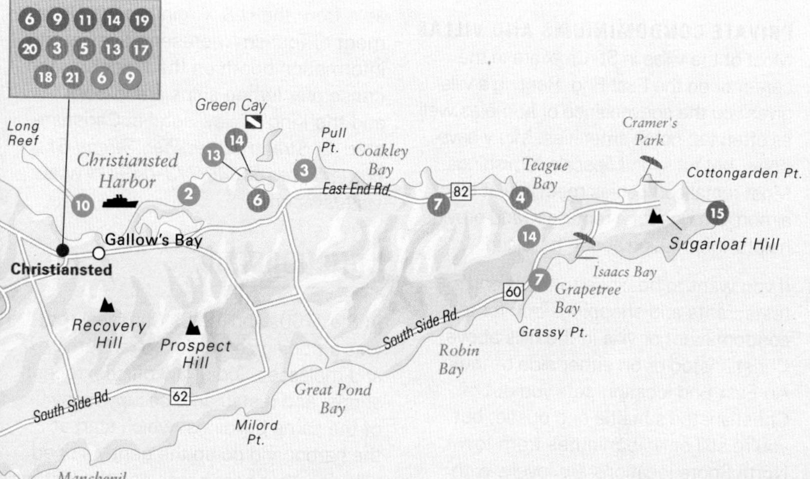

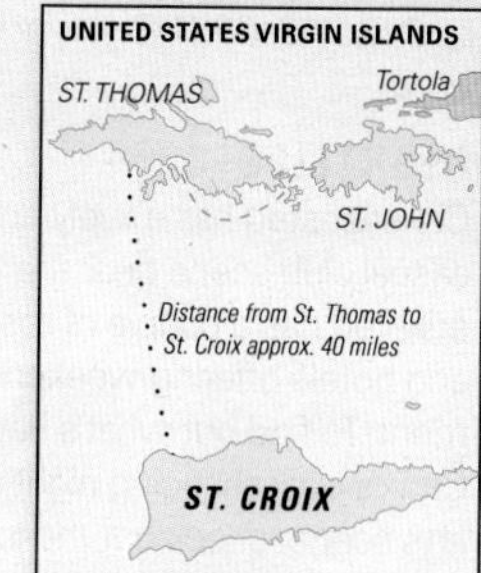

1
2
3
4
5

- 10 Louie and Nachos Beach Bar A3
- 11 Martha's Deli D3
- 12 Mt. Pellier Domino Club B2
- 13 Nate's Boathouse E2
- 14 The New Deep End Bar & Grill F2
- 15 Off the Wall C2
- 16 Polly's at the Pier A3
- 17 Rum Runners E2
- 18 Savant E2
- 19 Six Nine Restaurant and Bar A3
- 20 Spratnet Beach Bar ... B2
- 21 Too.Chez E2
- 22 Turtle's Deli and BBQ ... A3

Quick Bites

- 1 Armstrong's Homemade Ice Cream A3
- 2 Nidulari Artisan Bakery A3

Hotels

- 1 Arawak Bay: The Inn at Salt River ... D2
- 2 The Buccaneer E2
- 3 Carambola Beach Resort and Spa B2
- 4 Club St.Croix D2
- 5 Colony Cove D2
- 6 Company House Hotel . E2
- 7 Divi Carina Bay Resort and Casino G2
- 8 The Fred A3
- 9 Hotel Caravelle E2
- 10 Hotel on the Cay E2
- 11 The Palms at Pelican Cove D2
- 12 Sand Castle on the Beach A3
- 13 Tamarind Reef Resort .. F2
- 14 Villa Madeleine G2
- 15 Waves Cane Bay C1

air conditioners drown out any noise. Solitude is guaranteed at hotels and inns outside Christiansted and those on the outskirts of sleepy Frederiksted.

PRIVATE CONDOMINIUMS AND VILLAS
Most of the villas in St. Croix are in the center or on the East End. Renting a villa gives you the convenience of home as well as often top-notch amenities. Many have pools, hot tubs, and upscale furnishings. Most rental companies meet you at the airport, arrange for a rental car, and provide helpful information about the island.

If you want to be close to the island's restaurants and shopping, look for a condominium or villa in the hills above Christiansted or on either side of town. An East End location gets you out of Christiansted's hustle and bustle, but you're still only 15 minutes from town. North Shore locations are lovely, with gorgeous sea views and lots of peace and quiet. Frederiksted's small but charming downtown is within walking distance of several small hotels and inns.

RENTAL CONTACTS Vacation St. Croix. ✉ *400 La Grande Princess, Christiansted* ☎ *340/718–0361* 🌐 *www.vacationstcroix.com.*

NIGHTLIFE
Christiansted has a lively and eminently casual club scene near the waterfront. Frederiksted has a couple of restaurants, bars, and hotels offering weekend entertainment. To find out what's happening in St. Croix's ever-changing nightlife and eclectic arts scene, check out the local newspapers—*V.I. Daily News* and *St. Croix Avis.*

SHOPPING
Although the shopping on St. Croix isn't as varied or extensive as that on St. Thomas, the island does have several small stores with unusual merchandise. St. Croix shop hours are usually Monday through Saturday 9 to 5, but there are some shops in Christiansted open in the evening. Stores are often closed on Sunday.

VISITOR INFORMATION
St. Croix Visitor Center
VISITOR CENTER | Friendly advice as well as useful maps and brochures are available from the U.S. Virgin Islands Department of Tourism representatives at the information booth on the Fredericksted cruise pier (when ships are in port) and the King's Alley Hotel in Christiansted. ✉ *Strand Street Pier, Strand St., Frederiksted* ☎ *340/773–0495* 🌐 *www.visitusvi.com.*

Christiansted

In the 1700s and 1800s Christiansted was a trading center for sugar, rum, and molasses. Today law offices, tourist shops, and restaurants occupy many of the same buildings, which start at the harbor and go up the gently sloped hillsides. Your best bet to see the historic sights in this Danish-style town is in the morning, when it's still cool, although many buildings offer shade provided by historic arcaded walkways. Break for lunch at an open-air restaurant before exploring the many shopping opportunities. The city is the undisputed nightlife capital of St. Croix.

 Sights

★ D. Hamilton Jackson Park
CITY PARK | When you're tired of sightseeing, stop at this shady park on the street side of Fort Christiansvaern for a rest. It's named for a famed labor leader, judge, and journalist who started the first newspaper not under the thumb of the Danish crown (his birthday, November 1, is a territorial holiday celebrated with much fanfare in St. Croix). Public restrooms are available. ✉ *Between Fort Christiansvaern and Danish Customs House, Christiansted.*

Fort Christiansvaern is a National Historic Site.

★ Fort Christiansvaern

MILITARY SIGHT | FAMILY | The large yellow fortress dominates the waterfront. Because it's so easy to spot, it makes a good place to begin a walking tour. In 1749 the Danish built the fort to protect the harbor, but the structure was repeatedly damaged by hurricane-force winds and had to be partially rebuilt in 1771. It's now a National Historic Site, the best preserved of the few remaining Danish-built forts in the Virgin Islands. The park's visitor center is here, and rangers are on hand to answer questions. ✉ *Hospital St., Christiansted* ☎ *340/773–1460* 🌐 *www.nps.gov/chri* 🎟 *$7.*

Government House

GOVERNMENT BUILDING | One of the town's most elegant structures was built as a home for a Danish merchant in 1747. Today it houses offices and serves as the residence of the governor of the Virgin Islands. A sweeping staircase leads to a second-story ballroom, still used for official government functions. Out front, the traditional red Danish guard booth with its pointed top used to be a popular photo op, but it's now inaccessible to the public for security reasons. ✉ *105 King St., Christiansted* ☎ *340/773–1404.*

Old Danish Customs House

HISTORIC SIGHT | FAMILY | Built in 1830 on foundations that date from a century earlier, the historic building, which is near Fort Christiansvaern, originally served as both a customs house and a post office. In 1926 it became the Christiansted Library, and it's been a national park facility since 1972. It's closed to the public, but the sweeping front steps make a nice place to take a break. ✉ *King St., Christiansted* ☎ *340/773–1460* 🌐 *www.nps.gov/chri.*

Scale House

HISTORIC SIGHT | FAMILY | This 1856 building on the Christiansted waterfront was once where goods passing through the port were weighed and inspected. Visitors can see an old Danish scale on the ground floor. ✉ *King St., Christiansted* ☎ *340/773–1460* 🌐 *www.nps.gov/chri.*

★ Steeple Building
HISTORY MUSEUM | The first Danish Lutheran church on the island when it was built in 1753, the Steeple Building has been given new life as a museum with archaeological artifacts and exhibits on plantation life, the architectural development of Christiansted, the island's native inhabitants, and one-time St. Croix resident Alexander Hamilton. As of this writing, however, the building was closed for roof repairs. Admission, when it's open, is included in the price of visiting Christiansted National Historic Site. ✉ *Church St., Christiansted* ☎ *340/773–1460* 🌐 *www.nps.gov/chri* 🎫 *$7.*

 Restaurants

Café Christine
$$ | FRENCH | At this local lunchtime favorite the presentation is as dazzling as the food and the tropical artwork hanging in the dining room. The small menu changes daily, but look for dishes like croque monsieur or madame, a homemade falafel pita with local tomatoes and pickled onions drizzled with cucumber yogurt sauce, and daily quiche specials. **Known for:** daily changing menu; perfect lemon tart; views of historic Christiansted. $ *Average main: $14* ✉ *Apothecary Hall Courtyard, 6 Company St., Christiansted* ☎ *340/713–1500* 💳 *No credit cards* ⏲ *Closed Sat.–Mon.*

★ 40 Eats and Drinks
$$$ | ECLECTIC | This trendy place is small and cozy with a casual atmosphere. The menu selections include fresh fish prepared in creative ways, Italian specialties, and salads made with fresh local greens—check the daily specials on the blackboard. **Known for:** craft cocktails; creative seafood dishes; macaroni and cheese. $ *Average main: $25* ✉ *40 Strand St., Christiansted* ☎ *340/692–0524* 🌐 *www.facebook.com/40strandeatery.*

Martha's Deli
$$ | CARIBBEAN | This modest storefront eatery fills up with locals getting to-go orders of the restaurant's traditional Crucian breakfast, including salt fish, johnnycakes, eggs, cucumber salad, sautéed spinach, and—in a nod to the island's Danish heritage—herring. Lunch options include chicken, shrimp, and fish rotis, and a popular vegetable lentil soup. **Known for:** delicious lentil soup; traditional Crucian breakfast; numerous roti options. $ *Average main: $13* ✉ *300 Peters Rest, Christiansted* ☎ *340/773–6054* ⏲ *Closed Sun. and Mon.*

Nate's Boathouse
$$$ | ECLECTIC | Serving breakfast, lunch, and dinner indoors and out, the dockside spot has something for everyone on its extensive menu. Dinner can be as fancy as tilapia and garlic shrimp with mushrooms, white wine, and garlic butter, or as basic as a burger or chicken sandwich. **Known for:** Sunday brunch; Happy hour drinks specials; extensive menu. $ *Average main: $26* ✉ *1201 King Cross St., at the boardwalk, Christiansted* ☎ *340/692–6283* 🌐 *www.natesboathouse.com.*

★ Rum Runners
$$$ | ECLECTIC | FAMILY | Sitting right on the Christiansted boardwalk behind the Hotel Caravelle, Rum Runners serves a little bit of everything, including a to-die-for tropical salad topped with fresh local mango (in season) or pineapple. Heartier fare includes ribs and lime shrimp and spaghetti tossed with crab and bacon. **Known for:** boardwalk location; stellar views; local hangout. $ *Average main: $30* ✉ *Hotel Caravelle, 1044 Queen Cross St., Christiansted* ☎ *340/773–6585* 🌐 *www.rumrunnersstcroix.com* ⏲ *Closed Tues. and Wed.*

★ Savant
$$$$ | ECLECTIC | One of those small but special spots that everyone loves, including critics who regularly rank it among the Caribbean's best restaurants, this lively spot relies on local ingredients in its

fusion of Mexican, Thai, and Caribbean dishes that can include anything from Thai curry with chicken to a fillet of beef stuffed with portobello mushrooms and goat cheese. You can't go wrong with the daily egg roll special or the catch of the day. **Known for:** courtyard dining; bustling atmosphere; creative fusion fare. *$ Average main: $35 ✉ 4C Hospital St., Christiansted ☎ 340/713–8666 🌐 www.savantstx.com ⏲ Closed Sun. No lunch.*

Too.Chez

$$$ | **FRENCH** | This beautiful courtyard restaurant serves French-inspired American cuisine; the barbecued ribs are excellent, and you can do a partially healthy offset by ordering the roasted Brussels sprouts dip and scooping it onto flatbread. Don't skip the desserts, particularly the apple crisp topped with house-made vanilla ice cream. **Known for:** creative Caribbean cuisine; desserts that are worth the calories; courtyard dining. *$ Average main: $28 ✉ 53 King St., Christiansted ☎ 340/713–8888 🌐 www.toochezstx.com ⏲ Closed Sun. and Mon.*

Hotels

Company House Hotel

$ | **HOTEL** | This high-end boutique hotel seamlessly blends with the traditional Danish buildings on one of Christiansted's most historic streets. **Pros:** air-conditioned rooms; in the heart of Christiansted; quaint courtyard pool. **Cons:** no restaurant; busy location; street noise can be an issue. *$ Rooms from: $244 ✉ 2 Company St., Christiansted ☎ 340/773–1377 🌐 www.hotelcompanyhouse.com ⇆ 33 rooms 🍽 No Meals.*

Hotel Caravelle

$ | **HOTEL** | A stay at the Caravelle, which is near the harbor, puts you at the waterfront end of a pleasant shopping arcade and steps from shops and restaurants. **Pros:** parking on-site; good restaurant; convenient location. **Cons:** busy neighborhood; pool closed for renovations as of this writing; no beach. *$ Rooms from: $169 ✉ 44A Queen Cross St., Christiansted ☎ 340/773–0687 🌐 www.hotelcaravelle.com ⇆ 43 rooms 🍽 No Meals.*

Hotel on the Cay

$ | **RESORT** | Hop on the free ferry to reach this peaceful time-share resort in the middle of Christiansted Harbor and offering pleasantly furnished rooms with harbor views, balconies or patios, and kitchenettes for times when you don't want to eat at the hotel's beach bar. **Pros:** lovely beach; quiet; convenient location. **Cons:** no parking; could use renovating; accessible only by a short ferry ride. *$ Rooms from: $247 ✉ Protestant Cay, Christiansted ☎ 340/773–2035, 855/654–0301 🌐 www.hotelonthecay.com ⇆ 54 rooms 🍽 No Meals.*

Nightlife

BARS

The Beach Bar at Hotel on the Cay

THEMED ENTERTAINMENT | For a mini adventure in downtown Christiansted, hop the two-minute ferry to this hotel bar on Protestant Cay for trivia Wednesdays, live music on weekends, and periodic Tiki Tuesday parties with a luau-style buffet, steel pan bands, fire dancers, and moko jumbie performers. The beach bar is open until 10, and the ferry from the Christiansted boardwalk—normally $5 per person for non–hotel guests—is free after 5 pm. *✉ Protestant Cay, Christiansted ☎ 340/773–2035 🌐 www.hotelonthecay.com.*

Breakers Roar Tiki Bar

BARS | Classic rum-based drinks in decorative tiki glasses (think: zombies, mai tais and hurricanes) star at this dark, atmospheric bar with indoor and outdoor space. For something local, try the Iloilo, made with Mutiny vodka, or the Merciful Mistress, a tiki drink built around light Cruzan Diamond Estate rum. Small plates are available for noshing, including a pupu platter, of course. *✉ The*

King Christian Hotel, 1102 King's Wharf, Christiansted ☎ 340/773–6330 🌐 www.breakersroar.com.

★ Brew STX

LIVE MUSIC | Locals and visitors come here to drink freshly brewed mango lager and listen to live music several nights a week. Oh, and there are crab races on Mondays. A nice selection of appetizers and sandwiches, plus shareable build-your-own salads make this waterfront microbrewery a fun place to nosh while you work your way through beer flights and people-watch on the boardwalk. ✉ *Boardwalk at King's Alley, 55 A&B King's Alley, Christiansted* ☎ *340/719–6339* 🌐 *www.brewstx.com.*

Shopping

In Christiansted the best shopping areas are the **Pan Am Pavilion** and **Caravelle Arcade,** off Strand Street, and along **King** and **Company streets.** These streets give way to arcades filled with boutiques. The **Gallows Bay** shopping area has a few stores and eateries in a quiet neighborhood.

BOOKS

Undercover Books

BOOKS | This well-stocked independent bookseller sells Caribbean-themed books as well as the latest good reads. Saturday morning (11:30 am) story hour is a good rainy-day activity for kids, and frequent book-signing events feature local authors, many of whom also participate in the annual St. Croix Literary Festival, which takes place in April. The store is in the Gallows Bay shopping area. ✉ *5030 Anchor Way, Suite 11, Gallows Bay* ✣ *Across from the post office* ☎ *340/719–1567* 🌐 *www.undercoverbooksstcroix.com.*

CLOTHING

From the Gecko Boutique

MIXED CLOTHING | This store sells the most stylish men's and women's clothes on St. Croix, including a selection of fair trade and organic clothing, smart handbags, hats, swimwear, CBD products, and star-shaped paper lanterns. Bright, island-friendly colors rule the racks here. ✉ *55 Company St., Suite 1, Christiansted* ☎ *340/778–9433* 🌐 *www.fromthegecko.com.*

★ Hotheads Boutique

MIXED CLOTHING | As the name implies, this small store sells hats, yes, but they're often perched on top of cotton shifts, comfortable shirts, and trendy tropical wear from designers like Sigrid Olsen, Cenia, THML, and Anne Cole Resort. If you forgot your bathing suit, Hotheads has a good selection. ✉ *1244 Queen Cross St., Christiansted* ☎ *340/773–7888.*

Susan Mango

WOMEN'S CLOTHING | Austin native and fashion wholesaler Susan Connett brings her sense of style to St. Croix with a dazzling variety of resort wear, beach-wear, and fabrics sourced from women producers in Bali, Africa, Guatemala, and elsewhere. Come on Wednesday for free interior design advice from the owner. ✉ *54 King St., Christiansted* ☎ *512/689–7049.*

GIFTS

Many Hands

SOUVENIRS | This shop sells pottery in bright colors, paintings of St. Croix and the Caribbean, prints, and maps. They are all made by local artists, and they all make for perfect take-home gifts.

■ TIP→ The owners ship all over the world. ✉ *6 Pan Am Pavilion, 1102 Strand St., Christiansted* ☎ *340/773–1990.*

Mitchell-Larsen Studio

SOUVENIRS | This glass gallery offers an interesting amalgam of carefully crafted glass plates, suncatchers, and more. The pieces, all made on-site by St. Croix glassmaker Jan Mitchell Larsen, are often whimsically adorned with tropical fish, flora, and fauna. Photography from Steffen Larsen also is on display and for sale. ✉ *2000 Company St., Christiansted* ☎ *340/719–1000* 🌐 *www.mitchelllarsen-studio.com.*

Purple Papaya Souvenir and Gift Shop

SOUVENIRS | The largest store in downtown Christiansted is stuffed with every type of souvenir imaginable (tacky and otherwise). This is the place to go for St. Croix T-shirts, sandals, sunglasses, swimsuits, and beach towels as well as trinkets like shot glasses, coffee mugs, and magnets. ✉ *39 Strand St., Christiansted* ☎ *340/713–9412.*

JEWELRY

★ Crucian Gold

JEWELRY & WATCHES | St. Croix native Brian Bishop's trademark piece is the Turk's Head ring (a knot of interwoven gold strands). The family tradition continues with his kids, Nathan and Therese, creating contemporary sterling and gold pendants, rings, and earrings, necklaces, and pendants. Stop by to meet the Bishops, browse the jewelry, and "Feel the Love."✉ *1112 Strand St., Christiansted* ☎ *340/244–2996, 877/773–5241* 🌐 *www.cruciangold.com.*

★ ib designs

JEWELRY & WATCHES | This small shop showcases the handcrafted jewelry of local craftsman and "Island Boy" Whealan Massicott, including his signature, "infinity" style Crucian hook bracelet. Whether in silver or gold, the designs are simply elegant. ✉ *2108 Company St., Christiansted* ☎ *340/773–4322* 🌐 *www.ibdesignsvi.com.*

Oceanique Creations

JEWELRY & WATCHES | Chaney is jewelry made from shards of the antique Danish pottery that's found all over St. Croix; local residents find it in the ocean or buried in the ground and sell it to the owners of this Christiansted jewelry shop, who clean it, polish it, wrap it in silver wire, and sell it as earrings, necklaces, and bracelets. Seaglass jewelry is also sold here; like chaney, it's made in St. Croix. ✉ *1000 King St., Suite 1G, Christiansted* ☎ *305/438–3012* 🌐 *www.chaneychicks.com.*

Sonya Ltd.

JEWELRY & WATCHES | This boutique was founded by Crucian designer Sonya Hough, who invented the popular hook bracelet (wear the hook facing out if you're "available," inward if you're attached). Bracelets are priced from about $65 and up, depending on size and materials. In addition to the original silver and gold hooks in a variety of diameters, the shop sells variations that incorporate hurricane symbols, dolphins, hibiscus flowers, and infinity symbols. If you're going to splurge on one nice souvenir in St. Croix, make it a hook bracelet and you'll be recognized as an honorary Crucian whenever you wear it. ✉ *2101 Company St., Christiansted* ☎ *340/773–8924* 🌐 *www.sonyaltdstore.com.*

Under the Sun VI

JEWELRY & WATCHES | Designer Rob Low and the jewelers at Under the Sun VI can create one-of-a-kind pieces to your design. The shop specializes in gold jewelry but also carries diamonds, emeralds, rubies, and sapphires, and jewelry made from Crucian chaney and Dominican larimar. ✉ *1102 Strand St., Christiansted* ☎ *340/773–0365* 🌐 *www.underthesunvi.com.*

LIQUOR AND TOBACCO

Baci Duty Free

DUTY-FREE | The walk-in humidor here has a good selection of Arturo Fuente, Partagas, Padron, and Macanudo cigars. Baci also carries high-end liquor; sleek watches from Tissot, Frederick Constance, Alpina, Mido, Luminox, Citizen, and Bering; Steiner binoculars from Germany; and fine jewelry. ✉ *1235 Queen Cross St., Christiansted* ☎ *340/773–5040* 🌐 *www.facebook.com/bacidutyfree.*

West of Christiansted

Reef-protected Christiansted Bay stretches westward to Salt River Bay, Christopher Columbus's 1492 landing site on St. Croix. The quiet west side of the bay is dotted with small resorts and beach condos, while local restaurants (and one of the island's two McDonalds) are scattered along Northside Road. The coastal Estate Little Princess Plantation is a 1730s sugar plantation maintained by the Nature Conservancy. It's currently closed to the public.

Hotels

Club St. Croix

$ | **HOTEL** | **FAMILY** | Sitting beachfront just outside Christiansted, this condominium complex faces a lovely stretch of sand and also has a pool. **Pros:** beachfront location; good restaurant; full kitchens. **Cons:** need car to get around; no meals included; sketchy neighborhood. *Rooms from: $215 ✉ 3280 Golden Rock, Estate Golden Rock ☎ 340/718–9150, 800/524–2025 www.antillesresorts.com 50 apartments No Meals.*

Colony Cove

$ | **HOTEL** | **FAMILY** | In a string of condominium complexes, Colony Cove lets you experience comfortable beachfront living, offering large units that all have two bedrooms, two bathrooms, and washer–dryer combos—it's a good choice for families. **Pros:** beachfront location; swimming pool; good views. **Cons:** need car to get around; no meals included; sketchy neighborhood. *Rooms from: $240 ✉ 3221 Golden Rock, Estate Golden Rock ☎ 340/718–1965, 800/524–2025 www.antillesresorts.com 62 apartments No Meals.*

The Palms at Pelican Cove

$ | **RESORT** | A 10-minute drive from Christiansted's interesting shopping and restaurants, this resort, with its eclectic mix of guests, sits on a gorgeous strand of white sand, its beachfront rooms with clean, modern designs, dark-wood furnishings, framed tropical photos, and tile floors. **Pros:** nice beach; good restaurant; friendly staff. **Cons:** need car to get out and about; no meals included; neighborhood not the best. *Rooms from: $225 ✉ 4126 La Grande Princess, La Grande Princesse ☎ 340/718–8920, 800/548–4460 info@palmspelican-cove.com www.palmspelicancove.com 38 rooms No Meals.*

Shopping

FOOD

Pueblo

SUPERMARKET | This chain supermarket carries dry goods, fresh produce, meat, and seafood. There are two locations in greater Christiansted—in Orange Grove, which is closer to downtown, and La Reine. *✉ Golden Rock Shopping Center, Rte. 75, Christiansted ☎ 340/718–0118 www.wfmpueblo.com.*

East End

An easy drive along flat, well-marked roads to St. Croix's eastern end takes you through some choice real estate. Ruins of old sugar estates dot the landscape. You can make the entire loop on the road that circles the island in about an hour, a good way to end the day. But there are also enough nice beaches, easy walks, and lunch spots to spend a full day. Point Udall, at the eastern tip of St. Croix, is the first place the sun rises on U.S. land (at least in the Western Hemisphere).

Sights

★ Buck Island Reef National Monument

ISLAND | This national monument has pristine beaches that are just right for sunbathing, but there's also some shade for those who don't want to fry. The snorkeling trail set in the reef allows close-up study of coral formations and tropical fish. Overly warm seawater temperatures have led to a condition called coral bleaching that has killed some of the coral. The reefs are starting to recover, but how long it will take is anyone's guess. There's a hiking trail to the island's highest point (328 feet) and an overlook where you are rewarded for your efforts by spectacular views of St. John. Charter-boat trips leave daily from the Christiansted waterfront or from Green Cay Marina, about 2 miles (3 km) east of Christiansted. Big Beard's Adventure Tours, Caribbean Sea Adventures, and Buck Island Charters offer half- and full-day trips. ✉ *Off East End of St. Croix* ☎ *340/773–1460* 🌐 *www.nps.gov/buis.*

Point Udall

VIEWPOINT | This rocky promontory, marked by a large stone sundial sculpture, is the easternmost point in the United States; it's about a half-hour drive from Christiansted. A paved road takes you to an overlook with glorious views; it's an especially popular gathering spot on New Year's Day for those who want to be the first to greet the first sunrise of the year. Adventurous visitors can hike down to the pristine beach below. On the way back to town, look for the Castle Aura, an enormous Moorish-style mansion. It was built by the late Nadia Farber, the former Contessa de Navarro, and an extravagant local character. ✉ *Rte. 82, Whim.*

Beaches

★ Buck Island

BEACH | Part of Buck Island Reef National Monument, this is a must-see for anyone in St. Croix. The beach is beautiful, but its finest treasures are those you can see when you plop off the boat and adjust your mask, snorkel, and fins to swim over colorful coral and darting fish. Don't know how to snorkel? No problem—the boat crew will have you outfitted and in the water in no time. Take care not to step on those black-pointed spiny sea urchins or touch the mustard-color fire coral, which can cause a nasty burn. Most charter-boat trips start with a snorkel over the lovely reef before a stop at the island's beach. A hike leads uphill to an overlook for a bird's-eye view of the reef below. **Amenities:** none. **Best for:** snorkeling; swimming. ☎ *340/773–1460* 🌐 *www.nps.gov/buis.*

Restaurants

Duggan's Reef

$$$$ | SEAFOOD | Boston native Frank Duggan left the cold of the Northeast for St. Croix decades ago and never looked back, opening a beachfront restaurant on Teague's Bay that lures locals, visitors, and the occasional celebrity with a mixed menu of steaks and seafood. The signature dish is a nod to the Duggan family's Irish roots—Caribbean lobster sautéed in whiskey. **Known for:** lobster dishes; waterfront setting; surf-and-turf fare. $ *Average main: $33* ✉ *5A Teague Bay, Teague's Bay* ☎ *773–9800* 🌐 *www.duggansreefstx.com* 🕒 *Closed Sun. and Mon.*

The Galleon

$$$ | ECLECTIC | This popular dockside restaurant is the place to get off-the-boat seafood and Southern soul food in St. Croix—chef-owner Charles Mereday is a graduate of the Charleston, S.C., branch of Johnson and Wales University, after all. But you'll also find hand-cut steaks alongside island favorites like curried chicken and mango mahimahi. **Known for:** marina views; shrimp and grits; island classics. $ *Average main: $30* ✉ *Tamarind Reef Resort, Green Cay Marina off Rte. 82, Annas Hope* ☎ *340/244–6007* 🌐 *www.thegalleonstcroix.com* 🕒 *Closed Sun. and Mon. No lunch.*

★ Goat Soup and Whiskey

$$$ | ECLECTIC | The unlikely third location of a small string of same-named restaurants—the others are in Keystone, Colo. and Put-in-Bay, Ohio—this stylish open-air dining room overlooks the pool of a condo complex. The lunch menu includes a variety of burgers and sandwiches (yes, a lamb burger is an option), while dinner is a mix of hand-cut steaks and pasta dishes. **Known for:** attractive dining room; affordable lunch options; hand-cut steaks and goat stew. *Average main: $30 5000 Estate Coakley Bay, Christiansted 340/773–3333 www.soupandwhiskey.com Closed Wed.*

The New Deep End Bar & Grill
$$$ | ECLECTIC | A favorite with locals and vacationers, this poolside restaurant serves up salads, burgers, sandwiches, and seafood, as well as delicious pasta dishes and popular salads. Come for disco bingo on Thursday with dancing between games, the West Indian Carnival on Fridays, Sunday brunch, and live music on weekends. **Known for:** Sunday brunch; lively atmosphere; beach setting. *Average main: $23 Tamarind Reef Resort, 5001 Estate Southgate, Annas Hope 340/718–7071 www.newdeepend.com.*

Hotels

★ The Buccaneer
$$ | RESORT | FAMILY | Aimed at travelers who want everything at their fingertips, this family-friendly resort has sandy beaches, multiple restaurants, golf, tennis, a spa, and swimming pools. **Pros:** nice golf course; beachfront location; numerous activities. **Cons:** need car to get around; insular environment; pricey. *Rooms from: $320 5007 Estate Shoys, Shoys 340/712–2100, 800/255–3881 www.thebuccaneer.com 139 rooms Free Breakfast.*

Divi Carina Bay Resort and Casino
$$$$ | RESORT | An oceanfront location, one of the island's only casinos, and plenty of activities make this resort a reliable option for adults (guests must be 18 and over). **Pros:** on-site casino; spacious beach; good restaurant. **Cons:** staff can seem chilly; many stairs to climb; need car to get around. *Rooms from: $525 5025 Turner Hole Rd., Estate Turner Hole 340/773–9700, 800/367–3484 www.diviresorts.com 200 units All-Inclusive.*

Tamarind Reef Resort
$$ | HOTEL | Spread out along a sandy beach, these low-slung buildings offer casual comfort and appeal to independent travelers who want the option to eat in or out, as rooms have basic kitchenettes. **Pros:** good snorkeling; tasty restaurant; rooms have kitchenettes. **Cons:** need car to get around; there's a walk to the restaurants; motel-style rooms. *Rooms from: $308 5001 Tamarind Reef, off Rte. 82, Cotton Valley 340/718–4455, 800/619–0014 www.tamarindreefresort.com 40 rooms No Meals.*

Villa Madeleine
$$ | HOTEL | If you like privacy and your own private pool, you'll like Villa Madeleine, where villas flow downhill from a West Indian plantation greathouse. **Pros:** private pools; pleasant decor; full kitchens. **Cons:** no beachfront; need car to get around; lower units sometimes lack views. *Rooms from: $285 Off Rte. 82, Teague's Bay 340/690–3465 www.villamadeleine-stcroix.com 43 villas No Meals.*

Nightlife

Divi Carina Bay Casino
GATHERING PLACES | The larger of St. Croix's two casinos (the other is in downtown Christiansted) is located across the street from the Divi Carina Bay resort. For a night out on the island's East End the casino has reel-type slot machines, video poker, and table games including blackjack, poker, roulette, and craps. Guests of the all-inclusive Divi Carina Bay eat and drink free at the Carina Cafe. *25 Rte. 60, Estate Turner Hole 340/773–7529 www.divicarina.com.*

Ziggy's Island Market

GATHERING PLACES | A town in the U.S. that claimed a gas station as its best party scene would be a laughingstock, but Ziggy's is a point of pride for East End residents on St. Croix. A place to fuel up and pick up groceries by day, Ziggy's transforms into a quirky nightlife spot with hot BBQ food and a lively bar scene where the music pumps well into the evening. ✉ *5088 Estate Solitude, Cotton Valley* ☎ *340/773–8382.*

Shopping

FOOD

Seaside Market and Deli

SUPERMARKET | Although it's on the small side, this market has good-quality deli items, local produce, West Indian prepared foods, a florist, a bakery, and a pastry shop. ✉ *2001 Mount Welcome Rd., Christiansted* ☎ *340/719–9393* 🌐 *www.seasidemarketstx.com.*

Mid Island

A drive through the countryside between St. Croix's two big towns takes you past ruins of old plantations, many bearing whimsical names (Morningstar, Solitude, Upper Love). The traffic moves quickly—by island standards—on the main roads, but you can pause and poke around if you head down some side lanes. It's easy to find your way west, but driving from north to south requires good navigation. Don't leave your hotel without a map. Allow an entire day for this trip, so you'll have enough time for a swim at a north-shore beach. Although you can find lots of casual eateries on the main roads, pick up a picnic lunch if you plan to head off the beaten path.

Sights

Captain Morgan Distillery

DISTILLERY | The base for Captain Morgan–brand rum is made from molasses at this massive, industrial-scale distillery. The tour includes exhibits on island and rum history, a movie about the process, and a tram ride through the distillery. An extensive gift shop features a wide variety of branded clothing and keepsakes as well as rum for purchase. The tour ends with tastings of the many varieties of Captain Morgan rum (the original spiced, white, aged, dark, and fruit flavored) plus two cocktails. ✉ *Melvin Evans Hwy. and Rte. 66, Annaberg and Shannon Grove* ☎ *340/713–5654* 🌐 *www.captainmorganvisitorcenter.com* 🎫 *$10* ⏲ *Closed weekends.*

★ Cruzan Rum Distillery

DISTILLERY | A tour of this distillery, established in 1760, culminates in a rum tasting, all of which are sold here at good prices—including more than a dozen flavored rums you'll find in popular St. Croix cocktails like the Cruzan Confusion. The distillery is also the best place to pick up a bottle or two of Cruzan's premium single-barrel and Estate Diamond rums. It's worth a stop to look at the charming old buildings and learn about the distillation process, even if you're not a rum connoisseur. ✉ *3A Estate Diamond, Frederiksted* ☎ *340/692–2280* 🌐 *www.cruzanrum.com* 🎫 *$10* ⏲ *Closed Sun.*

Estate Whim Museum

HISTORIC HOME | **FAMILY** | The restored estate, with a windmill, cookhouse, and other buildings, gives a sense of what life was like on St. Croix's sugar plantations in the 1800s. The oval-shape greathouse has high ceilings and antique furniture and utensils. Notice its fresh, airy atmosphere—the waterless stone moat around the greathouse was used not for defense, but for circulating cooling air. The estate produced sugar and molasses from 1767 to 1934, first with animal power, then wind, and finally with a steam engine to crush the cane. If you have kids, the grounds are the perfect place for them to run around, perhaps while you browse in the museum gift shop or attend a food demonstration using the still-functioning ovens in the cookhouse. It's just outside of Frederiksted. *Rte. 70, Whim* *340/772–0598* *www.stcroixlandmarks.org* *$10.*

★ St. George Village Botanical Garden

GARDEN | At this 17-acre estate, fragrant flora grows amid the ruins of a 19th-century sugarcane plantation (the former overseer's house has been left open to the elements as a habitat for native fruit bats). There are miniature versions of each ecosystem on St. Croix, from a semiarid cactus grove to a verdant rain forest, along with hiking trails, a small museum, and a collection of seashells. The garden's orchid and bromeliad blooms are impressive. *127 Estate St. George, Estate Saint George* *Turn north at sign* *340/692–2874* *www.sgvbg.org* *$10.*

Restaurants

★ La Reine Chicken Shack

$$ | **CARIBBEAN** | This barnlike "Crucian-Rican" restaurant is often the first stop that locals make before heading to the airport and after arriving back home. Out back, dozens of chickens slowly rotate on a giant rotisserie; in front, regulars and a smattering of in-the-know visitors queue up for the juicy birds, traditional johnnycakes, and local food like stewed oxtail and conch in butter sauce. **Known for:** local vibe; finger-licking-good rotisserie chicken; traditional johnnycakes. *Average main: $15* *24 Slob A-B Estate, La Reine* *340/778–5717* *Closed Sun.*

Mt. Pellier Domino Club

$ | **CARIBBEAN** | You don't have to eat like a pig at this West End restaurant and bar in the rain forest, but you can feed a whole can of beer to one. The giant hogs residing here have developed a taste for the suds, and for $3 you can buy a nonalcoholic beer and offer it up to a pig who will crush the can in its powerful jaws, chug down the ingredients, and spit out the crushed aluminum when done. **Known for:** "mamajuana," a mix of Cruzan rum, honey, roots, leaves, and spices alternatively touted for its hallucinogenic and aphrodisiacal qualities; beer-drinking pigs; local daily specials. *Average main: $6* *Mahogany Rd., Montpellier* *340/626–8116* *www.dominoclubstcroix.com.*

Shopping

FOOD

The Market St. Croix

SUPERMARKET | This supermarket has a good selection of Middle Eastern foods and island-sourced products, in addition to the usual grocery-store items. *14 Plessen, Frederiksted* *340/719–1870* *www.themarketvi.com.*

Plaza Extra East

SUPERMARKET | This full-service supermarket stocks both locally grown and imported produce as well as deli items, specialty foods, duty-free liquor, and pharmacy needs. Perky's Pizza is located here, too. *Rte. 70, Sion Farm* *340/778–6240* *www.plazaextraeast.com.*

Frederiksted and Environs

St. Croix's second-largest town, Frederiksted, was founded in 1751. Just as Christiansted is famed for its Danish buildings, Frederiksted is known for its Victorian architecture. A stroll around its historic sights will take you no more than an hour. Allow a little more time if you want to duck into the few small shops. One long cruise-ship pier juts into the sparkling sea; it's the perfect place to start a tour of this quaint town.

VISITOR INFORMATION

CONTACTS Frederiksted Visitor Center. ✉ *Pier Strand St., Frederiksted.*

Sights

Caribbean Museum Center for the Arts

ART MUSEUM | Sitting across from the waterfront in a historic building, this small museum hosts an always-changing roster of exhibits and also houses a bookstore and a gift shop. Some works are cutting-edge multimedia efforts that you might be surprised to find in such an out-of-the way location. Openings are popular events, as are the occasional jazz concerts presented in the upstairs galleries. The back courtyard is a peaceful space, where sculptures and statues are on display; free Wi-Fi is an added inducement to linger. ✉ *10 Strand St., Frederiksted* ☎ *340/772–2622* 🌐 *www.cmcarts.org* 🎫 *Free* ⏲ *Closed Sun. and Mon.*

Fort Frederik

MILITARY SIGHT | **FAMILY** | On July 3, 1848, some 8,000 slaves marched on this fort to demand their freedom. Danish governor Peter von Scholten, fearing they would burn the town to the ground, stood up in his carriage parked in front of the fort and granted their wish. The fort, completed in 1760, has walls constructed of coral and rubble bound together with molasses, a testament to the ingenuity and durability of 18th-century engineering. Climb the battlements for great views of the cruise dock and the Caribbean Sea. Inside, a museum includes exhibits on the slave trade, moko jumbies, seashells and seaglass, indigenous artifacts from Salt River Bay, and local mahogany furniture. ✉ *Waterfront, Frederiksted* 🌐 *www.nps.gov/places/fort-frederiksted-usvi.htm* 🎫 *$7* ⏲ *Closed weekends.*

Little La Grange Farm and Lawaetz Museum

FARM/RANCH | For a trip back in time, tour this circa-1750 farm in a valley at La Grange. Tours include the lovely two-story house, aqueducts once used to transport water and cane juice, and the Little La Grange Farm, which produces organic crops for sale through the Ridge to Reef program. The greathouse includes the four-poster mahogany bed 19th-century owner Carl Lawaetz shared with his wife, Marie, the china Marie painted, family portraits, and the fruit trees that fed the family for several generations. Initially a sugar plantation, the farm was subsequently used to raise cattle and grow produce. ✉ *Rte. 76 (Mahogany Rd.), Estate Little La Grange* ☎ *340/473–1557* 🌐 *www.ridge2reef.org/little-lagrange-farm.html* 🎫 *$15* ⏲ *Closed Sun.–Tues., Thurs.–Fri.*

Sandy Point National Wildlife Refuge

WILDLIFE REFUGE | Located at the western tip of St. Croix, this 383-acre wildlife sanctuary provides critical habitat for leatherback, green, and hawksbill sea turtles, which nest on the refuge's long, sandy beaches. The beaches are open to visitors when not occupied by turtles. The mangrove-fringed West End Salt Pond, which lies partly within the refuge's boundaries, is a bird-watcher's delight. ✉ *Veterans Shore Dr., Hesselberg* ☎ *340/773–4554* 🌐 *www.fws.gov/refuge/sandy_point* ⏲ *Closed weekdays and during turtle nesting season (Apr.–Aug.).*

Beaches

West End beaches

BEACH | There are several unnamed beaches along the coast road north of Frederiksted, but it's best if you don't stray too far from civilization. Most vacationers plop down their towel near one of the casual restaurants spread out along Route 63. The beach at the Rainbow Beach Club, a five-minute drive outside Frederiksted, has the lively Rhythms beach bar, a casual restaurant decorated with license plates from around the world, and West End Watersports, which rents Jet Skis, Flyboards, and stand-up paddleboards by the half hour and beach chairs and umbrellas by the day. The

Some of St. Croix's best beaches are on the West End of the island around Frederiksted.

beach is broad and sandy, the waters clear and calm. If you want to be close to the cruise-ship pier, just stroll on over to the adjacent sandy beach in front of Fort Frederik. On the way south out of Frederiksted, the stretch near Sandcastle on the Beach hotel is also lovely. **Amenities:** food and drink; water sports. **Best for:** snorkeling; swimming; walking. ⊠ *Rte. 63, north and south of Frederiksted, Frederiksted.*

 Restaurants

Beach Side Café

$$$ | **ECLECTIC** | Sunday brunch is big here, but locals and visitors also flock to this oceanfront bistro at the Sand Castle on the Beach resort for lunch and dinner. Both menus include burgers and salads, but at dinner the daily pasta specials shine. **Known for:** weekend brunch; oceanfront setting; seafood chowder. [$] *Average main: $22* ⊠ *Sand Castle on the Beach, 127 Smithfield, Frederiksted* ☎ *340/772–1266* ⊕ *www.sandcastleonthebeach.com.*

Louie and Nachos Beach Bar

$$ | **MEXICAN** | The fare served here is the farthest thing from traditional Mexican food—in addition to the usual ingredients you can get a taco stuffed with buffalo chicken, or jambalaya, and vegan options are available, too. The bar and restaurant are one story up, so the views of the beach and surf are nice. **Known for:** great ocean views; inventive tacos; Orange Crush cocktails. [$] *Average main: $12* ⊠ *37 Strand St., Frederiksted* ☎ *340/772–5151* ⊕ *www.louieandnachos.com.*

★ **Polly's at the Pier**

$$ | **ECLECTIC** | With an emphasis on fresh ingredients, this casual spot right on the waterfront serves delicious fare, starting with the BELT (bacon, egg, lettuce, and tomato) breakfast sandwich and continuing with gourmet grilled-cheese sandwiches with delicious additions like basil, Bosc pears, and avocado at lunch. Salads are a specialty, and many are made with local Bibb lettuce and organic mixed greens. **Known for:** neighborhood ambience; local ingredients; waterfront location. [$] *Average*

main: $13 ✉ 3 Strand St., Frederiksted ☎ 340/719–9434 🌐 www.pollysatthepierst-croix.com ⏲ No dinner.

Six Nine Restaurant and Bar

$$$ | **ECLECTIC** | Tucked away in a quiet courtyard a few steps from the Frederiksted Pier, this indoor-outdoor restaurant is a rarity on St. Croix: an eatery with a sommelier and about 20 wines by the glass. Steaks and seafood entrées are the top draw at dinner, while a lighter menu of sandwiches, tacos, and wraps is offered at lunch. **Known for:** bagels and lox at Sunday brunch; stellar wine selection; lovely courtyard. *Average main: $25 ✉ 69A King St., Frederiksted ☎ 340/772–6969 🌐 www.sixninestx.com ⏲ Closed Mon. No dinner Sun.*

Turtle's Deli and BBQ

$$ | **SANDWICHES** | **FAMILY** | Huge sandwiches at this tiny spot start with homemade bread and can be as basic as turkey and cheddar or as imaginative as the Beast, piled high with hot roast beef, raw onion, and melted Swiss cheese with horseradish and mayonnaise. Barbecue—including pulled pork, chicken, and brisket plates—is another highlight. **Known for:** ample shaded outdoor seating; good-size portions; barbecue. *Average main: $15 ✉ 625 Strand St., Frederiksted ☎ 340/772–3676 ⏲ No dinner.*

Coffee and Quick Bites

Armstrong's Homemade Ice Cream

$ | **ICE CREAM** | **FAMILY** | This family-run business has been using the same Danish ice-cream recipe with local flavorings since 1900. Stop in for a sweet treat that includes a wide variety of tropically flavored homemade ice cream—almond, ginger, peanut, coconut, pumpkin—plus seasonal varieties like gooseberry, guava, mango, soursop, and passion fruit. **Known for:** ice cream for breakfast is always an option; house-made ice cream; interesting seasonal flavors. *Average main: $5 ✉ 78-B Whim, Queen Mary Hwy., Whim ☎ 340/772–1919 🌐 www.facebook.com/armstrongshomemadeice-cream ⏲ Closed Sun.*

★ Nidulari Artisan Bakery

$$ | **BAKERY** | A distinctive gypsy cart on the side of Mahogany Road (Route 76) spills open with fresh baked breads, tarts, sandwiches, and toasties with unusual fillings like black bean hummus or homegrown banana. The farm-to-table menu, which changes daily to reflect what's available, includes local fare, Indian curries, British-influenced dishes, and Southern comfort food. **Known for:** everything is made from scratch; goods baked in a traditional brick oven; chocolate made from local ingredients. *Average main: $15 ✉ Little La Grange Village, 9 Little La Grange, Mahogany Rd., Frederiksted ☎ 978/850–2924 🌐 www.nidulari.com ▭ No credit cards ⏲ Closed Mon., Tues., Thurs., and Fri.*

Hotels

★ The Fred

$ | **HOTEL** | This boutique hotel on the Frederiksted waterfront saucily beckons you to "Sleep with Fred" in one of a dozen bright and stylishly appointed guest rooms housed in a quartet of new and restored colonial buildings. **Pros:** spacious rooms; waterfront location; LGBTQ-friendly. **Cons:** not kid-friendly; tiny spa; beach is a mix of sandy and rocky sections. *Rooms from: $220 ✉ 605 Strand St., Frederiksted ☎ 340/777–3733 🌐 www.sleepwithfred.com 23 rooms No Meals.*

★ Sand Castle on the Beach

$ | **RESORT** | Right on a gorgeous stretch of white beach, the adults-only Sand Castle has a tropical charm that harks back to a simpler time in the Caribbean; its nearness to Frederiksted's interesting dining scene is also a plus. **Pros:** LGBTQ-friendly; on the beach; good food. **Cons:** small pool; no guests under age 18; some rooms are small or lack views. [$] *Rooms from: $219* ✉ *127 Smithfield, Frederiksted* ☎ *340/772–1205* 🌐 *www.sandcastleonthebeach.com* *25 units* *No Meals.*

★ **Leatherback Brewing**
BREWPUBS | St. Croix's first large-scale brewing operation has a plant and tasting room near the oil refinery by the airport; drop by to try some of the more than two dozen beers produced here, including the popular Island Life lager and a saison inspired by local bush tea and flavored with basil, lemongrass, ginger, and sorrel. The kitchen serves appetizers, wraps, pizzas, and calzones.

TIP→ You can find the beers at bars throughout the USVI and BVI, but they can't be shipped to the mainland. ✉ *William Roebuck Industrial Park, 9902 Industrial Park, off Melvin H. Evans Hwy., Frederiksted* ☎ *340/277–2337* 🌐 *www.leatherback-brewing.com.*

Lost Dog Pub
BARS | There's nothing fancy about this downtown Frederiksted bar, and that's just as the locals like it. Trivia and karaoke nights are popular, as is the pizza and pasta coming out of the kitchen. The courtyard out back is a jumble of mismatched tables, but the outdoor bar has affordable drinks and the atmosphere is surprisingly family-friendly. ✉ *12 King St., Frederiksted* ☎ *340/772–3526.*

Tap Deck Bar and Billiards
BARS | A stairway from a quiet courtyard leads up to this unassuming bar just off the Frederiksted waterfront and offering pool tables, and a food menu of cheese plates, poke bowls, salads, and flatbreads. Drink service can stretch from happy hour into the wee hours depending on the crowd; in addition to a good rum and whiskey selection, the bar offers a traditional absinthe pour for the adventurous. ✉ *1D Strand St., Frederiksted* ☎ *340/773–5227* 🌐 *www.tapdeckstx.com.*

The best shopping in Frederiksted is along **Strand Street** and on the side streets and alleyways that connect it with **King Street.** Some stores close on Sundays except when cruise ships are in port.

GIFTS

Franklin's on the Waterfront
HOUSEWARES | Jewelry by Dune made from St. Croix sand is featured among the gift items at this downtown Frederiksted boutique, which also sells locally made soaps, candles, and artwork. ✉ *4 Strand St., Frederiksted* ☎ *340/473–0222* 🌐 *www.facebook.com/franklinsonthewaterfront.*

North Shore

Diving is the main draw on St. Croix's north shore, home to the famous Cane Bay Wall, which plunges away from the reef off of the pleasant arc of beach known as Cane Bay; the bay is home to several small bars and inns. The Salt River Bay, a U.S. national park, is a protected estuary with a bioluminescent bay; Christopher Columbus landed nearby in 1493, but was driven off by local Carib warriors.

Annaly Bay Tide Pools
NATURE SIGHT | Tricky to reach and at times too dangerous to attempt, the Annaly Bay Tide Pools are nonetheless well worth the effort when conditions are safe to experience these natural pools. Usually sheltered from the surf by a solid wall of volcanic rock, the tide pools are a blissful oasis even if they can get crowded at times. The 2½-mile out-and-back hike in on the Trumbull Trail, which begins near the entrance of the

Carambola Beach Resort, and has some moderate elevation gain with some nice views of the coast. The tricky part is navigating the scramble on a sharp and narrow ledge over breaking surf to get to the pools themselves. If you don't want to do the hike, Tan Tan Tours can get you there by Jeep. Just steer clear when the weather and tides are rough. ✉ *Trailhead by Carambola Beach Resort, Rte. 80, Estate Davis Bay, Estate Fountain, Estate Fountain.*

Estate Mount Washington Plantation
RUINS | Several years ago, while surveying their property near Frederiksted, Anthony and Nancy Ayer discovered the ruins of a circa-1750 sugar plantation beneath the rain forest brush. The grounds have since been cleared and opened to the public. The estate is private property, but the owners allow visitors to take a self-guided walking tour of the mill, the rum distillery, and other ruins. An oversize wind chime ringing softly in the breeze and a stone-lined labyrinth create a sense of serenity. ✉ *Rte. 63, Estate Mount Washington and Washington Hill.*

Mt. Eagle
MOUNTAIN | At 1,165 feet, this is St. Croix's highest peak. Determined hikers can follow a dirt path to the summit, or take a jeep tour with Tan Tan Tours. Route 78 (Scenic Road) climbs the shoulder of the mountain to the trailhead; use your GPS to locate the exact trailhead. ✉ *Rte. 69, Estate Fountain.*

Salt River Bay National Historical Park and Ecological Preserve
NATURE PRESERVE | If you want to learn more about St. Croix's indigenous Carib people while appreciating beautiful preserves that protect endangered species, head to this joint national and local park. Christopher Columbus's men skirmished with the Carib people here in 1493, on his second visit to what he deemed the New World. The peninsula on the bay's east side is named for the event: Cabo de las Flechas (Cape of the Arrows). A ball court, used by the Caribs in religious ceremonies, was discovered at the spot where the taxis park. Take a short hike up the dirt road to the ruins of an old earthen fort for great views of Salt River Bay. The area also encompasses a coastal estuary with the region's largest remaining mangrove forest, a submarine canyon, and several endangered species, including the hawksbill turtle and the roseate tern. The water at the beach can be on the rough side, but it's a nice place for sunning when the turtles aren't nesting. Local tour companies offer tours, including to a pair of bioluminescent bays, by kayak and pontoon boat. The park visitor center has been closed since Hurricane Maria damaged it in 2017. ✉ *Rte. 75 to Rte. 80, Estate Salt River* ☎ *340/773–1460* 🌐 *www.nps.gov/sari.*

Cane Bay
BEACH | On the island's breezy North Shore, Cane Bay does not always have gentle waters but the scuba diving and snorkeling are wondrous. You can see elkhorn and brain corals, and less than 200 yards out is the drop-off called the Cane Bay Wall. Make Cane Bay an all-day destination by combining a dive with food and drinks at the casual bars and restaurants that line the waterfront, including the excellent AMA at Cane Bay. **Amenities:** food and drink. **Best for:** snorkeling; swimming. ✉ *Rte. 80, Cane Bay* ✣ *About 4 miles (6 km) west of Salt River.*

★ AMA at Cane Bay
$$$ | **CARIBBEAN** | This waterfront restaurant on the back deck of the Waves at Cane Bay hotel serves sustainably sourced Caribbean-American food that pairs wonderfully with the creative craft cocktails, such as the Old Cuban made with 18-year-old Matusalem rum and

Champagne. The dining room overlooks Cane Bay, a perfect backdrop to try the lobster pappardelle, local ceviche, or the catch of the day. **Known for:** creative cocktails; location overlooking Cane Bay; sustainable seafood from local purveyors. *Average main: $30* *Waves at Cane Bay, 112C Cane Bay, Cane Bay* *340/227–3432* *www.amacanebay.com* *Closed Sun. and Mon.*

The Landing Beach Bar
$$ | **SEAFOOD** | Grilled mahimahi sandwiches, falafel, tacos, and burgers are among the favorites at this open-air bar across the street from Cane Bay beach. Some dishes are prepared using local Leatherback beer, which is available behind the bar. **Known for:** ocean views; fresh-off-the-boat seafood; live music. *Average main: $15* *110c Cane Bay, Cane Bay* *340/718–0362* *www.thelanding-beachbar.com* *Closed Tues.*

Off the Wall
$$ | **AMERICAN** | Divers fresh from a plunge at the North Shore's popular Cane Bay Wall gather at this breezy spot on the beach, where sunsets are celebrated with a toast at the bar and the winter months offer the possibility of whale sightings offshore. The menu includes deli sandwiches, burgers, and hot dogs, but the stars are the calzones and pizzas, which run the gamut from vegetarian to meat-lovers. **Known for:** pizza and calzones; hammocks on the beach; friendly beach bar. *Average main: $20* *Rte. 80, Cane Bay* *340/718–4771* *www.otwstx.com* *Closed Fri.*

Spratnet Beach Bar
$$ | **CARIBBEAN** | A casual beach bar with a local vibe, the Spratnet is presided over by owner Calvin Belle, who usually occupies a bar stool and is happy to pour you a shot of homemade mamajuana (he calls his "papawana"), a potent rum drink infused with island roots and spices. Menu favorites include red snapper and a Sunday pig roast, and there's live music on weekends. **Known for:** conversing with locals; Sunday pig roasts; live music on weekends. *Average main: $16* *Cane Bay Rd., Cane Bay* *340/718–8485* *Closed Mon.*

Hotels

Arawak Bay: The Inn at Salt River
$ | **B&B/INN** | With stellar views of St. Croix's North Shore and an affable host, this 15-room hotel allows you to settle into island life at a price that doesn't break the bank. **Pros:** 20 minutes from Christiansted; stunning views; reasonable rates. **Cons:** no beach nearby; pool is small; can be some road noise. *Rooms from: $160* *62 Salt River Rd, Estate Salt River* *888/772–1684* *www.arawakhotelstcroix.com* *15 rooms* *Free Breakfast.*

Carambola Beach Resort and Spa
$$ | **RESORT** | This expansive Marriott-branded resort has a stellar beach and peaceful ambience as well as standalone rooms with terra-cotta floors, ceramic lamps, mahogany ceilings and furnishings, and rocking chairs. **Pros:** close to golf; lovely beach; relaxing atmosphere. **Cons:** limited amenities; ongoing renovations as of this writing; remote location. *Rooms from: $299* *Rte. 80, Estate Davis Bay, Estate Fountain* *340/778–3800, 888/503–8760, 800/627–7468* *www.marriott.com* *151 rooms* *No Meals.*

Waves Cane Bay
$$ | **HOTEL** | The famed Cane Bay Wall is just offshore from this boutique hotel, giving it an enviable location. **Pros:** beaches nearby; great diving; restaurants nearby. **Cons:** bland decor; on main road; need car to get around. *Rooms from: $322* *Rte. 80, 112C Cane Bay, Cane Bay* *340/718–1815* *www.thewaves-canebay.com* *11 rooms* *No Meals.*

Activities

BOAT TOURS

Almost everyone takes a day trip to Buck Island aboard a charter boat. Most leave from the Christiansted waterfront or from Green Cay Marina and stop for a snorkel at the island's eastern end before dropping anchor off a gorgeous Turtle Beach for a swim, a hike, and lunch. Sailboats can often stop right at the beach; a larger boat might have to anchor a bit farther offshore. A full-day sail runs about $120 for adults, with lunch included on most trips. A half-day sail costs about $85.

Big Beard's Adventure Tours

SAILING | Catamarans that depart from the Christiansted waterfront whisk you to Buck Island for half- and full-day snorkeling tours. The 42-foot *Adventure* has a glass viewing platform for those who want to see the fish but don't want to get in the water. The full-day tour on the *Renegade* concludes with dropping anchor at a private beach for an all-you-can-eat-and-drink barbecue. Sunset sails also are offered. ✉ *1247 Queen Cross St., Christiansted* ☎ *340/773–4482* 🌐 *www.bigbeards.com.*

Buck Island Charters

SAILING | Scheduled half-day trips to Buck Island on the trimaran *Teroro II* leave Green Cay Marina in the morning and afternoon. Bring your own lunch and drinks; cost is $85 for adults. Private charters for up to 10 passengers are also available on the 38-foot trimaran *Dragonfly.* ✉ *Green Cay Marina, Annas Hope* ☎ *340/718–3161* 🌐 *www.facebook.com/buckislandcharters.*

Caribbean Sea Adventures

SAILING | With boats leaving from the Christiansted waterfront, Caribbean Sea Adventures has both half- and full-day trips to Buck Island. Sunset sails and fishing excursions are also available. ✉ *Christiansted Boardwalk, 59 Kings Wharf, Christiansted* ☎ *340/773–2628* 🌐 *www.caribbeanseaadventures.com.*

Lyric Sails

ADVENTURE TOURS | This sailing adventure on a 63-foot, custom-built catamaran called the *Jolly Mon* features live musical entertainment from local performers Monday to Thursday and Saturdays. Visitors can choose a private day sail or a sunset sail. ✉ *1D Strand St., Christiansted* ☎ *340/201–5227* 🌐 *www.lyricsails.com.*

Schooner Roseway

SAILING | A Grand Banks schooner may seem to be a fish out of water in the Caribbean, but the triple red sails of the *Roseway* make her an instantly recognizable sight off the shores of St. Croix. Built in 1925 and serving as a pilot boat until 1972, the Roseway is now an experiential classroom for the World Ocean School but also sets off for two-hour sunset sails from Christiansted. ✉ *9B Hospital St., Christiansted* ☎ *340/626–7877* 🌐 *www.worldoceanschool.org.*

DIVING AND SNORKELING

At **Buck Island,** a short boat ride from Christiansted or Green Cay Marina, the reef is so impressive that it's been protected as a national monument. You can dive right off the beach at **Cane Bay,** which has a spectacular drop-off called the Cane Bay Wall. Dive operators also do boat trips along the wall, usually leaving from Salt River or Christiansted. **Frederiksted Pier** is home to a colony of seahorses, creatures seldom seen in the waters of the Virgin Islands. At **Green Cay,** just outside Green Cay Marina in the East End, you can see colorful fish swimming around the reefs and rocks. Two exceptional North Shore sites are **North Star** and **Salt River,** which you can reach only by boat. At Salt River you can float downward through a canyon filled with colorful fish and coral.

The island's dive shops take you out for one- or two-tank dives. Plan to pay about $95 for a one-tank dive and $130 for a two-tank dive, including equipment and an underwater tour. All companies offer certification and introductory courses called resort dives for novices.

The 18-hole Buccaneer Golf Course features views of the Caribbean from 13 of its holes.

Which dive outfit you pick usually depends on where you're staying. Your hotel may have one on-site. If so, you're just a short stroll away from the dock. If not, other companies are close by. Where the dive boat goes on a particular day depends on the weather, but in any case, all St. Croix dive sites are special. All shops are affiliated with PADI, the Professional Association of Diving Instructors.

★ Cane Bay Dive Shop

SCUBA DIVING | This Frederiksted shop is the place to go if you want to do a snorkel tour, shore dive, or boat dive along the North Shore, including the famous Cane Bay Wall, or to see the seahorses under the Frederiksted Pier. ✉ *2 Strand St., Frederiksted* ✣ *Across from cruise pier* ☎ *340/772–0715* 🌐 *www.canebay-scuba.com.*

Dive Experience

SCUBA DIVING | Convenient for those staying in Christiansted, Dive Experience runs trips to the North Shore walls and reefs, the Frederiksted Pier, and night dives, in addition to offering the usual certification and introductory classes. You also can help control the population of invasive lionfish by signing up for a spearfishing hunt. It's a PADI Five Star facility. ✉ *1000 King St., Suite 6, Christiansted* ☎ *340/773–3307, 800/235–9047* 🌐 *www.divexp.com.*

St. Croix Ultimate Bluewater Adventures

SCUBA DIVING | This company can take you to your choice of more than 75 dive sites; it also offers a variety of packages that include hotel stays, stylish and comfortable island wear, and dive gear available at the dive shop. Two locations—in downtown Christiansted and downtown Frederiksted—plus two dive boats make this one of the more versatile dive operations on the island. They offer a wide variety of dive training classes, too. ✉ *81 Queen Cross St., Suite 14, Christiansted* ☎ *340/773–5994* 🌐 *www.stcroixscuba.com.*

FISHING

Since the early 1980s, some 20 world records—many for blue marlin—have been set in these waters. Sailfish, skipjack, bonito, tuna, and wahoo are abundant. A charter runs about $750 for a half-day (for up to six people), with most boats going out for four-, six-, or eight-hour trips.

Captain Cook Charters

FISHING | This outfitter offers 4- to 10-hour fishing trips to troll for mahimahi, wahoo, tuna, and billfish on the 33-foot sportfisher *Hook 'n Cook.* ✉ *Green Cay Marina, Christiansted* ☎ *979/216–7018* 🌐 *www.stcroixfishingadventures.com.*

Gone Ketchin'

FISHING | Captain Grizz, a true old salt, heads half- ($500), three-quarter ($700), and full-day ($900) fishing charter trips to troll for marlin, wahoo, mahimahi, king mackerel, barracuda, and tuna. ✉ *Salt River Marina, Rte. 80, Estate Salt River* ☎ *340/713–1175, 340/998–2055* 🌐 *www.goneketchin.com.*

St. Croix Inshore Fishing Charters

FISHING | Deep sea fishing is imbued with a sense of adventure, but there's plenty of great angling to be had within sight of land in St. Croix, too. St. Croix Inshore Fishing Charters organizes trips in pursuit of shallow-water fish like tarpon, bonefish, and snook. Charter rates are $450 for one hour and $600 for six hours. The 21-foot *Always Sum-Ting*fishing boat put in at the Molasses Pier Boat Ramp between the airport and the Hovensa refinery. ✉ *Molasses Pier, Anguilla* ☎ *340/514–6078* 🌐 *www.fishstcroix.com.*

GOLF

★ Buccaneer Golf Course

GOLF | This 18-hole resort course, designed by Bob Joyce in 1973, is close to Christiansted and features views of the Caribbean from 13 of its holes. Golf lessons and club and cart rentals are available, and the pro shop also has a golf simulator. Walking the course after play has ended for the day is a popular evening pastime among Buccaneer resort guests. ✉ *Rte. 82, Shoys* ☎ *340/712–2144* 🌐 *www.thebuccaneer.com* 🎫 *$70 for 18 holes; $55 for 9 holes; additional $15–$25 for cart rental.* ⛳ *18 holes, 5,688 yards, par 70.*

Carambola Golf Club

GOLF | Golfers will enjoy the exotic beauty of this difficult course in the Carambola Valley designed by Robert Trent Jones Sr., because they might not enjoy their score. An extra sleeve of balls might also be required. The long water holes never return splash balls, and the rough surrounding jungle seldom does. Most fairways are forgiving with ample landing area, but the length of many holes makes playing this par 72 course challenging. ✉ *72 Estate River, Estate River* ☎ *340/778–5638* 🌐 *www.golfcarambola.com* 🎫 *$115 with cart* ⛳ *18 holes, 5727 yards, par 72.*

Reef Golf Course

GOLF | If you want to enjoy panoramic Caribbean views without paying big greens fees, the public, 9-hole Reef Golf Course on the island's East End is the place to go. The course design is basic, but the views from the hillside are spectacular. Trees on this course very seldom enter into play, and sand traps are absent. The 7th hole with its highly elevated tee is the most interesting. No good with a club in your hand? Try 18 holes of disc (Frisbee) golf, instead, or grab a racquet for a game of tennis or pickleball. ✉ *Rte. 82, Teague's Bay* ☎ *340/773–8844* 🎫 *$20 greens fee for nine holes, $10 for cart* ⛳ *9 holes, 2,395 yards, par 35.*

GUIDED TOURS

Joseph's VIP Taxi Tours

DRIVING TOURS | Guided island van tours are available with expert commentary on the sights, history, and culture of St. Croix. The cost is $200 for three hours or $350 for a full day with up to six passengers, plus $50 each additional passenger. ✉ *Christiansted* ☎ *340/277–6133* ✉ *shaggy95144@gmail.com.*

Sweeny's St. Croix Safari Tours

DRIVING TOURS | These open-air (but covered) safari truck tours of St. Croix depart from Christiansted and last about five hours. Costs run from $71 per person, plus admission to attractions like the St. George Village Botanical Garden and feeding beer to the pigs at the Mount Pellier Domino Club. ✉ *Christiansted* ☎ *340/773–6700* 🌐 *www.gotostcroix.com.*

HIKING

Crucian Heritage And Nature Tourism (CHANT)

HIKING & WALKING | CHANT runs several educational tours focused on St. Croix's natural and cultural heritage, including 2½-hour historic walking tours of Frederiksted on Wednesdays, and a Christiansted tour on Tuesdays that focuses on Alexander Hamilton, who lived in St. Croix as a teenager. A half-day tour of Maroon Ridge, which explores hideouts used by escaped slaves, is offered by appointment. CHANT's cultural center in downtown Frederiksted has exhibits of local art. ✉ *217 Custom House St., Frederiksted* ☎ *340/277–4834* 🌐 *www.chantvi.org.*

HORSEBACK RIDING

Paul and Jill's Equestrian Stables

HORSEBACK RIDING | From Sprat Hall, just north of Frederiksted, co-owner Jill Hurd will take you through the rain forest, across the pastures, along the beaches, and through valleys—explaining the flora, fauna, and ruins on the way. A 1½-hour morning or afternoon group ride costs $150. ✉ *Sprat Hall, Rte. 58, Frederiksted* ☎ *340/332–0417* 🌐 *www.paulandjills.com.*

KAYAKING

Sea Thru Kayak VI

KAYAKING | These tours of Salt River Bay use transparent kayaks so paddlers can see the marine life passing below their boat, including the tiny glowing dinoflagellates that light up St. Croix's bioluminescent bay. Stand-up paddleboard tours also are offered. ✉ *Salt River Marina, Rte. 80, Estate Salt River* ☎ *340/244–8696* 🌐 *www.seathrukayaksvi.com.*

Virgin Kayak Tours

KAYAKING | Virgin runs guided daytime, sunset, and evening kayak trips on Salt River Bay, including tours to see the bay light up with bioluminescent marine life on moonless nights. Other options include daytime ecological and history tours of the bay where Columbus landed and encountered indigenous Carib inhabitants, and sunset and moonlight tours. The company also rents kayaks and SUPs so you can tour around by yourself for a half or full day. Tours start at $60. ✉ *Rte. 80, Salt River Marina, Estate Salt River* ☎ *340/514–0062* 🌐 *www.virginkayaktours.com.*

ZIP LINING

Carambola Zip Line

ZIP LINING | **FAMILY** | St. Croix's newest and most thrilling attraction starts with a bumpy drive up the side of the Carambola Valley, with occasional stops for Instagram-worthy shots of the Carambola Golf Course and the Carambola Beach Resort from high above. Expert and friendly guides ease guests into the experience with a brief safety lesson before clipping into the first of the course's three ziplines, the 518-foot "Mongoose." It only gets longer and steeper from there—the Gauntlet runs 2,374 feet and drops more than 205 feet, with your suspended body reaching speeds of more than 30 mph. ✉ *1-C Estate River, Estate River* ☎ *340/244–1464* 🌐 *www.carambolazipline.com.*

Index

A

Abacus (Grand Cayman) ×, *303*
AC Hotel Kingston (Jamaica) , *551*
Admiral's Inn (Antigua) , *112*
Agua (Grand Cayman) ×, *303*
Agua Mania Adventures (St. Maarten and St. Martin), *817*
Ajoupa-Bouillon (Martinique), *607*
Alcazar de Colón (castle; Dominican Republic), *385*
Alexander Hamilton Birthplace (Nevis), *724*
Alfie's in Aruba (bar), *141*
Alfred's Ocean Palace (bar, *Jamaica), 567*
Alhambra Casino (Aruba), *143*
Alina (St. Maarten and St. Martin) ×, *796*
All Saints Episcopal Church (St. Thomas), *878*
Alto Vista Chapel (Aruba), *156*
Altos de Chavón (Dominican Republic), *396*
Altos de Chavón Amphitheater (Dominican Republic), *396*
AMA at Cane Bay (St. Croix) ×, *937–938*
Amalia Cafe (St. Thomas) ×, *883*
Amanyara (Providenciales) , *843*
Amstar DMC–Apple Vacations (tours; Dominican Republic), *435*
Andromeda Botanic Gardens (Barbados), *204*
Anegada (British Virgin Islands), *278–281*
Anegada Reef Hotel Restaurant ×, *279*
Anguilla, *14, 70–94*
beaches, 76, 80–81
festivals and seasonal events, 72, 92
health and safety, 75
lodging, 75, 86–89
nightlife and the arts, 89–90
price categories, 76
restaurants, 81–86
shopping, 90–92
sports and activities, 36, 92–94
transportation, 74–75
visitor information, 76
Anguilla Sands and Salts (shop), *90*
Animal Flower Cave (Barbados), *204*
Annaberg Plantation (St. John), *909–910*
Annaly Bay Tide Pools (St. Croix), *936–937*
Annandale Waterfall & Forest Park (Grenada), *451*
Anna's Art Gallery (Providenciales), *839*
Anse Chastanet (Saint Lucia), *764–765*
Anse Cochon (Saint Lucia), *765*
Anse de Grande Saline (St. Barthélemy), *31, 693*
Anse de Toiny (St. Barthélemy), *689–690*
Anse des Pitons (Saint Lucia), *765*
Anse Marcel Beach (St. Maarten and St. Martin), *807*
Anse Marcel Beach (St. Maarten and St. Martin) ×, *807*
Antigua and Barbuda, *14, 96–124*
beaches, 108–109, 124
festivals and seasonal events, 98, 103
health and safety, 101
lodging, 101–102, 111–116, 124
nightlife and the arts, 117
price categories, 102
restaurants, 109–111
shopping, 117–119
sports and activities, 119–123
tours, 102, 120
transportation, 99, 101
visitor information, 102
weddings, 102
Antillia Brewing Company (Saint Lucia), *753*
Apolline (Martinique) ×, *592*
Appleton Estate (Jamaica), *555*
Aquadilla (Puerto Rico), *663–664*
Aquafari (watersports; Curaçao), *374*
Aquarium de la Guadeloupe, *486*
Aquarium Restaurant (Grenada) ×, *455*
Arashi Beach (Aruba), *156*
Arecibo (Puerto Rico), *659–660*
Arikok National Park and environs (Aruba), *159–160*
Art Cave Francis Sling (Curaçao), *355*
ArtisA (arts center; Aruba), *158*
Aruba, *16, 126–166*
beaches, 131, 138, 144, 149, 151, 156, 157–158
festivals and seasonal events, 34, 128
health and safety, 131
lodging, 132, 140–141, 146–148, 152–154, 159
money matters, 128
nightlife and the arts, 131, 141, 154–155
price categories, 131
restaurants, 131–133, 138–140, 144–146, 151–152, 157, 158
shopping, 133, 135, 141–143, 148, 155
sports and activities, 36, 160–166
tours, 133–134, 157, 163–164
transportation, 130–131
visitor information, 134
weddings, 134
Aruba Active Vacations, *166*
Aruba Aloe Museum & Factory, *135*
Aruba Downtown Trolley, *133*
Aruba Ocean Villas , *159*
Aruba Ostrich Farm, *160*
Aruba Walking Tours, *133*
Aruba Watersports Center, *165*
At Sea (Bonaire) ×, *228*
Aurora International Golf Club (Anguilla), *33, 93*
Avila Beach Hotel (Curaçao) , *359–360*

B

Baby Beach (Aruba), *157–158*
Bàcaro (Grand Cayman) ×, *303*
Bacchus (St. Maarten and St. Martin) ×, *809*
Baci Ristorante (Providenciales) × 840
Bagatelle St. Barth ×, *682, 684*
Baie Longue (St. Maarten and St. Martin), *814–815*
Baie Nettlé (St. Maarten and St. Martin), *807–808*
Baie Orientale (St. Maarten and St. Martin), *812–814*
Bajo el Sol Gallery, Art Bar & Rum Room (St. John), *908*
Balaclava Jewellers (Grand Cayman), *314*
Balata (Martinique), *605–606*
Balls and Wine (St. Maarten and St. Martin) ×, *799*
Bamboo House (St. Maarten and St. Martin) ×, *799–800*
Bananakeet Cafe (Tortola) ×, *258*
Bananas (St. Kitts) ×, *728*
Bank of Jamaica Money Museum, *546*
Bannister Hotel &Yacht Club, The (Dominican Republic) , *425–426*
Baoase (Curaçao) , *360*
Bar at Ave, The (Grand Cayman), *313*
Barbados, *16, 168–214*
beaches, 174, 183, 185, 189–190, 193, 194, 196, 201, 206
festivals and seasonal events, 34
health and safety, 174–175
lodging, 175–176, 183, 188–189, 190–192, 194, 196, 198–201, 203–204, 207
money matters, 170
nightlife and the arts, 176, 185, 193, 194, 201
price categories, 176
restaurants, 177, 183, 185, 188, 190, 193–194, 195–196, 197–198, 201, 203, 206–207, 209–210
shopping, 177–178, 185, 189, 193, 201
sports and activities, 36, 210–214
tours, 178
transportation, 173–174
visitor information, 178–179
weddings, 179
Barbados Blue (dive site), *210–211*
Barbados Golf Club, *33*
Barbados Hiking Association, *212*
Barbados Military Cemetery, *179*
Barbados Museum & Historical Society, *179*
Barbados Turf Club, *179, 182*
Barbados Wildlife Reserve, *204–205*
Barbuda, *14, 123–124.* ⇨ *See also Antigua and Barbuda*
Bario Urban Street Food (Curaçao) ×, *358*
Barclays Park (Barbados), *205*
Barefoot (Aruba) ×, *138*

Barre de l'Isle Forest Reserve (Saint Lucia), *771*
Bas du Fort (Guadeloupe), *489*
Basilica Catedral Menor Santa Maria de la Encarnación (Dominican Republic), *385*
Basse-Pointe (Martinique), *608*
Basse-Terre (Guadeloupe), *494–500*
Baths Beach, The (Virgin Gorda), *268*
Baths National Park, The (Virgin Gorda), *30, 265*
Bay Bistro (Providenciales) ✕, *834*
Bayahibe (Dominican Republic), *398–399*
Bayamón (Puerto Rico), *643–644*
Beaches, *30–31.* ⇨ *See also under specific islands*
Beaches Turks & Caicos Resort Villages & Spa (Providenciales), *836*
Beer, *47*
Belair (Grenada), *465, 467*
Belgian Chocolate Factory (St. Thomas), *886*
Bella Luna Ristorante & Pizzeria (Providenciales) ✕, *834*
Belle Mont Farms on Kittitian Hill (St. Kitts), *718*
Bellefontaine (Martinique), *611*
Belmond Cap Juluca (Anguilla), *87*
Belmond La Samanna (St. Maarten and St. Martin), *815*
Betty's Hope Sugar Plantation (Antigua), *103*
Bibliothèque Schoelcher (Martinique), *589*
Big Blue Collective (tours; Turks and Caicos), *846*
Big Fish (St. Maarten and St. Martin) ✕, *797–798*
Bight, The (Providenciales), *828–829, 832*
Bight Beach, The (Providenciales), *828*
Billini Hotel (Dominican Republic), *388*
Bitter End Yacht Club (Virgin Gorda), *271*
Black Rocks (lava deposits; St. Kitts), *709*
Blanchard's (Anguilla) ✕, *82*
Bloody Bay Wall (Little Cayman), *341*
Blowholes (Grand Cayman), *318*
Blue by Eric (Grand Cayman) ✕, *305*
Blue Hole Mineral Spring (Jamaica), *560*
Blue Lagoon (Jamaica), *541–542*
Blue Mountains (Jamaica), *554–555*
Blue Waters Divers (Grand Turk), *862*
Blue Waters Resort & Spa (Antigua), *112*
Blues Caribbean Kitchen (Curaçao) ✕, *358–359*
Boardwalk Boutique Hotel Aruba, *152–153*
Boat races (Anguilla), *92*
Bob Marley Mausoleum (Jamaica), *530–531*
Bob Marley Museum (Jamaica), *546*
Boca Chica (Dominican Republic), *395–396*
Bochincha Container Yard (Aruba), *141*
Bodden Town (Grand Cayman), *316*
BodyHoliday Saint Lucia, *750*
Bohio Dive Resort (Grand Turk), *861*
Boiling Hole (South Caicos), *856*
Bolt, Usain, *553*
Bon Sea Semi-Submarine (Bonaire), *224*
Bonaire, *16, 216–240*
beaches, 227–228
festivals and seasonal events, 218
health and safety, 221
lodging, 221, 230–234
money matters, 218
nightlife and the arts, 234–235
price categories, 221
restaurants, 228–230
shopping, 235
sports and activities, 36, 225, 235–240
tours, 240
transportation, 220–221
weddings, 221
Bonaire Landsailing Adventures, *240*
Bonaire Marine Park, *224*
Bonaire Oceanfront Apartments, *231*
Bonaire Tours & Vacations, *239*
Booby Pond Nature Reserve (Little Cayman), *341*
Boolchard's Digital World (shop; Aruba), *142*
Boquerón (Puerto Rico), *663*
Bosque Estatal de Guánica (Puerto Rico), *669*
Botanical Gardens of Nevis, *724–725*
Bottom Bay Beach (Barbados), *30, 195*
Bouillante (Guadeloupe), *496–497*
Brac Parrot Reserve (Cayman Brac), *331*
Brandywine Estate (Tortola) ✕, *252*
Brass Boer (Bonaire) ✕, *229*
Brasserie, The (Grand Cayman) ✕, *293*
Breathless Punta Cana Resort & Spa (Dominican Republic), *403*
Bridgetown (Barbados), *179, 182–185*
Brimstone Hill (St. Kitts), *709, 711*
British Virgin Islands, *14, 242–282*
beaches, 255, 256, 257–258, 268, 272, 274, 279
festivals and seasonal events, 244
health and safety, 246–247
lodging, 247, 253, 256, 259–260, 264, 269–270, 271, 273, 277, 281, 282
money matters, 244
nightlife and the arts, 254, 260, 270, 271–272, 277–278
price categories, 2472
restaurants, 252–253, 255–256, 258–259, 268–269, 271, 274–277, 279–280, 282
shopping, 255–256, 270, 272
sports and activities, 36, 261–264, 273, 278, 281
transportation, 246
visitor information, 248
weddings, 248
Buccaneer, The (St. Croix), *930*
Buccaneer Golf Course (St. Croix), *33, 941*
Buck Island Reef National Monument (St. Croix), *928–929*
Bucuti & Tara Beach Resorts (Aruba), *146–147*
Bugaloe Bar & Grill (Aruba), *154*
Bugaloos (Providenciales) ✕, *843*
Bushbar (Jamaica) ✕, *543*
Bushiribana Gold Mine Ruins (Aruba), *149*
Bushy Park Barbados, *194*
Butterfly Farm (Aruba), *149*

C

Cabarete (Dominican Republic), *415–418*
Cabrera (Dominican Republic), *418–420*
Cadushy Distillery and Gardens (Bonaire), *224–225*
Café Celeste at Malliouhana (Anguilla) ✕, *82*
Café Cuatro Sombras (Puerto Rico) ✕, *629*
Caicos Bakery (Providenciales) ✕, *835*
Caicos Café Bar and Grill (Providenciales) ✕, *834*
Caicos Dream Tours (boating; Providenciales), *844*
Calabash Cove Resort & Spa (Saint Lucia), *750*
Calabash Luxury Boutique Hotel (Grenada), *457*
California Dunes (Western Tip; Aruba), *148, 156–157*
California Lighthouse (Aruba), *156*
Calle Las Damas (Dominican Republic), *385*
Callwood Distillery (Tortola), *257*
Camana Bay Observation Tower (Grand Cayman), *302*
Cane Bay Dive Shop (St. Croix), *940*
Cane Garden Bay (Tortola), *257*
Cane Garden Bay Beach (Tortola), *257–258*
Cap Maison (Saint Lucia), *751*
Capilla de Porta Coeli (Puerto Rico), *670*
Capriccio (Bonaire) ✕, *229*
Captain Don's Habitat Dive Shop (Bonaire), *238*
Captain Morgan Distillery (St. Croix), *931*
Cardinal Arthur (bird watching; Middle Caicos), *855*
Careenage, The (Barbados), *182*
Caribbean Club (Grand Cayman), *309*
Caribbean Museum Center for the Arts (St. Croix), *933*
Carib's Leap (Grenada), *451*
Carlisle Bay (Antigua), *112*

Carnival, *34–35, 65–67*
Carolina (Puerto Rico), *642–643*
Carriacou (Grenada), *465–471*
Carriacou Historical Society & Museum (Grenada), *467*
Casita Miramar (Puerto Rico) ✕, *638*
Casa Alcaldia de San Juan (Puerto Rico), *628*
Casa Bacardí (Puerto Rico), *644*
Casa Blanca (Puerto Rico), *628*
Casa Bonita Tropical Lodge (Dominican Republic) 🏨, *393*
Casa Colonial Beach & Spa (Dominican Republic) 🏨, *413*
Casa Cortés ChocoBar (Puerto Rico) ✕, *631*
Casa de Arte de Sosúa (Dominican Republic), *414*
Casa de Campo (Dominican Republic) 🏨, *27, 32*
Casa de Campo Marina (Dominican Republic), *431*
Casa de Campo Resort (Dominican Republic), *431*
Casa 43 Mexican Kitchen and Tequilla Bar (Grand Cayman) ✕, *305*
Casa Museo General Gregorio Luperón (Dominican Republic), *411*
Casa Wiechers Villaronga (Puerto Rico), *667*
Casas del XVI (Dominican Republic) 🏨, *388*
Cascade aux Ecrevisses (Guadeloupe), *497*
Casibari and Ayo Rock Formations, *160*
Castillo San Cristóbal (Puerto Rico), *628*
Castillo San Felipe del Morro (Puerto Rico), *628*
Castries (Saint Lucia), *752–753, 756–760*
Castries Central Market (Saint Lucia), *753*
Cataño and Bayamón (Puerto Rico), *643–644*
Catalonia Royal Bávaro (Dominican Republic) 🏨, *403–404*
Catedral de San Juan Bautista (Puerto Rico), *628–629*
Cathedral of the Immaculate Conception (Grenada), *447*
Cathedral of the Immaculate Conception (Saint Lucia), *753*
Cathedral of St. John the Divine (Antigua), *103*
Cathedral of Thorns (arts center; Curaçao), *355*
Cathédrale de St-Pierre et St-Paul (Guadeloupe), *483*
Catherineberg Ruins (St. John), *913*
Cattlewash Beach (Barbados), *206*
Caves, The (Jamaica) 🏨, *564*
Caves Restaurant, The (Jamaica) ✕, *27, 560*
Cayo Icacos (Puerto Rico), *650*
Cayo Levantado (Dominican Republic), *424*
Cayman Brac (Cayman Islands), *331–337*
Cayman Brac Museum, *331, 333*
Cayman Islands, *12, 284–342*
beaches, 289, 293, 299, 302–303, 315, 319, 333–334, 339
festivals and seasonal events, 286
health and safety, 289
lodging, 289, 294–295, 302, 309–312, 320, 334–335, 340
money matters, 286
nightlife and the arts, 290, 295–296, 302, 312–313, 320–322, 335
price categories, 290
restaurants, 290, 293–294, 301–302, 303, 305–309, 315–316, 319–320, 334, 339–340
shopping, 290–291, 296–298, 314, 336
sports and activities, 36, 322–325, 336–337, 341–342
tours, 327
transportation, 287–289
visitor information, 291
weddings, 291
Cayman Islands Brewery (Grand Cayman), *318*
Cayman Islands National Museum (Grand Cayman), *292*
Cayman Kayaks (Grand Cayman), *328*
Cayman Spirits/Seven Fathoms Rum (Grand Cayman), *292*
Cayman Turtle Centre (Grand Cayman), *298–299*
Celine Charters (St. Maarten and St. Martin), *817*
Cellar 8 (Jamaica) ✕, *550*
Central Interior (Barbados), *207–210*
Centro Ceremonial Indigena de Tibes (Puerto Rico), *667*
Centro León (Dominican Republic), *420*
Ceviche 91 (Curaçao) ✕, *359*
Chalk Sound (Providenciales), *832–833*
Chalk Sound National Park (Providenciales), *832*
Chalky Mount (Barbados), *205*
Champers (Barbados) ✕, *188*
Charlotte Amalie (St. Thomas), *878–887*
Château Murat (Guadeloupe), *501*
Château Mygo House of Seafood (Saint Lucia) ✕, *760–761*
Cherry Tree Hill (Barbados), *205*
Cheshire Hall (Providenciales), *841*
Cheval Blanc St-Barth Isle de France (St. Barthélemy) 🏨, *692*
CHIC Punta Cana by Royalton (Dominican Republic) 🏨, *404*
Chichi Shop Punda (Curaçao), *362*
Children, attractions for, *38–39*
Children's Museum Curaçao, *355*
Chill-Pops Gourmet Paletas (Jamaica) ✕, *560–561*
Chophouse, The (Aruba) ✕, *144*
Chrishi Beach Club (Nevis), *733*
Christiansted and environs (St. Croix), *922–930*
Christoffel National Park (Curaçao), *369*
Christopher (St. Barthélemy) ✕, *695*
Chukka Good Hope Estate (amusement park; Jamaica), *528–529*
Clear Kayak Aruba, *165*
Cliff at Cap, The (Saint Lucia) ✕, *749*
Club Med Buccaneer's Creek (Martinique) 🏨, *603*
Club Med La Caravelle (Guadeloupe) 🏨, *492*
Club Med Punta Cana (Dominican Republic) 🏨, *404*
Club Seaborne (Puerto Rico) 🏨, *657*
Coal Pot Restaurant, The (Saint Lucia) ✕, *756*
Cobblers Cove (Barbados) 🏨, *26, 203*
Coccoloba (Grand Cayman) ✕, *306*
Cockburn Harbour (South Caicos), *856*
Cockburn Town (Grand Turk), *857–860*
Coco Bistro (Providenciales) ✕, *834*
Coco Hill Forest (Barbados), *207*
CocoMaya (Virgin Gorda) ✕, *268*
Coconut Beach Restaurant (Grenada) ✕, *455*
Cocovan (Providenciales) ✕, *835–836*
Codrington Theological College (Barbados), *205*
Colombier (St. Barthélemy), *690*
Colony Club (Barbados) 🏨, *198*
Competitions des Boeufs Tirants (Guadeloupe), *501*
Conch Bar Caves (Turks and Caicos), *854*
Conch Shell Mounds (Anegada), *279*
Concord Falls (Grenada), *452*
Condado (Puerto Rico), *634–635, 638*
Contacts, *68*
Cooper Island (British Virgin Islands), *281–282*
Cooper Island Beach Club 🏨, *282*
Copamarina Beach Resort & Spa (Puerto Rico) 🏨, *670*
Copper Mine National Park (Virgin Gorda), *265*
Coral Bay and environs (St. John), *913–918*
Coral Beach Club (St. Maarten and St. Martin) 🏨, *798*
Coral Reef Club (Barbados) 🏨, *198*
Coral World Ocean Park (St. Thomas), *887*
Corossol (St. Barthélemy), *690*
Country Club at Sandy Lane (golf course; Barbados), *212*
Crackpot Kitchen (Providenciales) ✕, *834–835*
Craft F&B Co. (Grand Cayman) ✕, *306*
Crane, The (Barbados) 🏨, *196*
Crane and the Southeast (Barbados), *194–196*
Crane Beach (Barbados), *195*

Crucian Gold (shop; St. Croix), *927*
Cruz Bay (St. John), *902–903, 906–909*
Cruzan Rum Distillery (St. Croix), *931*
Crystal Caves (Grand Cayman), *318*
Cuba's Cookin' (Aruba) ✕, *139*
Cuisine, *41–47, 321, 387, 612*
Culebra (Puerto Rico), *656–658*
Cunucu Houses (Aruba), *134*
Cupecoy (St. Maarten and St. Martin), *795*
Cupecoy Beach (St. Maarten and St. Martin), *795*
Curaçao, *16–17, 344–374*
beaches, 349, 371–372
festivals and seasonal events, 35, 346, 361
health and safety, 352
lodging, 352, 359–361, 366, 372–373
money matters, 346
nightlife and the arts, 352, 361–362, 366
price categories, 352
restaurants, 353, 358–359, 365, 373
shopping, 353, 357, 362, 367, 372–373
sports and activities, 36, 362–364, 367–368, 374
tours, 354, 363–364, 368, 374
transportation, 348–349
visitor information, 354
Curaçao Marriott Beach Resort , *360*
Curaçao Museum (Het Curacaosch Museum), *355, 357*
Curaçao Sea Aquarium, *364*
CurAloe Plantation & Factory (Curaçao), *365*
Curtain Bluff (Antigua) , *27, 113*
C/X Culinary Experience (Dominican Republic) ✕, *402*
Cynthia's Talk of the Town (St. Maarten and St. Martin) ✕, *809*
Cyparis Express (Martinique), *606, 607*

D

D. Hamilton Jackson Park (St. Croix), *922*
Da Conch Shack (Providenciales) ✕, *843*
Da Vinci Ristorante (Aruba) ✕, *151*
Dasheene (Saint Lucia) ✕, *767*
De La Grenada Industries, 452
De Palm Private Island (Aruba), *135*
De Palm Tours (Aruba), *163–164*
Delfins Beach Resort (Bonaire) , *232*
Den Paradera (Curaçao), *365*
DePalm Pleasure Sail & Snorkeling (Aruba), *163*
Depaz Distillery (Martinique), *607*
Derek Walcott Square (Saint Lucia), *753*
Desecheo Island (Puerto Rico), *661*
Deshaies (Guadeloupe), *498–500*
Devil's Bridge (Antigua), *103*
Devon House (Jamaica), *546*
Diamond Chocolate Factory (Jouvay Chocolate; Grenada), *452*
Diamond Falls Botanical Gardens & Mineral Baths (Saint Lucia), *762*
Diamond Rock (Martinique), *602*
Distrito T-Mobile (Puerto Rico), *638*
Dive Curaçao, (dive center), *363*
Dive Friends Bonaire, *238*
Dive Provo (Providenciales), *847*
Dive Saint Lucia, *773*
DiveTech (Grand Cayman), *324*
Divi Aruba All-Inclusive , *146*
Divi Aruba Phoenix Beach Resort , *153*
Divi Little Bay Beach Resort (St. Maarten and St. Martin) , *802*
Diving and snorkeling, *36–37*
Dolphin Academy (Curaçao), *365*
Dolphin Cove (Jamaica), *532*
Domaine de Vanibel (Guadeloupe), *495*
Dominican Republic, *13, 376–436*
beaches, 395, 398–399, 401–402, 412, 413–416, 419, 422, 424, 426–427
festivals and seasonal events, 34, 378
health and safety, 382
lodging, 383, 388, 389–390, 391, 393, 397, 399, 403–408, 412–413, 415, 417, 419, 423–424, 425–426, 427
money matters, 378
nightlife and the arts, 383–384, 389, 390, 393, 408–409, 417–418, 424
price categories, 383
restaurants, 382–383, 387, 389, 391, 395–397, 402, 412, 415, 416–417, 420, 423, 425, 427
shopping, 384, 389, 390–391, 397–398, 409
sports and activities, 428–436
tours, 429, 431, 433, 435–436
transportation, 380–382
visitor information, 384
weddings, 384
Donkey Sanctuary Aruba, *160*
Donkeys of Bonaire, *233*
Dorado (Puerto Rico), *658–659*
Dorado Beach, A Ritz-Carlton Reserve (Puerto Rico) , *659*
Double Header Sportfishing (St. Thomas), *898*
Dragon Cay Resort (Middle Caicos) , *854*
Drake's Seat (overlook; St. Thomas), *894*
DreadHop Brewing (Barbados), *193*
Dreamcatcher, The (Puerto Rico) , *641*
Dreamer Catamaran Cruises (Jamaica), *575*
Driftwood Charters (Aruba), *164*
Druif Beach (Aruba), *143–148*
Dubuc Castle (Martinique), *610*
Dunn's River Falls & Park (Jamaica), *533*
Dunn's River Falls Beach (Jamaica), *536*
Dutch Pancakehouse, The (Aruba) ✕, *139*
Dutch Side (St. Maarten and St. Martin), *789–802, 812*

E

Eagle Beach (Aruba), *30, 143–148*
East Bay Resort (South Caicos) , *856*
East Coast (Barbados), *204–207*
East End (Curaçao), *364–368*
East End (Grand Cayman), *318–331*
East End (St. Croix), *928–931*
East End (St. Thomas), *887–891*
ECO Lifestyle + Lodge (Barbados) , *205*
Eden Brown Estate (Nevis), *726*
Eden Rock St. Barths , *696–697*
Edmund Forest Reserve (Saint Lucia), *762*
Educators Park (St. Thomas), *878, 881*
876 Beach Club (Jamaica), *529*
El Capitolio (Puerto Rico), *634*
El Quenepo (Puerto Rico) ✕, *654*
El Yunque (Puerto Rico), *645, 648*
Elements (Aruba) ✕, *144*
Elvis' Beach Bar (Anguilla) ✕, *83, 90*
Emancipation Garden (St. Thomas), *881*
Emancipation Park (Jamaica), *546–547*
Emancipation Statue (Barbados), *182*
Emergencies, *54, 60*
Emilio's (St. Maarten and St. Martin) ✕, *792*
Epic Tours (Bonaire), *236*
Estate Mount Washington Plantation (St. Croix), *937*
Estate Whim Museum (St. Croix), *931–932*
Estela (Puerto Rico) ✕, *661*
Evita's Italian Restaurant (Jamaica) ✕, *537*
Excellence Oyster Bay (Jamaica) , *530*
Excellence Punta Cana (Dominican Republic) , *405*

F

Fairmont El San Juan Hotel (Puerto Rico) , *642*
Fairview Great House & Botanical Gardens (St. Kitts), *711*
Fajardo (Puerto Rico), *649–652*
Falmouth (Antigua), *103, 106*
Falmouth (Jamaica), *528–530*
Farley Hill National Park (Barbados), *205*
Faulkner House Museum (Anegada), *279*
Fern Gully (Jamaica), *533*
Festivals and seasonal events, *65–67.* ⇨ *See also under specific islands*
Fig Tree Drive (Antigua), *106*
Firefly Estate (Jamaica), *533*
Flamands (St. Barthélemy), *691–692*
Flamingo Adventure Golf (Bonaire), *225*
Flamingo Divers (Providenciales), *847*
Flamingo Pond (North Caicos), *852–853*

Floating Market (Curaçao), *357*
Flower Forest Botanical Gardens (Barbados), *207, 209*
Floyd's Pelican Bar (Jamaica) ✕, *557*
Flying Fishbone (Aruba) ✕, *158*
Folkestone Marine Park and Museum (Barbados), *196*
Folly Lighthouse (Jamaica), *542*
Folly Ruins (Jamaica), *542*
Fond Doux Eco Resort (Saint Lucia) ▦, *768–769*
Fond Doux Estate (Saint Lucia), *762*
Foodies (Bonaire) ✕, *229*
Forêt de Montravail (Martinique), *602*
Ft. Ashby (Nevis), *726*
Fort Burt (Tortola), *249*
Fort Charles (Jamaica), *554*
Fort Charlotte (Saint Lucia), *753*
Fort Christian (St. Thomas), *881*
Fort Christiansvaern (St. Croix), *923*
Fort-de-France (Martinique), *587–594*
Ft. Fleur d'Épée (Guadeloupe), *489*
Ft. Frederick (Grenada), *447*
Fort Frederik (St. Croix), *933*
Ft. George (Antigua), *106*
Ft. George (Grenada), *447, 450*
Fort Louis (St. Maarten and St. Martin), *803*
Fort Napoléon des Saintes (Guadeloupe), *506*
Fort Nassau Restaurant (Curaçao) ✕, *359*
Fort Recovery (Tortola), *255*
Fort Recovery Beachfront Villas and Suites (Tortola) ▦, *256*
Fort St-Louis (Martinique), *589*
Fort Zoutman (Aruba), *135*
Fothergills Nevisian Heritage Village, *726*
40 Eats and Drinks (St. Croix) ✕, *924*
Four Seasons Golf Course (Nevis), *32, 735*
Four Seasons Resort Nevis ▦, *731*
Foxy's Taboo (Jost Van Dyke) ✕, *275*
Franklin D. Roosevelt Memorial Park (St. Thomas), *881*
Fred, The (St. Croix) ▦, *935*
Frederick Evangelical Lutheran Church (St. Thomas), *881*
Frederiksted and environs (St. Croix), *932–936*
Free Walking Tours (Curaçao), *364*
French Cul de Sac (St. Maarten and St. Martin), *806–807*
French Heritage Museum (St. Thomas), *894*
French Side (St. Maarten and St. Martin), *802–818*
Frenchtown (St. Thomas), *894*
Friar's Boy Beach Café (St. Maarten and St. Martin) ✕, *803, 805*
Friends of the Park Store St. John), 908
Friends of the Virgin Islands National Park (St. John), *917*
Frigate Bird Sanctuary (Barbuda), *124*
Fromage Bistro (Jamaica) ✕, *550*
Fruit Bowl (grocery; St. Thomas), *893*
Fusion Restaurant Wine & Piano Bar (Aruba) ✕, *145*

G

Galerias at Puntacana Village (Dominican Republic), *409*
Gallery Alma Blou (Curaçao), *362*
Gallery Camille Pissarro (St. Thomas), *881*
Galley Bay Resort & Spa (Antigua) ▦, *26, 114*
Gallows Point Resort (St. John) ▦, *906*
Garrison, The (Barbados), *179, 182–185*
Gazcue (Dominican Republic), *391, 393*
Geejam (Jamaica) ▦, *544*
George Town (Grand Cayman), *291–298*
Gladys B. Howard Little Cayman National Trust Visitors Centre, *338*
Gladys' Cafe (St. Thomas) ✕, *883*
Glistening Waters (Jamaica), *529*
Gloria-Movies, Entertainment, Dining & Play (Aruba), *143*
Gloria's Seafood City (Jamaica) ✕, *550–551*
Go Golf Tours (GGT; Dominican Republic), *435–436*
Goat Soup and Whiskey (St. Croix) ✕, *929–930*
GoldenEye (Jamaica) ▦, *539*
Golf, *32–33*
Golf Links at Royal Isabela (Puerto Rico), *33, 665*
Gorda Peak National Park (Virgin Gorda), *272*
Gotomeer (Bonaire), *225*
Gouverneur (St. Barthélemy), *692*
Gouverneur de Rouville Restaurant & Café (Curaçao) ✕, *359*
Gouyave Nutmeg Processing Station (Grenada), *452*
Government House (St. Croix), *923*
Government House (Saint Lucia), *753, 756*
Government House (St. Thomas), *881*
Grace Bay (Providenciales), *833–840*
Grace Bay Beach (Providenciales), *833*
Graceway IGA (shop; Providenciales), *832*
Gran Ventana Beach Resort (Dominican Republic) ▦, *413*
Grand Anse (Grenada), *452*
Grand Anse Beach (Grenada), *454*
Grand Case (St. Maarten and St. Martin), *808–811*
Grand Cayman–Eastern Districts (Cayman Islands), *314–331*
Grand Cayman–West Section (Cayman Islands), *291–314*
Grand Cul de Sac (St. Barthélemy), *692–693*
Grand Étang National Park & Forest Reserve (Grenada), *453, 455*
Grand Old House (Grand Cayman) ✕, *294*
Grand Palladium Lady Hamilton Resort & Spa (Jamaica) ▦, *525*
Grand Turk (Turks and Caicos), *856–863*
Grand Turk Lighthouse (Turks and Caicos), *860*
Grande Saline (St. Barthélemy), *693–694*
Grande-Terre (Guadeloupe), *483, 486–494*
Grappa (Puerto Rico) ✕, *658*
Great Harbour Beach (Jost Van Dyke), *274*
Greater Antilles, *13*
Green Grotto Caves (Jamaica), *531*
Greenwood Great House (Jamaica), *521–522*
Grenada, *17, 438–472*
beaches, 444, 452, 453, 454–455, 468, 472
festivals and seasonal events, 35, 440
health and safety, 444
lodging, 444–445, 456–460, 469–470, 472
money matters, 440
nightlife and the arts, 445, 460
price categories, 445
restaurants, 445–446, 450, 455–456, 468–469, 472
shopping, 446, 450–451, 460–461
sports and activities, 37, 461–465, 470–471, 472
tours, 463–465, 471, 472
transportation, 442–444
visitor information, 446
weddings, 447
Grenville Nutmeg Processing Station (Grenada), *453*
Guadeloupe, *14, 474–510*
beaches, 479, 489, 490, 492, 494, 496, 499, 502, 506
festivals and seasonal events, 35, 476, 501
health and safety, 479
lodging, 479–480, 488, 491, 492–493, 496, 497–498, 499–500, 502–504, 506–507
money matters, 476
nightlife and the arts, 480, 488, 491, 492
price categories, 480
restaurants, 480, 482, 483, 487–488, 490–491, 492, 496–497, 499, 502, 506
shopping, 482, 486, 489, 490, 493, 494, 504, 507
sports and activities, 37, 508–510
transportation, 478–479
visitor information, 482
weddings, 482
Guana Island (British Virgin Islands), *282*
Guana Island Resort (British Virgin Islands) ▦, *282*
Guanahani Restaurant and Bar (Grand Turk) ✕, *861*
Guánica (Puerto Rico), *669–670*
Gun Hill Signal Station (Barbados), *209*
Gustavia (St. Barthélemy), *682–689*

H

Habitation Bellevue Distillery (Guadeloupe), *501*
Habitation Céron (Martinique), *613*
Habitation Clément (Martinique), *594*
Habitation Simon A1710 (Martinique), *594*
Hacienda Tamarindo (Puerto Rico) 🏨, *655*
Half Moon Bay (Providenciales), *842*
Hang Out Beach Bar (Bonaire) ✕, *229*
Harbour Village Beach Club (Bonaire) 🏨, *232*
Hard Rock Hotel & Casino Punta Cana (Dominican Republic) 🏨, *405*
Harmony Beach Park (Jamaica), *523*
Harrison's Cave (Barbados), *209*
Hassel Island (St. Thomas), *882*
Hastings (Barbados), *185, 188–189*
Hato Caves (Curaçao), *369*
Hato Rey (Puerto Rico), *639–640*
Health and safety, *56.* ⇨ *See also under specific islands*
Hebrew Congregation of St. Thomas, *882*
Hendo's Hideout (Jost Van Dyke) ✕, *275*
Her Majesty's Prison (Grand Turk), *857*
Her Majesty's Prison Museum (Tortola), *249*
Heritage House (Cayman Brac), *333*
Heritage Museum Collection (Anguilla), *76*
Heritage Quay (Antigua), *106*
Hermitage (Nevis) 🏨, *732*
Hermitage Plantation Inn (Nevis) ✕, *728–729*
Hermosa Cove (Jamaica) 🏨, *539*
Heywoods Beach (Barbados), *201*
Hibernia Restaurant and Art Gallery (Anguilla) ✕, *83*
High North Nature Reserve (Grenada), *467*
Hodelpa Nicolas de Ovando (Dominican Republic) 🏨, *388*
Hog Heaven (Virgin Gorda) ✕, *271*
Holetown and environs (Barbados), *196–201*
Holiday Inn Resort Aruba 🏨, *153*
Hollywood Beach Suites (North Caicos) 🏨, *853–854*
Holywell Pak (Jamaica), *554*
Hope Royal Botanic Gardens (Jamaica), *547*
Hope Zoo (Jamaica), *547*
Horny Toad, The (St. Maarten and St. Martin) 🏨, *801*
Horse Ranch Bonaire, *239*
Hôtel Barrière Le Carl Gustaf (St. Barthélemy) 🏨, *686*
Hotel El Convento (Puerto Rico) 🏨, *632*
Hotel La Plantation (St. Maarten and St. Martin) 🏨, *814*
Hôtel Le Toiny (St. Barthélemy) 🏨, *689–690*
Hôtel L'Esplanade (St. Maarten and St. Martin) 🏨, *810*
Hotel Manapany (St. Barthélemy) 🏨, *697*
Hotel Plein Soleil (Martinique) 🏨, *595*
Hotel Riu Palace Macao (Dominican Republic) 🏨, *405–406*
House, The (Barbados) 🏨, *199*
Hunte's Gardens (Barbados), *209*
Hyatt Regency Casino (Aruba), *149*
Hyatt Zilara Rose Hall (Jamaica) 🏨, *527*

I

Ib designs (shop; St. Croix), *927*
Iberostar Grand Bávaro Hotel (Dominican Republic) 🏨, *406*
Iglesia Santa Bárbara (Dominican Republic), *386*
Iguana Mama (tours; Dominican Republic), *429*
Il Pasticcio (Dominican Republic) ✕, *420*
Iles des Saintes (Guadeloupe), *504–510*
Ilet Pinel (St. Maarten and St. Martin), *806*
Îlets Pigeon (Guadeloupe), *496*
Imagine (club; Dominican Republic), *409*
Immunizations, *56*
Independence Square (St. Kitts), *712*
Indigo (Providenciales) ✕, *828*
Indigo Blue (shop; Nevis), *734*
Indigo Divers (Grand Cayman), *324–325*
Infini (Aruba) ✕, *145*
Infiniti Restaurant & Raw Bar (Providenciales) ✕, *835*
Institute of Jamaica, *547*
Institute for Hispanic Culture (Dominican Republic), *386*
Interpretation Center Paul Gauguin (Martinique), *611–612*
Isabela (Puerto Rico), *664–665*
Isla Catalina (Dominican Republic), *398*
Isla Culebrita (Puerto Rico), *656*
Isla Saona (Dominican Republic), *398*
Isla Verde and Carolina (Puerto Rico), *642–643*
Island Harbour (Anguilla), *80*
Island Routes Caribbean Adventures (Jamaica), *572*
Island Vibes (boating; Providenciales), *844*
Isle Grande (Puerto Rico), *638*
It Rains Fishes (Bonaire) ✕, *230*
Italian Job, The (Jamaica) ✕, *543*
Ivan's Bar & Restaurant (Jamaica) ✕, *561*
Izi Ristorante Italiano (St. Maarten and St. Martin) ✕, *800*

J

J.R. O'Neal Botanic Gardens (Tortola), *249*
Jacala Beach Restaurant (Anguilla) ✕, *83*
Jack Sprat Restaurant (Jamaica) ✕, *557*
Jackson Wall (Little Cayman), *342*
Jacques Waterfront Dining (Saint Lucia) ✕, *749*
Jade Mountain (Saint Lucia) 🏨, *26, 769*
Jakes Hotel (Jamaica) 🏨, *557, 559*
Jamaica, *13, 512–576*
beaches, 517, 522–523, 529, 531, 536, 540, 542–543, 556–557, 560
festivals and seasonal events, 35, 514, 517–518
health and safety, 518
lodging, 518–519, 525–528, 530, 532, 538–541, 544–545, 551–552, 555, 557, 559, 563–565, 567
money matters, 514
nightlife and the arts, 519, 528, 541, 552, 567
price categories, 519
restaurants, 519–520, 523, 525, 529–530, 531–532, 536–538, 543–544, 550–551, 554, 555, 557, 560–562
shopping, 520, 541, 545, 552–553, 567–568
sports and activities, 568–576
tours, 521, 571–574
transportation, 516–517
visitor information, 521
weddings, 521
Jamaica Standard Products Coffee Factory, *555–556*
Jamaica Swamp Safari Village, *529*
Jamaican Jazz and Blues (festival), *517–518*
Jamaican Rum Festival, *518*
Jardin Botanique de Deshaies (Guadeloupe), *498*
Jardin de Balata (Martinique), *605–606*
Jibe City (windsurfing; Bonaire), *240*
Jolly Pirates (Aruba), *161*
Jost Van Dyke (British Virgin Islands), *273–278*
Jumby Bay Island (Antigua) 🏨, *27, 115*
Junior's Glass Bottom Boat (Anguilla), *94*
JW Marriott Santo Domingo (Dominican Republic) 🏨, *390*

K

Karel's Beach Bar (Bonaire), *234*
Kate Design (shop; St. Kitts), *720*
Kay's Fine Jewelry (shop; Aruba), *142*
Kenny's Italian Cafe (Jamaica) ✕, *561–562*
Kew (North Caicos), *853*
King's Casino (Antigua), *108*
Kingston (Jamaica), *545–563*
Kome (Curaçao) ✕, *359*

Konoko Falls and Park (Jamaica), *533*
Kool Runnings Adventure Park (Jamaica), *560*
Kralendijk (Bonaire), *225*
Kreol West Indies (museum; Guadeloupe), *501*
Kukoo Kunuku Party & Foodie Tours (Aruba), *133–134*
Kunuku Aqua Funpark (Curaçao), *369*

L

L & L Rum Shop (Nevis), *734*
La Belle Creole (Grenada) ✕, *455–456*
La Cabane (Barbados) ✕, *197*
La Cana Golf Club (Dominican Republic), *33, 435*
La Case d L'Isle (St. Barthélemy) ✕, *691*
La Cigale (St. Maarten and St. Martin) ✕, *808*
La Concha–A Renaissance Resort (Puerto Rico) 🏨, *635*
La Créole Beach Hotel & Spa (Guadeloupe) 🏨, *488*
La Désirade (Guadeloupe), *503*
La Distillerie J.M. (Martinique), *608–609*
La Estación (Puerto Rico) ✕, *650*
La Factoria (bar; Puerto Rico), *632–633*
La Fortaleza (Puerto Rico), *629*
La Marocain (St. Maarten and St. Martin) ✕, *805*
La Playa Orient Bay (St. Maarten and St. Martin) 🏨, *814*
La Playita (Dominican Republic), *426*
La Reine Chicken Shack (St. Croix) ✕, *932*
La Romana (Dominican Republic), *396–398*
La Sagesse Restaurant (Grenada) ✕, *456*
La Savane (Martinique), *589*
La Savane des Esclaves (Martinique), *598*
La Suite Villa (Martinique) 🏨, *599–600*
La Toubana Hôtel & Spa (Guadeloupe) 🏨, *493*
Ladera Resort (Saint Lucia) 🏨, *769*
Laguna Dudú (Dominican Republic), *418–419*
Laluna (Grenada) 🏨, *458*
Landhuis Chobolobo (Curaçao), *357*
Landings Resort & Spa, The (Saint Lucia) 🏨, *751*
Las Brisas Restaurant and Bar (Providenciales) ✕, *833*
Las Croabas (Puerto Rico), *650*
Las Galeras (Dominican Republic), *426–427*
Las Terrenas (Dominican Republic), *422–424*
L'Astrolabe (St. Maarten and St. Martin) ✕, *813*
Laura Herb & Spice Garden (Grenada), *453*
L'Azure (Barbados) ✕, *195*
Leatherback Brewing (St. Croix), *936*
Le Barthélemy Hotel & Spa 🏨**, 690**
Le Carbet (Martinique), *611–612*
Le Centre de Découverte des Sciences de la Terre (Martinique), *607*
Le Diamant (Martinique), *602–603*
Le François (Martinique), *594–595*
Le Gosier (Guadeloupe), *486–488*
Le Marin (Martinique), *603*
Le Morne Rouge (Martinique), *608*
Le Moule (Guadeloupe), *488–489*
Le Musée Territorial, Wall House (St. Barthélemy), *682*
Le Petibonum (Martinique) ✕, *612*
Le Petit Collectionneur (St. Barthélemy), *682*
Le Petit Hotel (St. Maarten and St. Martin) 🏨, *810*
Le Plein Soleil Restaurant (Martinique) ✕, *595*
Le Prêcheur (Martinique), *613*
Le Sélect (bar; St. Barthélemy), *686*
Le Sereno (St. Barthélemy) 🏨, *693*
Le Temps des Cerises (St. Maarten and St. Martin) 🏨, *811*
Le Ti St. Barth Caribbean Tavern (St. Barthélemy) ✕, *695*
Le Village St. Barth Hotel 🏨**, 897**
Le Zandoli (Martinique) ✕, *599*
Le Zawag (Guadeloupe) ✕, *487*
Legislature Building (St. Thomas), *882*
Les Ballades du Delphis (sailing; Martinique), *614*
Les Chutes du Carbet (Guadeloupe), *497*
Les Fonds Blancs (Martinique), *594*
Les Mamelles (Guadeloupe), *496*
Les Trois-Îlets (Martinique), *595, 598–601*
L'Escargot (Jamaica) ✕, *531*
L'Esprit (St. Barthélemy) ✕, *693–694*
Lesser Antilles and Leeward Islands, *14–15*
Lime Inn (St. John) ✕, *903*
Lime Out (St. John) ✕, *914–915*
L'Isola (St. Barthélemy) ✕, *684–685*
Little Bay (St. Maarten and St. Martin), *802*
Little Cayman (Cayman Islands), *338–342*
Little Cayman Museum, *338*
Little Cayman Research Center, *338–339*
Little Dix Bay Pavilion (Virgin Gorda) ✕, *268*
Little Havana (bar; Bonaire), *235*
Little La Grange Farm and Lawaetz Museum (St. Croix), *933*
Lobster Dave Seafood Restaurant (Jamaica) ✕, *537*
Lodging. ⇨ **See under specific islands**
Lone Star (Barbados) ✕, *197*
Lorient (St. Barthélemy), *694–695*
Los Haitises National Park (Dominican Republic), *424–425*
Loterie Farm (St. Maarten and St. Martin), *812*
Lovango Cay (St. John), *912–913*
Love Villas (Grand Turk) 🏨, *859*
Lovers Leap (Jamaica), *556*
Lovers National Park & Bird Sanctuary (Grenada), *453*
Luca (Grand Cayman) ✕, *306–307*
Lucia (Dominican Republic) ✕, *412*
Luna Restaurant & Tapas Bar (Nevis) ✕, *729*
Luquillo (Puerto Rico), *648–649*

M

Maca Bana (Grenada) 🏨, *458*
Macabuca Oceanside Tiki Bar (Grand Cayman), *302*
Macouba (Martinique), *608–609*
Madero Ocean Club (Curaçao) ✕, *365*
MADMI (Museum of Art & Design Miramar; Puerto Rico), *638*
Mafolie Hotel (St. Thomas) 🏨, *884*
Magens Bay (St. Thomas), *895*
Magic Moments (cruise; St. Thomas), *896–897*
Maho (St. Maarten and St. Martin), *796–797*
Malcolm Guishar Recreational Park (Nevis), *726*
Malliouhana, An Auberge Resort (Anguilla) 🏨, *88*
Mambo Beach Boulevard (amusement park; Curaçao), *366*
Mamiku Gardens (Saint Lucia), *771*
Manchebo Beach (Aruba), *143–148*
Mandeville (Jamaica), *556*
Mangazina di Rei Cultural Park (Bonaire), *225*
Mango (Nevis) ✕, *729*
Mango Reef (Providenciales) ✕, *841*
Mangrove Beach Corendon Curacao All-Inclusive Resort 🏨**, 360**
Manman'dlo the Siren (Guadeloupe) ✕, *502*
Manta House (Grand Turk) 🏨, *859*
Margaritaville Montego Bay (Jamaica) ✕, *523*
Margaritaville Negril (Jamaica) ✕, *562*
Margaritaville Vacation Club by Wyndham (St. Thomas) 🏨, *887*
Maria Islands Nature Reserve (Saint Lucia), *771*
Marie-Galante (Guadeloupe), *500–504*
Marigot (St. Maarten and St. Martin), *802–803, 805–806*
Marigot Bay (Saint Lucia), *760–761*
Mario Bistro (St. Maarten) ✕, *795*

Maritime Museum (Curaçao), *357*
Market Square (Grenada), *451*
Marmalade (Puerto Rico) ✕, *631*
Martha Brae River (Jamaica), *529*
Martinique, *17, 578–616*
beaches, 584, 598–599, 602–603, 604–605, 611
festivals and seasonal events, 34, 580
health and safety, 585
language, 612
lodging, 585–586, 592–593, 595, 599–600, 603, 604, 608, 610, 611
money matters, 580
nightlife and the arts, 586, 593, 600–601, 604, 611
price categories, 586
restaurants, 584–585, 591–592, 595, 599, 603, 605, 611, 612
shopping, 586–587, 593–594, 601
sports and activities, 613–616
transportation, 582–584
visitor information, 587
weddings, 587
Mask-Mopa Mopa Art (shop; Aruba), *143*
Maundays Bay (Anguilla), *81*
Meads Bay (Anguilla), *81*
Megaliths of Greencastle Hill (Antigua), *106*
Memorial Moravian Church (St. Thomas), *882*
Meridian Club, Turks & Caicos 🏨, *851–852*
Miami Beach (Barbados), *193*
Mid Island (St. Croix), *931–932*
Mid Island (St. John), *913*
Middle Caicos (Turks and Caicos), *854–855*
Mikvé Israel-Emanuel Synagogue (Curaçao), *357*
Miramar and Isle Grande (Puerto Rico), *638*
Miss Ann Boat Trips (Curaçao), *368*
Miss T's Kitchen (Jamaica) ✕, *537*
Mission House (Grand Cayman), *316*
Mr. Grouper's (Providenciales) ✕, *828*
Monasterio de San Francisco (Dominican Republic), *386*
Money matters, *58.* ⇨ *See also under specific islands*
Mont Pelée (Martinique), *608*
Montego Bay (Jamaica), *521–528*
Montpelier Plantation & Beach (Nevis) 🏨, *732–733*
MooMba Beach Bar (Aruba), *154*
Moon Palace Jamaica 🏨, *540*
Morgan Lewis Windmill (Barbados), *205–206*
Morgan Resort & Spa, The (St. Maarten and St. Martin) 🏨, *796*
Morgan's Seafood Restaurant (Grand Cayman) ✕, *307*
Morne-à-l'Eau (Guadeloupe), *494*
Morne Coubaril (Saint Lucia), *764*
Mt. Eagle (St. Croix), *937*
Mount Gay Rum Visitors Centre (Barbados), *182*
Mount Healthy National Park (Tortola), *260*
Mt. Hooiberg (Aruba), *158*
Mountain Top (St. Thomas), *894*
Mudjin Bar and Grill (Middle Caicos) ✕, *854*
Mullet Bay Beach (St. Maarten and St. Martin), *31, 795*
Mundo Bizarro (club; Curaçao), *361*
Murphy's West End Restaurant (Jamaica) ✕, *562*
Musée Camélia Costumes et Traditions (Guadeloupe), *486*
Musée d'Archéologie Précolombienne et de Préhistoire (Martinique), *589, 591*
Musée de la Pagerie (Martinique), *595, 598*
Musée d'Histoire et d'Ethnographie (Martinique), *591*
Musée du Café/ Café Chaulet (Guadeloupe), *495*
Musée du Père Pinchon (Martinique), *591*
Musée Volcanologique Franck Perret (Martinique), *607–608*
Museo Castillo Serrallés (Guadeloupe), *483*
Museo Castillo Serrallés (Puerto Rico), *667*
Museo de Ámbar Dominicano (Dominican Republic), *411*
Museo de Arte Contemporáneo de Puerto Rico, *639*
Museo de Arte de Ponce (Puerto Rico), *667–668*
Museo de Arte de Puerto Rico, *639–640*
Museo de Historia, Antropología y Arte (Puerto Rico), *643*
Museo de la Historia de Ponce (Puerto Rico), *668*
Museo de las Américas (Puerto Rico), *629*
Museo Judio Sosúa (Dominican Republic), *414*
Museum of Antigua and Barbuda, *106*
Museum of Nevis History, *726–727*
Myett's Garden & Grille Restaurant (Tortola), *260*
Mystic Mountain (Jamaica), *536*

N

Naca'n (Dominican Republic) ✕, *387*
National Gallery of Jamaica, *547*
National Gallery of the Cayman Islands (Grand Cayman), *292*
National Museum (St. Kitts), *712*
National Park Shete Boka (Curaçao), *369, 371*
National Stadium of Jamaica *483*
National Trust for the Cayman Islands (Grand Cayman), *292*
Negril (Jamaica), *559–568*
Negril Beach (Jamaica), *31*
Neisson Distillery (Martinique), *612*
Nelson's Dockyard (Antigua), *106–107*
Neptune's Lookout (St. John), *913*
Neptune's Treasure (Anegada) ✕, *279*
Nevis, *15, 702–708, 724–736.* ⇨ *See also St. Kitts and Nevis*
Nevis Adventure Tours, *735*
Nevis Hot Springs, *727*
Nevis Sun Tours, *736*
Nidulari Artisan Bakery (St. Croix) ✕, *934*
Nightlife and the arts. ⇨ **See under specific islands**
1919 Restaurant (Puerto Rico) ✕, *634*
99 Steps (staircase street; St. Thomas), *882*
Nonsuch Bay Resort (Antigua) 🏨, *115*
Noord (Aruba), *148–155*
Norman Island (British Virgin Islands), *282*
North Beach (Salt Cay), *863*
North Caicos (Turks and Caicos), *852–854*
North Side (Grand Cayman), *315–316*
North Shore (St. Croix), *936–942*
North Shore (St. John), *909–912*
North Shore Shell Museum (Tortola), *257*

O

Ocean Encounters (diving; Curaçao), *367*
Ocean Frontiers (diving; Grand Cayman), *325*
Ocean Park (Puerto Rico), *641–642*
Ocean Terrace Inn (St. Kitts) 🏨, *718*
Ocean World Adventure Park (Dominican Republic), *411–412*
Oceana Restaurant & Bistro (St. Thomas) ✕, *895*
Oceanaire Bistro (Salt Cay) ✕, *864*
Ocho Rios (Jamaica), *532–541*
Octopus Aruba, *164*
Oistins (Barbados), *192–194*
Oistins Fish Fry (Barbados), *193*
Old Danish Customs House (St. Croix), *923*
Old Government House Museum (Tortola), *252*
Old Quarry Golf Course (Curaçao), *367–368*
Old Road (St. Kitts), *712*
Old San Juan (Puerto Rico), *625, 628–634*
Old Stone Farmhouse (St. Thomas) ✕, *889*
O:live Boutique Hotel (Puerto Rico) 🏨, *635*
Oliver's (Grenada) ✕, *456*

Omar's Cafe (Tortola) ✕, *255–256*
On The Dune (Nevis) ✕, *729*
1,000 Steps (Bonaire), *225–226*
Oranjestad (Aruba), *134–135, 138–143*
Orega (St. Barthélemy) ✕, *684*
Orléans (St. Maarten and St. Martin), *811*
Ostrich Farm (Curaçao), *365*
O2 Beach Club and Spa (Barbados), *191*
Owen Island (beach; Little Cayman), *339*
Ox-pulling competition (Guadeloupe), *501*
Oyster Pond (St. Maarten and St. Martin), *797–798*

P

Paddle Barbados, 214
Palm Beach (Aruba), *148–155*
Palm Court at Orient Beach Hotel (St. Maarten and St. Martin), *814*
Palm Heights (Grand Cayman), *311*
Palms, The (Providenciales), *837*
Pantheon de la Patria (Dominican Republic), *386*
Paradise Beach (Grenada), *468*
Paradisus Palma Real (Dominican Republic), *407*
Parc Cultural Aimé Césaire (Martinique), *591*
Parc National de la Guadeloupe, *497*
Parham (Antigua), *108*
Parliament Buildings (Barbados), *182*
Parque Colón (Dominican Republic), *386*
Parque de Bombas (Puerto Rico), *668*
Parque de las Cavernas del Río Camuy (Puerto Rico), *660*
Parque Nacional Isabel de Torres (Dominican Republic), *412*
Parrot Cay Resort (Turks and Caicos), *850–851*
Paseo de la Princesa (Puerto Rico), *629*
Paseo Herencia (Aruba), *155*
Passions on the Beach (Aruba) ✕, *145*
Passports, *59*
Patio 15 (Aruba) ✕, *139*
Pavilion, The (St. Kitts) ✕, *716*
Peace Hill (St. John), *910*
Pearls Airport (Grenada), *453*
Pebbles Beach (Barbados), *183*
Pedro St. James Castle (Grand Cayman), *316*
Pelican Key (St. Maarten and St. Martin), *798–799*
Peter Tosh Museum (Jamaica), *547*
Petite Martinique (Grenada), *471–472*
Petite Pump Room (St. Thomas) ✕, *884*
Phantasea Tropical Botanical Garden (St. Thomas), *894*
Philipsburg (St. Maarten and St. Martin), *789, 792–795*
Philip's Animal Garden (Aruba), *149*
Piantini (Dominican Republic), *389–391*
Pic Paradis (St. Maarten and St. Martin), *811–812*
Piedra So (golf; Bonaire), *239*
Pier 1 (Jamaica) ✕, *523*
Pigeon Island National Landmark (Saint Lucia), *748*
Pillory Beach (Grand Turk), *860–861*
Pinchos Grill & Bar (Aruba) ✕, *139–140*
Pine Cay (Turks and Caicos), *851–852*
Pink Beach (Antigua and Barbuda), *30*
Pink Plantation House, The (Saint Lucia) ✕, *756*
Pinney's Beach (Nevis), *31*
Pirates Point Restaurant (Little Cayman) ✕, *339–340*
Pirates Point Resort (Little Cayman), *340*
Pitons, The (Saint Lucia), *764*
Pizza Pi (St. Thomas) ✕, *889*
Plasa Bieuw (Old Market; Curaçao), *357*
Playa Blanca (Dominican Republic) ✕, *402*
Playa Borinquen (Puerto Rico), *663–664*
Playa Colorado (Dominican Republic), *426*
Playa Cosón (Dominican Republic), *422*
Playa Dorada (Dominican Republic), *413–414*
Playa Flamenco (Puerto Rico), *31, 657*
Playa Grande (Dominican Republic), *419*
Playa Mar Chiquita (Puerto Rico), *658*
Playa Peña Blanca (Puerto Rico), *664*
Playa PortoMari (Curaçao), *30, 372*
Plaza Colón (Puerto Rico), *629*
Plaza Beach & Dive Resort Bonaire, *232*
Plaza de Armas (Puerto Rico), *629–630*
Plaza de España (Dominican Republic), *386–397*
Plaza del Mercado (Puerto Rico), *640*
Point of Sand (beach; Little Cayman), *339*
Point Udall (St. Croix), *929*
Pointe-à-Pitre (Guadeloupe), *483, 486–488*
Pointe des Châteaux (Guadeloupe), *489–490*
Pointe du Bout (Martinique), *598*
Pointe Milou (St. Barthélemy), *695*
Polly's at the Pier (St. Croix) ✕, *934–935*
Ponce (Puerto Rico), *665–668*
Port Antonio (Jamaica), *541–545*
Port Louis (Guadeloupe), *494*
Port Royal (Jamaica), *553–554*
Port Zante (St. Kitts), *712*
Portland Cliff Hanger (Jamaica) ✕, *543*
Potcake (dog adoption; Turks and Caicos), *837*
Presqu'île du Caravelle (Martinique), *610*
Primo Bar & Bistro (Barbados) ✕, *190*
Princess Diana Beach (Barbuda), *124*
Providenciales (Turks and Caicos), *827–850*
Provo Golf Club (Turks and Caicos), *33, 848*
Poza de las Mujeres (Puerto Rico), *658*
Public Market (Antigua), *103*
Puerto de Tierra (Puerto Rico), *634*
Puerto Mosquito Bioluminescent Bay (Puerto Rico), *653*
Puerto Plata (Dominican Republic), *411–413*
Puerto Rico, *13, 618–670*
beaches, 623, 635, 641, 642, 649, 650, 653–654, 657, 658, 661–662, 663–664, 668–669
festivals and seasonal events, 35, 620
health and safety, 624
lodging, 624, 631–632, 635, 641–642, 643, 644–645, 651, 654–655, 657, 659, 662, 665, 669, 670
money matters, 620
nightlife and the arts, 624–625, 633–634
price categories, 624
restaurants, 623–624, 630–631, 635, 638, 640, 641, 642, 644, 649, 650–651, 654, 657, 658–659, 662, 664–665, 669
shopping, 625, 633–634, 638
sports and activities, 37, 634, 649, 651–652, 655, 657–658, 659, 662, 665
transportation, 622–623
visitor information, 625
Puerto Seco Beach (Jamaica), *531*
Punda Thursday Vibes (festival; Curaçao), *361*
Punta Cana (Dominican Republic), *399, 401–409*
Punta Espada Golf Course (Dominican Republic), *435*
Purebeach (bar; Aruba), *155*
Pyratz Gourmet Sailing (St. Maarten and St. Martin), *815*

Q

Queen Elizabeth II Botanic Park (Grand Cayman), *314–315*
Queen Emma Bridge (Curaçao), *357–358*
Queen's Park and Queen's Park Gallery (Barbados), *182–183*
Quinta del Carmen (Aruba) ✕, *151–152*
Quito's Gazebo (Tortola) ✕, *258*
Quito's Inn (Tortola), *260*

R

R Hotel Kingston (Jamaica), *551*
R&I PATTON goldsmithing (shop; St. John), *909*
Rabot Hotel (Saint Lucia), *769*
Rabot Restaurant (Saint Lucia) ✕, *767*
Radisson Blu Aruba, *154*
Ragazzi (Grand Cayman) ✕, *307*
Ragged Point (Barbados), *194*

Rainbow Cafe & Beach Bar (St. Maarten and St. Martin) ✕, *810*
Rainforest Adventures St. Maarten (St. Maarten and St. Martin), *789, 792*
Rancho La Ponderosa (Aruba), *165*
Rancho Loco (Aruba), *165*
Reach Falls (Jamaica), *542*
Rebel Salute (festival; Jamaica), *518*
Red Hook (St. Thomas), *887*
Red Sail Sports Aruba, *164*
Redcliffe Quay (Antigua), *108*
Reduit Beach (Saint Lucia), *31, 748–749*
Reef Bay Trail (St. John), *913*
Refugio Nacional de Vida Silvestre de Culebra (Puerto Rico), *656*
Regency Bar and Lounge (Jamaica), *552*
Reggae Sunfest (festival; Jamaica), *518*
Renaissance Mall (Aruba), *142*
Renaissance Marketplace (Aruba), *135, 142*
Reserva Natural Las Cabezas de San Juan (Puerto Rico), *650*
Restaurants. ⇨ **See under specific islands**
Rhodes Restaurant (Grenada) ✕, *456*
Rhum de Père Labat Distillery, Domaine Poisson (Guadeloupe), *501*
Rick's Cafe (Jamaica) ✕, *562–563*
Rincón (Bonaire), *226*
Rincón (Puerto Rico), *660–662*
Rio Grande (Jamaica), *542*
Río Grande (Puerto Rico), *644–645*
Río Piedras (Puerto Rico), *643*
Ritz-Carlton Aruba, *154*
Ritz-Carlton Grand Cayman, The, *311*
Ritz-Carlton Turks & Caicos, *836*
River Antoine Rum Distillery (Grenada), *453–454*
Rockhouse Hotel (Jamaica), *565*
Rockhouse Restaurant (Jamaica) ✕, *563*
Rocklands Bird Sanctuary (Jamaica), *522*
Rockley (Barbados), *185, 188–189*
Rodney Bay and the North (Saint Lucia), *748–752*
Ron del Barrilito (Puerto Rico), *644*
Rooi Lamoenchi Kunuku (Bonaire), *226*
Romney Manor (St. Kitts), *712*
Rose Hall Great House (Jamaica), *522*
Rosewood Le Guanahani St. Barth, **693**
Rosewood Little Dix Bay (Virgin Gorda), *270*
Round Hill Hotel and Villas (Jamaica), *27, 527*
Route to Grand' Rivière (Martinique), *609*
Royal Isabela (Puerto Rico), *665*
Royalton Negril (Jamaica), *565*
Rue Victor Schoelcher (Martinique), *591*
Rum, *46*
Rum Runners (St. Croix) ✕, *924*
Runaway Bay (Jamaica), *530–532*

S

Safety, 56. ⇨ **See also under specific islands**
Sage Mountain National Park (Tortola), *260–261*
Sailrock Resort (South Caicos), *856*
St. Barthélemy, *14, 672–700*
beaches, 677, 680, 682, 684, 690, 692, 693, 694, 696
festivals and seasonal events, 674
health and safety, 681
lodging, 680–681, 686, 689–690, 692–693, 694, 695, 696–697
money matters, 674
nightlife and the arts, 681, 686, 697
price categories, 680
restaurants, 680, 682, 684–685, 689, 690, 692, 693–694, 696
shopping, 681, 686–689, 693, 694–695, 698–699
spas, 695
sports and activities, 699–700
tours, 700
transportation, 676–677, 682
visitor information, 682
St-Claude (Guadeloupe), *497–498*
St. Croix, *918–942.* ⇨ *See also United States Virgin Islands*
St-François (Guadeloupe), *489–491*
St. George Village Botanical Garden (St. Croix), *932*
St. George's (Grenada), *447, 450–451*
St. George's Anglican Church (St. Kitts), *712*
St. George's Methodist Church (Grenada), *450*
St. James Distillery & Rum Museum (Martinique), *610*
St-Jean (St. Barthélemy), *695–699*
St. John, *899–918.* ⇨ *See also United States Virgin Islands*
St. John's Figtree Church (Nevis), *727*
St. Kitts and Nevis, *15, 702–736*
beaches, 713–714, 727–728
festivals and seasonal events, 704
health and safety, 708
lodging, 708, 717–719, 731–733
money matters, 704
nightlife and the arts, 719–720, 733–734
price categories, 708
restaurants, 708, 714–717, 728–729, 731
shopping, 720–721, 734
sports and activities, 721–724, 734–736
tours, 723, 736
transportation, 706–707
visitor information, 708
weddings, 708
St. Kitts Eco Park, *712–713*
St. Kitts Scenic Railway, *713*
St. Lawrence Gap (Barbados), *189–192*
St-Louis Cathedral (Martinique), *591*
Saint Lucia, *17, 738–778*
beaches, 744–745, 748–749, 756, 760, 764–765
festivals and seasonal events, 34, 745
health and safety, 745
language, 759
lodging, 745–746, 750–752, 756–758, 761, 768–770, 771–772
money matters, 740
nightlife and the arts, 752
price categories, 746
restaurants, 745–747, 749–750, 756, 760–761, 765, 767
shopping, 747, 752, 758–760, 770
sports and activities, 37, 772–778
tours, 775–776
transportation, 743–744
visitor information, 747
weddings, 747
Saint Lucia Distillers Group of Companies, *760*
Saint Lucia National Trust, *776*
St. Maarten and St. Martin, *15, 780–818*
beaches, 786, 792, 795, 796, 797, 802, 803, 806, 807, 809, 811, 812–813, 814–815
festivals and seasonal events, 35, 782
lodging, 787–788, 793, 795, 796–797, 798–799, 801–802, 806–807, 810–811, 814, 815
money matters, 782
nightlife and the arts, 788, 794, 797, 799, 802
price categories, 787
restaurants, 786–787, 792–793, 795, 796, 797–798, 803, 805, 807, 808, 809–810, 811, 813–814
shopping, 789, 794–795, 805–806, 811, 814
sports and activities, 815–818, 855
transportation, 784–785
visitor information, 789
weddings, 789
St. Maarten Museum, *792*
St. Michael's Cathedral (Barbados), *183*
St. Nicholas Abbey (greathouse; Barbados), *206*
St-Pierre (Martinique), *606–608*
St. Regis Bahia Beach Resort (Puerto Rico), *645*
St. Thomas, *873–899.* ⇨ *See also United States Virgin Islands*
St. Thomas Anglican Church (Nevis), *727*
St. Thomas Historical Trust Museum, *882–883*
St. Thomas Reformed Church, *883*
Ste-Anne (Guadeloupe), *492–494*
Ste-Anne (Martinique), *603–604*
Ste-Luce (Martinique), *604–605*
Ste-Marie (Martinique), *609–610*
Ste-Rose (Guadeloupe), *496*
Saints Peter and Paul Cathedral (St. Thomas), *882*
Salt Cafe (Barbados) ✕, *188*
Salt Cay (Turks and Caicos), *863–864*
Salt Cay Divers (Turks and Caicos), *864*

Salt Pans (Bonaire), *226*
Salt Plage (bar; St. Kitts), *719–720*
Salt River Bay National Historical Park and Ecological Preserve (St. Croix), *937*
Salto el Limón Waterfall (Dominican Republic), *422*
Samaná Peninsula (Dominican Republic), *420–427*
Sambil Mall (Curaçao), *372–373*
San Germán (Puerto Rico), *670*
San Juan (Puerto Rico), *625–644*
San Nicolas (Aruba), *157–159*
San Nicolas Art Walk (Aruba), *157*
Sand Bar (Grand Turk) ✕, *859*
Sand Bar Eden Rock (St. Barthélemy) ✕, *696*
Sand Castle on the Beach (St. Croix) 🏨, *935–936*
Sandals Grande Saint Lucia 🏨, *752*
Sandals Grenada 🏨, *459*
Sandals Halcyon Beach Resort & Spa (Saint Lucia) 🏨, *757*
Sandals Royal Plantation (Jamaica) 🏨, *541*
Sandals South Coast (Jamaica) 🏨, *559*
Sandpiper Hotel, The (Barbados) 🏨, *200*
Sandy Ground (Anguilla), *76*
Sandy Island (Anguilla), *93*
Sandy Island (Grenada), *468*
Sandy Lane Country Club (Barbados), *32*
Sandy Point National Wildlife Refuge (St. Croix), *933*
Santa Bárbara de Samaná (Dominican Republic), *424–426*
Santiago (Dominican Republic), *419–420*
Santo Domingo (Dominican Republic), *384–393*
Santurce and Hato Rey (Puerto Rico), *639–640*
Sapodilla Hill (Providenciales), *832*
Savaneta (Aruba), *157–159*
Savant (St. Croix) ✕, *924–925*
Scale House (St. Croix), *923*
Scape Park at Cap Cana (Dominican Republic), *401*
Schoelcher (Martinique), *591*
Scotchies Montego Bay (Jamaica) ✕, *525*
Screaming Eagle Restaurant Aruba ✕, *145*
Scrub Island Resort, Spa and Marina (Tortola) 🏨, *264*
SCUBA SHACK – Shoal Bay Scuba and Watersports (Anguilla), *93*
Sea Shed (Barbados) ✕, *198*
Secrets Royal Beach Punta Cana (Dominican Republic) 🏨, *407*
Señor Paleta (Puerto Rico) ✕, *631*
Serena's Art Factory (Curaçao), *367*
Serendipity (St. Kitts) ✕, *716*
Serenity at Coconut Bay (Saint Lucia) 🏨, *772*
Seru Largu (Bonaire), *226*
Seven (Grand Cayman) ✕, *307–308*
Seven Mile Beach (Grand Cayman), *30, 302–314*
Seven Mile Beach (Jamaica), *560*
Seven Stars (Providenciales) 🏨, *838*
Shaggy and Friends (festival; Jamaica), *518*
Sharkies Seafood Restaurant (Jamaica) ✕, *531–532*
Sheer Rocks (Antigua) ✕, *111*
Shellona (St. Barthélemy) ✕, *685*
Shirley Heights (Antigua), *108*
Shirley Heights Lookout (bar; Antigua), *117*
Shiva's Gold and Gems (shop; Aruba), *155*
Shoal Bay (Anguilla), *80–81*
Shops at Alhambra Mall, The (Aruba), *148*
Siboney Beach Club (Antigua) 🏨, *115*
Simpson Bay (St. Maarten and St. Martin), *799–802*
Simpson Bay Resort and Marina (St. Maarten and St. Martin) 🏨, *798–799*
Six Senses Spa (Dominican Republic), *436*
Skinny Legs (St. John) ✕, *915*
Skyride to Paradise Point (St. Thomas), *892*
Slave Huts (Bonaire), *226*
Sloop Jones (shop; St. John), *915*
Soggy Dollar Bar (Jost Van Dyke) ✕, *275*
Somerset, The (Providenciales) 🏨, *838–839*
Somerset Falls (Jamaica), *542*
Somewhere Café and Lounge (Providenciales) ✕, *829*
Sonesta Ocean Point (St. Maarten and St. Martin) 🏨, *796*
Soper's Hole (Tortola), *255*
Sophia's Bar & Grill (SBG; Dominican Republic) ✕, *389*
Sosúa (Dominican Republic), *414–415*
Soufrière and Southwest Coast (Saint Lucia), *761–770*
South Caicos (Turks and Caicos), *855–856*
South Coast (Jamaica), *555–559*
South Coast Bar and Grill (Grand Cayman), *321*
South Point area (Barbados), *192–194*
South Point Lighthouse (Barbados), *193*
Southeast Shore (St. Thomas), *892–894*
Southern Cross Club (Little Cayman) 🏨, *340, 342*
South West Collective (bar; Grand Cayman), *295–296*
Spanish Town (Virgin Gorda), *265*
Speightown (Barbados), *201*
Spice Island Beach Resort (Grenada) 🏨, *459–460*
Spice Mill (St. Kitts) ✕, *716–717*
Sports and activities. ⇨ **See specific sports; under specific islands**
Steeple Building (St. Croix), *924*
Stellaris Casino (Aruba), *149*
Stingray City (dive site; Grand Cayman), *322*
Stingray City Sandbar (snorkeling site; Grand Cayman), *329*
Strawberry Hill (Jamaica) ✕, *555*
Strawberry Hill Hotel (Jamaica) 🏨, *555*
Sublime Samaná (Dominican Republic) 🏨, *423*
Substation Curaçao (submarine), *368*
Sugar Beach, A Viceroy Resort (Saint Lucia) 🏨, *770*
Sugar Mill Hotel (Tortola) 🏨, *260*
Sugar Mill Restaurant (Tortola) ✕, *259*
Sulpher Springs Park (Saint Lucia), *764*
Sun Charters (schooner; Providenciales), *845*
Sun Dog Café (St. John) ✕, *912*
Sunscape Curaçao Resort, Spa & Casino 🏨, *361*
Sunshine's (Nevis) ✕, *730*
Super Food Plaza (Aruba), *148*
Susannaberg Ruins & Neptune's Lookout (St. John), *913*
Sweetfield Manor (Barbados) 🏨, *184*
Synagogue Historic District (Barbados), *183*

T

T.H. Palm & Company (shop; Aruba), *155*
Taikun (Grand Cayman) ✕, *308*
Tamarijn Aruba All-Inclusive Beach Resort 🏨, *148*
Tamarin St. Barth 🏨, *694*
Tao (Saint Lucia) ✕, *749*
Tartane (Martinique), *610–611*
Taste My Aruba ✕, *140*
Telephones, *59*
Tensing Pen Resort (Jamaica) 🏨, *567*
Terra Nova All Suite Hotel (Jamaica) 🏨, *552*
Terre-de-Haut (Guadeloupe), *504, 506–510*
Three Mary Cays (North Caicos), *853*
Ti Kaye Resort & Spa (Saint Lucia) 🏨, *770*
Tiami Catamaran Cruises (Barbados), *213*
Tides, The (Barbados) ✕, *198*
Tin Box (Puerto Rico) ✕, *653*
Top Carrot (St. Maarten and St. Martin) ✕, *801*

Tortola (British Virgin Islands), *248–264*
Tortola Pier Park, *252*
Tortuga Bay (Dominican Republic) ⌂, *408*
Tranquility Beach (Anguilla) ⌂, *89*
Tranquilo Charters Aruba, 161
Transportation, *52–54.* ⇨ *See also under specific islands*
Trench Town Culture Yard Museum (Jamaica), *547*
Tres Sirenas (Puerto Rico) ⌂, *662*
Trident Freedivers (Barbados), *211*
Trident Hotel (Jamaica) ⌂, *545*
Tropical Travel (Bonaire), *239*
Trunk Bay Beach (St. John), *911*
Tryall Club Golf Course (Jamaica), *32*
Turks and Caicos Islands, *13, 820–864*
beaches, 828, 832–833, 842–843, 860–861, 863
festivals and seasonal events, 822
health and safety, 826
lodging, 826, 828, 829, 832, 836–839, 841, 843, 850–852, 853–854, 855, 856, 859–860, 861, 864
money matters, 822
nightlife and the arts, 839, 843, 861
price categories, 826
restaurants, 828–829, 833, 834–836, 830–841, 843, 853, 855, 856, 859, 861, 864
shopping, 832, 839–840, 843, 852, 861
spas, 840
sports and activities, 37, 844–850, 861–863, 864
tours, 826
transportation, 824–825
visitor information, 826–827
weddings, 827
Turks and Caicos National Museum (Grand Turk), *857, 859*
Turks Head Inne (Grand Turk) ⌂, *860*
Turks Kebab (Providenciales) ✕, *835*
Turtle Cove (Providenciales), *840–841*
Twist of Flavors (Aruba) ✕, *145–146*
Tyrrel Bay (Grenada), *467*

U

United States Virgin Islands, *15, 866–942*
beaches, 874–875, 887–889, 895, 900, 910–911, 913–914, 919, 929, 933–934, 937
festivals and seasonal events, 868
health and safety, 872
lodging, 872, 875, 878, 884–885, 890, 893, 896, 901–902, 903, 906, 912, 913, 919, 922, 925, 928, 930, 935–936, 938
money matters, 868
nightlife and the arts, 878, 884, 891, 893, 902, 907, 915, 922, 925–926, 930–931, 936
price categories, 873
restaurants, 875, 883–884, 889, 892, 895–896, 900, 903, 912, 914–915, 919, 924–925, 929–930, 932, 934–935, 937–938
shopping, 878, 885–887, 891, 893–894, 907–909, 915, 922, 926–927, 928, 931, 932, 936
sports and activities, 37, 896–899, 916–918, 939–942
tours, 879, 896, 898, 939, 941–942
transportation, 870–872
visitor information, 873, 922
weddings, 873

V

Veya and Meze at Veya (Anguilla) ✕, *86*
Vieques (Puerto Rico), *37, 652–655*
Vieques National Wildlife Refuge (Puerto Rico), *653*
Vieux Fort and the East Coast (Saint Lucia), *770–772*
Vieux-Habitants (Guadeloupe), *495*
Villa rentals, *62–63*
Village Bar at Lemon Arbour, The (Barbados) ✕, *209–210*
VIP Diving (Bonaire), *238–239*
Virgin Gorda (British Virgin Islands), *264–273*
Virgin Islands Children's Museum (St. Thomas), *892*
Virgin Islands National Park (St. John), *902*
Visas, *59*
Visitor information, *59–60, 68.* ⇨ *See also under specific islands*
Voilà by Lilee (Jamaica) ✕, *557*

W

Wades Green (North Caicos), *853*
Washington Slagbaai National Park (Bonaire), *226–227*
Water Department Barbecue (Nevis), *734*
Weddings, *64.* ⇨ *See also under specific islands*
Weibel Museum (St. Thomas), *883*
Welchman Hall Gully (Barbados), *209*
West Bay (Cayman Islands), *298–302*
West Dock Island Grill Beach Bar (Aruba), *141*
West End (Curaçao), *368–374*
West End (St. Thomas), *894–899*
West Indies Wine Company (bar; Grand Cayman), *313*
Westerhall Estate (Grenada), *454*
Western Tip (California Dunes; Aruba), *148, 156–157*
Westin Grand Cayman Seven Mile Beach Resort & Spa ⌂, *312*
Whale Museum & Nature Center (Dominican Republic), *425*
Whale Samaná (Dominican Republic), *433*
White Bay Beach (Jost Van Dyke), *274*
Willemstad (Curaçao), *354–364*
Willemstoren Lighthouse (Bonaire), *227*
Wind Creek Crystal Casino (Aruba), *135, 138*
Windows on Aruba ✕, *146*
Windward (Grenada), *467*
Windward Islands and the ABCs, *16–17*
Wonky Dog, The (Anegada) ✕, *280*
Worthing (Barbados), *185, 188–189*
Worthing Square Food Garden ✕, *196*
Wreck of the Ten Sails Park (Grand Cayman), *318*
Wymara Resort & Villas (Providenciales) ⌂, *829, 832*

Y

Y.S. Falls (Jamaica), *556*
Yaaman Adventure Park (Jamaica), *536*
Yoda Guy Movie Exhibit (St. Maarten and St. Martin), *792*

Z

Zaka Art Café (Saint Lucia) ✕, *768*
Zanzibar (Martinique) ✕, *603*
Zee Best (St. Maarten and St. Martin) ✕, *801*
Zimbali's Mountain Cooking Studio (Jamaica) ✕, *563*
Zoëtry Agua Punta Cana (Dominican Republic) ⌂, *26*
Zoëtry Curaçao Resort & Spa ⌂, *372*
Zozo's H2O (St. John) ✕, *912*

Photo Credits

Front Cover: RobertHarding/ Alamy Stock Photo [Description: Palm Beach, Aruba, Netherlands Antilles, Caribbean]. **Back cover, from left to right:** Loneroc/Shutterstock. Blacqbook/Shutterstock. Raffles Hotels and Resorts. **Spine:** Natchapon L./Shutterstock. **Interior, from left to right:** Zstock/Shutterstock (1). SeanPavonePhoto/iStockphoto (2-3). NorthJoe,[CC BY 2.0]/Flickr (5). **Chapter 1: Experience the Caribbean:** BlueOrange Studio/Shutterstock (8-9). Jo Ann Snover/dreamstime (18-19). Cathy Church/Cayman Islands (19). Barbados Golf Club (19). Dominican Republic Ministry of Tourism (20). Don Cristian Ramsey/shutterstock (20). Ilona Roco/shutterstock (20). Thierry dehove/shutterstock (20). EQRoy/shutterstock (21). Deep Blue Publications Ltd (21). Anguilla Tourist board (22). CathyRL/Shutterstock (22). Simon Dannhauer/shutterstock (22). Lisafx/istockphoto (22). Mandritoiu/shutterstock (23). Asher Hung/BVI Tourist Board (23). St. Barts Tourism (23). OkFoto/shutterstock (23). Dennisvdw/istockphoto (24). Grandrouge/Shutterstock (24). Elijah Lovkoff/shutterstock (25). Jade Mountain Resort (26). Alexis Andrews/Galley Bay Resort &Spa (26). Zoëtry Agua Punta Cana (26). Nicksmithphotography.com (26). Round Hill Hotel and Villas (27). Oetker Collection's Jumby Bay Island (27). Casa de Campo Resort & Villas (27). Islandoutpost (27). Antigua & Barbuda Tourism Authority (28). Discover Dominica Authority (28). Dominican Republic Ministry of Tourism (28). AntiguaAndBarbudaTourismAuthority_photo03 (29). AntiguaAndBarbudaTourismAuthority_photo02 (29). Filip Fuxa/shutterstock (30). Lorenzo Mittiga (30). Eduardo Gato (30). Alexander Shalamov/Dreamstime.com (31). Lucky-photographer/ Shutterstock(31). Kim Sargent (32). Paul Needham/Flickr (32). LC Lambrecht/Dominican Republic Ministry of Tourism (32). Kelly Fajack/Four Seasons Resort Nevis (32). Steve Simonsen/The Buccaneer (33). Gary James/Provo Golf Club (33). Royal Isabela (33). Envisionworks (33). Hopsalka/iStockphoto (34). SvetlanaSF/shutterstock (35). BlueOrange Studio/shutterstock (36). John A. Anderson/Shutterstock (37). Heeb Christian/Agefotostock (40). Nico Tondini/Agefotostock (41). Dom/Shutterstock (41). Dom/Shutterstock (41). Rohit Seth/Shutterstock (42). Kobako,[CC BY-SA 2.5]/wikipedia.org (42). Karen Wunderman/Shutterstock (43). Midori,[CC BY-SA 2.5]/wikipedia.org (43). Mulling it Over/Flickr (43). Stu_spivack/Flickr (43). Arkady/Shutterstock (44). Ahnhuynh/Shutterstock (44). Mlvalentin/wikipedia.org (44). Sakurai Midori, [CC BY-SA 2.5]/wikipedia.org (44). HLPhoto/Shutterstock (45). Cck/Flickr (45). Elena Elisseeva/Shutterstock (45). Only Fabrizio/ Shutterstock (45). Yosoynuts,[CC BY-ND 2.0]/Flickr (46). Ingolf Pompe/ Agefotostock (46). Charles Tobias (46). Havana Club Anejo Oro (46). Cogdogblog/Flickr (47). Robert S. Donovan/Flickr (47). NorthJoe,[CC BY 2.0]/Flickr (47). Pocketwiley,[CC BY 2.0]/Flickr (47). Granstrom/wikipedia.org (47). Richard Ellis / Alamy Stock Photo (48). **Chapter 3: Anguilla:** HubertHaciski/Shutterstock (69). DiegoMariottini/Shutterstock (77). EQRoy/Shutterstock (84). The Leading Hotels of the World (86). **Chapter 4: Antigua and Barbuda:** Alexander Shalamov/Dreamstime (95). Gemma Fletcher/Shutterstock (100). Chiara Magi/Shutterstock (107). Curtain Bluff (113). **Chapter 5: Aruba:** Sergey02/iStockphoto (125). Byvalet/Shutterstock (138). LittlenySTOCK/Shutterstock (146). Aruba Tourism Authority (162). **Chapter 6: Barbados:** Barbados Tourism Marketing Inc (167). Hwinther/Barbados Tourism Marketing Inc (175). Richard Semik/Dreamstime (192). Ed Rhodes / Alamy Stock Photo (195). Courtesy of Coral Reef Club (197). Fairmont Hotels & Resorts (199). **Chapter 7: Bonaire:** Gail Johnson/Shutterstock (215). Harbour Village Beach Club (234). Michelle Peters/Shutterstock (236). **Chapter 8: British Virgin Islands:** Thomas Kloc/Shutterstock (241). BlueOrange Studio/Shutterstock (249). Gem Russan/Shutterstock (254). FB-Fischer FB-Fischer/imagebroker.net/photolibrary.com (265). NAPA/Shutterstock (275). Bunchie VI/Shutterstock (280). **Chapter 9: Cayman Islands:** Ethan Daniels/Shutterstock (283). Jan Schneckenhaus/ Shutterstock (299). Don McDougall/Cayman Islands Department of Tourism (310). Von Hughes-Stanton/Shutterstock (319). Corbis (Own) (324). Michelle de Villiers/Shutterstock (329). **Chapter 10: Curaçao:** Philip Coblentz/Digital Vision (Own) (343). Curacao Tourist Board (358). Naturepics_li/iStockphoto (363). NaturePicsFilms/Shutterstock (370). Simon Dannhauer/iStock (373). **Chapter 11: Dominican Republic:** Dominican Republic Ministry of Tourism (375). Harry Pujols, [CC BY 2.0]/flickr (397). Tedmurphy, [CC BY 2.0]/flickr (406). Bildagentur Zoonar GmbH/Shutterstock (418). Blaz Dobravec/Shutterstock (422). **Chapter 12: Grenada:** Grenada Tourism Authority (437). Grenada Board of Tourism (464). Lisa Belle Larsen/Shutterstock (467). **Chapter 13: Guadeloupe:** Pays Guadeloupe/ Shutterstock (473). Tristan Deschamps/F1 Online (481). Oliver Hoffmann/Shutterstock (487). La Toubana Hotel (493). Philippe Giraud (498). Vouvraysan/Shutterstock (500). **Chapter 14: Jamaica:** Mbrand85/Shutterstock (511). Nigel D. Lord/Round Hill Hotel and Villas (526). Zaschnaus/Dreamstime (539). Ralfliebhold/Dreamstime (561). Kim Sargent (573). **Chapter 15: Martinique:** Photoshooter2015/Shutterstock (577). AIDAsign/Shutterstock (602). Frameme,[CC BY-SA 2.5]/wikipedia.org (605). Pack-Shot/Shutterstock (606). Luc Olivier/ Martinique Tourist Board (609). Luc Olivier/ Martinique Tourist Board (615). **Chapter 16: Puerto Rico:** Sorin Colac/Dreamstime (617). Tomás Fano/Flickr (630). Hotel El Convento (632). Thomas Hart Shelby (639). Dennis van de Water/Shutterstock (645). CindyLeighDesign/iStockphoto (652). Tres Sirenas Beach Inn (661). Fortherock/Flickr (668). **Chapter 17: St. Barthélemy:** Sean Pavone/Shutterstock (671). Christian Wheatley/iStockphoto (683). Leonard Zhukovsky/Shutterstock (685). Joe Benning/Shutterstock (687). Restaurant Le Gaiac (691). Photostravellers/Shutterstock (696). **Chapter 18: St. Kitts and Nevis:** NAPA/Shutterstock (701). Roger Brisbane, Brisbane Productions (711). OBrien (717). EQRoy/Shutterstock (725). Peter Peirce (732). **Chapter 19: Saint Lucia:** Inga Locmele/Shutterstock (737). Sandals Resorts (757). Sandals Resorts (758). Chris Harwood/Shutterstock (763). Ladera (767). Joe McNally/Jade Mountain (768). Saint Lucia Tourist Board (774). **Chapter 20: St. Maarten and St. Martin:** Multiverse/Shutterstock (779). Sean Pavone/Shutterstock (805). Steve Heap/Shutterstock (808). Chris Floyd (813). **Chapter 21: Turks and Caicos Islands:** Turks & Caicos Islands Tourist Board (819). Jsnover | Dreamstime.com (842). Turks And Caicos Tourist Office (846). Provo Golf Club (849). Como Hotels and Resorts (851). Ramunas/Dreamstime (862). **Chapter 22: United States Virgin Islands:** Walleyelj/Dreamstime (865). Jiawangkun/Dreamstime (879). Coral World Ocean Park, St. Thomas (888). Elijah Lovkoff/Shutterstock (891). SeanPavonePhoto/iStockphoto (907). EQRoy/Shutterstock (911). Big Blink Creative/Shutterstock (923). Bill Ross/Flirt Collection/photolibrary.com (934). Steve Simonsen (940).

*Every effort has been made to trace the copyright holders, and we apologize in advance for any accidental errors. We would be happy to apply the corrections in the following edition of this publication.

Notes

Notes

Fodor's ESSENTIAL CARIBBEAN

Publisher: Stephen Horowitz, *General Manager*

Editorial: Douglas Stallings, *Editorial Director*, Jill Fergus, Amanda Sadlowski, *Senior Editors*; Kayla Becker, Alexis Kelly, *Editors;* Angelique Kennedy-Chavannes, *Assistant Editor*

Design: Tina Malaney, *Director of Design and Production*; Jessica Gonzalez, *Graphic Designer;* Erin Caceres, *Graphic Design Associate*

Production: Jennifer DePrima, *Editorial Production Manager*, Elyse Rozelle, *Senior Production Editor;* Monica White, *Production Editor*

Maps: Rebecca Baer, *Senior Map Editor*, Mark Stroud (Moon Street Cartography), David Lindroth, *Cartographers*

Photography: Viviane Teles, *Senior Photo Editor;* Namrata Aggarwal, Payal Gupta, Ashok Kumar, *Photo Editors;* Eddie Aldrete, *Photo Production Intern*

Business and Operations: Chuck Hoover, *Chief Marketing Officer*, Robert Ames, *Group General Manager*, Devin Duckworth, *Director of Print Publishing*

Public Relations and Marketing: Joe Ewaskiw, *Senior Director of Communications and Public Relations*

Fodors.com: Jeremy Tarr, *Editorial Director;* Rachael Levitt, *Managing Editor*

Technology: Jon Atkinson, *Director of Technology;* Rudresh Teotia, *Lead Developer*

Writers: Diane Bair, Carol M. Bareuther, Amber Love Bond, Susan Campbell, Riselle Celestina, Mechi Annais Estevez Cruz, Bob Curley, Tracy Laville, Sara Liss, Sheri-kae McLeod, Sheryl Nance-Nash, Akiera Paterson, Paulina Salach, Alicia Simon, Lee Yeaman, Jane E. Zarem

Editors: Kayla Becker, Alexis Kelly, Andrew Collins

Production Editor: Jennifer DePrima

3rd Edition

ISBN 978-1-64097-519-4

ISSN 2471-9064

PRINTED IN THE UNITED STATES OF AMERICA

10 9 8 7 6 5 4 3 2 1

About Our Writers

Diane Bair is an award-winning travel journalist whose work has appeared in national magazines, online, and in major daily newspapers, including frequent stories for *The Boston Globe.* She's also co-authored (with Pamela Wright) more than two dozen books on travel, outdoor recreation, and wildlife-watching. Seeing all of the inhabited Caribbean islands is a life goal and she's getting close to reaching it. She updated the Saint Lucia chapter. Follow her on Instagram @dianebairtravel.

St. Thomas–based writer and dietitian **Carol M. Bareuther** writes for several regional and national magazines, such as *Destinations, Discover St. Thomas–St. John, Southern Boating, Produce Business,* and *All At Sea.* She's the author of two books, including *Virgin Islands Cooking.* She updated the St. Thomas and St. John sections of the U.S.V.I. chapter.

Amber Love Bond is a Miami-based food + beverage and travel writer who is always on the go. After a decade-long career in corporate finance, she stumbled upon her passion for writing about the world around and hasn't looked back since. Amber contributes to over a dozen print and digital publications including *American Way, Eater, Tasting Panel Magazine,* and more. You can find her at the opening of every restaurant, sipping cocktails at Miami's coolest bars, or hanging out on the beach with her laptop in tow. She updated St. Kitts and Nevis.

Susan Campbell is an award-winning travel-and-lifestyle writer specializing in the Dutch Caribbean. She has hundreds of articles to her credit about Aruba, Bonaire, Curacao, and St. Maarten in over 22 major national and international print and web outlets as well as on-island magazines. When Susan isn't seeking the best hot spots in the tropics, she is reporting about the highlights of her hometown in Montreal. She updated the Aruba, Bonaire, and Curacao chapters.

Riselle Celestina is a Caribbean travel writer, blogger, and video maker based on the island of St. Maarten. Her passion for and knowledge of the Caribbean region makes her a fan favorite on social media and on her YouTube channel for Caribbean travel tips and suggestions. Her travel stories have been published in *Insider Travel, Visit St. Maarten, Afar, Mélange Travel & Lifestyle,* and in the *Winair In-Flight Magazine* among others. You can read her travel stories here: www.thetravelingislandgirl.com

Mechi Annaís Estévez Cruz is a mixed afroindigenous Dominican storyteller and decolonial activist based in Samaná, Dominican Republic. Primarily a grassroots organizer with 10 years of experience in tourism, Mechi's current work focuses on uplifting ancestral knowledge, practices, and history on a local and international level. Their writing has appeared in *Fodor's, The Paris Review,* and *Remezcla* among others. They updated the Dominican Republic chapter.

Bob Curley is a freelance travel writer specializing in the Caribbean and whose work has appeared in *Coastal Living, AFAR, USA Today,* and scores of other publications. He updated the BVI chapter and the St. Croix section of the U.S.V.I. chapter. Follow Bob on Instagram @gocaribbean and at 🌐 *www.honestraveler.com.*

Tracy Laville is a writer and a visual storyteller based on St. Maarten. She tells stories about culture and travels and has worked closely with the French Tourist Bureau to portray the authenticity of St. Martin. She updated the Martinique chapter.

About Our Writers

Trilingual in English, Hebrew, and Farsi, **Sara Liss** started her career in journalism in the Middle East, where she was a reporter for the Associated Press's Jerusalem bureau and *Time Out Istanbul*. She now resides in Surfside near Miami Beach with her family and has contributed to publications including *Condé Nast Traveler*, *The Miami Herald*, and *Departures*. Her first cookbook, *Miami Cooks*, was released in 2020. Sara updated the Cayman Islands. Follow her on Instagram @Slissmia.

As a native of Jamaica and what the locals call a "dry land tourist," **Sheri-kae McLeod** has always been fascinated with exploring her beautiful home island and showcasing the best of Jamaica through travel media. She has worked for several local, regional and international media publications and marketing companies in the capacity of journalist, writer, editor, and digital content creator. She updated the Jamaica and Turks & Caicos chapters. You can connect with Sheri-kae on Instagram at @shaaeex.

Sheryl Nance-Nash, a New York-based freelance journalist, loves to write about the intersection of travel, history, wellness, art and culture. Her work has appeared on *Condé Nast Traveler*, *The Daily Beast*, *Afar*, *Newsweek.com*, and *Global Traveler*, among others. Sheryl updated the St. Barth chapter.

As an avid nature lover, **Akiera Paterson** especially enjoys traveling throughout the Caribbean, being from the beautiful spice isles of Grenada, Carriacou, and Petite Martinique. She updated the Grenada chapter of Caribbean.

A culinary and travel entrepreneur, **Paulina Salach** is the co-founder of Puerto Rico Restaurant Week and Spoon Food Tours, a food tour company based in San Juan. She is also a licensed publicist, culinary consultant, event producer, and social media manager. In 2014, she was one of the hosts of the Saborea food festival held in San Juan. Paulina has contributed to *Have Fork Will Travel*, a handbook for food and drink tourism. She is a native of Poland and has lived in Barcelona, New York City, and currently resides in Puerto Rico. She updated the Puerto Rico chapter.

Alicia Simon is a New York native, Antigua-based journalist, literary writer, and award-winning screenwriter. Her work has been published by *The Antigua Observer*, Visit Antigua & Barbuda, *Business Focus Antigua*, *Fodor's*, and more. Specializing in feature writing, Alicia strives to add a human face to stories about travel, finance, and the arts. On her off time, you'll find her amassing her collection of exotic houseplants with her rambunctious sons. She updated the Antigua and Barbuda chapter.

Lee Yeaman is a travel and lifestyle writer from Scotland. Her work has featured in several major national and international print and web publications. Lee travels with her young son Leo and after spending a year in Barbados, she is on a mission to help other parents realize their travel dreams. Lee updated the Barbados chapter. You can follow her on Instagram @thegoddessclan.

Jane E. Zarem travels frequently to the Caribbean from her Connecticut home. Over the years, she has contributed to numerous Fodor's guides in addition to Caribbean—among them New England, USA, Cape Cod, and In Focus Barbados and St. Lucia. She updated the Experience, Travel Smart, and Guadeloupe chapters.

Several Caribbean destinations were updated but appear only on www.fodors.com. **Susan Campbell** updated Saba. **Vernon O'Reilly-Ramesar** updated Trinidad and Tobago. **Alicia Simon** updated Montserrat. **Jane E. Zarem** updated Dominica, St. Vincent & Grenadines, and Statia.